Management Science

Management Science

Terry L. Dennis
Rochester Institute of Technology

Laurie B. Dennis
RIT Research Corporation

West Publishing Company
St. Paul   New York   Los Angeles   San Francisco

Copyeditor: Joan Callahan Compton
Design: John Rokusek
Artwork: Alexander Teshin and Associates
Composition: Beacon Graphics
Indexing: Schroeder Editorial Services
Cover Image and Design: David Farr, ImageSmythe, Inc.

COPYRIGHT ©1991   By WEST PUBLISHING COMPANY
50 W. Kellogg Boulevard
P.O. Box 64526
St. Paul, MN 55164-1003

98 97 96 95 94 93 92 91   8 7 6 5 4 3 2 1 0
Library of Congress Cataloging–in–Publication Data

Dennis, Laurie B.
  Management science / Laurie B. Dennis, Terry L. Dennis.
    p. cm.
  Includes bibliographical references and index.
  ISBN 0-314-76644-8
  1. Management science. I. Dennis, Terry L. II. Title.
T56.D379 1991
658--dc20

90–43804
CIP

To Matt, Sara, and Rachel

Table of Contents

Chapter 8

NETWORK MODELS 253

Chapter 9

INTEGER PROGRAMMING 304

Chapter 10

GOAL PROGRAMMING 348

Chapter 11

PROJECT SCHEDULING WITH PERT/CPM 382

Chapter 12

INVENTORY MANAGEMENT 444

Chapter 13

DECISION ANALYSIS 493

Chapter 14

QUEUING ANALYSIS 543

Chapter 15

SIMULATION 586

APPENDICES

INDEX I–1

Preface

We believe that management science should be taught as part of the managerial decision making process, not as an applied mathematics course. Thus, the introductory chapter of this book is not a throwaway, but rather an essential introduction to the course. The models and techniques presented in succeeding chapters can then be recognized as useful tools that provide information vital for informed and economically rational decision making. In turn, to use these tools effectively, the decision maker must be able to recognize and model the problem before determining a solution or making a decision. Thus, problem recognition and model formulation take their rightful place as essential components in the problem-solving/decision making process.

In the best of all possible situations, a student learns not only the theoretical underpinnings and computational mechanics of the specific technique, but also problem recognition (including the assumptions to be met) and problem formulation (with ample opportunity for practice). This would include looking at a variety of real-world applications and situations. In this best of worlds, the student would also have the opportunity to practice using some of the better known and most often used commercial computer packages. However, in the more common, less than perfect classroom situation, much of the time is spent learning theoretical background and computational procedures. This oversimplified scenario, happily, is rapidly fading. With more and more computer packages available for classroom use, professors are able to spend more time on formulation and on analyzing solutions to be used in making decisions. Professors can now bring real-life experiences, cases, applications, and problems to the class for discussion, can pose the what-if questions that affect decisions, and can give sufficient amounts of time to practicing formulations and to analyzing results. No textbook can do this as effectively as the individual teacher. Moreover, an introductory survey textbook cannot cover each model in depth. At its best, a textbook should explain the basics to the student well enough so that the professor is free to concentrate on bringing his or her experience and expertise to the subject, adding depth and breadth.

Since the publication of our *Microcomputer Models for Management Decision Making* book and software, we have heard from many users that it has changed the way they now teach management science—allowing them ample time to formulate an ever-increasing variety of more complicated problems and time to really look at and analyze the results. Since they are free of the computational burden, there is greater opportunity to discuss what is actually happening in the solution. For instance, with LP, it is possible to examine each tableau and explain what is happening with each iteration. The student still learns simplex, but is not responsible for the computations.

In structuring this textbook, we were mindful of users' comments, our own teaching experiences, and a recent AACSB committee report recommending greater use of computerized algorithms and case studies for the effective teaching of management science. Thus, we have tried to emphasize problem recognition, model formulation, and the decision making context of each model and have presented both manual and computer solution procedures for each technique. To emphasize our belief in the importance of computer solutions in the classroom, we have included a Linear Programming Computer Solutions chapter as well as a chapter on the simplex method. This is not to negate the importance of learning simplex. It merely reflects a personal shift in emphasis and offers an alternative approach to teaching the course. The two chapters can in fact be taught in reverse order. It is also possible to eliminate one or the other, but we do not recommend it.

Because we feel that management science is a tool to be used in making decisions, we have included a Focus on Decision Making section in each chapter (treating all linear programming chapters as one). Here we have raised questions about what happens after the computer or algorithm provides an answer to a specific problem. In this What Happens Next section, we want the student to think about the qualitative as well as quantitative aspects of the decision.

We also feel very strongly that students need to see that the management science discipline and tools are both useful and used. To that end, we have included at the end of most chapters a real-world application taken primarily from recent *Interfaces*. Moreover, students must recognize the role of these models as a tool, one input in the decision making process. Therefore, some of the applications reveal that frequently a situation requires the use of a combination of procedures and that the models must be tailored to fit each unique situation.

We have written this text for the student—for whom the material presented is probably brand new, a little strange, and perhaps intimidating. We have tried to make our presentation as clear and intelligible as possible (frequently saying the same thing in more than one way) so that the student can learn from the textbook as well as from the classroom experience. Students need both. We have also tried to write as we have taught, starting with an objective, a definition of what is going to happen, and moving from the general to the specific. Some texts begin each chapter or topic with a short case, scenario, or example and relate the solution technique to this specific situation. This is not our approach. We have found that this approach frequently ignores variations or considerations not included in the given scenario. This may leave learners unable to handle problems that vary in any way from the example. Students do not fully understand the model or technique being discussed, but they can solve any problem that looks just like the one explained. Thus, although we begin each chapter with a scenario to introduce the problem type that can be solved, we do not teach the technique only for that particular problem. We first present a comprehensive overview of the subject, including the underlying assumptions and components of the model, and then discuss the solution procedures used to solve problems of this type. At this point, the introductory example is used for clarification and specificity. We then discuss special cases and problems, computer solutions for these problems, and specific applications. This is our general approach. Obviously, the structure of each chapter has been dictated to some extent by the model being discussed. Finally, we believe that, as with any textbook, this text should be only one part of the instructional framework within which the student learns management science.

To the best of our knowledge, the programs that accompany this book run on all IBM PC/XT compatible microcomputers. Most of these programs are modifications of the programs which have been used successfully by students since 1984.

We would like to take this opportunity to thank Patrick J. Fitzgerald, who provided the encouragement and support necessary for us to undertake this project. We also want to thank Paul Kingston of IBM for providing the MPSX/370 example output. We would also like to thank Dick Fenton, Nancy Hill-Whilton, Tom Modl, John Rock, and Lucinda Gatch of West Publishing Company. Finally, we thank Tim McGrath, SUNY-Plattsburg; Yasemin Aksoy, Tulane University; Edward K. Baker, University of Miami; James A. Bartos, The Ohio State University; William R. Benoit, Plymouth State College; Anthony E. Bopp, James Madison University; William H. Collins, East Carolina University; Richard J. Coppins, Virginia Commonwealth University; Connie Edwards, Auburn University; David L. Eldredge, Murray State University; Dale R. Fox, University of Tennessee—Knoxville; Dennis Geyer, Golden Gate University; Edward Gillenwater, University of Mississippi; Wesley Green, Ashland University; Richard Gunther, California State University-Northridge; Donald L. Haney, St. Mary's University; Don Harnett, Indiana University; Larry Jacobs, University of North Florida; Jooh Lee, Glassboro State University; Charles E. Leinart, Metropolitan State College; Robert Markland, University of South Carolina; David G. Martin, St. Bonaventure University; Robert W. Metzger, Central Michigan University; Michael Mogavero, Alfred University; Carl H. Naeher, SUNY-Buffalo; Ata Nahouraii, Indiana University of Pennsylvania; Sanjeev Phukan, Bemidji State University; James A. Pope, Old Dominion University; Harold Rahmlow, St. Joseph's University; Susan Reiland; Don Robinson, Illinois State University; Andrew Seila, The University of Georgia; Robert Schellenberger, East Carolina University; Larry Scheuermann, University of Southwestern Louisiana; Ernest Teagarden, Dakota State University; Jack Yurkiewicz, Pace University; Don Ziegenbein, University of Maine, Orono; who were involved in the review of this text and the computer programs.

Management Science comes with the following supplements:

Instructor's Manual, which includes lecture notes and solutions to all problems.
Transparency Masters of key in-text art, as well as LINDO & STORM output.
Test Bank by Dave Martin, St. Bonaventure University, which includes multiple choice, true/false, short answer, and computational problems, and a listing of most appropriate problems for computer work.
Computerized Testing.
Study Guide by Rich Coppins, Virginia Commonwealth University, which includes key concepts with numbered references to worked examples and problems, chapter reviews, chapter checkpoints, study hints, true/false questions, five worked examples, ten problems (including challenge problems and computer-appropriate problems), and an end-of-book answer section.

Management Science

Introduction: The Management Science Approach to Decision Making

By the end of this chapter, you should be able to:

1

relate management to decision making and describe the manager's role in decision making;

2

relate decision making to problem solving;

3

describe the decision making/problem solving processes;

4

define and explain the term management science, identifying its characteristics;

5

describe the management science approach;

6

explain what a model is, types of models used, and their role;

7

describe the structure of a mathematical model, including a discussion of the component parts.

This is an introductory management science textbook. **Management science** is a rational, systematic approach to problem solving that employs quantitative analysis to help managers make decisions. A variety of quantitative techniques have been developed to help solve specific types of standard problems. In this book, you will be introduced to some of these techniques. However, these techniques are only one component of a discipline that provides a logical framework for decision making. Therefore, this book is really about making decisions and solving problems, using a scientific approach and quantitative analysis. This chapter serves as an introduction to management science and to the role of management science and quantitative models in decision making.

1.1 *DECISION MAKING/PROBLEM SOLVING*

Decision making is a part of life, something we do numerous times daily, automatically, subconsciously, without really identifying it as decision making—should I get out of bed today, should I have the tuna or egg salad. Such trivial decisions are arrived at in a variety of ways, usually intuitively or from experience, (if I don't get up I'll lose my job, the tuna wasn't good last time). Some decisions are recognized as being more important—should I major in mechanical engineering or accounting, should I buy a house or stay in an apartment. Some decisions we recognize as very important problems—I just lost my job, what do I do now. With these kinds of decisions we try to be more logical or rational. We make lists, pro and con. We consider the alternatives. In fact, formally or informally we go through a decision-making process. We may even quantify the decision (it costs more to buy than to rent, but when I consider tax benefits...). Making decisions, some important, some everyday matter of fact, is a major responsibility of management. Managers are decision makers who approach decision making in much the same way.

The Manager As a Decision Maker

To manage means to direct, control, or administer. To manage a firm or an organization involves planning, organizing, and controlling operations in an efficient and effective way to reach an objective. Here, we are defining operations as a basic input-output system. The output is determined by the nature of the inputs and the transformation process. Output can be changed by manipulating either/or both the inputs and the processing. Managers make the system work. They make the decisions that determine the inputs, and they select the processes that will best achieve the desired objective given any constraints.

The decision is a conclusion or the end point of a process. The process begins whenever a manager observes a problem, determines that there is a conflict or adversarial situation, or must make a choice from among alternatives. A problem is perceived or recognized to exist whenever there is a substantial difference between expectation and realization. This problem orientation is central to a quantitative approach to decision making. The manager makes the decisions that alleviate the perceived problem.

Both the decision making and problem solving responsibilities of management have been discussed as almost equivalent terms. For our purposes, we will define the entire process as problem solving. Decision making ends with a recommendation that will solve the problem. Problem solving includes implementing this recommendation.

The Decision-Making Process

We are concerned with the way decisions are made. Whether it is done consciously or unconsciously, formally or informally, the decision-making process or pattern usually takes the following form: (1) The problem is clearly identified and defined. This means to recognize and state both the objective or goal to be achieved and any constraints. (2) Data are collected. (3) Alternative courses of action are identified. (4) The data are analyzed and the alternatives are evaluated. (5) A decision is made based on this analysis and evaluation. Once the decision is made, the next step is to implement the results. This process can be in either a qualitative or a quantitative form.

Qualitative decision making relies on personal judgement (intuition) or past experience with similar problems (standard operating procedure). Frequently, such an approach or "feel" for a situation is sufficient for making a decision. In many ways, decision making is a talent acquired with experience. Problems can be approached and successfully solved using creativity, judgement, experience, and intuition. These subjective, qualitative factors are an inherent and vital component of good decision making.

Quantitative Tools in Decision Making

However, there are occasions when a more systematic and quantitative approach to decision making is desirable and more helpful. There are times when a problem is unusually complicated and multifaceted, involving many variables and many departments or divisions. It is not possible to reach an intuitive decision or to achieve an understanding of the problem. A systematic approach usually provides a better solution for such a problem. This is also true with problems that have not been encountered frequently (lack experience) and with problems where an error would be extremely costly.

The business world is a complex place, which complicates decisions and the decision-making process. The environment in which decisions must be made and in which managers must operate is changing rapidly. Advances in technology require changes in management practices. Complex technological environments, with more alternatives, greater uncertainty, higher cost for errors, and greater difficulty in predicting consequences make it more difficult and riskier to rely on intuitive decision making. The decision maker has a better chance of making a proper decision by using quantitative tools. Management science provides these quantitative procedures, processes, and techniques. Some standard management science techniques have been developed that can be used to solve problems that fit into a standard classification. Managers are becoming more sophisticated, recognizing that successful solutions are reached through a combination of qualitative and quantitative factors.

1.2 *MANAGEMENT SCIENCE/OPERATIONS RESEARCH*

In this text, the terms management science (MS) and operations research (OR) are considered nearly equivalent. We use the term management science throughout the text, while recognizing that historically OR came first. Management science has developed as an interdisciplinary field, an approach to problem solving that uses elements of such disciplines as mathematics, engineering, science, economics, and computer science.

Management science provides an approach for solving quantifiable problems. This approach uses quantitative tools and scientific methodology to provide a rational way to make decisions. It applies scientific methodology to management problems in order to develop and evaluate solutions. However, management science is more than a collection of mathematically oriented tools and techniques developed for the solution of management problems. It is a strategy for approaching problems in a logical, consistent, and systematic manner. This strategy for problem solving is as important as the knowledge of the mechanics of the mathematical techniques used to solve the problem.

The Evolution of MS/OR

It is impossible to pinpoint the exact birth date of management science. Instances in which scientific methodology seems to have been applied to management problems were recorded thousands of years ago. In Chapter 18 of the Book of Exodus,

Jethro is said to have written a treatise on the principles of organization. In the fifteenth century, Venetian shipbuilders used an assembly line to recondition and refit ships. However, not until the industrial revolution do we see a consistently scientific approach to management. In the late nineteenth century, Frederick W. Taylor questioned management's assumption that the largest shovel a man could fill and carry was the size of shovel that would maximize profit. Taylor devised a series of experiments to discover what variables were really relevant for this productivity problem. Productivity rose when he implemented his discovery that total weight (shovel + ore) was the only relevant variable: workers became fatigued less quickly when total weight was lowered. This example of formalized scientific management marked the beginning of industrial engineering as a profession, and earned Taylor the title "father of scientific management." A contemporary of Taylor's, Henry L. Gantt, refined scientific management by taking a broader point of view. While Taylor was primarily interested in the best way to accomplish a single task, Gantt looked at the various steps in a complete operation.

This early stage in the development of MS was important. The shift from improving the performance of specific tasks to considering broader overall operations, combined with a multidisciplinary approach, signaled the emergence of management science. While it is not possible to identify the first true application of MS, it is possible to site the work of several pioneers working in the early decades of the twentieth century. In 1914, an Englishman, Frederick W. Lanchester, attempted to quantify military operations, predicting the outcome of battles based on the numerical strength of personnel and weaponry. Lanchester is important because he developed a predicting equation to model a real life situation and tested the model against that situation. Several other pioneers during this time include: Ford W. Harris, who published a simple economic lot size formula as a model for inventory control; A. K. Erlang, whose formulas founded modern queuing or waiting line theory; Walter Shewhart, whose application of statistical inference introduced the concept of quality control charts; and Horace C. Levinson, who studied the relationship between advertising and sales and the effect of customers' income and home location on purchases. These pioneers recognized the necessity of using specialists from a variety of fields, working together in research teams, to experiment with entire systems, rather than with single elements of a system.

However, despite these advances in the scientific, multidisciplinary approach to management problems, MS did not emerge as a recognized discipline until World War II. By 1939, the British had the nucleus of an "operational research" organization, a team of specialists assembled to investigate the use of radar. The British increasingly called on experts from various disciplines to study military problems such as civilian defense and antisubmarine warfare. The most famous of these groups, Blackett's Circus, under the direction of the celebrated physicist and Nobel Laureate, P.M.S. Blackett, included three physiologists, two mathematical physicists, one astrophysicist, one army officer, one surveyor, one general physicist, and two mathematicians. This team approach became characteristic of MS.

The success of these British OR groups in helping to win the Battle of Britain influenced the U.S. military in its decision to include such groups on its staff. American military leaders considered the work of these "operations research" groups too important to disband after the war. The Army continued its OR functions through the Operations Research Office, the Navy established the Operations Evaluation Group, and the Air Force continued its groups as part of the Operations Analysis Division.

Despite the use of MS by the military establishment, MS methodology was largely ignored by industry in the United States. Managers had seen many fads come and go and were not willing to jump at another one. Moreover, communication between scientists and managers was difficult, with many managers not convinced of the reliability of the scientists. Not until some of the formerly "top secret" applications were released and a few companies tried MS with great success, did its value begin to be recognized. The situation was different in Great Britain. The nationalization of certain key industries provided an excellent opportunity for operations research techniques and offered the chance to experiment on whole industries. Two important events helped further its acceptance and adoption by American industry. In 1947, Dantzig developed the simplex solution to linear programming. This method of determining the optimal allocation of scarce resources was both relevant and profitable to industry. Of even greater importance for the acceptance of MS was the development and production of high-speed electronic computers. Computers became invaluable tools for the management science profession because of their ability to perform rapidly and reliably functions and calculations that were previously impossible or unprofitable. As a result of these developments, management science was recognized as having value for business and industry.

The MS discipline has developed rapidly since its acceptance in the 1950s. Moreover, the scope of the problems addressed by management science professionals has expanded. A measure of its formalization has been the establishment and proliferation of professional associations and publications. Special historical note (and not intended in any way to be all inclusive) are: Operational Research Society (British 1950); Operations Research Society of America (ORSA) (1952), which publishes the journal *Operations Research*; The Institute of Management Science (TIMS) (United States 1953), which publishes the journal *Management Science*; and the Decision Sciences Institute, formerly American Institute of Decision Sciences, (United States 1969). Today ORSA/TIMS cooperate to publish *Interfaces*.

By the end of the 1950s, many of the MS tools were well developed. Most applications focused on well-defined, specialized problems. In the 1960s and 1970s, management science dealt with more realistic and less well-structured problems. Decision analysis began to be recognized as a process for dealing with decisions that must be made under uncertainty. Use of management science has now expanded into large social and urban systems such as criminal justice systems and education. MS is increasingly concerned with the management information systems (MIS) interface, which has resulted in a special kind of information system, a decision support system.

The continued growth and change in management science as an approach to problem solving has resulted in both increased numbers of academic courses being offered to greater numbers of students, and to changes in the way these courses are designed and taught. Management science courses are no longer viewed as applied math courses concentrating on mathematical algorithms used to reach a solution. Instead they are recognized as problem-solving courses with the emphasis shifting toward developing problem solving and model formulation skills.[1]

---

[1] Two articles on this subject are: Borsting, Jack R., et al. "A Model for a First Course in Management Science/ Operations Research." *Interfaces*, 18:(September–October), 72–80, 1988. Samson, Danny. (Comment on the Paper by Borsting, et al.) "A Model for a first MBA Course in Management Science/Operations Reasearch." *Interfaces*, 18:November–December), 123–127, 1988.

Characteristics of Management Science

Thus far, we have defined management science as a systematic, rational approach to decision making. We now turn our attention to the characteristics of management science: scientific method, systems approach, interdisciplinary/team approach, problem orientation using mathematical models, and computer use. These characteristics help describe the discipline and enable us to understand the context or environment in which MS helps solve problems.

The Scientific Method

A basic characteristic of MS is its application of the scientific method to decision making. The scientific method involves the following step-wise approach to problem solving.

1. Observation: A problem is recognized.
2. Definition: The situation is analyzed and the problem is distinguished from its symptoms.
3. Formulation of an hypothesis: Based on observation and examination of the system, a description of the factors involved and their interaction and interrelationship can be formulated and an optimal solution can be conceived.
4. Experimentation: Means and methods for testing the hypothesis are devised and executed.
5. Verification: The results of the experimentation are analyzed.

The management science approach is built on the premise that a significant portion of decision making consists of identifying and analyzing the problem, recognizing the relationships among the factors, and isolating those factors over which the decision maker has control. There is a striking similarity between the first three steps of the scientific analysis and the MS decision making premise. However, a manager is more likely to perform these steps in an informal manner than would a scientist. The hypotheses produced may be more intuitive than explicit. The final two steps, experimentation and verification are more complex and difficult to control in the real world than in a controlled laboratory environment. These will be discussed in greater detail later. First, let's look at an example of a problem approached in this systematic manner, emphasizing observation, definition, and hypothesis.

Example Problem

A small food processing plant makes a grape drink. The manager has noticed that while sales are increasing annually, profits are not increasing in proportion to sales. After checking accounting data for the past five years, the manager is able to confirm that in the past year, profit margins have not, in fact, kept pace with sales growth. Special promotional pricing might be one reason for both increased sales and smaller profit margins. Another reason might be increased costs. After further investigation, the manager discovers that the latter has, in fact, occurred. Costs have increased more rapidly than prices, shrinking the profit margin on this product. The increased costs could be a result of increased production costs caused by declining productivity (necessitating more labor per unit) or increased labor costs (higher wages or benefits), or they could be the result of increased costs in raw materials. Further investigation showed the manager that production costs had not increased significantly; however, the cost of raw materials had. The grape drink was formulated using water, sugar, and grape concentrate. Analysis of these costs revealed that the cost of sugar had increased at a rate double that of the increases in the price the company was charging for the drink. The manager can now clearly define the problem as one of shrinking profit margins caused by the rapid increase in sugar prices.

Once the problem has been identified, the manager can formulate an hypothesis that can be tested. (Note that in identifying the problem, the manager has really tested several preliminary hypotheses or considered various alternatives.) Since the cost of sugar is beyond the control of the manager (we will assume that shopping for another supplier will not yield lower sugar costs in this case), the manager may hypothesize that a different product formulation, which requires less sugar might solve this problem. Note there may have been alternative hypotheses that the manager could have formulated, for example, the introduction of a cheaper sugar substitute would solve the problem. There are many more factors involved in this type of problem. For example, choosing to try a new product formulation could require such things as test marketing the new product, a new advertising campaign, new packaging or labeling, new or different production facilities, and so on. All of these changes will have to be considered. Once the manager has formulated the hypothesis, it can be tested through experimentation, trial and error, or mathematical modeling.

A Systems Approach

A second fundamental characteristic of management science is its systems approach. A **system** can be thought of as a whole, comprising interrelated parts that are intended to accomplish a clearly defined objective.

This term is used to define or describe many units in our society today, including stereo, school, and computer systems. Each of these is a whole comprised of interrelated parts, each functioning independently, but with a clearly defined goal. A stereo system can be viewed with its tuner, turntable, cartridge, cassette player, and speakers as a system designed to interact to give great sound.

Systems may be classified as either open or closed. Open systems interact with their environment; closed systems are self-contained. Systems may be viewed as having three distinct components: (1) inputs: elements that come either from within the system or from the outside environment; (2) processes: elements necessary to convert inputs into outputs; and (3) outputs: the result or finished product. In an FM stereo system, the inputs include the FM signal in the air waves and a prerecorded tape. The processes include the selection by the tuner of the appropriate station signal and the conversion of the magnetic impulses to electronic signals by the tape head. The outputs can be the magnificent sound of a Beethoven symphony or the faithful reproduction of a rock concert.

All systems are also subsystems, that is, a system is contained within some larger system. This in turn is contained within some larger system, and so on. Each component of the stereo in our example is a subsystem of the whole system. Systems are hierarchical, meaning there are levels of systems. System components are usually connected by some type of feedback device. Systems are also surrounded by an environment. The environment includes those elements outside the system that influence the system's performance and its ability to attain it's objective. The environment describes those variables (legal, political, economic) that cannot be controlled or manipulated. They definitely play a part in the achievement of the system's objectives. In the stereo system, the quality of the recording, the strength of the signal, and the FCC regulations are elements of the environment. Feedback is simply that flow of information to the decision maker about the output. Using this information the decision maker can make changes in inputs and processes. Figure 1.1 represents a complete system.

By viewing the organization as a system, individual parts can be considered in relation to the whole. This systems approach is important. It allows us to recognize that a decision made in one part has an impact on other parts. The good of the whole may not necessarily be derived from the greatest good for an individual part. Determining the best solution for one component or subsystem may not necessarily result in the best or optimal solution for the organization as a whole. Optimization and suboptimization will be discussed in greater detail when solutions to problems are discussed later.

Interdisciplinary/Team Approach

There are two forces at work in organizations that necessitate the frequent use of a team approach to solving managerial problems: the complexity of managerial problems and the high degree of specialization required of managers. Many problems have physical, economic, sociological, engineering, and mathematical aspects. They frequently involve many departments or functional areas. Most managers cannot be expected to have expertise in all of these areas. By bringing together a team with a variety of experience and expertise, managers can analyze and approach problems from a variety of directions. Each team member can analyze the problem and relate it to his or her own discipline, determining if this particular problem can be solved using a solution method from that field. The pool of possible solution approaches and methodologies is enlarged and all aspects of the problem are considered. For example, in the grape drink problem, the manager could have worked with accounting, purchasing, market research, marketing, quality control, production, and packaging to analyze the problem.

We need to be aware that the team approach is not without problems and does not always offer the best approach. Committees or teams may be inefficient, suffer from poor communication, or result in a compromise instead of an optimal decision. In short, the team approach can show all the weaknesses and deficiencies of a poorly organized and inefficiently run committee. While the team approach is a characteristic of the management science approach, many problems are simple enough to be solved by a single individual who is knowledgeable about management science techniques and computer solutions.

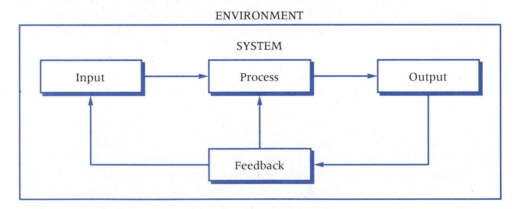

Figure 1.1 The System and Its Environment

Problem Orientation: Use of Mathematical Models

The decision making/problem solving process is initiated with the recognition of a problem. Analysis of any problem takes two forms, qualitative and quantitative, each providing important information. Our concern is with that part of MS that concentrates on the quantitative data associated with the problem, that is, problems that are quantifiable. Once a problem has been observed, analyzed, and defined, it has to be solved. Mathematical models and computers provide the techniques and tools to solve the problems. If the problem is recognized as a fairly standard one, then it can be solved using standard tools that have been developed. These tools include management science techniques and/or standard tools borrowed from other disciplines. For more complex, non-standard problems, the management scientist or manager may have to build the tool. Managers must be familiar with available tools.

A **model** is an abstraction of an object or real world phenomenon. It is a simplified representation of reality that accurately displays the key properties of the object it is representing. A mathematical model, the type we are interested in, is a formal structure that creates the framework within which a problem can be analyzed. A mathematical model attempts to represent a given problem by equations and other mathematical statements. It translates the essential features of the situation into mathematical symbols. Modeling is the backbone of management science. However, building models is a difficult process, which requires both accuracy and simplicity. This will be discussed it in depth later.

Use of Computers

Management science has increasingly become associated with the use of computers. In fact, the development of management science is directly related to the development of the computer and the use of computers is a fundamental characteristic of management science. Computers offer a fast, accurate, relatively inexpensive, and flexible means of solving complicated, multifaceted managerial decision problems.

Many quantifiable managerial problems are extremely complex, involving numerous interrelated components or variables. The solution of such problems can be amazingly difficult, and the computational burden can be enormous. A manual approach to the analysis and solution of such problems can be impractical. The use of computers has made the solution of mathematically complex problems practical. Problems that took weeks or months to solve manually can now be solved in minutes or seconds by computer.

Computers are used for more than the quick execution of cumbersome calculations. They are also used in data analysis and model validation. And computers are extremely valuable in helping managers understand and use the model results, allowing "what if?" kinds of analysis that can be performed quickly and easily. The use of computers to help in managerial problem solving is not limited to custom software, specifically written for MS techniques. Over the counter software is being used to solve problems and to do quick "what if?" analyses. Figure 1.2 illustrates the use of a spreadsheet package to evaluate the impact of a 5 percent change in labor costs per unit and a 10 percent change in material costs on an example Income Statement.

We will rely heavily on computer solutions for the models introduced in this text. Students should learn to recognize and define the problem, be able to formulate the model correctly, understand the solution process, and learn to use the computer solutions in the most effective manner.

```
BASE MODEL                          INCREASES IN MATERIAL &
                                    LABOR COSTS

Per Unit Costs:                     Per Unit Costs:
-------------------                 -------------------
Material                  $2.40     Material                  $2.64
Labor                     $3.25     Labor                     $3.41

Sales (units)           300,000     Sales (units)           300,000

Revenue              $4,200,000     Revenue              $4,200,000
Cost of Goods Sold                  Cost of Goods Sold
  Materials             720,000       Materials             792,000
  Labor                 975,000       Labor               1,023,000
Total CGS             1,695,000     Total CGS             1,815,000
                      ----------                          ----------
Gross Profit         $2,505,000     Gross Profit         $2,385,000

Expenses                            Expenses
  Administration        252,000       Administration        252,000
  Sales                  42,000       Sales                  42,000
  Advertising           350,000       Advertising           350,000
                        -------                             -------
Total Expenses         $644,000     Total Expenses         $644,000

Profit Before Taxes  $1,861,000     Profit Before Taxes  $1,741,000
Taxes (@52%)            967,720     Taxes (@52%)            905,320
                     ==========                          ==========
Net Profit             $893,280     Net Profit             $835,680
```

Figure 1.2 Spreadsheets Showing "What If?" Analysis

1.3 *THE MANAGEMENT SCIENCE PROCESS*

The management science process provides managers with a quantitative basis for problem solving. This systematic approach, which closely parallels the scientific method, follows an ordered set of steps.

1. observation
2. problem definition/classification
3. model formulation/construction
4. data selection/preparation
5. solution
6. validation/analysis
7. implementation

Figure 1.3 compares the decision making process and the scientifc method. Each of the steps will be analyzed individually.

Observation

Management science is problem oriented. The decision making/problem solving process is initiated with the recognition of the problem. Recall from a previous discussion of problem solving that problems are not necessarily the result of a crisis situation. A problem is recognized whenever there is a substantial difference between expectation and realization. The system must be continuously, closely, and

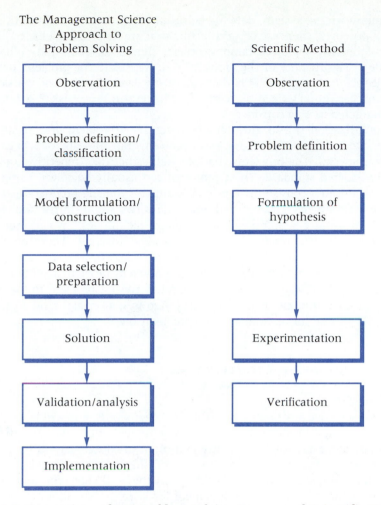

Figure 1.3 Comparison of MS Problem-Solving Process and Scientific Method

consistently observed so that a problem can be recognized and identified as soon as it occurs or is anticipated. This is important, since not all problem situations are reactive. Observation can be relatively easy, involving, for example, visitations and/or conferences with department heads. Or it can be difficult and complex, involving research and data gathering to monitor the systems. However observation is handled, it is an important step, requiring management to recognize the importance of observing and monitoring the system.

Problem Definition/Classification

An improperly defined problem can easily result in an inappropriate or incorrect solution. Definition is a way of conceptualizing or seeing a problem, a way of distinguishing the problem from its symptoms. In definition, the parameters of the problem are clearly recognized and established. Defining a problem requires defining the system, the purpose or objective to be achieved, and any constraints or limitations that have to be considered. With some complicated problems, having many interrelated parts, this is often a difficult step. However, in the process of observing and monitoring a system, data are being gathered that can help in this definition step. Moreover, there are certain factors that are helpful in defining the problem. The following questions among others, should be answered. What is the magnitude or significance of the problem? Can we isolate the problem area? What is the objective to be achieved? Is there any time dependency to be considered? Is the system best characterized as "certain," "uncertain," or "risk"? Are there any special characteristics to consider?

Conceptualization is also an attempt to identify a problem and an attempt to classify it into a definable category. Most problems fall into one of two categories, standard or special. The problems that are well-structured, repetitive, or are routine are considered standard. These problems can usually be solved using a series of routinely repeated consistent steps. For example, monthly production schedules, sales route assignments, and optimal order quantities are all fairly standard problems that can usually be handled with standard techniques. Special problems are those that are ill-structured, nonrecurrent, and/or different. These problems are not generally solved using a standard technique. Classification of standard problems also requires identifying the specific prototype or problem solving technique. Definition and classification is not an attempt to twist a problem to make it conform to a given technique. It is a necessary step in conceptualizing a problem so that a model can be formulated and the problem solved.

Model Formulation/Construction

Models—Definition and Type

A model is a selective abstraction of reality. In other words, a model is a representation that simplifies, idealizes, and abstracts some real entity. We are all familiar with models. Some are used frequently and often unconsciously in basic problem solving situations. Models come in all sizes and shapes, and in varying degrees of accuracy and complexity such as the chart on the wall that represents the fund raising goal achieved, the Income Statement for last year, the diorama of the Civil War battle, Einstein's theorem $e = mc^2$, the scale drawing of the kitchen to be redecorated, and the mental picture of our perfect job. These models all have something in common. They simplify reality by ignoring or assuming away irrelevant, extraneous factors. Moreover, they help us to better understand a problem.

Several different kinds of models exist, with varying degrees of abstraction. However, they all belong to one of three basic types or forms: iconic, analog, or mathematical (listed in progressive degree of abstraction). An **iconic model** is a physical representation of a real object. A child's model car, the scale model mockup of a newly designed airplane used in testing, the scale drawing of a room, the Civil War diorama, and a photograph, are all everyday examples of iconic models. An **analog model** is also physical in form. However, it does not have the same physical appearance as the object being modeled. Instead, it substitutes one property for another to convey meaning and can represent dynamic situations statically. Among the most commonly recognized analog models are the speedometer, with the needle position representing speed, and a thermometer representing temperature. The fund raising chart, a diagram of the problem solving process, and a flow chart representing a program or process are also analog models. **Mathematical** or **symbolic models** attempt to represent reality by means of symbols and mathematical relationships, that is, by equations and other mathematical statements. An equation showing the relationship between rate of pay, hours worked, and wages ($W = r \times H$), where W represents wages, r represents hourly rate of pay, and H represents hours worked is a very simple mathematical model. Mathematical models create the framework within which problems can be analyzed. The mathematical symbols and expressions can be manipulated in ways that the actual problem components cannot. By studying and analyzing the model, conclusions about the real situation can be drawn.

Mathematical models are classified as **descriptive** or **normative**. Descriptive models, representing a relationship, but not indicating any course of action, are useful in predicting the behavior of a system. They do not identify the best course of action, only what is likely to happen. The simple wage relationship is a descriptive model. Normative models prescribe the course of action that should be undertaken to achieve the defined objective. These model are optimization models and are prescriptive. A transportation model that gives the best or optimum number of units to ship from each source to each destination, from among several sources and destinations, in order to minimize transportation costs is a normative model.

Within these two classifications, there are several subclassifications into which models are usually categorized: deterministic versus stochastic; linear versus nonlinear; static versus dynamic; or simulation models. These classifications will be discussed in later chapters.

Constructing or Building a Model

Model building is as much art as it is science, requiring the difficult task of balancing simplicity with accuracy. It demands understanding the problem well enough to be able to abstract it to a mathematical form, one that is detailed enough to represent the essential components and at the same time simple enough to be manageable.

There are no kits, no rules or set of instructions for building a quantitative model. There are no lists of component parts that must be included, no one way that always works, and not necessarily only one way to construct a model for a particular problem. There are some guidelines that can be useful. However, even these are more helpful for certain types of problems than for others.

Once the model has been conceptualized and verbally defined, building the model becomes a matter of abstracting this definition into mathematical symbols and relationships. Once we understand that the model has to represent the interrelated parts of the problem, we can think in terms of what exactly those parts are and just how they are related. The model should indicate the outcome or objective being sought, designate those unknown quantities that are to be determined in the solution (the decision variables), and selectively describe the environment.

The model builder, therefore, first has to designate several sets of variables. (1) **Decision variables** represent the unknown quantities that are to be determined in the solution. These are independent variables that are controllable by the decision maker, and represent factors where a choice must be made. The decision maker can manipulate these factors. They are usually denoted by any letter of the alphabet, A, B, C, X, ... or by a letter with a subscript, X_1, X_2, X_3, etc. The coefficients for these decision variables are called **parameters**, and they describe the relationship between the decision variables. For example $20X = 45Y$ shows the value of X relative to the value of Y. They remain constant for the problem. (2) **Uncontrollable variables** represent factors that affect the result, but are not under the control of the decision maker. These are generally independent environmental inputs that cannot be manipulated or specified by the decision maker. For example, tax laws and prices set by suppliers are out of the control of the decision maker. Frequently uncontrollable variables take the form of parameters in the model. (3) **Dependent variables** represent the outcome, output, or objective to be achieved. They are subject to or dependent upon the occurrence of another event or the value of another variable. In the equation $Y = 5X^2 - 10X + 35$, Y is dependent upon the value of X.

The model builder also has to show the structure of the model. The components that have been expressed as variables have to be tied together by sets of mathematical expressions (equations or inequalities) to form a system. Figure 1.4 shows the structure of a model.

Additonally, the model builder has to show the mathematical relationships in the model. In many managerial models these relationships include two parts, the **objective function** and the **constraints**. The objective function defines the effectiveness of the model as a function of the decision variables. In other words, the objective function expresses the outcome or objective variable (dependent variable) as it relates to the decision variables (indenpendent variables). For instance, $R = aX + bY$ is an objective function showing the revenue (R) achieved from the sale of two products (X and Y), each sold at a different price (a and b).

Constraints express the limitations or restrictions that occur in the problem. That is, constraints show the restrictions imposed on the system that limit the permissible (feasible) values that the decision variables can take. Constraints ensure that the solution satisfies the uncontrollable, environmental factors dictated by the problem. For instance, in the revenue example, there could be a production restriction that limits the quantity that can be produced. The equation $X < 50$ means that fewer than 50 units of product X could be manufactured. A sales study that indicates that no more than 75 units of both X and Y can be sold in the given time period can be represented as $X + Y \leq 75$.

The problem definition stage usually identifies each of these verbally. The success of the quantitative approach to problem solving depends on how accurately these elements can be expressed mathematically and how well they can be tied together by sets of mathematical expressions.

Once the model has been constructed, it has to be validated. The validity of a model indicates how well it represents reality. It is necessary to discover whether

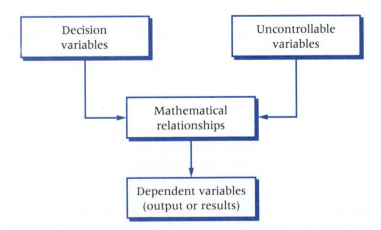

Figure 1.4 Model Structure

the model is internally correct. Validation will be discussed after the solution procedure is described.

Data Selection/Preparation

Data selection is both a continuation of a process that was begun with monitoring the system and observing a problem and also a separate, distinct step. It is imperative to recognize that the management science problem solving approach is a process and not just a set of distinct and separate steps. Data are collected from records, meetings, data banks, studies, and so on. From this mass, the data appropriate to or required by the model must be selected and/or prepared. The data that are to be selected refer to the values of the uncontrollable inputs, all of which must be specified before the model can be analyzed and solved. When these input values are not readily available, usually with large problems, the model is developed using a standard notation (symbols) to represent these variables and the data collection will indeed be a separate step. Data collection is not a trivial step that can be relegated to a clerical staff. It is a critical part of quantitative analysis, and the possibility for error in data collection, especially for a problem involving hundreds of decision variables and thousands of data elements, is great. An error in the data resulting in an incorrect solution can be costly.

Solution

Finding a solution to the model and therefore, probably to the problem, means determining the values for the decision variables, which achieve the desired objective or output level. Therefore, the decision makers have to specify or define an acceptable output level and select a solution process that will achieve that output level. We have to emphasize once again that solution procedures to standard problems (the ones we will be dealing with) are already well developed. Computer codes exist that solve these problems quickly and accurately. Most techniques introduced in this text have a corresponding computer solution. However, we are discussing solution processes and desirable outputs because it is important to understand some of the concepts and methodologies involved in order to better understand what is happening. This is especially important when it comes to understanding and using computer results.

Solutions are generally classified as follows: **feasible**, those that satisfy all the requirements and constraints of the system, versus **infeasible**, those violating one or more of these restrictions; **optimal**, best possible solution, versus **nonoptimal**; **unique**, the only existing optimal solution, versus **multiple**, having two or more optimal solutions that can be identified. Each is discussed as it applies in succeeding chapters.

Solution Techniques

Solution processes and procedures can be separated into one of four categories: (1) complete enumeration, (2) algorithms, (3) heuristics, and (4) simulation. Complete **enumeration** involves checking every possible value of the decision variables, to find the optimal solution which is a time consuming, tedious, and frequently an impossible approach. Algorithms provide a set of procedures, a step-by-step process, for finding the optimal solution. An **algorithm** is a progressive trial-and-error approach that checks only a portion of the feasible solutions, improving each solution until the best one is found. An algorithm is developed for a given model and will usually work only in solving a problem with those specific characteristics. Both complete enumeration and algorithms attempt to find an optimal solution. The **heuristic** process is a step-by-step procedure that relies on logical (empirical or intuitive) rules to arrive at a "good enough" solution. This process moves from one solution point to another, following the search rule being used, in such a way that the model objective, or the solution is improved with each move. When no further improvement can be made, an approximate solution has been achieved. Heuristics are usually used on extremely complex problems and depend on the specific problem. A **simulation** imitates the behavior of the problem for a given, defined set of input conditions. In an attempt to analyze a problem in order to determine the best course of action, not necessarily the optimal solution, model behavior is studied under varying inputs. A solution that provides the desired level of results is then selected. Heuristics and simulations provide nonoptimal or approximate solutions. Figure 1.5 shows another way of classifying solution techniques. Some solution techniques can be classified in more than one way. The categories are not mutually exclusive. Furthermore, this table is not meant to be all inclusive.

Output Levels

The decision maker must select a solution procedure that can achieve the output or result level desired. What is being sought? Do we want the very best solution or will any acceptable solution be good enough? This decision regarding the acceptability of a result level, frequently referred to as "**principle of choice**," is important to us. It can help in the selection of a solution procedure. We are interested in the decision to attain either an optimal solution, or a satisfactory (good enough) solution.

Optimization, attaining the best of all possible alternatives, requires examining all alternatives and proving that the one selected gives the best results. Optimization prescribes a course of action designed to attain the objective being sought. Normative models are designed to optimize objectives. While the term optimization is used, we are actually describing what is called **constrained optimization**. Most problems must be solved within certain limits or constraints. For example, production may be limited by plant capacity, or machines can be scheduled for a maximum of 24 hours per day. When we use the term optimization, we are discussing optimization within the limits imposed by the situation.

There are other limits on "optimal" solutions as well. A decision made in one sector of a system may significantly affect other areas. Using optimization requires the decision maker to consider the impact of each course of action on the entire system or organization. For example, reducing the number of repair parts held in stock may reduce the carrying costs for the maintenance department, thereby optimizing that department's cost cutting efforts. However, if production equipment is down for long periods of time while maintenance waits for parts, the money lost by the organization as a whole may more than offset the gains made by maintenance. An optimizing decision that has a greater negative impact on the rest of the organization is called **suboptimal** and the process of optimizing for one part of the organization without regard to the total organization is called **suboptimization**. While such a decision may be inferior or harmful, it is not necessarily so. It may provide a practical way to first approach a problem. After analyzing a subsystem and reaching a tentative conclusion or solution, management can then test its

Linear Programming	Network	Inventory	Stochastic	Special Purpose Algorithms	Nonlinear
Linear programming	Network flow models	Deterministic demand	Decision theory	Assignment models	Dynamic programming
Integer programming	PERT/CPM	Stochastic demand	Markov analysis	Transportation models	Calculus
Goal programming	Transshipment models	MRP	Queuing	Transshipment models	Nonlinear programming
Transshipment models	Transportation		Forecasting	Network flow models	EOQ Inventory models
Transportation	Assignment		Simulation		
			Game theory		
			Stochastic inventory models		

Figure 1.5 Management Science Techniques

effect on the system. If no significant dangers can be seen, the solution can be considered optimal for the system.

For solutions of the "good enough" type, the decision maker establishes a desired level to be achieved and then searches the alternatives to find one that meets this objective. For instance, a buyer searching for rental properties may have a list of desired factors, including condition, price, location, and income potential. The buyer then searches the available listings (the alternatives) to find one that satisfies his or her goals. If none exists, the buyer may have to change the level of aspiration. The alternative selected is not necessarily the optimal choice, since the decision maker is searching the system only for specific or given conditions. Those techniques described as descriptive use this principle of choice.

We have described optimal decisions and "good enough" decisions. It should be emphasized that optimal is not always "best" in practice. The solution to the problem is based on the solution to the model that was constructed to represent the problem. A model is not reality; a model is a selective representation of reality. The decision is best only within the limited confines of the model and no model can completely capture the real world. In addition, a decision is made and the problem is solved using both quantitative and qualitative factors. There are times when an optimum quantitative solution to a model may not be the right or best decision.

The reason may be the cost involved, difficulty of implementation, political factors, economic environment, or other factors. For example, firing the lazy clerk would be best for profits, but the manager knows that the clerk is the owner's favorite nephew. Based on experience or intuition, managers may decide to modify a quantitative solution to arrive at what they consider a better, more practical decision.

Validation/Analysis

Once a model is capable of yielding a solution, the model must be **validated**. The model has to be tested to see how well it represents reality. Several procedures can be used to accomplish this step. The decision maker can examine the results from several inputs to see if they are reasonable or logical, based on experience. A model can also be tested using a small sized problem, which has known or expected solutions. Frequently, a problem or information from a prior situation is used and the results compared with what actually occurred. If the model does not provide satisfactory results, adjustments must be made.

Another way of analyzing a model and testing its usefulness and accuracy is to alter the inputs to the model and observe what happens to the output. This is a very general description of **sensitivity analysis**, a way of doing a "what if?" analysis (what happens if . . .). The purpose of sensitivity analysis is to determine the effect of changes in the input (independent variables) on the output (the dependent variables). Sensitivity analysis will be discussed in later chapters.

Implementation

The problem solving process does not end with the decision or solution generated by the model. Problem solving includes implementing the decision. Frequently this is an extremely difficult process. The new procedure often meets with resistance which is the result of reluctance to change, misunderstanding, and/or mistrust. All of the issues discussed under "best decision" are also at work here. The model builder and the decision maker must work together from the beginning to be sure all conditions are defined and all assumptions are understood. The entire process should be well-documented. Implementation requires good communication throughout the entire process. It may also require user education and a publicity campaign to keep management informed. Actual implementation also requires a feedback mechanism for evaluation.

1.4 *THE USE OF THE MANAGEMENT SCIENCE PROCESS AND TECHNIQUES*

In the preceding sections, we emphasized that management science provides a logical, systematic framework for making decisions and solving problems. We have also indicated that it is neither universally applicable nor always the decision making method of choice. We need to examine, once again, the specific strengths and limitations of management science.

Management science is useful primarily because it forces decision makers to approach a problem in a rational and consistent manner. Problems are required to be clearly defined, not only to explicitly identify the objective being sought and the decision variables that influence the objective, but also to analyze and define all the interactions and interrelationships between the variables. It encourages communication within the organization and better monitoring of the system. Using models can be less costly, because the experimentation is performed on and with models and not on the actual system. Solutions are quickly and accurately generated by computer, and the best available solution can often be more readily identified. The MS process and the computer solutions allow large numbers of alternatives to be examined relatively inexpensively, and provides for easier "what if" types of analysis of the solution.

The use of management science is limited because (1) there are questions concerning how well a model which simplifies complex situations can represent reality, (2) the cost of developing and implementing a model may outweigh the savings gained by using the model. Many managerial decision making situations can be handled without the use of sophisticated models, and (3) there may be a lack of acceptance or understanding by some decision makers.

Real World Use of Management Science

Is management science a collection of tools or an applied math course taught in colleges and universities but ignored in the real world? Table 1.1 shows the result of a study by Shannon, Long, and Buckles,[2] in which practitioners from government, industry, and academia were asked to indicate both familiarity with and usage of various quantitative methods.

As can be seen from the survey, not all management science techniques are equally used by organizations. Indeed, not all MS techniques are equally useful. A more recent study, a survey of corporate executives, conducted in 1983 by

Table 1.1 Survey Results Showing Familiarity with, Usefulness, and Usage of Management-Science Techniques

Technique	Familiarity Rank	Utility Rank	% Usage
Linear Programming	1	2	83.8%
Simulation	2	1	80.3
Network Analysis	3	4	58.1
Queuing Theory	4	7	54.7
Decision Trees	5	3	54.7
Integer Programming	6	6	38.5
Replacement Analysis	10	5	38.5
Dynamic Programming	7	11	32.5
Markov Processes	9	10	31.6
Nonlinear Programming	8	9	30.7
Goal Programming	12	8	20.5
Game Theory	11	12	13.7

[2]Shannon, R. E., S. S. Long, and B. P. Buckles. "Operations Research Methodologies in Industrial Engineering: A Survey." Reprinted from *AIIE Transactions*, Volume 12 No. 4. Copyright Institute of Industrial Engineers, 25 Technology Park/Atlanta, Norcross, GA 30092.

Table 1.2 Survey Results Showing Frequency of Use of Management-Science Techniques

Technique	Frequent or Moderate Use (% of Respondents)
Statistical Analysis	98.4%
Computer Simulation	87.1
CPM/PERT	74.2
Linear Programming	74.2
Queuing Theory	59.7
Nonlinear Programming	46.8
Dynamic Programming	38.7
Game Theory	30.6

Forgionne,[3] provides results similar to the earlier Shannon, Long, and Buckles study. The results as presented in Table 1.2 indicate the frequency of use of eight techniques.

It appears from these surveys that the most frequently used management science techniques are simulation, linear programming, and PERT/CPM (network analysis). A more recently published longitudinal study conducted over a ten-year period also showed that OR practitioners found statistical analysis, computer simulation, and linear programming to be among the four most useful quantitative techniques.[4] Obviously, there is value in learning these specific mangement science techniques. However, we emphasize that management science is not merely a collection of tools and mathematical techniques. Rather it provides an approach to problem solving. Studying the techniques, even the ones with limited applicability, may offer clues, valuable insights, or unique ways of approaching a problem.

1.5 *CONCLUDING REMARKS: THE MANAGER REVISITED*

The manager is responsible for making the final, best decision. Management science provides an approach and some tools to help managers make better decisions. While the focus of this text is on specific, simplified problem situations, and uses certain standard techniques and computer-based tools, it is not intended to present MS and the quantitative approach as a substitute for good management. The manager uses the quantitative output as one part of the total data used in making the decision. MS offers a framework in which to make these decisions. The MS approach requires the manager to help define and conceptualize the problem situation, evaluate the model being used, and then interpret the results. In making the final decision, this result has to be considered and combined with more subjective factors, for example, intuition and executive judgement, to arrive at a best decision.

[3]Reprinted by permission of G. Forgionne, "Corporate Management Science Activities: An Update," *Interfaces*, 13(3), June 1983. Copyright 1983 The Institute of Management Sciences, 290 Westminster Street, Providence, RI 02903.
[4]Reprinted by permission of John L. Harpell, Michael S. Lane, and Ali H. Mansour. "Operations Research in Practice: A Longitudinal Study," *Interfaces*, 19, May–June 1989. Copyright 1989, The Institute of Management Sciences.

CITGO PETROLEUM CORPORATION[5]

In 1983, Citgo Petroleum Corporation was acquired by Southland Corporation as part of Southland's effort to integrate vertically. Citgo is one of the nation's largest industrial companies, with 1985 sales in excess of $4 billion. Through its 7-Eleven convenience stores, Southland retails over two billion gallons of gasoline per year. Southland was determined to establish management priorities and procedures that would make Citgo successful in the downstream petroleum business (refining and marketing), and at the same time supply its 7-Eleven stores with quality motor fuels. Success would require transforming Citgo from an integrated oil company which produced its own crude oil to an independent refiner and marketer of petroleum products. This would mean fundamentally changing the basis for Citgo's decision making, making it more responsive to the market and less driven by the refining of crude oil. To accomplish this, Southland management first established Citgo as a wholly-owned subsidiary with full debt load both to insure that Citgo would make a profit independent of Southland's gasoline retailing business and to provide economic survival as a basic motivation for improvements in their operation. Second, Southland created a task force charged with the task of holistically exploring ways to improve Citgo's profitability.

The task force began in August 1983 with an evaluation of the downstream petroleum industry. The task force concluded that as a result of certain environmental changes that had been occurring during the past 15 years, the industry was in the midst of an information explosion. Among the changes and the consequences noted were (1) an increased emphasis on making a profit from downstream operations. This profit objective requires addressing such issues as which markets to serve, how to serve them, what products to sell, what price to charge, and where to buy the product—all of which require much more data and better management science tools. (2) a number of new sources of crude oil and refined product, including significant amounts bought on spot markets and crude purchased on the futures market. Petroleum companies need to keep track of many potential sources of crude and product, which requires good decision support systems. (3) the price-volume relationship becoming more elastic as the commodity nature of the product is increasing and marketing power is shifting from the refiner to the wholesale distributor. Therefore, to generate day-to-day profits requires gathering and analyzing large amounts of information in order to control terminal inventories and coordinate refinery production and product purchases. (4) the cost of financing working capital, which increased dramatically (20 to 40-fold) since 1972. This significantly altered the cost of supplying product to a customer and made the difference between making a profit or showing a loss in the high-volume, low-profit margin downstream industry. To reduce working capital, inventories had to be reduced and credit terms had to be tightened. These changes increased decision making needs. The industry-

[5]Reprinted by permission of Darwin Klingman, Nancy Phillips, David Steiger, and Warren Young, "The Successful Deployment of Management Science throughout Citgo Petroleum Corporation," *Interfaces*, 17, January–February 1987. Copyright 1989, The Institute of Management Sciences.

wide information explosion works to overload the decision making capabilities of many downstream companies and provide a competitive edge to those companies able to harness it. As a result of this industry evaluation, the task force adopted two interrelated goals: (1) to provide Citgo decision makers with the best possible management science tools to gather and analyze the information required for economically rational decision making. (2) to identify and implement the organizational changes necessary for utilizing management science effectively.

With these goals in mind, the task force, working with Citgo's management, identified both the areas where harnessing the information explosion could be significantly beneficial (a total of $55 to $60 million per year) and the tools that could be used to realize this potential profit improvement. In 1984–1985, the task force developed various strategies that involved combining profit center focus, mathematical programming, organizational theory, artificial intelligence, expert systems, decision support systems, and forecasting techniques with the latest information systems technologies.

Among the areas identified for implementing organizational changes and mangement science tools were the crude oil acquisition and refining areas. As with many integrated oil companies, the refinery was operated using a strategy of minimizing incremental costs as opposed to optimizing profit. The task force wanted to establish procedures, tools, and an organizational culture based on economically rational decision making, which would involve manufacturing for profit. The actions taken by the task force to improve decision-making capabilities and reduce costs were rooted in the conviction that refining is an information-processing activity. Therefore, the task was to establish data highways for both data acquisition and dissemination and data repositories for convenient access to all data, and then to fuse the data and data gathering systems with management science techniques to provide accurate, timely, and useful information for decision making. After determining the major operating costs, it was recognized that the best tool for helping management control the three largest operating costs is a refinery linear programming (LP) system. However, the quality of the decision information provided depends not only on the quality of the model and its use, but also on the quality of the input data. An audit to determine the quality of Citgo's refinery LP system and its associated data revealed many weaknesses in both the data and the refinery LP system. Much of the data on costs, unit yields, and crude assays were inaccurate and out of date. Steps to correct this included creation of a physical measurement data base using a modern data base management system and replacing the optimization software in the refinery LP system with IBMs MPSX linear programming system for optimization. Next the LP model itself was carefully evaluated to determine where it could be improved, resulting in the addition of several enhancements. The new model was validated and calibrated and ultimately recalibrated and completed. The refinery LP system is now used routinely to provide critical decision information in several areas, including crude selection and acquisition economics, refinery run levels and product component production levels.

Additional mangement-science tools and organizational changes implemented in the manufacturing area included: process control equipment and nonlinear optimization models to measure and optimize energy utilization; procedures to evaluate operator performance and train operators on the process control equipment; a maintenance information system at the refinery; and a PC-based scheduling system to schedule delivery and distribution of crude oil from the storage tank farm into the refinery. As a result of these changes in the manufacturing area, the Lake Charles refinery is highly versatile and efficient. The refinery is highly flexible, and production runs can be tailored to meet the market conditions. Citgo management estimates that the overall benefits of the manufacturing changes coupled with effective mangement usage were approximately $50 million in 1985.

A second area identified by the task force for the application of new tools and organizational changes was in strategic and operational market planning. The task force developed a system called TRACS (Tracking, Reporting, and Aggregation of Citgo Segmented Sales) to evaluate the profitability of existing markets. TRACS is a sophisticated data base management system coupled with rule-based artificial intelligence which provides an economic comparison between potential selling options and distribution channels. The task force also applied new tools and concepts for information gathering and analysis in market planning. Prior to the implementation of the new management-science tools, each department collected, organized, and stored its own operational data. As a result, different departments often made operational decisions that were nonoptimal or even conflicting. To begin the process of breaking down departmental information walls, a corporate-wide, on-line production acquisition and supply system (PASS) was developed. PASS is a management data base implemented using a state-of-the-art data base management system, ADABAS, was developed. PASS contains up-to-date operational information on such items as sales, inventory, trades, and exchanges for all refined products, past, present, and future. Since PASS provided an amount of information too massive to be fully analyzed by one decision maker or a group of decisoin makers, the task force developed the SDM system, an optimization-based supply, distribution, and marketing model in order to use this data to make economically rational decisons. The system is used by top mangagement to make many operational decisions, such as where to sell products, what price to charge, where to buy or trade product, how much product to hold in inventory, and how much product to ship by each mode of transportation.

The refinery LP system and the SDM system, which are linked together by the spot price forecast, serve as the primary corporate operational-planning tools, providing information about material balances and make or buy planning that is based on forecasts and operational data. In addition, they provide a holistic view of the corporation from crude acquisition through product sales. These systems and their associated data bases provide management with accurate and timely data and powerful planning support.

Several organizational changes were made to facilitate the cross-functional coordination and implementation of the operational tools recommended by the task force. These included creating and filling new positions, and departments to improve communication and coordination of information flow.

Finally, the task force analyzed Citgo's cash flow cycle to determine the most effective tools to gather and analyze information to help control working capital. Analysis indicated a significant potential for savings associated with the selection and purchase of products and crude oils. Both the LP model and the SDM model provide detailed and integrated information on optimal quantities and qualities to be purchased. The control of product and crude oil payables was improved by the incorporation of a payable float optimization system into the corporate payables system. In addition, since terminal inventories and exchange imbalances represent the largest component of Citgo's working capital, the task force implemented the TRACS system and the SDM optimization models to provide management with the necessary control information. These systems helped management reduce product inventories by $116 million.

The benefits of these integrated information-gathering systems, data base management systems, forecasting models, optimization-based decision support systems, artificial-intelligence-based evaluation systems, and organizational changes have been numerous. They include improved communication and coordination between supply, distribution, marketing, and refining groups; improved data; reduced inventories; elimination of unnecessary product terminals; improved management of exchange agreements and purchase/sale/trade agreements; added insights into pricing strategies; better forecasts; and economically rational decision making. Citgo management estimates that the effective usage of these tools improved marketing profits by $2.5 million and refining profits by $50 million in 1985. Working capital requirements were reduced by $150 million, with resulting reduced interest expenses of approximately $18 million. The total dollar benefits in 1985 were approximately $70 million.

GLOSSARY

algorithm systematic solution procedure; a sequence of well-defined steps leading to a solution

analog model physical model that does not have the same physical appearance as the object being modeled; substitutes one property for another

constrained optimization obtaining the best possible solution, given restrictions or limitations imposed on the system; optimization of the objective subject to constraints

constraints limitations or restrictions that occur in a problem, i.e., constraints show the restrictions imposed on the system that limit the permissible (feasible) values the decision variables can take; mathematical statement (equality or inequality) representing requirements or restrictions that must be met

decision variables unknown quantities to be determined in the solution of a problem; variables or factors under the control of the decision maker

dependent variables subject to or dependent upon the occurrence of another event or the value of another variable

descriptive model models that represent a relationship, but do not indicate any course of action, they do not identify a "best" course of action but rather describe how a system operates

enumeration numerical solution technique that involves checking every possible value of the decision variables, to find the optimal solution

feasible solution a solution satisfying all the requirements and constraints of the system; an allowable decision

heuristic a procedure that relies on logical (empirical or intuitive) rules to arrive at a "good enough" solution

iconic model physical representation of a real object

independent variables unknowns that are not dependent on value of another variable

infeasible solution a solution violating one or more of the system's constraints; not acceptable

management science a rational, systematic approach to problem solving/decision making; a quantitative approach that can be used to make better decisions

mathematical model system of mathematical symbols and expressions representing a real situation

model an abstraction of reality; simplified representation of a real object or situation

multiple optimal solutions having two or more optimal solutions that can be identified; also referred to as alternate optimal solutions

nonoptimal solution any feasible solution that is not optimal

normative model a model that prescribes the course of action that should be undertaken to achieve the defined objective

objective function mathematical relationship representing the objective of a problem; measures the effectiveness of proposed solutions

operations research application of scientific approach to managerial decision making; here, basically the same as management science

optimal solution the best possible solution

optimization finding the best possible solution

parameters the coefficients of the decision variables, constants that describe the relationship among the decision variables and whose values govern the particular solution to a problem

principle of choice criterion used to determine the acceptability of a result level

sensitivity analysis the manner in which output (solution) is affected by changes in the input (independent variables); a way of doing a "what if?" analysis (what happens if . . .)

simulation an imitation of reality; a mathematical replication that will act like a real situation in certain specified respects

suboptimization selection of solution that is best possible one for a subsystem but not necessarily for the entire system

system a set of elements that are related in such a way as to form a whole, i.e., a unit, comprised of interrelated parts that are intended to accomplish a specific objective

uncontrollable variables independent variables, representing factors that affect the result, but which are not under the control of the decision maker; usually environmental factors

unique solution the only existing optimal solution

validation process of testing a model to see how well it represents reality and to make sure the results are correct

REVIEW QUESTIONS

1. Describe the decison-making process and discuss the manager's role in making decisions. Give an example of a decision that can be quantified and one that is primarily a qualitative decision.
2. How would you define a managerial problem? How or when can a managerial problem be recognized?

3. What is the difference between decision making and problem solving?
4. Define the term management science.
5. What are the chief characteristics of the management science approach?
6. How can the scientific method be applied to management science, which is not a pure science and whose environment cannot be controlled in a laboratory situation?
7. How does the "systems approach" apply to management science? What are the advantages of adopting this systems perspective in making decisions?
8. We have given an ordered set of steps for the management science problem solving process. What are they?
9. What is the importance of the problem definition stage in this process?
10. Give an explanation of the term model and explain the difference between the three types described in the text.
11. How is the model used in solving problems? What does it mean to "solve a model"?
12. Explain how a model is constructed, including a discussion of component parts, structure, and relationships.
13. What is meant by objective function? Constraints? How are decision variables and objective function related? What is meant by constrained optimization? Give an example.
14. Distinguish between model results that recommend a decision and model results that are descriptive. Discuss the concept of a "best" solution. What is the role of the manager in making the decision?
15. Why is it necessary to specify a desired result level? Give an example that illustrates the difference between optimization and suboptimization.
16. What is the difference between numerical and analytical solution techniques? Give an example of each.
17. What is an algorithm?
18. What does "validate a model" mean? Describe ways that this can be done.
19. What is implementation?
20. What are some factors that limit the use or application of management science?

Linear Programming: Introduction and Model Formulation

By the end of this chapter, you should be able to:

1

recognize that for a given problem the underlying assumptions of
an LP problem have been met, and the problem can be solved using
linear programming;

2

analyze the problem, verbally defining the objective function and
the constraints;

3

formulate simple LP models from example problems.

In this chapter we introduce one of the most useful and frequently used problem solving tools, linear programming (LP). This introduction includes both a discussion of the requirements and underlying assumptions of a linear programming problem and a description of the structure of an LP problem. Further, expanding upon the Chapter 1 introduction to model building, we present a more detailed and specific description of the LP model and its formulation. We have included several example problems that not only demonstrate the modeling process, but also provide an opportunity, through practice and repetition, to become familiar and comfortable with formulating LP models.

Turbo Inc.

Turbo Inc. is a small machining company that produces multiblade impellers used in pumps and blowers. George Milopolis, the production manager for Turbo, is preparing the production schedule for the coming month for two heavy-duty blower impellers. These impellers are machined from steel blanks and then heat treated for extra strength. One of the impellers also has a special teflon hub liner installed. George is having difficulty with the schedule this month. Normally, Turbo uses the orders received from manufacturers to determine the number of each type of impeller to produce. Recently, however, the company signed an agreement with a distributor to sell all impellers through that distributor. This will allow Turbo more flexibility, because the distributor has a larger market for both types of impellers. This means that George no longer schedules production just to fill orders and he is now free to produce any combination of these products. However, management has informed him that he should now attempt maximize the profit contribution on these products, even if it means producing only one type of impeller. In making this decision, George knows that production is limited by the amount of machining and heat treating time available for these products. He also knows that the teflon hub liners are available only in limited quantities. In addition, the contribution toward profit is different for each impeller type.

This is an example of a problem that can be solved using linear programming. We will return to this problem later in the chapter.

2.1 *AN INTRODUCTION TO LINEAR PROGRAMMING*

Linear programming is a mathematical solution technique that enables managers to make decisions concerning the best use of an organization's resources. It is used for the allocation of restricted or constrained resources in an attempt to achieve a single objective, that is, to solve the problem of allocating limited resources among competing activities in order to optimize some objective. LP is widely used by organizations wishing to maximize or minimize some quantity (such as profit or costs) in the presence of constrained resources that limit the pursuit of this objective. Such allocation problems are common in organizations and their solution can be extremely difficult because of the possibility of multiple solutions. LP offers an efficient way to reach an optimal solution in these problems.

The name, linear programming, does not refer to a computer program. Rather, it describes a direct and proportional relationship between two or more variables and a mathematical solution technique, consisting of a set of predetermined repetitive steps. LP is a component of a more generalized field of solution techniques, mathematical programming, and is frequently identified as a constrained optimization model.

Applications

LP is used by numerous diverse organizations, industrial, agricultural, military, and so on, for a broad range of applications. The most common and frequent use is in the area of product mix, involving the allocation of limited resources in the manufacture of selected products in order to either minimize cost or maximize profit. For example, George Milopolis must determine how many of each of two special impellers to manufacture in order to maximize Turbo's profit. The contribution toward profit varies for each impeller. Because each one has specific machining and heat treatment requirements, and the amount of time available for machining and heat treating is restricted, simply producing only the more profitable of the two impellers may not be optimal. Turbo might find the right combination (product mix) through trial and error, since it is a small problem. However, LP can be used more efficiently to find the optimal solution.

LP has also been used effectively in such widely diverse applications as media selection or marketing strategy, portfolio selection, assignment or labor problems, transportation problems, ingredient and blending problems, and goal planning. We will provide multiple example problems to demonstrate a variety of these uses.

2.2 *CHARACTERISTICS AND ASSUMPTIONS OF LINEAR PROGRAMMING PROBLEMS*

A linear programming problem must contain: (1) an objective to be achieved optimally (maximized or minimized); (2) resources that are constrained or in limited supply and need to be allocated among competing activities; (3) interaction between variables such that there are alternative courses of action or a variety of solutions available; (4) linearity or direct relationship among the variables, meaning that both the objective and the constraints can be stated mathematically as a linear function.

Assumptions

These characteristics imply specific, basic assumptions that are necessary for a problem to be categorized as an LP problem. If these conditions are not met, the problem cannot be formulated as an LP model and solved using linear programming. These assumptions limit the applicability of LP.

Basically, it is assumed (1) that there is a single goal, which can be stated verbally and represented mathematically as a linear objective function; (2) that the restrictions (constraints) are also linear; (3) that all the parameters are static and are known with certainty over the problem's time frame.

The assumption of certainty requires that exact values for all parameters be assigned. If the exact numerical values cannot be determined, reliable, informed estimates are often used. In the inequality $45X + 62Y \leq 450$, the parameters 45, 62, and 450 are constants. Their exact values are known. The inequality $c_1X + 62Y \leq 450$ could not be used because "c_1" is unknown.

The assumption of linearity requires that all coefficients are constants, all variables have an exponent of one, that there are no products or quotients of variables, and that there are no exponential, trigonometric, or logarithmic terms.

$$2X + 3Y = 45 \quad \text{is linear}$$

$$4XY = 65 \quad \text{is not linear}$$

$$16X^2 + 22Y = 246 \quad \text{is not linear}$$

Linearity describes a stable relationship between dependent and independent variables. A linear expression containing two variables can be expressed graphically by a straight line. For example, the linear expression

$$c_1\mathbf{x}_1 + c_2\mathbf{x}_2 = b$$

where

$$c_1, c_2 \quad \text{and} \quad b \quad \text{are constants}$$

$$\mathbf{x}_1 \quad \text{and} \quad \mathbf{x}_2 \quad \text{are decision variables}$$

represents a straight line.

The assumptions of additivity, divisibility, and proportionality (all properties of linearity) help clarify the meaning and implications of linearity. Additivity assumes that the total value of the objective function, or the total utilization of each resource, is equal to the sum of its component parts. For example, if it takes five hours to assemble one unit of product A and three hours to assemble one unit of product B, it takes eight hours of the resource assembly time to produce one unit of each product. The whole is equal to the sum of the parts. If A is a variable used to represent units of product A, and B is a variable used to represent units of product B, this relationship can be stated using the equation $5A + 3B = 8$.

Divisibility assumes that all of the unknown variables are continuous. This means that they can take any fractional value or assume any real value in a continuous range. For example, variable A can take any value along the continuum $5 \ldots 6$. Thus, A can be 5, 5.33, 5.465, 5.698, and so on. LP does not necessarily provide integer solutions. If integer solutions are required and simply rounding the LP solution to get an approximate (though maybe not optimal) solution is not satisfactory, there is another more appropriate technique, integer linear programming, which will be presented in a later chapter.

Proportionality requires that the value of the objective function, or of the resources utilized, is in direct proportion to the value of the decision variables (those variables whose value is being determined in the problem). For example, if it takes five hours of assembly time to assemble one unit of product A, it will take 20 hours of assembly time to assemble four units of product A and 500 hours to assemble 100 units. This means that there are no special start up costs or economies of scale that affect the value of the decision variable.

There is also a nonnegativity assumption disallowing negative variable values. For example, it is not possible to produce −4 units of a product. Values in LP problems must be greater than or equal to 0 (≥ 0).

2.3 *LINEAR PROGRAMMING MODEL FORMULATION*

Once a problem has been identified as a linear programming problem, an LP model must be built or formulated in order to eventually solve the problem. The model provides the means for analyzing and studying the problem and allows for the examination of various solutions. Being able to formulate the model indicates an understanding of the real problem. It means that the real problem can be stated in a way that can be analyzed and solved mathematically. Formulating the model simply means stating the problem in some standard form using mathematical symbols to represent the objective function and the constraints of the problem. Model formulation is an extremely important and absolutely essential initial step for problem solution, but it is often the most difficult step. It is by far more art than science, requiring human insight and reasoning. It is the step that has not yet been computerized. We will provide some guidelines and demonstrate the process with several examples. We will then give you problems for practice. Experience in formulating these models is an important factor in seeing and thinking through linear programming problems.

Components

An LP model consists of three components, decision variables, objective function, and constraints. These components were introduced earlier in general terms. These will now be described in greater detail.

Decision variables are those variables whose quantities are under the control of management, for example, units to be produced or resources to be allocated. The values of these variables are determined when the LP model is solved. The decision variables identify what is being sought in the problem. These must be correctly defined, since they identify what decisions must be made in order to achieve the objective.

The **objective function** is a mathematical statement of a single objective or goal to be achieved. It describes the goal as a linear relationship in terms of the decision variables. This goal will always be maximized or minimized. If Z is used to express profit and C to express cost, the following are examples of objective functions:

$$Z = \text{MAX } 5X_1 + 6X_2$$

$$Z = \text{MAX } 25X_1 + 36X_2 + 10X_3$$

$$C = \text{MIN } 89X_1 + 46X_2$$

In the remainder of this text, we will use the expression MAX $5X_1 + 6X_2$ in place of the more precise mathematical function.

Constraints are mathematical statements, in the form of linear equations and/or inequalities, which represent the restrictions in the problem. These constraints, which express resource limitations, quantity requirements, guidelines and regulations, and so on, are not controlled by management. The optimization of the objective function is achieved subject to these constraints. In the mathematical expression, all decision variables must be on the left-hand side and the constants must be on the right-hand side (which will be referred to in later chapters as RHS). Since, as we have stated previously, values in LP problems must be greater than or equal to 0 (nonnegative), it is also necessary, when modeling the problem, to include the nonnegativity constraints, expressed as $X_1, X_2 \geq 0$, rather than $X_1 \geq 0$ and $X_2 \geq 0$. Constraint statements take the form

Subject to

$$2X_1 + 3X_2 \leq 35$$

$$8X_1 + 7X_2 \leq 95$$

$$X_1 \qquad \geq 5$$

$$X_1, X_2 \geq 0$$

While the examples here show subscripted X as the variables, any variable names may be selected. In fact it may be helpful to select letters that are mnemonically meaningful, as we will show in the next section.

To help you get an understanding for these LP model components and for approaching an LP problem, we will demonstrate and explain in detail the formulation of an LP model for some example problems. These have been selected to familarize you with some of the applications of LP.

In constraints, all numbers greater than 999 are shown without commas. (For example, 45,000 will be shown as 45000.)

2.4 *LP DEMONSTRATION PROBLEMS AND APPLICATIONS*

For our first example, the Turbo problem is used. This is an example of a class of problems referred to as product mix problems.

A Product Mix Problem

Turbo produces multiblade impellers. George has to schedule the production of two special impellers, designated the Homeowner and the Professional. Production resources are limited and it is critical that profit from these two products be maximized. Each impeller is machined in the machining department and then heat treated for additional strength. Each Homeowner requires 1 hour of machining time and each Professional requires 2 hours. Each Homeowner must be heat treated for 4 hours and each Professional for 3 hours. Current production control figures show there are 80 hours of machining time available per day and the equivalent of 180 hours of oven time for heat treating. The Professional also requires a special teflon hub liner. Turbo can obtain a maximum of 36 of these teflon liners per day. The accounting department has informed George that each Homeowner contributes $15 per unit toward profit while each Professional contributes $12 per unit. George must use this information to decide how many of each impeller to produce.

Formulation

Analysis The first step in any formulation is to analyze the problem. In order to correctly formulate the problem, it is necessary to understand the problem and recognize the decision being made clearly enough to state the decision variables, objective function, and the constraints verbally. In this problem, George must decide how many of each impeller to manufacture each day in order to maximize profit. What is the objective? Turbo wishes to maximize its profit from the sale of the two impellers, the Homeowner at a per unit profit of $15 and the Professional at a per unit profit of $12. This is a statement of the objective (note, it is not a statement of the objective *function*). Later, we will restate this to make it a mathematical function. What are the decision variables? In this case George wishes to determine the number of units of the Homeowner impeller to produce daily and the number of units of the Professional impeller to produce daily.

The amount of time available for machining and heat treating the impellers is limited, and the supply of a part required by one of the impellers is restricted. Therefore, there are constraints on the system. There are only 80 hours of machining time available for production of impellers. This time must be allocated or divided between the two impeller models, each of which requires a different amount. It takes one hour of machining time for each Homeowner produced and two hours for each Professional. Furthermore, total available heat treatment time is limited to 180 oven hours, with each Homeowner requiring four hours in the oven and each Professional requiring three. Additionally, the special hub liner needed by the Professional is in short supply, with no more than 36 liners available per day. From these facts, it is possible to construct the constraint statements.

The decision variables In this case (as already shown) the decision variables are

H = The number of Homeowner impellers to be produced daily.

P = The number of Professional impellers to be produced daily.

The objective function The objective function should evaluate the profit potential of any proposed production mix. In this case, Turbo wishes to maximize profit from the sale of the Homeowner and the Professional impellers, which contribute $15 and $12 per unit, respectively, toward profit. Specifically, George wishes to determine how many of each model to produce daily in order to maximize profit. The daily profit from the Homeowner model can be represented by 15H (the per unit profit times the number of units produced). The daily profit from the Professional model can be represented by 12P (the per unit profit times the number of units produced). The total daily profit realized is the sum of these two, 15H + 12P. This statement will allow Turbo to evaluate any combination of impellers produced. Since Turbo wishes to maximize the profit, the objective function can be expressed as

$$\text{MAX } 15H + 12P$$

The constraints The limitations on the system have been shown to be limited availability of machine time, limited oven time for heat treatment, and a restricted supply of a required part.

Machining time Both impellers, Homeowner and Professional, require machining (one hour and two hours per unit, respectively). Total machining time used per day can not exceed 80 hours, that is, machining time ≤ 80. This is an inequality (less than or equal to), because it is not required that available machining time be used to capacity. On a daily basis, the Homeowner requires a total machining time of H hours (1H) and the Professional requires 2P hours. These are arrived at by multiplying the per unit time required by the number of units produced. The machining time constraint is the sum of these two times, not to exceed the 80 hours available. The machining constraint is expressed as

$$H + 2P \leq 80$$

Oven time for heat treatment Both impellers require heat treatment in ovens with a total time availability of 180 hours (≤ 180) per day. The Homeowner requires 4H hours of oven time (4 hours per unit times the number of units produced daily). The Professional requires a total of 3P oven hours (3 hours per unit times P units produced daily). Thus, the oven time constraint is stated

$$4H + 3P \leq 180$$

Restricted part availability Since the hub liners for the Professional are available only in a limited quantity (≤ 36), the number of units of the Professional produced per day is similarly restricted to 36 or fewer. This constraint is stated

$$P \leq 36$$

Nonnegativity constraint It is impossible to produce a negative number of impellers. However, it is possible to produce no units of either one or the other. Therefore, H and P must be nonnegative numbers. That is, H and P must have zero or positive values. This constraint is expressed

$$H \geq 0$$

$$P \geq 0$$

or

$$H, P \geq 0$$

In most computer programs available, the nonnegativity constraints are automatically included, and thus, do not have to be entered. However, it is a good idea to get in the habit of remembering to include them in the model formulation.

Final LP formulation In summary, the problem is to find the daily production plan that will maximize profit. Thus, the final model formulation for this problem is

$$MAX \quad H + 12P$$

subject to

$$H + 2P \leq 80 \quad \text{[machining]}$$
$$4H + 3P \leq 180 \quad \text{[heat treating]}$$
$$P \leq 36 \quad \text{[teflon hub liners]}$$
$$H, P \geq 0$$

In this formulation, notice that all decision variables are on the left-hand side (LHS) and all constants are on the right-hand side (RHS). Note also that all constraints do not have to be in the same terms or units of measure (dollars, hours, hub liners, etc.). However, for each specific constraint, the units on LHS and RHS must be consistent.

At this point, we are interested only in model formulation. Solution methodology will be discussed in future chapters. (However, it is a fairly simple matter to find the solution by using the LP program on the computer disk that accompanies this book.)

A Blending Problem

Door-2-Door Products blends its own all-purpose liquid cleanser, composed of three ingredients: detergent, ammonia, and lemon concentrate. Each gallon of cleanser must contain at least 10 percent but no more than 15 percent ammonia. In addition, each gallon must contain at least 2 percent but not more than 5 percent lemon concentrate. Door-2-Door estimates it will need 200,000 gallons of the cleanser to meet monthly demand. The cleanser is produced by blending bulk cleansers, which Door-2-Door obtains from two different suppliers. Supplier A sells Door-2-Door a cleanser which is 80 percent detergent and 20 percent ammonia for $1.10 per gallon. Supplier B sells a cleanser which is 90 percent detergent, 5 percent ammonia, and 5 percent lemon concentrate for $1.35 per gallon. Door-2-Door wants to minimize the cost of producing its cleanser. The firm's accountants have stated that production costs are relatively fixed and that the only variable costs are those of the ingredients used in its cleanser.

Formulation

Analysis In this problem, Door-2-Door must decide how much bulk cleanser to purchase from supplier A (at $1.10/gal) and how much bulk cleanser to purchase from supplier B (at $1.35/gal) in order to minimize the cost of blending their own cleanser. What is the objective? Door-2-Door wishes to minimize the cost of blending its own cleanser, which is made from two bulk cleansers, one costing $1.10 per gallon and one costing $1.35 per gallon. What is being sought? Door-2-Door wants to identify the amount of each bulk cleanser to purchase.

The constraints reflect the need to produce a specific number of gallons (200,000) and the requirement for product consistency (per gallon ammonia content between 10 and 15 percent and lemon concentrate content between 2 and 5 percent). Blending problems are sometimes a little more difficult to analyze and visualize than the simple product mix problem presented first. Table 2.1, shows the cost and composition of each bulk cleanser, and Figure 2.1, shows the problem graphically.

The decision variables For the Door-2-Door blending problem, the decision variables are

A = the quantity in gallons of bulk cleanser A (80% detergent, 20% ammonia) to purchase

B = the quantity in gallons of bulk cleanser B (90% detergent, 5% ammonia, 5% lemon) to purchase

The objective function Door-2-Door would like to pay as little as possible (minimize the cost) for the bulk cleansers used in making their own cleanser. The total cost is the sum of the individual costs. The cost of bulk cleanser A is its cost

Table 2.1 Cost and Composition per gallon

Bulk cleanser	Cost	Detergent (%)	Ammonia (%)	Lemon (%)
A	$1.10	80	20	0
B	$1.35	90	5	5

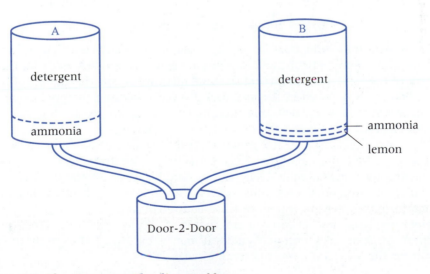

Figure 2.1 The Detergent Blending Problem

per gallon times the number of gallons purchased, \$1.10 times variable A (1.10A). The cost of bulk cleanser B then is \$1.35 times variable B (1.35B). Therefore, the objective function, to minimize total cost is expressed

$$\text{MIN } 1.10A + 1.35B$$

The constraints   The constraints on this system are 1. the amount that must be produced to meet demand for the month, 2. consistency requirements for ammonia, 3. consistency requirements for lemon concentrate.

The demand constraint   200,000 gallons of cleanser, blended from bulk cleanser A and bulk cleanser B, must be produced. Assuming that Door-2-Door will produce exactly 200,000 gallons, the constraint, an equality, is expressed

$$A + B = 200000$$

The ammonia requirement   Each gallon of Door-2-Door cleanser must contain at least 10 percent, but not more than 15 percent ammonia. This requires some thought. First, it might be easier to visualize this as two constraints, one requiring a minimum amount of ammonia ($\geq 10\%$), and one setting a maximum limit on the quantity of ammonia ($\leq 15\%$). Next, it is necessary to convert the per gallon ammonia requirement to its equivalent number of gallons in the total produced (200,000). For a product containing at least 10 percent ammonia, this would be at least 20,000 gallons ($\geq 20,000$). For a blend containing a maximum of 15 percent ammonia, this would be an amount not to exceed 30,000 gallons ($\leq 30,000$). It is also necessary to take into account that each bulk product contains a different percentage of ammonia (.20A and .05B) and only one of them, product B, contains lemon. This influences the decision in several ways. If only product B (the more expensive product) were used because it contains lemon, it would violate the requirement for a minimum of 20,000 gallons of ammonia (5 percent times 200,000 equals 10,000). Using all of product A (the less expensive product) will not work either. Not only does it not contain any lemon concentrate, but 20 percent of 200,000 exceeds 30,000 gallons, the maximum allowable amount of ammonia. These constraints can be expressed

$$.20A + .05B \geq 20000 \qquad \text{(minimum of 10\% ammonia)}$$

$$.20A + .05B \leq 30000 \qquad \text{(maximum of 15\% ammonia)}$$

These constraints could have been expressed in another way. The minimum amount of ammonia (10%) could have been written as $\geq .10(A + B)$ (at least 10 percent of the total quantity, where the total quantity equals the gallons of A and the gallons of B included in the mixture). However, because the production constraint was A + B = 200,000, this quantity can be substituted for the expression A + B, giving us $\geq .10(200,000)$ or $\geq 20,000$ (as shown).

The lemon requirement   Each gallon of Door-2-Door cleanser must contain at least 2 percent but not more than 5 percent lemon concentrate. Again, we convert this to the total gallon equivalency (2 percent of 200,000 = 4000). This is very similar to the ammonia constraints. However, only product B contains lemon and it contains only 5 percent lemon, which is equivalent to the maximum percentage of lemon the final product can contain, that is, if all product B were used, the upper limit on lemon concentrate would still not be exceeded. Thus, only the constraint for the lower limit has to be expressed

$$.05B \geq 4000$$

The nonnegativity constraints indicate that there can be no negative amounts of an ingredient in the cleanser.

$$A, B \geq 0$$

Final LP formulation The linear programming model for the Door-2-Door problem can be summarized

$$
\begin{array}{lll}
\text{MIN} & 1.10A + 1.35B & \\
\text{subject to} & & \\
& A + \quad B = 200000 & \text{[product demand]} \\
& .20A + .05B \geq 20000 & \text{[minimum ammonia]} \\
& .20A + .05B \leq 30000 & \text{[maximum ammonia]} \\
& \quad\quad .05B \geq 4000 & \text{[minimum lemon]} \\
& A, B \geq 0 &
\end{array}
$$

An Investment Problem

Mr. Rulan, investment manager for ABC Investment Company has up to $800,000 to invest in new "hi-tech" stock issues. Information on the four stocks ABC has selected for further consideration is summerized as follows:

Stock	Dividend	Expected growth (%)	Cost/Share
A	1.20	25	30
B	.50	22.5	40
C	1.05	24	35
D	0	30	50

Mr. Rulan knows that ABC desires to obtain the maximum possible growth in the dollar value (excluding dividends) of this portfolio over the coming year. The company also desires at least $20,000 in annual dividend income from this portfolio. In order to lessen the risk involved in the portfolio, it has been decided that dollars invested in stock D (considered a high-risk stock) cannot exceed 60 percent of the dollar amount invested in stock A (considered a low risk). Mr. Rulan, for personal reasons, wishes at least 10 percent of the total dollar investment be invested in stock B.

Formulation

Analysis ABC must decide how much, if any, of its $800,000 to invest in each of four different stocks in order to maximize growth, that is, ABC must decide how much to invest in stock A (expected growth of 25 percent), in stock B (an expected growth of 22.5 percent), in stock C (expected growth of 24 percent), and in stock D (expected growth of 30 percent) in order to achieve maximum growth in the dollar value of this portfolio. The objective is to maximize growth in the dollar value of this portfolio (each stock having a different expected growth), and ABC is seeking to identify how much to invest in each of the four stocks (what is the objective, and what is being sought?).

The constraints reflect company guidelines and restrictions for this investment, a requirement of a minimum dividend return ($\geq$ $20,000), a restriction on the investment in high-risk stock D (not to exceed 60 percent of the dollar investment in a low-risk stock A), and a requirement of a minimum purchase (number of shares $\geq$ 100) of stock B.

The decision variables   The four decision variables in this model, representing the dollar amount invested in each of the four alternative stocks, are

$$A = \text{the amount (\$) invested in stock A}$$

$$B = \text{the amount (\$) invested in stock B}$$

$$C = \text{the amount (\$) invested in stock C}$$

$$D = \text{the amount (\$) invested in stock D}$$

The objective function   The objective is to maximize the growth from the investment in the four alternative stocks. The total expected return in dollar amounts is the sum of the individual expected returns. The total return for each alternative is the dollar amount invested times the expected growth for that alternative. Therefore, the total expected return on an investment in stock A is .25A. In stock B, the total expected return is .225B, in stock C it is .24C, and .3D for stock D. The objective function, the total of these individual returns, is

$$\text{MAX } .25A + .225B + .24C + .3D$$

The constraints   The constraints on this system include the amount that is available for investment, the requirement of a minimum dividend return, the requirement that a minimum number of shares of a specific stock be purchased, and the restriction on the amount that can be invested in a high-risk stock relative to the amount invested in a low-risk stock.

The amount available for investment is $800,000. The sum of the amounts invested in the four alternatives must be less than or equal to $800,000 ($\leq$ 800000). The first constraint, then is expressed

$$A + B + C + D \leq 800000$$

The minimum dividend return constraint is not quite as straight forward. The total dividend is the sum of the individual dividends. This total must be at least $20,000 ($\geq$ 20,000). Dividends are figured by multiplying the dividend per share ($1.20, $.50, $1.05, or 0) times the number of shares. To find the number of shares of each stock purchased, it is necessary to divide the dollar amount invested in that stock (A, B, C, or D) by the corresponding cost per share ($30, 40, 35, or 50, respectively). In other words, the dividend yield for each of the four stocks is equal to the dividend per share times the dollar amount invested in that stock divided by the cost per share. The total divided for stock A can be expressed by the equation (A/30) $\times$ 1.2, for B it is (B/40) $\times$ .5, and for C it is (C/35) $\times$ 1.05. There is no dividend for D. The total dividend constraint therefore, becomes

$$\frac{1.2A}{30} + \frac{.5B}{40} + \frac{1.05C}{35} \geq 20000$$

This can be rewritten as

$$(^{1.2}\!/_{30})A + (^5\!/_{40})B + (^{1.05}\!/_{35})C \geq 20000$$

However, this is not exactly in the usual or standard LP form. Simplifying (by dividing each dividend by the cost per share of that stock) gives us the more recognizable constraint form

$$.04A + .0125B + .03C \geq 20000$$

The constraint restricting the amount invested in the high-risk stock D also requires some thought. The dollar amount invested in stock D must be less than or equal to (not to exceed) 60 percent of the dollar amount invested in stock A. This can be expressed

$$D \leq .6A$$

But again, it is not in the required form with all decision variables on the left-hand side. Subtracting .6A from both sides gives us the acceptable constraint.

$$-.6A + D \leq 0$$

The final constraint, the dollar investment in stock B must be at least 10 percent of the total investment, can be expressed as

$$B \geq .10(A + B + C + D)$$

While $A + B + C + D \leq 800,000$ is known from the first constraint, it is not possible simply to substitute 10 percent of 800,000 or 80,000 in this case, since Mr. Rulan does not have to invest the total amount (although it is logical that he probably will, since he wishes to maximize dollar growth). All decision variables must be on the left-hand side of the inequality. Thus, subtracting the RHS value from both sides,

$$B - .10(A + B + C + D) \geq 0$$

and then multiplying the total investment expression by .10,

$$B - .1A - .1B - .1C - .1D \geq 0$$

and combining like terms, results in the final form of this constraint

$$-.1A + .9B - .1C - .1D \geq 0$$

Final LP formulation The final LP model for the ABC Investment Company is

MAX .25A + .225B + .24C + .30D

subject to

A +	B +	C +	D ≤ 800000	[total investment]
.04A +	.0125B +	.03C	≥ 20000	[min dividend]
−.6A +			D ≤ 0	[max stock D]
−.1A +	.9B −	.1C −	.1D ≥ 0	[min stock B]

$$A, B, C, D \geq 0$$

A Marketing Problem

Discount Distributors uses bulk mailings, newspaper ads, and television ads to promote its merchandise. Mailings are sent to 20,000 people, newspaper ads reach 25,000 people, and TV ads are seen by 50,000. Mailings cost $500, newspaper ads are $600 per ad, and TV advertising is $2000 an ad. Market research has shown that the mailings tend to be ineffective if used more than once per quarter. Discount wishes to place at least 10 newspaper ads per quarter, since this guarantees them better ad placement in the paper. Finally, Discount's Art Department estimates it takes 30 hours to prepare and mail a flyer for the bulk mailings, 5 hours to prepare a newspaper ad, and 15 hours for each TV ad. The Art Department currently has 260 hours available per quarter. Taking all of this data into account, Ms. Rakel, Marketing Manager for Discount must prepare an advertising plan for the coming quarter, such that the largest possible audience is reached without exceeding the department's $24,000 quarterly budget.

Formulation

Analysis   Ms. Rakel's objective is to reach as many people as possible with Discount's advertising campaign, which makes use of three distribution channels (mailings, newspaper ads, and TV ads) each reaching a different number of people (20,000, 25,000, and 50,000, respectively). What is being sought is the number of mailings, the number of newspaper ads, and the number of TV ads to be used to reach the greatest number of people. However, this decision is influenced or constrained both by budget restrictions ($\leq$ \$24,000) and by availability of time in the art department ($\leq$ 260 hours). It is further constrained by her wish to place at least 10 newspaper ads ($\geq$ 10) in order to insure better ad placement, and market research that indicates mailings should not exceed one per quarter ($\leq$ 1). Newspaper ads and TV ads may be placed in different sections or time spots, and therefore, may be noticed by different people each time they are run (with some unavoidable duplication). However, the mailings use the same mailing list, and thus are seen by the same people.

The decision variables   For this model, there are three decision variables representing the number of each type of advertising or promotion used.

$$M = \text{the number of bulk mailings used}$$

$$N = \text{the number of newspaper ads used}$$

$$T = \text{the number of TV ads used}$$

The objective function   Discount desires to reach as many people as possible through its advertising, that is, Discount wishes to maximize its audience exposure. This can be determined by summing the number reached via each of the three choices. The number reached by each source is found by multiplying the number reached by that channel by the number of times that channel is used. For example, if each bulk mailing ad reaches 20,000 people, then two bulk mailing ads reach 40,000 people, and M bulk mailing ads reach 20,000M people. The objective function can be expressed

$$\text{MAX } 20000M + 25000N + 50000T$$

The constraints   There are four constraints in this model, reflecting the limited budget, art department time, minimum number of newspaper ads, and maximum number of bulk mailings.

The budget constraint must show that the total cost (the sum) for the three options is less than or equal to the available $24,000 (it is not necessary to spend it all). The cost for each option is equal to its unit cost (cost each time) times the number of times that option is utilized. For example, since each newspaper ad costs $600, three ads cost $1800, and N ads cost $600N. The constraint is

$$500M + 600N + 2000T \leq 24000$$

The constraint reflecting that art department time is restricted to 260 hours is constructed in the same way. One bulk mailing takes 30 hours of time. Therefore, 30M represents the amount spent on bulk mailing. Similarly, 5N and 15T represent, respectively, the time spent on newspaper ads and TV ads. The constraint then is expressed

$$30M + 5N + 15T \leq 260$$

The final two constraints reflect the number of newspaper ads and bulk mailings that are desirable. Discount would like to place at least 10 newspaper ads and keep bulk mailings to a maximum of one. It is not possible to place a fraction of an ad or do part of a mailing. This means either rounding any fractional values or solving for integer values only. Optimal integer LP solutions will be discussed in a later chapter. For now, we are concerned only with LP model formulation, and the model formulation is independent of its solution. These constraints are expressed

$$N \geq 10$$

$$M \leq 1$$

However, notice the difference it would make if the bulk mailing constraint were made equal to one, instead of less-than-or-equal-to one. That would mean a bulk mailing would have to be used. The option not to use a mailing would be eliminated.

Final LP formulation   The complete linear programming model for this problem is expressed as

MAX $20000M + 25000N + 50000T$

subject to

$500M +$	$600N +$	$2000T \leq 24000$	[budget $]
$30M +$	$5N +$	$15T \leq 260$	[art dept hours]
	N	≥ 10	[min # newspaper ads]
M		≤ 1	[max # bulk mailings]
	$M, N, T \geq 0$		[max # bulk mailings]

A Scheduling Problem

The All Day Grocery Store provides 24-hour service for its customers. Because of different shopping patterns, All Day has found it needs the following number of clerks, at a minimum, for each time period:

Time	Clerks
12–4 AM	2
4–8 AM	4
8 AM–12 PM	8
12–4 PM	7
4–8 PM	10
8 PM–12 AM	5

There are six work shifts each day (beginning at midnight, 4 and 8 AM, noon, 4 and 8 PM). All clerks work 8-hour shifts. All Day's manager must set up a schedule for his clerks which will cover customer demand while keeping overall staffing needs to a minimum.

Formulation

Analysis This is not necessarily an easy problem to see immediately. Figure 2.2 describes the scheduling concept.

The starting hours of each shift are shown across the horizontal axis. The hours at work are shown vertically. The shading shows the eight hours at work for each starting time. The combination of eight-hour work blocks with shifts starting every four hours results in overlapping. Clerks who start work in one shift are still working when the next shift begins. All Day wants to set up a schedule, specifying how many clerks to have arrive at each shift, that minimizes the total number of people used in a day. This will become the objective function, stated in terms of number of clerks per shift. At the same time, All Day has to have a minimum number on duty each four-hour period in order to meet customer demands. These staffing requirements will be the constraints on the system.

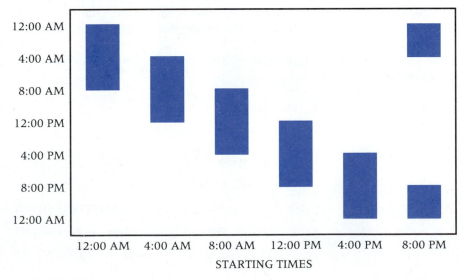

Figure 2.2 Scheduling Problem

The decision variables The decision variables are taken from Figure 2.2, that is, the decision variables represent the number of clerks starting at each shift.

$$A = \text{number of clerks beginning work at 12 midnight}$$

$$B = \text{number of clerks beginning work at 4 AM}$$

$$C = \text{number of clerks beginning work at 8 AM}$$

$$D = \text{number of clerks beginning work at 12 noon}$$

$$E = \text{number of clerks beginning work at 4 PM}$$

$$F = \text{number of clerks beginning work at 8 PM}$$

The objective function The objective is to minimize the total number of clerks used in a 24-hour period. The total is the sum of the clerks beginning work each shift.

$$\text{MIN } A + B + C + D + E + F$$

The constraints The constraints reflect the staffing requirements that are caused by shopping patterns that have been observed. Each constraint will show the minimum number of clerks who should be at work during that four-hour period. However, because each clerk works an eight-hour period, the number of clerks at-work during any given four hour shift is represented by the people who start at that time and the people who started the previous four-hour shift and are still at work (to complete their eight-hour block). For example, looking at Figure 2.2, we can see that from 4 AM to 8 AM, those at work include the clerks who began work at midnight (decision variable A) and those clerks who began work at 4 AM (decision variable B). According to observed shopper pattern, the time from 4 to 8 AM requires a minimum of four clerks on duty. This constraint can be expressed $A + B \geq 4$. The other constraints can be constructed in the same manner. The time period from midnight to 4 AM might require a little more thought, since it is not shown directly (the 8-hour block is split). However the reasoning is the same. Those working from midnight to 4 AM include both those who begin at midnight (A) and those who start at 8 PM (F). The midnight to 4 AM shift requires two clerks. Therefore, the constraint can be expressed $F + A \geq 2$ or $A + F \geq 2$. The complete formulation of the constraints is

$$A + B \geq 4$$

$$B + C \geq 8$$

$$C + D \geq 7$$

$$D + E \geq 10$$

$$E + F \geq 5$$

$$A + F \geq 2$$

Final LP formulation Once this problem can be visualized, it is fairly easy to formulate. The complete model is shown as follows:

$$\text{MIN } A + B + C + D + E + F$$

subject to

$$A + B \geq 4 \qquad [\text{4--8 AM}]$$

$$B + C \geq 8 \qquad [\text{8 AM--12 PM}]$$

$$C + D \geq 7 \qquad [12 \text{ PM–4 PM}]$$

$$D + E \geq 10 \qquad [4 \text{ PM–8 PM}]$$

$$E + F \geq 5 \qquad [8 \text{ PM–12 AM}]$$

$$A + F \geq 2 \qquad [12 \text{ AM–4 AM}]$$

$$A, B, C, D, E, F \geq 0$$

A Production Scheduling Problem

Woodline Products manufactures a TV-VCR stand (some assembly required). Demand for this product varies widely from week to week, as shown in the following table:

Week	Demand
1	5000
2	7500
3	6000
4	5500
5	8000
6	4000

Mr. Jaworski, production manager for this product line, wishes to prepare a production schedule for the next six weeks that will meet demand while minimizing per unit production and inventory costs. The plant's production capacity for this product is 6000 units per week, although it is possible to produce an additional 1000 units per week by scheduling overtime. Any units produced, but not shipped are placed in inventory. Mr. Jaworski knows it costs Woodline $26 per unit produced during regular hours and $31 per unit for any units produced using overtime. It is also estimated that units remaining in inventory at the end of a week have a carrying cost of $1.50 per unit. There are currently 1600 units in inventory and the company has a policy of maintaining an ending inventory of at least 500 units each week.

Formulation

Analysis Mr. Jaworski's objective is to minimize his total production and inventory costs for this line over the next six weeks while still meeting weekly demand. What must be decided are the number of units to be produced each week during regular hours, the number of units to be produced on overtime, and the number of units that will remain in inventory at the end of each week. These decisions are constrained by the weekly demand, the maximum production capacities, and the minimum ending inventory desired.

The decision variables For this problem, there are three basic variables representing normal production, overtime production, and ending inventory. However, since these variables are required for each week and Mr. Jaworski is scheduling for the next six weeks, there will be a total of 18 variables. These variables can be represented by

P_i = the number of units produced on regular time in week i

O_i = the number of units produced on overtime in week i

I_i = the number of units in inventory at the end of week i

where

$$i \text{ varies from 1 to 6.}$$

The objective function   Mr. Jaworski wishes to minimize his total production and inventory costs over the next six weeks. Since he knows the cost per unit for production and inventory, the objective function can be expressed

$$\text{MIN } 26\,P_i + 31\,O_i + 1.50\,I_i$$

or

$$\text{MIN } 26P_1 + 26P_2 + 26P_3 + 26P_4 + 26P_5 + 26P_6 + 31O_1 + 31O_2 + 31O_3 + 31O_4 + 31O_5 + 31O_6 + 1.5I_1 + 1.5I_2 + 1.5I_3 + 1.5I_4 + 1.5I_5 + 1.5I_6$$

The constraints   There are four sets of constraints for this problem. They reflect the regular weekly production capacity, the overtime weekly production capacity, the desired weekly ending inventory, and the weekly demand. The regular production capacity constraints can be expressed by the generalized term

$$P_i \leq 6000$$

The overtime production capacity constraints can be expressed by

$$O_i \leq 1000$$

The minimum desired ending inventory constraints can be expressed by

$$I_i \geq 500$$

In each case, there are six constraints, one for each week.

The weekly demand constraints must reflect the fact that the units available from the previous week's ending inventory or this weeks production must equal the units shipped or placed in inventory at the end of the week. This can be expressed as a **balance equation**

$$\begin{bmatrix} \text{ending} \\ \text{inventory} \\ \text{from} \\ \text{previous} \\ \text{week} \end{bmatrix} + \begin{bmatrix} \text{units} \\ \text{produced on} \\ \text{regular time} \end{bmatrix} + \begin{bmatrix} \text{units} \\ \text{produced on} \\ \text{overtime} \end{bmatrix} = \begin{bmatrix} \text{demand} \\ \text{for this} \\ \text{week} \end{bmatrix} + \begin{bmatrix} \text{ending} \\ \text{inventory} \\ \text{for this} \\ \text{week} \end{bmatrix}$$

which can be expressed in terms of the decision variables as

$$I_i - 1 + P_i + O_i = D_i + I_i$$

Demand for each week (D_i) is given and can, therefore, be treated as a constant. Rearranging the equation, the general constraint can be expressed as

$$P_i + O_i + I_{i-1} - I_i = D_i$$

The ending inventory for week zero is the beginning inventory for week one. This is known to be 1600 units and can be treated as a constant. Thus, for week one, the constraint is

$$P_1 + O_1 + 1600 - I_1 = 5000$$

or

$$P_1 + O_1 - I_1 = 3400$$

Final LP formulation The complete LP model for this problem can be expressed as

$$\text{MIN } 26P_1 + 26P_2 + 26P_3 + 26P_4 + 26P_5 + 26P_6 + 31O_1 + 31O_2$$
$$+ 31O_3 + 31O_4 + 31O_5 + 31O_6 + 1.5I_1 + 1.5I_2 + 1.5I_3$$
$$+ 1.5I_4 + 1.5I_5 + 1.5I_6$$

subject to

$$P_1 \leq 6000$$
$$P_2 \leq 6000$$
$$P_3 \leq 6000$$
$$P_4 \leq 6000 \quad \text{[production capacity]}$$
$$P_5 \leq 6000$$
$$P_6 \leq 6000$$

$$O_1 \leq 1000$$
$$O_2 \leq 1000$$
$$O_3 \leq 1000$$
$$O_4 \leq 1000 \quad \text{[overtime production capacity]}$$
$$O_5 \leq 1000$$
$$O_6 \leq 1000$$

$$I_1 \geq 500$$
$$I_2 \geq 500$$
$$I_3 \geq 500$$
$$I_4 \geq 500 \quad \text{[minimum inventory]}$$
$$I_5 \geq 500$$
$$I_6 \geq 500$$

$$P_1 + O_1 - I_1 = 3400$$
$$P_2 + O_2 + I_1 - I_2 = 7500$$
$$P_3 + O_3 + I_2 - I_3 = 6000 \quad \text{[balance equation, to}$$
$$P_4 + O_4 + I_3 - I_4 = 5500 \quad \text{insure that weekly demand}$$
$$P_5 + O_5 + I_4 - I_5 = 8000 \quad \text{is met]}$$
$$P_6 + O_6 + I_5 - I_6 = 4000$$
$$P_i, O_i, I_i \geq 0$$

Note that while this formulation will yield production and inventory levels for the next six weeks, only the schedule for week one will be implemented immediately. The schedules for the remaining weeks may be considered tentative. They may change as additional information becomes available or demand is revised.

2.5 *LP MODEL FORMULATION GUIDELINES: A SUMMARY*

Formulating the LP model, and doing it correctly, is the essential step in solving LP problems. Now that you are more familiar with LP problems, and have some practice with the example problems, we will present a summary of the formulation process. Keep in mind that these are just guidelines. Model formulation is part science and part art.

1. Analyze the problem, and make sure that you understand precisely what is being decided, that is, what decision is being made. Be sure you can state the objective clearly. Is it a maximization or a minimization problem? What exactly is being sought? Can you state it in your own words?
2. Determine the decision variables, and identify the variables whose values you are seeking. It is important to remember that the optimum value of the decision variables provides the answer to the problem. Incorrectly identifying these variables invalidates the model.
3. Represent the objective as a mathematical function, that is, express the objective function as a linear expression involving the decision variables. The objective (to maximize or minimize) is described in terms of the decision variables. This expression should evaluate the effectiveness of any solution to the problem.
4. Identify the constraints and express them as linear expressions (again involving the decision variables). There must be a constraint for each limitation, requirement, regulation, condition, demand, rule, and so on, that in any way restricts or defines the availability of the resources. Each decision variable that affects a given resource must be included in that constraint.
5. Finally, collect all relevant data, remembering that all parameters must be constants. All data must be complete and reliable. If exact values are not available, informed estimates may have to be used.

2.6 *FOCUS ON DECISION MAKING: A PREVIEW*

This chapter focuses on linear programming problem formulation. Chapters 3 through 6 are a unit that introduce LP and illustrate LP solution processes. Beginning with Chapter 6, most chapters will include a section entitled, "Focus on Decision Making," which includes a problem, its formulation and computer solution, an analysis of the computer output and results, and a discussion of what happens after a quantitative solution is determined. This section is designed to illustrate that, given the correct identification of a problem-type and its proper formulation, a problem is usually easily solved using a computer software package. Moreover, this section serves to show that this solution is only one part of the decision-making process. In this section, we preview this feature using the production scheduling problem already formulated in the chapter.

Recall that Mr. Jaworski is attempting to schedule production of a TV-VCR stand for Woodline Products for a six-week period. His objective is to meet demand for this product while minimizing production and inventory costs. The problem formulation is repeated

$$\text{MIN } 26P_1 + 26P_2 + 26P_3 + 26P_4 + 26P_5 + 26P_6 + 31O_1 + 31O_2 + 31O_3 + 31O_4$$
$$+ 31O_5 + 31O_6 + 1.5I_1 + 1.5I_2 + 1.5I_3 + 1.5I_4 + 1.5I_5 + 1.5I_6$$

subject to

$$P_1 \le 6000$$
$$P_2 \le 6000$$
$$P_3 \le 6000$$

$$P_4 \leq 6000$$
$$P_5 \leq 6000$$
$$P_6 \leq 6000$$
$$O_1 \leq 1000$$
$$O_2 \leq 1000$$
$$O_3 \leq 1000$$
$$O_4 \leq 1000$$
$$O_5 \leq 1000$$
$$O_6 \leq 1000$$
$$I_1 \geq 500$$
$$I_2 \geq 500$$
$$I_3 \geq 500$$
$$I_4 \geq 500$$
$$I_5 \geq 500$$
$$I_6 \geq 500$$
$$P_1 + O_1 - I_1 = 3400$$
$$P_2 + O_2 + I_1 - I_2 = 7500$$
$$P_3 + O_3 + I_2 - I_3 = 6000$$
$$P_4 + O_4 + I_3 - I_4 = 5500$$
$$P_5 + O_5 + I_4 - I_5 = 8000$$
$$P_6 + O_6 + I_5 - I_6 = 4000$$
$$Pi, Oi, Ii \geq 0$$

Once this problem has been formulated into the LP model, a computer program can be used to solve it. Computer solutions are discussed in Chapter 6. However, the computer solution to this problem obtained using the Dennis & Dennis software is included here, as both a preview and as an illustration of the ease with which a solution may be obtained. The figure below contains both the input summary and output/solution.

```
HERE IS WHAT YOU ENTERED:

0    MIN  26P1+26P2+26P3+26P4+26P5+26P6+31O1+31O2+31O3
     +31O4+31O5+31O6+1.5I1+1.5I2+1.5I3+1.5I4+1.5I5+1.5I6
   SUBJECT TO:
1      1P1≤ 6000
2      1P2≤ 6000
3      1P3≤ 6000
4      1P4≤ 6000
5      1P5≤ 6000
6      1P6≤ 6000
7      1O1≤ 1000
8      1O2≤ 1000
9      1O3≤ 1000
10     1O4≤ 1000
11     1O5≤ 1000
12     1O6≤ 1000
```

```
13      1I1≥ 500
14      1I2≥ 500
15      1I3≥ 500
16      1I4≥ 500
17      1I5≥ 500
18      1I6≥ 500
19      1P1+1O1−1I1= 3400
20      1P2+1O2+1I1−1I2= 7500
21      1P3+1O3+1I2−1I3= 6000
22      1P4+1O4+1I3−1I4= 5500
23      1P5+1O5+1I4−1I5= 8000
24      1P6+1O6+1I5−1I6= 4000

AFTER 22 ITERATIONS,
THIS SOLUTION IS OPTIMAL:

VARIABLE          QUANTITY
--------          --------
   P1               5900
   P2               6000
   P3               6000
   P4               6000
   P5               6000
   P6               4000
   O5               1000
   I1               2500
   I2               1000
   I3               1000
   I4               1500
   I5                500
   I6                500
   S1                100
   S6               2000
   S7               1000
   S8               1000
   S9               1000
   S10              1000
   S12              1000
   S13              2000
   S14               500
   S15               500
   S16              1000

OPTIMAL Z = 922899.9
```

Interpretation and Analysis of the Results

The solution portion of the computer results shown tells Mr. Jaworski that the production schedule should be set at 5900 units the first week ($P1 = 5900$), 6000 units for the second through fifth weeks, and 4000 units for the sixth week. It also indicates that overtime production of 1000 units will be needed in the fifth week ($I5 = 1000$). Inventory levels will be 2500, 1000, 1000, 1500, 500, and 500 units in weeks one through six, respectively. The overall cost of this schedule is $922,900 (922899.9) over the six-week period. The meaning of the S1 to S16 variables will be explained in later chapters.

What Happens Next

This solution becomes an input in Mr. Jaworski's decision making process. He can adopt this schedule knowing that it will meet demand for the product while minimizing the associated production and inventory costs. However, as noted earlier in the chapter, only the schedule for week one would be implemented immediately. The schedules for weeks two through six would remain tentative and could change with changes in the problem parameters or as demand information is revised or updated. If demand for week seven were to exceed the normal production capacity of 6000 units, Mr. Jaworski would most likely want to increase production in week five from its currently scheduled 4000 units. Since Mr. Jaworski is operating in a dynamic environment, he would probably reformulate the problem incorporating new data and rerun it on a periodic basis. If there are no parameter changes or dramatic increases in demand in future weeks, a new schedule might be run every three weeks. This would allow adequate time to adjust production schedules as needed.

2.7 CONCLUDING REMARKS

Linear programming is a technique used for allocating scarce resources among competing activities so that a single objective is optimized (either maximized or minimized). LP is widely used, by a variety of organizations, for myriad applications—some of which have been shown in the example problems. With ever increasing availability of easy to use, fast and reliable computer solutions for LP problems, correctly formulating the model has become the single most important step in the solution process.

It is important for the decision maker to recognize that if the problem at hand does not meet the underlying assumptions and fit the characteristics of an LP problem, then LP may not be the proper solution technique. At least the decision maker must be aware of the implications of using LP under such circumstances. For example, if a noninteger solution is unacceptable, is a rounded, though perhaps nonoptimal solution acceptable? If not, a more time-consuming and perhaps costlier solution procedure will be necessary. Integer linear programming will be covered in a later chapter. Is the data associated with the problem static? The optimal solution determined using LP may not remain optimal when the data change. We will discover more about this in the discussion of sensitivity analysis in Chapter 5.

In this chapter we focused on the formulation of LP models. In Chapters 3 through 6 solving LP problems will be discussed. The primary solution technique for LP problems is an iterative algorithm known as the simplex method. This algorithm is discussed in Chapter 4. The simplex method or some variation, for example, the two phase simplex method, is the algorithm used by most LP computer programs. The graphical approach, which we discuss in Chapter 3 as a method of visualizing LP problems and their solutions, can be used to solve simple problems with two decision variables. However, it is generally impractical as a solution method for real problems, since most real-world LP problems have more than two variables. A new technique, known as Karmarkar's algorithm, was introduced in 1984 by N. Karmarkar.[1] Karmarkar's algorithm is more complex than the simplex method, but does save computer time on some LP problems. For a further discussion of Karmarkar's algorithm, see J. N. Hooker's article.[2]

Today virtually all LP problems are solved using one of a variety of available computer programs. The use of computer solution techniques is discussed in Chapter 6. Any of the example problems or end-of-chapter problems from this chapter can be easily solved on a PC using the D&D LP computer program which accompanies this text.

Management Science Application _____

WELLBORN CABINET, INC.[3]

In 1986, the Auburn University Technical Assistance Center undertook a project with Wellborn Cabinet Inc., aimed at developing an optimal wood procurement policy. Wellborn Cabinet Inc., is a manufacturer of kitchen cabinets with 375 employees and annual sales of $16,000,000. The company, located in Alabama, has a wood cabinet assembly plant that includes a rough mill for producing blanks (wood cabinet components), a sawmill, and four dry kilns. The company purchases approximately $1,400,000 worth of solid wood raw materials in the form of #1 and #2 grade hardwood logs and #1 and #2 common grade lumber (dry and green). On an annual basis, the plant was using about 3,700,000 board feet of lumber.

The domestic cabinet industry has experienced steady growth over the past two decades as a result of the growth in the new housing industry and an active remodeling market. Industry estimates project a growth in cabinet production from 44 million units in 1986 to over 50 million cabinets in 1990. This market is very competitive, placing constant pressure on manufacturers to offer quality products at competitive prices. Because cabinet manufacturing is basically an assembly operation, raw material procurement policies play a major part in the determination of product quality and cost. Wood raw materials constitute approximately 45 percent of the total cabinet material cost.

Approximately three-quarters of the company's lumber comes from logs processed at the company's sawmill. The remainder is purchased from outside sources. The sawmill has the capacity to process up to 1500 logs with small-end diameters of 9 to 22 inches during a 5-day work week. Green lumber must be dried in the kilns before it can be used. The kilns have a total capacity of 90,000 board feet per 9-day drying cycle. Dry lumber is then planed and converted into blanks at the rough mill. There are approximately 130 different-sized blanks used in the company's products. All blank sizes are cut every week. The number of blanks obtained from dry lumber is a function of the blank size being cut and the size of the lumber. While the size of

[1]Karmarkar, N. "A New Polynomial Time Algorithm for Linear Programming." *Combinatorica*, 4(4): 373–95, 1984.
[2]Hooker, J. N. "Karmarkar's Linear Programming Algorithm." *Interfaces*, 16(July–August) 75–90, 1986.
[3]Reprinted by permission of Honorio F. Carino, and Clinton H. LeNoir, Jr. "Optimizing Wood Procurement in Cabinet Manufacturing." *Interfaces*, 18, 10–19 (March-April, 1988), Copyright 1988, The Institute of Management Sciences.

the lumber produced at the sawmill can be controlled, lumber purchased from suppliers is in mill-run (random) sizes and not, therefore, a controllable input.

At the time of the technical assistance project, about 65 percent of the total volume of logs being purchased were grade #1. Of the 27 percent of the lumber purchased from outside suppliers, most was #1 common. Ninety-five percent of the dry lumber and 70 percent of the green lumber purchased was #1 common. The remainder was #2 common.

An Auburn University technical assistance group applied linerar programming to determine the optimum wood procurement policy for the Wellborn company. The LP model of the blank production system was designed to minimize the total cost of producing blanks during the work week. The constraints included the capacities of the sawmill and the dry kilns, the number of blanks required by manufacturing, the supply of raw materials, and the capacity of the rough mill. Input data included the size (diameter and length) of logs, estimates of the volume and grade yield of input logs (from a regression equation), the number of blanks required, the maximum throughput of the sawmill, the aggregate capacity of the dry kilns, the delivered cost of logs and lumber, the cost of converting logs into lumber, the cost of drying lumber, the cost of converting dry lumber into blanks, and the weekly blank requirements by size.

The results from the LP model indicated that the company could minimize the total cost of blank production by purchasing only #2 grade logs with a small end diameter between 9 and 15 inches and #2 common green lumber. Using the recommended purchase policy, the company would be expected to save approximately 32 percent of its wood raw material costs or about $412,000 annually.

GLOSSARY

additivity assumption assumption in LP that the total value of the objective function or the total utilization of each resource is equal to the sum of its component parts

balance equation form of a constraint equation which expresses input equal to output or supply equal to demand

certainty assumption in LP that all data involved (parameters) in a problem are known exactly (with certainty)

constraint mathematical statement (equality or inequality) of the restrictions in an LP problem that represent resource limitations or requirements

decision variables those variables, under the control of management, whose value, when determined, represent the solution to a given LP problem

divisibility assumption in LP that all resources are divisible into fractional values, that is, that they can assume any value along a continuous range

linear programming mathematical technique for finding the best use (allocation) of resources subject to restrictions (constraints)

linearity assumption in LP that all variables appear in separate terms, all coefficients are constants, and all variables are raised to the first power (all variables have exponent of one)

nonnegativity constraints condition or assumption in LP that disallows negative values for variables, that is, a stipulation that decision variables must have nonnegative (positive or zero) values

objective function mathematical statement of the single objective or goal to be achieved optimally in LP

parameters constants that describe the relationship between the decision variables; the coefficients that remain constant for the problem

proportionality assumption assumption in LP that the value of the objective function, or of the resources utilized, is in direct proportion to the values of the decision variables, such that a change in the value of an independent variable results in a constant change in the value of the dependent variable

PROBLEMS

1. Woodco manufactures two chairs, models A and B. The profit per chair, wood, labor, and brass fasteners required are listed with the availability of each resource.

Line	Wood (bd ft)	Labor (hr)	Fasteners	Profit
A	20	2	2	$15
B	32	2	8	35
Monthly availability	10,000	800	2000	

Formulate the monthly production schedule that will maximize Woodco's profits.

2. How would the problem formulation for question 1 change if Woodco simply wanted to produce the largest number of chairs possible per month? Based on the data given, which line of chairs would be most likely to be produced? Why?

3. A company produces two products, X and Y. Each unit produced must be processed on three assembly lines. The required production time for each product is shown in the following table:

Product	Line 1	Line 2	Line 3
X	3 hr	2 hr	4 hr
Y	3	3	2
Total hours available	45	48	54

Product X has a profit of $6 and product Y a profit of $4. The company wishes to maximize profit. Formulate the LP model that will achieve this objective.

4. The Acme Novelties Co. produces two stuffed animals, a bear and a cuddle pup, each with the same material. The materials used are an acrylic fake fur and a foam filling. The resource requirements for each animal and the total resources available are shown.

Product	Resource Requirements	
	Fur (yd)	Filling (lb)
Bear	$1\frac{1}{2}$	2
Cuddle pup	2	$2\frac{1}{4}$
Total resources	50 yd	65 lb

Each bear has a $5.50 profit and each cuddle pup a $3.00 profit. Formulate a linear-programming model to determine the numer of each type of animal to produce to maximize Acme's profits.

5. Savoy Sausages produces a special bulk sausage for a pancake restaurant franchise. The sausage is produced in 2500 pound batches, is a mixture of pork, at a cost of $3 per pound, beef at $5 per pound, and cereal at $1.75 per pound. According to the franchise specifications, each batch must contain at least 600 pounds of pork and at least 1200 pounds of beef. The mix cannot contain more than 900 pounds of cereal. The company wants to find the optimal mix of ingredients. Formulate a linear programming model that will achieve this objective.

6. The Stereo Shop assembles tuner/amplifiers, turntables, and speakers into "starter systems." It offers two basic systems, economy and basic. The economy system has only the tuner/amplifier and two speakers, while the basic system also includes a turntable. The Stereo Shop estimates it makes $50 on each economy system and $70 on each basic system. The shop currently has 100 tuner/amplifiers, 40 turntables, and 180 speakers available. There are also 120 labor hours available. It takes 60 minutes to assemble an economy system and 90 minutes to assemble a basic system. If the Stereo Shop can sell all of the systems it assembles, formulate a linear programming model that will help management decide how many units of each system to assemble to maximize profit.

7. A clothing manufacturer makes football jerseys and soccer shirts for youth teams. The major resources used are material, numerals, and labor. Football jerseys require 8 square feet of material, soccer shirts 5 square feet. Both jerseys and shirts require two numerals. It takes two hours to make a football jersey and three hours to make a soccer shirt. The company currently has 215 square yards of material, 600 numerals, and 685 hours of labor available. Each football jersey yields a profit of $6 and each soccer shirt $4.50. Formulate the LP model for the correct production mix.

8. A plastic manufacturer has contracted to deliver 6 tons of plastic to a television cabinet fabricator each month. The contract can be filled with either or both of two types of plastic, X13 or Y25. It takes 4 days to produce a ton of X13 and 2 1/2 days to produce a ton of Y25. The plant can allocate only 21 days of production time to this contract. Because of resource limitations, the plant can produce only 4 tons of X13 and 4 tons of Y25. Manufacturing costs are $60 per ton for X13 and $120 per ton for Y25. Formulate the LP model that will help this manufacturer to schedule the production of these two plastics.

9. The ABC Company sells two types of porch furniture, gliders and chairs. It makes a profit of $100 on each glider and $40 on each chair. Each glider requires 40 square feet of display space and each chair redquires 25 square feet of display space. It takes 1 1/2 hours to assemble a glider and 2/3 hour to assemble a chair. ABC has 900 square feet of display space and 30 hours of labor available for assembly. The sales manager wants at least two chairs displayed for every glider displayed. Formulate the LP model that will allow ABC to determine the number of gliders and chairs to display, if they wish to maximize their profit.

10. Acme Investment Company just received an investment order from a customer. The customer specified that the investment must be in one or more of three stocks. The information on each stock is shown. The customer wishes

Acme to invest $600,000 in such a way that the growth in the portfolio's dollar value is maximized.

Stock	Price	Expected Growth	Dividend
Hi-Tech Co.	$60	8%	$2.00
Sky Aerospace	80	12	1.20
Grandma's Rockers	20	2	4.00

The customer has placed the following restrictions on Acme:

(a) no more than 3000 shares of Sky Aerospace may be purchased
(b) the total annual dividend from all stocks must be at least $15,000.

Acme wishes to decide how many shares of each stock to purchase. Formulate an LP model that will help them.

11. Copper Clad Cookware manufactures three types of copper clad cookware, an 8 inch skillet, a 12 inch skillet, and a 2-quart pan. Production requirements, profits, material, and labor availability are shown.

Item	Profit/unit	Copper (lb)	Labor (hr)
8" skillet	$1.40	.5	1
12" skillet	.90	.6	1.5
2 quart pan	1.10	.4	.5
Available/month		48 lb	90 hr

Assuming Copper Clad can sell all of the cookware it manufactures each month and it wishes to maximize its profits, formulate an LP model to help it determine its optimal product mix.

12. Fred's Refuse Collection is considering opening a new pickup route. The new route would require a truck capacity of 77,100 cubic feet. Fred can purchase two types of trucks. Data on the trucks are shown as follows:

Truck	Cost	Capacity	Men Required	Space Required
Mainliner	$60,000	6180	3	700
Lowboy	24,000	2200	1	200

Capacity is given in cubic feet and space required in square feet. Fred currently has 36 qualified applicants and 8000 square feet of parking space available for additional trucks. If Fred wishes to minimize his total truck investment, formulate the LP model to help Fred decide how many of each type of truck he should buy.

13. How would the problem formulation for Fred's Refuse Collection (problem 12) change if it cost Fred $300 for each applicant he had to hire and train?

14. Flash Skateboards manufactures three models, Beginner, Racer, and Hot Dog. Flash makes $6 profit on each Beginner, $8 on each Racer, and $9 on each Hot Dog. The Beginner and Racer each require 1 pound of fiberglass and the Hot Dog 2 pounds. The Beginner and Hot Dog require 1 hour of manufacturing labor, while the Racer requires 2 hours. The Beginner requires 1 hour of finishing time, the Racer 1.4 hours, and the Hot Dog 2 hours. Flash has

70 pounds of fiberglass, 90 hours of manufacturing time, and 80 hours of finishing time available for the week. If Flash can sell all of the skateboards it produces and wishes to maximize profits, formulate the LP model which would help the company determine its weekly production schedule.

15. The ABC advertising agency has been hired to promote a new product. Their advertising options are listed the following in the table.

	Cost per ad	Estimated audience reached per ad	Number of spots available
Radio	$ 1,000	8,000	8
Day-time TV	5,000	25,000	5
Prime-time TV	17,000	60,000	3
Newspaper	500	4,000	20

The client wishes to reach as large an audience as possible, but doesn't wish to spend more than $60,000. The client has also specified at least one ad must be placed in each medium (radio, TV, and newspaper) and that newspaper ads cannot exceed 60 percent of the total number of ads placed. Formulate this LP model.

16. Assume the client in problem 15 wishes to spend as little as possible to reach an audience of at least 211,000 people. How would this change the problem formulation?

17. Wilson Wine Company has decided to add a line of wine coolers to its regular wines. It will add two brands, Lite Cooler and Regal Cooler. Both brands include wine, lemon juice, and lime juice. Regal also includes grapefruit juice. Each gallon of Lite will contain 4 ounces of lemon juice and 2 ounces of lime juice. Each gallon of Regal will contain 3 ounces of lemon juice, 3 ounces of lime juice, and 4 ounces of grapefruit juice. Wilson has 1200 ounces of lemon juice, 1000 ounces of lime juice, and 1100 ounces of grapfruit juice available. Market estimates indicate that Wilson can sell at least 150 gallons of Lite at a profit of $2.60 per gallon and at least 100 gallons of Regal at a profit of $3.10 per gallon. Formulate the LP model for this problem.

18. The XYZ Corporation produces two products, A and B. Product A yields a profit of $8 per unit and product B yields a profit of $6 per unit. Both products must pass through two work centers, fabrication and assembly. Product A requires 2 hours in fabrication and 3 hours in assembly. Product B requires 3 hours in fabrication and 1 hour in assembly. XYZ currently has 400 hours of fabrication time and 300 hours of assembly time available. What production schedule would be appropriate for each product if XYZ wishes to maximize its profits and can sell all of either product produced?

19. Assuming XYZ workers in problem 18 can be assigned to either department, how should the 700 available hours be allocated between the fabrication and assembly departments if XYZ still wishes to maximize its profits?

20. Assume XYZ (problem 19) has a contract calling for 100 units of each product. If these units cannot be produced on regular time, XYZ can add up to 300 hours of overtime in the fabrication deparment and up to 200 hours in the assembly department. Because of the additional labor costs, however, the profit per unit for either product produced on overtime is reduced by $2 per unit. Formulate the LP model to determine the optimal production schedule.

21. The Hospitality Host at the Convention Center is preparing for the Fourth of July pops concert. Experience has taught him that a great deal of wine is

consumed on this particular evening. He knows that at this time of the year the light-white wine and the chablis will be most popular. Based on his experience, he estimates no more than 750 bottles of chablis and no more than 650 bottles of the light white can probably be sold. However, his contract with the winery requires that he purchase at least 300 bottles of their new summer pink. He has a storage capacity for only 1500 bottles at the facility. If he makes a profit of $2 per bottle on Light White, $1.70 per bottle on Chablis, and $1.25 per bottle on Summer Pink, formulate the LP model which will help him to determine the number of bottles of each type of wine to purchase in order to maximize his profits.

22. At the last minute, the Hospitality Host for the pops concert is offered 200 bottles of champagne by the winery. The champagne would cost $5 per bottle and sell for $7.50. If he feels the champagne would sell, how would this change the LP model formulated in the previous problem?

23. The Powers family has 500 acres of their farm land on which they plant corn and pumpkins to sell in their farm market. Each acre of corn costs $100 to plant, cultivate and harvest, while each acre of pumpkins cost $75. The Powers have a budget of $40,000 to spend on these crops. Each acre of corn yields a profit of $250, while each acre of pumpkins yields a profit of $125. Because of the good will of the community from a "pumpkin festival" and school visits to the pumpkin patch, the Powers want to plant at least 100 acres of pumpkins. The Powers want to know how many acres of each crop to plant to maximize profit. Formulate an LP model to solve this problem.

24. Recreational Vehicles, a bicycle shop in East Rochester, NY, is opening a second store in Gates. The manager, Bill Hoffrey, must decide how many touring, racing, and trail models to order from the manufacturer, Swift Inc., for the summer season. Each touring model costs $225, each racer $350, and each trail bike costs $435. He has a total budget of $12,000 to purchase the bikes. The tour bike sells for $400, the racer sells for $500, and the trail bike sells for $650. Space in the shop for display and storage is limited to 500 square feet. The trail bike requires 20 square feet of space, the racer 14 square feet, and the touring bike 16 square feet. Maximum demand is 15 for the touring bike, 20 for the racer, and 10 for the trail bike for the coming season. Bill wants to know how many bikes of each type to stock in order to maximize his profit. Formulate an LP model for this problem.

25. Hike & Grow camp for adolescents sends campers on various 1-, 2-, and 3-day hiking trips. Among the provisions each camper receives is a 16 ounce trail package of dried fruits and seeds which meets minimum daily requirements for vitamins A, C, and D, iron, and potassium (one package for each day of the hike). Hike & Grow packs its own mix, comprised of raisins, dried bananas, coconut, and sunflower seeds. The vitamin/mineral requirements and contributions are as follows:

| Vitamins/minerals | Contributions (mg/o) | | | | |
	Raisins	Bananas	Coconut	Seeds	MDR
A	2	3			16
C	3		1	1	18
D		2	2	1	15
iron	3		2	1	22
potassium		4		3	17

The cost per ounce of raisins is 4 cents, cost per ounce of dried banana is 3 cents, cost per ounce of coconut is 6 cents, and the cost per ounce of sunflower seed is 2 cents. The dietician making up the 16-ounce package needs to minimize the cost yet meet the MDR. Formulate the LP model to solve this problem.

26. The camp director has decided to add 1 ounce of dried apples and 2 ounces of chocolate chips to the trail mix to improve its flavor. Apples, which provide 2 mg of vitamin A per ounce, cost 3 cents per ounce. Chocolate chips cost 5 cents per ounce. The total mix will still weigh only 16 ounces. How would this change the LP model formulated in the previous problem if the objective is still to minimize cost?

27. The Denneco Construction Company has just purchased a 400,000 square foot warehouse which it plans to convert into condominiums. There will be three different units: deluxe units, 2000 square feet in size; 2-bedroom units, 1200 square feet in size; and 3-bedroom units, 1500 square feet in size. Denneco estimates it will make a profit of $20,000 on each deluxe unit, $7000 on each 2-bedroom unit, and $12,000 on each 3-bedroom unit. Market research shows that Denneco can probably sell no more than 30 deluxe units. As a part of the purchase agreement, Denneco agreed that at least 20 percent of the units would be the lower cost 2-bedroom units. To maintain a high class image, however, Denneco knows that the 2-bedroom units cannot exceed 40 percent of the total number of units built. Also included in the sales agreement was a clause giving the seller the right to purchase 10 deluxe units and 10 3-bedroom units for later resale. Formulate the LP model which will help Denneco decide how many of each type of unit to construct.

28. Best Home Products has decided to open four new sales regions in the eastern United States: the North East, Central, D.C. area, and South East regions. Management must now decide how many sales people to allocate to each of these regions. They have 95 people waiting to be assigned. Estimated sales revenue per salesperson for each region has been projected as follows: North East—$80,000, Central—$150,000, D.C. area—$180,000, and South East—$100,000. Annual expenses budgeted per salesperson by region are estimated to be: North East—$10,000, Central—$18,000, D.C. area—$12,000, and South East—$10,000. The company has $1,500,000 budgeted for expenses for the year. Initially, each new sales region should have at least 15 salespeople. However, because of its size, the D.C. area region cannot support more than 20 salespeople. How many salespeople should be assigned to each region to maximize total sales revenue?

29. How would the problem formulation for Best Home Products (problem 28) change if the company wishes to maximize total contribution to profit?

30. Paul's Plantfood Company produces three brands of plant food, Fast Grow, Green Thumb, and Miracle Green, manufactured at plants in Fairport, NY and Bradenton, Florida. The plant in Fairport has a production capacity of 3000 pounds weekly. The plant in Bradenton can produce 5000 pounds weekly. The combined weekly budget for both plants is $25,000. Sales records show a weekly demand of 3000 pounds for Fast Grow, 2500 pounds for Green Thumb, and 2000 pounds for Miracle Green. Fast Grow costs $2.00 per pound to produce at Fairport and $1.50 at Bradenton. Green Thumb costs $1.50 per pound to produce at Fairport and $1.25 at Bradenton. Miracle Green costs $2.00 per pound to produce at Fairport and $1.40 at Bradenton. Selling prices

are $6.50 per pound of Fast Grow, $5.00 per pound of Green Thumb, and $5.50 per pound of Miracle Green. Paul wants to know the number of pounds of each plant food to produce at each plant in order to maximize profit. Formulate a linear programming model for this problem.

31. The Wexler Widget Company just received a contract to produce 6000 R24 widgets over a 3-month period. Wexler must deliver 1500 R24s in January, 2500 in February, and 2000 in March. Wexler can schedule 1800 hours of regular labor per month and up to 400 hours of overtime labor per month. It costs $8 per regular hour and $12 per overtime hour. Any widgets not shipped in the month produced must be stored in a warehouse at a cost of $3 per unit per month. If it takes 1 hour to produce a R24 widget, how many hours of regular and overtime work should be scheduled each month to meet the contract at a minimum cost?

32. The Megacity Power Company (MPC) wishes to schedule its workforce for the coming month. Employees work 8-hour shifts beginning at 8 AM, 12 AM, 4 PM, 8 PM, and 12 AM. All but the late shift (12 AM to 8 AM) overlap the next shift by 4 hours. Based on past experience, the following number of workers will be needed during the times shown:

Hours	Workers required
12 AM- 8 AM	6
8 AM-12 PM	10
12 PM- 4 PM	16
4 PM- 8 PM	18
8 PM-12 AM	8

How many workers should be scheduled to report for each of the five shifts if MPC wishes to minimize its total workforce?

33. The Party Mix Company packages and sells four types of party packages: pretzels, peanuts, chex and nuts, and a party mix. The packages are sold in 8-ounce plastic soft packs. The profits per package are shown as follows:

Package	Profit/package	Contents
Pretzels	30¢	Pretzels only
Peanuts	45¢	Peanuts only
Chex & nuts	26¢	15% peanuts, remainder chex cereals
Party mix	54¢	20% pretzels, 10% peanuts, remainder chex cereals

If PMC has 200 pounds of pretzels, 400 pounds of peanuts, and 500 pounds of chex cereals, how many packages of each type of product should it produce if it can sell all it produces.

34. The Tropical Fruit Company (TFC) supplies fruit juice and fruit juice blends to restaurants in the Southeast. TFC's juices and profit contributions per ounce are as follows: orange (7¢), grapefruit juice (7¢), tangerine (6¢), pineapple (9¢), guava (11¢), and mango (13¢). TFC's blended juices and profit contribution per ounce are: orange/pineapple (11¢), Tropical Delight—tangerine, guava, and mango (9¢), and Tropical Breeze—all six juices (10¢). The orange/pineapple blend is 60 percent orange juice and 40 percent pineapple juice. Tropical Delight is 50 percent tangerine juice, 30 percent guava juice, and 20 percent mango juice. Tropical Breeze is 30 percent pineapple

juice, 25 percent orange juice, 20 percent tangerine juice, 10 percent guava juice, 10 percent mango juice, and 5 percent grapefruit juice. The company has 200 gallons of pineapple juice, 200 gallons of tangerine juice, 300 gallons of orange juice, 250 gallons of grapefruit juice, 150 gallons of guava juice, and 100 gallons of mango juice on hand. All of TFC's products are sold by the gallon. The mango and guava juices are also available in half-gallon sizes. The company has back orders for 30 gallons of pineapple juice, 20 half-gallons of mango juice, and 25 half-gallons of guava juice that must be filled from current supplies. TFC management wishes to determine how many containers of each product to prepare to maximize its profits.

35. Acme Electronics produces a component used in a variety of small electrical appliances. Mr. Jacoby, production manager for this product line, wishes to prepare a production schedule for the next 7 weeks that will meet demand while minimizing per unit production and inventory costs. Demand for the component varies widely from week to week as shown by the contract figures in the following table:

Week	Demand
1	30,000
2	45,000
3	35,000
4	33,000
5	48,000
6	24,000
7	32,000

At full capacity during regular operating hours, Acme can produce 35,000 of these components per week. It costs Acme $3.60 per component produced during regular hours. Another 10,000 units per week can be produced by scheduling overtime. Components produced on overtime cost $5.20 per unit. Units produced during the week are shipped at the end of the week to fill existing orders. Any excess units are placed in inventory. Components placed into inventory incur a 40 cents per item per week carrying cost. There are currently 9000 components in inventory and the company has a policy of maintaining an ending inventory of at least 3000 components per week to cover special rush orders. Formulate this problem so that Mr. Jacoby can schedule production in such a way as to minimize total production and inventory costs.

Chapter

3

Graphical Linear Programming

By the end of this chapter, you should be able to:

1

plot the linear programming constraints graphically;

2

identify the area of feasible solutions or feasible region;

3

plot the LP objective function;

4

determine the optimal solution to simple problems graphically;

5

rewrite an LP model in standard form;

6

recognize graphical LP problems that have alternate optimal
solutions, are infeasible, or are unbounded.

In this chapter, we introduce the graphi-
cal approach to solving LP problems. The major purpose of the graphical approach
is that it helps to increase understanding of the more complex solution processses
that are introduced in later chapters.

3.1 *INTRODUCTION TO THE GRAPHICAL SOLUTION METHOD*

The **graphical solution method** gives a visual representation of the LP model. It
shows which solution points meet each constraint and which points do not. Once
all of the acceptable solution points have been defined using the graphical method,
the objective function can be plotted and the optimal solution point can be determined through an interpretation of the graph.

The beginning point for the graphical approach is the LP model. We will use the
model formulated in Chapter 2 for Turbo Inc. Recall that Turbo was manufacturing two different impellers for heavy-duty blowers, the Homeowner model and the
Professional model. Each Homeowner contributed $15 toward profit and each Pro-
fessional $12. The Homeowner required 1 hour of machining time and the Profes-
sional 2 hours, with a total of 80 machining hours available per day. In addition,
the Homeowner required 4 hours of heat treating and the Professional 3 hours,
with 180 hours of oven time available per day. Each Professional also required a

special teflon hub, but Turbo could obtain only 36 per day. Formulating this problem to maximize total profit contribution resulted in the following model:

$$\text{MAX } 15H + 12P$$

subject to

$$1H + 2P \le 80$$

$$4H + 3P \le 180$$

$$1P \le 36$$

$$H, P \ge 0$$

The objective function to this problem shows the relationship between units of the Homeowner model (H) and Professional model (P) produced each day and profit contribution. The first constraint represents the machining time, the second the oven time, and the third the teflon hubs. The last constraint, $H, P \ge 0$, is the non-negativity constraint, which indicates the solution values must lie above the H-axis and to the right of the P-axis.

Plotting the Constraints

The first step in the graphic solution procedure is to plot each constraint equation on the graph. For clarity, we will show each constraint plotted separately and then combine them on one graph. H will be placed on the horizontal axis (H-axis) and P on the vertical axis (P-axis). The machining constraint will be plotted first.

$$1H + 2P \le 80$$

The easiest way to plot the constraints is to consider only the equality portion of the constraint ($1H + 2P = 80$), and to determine the H-axis and P-axis intercepts for this line. The point where the line intercepts the H-axis can be determined by setting the value of P to zero and solving for the value of H:

$$1H + 2(0) = 80$$

$$H = 80$$

Thus, a point is plotted at $H = 80$ (and $P = 0$) on the H-axis. Moving to the P-axis, where the value of H is zero, the value of P can be determined:

$$1(0) + 2P = 80$$

$$2P = 80$$

$$P = 40$$

Thus, a point can be plotted on the P-axis at $P = 40$ (and $H = 0$). Given that the equation is linear, these two points can now be connected with a straight line, as shown in Figure 3.1(a). Since the constraint was plotted as an equation, the next step is to determine on which side of this line the points less than 80 lie. This can be accomplished by examining the values on one of the axes. On the H-axis, all values less than 80 lie to the left of the intercept point. Therefore, points to the left of the line (under) will satisfy the constraint.

The shaded area in Figure 3.1(b) represents the set of all nonnegative points which satisfy this constraint, i.e., all nonnegative points which lie on or under this constraint.

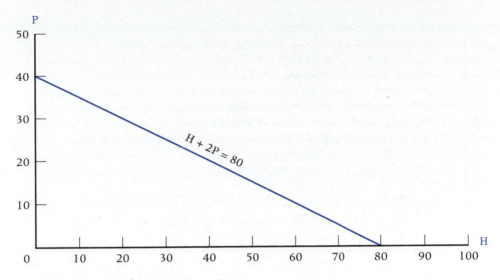

Figure 3.1(a) Machining Constraint

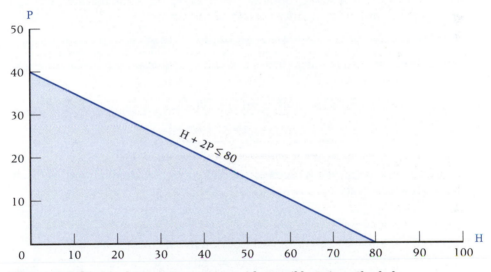

Figure 3.1(b) Machining Constraint with Feasible Points Shaded

Any point on the line will give a combination of Homeowner and Professional impellers that will require exactly 80 hours of machining time. Any point below the line, such as point X in Figure 3.2 (H = 10 and P = 10), will require less than 80 hours of machining time $(1H + 2P = 1 \times 10 + 2 \times 20 = 30)$. Any point above the line, such as point Y in Figure 3.2 (H = 30 and P = 40), will require more than 80 hours of machining time $(1H + 2P = 1 \times 30 + 2 \times 80 = 110)$. Any point on or under the line is an acceptable or feasible solution point, whereas any point above the line exceeds the available hours and therefore is referred to as an infeasible solution point.

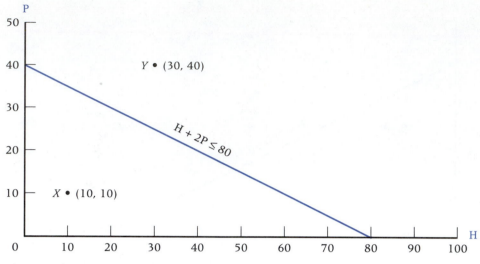

Figure 3.2 Example Points

The heat treating constraint can now be plotted in the same manner. The constraint is expressed by the equality portion of the constraint

$$4H + 3P = 180$$

On the H-axis, zero can be substituted for P and the equation solved for the H-axis intercept:

$$4H + 3(0) = 180$$
$$4H = 180$$
$$H = 45$$

After plotting the point (45,0), we move to the P-axis, set H equal to 0, and solve for the P-axis intercept:

$$4(0) + 3P = 180$$
$$3P = 180$$
$$P = 60$$

Once the point (0,60) is plotted, the two points can be connected with a straight line as shown in Figure 3.3. Again, the shaded area represents points that satisfy the inequality. This figure illustrates the limitations imposed by the heat treating department. Any combination of Homeowner and Professional impellers represented by a point on or under this constraint line can be produced.

The third constraint, representing the teflon hubs, can be represented by a straight horizontal line at P = 36, as shown in Figure 3.4. Because this constraint is P ≤ 36, any number of Professional models between 0 and 36 (the shaded area) can be produced.

Although we have shown each of the above constraints separately, normally they are all placed on the same graph, as shown in Figure 3.5. Since any impellers manufactured must pass through both the machining and heat treating depart-

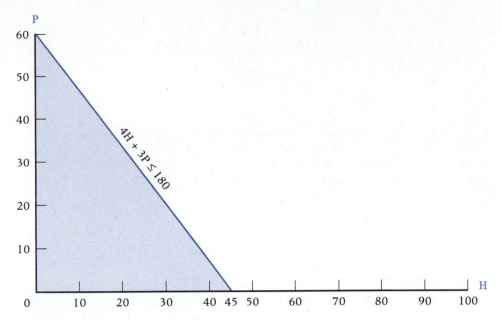

Figure 3.3 Heat Treat Constraint

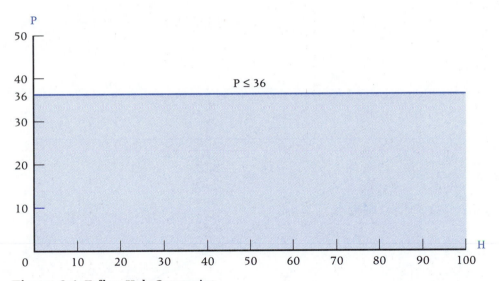

Figure 3.4 Teflon Hub Constraint

ments, and the Professional models must also have the teflon hub, Turbo can manufacture any number of Homeowner and Professional models that conforms to all of these constraints simultaneously. These points are in the shaded area of Figure 3.5.

Feasible Region

The area defining the set of feasible solution points (acceptable solutions) is known as the **feasible region**, or area of feasible solutions, and is shown as the heavily shaded area in Figure 3.6. Any point outside this region or area, such as point E or

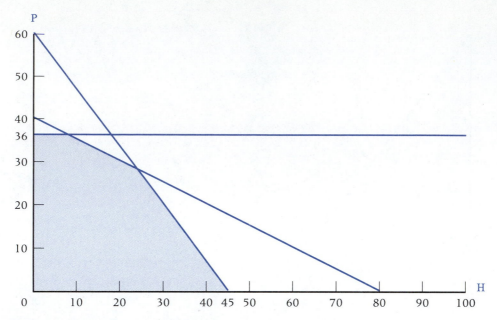

Figure 3.5 All Constraints Plotted

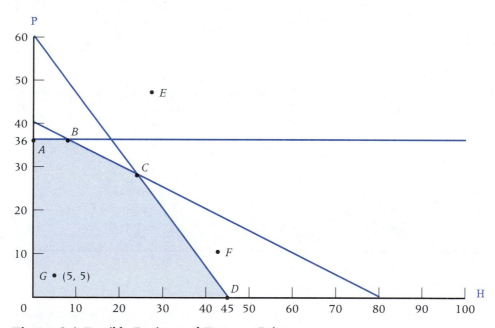

Figure 3.6 Feasible Region and Extreme Points

F, represents a combination of Homeowner and Professional models that violates one or more of the stated constraints and is therefore defined as infeasible, or an infeasible solution.

Point G (5, 5) lies inside the area and is a feasible solution. The objective, however, is to find the optimal solution. By inspection of the graph, you can see that there are other feasible points that allow greater production, and greater profit, than point G. The boundary on feasible points is the edge of the feasible region.

Points A, B, C, and D all lie at the edge of the feasible region and are known as **extreme points**. They represent the intersections of the problem constraints. An optimal solution occurs at one of these points. (The origin also is an extreme point on the feasible region, but is not discussed since it cannot be an optimal solution to a maximization problem.)

The value of the objective function can be determined at each of these extreme points by determining the value of H and P at each point and substituting these values back into the objective function. The following table shows the values at each extreme point and the corresponding value of the objective function (15H + 12P):

Extreme Point	Variable Values	Objective Function Values
A	H = 0, P = 36	432
B	H = 8, P = 36	552
C	H = 24, P = 28	696
D	H = 45, P = 0	675

Since the optimal solution occurs at the point where the value of the objective function is maximized, the optimal solution occurs at point C, where the value of the objective function is $696. Point C designates the point on the graph where H = 24 and P = 28. However, enumerating all extreme point values is an inefficient solution method. We will now show how the optimal solution is found without this enumeration.

Plotting the Objective Function

The objective function for this problem (MAX 15H + 12P) gives the relationship between the decision variables and total profit contribution. If an arbitrary total profit figure is selected (e.g., $180) and the objective function is set equal to that value, the objective function can also be plotted:

$$15H + 12P = 180$$

Solving for the axis intercepts gives H = 12 when P = 0 and P = 15 when H = 0. This objective function is drawn as a dotted line to distinguish it from the constraint lines, as shown in Figure 3.7. Any combination of Homeowner and Professional impellers that lies on this line will yield a profit contribution of exactly $180.

If the objective function is set equal to $360 and solved again, H = 24 when P = 0 and P = 30 when H = 0. Notice that, when the value of the objective function is doubled, the axis intercepts also double. This line (15H + 12P = 360) can also be plotted on the graph as shown in Figure 3.8. Any point on this line represents a combination of Homeowner and Professional impellers that will provide a profit contribution of exactly $360.

Two observations can be made about these lines. First, they are parallel, since they both have the same slope. Second, as the lines move further from the origin, the value of the objective function increases. Thus, a number of such objective functions could be drawn on the graph, each one parallel to the previous one and each increasing in value as it moves further from the origin. In economic terms, such lines are called **isoprofit lines**.

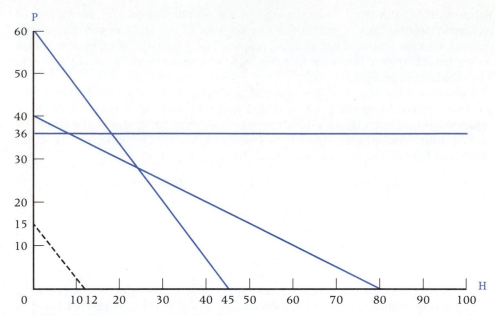

Figure 3.7 $180 Objective Function Plotted

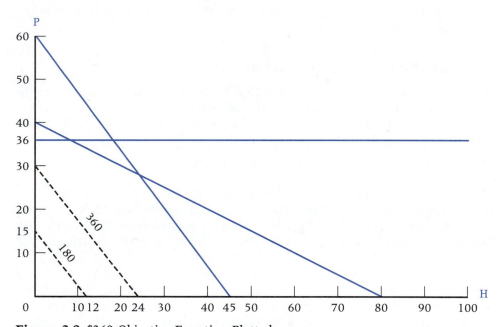

Figure 3.8 $360 Objective Function Plotted

There is no need to draw a large number of these isoprofit lines. Whenever an isoprofit line passes through the feasible region, it indicates there are additional solutions that give a greater profit contribution. Since the optimal solution occurs at an extreme point, we look for an isoprofit (objective function) line that is just touching or tangent to the feasible region. At this point of tangency, a feasible solution exists that is also optimal, since the isoprofit line cannot be moved further without moving it totally into the infeasible range. Thus, there is no need to draw several isoprofit lines. If we can draw one line on the graph and then determine from that line where a parallel line would be tangent to the area of feasible solutions, that point of tangency will be the optimal solution.

Since the isoprofit line is used to determine the point of tangency, we need a value that results in an isoprofit line that lies very close to the edge of the area of feasible solutions. Arbitrarily selecting such a value is not always an easy task. A slightly different approach can be used to avoid this selection problem, as discussed in the next section.

Using a Multiplier to Place an Objective Function on the Graph

In the example, the objective function was first set equal to the product of the decision variable coefficients:

$$15H + 12P = (15 \times 12)$$

That gave the intercepts $(0, 15)$ and $(12, 0)$. When that value was doubled, the intersect values doubled. This operation is equivalent to multiplying the product of the coefficients by 2:

$$15H + 12P = (15 \times 12) \times 2$$

Now if the product of the two coefficients is set equal to a constant, CNST, and the multiplier (2) is set equal to m, the equation can be rewritten as

$$15H + 12P = CNST \times m$$

If m is assumed to be equal to 1, the intersect value of each variable is equal to the coefficient of the other variable; that is, $H = 12$ when $P = 0$ and $P = 15$ when $H = 0$. These points can be marked on the axis and used to determine where a line connecting these points will fall, relative to the feasible region.

If an isoprofit line further from the origin is desired, each intersect value can be multiplied by a value m to obtain new intersect points. A multiplier of 2 will give intersects of $H = 24$ and $P = 30$; a multiplier of 3 yields intersects of $H = 36$ and $P = 45$. If the original isoprofit line would lie too far outside the feasible region, a fractional multiplier could be used. For example, a multiplier of $\frac{1}{3}$ would give intersects of $H = 4$ and $P = 5$. In the example problem, a multiplier of 4 would give intersects of $H = 48$ and $P = 60$. Plotting this isoprofit line shows that a line parallel to this line should be tangent to the feasible region at point C, as in Figure 3.9.

Once point C is determined to be the optimal solution point, the H and P (X and Y) coordinates for this point can be found. If the graph has a large enough scale and is drawn carefully, vertical and horizontal lines can be drawn from the point to the H and P axes to determine the values $H = 24$ and $P = 28$, as shown in Figure 3.10. Substituting these points into the objective function gives the value $696. Thus, the point of tangency gives the same optimal solution as the enumeration of the extreme points, but without all the accompanying calculations. If the scale of the graph does not permit the coordinates to be read accurately, they can be determined by treating the inequalities as equalities and solving the two constraints that intersect at the optimal point simultaneously. This procedure should be familiar, but is discussed below for review.

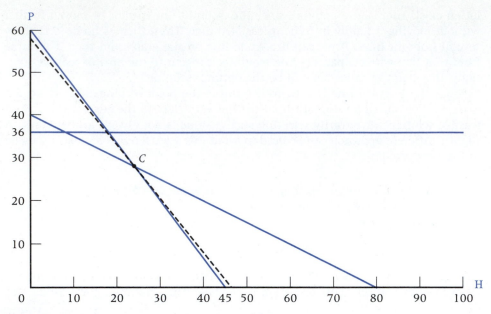

Figure 3.9 Determining a Point of Tangency

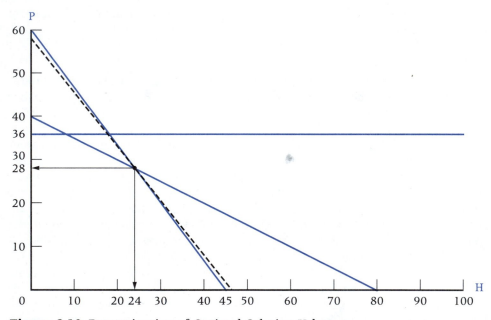

Figure 3.10 Determination of Optimal Solution Values

Determining the Intersect of Two Equations

Frequently, an optimal point cannot be read accurately from a graph. In this problem, the constraints which intersect at the optimal point are

$$[1] \quad 1H + 2P \leq 80$$

and $\qquad [2] \quad 4H + 3P \leq 180$

These constraints are known as **binding constraints** because the optimal solution point lies at their intersection. They determine (limit) the optimal solution point. Constraints that do not pass through the optimal solution point are **nonbinding**.

We will convert both inequalities to equalities (since the optimal point lies *on* the lines, not below them) and perform **elementary row operations** (multiplying or dividing all terms in the inequality by a constant) to solve. Multiplying the first constraint by 4 gives $4H + 8P = 320$. Subtracting the second constraint equation from this equation and solving for P,

$$[1] \quad 4H + 8P = 320$$
$$[2] \quad -(4H + 3P = 180)$$
$$5P = 140$$
$$P = {}^{140}\!/_{5} = 28$$

yields P = 28. This value can be substituted back into either of the original constraint equations to solve for H:

$$1H + 2(28) = 80$$
$$1H + 56 = 80$$
$$1H = 80 - 56 = 24$$

Thus, the intersect coordinates are H = 24 and P = 28. These values can be substituted into the objective function to determine the maximum profit contribution:

$$15(24) + 12(28) = 360 + 336 = 696$$

The solution says that Turbo will achieve a maximum profit contribution of $696 if it produces 24 Homeowner and 28 Professional impellers.

Note, however, that this solution gives the point of intersection of two constraint lines. If the constraints do not intersect at the optimal point, the answer will not be the optimal solution to the problem. The optimal solution is determined graphically, and this procedure is used only to verify or determine the precise values.

Summary of the Graphical Solution Procedure

To solve a linear programming problem graphically, we use the following algorithm:

1. Formulate the LP model.
2. Plot each constraint on graph paper by finding the points where that constraint, when treated as an equality, intercepts each axis, and then connecting those points with a straight line.
3. Once all the constraints have been plotted, determine the feasible region (that area bounded by and conforming to the inequalities).
4. Plot the objective function as a dotted line by determining the axis intercepts and then using an appropriate multiplier so that the objective function is somewhat near the edge of the feasible region.
5. Determine where a line parallel to the plotted objective function would be tangent to the feasible region. This point is the optimal solution.

6. Read the values (coordinate points) of the optimal solution point from the graph's axes, or solve for them using the appropriate constraint equations.
7. Substitute the solution values into the objective function to determine the optimal value of the objective function.

3.2 SLACK AND SURPLUS VARIABLES AND THE STANDARD FORM

Sometimes an optimal solution does not use all of an available resource. The remaining quantity of this resource is referred to as slack. At other times, an optimal solution exceeds a stated requirement; for example, at least 10 units must be produced. When this happens, the amount by which the requirement is exceeded is called a surplus. In maximization problems, slack may occur with a less-than-or-equal-to constraint, and surplus may occur with a greater-than-or-equal-to constraint. The amount of slack or surplus associated with any constraint can be determined by changing the constraint inequality to an equality through the addition of a slack or surplus variable. When all model constraints are changed in this manner, the problem is said to be in **standard form**. The letter S is used to represent slack and/or surplus variables, with subscripts to distinguish between them. S_1 denotes the slack in constraint 1, S_2 is the slack in constraint 2, and so on.

Recall that the optimal solution point lies at the intersection of two or more constraints. Thus, slack and surplus are zero for binding constraints. Similarly, all non-binding constraints have a nonzero slack or surplus value.

We will use the Turbo problem to illustrate the conversion of an LP model to its standard form. The original model was formulated as:

$$MAX\ 15H + 12P$$

subject to

$$1H + 2P \leq 80 \quad \text{[machining hours]}$$
$$4H + 3P \leq 180 \quad \text{[heat treating hours]}$$
$$1P \leq 36 \quad \text{[hub liners]}$$
$$H, P \geq 0$$

Since all of the original constraints are less-than-or-equal-to constraints, we can rewrite them as equalities by including **slack variables**. Using S_1 to represent the unused machining hours, S_2 to represent the unused heat treating hours, and S_3 to represent unused hub liners, the model can now be expressed in its standard form:

$$MAX\ 15H + 12P + 0S_1 + 0S_2 + 0S_3$$

subject to

$$1H + 2P + 1S_1 \qquad\qquad = 80$$
$$4H + 3P + \qquad 1S_2 \qquad = 180$$
$$1P + \qquad\qquad 1S_3 = 36$$
$$H, P, S_1, S_2, S_3 \geq 0$$

Note that the slack variables are added to the objective function as well. Since they provide no contribution to profit, they have coefficients of zero (0).

Substituting the optimal solution point values found previously (H = 24, P = 28) into the standard form of this problem and solving gives the following values:

$$S_1 = 0$$

$$S_2 = 0$$

$$S_3 = 8$$

Thus, by converting the model to its standard form and substituting the optimal values, we can determine the value of all slack variables. These values represent the amount of unused resource associated with each constraint. The binding constraints (machining and heat treating) have zero slack. The third constraint (hub liners) is nonbinding. At the optimal production level, there are eight unused hub liners.

Some problems may have greater-than-or-equal-to constraints. For example:

$$2X_1 + 3X_2 \geq 12$$

To change this inequality to the standard form, a **surplus variable** is subtracted from the left-hand side of the inequality to change it to an equality. In the following equation, S_1 represents a surplus variable:

$$2X_1 + 3X_2 - S_1 = 12$$

If the optimal solution were $X_1 = 4$ and $X_2 = 2$, the value of S_1 could be determined through substitution:

$$2(4) + 3(2) - S_1 = 12$$

$$8 + 6 - S_1 = 12$$

$$S_1 = 14 - 12$$

$$S_1 = 2$$

This solution implies that a surplus of 2 exists; a minimum LHS value of 12 is required by the constraint, and the LHS value for the optimal solution is 14.

Thus, when changing a less-than-or-equal-to constraint to the standard form, a slack variable is added; and when changing a greater-than-or-equal-to constraint to the standard form, a surplus variable is subtracted. Since the letter S is used for both slack and surplus variables, subscripts can be used to distinguish among the various constraints. If the first constraint requries the addition of a slack variable, it is called S_1. If the second constraint requires the subtraction of a surplus variable, it is called S_2. Constraints represented by equalities need neither a slack nor a surplus variable, since they are already in the standard form.

3.3 *SOLVING MINIMIZATION PROBLEMS GRAPHICALLY*

In the Turbo problem, we were looking for a solution that maximized the contribution to profit. The graphical method can also be used to solve problems that attempt to minimize the objective function. Consider the problem given below:

$$\text{MIN } 5X + 7Y$$

subject to

$$3X + 5Y \geq 30$$
$$6X + 2Y \geq 24$$
$$X + Y \geq 8$$
$$X,Y \geq 0$$

Following the normal solution precedure used for maximization problems, first we plot the constraints. The first constraint intersects the X axis at X = 10, Y = 0 and the Y axis at X = 0, Y = 6. Since this is a greater-than-or-equal-to constraint, solution points must lie on or above this line to be feasible. This constraint is shown graphically in Figure 3.11. The second constraint gives the axis points X = 4, Y = 0 and X = 0, Y = 12. Again, feasible points must be on or above the line. This constraint is shown in Figure 3.12. The third constraint gives the axis points X = 8, Y = 0 and X = 0, Y = 8, as shown in Figure 3.13. Again, all constraints normally are plotted on the same graph, but they are shown separately in the previous figures for clarity. The constraints are combined in Figure 3.14, with the area of feasible solutions shaded. The objective function can now be plotted. Since cost is being minimized in this problem, the objective function represents an **isocost** rather than an isoprofit line. Although the isoprofit line is extended as far from the origin as possible in order to maximize profit, an isocost line should be as close to the origin as possible (and tangent to the area of feasible solutions), since this point of tangency represents the minimum cost solution.

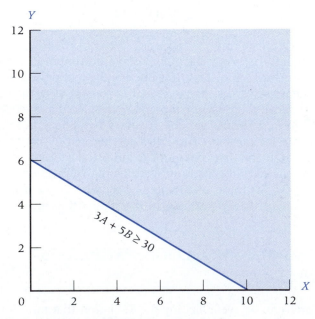

Figure 3.11 Minimization Problem—First Constraint

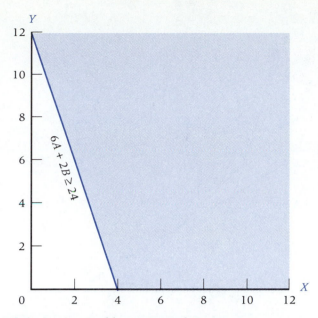

Figure 3.12 Minimization Problem—Second Constraint

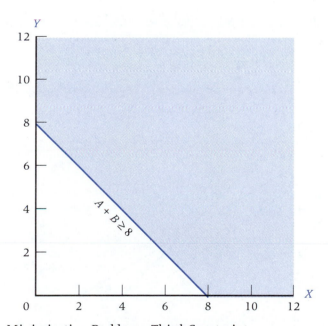

Figure 3.13 Minimization Problem—Third Constraint

Following the procedure outlined earlier in the chapter, we let X = 7 when Y = 0 and Y = 5 when X = 0. These points give an isocost line that lies fairly near the feasible region, so it is not necessary to use a multiplier in this problem to adjust its location. Figure 3.15 illustrates this fact. The graphic solution in Figure 3.15

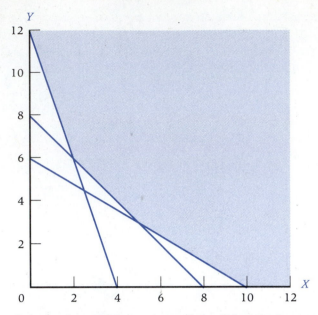

Figure 3.14 Minimization Problem—Area of Feasible Solutions

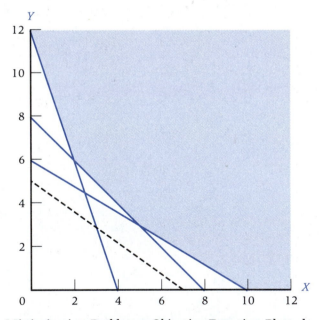

Figure 3.15 Minimization Problem—Objective Function Plotted

shows that a line parallel to the present isocost line would be tangent to the area of feasible solutions at point $(5, 3)$. The optimal solution to this problem, therefore, is $X = 5$, $Y = 3$, and the value of the objective function is $5(5) + 7(3)$ or 46.

Thus, the solution procedure for a minimization problem is similar to that for a maximization problem. The basic differences are (1) that the objective function is represented by an isocost line rather than an isoprofit line; and (2) that the point of tangency with the feasible region lies as close to the origin as possible, since iso-cost lines closer to the origin have smaller values.

Handling a Problem with Unusual Constraints

The example problems solved thus far have been fairly straightforward in terms of graphing the constraints and identifying the area of feasible solutions. Let's vary the constraints slightly in the minimization problem we just solved:

$$\text{MIN} \quad 5X + 7Y$$

subject to

[1]	$3X + 5Y \geq 30$
[2]	$6X \geq 24$
[3]	$4X \geq 2Y$
[4]	$X \leq 8$
	$X, Y \geq 0$

Before, we can solve this problem, we must restate the third constraint, since constraints must have all decision variables on the LHS of the constraint and all constants on the RHS. In this case, the term 2Y can be moved to the LHS by subtracting it from both sides, giving the constraint

$$[3] \quad 4X - 2Y \geq 0$$

Now we can follow the normal procedure for solving problems graphically, beginning with the determination of the intersect points and the plotting of each constraint. The first constraint intersects the X-axis at X = 10 and the Y-axis at Y = 6. Since the constraint is greater-than-or-equal, all feasible solutions must lie on or above this line, as shown in Figure 3.16. The second constraint intersects the

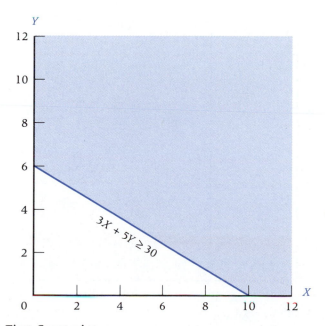

Figure 3.16 First Constraint

X axis at X = 4, represented by a vertical line with the feasible area to the right of it. This constraint is shown in Figure 3.17. The third constraint must be handled differently, because one of the variables has a negative coefficient. This constraint will have a positive slope and not intersect both axes in this quadrant. Treating the inequality like an equality gives

$$4X - 2Y = 0$$

Substituting 0 for X and solving gives Y = 0. Thus, this constraint begins at the origin (X = 0, Y = 0). For the second point, an arbitrary value is selected for either X or Y and substituted into the equation. If, for example, X is set equal to 1, then Y must equal 2:

$$4(1) - 2Y = 0$$

$$-2Y = -4$$

$$2Y = 4$$

$$Y = 2$$

This point can be plotted on the graph and a line drawn from the origin through it (and extend it further). Because the inequality was greater-than-or-equal-to zero, the feasible area in this case lies below the line. When Y = 2, X may equal 1, 2, 3, and so on, as shown in Figure 3.18.

The fourth constraint produces a vertical line at X = 8. Since this constraint is less-than-or-equal, the feasible points must lie to the left of this line, as shown in Figure 3.19.

Again, the constraints normally are all put on the same graph. They have been shown separately here for purposes of clarity. Combining these constraints in Figure 3.20 yields the feasible region for this problem.

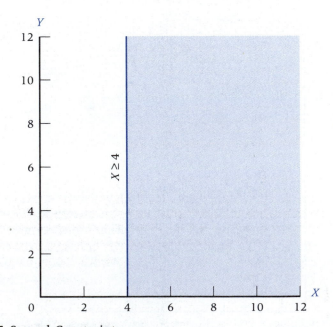

Figure 3.17 Second Constraint

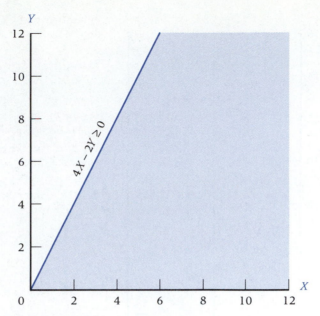

Figure 3.18 Third Constraint

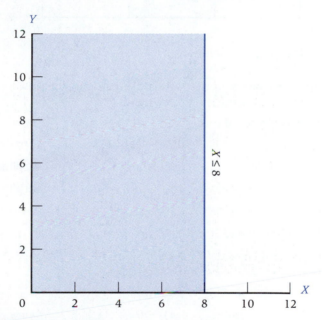

Figure 3.19 Fourth Constraint

The objective function can not be plotted (an isocost line). This line is identical to the one used in the previous example, since the objective function did not change. Figure 3.21 (on page 81) shows this isocost line on the graph. Figure 3.21 shows that the point of tangency occurs at X = 4, Y = 3.6. Substituting these values back into the objective function yields a value of 45.2.

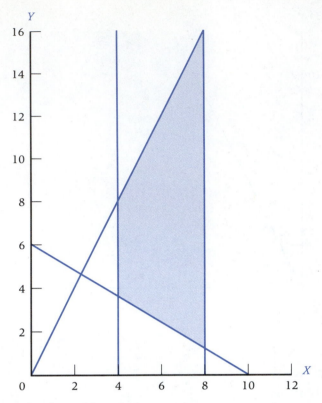

Figure 3.20 Area of Feasible Solutions

Converting the constraints to the standard form and substituting the solution values into the equations yields the following results.

Constraints expressed in standard form:

$$3X + 5Y - 1S_1 + 0S_2 + 0S_3 + 0S_4 = 30 \quad (S_1 = \text{surplus})$$

$$6X \quad + 0S_1 - 1S_2 + 0S_3 + 0S_4 = 24 \quad (S_2 = \text{surplus})$$

$$4X - 2Y + 0S_1 + 0S_2 - 1S_3 + 0S_4 = 0 \quad (S_3 = \text{surplus})$$

$$X \quad + 0S_1 + 0S_2 + 0S_3 + 1S_4 = 8 \quad (S_4 = \text{slack})$$

Substituting the optimal values for X and Y:

constraint 1: $3(4) + 5(3.6) - S_1 = 30$

$12 + 18 - S_1 = 30$

$S_1 = 0$

constraint 2: $6(4) - S_2 = 24$

$24 - S_2 = 24$

$S_2 = 0$

constraint 3: $4(4) - 2(3.6) - S_3 = 0$

$16 - 7.2 - S_3 = 0$

$S_3 = 8.8$

constraint 4: $4 + S_4 = 8$

$S_4 = 4$

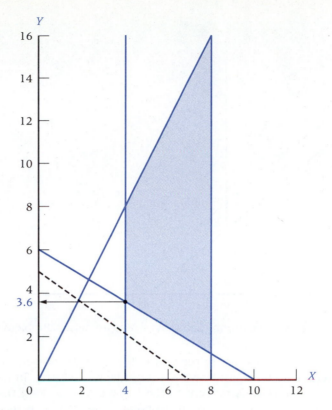

Figure 3.21 Objective Function Plotted

Thus, surplus variables S_1 and S_2 are equal to zero, surplus variable S_3 is equal to 8.8, and slack variable S_4 is equal to 4. Constraints 1 and 2 have no surplus values because they are binding. The surplus in constraint 3 implies that enough X and Y are used to exceed that requirement by 8.8 units. The slack in constraint 4 indicates that four units of that resource remain, i.e., not all of the original eight units were used.

3.4 *ALTERNATE OPTIMAL SOLUTIONS*

In some cases, the objective function, when plotted as an isoprofit or isocost line, is parallel to a binding constraint. When that happens, the optimal objective function is tangent to the area of feasible solutions all along the edge of the area rather than at a single point. Figure 3.22 illustrates this situation for the problem

$$\text{MAX} \quad 10X + 12Y$$

subject to

$$2X \quad\quad\quad \geq \quad 12$$
$$5X + 6Y \leq 270$$
$$X \quad\quad\quad \leq \quad 36$$
$$X, Y \geq 0$$

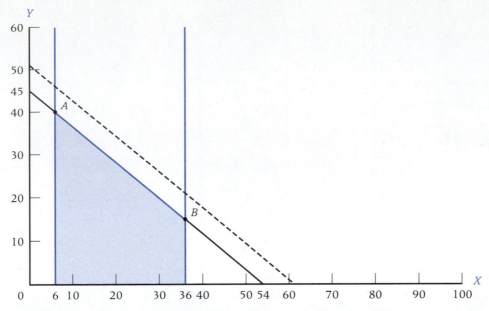

Figure 3.22 Alternative Optimal Solutions—Maximization Problems

The parallel isocost line appears in the figure; the optimal (tangent) isocost line is superimposed on the constraint line and cannot be seen clearly. In the figure, the optimal objective function is tangent to the feasible region along the edge represented by the line from point A (6, 40) to point B (36, 15). This means that any point on that line (A to B) is an optimal solution, producing the same value for the objective function (540). We describe this problem as having **alternate optimal solutions**. In other words, there are multiple or alternate solutions that are optimal in terms of maximizing or minimizing the value of the objective function.

3.5 *PROBLEMS THAT CAN'T BE SOLVED*

Occasionally, a LP problem cannot be solved graphically. There are two types of problems that have no optimal solution. The first is called an infeasible problem and the second an unbounded problem.

Infeasible Problems

An **infeasible problem** is one that has no common area of feasible solutions. The following problem would be infeasible:

$$\text{MAX } 2X_1 + 5X_2$$

subject to

$$4X_1 + 6X_2 \leq 240$$

$$3X_1 + 2X_2 \geq 240$$

$$X_1, X_2 \geq 0$$

The graphical solution in Figure 3.23 reveals that there is no common point that is both below the first constraint and above second. Thus, this problem is an infeasible problem. Problems are infeasible only when the constraints imposed upon the solution cannot possibly be met.

Unbounded Problems

An **unbounded problem** is one that has no binding limits; that is, the area of feasible solutions allows one or more of the decision variables to be infinite. The following problem is unbounded:

$$MAX\ 2X_1 + 5X_2$$

subject to:

$$X_1 + X_2 \geq 20$$
$$X_2 \leq 15$$
$$X_1, X_2 \geq 0$$

The graphical solution shown in Figure 3.24 reveals that the area of feasible solutions has no boundary on the right-hand side, so that it appears possible to produce an infinite amount of X_1. Since an infinite amount of any product cannot actually be produced in a finite amount of time, the existence of an unbounded problem typically indicates that a constraint was omitted when the problem was originally stated (e.g., there are only 24 hours per day). There are no true unbounded problems in actuality, but there may be problems for which a constraint

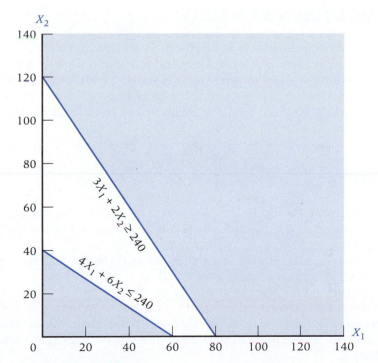

Figure 3.23 Infeasible Problem

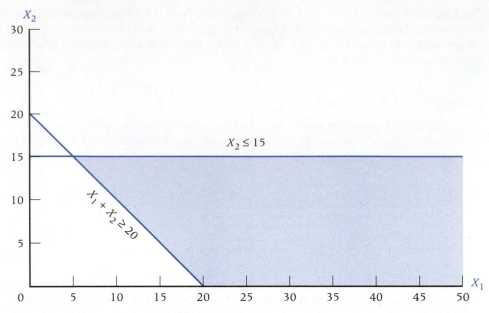

Figure 3.24 Unbounded Problem

was not stated in the original problem formulation. Thus, when you find that a problem is unbounded, reexamine the problem formulation to discover the missing constraint.

3.6 *CONCLUDING REMARKS*

Once linear programming problems have been formulated, they can be solved. Although the graphical approach is not a practical solution method for most LP problems, it does provide a visual representation of simple LP problems and serves as a basis for understanding the more complex procedures discussed in Chapters 4 and 5. Realistically, graphical solutions are limited to small problems with two decision variables.

GLOSSARY

alternate optimal solutions situation where more than one optimal solution exists; occurs when the objective function is parallel to one of the binding constraint lines

binding constraint constraint that passes through the optimal solution point; has no slack or surplus associated with it

extreme points points that lie at the intersection of two or more constraints within the feasible region

feasible region the solution space that satisfies all the constraints simultaneously

elementary row operations an equality or inequality is multiplied or divided by a constant

feasible solution any solution that meets both the constraint limitations and the nonnegativity requirements

graphical solution method method of solving LP problems with two variables in which the constraints are plotted to define an area of feasible solutions, and the objective function is then plotted to determine a point of tangency between the objective function and the area of feasible solutions; this point is the optimal solution

infeasible problem a problem that has no points that meet all of the constraint requirements and which satisfy the nonnegativity requirement

infeasible solution a solution that does not meet all of the constraint requirements, or that produces a negative solution point

isocost lines a set of lines plotted on the graph that have the same slope and represent the different cost levels associated with various decision variable values

iosprofit lines a set of lines plotted on the graph that have the same slope and represent the different profit levels associated with various decision variable values

nonbinding constraint constraint that does not pass through the optimal solution point; nonzero slack or surplus values associated with it

slack variable a variable that represents the amount of unused resource available when an optimal solution has been reached; represented by a subscripted letter S

standard form an LP model with slack and/or surplus variables added, so that all the constraints are expressed as equalities with all the decision variables on the LHS and the constants on the RHS

surplus variable a variable that represents the amount by which a greater-than constraint has been exceeded when an optimal solution is reached; represented by a subscripted letter S

unbounded problem an LP problem that allows for an infinite quantity of one or more of the decision variables in the optimal solution; that is, one or more of the decision variables are unconstrained

PROBLEMS

1. Graph each of the following constraints. Indicate the feasible region for each constraint.

   a. $3X_1 + 5X_2 \leq 75$
   b. $2X_1 + 3X_2 \geq 30$
   c. $4X_1 + 2X_2 = 16$
   d. $5X_1 \leq 35$
   e. $-3X_1 + 4X_2 \geq 24$
   f. $7X_1 - 4X_2 \leq 56$

2. Graph the following constraints. Indicate the feasible region for these constraints and determine the values for each of the extreme points.

$$5X_1 + 4X_2 \leq 40$$
$$3X_1 + 5X_2 \leq 30$$
$$10X_2 \leq 50$$
$$X_1, X_2 \geq 0$$

3. What is the optimal solution to problem 2 if the objective function is (MAX):

   a. $3X_1 + 2X_2$
   b. $X_1 + 2X_2$
   c. $7X_1 + 9X_2$

4. A manager has formulated the following LP product mix problem. Solve this problem graphically.

$$MAX\ 4X_1 + 5X_2$$

subject to
$$4X_1 + 2X_2 \leq 120$$
$$3X_1 + 6X_2 \leq 180$$
$$X_1, X_2 \geq 0$$

5. Solve the following LP problem graphically.

$$MAX\ X_1 + 5X_2$$

subject to
$$X_1 + 2X_2 \leq 40$$
$$3X_1 + X_2 \leq 45$$
$$X_1, X_2 \geq 0$$

6. Solve the following LP problem graphically.

$$MAX\ 5X_1 + 3X_2$$

subject to
$$3X_1 \qquad \leq 18$$
$$2X_2 \leq 8$$
$$2X_1 + 3X_2 \leq 18$$
$$X_1, X_2 \geq 0$$

7. Solve the following LP problem graphically.

$$MAX\ 30X_1 + 18X_2$$

subject to
$$2X_1 + 3X_2 \leq 9$$
$$12X_1 + 9X_2 \geq 36$$
$$2X_1 + 4X_2 \geq 12$$
$$X_1, X_2 \geq 0$$

8. The Door-2-Door Products problem (example blending problem, Chaper 2) was formulated as follows:

$$MIN\ 1.10A + 1.35B$$

subject to
$$A + B = 200000$$
$$.20A + .05B \geq 20000$$

$$.20A + .05B \leq 30000$$
$$.05B \geq 4000$$
$$A, B \geq 0$$

Determine the optimal number of gallons of cleanser to purchase from suppliers A and B by solving this problem graphically.

9. The Stereo Shop (Chapter 2, problem 6) wishes to determine the number of economy and basic stereo systems it should assemble to maximize its profits. Solve this problem graphically.

10. Solve the following LP problem graphically.

$$\text{MAX } 5X_1 + 7X_2$$

subject to
$$2X_1 + 2X_2 \leq 16$$
$$12X_1 + 7X_2 \leq 84$$
$$3X_1 + 6X_2 \leq 36$$
$$X_1, X_2 \geq 0$$

11. Solve the following LP problem graphically.

$$\text{MAX } 6X_1 + 6X_2$$

subject to
$$X_1 \leq 50$$
$$2X_2 \leq 80$$
$$0.5X_1 + X_2 \leq 50$$
$$X_1, X_2 \geq 0$$

12. The clothing manufacturer (Chapter 2, problem 7) wishes to determine the number of football jerseys and soccer shirts to produce to maximize profits. Solve this problem graphically.

13. Wexler Electronics produces two specialty radios. The regular model is an AM/FM radio; the deluxe model also includes a tape player. Wexler is planning its production schedule for the coming week (40 hours). A regular radio requires 20 minutes of assembly time and a deluxe radio requires 30 minutes of assembly time. Wexler has 110 AM/FM receivers and 40 tape players on hand for the coming week; all other parts are available in larger quantities. Wexler makes $12 profit on a regular radio and $15 profit on a deluxe radio. Solve this problem graphically.

14. Consider the following LP problem:

$$\text{MAX } 6X_1 + 4X_2$$

subject to
$$X_1 + 2X_2 \leq 6$$
$$2X_1 + 3X_2 \leq 12$$
$$3X_1 + 3X_2 \leq 12$$
$$X_1, X_2 \geq 0$$

15. Solve the following LP problem graphically.

$$\text{MAX } 3X_1 + 6X_2$$

subject to

$$X_1 + X_2 \le 20$$
$$-2X_1 + 4X_2 \le 50$$
$$5X_1 + 3X_2 \le 75$$
$$X_1, X_2 \ge 0$$

16. Solve the following LP problem graphically.

$$\text{MAX } 2X_1 + X_2$$

subject to

$$2X_1 + 2X_2 \le 32$$
$$X_1 = 10$$
$$4X_1 + 6X_2 \ge 48$$
$$X_1, X_2 \ge 0$$

17. Solve the following LP problem graphically.

$$\text{MAX } 5X_1 + 10X_2$$

subject to

$$X_1 \le 15$$
$$X_2 \le 12$$
$$3X_1 + 3X_2 = 54$$
$$X_1, X_2 \ge 0$$

18. The plastics manufacturer discussed in Chapter 2, problem 8, wishes to find the optimal production schedule for his two products. Solve this problem graphically.

19. The ABC Company (Chapter 2, problem 9) must decide how many gliders and chairs to display on its showroom floor. Determine the optimal display graphically.

20. Solve the following LP problem graphically.

$$\text{MAX } 6X_1 + 4X_2$$

subject to

$$X_1 + X_2 \le 18$$
$$3X_1 + 1.5X_2 \le 45$$
$$2X_1 \ge 9$$
$$3X_2 \ge 36$$
$$X_1, X_2 \ge 0$$

21. Solve the following LP problem graphically.

$$\text{MIN } 3X_1 + 4X_2$$

subject to

$$6X_1 + 3X_2 \ge 210$$
$$2X_1 + 4X_2 \ge 160$$
$$X_1, X_2 \ge 0$$

22. Solve the following LP problem graphically.

$$\text{MIN } 5X_1 + 4X_2$$

subject to
$$\begin{aligned} X_1 + X_2 &\geq 8 \\ X_1 + 3X_2 &\geq 12 \\ 3X_1 + X_2 &\geq 12 \\ X_1, X_2 &\geq 0 \end{aligned}$$

23. Consider the following LP problem:

$$\text{MIN } 9X_1 + 6X_2$$

subject to
$$\begin{aligned} X_1 + X_2 &\geq 5 \\ 2X_1 + X_2 &\geq 6 \\ X_2 &\leq 2 \\ X_1, X_2 &\geq 0 \end{aligned}$$

a. Convert this problem to the standard form.
b. Solve the problem graphically.
c. State the slack or surplus values associated with each constraint.

24. Convert the following problem to the standard form.

$$\text{MAX } X_1 + X_2 + X_3$$

subject to
$$\begin{aligned} 3X_1 + 4X_2 + 2X_3 &\leq 100 \\ 5X_1 + 3X_2 + 6X_3 &\leq 160 \\ 4X_1 + 5X_3 &\geq 85 \\ X_1, X_2, &\geq 0 \end{aligned}$$

25. Solve the following LP problem graphically.

$$\text{MIN } 10X_1 + 10X_2$$

subject to
$$\begin{aligned} X_1 + 3X_2 &\leq 65 \\ 2X_1 - 2X_2 &= 30 \\ 6X_1 + 2X_2 &\geq 120 \\ X_1, X_2 &\geq 0 \end{aligned}$$

26. Solve the following LP problem graphically.

$$\text{MIN } 7X_1 + 8X_2$$

subject to
$$\begin{aligned} 7X_1 &\leq 70 \\ 5X_1 + 15X_2 &\geq 45 \\ 8X_1 + 8X_2 &\geq 50 \\ X_1, X_2 &\geq 0 \end{aligned}$$

27. Convert the following problem to the standard form.

$$\text{MIN } 10A + 13B + 9C$$

subject to

$$
\begin{aligned}
5A + 7B + 6C &\geq 75 \\
4B + 5C &\geq 48 \\
3A + 5B + 4C &\leq 120 \\
2A + 3B &= 65 \\
A, B, C &\geq 0
\end{aligned}
$$

28. Solve the following LP problem graphically.

$$\text{MIN } 7.5X_1 + 6X_2$$

subject to

$$
\begin{aligned}
6X_1 + 7X_2 &\leq 63 \\
8X_1 + 7.5X_2 &\geq 45 \\
2X_1 + X_2 &\geq 8 \\
X_1 + 4X_2 &\geq 12 \\
X_1, X_2 &\geq 0
\end{aligned}
$$

29. The manager of a local store purchases two products that are sold both separately and in a mixture. He has formulated the following LP model, which represents his total cost for these products and the constraints he must meet. Determine graphically the optimal amount of each product he should purchase.

$$\text{MIN } 7X_1 + 9X_2$$

subject to

$$
\begin{aligned}
3X_1 &\geq 240 \\
5X_2 &\geq 300 \\
2X_1 + 2X_2 &\geq 300 \\
3X_1 + 4X_2 &\leq 600 \\
X_1, X_2 &\geq 0
\end{aligned}
$$

30. Solve the following LP problem graphically.

$$\text{MIN } X_1 + X_2$$

subject to

$$
\begin{aligned}
3.5X_1 + 3X_2 &\leq 21 \\
X_1 + 2X_2 &\geq 8 \\
X_1 &\geq 3 \\
X_1, X_2 &\geq 0
\end{aligned}
$$

31. Wilson Wine (Chapter 2, problem 17) must determine the optimal number of gallons of wine cooler to produce to maximize its expected profit. Solve this problem graphically.

32. Solve the following LP problem graphically.

$$\text{MAX } 3X_1 + 4X_2$$

subject to
$$2X_1 + 3X_2 \geq 60$$
$$5X_2 \leq 150$$
$$10X_1 + 6X_2 \geq 150$$
$$X_1, X_2 \geq 0$$

33. The Powers family (Chapter 2, problem 23) wishes to determine the optimal number of acres of corn and pumpkins to plant in order to maximize its profits. Find this solution graphically.

34. Solve the following LP problem graphically.

$$\text{MAX } 5X_1 + 5X_2$$
subject to
$$3X_1 + 4X_2 \leq 96$$
$$5X_1 + 2X_2 \leq 100$$
$$X_2 \leq 45$$
$$3X_1 \geq 20$$
$$X_1, X_2 \geq 0$$

35. Solve the following LP problem graphically.

$$\text{MAX } X_1 + X_2$$

subject to
$$5X_1 + 5X_2 \leq 200$$
$$12X_1 + 4X_2 \leq 300$$
$$2X_1 + X_2 \geq 100$$
$$X_1, X_2 \geq 0$$

36. Solve the following LP problem graphically.

$$\text{MAX } 3X_1 + 2X_2$$

subject to
$$2X_1 - 2X_2 \leq 80$$
$$-2X_1 + 3X_2 \leq 90$$
$$X_1 + X_2 \leq 55$$
$$X_1, X_2 \geq 0$$

37. Solve the following LP problem graphically.

$$\text{MAX } 6X_1 + 4X_2$$

subject to
$$12X_1 + 3X_2 \leq 480$$
$$3X_1 + 5X_2 \leq 375$$
$$9X_1 + 6X_2 \leq 450$$
$$X_1, X_2 \geq 0$$

Chapter

4

Simplex Linear Programming

By the end of this chapter, you should be able to:

1

recognize what is taking place (mathematically) in the simplex solution process;

2

determine the optimal solution values and shadow prices from the final simplex tableau;

3

understand the meaning of the term shadow prices;

4

understand how to change a basic LP model into tableau form through the addition of slack, surplus, or artificial variables to facilitate the simplex solution procedure; and

5

understand how to recognize infeasible, unbounded, and degenerate problems.

In this chapter we continue our discussion of linear programming. In Chapter 2 we introduced LP as a widely used mathematical technique for solving constrained optimization problems. In Chapter 3 we introduced the graphical solution method for linear programming problems. We explained, however, that the graphical procedure has limited practical use and was introduced primarily to give you a visual representation of the solution to an LP problem. It is easier to understand what is meant by an area of feasible solutions or extreme points when you can see them. In this chapter, we will introduce an algorithm known as simplex LP, or the simplex method, which can be used to solve LP problems mathematically. This algorithm uses an iterative algebraic solution procedure that begins at the origin and examines successive adjacent extreme points until an optimal solution is found.

Bob Adams Jewelry

Bob Adams Jewelry manufactures inexpensive gold-filled pendants and pins and sells them to several area discount jewelry and department stores. This jewelry is made using gold, silver, and a base metal. Each pendant requires 4.5 grams of gold, 3 grams of silver, and 4 grams of the base metal. Each pin requires 2 grams of gold, 5 grams of silver, and 4 grams of the base metal. Bob finds he has no problem selling his entire daily output, regardless of the mix of pendants and pins. He currently makes an $8.00 profit on each pendant and a $10.00 profit on each pin. Output is limited only by the quantities of materials he has available. Bob typically has 36 grams of gold, 45 grams of silver, and 40 grams of base metal available each day.

By now you recognize this as a simple LP problem. As we discuss the simplex solution procedure in this chapter, we will refer to Bob Adams' problem.

4.1 *INTRODUCTION TO THE SIMPLEX METHOD*

The **simplex method** is an iterative algebraic solution procedure that begins at an initial solution point (equivalent to the graphical origin) and examines successive adjacent extreme points until the optimal solution is found. Because the graphical procedure makes the solution process easier to understand (visualize), we will first illustrate the simplex solution steps by comparing them to a graphic solution.

Recall that the usual procedure with any problem is to analyze it and then formulate it. In this chapter, however, our emphasis is on the solution of the problem rather than its formulation. Thus, we will begin with the following LP formulation of the Bob Adams jewelry problem and its graphic solution, which is shown in Figure 4.1. X_1 represents pendants, and X_2 stands for pins.

$$\text{MAX } 8X_1 + 10X_2$$

subject to

$$4.5X_1 + 2X_2 \leq 36$$

$$3X_1 + 5X_2 \leq 45$$

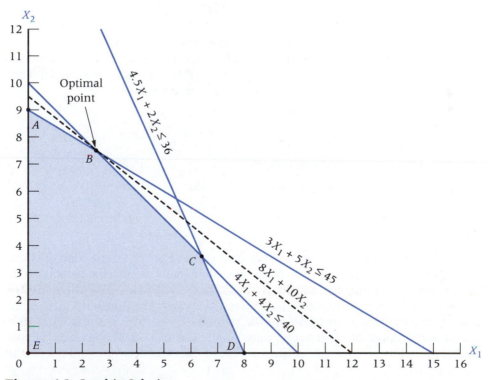

Figure 4.1 Graphic Solution

$$4X_1 + 4X_2 \leq 40$$

$$X_1, X_2 \geq 0$$

The feasible region has been shaded and the feasible extreme points have been labeled A, B, C, D, and E. The optimal solution is point B, where $X_1 = 2.5$ and $X_2 = 7.5$. The value of the objective function at this point is $95. It may seem impractical to suggest that Bob make 2.5 pendants and 7.5 pins per day. If, however, partially finished jewelry is treated as work in process, the solution can be interpreted as producing 5 pendants and 15 pins every two days.

4.2 *ALGEBRAIC SOLUTION OF EXTREME POINT VALUES*

The simplex algorithm solves LP problems through an iterative algebraic solution procedure, which begins at an initial solution point and examines successive adjacent extreme points until the optimal solution is found. To illustrate this procedure, we will first look at an algebraic solution, relating its steps to the graphic solution already obtained. Thus we can see how to determine *specific* extreme points algebraically without having to find them through a trial-and-error method. Remember, we are solving for specific points that we have already pictured graphically, in an attempt to relate the two methods and to clarify the simplex method. We will then see how the initial simplex tableau is set up, and learn the steps of the iterative simplex procedure that will be used to solve the problem.

Algebraic Solution Overview

Because the simplex solution procedure examines only extreme points, it uses equalities rather than inequalities. These equalities can be obtained by converting the LP model to the standard form. The slack variables that have been added represent unused or available quantities of the three resources.

$$\text{MAX } 8X_1 + 10X_2 + 0S_1 + 0S_2 + 0S_3$$

subject to

$$4.5X_1 + 2X_2 + 1S_1 \qquad\qquad = 36$$

$$3X_1 + 5X_2 \qquad + 1S_2 \qquad = 45$$

$$4X_1 + 4X_2 \qquad\qquad + 1S_3 = 36$$

$$X_1, X_2, S_1, S_2, S_3 \geq 0$$

Since the extreme points occur either on an axis or at the intersection of two or more constraints, these intersect points (and, therefore, the extreme points) can be determined by solving the equations simultaneously. In this case there are five variables (two decision variables and three slack variables) and only three equations. The letter n is used to denote the number of variables and the letter m to denote the number of constraints; thus, n = 5 and m = 3. The simplex method begins the solution process by setting n − m of the variables equal to zero. In this

case, two variables must be set equal to zero. The choice of these variables is arbitrary. If the origin (point E) is selected as a starting point, the decision variables
X_1 and X_2 are set equal to zero, thus reducing the constraint equations to:

$$S_1 = 36$$

$$S_2 = 45$$

$$S_3 = 40$$

At point E no products are being produced and, therefore, no resources are being
used. Thus, the slack variables are equal to the original resource quantities.

In general, whenever there are n variables and m constraints, where m is less
than n, n − m variables must be set equal to zero before the problem can be solved
algebraically. When this is done, the variables set equal to zero are known as **nonbasic variables** and the remaining variables are **basic variables.** The solution
derived from this step, setting n − m variables equal to zero, is called a **basic solution.** Thus, in the example, there were five variables and three constraints, so
there were three basic variables and two (n − m or 5 − 3) nonbasic variables. Basic solutions can be either feasible or infeasible, depending upon whether they lie
inside or outside the area of feasible solutions. **Basic feasible solutions** are solutions to the problem that also meet the nonnegativity requirements. Solutions that
do not meet the nonnegativity requirement are known as infeasible solutions. The
graphic solution for this problem is repeated in Figure 4.2. The extreme points are
lettered A through E. Note that the origin, which corresponds to the basic solution
above, is labelled as point E.

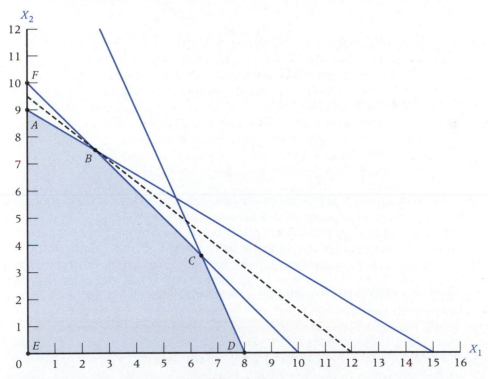

Figure 4.2 Graphical Area of Feasible Solutions

Since the simplex method solves for adjacent points, we will select a point on the graph adjacent to the origin (point E) and solve for its value. Of the available choices, points A and D, we arbitrarily select point A. Since point A is the intersection of constraint 2 and the X_2 axis, X_1 is zero, and S_2 (the slack variable associated with constraint 2, silver) is also zero. (Without the graph as a point of reference, we might not have selected these variables specifically to set equal to zero.) By substituting $X_1 = 0$ and $S_2 = 0$ into constraint equation 2, we can find the value of X_2.

$$[2] \quad 3X_1 + 5X_2 + 1S_2 = 45$$
$$3(0) + 5X_2 + 1(0) = 45$$
$$5X_2 = 45$$
$$X_2 = 9$$

We then use this value ($X_2 = 9$) in the solution of equations 1 and 3.

$$[1] \quad 4.5X_1 + 2X_2 + 1S_1 = 36$$
$$4.5(0) + 2(9) + 1S_1 = 36$$
$$18 + S_1 = 36$$
$$S_1 = 36 - 18$$
$$S_1 = 18$$
$$[3] \quad 4X_1 + 4X_2 + 1S_3 = 40$$
$$4(0) + 4(9) + 1S_3 = 40$$
$$36 + S_3 = 40$$
$$S_3 = 40 - 36$$
$$S_3 = 4$$

Thus, the basic solution at point A is

$$X_2 = 9$$
$$S_1 = 18$$
$$S_3 = 4$$

Since the nonnegativity requirements are met, this is a basic feasible solution. The value of the objective function at this point is 90 ($\$10 \times 9$ pins).

The points adjacent to point A are points B and F. Point F is not in the feasible region, so we select point B. The values at point F could be found algebraically, but the solution would not be feasible. At point B, the intersection of constraints 2 and 3, both S_2 and S_3 are equal to zero (since there is no slack at any point *on* a constraint line). Substituting $S_2 = 0$ and $S_3 = 0$ into constraints 2 and 3 yields two equations with two unknowns:

$$[2] \quad 3X_1 + 5X_2 + 1S_2 = 45$$
$$3X_1 + 5X_2 + 1(0) = 45$$
$$3X_1 + 5X_2 = 45$$

$$[3] \quad 4X_1 + 4X_2 + 1S_3 = 40$$

$$4X_1 + 4X_2 + 1(0) = 40$$

$$4X_1 + 4X_2 = 40$$

We now solve these two equations simultaneously to obtain the value of X_2. Multiplying equation [2] by 4 yields

$$[2] \quad 4 \times (3X_1 + 5X_2 = 45) => 12X_1 + 20X_2 = 180$$

and multiplying equation [3] by 3 yields

$$[3] \quad 3 \times (4X_1 + 4X_2 = 40) => 12X_1 + 12X_2 = 120$$

Subtracting equation [3] from equation [2],

$$[2] \quad 12X_1 + 20X_2 = 180$$

$$[3] \quad -(12X_1 + 12X_2 = 120)$$

$$0 \ + \ 8X_2 = \ 60$$

$$X_2 = {}^{60}\!/_8 = 7.5$$

it can be determined that $X_2 = 7.5$. Substituting this value back into equation [3] and solving,

$$[3] \quad 4X_1 + 4X_2 = 40$$

$$4X_1 + 4(7.5) = 40$$

$$4X_1 + 30 = 40$$

$$X_1 = 40 - 30 = 10$$

$$X_1 = {}^{10}\!/_4 = 2.5$$

gives $X_1 = 2.5$. The value of the objective function at point B is 95 ($8 \times 2.5 + 10 \times 7.5$). Substituting these values into constraint equation [1] gives the value for S_1:

$$[1] \quad 4.5X_1 + 2X_2 + 1S_1 = 36$$

$$4.5(2.5) + 2(7.5) + S_1 = 36$$

$$11.25 + 15 + S_1 = 36$$

$$26.25 + S_1 = 36$$

$$S_1 = 36 - 26.25$$

$$S_1 = 9.75$$

The basic solution at point B is

$$X_1 = 2.5$$

$$X_2 = 7.5$$

$$S_1 = 9.75$$

The nonnegativity requirement has been met, so this is a basic feasible solution. We could determine the values at points C and D on the graph next; however, since this problem has already been solved graphically and point B is known to be the optimal solution, there is no point in continuing. The purpose of this procedure was to demonstrate that the values of the extreme points can be determined algebraically.

4.3 *THE SIMPLEX TABLEAU*

The simplex method uses the algebraic solution procedure to solve for adjacent extreme point values in a systematic manner. In other words, the simplex procedure solves sets of simultaneous equations to find the values of the basic variables at given extreme points. It is not necessary to have a graphic representation of the feasible region as a guide before solving the problem. In fact, it is usually impossible to have a graphic solution, because the number of decision variables normally exceeds two. The simplex method automatically selects the adjacent extreme points, ignoring all infeasible points along the way.

Creating the Initial Simplex Tableau

The simplex method uses a tableau to represent the data. The first or beginning tableau is called the **initial tableau.** It has a row of objective function coefficients; a row of variable names $(A, B, X_1, X_2,$ etc.) listing all decision and slack variables found in the problem; and then one row for each constraint equation. Thus, the example problem

$$\text{MAX } 8X_1 + 10X_2 + 0S_1 + 0S_2 + 0S_3$$

subject to

$$4.5X_1 + 2X_2 + 1S_1 \qquad\qquad = 36$$

$$3X_1 + 5X_2 \qquad + 1S_2 \qquad = 45$$

$$4X_1 + 4X_2 \qquad\qquad + 1S_3 = 40$$

$$X_1, X_2, S_1, S_2, S_3 \geq 0$$

would appear in the tableau as

C_j	BASIC VAR	8 X_1	10 X_2	0 S_1	0 S_2	0 S_3	RHS
		4.5	2	1	0	0	36
		3	5	0	1	0	45
		4	4	0	0	1	40

Note that all of the variable names are listed in the second row of the tableau, with each variable's objective function coefficient above it and its constraint equation coefficients below it. The RHS values are listed on the right-hand side of the tableau. Each row represents one of the constraint equations. The values in each row of the tableau are the coefficient values from the corresponding constraint, and the RHS value is the right-hand side of the constraint. The top row has been labelled the C_j row. The letter C stands for the objective function coefficient and the subscript j represents the jth column in the tableau. Thus, $C_1 = 8$, $C_2 = 10$, $C_3 = 0$, and so on. Remember that the slack variables S_1, S_2, and S_3 have objective function coefficients of zero because resources contribute toward profit only when they are used to produce products, not when they are left unused.

Each tableau column has the name of the variable that is in that column; for example, the first column is the X_1 column and the third is the S_1 column. The S_1, S_2, and S_3 columns are known as **unit columns.** A unit column is a column that has a coefficient of 1 in one row and zero coefficients in all of the remaining rows. There must be one unit column for every constraint row in the tableau. Since there are three rows in this tableau, there must be three unit columns. The coefficient of 1 always occurs where the row representing a basic variable and the column for that variable intersect. The unit columns, taken together, form a unit or identity matrix—a matrix with elements of 1 on the diagonal and zero everywhere else.

The initial simplex tableau is equivalent to the graphical solution at point E, the origin, where X_1 and X_2 are equal to zero. When we solved for this point algebraically, the basic solution was

$$S_1 = 36$$

$$S_2 = 45$$

$$S_3 = 40$$

Variables that occur in a basic solution are referred to as **basic variables.** In the above solution, therefore, S_1, S_2, and S_3 are the basic variables. Since the simplex solution procedure always begins at the graphic origin—the point where all decision variables are equal to zero—and since there must be m basic variables (one for each constraint row), the slack variables S_1, S_2, and S_3 are the basic variables in the initial tableau. In the initial tableau, the basic variables for each row can be determined easily by looking at the coefficients for the slack and surplus variables. If the coefficient is $+1$ in a unit column, that variable is the basic variable for that row. The 1 value in the unit column always occurs at the point where the basic variable for that row is the same as the column variable. Thus, looking at the slack variables and their coefficients, we can see that S_1, S_2, and S_3 are the basic variables.

$$
\begin{array}{cccc}
\textit{BASIC VAR} & S_1 & S_2 & S_3 \\
 & | & | & | \\
S_1 \longleftarrow & 1 & 0 & 0 \\
S_2 \longleftarrow & 0 - & 1 & 0 \\
S_3 \longleftarrow & 0 - & 0 - & 1 \\
\end{array}
$$

Adding the initial basic variables to the tableau, and copying their objective function coefficients to the left of each basic variable, gives the following tableau:

C_j	BASIC VAR	8 X_1	10 X_2	0 S_1	0 S_2	0 S_3	RHS
0	S_1	4.5	2	1	0	0	36
0	S_2	3	5	0	1	0	45
0	S_3	4	4	0	0	1	40

The basic variables are variables with solution values in the tableau. The values of the basic variables appear in the RHS column. Thus the above tableau shows that

BASIC VAR		RHS
S_1	=	36
S_2	=	45
S_3	=	40

At this point, there are 36 unused or slack units of resource 1, 45 units of resource 2, and 40 units of resource 3. In other words, no products are being produced at this point, but all of the resources are available.

Recall that X_1 and X_2, the nonbasic variables, are both equal to zero. This follows from the fact that n − m (5 − 3) variables are always equal to zero and there are already three variables in the tableau. In any problem, all nonbasic variables have a value of zero. Examining the tableau column associated with nonbasic variable X_1,

Row	X_1
S_1	4.5
S_2	3
S_3	4

we see that the X_1 column indicates how many units of each constraint resource ($S_1, S_2,$ or S_3) are used to produce one unit of X_1. Thus, 1 unit of X_1 requires 4.5 units of resource 1 (S_1), 3 units of resource 2 (S_2), and 4 units of resource 3 (S_3). In economic terms, these coefficients represent the marginal rate of substitution between the basic variables and the column variables. The column associated with nonbasic variable X_2 yields the same type of information:

Row	X_2
S_1	2
S_2	5
S_3	4

The X_2 column values show that, to produce 1 unit of X_2, we need 2 units of resource 1 (S_1), 5 units of resource 2 (S_2), and 4 units of resource 3 (S_3).

Taking the contribution value of each basic variable (0 from the objective function coefficient) and multiplying it by the units of each resource required to produce a unit of a decision variable, and then adding those results, yields the profit forgone by producing one unit of that nonbasic variable. For example, for X_1,

VAR	C_j		X_1		Profit Forgone
S_1	0	×	4.5	=	0
S_2	0	×	3	=	0
S_3	0	×	4	=	0
			Total	=	0

the additional cost is zero. For X_2,

VAR	C_j		X_2		Profit Forgone
S_1	0	×	2	=	0
S_2	0	×	5	=	0
S_3	0	×	4	=	0
			Total	=	0

the profit forgone is also zero. Why is the forgone profit associated with producing an additional unit of either of these products zero? Because the resources are already available (and idle). If one unit of X_1 is added to the solution, the value of the objective function increases by 8 since each unit of X_1 has a profit contribution of $8. If the profit forgone by adding this extra unit is zero (as determined in the previous calculations), then the net improvement in the objective function would be $8 - 0$ or 8. Adding one unit of X_2 increases the objective function by 10. With a forgone profit of zero, the net improvement for a unit of X_2 would be $10 - 0$ or 10.

We can incorporate these calculations into the tableau by adding two more rows: a Z_j row that contains the profit forgone by adding one unit of a nonbasic variable, and a $C_j - Z_j$ row that contains the net improvement value for each nonbasic variable. The Z_j and $C_j - Z_j$ values are also calculated for the basic variables. Multiplying the objective function coefficients by the RHS values and summing the results yields the value of the objective function at this solution point. For example:

VAR	C_j		RHS		Profit Forgone
S_1	0	×	36	=	0
S_2	0	×	45	=	0
S_3	0	×	40	=	0
			Total	=	0

These calculations (the basic variable coefficients from the leftmost tableau column times the column values for the jth column) give the Z_j row for the tableau:

C_j	BASIC VAR	8 X$_1$	10 X$_2$	0 S$_1$	0 S$_2$	0 S$_3$	RHS
0	S_1	4.5	2	1	0	0	36
0	S_2	3	5	0	1	0	45
0	S_3	4	4	0	0	1	40
	Z_j	0	0	0	0	0	0

We then determine the $C_j - Z_j$ row by subtracting these Z_j values from the C_j values (top row of the tableau) for each column:

C_j	BASIC VAR	8 X$_1$	10 X$_2$	0 S$_1$	0 S$_2$	0 S$_3$	RHS
0	S_1	4.5	2	1	0	0	36
0	S_2	3	5	0	1	0	45
0	S_3	4	4	0	0	1	40
	Z_j	0	0	0	0	0	0
	$C_j - Z_j$	8	10	0	0	0	

This completes what is referred to as the **initial simplex tableau.** The tableau that the simplex method uses to represent the data always takes the following form:

C_j		Objective Function (OF) Coefficients	
	BASIC VAR	List of Variables	RHS
Basic Variable OF Coef	Basic Variables	Matrix (Constraint) Coefficients	RHS Values
	Z_j	Forgone Profit	OF Value
	$C_j - Z_j$	Net Improvement	

4.4 *THE SIMPLEX SOLUTION PROCEDURE*

The initial simplex tableau is always the starting point in the simplex method. As stated previously, this method uses an iterative procedure to move to an adjacent extreme point. It makes the move by substituting a nonbasic variable for an existing basic variable; that is, it changes the solution by changing one of the basic variables. Recall that in this specific problem, X_1 represents the number of pendants produced and X_2 the number of pins produced, and that the three resources are gold, silver, and base metal in grams. In the following discussion, we will refer to products only as X_1 and X_2 and to the resources only as resource 1, 2, or 3.

Determining Which Variable Will Enter the Tableau

The initial simplex tableau is the starting point. It corresponds to the graphical point at the origin, where all of the decision variables are zero (nonbasic). To proceed to the next solution point, the variable entering the tableau (the variable being substituted for an existing basic variable) must be selected. This is done by examining the $C_j - Z_j$ row. Since this row shows the net improvement in profit for each variable, the variable that yields the largest improvement per unit is selected. In this case, the appropriate variable is X_2, with an improvement value of $10. The column associated with the entering variable is known as the **pivot column.**

Determining Which Variable Will Leave the Tableau

After selecting the variable that will enter the tableau, the variable to be replaced (leaving the tableau) must be determined. In this case, unused resources are being replaced with units of a product; that is, slack resources are being used to make a product. This process will result in more units of the product and fewer units of the resources. And because each additional unit produced adds to the profit contribution, the resources are used continuously to make additional units of product X_2 until one resource is used up. The coefficients of the X_2 column

$$X_2$$

$$2$$
$$5$$
$$4$$

show that the addition of one unit of X_2 requires two units of resource 1, five units of resource 2, and four units of resource 3. The current quantities of these resources appear as slack values in the RHS column of the tableau.

RHS

36

45

40

There are 36 units of resource 1, and each unit of X_2 requires two units of this resource. Thus, a maximum of 18 units of X_2 can be produced (the RHS value, 36, divided by the coefficient, 2). We can determine the maximum number of X_2 units that can be produced by taking the ratio of the RHS value to the coefficient for each row:

$$[S_1] \quad 36/2 = 18$$

$$[S_2] \quad 45/5 = 9$$

$$[S_3] \quad 40/4 = 10$$

This result indicates that there is enough resource 1 to make 18 units of X_2, enough resource 2 to make nine units of X_2, and enough resource 3 to make 10 units of X_2. Because a combination of all three resources is required to produce units of X_2, the second constraint obviously limits production to a maximum of nine units. When nine units of X_2 are produced, all available units of resource 2 are exhausted and the slack for that resource is equal to zero. Thus, we substitute units of product X_2 for units of resource 2 until S_2 becomes zero and nonbasic. This result indicates that when X_2 enters the tableau, S_2 leaves. The row that limits or constrains the entering variable (the row with the smallest ratio) is known as the **pivot row**. This resource is also said to be **binding** upon the solution value, because it limits the value the solution can take. The coefficient at the intersection of the pivot column and the pivot row is called the **pivot element.** In this example, the pivot element is 5 (at the intersection of the X_2 column and the S_2 row).

pivot element

C_j	BASIC VAR	8 X_1	10 X_2	0 S_1	0 S_2	0 S_3	RHS	Ratio	
0	S_1	4.5	2	1	0	0	36	18	
0	S_2	3	5	0	1	0	45	9	← pivot row
0	S_3	4	4	0	0	1	40	10	
	Z_j	0	0	0	0	0	0		
	$C_j - Z_j$	8	10	0	0	0			

↑ pivot column

Calculating the New Pivot Row

Once X_2 enters the tableau and S_2 leaves, the new coefficients and RHS values for the tableau must be calculated. We begin by replacing S_2 with X_2 in the new tableau:

C_j	BASIC VAR	8 X_1	10 X_2	0 S_1	0 S_2	0 S_3	RHS
0	S_1						
10	X_2						
0	S_3						
	Z_j						
	$C_j - Z_j$						

When X_2 enters the tableau, the X_2 column must be a unit column; that is, it must have a coefficient of 1 at the intersection of the second (X_2) row and the X_2 column and zero in all other rows. To achieve this result, we divide each element (coefficient) in the pivot row by the pivot element value, 5. This gives the values shown in the new tableau's X_2 (pivot) row (including the value of 1 at the intersection of the X_2 column and the new X_2 row). Note that the RHS value is also divided by the intersect element, and that this result is equal to the maximum number of X_2s that can be produced (as determined previously). We will leave the values in fractional form throughout this example. Actual results can be in fraction or decimal form.

C_j	BASIC VAR	8 X_1	10 X_2	0 S_1	0 S_2	0 S_3	RHS
0	S_1						
8	X_2	$3/5$	1	0	$1/5$	0	9
0	S_3						
	Z_j						
	$C_j - Z_j$						

Calculating the Remaining Tableau Row Values

Remember, since X_2 is now in the tableau, the X_2 column must be converted to a unit column. The unit value (1) is already at the intersection of the X_2 row and the X_2 column. The remaining rows must now be changed in such a way that their X_2 column values are all zero. We can achieve this result by performing elementary row operations on those rows and the new pivot row. This procedure is similar to solving equations simultaneously, where one variable is removed from the equations. For example, in solving the equations

$$[1] \quad 3A + 8B = 90$$
$$[2] \quad A + 2B = 20$$

simultaneously, we multiply equation [2] by 3

$$[2] \quad 3 \times (A + 2B = 20) => 3A + 6B = 60$$

and then subtract the result from equation [1] to determine the value of B:

$$[1] \qquad 3A + 8B = 90$$
$$[2] \qquad -(3A + 6B = 60)$$
$$ 0 \qquad 2B = 30$$
$$B = {}^{30}\!/_{2} = 15$$

We use this procedure to convert the remaining row elements in the pivot column to zero, making it a unit column. That is, we multiply the new pivot row by a constant, K, and then subtract the resulting values from the initial values in the row being converted. This procedure is described in detail for the conversion of the S_1 row.

The S_1 row in the initial tableau is

	X_1	X_2	S_1	S_2	S_3	RHS
[S_1]	$\frac{1}{2}$	2	1	0	0	36

which can be rewritten as

$$[S_1] \qquad \tfrac{1}{2}X_1 + 2X_2 + 1S_1 + 0S_2 + 0S_3 = 36$$

It is necessary to change the coefficient at the intersection of the X_2 column and the S_1 row from 2 to zero (0). The new pivot row can also be rewritten as

$$[X_2] \qquad \tfrac{3}{5}X_1 + 1X_2 + 0S_1 + \tfrac{1}{5}S_2 + 0S_3 = 9$$

The coefficient of X_2 in the X_2 row is 1. If we multiply this row by 2 and subtract the result from the S_1 row, the resulting X_2 coefficient is zero. Thus, the multiplier constant K is equal to 2. Multiplying the X_2 row by 2 yields

$$[X_2] \qquad 2 \times (\tfrac{3}{5}X_1 + X_2 + 0S_1 + \tfrac{1}{5}S_2 + 0S_3 = 9)$$
$$=> \tfrac{6}{5}X_1 + 2X_2 + 0S_1 + \tfrac{2}{5}S_2 + 0S_3 = 18$$

Subtracting this resulting X_2 row from the [S_1] row results in an equation with the desired zero coefficient for X_2 (row [S_1']).

$$[S_1] \qquad \tfrac{1}{2}X_1 + 2X_2 + 1S_1 + 0S_2 + 0S_3 = 36$$
$$[X_2] \qquad -(\tfrac{6}{5}X_1 + 2X_2 + 0S_1 + \tfrac{2}{5}S_2 + 0S_3 = 18)$$
$$[S_1'] \qquad {}^{33}\!/_{10}X_1 + 0 \quad + 1S_1 - \tfrac{2}{5}S_2 + 0S_3 = 18$$

The same result can be obtained in tableau form by multiplying the elements of the new pivot row by 2 and subtracting the result from the old S_1 row:

	X_1	X_2	S_1	S_2	S_3	RHS
[S_1]	$\frac{1}{2}$	2	1	0	0	36
[X_2]	$-(\frac{6}{5}$	2	0	$\frac{2}{5}$	0	18)
[S_1']	$^{33}\!/_{10}$	0	1	$-\frac{2}{5}$	0	18

These same calculations can also be shown by displaying each row element in a vertical column:

S_1 Row Values	Multiplier K			New X_2 Row Values		Result (New Row Values)
$\frac{9}{2}$	–	(2	×	$\frac{3}{5}$)	=	$\frac{33}{10}$
2	–	(2	×	1)	=	0
1	–	(2	×	0)	=	1
0	–	(2	×	$\frac{1}{5}$)	=	$-\frac{2}{5}$
0	–	(2	×	0)	=	0
36	–	(2	×	9)	=	18

These values can now be entered into the tableau for the new S_1 row.

C_j	BASIC VAR	8 X_1	10 X_2	0 S_1	0 S_2	0 S_3	RHS
0	S_1	$\frac{33}{10}$	0	1	0	0	36
10	X_2	$\frac{3}{5}$	1	0	$\frac{1}{5}$	0	9
0	S_3						
	Z_j						
	$C_j - Z_j$						

Now consider the S_3 row from the initial tableau.

	X_1	X_2	S_1	S_2	S_3	RHS
[S_3]	4	4	0	0	1	40

The intersect of the S_3 row and the X_2 column is 4. To change this value to zero, the X_2 row values can be multiplied by 4 and the resulting X_2 row subtracted from the S_3 row. We show this in the column format.

S_3 Row Values	Multiplier K			New X_2 Row Values		Result (New Row Values)
4	–	(4	×	$\frac{3}{5}$)	=	$\frac{8}{5}$
4	–	(4	×	1)	=	0
0	–	(4	×	0)	=	0
0	–	(4	×	$\frac{1}{5}$)	=	$-\frac{4}{5}$
1	–	(4	×	0)	=	1
40	–	(4	×	9)	=	4

Substituting these values into the tableau completes the row values for the new tableau.

C_j	BASIC VAR	8 X_1	10 X_2	0 S_1	0 S_2	0 S_3	RHS
0	S_1	$\frac{33}{10}$	0	1	0	0	36
10	X_2	$\frac{3}{5}$	1	0	$\frac{1}{5}$	0	9
0	S_3	$\frac{8}{5}$	0	0	$-\frac{4}{5}$	1	4
	Z_j						
	$C_j - Z_j$						

The purpose of using these elementary row operations is to transform the X_2 column to a unit column. To do so, the X_2 column elements for the first and third rows must be changed to zero. Since the X_2 coefficient in the new pivot row is 1, if the multiplier (K) is set equal to the X_2 coefficient in the original row, it will always result in new X_2 coefficients of zero. In the case of the S_1 row, a zero was obtained in the pivot column by multiplying the new pivot row by the value of the coefficient at the intersection of the pivot column and the old row (2) and subtracting the result from the original row. In the S_3 row, the multiplier was 4. Thus, the multiplier is always equal to the coefficient at the intersection of the row being recalculated and the pivot column.

This procedure can be generalized into the following rule for calculating new row coefficients and RHS values, for all rows except the pivot row:

For each element in the row including the RHS value, the new element value equals:

$$\begin{array}{ccccc} \text{old row value} & & \text{value of coefficient} & & \text{value of jth} \\ & - & \text{at intersect of old} & \times & \text{element in the} \\ \text{(column j)} & & \text{row and pivot column} & & \text{new pivot row} \end{array}$$

Once the new tableau row values have been calculated, the Z_j and $C_j - Z_j$ row values can be calculated. Remember that the Z_j values are obtained by multiplying the appropriate C_j value times the corresponding row coefficient for a given column (the jth column), and then summing those products. For example:

VAR	C_j		X_1		Profit Forgone	
S_1	0	×	$^{33}\!/_{10}$	=	0	
X_2	10	×	$^3\!/_5$	=	6	X_1 column (j = 1)
S_3	0	×	$^8\!/_5$	=	0	
					6	

VAR	C_j		X_2		Profit Forgone	
S_1	0	×	0	=	0	
X_2	10	×	1	=	10	X_2 column (j = 2)
S_3	0	×	0	=	0	
					10	

VAR	C_j		S_1		Profit Forgone	
S_1	0	×	1	=	0	
X_2	10	×	0	=	0	S_1 column (j = 3)
S_3	0	×	0	=	0	
					0	

VAR	C_j		S_2		Profit Forgone	
S_1	0	×	0	=	0	
X_2	10	×	$^1\!/_5$	=	2	S_2 column (j = 4)
S_3	0	×	$-^4\!/_5$	=	0	
					2	

VAR	C_j		S_3		Profit Forgone	
S_1	0	×	0	=	0	
X_2	10	×	0	=	0	S_3 column (j = 5)
S_3	0	×	1	=	0	
					0	

Adding these values to the Z_j row and then subtracting them from the C_j row to determine the $C_j - Z_j$ row completes the second tableau:

C_j	BASIC VAR	8 X_1	10 X_2	0 S_1	0 S_2	0 S_3	RHS
0	S_1	$33/10$	0	1	0	0	18
10	X_2	$3/5$	1	0	$1/5$	0	9
0	S_3	$8/5$	0	0	$-4/5$	1	4
	Z_j	6	10	0	2	0	90
	$C_j - Z_j$	2	0	0	−2	0	

The basic variables in the solution in this tableau are S_1, X_2, and S_3. The RHS values indicate that we are making 9 units of X_2 and have 18 units of S_1 (slack or unused resource 1) and 4 units of S_3 (slack units of resource 3) still available. The Z_j value for the RHS shows that the value of the objective function at this point is 90.

The next step is to check this solution to see if it is optimal. Optimality can be determined by examining the $C_j - Z_j$ row for possible profit improvement. The X_1 column has a $C_j - Z_j$ value of 2, indicating that, for every additional unit of X_1 produced, profit contribution can be increased by \$2. This solution is not optimal, since further profit improvement is possible. Once it has been determined that a nonoptimal solution exists, the simplex iteration process is repeated; that is, the variable that enters the tableau (the pivot column) and the variable that leaves the tableau (the pivot row) are determined, and the new tableau values are calculated. This procedure continues until the $C_j - Z_j$ row shows that there is no further improvement to be made. At that point, an optimal solution exists.

This repetitive search for an optimal solution is known as an **iterative** solution procedure. Each successive tableau improves upon the prior solution until the final, optimal solution is reached.

Continuing with the example, we examine the second tableau to determine the pivot column. The largest $C_j - Z_j$ value, 2, is found in the X_1 column. This means X_1 will enter the tableau in the next iteration. Dividing the RHS values by the coefficients from X_1 column

$$[S_1] \quad 18/33/10 \quad = \quad 180/33 = 60/11$$

$$[X_2] \quad 9/3/5 \quad = \quad 45/3 = 15$$

$$[S_3] \quad 4/8/5 \quad = \quad 20/8 = 5/2$$

reveals that the S_3 row is the most constraining, because it yields the smallest nonnegative ratio. Thus, the S_3 row is the new pivot row. The pivot element (found at the intersection of the X_1 column and the S_3 row) is $8/5$. Dividing the elements of the S_3 row by $8/5$ produces the elements of the new X_1 row in the third tableau.

$$^8\!/_5 / ^8\!/_5 = 1$$

$$0 / ^8\!/_5 = 0$$

$$0 / ^8\!/_5 = 0$$

$$-^4\!/_5 / ^8\!/_5 = -\tfrac{1}{2}$$

$$1 / ^8\!/_5 = \tfrac{5}{8}$$

$$4 / ^8\!/_5 = \tfrac{5}{2}$$

Substituting X_1 for S_3 and entering these values, we have

C_j	BASIC VAR	8 X_1	10 X_2	0 S_1	0 S_2	0 S_3	RHS
0	S_1						
10	X_2						
8	X_1	1	0	0	$-\tfrac{1}{2}$	$\tfrac{5}{8}$	$\tfrac{5}{2}$
	Z_j						
	$C_j - Z_j$						

Following the same elementary row procedure outlined previously, we can determine the new S_1 and X_2 row values. A zero value can be obtained for the X_1 column and S_1 row intersect by multiplying the new pivot row by the intersect element of 33/10 and subtracting it from the old S_1 row. Using the general rule we formulated, the calculations to determine the new S_1 row are:

Old S_1 Values		Intersect Coefficient		Corresponding Pivot Row Element		Result (New S_1 Row Values)
$^{33}\!/_{10}$	$-$	$(^{33}\!/_{10}$	$\times$	$1)$	$=$	0
0	$-$	$(^{33}\!/_{10}$	$\times$	$0)$	$=$	0
1	$-$	$(^{33}\!/_{10}$	$\times$	$0)$	$=$	1
0	$-$	$(^{33}\!/_{10}$	$\times$	$-\tfrac{1}{2})$	$=$	$^{33}\!/_{20}$
0	$-$	$(^{33}\!/_{10}$	$\times$	$\tfrac{5}{8})$	$=$	$-^{33}\!/_{16}$
18	$-$	$(^{33}\!/_{10}$	$\times$	$\tfrac{5}{2})$	$=$	$^{39}\!/_{4}$

The X_2 row can now be calculated. The intersect value here is 3/5, so the calculations are:

Old X_2 Values		Intersect Coefficient		Corresponding Pivot Row Element		Result (New X_2 Row Values)
$\tfrac{3}{5}$	$-$	$(\tfrac{3}{5}$	$\times$	$1)$	$=$	0
1	$-$	$(\tfrac{3}{5}$	$\times$	$0)$	$=$	1
0	$-$	$(\tfrac{3}{5}$	$\times$	$0)$	$=$	0
$\tfrac{1}{5}$	$-$	$(\tfrac{3}{5}$	$\times$	$-\tfrac{1}{2})$	$=$	$\tfrac{1}{2}$
0	$-$	$(\tfrac{3}{5}$	$\times$	$\tfrac{5}{8})$	$=$	$-\tfrac{3}{8}$
9	$-$	$(\tfrac{3}{5}$	$\times$	$\tfrac{5}{2})$	$=$	$^{15}\!/_{2}$

Adding these new row values to the third tableau gives

C_j	BASIC VAR	8 X_1	10 X_2	0 S_1	0 S_2	0 S_3	RHS
0	S_1	0	0	1	$33/20$	$-33/16$	$39/4$
10	X_2	0	1	0	$1/2$	$-3/8$	$15/2$
8	X_1	1	0	0	$-1/2$	$5/8$	$5/2$
	Z_j						
	$C_j - Z_j$						

Calculating the Z_j and $C_j - Z_j$ values, completes the third tableau.

C_j	BASIC VAR	8 X_1	10 X_2	0 S_1	0 S_2	0 S_3	RHS
0	S_1	0	0	1	$33/20$	$-33/16$	$39/4$
10	X_2	0	1	0	$1/2$	$-3/8$	$15/2$
8	X_1	1	0	0	$-1/2$	$5/8$	$5/2$
	Z_j	8	10	0	1	$10/8$	95
	$C_j - Z_j$	0	0	0	-1	$-10/8$	

At this point, 2.5 ($5/2$) units of X_1 and 7.5 ($15/2$) units of X_2 are being produced, and 9.75 ($39/4$) units of resource 1 (S_1) remain. The value of the objective function is 95. In the $C_j - Z_j$ row, all net improvement values are either zero or negative, meaning no further improvement can be made and, therefore, this solution is optimal. The values of S_2 and S_3 are zero, since they are not in the tableau (they are nonbasic variables). Thus, the simplex solution shows that Bob's optimal product mix is 2.5 pins and 7.5 pendants per day, as discussed earlier. This solution also shows that there will be 9.75 grams of unused gold each day. This result suggests that Bob should reduce the amount of gold he purchases daily by this amount.

Summary of Steps in the Simplex Method

The steps in the simplex solution procedure can be summarized:

1. Set up the initial tableau.
2. Calculate the Z_j and $C_j - Z_j$ values.
3. Check for optimality. If an optimal solution has been reached, stop. If an optimal solution has not been reached, determine the variable entering the tableau (pivot column) by selecting the variable with the best net improvement value ($C_j - Z_j$ values).
4. Determine the variable leaving the tableau (pivot row) by selecting the row with the smallest ratio of RHS value to pivot column element.
5. Calculate the values for the new pivot row by dividing all of the elements in the old pivot row by the pivot element (the value at the intersection of the pivot column and the pivot row).
6. Calculate the new values for the remaining rows. For each row, this is accomplished by taking the existing row values and subtracting the product of the intersect value (the coefficient at the intersection of the row and the pivot

column) and the coefficient from the new pivot row (for each corresponding column).

7. Repeat the process beginning at step 2.

4.5 *SHADOW PRICES*

The final simplex tableau gave the solution values for the basic variables and the value of the objective function ($X_1 = 2.5$, $X_2 = 7.5$, $S_1 = 9.75$, and $Z_{max} = 95$). There is, however, additional information to be gained from the tableau, which is repeated below.

C_j	BASIC VAR	8 X_1	10 X_2	0 S_1	0 S_2	0 S_3	RHS
0	S_1	0	0	1	$33/20$	$-33/16$	$39/4$
10	X_2	0	1	0	$1/2$	$-3/8$	$15/2$
8	X_1	1	0	0	$-1/2$	$5/8$	$5/2$
	Z_j	8	10	0	1	$10/8$	95
	$C_j - Z_j$	0	0	0	-1	$-10/8$	

The $C_j - Z_j$ row values for the decision variables indicate how much additional profit can be made by adding additional units of these variables to the final solution. Because both X_1 and X_2 are basic variables, the $C_j - Z_j$ values are zero.

The column coefficients for the nonbasic variables (S_2 and S_3) indicate the rate of substitution between those variables (resources) and the basic variables. For example, the S_2 column

$$S_2$$

$[S_1]$	$33/20$
$[X_2]$	$1/2$
$[X_1]$	$-1/2$

shows that, if one additional unit of resource 2 is added, the result is the production of 1/2 unit more of X_2, and 1/2 unit less of X_1, and the use of 33/20 unit more of resource 1. Since each unit of X_2 is worth \$10, each unit of X_1 is worth \$8, and each unit of S_1 has a zero value, \$5.00 is gained from the additional production of X_2 (10 × 1/5 = 5), but \$4.00 is lost from the decreased production of X_1 (8 × $-1/2 = -4$). The result is a net gain of \$1.00 for each unit of resource 2 that is added. The rates of substitution work in both directions; reducing resource 2 by one unit results in a loss of \$1.00 per unit. Note that these values correspond to the values already calculated in the Z_j row, and are referred to as **shadow prices** for the nonbasic variables.

A shadow price is the relative worth of one unit of a particular resource. The shadow prices show how much the objective function changes if one unit or one more unit of a particular resource is available. Thus, the Z_j row values for the non-basic variables give the shadow prices for the resources; in other words, they indicate how a reduction in the original RHS value of one unit would affect the overall value of the objective function. The shadow price of 1 for the second constraint (represented by variable S_2) indicates that, if the number of available units is reduced from 45 to 44, the optimal value of the objective function is reduced by $1.00. The reverse is also true: if one unit of this resource is added, the value of the objective function increases by $1.00. This result is due to the rate of substitution between variables, as discussed previously. The shadow price reflects the relationship between a change in one unit of a resource and the corresponding change in the value of the objective function.

The shadow price for the first constraint (a basic variable) indicates that, if the number of units of this resource were reduced from 36 to 35, the profit contribution would not be reduced. This makes sense, since there are 9.75 unused (slack) units of this resource at the optimal solution point. Decreasing the original value by 1 would still leave 8.75 unused units, and increasing the original value by 1 would simply increase the number of unused units. In either case, the objective function would not change because this constraint is not binding.

Shadow price values can be used to make decisions that affect the original RHS values of the constraints. If the RHS value for either constraint 2 or constraint 3 can be increased by one unit, constraint 3 should be chosen since the value of the additional unit of that resource is greater (1.25 versus 1.00). This holds true as long as the additional cost of that marginal unit is less than the expected gain of 1.25. Thus, for Bob Adams, silver has a shadow price of $1 per gram and the base metal has a shadow price of $1.25 per gram. It is important to note that these shadow prices are not the prices Bob pays for these resources; rather, they represent the marginal profit value of these resources to Bob.

There are two important points to remember, however. First, constraints have shadow prices associated with them because they are binding. If the amount of a resource (its RHS value) is increased sufficiently, a point could be reached where the constraint is no longer binding. For example, if constraint 3 were increased by 5 units, to 45, that constraint would no longer be binding and there would be slack or unused units of that resource. Thus, the shadow prices apply only within a certain range of values. Once that range is exceeded in either direction, the shadow price changes. (Chapter 5 explains how to determine the range over which the shadow price applies.) The second point to remember is that, because of the interrelationship between the constraints, it might not be possible to increase both resources simultaneously and achieve the expcted increase in the objective function. Changing the value of one constraint's RHS could have an impact upon the shadow price of another constraint. Also, any change in the RHS of a constraint, while reflected in the value of the shadow price, changes the optimal solution in terms of both the decision variable values and the value of the objective function.

4.6 EQUALITY AND GREATER-THAN CONSTRAINTS

In the example problem, all of the constraints were less-than-or-equal-to constraints. We converted them to equalities by adding slack variables. There are two situations where further modifications must be made before the problem can be solved using the simplex method.

Equality Constraints

If the constraint is an equality, for example,

$$2X + 4Y = 50$$

there is no need to add a slack variable to change an inequality to an equality. But when we set the decision variables equal to zero initially, the result is

$$2(0) + 4(0) = 50$$

$$0 = 50$$

which cannot possibly be true. To ensure that the decision variables can take a value of zero, we add a third variable to the initial constraint equation. This third variable is added only to allow the problem to be solved initially, and should not appear in the final solution. This variable is an **artificial** or imaginary variable, **A**, and is added to any equality constraints that occur in the model. This procedure gives the equation

$$2X + 4Y + A_1 = 50$$

and when the decision variables are set equal to zero, results in

$$2(0) + 4(0) + A_1 = 50$$

$$A_1 = 50$$

This artificial variable has been given a subscript to distinguish it from other possible artificial variables (just as we added subscripts to all the slack variables). Since the coefficient for A_1 in this equation is 1, and A_1 will have a coefficient of 0 in all other constraints, the A_1 column is a unit column and therefore a basic variable in the initial solution.

A_1 cannot have nonzero value in the final solution, however, since it is imaginary. Steps must be taken, therefore, to ensure that it will have a zero value. This can be accomplished by assigning a very large negative number as the objective function coefficient for any artificial variables, thus producing negative objective function values as long as any artificial variables remain in the solution. Since we are attempting to maximize the objective function, an optimal solution will not occur as long as any artificial variables with nonzero values remain in the tableau. Because large numbers can be cumbersome to write and work with in several tableaus, the process can be simplified by assigning the artificial variables the objective function coefficient $-M$, where M is an extremely large number.

Greater-than-or-equal-to Constraints

The second situation that will not solve initially is the greater-than-or-equal-to constraint. For example:

$$5X + 7Y \geq 90$$

$$0 + 0 \geq 90$$

$$0 \geq 90$$

With these constraints, a surplus variable is subtracted when converting to the standard form:

$$5X + 7Y - S_1 = 90$$

But when X and Y are set equal to zero and the equation is solved, the result is

$$5(0) + 7(0) - S_1 = 90$$

$$-S_1 = 90$$

$$S_1 = -90$$

which violates the nonnegativity constraint. Thus, in order to set all decision variables equal to zero and solve the initial tableau, an artificial variable must also be added to a greater-than-or-equal-to constraint to allow the initial tableau to be solved.

$$5X + 7Y + A_1 - S_1 = 90$$

When the decision variables are set equal to zero, the result is

$$5(0) + 7(0) + A_1 - S_1 = 90$$

$$A_1 - S_1 = 90$$

Setting the surplus variable equal to zero (if both decision variables are equal to zero, there is obviously no surplus), the artificial variable takes a value of 90.

$$A_1 - 0 = 90$$

$$A_1 = 90$$

The artificial variable would have an objective function coefficient value of $-M$; the surplus variable, like the slack variables we dealt with before, would have an objective function coefficient of zero, since it neither adds to nor subtracts from the value of the solution. Note that, when we add an artificial variable and subtract a surplus variable, the artificial variable still has a coefficient of 1 in the initial tableau and therefore is a basic variable. The surplus variable has a coefficient of -1 and is not a basic variable in the initial solution.

The steps necessary to move from constraints stated in model form to those in the tableau or tableau form can be summarized as follows:

1. If the original constraint is less-than-or-equal, add a slack variable S_j, with an objective function coefficient of 0.
2. If the original constraint is an equality, add an artificial variable, A_j, with an objective function coefficient of $-M$ (a large negative value).
3. If the original constraint is greater-than-or-equal-to, add an artificial variable and subtract a surplus variable. The artificial variable should have an objective function coefficient of $-M$ and the surplus variable an objective function coefficient of 0.

4.7 *MINIMIZATION PROBLEMS*

There are two popular approaches for using the simplex method to solve minimization problems. The first involves revising the simplex method and selecting the $C_j - Z_j$ value that represents the greatest cost reduction (the most negative number) when determining the entering variable. This continues until all $C_j - Z_j$ values are greater-than-or-equal-to zero. The second technique multiplies the objective function by -1 and solves the problem as a maximization problem. We will demonstrate the first approach using the following example problem:

Bill's Lemonade, Inc.

Bill's Lemonade, Inc. sells premixed lemonade in plastic pouches to grocery stores. Bill purchases lemon concentrate from two different suppliers, X and Y. He mixes the concentrate with water to make lemonade, then packages and labels the product. Bill finds he must have 4 ounces of concentrate for each 12-ounce pouch. While the lemonade is mixed in 100-gallon batches, all cost accounting is on a per pouch basis. Concentrate X is stronger and costs 7 cents per ounce, whereas concentrate Y costs 5 cents per ounce. The strength of a concentrate is measured in flavor units: X has 9 flavor units per ounce, but Y has only 6. Each pouch of lemonade sold must have at least 30 flavor units to be acceptable to Bill's customers. Each concentrate also has a different amount of vitamin C. Bill has found that his customers equate vitamin C with good health, and he wants to advertise that each package contains the minimum daily requirement of 60 units. Concentrate X has 14 units and Y 20 units per ounce. Bill is about to place an order for concentrate and wishes to know how many ounces of each concentrate he should use per pouch.

Bill needs to know how much of each concentrate he should order. Since Bill is an astute businessman, he also wishes to minimize his cost. Thus, his decision variables are X, the ounces of concentrate X; and Y, the ounces of concentrate Y. The objective function for this model, on a per package basis, is

$$\text{MIN } 7X + 5Y$$

and the constraints are

$$X + Y = 4 \quad \text{(total ounces per pouch)}$$
$$9X + 6Y \geq 30 \quad \text{(flavor units per pouch)}$$
$$14X + 20Y \geq 60 \quad \text{(vitamin C units)}$$
$$X, Y \geq 0 \quad \text{(nonnegativity)}$$

Thus, the LP model is

$$\text{MIN } 7X + 5Y$$
$$\text{subject to}$$
$$X + Y = 4$$
$$9X + 6Y \geq 30$$
$$14X + 20Y \geq 60$$
$$X, Y \geq 0$$

Because Bill is attempting to minimize the value of the objective function in this case, $+M$ coefficients are used for the artificial variables (very large costs). Converting the constraints to equalities in tableau form yields

$$X + Y + A_1 = 4$$
$$9X + 6Y + A_2 - S_1 = 30$$
$$14X + 20Y + A_3 - S_2 = 60$$
$$X, Y, A_1, A_2, A_3, S_1, S_2 \geq 0$$

Adding the slack, surplus, and artificial variables to the objective function gives

$$\text{MIN } 7X + 5Y + MA_1 + MA_2 + 0S_1 + MA_3 + 0S_2$$

Entering these values into the initial tableau gives

C_j	BASIC VAR	7 X	5 Y	M A_1	M A_2	0 S_1	M A_3	0 S_2	RHS
M	A_1	1	1	1	0	0	0	0	4
M	A_2	9	6	0	1	−1	0	0	30
M	A_3	14	20	0	0	0	1	−1	60
	Z_j	24M	27M	M	M	−M	M	−M	94M
	$C_j - Z_j$	7−24M	5−27M	0	0	M	0	M	

In this case, the value of the objective function, 94M, represents the total cost at this point. The objective is to reduce it as much as possible. If this were a maximization problem, the $C_j - Z_j$ row would represent profit improvement; in this case, it represents cost improvement (reduction), or change in cost per unit of each variable. Since the initial cost is very high and we want it to go down, we select the variable with the largest (absolute) negative value. In this case, variable Y with a cost improvement of 5−27M is the largest (absolute) negative value. For each unit of Y added to the solution, the cost can be expected to drop by 27M−5 (cents). Thus, variable Y enters the solution in the next tableau.

We determine the pivot row just as we did with maximization problems, by finding the minimum ratio of RHS value to pivot column coefficient. Those ratios are

$$[A_1] \qquad ^4/_1 = 4$$

$$[A_2] \qquad ^{30}/_6 = 5$$

$$[A_3] \qquad ^{60}/_{20} = 3$$

Thus, the A_3 row is the pivot row; variable Y enters the tableau, replacing variable A_3 in the next tableau. The row calculation procedures are exactly the same in minimization problems as in maximization problems and, therefore, will not be enumerated. The second tableau is

C_j	BASIC VAR	7 X	5 Y	M A_1	M A_2	0 S_1	M A_3	0 S_2	RHS
M	A_1	.3	0	1	0	0	−.05	.05	1
M	A_2	4.8	0	0	1	−1	−.3	.3	12
5	Y	.7	1	0	0	0	.05	−.05	3
	Z_j	5.1M +3.5	5	M	M	−M	−.35M +.25	.35M −.25	13M + 15
	$C_j - Z_j$	3.5 −5.1M	0	0	0	M	.65M −.25	−.35M +.25	

The $C_j - Z_j$ row in this solution still has negative values, indicating this solution is not optimal. The X column has the largest (absolute) negative value in the $C_j - Z_j$ row (3.5 − 5.1M), and thus X will enter the tableau. Calculating the ratios determines that variable A_2 will leave the tableau.

$$^1/_3 = 3.333$$

$$^{12}/_{4.8} = 2.4$$

$$^3/_7 = 4.2857$$

Performing the necessary calculations would give the third tableau.

C_j	BASIC VAR	7 X	5 Y	M A_1	M A_2	0 S_1	M A_3	0 S_2	RHS
M	A_1	0	0	1	−.06	.06	−.03	.03	.25
7	X	1	0	0	.21	--.21	−.06	.06	2.5
5	Y	0	1	0	−.15	.15	.09	−.09	1.25
	Z_j	7	5	M	−.06M +.72	.06M −.72	−.03M +.03	.03M −.03	.25M +23.75
	$C_j - Z_j$	0	0	0	.06M −.72	.72 −.06M	.03M −.03	.03 −.03M	

The $C_j - Z_j$ row still has negative values. Therefore, an optimal solution has not been reached. The largest absolute negative value (.72 − .06M), indicates that S_1 will enter the tableau, and the ratios indicate A_1 will leave the tableau. Note that the X row has a negative coefficient (−.21). This implies a negative rate of substitution. As S_1 increases, the value of X will also increase. The fourth tableau is

C_j	BASIC VAR	7 X	5 Y	M A_1	M A_2	0 S_1	M A_3	0 S_2	RHS
0	S_1	0	0	16	−1	1	−.5	.5	4
7	X	1	0	3.33	0	0	−.17	.17	3.33
5	Y	0	1	−2.33	0	0	.17	−.17	.667
	Z_j	7	5	11.67	0	0	−.33	.33	26.67
	$C_j - Z_j$	0	0	M −11.67	M	0	M +.33	−.33	

The fourth tableau is still not an optimal tableau, since the $C_j - Z_j$ value for S_2 is −.33. S_2 will enter the tableau and S_1 will leave, giving the fifth tableau.

C_j	BASIC VAR	7 X	5 Y	M A_1	M A_2	0 S_1	M A_3	0 S_2	RHS
0	S_1	0	0	32	−2	2	−1	1	8
7	X	1	0	−2	.33	−.33	0	0	2
5	Y	0	1	3	−.33	.33	0	0	2
	Z_j	7	5	1	.667	−.667	0	0	24
	$C_j - Z_j$	0	0	M − 1	M − .67	.667	M	0	

The $C_j - Z_j$ row for this tableau shows that all $C_j - Z_j$ values are now positive. An optimal solution has finally been reached. Bill should use 2 ounces of concentrate X and 2 ounces of concentrate Y, with a minimum cost of 24 cents per package. The S_1 value of 8, a surplus value for the second constraint, indicates there is a surplus of 8 flavor units.

Thus, minimization problems are solved in the same manner as maximization problems, except that the $C_j - Z_j$ value that reduces the value of the objective function the most is selected. Although this minimization problem has artificial variables in it with M coefficients, you might also encounter artificial variables in maximization problems, since they are added to any equal-to or greater-than-or-equal-to constraints. Some computer programs solve minimization problems by multiplying the objective function by -1 and then treating the problem as a maximization problem, or conversely, by multiplying the objective function of a maximization problem by -1 and treating it as a minimization problem.

4.8 *SPECIAL CONSIDERATIONS WHEN SOLVING LP PROBLEMS*

In Chapter 3, we showed that it is possible to have infeasible problems and unbounded problems, although both are usually caused by improper problem formulation. While it is easy to recognize those situations when they are displayed graphically, it is also possible to identify them when they occur in a simplex tableau. In this section we will discuss these special problems, as well as how to deal with ties in the $C_j - Z_j$ values, ties in the ratios used to determine the leaving variable (pivot row), and alternate optimal solutions.

Infeasible Problems

An infeasible problem is a problem that does not have an area of feasible solutions that satisfies all constraints simultaneously. Infeasible problems usually occur when a problem has both less-than-or-equal-to and greater-than-or-equal-to constraints with no area of overlap. In the simplex tableau, and infeasible problem can be identified when the $C_j - Z_j$ row indicates that an optimal solution has been found and an artificial variable still remains in the tableau with a value greater than zero.

In Chapter 3, we used the problem

$$\text{MAX } 2X_1 + 5X_2$$

subject to

$$X_1 + 2X_2 \leq 50$$

$$3X_1 + X_2 \geq 200$$

$$X_1, X_2 \geq 0$$

to demonstrate infeasibility graphically. Figure 4.3 shows the final simplex tableau for this problem.

C_j	BASIC VARIABLE	2 X_1	5 X_2	0 S_1	$-M$ A_1	0 S_2	RHS
2	X_1	1	2	1	0	0	50
$-M$	A_1	0	-5	-3	1	-1	50
	Z_j	2	$4 + 5M$	$2 + 3M$	$-M$	M	$100 - 50M$
	$C_j - Z_j$	0	$1 - 5M$	$-2 - 3M$	0	$-M$	

Figure 4.3 Final Tableau of Infeasible Problem

In this tableau, all the $C_j - Z_j$ values are negative or zero, indicating an optimal solution has been reached; but the artificial variable A_1 remains in the tableau with a value of 50. This indicates that the problem is infeasible. (Mathematically, the constraint evaluates as $3(50) + 0 \geq 200$, which is not feasible.) Given the large negative coefficient assigned to the artificial variable (A_1), the only time the artificial variable remains in the solution is when no feasible alternative solution exists. Thus whenever an artificial variable with a nonzero value remains in the final solution, it indicates an infeasible problem.

Unbounded Problems

An unbounded problem is a problem that has no limit on the quantity of one or more of the variables. That would mean, for example, that it is possible to produce an infinite amount of some product. Like infeasible problems, most unbounded problems result from improper formulation of the original problem. Usually unbounded problems occur when a constraint has been omitted. In the simplex tableau, an unbounded problem can be identified by a pivot column that has no values greater than zero.

Again, drawing from Chapter 3, we will use the following problem to illustrate an unbounded problem:

$$\text{MAX } 2X_1 + 5X_2$$

subject to

$$X_2 \leq 15$$

$$X_1 + 3X_2 \geq 60$$

$$X_1, X_2 \geq 0$$

Figure 4.4 shows the final tableau for this problem. Note that this final tableau is not the optimal solution point, but the point at which we discover that the problem is unbounded.

In this tableau, the $C_j - Z_j$ value for the S_2 column has the largest positive value, making the S_2 column the pivot column. However, the pivot column has coefficient values of 0 and -1. These values imply that X_2 will not decrease as S_2 increases and that X_1 will increase as S_2 increases (a negative rate of substitution). This suggests X_1 may approach infinity and that the problem is unbounded. Thus, the lack of positive values in the S_2 column indicates that this problem is an unbounded problem.

C_j	BASIC VARIABLE	2 X_1	5 X_2	0 S_1	$-M$ A_1	0 S_2	RHS
5	X_2	0	1	1	0	0	15
2	X_1	1	0	-3	1	-1	15
	Z_j	2	5	-1	2	-2	105
	$C_j - Z_j$	0	0	1	$-M - 2$	2	

Figure 4.4 Final Tableau of Unbounded Problem

Two or More Variables That May Enter the Tableau

In some cases, two or more variables may have identical $C_j - Z_j$ values. If these values determine the pivot column, only one column may be selected. The choice is made arbitrarily, as shown in Figure 4.5, where variables X_1, and X_3 both have a value of 2. It will make absolutely no difference in the final solution.

Degenerate Problems

Occasionally, when determining the pivot row, two or more rows may have the same minimum ratio value. This situation implies that three or more constraints are intersecting at the same point. When this happens, one of the tied variables is arbitrarily selected to leave the tableau. The variable not selected to leave the tableau will then have a value of zero in the next tableau, even though it is a basic variable. When this occurs (when a basic variable in a basic feasible solution has a value of zero), the problem is called a degenerate problem. Figure 4.6 illustrates a situation where degeneracy occurs. The X_1 column is the pivot column in this tableau. Dividing the RHS values by the X_1 column coefficients produces a tie between the S_2 and X_3 rows as the pivot row.

C_j	BASIC VARIABLE	3 X_1	5 X_2	4 X_3	0 S_1	0 S_2	0 S_3	RHS
0	S_2	.4	0	0	.5	1	0	2
5	X_2	.2	1	.4	.6	0	0	5
0	S_3	.4	0	1	−.4	0	1	4
	Z_j	1	5	2	3	0	0	25
	$C_j - Z_j$	2	0	2	−3	0	0	

Figure 4.5 Two Variables Which May Enter the Next Tableau

C_j	BASIC VARIABLE	3 X_1	5 X_2	4 X_3	0 S_1	0 S_2	0 S_3	RHS
0	S_2	.2	0	0	2	1	.2	2
5	X_2	.2	1	0	1	0	.1	5
4	X_3	.4	0	1	1	0	.4	4
	Z_j	2.6	5	4	9	0	2.1	41
	$C_j - Z_j$	0.4	0	0	−9	0	−2.1	

Figure 4.6 Tableau of a Degenerate Problem

$$[S_2] \quad 2/ .2 = 10$$

$$[X_2] \quad 5/ .2 = 25$$

$$[S_3] \quad 4/ .4 = 10$$

Figure 4.7 shows the next tableau when S_2 is selected as the pivot row.

In this tableau, the value of X_3, which was tied with row S_2 in the tableau in Figure 4.6, now has a value of zero although it is still a basic variable in the tableau. Degeneracy is not a major problem in solving problems using the simplex method in most cases. In rare instances, the simplex procedure enters an endless loop, where two variables alternate entering and leaving the basic solution. There are tie-breaking rules to prevent this result, but they are beyond the scope of this text. When we check the $C_j - Z_j$ row for optimality, we know we have an optimal (maximization) solution when all the $C_j - Z_j$ values are less than or equal to zero. Some problems, however, have more than one optimal solution. We identify these solutions as having **alternate optimal** solutions or **alternate optima.** Consider the tableau shown in Figure 4.8. Variable X_1, a nonbasic variable, has a $C_j - Z_j$ value of zero. This implies that, if X_1 enters the tableau, the value of the objective function will change by a zero amount (or not at all). Thus another optimal solution with variable X_1 in that solution must exist. This result usually occurs when the objective function has the same slope as one of the constraints. Thus, alternate optimal solutions exist whenever a nonbasic variable has a $C_j - Z_j$ value of zero in an optimal solution.

C_j	BASIC VARIABLE	3 X_1	5 X_2	4 X_3	0 S_1	0 S_2	0 S_3	RHS
3	X_1	1	0	0	10	5	1	10
5	X_2	0	1	0	−1	−1	−.1	3
4	X_3	0	0	1	−4	−2	0	0
	Z_j	3	5	4	11	2	2.5	45
	$C_j - Z_j$	0	0	0	−11	−2	−2.5	

Figure 4.7 Tableau of Degenerate Problem

C_j	BASIC VARIABLE	3 X_1	5 X_2	4 X_3	0 S_1	0 S_2	0 S_3	RHS
0	S_2	.3	0	0	2	1	.2	6
5	X_2	.2	1	0	−1	0	.1	4
4	X_3	.5	0	1	2	0	.4	8
	Z_j	3	5	4	3	0	2.1	52
	$C_j - Z_j$	0	0	0	−3	0	−2.1	

Figure 4.8 Example Alternate Optimal Solution

4.9 COMPUTER SOLUTIONS

In addition to providing output summaries for problems, many computer programs also enable the user to see tableaus as they are calculated. Figure 4.9 shows the output when the "ALL TABLEAUS" option is selected, using the program that accompanies this book.

Note that all values are displayed decimally and that some rounding does occur.

TABLEAU NUMBER 1

C(j)		8	10	0	0	0	
	Basis	X1	X2	S1	S2	S3	RHS
0	S1	4.5	2	1	0	0	36
0	S2	3	5	0	1	0	45
0	S3	4	4	0	0	1	40
	Z	0	0	0	0	0	0
	C - Z	8	10	0	0	0	

Press any key to continue

TABLEAU NUMBER 2

C(j)		8	10	0	0	0	
	Basis	X1	X2	S1	S2	S3	RHS
0	S1	3.3	0	1	-.4	0	18
10	X2	.6	1	0	.2	0	9
0	S3	1.6	0	0	-.8	1	4
	Z	6	10	0	2	0	90
	C - Z	2	0	0	-2	0	

Press any key to continue

TABLEAU NUMBER 3

C(j)		8	10	0	0	0	
	Basis	X1	X2	S1	S2	S3	RHS
0	S1	0	0	1	1.25	-2.063	9.75
10	X2	0	1	0	.5	-.375	7.5
8	X1	1	0	0	-.5	.625	2.5
	Z	8	10	0	1	1.25	95
	C - Z	0	0	0	-1	-1.25	

Press any key to continue

Figure 4.9 Computer Tableau Output

4.10 *CONCLUDING REMARKS*

A great deal of time in this chapter has been spent on the simplex method. The basic intent is to acquaint the reader with the mathematics behind the solution technique. In solving real-world problems, however, the simplex method may require hundreds or even thousands of calculations before an optimal solution is obtained. Many computer programs are available commercially to solve LP problems, thus relieving managers of the lengthy and tedious computations. Nowadays, a manager who solves a linear programming problem without using a computer is the exception. Although we assume the reader will use one of these programs, we have included this chapter to provide a better understanding of the underlying concepts. Thus, our intention has been to make you aware of what the computer is doing, rather than to enable you to perform these calculations yourself.

GLOSSARY

alternate optima a condition where more than one optimal solution exists for an LP problem; also known as alternate optimal solution

artificial variable an imaginary variable, represented by A, which is added to equality and greater-than-or-equal-to constraints so that the simplex method can set all decision variables equal to zero initially and still find a feasible solution

basic feasible solution a basic solution where all of the solution values satisfy all constraint and nonnegativity requirements, i.e., all of the solution values are feasible

basic solution a solution to a linear programming problem in which a number of variables equal to the number of constraints in the problem have solution values, and the remaining variables are set equal to zero; in a problem with n variables and m constraints where $n > m$, the basic solution is obtained by first setting $n - m$ variables equal to zero and then solving for the values of the remaining (nonzero) variables

basic variables variables that are included in the tableau of a simplex solution, usually with nonzero values; there should be one basic variable for every constraint in the LP model

C_j represents the objective function coefficient for the jth column in the simplex tableau

$C_j - Z_j$ represents the row that shows the net improvement in the value of the objective function with the addition of one unit of the variable represented by the jth column

degeneracy the condition that exists when a basic variable has a zero value; this condition occurs when the ratios used to detemine the pivot row result in a tie between two or more variables

identity matrix a matrix of coefficients that has unity values (ones) on the diagonal and all the remaining values are zero

initial tableau also known as the initial simplex tableau, is the first or beginning tableau in the simplex method and corresponds to a point where all decision variables are equal to zero

iterative a solution that follows a repetitive procedure until an optimal solution is found

M a very large value assigned as a coefficient for artificial variables to ensure that they do not remain in the optimal simplex solution; in maximization problems, the coefficient $-M$ is assigned, while in minimization problems, the coefficient $+M$ is used

nonbasic variables variables that are not basic variables in the final simplex tableau; nonbasic variables must be equal to zero in the final solution

pivot column the column that determines which variable will enter the tableau in the next simplex iteration

pivot element the coefficient at the intersection of the pivot column and the pivot row

pivot row the row that determines which variable will leave the tableau in the next simplex tableau; the one that is most constraining on the entering variable

shadow price indicates the relative worth of one unit of a resource

simplex method an algorithm for solving linear programming problems; uses an iterative algebraic solution procedure, beginning at the origin and examining successive adjacent extreme points until an optimal solution is found

unit column a column with a coefficient of one (1) in one row and zero in all remaining rows

Z_j indicates the cost incurred if one unit of the jth variable is added to the solution

PROBLEMS

1. The manager of a plant producing three products has formulated the following product mix problem:

$$\text{MAX } 5X_1 + 3\tfrac{1}{2}X_2 + 3X_3$$

subject to

$$
\begin{aligned}
2X_1 + X_2 + 3X_3 &\leq 500 \\
8X_1 + 10X_2 + 16X_3 &\leq 2150 \\
X_1, X_2, X_3 &\geq 0
\end{aligned}
$$

Solve this problem using the simplex algorithm.

2. Given the following problem:

$$\text{MAX } 4X_1 + 5X_2 + 3X_3$$

subject to

$$
\begin{aligned}
X_1 + 2X_2 + 3X_3 &\leq 12 \\
2X_1 + X_2 &\leq 6 \\
X_1, X_2 &\geq 0
\end{aligned}
$$

   a. Convert the problem to the standard form.
   b. Solve this problem using the simplex algorithm.

3. Given the following problem:

$$\text{MAX } 6X_1 + 2X_2 + 5X_3$$

subject to

$$
\begin{aligned}
2X_1 + X_2 + 3X_3 &\leq 40 \\
6X_1 + 2X_2 + X_3 &\geq 20
\end{aligned}
$$

$$X_1 + X_2 + X_3 = 12$$
$$X_1, X_2, X_3 \geq 0$$

a. Convert the problem to the standard form.
b. Solve this problem using the simplex algorithm.

4. Set up the initial simplex tableau for the following LP model (do not solve):

$$MAX\ 5X_1 - 3X_2 + 4X_3 + 2.5X_4$$

subject to

$$
\begin{aligned}
3X_1 + 2X_2 + X_3 + 3X_4 &\leq 60 \\
2X_1 + 4X_2 \qquad - 3X_4 &\leq 50 \\
-4X_1 + 3X_2 + 5X_3 + 4X_4 &\geq 35 \\
X_1 \qquad + 2X_3 + X_4 &\geq 16 \\
X_1, X_2, X_3, X_4 &\geq 0
\end{aligned}
$$

5. Set up the initial simplex tableau for the following LP model (do not solve):

$$MIN\ 6A + 7B + 4C + 5D$$

subject to

$$
\begin{aligned}
3A + 4B \qquad\qquad &\geq 28 \\
A \qquad + 3C + 2D &= 25 \\
2A + 3B \qquad + 4D &\geq 16 \\
5A + 2B + 2C \qquad &= 37 \\
A, B, C, D &\geq 0
\end{aligned}
$$

6. Given the following problem:

$$MAX\ 6X_1 + 5X_2$$

subject to

$$
\begin{aligned}
1.5X_1 + 2X_2 &\leq 30 \\
8X_1 + 4X_2 &\leq 80 \\
X_1, X_2 &\geq 0
\end{aligned}
$$

a. Convert the problem to the standard form.
b. Solve this problem using the simplex algorithm.

7. Door-2-Door Products (Chapter 2, example blending problem) blends its own all-purpose liquid cleanser from bulk cleansers purchased from two suppliers, A and B. The LP model for this problem is:

$$MIN\ 1.10A + 1.35B$$

subject to

$$
\begin{aligned}
A + \quad B &= 200000 \\
.20A + .05B &\geq 20000 \\
.20A + .05B &\leq 30000 \\
.05B &\geq 4000 \\
A, B &\geq 0
\end{aligned}
$$

Solve this problem using the simplex algorithm.

8. Solve the following problem using the simplex algorithm:

$$\text{MIN } 4A + 6B$$

subject to
$$4A + 6B \geq 12$$
$$4A + 2B \geq 18$$
$$A, B \geq 0$$

9. Consider the following problem:

$$\text{MIN } 5X_1 + 6X_2$$

subject to
$$3X_1 + 6X_2 \geq 18$$
$$4X_1 + 2X_2 \geq 18$$
$$X_1, X_2 \geq 0$$

a. Solve the problem graphically.
b. Find the optimal solution using the simplex algorithm.
c. Compare the value of the basic variables in each tableau with the graphic extreme points.
d. Determine the shadow prices for each constraint.

10. Consider the following problem:

$$\text{MAX } A + 3B + 2C + 5D$$

subject to
$$A - B + 2C + D = 6$$
$$3A + B + 3C + D = 10$$
$$6A + 10B + 4D \leq 32$$
$$A, B, C, D \geq 0$$

a. Solve this problem using the simplex algorithm.
b. Which constraints are binding upon the optimal solution?
c. What are the reduced costs for the nonbasic variables?
d. What are the shadow prices associated with each constraint?
e. If you could obtain one additional unit of one constraint, which constraint would you choose? Why?

11. Consider the following problem:

$$\text{MAX } 5X_1 + 5X_2 + 4X_3 + 6X_4$$

subject to
$$3X_1 + 5X_2 + 2X_3 + 4X_4 \leq 224$$
$$-2X_1 + 4X_2 + 2X_3 + 4X_4 \leq 184$$
$$10X_1 + 8X_2 + 10X_3 - 10X_4 \leq 280$$
$$X_1, X_2, X_3, X_4 \geq 0$$

a. Solve this problem using the simplex algorithm.
b. Which constraints are binding upon the optimal solution?
c. What are the reduced costs for the nonbasic variables?

d. What are the shadow prices associated with each constraint?

e. If you could obtain one additional unit of one constraint, which constraint would you choose? Why?

12. Hyper Fast Computers manufacturers IBM-compatible personal computers. Hyper Fast makes three PC models: a Desktop-386, a Desktop-286, and a Laptop-286. Because of limited production facilities, Hyper Fast cannot produce more than 100 desktop models or more than 60 laptop models per month. Hyper Fast also has a limited supply of CPU chips (80286 and 80386) available for the coming month. It has 45 80386 chips and 120 80286 chips for the month. The Desktop-386 model requires 4 hours of assembly time, the Desktop-286 model requires 3 hours of assembly time, and the Laptop-286 model requires 2½ hours of assembly time. Hyper Fast has 290 hours of assembly time available for the coming month. Hyper Fast estimates it makes $1,250 profit on a Desktop-386, $900 profit on a Desktop-286, and $800 profit on a Laptop-286.

a. Formulate this problem as a profit maximization problem.
b. Solve the problem.
c. Identify the binding constraints for this problem.
d. What are the shadow prices associated with each of these constraints?

13. Given the following simplex tableau:

C_j	BASIC VAR	3 A	4 B	2 C	0 S_1	0 S_2	0 S_3	RHS
		-1	0	4	1	0	-6	12
		0	0	3	0	1	-4	13
		1	1	0	0	0	1	18
	Z							
	C − Z							

a. Is this problem a maximization or minimization problem?
b. Which variables are basic?
c. Complete the tableau.
d. Identify the pivot column and the pivot row.
e. Find the optimal solution to this problem.

14. Given the following simplex tableau:

C_j	BASIC VAR	4 A	6 B	M A_1	0 S_1	M A_2	0 S_2	RHS
		1	1.5	.25	$-.25$	0	0	3
		0	-4	-1	1	1	-1	6
	Z							
	C − Z							

a. Is this problem a maximization or minimization problem?
b. Which variables are basic?
c. Complete the tableau.

d. Identify the pivot column and the pivot row.

e. Find the optimal solution to this problem.

15. Given the following simplex tableau:

C_j	BASIC VAR	1 A	3 B	2 C	5 D	$-M$ A_1	$-M$ A_2	0 S_1	RHS
		.5	.25	1	.5	.125	0	0	3.2
		0	2.5	0	3	$-.25$	1	0	.4
		0	0	0	0	$-.5$	0	1	28
	Z								
	C − Z								

a. Is this problem a maximization or minimization problem?

b. Which variables are basic?

c. Complete the tableau.

d. Identify the pivot column and the pivot row.

e. Find the optimal solution to this problem.

16. Given the following simplex tableau:

C_j	BASIC VAR	5 A	6 B	5 C	4 D	0 S_1	0 S_2	0 S_3	RHS
		1	0	.2	0	.2	0	$-.2$	4
		0	0	1	1	$-.2$	.133	.367	30
		0	1	.6	0	.2	$-.067$	$-.033$	10
	Z								
	C − Z								

a. Is this problem a maximization or minimization problem?

b. Which variables are basic?

c. Complete the tableau.

d. Is this solution optimal?

e. State the optimal solution to this problem (in terms of variable quantities, reduced costs and shadow prices).

f. Which constraints are binding on this solution?

g. How would the value of the objective function change if four units of product C were added to the solution?

17. Given the following tableau:

C_j	BASIC VAR	1 A	5 B	3 C	0 S_1	0 S_2	0 S_3	RHS
		2	0	5	1	0	-6	20
		0	0	3	0	1	-4	12
		1	1	0	0	0	1	18
	Z							
	C − Z							

a. Which variables are basic?
b. Complete the tableau.
c. Identify the pivot column and the pivot row.
d. This tableau presents a special type of LP problem. Identify that problem.

18. Given the following tableau:

C_j	BASIC VAR	6 A	5 B	3 C	0 S_1	$-M$ A_1	0 S_2	RHS
		1	0	1	2	0	3	45
		0	0	0	0	1	0	10
		0	1	1	-1	0	0	25
	Z							
	C − Z							

a. Which variables are basic?
b. Complete the tableau.
c. Is this solution optimal?
d. This tableau presents a special type of LP problem. Identify that problem.

19. Given the following tableau:

C_j	BASIC VAR	2 A	4 B	4 C	0 S_1	0 S_2	0 S_3	RHS
		2	0	-3	1	0	-3	100
		0	0	-1	0	1	-2	150
		1	1	0	0	0	2	200
	Z							
	C − Z							

a. Which variables are basic?
b. Complete the tableau.
c. Identify the pivot column and the pivot row.
d. This tableau presents a special type of LP problem. Identify that problem.

20. Given the following tableau:

C_j	BASIC VAR	8 A	6 B	7 C	0 S_1	0 S_2	0 S_3	RHS
		0	0	3	1	0	2	20
		0	0	-1	0	1	-3	75
		1	.75	2	0	0	2	80
	Z							
	C − Z							

a. Which variables are basic?
b. Complete the tableau.

c. Is this solution optimal?

d. This tableau presents a special type of LP problem. Identify that problem.

21. The Party Mix Company packages and sells four types of party packages: pretzels, peanuts, chex and nuts, and party mix. The products are sold in 8-ounce plastic soft-packs. The profit contributions per package are shown below.

Package	Profit/package	Contents
Pretzels	30¢	Pretzels only
Peanuts	45¢	Peanuts only
Chex & nuts	26¢	15% peanuts, remainder chex cereals
Party mix	54¢	20% pretzels, 10% peanuts, remainder chex cereals

a. If PMC has 215 pounds of pretzels, 400 pounds of peanuts, and 525 pounds of chex cereals, how many packages of each type of product should it produce if it can sell all it produces?

b. Which constraints (ingredients) are binding?

c. How much should Party Mix be willing to pay (per pound) for additional quantities of each ingredient?

Consultant's Report ───────────────────────────────

SAM'S SECURITY SERVICES

Sam's Security Services offers special courier and armored car services to local businesses and banks in the Los Angeles area. Sam has been in business since 1972 and has established and excellent reputation for speed of delivery, reliability, and security. Because of this excellent record, Sam finds the demand for his services currently exceeds his ability to provide them, and he must turn down some jobs each day.

Sam began the business with one station wagon and one armored mini-van. Over the years he has added vehicles as his business has grown, and he now uses three types of vehicles: station wagons, for most courier services; armored mini-vans, to transport cash and other valuable commodities; and the traditional armored truck, to transport large amounts of cash between businesses and banks. Sam currently has five station wagons, eight mini-vans, and three armored trucks. All vehicles are equipped with two-way radios that allow communications with the dispatcher or the local police department. Each vehicle must have a specially licensed and bonded armed driver. In addition, each mini-van has an armed guard who accompanies the driver, and each armored truck has two armed guards. Unfortunately, due to some recent retirements and employee relocations, Sam has only thirteen drivers and ten guards on his payroll. He is currently attempting to replace personnel in both categories, but since drivers and guards must be bondable and qualified marksmen, this task is difficult.

Sam estimates that the company grosses an average of $250 per day on each station wagon, $350 per day on each mini-van, and $500 per day on each armored truck. Depreciation on the vehicles is estimated at $10 per day per station wagon,

$15 per day per mini-van, and $25 per day per armored truck. Insurance costs are $5, $10, and $15 per day per vehicle, respectively. Maintenance and gasoline costs are based upon daily use and are estimated to be $10 per day for the station wagons, $20 per day for the mini-vans, and $35 per day for the armored trucks. Drivers are each paid $100 per day, and guards are each paid $65 per day. Dispatcher and office costs are estimated at $210 per day. Because Sam is currently turning down jobs for all three types of vehicles due to his lack of drivers and guards, he wonders if there is some special combination of vehicles that would give him the greatest profit per day.

You have been hired as a management consultant to help Sam by applying management science techniques to his special problem. Prepare a report for Sam's Security Services that addresses:

1. The number of each type of vehicle he should place in service each day to maximize his profits, and the amount of profits he can expect to achieve.
2. The amount by which daily profits can be increased if Sam is able to hire additional drivers for his vehicles.
3. The amount by which daily profits can be increased if Sam is able to hire additional armed guards.
4. The types of vehicles Sam should add to his fleet if he decides to expand the number of vehicles he currently owns, and how these additions will affect his profits.

5

Sensitivity Analysis and Duality

By the end of this chapter, you should be able to:

1

perform sensitivity analysis on the objective function coefficients of basic variables;

2

perform sensitivity analysis on the objective function coefficients of nonbasic variables;

3

perform sensitivity analysis on the RHS values of the constraints;

4

determine the impact of a new variable on the LP solution;

5

determine the impact of a new constraint on the LP solution;

6

convert a primal problem to a dual problem; and

7

interpret the results of the dual solution.

In this chapter we introduce two linear programming–related topics: sensitivity analysis and duality. Sensitivity analysis, or postoptimality analysis, assesses the impact of changes in the problem parameters upon the optimal LP solution. Duality, an alternate approach to formulating and solving LP problems, provides the basis for understanding the concept of shadow prices.

Wilson Electronics

Wilson Electronics is a small, family-owned company located in Sarasota, Florida. The company was founded in 1975 to assemble electronic components on a sub-contract basis. Originally, Wilson performed a wide variety of small assembly jobs for a number of local manufacturers. Currently, however, the company's subcontracting is limited to two computer components. Assembling these components has provided a relatively stable, long-term opportunity for Wilson. Component 1 passes through three assembly centers; Component 2 passes through two assembly centers. The profit per unit is $5 for Component 1 and $4 for Component 2. Component 1 requires 2, 9, and 2 minutes of assembly time in the three centers respectively. Component 2 requires 4 minutes in the first center and 6 minutes in the second center, and does not pass through the third center. There are currently 300, 630, and 120 minutes per day available in the respective centers.

A local college student, working in Wilson's production planning department over the summer, used linear programming to determine the optimal production mix for these components. Max Fuller, production manager, uses these results as the basis for his production planning on these two components. While the parameters of this problem have remained constant over the past year, Max is concerned about how a change in the profit contributions would impact the optimal solution. In recent weeks there has been some discussion concerning changes in computer prices.

This is another example of a simple product-mix LP problem. We will return to it later in the chapter to illustrate how sensitive the LP optimal solution is to changes in the objective function coefficients, and how Max can make use of this information.

5.1 *AN INTRODUCTION TO SENSITIVITY ANALYSIS*

The optimal solution to an LP problem provides the user with the decision variable values, the value of the objective function, and the shadow or dual prices. These solution values are based on the assumption that the input parameters are constant. But what happens when a parameter value changes? Do any or all of the solution values change? Does the problem have to be resolved before further decisions can be made? How sensitive is the solution to parameter changes? In other words, do slight parameter changes cause no change, minor changes, or major changes in the solution values? **Sensitivity analysis,** or postoptimality analysis, provides an answer to these questions.

Sensitivity is a matter of degree. Some problem solutions are relatively sensitive to changes in the input parameters. In these cases, changing the input parameters significantly affects the optimal solution. When solutions are relatively insensitive, however, changing input parameters has little effect on the optimal solution.

It is important for a manager to know not only the optimal solution to a problem, but also how sensitive that solution is to possible parameter changes (or errors in the original parameter estimates). If the solution is relatively insensitive to parameter changes, the previous solution (and the resulting decision) may still be acceptable. But if the solution is relatively sensitive to parameter changes, it may necessitate reformulating and resolving the problem. In this chapter, we will examine sensitivity analysis in greater detail as it relates to four types of parameter changes:

1. Changes in the objective function values for basic variables.
2. Changes in the objective function values for nonbasic variables and the introduction of new decision variables into the problem.
3. Changes in the original RHS values (that is, changes in the quantities of resources available).
4. The addition of new constraints into the problem.

Although most sensitivity analysis makes use of data provided by the final simplex tableau, we will introduce each topic with a brief graphical example to provide a simple, visual explanation of the underlying principles involved. We will then move to the mathematical solution using the simplex data. Computer-based sensitivity analysis is described in Chapter 6.

5.2 *CHANGES IN OBJECTIVE FUNCTION VALUES FOR BASIC VARIABLES*

Consider the following LP formulation of Wilson Electronic's production planning problem, where X_1 represents Component 1 and X_2 Component 2:

$$\text{MAX } 5X_1 + 4X_2$$

subject to

$$2X_1 + 4X_2 \leq 300 \quad \text{[assembly center 1]}$$

$$9X_1 + 6X_2 \leq 630 \quad \text{[assembly center 2]}$$

$$2X_1 \qquad\quad \leq 120 \quad \text{[assembly center 3]}$$

$$X_1, X_2 \geq 0$$

Graphic Solution

The graphic solution to this problem is shown in Figure 5.1. The optimal solution to this problem occurs at point B, where $X_1 = 30$ and $X_2 = 60$, with a Zmax value of 390. How would this solution be affected by a change in the objective function coefficients? If the coefficients changed such that the slope of the objective function were relatively flat, as shown in Figure 5.2a, the optimal solution would change to point A, where $X_1 = 0$ and $X_2 = 75$. (The new Zmax value cannot be determined without knowing the specific values of the new objective function co-

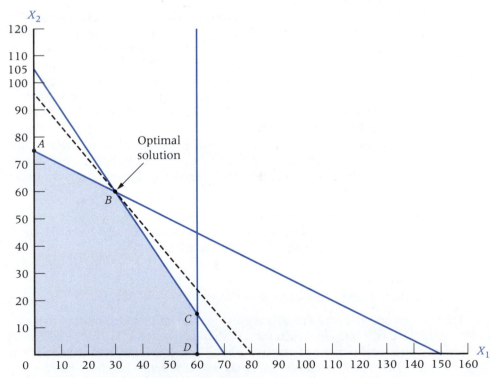

Figure 5.1 Graphic Solution to LP Problem

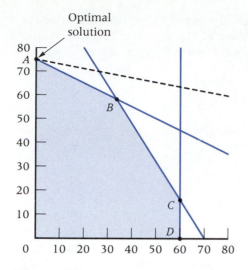

Figure 5.2a

Figure 5.2b

efficients.) If the coefficients changed such that the slope of the objective function were much more vertical, as shown in Figure 5.2b, the optimal solution would change to point C, where $X_1 = 60$ and $X_2 = 15$. Thus, when the slope of the objective function becomes flatter than the slope of constraint 1 or steeper than the slope of constraint 2, the optimal solution changes. But as long as the slope of the objective function is such that the objective function falls between those two constraints (as shown originally in Figure 5.1), the optimal solution ($X_1 = 30$, $X_2 = 60$) does not change. The slopes of the constraint equations can be determined by altering their form to the more familiar equation for a straight line,

$$Y = aX + b$$

where a is the slope and b is the Y-axis intercept. Rearranging constraint 1

$$2X_1 + 4X_2 \leq 300$$

$$4X_2 \leq -2X_1 + 300$$

$$X_2 \leq -\tfrac{1}{2}X_1 + 75$$

we see that it has a slope of $-\tfrac{1}{2}$. Rearranging constraint 2

$$9X_1 + 6X_2 \leq 630$$

$$6X_2 \leq -9X_1 + 630$$

$$X_2 \leq -\tfrac{3}{2}X_1 + 105$$

gives the slope $-\tfrac{3}{2}$. We can state the slope of the objective function in terms of the coefficients C_1 and C_2 (5 and 4 in this problem):

$$C_1(X_1) + C_2(X_2) = \text{constant}$$

$$C_2(X_2) = -C_1(X_1) + \text{constant}$$

$$X_2 = {}^{C_1}\!/_{C_2}(x_1) + \text{constant}$$

Since the slope of the objective function can be expressed as $-{}^{C_1}\!/_{C_2}$, the optimal solution does not change as long as

$$-\tfrac{3}{2} \leq -{}^{C_1}\!/_{C_2} \leq -\tfrac{1}{2}$$

If we hold coefficient C_1 constant (at its original value of 5), we can determine the range of values for C_2 that will keep the slope of the objective function within these limits. The algebraic calculations are shown below for each side of the range.

$$-\tfrac{3}{2} \leq -\tfrac{5}{C_2} \qquad -\tfrac{5}{C_2} \leq -\tfrac{1}{2}$$

$$-\tfrac{3}{2} C_2 \leq -5 \qquad -5 \leq -\tfrac{1}{2} C_2$$

$$-C_2 \leq -5(\tfrac{3}{2}) \qquad -2(5) \leq -C_2$$

$$-C_2 \leq -\tfrac{10}{3} \qquad -10 \leq -C_2$$

$$C_2 \geq \tfrac{10}{3} \qquad 10 \geq C_2$$

$$10 \geq C_2 \geq \tfrac{10}{3}$$

These calculations indicate that, if C_1 is held constant at 5, the value of C_2 can vary between $\tfrac{10}{3}$ and 10 without causing the optimal solution to change. Obviously, if C_2 changes from 4 to 8, the value of the objective function changes from 390 to 630 ($5 \times 30 + 8 \times 60 = 150 + 480 = 630$), but the values of the basic variables ($X_1 = 30$ and $X_2 = 60$) remain unchanged.

The value of C_2 can then be held constant at 4 to determine the range for C_1.

$$-\tfrac{3}{2} \leq -\tfrac{C_1}{4} \qquad -\tfrac{C_1}{4} \leq -\tfrac{1}{2}$$

$$-\tfrac{3}{2}(4) \leq -C_1 \qquad -C_1 \leq -\tfrac{1}{2}(4)$$

$$-6 \leq -C_1 \qquad -C_1 \leq -2$$

$$6 \geq C_1 \qquad C_1 \geq 2$$

$$6 \geq C_1 \geq 2$$

Thus, with C_2 constant at 4, as long as the value of C_1 is between 2 and 6, the values of the basic variables does not change.

Tabular Solution

The graphic solution was used to illustrate the determination of ranges for the objective function coefficients of basic variables only because it provides a visual representation of the range. In actual practice, the range of values for the objective function coefficients is determined using the data from the final simplex tableau. The final tableau for this problem is

C_j	BASIC VAR	5 X_1	4 X_2	0 S_1	0 S_2	0 S_3	RHS
0	S_3	0	0	$\tfrac{1}{2}$	$-\tfrac{1}{3}$	1	60
4	X_2	0	1	$\tfrac{3}{8}$	$-\tfrac{1}{12}$	0	60
5	X_1	1	0	$-\tfrac{1}{4}$	$\tfrac{1}{6}$	0	30
	Z_j	5	4	$\tfrac{1}{4}$	$\tfrac{1}{2}$	0	390
	$C_j - Z_j$	0	0	$-\tfrac{1}{4}$	$-\tfrac{1}{2}$	0	

To determine the range using the tableau figures, the amount that the objective function coefficients can change without changing the RHS values must first be determined. Recall from Chapter 4 that this is the optimal solution. The RHS value does not change as long as the $C_j - Z_j$ row values are negative. Thus, values for the objective function coefficients must be determined such that $C_j - Z_j \leq 0$ for each nonbasic variable. To do this, we can substitute the variable C_1 for the coefficient value of 5 in the tableau. Z_j is then calculated for the S_1 column.

| | | Col | |
C_j	VAR	S_1	$C_j \times S_1$
0	S_3	$\frac{1}{2}$	0
4	X_2	$\frac{3}{8}$	$\frac{3}{2}$
C_1	X_1	$-\frac{1}{4}$	$-\frac{1}{4} C_1$
			$\frac{3}{2} - (\frac{1}{4})(C_1)$

Substituting this Z_j value into the equation $C_j - Z_j \leq 0$ gives

$$0 - (\tfrac{3}{2} - (\tfrac{1}{4})(C_1)) \leq 0$$

$$-\tfrac{3}{2} + (\tfrac{1}{4})C_1 \leq 0$$

$$(\tfrac{1}{4})C_1 \leq \tfrac{3}{2}$$

$$C_1 \leq 6$$

The same calculations can then be performed for the S_2 column.

| | | Col | |
C_j	VAR	S_2	$C_j \times S_2$
0	S_3	$-\frac{1}{3}$	0
4	X_2	$-\frac{1}{12}$	$-\frac{1}{3}$
C_1	X_1	$\frac{1}{6}$	$\frac{1}{6}(C_1)$
			$\frac{1}{6}(C_1) - \frac{1}{3}$

Substituting into $C_j - Z_j \leq 0$ gives the following result.

$$0 - ((\tfrac{1}{6})C_1 - \tfrac{1}{3}) \leq 0$$

$$-(\tfrac{1}{6})C_1 + \tfrac{1}{3} \leq 0$$

$$-(\tfrac{1}{6})C_1 \leq -\tfrac{1}{3}$$

$$-C_1 \leq -2$$

$$C_1 \geq 2$$

This calculation must be performed for each nonbasic variable (excluding artificial variables). Once all the calculations are completed, the most constraining values are used to determine the range for C_1. In this case, there is only one upper limit ($C_1 \leq 6$) and one lower limit ($C_1 \geq 2$), so the range for C_1 is

$$6 \geq C_1 \geq 2$$

which is the same range that was found when solving graphically.

The process is then repeated using C_2. The S_1 column yields

C_j	VAR	Col S_1	$C_j \times S_2$
0	S_3	$\frac{1}{2}$	0
C_2	X_2	$\frac{3}{8}$	$(\frac{3}{8})C_2$
5	X_1	$-\frac{1}{4}$	$-\frac{5}{4}$
			$(\frac{3}{8})C_2 - \frac{5}{4}$

$$0 - ((\tfrac{3}{8})C_2 - \tfrac{5}{4}) \le 0$$

$$-(\tfrac{3}{8})C_2 + \tfrac{5}{4} \le 0$$

$$-(\tfrac{3}{8})C_2 \le -\tfrac{5}{4}$$

$$-C_2 \le -(\tfrac{5}{4})(\tfrac{8}{3})$$

$$C_2 \ge {}^{10}\!/_3$$

and the S_2 column yields

C_j	VAR	Col S_2	$C_j \times S_2$
0	S_3	$-\frac{1}{3}$	0
C_2	X_2	$-\frac{1}{12}$	$-(\frac{1}{12})C_2$
5	X_1	$\frac{1}{6}$	$\frac{5}{6}$
			$\frac{5}{6} - (\frac{1}{12})C_2$

$$0 - (\tfrac{5}{6} - (\tfrac{1}{12})C_2) \le 0$$

$$-\tfrac{5}{6} + \tfrac{1}{12}C_2 \le 0$$

$$(\tfrac{1}{12})C_2 \le \tfrac{5}{6}$$

$$C_2 \le 10$$

Thus, the range for C_2 is

$$10 \ge C_2 \ge {}^{10}\!/_3$$

which also corresponds to the range obtained graphically. This answers part of Max Fuller's question posed earlier for Wilson Electronics. If the profit contribution of Component 1 changes, the optimal solution remains $X_1 = 30$ and $X_2 = 60$ as long as that profit contribution remains between \$2 and \$6. If the profit contribution of Component 2 changes, the optimal solution remains unchanged as long as that profit contribution remains between \$3.33 and \$10.

In some cases, several nonbasic variables give limits for an objective function coefficient; for example, $C_3 \le 3$ and $C_3 \le 5$. In this case, the more binding limit, $C_3 \le 3$ is selected. Obviously, any value of $C_3 \le 3$ is also ≤ 5. In other cases there may not be an upper or lower limit. This result occurs when all of the C_j coefficients fall on either the upper or lower side of the original value. For example, if there were two nonbasic columns and the calculations resulted in $C_j \ge 3$ and $C_j \ge 9$, with no $C_j \le$ values, the lower limit would be $C_j \ge 9$, but there would be no upper limit. In those cases, this is simply indicated as NO LIMIT. Thus, a range of

$$12 \ge C_3 \ge \text{NO LIMIT}$$

implies that the optimal solution does not change as long as the value of C_3 is less than or equal to 12, and that there is no lower limit. This is likely to happen when there is a constraint such as $X_3 \geq 10$ and the value of X_3 equals 10 in the optimal solution. Reducing the value of C_3 does not cause the X_3 to leave the tableau, because that would violate the constraint. A problem with no upper limit (NO LIMIT $\geq C_3 \geq 4$) implies an optimal solution at a point where the maximum amount of X_3 is in the solution, and raising the coefficient does not cause any more to be added.

Recall that these ranges indicate what values the objective function coefficients can take without changing the solution values for basic variables, *assuming all other objective function coefficients and other parameters are held constant*. Changing an objective function coefficient will, however, change the value of the objective function.

5.3 *CHANGES IN OBJECTIVE FUNCTION VALUES FOR NONBASIC VARIABLES*

The above solution procedure gives objective function coefficient ranges for basic variables, but it does not give ranges for nonbasic variables. Ranges for basic variable coefficients indicate the ranges over which the basic variable solution values do not change. Nonbasic variables are equal to zero; therefore, the range of objective function coefficients for nonbasic variables indicates a range over which those variables remain nonbasic, i.e., the solution values remain unchanged. Consider the following final tableau:

C_j	BASIC VAR	5 X_1	4 X_2	2 X_3	0 S_1	0 S_2	0 S_3	RHS
0	S_3	0	0	-1	$\frac{1}{2}$	$-\frac{1}{3}$	1	60
4	X_2	0	1	$\frac{1}{2}$	$\frac{3}{8}$	$-\frac{1}{12}$	0	60
5	X_1	1	0	$\frac{1}{2}$	$-\frac{1}{4}$	$\frac{1}{6}$	0	30
	Z_j	5	4	$\frac{9}{2}$	$\frac{1}{4}$	$\frac{1}{2}$	0	390
	$C_j - Z_j$	0	0	$-\frac{5}{2}$	$-\frac{1}{4}$	$-\frac{1}{2}$	0	

In this tableau, X_3 is a nonbasic variable that remains nonbasic as long as its $C_j - Z_j$ value is $\leq$ zero. If the value of C_3 is lowered (from its original value of 2, as shown in the tableau above), the $C_j - Z_j$ value becomes smaller, since the Z_j value remains 4 1/2 (as shown in the tableau). Thus, there is no lower limit on C_3. In determining the upper limit, we can substitute the variable C_3 for the objective function value of 2 in the equation $C_j - Z_j \leq 0$, yielding

$$C_3 - \frac{9}{2} \leq 0$$

$$C_3 \leq \frac{9}{2}$$

Thus, the range for C_3 is

$$\frac{9}{2} \geq C_3 \geq \text{NO LIMIT}$$

Note that the upper limit for C_3 is equal to the Z_j value for X_3. The upper limit for a nonbasic variable is always equal to its Z_j value. The lower limit for a nonbasic variable is always unlimited (NO LIMIT).

5.4 *THE ADDITION OF A NEW VARIABLE*

In some cases, it may be desirable to introduce an entirely new variable into a problem. Sensitivity analysis can also be used to analyze its effect upon the current optimal solution. The final tableau used in determining the objective function coefficient ranges for the basic variables is reproduced below.

C_j	BASIC VAR	5 X_1	4 X_2	0 S_1	0 S_2	0 S_3	RHS
0	S_3	0	0	$\frac{1}{2}$	$-\frac{1}{3}$	1	60
4	X_2	0	1	$\frac{3}{8}$	$-\frac{1}{12}$	0	60
5	X_1	1	0	$-\frac{1}{4}$	$\frac{1}{6}$	0	30
	Z_j	5	4	$\frac{1}{4}$	$\frac{1}{2}$	0	390
	$C_j - Z_j$	0	0	$-\frac{1}{4}$	$-\frac{1}{2}$	0	

We are considering the introduction of a new variable X_3, with an objective function coefficient of 3. Production data indicates this variable requires 3 units of resource 1, 7.5 units of resource 2, and no units of resource 3. To produce one unit of this new variable, therefore, requires 3 units of S_1 and 7.5 units of S_2. The shadow price for S_1 ($\frac{1}{4}$ or 0.25 from the tableau) indicates that reducing S_1 by 3 units (to add 1 unit of X_3) reduces the objective function by $\frac{1}{4}$ per unit or $\frac{3}{4}$ in total ($3 \times \frac{1}{4} = \frac{3}{4}$). And since the shadow price for S_2 is $\frac{1}{2}$, and 7.5 units of S_2 are needed to add a unit of X_3, the objective function is further reduced by 3.75 ($7.5 \times \frac{1}{2} = 3.75$). Thus, removing sufficient resources from the current solution to produce one unit of X_3 causes a reduction of 4.50 (.75 + 3.75) in the objective function value. There is also an increase in the objective function caused by the addition of one unit of X_3 with a C_3 (objective function coefficient) value of 3. The net change is $3 - 4\frac{1}{2}$ or $-1\frac{1}{2}$. This result suggests that the new variable should not be added—or at least would not be a basic variable—unless its objective function coefficient is at least $4.50.

5.5 *CHANGES IN THE RHS VALUES*

As we have seen previously, changes in the RHS values—which reflect changes in the amounts of resources available—cause the optimal solution values and the value of the objective function to change. The change in the value of the objective function can be predicted from the shadow price associated with the resource being changed. Thus, the resource shadow prices indicate how much the value of the objective function is increased by the addition of more units of a resource, or how much the objective function value is decreased if fewer units of a resource were available. But these gains or losses cannot be incurred indefinitely. There are finite limits on the amount a resource can be increased or decreased and still remain binding upon the solution. Sensitivity analysis of the RHS values enables those limits to be determined. The graphic solution to the example problem is repeated in Figure 5.3.

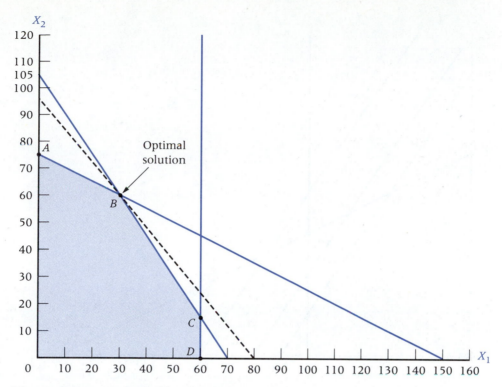

Figure 5.3 Example Problem Graphic Solution

Graphic Solution

The tableau solution to this problem indicates that constraint 1 has a shadow price of 25¢ and constraint 2 has a shadow price of 50¢. Thus, given the opportunity to expand one of the resources, we would choose to expand the number of units of resource 2, because we would realize an additional 50¢ for each unit added. Figure 5.4 illustrates the addition of 90 and 270 units of resource 2, increasing the original RHS value to 720 and 900 respectively.

Note that, when 90 units are added (constraint line L2'), the optimal solution shifts to point E ($X_1 = 45$ and $X_2 = 52.5$ with Zmax = 435). This is a $45 increase in Zmax (390 to 435), which is equivalent to 90 units at 50¢ each. But when 270 units are added (constraint line L2"), constraint 2 is no longer binding on the solution. The optimal solution shifts to point F ($X_1 = 60$ and $X_2 = 45$)—the intersection of constraints 1 and 3—with a Zmax value of 480. This outcome suggests that the shadow price of 50¢ applies only over a limited range of values for constraint 2. Sensitivity analysis on the RHS values aids in determining the range of values for the RHS over which the shadow price applies.

Since the shadow price is determined from the combination of X_1 and X_2 at a point where constraint lines 1 and 2 intersect, it should not change as long as the optimal solution remains at the intersection of those lines. In this problem, the intersect point can exist anywhere along the constraint 1 line, from point A on the X_2-axis to point F in Figure 5.5.

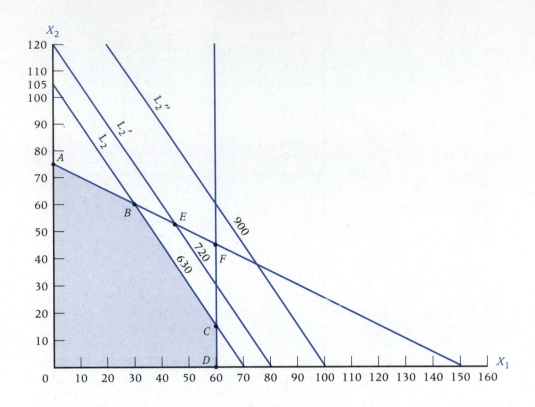

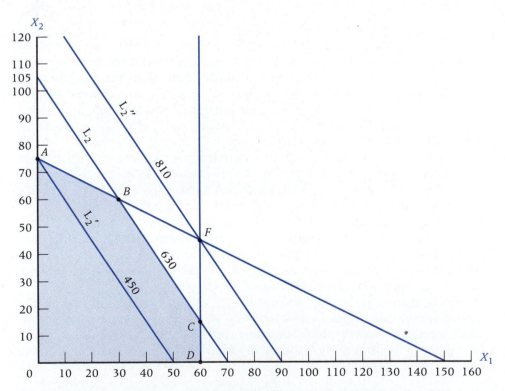

Figure 5.5 Range of Points Where the Shadow Price for Constraint 2 does not Change

Thus, the RHS value of constraint 2 can be increased up to 810 units, causing the line to shift upward to line L2'. Any additional units cause the line to shift beyond point F, the last point where constraint line 2 is binding upon the optimal solution. If the RHS value is decreased, it can be reduced until it reaches 450 units, which corresponds to line L2". Reducing the number of units further causes the line to drop below point A, the last point where constraint line 1 remains binding upon the optimal solution.

Figure 5.6 shows graphically the upper and lower limits (lines L1' and L1") for changes in the RHS values of constraint 1. The lower limit is at 180 units and the upper limit at 420 units.

Figure 5.7 shows the lower limit (L3") for constraint line 3. Because constraint 3 is not binding upon the optimal solution, L3 has a shadow price of zero. In the case of this constraint, therefore, the range of values over which the constraint remains nonbinding is being determined. Thus, reducing the RHS to 60 causes the constraint to become binding (intersect constraint lines 1 and 2 at point A). Note that there is no upper limit with constraint 3, since the constraint can be shifted an infinite distance to the right without affecting the optimal solution.

Tabular Solution

Like the earlier sensitivity analysis on the objective function coefficients, the graphical approach is useful to obtain a visual representation of the solution, but is too limited to be practical in most cases (it can be used only for problem with two vari-

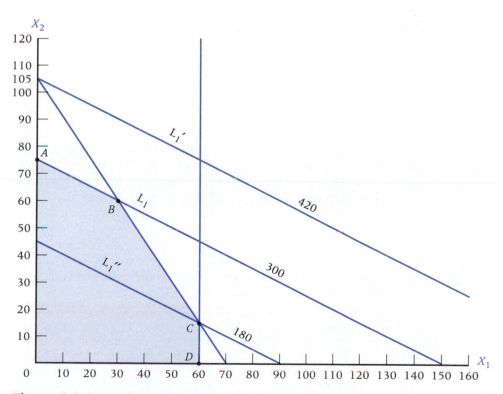

Figure 5.6 Constraint 1 RHS Range

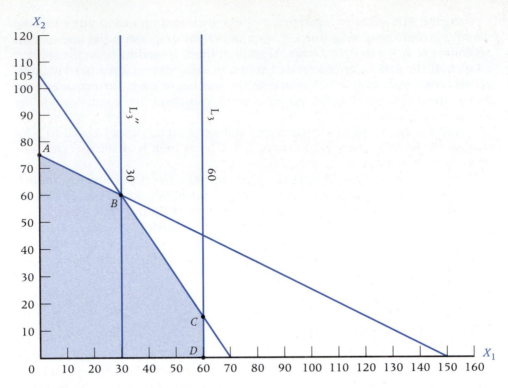

Figure 5.7 Constraint 3 RHS Range

ables). Therefore, we will look at a solution method that makes use of the data from the final tableau.

Basic Variable	S_2	RHS
S_3	$-\frac{1}{3}$	60
X_2	$-\frac{1}{12}$	60
X_1	$\frac{1}{6}$	30

The S_2 column represents the rates of substitution between the second constraint and the basic variables. For every unit of S_2 added, the amount of S_3 (slack units of resource 3) decreases by $\frac{1}{3}$ unit; the number of units of X_2 decreases by $\frac{1}{12}$ unit; and the number of units of X_1 increases by $\frac{1}{6}$ unit. Conversely, for every unit S_2 is decreased, the amount of S_3 increases by $\frac{1}{3}$ unit, X_2 increases by $\frac{1}{12}$ unit, and X_1 decreases by $\frac{1}{6}$ unit. There are limits to this substitution, however. Decreasing S_2 may cause a $\frac{1}{6}$ unit decrease in X_1, but since there are only 30 units of X_1 in this solution, X_1 cannot decrease by more than 30 units. This means S_2 cannot be decreased more than 180 units (30 divided by $\frac{1}{6}$) at this rate of substitution. Thus, if the current RHS values are divided by the rates of substitution, the results indicate the limits on the change in the number of units of S_2.

Basic Variable	RHS	S_2	Limit
S_3	60	$-\frac{1}{3}$	-180
X_2	60	$-\frac{1}{12}$	-720
X_1	30	$\frac{1}{6}$	180

Positive limits apply to reductions in S_2; negative limits apply to additions to S_2. Therefore, the upper and lower limits for the RHS values can be determined by subtracting the smallest absolute positive and negative limits (-180 [S_3] and 180 [X_1]) from the original RHS value. In this case, the original value is 630. This gives a lower limit of $630 - 180$, or 450, and an upper limit of $630 - (-180)$, or 810.

The same procedure can be used to determine the limits for constraint 1.

Basic Variable	RHS	S_1	Limit
S_3	60	½	120
X_2	60	⅜	160
X_1	30	$-¼$	-120

Lower Limit	Upper Limit	
300	300	[original RHS value]
-120	$-(-120)$	
180	420	

The lower limit is 180 units and the upper limit is 420 units.

Limits for constraint 3 (nonbinding) can be determined in the same manner.

Basic Variable	RHS	S_3	Limit
S_3	60	1	60
X_2	60	0	∞
X_1	30	0	∞

Lower Limit	Upper Limit
120	120
-60	[no negative value]
60	NO LIMIT

Note that, whenever there are no negative limits, there is no upper limit. Conversely, when there are no positive limits, the reverse is true: there are no lower limits.

Problems with = and ≥ Constraints

If the following constraints were added to the example problem

$$3X_1 + 3X_2 \geq 150$$

$$1X_2 = 60$$

the final tableau would change to:

| C_j | BASIC | 5 | 4 | 0 | 0 | 0 | $-M$ | 0 | $-M$ | |
	VAR	X_1	X_2	S_1	S_2	S_3	A_1	S_4	A_2	RHS
5	X_1	1	0	.5	0	0	0	0	-2	30
0	S_2	0	0	-4.5	1	0	0	0	12	0
0	S_3	0	0	-1	0	1	0	0	4	60
4	X_2	0	1	0	0	0	0	0	1	60
0	S_4	0	0	1.5	0	0	-1	1	-3	120
	Z_j	5	4	2.5	0	0	0	0	-6	390
	$C_j - Z_j$	0	0	-2.5	0	0	$-M$	0	$-M + 6$	

Sensitivity analysis on the RHS values for the first three constraints gives the following limits:

Lower Limit	Upper Limit
240	360
NO LIMIT	NO LIMIT
60	NO LIMIT

The fourth constraint, a greater-than-or-equal-to constraint, has two columns in the tableau: one for the artificial variable (A_1) and one for the surplus variable (S_4). Which column should be used to determine the limits? Since this ≥ constraint is below (less than) the optimal solution, there should be an upper limit but no lower limit. If the A_1 column were used, the upper limit would be 270 and there would be no lower limit. If the S_4 column were used, the lower limit would be 30 and there would be no upper limit. Thus, we use the artificial variable column values to determine the limits for ≥ constraints as follows:

Variable	RHS	A_1	Limit
X_1	30	0	∞
S_2	0	0	∞
S_3	60	0	∞
X_3	60	0	∞
S_4	120	-1	-120

Lower Limit	Upper Limit
150	150
[no positive value]	-120
NO LIMIT	270

The fifth constraint, an equality constraint, has only one column: the column for the artificial variable A_2. With only one column, the choice is easy. The A_2 column is used to determine the limits for the fifth constraint. The results are as follows:

Basic Variable	RHS	A_2	Limit
X_1	30	−2	−15
S_2	0	12	–
S_3	60	4	15
X_2	60	1	60
S_4	120	−3	−40

Lower Limit	Upper Limit
60	60
−15	−(−15)
45	75

Note that this example contains an unusual situation—variable S_2 is a basic variable with a value of zero. When a basic variable has a value of zero, it is ignored when calculating the RHS limits.

Other forms of sensitivity analysis have not been mentioned here: changes in constraint coefficients, the introduction of a new cosntraint, and the removal of an existing constraint. While the impact of some of these changes can be calculated (e.g., changes in constraint coefficients for nonbasic variables and the introduction of constraints that are not binding), usually it is necessary to resolve the modified problem to determine the impact of the remaining changes. Since there are computer programs that make this recalculation relatively easy, we will not discuss these topics.

5.6 DUALITY

Duality is a term applied to the fact that every LP problem can be expressed in two forms. The first or original form is called the **primal** or primal problem. The second form is called the **dual** or dual problem. When the primal form of the problem is solved a **primal solution** is obtained. Solving the dual form of the problem yields the **dual solution**. Thus, for every primal solution, there is also a dual solution. And since the primal and dual are the same problem expressed in two different forms, their solution values are closely related. The solution values of the primal solution are the shadow prices in the dual, and the shadow prices of the primal are the solution values of the dual. Moreover, the value of the objective function is the same for both forms of the solution.

The dual solution is important for two reasons. First, it provides a basis for understanding some of the economic relationships that exist in the LP solution, such as shadow prices and sensitivity analysis. And second, it allows some primal LP problems to be transformed into dual problems, which are easier to solve because they require fewer calculations before the final solution is reached.

We will return to the earlier example problem. Since this is the original problem, it is in what we referred to as the primal form.

$$MAX\ 5X_1 + 3X_2$$

subject to

$$2X_1 + 4X_2 \leq 300$$

$$9X_1 + 6X_2 \leq 630$$

$$2X_1 \qquad \leq 120$$

$$X_1, X_2 \geq 0$$

The solution determined for this problem is its primal solution.

Variable	Quantity
X_1	30
X_2	60
S_3	60

Zmax = 390

Variable	Shadow price
X_1	0
X_2	0
S_1	−.25
S_2	−.5
S_3	0

This problem will now be converted to its dual form.

Converting a Problem to the Dual Form

When converting a problem to its dual form, there are six basic rules which apply.

1. If the primal problem is maximization with all $\leq$ constraints, the dual is minimization with all $\geq$ constraints; conversely, if the primal is minimization with all $\geq$ constraints, the dual is maximization with all $\leq$ constraints.
2. The number of decision variables in the dual problem is equal to the number of constraints in the primal problem.
3. The number of constraints in the dual problem is equal to the number of decision variables in the primal problem (with certain exceptions, which will be noted later). Each dual decision variable corresponds to the value of one unit of that particular resource (the resource's shadow price).
4. The objective function coefficients in the dual problem are equal to the RHS values in the primal problem.
5. The RHS values in the dual problem are equal to the objective function coefficients in the primal problem.
6. If the primal constraints are $\leq$, the dual constraints are $\geq$; if the primal constrains are $\geq$, the dual constraints are $\leq$.
7. If we refer to the constraint coefficients as a_{ij} where i = row and j = column, then a_{ij} in the dual problem equals a'_{ji} from the original problem, i.e., $a_{12} = a'_{21}$.

Applying these rules:

1. The primal problem is maximization; therefore, the dual is minimization.
2. The primal problem has three constraints, so the dual problem has three decision variables. We will label these variables Y_1, Y_2, and Y_3.

3. The primal problem has two decision variables, so the dual has two constraints.
4. The primal RHS values are 300, 630, and 120. These values become the objective function coefficients in the dual. Since the dual is a minimization problem (rule 1), the objective function is:

$$\text{MIN } 300Y_1 + 630Y_2 + 120Y_3$$

5. The objective function coefficients in the primal are 5 and 4. These become the RHS values in the dual.
6. The primal problem has two decision variables. Thus, the dual has two constraints (rule 2). The original constraints are $\leq$ constraints. In the dual, the constraints are $\geq$ constraints (rule 6). The constraints have RHS values of 5 and 4, the objective function values from the primal problem (rule 5).

$$\geq 5 \quad \text{[constraint 1]}$$

$$\geq 4 \quad \text{[constraint 2]}$$

7. The constraint coefficients in the primal problem are

	$j = 1$	$j = 2$
$i = 1$	2	4
$i = 2$	9	6
$i = 3$	2	0

Thus, the primal coefficients are

$$a_{11} = 2 \quad a_{12} = 4$$

$$a_{21} = 9 \quad a_{22} = 6$$

$$a_{31} = 2 \quad a_{32} = 0$$

Transposing gives dual coefficients of

	$j = 1$	$j = 2$	$j = 3$
$i = 1$	2	9	2
$i = 2$	4	6	0

or

$$a'_{11} = 2 \quad a'_{12} = 9 \quad a'_{13} = 2$$

$$a'_{21} = 4 \quad a'_{22} = 6 \quad a'_{23} = 0$$

Thus, the constraints are

$$2Y_1 + 9Y_2 + 2Y_3 \geq 5$$

$$4Y_1 + 6Y_2 + 0Y_3 \geq 4 \quad [4Y_1 + 6Y_2 \geq 4]$$

Pulling this all together yields the dual problem

$$\text{MIN } 300Y_1 + 630Y_2 + 120Y_3$$

subject to

$$2Y_1 + 9Y_2 + 2Y_3 \geq 5$$
$$4Y_1 + 6Y_2 \geq 4$$
$$Y_1, Y_2, Y_3 \geq 0$$

Interpretation of the Dual Problem

Dual variables reflect an economic relationship between the primal decision variables and the resources. In the primal, constrained resources are used to produce products (X_1 and X_2). The objective of the primal problem is to maximize profits. In the dual, the decision variables represent the marginal value of the resources used to produce products X_1 and X_2. The objective is to minimize the total value of the resources used. Thus, Y_1 is the marginal value of resource 1, Y_2 is the marginal value of resource 2, and Y_3 is the marginal value of resource 3. The constraints represent the marginal value of the resources used to produce a particular product. It takes two units of resource 1, nine units of resource 2 and two units of resource 3 to produce one unit of X_1. The value of the resources used must be greater than or equal to 5, the marginal profit of product X_1. The Y_i values represent value added or profit potential rather than cost.

Interpretation of the Dual Solution

The computer solution to this dual problem is shown in Figure 5.8. The optimal quantities are $Y_1 = 0.25$, $Y_2 = 0.5$, and (since Y_3 is a nonbasic variable) $Y_3 = 0$. This result indicates that one unit of Y_1 is worth 25¢ and one unit of Y_2 is worth 50¢. Recall that these values are the same ones obtained as shadow prices for the con-

```
        THIS SOLUTION IS OPTIMAL:

        VARIABLE            QUANTITY
        ------------        ------------
           Y1                  .25
           Y2                  .5
        OPTIMAL Z = 390

        VARIABLE            SHADOW PRICE
        ------------        ------------
           Y1                   0
           Y2                   0
           Y3                  -60
           S1                  -30
           S2                  -60
```

Figure 5.8 Computer Solution to Dual Problem

straints in the primal problem. The objective function value of 390 is also the same, as it should be. The dual shadow prices (ignoring the negative sign) are $Y_3 = 60$, $S_1 = 30$, and $S_2 = 60$. S_1 represents constraint 1 (X_1 in the dual) and S_2 represents constraint 2 (X_2 in the dual). These are the solution values for X_1 and X_2 in the primal problem. The shadow prices in the dual, therefore, correspond to the values of the basic variables in the primal solution ($S_3 = 60$, $X_1 = 30$, and $X_2 = 60$). Thus the dual solution provides the same information as the primal solution, but in a different form. The final tableau for the dual problem, with the artificial variable columns omitted, is shown in Figure 5.9. The substitution rates between Y_1 and Y_2 and Y_3, S_1, and S_2 are summarized in the table below:

	Y_3	S_1	S_2
Y_1	$-.5$	$.25$	$-.375$
Y_2	$.333$	$-.167$	$.083$

In the final tableau of the primal problem, the substitution rates are

	S_1	S_2
S_3	$.5$	$-.333$
X_1	$-.25$	$.167$
X_2	$.375$	$-.083$

Note that the substitution rates are identical in value, but that the signs are reversed. The signs differ only because of the interpretation placed on the values; in reality they may be treated as identical.

5.7 FORMULATING DUAL PROBLEMS—OTHER CONSIDERATIONS

It is easiest to change problems from primal form to the dual form when the primal problem is in the form of a maximization problem subject to all less-than-or-equal-to constraints, or a minimization problem subject to all greater-than-or-equal-to constraints. But not all problems take one of these two forms. In the following sections, we will deal with variations on these forms.

```
TABLEAU NUMBER 3

C(j)   BASIC | 300  630   120      0       0
        VAR  | Y1   Y2    Y3      S1      S2   | RHS
       -----------------------------------------------
 630    Y2   | 0    1    .333   -.167    .083 | .5
 300    Y1   | 1    0    -.5     .25    -.375 | .25
       -----------------------------------------------
        z    | 300  630   60     -30     -60  | 390
       C - z | 0    0     60      30      60  |
```

Figure 5.9 Dual Solution Final Tableau

Maximization Problem with Greater-Than-Or-Equal-To Constraint(s)

Assume we have the following primal problem:

$$\text{MAX } 3X_1 + 5X_2 + 4X_3$$

subject to

$$6X_1 + 4X_2 + 5X_3 \leq 85$$
$$5X_1 + 7X_2 + 5X_3 \geq 100$$
$$2X_1 + \qquad\quad 2X_3 \leq 40$$
$$X_1, X_2, X_3 \geq 0$$

This problem would be in the proper form if the second constraint were a less-than-or-equal-to constraint. This constraint can be converted by multiplying it by -1. This changes the constraint to

$$-5X_1 - 7X_2 - 5X_3 \leq -100$$

We can ignore the negative right-hand side for the moment, since we are not attempting to solve this problem. The problem is now in the form

$$\text{MAX } 3X_1 + 5X_2 + 4X_3$$

subject to

$$6X_1 + 4X_2 + 5X_3 \leq 85$$
$$-5X_1 - 7X_2 - 5X_3 \leq -100$$
$$2X_1 + \qquad\quad 2X_3 \leq 40$$
$$X_1, X_2, X_3 \geq 0$$

which can be converted to the following dual problem:

$$\text{MIN } 85Y_1 - 100Y_2 + 40Y_3$$

subject to

$$6Y_1 - 5Y_2 + 2Y_3 \geq 3$$
$$4Y_1 - 7Y_2 \qquad\quad \geq 5$$
$$5Y_1 - 5Y_2 + 2Y_3 \geq 4$$
$$Y_1, Y_2, Y_3 \geq 0$$

Thus, greater-than-or-equal-to constraints in maximization problems (or less-than-or-equal-to constraints in minimization problems) can be converted to the proper form by multiplying them by -1.

Equality Constraints

Consider the following primal problem:

$$\text{MAX } 3X_1 + 5X_2$$

subject to

$$2X_1 + 3X_2 \leq 8$$
$$5X_1 + 4X_2 = 9$$
$$X_1 + X_2 \leq 3$$
$$X_1, X_2 \geq 0$$

In this case, the second constraint is an equality. Two similar approaches can be used to convert equality constraints into the dual form. The first begins by expressing the equality constraint as two constraints:

$$[1] \quad 5X_1 + 4X_2 \leq 9$$
$$[2] \quad 5X_1 + 4X_2 \geq 9$$

These constraints yield the same results as the equality constraint, since the only solution that satisfies both constraints occurs when $5X_1 + 4X_2 = 9$. Constraint [2] can then be converted to a less-than-or-equal-to constraint by multiplying it by -1. This step gives the primal problem in the following form:

$$\text{MAX } 3X_1 + 5X_2$$

subject to

$$2X_1 + 3X_2 \leq 8 \quad [1]$$
$$5X_1 + 4X_2 \leq 9 \quad [2a]$$
$$-5X_1 - 4X_2 \leq -9 \quad [2b]$$
$$X_1 + X_2 \leq 3 \quad [3]$$
$$X_1, X_2 \geq 0$$

The fact that there are four constraints suggests that there must be four variables in the dual formulation. But the constraints [2a] and [2b] are really reformulations of the original equality constraint. This problem can be dealt with by introducing variable $Y_{2'}$ for constraint [2a] and variable $Y_{2''}$ for constraint [2b]. The dual formulation would then be

$$\text{MIN } 8Y_1 + 9Y_{2'} - 9Y_{2''} + 3Y_3$$

subject to

$$2Y_1 + 5Y_{2'} - 5Y_{2''} + 1Y_3 \geq 3$$
$$3Y_1 + 4Y_{2'} - 4Y_{2''} + 1Y_3 \geq 5$$
$$Y_1, Y_{2'}, Y_{2''}, Y_3 \geq 0$$

and the actual solution value or shadow price for the equality constraint would be the combination of $Y_{2'}$ and $Y_{2''}$.

The second approach introduces an unrestricted variable (in this case Y_2) when an equality constraint is encountered. An unrestricted variable does not have to meet the nonnegativity restriction; it can be either positive or negative. The dual formulation would then be

$$\text{MIN } 8Y_1 + 9Y_2 + 3Y_3$$

subject to

$$2Y_1 + 5Y_2 + 1Y_3 \geq 3$$
$$3Y_1 + 4Y_2 + 1Y_3 \geq 5$$
$$Y_1, Y_3 \geq 0 \quad Y_2 \text{ unrestricted}$$

Since the simplex procedure will not solve problems with unrestricted variables, however, we need to modify the problem before solving it using simplex. We can set the Y_2 variable equal to the difference between two variables, $Y_{2'}$ and $Y_{2''}$

$$Y_2 = Y_{2'} - Y_{2''}$$

where $Y_{2'}$ and $Y_{2''}$ both meet the nonnegativity requirement. These variables can then be substituted into the LP model for Y_2, yielding the same result as the first approach discussed.

$$\text{MIN } 8Y_1 + 9Y_{2'} - 9Y_{2''} + 3Y_3$$

subject to

$$2Y_1 + 5Y_{2'} - 5Y_{2''} + 1Y_3 \geq 3$$
$$3Y_1 + 4Y_{2'} - 4Y_{2''} + 1Y_3 \geq 5$$
$$Y_1, Y_{2'}, Y_{2''}, Y_3 \geq 0$$

Minimization Primal Problem

Although there is nothing special or exceptional about a minimization primal problem, the dual formulation of a minimization problem will be shown since it differs from the previous examples. Consider the following primal problem:

$$\text{MIN } 3X_1 - 4X_2 + 5X_3$$

subject to

$$2X_1 + 3X_2 + 3X_3 \geq 27$$
$$X_1 - \quad\quad X_3 \geq 0$$
$$4X_1 + 2X_2 + 4X_3 \leq 55$$
$$X_2 \quad\quad \leq 4$$
$$X_1, X_2, X_3 \geq 0$$

Constraints 3 and 4 are first converted to the greater-than-or-equal-to form.

$$(4X_1 + 2X_2 + 4X_3 \leq 55) \times -1 \Rightarrow -4X_1 - 2X_2 - 4X_3 \geq -55$$
$$(X_2 \leq 4) \times -1 \Rightarrow -X_2 \geq -4$$

This gives the primal problem

$$\text{MIN } 3X_1 - 4X_2 + 5X_3$$

subject to

$$2X_1 + 3X_2 + 3X_3 \geq 27$$
$$X_1 \qquad - X_3 \geq 0$$
$$-4X_1 - 2X_2 - 4X_3 \geq -55$$
$$-X_2 \qquad \geq -4$$
$$X_1, X_2, X_3 \geq 0$$

which can then be changed to the following dual problem:

$$\text{MAX } 27Y_1 + 0Y_2 - 55Y_3 - 4Y_4$$

subject to

$$2Y_1 + Y_2 - 4Y_3 \qquad \leq 3$$
$$3Y_1 - \qquad 2Y_3 - Y_4 \leq -4$$
$$3Y_1 + Y_2 - 4Y_3 \qquad \leq 5$$
$$Y_1, Y_2, Y_3, Y_4 \geq 0$$

Since this gives a negative right-hand-side value, multiplying the second constraints by -1 gives the following dual formulation:

$$\text{MAX } 27Y_1 + 0Y_2 - 55Y_3 - 4Y_4$$

subject to

$$2Y_1 + Y_2 - 4Y_3 \qquad \leq 3$$
$$-3Y_1 + \qquad 2Y_3 + Y_4 \geq 4$$
$$3Y_1 + Y_2 - 4Y_3 \qquad \leq 5$$
$$Y_1, Y_2, Y_3, Y_4 \geq 0$$

5.8 CONCLUDING REMARKS

Sensitivity or postoptimality analysis provides the decision maker with additional information, revealing the sensitivity of the optimal solution to changes in problem parameters. The changes can be in the objective function coefficients or in the constraint RHS values, and are caused by a number of factors. They could be the result of errors in the original parameter estimates or environmental changes beyond the control of the decision maker. In some situations, the changes are tentative considerations that will be implemented only if the analysis indicates acceptable results.

Duality addresses the fact that every problem can be expressed in two distinct forms, a primal and a dual. Both solve the same problem, but from a different perspective. The dual provides a basis for understanding some of the economic relationships that exist in any LP solution.

Together, sensitivity analysis and duality can often provide the manager with information that is as important as the information gained from the solution of the original LP problem. The manager who understands the marginal rates of substitution between variables, shadow prices and dual prices, and the marginal values determined in the solution of the dual problem has a firm grasp of the principles of linear programming. These concepts are often given less attention than they merit.

Management Science Application

WELLBORN CABINET REVISITED[1]

The use of an LP model to optimize a wood procurement policy for Wellborn Cabinet, Inc. was discussed in the application at the end of Chapter 2. The company purchased #2 green lumber or #2 logs, which varied from 8 to 14 feet in length and from 9 to 15 inches in diameter. The shadow prices for the various sizes of logs (constraints for the original problem) included the following information:

Diameter (in)	Length	Shadow Price
9	12	−12.55
9	14	−37.08
10	12	−15.97
10	14	−31.88
.	.	.
.	.	.
14	10	0.00
14	12	−0.86
15	8	−0.42

From this information it was determined that, when additional logs had to be obtained, it was to the company's advantage to purchase 14-foot logs with smaller diameters (9 or 10 inches) rather than shorter logs with larger diameters (14 or 15 inches). The cost of producing blanks could be reduced by $37.08 for each log measuring 9 inches by 14 feet; a 15-inch-by-8-foot log reduced the cost only by $0.42. Thus, the shadow prices for the various log sizes indicated the logs to purchase as needs increased.

Sensitivity analysis of the objective function coefficients indicated that the optimal purchase policy would not change over a $5 range in prices for logs and a $4 range for lumber. It also indicated that #1 grade dry lumber, which was not purchased under the optimal purchase policy, should not be purchased even if the price of that lumber was reduced by up to 20 percent.

Sensitivity analysis on the RHS values indicated that the kilns used for drying green lumber, which were currently being used at capacity, could be increased in number to reduce costs further. It was determined that a 22 percent increase in dry kiln capacity, needed to increase blank output to 25 MBF per week, would be cost effective.

[1]Reprinted with permission of Honorio F. Carino and Clinton H. LeNoir, Jr., "Optimizing Wood Procurement in Cabinet Manufacturing," *Interfaces*, 18 (March–April, 1988): 10–19. Copyright 1988, The Institute of Management Sciences.

Thus, the shadow prices associated with the problem constraints and sensitivity analysis on the objective function coefficients and RHS values provided information that the company's management could use when making additional purchase decisions or capacity expansion decisions.

GLOSSARY

dual problem associated alternate LP problem; every linear programming maximization problem has an associated minimization problem, and every minimization problem has an associated maximization problem

objective function coefficient ranges range of values the objective function coefficient for a decision variable can take without changing the LP solution values

primal problem original form that an LP problem takes

RHS ranges range of values that the RHS values can take without changing the value of the shadow price for that particular constraint

sensitivity analysis determination of effect of parameter changes upon the LP solution values; also referred to as postoptimality analysis

unrestricted variable a variable that is not constrained by the non-negativity restriction, i.e., the variable can have a positive or negative solution value

PROBLEMS

1. Given the following problem:

$$\text{MAX } X_1 + X_2$$

subject to
$$2X_1 + 4X_2 \leq 48$$
$$8X_1 + 6X_2 \leq 96$$
$$X_1 \qquad \leq 9$$
$$X_1, X_2 \geq 0$$

   a. Solve the problem graphically.
   b. Determine the objective function coefficient ranges algebraically.

2. If the objective function coefficient for X_2 is increased to 1.5, do the solution values change?

3. If the objective function in problem 1 changed to

$$\text{MAX } 20X_1 + 12X_2$$

   a. Determine the optimal solution graphically.
   b. Determine the ranges of values for the objective function coefficients algebraically.

4. **a.** If the RHS value for the first constraint in problem 1 is increased to 60, would you expect the shadow price for that constraint to change? Explain graphically.
   b. If the RHS value for the first constraint in problem 1 is increased to 72, would you expect the shadow price for that constraint to change? Explain graphically.

5. Given the following final maximization tableau

Cj	BASIC VAR	3 X₁	4 X₂	0 S₁	0 S₂	0 S₃	RHS
4	X₂	0	1	.4	−.1	0	8
3	X₁	1	0	−.3	.2	0	9
0	S₃	0	0	−.4	−.4	1	4
	Z	3	4	.7	.2	0	59
	C − Z	0	0	−.7	−.2	0	

determine the ranges of objective function coefficients.

6. Given the following information from problem 5, if the original RHS values were 50, 120, and 72, determine the ranges of RHS values.

7. Given the following final maximization tableau

Cj	BASIC VAR	1 X₁	2 X₂	0 S₁	0 S₂	RHS
1	X₁	1	0	.179	−.143	8
2	X₂	0	1	−.071	.107	6
	Z	1	2	.036	.071	20
	C − Z	0	0	−.036	−.071	

determine the ranges of objective function coefficients.

8. Given the information from problem 7, if the original RHS values were 192 and 184, determine the ranges of RHS values.

9. Given the following final maximization tableau

Cj	BASIC VAR	12 X₁	14 X₂	0 S₁	0 S₂	0 S₃	RHS
14	X₂	0	1	.25	−.167	0	5
12	X₁	1	0	−.125	.25	0	12.5
0	S₃	0	0	−.25	.167	1	11
	Z	12	14	2	.667	0	220
	C − Z	0	0	−2	−.667	0	

determine the ranges of objective function coefficients.

10. Given the information from problem 9, if the original RHS values were 80, 90, and 16, determine the ranges of RHS values.

11. Given the following final maximization tableau

Cj	BASIC VAR	3 X₁	5 X₂	4 X₃	0 S₁	0 S₂	0 S₃	
0	S₁	−4	0	0	1	−.75	−.5	3
5	X₂	1	1	0	0	.25	−.5	3
4	X₃	1	0	1	0	0	1	5
		9	5	4	0	1.25	1.5	35
		−6	0	0	0	−1.25	−1.5	

determine the ranges of objective function coefficients.

12. Given the information from problem 11, if the original RHS values were 22, 22, and 5, determine the ranges of RHS values.

13. Given the following problem:

$$\text{MAX } 5A + 4B$$

subject to

$$2A + 4B \leq 300$$
$$9A + 6B \leq 930$$
$$2A \quad\;\; \leq 120$$
$$A, B \geq 0$$

a. Solve the problem.
b. Determine the ranges for the objective function coefficients.
c. Determine the ranges for the RHS values.

14. Given the following problem:

$$\text{MAX } 6X_1 + 8X_2$$

subject to

$$X_1 + 3X_2 \leq 150$$
$$4X_1 + 2X_2 \leq 200$$
$$2X_1 \quad\;\; \leq 80$$
$$X_1, X_2 \geq 0$$

a. Solve the problem.
b. Determine the ranges for the objective function coefficients.
c. Determine the ranges for the RHS values.

15. Given the following final tableau:

Cj	BASIC VAR	5 X_1	4 X_2	0 S_1	0 S_2	0 S_3	$-M$ A_1	0 S_4	RHS
0	S_3	0	0	.5	$-.333$	1	0	0	60
0	S_4	0	0	.375	.25	0	-1	1	90
5	X_1	1	0	$-.25$	.167	0	0	0	30
4	X_2	0	1	.375	$-.083$	0	0	0	60
	Z	5	4	.25	.5	0	0	0	390
	C $-$ Z	0	0	$-.25$	$-.5$	0	$-M$	0	

a. Is this problem a maximization or a minimization problem? How can you tell?
b. Explain whether each constraint is a $\leq$, $=$, or $\geq$ constraint. (Assume all slack, artificial, and surplus variables are added in order as needed.)
c. Find the ranges for the objective function coefficients.
d. If the original RHS values in the constraints were 300, 620, 120, and 180, determine the ranges for the RHS values.

16. Given the following final tableau:

Cj	BASIC VAR	3 X₁	2 X₂	4 X₃	0 S₁	0 S₂	0 S₃	RHS
2	X_2	.667	1	0	.333	0	−.667	20
0	S_2	−.067	0	0	−.333	1	−.533	64
4	X_3	.8	0	1	0	0	.4	72
	Z	4.533	2	4	.667	0	.267	328
	C − Z	−1.533	0	0	−.667	0	−.267	

a. Is this problem a maximization or a minimization problem? How can you tell?
b. Explain whether each constraint is a ≤, =, or ≥ constraint. (Assume all slack, artificial, and surplus variables are added in order as needed.)
c. Find the ranges for the objective function coefficients.
d. If the original RHS values in the constraints were 420, 300, and 180, determine the ranges for the RHS values.

17. Given the following Dennis & Dennis computer solution:

```
         VARIABLE              QUANTITY
         --------              --------

           X1                     9
           X3                    12
           S2                    50
           S4                     5
         OPTIMAL Z = 3000

         VARIABLE            SHADOW PRICE
         --------            ------------

           X1                     0
           X2                    -6
           X3                     0
           S1                   -15
           S2                     0
           S3                   -12
           S4                     0
```

a. State the optimal solution to this problem in terms of all decision and slack variables.
b. How many constraints are there in this problem?
c. If the objective function coefficient for decision variable X_1 is 200, what is the objective function coefficient for decision variable X_3?
d. What constraints are binding upon this solution? How can you tell?
e. Explain the meaning of the shadow prices shown in this solution.

18. Given the following computer solution:

```
            VARIABLE         QUANTITY
            --------         --------

              X2               100
              X3               100
              S1               600
          OPTIMAL Z = 6800

            VARIABLE       SHADOW PRICE
            --------       ------------

              X1               0
              X2               0
              X3               0
              S1               0
              S2              -8
              S3              -5.5
```

a. If you could add one more unit to one of the constraints, which one would it be? Why?

b. If a friend of yours told you he solved the problem without a computer and got the answer $X_1 = 200$, $X_2 = 100$, and $Z = 6800$, would you believe this answer could be possible?

19. Given the following computer solution:

```
            VARIABLE         QUANTITY
            --------         --------

              X1                35
              X3                60
              S3                25
          OPTIMAL Z = 850

            VARIABLE       SHADOW PRICE
            --------       ------------

              X1                0
              X2              -2.75
              X3                0
              S1              -3.75
              S2              -4.5
              S3                0
```

SENSITIVITY ANALYSIS OF OBJECTIVE FUNCTION COEFFICIENTS

VARIABLE NAME	LOWER LIMIT	ORIGINAL VALUE	UPPER LIMIT
X1	2	5	10
X2	NO LIMIT	8	14
X3	6	12	20

```
          SENSITIVITY ANALYSIS OF RIGHT HAND SIDE RANGES

                      LOWER     ORIGINAL    UPPER
          CONSTRAINT  LIMIT      VALUE      LIMIT
          ----------  -----     --------    -----
              1        300        550        600
              2        200        320        500
              3        400        500      NO LIMIT
```

a. If we could add one more unit to one of the constraints, which one would you choose? Why?

b. If we reduced production of decision variable X_1 by 5 units without increasing the production of any other variables, how would the overall profit be affected?

c. If we produced fthe more units of decision variable X_2, how would the overall profit change?

d. If we could add 100 units of resource 2, how would the overall profit be affected?

e. If we could add 50 units of resource 3, how would the overall profit be affected?

f. If we could add 200 units of resource 2, how would the overall profit be affected?

20. Write the dual formulation for the following LP problem.

$$MAX\ 3X_1 + 5X_2$$

subject to
$$6X_1 + 4X_2 \leq 200$$
$$4X_1 + 7X_2 \leq 210$$
$$X_1, X_2 \geq 0$$

21. Solve both the primal and dual problems from problem 20. Compare both answers.

22. Write the dual formulation for the following LP problem.

$$MAX\ 4X_1 + 6X_2 + 5X_3$$

subject to
$$3X_1 + 7X_2 + 6X_3 \leq 500$$
$$5X_1 + 5X_2 + 4X_3 \leq 480$$
$$6X_2 + 6X_3 \leq 330$$
$$X_1, X_2, X_3 \geq 0$$

23. Solve the dual problem from problem 22.

24. Write the dual formulation for the following LP problem.

$$MAX\ 5X_1 + 6X_2$$

subject to
$$3X_1 + 6X_2 \leq 100$$
$$5X_1 + 4X_2 \leq 110$$
$$2X_1 + 2X_2 \geq 90$$
$$X_1, X_2 \geq 0$$

25. Solve both the primal and dual problems from problem 24. Are the results consistent with the chapter discussion?

26. Write the dual formulation for the following LP problem.

$$\text{MAX } X_1 + 2X_2 + 1.5X_3$$

subject to
$$
\begin{aligned}
9X_1 + 7X_2 + 8X_3 &\le 400 \\
4X_1 + 5X_2 + 3X_3 &\ge 120 \\
6X_1 + 11X_2 + 9X_3 &\le 540 \\
X_1, X_2, X_3 &\ge 0
\end{aligned}
$$

27. Write the dual formulation for the following LP problem.

$$\text{MIN } X_1 + X_2 + X_3 + X_4$$

subject to
$$
\begin{aligned}
4X_1 + 3X_2 + 3X_4 &\ge 12 \\
2X_2 + 5X_3 + 4X_4 &\ge 15 \\
X_1 &\ge 2 \\
2X_3 + 3X_4 &\ge 10 \\
X_1, X_2, X_3, X_4 &\ge 0
\end{aligned}
$$

28. Write the dual formulation for the following LP problem.

$$\text{MAX } 12A + 9B + 15C + 11D$$

subject to
$$
\begin{aligned}
14A + 12B + 16C + 13D &\le 1200 \\
3A + 4C &\ge 300 \\
15A + 10B + 18C + 10D &\le 1100 \\
B + 2D &= 600 \\
A, B, C, D &\ge 0
\end{aligned}
$$

29. Solve the dual problem formulated in problem 26. Interpret the meaning of the solution values.

30. Write the dual formulation for the following LP problem.

$$\text{MAX } 5X_1 + 4X_2$$

subject to
$$
\begin{aligned}
2X_1 + 4X_2 &\le 300 \\
9X_1 + 6X_2 &\le 630 \\
2X_1 &\le 120 \\
3X_1 + 3X_2 &\ge 150 \\
X_2 &= 60 \\
X_1, X_2 &\ge 0
\end{aligned}
$$

31. Solve the dual problem formulated in problem 30. Interpret the results of the dual solution.

Chapter
6

Linear Programming Computer Solutions

By the end of this chapter, you should be able to:

1

input an LP problem into the computer;

2

obtain and interpret a computer solution, including the solution
values and the meaning of shadow or dual prices; and

3

be able to interpret computer output relating to sensitivity analysis.

The three preceding chapters were designed to give the reader a basic understanding of LP solution techniques. An awareness of the theoretical basis and computational procedures of LP is important if the model is to be used most effectively. In the real world, however, LP problems are solved using a computer program. In this chapter we focus on the use of computer programs to solve LP problems. LP software packages use some version of the simplex algorithm described in Chapter 4. Karmarkar's algorithm, discussed briefly in Chapter 2, might prove superior to simplex for some types of LP problems. In this event, Karmarkar's algorithm may replace simplex in some future software packages. The LP program that accompanies this book uses simplex, and is intended to be a learning tool rather than a commercial LP program. It will easily solve the problems in this book and provide the user with experience using the computer to solve LP problems—experience that can later be transferred to most commercial LP programs.

6.1 *AN INTRODUCTION TO COMPUTER SOLUTIONS*

In Chapter 1, we pointed out that the computer has had a major impact upon the field of management science, allowing both faster solutions and the capability of solving much larger problems. Linear programming has benefited greatly from this move toward computerized solution procedures. The computer and the easy availability of LP software in all size and price ranges has made this technique available to increasing numbers of users. Moreover, problems that were for all practical purposes unsolvable because of their size or complexity can now be solved. Within the limits of the computer and software, it is possible to solve any feasible LP problem that can be formulated by the user.

Hundreds of LP programs are available today, from large mainframe programs, which can solve problems with tens of thousands of variables and constraints, to small PC programs. The programs differ principally in their features, methods of data input, flexibility, and the size of the problems that can be solved. While the data **input** methods and the **output** (solution) displays differ from program to program, there are basic similarities. The basic input generally includes: (1) identification of the problem as maximization or minimization; (2) the objective function, including the variable coefficients and names (some programs assign names); (3) the problem constraints, including variable coefficient, type of constraint ($\geq$, $=$, $\leq$), and RHS value for each constraint. There is no standard input for interactive LP software, but all the inputs listed above are included. Many interactive programs enable the user to input the LP model by row, in the same form it is written by hand on a piece of paper. There is a standard input format, known as MPS, for mainframe batch-oriented LP software. It includes the same data and a problem name.

The following section explains the solution of an LP problem using the Dennis & Dennis software included with this book. In section 6.3, we show input and output for the same problem using two other programs, LINDO and MPSX, for comparison purposes. Appendix E contains a brief summary of input/output instructions for using the Dennis & Dennis software.

It is important to remember that, while the computer brings speed to the solution process, performing thousands of calculations per second, the most important part of the solution process is still the problem formulation discussed in Chapter 2. If the problem is not formulated correctly (into an LP model), the solution will be meaningless. The computer will give you the wrong answer—quickly.

6.2 *COMPUTER SOLUTION OF AN LP PROBLEM*

In Chapter 2 we formulated an LP model for ABC Investment Company to help the manager, Mr. Rulan, decide how much to invest in each of four stocks, A, B, C, and D. The LP model is shown below.

MAX .25A + .225B + .24C + .30D

subject to

A +	B +	C +	D $\leq$ 800000	[total $ amount]
.04A +	.0125B +	.03C	$\geq$ 20000	[minimum dividend]
−.6A		+	D $\leq$ 0	[balance risk]
−.1A +	.9B −	.1C −	.1D $\geq$ 0	[stock B $\geq$ 10%]
		A, B, C, D $\geq$	0	[nonnegativity]

Although most real-world problems are much larger, we will use this problem to demonstrate the computer solution because it has already been formulated. Its small size makes the example displays relatively simple and easy to understand.

Input

As we indicated previously, any program must know whether the problem is a maximization or minimization problem; how many variables and constraints the problem has; the objective function coefficients for the variables; the constraint coefficients and RHS values; and whether each constraint is an equality (=) or inequality (≤ or ≥). The Dennis & Dennis software demonstrated here allows either free form or tabular (spreadsheet) entry for the model. The free form entry format is used in this example. Figure 6.1 shows the data input for this problem. Prompts are shown in color and user inputs in normal print. Notice that the data is entered by row as it would be written, and that nonnegativity constraints are not entered (nonnegativity is assumed by the program).

Each program has various optional features available. Since these features, such as error correction routines or the ability to name constraints, are program-specific, they are not discussed here. The user should simply be aware that some programs require additional or optional input or responses to deal with these features.

Output

Once the input has been completed, the computer program solves the problem and displays the solution in an output summary. As indicated previously, computer output for an LP problem includes, at a minimum, a list of the variables and their corresponding solution values along with the value of the objective function. The ouput from most programs also includes the variables and their shadow or dual prices. The output for this problem is shown in Figure 6.2 and is interpreted in the next section. Sensitivity analysis output is discussed separately in section 6.4.

Interpretation of Results

It is easy to interpret results from a computer output, because the results are usually in summary form. The user must, of course, know what information is being sought and what information is being provided by the software.

```
TYPE OF PROBLEM:  MAX/MIN

ENTER OBJECTIVE FUNCTION
MAX .25A+.225B+.24C+.3D

ENTER THE CONSTRAINTS, ONE PER LINE, HERE. AFTER YOU HAVE ENTERED
THE LAST CONSTRAINT, ENTER THE WORD GO.

1   A+B+C+D<800000
2   .04A+.0125B+.03C>20000
3   −.6A+D<0
4   −.1A+.9B−.1C−.1D>0
5   GO
```

Figure 6.1 LP Model Input

```
            AFTER 4 ITERATIONS
            THIS SOLUTION IS OPTIMAL:

            VARIABLE        QUANTITY
            ---------       --------
               A            475000
               B             80000
               D            245000
               S3            40000


            OPTIMAL Z = 210250


            Press any key to continue


            VARIABLE       SHADOW PRICE
            ---------      ------------
               A               0
               B               0
               C               .022
               D               0
               S1              .294
               S2             1.25
               S3              0
               S4              .059

    DO YOU WANT TO DO SENSITIVITY ANALYSIS? (YES/NO)
```

Figure 6.2 Computer Solution Output for ABC Investment

In the Dennis & Dennis software output, the first section of the output summary gives the solution values for the decision variables and any slack or surplus variables and the value of the objective function. Figure 6.3 shows that, for the ABC Investment problem, stocks A, B, and D should be purchased, since these were the variable names used for those stocks. The S_3 variable is a slack variable associated with the third constraint. Any variable not listed in the computer output has a zero value.

```
    VARIABLE                                       QUANTITY
    ---------                                      --------

       A        -indicates stocks                  475000
       B         A, B, and D should                 80000
       D         be purchased.                     245000

       S3                                           40000

    OPTIMAL Z = 210250
```

Figure 6.3 First Output Summary ABC Investment

The quantity column indicates how many dollars should be invested in each stock. This solution can be interpreted as follows: purchase $475,000 worth of stock A, $80,000 worth of stock B, and $245,000 worth of stock D. Since decision variable C (stock C) is not included in the output, its value is zero. The "OPTIMAL Z" value of 210250 is the computed optimal value of the objective function—$210,250.

Recall that, when an LP problem is converted to the standard form, slack or surplus variables are added to the inequalities to make them equalities, and that the value of those slack or surplus variables can be determined. In this problem, there are four inequality constraints. Thus there are four slack or surplus variables, identified as S_1, S_2, S_3, and S_4. Since slack variables are added to less-than-or-equal-to constraints and surplus variables are added to greater-than-or-equal-to constraints, variables S_1 and S_3 are slack variables and variables S_2 and S_4 are surplus variables. In the solution, the slack variable S_3 has a solution value of 40,000. The third constraint in this problem is formulated such that the amount invested in stock D cannot exceed 60 percent of the amount invested in stock A. This was originally stated as

$$D \leq .6A$$

In standard form, this constraint becomes

$$D - .6A + S_3 = 0$$

By substituting the solution values into this equation, we can determine the value of S_3.

$$245,000 - .6(475,000) + S_3 = 0$$
$$245,000 - 285,000 + S_3 = 0$$
$$-40,000 + S_3 = 0$$
$$S_3 = 40,000$$

Thus, this constraint has been satisfied with 40,000 units to spare, which is what the $S_3 = 40,000$ in the output indicates. The third constraint has a slack of 40,000 units. This result indicates an additional $40,000 can be invested in stock D without violating the third constraint. Again, the absence of variables S_1, S_2, and S_4 from the solution indicates they have values of zero in the optimal solution.

The second part of the output summary lists variables and dual or shadow prices or reduced costs. Dual or shadow prices exist for each slack or surplus variable; reduced costs exist for all decision variables (although variables with nonzero solution values have reduced costs of zero). While dual and/or shadow prices are explained in detail in Chapter 4, we have included a brief review here to help the reader relate these concepts to the computer output. Recall that dual prices reflect the change in the objective function value resulting from a one-unit change (increase) in the RHS value of the constraint associated with that particular slack or surplus variable. Reduced costs indicate the amount by which the objective function coefficient for a particular decision variable must change before that variable can have a positive solution value in the optimal solution. Figure 6.4 shows this output for the ABC Investment problem. This table can be divided into two sections, one with variables A through D (decision variables) and the other with variables S_1 through S_4 (slack or surplus variables). For the first part of the table (variables A–D), the value of the dual or shadow price indicates how much the

VARIABLE	DUAL OR SHADOW PRICE
A	0
B	0
C	.022
D	0
S1	.294
S2	1.25
S3	0
S4	.059

Figure 6.4 Second Output Summary for ABC Investment

value of the objective function (210250) would change if one unit of a variable not currently in the solution were substituted into the solution shown. Variables already in the solution always have shadow prices of zero. In this problem, stock C has a shadow price of .022. Since no stock C is currently being purchased, to buy one dollar's worth of stock C, we must replace one dollar's worth of some combination of stocks A, B, and D. The net effect of this replacement would be a loss of .022 (a reduction of the value of the objective function by 2.2¢ for every dollar invested in stock C).

For the second part of the table (variables S_1–S_4), the dual or shadow prices indicate how much the objective function would change if the indicated constraint were tightened by one unit. For example, constraint 1 limits the total dollar investment to $800,000. Variable S_1, associated with this constraint, has a shadow price of .294. This indicates that, for every dollar *less* than the original $800,000 that ABC invests, the value of the objective function is reduced by $.294. The reverse is also true: for every extra dollar ABC invests, the value of the objective function is increased by $.294. This change in the objective function value results from the purchase of fewer shares with a lower investment, or more shares with a higher investment. A change in the total dollar investment also would result in a slightly different combination of stocks.

The S_2 variable, a surplus variable associated with the minimum dividend (second) constraint, has a shadow price of 1.25. For every dollar the required minimum dividend is tightened, the value of the objective function is reduced by $1.25. Note, however, that since this constraint specifies a minimum dividend (it is a ≥ constraint), tightening the constraint means increasing the required dividend by $1.00 (to $20,001). Again, the reverse is also true; relaxing the constraint by $1.00 allows the objective function to be increased by $1.25.

The S_3 variable, a slack variable associated with the risk (third) constraint, has a shadow price of zero. Tightening this constraint has no effect at all on the objective function, since the first part of the output showed that there are 40,000 dollars worth of slack associated with this constraint ($S_3 = 40,000$).

The S_4 variable, a surplus variable associated with the percent of the total purchase represented by stock B (fourth) constraint, has a shadow price of .059. Tightening this constraint means increasing the required amount of stock B that must be purchased. For every extra dollar spent on stock B, the value of the objective function decreases by $.059; and for every dollar less spent on stock B (which would imply relaxing the 10 percent minimum requirement), the objective function increases by $.059. Again, this result occurs when a dollar's worth of other stocks with higher yields is substituted for stock B, resulting in a slight change in the solution values.

Thus, for the decision variables, the dual or shadow prices indicate how much the objective function is reduced by the addition of one unit of a variable not currently in the solution. The dual or shadow prices for the S (slack or surplus) variables indicate the amount the objective function value changes if the associated constraints are tightened or relaxed—on a per unit basis. Tightening the constraint reduces the objective function value; relaxing the constraint increases the objective function value.

6.3 SENSITIVITY ANALYSIS WITH COMPUTER SOLUTIONS

The concept of sensitivity analysis was presented in Chapter 5. In this section, we discuss it in terms of computer solutions. This discussion assumes the reader is familiar with sensitivity analysis concepts as they apply to objective function coefficient ranges and RHS ranges. Recall that sensitivity analysis provides additional information on how responsive the solution values (quantities and shadow prices) are to changes in the problem parameters. Computerized sensitivity analysis normally determines a range of values for each objective function coefficient and each right-hand-side value. The objective function coefficient range indicates the amount an objective function coefficient can change without affecting the decision variable quantities in the solution. The right-hand-side ranges indicate, for each constraint, the amount the original RHS value can change without affecting the shadow price for that constraint.

Objective Function Coefficients

Figure 6.5 shows the sensitivity analysis output for the objective function coefficients for the ABC Investment problem. This output gives the values of the lower limit, the original objective function value, and the upper limit for each decision variable. The solution indicates that, as long as the growth rate for stock A is somewhere between the lower limit of .22 (22 percent) and the upper limit of .3 (30 percent), the solution values for the decision variables do not change. This

```
      SENSITIVITY ANALYSIS OF OBJECTIVE FUNCTION COEFFICIENTS

   VARIABLE          LOWER         ORIGINAL         UPPER
   NAME              LIMIT           VALUE          LIMIT
   --------        ---------       --------        -------
      A               .22             .25            .3
      B             -2.716           .225           .284
      C            NO LIMIT          .24            .26
      D               .25             .3           NO LIMIT
```

Figure 6.5 Sensitivity Analysis of Objective Function Coefficients

range is based upon the assumption that the original values for the remaining stocks do not change. In other words, the objective function value for stock A can vary over this range while the other values are held constant.

The objective function coefficient of stock B can vary from −2.716 (−271.6 percent) to .284 (28.4 percent). The negative lower limit reflects the fact that Mr. Rulan specified that stock B must comprise 10 percent of the investment. Thus, stock B would be purchased even if it were declining in value (had a negative growth rate).

Stock C has no lower limit (NO LIMIT). Currently, no stock C is being purchased; its growth rate is too low to make it attractive. Thus, lowering the growth rate has no effect—it still won't be purchased. If, however, its growth rate were raised to the upper limit, .26 (26 percent), it would become an attractive investment and Mr. Rulan should consider purchasing it. The objective function coefficient range of a variable not currently in the solution, therefore, denotes the range of coefficient values over which the variable will remain *not* in the solution.

Stock D has a range of .25 (25 percent) to NO LIMIT. This suggests that, if the growth rate for this stock were reduced below 25 percent, it would no longer be an attractive purchase. No upper limit (NO LIMIT) implies that the growth rate can be increased (without limit) without changing the value of the decision variables. No increase in the growth rate for stock D can induce Mr. Rulan to purchase more of this stock, because he is currently buying as much stock D as he possibly can under the existing constraints.

Right-Hand-Side Values

Figure 6.6 shows the output for sensitivity analysis of the right-hand-side values. This output includes a lower limit, the original RHS value, and an upper limit for each constraint.

Constraint 1 limits the total investment to $800,000 and has a shadow price of $.294 as explained previously. This shadow price remains unchanged for total investment amounts between $536,912.75 and $842,105.26.

Constraint 2 requires total dividend payments of $20,000 and has a shadow price of $1.25. This shadow price remains unchanged for dividend amounts between $19,000 and $29,800.

Constraint 3 limits the risk of the investment by requiring that the amount invested in stock D be less than 60 percent of the amount invested in stock A. It has a shadow price of zero. Since the value of S_3 in the optimal solution demonstrated that

```
        SENSITIVITY ANALYSIS OF RIGHT-HAND-SIDE RANGES

                      LOWER        ORIGINAL       UPPER
        CONSTRAINT    LIMIT          VALUE        LIMIT
        ----------   --------      --------      --------
            1        536912.75      800000      842105.26
            2          19000         20000        29800
            3         -40000            0        NO LIMIT
            4        -79999.99         0         356363.63
```

Figure 6.6 Sensitivity Analysis of the RHS Values

this constraint had been met with $40,000 to spare, the lower limit indicates the amount invested in stock A can be decreased by 40,000 without affecting the shadow price. An upper limit of NO LIMIT shows that this constraint has already been met with the current RHS value of zero. Increasing its value simply increases the amount by which the requirement is exceeded, without affecting the shadow price.

Constraint 4 specifies that stock B must make up at least 10 percent of the amount invested in all four stocks. It has a shadow price of $.059. This shadow price remains unchanged for RHS values between a lower limit of −$80,000 (shown in Figure 6.6 as −79999.99 because of a sight error in the precision of the PC's solution) and an upper limit of $356,363.63. Recall that these values represent the RHS of the inequality

$$-.1A + .9B - .1C - .1D \geq 0$$

which can be restated as

$$B \geq .1(A + B + C + D)$$

or

$$\frac{B}{A + B + C + D} \geq .1$$

which represents the amount invested in stock B as a percentage of the total investment. If the total investment is assumed to be $800,000, the left side of this inequality can be expressed as

$$\frac{B}{800,000}$$

which can be defined as a new variable, B%, which represents the percent of the total invested in stock B. Using this notation, the lower limit can be expressed as

$$B\% \geq .1 + \frac{-80,000}{800,000}$$

or

$$B\% \geq .1 - .1 \geq 0$$

Thus, the lower limit represents a zero percent investment in stock B. In like manner, the upper limit can be expressed as

$$B\% \geq .1 + \frac{356,363.63}{800,000}$$

or

$$B\% \geq .1 + .44545 \geq .54545$$

This represents an upper limit of 54.5 percent. This means the shadow price for this constraint will remain unchanged if the amount invested in stock B is between 0 percent and 54.5 percent of the total investment.

In summary, sensitivity analysis provides additional information for the manager. The objective function ranges indicate the range of values that each decision variable's objective function coefficient can take without changing the values (quantities) of the decision variables in the optimal solution. The right-hand-side ranges indicate the amount that a particular constraint can be tightened or relaxed without affecting its shadow price. With this information, the manager does not have to recalculate the optimal solution each time one of these parameters changes.

In the next section, we introduce two additional LP programs to demonstrate input and output similarities and differences. These programs were selected to emphasize the real world applicability of LP by using real world packages.

6.4 ADDITIONAL COMPUTER INPUT AND SOLUTIONS (OPTIONAL)

In section 6.2, we showed the computer input and output (solutions) for the Dennis & Dennis LP computer program. Recall that most programs require similar input and provide similar output, with some variations in format. This section illustrates that similarity by showing input and output for the ABC Investment Company using two readily available programs, LINDO/PC and IBM's MPSX/370. LINDO (Linear, Interactive, and Discrete Optimizer) is an interactive program that is available in both mainframe and PC versions. MPSX/370 (Mathematical Programming System eXtended) is a batch input program, designed to solve large, complex LP problems on the mainframe computer. The use of MPSX/370 on a problem of this small size is equivalent to using a power saw to cut a pencil in half; however, for comparison purposes, we continue to use the ABC Investment problem.

LINDO/PC Input and Output

Figure 6.7 shows the problem input. LINDO prompts are shown in color, user input in normal print. The input takes the following form. LINDO/PC prompts the user with a colon (:) to indicate it is ready for instructions. At this point, the user enters the objective function, beginning with "MAX." LINDO then responds with a question mark, indicating it needs additional input. The user enters "ST" (for subject to) to tell LINDO that the objective function has been completed and that constraints will follow. Then the user enters the constraints one per line, and types the word "END" to tell LINDO the input has been completed. LINDO responds with a warning concerning the size of the values and another colon, indicating it is ready for the next command. The warning is included because the small coefficients,

```
: MAX .25A+.225B+.24C+.3D
? ST
? A+B+C+D<800000
? .04A+.0125B+.03C>20000
? −.6A+D<0
? −.1A+.9B−.1C−.1D>0
? END
 WARNING: PROBLEM IS POORLY SCALED. THE UNITS
 OF THE ROWS AND VARIABLES SHOULD BE CHANGED SO
 THE COEFFICIENTS COVER A MUCH SMALLER   RANGE.
:
```

Figure 6.7 LINDO/PC Input

such as .0125, in combination with the large RHS values, such as 800000, can sometimes produce values that exceed the number of significant digits used by the computer.

The command "GO" causes LINDO to solve the problem and display the output. Figures 6.8 and 6.9 show the problem solution and sensitivity analysis output. Responding to the prompt with a "Y" or "YES" causes LINDO to perform sensitivity analysis and output the resulting ranges. The slight variations between some of the

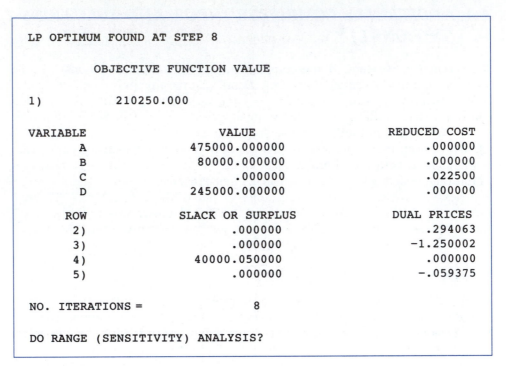

```
LP OPTIMUM FOUND AT STEP 8

         OBJECTIVE FUNCTION VALUE

1)          210250.000

VARIABLE              VALUE            REDUCED COST
    A            475000.000000            .000000
    B             80000.000000            .000000
    C                 .000000             .022500
    D            245000.000000            .000000

   ROW         SLACK OR SURPLUS          DUAL PRICES
    2)               .000000             .294063
    3)               .000000           -1.250002
    4)          40000.050000             .000000
    5)               .000000            -.059375

NO. ITERATIONS =                8

DO RANGE (SENSITIVITY) ANALYSIS?
```

Figure 6.8 LINDO/PC Solution Output

```
RANGES IN WHICH THE BASIS IS UNCHANGED:

                         OBJ COEFFICIENT RANGES
VARIABLE      CURRENT        ALLOWABLE        ALLOWABLE
              COEF           INCREASE         DECREASE
    A          .250000        .050000          .030000
    B          .225000        .059375         2.940625
    C          .240000        .022500         INFINITY
    D          .300000       INFINITY          .050000

                         RIGHTHAND SIDE RANGES
   ROW        CURRENT        ALLOWABLE        ALLOWABLE
              RHS            INCREASE         DECREASE
    2     800000.000000    42105.320000     263087.200000
    3      20000.000000     9799.998000       1000.001000
    4          .000000      INFINITY         40000.050000
    5          .000000    356363.600000      80000.000000
```

Figure 6.9 LINDO/PC Sensitivity Analysis Output

LINDO values and those shown earlier are the result of rounding. For example, the computer program that accompanies this book gives a value of 40,000 for the slack associated with the third constraint; LINDO gives a value of 40,000.05. Note that LINDO labels the objective function as row 1. Thus, the LINDO output for rows 2 through 5 are associated with constraints 1 through 4. LINDO also gives allowable increases and decreases for sensitivity analysis rather than upper and lower limits, and uses INFINITY rather than NO LIMIT.

MPSX/370 Input and Output

IBM's MPSX/370 program is a popular mainframe program capable of dealing with very large and complex problems. In fact, solving the example problem used here with MPSX/370 is really an inappropriate use of this program. MPSX/370 is designed to solve problems with hundreds or even thousands of variables and constraints. It is included here because it is batch-oriented, and to acquaint the reader with the very different input(s) required and the form the output may take. Since the input and output data can easily require several pages, only a portion is shown here. The input for the MPSX/370 program is in two separate sections. The first describes the data that will be used in the problem (variable names, coefficients, and RHS values). The second is a control program that is compiled and run with the MPSX program. Figure 6.10 gives an example of the data file. Notice that the

```
NAME                  ABC. INV
ROWS
 N        GROWTH
 L        INVEST
 G        DIVIDEND
 L        HIRISK
 G        BMIN
          COLUMNS
          STOCKA        GROWTH              .25000
          STOCKA        INVEST             1.00000
          STOCKA        DIVIDEND            .04000
          STOCKA        HIRISK        -     .60000
          STOCKA        BMIN          -     .10000
          STOCKB        GROWTH              .22500
          STOCKB        INVEST             1.00000
          STOCKB        DIVIDEND            .01250
          STOCKB        BMIN                .90000
          STOCKC        GROWTH              .24000
          STOCKC        INVEST             1.00000
          STOCKC        DIVIDEND            .03000
          STOCKC        BMIN          -     .10000
          STOCKD        GROWTH              .30000
          STOCKD        INVEST             1.00000
          STOCKD        HIRISK             1.00000
          STOCKD        BMIN          -     .10000
RHS
          RHS           INVEST        800000.00000
          RHS           DIVIDEND       20000.00000
ENDATA
```

Figure 6.10 MPSX/370 Data Input

data is in the MPS batch input form mentioned earlier. The input begins with the program name (ABC.INV). The ROWS section includes the rows in the LP model (N = objective function, L = ≤ constraint, and G = ≥ constraint) and a row name, such as GROWTH. The COLUMNS section contains the variable name and its coefficient for each associated row. The RHS section gives RHS values for each named row. Rows not included have RHS values of zero. Figure 6.11 is an example of the control program. This listing contains instructions that tell the program what it is expected to do, using MPSX specific instructions. Figure 6.12 shows part of the output for this problem. This introduction will not enable the reader to use MPSX. It is also probable that most users will never use MPSX themselves (even if their companies do). The reader should be aware, however, that these programs exist and are commonly used on real-world problems.

Since this output format differs somewhat from that of the previous programs, we will give a brief explanation. In SECTION 1, the value of the objective function (GROWTH) is 210250. The "SLACK ACTIVITY" value for HIRISK shows that this constraint has a value of 40000 in the final solution. The "DUAL ACTIVITY" column contains the shadow prices. Constraint 1 has a shadow price of 29.406¢, constraint 2 has a shadow price of $1.25, constraint 3 has a shadow price of zero, and constraint 4 a shadow price of 5.937¢. The "ACTIVITY" column for SECTION 2 of the output gives the solution values for the decision variables. The column values show that the optimal decision is to purchase $475,000 worth of stock A, $80,000 worth of stock B, no stock C, and $245,000 worth of stock D. The "REDUCED COST" column indicates that all decision variables have shadow prices of zero, with the exception of stock C, which has a value of 2.25¢.

We have included the inputs and outputs from LINDO/PC and MPSX/370 in this chapter to acquaint the reader with two popular programs and to illustrate the similarities and differences in input and output. Because of its ability to handle larger

```
    MPSX/370 R1.7 MPSCL COMPILATION

        0001                PROGRAM
        0002                INITIALZ
        0210                TITLE ('ABC INVESTMENT')
        0211                MOVE (XDATA, 'ABC.INV')
        0212                MOVE (XPBNAME, 'ABC')
        0213                CONVERT ('SUMMARY')
        0214                MOVE (XOBJ,'GROWTH')
        0215                MOVE (XRHS,'RHS')
        0216                SETUP ('MAX')
        0217                BCDOUT ('ONE')
        0218                PICTURE
        0219                OPTIMIZE
        0450                SOLUTION
        0451                STATUS
        0452                EXIT
        0453                PEND
```

Figure 6.11 MPSX/370 Control Program

```
SECTION 1 - ROWS

NUMBER ...ROW   ...ACTIVITY...    SLACK ACTIVITY   DUAL ACTIVITY

     1  GROWTH     210250.00000    210250.00000-      1.00000
     2  INVEST     800000.00000          .             .29406-
     3  DIVIDEND    20000.00000          .            1.25000
     4  HIRISK      40000.00000     40000.00000          .
     5  BMIN            .                 .             .05937


SECTION 2 - COLUMNS

NUMBER  .COLUMNS  ...ACTIVITY...    ..INPUT COST..  .REDUCED COST.
     6  STOCKA     475000.00000        .25000           .
     7  STOCKB      80000.00000        .22500           .
     8  STOCKC          .              .24000           .02250-
     9  STOCKD     245000.00000        .30000           .
```

Figure 6.12 MPSX/370 Partial Solution Output

and more complex problems, MPSX/370 requires more input data. But all three programs provide the same basic solution values, with slight variations caused by rounding. These programs are representative of most programs available today.

Focus on Decision Making

Maxgood House Coffee Company produces four varieties of ground coffee, all of which are sold in 1-pound vacuum bags. These coffees are Jamaican, Peruvian, Columbian, and Superior Blend; the latter is a blend of Jamaican, Peruvian and Columbian beans. The Superior Blend contains 25 percent Jamaican beans, 35 percent Peruvian beans, and 40 percent Columbian beans. Currently, Maxgood can sell all of each type of coffee that it can produce, although its wholesalers have specified that at least 25 percent of all coffee they buy must be the Special Blend.

The table below shows the number of pounds of each type of bean that the Maxgood coffee buyers can obtain for the coming month, and the price per pound.

Country of Origin	Pounds Available per Month	Price per Pound
Jamaican	80,000	$ .50
Peruvian	94,000	.60
Columbian	130,000	.75

Maxgood sells its coffees to wholesalers at the following prices (per pound): Jamaican, $1.50; Peruvian, $1.65; Columbian, $1.95; and Special Blend, $1.80.

The company has the capacity to grind and package 400,000 pounds of coffee per month. Blending capacity is limited to 90,000 pounds per month. Maxgood has no loss of weight in either the grinding or blending processes; in other words, 1 pound of coffee beans yields 1 pound of ground coffee. Preprinted vacuum bags cost $.04 each. Labor costs are estimated to be $.26 per pound for the non-blended coffees and $.41 per pound for the blended coffees.

Maxgood management is trying to decide how many pounds of each type of coffee to have the buyers purchase, and how many pounds of each type of coffee they should produce and ship to their wholesalers. Maxgood's coffee buyers have also informed management that an additional 70,000 pounds of Columbian beans are available, but at a cost of $.95 per pound (a premium of $.20 per pound).

Data Preparation/Problem Formulation

Given the differential selling prices and costs, Maxgood should attempt to produce the combination of coffees that will maximize its monthly profit contribution. Given the data, monthly profit contribution per pound can be determined as:

	Jamaican	Peruvian	Columbian	Special Blend
Selling Price	$1.50	$1.65	$1.95	$1.80
Bean costs	.50	.60	.75	.635*
Bags	.04	.04	.04	.04
Labor costs	.26	.26	.26	.41
Total costs	.80	.90	1.05	1.085
Profit/pound	$ .70	$ .75	$ .90	$ .785

*Calculated as: .50(25%) + .60(35%) + .75(40%) = .635

By determining the amount of each type of coffee to produce in order to maximize profit contribution, Maxgood is also determining the quantity of each type of coffee bean that should be purchased by the buyers.

The decision variables for this problem (J, P, C, SB) represent the pounds of each type of coffee produced. The objective function can be stated as

$$MAX\ .70J + .75P + .90C + .785SB$$

The constraints for the pounds of each type of bean available can be expressed as the pounds of beans used in pure or nonblended coffee plus the pounds of that particular bean used in the special blend. Thus, Jamaican beans would be used for Jamaican coffee (100%) and for special blend (25%). The constraint for Jamaican beans would be

$$J + .25SB \leq 80000$$

The grinding capacity can be stated as

$$J + P + C + SB \leq 400000$$

and the blending capacity as

$$SB \leq 90000$$

We can state the specification that at least 25 percent of the coffee produced must be special blend:

$$SB \geq .25(J + P + C)$$

which can be restated

$$-.25J - .25P - .25C + .75SB \geq 0$$

Thus, the complete formulation would be

$$\text{MAX } .7J + .75P + .9C + .785SB$$

subject to

$$J + \qquad\qquad\qquad .25SB \leq 80000$$

$$P + \qquad\qquad .35SB \leq 94000$$

$$C + \quad .4SB \leq 130000$$

$$J + \quad P + \quad C + \quad SB \leq 400000$$

$$SB \leq 90000$$

$$-.25J - .25P - .25C + .75SB \geq 0$$

$$J, P, C, SB \geq 0$$

Computer Solution

Entering this problem into the computer and solving yields the following results:

```
AFTER 4 ITERATIONS,
THIS SOLUTION IS OPTIMAL:


VARIABLE        QUANTITY
----------      ----------
   J            61000
   P            67400.003
   C            99600
   SB           76000.001
   S4           95999.996
   S5           13999.999


OPTIMAL Z = 242550


VARIABLE        SHADOW PRICE
----------      ------------
   J                 0
   P                 0
   C                 0
   SB                0
   S1               -.697
   S2               -.747
   S3               -.897
   S4                0
   S5                0
   S6               -.013
```

Interpretation and Analysis of the Results

This solution indicates that Maxgood will maximize its profit contribution if it produces 61,000 pounds of Jamaican coffee, 67,400 pounds of Peruvian, 99,600 pounds of Columbian, and 76,000 pounds of Special Blend. Total profit contribution will be $242,550 for the month. Note that these answers have been rounded from those shown in the computer solution. In this case, rounding does not violate any of the constraints. The answers reflect the lack of precision imposed by the PC and the compiler.

We can determine the number of pounds of each type of bean to purchase in one of two ways. First, we can use the solution numbers to calculate the number of pounds. For example, $J = 61,000$ pounds of Jamaican beans and $SB = 76,000$ pounds of Special Blend. Since the Special Blend is 25 percent Jamaican beans, this means that Maxgood should purchase $61,000 + .25(76,000)$ or 80,000 pounds of Jamaican beans. The second method is easier: S_1 represents the slack associated with Jamaican beans. Since S_1 is equal to zero in the final solution (it is nonbasic), all 80,000 pounds of the Jamaican beans are used in the optimal solution and should, therefore, be purchased. S_2 and S_3 are also equal to zero, implying that all 94,000 pounds of Peruvian beans and 130,000 pounds of Columbian beans should be purchased.

The optimal solution also shows S_4 equals 96,000 and S_5 equals 14,000. S_4, a slack variable associated with the fourth constraint (grinding capacity), indicates that the company has an additional 96,000 pounds of (unused) grinding capacity. S_5, a slack variable associated with the fifth constraint (blending capacity), indicates that Maxgood could blend an additional 14,000 pounds of Special Blend.

In order to determine whether or not to purchase additional Columbian beans at a cost of $.95 per pound, it is necessary to examine the shadow price associated with the slack variable for Columbian beans, S_3. S_3 has a shadow price of $.897. This indicates that the value of the objective function (profit contribution) can be increased by $.897 for each additional pound of Columbian beans that can be obtained. Since the normal cost of Columbian beans ($.75 per pound) is already included in the profit contribution determination, this shadow price should be compared with the premium paid for an additional pound of Columbian beans ($.20 per pound). This indicates that adding Columbian beans would be worthwhile, since an additional pound of Columbian beans would net an additional profit contribution of $.697 per pound.

Once this determination is made, the next question is "How many additional pounds should be purchased?" This can be determined by requesting and examining the sensitivity analysis output for this problem.

SENSITIVITY ANALYSIS OF RIGHT HAND SIDE RANGES

CONSTRAINT	LOWER LIMIT	ORIGINAL VALUE	UPPER LIMIT
1	14933.33	80000	136000
2	20136.98	94000	150000
3	19333.34	130000	186000
4	304000	400000	NO LIMIT
5	76000	90000	NO LIMIT
6	−76000	0	14000

The upper limit of the RHS range for constraint 3 (Columbian beans) is 186,000. This indicates that the shadow price only holds up to a maximum of 186,000 pounds, or an addition of 56,000 pounds. Thus, Maxgood management should authorize the buyer to purchase 56,000 of the available 70,000 pounds at the offered price. This will increase the monthly profit contribution by approximately $30,032 (56,000 × 0.697).

6.5 *CONCLUDING REMARKS*

This chapter is important because most, if not all, real-world LP problems are solved using computer programs. Computers and these programs enable managers to obtain relatively fast, accurate solutions to large or complex problems that would otherwise be impractical to solve. While data collection and model formulation were not stressed in this chapter, it should be obvious that improper data collection or improper formulation results in an incorrect answer, no matter what program is used. The computer is a powerful tool; managers who do not take advantage of it place themselves at a significant disadvantage.

Management Science Application

SCHOOL BUS SCHEDULING USING LINEAR PROGRAMMING[1]

Transporting children to and from school each day is a major cost for many school districts. The rising cost of buses and increases in drivers' salaries make efficient scheduling of school buses an important issue for many school districts. A study of student busing in New Haven, Connecticut was undertaken in an attempt to design and validate a model that would help school districts reduce the cost of busing. A linear programming model was developed that minimized the number of school buses needed to meet the city's busing requirements.

The problem had two components: routing and scheduling. Routing involved the determination of the route each bus would follow as it picked up children and took them to school in the morning or took them home from school in the afternoon. Scheduling involved the assignment of particular buses to specific routes. In some cases, buses could be assigned to more than one route. New Haven determined both routes and schedules, which were

[1]Barry Shore, *Quantitative Methods for Business Decisions: Text and Cases* (New York: McGraw-Hill, 1978), pp. 196–200. Reprinted by permission of McGraw-Hill.

then followed by the private busing company. The linear programming model focused on the scheduling component of the problem. Routes were accepted as previously determined by the city.

The scheduling problem was divided into two problems, one for the morning schedule and one for the afternoon schedule. A major component of the morning scheduling problem was the arrival of buses at particular schools within a specified time window. For example, buses dropping off students at an elementary school might be expected to arrive at the school between 8:00 AM and 8:15 AM. In New Haven, the allowable time windows for each school were established based upon discussions between school principals, who preferred not to have students dropped off too early, and the scheduler, for whom wider time windows meant more flexibility. The researchers found that the afternoon problem was actually less constraining than the morning problem. Most of the schools began around the same time in the morning, but variations in the length of the school day among schools, and faster bus speeds due to lighter afternoon traffic, allowed the afternoon schedule to be covered by fewer buses.

Data was gathered by estimating route distances using a map wheel and by riding school buses. It was found that actual travel times could be estimated by assuming constant travel speeds, both along the routes and from the end of the routes to the destination schools. Buses averaged 13 miles per hour along their routes in the morning and 14.5 miles per hour from the end of their routes (the point where the last student was picked up) to the destination schools.

In developing the model, arrival times were changed from a continuous variable to a discrete variable by requiring that the buses arrive at one of K specified times within the school's time window. The model was run twice, once with only two allowable arrival times and a second time with four allowable arrival times. While the problem is actually an integer linear programming problem, since the city can rent only whole buses for the year, the problem was solved for the LP relaxation solution. If the optimal LP solution contained fractional buses (e.g., 27.75 buses), a constraint was added, specifying that the total number of buses was equal to 28. The model was used to determine the number of buses needed in New Haven for the 1976–1977 school year, which included 27 schools and 84 routes. It was then used for the 1980–1981 school year, which included 37 schools and 102 routes.

When the model was applied to the 1976–1977 school year, the optimal solution indicated that 28 buses were necessary to cover the schedule with two arrival times, or 27 buses with four arrival times. This result compared to 38 buses actually used in that year. The city of New Haven rents buses with drivers from a private firm at the cost of $20,000 per year per bus. Had this model actually been used, the resulting savings would have been $220,000 or a 29 percent cost savings. In the 1980–1981 school year, the model indicated that 30 buses would be needed with either two or four arrival times, although the model with four arrival times was not an all-integer solution. The all-integer solution was not found for the four-arrival time problem because the model exceeded the capacity of the computer being used and would have required software modification to solve. The actual school plan called for 37 buses. Thus, the model provided a solution that reduced the cost of busing by 23.3 percent. While no specific data are available at this time on the extent to which this model is being employed, the methods developed in this study have been used by the Las Vegas County School System.

GLOSSARY

input data that must be entered into the computer before a solution can be obtained
output data provided by the computer when the program is run
software computer programs

PROBLEMS

1. Mr. Rulan, investment manager for ABC Investment Company (example problem), must decide how many dollars to invest in each of four stocks. The customer has decided to invest up to $1,000,000, but has specified that 20 percent of the investment must be in stock B. All other requirements remain unchanged. Mr. Rulan has reformulated this problem as follows:

$$\text{MAX } .25A + .225B + .24C + .30D$$

subject to

$$A + B + C + D \le 1000000$$
$$.04A + .0125B + .03C \ge 20000$$
$$-.6A + D \le 0$$
$$-.2A + .8B - .2C - .2D \ge 0$$
$$A, B, C, D \ge 0$$

Determine the optimal solution to this problem.

2. Hyper Fast Computers (Chapter 4, problem 12) manufactures IBM-compatible personal computers. Hyper Fast makes three PC models: a Desktop-386, a Desktop-286, and a Laptop-286. Because of limited production facilities, Hyper Fast cannot produce more than 100 desktop models or more than 60 laptop models per month. Hyper Fast also has a limited supply of CPU chips available for the coming month. It has 45 80386 chips (used in the Desktop-386) and 120 80286 chips (used in the Desktop-286 and Laptop-286) for the month. The Desktop-386 model requires 4 hours of assembly time, the Desktop-286 model requires 3 hours of assembly time, and the Laptop-286 model requires 2½ hours of assembly time. Hyper Fast has 290 hours of assembly time available for the coming month. Hyper Fast estimates it makes $1,250 profit on a Desktop-386, $900 profit on a Desktop-286, and $800 profit on a Laptop-286.

   a. Determine the optimal product mix.
   b. Which resources are binding?
   c. How much should Hyper Fast be willing to pay for additional assembly hours? Extra 80286 chips? Extra 80386 chips?

3. Discount Distributors (Chapter 2, example problem) must determine the best way to promote its merchandise. The LP model has been formulated as:

$$MAX\ 20000M + 25000N + 50000TV \leq 24000$$

subject to

$$
\begin{aligned}
500M +\ &600N +\ 2000TV \leq 24000 \\
30M +\ &5N +\ 15TV \leq 260 \\
&N\quad\quad\quad \geq 10 \\
M\quad\quad &\quad\quad\quad\quad \leq 1 \\
&M, N, TV \geq 0
\end{aligned}
$$

Determine an advertising plan for Discount that maximizes the audience reached without exceeding the advertising budget of $24,000.

4. Denneco Construction (Chapter 2, problem 27) has purchased a warehouse that it plans to convert into three types of condominium units. Prior to beginning construction, however, the company was able to purchase a connecting annex building that increases the available footage by 20,000 square feet. Determine the optimal conversion plan for this project.

5. Given the following computer solution:

VARIABLE	QUANTITY
A	15
C	8
D	20
S2	14

OPTIMAL Z = 40

VARIABLE	REDUCED COST/ SHADOW PRICE
A	0
B	2.5
C	0
D	0
S1	1.75
S2	0
S3	3

a. Which variables are basic?
b. Which constraints (resources) are binding?
c. What will be the value of the objective function if one unit of variable B is added to the solution?

6. XYZ Corporation produces two products, A and B. Product A yields a profit contribution of $8 per unit and product B yields a profit contribution of $6 per unit. XYZ currently has a contract calling for the delivery of 100 units of each product. These units can be produced on regular time or overtime, but must pass through both the fabrication and assembly departments. There are 700 hours of regular time that can be allocated between the departments. In

addition, up to 300 overtime hours can be assigned in the fabrication department and 200 overtime hours in the assembly department. Product A requires 2 hours in fabrication and 3 hours in assembly. Product B requires 3 hours in fabrication and 1 hour in assembly. Using overtime to produce units reduces their profit contribution by $2 each. Determine the optimal number of units of each product to produce, the number of regular hours that should be assigned to each department, and the number of overtime hours to be allocated to each department.

7. Best Home Products (Chapter 2, problem 28) is opening four new sales regions. Determine the optimal number of salespeople to assign to each region.

8. The manager for the All Day Grocery Store (Chapter 2, example problem) must set up a schedule for his clerks that will cover customer demand while keeping overall staffing needs to a minimum. Find the optimal solution for this manager.

9. Given the following LINDO/PC output:

OBJECTIVE FUNCTION VALUE

1)	415.500000	

VARIABLE COST	VALUE	REDUCED
A	68.500000	.000000
B	42.000000	.000000
C	.000000	.300000

ROW PRICES	SLACK OR SURPLUS	DUAL
2)	.000000	.200000
3)	161.000000	.000000
4)	.000000	.550000
5)	77.000000	.000000
6)	7.000000	.000000

a. Which variables are basic?
b. Which constraints (resources) are binding?
c. What will the value of the objective function be if one unit of variable C is added to the solution.

10. Mr. Jaworski, production manager for Woodline Products (Chapter 2, example problem) must prepare a production schedule for the next six weeks that will meet demand while minimizing per unit production and inventory costs. Determine the optimal least cost schedule for Mr. Jaworski.

11. Paul's Plantfood Company (Chapter 2, problem 30) produces three brands of plant food at two different factories. Paul wishes to determine the number of pounds of each type of plantfood to produce at each factory in order to maximize his profits. Determine the solution to this problem.

12. Shark Electronics manufactures four compact disk players: the remote-control model CD48; the full-function infrared remote control model CD58; the six-disk remote model CD68; and the portable model CD78. The assembly process requires assembly at five workstations, as follows:

Time at Work Station (Minutes)					
Model	1	2	3	4	5
CD48	3	2	4	3	6
CD58	4	3	2	2½	7
CD68	4	2½	5	1	7
CD78	2½	1½	6	2	0

A maximum of eight hours is available each day at each of the five work stations.

If Shark makes a profit of $33 for each model CD48, $30 for each model CD58, $50 for each model CD68, and $35 for each model CD78, how many of each model should be produced each day in order to maximize profit? (Assume Shark can sell all of each model it produces.)

13. Shark Electronics (problem 12) sales figures for the last quarter indicate that models CD48 and CD78 are the best-selling models. The outlets purchasing Shark's CDs are still willing to purchase all units produced, but have specified that at least 60 percent of the models delivered should be the more popular models. Determine the optimum number of each model to produce each day in order to maximize profits.

14. Shark Electronics (problem 12) has a company policy to balance workloads on all assembly jobs. Therefore, management wants to schedule work so that no assembler at any workstation has a workload that exceeds other workstations by more than 0.5 hour per day. Thus, during an 8 hour day, all assemblers must be assigned at least 7.5 hours of work. Does this policy change the solution to problem 12?

15. Superior Foods has introduced a line of specialty coffees (mocha, vanilla bean, etc.) that has become very popular. Superior researchers are currently developing a "master blend," which they intend to sell at a lower cost than any brand currently on the market. Coffee is judged on its flavor, aroma, and color. The master blend will be made from Jamaican, Peruvian, and Columbian coffees. Each coffee is rated on a scale of 1 to 10 for flavor, aroma, and color. Jamaican beans cost $.80 per pound, have a flavor rating of 8.2, an aroma rating of 7.1, and a color rating of 4. Peruvian beans cost $.60 per pound, have a flavor rating of 7, an aroma rating of 6, and a color rating of 7.5. Columbian beans cost $.95 per pound, have a flavor rating of 9.5, an aroma rating of 5, and a color rating of 6.2. Market research indicates that coffees sell best when the flavor rating is at least 8.5, the aroma rating is at least 6, and the color rating is at least 5. How many pounds of each type of bean should Superior purchase if they wish to produce at least 60,000 pounds of their master blend? (Assume no weight loss in grinding or mixing the beans.)

16. How does the solution to problem 15 change if Superior Foods wishes to produce at least 100,000 pounds of its master blend, but only 35,000 pounds of Columbian beans are available?

17. Superior Foods (problem 15) wishes to produce 100,000 pounds of its master blend coffee. It currently has 60,000 pounds of Jamaican beans, 50,000 pounds of Peruvian beans, and 60,000 pounds of Columbian beans available. All available beans were purchased at regular prices ($.80, $.60, and $.95 per pound). Superior wholesales the master blend for $2.10 per pound. Superior has found that its coffee beans lose their flavor when stored too long. There

fore, all coffee beans not used in its current production (exactly 100,000 pounds of master blend) will be sold at $.20 a pound below their original cost. Determine the blending that will maximize profits.

18. The ABC advertising agency (Chapter 2, problem 15) has been hired to promote a new product. ABC wishes to select from among four advertising options in a way that will reach as large an audience as possible, without spending more than $200,000. Recently, however, advertisers have discovered that prime-time TV ads reach 80,000 people rather than 60,000. Because of this increase in the audience, the cost of these ads has been increased to $17,000. Other figures remain unchanged. Determine the optimal advertising plan for ABC.

19. Hike and Grow camp (Chapter 2, problem 25) provides a trail mix to all campers departing on hiking trips. The dietician wishes to mix the four available ingredients so that various minimum daily requirements are met at minimum cost. Determine the optimal mixture for the dietician.

20. Interpret the following computer output:

SENSITIVITY ANALYSIS OF OBJECTIVE FUNCTION COEFFICIENTS

VARIABLE NAME	LOWER LIMIT	ORIGINAL VALUE	UPPER LIMIT
A	-2	5	6.333
B	0	6	8
C	NO LIMIT	5	8.6
D	3.273	4	11

SENSITIVITY ANALYSIS OF RIGHT-HAND-SIDE RANGES

CONSTRAINT	LOWER LIMIT	ORIGINAL VALUE	UPPER LIMIT
1	92	112	262
2	-85	140	290
3	10.18	92	112

21. Interpret the following computer output:

SENSITIVITY ANALYSIS OF OBJECTIVE FUNCTION COEFFICIENTS

VARIABLE NAME	LOWER LIMIT	ORIGINAL VALUE	UPPER LIMIT
A	NO LIMIT	1	3.4
B	-1	3	NO LIMIT
C	-1	2	14
D	.2	5	NO LIMIT

SENSITIVITY ANALYSIS OF RIGHT-HAND-SIDE RANGES

CONSTRAINT	LOWER LIMIT	ORIGINAL VALUE	UPPER LIMIT
1	1.33	6	9.33
2	7.14	10	17
3	4	32	52

22. Power's Farm Market purchases grapes from Casa Larga Vineyards. Some of these grapes are sold at the market, some are used to make grape pies that are sold to market customers, and some are used to produce private label "fruit only" grape spread, sold at both the market and other retail locations. Grapes used to make jelly are graded as A, B, or C, with grade A the highest quality. Grade A grapes are sweeter and unblemished; grade B grapes are less sweet and have some blemishes. Grade C grapes are usually slightly damaged (either by nature or in picking). The main quality considerations for jelly are sweetness and clarity. Because of blemishes, grade C grapes result in a cloudy jelly. The cost per quart of the grapes are $.75, $.60, and $.25 for grades A, B, and C respectively. The grapes are given both a sweetness rating (based on sugar content) and clarity ratings. The sweetness ratings are on a scale of 1 to 10, with 10 the highest rating. The sweetness ratings for the current crop are 9.8, 8.2, and 9.0 for grades A, B, and C respectively. The clarity ratings, on a scale of 1 to 5 (with 1 the best clarity rating), are 1.8, 2.2, and 3.5 for grades A, B, and C respectively. The jelly must have a sweetness rating between 9 and 9.5 and the clarity rating can be no greater than 2.1. Each quart of grapes yields two 8-ounce jars of jelly, with each jar selling for $1.95. If Power's wishes to minimize the cost of grapes used in the jelly, what is the best way to blend each 8-ounce jar?

23. The price of grapes in problem 22 has dropped dramatically. The cost per quart is now $.50, $.40, and $.07 for grades A, B, and C respectively. Power's private label "fruit only" grape spread is in great demand at a large number of specialty stores. Power's has orders for 10,000 8-ounce jars of the grape spread. Processing costs are $.10 per jar. Powers still wishes to minimize cost. How many quarts of each grade must be purchased to produce 10,000 jars at minimal cost?

24. Windsor Shirt Company is a factory outlet store that sells men's and women's shirts at discount prices. There are three full-time employees—a manager and two assistant managers. The remaining employees are all part-time. These employees are scheduled in 3-hour shifts. On Saturday, the busiest day, the store is open from 10 AM to 9 PM. Management wants to schedule part-time employees so as to minimize labor costs while still providing sufficient coverage for good customer service. The average wage rate for part-time employees is $3.50 per hour. The total number of employees needed at various time periods throughout the day is given in the following table:

Time	Part-time Employees Needed
9:30-10:30	2
10:30-11:30	3
11:30-12:30	5
12:30- 1:30	5
1:30- 2:30	5
2:30- 3:30	4
3:30- 4:30	4
4:30- 5:30	3
5:30- 6:30	3
6:30- 7:30	5
7:30- 8:30	3
8:30- 9:30	2

One full-time employee comes in at 9:30 AM to open the store and works until 4:00 PM (with a one-half hour unpaid lunch break at 12:30). A second full-time employee arrives at 3:00 PM and works until 9:30 PM (with a one-half hour unpaid dinner break at 5:30). Kathy Lindsey, the store manager, has to develop a minimum cost schedule for the part-time employees for Saturdays.

a. Determine the appropriate minimum cost schedule.
b. If part-time employees can be scheduled for up to six hours per shift on Saturdays, how would this change the schedule determined in part (a)?

25. The Tropical Fruit Company supplies fruit juice and fruit juice blends to restaurants in the Southeast. TFC's juices and profit contributions per ounce are as follows: orange ($.07), grapefruit juice ($.07), tangerine ($.06), pineapple ($.09), guava ($.11), and mango ($.13). TFC's blended juices and profit contribution per ounce are: orange/pineapple ($.11), Tropical Delight—tangerine, guava, and mango ($.09), and Tropical Breeze—all six juices ($.10). The orange/pineapple blend is 60 percent orange juice and 40 percent pineapple juice. Tropical Delight is 50 percent tangerine juice, 30 percent guava juice, and 20 percent mango juice. Tropical Breeze is 30 percent pineapple juice, 25 percent orange juice, 20 percent tangerine juice, 10 percent guava juice, 10 percent mango juice, and 5 percent grapefruit juice. The company has 200 gallons each of pineapple and tangerine juice, 300 gallons of orange juice, 250 gallons of grapefruit juice, 150 gallons of guava juice, and 100 gallons of mango juice on hand. All of TFC's products are sold by the gallon. The mango and guava juices are also available in half-gallon sizes. The company has back-orders for 30 gallons of pineapple juice, 20 half-gallons of mango juice, and 28 half-gallons of guava juice that must be filled from current supplies. TFC management wishes to determine how many containers of each product to prepare to maximize its profits.

a. Solve this problem.
b. Determine the shadow prices for each type of fruit juice.
c. Perform sensitivity analysis to determine the ranges for the objective function coefficients and the right-hand sides.

26. Acme Electronics produces a component used in a variety of small electrical appliances. Mr. Jacoby, production manager for this product line, wishes to prepare a production schedule for the next seven weeks that will meet demand while minimizing per unit production and inventory costs. Demand for the component varies widely from week to week, as shown by the contract figures in the following table:

Week	Demand
1	32,000
2	44,000
3	27,000
4	31,000
5	48,000
6	29,000
7	46,000

At full capacity during regular operating hours, Acme can produce 35,000 of these components per week. It costs Acme $2.60 per component produced during regular hours. Another 10,000 units per week can be produced by scheduling overtime. Components produced on overtime cost $3.10 per unit. Units produced during the week are shipped at the end of the week to fill existing orders. Any excess units are placed in inventory. Components placed into inventory incur a $.25 per item per week carrying cost. There are currently 9,000 components in inventory, and the company has a policy of maintaining an ending inventory of at least 3,000 components to cover special rush orders. Formulate and solve this problem so that Mr. Jacoby can schedule production in such a way as to minimize total production and inventory costs.

27. Kober, Inc., a manufacturer of athletic equipment, has developed a new walking shoe named the Traveller that it would like to introduce to the public. The total advertising budget for this product has been set at $360,000. Kober management wants to spend this money in such a way as to maximize potential sales. Market research indicates that those people in the over-$30,000 income bracket are twice as likely to buy the shoe. A media blitz is planned for the final week of the NCAA basketball tournament. The selected media have been narrowed to TV; two small specialty magazines aimed at walkers and joggers; and a leading news magazine. (Market research also indicates people subscribing to the specialty magazines are three times as likely to buy the shoe. This result is independent of income; readers of these magazines earning over $30,000 are six times as likely to purchase the shoe.) Three-fourths of the advertising budget will be designated for this week. Each unit of TV time during the week will reach 70 million people, half of whom earn over $30,000 annually. Each unit of advertising time on TV during the tournament costs $160,000. Market research shows that one advertisement will be noticed by 60 percent of the viewer audience, while two advertisements will be noticed by the total viewer audience. Specialty magazine A reaches 4 million people, 3 million of whom are in the over-$30,000 income bracket. Specialty magazine B reaches 3 million people, two-thirds of whom are in the over-$30,000 income bracket. One unit of advertising in specialty magazine A costs $25,000 and one unit of advertising in specialty magazine B costs $20,000. News magazine C reaches 10 million people each week, three-fourths of whom are in the over-$30,000 income bracket. News magazine D reaches 9 million people, two-thirds of whom are in the over-$30,000 income bracket. News magazine E has 7.5 million readers, half of whom are in over-$30,000 income bracket. Each advertising unit in magazines C and D costs $65,000. An advertising unit in magazine E costs $45,000. Kober does not want to place more than one ad in each magazine during the week. What is the best selection of media that Kober management can make to reach the most potential buyers during that week?

28. The marketing vice-president at Kober, Inc. (problem 27) and the sales manager at news magazine E are old friends. Because of this friendship, news magazine E offers Kober a special package for the introduction of this new shoe. If Kober agrees to purchase an advertisement in the news magazine (at $45,000), the magazine will give Kober a free advertisement in a new magazine (F) being released by the same publisher. It is estimated that this new magazine will reach 4 million people, all of whom earn over $30,000. Does this offer change the optimal solution found in problem 27 and if so, how?

29. Plastico Company makes a variety of molded plastic items used by the automobile industry. Recently, Plastico decided to add a small line of plastic shelves and tables that will be sold through a large discount store. The company plans to make the following six items: a two-shelf unit, a three-shelf unit, a four-shelf unit, a 14-inch table, a 16-inch table, and a planter table (12 × 36 inches). Profit contributions on these items are estimated to be $6, $7.60, $8.70, $3.00, $4.00, and $7.35 respectively. The products all require existing operations within the plant: molding, trimming and finishing, and packaging. All products will be made from the same raw materials. The following table shows the times (in minutes) and amounts of raw material (in pounds) required for each product:

Product	Molding	Trimming & Finishing	Packaging	Raw Material (pounds)
2-shelf	11	12	3	4
3-shelf	13	16	4	6
4-shelf	15	20	5	8
14" table	8	5	2	2.5
16" table	8	7	2	3
planter	12	10	4	5.5

There are currently 10 hours of molding time, 12 hours of trimming and finishing time, and 3 hours of packaging time available. There are 255 pounds of raw materials available. Assuming Plastico can sell all of any product they produce, what would their product mix be if they wish to maximize profit contribution?

Consultant's Report _____

Vista Properties, Inc.[2]

Vista Properties is a real estate development company currently facing several problems in the design and construction of a large shopping center. The company already owns 140,000 square feet of land on which this center will be built, and it has an option to buy an additional 20,000 square feet of adjoining land. One problem is whether this option should be exercised. The second problem concerns the use of the available space. What kind of stores should be included in the shopping center, and how much of this available space should be allocated to each of them?

Company Background

Vista Properties was founded in 1963 by Ted Wasser. Although the company emphasizes primarily the development of shopping centers, it has occasionally built condominiums.

Vista has had an enviable record. With the exception of one condominium project, it has earned substantial profits on all its investments. Mr. Wasser credits this success to his team of qualified managers, who carefully screen an average of 40 projects before one is undertaken.

Especially useful during the screening phase is the demographic information provided by Data Profile, Inc. For $130, a complete printout of demographic data is supplied from Data Profile's computer. These data are based on the most recent

[2]Arthur J. Swersey and Wilson Ballard, "Scheduling School Buses," *Management Science*, 30 (July, 1984), 844-853.

census information. Included are the number of people within a given radius of the proposed site, growth rates, annual incomes, number of children, whether or not they own a house, education, and so on. From these data Vista's management can proceed to make several key estimates for the proposed site.

After the site is chosen, Vista architects develop plans for the outside and inside of the complex. In the last five years considerable effort has been directed at blending the buildings and parking facilities with their environment.

Once the project is begun, tight cost controls are imposed. Every effort is made to complete the project within the allocated budget.

After the project is completed and after the tenants have moved into their stores, Vista's management job still continues. It coordinates promotional campaigns for its tenants including advertising, dollar days, fairs, and concerts.

Vista's interest is to make the property valuable by building up the sales level of its tenants.

After this phase of rapid growth is over, Vista usually sells the property at a considerable profit. In general the shopping center is sold seven years after it is opened.

Midvale Shopping Center

The Midvale Shopping Center project passed the screening phase some 12 months ago. At that time 140,000 square feet of land were purchased.

The shopping center is located 25 miles west of a major metropolitan area and is 5 miles from its closest competitive center. Demographic data show this to be a rapidly growing area.

Construction is scheduled to be started in six months and will cost $6 per square foot. This figure does not include interior finishing work but does include the cost of parking space which is required for each square foot of interior space.

Of the 140,000 square feet of land available no more than 45,000 square feet of floor space can be used according to local zoning restrictions. The rest must be used for parking and aesthetic purposes.

The problem which the company now faces is to determine how this 45,000 square feet of space is to be divided. There are 12 possible types of stores which can be included. The list is given in Exhibit A. Since certain types of stores are considered essential, the list is divided into groups and each group has a minimum number of square feet. In group A, however, it is considered essential to have both a supermarket and a discount department store. Each of these must have at least 10,000 square feet. To prevent unreasonably large stores, maximum sizes are also given in Exhibit A.

Once it is determined how the space is to be divided, it is very unlikely that any difficulty will be encountered in obtaining tenants. Since there is a broad market for shopping center space within a reasonable distance, the rental fees are market-determined and will be readily accepted by the tenants. It is expected, therefore, that there will be no negotiation on price.

The criterion by which a shopping center is judged is the present value of its after-tax flows. These flows are shown in column 2 of Exhibit A. They represent the present value of rent revenues less fixed charges, depreciation, and taxes over the seven-year life of the project. To this is added the projected sale price of the property when it is sold. The figures are given on a per-square-foot basis and do not include interior improvements. Mr. Wasser has argued, however, that the net of these two figures should be used. The cost of interior improvements is given in column 1 of Exhibit A.

Vista's available capital for financing interior improvement is limited to $450,000. It is unlikely that any additional funds could be acquired.

An essential financial consideration for these centers is that the guarantee rent must cover the fixed charges including interest charges on the debt. Each tenant must sign a lease which guarantees Vista a fixed rental payment each year. In addition, if the tenants' sales revenue exceeds a certain level, a percentage (6 percent) of this excees is paid to Vista. The guarantee rents for each type of store are given in column 3 of Exhibit A. Fixed charges are estimated to be $125,000.

The Option

Vista has an option to purchase 20,000 square feet of land adjacent to its present parcel. Only 6,000 square feet can be used for stores. The option will expire in 3 months and carries a price of $10 per square foot of land.

Capital outlay for this additional parcel has been computed in the following way:

Land costs: $10 per square foot × 20,000 square feet	= $200,000
Construction costs: $6 per square foot × 6000 square feet	= 36,000
Interior improvements (average): $10 per square foot × 6000 square feet	= 60,000
Total Capital Required	$296,000

To raise this capital, Mr. Wasser would borrow as much as possible and then issue common stock for the remainder. This would add $29,000 per year to his fixed charges, assuming an average capital cost of slightly less than 10 percent.

Exhibit A Shopping Center Data

Group	Type of store	Cost of interior improvements[1]	Present value[1]	Guarantee rent[1]	Group min[2]	Store max[2]
A	1 Supermarket	9	60	3.2	20	20.0
	2 Discount store	13	80	4.1		20.0
B	3 Fabric	12	45	3.0	2	0.9
	4 Women's specialty	8	50	3.2		3.0
	5 Men's specialty	7	48	3.2		2.0
C	6 Hardware	6	50	3.0	2	4.0
	7 Drug	7	46	3.1		1.6
D	8 Gift	8	35	2.5	2	3.0
	9 Bakery (sales only, no baking)	9	50	2.4		1.3
	10 Ice cream/sandwich	10	40	2.6		1.5
	11 Music and hi-fi	7	46	2.3		1.5
	12 Barber	11	35	3.0		1.0

[1]Dollars per square foot
[2]Thousand of square feet

You have been hired as a consultant to help Mr. Wasser by applying management science techniques to this particular problem. Prepare a report for Vista Properties, Inc. that addresses:

1. The stores that should be included in the complex, the number of square feet that should be allocated for each store, and the expected annual revenue.
2. A recommendation regarding the purchase option, including its impact upon the stores to be included, the square foot allocations, and the expected annual revenue.

Transportation and Assignment

By the end of this chapter, you should be able to:

1

recognize transportation and assignment problems;

2

formulate them using LP and the transportation or assignment tableau;

3

solve transportation and assignment problems using a computer program, LP, and the special purpose algorithms.

The transportation and assignment models introduced in this chapter are special applications of linear programming. These models, also called distribution models or linear programming network models, deal with physical allocations. The transportation model is used to determine the best allocation of a product from its point of origin to its point of demand; that is, to select the shipping route that will optimize a given objective (usually to minimize total shipping costs). The assignment model is concerned with optimal one-to-one allocations, such as assigning candidates to positions, sales people to territories, or jobs to machines.

These problems can be formulated and solved as LP problems using simplex or the LP computer solutions introduced earlier, but special-purpose transportation and assignment algorithms are easier and computationally more efficient to use. In this chapter we will demonstrate the LP formulation of these problems and then discuss the more efficient special-purpose algorithms. In this way you should gain a better understanding of the components of the problems and a feel for what is happening in the solution. We will also demonstrate the practicality of using computer solutions for larger-scale problems, and introduce some problems that can be solved using a transportation algorithm even though they are not obviously distribution problems.

Fresh Fish, Fast Frozen

Fresh Fish, Fast Frozen ships frozen North Atlantic whitefish from their plants to warehouses in the Northeast for later distribution to specialty stores and restaurants in the Midwest. The fish is fast-frozen at harbor sites along the Northeast seacoast.

FFFF now has plants in Boothbay Harbor, Maine; Gloucester, Massachusetts; and Mystic, Connecticut. Their warehouses are located in Burlington, Vermont; Syracuse, New York; Jamestown, New York; and Harrisburg, Pennsylvania. Currently the plant in Boothbay Harbor is able to supply 300 tons of fish weekly, Gloucester supplies 500 tons weekly, and Mystic freezes 450 tons weekly. The weekly demand in tons at each warehouse is known to be: Syracuse—350, Burlington—400, Jamestown—300, and Harrisburg—200. Per unit shipping cost along each route depends directly upon distance (including driver costs and fuel costs) and such costs as tolls and local road use taxes. FFFF has figured the costs to be as follows: from Boothbay Harbor to Syracuse $20, to Burlington $27, to Jamestown $35, to Harrisburg $15; from Gloucester to Syracuse $18, to Burlington $31, to Jamestown $23, and to Harrisburg $19; from Mystic to Syracuse $12, to Burlington $17, to Jamestown $14, and to Harrisburg $28. Faced with rising shipping costs, FFFF management is in the process of selecting shipping routes that will minimize their transportation costs.

7.1 *AN INTRODUCTION TO THE TRANSPORTATION PROBLEM*

Transportation problems have certain unique characteristics. Basically, **transportation problems** are concerned with selecting routes for transporting a homogeneous product from a number of sources to a number of destinations. The supply and demand quantities are known and are assumed to be constant. The per unit shipping costs from each source to each destination are also known and assumed to be constant. Usually (not always) the objective is to find the lowest total shipping cost. Obviously this has to be done without violating the supply and demand constraints. Thus, we can recognize the components of a transportation problem as (1) a limited supply available at a number of sources, (2) a fixed demand required at a number of destinations, (3) given supply and demand quantities that are assumed to be constant, and (4) known per-unit shipping costs for each route (source to destination). It is also assumed that there are no shipments between sources or between destinations.

Solving Transportation Problems

Transportation problems can be solved using either LP or special-purpose algorithms that take advantage of their network structure, thus permitting solution by computational procedures that are more efficient, streamlined versions of simplex. In this chapter, we are concerned primarily with describing solution by special-purpose algorithms. These procedures ususally cut computation time and enable us to solve larger problems that might otherwise be unsolvable.

In general, transportation problems are solved using an iterative technique in which the model is formulated and an initial feasible solution is developed and tested for optimality. If it is not optimal, it is progressively improved until optimality is achieved. The calculations required are generally quite simple. We will begin by demonstrating the model formulation using the Fresh Fish, Fast Frozen (FFFF) problem introduced earlier.

The information culled from the problem can be arranged in the following tables to enable us to see it better:

Supply		Demand	
Boothbay Harbor	300	Syracuse	350
Gloucester	500	Burlington	400
Mystic	450	Jamestown	300
		Harrisburg	200

Per Unit Shipping Costs for Each Route

Boothbay Harbor		*Gloucester*		*Mystic*	
to:		to:		to:	
Syracuse	$20	Syracuse	$18	Syracuse	$12
Burlington	$27	Burlington	$31	Burlington	$17
Jamestown	$35	Jamestown	$23	Jamestown	$14
Harrisburg	$15	Harrisburg	$19	Harrisburg	$28

This problem can be represented graphically as a network. Figure 7.1 shows the various transportation routes, supply sources, demand destinations, and shipping costs for each route. In Chapter 10, we will discuss such networks and network models in detail.

7.2 *MODEL FORMULATION OF TRANSPORTATION PROBLEMS*

Since transportation is a special application of linear programming, we will first formulate the FFFF problem as an LP model because of its familiarity.

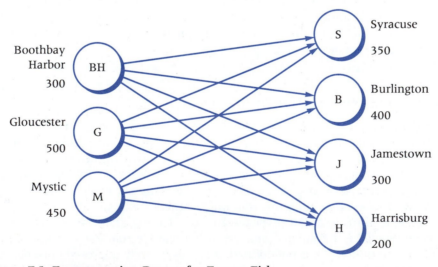

Figure 7.1 Transportation Routes for Frozen Fish

LP Formulation

The objective in this problem is to minimize total shipping cost. The objective function can be stated as the per-unit shipping cost multiplied by the quantity shipped, for each of the shipping routes (from each source, i, to each destination, j). The quantities shipped are designated X_{ij} for each $i = 1, 2, 3, \ldots m$ and each $j = 1, 2, 3, \ldots n$ as follows:

X_{11} = Quantity shipped from Boothbay Harbor to Syracuse
X_{12} = Quantity shipped from Boothbay Harbor to Burlington
X_{13} = Quantity shipped from Boothbay Harbor to Jamestown
X_{14} = Quantity shipped from Boothbay Harbor to Harrisburg
X_{21} = Quantity shipped from Gloucester to Syracuse
X_{22} = Quantity shipped from Gloucester to Burlington
X_{23} = Quantity shipped from Gloucester to Jamestown
X_{24} = Quantity shipped from Gloucester to Harrisburg
X_{31} = Quantity shipped from Mystic to Syracuse
X_{32} = Quantity shipped from Mystic to Burlington
X_{33} = Quantity shipped from Mystic to Jamestown
X_{34} = Quantity shipped from Mystic to Harrisburg

Shipping routes are source to destination; for example, X_{11} is the route from source 1, Boothbay Harbor, to destination 1, Syracuse. Thus the rather long objective function is stated

$$\text{MIN } 20X_{11} + 27X_{12} + 35X_{13} + 15X_{14} + 18X_{21} + 31X_{22} + 23X_{23} +$$
$$19X_{24} + 12X_{31} + 17X_{32} + 14X_{33} + 28X_{34}$$

The constraints in a transportation problem are of two general types, supply and demand. In this problem, since supply equals demand, the constraints are equalities and are stated as follows:

Supply Constraints

$$X_{11} + X_{12} + X_{13} + X_{14} = 300$$

$$X_{21} + X_{22} + X_{23} + X_{24} = 700$$

$$X_{31} + X_{32} + X_{33} + X_{34} = 400$$

Demand Constraints

$$X_{11} + X_{21} + X_{31} = 200$$

$$X_{12} + X_{22} + X_{32} = 450$$

$$X_{13} + X_{23} + X_{33} = 350$$

$$X_{14} + X_{24} + X_{34} = 400$$

The complete LP formulation is

$$\text{MIN } 20X_{11} + 27X_{12} + 35X_{13} + 15X_{14} + 18X_{21} + 31X_{22} + 23X_{23} +$$
$$19X_{24} + 12X_{31} + 17X_{32} + 14X_{33} + 28X_{34}$$

Subject to

$$X_{11} + X_{12} + X_{13} + X_{14} = 300$$

$$X_{21} + X_{22} + X_{23} + X_{24} = 500$$

$$X_{31} + X_{32} + X_{33} + X_{34} = 450$$

$$X_{11} + X_{21} + X_{31} = 350$$

$$X_{12} + X_{22} + X_{32} = 400$$

$$X_{13} + X_{23} + X_{33} = 300$$

$$X_{14} + X_{24} + X_{34} = 200$$

$$X_{11}, X_{12}, X_{13}, X_{14}, X_{21}, X_{22}, X_{23}, X_{24}, X_{31}, X_{32}, X_{33}, X_{34} \geq 0$$

Figure 7.2 shows the computer solution to this problem. The optimal solution has a cost of \$22,650, with 6 of 12 possible routes used. Variable A5 is an artificial variable with a value of 0. Since all variables have coefficients of 1 and all RHS values are whole numbers, the solution values are all integer values.

The Transportation Tableau

The transportation model can also be formulated (or displayed) in tabular form. The **transportation tableau** provides a convenient, concise framework for presenting all the relevant data. Further, it provides a "visual" representation of the problem. For computer solutions, it helps ensure that the necessary data are available for input. For manual solutions—especially for small, daily problems that can be solved quickly and relatively painlessly with the transportation algorithms—it also serves to facilitate the search for progressively better solutions.

Explanation of the Tableau

The tableau shows the supply at each source and the demand at each destination. Sources are represented by rows. Destinations are represented by columns. The

```
            AFTER 14 ITERATIONS,
        THIS SOLUTION IS OPTIMAL:

        VARIABLE        QUANTITY
        --------        --------

          BHB             100
          BHH             200
          GS              350
          GJ              150
          MB              300
          MJ              150
          AS                0
        OPTIMAL  Z = 22650
```

Figure 7.2 Solution to Frozen Fish Problem

cells formed by the rows (sources) and columns (destinations) represent a route from each source to each destination. The number in the upper right-hand corner of each cell is the per-unit cost of sending the item along that route. Table 7.1 shows the general form for the transportation tableau.

Specifically:

Left side: The sources of supply are listed on the left side, with each row representing one source.

Right side: The supplies available at each source (capacity or supply constraints) are listed in the right-most column.

Top Row: The destinations, points of demand, are listed along the top row, with each column representing one destination.

Bottom Row: The requirements for each destination (demand constraints) are listed here.

Table: The center of the table is composed of cells, formed by the rows and columns, which represent the shipping routes, one for each source to each destination. They are designated by the row and column numbers (cell 1,1 is in row 1, column 1). Each cell also shows, in the upper right-hand corner, the corresponding per-unit shipping cost. This is shown in Table 7.1 as C_{11} in cell 1,1. Each cell also contains a decision variable, representing the quantity to be shipped along that route. In Table 7.1, cell 1,1 contains the decision variable X_{11}—the quantity to be shipped from source 1 to destination 1.

Table 7.2 shows the transportation tableau for the FFFF problem.

Notice that each row represents a supply constraint and each column represents a demand constraint. Also note that supply exactly equals demand. This is known as a **balanced problem.** Problems with supply exceeding demand or demand exceeding supply are unbalanced problems. Before solving unbalanced problems, they must be changed to balanced problems through the addition of a dummy (imaginary) row or column. This will be explained in greater detail in section 7.5.

Table 7.1 Transportation Tableau

From source	To destination			
	1	2	3	Supply
1	C_{11} X_{11}			
2				
3				
Demand				Total Supply Total Demand

Table 7.2 Transportation Tableau for Frozen Fish Example

To From	Syracuse 1		Burlington 2		Jamestown 3		Harrisburg 4		Supply
Boothbay Harbor 1		20		27		35		15	300
Gloucester 2		18		31		23		19	500
Mystic 3		12		17		14		28	450
Demand	350		400		300		200		1250 1250

7.3 *DEVELOPING AN INITIAL SOLUTION*

An initial feasible solution is any allocation that satisfies all of the requirements of the problem, while not violating any of the constraints. All supplies are allocated and all demands are met. This initial solution provides the starting point from which improvement in the objective function can be made. From among several methods available for finding an initial solution, we have chosen to present two: the Northwest Corner Rule and a Minimum Cell or Least Cost Method.[1]

Northwest Corner Rule

The Northwest Corner Rule is a systematic, mechanical method for finding an initial solution that does not take cost into consideration when making an allocation to a cell. It does, however, offer the advantage of being quick and extremely easy to use. We will begin our explanation with an overview of the procedure, and then apply it specifically to the FFFF problem.

The NW Corner Method begins in the upper left-hand cell, the "northwest" corner of the tableau. As many units as possible are allocated to that route. This allocation is the smaller amount of either the row supply or the column demand. The amount allocated will either exhaust the supply in the row or meet the demand in the column. It cannot exceed either or the constraint will be violated. Next, that allocated amount is subtracted from the demand column and the row supply. Subsequent allocations are made to an adjacent cell, which may be one cell to the right, down one cell, or to the right and down one, depending upon the supply available or the demand yet to be met. Demands are satisfied by moving in a sequential manner left to right, while supplies are depleted by moving from top to bottom. Each allocation eliminates a row or column and reduces the number of feasible cells remaining. In effect, each allocation gives us a new table with a new NW corner. Allocations are made sequentially to each new NW corner.

---

[1]If the reader is interested in learning about Vogel's Approximation Method (VAM), another initial solution method, see Fredrick S. Hiller and Gerald J. Lieberman, *Introduction to Operations Research,* 4th ed. (Oakland, CA: Holden-Day, Inc., 1986). 200–202.

Now using the FFFF example, Table 7.3, let's see how this works. Beginning in the upper left-hand corner (cell 1,1), as many units (tons) are allocated as possible. This will be the smaller of the demand (350) and the supply (300), therefore, 300 tons are allocated. The constraints are not violated and the supply is exhausted at Boothbay Harbor. Table 7.3 also shows the allocation subtracted from the row and column. In order to keep track of things, we can draw a line through the remainder of this row to indicate that no further allocations can be made from Boothbay Harbor.

Now we make allocation to a feasible adjacent cell. In this case, since the supply in this row has been exhausted, it is necessary to move down one row. This is now the current NW corner. Fifty units, the smaller of the row supply or column demand, are allocated to cell 2,1. We subtract the allocations from the row and column and cross out the remaining cells in that column, since the demand at Syracuse has now been met. This is shown in Table 7.4.

Table 7.3 Initial Allocation to Northwest Corner Frozen Fish

To \ From	Syracuse 1	Burlington 2	Jamestown 3	Harrisburg 4	Supply
Boothbay Harbor 1	20 300	27	35	15	~~300~~ 0
Gloucester 2	18	31	23	19	500
Mystic 3	12	17	14	28	450
Demand	50 ~~350~~	400	300	200	1250 1250

Table 7.4 Second NW Allocation: Frozen Fish Example

To \ From	Syracuse 1	Burlington 2	Jamestown 3	Harrisburg 4	Supply
Boothbay Harbor 1	20 300	27	35	15	~~300~~ 0
Gloucester 2	18 50	31	23	19	~~500~~ 450
Mystic 3	12	17	14	28	450
Demand	50 ~~350~~ 0	400	300	200	1250 1250

Since the demand at Syracuse (column 1) has been met and there are still units available at Gloucester, we make the next allocation (400 units) to cell 2,2. This is the next available NW corner. This allocation satisfies demand at Burlington and reduces the supply from Gloucester to 50, as shown in Table 7.5.

Demand has been satisfied in columns 1 and 2, and supply has been used up in row 1. The area of feasible cells has shrunk to 4 cells: 2,3; 2,4; 3,3; and 3,4. We continue making allocations to the new NW corner. Since the supply from Gloucester has not been exhausted, we make the next allocation to the cell to the right, 2,3. Fifty units will deplete the supply at Gloucester. The final two allocations are made to 3,3 and 3,4. Table 7.6 shows the fourth and fifth allocations. This tableau represents the initial feasible solution. The cells that have allocations are referred to as **occupied cells.** All demands have been met and all supplies have been exhausted; the sum of allocations in each column equals the demand for that column, and the sum of allocations in each row equals the supply available for that row.

Table 7.5 Third NW Allocation: Frozen Fish Example

To \ From	Syracuse 1	Burlington 2	Jamestown 3	Harrisburg 4	Supply
Boothbay Harbor 1	20 / 300	27	35	15	300 / 0
Gloucester 2	18 / 50	31 / 400	23	19	500 / 450 50
Mystic 3	12	17	14	28	450
Demand	350 50 0	400 0	300	200	1250 / 1250

Table 7.6 Initial Feasible Solution

To \ From	Syracuse 1	Burlington 2	Jamestown 3	Harrisburg 4	Supply
Boothbay Harbor 1	20 / 300	27	35	15	300 / 0
Gloucester 2	18 / 50	31 / 400	23 / 50	19	500 / 450 50 0
Mystic 3	12	17	14 / 250	28 / 200	450 / 0
Demand	350 50 0	400 0	250 300 0	200 0	1250 / 1250

We compute the transportation cost (total shipping cost) of this solution by multiplying the per-unit shipping cost for each occupied cell (route chosen) by the allocation made to that cell.

$$20(300) + 18(50) + 31(400) + 23(50) + 14(250) + 28(200) = 29,550$$

Figure 7.3 summarizes the route allocations and the costs.

Northwest Corner is a systematic approach to finding an initial solution and is relatively easy to use. Since this approach does not consider cost in making allocations, however, it is unlikely that this initial solution will be optimal. Next, we will examine an initial solution procedure that does take cost into consideration, and usually yields a better solution.

Least Cost Method

The Least Cost Method (also called minimum cell, or minimum cost) is one of several methods that try to use costs to arrive at an initial solution. It is an intuitive approach, heuristic in nature, that proceeds logically, making allocations to cells with the lowest costs, until all demand is satisfied and supplies are depleted. Accordingly, as much as possible is allocated to the cell having the minimum cost. A tie (more than one cell with the same cost) is broken arbitrarily. The amount allocated is sufficient to exhaust either the corresponding supply or demand (obviously the smaller of the two amounts). The next allocation is made to the cell with the least cost that has not been eliminated. The process is repeated until all possible allocations have been made. We will use our Frozen Fish example to demonstrate this method and compare the results with those obtained using Northwest Corner.

The lowest cost in the tableau is $12, in cell 3,1. Thus, an initial allocation of 350 tons is made to cell 3,1, satisfying demand at Syracuse and reducing the supply at Mystic to 100. The initial allocation is shown in Table 7.7. The routes 1,1 and 2,1 can no longer be considered, and will not be used in the initial solution. Cell 3,3 is now the least cost cell. We make an allocation of 100 units to this route, because only 100 units remain available at Mystic. This allocation depletes the supply for row 3, as shown in Table 7.8. The crossed out areas are those routes that can no longer be used.

The next allocation, 200 units, is made to cell 1,4, with the least cost of 15. This meets the demand at Harrisburg and reduces the supply available at Boothbay Harbor to 100. We make the fourth allocation, 200 units, to cell 2,3, satisfying demand

Figure 7.3 NW Corner Initial Solution Cost

Route	Pounds of Fish	Cost/lb	Cost
Bar Harbor to Syracuse (1, 1)	300	$20	$ 6,000
Gloucester to Syracuse (2, 1)	50	18	900
Gloucester to Burlington (2, 2)	400	31	12,400
Gloucester to Jamestown (2, 3)	50	23	1,150
Mystic to Jamestown (3, 3)	250	14	3,500
Mystic to Harrisburg (3, 4)	200	28	5,600
Total Cost			$29,550

Table 7.7 Initial Least Cost Cell Allocation

To / From	Syracuse 1	Burlington 2	Jamestown 3	Harrisburg 4	Supply
Boothbay Harbor 1	20	27	35	15	300
Gloucester 2	18	31	23	19	500
Mystic 3	12 350	17	14	28	4̶5̶0̶ 100
Demand	0 3̶5̶0̶	400	300	200	1250 1250

Table 7.8 Second Allocation to Least Cost Cell

To / From	Syracuse 1	Burlington 2	Jamestown 3	Harrisburg 4	Supply
Boothbay Harbor 1	20	27	35	15	300
Gloucester 2	18	31	23	19	500
Mystic 3	12 350	17	14 100	28	4̶5̶0̶ 1̶0̶0̶ 0
Demand	0 3̶5̶0̶	400	200 3̶0̶0̶	200	1250 1250

at Jamestown and reducing the supply from Gloucester to 300. Table 7.9 shows these two allocations. Note that, with four allocations made, there are only two available cells remaining, 1,2 and 2,2.

The fifth allocation, 100 units, is made to cell 1,2 with the current least cost of 27. This exhausts supply at Boothbay Harbor. Finally, we allocate 300 units to the remaining available cell, 2,2. The initial solution is shown in Table 7.10. All demands have been satisfied. All supplies have been used up. This can be verified by adding up the allocations in each column and in each row.

The total cost of this solution is $25,200, as compared to the $29,550 cost of the NW corner solution and $22,650 optimal cost. Figure 7.4 shows the routes used with this solution and the associated costs. The initial solution arrived at using the least cost method usually is closer to optimal and requires fewer iterations to achieve optimality.

Once an initial solution has been found, it is necessary to test to see if this is the best solution and then, if the solution is not optimal, to generate an improved solution.

Table 7.9 Third and Fourth Allocations to Least Cost Cells

To From	Syracuse 1	Burlington 2	Jamestown 3	Harrisburg 4	Supply
Boothbay Harbor 1	20	27	35	15	~~300~~ 100
Gloucester 2	18	31	23 200	19	~~500~~ 300
Mystic 3	12 350	17	14 100	28	~~450~~ ~~100~~ 0
Demand	0 ~~350~~	400	~~200~~ 0 ~~300~~	0 ~~200~~	1250 1250

Table 7.10 Initial Solution by Least Cost Method

To From	Syracuse 1	Burlington 2	Jamestown 3	Harrisburg 4	Supply
Boothbay Harbor 1	20	27 100	35	15 200	~~300~~ ~~100~~ 0
Gloucester 2	18	31 300	23 200	19	~~500~~ ~~300~~ 0
Mystic 3	12 350	17	14 100	28	~~450~~ ~~100~~ 0
Demand	0 ~~350~~	0 ~~400~~	~~200~~ 0 ~~300~~	0 ~~200~~	1250 1250

Figure 7.4 Least Cost Initial Solution Cost

Route	Pounds of Fish	Cost/lb	Cost
Boothbay Harbor to Burlington (1, 2)	100	$27	$ 2,700
Boothbay Harbor to Harrisburg (1,4)	200	15	3,000
Gloucester to Burlington (2, 2)	300	31	9,300
Gloucester to Jamestown (2, 3)	200	23	4,600
Mystic to Syracuse (3, 1)	350	12	4,200
Mystic to Jamestown (3, 3)	100	14	1,400
Total Cost			$25,200

7.4 *TESTING FOR OPTIMALITY AND GENERATING AN IMPROVED SOLUTION*

Two solution methods are used to test for optimality and to generate an improved solution: the stepping stone method and the MODI method. Both methods systematically examine unused shipping routes, which are represented in the tableau by unoccupied cells (or **empty cells**), to determine whether using any of these routes would result in lower total costs (or higher total profits). If such a route is found, as many units as possible are allocated to it. This results in a new solution, which is then evaluated for optimality. The process is repeated until no better route exists. In the transportation tableau, occupied cell quantities are basic variable values and empty cells are nonbasic variable values (zero).

We will discuss both the stepping stone method and the MODI method in greater detail in the following sections. With either procedure, in order to test a solution for optimality, the number of occupied cells must be equal to the total number of rows plus columns minus 1:

$$\text{number of occupied cells} = m + n - 1$$

If this condition or rule is not met, the solution is **degenerate.** We will discuss **degeneracy** and how to handle it later in the chapter. Both of the initial solutions generated for the example problem conform to this rule: 3 rows + 4 columns − 1 = 6 occupied cells. We begin with the stepping stone method.

Stepping Stone Method

In order to evaluate an unused route, the net impact on the total cost of using that route must be determined. This is accomplished by evaluating costs on a per-unit basis as one unit is transferred from an existing route (occupied cell) to an unused route (empty cell). This involves calculation of what is called a cell evaluator or cost index value for the unused cell. A **cell evaluator** indicates the cost change that results from the addition of one unit to that cell. The transfer or shift of units from one cell to another is subject to supply and demand constraints and involves a minimum of four cells. The number of cells involved in a transfer is always an even number. All empty cells are evaluated. We will examine this technique in detail using the initial solution to the FFFF problem generated using the least cost method, repeated in Table 7.11.

There are six empty cells to be evaluated: 1,1; 1,3; 2,1; 2,4; 3,2; and 3,4. Although cell 1,1 is a logical starting point, we will evaluate cell 3,2 first for demonstration purposes because the evaluation is less complicated. Thus, we allocate one unit to cell 3,2. This allocation violates the demand in column 2 (401 units) and the supply in row 3 (451 units). Clearly, if there is to be a transfer or shifting of allocations, we must adjust other affected cells to maintain demand and supply requirements. First we trace a path showing the possible transfer or shift in allocations. The path follows a direct route from the empty cell via occupied cells back to the same empty cell. This is referred to as a stepping stone path and is a **closed loop.** There are certain guidelines for drawing these paths.

1. Begin with an empty cell and move to an occupied cell, using only horizontal or vertical movements. Diagonal moves are not allowed.
2. Use the most direct route to return to the cell being evaluated. It may be necessary to step over or skip occupied cells. Empty cells are always skipped. This is analogous to using stepping stones to cross a pond. The empty cells represent-

Table 7.11 Least Cost Method Initial Solution

To From	Syracuse 1	Burlington 2	Jamestown 3	Harrisburg 4	Supply
Boothbay Harbor 1	20	27 100	35	15 200	300
Gloucester 2	18	31 300	23 200	19	500
Mystic 3	12 350	17	14 100	28	450
Demand	350	400	300	200	1250 1250

water and should not be stepped into. The occupied cells represent stepping stones. Skipped-over cells are not affected or changed in this process. Corners or 90° turns in the path can occur only at occupied cells and at the empty cell being evaluated. The loop can cross over itself, but there is always an even number of cells in a path, with a minimum of four.

3. Assign plus (+) and minus (−) signs alternately at each corner cell of the path. In any row or column there must be exactly one plus and one minus. Begin with a plus (+) in the empty cell being evaluated. These signs represent the addition or subtraction of one unit to or from a cell. The balance of plus and minus signs in the closed loop assures that the constraints have not been violated.

In Table 7.12, a plus sign has been entered in cell 3,2, indicating the addition of one unit to this cell. This is the start of the path. However, adding one unit to that cell violates both the column and row constraints. As we trace the path, we will demonstrate how to adjust the allocations so that the net gain in either a row or column is zero and no constraints are violated.

Now we can draw the stepping stone path. Starting with cell 3,2, the cell being evaluated, we draw a vertical line to the occupied cell 2,2. A minus sign is entered

Table 7.12 Evaluation of Cell 3,2

To From	Syracuse 1	Burlington 2	Jamestown 3	Harrisburg 4	Supply
Boothbay Harbor 1	20	27 100	35	15 200	300
Gloucester 2	18	31 300 −	23 200 +	19	500
Mystic 3	12 350	17 ① +	14 100 −	28	450
Demand	350	400	300	200	1250 1250

there, indicating the subtraction of one unit from its current allocation. Column 2 demand has not been violated: $100 + 299 + 1 = 400$. The supply for row 2 has been changed, however, violating the supply constraint. Since one unit must now be added to an occupied cell in that row, we draw a horizontal line to cell 2,3, where a plus (+) sign is entered. This balances the supply constraint, but violates the demand constraint for column 3. Drawing a vertical line down to cell 3,3 and entering a minus to represent the subtraction of one unit from that cell remedies the situation. Notice that, when this unit is subtracted from 3,3, the supply constraint is not violated, since one unit has already been added to this row in cell 3,2, the starting point. This completes the path, closing the loop. There are no change in supplies or demands.

This path involved just four adjacent cells (which is why cell 3,2 was selected as the first cell for evaluation). Not all paths are this easy to trace. It may help to realize that, in a given solution (for a non-degenerate problem), there is only one possible path for each empty cell (although the path may be drawn in either a clockwise or counterclockwise direction).

In evaluating a cell, we examine increases and decreases in costs that result from this shifting process. The cell evaluator represents the net change in total costs. This reallocation increased the cost at cell 3,2 by $17, reduced cost at cell 2,2 by $31, increased cost at cell 2,3 by $23, and reduced cost at cell 3,3 by $14. The net result is a reduced cost of $5.

$$\begin{array}{cccc} 3,2 & 2,2 & 2,3 & 3,3 \\ +17 & -31 & +23 & -14 = -5 \end{array}$$

In other words, the value of a cell evaluator is found by subtracting the sum of the per-unit shipping costs in the losing cells (cells with minus signs) from the sum of the per-unit shipping costs in the gaining cells (cells with plus signs).

By shipping one ton of frozen fish from Mystic to Burlington, an unused route, FFFF can reduce total shipping costs by $5 per ton. This result indicates that the current solution can be improved and is therefore not optimal. It is necessary to continue evaluating unused cells until all the empty cells have been tested before selecting the one that will most improve the solution.

We will evaluate empty cell 1,1 next. Table 7.13 shows the more complicated closed path for this evaluation, involving six cells.

Table 7.13 Evaluation of Cell 1, 1

To / From	Syracuse 1	Burlington 2	Jamestown 3	Harrisburg 4	Supply
Boothbay Harbor 1	+ ←—20— ①	— — 27 / 100	35	15 / 200	300
Gloucester 2	18	+ ←—31— 300	— 23 / 200	19	500
Mystic 3	— —12 350	—17—	→+ 14 / 100	28	450
Demand	350	400	300	200	1250 / 1250

Notice that, in each row and column, there is exactly one plus (+) and one minus (−). Corners occur only at occupied cells, and none of the constraints has been violated. The total cost impact of this path is +3:

$$
\begin{array}{cccccc}
1,1 & 1,2 & 2,2 & 2,3 & 3,3 & 3,1 \\
+20 & -27 & +31 & -23 & +14 & -12 = 3
\end{array}
$$

For each unit shipped along this route there would be an increased cost of $3. Thus, a move to this route will increase the total cost, which is undesirable in the minimization problem.

The closed loops and computations for the remaining four empty cells, 2,1; 3,4; 1,3; and 2,4 are shown in Tables 7.14 through 7.17.

Table 7.14 Evaluation of Cell 2,1

To From	Syracuse 1	Burlington 2	Jamestown 3	Harrisburg 4	Supply
Boothbay Harbor 1	20	27 100	35	15 200	300
Gloucester 2	+ ←18 ①	31 300	23 200	19	500
Mystic 3	12 350	17	14 100	28	450
Demand	350	400	300	200	1250 1250

$$
\begin{array}{cccc}
2,1 & 2,3 & 3,3 & 3,1 \\
+18 & -23 & +14 & -12 = -3
\end{array}
$$

Table 7.15 Evaluation of Cell 3,4

To From	Syracuse 1	Burlington 2	Jamestown 3	Harrisburg 4	Supply
Boothbay Harbor 1	20	+ ←27 100	35 200	15	300
Gloucester 2	18	31 300	23 200	19	500
Mystic 3	12 350	17	14 100	+ ① 28	450
Demand	350	400	300	200	1250 1250

$$
\begin{array}{cccccc}
3,4 & 3,3 & 2,3 & 2,2 & 1,2 & 1,4 \\
+28 & -14 & +23 & -31 & +27 & -15 = 18
\end{array}
$$

Table 7.16 Evaluation of Cell 2,4

To From	Syracuse 1	Burlington 2	Jamestown 3	Harrisburg 4	Supply
Boothbay Harbor 1	20	+ ← 27 100	35	15 200	300
Gloucester 2	18	31 300	23 200	+ ① 19	500
Mystic 3	12 350	17	14 100	28	450
Demand	350	400	300	200	1250 1250

$$\begin{array}{cccc} 2,4 & 2,2 & 1,2 & 1,4 \\ +19 & -31 & +27 & -15 = 0 \end{array}$$

Table 7.17 Evaluation of Cell 1,3

To From	Syracuse 1	Burlington 2	Jamestown 3	Harrisburg 4	Supply
Boothbay Harbor 1	20	27 100	+ ① 35	15 200	300
Gloucester 2	18	+ ← 31 300	23 200	19	500
Mystic 3	12 350	17	14 100	28	450
Demand	350	400	300	200	1250 1250

$$\begin{array}{cccc} 1,3 & 2,3 & 2,2 & 1,2 \\ +35 & -23 & +31 & -27 = 16 \end{array}$$

The results of these evaluations are summarized as follows and shown in Table 7.18.

Empty Cell	Cell Evaluator
1,1	3
1,3	16
2,1	−3
2,4	0
3,2	−5
3,4	18

A negative cell evaluator indicates that an allocation made to that cell would result in a reduced cost, the objective in a minimization problem. A positive cell evaluator

Table 7.18 Evaluation of Empty Cells

To From	Syracuse 1	Burlington 2	Jamestown 3	Harrisburg 4	Supply
Boothbay Harbor 1	20 3	27 100	35 16	15 200	300
Gloucester 2	18 −3	31 300	23 200	19 0	500
Mystic 3	12 350	17 −5	14 100	28 18	450
Demand	350	400	300	200	1250 1250

indicates that the solution value would increase in value, the objective in a maximization problem. A zero indicates the existence of another solution just as good as the current one; however, an allocation to this cell results in no change in the total solution value. A zero cell evaluator in the optimal solution indicates that there is an alternate optimal solution (or multiple optimal solutions) available; that is, the value would be the same, but different routes would be involved.

In this example there are two cells with negative cell evaluators, 2,1 and 3,2, indicating that the current solution is not optimal. If one or more of the cell evaluators is negative (in a minimization problem), the existing solution is not optimal.

Developing an Improved Solution Using Stepping Stone

Improving a nonoptimal solution requires identifying the empty cell to be occupied (the incoming cell) and then developing the improved solution by shifting as many units as possible along the path to that cell. In a minimization problem, the entering cell is the cell with the most negative cell evaluator, that is, the cell that will decrease the per unit cost the most. In this problem, cell 3,2 with a cell evaluator of −5 is the incoming cell. If there were a tie between two or more cells with the same value, either one could be selected. The choice is arbitrary. Since cost is decreased on a per-unit basis, as many units as possible should be reallocated. The quantity is determined by comparing the allocations in all of the losing (−) cells *on this path*. Logically, the smallest amount in these losing cells is the quantity to be shifted. Shifting any larger amount would violate a constraint, since it is not possible to shift more units than are available. This quantity is then added to the gaining (+) cells in this loop and subtracted from the losing (−) cells in the loop. One of the losing cells will become empty. In the example problem there are 300 units in cell 2,2 and 100 units in 3,3. Shifitng 100 units along this loop gives the result shown in Table 7.19. Shifting 300 units would have resulted in 100 − 300 = −200 units in cell 3,3—but it's not possible to ship −200 tons of fish! Remember, shifts are made only along the closed loop and only one transfer is made for each iteration. Note that, in the new solution, cell 3,3 becomes empty.

Once again it is necessary to determine whether or not this solution is optimal. This requires repeating the procedure; drawing the closed paths for each empty cell; computing the cell evaluators; and, if necessary, transferring an allocation

Table 7.19   Improved Solution

To \ From	Syracuse 1		Burlington 2		Jamestown 3		Harrisburg 4		Supply
Boothbay Harbor 1		20	100	27		35	200	15	300
Gloucester 2		18	– 300 – 100 = 200	31	+ 200 + 100 = 300	23		19	500
Mystic 3	350	12	+ 0 + 100 = 100	17	– 100 – 100 = 0	14		28	450
Demand	350		400		300		200		1250 / 1250

from an occupied cell to the empty cell entering the next improved solution. Each new solution represents one iteration of the stepping stone method. Table 7.20 shows the cell evaluator values for these empty cells.

When tracing closed loops, it may be necessary to skip over occupied cells as well as unoccupied cells (as in the evaluation of cells 1,1; 2,4; and 3,4). Also, remember that corners or turns can occur only at occupied cells. That is a good way to tell if the path is correct. If there is no occupied cell at which to turn, it means the line is not being drawn correctly.

Since there are still negative cell evaluators, we have not achieved an optimal solution. Cell 2,1, with a cell evaluator of −8, is the cell with the most negative evaluator. Two hundred units are allocated to that cell. Table 7.21 shows this improved solution, after we add the 200 units to the gaining cells and subtract them from the losing cells on the closed path.

Thus, it is necessary to repeat the procedure of testing for optimality and transferring an allocation if necessary to improve the solution. Imagine what it would be like with a very large problem, requiring many iterations. The calculations are

Table 7.20   Cell Evaluators

To \ From	Syracuse 1		Burlington 2		Jamestown 3		Harrisburg 4		Supply
Boothbay Harbor 1		20	100	27		35	200	15	300
	−2				+16				
Gloucester 2		18	200	31	300	23		19	500
	−8						0		
Mystic 3	350	12	100	17		14		28	450
					+5		+23		
Demand	350		400		300		200		1250 / 1250

Table 7.21 Improved Solution Iteration 2

To \ From	Syracuse 1	Burlington 2	Jamestown 3	Harrisburg 4	Supply
Boothbay Harbor 1	20	27 — 100	35	15 — 200	300
Gloucester 2	18 — 200	31	23 — 300	19	500
Mystic 3	12 — 150	17 — 300	14	28	450
Demand	350	400	300	200	1250 / 1250

simple, the procedure straightforward and easy, but it can be time-consuming. In Table 7.22 we show one of the traced loops to demonstrate a loop crossing over itself. The results of these evaluations are summarized in Table 7.23. Table 7.24 shows the improved solution, shifting 150 units (the smaller amount in the two losing cells involved) along the closed loop $3,3-3,1-2,1-2,3$.

Testing this solution for optimality gives the results shown in Table 7.25. All the cell evaluators are positive, indicating an optimal solution. The total cost (the per-unit shipping costs multiplied by the cell allocations) is

$$27(100) + 15(200) + 18(350) + 23(150) + 17(300) + 14(150) = \$22{,}650$$

as compared to the initial least cost solution of \$25,200.

Thus, as we have seen, the stepping stone method is a sequential procedure that begins with an initial feasible solution and uses a search and evaluation technique to find the optimal solution. Each step requires the introduction into the solution

Table 7.22 Evaluation of Cell 1, 3 showing loop crossing itself

To \ From	Syracuse 1	Burlington 2	Jamestown 3	Harrisburg 4	Supply
Boothbay Harbor 1	20	– 27 — 100	+ ① 35	15 — 200	300
Gloucester 2	+ 18 — 200	31	– 23 — 300	19	500
Mystic 3	– 12 — 150	+ 17 — 300	14	28	450
Demand	350	400	300	200	1250 / 1250

1, 3	2, 3	2, 1	3, 1	3, 2	1, 2
+35	−23	+18	−12	+17	−27 = 8

Table 7.23 Cell Evaluators for Iteration 3

To / From	Syracuse 1	Burlington 2	Jamestown 3	Harrisburg 4	Supply
Boothbay Harbor 1	20 / −2	100 / 27	35 / +8	200 / 15	300
Gloucester 2	200 / 18	31 / +8	300 / 23	19 / +8	500
Mystic 3	150 / 12	300 / 17	14 / −3	28 / +23	450
Demand	350	400	300	200	1250 / 1250

Table 7.24 Improved Solution Iteration 3

To / From	Syracuse 1	Burlington 2	Jamestown 3	Harrisburg 4	Supply
Boothbay Harbor 1	20	100 / 27	35	200 / 15	300
Gloucester 2	350 / 18	31	150 / 23	19	500
Mystic 3	12	300 / 17	150 / 14	28	450
Demand	350	400	300	200	1250 / 1250

Table 7.25 Cell Evaluators for Iteration 4

To / From	Syracuse 1	Burlington 2	Jamestown 3	Harrisburg 4	Supply
Boothbay Harbor 1	20 / +1	100 / 27	35 / +11	200 / 15	300
Gloucester 2	350 / 18	31 / +5	150 / 23	19 / +5	500
Mystic 3	12 / +3	300 / 17	150 / 14	28 / +23	450
Demand	350	400	300	200	1250 / 1250

of an empty cell, a route not currently being used, and the subsequent, concurrent elimination of an occupied cell, a route in the current solution. We then evaluate the per-unit cost of introducing each unused cell. Stepping stone is useful because it provides an easy-to-follow, physical representation of what is happening. Note that the cell evaluators for each iteration are the dual or shadow prices that would be obtained in the simplex tableaus, as discussed previously. The MODI method presented next offers an easier way to compute the cell evaluator values.

MODI (Modified Distribution Method)

MODI is a modified version of stepping stone in which the optimality test involves a different approach for calculating the cell evaluators. The evaluator values are determined mathematically without having to draw the closed loops for each empty cell. In MODI only one closed path is drawn—after the unused cell with the best cell evaluator has been identified. This path is used to determine the maximum amount that can be transferred to the entering cell and those cells involved in the shifting process. Once again, the procedure requires that each feasible solution is not degenerate; that is, each solution being tested must have m + n − 1 occupied cells.

MODI uses a two-step procedure for finding cell evaluators. The first step is to compute an index value for each row and each column in the transportation tableau. In the second step, these values are used to compute the cell evaluators for each unoccupied cell. To determine an index for each row, R_i for i = 1, 2, ... m, and each column, K_j for j = 1, 2, ... n, the formula

$$C_{ij} = R_i + K_j$$

is used for every occupied cell, where C_{ij} is the cost associated with cell i, j. To see how this works, we will look at our previous problem, beginning with the least cost initial solution shown in Table 7.26, with the row and column indicators added.

Table 7.26 Initial Solution by Least Cost Method

	To From	K_1 Syracuse 1		K_2 Burlington 2		K_3 Jamestown 3		K_4 Harrisburg 4		Supply
R_1	Boothbay Harbor 1		20	100	27		35	200	15	300
R_2	Gloucester 2		18	300	31	200	23		19	500
R_3	Mystic 3	350	12		17	100	14		28	450
	Demand	350		400		300		200		1250 1250

The occupied cells (the routes being used) give us the following expressions:

Shipping Cost	Expression	
(C_{12})	$R_1 + K_2 = 27$	[1]
(C_{14})	$R_1 + K_4 = 15$	[2]
(C_{22})	$R_2 + K_2 = 31$	[3]
(C_{23})	$R_2 + K_3 = 23$	[4]
(C_{31})	$R_3 + K_1 = 12$	[5]
(C_{33})	$R_3 + K_3 = 14$	[6]

The significance of the R and K values is not their absolute values but their relative value. We are interested in comparing the figures, not in the numerical value itself. There are six equations with seven unknowns. To solve these equations, we arbitrarily assign a value to one of the unknowns and then use the equations to solve for the other values. We will arbitrarily assign R_1 a value of zero ($R_1 = 0$). This value can then be substituted into equation [1] to obtain a value for K_2,

$$0 + K_2 = 27$$

$$K_2 = 27$$

and into equation [2], to obtain a value for K_4.

$$0 + K_4 = 15$$

$$K_4 = 15$$

The value of K_2 (27) can then be substituted into equation [3] to obtain the value of R_2.

$$R_2 + 27 = 31$$

$$R_2 = 31 - 27 = 4$$

Substituting this value into equation [4] gives the value of K_3,

$$4 + K_3 = 23$$

$$K_3 = 23 - 4 = 19$$

which can then be used in equation [6] to obtain the value of R_3.

$$R_3 + 19 = 14$$

$$R_3 = 14 - 19 = -5$$

Substituting this value into equation [5] yields the value for K_1.

$$-5 + K_1 = 12$$

$$K_1 = 12 + 5 = 17$$

The value of all of the row and column indices are summarized here:

Row Index	Column Index
$R_1 = 0$	$K_1 = 17$
$R_2 = 4$	$K_2 = 27$
$R_3 = -5$	$K_3 = 19$
	$K_4 = 15$

In step two, cell evaluators for the empty cells are calculated. For each unused cell, the cell evaluator can be determined by using the equation

$$e_{ij} = C_{ij} - R_i - K_j$$

The process described above can be used to determine the cell evaluators for each of the unoccupied cells. These calculations are shown below and summarized in Table 7.27.

Cell	Expression					Value
1, 1	$e_{11} = C_{11}$ −	R_1 −	K_1			
	20 −	0 −	17	=		3
1, 3	$e_{13} = C_{13}$ −	R_1 −	K_3			
	35 −	0 −	19	=		16
2, 1	$e_{21} = C_{21}$ −	R_2 −	K_1			
	18 −	4 −	17	=		−3
2, 4	$e_{24} = C_{24}$ −	R_2 −	K_4			
	19 −	4 −	15	=		0
3, 2	$e_{32} = C_{32}$ −	R_3 −	K_2			
	17 − (−5) −	27		=		−5
3, 4	$e_{34} = C_{34}$ −	R_3 −	K_4			
	28 − (−5) −	15		=		18

If you check these cell evaluators with those obtained earlier using the stepping stone method, you will find they are exactly the same, as they should be since MODI is simply an alternative calculation method. Now that you have seen the algebraic solution method, you will undoubtedly recognize that, with some practice, you can calculate R and K values directly on the tableau.

From this point on, once the cell evaluators have been computed, the procedure for developing an improved solution is identical to the improvement procedure described with stepping stone. The next step, if the solution is not optimal, is to determine the incoming cell. We find the stepping stone closed loop and determine

Table 7.27 First Iteration Cell Evaluators Using MODI

		K_1	K_2	K_3	K_4	
	To From	Syracuse 1	Burlington 2	Jamestown 3	Harrisburg 4	Supply
R_1	Boothbay Harbor 1	20 +3	27 100	35 +16	15 200	300
R_2	Gloucester 2	18 −3	31 300	23 200	19 0	500
R_3	Mystic 3	12 350	17 −5	14 100	28 +18	450
	Demand	350	400	300	200	1250 1250

the number of units being reallocated on that loop. After the reallocation, we evaluate this improved solution. The process is repeated until an optimal solution is determined.

Summary of Stepping Stone and MODI Methods

Stepping Stone

1. Using the current solution, trace a closed loop for each empty cell and determine the marginal cost of introducing each unused route into the solution.
2. If the solution is not optimal, allocate as much as possible to the empty cell that is entering the solution and adjust the other allocations along this path. For a minimization problem, a solution is optimal if all the cell evaluators are greater than or equal to $0 (\geq 0)$. The entering cell is the one with the most negative cell evaluator, i.e., the one with the greatest net decrease in cost.
3. Return to step 1.

MODI

1. Using the current solution, compute R and K values for each row and column by using the formula $R_i + K_j = C_{ij}$ with each occupied cell.
2. Calculate the cell evaluator for each empty cell, using the formula $e_{ij} = C_{ij} - R_i - K_j$.
3. If the solution is not optimal, allocate as many units as possible to the empty cell with the best cell evaluator value, using the stepping stone path for that cell. For a minimization problem, a solution is optimal if all the cell evaluators are greater than or equal to $0 (\geq 0)$.
4. Return to step 1.

7.5 *SPECIAL SITUATIONS IN TRANSPORTATION PROBLEMS*

Unbalanced Problems

Recall that, in an unbalanced transportation problem, total supply does not equal total demand. The special-purpose algorithms just discussed require a balanced tableau. In general, unbalanced problems are balanced artificially with the addition of either a **dummy destination** (column) or a **dummy supply** (row). When supply is greater than demand, not all of the supply is shipped. A dummy destination, a fictitious column, is added to absorb the excess supply. When demand is greater than supply, not all the demand can be met. The problem is balanced by adding a dummy source, a fictitious row, to meet the excess demand. In either case, the per-unit shipping cost is 0, for obviously nothing is really shipped along this route. When using the least cost method to make initial allocations, zero costs in a dummy row or column should be ignored.

For example, let's change the Frozen Fish example to demonstrate how to balance an unbalanced problem with the addition of an imaginary source or destination, a dummy row or column. Recall that, in the original tableau, total supply equaled total demand, $1250 = 1250$. If the demand at Syracuse were changed from 350 to 450 units, the tableau would be unbalanced, with an excess demand of 100 units (demand greater than supply).

To balance the tableau, we add a dummy row—a fictitious source whose supply equals the difference between total actual demand and total actual supply. The per-unit shipping cost is zero, since there will not be any actual shipments along this route. Table 7.28 shows this addition. Any supply allocated from this source is really unmet demand. The addition of the dummy source allows a solution to be found that will enable management to supply as much as possible of the demand at minimum cost.

If the supply at Mystic were changed from 450 to 650 units with no change in the original demand, the tableau would be unbalanced with an excess supply of 200 units. There are now 200 tons of frozen fish that will not be shipped. We can balance this table by adding a fictitious destination, a dummy column, with a demand equal to the excess supply as shown in Table 7.29. This dummy destination absorbs the unshipped supply. The shipping cost is again set at zero. When the solution is found, the decision maker can tell not only the optimal shipping route, but also which plant should not be utilized at full capacity.

Table 7.28 Tableau with Dummy Row

To From	Syracuse 1	Burlington 2	Jamestown 3	Harrisburg 4	Supply
Boothbay Harbor 1	20	27	35	15	300
Gloucester 2	18	31	23	19	500
Mystic 3	12	17	14	28	450
Dummy	0	0	0	0	100 (excess)
Demand	450	400	300	200	1350 1350

Table 7.29 Tableau with Dummy Column

To From	Syracuse 1	Burlington 2	Jamestown 3	Harrisburg 4	Dummy	Supply
Boothbay Harbor 1	20	27	35	15	0	300
Gloucester 2	18	31	23	19	0	500
Mystic 3	12	17	14	28	0	650
Demand	450	400	300	200	(excess) 200	1450 1450

Maximization Problems

In our discussion of solution procedures, we have emphasized minimization problems, touching briefly on certain differences in solving problems with a maximization objective. There are two general approaches to a maximization problem. One requires that the signs of the objective function values be changed; for example, all shipping costs with a positive sign ($+$) are changed to negative ($-$), and the problem is treated as a minimization problem. Computer solutions to transportation problems are program specific. Many require only that you indicate whether the problem is a maximization or minimization problem.

In the second approach, the same solution procedure is used with one fundamental difference: the cell evaluators are recognized as marginal returns instead of marginal costs, and the largest return is being sought. Thus for the initial solution, the least cost method becomes the highest return method and allocations are made sequentially to the available cells with highest return or profit. The test for optimality determines whether an allocation to an unused cell results in a higher return, that is, a positive cell evaluator. A positive cell evaluator indicates that the solution value would increase. The allocation is made to the cell with the largest marginal return (positive cell evaluator). If all the unused routes have cell evaluators less than or equal to zero, then an optimal solution has been found.

Restricted Route

There are situations when certain routes are prohibited or unacceptable; in other words, units cannot be shipped from a given source to a specific destination. It must then be insured that, in the optimal solution, no units are allocated to that cell (route). In formulating the transportation problem, this is handled by assigning an arbitrary value, designated as M, to that cell. For a minimization problem, this value represents a very large cost, while in a maximization problem, it is an extremely negative return. When the cell with M is evaluated, its prohibitive value (extremely high cost or negative return) keeps it from being selected as the entering variable. This is the same principle presented in the discussion of the simplex tableau, wherein we assigned a very large coefficient of M to an artificial variable to force it out of the final solution.

Degeneracy

A feasible solution is termed degenerate when there are fewer than $m + n - 1$ occupied cells. This condition can arise in the initial feasible solution or in any intermediate feasible solution. Neither stepping stone nor MODI will work with a degenerate solution. With a degenerate tableau not all the closed paths necessary for the stepping stone method can be traced, nor can all the $C_{ij} = R_i + K_j$ be calculated for the MODI method. Table 7.30 shows an initial solution determined using NW corner. With three rows and three columns, there should be five occupied cells ($3 + 3 - 1 = 5$). Since there are only four, the solution is degenerate.

To solve a transportation problem in which degeneracy occurs, one of the empty cells must be treated as an occupied cell. Thus, a zero (0) is allocated to an unoccupied cell. The zero shows that no real allocation has been made, but it indicates that the cell will be treated as occupied when determining stepping stone paths or MODI formulas. It is necessary to select a cell that allows the stepping stone and

Table 7.30 Degenerate Solution

From \ To	1	2	3	SUPPLY
1	24 75	54 25	70	100
2	36	62 50	46	50
3	40	34	28 100	100
DEMAND	75	75	100	250 250

MODI methods to work. This means that the cell will allow the stepping stone paths to be completed, or the R and K indicators to be calculated. In this example, we need an occupied cell to create a closed loop with cell 3, 3. Placing a zero in any one of four cells (3, 1), (3, 2), (1, 3), or (2, 3) will allow this loop. There is rarely a tableau in which one and only one cell can close a loop. In this case, cell 3, 1 is arbitrarily chosen for the zero allocation, as shown in Table 7.31. The stepping stone paths and cell evaluations for this new tableau are

$$
\begin{array}{llllll}
1,1 = & 1,3 & 3,3 & 3,1 & 1,1 & \\
 & +70 & -28 & +40 & -24 = & 58 \\[6pt]
2,1 = & 2,1 & 1,1 & 1,2 & 2,2 & \\
 & +36 & -24 & +54 & -62 = & 4 \\[6pt]
2,3 = & 2,3 & 3,3 & 3,1 & 1,1 & 1,2 \quad 2,2 \\
 & +46 & -28 & +40 & -24 & +54 \quad -62 = \quad 36 \\[6pt]
3,2 = & 3,2 & 3,1 & 1,1 & 1,2 & \\
 & +34 & -40 & +24 & -54 = & -36
\end{array}
$$

Table 7.31 Degenerate Solution with Artificially Designated Cell

From \ To	1	2	3	SUPPLY
1	24 75	54 25	70	100
2	36	62 50	46	50
3	40 0	34	28 100	100
DEMAND	75	75	100	250 250

This solution is not optimal. Therefore, we must make an allocation to the cell with the smallest cell evaluator, cell 3,2. In this case, the losing cell having the least number of available units is cell 3,1, with zero (0) units. It is not always true that the cell with the artificially designated allocation will be on the closed loop for the entering cell, but it does give us a chance to illustrate what happens in this case. The resulting tableau is shown in Table 7.32. There are still five occupied cells since cell 3,2 is considered occupied. A zero transfer results in the 0 being moved to the cell representing the entering cell. Thus, an iteration is passed through without changing the value of the solution. Testing once again for optimality results in the following marginal costs (cell evaluators):

$$1,3 = 22$$
$$2,1 = 4$$
$$2,3 = -10$$
$$3,1 = 36$$

Cell 2,3 is the entering cell; cell 2,2, with 50 units, is the losing cell. The improved solution is shown in Table 7.33.

Table 7.32 Improved Solution After Zero (0) Transfer

From \ To	1	2	3	SUPPLY
1	24 \ 75	54 \ 25	70	100
2	36	62 \ 50	46	50
3	40	34 \ 0	28 \ 100	100
DEMAND	75	75	100	250 \ 250

Table 7.33 Improved Solution

From \ To	1	2	3	SUPPLY
1	24 \ 75	54 \ 25	70	100
2	36	62	46 \ 50	50
3	40	34 \ 50	28 \ 50	100
DEMAND	75	75	100	250 \ 250

Degeneracy can occur not only in the initial feasible solution but also at any intermediate solution. In the adjustment (shifting) process, it is possible for two or more cells to lose all units and become zero. Recall that the shifting units are subtracted from losing cells on the path and that the cell with the smaller amount leaves the solution. In this case, the solution approach is the same; that is, zero units are artificially allocated to the newly vacated cell to allow the problem to be solved. If by chance two or more cells on the path have the same allocation, the allocation of each will decrease to zero and the solution becomes degenerate. This is remedied by placing as many zeros as necessary (to make the solution nondegenerate) in the cells that have just become zero. For example, if two cells become zero, we artificially assign a zero allocation to one of them (remember, one of the cells had to leave the solution). If three cells become zero, we would place zeros in two of the cells just vacated. The problem is then solved as usual.

7.6 *COMPUTER SOLUTIONS TO TRANSPORTATION PROBLEMS*

The special transportation algorithms are not difficult to use, since they require only simple computations. It is easy to see, however, even from a small example, that the process can become complicated and time consuming as problems become larger and more complex. Computer solutions eliminate these difficulties. Since transportation problems are specialized LP problems, they can be solved using an LP computer package. However, there are computer programs available that make use of the special structure of the transportation problem. These programs are especially helpful for the larger, more complex problems that are likely to be encountered in what we call "the real world." To demonstrate the efficiency of computer solutions, let's look at a slightly larger version of the Frozen Fish Problem.

An Expanded Frozen Fish Problem

FFFF has expanded, acquiring five more processing plants and seven more distribution centers. The information concerning supplies, demands, and per-unit shipping costs are shown below. The processing plants are now designated as S1 through S8, and the distribution centers are designated D1 through D11.

Supply		*Demand*	
Plant	Quantity	Center	Quantity
S1	300	D1	350
S2	500	D2	400
S3	450	D3	300
S4	450	D4	200
S5	425	D5	225
S6	375	D6	375
S7	600	D7	350
S8	350	D8	150
		D9	250
		D10	300
		D11	325

Per Unit Shipping Costs

	D1	D2	D3	D4	D5	D6	D7	D8	D9	D10	D11
S1	20	27	28	25	20	21	18	24	23	22	26
S2	18	24	23	19	19	18	16	17	23	18	20
S3	14	17	15	18	20	16	18	19	23	15	17
S4	13	12	12	14	16	17	15	18	14	19	17
S5	35	32	30	29	31	28	31	32	33	29	28
S6	20	18	17	17	19	18	20	20	16	21	20
S7	27	31	25	23	24	26	22	23	23	25	24
S8	26	23	19	18	19	20	23	20	21	24	19

Obviously, this problem is a little more difficult to solve by visual inspection or intuition. It could also get a bit messy and long using the stepping stone method. Figure 7.5 shows the computer solution. This output, which is in the form of the transportation tableau, shows the shipping routes to use and the optimal allocation along these routes.

```
OPTIMAL ALLOCATION:


              D1     D2     D3     D4     D5     D6     D7     D8

    S1        0      0      0      0      200    0      100    0
    S2        0      0      0      0      0      300    0      0
    S3        350    0      0      0      0      0      0      0
    S4        0      400    50     0      0      0      0      0
    S5        0      0      0      0      0      75     0      0
    S6        0      0      125    0      0      0      0      0
    S7        0      0      0      200    0      0      250    150
    S8        0      0      125    0      25     0      0      0

  DEMAND      350    400    300    200    225    375    350    150


              D9     D10    D11    DUMMY  SUPPLY

    S1        0      0      0      0      300
    S2        0      200    0      0      500
    S3        0      100    0      0      450
    S4        0      0      0      0      450
    S5        0      0      125    225    425
    S6        250    0      0      0      375
    S7        0      0      0      0      600
    S8        0      0      200    0      350

  DEMAND      250    300    325    225

MIN SOLUTION VALUE = 58525
```

Figure 7.5 D&D Computer Solution

7.7 *APPLICATIONS OF THE TRANSPORTATION MODEL*

The utility of the transportation model can be demonstrated in its application to "transportation-like" problems. Many problems in production planning, scheduling, and inventory can be formulated as transportation problems. To illustrate this, we will look at two applications of the transportation model.

Production Planning Problems

Problem 1

Specialty Sportswear produces fleece sport tops in three styles at plants in four locaitons, 1, 2, 3, and 4. With the current craze for novelty fleecewear, demand exceeds monthly production capacity. Monthly capacities of the plants are 53,000, 35,000, 46,000, and 59,000 respectively. Monthly demand for the three styles (which we will call a, b, and c) are 75,000, 65,000, and 62,000. Profits per top at each plant are as follows:

| | STYLE | | |
PLANT	a	b	c
1	5.00	7.00	3.25
2	4.25	6.50	10.00
3	8.00	2.75	4.50
4	1.50	9.00	4.75

Specialty must decide how many tops of each type to produce in each plant to maximize profit.

We can formulate this problem as a transportation problem if we consider the manufacturing plants as sources, with the capacity as supply, and the styles as destinations with a given demand. Table 7.34 shows this problem formulated and

Table 7.34 Specialty Sportswear Transportation Tableau

From (plant)	To (style) a	b	c	Supply (in 1000's)
1	5	7	3.25	53
2	4.25	6.50	10	35
2	8	2.75	4.50	46
4	1.50	9	4.75	59
Demand (in 1000's)	74	68	62	193 / 204

```
OPTIMAL ALLOCATION:

                    a      b      c      SUPPLY

        1           28     9      16     53
        2           0      0      35     35
        3           46     0      0      46
        4           0      59     0      59
        DUMMY       0      0      11     11
        _____

        DEMAND      74     68     62
        SOLUTION VALUE=1504
```

Figure 7.6 Computer Solution

set up as a transportation tableau. Note that this is an unbalanced problem, and that it is a maximization problem. The computer solution is shown in Figure 7.6.

Because the problem is unbalanced, with demand exceeding supply by 11,000 units, we added a dummy row. Specialty will manufacture only 51,000 of the 62,000 required for style c in order to obtain the maximum profit of $1,504,000.

Many production planning problems are not quite as simple as the one just presented. Production schedules are frequently set up on for longer periods (e.g., quarterly) rather than on a weekly or monthly basis. Any mismatch of capacity and demand can be handled through inventory. However, there is usually a holding cost for maintaining inventory. In this kind of production planning problem, it is necessary to figure out how to use the available capacity to meet both present and future needs, considering both production and holding costs. The next example will demonstrate how this kind of problem can be formulated as a transportation problem.

Problem 2

ABCO manufactures central air conditioning units. Demand for these units increases in the spring of each year, but production capacity, from both regular working hours and overtime hours, remains constant. During regular hours 400 units can be produced a month. Overtime hours can add a maximum of 75 units each month. It costs ABCO $70 for each unit produced during regular hours and $100 per unit using overtime. Inventory costs are $15 per month. ABCO wishes to set up a spring quarter production schedule that will minimize total production cost. The quarter has the following anticipated demand: 300 units in April, 450 units in May, and 600 units in June.

June demand cannot be met by June production. ABCO must decide how to use the available capacity to meet both current demand (demand each month) and future demand at minimum cost. Both production costs and inventory holding costs must be considered. Thus, units produced and shipped in the same month cost $70.00. Units shipped in the month after production cost $85 ($70 production cost + $15 holding cost). ABCO adds holding costs for each month the stock is held in inventory. Table 7.35 displays these data. This table is easily converted to the tableau form shown in Table 7.36 and solved as a transportation problem.

Table 7.35 ABCO Production Planning Problem

TO / FROM	Units shipped in: April	May	June	Capacity
(production)				
April—reg hours	70	85	100	400
April—overtime	100	115	130	75
May—reg hours	M	70	85	400
May—overtime	M	100	115	75
June—reg	M	M	70	400
June—overtime	M	M	100	75
				1425
Demand	300	450	600	1350

Table 7.36 ABCO Production Planning Tableau

TO / FROM	April	May	June	Dummy	Supply (Capacity)
April—reg hours	70	85	100	0	400
April—overtime	100	115	130	0	75
May—reg hours	M	70	85	0	400
May—overtime	M	100	115	0	75
June—reg hours	M	M	70	0	400
June—overtime	M	M	100	0	75
Demand Units shipped	300	450	600	75	1425 1425

Capacity for each month, divided into regular and overtime capacity, is represented by the rows. Demand for each month is represented by columns. Costs are shown as the sum of the production cost and holding cost. The shaded area of the tableau represents infeasible schedules, such as units produced in May but shipped in April. (Note: This might be feasible when backorders, with associated costs, are allowed. Although backorders can be seen as a way of satisfying present demand with future capacity, in this example backorders are not allowed.) We can force the solution procedure to treat these cells as infeasible (prohibited or unacceptable routes, if you prefer) by assigning them a very high cost, such as M. The solution is shown in Figure 7.7. This solution indicates that 400 units should be produced in April during regular hours, with 300 shipped in May and 100 going into storage

```
OPTIMAL ALLOCATION:
              April    May    June    DUMMY    SUPPLY

   Apr-r      300       50      50       0        400
   Apr-o        0        0       0      75         75
   May-r        0      400       0       0        400
   May-o        0        0      75       0         75
   June-r       0        0     400       0        400
   June-o       0        0      75       0         75

   DEMAND     300      450     600      75
SOLUTION VALUE=102375
```

Figure 7.7 ABCO Production Planning Solution

(50 are shipped in May and 50 in June). The 75 shown for production during over-time hours in April are not really produced; this is the dummy demand required to balance the problem, since supply (production capacity) exceeds demand. In May 400 units are produced during regular hours, 75 during overtime. Of these, 450 units are shipped, 50 from inventory. In June 475 units are produced, 400 from regular hours and 75 overtime. To meet the 600 unit demand in June requires these 475 units and the 50 unit inventory from April, and the 75 overtime units in inventory from May.

7.8 AN INTRODUCTION TO THE ASSIGNMENT PROBLEM

Assignment problems are concerned with an optimal one-to-one allocation or assignment of one set of objects to another set of objects. It is a problem of assigning n indivisible units to n tasks, such as sales people to territories or jobs to machines, in such a way as to optimize a given objective, such as minimizing total cost or maximizing total profit. The key constraint is that each object (person, unit, job) can be assigned to one and only one other object (task, job, machine). The easily recognizable characteristics of an assignment problem can be summarized as follows:

1. The objects to be assigned are indivisible (they cannot be divided among more than one task) and finite in number.
2. Objects have to be assigned on a one-to-one basis to other objects.
3. There is a known cost or payoff associated with each specific assignment.

Solving Assignment Problems

As we have mentioned previously, assignment problems can be solved as linear programming problems. The formulation is presented in the next section. As we will demonstrate, however, there exist special-purpose algorithms that allow more computationally efficient solutions of assignment problems. The emphasis in this chapter will be on one such algorithm, the Hungarian method. First, we will discuss the possibility of solving assignment problems as transportation problems.

Since the assignment problem is a special form of the transportation problem, in which the supply at each source and the demand at each destination is equal to one, it can also be solved using the transportation methods discussed previously. The transportation method, however, is not an efficient algorithm to use for an assignment problem. Recall that to use stepping stone or MODI, there have to be m + n − 1 occupied cells in a feasible solution in order to test it for optimality. With four sources and four destinations there would have to be seven occupied cells (4 + 4 − 1). Since assignments are made on a one-to-one basis in an assignment problem, only four assignments can be made (only four cells would be occupied). Thus, the initial solution and all improved solutions would be degenerate, requiring the addition of three zero cells to the solution. Assignment problems solved using any of the transportation techniques are always highly degenerate (having n − 1 degenerate cells). Coping with degeneracy at each solution makes transportation methods computationally inefficient, although it is possible to use computer solutions for transportation problems, because these generally handle degeneracy automatically.

Formulating Assignment Problems

To demonstrate the formulation and solution of assignment problems, we will use the following problem:

Speedy Parcel Service

Speedy Parcel Service, an express parcel service, also provides a local message delivery service. Messages are picked up and delivered within the city limits, with a two-hour delivery guarantee. Speedy dispatches messenger cars by radio and pays the drivers partly on the basis of mileage. At the present time, there are four calls for pickup and delivery (1, 2, 3, 4) and four cars (W, X, Y, Z) on the road that can be dispatched. The total driving distance, mileage to pickup spot plus mileage from pickup to destination, for each car is calculated as follows:

Car W to 1 = 8 miles		Car X to 1 = 15 miles	
2 = 20		to 2 = 16	
3 = 15		to 3 = 12	
4 = 17		to 4 = 10	
Car Y to 1 = 22 miles		Car Z to 1 = 25 miles	
to 2 = 19		to 2 = 15	
to 3 = 16		to 3 = 12	
to 4 = 30		to 4 = 9	

The Speedy dispatcher wants to determine which car to send for each delivery in order to minimize total mileage.

We will begin by briefly demonstrating the LP formulation of the parcel service example.

LP Formulation   The Speedy Parcel Service problem can be formulated as an LP problem as follows:

MIN $8W_1 + 20W_2 + 15W_3 + 17W_4 + 15X_1 + 16X_2 + 12X_3 + 10X_4 +$
$22Y_1 + 19Y_2 + 16Y_3 + 30Y_4 + 25Z_1 + 15Z_2 + 12Z_3 + 9Z_4$

subject to

$W_1 + W_2 + W_3 + W_4 = 1$

$X_1 + X_2 + X_3 + X_4 = 1$

$Y_1 + Y_2 + Y_3 + Y_4 = 1$

$Z_1 + Z_2 + Z_3 + Z_4 = 1$

$W_1 + X_1 + Y_1 + Z_1 = 1$

$W_2 + X_2 + Y_2 + Z_2 = 1$

$W_3 + X_3 + Y_3 + Z_3 = 1$

$W_4 + X_4 + Y_4 + Z_4 = 1$

all variables = 1 or 0

where each assignment is designated by the car letter, W, X, Y, Z, and the job number, 1, 2, 3, 4. Thus, the decision variables (16 in all) are W_1, W_2, W_3, W_4, X_1, $X_2, \ldots Z_4$ and represent assignments.

As in a transportation problem, the constraints represent supply and demand. Note, however, that each supply is one unit and each demand is one unit. Each car, such as car W, can supply only one pickup and delivery. Each job, such as job 1, requires only one pickup and delivery.

The Assignment Tableau   The assignment model can also be formulated in a tabular form that is similar to the one presented for transportation problems. This form provides a concise framework for the relevant data. In the assignment tableau, rows represent the units, such as persons, jobs, or cars to be assigned. These are analogous to the supply or source in the transportation tableau. Columns represent the task to which the units are assigned, such as machine, route, or territory. The assignment tableau does not have to show supplies available at each source, or demand at each destination. Because a one-to-one allocation is being made, supplies and demands are all represented as 1. The assignment cost (distance, time, money, etc.) for each specific assignment of unit to task is shown in the tableau cells. Assignment problems can be balanced or unbalanced. In a balanced problem, wherein the number of items to be assigned equals the number of items to which they are assigned, the number of rows is equal to the number of columns. That is, in a balanced problem m = n. To balance an unbalanced assignment tableau, dummy rows or columns (with zero cost or payoff) are added. Table 7.37 shows the Speedy Parcel Service problem in an assignment tableau.

7.9 *HUNGARIAN SOLUTION METHOD FOR ASSIGNMENT PROBLEMS*

The **Hungarian method** is a fast, simple, efficient algorithm for solving assignment problems. Basically, the Hungarian method requires us to calculate a table of opportunity costs or losses, called an opportunity cost table; determine if an opti-

Table 7.37 Assignment Tableau

Car	Jobs 1	2	3	4
W	8	20	15	17
X	15	16	12	10
Y	22	19	16	30
Z	25	15	12	9

mal assignment can be made; and then, if necessary, revise the opportunity cost table and again determine if an optimal solution can be made. The process continues until an optimal solution is made. The approach of the Hungarian method is to reduce the assignment cost table by a series of arithmetic operations, in order to create a table containing cells with zero opportunity costs (reduced costs of zero). The optimal assignment is ultimately reached by making assignments only to the cells with a zero opportunity cost. These reductions can be made without affecting the ultimate optimal solution. When subtracting or adding a constant, the absolute cost is changed, but not the relative cost. The concern here is with the costs relative to one another. The costs being compared are opportunity costs. However, these new reduced costs cannot be used to calculate the objective function, that is, the value of the optimum assignment. For this, the actual (absolute) values must be used.

The first step, then, is to develop a total opportunity cost table. **Opportunity cost** refers to the penalty or cost associated with any decision or action, or the opportunity that is sacrificed by taking that action instead of an alternative action. If we choose a particular course of action, we cannot take different action. For example, in Table 7.37, if car W is assigned to job 3, it cannot be assigned to job 1, the lowest cost assignment. This results in an increased relative cost of $7 ($15 − $8). Developing an opportunity cost table is a two-step procedure.

In the first step, we make row reductions. This is accomplished by subtracting the minimum value in each row from every value in that row. Note that we are working with one row at a time. Table 7.38 shows the Speedy Parcel Service tableau with the row reductions made.

Note that we subtracted the smallest number in each row from every other number in that row (8 from numbers in row W, 10 in X, 16 in Y, and 9 in Z). There is at least one zero for each row. In certain very rare instances, it is possible that the zeros in each row will be placed so that they also occur one in each column. In this case the next step is eliminated. (However, this is not likely to happen and column reductions will be necessary.)

Table 7.38 Speedy Parcel Tableau with Row Reductions

Car	Jobs 1	2	3	4
W	0	12	7	9
X	5	6	2	0
Y	6	3	0	14
Z	16	6	3	0

Column reductions are made in the same manner. We subtract the minimum value in each column (it will be a zero in some instances) from every value in that column. Table 7.39 shows the assignment table after these reductions are made. This is the total opportunity cost table. In columns 1, 3, and 4 a zero has been subtracted; in column 2 the value 3 was subtracted. There is now at least one zero in each column and each row. Where the zero was the minimum subtracted, there was obviously no change. Once the total opportunity cost table has been developed, we can begin making assignments wherever a zero is present. An optimal assignment occurs whenever unique assignments can be made, that is, whenever there is one and only one assignment to a zero cell per row and column so as not to violate the constraints. There is a zero in each row and each column, but in order to determine whether an optimal assignment can be made, we need to test for optimality.

The second step in the Hungarian method is to determine whether an optimal assignment can be made. If a zero assignment can be made to each row and each column, then the relative cost of the assignment is zero and the solution is optimal. There is a simple procedure to determine if there are enough zero cells to allow an optimal assignment. The test is to find the minimum number of horizontal and vertical (row and column) lines necessary to cross out all the zeros in the table. If the minimum number is equal to n, the number of rows or columns (equal to the number of assignments to be made), then an optimal assignment can be made. The table is "reduced." Table 7.40 shows the lines drawn for the Speedy Parcel Service problem.

Notice that the minimum number of lines required to cover all of the zeros here is three (there can be more than one way to draw the lines covering the zeros). Since we need to make four assignments (n = 4), we cannot yet make an optimal

Table 7.39 Total Opportunity Cost Table

Car	Jobs			
	1	2	3	4
W	0	9	7	9
X	5	3	2	0
Y	6	0	0	14
Z	16	3	3	0

Table 7.40 Lines Covering Zeros

Car	Jobs			
	1	2	3	4
W	0	9	7	9
X	5	3	2	0
Y	6	0	0	14
Z	16	3	3	0

assignment. Actually, in this particular case this is apparent from visual inspection of the assignment possibilities (the zeros). If car W is assigned to job 1, there is no difficulty. Then, if X is assigned to 4, and Y to 3, what happens to car Z? Job 4 is already taken. Job 2 is still unassigned. If Y is assigned to job 2, then job 3 cannot be assigned. Assignments must be made such that there is one and only one assignment in each row *and* each column; that is, assignments must be **unique assignments.** This completes one iteration of the solution procedure. The opportunity cost table needs to be revised.

To revise the table, we need to subtract the value of the minimum uncovered cell from every other uncovered cell *and* add it to those cells at the intersections of the lines covering the zeros. The other cells are left unchanged. In this example, the minimum value is 2 (at cell X,3). Subtracting it from the uncovered cells and adding it to the two intersections gives the table shown in Table 7.41.

This time it takes four lines to cover all of the zeros (there may be more than one way to draw the lines, but the number will always be the same). Since the number of lines is equal to the number of assignments to be made, we can make an optimal assignment. Four unique assignments are possible. Table 7.42 shows these lines.

The final step is to make the assignments. We can make one and only one assignment in each row or column. If only one solution exists, there is a quick method for making assignments: simply locate the row or column having only one zero, make that assignment, and then drop that row *and* column from the matrix. Repeat the procedure until all the assignments have been made. In the example, both row W and column 1 fit this criterion. W can be assigned to job 1, and row W and column 1 can be dropped from the table. Next, since column 2 has only one zero, we make an assignment to cell Y,2 and drop column 2 and row Y from the

Table 7.41 Further Reductions

		Jobs		
Car	1	2	3	4
W	0	7	5	9
X	5	1	0	0
Y	6	0	0	16
Z	16	1	1	0

Table 7.42 Next Set of Zero Covering Lines

		Jobs		
Car	1	2	3	4
W	0	9	7	9
X	5	3	2	0
Y	6	0	0	14
Z	16	3	3	0

matrix. Row Z has just one zero. Making the assignment to cell Z,4 eliminates row Z and column 4. That leaves one assignment to make at cell X,3. Table 7.43 shows the optimal assignments (or optimal solution).

To find the optimal solution value, we take the absolute cost of each assignment from the original tableau, as summarized below:

$$
\begin{array}{lll}
\text{Car W} \rightarrow \text{Job 1} = & 8 \text{ miles} \\
\text{Car X} \rightarrow \text{Job 3} = & 12 \text{ miles} \\
\text{Car Y} \rightarrow \text{Job 2} = & 19 \text{ miles} \\
\text{Car Z} \rightarrow \text{Job 4} = & 9 \text{ miles} \\
\hline
\text{Total} = & 48 \text{ miles}
\end{array}
$$

Alternate or **multiple optimal solutions** are very common in assignment problems. When this happens, some rows or columns have more than one zero. While alternative assignments may be possible, the solution total will be the same. The selection of assignments is arbitrary. For example, if the original table had contained the slightly different values shown in Table 7.44, multiple optimal solutions would exist. The second iteration, after all reductions are made, gives the result shown in Table 7.45.

Table 7.43 Further Reductions

Car	Jobs			
	1	2	3	4
W	1			
X			1	
Y		1		
Z				1

Table 7.44 Revised Assignment Tableau

Car	Jobs			
	1	2	3	4
W	8	20	15	17
X	15	16	12	10
Y	22	19	16	30
Z	25	14	11	9

Table 7.45 Final Tableau Revised

Car	Jobs			
	1	2	3	4
W	0	7	5	9
X	5	1	0	0
Y	8	0	0	16
Z	16	0	0	0

Table 7.46 Revised Problem Optimal
Solution (One Alternative)

Car	Jobs 1	2	3	4
W	1			
X				1
Y			1	
Z		1		

The same assignments which were made previously can be made here, but we can make others instead. Table 7.46 shows one alternative. Notice that the solution value remains unchanged.

$$\text{Car W} \rightarrow \text{Job 1} = \ 8 \text{ miles}$$

$$\text{Car X} \rightarrow \text{Job 4} = 10 \text{ miles}$$

$$\text{Car Y} \rightarrow \text{Job 3} = 16 \text{ miles}$$

$$\text{Car Z} \rightarrow \text{Job 2} = 14 \text{ miles}$$

$$\text{Total} = 48 \text{ miles}$$

Hungarian Method Summary

1. Starting with a balanced table, develop a total opportunity cost table by first reducing row values and then reducing column values. Subtract the minimum value in each row from each cell in that row. Then subtract the minimum value in each column from every cell in that column.
2. Test this table to see if an optimal assignment can be made. Use the minimum possible number of horizontal and vertical lines necessary to cross out the zero cells. If the number of lines = n, an optimal solution can be achieved. If not, reduce the table further by subtracting the minimum value in an uncovered cell from all other uncovered cells and add it to the cells where the lines intersect. Repeat the optimality test.
3. If an optimal assignment can be made, i.e., if the number of lines equals the number of rows or columns (n), make the assignments such that there is one assignment in each row and each column.

Solving Maximization Problems with the Hungarian Method

In order to solve a maximization problem, it is necessary to transform the problem into a minimization problem in such a way that the optimal solution to the new minimization problem is the same as the optimal solution to the initial maximization problem. There are several ways to do this. One way is to subtract each entry in the table from the maximum value in the table.

Again, it is necessary to think in terms of opportunity costs. In a maximization problem, with the cell value representing payoff, it is natural to choose the cell with the largest payoff. Selecting any other cell would have a "cost." This cost would be the difference between the value selected and the highest value that could have been chosen. Let's look again at the Speedy Parcel Service example, shown in Table 7.47. This time, however, the cell values represent the profit that would result if that particular assignment were made.

To transform this table to a minimization problem, we subtract each value in the original table from the largest value in the table (a profit of 30 in cell Y,4). The transformed table, shown in Table 7.48, is an opportunity cost table, and the Hungarian method can now be used to solve the problem. Once we have made the optimal assignments, we use the original profit values to calculate the value of the solution.

Handling Impossible Assignments

In some instances an assignment may be unacceptable. For some reason, a particular matchup is impossible. To handle this, a very high cost (M) or a very low payoff ($-M$) is assigned to that cell. It works to keep that cell out of the solution, as it did in transportation and simplex.

Table 7.47 Assignment Tableau–Maximization

	Jobs			
Car	1	2	3	4
W	8	20	15	17
X	15	16	12	10
Y	22	19	16	30
Z	25	14	11	9

Table 7.48 Transformation of a Maximization Problem to a Minimization Problem

	Jobs			
Car	1	2	3	4
W	22	10	15	13
X	15	14	18	20
Y	8	11	14	0
Z	5	16	19	21

Focus on Decision Making

In July of each year, James Burner, Director of Public Works for the city of Metropolis, is faced with the unpleasant but necessary task of awarding private snow removal contracts for the coming winter. Metropolis is located in upstate New York and is subject to frequent and heavy snowfalls. The city's Public Works Department has sufficient equipment and employees to clear the major streets and highways within the city. The Department has found, however, that it is more practical to hire private contractors to clear side streets and some of the smaller public parking areas. In the past, this practice has sometimes proved to be a major headache for the city. When the private contractors fail to clear all the streets assigned to them on a timely basis, not only is traffic in that neighborhood disrupted, but the residents complain loudly to the mayor's office and the newspapers. This creates a major political "hot potato," putting a great deal of pressure on the Director of Public Works.

Each year, private contractors submit bids for snow removal in designated sectors of the city. Mr. Burner reviews these bids and then awards contracts. While city regulations do not limit his selection to the low bidder for each sector, his objective is to minimize the overall snow removal costs for all sectors. In reviewing the past performance of the various private contractors, Mr. Burner has come to the conclusion that many of the problems result not from inability or incompetence, but because contractors are overcommitted. Contractors normally have few problems when the snowfall is average, but during severe snowstorms their equipment is often insufficient to keep up with the load. To deal with this problem, Mr. Burner has decided to award most contractors just one sector. He feels Anderson's Snow Removal Service, the largest private contractor, has the capacity to clear up to three sectors.

Data Preparation/Problem Formulation

The city is currently divided into eight sectors. The Department of Public Works has received bids from twelve private contractors. Mr. Burner had placed all bids for each sector on a large blackboard in his office and was attempting, by trial-and-error, to evaluate the bids when his administrative assistant, Cathy Hogan, looked at the blackboard and said, "Oh, an assignment problem. I had to do one of these in my evening MBA class last semester. The computer sure makes short work of these, doesn't it?" Mr. Burner responded, "It sure does. In fact, I was just about to have you work on this. Can you have a solution for me by this afternoon?" Cathy said, "Of course," and copied the following information from the board.

| Contractor | Sector | | | | | | | |
	1	2	3	4	5	6	7	8
Anderson	41	36	32	53	34	51	43	47
Snyder	38	35	30	48	33	43	46	49
Quinlin	42	43	38	50	33	48	42	51
Jackson	43	41	33	49	41	53	43	48
Colella	44	37	35	56	39	—	—	—
Campbell	43	—	—	47	40	41	37	45
Sweeney	39	40	36	52	32	49	—	—
Murillo	40	41	34	55	37	47	38	48
Washington	—	37	37	51	35	52	38	51
Gomez	43	39	34	52	36	50	43	54
Morgeiwcz	38	36	33	47	31	45	39	46
Franklin	42	38	33	50	38	49	40	—

(All figures are in thousands of dollars.)

Computer Solution

When Cathy entered the data, she realized that she had to make three separate entries for Anderson, since it was possible for that company to be awarded contracts for as many as three sectors. The computer provided the following optimal solution (dummy columns are not displayed):

OPTIMAL ASSIGNMENT:

	1	2	3	4	5	6	7	8
1	0	1	0	0	0	0	0	0
2	0	0	1	0	0	0	0	0
3	0	0	0	0	0	0	0	1
4	0	0	0	0	0	1	0	0
5	0	0	0	0	0	0	0	0
6	0	0	0	1	0	0	0	0
7	0	0	0	0	0	0	0	0
8	0	0	0	0	0	0	1	0
9	0	0	0	0	1	0	0	0
10	0	0	0	0	0	0	0	0
11	0	0	0	0	0	0	0	0
12	0	0	0	0	0	0	0	0
13	1	0	0	0	0	0	0	0
14	0	0	0	0	0	0	0	0

MIN SOLUTION VALUE = 314
ALTERNATE OPTIMAL SOLUTION EXISTS

Interpretation and Analysis of the Results

These results indicate that the city can keep costs to a minimum of $314,000 for the coming winter by assigning sectors 2, 3, and 8 to Anderson; sector 1 to Sweeney; sector 4 to Jackson; sector 5 to Morgeiwcz; sector 6 to Snyder; and sector 7 to Campbell. Quinlin, Colella, Murillo, Washington, Gomez, and Franklin are not awarded any contracts. By running subsequent solutions, Cathy also determined that the alternate optimal solutions result from entering Anderson three times and from the possible alternate dummy column assignments.

What Happens Next

After Mr. Burner reviewed the results with Cathy, he felt pleased that a minimum cost decision could be reached with so little effort. He also noted, however, that other factors might have to be considered when making the final decision. He knew that the six contractors not awarded a contract would be dissatisfied when they discovered that Anderson had received three contracts. Moreover, he recognized that, while the city had three sectors (6, 7, and 8) with predominantly Hispanic populations, none of the contracts would be going to either of the Hispanic contractors. This, he knew, could create political repercussions. Upon examining the results and bids, he also knew he could award one of Anderson's contracts to Murillo at an increase in cost of only $1,000. He decided to discuss this possibility further with the mayor's office.

7.10 CONCLUDING REMARKS

In this chapter we introduced two useful variations of the linear programming model: transportation and assignment models. These and other network problems that we will introduce in Chapter 8 are increasingly important to management science. Transportation models are concerned with the allocation of a product from its point of origin to its point of demand; assignment models are concerned with the optimal one-to-one allocation of one set of objects to another set of objects. However, allocation techniques have widespread applicability to "transportation-like" problems in production and scheduling. These applications greatly enhance the utility of these models. Because of their special structure, these problems can be presented in both a network and a tabular form, which makes them easier to visualize and also allows them to be solved using special algorithms that are faster and computationally much easier than LP. While the computations required by the special-purpose algorithms presented here are not difficult, they can become tiresome with very large problems. The availability of special software has made it increasingly easy and practical to solve distribution problems using a computer.

Management Science Application ————————————————————

THE ROYAL THAI NAVY[2]

Thailand, which has compulsory military service for all men, assigns those who live in the coastal provinces to the Royal Thai Navy. Men drafted into the Navy report first to a drafting center in their home locality, and are then transported by land vehicle to a naval base. Those from a northern province go to the main naval base in Satahep, near Bangkok. Those from a southern province are first brought overland to a branch naval base, and are then transported by ship to the main base. In the southern provinces there are 36 drafting centers and four branch bases. The Thai Navy must determine how many men from each drafting center to assign and transport to each branch base. Then, given a solution to this problem, it is necessary to determine which of the ships available at the main base to use, and how to route them in order to pick up and transport the men to the main branch. Because of the organizational structure of the Navy, these two decisions are made by different people in different places at different times. Thus, it is not possible to build a unified model to solve both problems simultaneously.

Solution of these problems was undertaken as a graduate school project at the University of Tennessee. To determine the optimal number of men to transport from each drafting center to each branch base, given the number of men at each drafting center, the capacity of each branch base, and the cost for transporting each man between each drafting center and each branch base, the class used a standard transportation model. The computer software selected was the GNET package in conjunction with a class-developed problem generator and report writer written in FORTRAN.

---

[2]Reprinted with permission of Paiboon Choypeng, Pojana Puakpong, and Richard E. Rosenthal, "Optimal Ship Routing and Personnel Assignment for Naval Recruitment in Thailand," *Interfaces*, 16 (July–August 1986): 47–52. Copyright (1986), The Institute of Management Sciences.

The second problem—the optimal deployment of the available fleet of ships to transport draftees to the main naval base—was solved as a vehicle routing problem using an integer programming model. The class used a set partitioning approach with a primary objective of minimizing the number of ships required for transporting all of the draftees. Distance minimization was used as a secondary, tie-breaking objective. At the time of the study, there were nine vessels of three different classes available for draftee transport. There was also a restriction, based on size, as to which ships were able to visit which bases. From this information, using complete enumeration, the class generated a list of 23 possible voyages. The integer programming model was solved using LINDO. A problem generator was written to generate the voyages and create the LINDO input automatically.

Results obtained by the mathematical programming models are felt to be superior to results obtained using the manual procedures that the Thai Navy traditionally employs. For example, in assigning draftees to a naval base, the usual procedure is to send each man to the nearest base. In some instances, however, base capacities have been exceeded and the Navy has had to transport men from oversubscribed bases to undersubscribed bases. The optimization model avoids the time delays and cost of these extra trips. Data are not yet available to determine how many voyages and kilometers could have been saved if the mathematical programming had been available for vehicle routing for the past few years. According to a Thai Navy captain, the results are superior to the results obtained through manual procedures. The Thai Navy is testing the suitability, feasibility, and acceptability of the model. If it works out, it will be applied and implemented.

GLOSSARY

assignment problem distribution problem with a one-to-one allocation of one set of objects to another set of objects; a special case of the transportation problem where all supplies and demands are equal to 1, and one and only one assignment can be made in any given row or column

assignment tableau tabular form in which an assignment problem is displayed; convenient, concise framework for presenting all the relevant data (rows represent objects to be assigned, columns represent objects to which assignments are to be made, and relevant costs are shown in the cells); used to facilitate solution

balanced problem physical allocation problem in which total supply is equal to total demand; in assignment problems the number of assignees is equal to the number of available assignments or jobs

cell intersection of a row and a column, representing a route from source i to destination j in a transportation problem or an assignment in an assignment problem

cell evaluator opportunity cost of shipping one unit via a route not currently being used; an improvement index representing the net change in cost that results when there is a one-unit reallocation to a presently unoccupied cell

closed loop path, showing the possible transfer of units or shift in allocations in a transportation table, that follows a direct route from the empty cell via occupied cells back to the same empty cell

degeneracy condition existing in a transportation tableau that has less than the required $m + n - 1$ occupied cells in solution

destination point of demand in a transportation problem; where the shipment is going

dummy rows and columns the rows, representing fictitious sources or objects awaiting assignment, or columns, representing destinations or jobs, that are added to balance a tableau

empty cell unused or unoccupied cells in a transportation table, representing an unused route

Hungarian method special-purpose algorithm designed to solve assignment problems

impossible assignment unacceptable assignment; cell in an assignment tableau to which no assignment can be made

least cost method technique that considers cost when determining an initial feasible solution to a transportation problem; makes allocations sequentially to the feasible cell having minimum cost

MODI special-purpose algorithm used to solve transportation problems; a modified version of the stepping stone method in which the cell evaluators used to test for optimality are calculated mathematically without having to draw the stepping stone path

multiple optimal solutions situation in transportation and assignment problems in which there exist more than one assignment or allocation pattern having the same optimal solution value

northwest corner method systematic, logical procedure for determining an initial solution to a transportation problem; allocations are made to current feasible NW corner of the tableau

occupied cell used cells in transportation tableau, representing route being used

opportunity cost penalty or cost associated with any decision or action; the cost of the opportunity that is sacrificed by taking one action instead of an alternative action

restricted route situation in a transportation problem in which a particular route(s) cannot be used; no allocations can be made along designated prohibited routes

source point of supply in transportation problem; place where shipment originates

stepping stone method special-purpose algorithm used to solve transportation problems; sequential procedure that begins with an initial solution, tests for optimality, and then (if necessary) improves the solution by reallocating items to a previously unused route

transportation problem special linear programming problem in which it is necessary to determine the best allocation of a product from its source, i, to its destination, j, selecting the shipping route pattern that will optimize a given objective

transportation tableau tabular form in which transportation problem is displayed; convenient, concise framework for presenting all the relevant data (rows represent sources, columns represent destinations, and cells show costs); used to facilitate solution

PROBLEMS

1. Given the following transportation tableau:

To From	1	2	3	Supply
A	33	21	26	500
B	31	12	20	800
C	15	24	30	600
Demand	750	350	800	

a. Find the minimum cost solution.
b. Is it balanced? How do you know?
c. Are there alternate optimals? How do you know?

2. Find the minimum cost solution for the following problem:

To From	A	B	C	D	Supply
1	12	9	15	21	150
2	18	15	9	12	240
3	15	12	30	24	120
4	21	24	9	12	270
Demand	225	165	150	240	

a. Is this problem balanced?
b. Are there alternate optimals?

3. Given the following tableau:

To From	A	B	C	D	E	F	Supply
1	15	25	40	60	70	85	150
2	20	35	50	65	75	90	375
3	60	50	45	35	20	10	225
4	30	54	20	25	30	54	300
5	40	50	60	50	40	30	675
6	35	25	30	40	50	60	600
Demand	525	150	300	450	750	150	

a. Determine the optimal allocation pattern to minimize total shipping cost.
b. Are there alternate optimals?
c. What happens to this pattern and cost if the shipping routes from 1 to A and 3 to F cannot be used?

4. In the following tableau, the coefficients represent a per-unit payoff. Find the maximum payoff solution to this problem.

To From	A	B	C	D	E	Supply
1	3.5	3	1	6	4.5	120
2	1.5	4.5	4	2.5	3	150
3	5	2	5.5	2.5	3	150
Demand	80	110	140	80	75	

5. Given the following table showing individuals to be assigned to projects and the attendant costs associated with each assignment:

Project

Person	A	B	C	D
Garner	7	8	8.50	7.60
Duane	11.20	12	11.80	10.50
VerKolen	5.80	6.40	7.25	8.40
Perez	5.60	6.80	8.10	10

determine the one-to-one assignment that will minimize total cost.

6. Given the following table showing jobs to be assigned to machines and the production cost of each assignment:

Machine

Job	1	2	3	4	5	6
A	36	38	32	40	35	31
B	25	22	29	24	27	26
C	30	35	22	31	33	36
D	41	43	47	42	39	22
E	37	34	26	41	23	41
F	22	27	30	20	46	33

a. Determine what jobs should be assigned to what machines to minimize production cost.
b. What happens if it is not possible to assign job A to machine 1?

7. Given a transportation problem with the following costs, supplies, and demands:

To From	A	B	C	D	Supply
1	50	75	30	45	200
2	65	80	40	60	190
3	40	70	50	55	220
Demand	130	160	190	130	

a. Find an initial solution using the northwest corner method.
b. Find an initial solution using the least cost method.
c. Compare the results.
d. Solve the problem using the stepping stone method.

8. Given the following tableau, find an initial solution using both the northwest corner and least cost methods and then use MODI to determine the minimum cost solution.

To From	A	B	C	Supply
1	5	7.5	3	105
2	6.5	8	4	60
3	4	7	5.5	180
Demand	120	135	90	

9. Answer the questions below, given the following tableau:

To From	A	B	C	Supply
1	30	25	M	2500
2	27.5	20	15	2000
3	22.5	17.5	15	750
4	10	37.5	7.5	1000
Demand	2250	1250	2250	

    a. What does the M coefficient signify?
    b. Balance the problem.
    c. Find an initial solution using NW corner.
    d. Is the solution degenerate?
    e. Solve the problem using any solution procedure.
    f. Which demand is not met?

10. Job Shop Manufacturing has four jobs to run. These jobs can be scheduled on any of three machines. The following table shows the cost associated with each particular assignment.

Machine

Job	A	B	C
1	15	19	25
2	22	18	29
3	31	17	14
4	18	37	12

    a. How do you balance this problem?
    b. What assignments minimize total production cost?
    c. What job will not be run?

11. Given this transportation problem with coefficients representing per unit profit:

To From	A	B	C	D	Supply
1	.05	.25	.15	.1	50
2	.2	.1	.1	.2	30
3	.15	.05	.1	.2	60
Demand	35	25	50	30	

a. Find an initial solution using the maximization equivalent to least cost (maximum payoff).

b. Solve the problem.

c. Are there alternative solutions?

12. Alvirez Computing has three programming jobs to be done and four programmers available. The department manager estimates it will take the programmers the following amount of time (in hours) to complete each job:

	A	B	C
Willis	5	8	6
Pastore	7	9	6
Ruiz	4	7	5
Jackson	6	8	7

Which programmer should be assigned to each job if management wishes to minimize total programming time spent?

13. Smith and Baxter has one salesperson available to cover each of its four sales territories. The sales manager estimates the following sales volumes (in thousands of dollars) for each salesperson and territory:

Territory

	East	South	North	West
Phil	112	96	118	106
Jane	118	106	122	110
Lavnar	100	110	92	98
Alicia	125	118	128	122

Which salesperson should the sales manager assign to each territory if he wishes to maximize total sales?

14. Given the following transportation table:

Customer

Plant	A	B	C	Supply
Evansville	7	8	9	150
Indianapolis	5	9	7	150
Calumet	6	8	5	250
Demand	200	200	150	

a. Determine an initial solution for this problem using the least cost method.

b. Find the optimal solution to this problem using stepping stone.

15. White Thumb Confections bakes pastries for sale at three area galleries and museums. Offerings are currently limited to four confections: Napoleons, eclairs, apple strudel, and cheesecake. White Thumb bakes 250 of each product daily for sale that day. Demand at each location is constant, regardless of the variety offered for sale that day, but profit per item varies with each location. Location 1 sells 125 items a day; location 2 sells 300; and location 3 sells 200. The per-unit profit of each item at each location is summarized as follows:

Item	Location	Profit/unit (in cents)
Napoleon	1	6
Napoleon	2	7.5
Napoleon	3	10
Eclair	1	6.5
Eclair	2	8.5
Eclair	3	9.5
Strudel	1	5.5
Strudel	2	8.5
Strudel	3	11
Cheesecake	1	7
Cheesecake	2	8
Cheesecake	3	9

White Thumb wishes to maximize its daily profit. How many of each item should be sent to each shop? Formulate this as a transportation problem. Solve using MODI (for the initial solution use maximum payoff).

16. Glen Brown Market Research has contracts for five new projects that now require directors. There are currently six possible choices for assignment to these projects. Time required for project completion is a factor in profit, and completion time is, in turn, a function of the experience and leadership style of the project director. The table below shows the directors who are available and their expected time of completion (in weeks) for each project.

			Project		
Director	1	2	3	4	5
Pederson	3.8	4.0	3.0	4.1	3.6
Ruiz	2.0	1.5	2.5	1.75	2.3
Murphy	2.7	3.6	1.6	2.9	3.1
Crestuk	4.3	4.6	7.1	4.4	2.6
Levy	3.7	3.2	2.1	4.3	1.7
Rullon	1.8	2.2	2.8	1.2	5.0

a. What assignments should be made so that total time of completion is minimized?

b. Who will not be assigned at this time?

c. Are there any changes if Ruiz cannot be assigned to project 2 and Murphy cannot take project 3?

17. Forsyth Manufacturing is attempting to determine an optimal production schedule for the next three months. Forsyth can produce 200 units per month on regular time at a cost of $18 per unit, and up to 80 additional units per month on overtime at a cost of $24 per unit. Forsyth also can purchase up to 50 units per month from a subcontractore at $28 per unit. Units not shipped in the month they are produced (or purchased) cost $3 per unit per month to store.

a. If demand is 250 units in month 1, 350 units in month 2, and 200 units in month 3, determine the production schedule for the three-month period that will minimize total cost.

b. If Forsyth has 100 units in inventory at the beginning of month 1 and wishes to have at least 50 units in inventory at the end of the third month, how will this affect your answer to part (a)? (Assume the storage cost on the 100 units currently in inventory will accrue in month 1, and the storage costs on the ending inventory will not accrue until month 4.)

18. White Thumb has four confections to be baked by three assistants. Experience shows that each assistant is more proficient at certain tasks. Thus, it takes each assistant a different amount of time to complete each product. Profit on each item is related in part to the time spent in preparation. White Thumb wishes to maximize profit from these confections. The payoff per assistant per item is summarized as follows:

Worker	Item	Profit (in cents)
1	Napoleon	10
1	Eclair	12
1	Strudel	6
1	Cheesecake	5
2	Napoleon	7
2	Eclair	15
2	Strudel	10
2	Cheesecake	5
3	Napoleon	11
3	Eclair	8
3	Strudel	7
3	Cheesecake	10

a. Find the optimal assignment for White Thumb.
b. Which confection will not be baked?
c. Formulate this as an LP problem.

19. The Maxima Company sells electronic components to four customers. Current demand from its customers exceeds the combined capacity of its three plants. Maxima's management must decide how many units it should supply to each customer. All customers pay a $42 per unit price (Maxima pays shipping costs), and all are given equal priority for the available components. Component costs vary from plant to plant because of differing labor and power costs. Production costs, capacities, shipping costs, and customer demand are shown below:

Plant	Per Unit Costs	Capacity
Tampa	12	6000
Fort Worth	13	5000
Columbus	15	8000

Customer

Plant	A	B	C	D
Tampa	14	20	10	24
Fort Worth	17	16	12	18
Columbus	13	18	6	21
Demand	4000	7000	6000	3000

How many units should Maxima ship from each plant to each customer if it wishes to maximize total profits? Which customer(s) will have unmet demand?

20. Acme Manufacturing uses four machines to manufacture four similar products. Each product can be produced by any of the four machines. Production costs vary among machines and products due to different machining times and scrap rates. Cost and monthly capacity and demand data are as follows:

Machine	Capacity	Product	Demand
A	300	R	450
B	500	S	200
C	200	T	250
D	400	U	400

Production cost/unit	Product			
Machine	R	S	T	U
A	3.80	3.60	3.70	3.55
B	3.75	3.65	3.60	3.50
C	3.65	3.75	3.80	3.60
D	3.75	3.60	3.90	3.50

a. Determine the optimal monthly production schedule for each machine.
b. Management has discovered that, because of fine adjustment problems, machine D cannot be used to produce products S or U. Does this alter the production schedule?
c. If management could repair the fine adjustment controls on machine D for a cost of $200, should they do so?

21. Steel Belt Corp. produces snowblower tires at two plants. The tires are then shipped to three warehouses. Plant capacities and warehouse demands are as follows:

Plant	Capacity	Warehouse	Demand
Akron	3000	Bangor	1800
Columbia	1600	Cleveland	1300

Production and shipping costs are as follows:

	Warehouse		
Plant	Bangor	Cleveland	Des Moines
Akron	9.10	8.60	8.85
Columbia	9.00	8.80	9.05

a. How many of these tires should be shipped from each plant to each warehouse if Steelbelt wishes to minimize costs?
b. Is this the only optimal distribution schedule?

22. A busy orthodontist has just introduced a new Office on Wheels to care for patients in rural areas. Three chairs are designated for use by three assistants who handle routine tasks (checkups, tightening bands, and instruction of patients in proper dental care). Each assistant can handle each task, however their times vary. If the objective is to see as many patients as possible, what are the best assignments, given the following estimates of numbers of patients seen per hour at each task?

		Task	
Assistant	Tighten bands	Checkups	Instruction
Kristen	6	10	4
Rachel	7	6	5
Sara	4	9	6

23. Newton is about to begin a preservation project in the heart of the old commercial district. Plans include turning a vacant lot into a park with a playground; tearing down a warehouse to build a mini-shopping mall; and preserving and refurbishing two townhouses (projects 3 and 4). Bids for the projects have been received from five contractors, as shown below:

Contractor	Project	Bid (in 100,000s)
A	1	1.5
A	3	2
A	4	3
B	1	1.75
B	2	4
B	3	1.5
B	4	3.25
C	2	4.25
C	3	2
C	4	2.75
D	1	1.8
D	2	3.75
D	3	1.8
D	4	3
E	1	1.45
E	3	1.75
E	4	2.9

In order for the city to qualify for a preservation grant, each project must be awarded to a different contractor; that is, each contractor can undertake one and only one project. What project should be assigned to which contractor in order to minimize total cost?

24. In a consolidation effort, a school district will bring together primary students from three small neighborhood schools into one central district school. There will be three first grades, two second grades, and one third grade. Currently, eight teachers are teaching at the primary grade level. They have been evaluated for overall effectiveness for each grade. The ratings are summarized below (5 is highly effective, 1 is ineffective).

	Grade		
Teacher	1	2	3
Wright	4.2	4.0	3.7
Perez	4.0	3.5	3.2
Garman	2.5	3.0	1.8
Mateo	2.0	2.5	2.8
Smithson	4.0	4.3	4.1
Sharp	3.6	2.4	2.5
Jacobs	1.9	2.6	4.0
Zenid	3.4	3.3	2.6

The school district would like to assign teachers to classes in a way that maximizes teaching effectiveness. What teachers should be teaching what level?

25. Solve the following linear programming problem:

$$MIN\ 8A_1 + 6A_2 + 10A_3 + 14A_4 + 12B_1 + 10B_2 + 6B_3 + 8B_4 + 10C_1 +$$
$$8C_2 + 20C_3 + 16C_4 + 14D_1 + 16D_2 + 6D_3 + 8D_4$$

subject to

$$A_1 + A_2 + A_3 + A_4 = 200$$
$$B_1 + B_2 + B_3 + B_4 = 320$$
$$C_1 + C_2 + C_3 + C_4 = 160$$
$$D_1 + D_2 + D_3 + D_4 = 360$$
$$A_1 + B_1 + C_1 + D_1 = 300$$
$$A_2 + B_2 + C_2 + D_2 = 220$$
$$A_3 + B_3 + C_3 + D_3 = 200$$
$$A_4 + B_4 + C_4 + D_4 = 320$$

Set this problem up as a transportation problem and solve.

26. ABCO desires to minimize the cost of shipping a product from three warehouses to four shops, given the following cost, supply, and demand data:

From	To				Supply
	1	2	3	4	
1	200	230	180	330	20
2	190	300	250	200	18
3	325	175	225	185	21
Demand	21	14	12	15	

a. Formulate the problem as an LP problem.

b. The route from warehouse 1 to shop 3 can no longer be used. Set up a transportation tableau that shows this restriction.

c. With this new information, solve the problem.

27. M & D confections produces candy that is sold as fund-raising ventures by school groups and service organizations. The candy is made at plants in Syracuse and White Plains, and is shipped (in case lots of 100 boxes) to distribution centers in five cities in the state. The Rochester warehouse requires 350 cases per month, Watertown 200, Plattsburgh 150, Olean 200, and NYC 800. The Syracuse facility can supply 1,000 cases per month. The White Plains plant produces 700 cases. The per-case shipping cost from each plant to each warehouse is shown below:

From	To	Cost
Syracuse	Rochester	$2.00
Syracuse	Watertown	5.00
Syracuse	Plattsburg	2.75
Syracuse	Olean	3.25
Syracuse	NYC	4.00
White Plains	Rochester	3.00
White Plains	Watertown	4.00
White Plains	Plattsburg	2.00
White Plains	Olean	3.25
White Plains	NYC	3.00

M & D Confections wants to determine the optimal shipping pattern to minimize total transportation cost.

a. Folmulate this as an LP problem.
b. Set up a transportation tableau.
c. Solve the problem.

28. During the Christmas shopping season, Discount Mart has four quick checkout counters open at all times. There are six clerks available now. Management must decide who to assign to which register. The assignments will be made on the basis of the numbers of customers served per hour. The number varies with the register because of specific register restrictions and requirements (no checks, credit card only, cash only, maximum number of items, etc.) and the ability of the individual cashier to handle these situations. The table below summarizes the number of customers that each cashier can handle at each register (based on past experience):

	Register			
Clerk	**1**	**2**	**3**	**4**
A	30	45	22	36
B	29	48	23	32
C	31	41	21	31
D	28	52	22	30
E	36	45	19	35
F	25	47	20	38

a. What assignment should be made to maximize the number of customers served?
b. Which clerks will not be assigned to one of these four registers?

29. Ye Olde Cheese Shoppe adds special kiosks to area shopping malls and stores during the fall and winter. Assistant managers from permanent locations are moved to manage these temporary spots. Six such assignments need to be made now. Management would like to keep its staff as happy as possible by assigning individuals to a location of their choice. Each temporary manager has been asked to rank the temporary assignments: 1 for first choice, 5 for "no way." Based on the rankings below, select two ways Ye Olde Cheese Shoppe can assign managers to make them happiest.

Mall Location

Manager	Perinton	Pittsford	Eastview	Midtown	Market Place	Irondequoit
Jones	1	2	3	5	4	6
Biorne	1	3	2	6	4	5
Kuehn	4	5	2	3	1	4
Carlsen	5	6	4	2	3	1
Jackson	5	6	1	4	2	3
Konecnty	6	4	5	2	3	1

How many of the assistant managers are assigned to their first choice?

Paul's Plant Food

In 1970, Paul Biorn took control of the family-owned fertilizer processing company. Shortly thereafter, he began producing three brands of plant food, Fast Grow, Green Thumb, and Miracle Green, under the name Paul's Plant Food Company. The introduction of these three products coincided nicely with the phenomenal increase in sales of decorative house plants, the surge in foundation plantings, and the rising number of home gardeners. As a result, profits from these products were outstanding. However, over the past five years, profits have been slowly decreasing. The declining profits have been attributed to a number of factors, including increased competition as new fertilizer and plant food producers enter the market and a backlash effect as some customers confuse the use of fertilizers with the use of pesticides and are opting for natural or organically grown foodstuffs.

These three plant foods are manufactured at plants in Fairport, New York, and Bradenton, Florida and are shipped to a central distribution center in Cincinnati, Ohio. The plant in Fairport has a production capacity of 9,000 pounds weekly. The plant in Bradenton can produce 15,000 pounds weekly. The combined weekly budget for both plants is $85,000. Sales records show a weekly demand of 9,000 pounds for Fast Grow, 7,500 pounds for Green Thumb, and 6,000 pounds for Miracle Green. Fast Grow costs $4.50 per pound to produce at Fairport and $3.00 at Bradenton. Green Thumb costs $3.50 per pound to produce at Fairport and $2.75 at Bradenton. Miracle Green costs $4.25 per pound to produce at Fairport and $4.65 at Bradenton. Selling prices are $9.00 per pound of Fast Grow, $7.50 per pound of Green Thumb, and $8.00 per pound of Miracle Green. It costs $0.12 per pound to ship the plant foods from Bradenton to Cincinnati and $0.10 per pound to ship from Fairport to Cincinnati.

The company wants to maximize the profit potential from these products and is considering various ways to reduce costs. Accordingly, Paul has asked the managers of marketing/distribution, sales, and production to provide a report outlining suggestions for reducing costs and increasing profits.

Dick Sonner, marketing/distribution manager, feels that cost savings can be made in the distribution and plant production area. At present, production at the Fairport plants is evenly divided among the three products (3,000 pounds each). Production at Bradenton is sufficient to meet remaining demand for each product. Dick feels this is wasteful. He feels production schedules should be altered to take advantage of the cost differentials that exist between plants for each product, and to take advantage of the differences in shipping costs. Under this plan, the company is currently spending $81,000 on production costs and $2,520 on shipping costs.

You have been hired as a consultant to help Paul by applying management science techniques to this particular problem. Prepare a report for Paul's Plant Food Company which addresses:

1. The amount of each type of plant food that should be produced at each plant.
2. The amount of idle capacity that will exist at each plant.
3. The optimal (minimum) cost associated with this recommendation.

8

Network Models

By the end of this chapter, you should be able to:

1

recognize a transshipment problem, a shortest route problem, a
minimal spanning tree problem, and a maximal flow problem;

2

formulate each of these as an LP problem;

3

recognize the difference between a capacitated and a
non-capacitated transshipment problem;

4

solve a non-capacitated transshipment problem as a transportation
problem;

5

solve shortest route, minimal spanning tree, and maximal flow
problems using a computer solution and/or manually.

In this chapter we present network or
network flow models, which are concerned with the flow of items through a system. Specifically, we will discuss solutions for shortest route, minimal spanning
tree, maximal flow, and transshipment problems, all of which can be viewed as
maximum flow/minimum cost problems. Since network models are all special
types of LP problems, we will demonstrate the LP formulations for each of these
problem types. Highly efficient special-purpose algorithms have been developed
that take advantage of the unique structure of network problems.

Network models are among the most popular and important types of optimization models used in management science today. Because networks can be represented in diagram form, they enable the decision maker to interpret a system
visually, thus improving understanding of the underlying problem. Furthermore,
many real-life problems can be modeled as networks. Many managerial problems
that might not initially appear to be networks can in fact be represented by networks in the abstract, thus taking advantage of highly efficient network algorithms to obtain an optimal solution. Moreover, very large, complicated problems
may contain subproblems with a network form. Recognizing and formulating the
problem as a network problem is not an easy, or trivial step. It is a crucial, often
time-consuming, painstaking process that requires great ingenuity and experience.

A Security System

The Longboat Key Club is an exclusive gulf-front resort on Longboat Key. Scattered among several pools, tennis courts, tropical gardens, and golf courses are private residences, a shopping mall, rental condominiums, restaurants, clubhouses, and a conference/visitor center. The resort is accessible only through a security checkpoint. Management is in the process of installing a new security system, including a television monitoring system, which will be connected to all residential, commercial, and recreational areas of the resort. To minimize disruption, management would like to use conduits (telephone and electricity) that are already in place. It is even more important to reduce installation cost by minimizing the total length of cable used. Management must therefore find a way to connect all these areas using the minimum amount of cable.

Later in the chapter we will return to this problem, which is an example of a minimal spanning tree problem.

8.1 *AN INTRODUCTION TO NETWORKS*

A **network** is an arrangement of **paths** or routes, connected at various points, through which items move from point to point (source to destination) along the connecting links. A network is graphically represented as a collection of **nodes** (the junction points) connected by **arcs** (the **branches** of the paths). In a network diagram, nodes are shown as numbered circles. Arcs or branches are lines between the nodes and are labeled by the nodes they join. For example, the following branch from node 1 to node 2

is designated 1,2. The arcs can be **directed** or **undirected;** that is, flow along the path can be in one given direction only (directed) or in either direction (undirected). The flow in the illustrated network is undirected. An arc can have values assigned, representing factors such as distance, cost, or length of time. Flow over the arcs can consist of many different kinds of things, such as gas through a pipeline, goods from factory to warehouse, or data from computer to computer. The amount of flow between the arcs is denoted by a variable, X_{ij}, for a flow from node i to node j. Flow also may be **capacitated;** in other words, there may exist capacity limits on the amount of flow allowed on any given arc. The per unit cost of flow over an arc is represented as C_{ij}.

Figure 8.1 shows the network diagram for the Fresh Fish, Fast Frozen transportation problem from the previous chapter, which we will now use to illustrate the components of a network diagram. Recall that FFFF wishes to minimize the cost of transporting frozen fish from three factory sites to four distribution centers. Management wishes to determine how much to ship over each route—that is, the flow over each arc (X_{ij})—in order to minimize the total cost. Nodes 1, 2, and 3 represent the processing plants. Nodes 4, 5, 6, 7 represent the distribution centers. The lines that connect processing plants with distribution centers are arcs or branches. Each arc represents a possible route. The per-unit cost of shipping along that route is shown above the line.

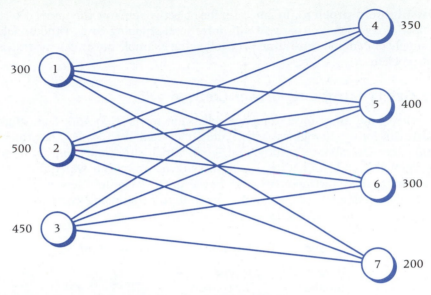

Figure 8.1 Network Diagram for the FFFF Problem

Solving Network Problems

Network models are formulated when the network structure (or component) has been recognized and drawn. For textbook problems, and for many small, simple, physical distribution problems, this is a relatively easy step. For many real-life problems, however, this is a difficult step that requires a great deal of experience. Network problems can be formulated as LP problems with an LP network form, a common thread that is helpful for both problem recognition and model formulation. We will stress this general form (and variations) as we present each model. Moreover, there are special-purpose algorithms for the shortest route, minimal spanning tree, and maximal flow models discussed in this chapter. Each of these will be discussed in the appropriate section.

Next we will introduce a class of network problem, the transshipment problem, that is similar to the transportation problem represented earlier.

8.2 *TRANSSHIPMENT PROBLEMS*

A **transshipment problem,** like the transportation problem, is concerned with allocating the flow of a given product in such a way as to minimize the total cost (maximum flow/minimum cost). In a transshipment problem, however, shipment is not restricted to a source-to-destination pattern (as it is in a transportation problem). A transshipment network contains three types of nodes: **source** nodes, **sink** (destination) nodes, and **transshipment nodes**. Transshipment nodes are nodes through which the flow can move, but these are neither sources nor sinks. A warehouse or regional distribution center is an example of a transshipment node. Arcs represent possible shipping routes between sources, transshipment points, and destinations (sinks). The supply available at each source is limited, and demand at each destination is known. If the amount that can be shipped along any route (the flow along a given arc) is restricted, the problem then becomes a **capacitated**

transshipment problem. In any case, the objective remains the same: determine the flow along each arc that will minimize total shipping cost, without violating any supply or demand constraints. The following example illustrates the transshipment problem.

The Gritty Sand and Gravel Company

The Gritty Sand and Gravel Company sells sand to the New York State Highway Department for use in highway repair and on icy state roads. GS&G has three production sites (Hamburg, Corning, and Troy), which ship sand monthly to one of two regional warehouses, Cicero and Tarrytown. From the warehouses, GS&G ships sand to three metropolitan areas in the state: Rochester, New York City, and Albany. The following tables list the per-unit (ton) shipping costs from site to warehouse and from warehouse to metropolitan, area:

Site	Warehouse	Per-unit Cost
Hamburg	Cicero	12
Hamburg	Tarrytown	15
Corning	Cicero	17
Corning	Tarrytown	24
Troy	Cicero	16
Troy	Tarrytown	14

Warehouse	City	Per-unit Cost
Cicero	Rochester	16
Cicero	NYC	20
Cicero	Albany	19
Tarrytown	Rochester	17
Tarrytown	NYC	14
Tarrytown	Albany	15

GS&G can supply 400 tons per month from Hamburg and Corning, and 100 tons from Troy. Demand is 450 tons in Rochester, 150 tons in NYC, and 300 tons in Albany. Gritty wants to minimize total shipping cost. What allocations should be made to achieve this objective?

Figure 8.2 shows the network diagram for this problem. Nodes 1, 2, and 3, representing the production sites, are the source or origin nodes. The number to the left of each node is the supply available at the site. Nodes 4 and 5, representing the warehouses, are transshipment nodes. Nodes 6, 7, and 8, representing the metropolitan areas, are destination nodes. The demand at each city is shown to the right of the node. Per-unit shipping cost between localities is shown above each arc.

Solving Transshipment Problems

The solution method for a transshipment problem depends upon whether or not the problem is capacitated. Both types of problem can be solved using LP. An uncapacitated transshipment problem can also be solved as a transportation problem using a transportation algorithm. In this section, we will begin with an uncapacitated problem and discuss both solution techniques. Then we will take a brief look at an LP formulation for a capacitated transshipment problem.

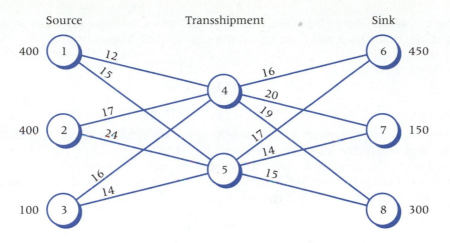

Figure 8.2 Network for the GS&G Transshipment Problem

LP Formulation of the GS&G Transshipment Problem

In a transshipment problem, the objective is to determine how much to ship along each arc (from i to j). Thus, there is one decision variable associated with each arc in the network (X_{ij}). In the GS&G problem, with 12 arcs, there are 12 decision variables. The cost of shipping one unit along each arc is C_{ij}; the total cost over that arc is $C_{ij}X_{ij}$. With the stated objective of minimizing cost, the objective function, expressed as the sum of the costs along the arcs, for this problem is

$$\text{MIN } 12X_{14} + 15X_{15} + 17X_{24} + 24X_{25} + 16X_{34} + 14X_{35} + 16X_{46} +$$
$$20X_{47} + 19X_{48} + 17X_{56} + 14X_{57} + 15X_{58}$$

Constraints express the flow balance through nodes, or the flow into a node minus the flow out of the node. There is a constraint associated with each node. It is also possible to have additional constraints, depending upon the problem requirements. For example, there can be limiting flow capacities on certain arcs.

Source node constraints must reflect the fact that the amount shipped out of a node is equal to (or less than) the supply available at that node; in other words, the constraint accounts for the supply at each source. The sum of the shipments out (the flow) must be less than or equal to ($\leq$) the supply at that source. Thus, for the GS&S problem, there are three constraints for the three source nodes. Each constraint reflects that shipments can be made to two transshipment nodes and that supply is equal to demand:

$$X_{14} + X_{15} = 400 \quad \text{[node 1]}$$
$$X_{24} + X_{25} = 400 \quad \text{[node 2]}$$
$$X_{34} + X_{35} = 100 \quad \text{[node 3]}$$

Destination node constraints account for the demand and must show that the amount shipped to that node equals the demand at that node. A transshipment problem can also be unbalanced, with the amount shipped being less than the demand. The sum of the shipments arriving at the destination must be less than or equal to ($\leq$) the demand. For the GS&G problem, shipments can arrive at the three destination nodes from two transshipment nodes. With supply equal to demand, the destination node constraints are expressed as follows:

$$X_{46} + X_{56} = 450 \quad \text{[node 6]}$$

$$X_{47} + X_{57} = 150 \quad \text{[node 7]}$$

$$X_{48} + X_{58} = 300 \quad \text{[node 8]}$$

The remaining two nodes in this problem are transshipment nodes. Shipments arrive and shipments leave, but none remain; that is, shipments flow through these nodes. The constraints must reflect that the sum of shipments arriving is equal to the sum of shipments departing (arrivals − departures = 0). The sum of shipments arriving at node 4 is expressed as

$$X_{14} + X_{24} + X_{34}$$

and the sum of shipments leaving node 4 is expressed as

$$X_{46} + X_{47} + X_{48}$$

Since no units remain in node 4, these are equal:

$$X_{14} + X_{24} + X_{34} = X_{46} + X_{47} + X_{48}$$

When expressed in standard form this becomes

$$X_{14} + X_{24} + X_{34} - X_{46} - X_{47} - X_{48} = 0 \quad \text{[node 4]}$$

Similarly, the constraint for node 5 is

$$X_{15} + X_{25} + X_{35} - X_{56} - X_{57} - X_{58} = 0 \quad \text{[node 5]}$$

The complete LP formulation for the GS&G problem is

$$\text{MIN } 12X_{14} + 15X_{15} + 17X_{24} + 24X_{25} + 16X_{34} + 14X_{35} + 16X_{46} + 20X_{47} + 19X_{48} + 17X_{56} + 14X_{57} + 15X_{58}$$

subject to

$$
\begin{aligned}
X_{14} + X_{15} &= 400 \\
X_{24} + X_{25} &= 400 \\
X_{34} + X_{35} &= 100 \\
X_{14} + X_{24} + X_{34} - X_{46} - X_{47} - X_{48} &= 0 \\
X_{15} + X_{25} + X_{35} - X_{56} - X_{57} - X_{58} &= 0 \\
X_{46} + X_{56} &= 450 \\
X_{47} + X_{57} &= 150 \\
X_{48} + X_{58} &= 300 \\
X_{ij} &\geq 0 \text{ for all i and j}
\end{aligned}
$$

Figure 8.3 shows the optimal solution, which is then summarized in Table 8.1.

In a transshipment problem, a wide variety of shipping patterns can occur. It is possible to have shipments between sources, between destinations, and from destination to source. Thus, it is possible to have nodes where items arrive, depart, and

```
           AFTER 11 ITERATIONS,
           THIS SOLUTION IS OPTIMAL:


           VARIABLE              QUANTITY
           --------              --------
             X14                    50
             X15                   350
             X24                   400
             X35                   100
             X46                   450
             X57                   150
             X58                   300
              A8                     0


           OPTIMAL Z = 27850
```

Figure 8.3 Optimal Solution GS&G Transshipment Problem

Table 8.1 Amounts Shipped Along Each Route

From	Node	To	Node	Amount Shipped
Hamburg	1	Cicero	4	50
Hamburg	1	Tarrytown	5	350
Corning	2	Cicero	4	400
Troy	3	Tarrytown	5	100
Cicero	4	Rochester	6	450
Tarrytown	5	NYC	7	150
Tarrytown	5	Albany	8	300

remain. In any event, there exists one constraint for each node. However, the constraint may contain more variables in order to reflect or expresses the balance of flow at that node. For source nodes, the sum of the shipments out minus the sum of the shipments in must be less than or equal to the supply available at that source. For the destination nodes, the sum of the shipments in minus the sum of the shipments out must be equal to or less than the demand. For transshipment nodes, the sum of shipments out always equals the sum of shipments in.

In the final LP formulation for this problem, notice that there are no more than two nonzero coefficients in each column, and that these nonzero coefficients are either $+1$ or -1. In general, these are common characteristics for LP formulations of network problems. An additional set of constraints sometimes is necessary to place capacities, U_{ij}, on the arcs.

Next, we will examine the solution of an uncapacitated transshipment problem as a transportation problem.

Formulation of a Transshipment Problem as a Transportation Problem
It is possible to convert an uncapacitated transshipment problem into an equivalent transportation problem, which can then be solved using the computationally efficient transportation algorithms. The conversion replaces the transshipment diagram, which has transshipment nodes, with a transportation network that has

Table 8.2 GS&G Transportation Tableau

From	To 6	To 7	To 8	Supply
1				400
2				400
3				100
Demand	450	150	300	

only origins and destinations. The now-familiar transportation tableau can then be set up. The supply from each source and the demand at each destination remain the same. Table 8.2 shows the transportation tableau for this problem without shipping costs entered.

Since the objective is cost minimization, it is reasonable to assume that all items shipped from an origin through a transshipment point to a destination will be shipped over the least-cost route. The transshipment nodes can be eliminated by selecting the least-cost shipping route (sequence of arcs) from each source to each destination. This solution gives the per-unit shipping cost for each route. In this problem, there are two possible routes from each source to each destination. For example, to go from Hamburg to Rochester (1—6) we can use either of two routes: $1 \rightarrow 4 \rightarrow 6$, or $1 \rightarrow 5 \rightarrow 6$. To go from Hamburg to NYC (1—7) there are also two route choices: $1 \rightarrow 4 \rightarrow 7$ or $1 \rightarrow 5 \rightarrow 7$. We determine the minimum cost of each by summing the costs of each arc on the path, as shown below:

$$\text{Path } 1 - 4 - 6$$
$$C_{14} + C_{46} = 12 + 16 = 28$$

$$\text{Path } 1 - 4 - 7$$
$$C_{14} + C_{47} = 12 + 20 = 32$$

$$\text{Path } 1 - 5 - 6$$
$$C_{15} + C_{56} = 15 + 17 = 32$$

$$\text{Path } 1 - 5 - 7$$
$$C_{15} + C_{57} = 15 + 14 = 29$$

Table 8.3 Summary of Least-Cost Routes from Each Source to Each Destination

Source Node	Transshipment Node	Destination Node	Cost
1	4	6	28
1	5	7	29
1	5	8	30
2	4	6	33
2	4	7	37
2	4	8	36
3	5	6	31
3	5	7	28
3	5	8	29

Table 8.4 Completed GS&G Transportation Tableau

| | To | | | |
From	6	7	8	Supply
1	28	29	30	400
2	33	37	36	400
3	31	28	29	100
Demand	450	150	300	

```
OPTIMAL ALLOCATION:

                6      7      8     SUPPLY
        1    |  50     50    300     400
        2    |  400    0      0      400
        3    |  0      100    0      100
     DEMAND  |  450    150    300

SOLUTION VALUE = 27850
```

Figure 8.4 Solution to GS&G Transportation Problem

Thus for 1— 6 the least cost is 28 and for 1— 7 the least cost is 29. This procedure is repeated for each source-to-destination route (nine in this tableau). The least-cost routes are summarized in Table 8.3. Table 8.4 shows the completed transportation tableau. Figure 8.4 shows the computer solution to this problem.

This solution shows the following shipping allocations:

Source 1–Destination 6	50 units
Source 1–Destination 7	50 units
Source 1–Destination 8	300 units
Source 2–Destination 6	400 units
Source 3–Destination 7	100 units
Cost =	$27,850

Note that this transportation solution does not provide the complete answer to the original problem, since it does not show which paths (and transshipment points) were used. To find how much to ship along each arc, it is necessary to return to the least-cost route calculations. These calculations show the transshipment node of each selected route and the arcs in each path. For example, the optimal transportation solution shows 50 units being shipped from Hamburg (1) to Rochester (6), that is, 50 units are shipped along route 1—6. Table 8.3, the summary of least-cost routes, indicates that route 1—6 goes through node 4. Thus, the route or path

Table 8.5 Summary of Optimal Shipping Allocations

From	Node	To	Node	Quantity
Hamburg	1	Cicero	4	50
Hamburg	1	Tarrytown	5	350
Corning	2	Cicero	4	400
Troy	3	Tarrytown	5	100
Cicero	4	Rochester	6	450
Tarrytown	5	NYC	7	150
Tarrytown	5	Albany	8	300

is 1–4–6. Fifty units are to be shipped via route 1–4, and then 50 units are to be shipped via route 4–6. This is summaried for all routes as follows:

Source 1–Destination 6   50 units
   Path 1–4–6 (arc 1–4 and arc 4–6)
Source 1–Destination 7   50 units
   Path 1–5–7 (arc 1–5 and arc 5–7)
Source 1–Destination 8   300 units
   Path 1–5–8 (arc 1–5 and arc 5–8)
Source 2–Destination 6   400 units
   Path 2–4–6 (arc 2–4 and arc 4–6)
Source 3–Destination 7   100 units
   Path 3–5–7 (arc 3–5 and arc 5–7)

The final step is to sum the allocations made to a particular arc in order to determine the total shipped along that arc. For example, 50 units and 400 units are shipped along arc 4–6, for a total of 450 units. We can use these same data to determine the number of units flowing through each transshipment node. For example, shipments from node 1 to node 6 and from node 2 to node 6 flow through node 4, for a total of 450 units (400 + 50). The optimal solution is shown in Table 8.5.

This method is fairly simple and convenient to use for small transshipment problems with simple route patterns. For large problems, with many, varied, and complicated routes, calculating the least-cost routes can be confusing and time-consuming. Linear programming often is easier in such a case. Finding the least-cost route is also a shortest-route problem. A computer solution for shortest route makes it easier to find the least-cost routes in complicated transshipment problems.

Thus far, we have been discussing transshipment problems that have no limits or upper bounds on the amount that can be shipped on any given branch. The flow along the arcs or through the nodes has not been capacitated. In the next section, we will briefly introduce the capacitated transshipment problem.

Solving Capacitated Transshipment Problems
In many real-world transshipment situations there are restrictions, limits or upper bounds on the amount that can be shipped over a given branch or through a specific intermediary point. In other words, capacities can exist on both transshipment nodes and on arcs or on each separately. A warehouse with a limited capacity represents a capacitated node. In a pipeline system that has pipes with varying diameters, a pipe with a smaller diameter represents a capacitated arc. Let's consider

what happens to our GS&G problem if we limit the number of units (tons) that can be handled by the warehouse in Cicero (transshipment node 4). In this case, there is a capacitated node.

Because of storm damage, the warehouse in Cicero can now handle no more than 350 tons of sand per month. If all other factors remain the same, how does this change affect the shipping allocations obtained earlier? Figure 8.5 repeats the network diagram for this problem, with the capacity limit shown below node 4.

The LP formulation remains the same, with one additional constraint to account for the limit at node 4. The sum of the arrivals at node 4 must be less than or equal to the capacity, in this case 350 tons. Thus we add the constraint

$$X_{14} + X_{24} + X_{34} \leq 350$$

The completed LP formulation is

$$\text{MIN } 12X_{14} + 15X_{15} + 17X_{24} + 24X_{25} + 16X_{34} + 14X_{35} + 16X_{46} +$$
$$20X_{47} + 19X_{48} + 17X_{56} + 14X_{57} + 15X_{58}$$

subject to

$$
\begin{aligned}
X_{14} + X_{15} &= 400 \\
X_{24} + X_{25} &= 400 \\
X_{34} + X_{35} &= 100 \\
X_{14} + X_{24} + X_{34} - X_{46} - X_{47} - X_{48} &= 0 \\
X_{15} + X_{25} + X_{35} - X_{56} - X_{57} - X_{58} &= 0 \\
X_{46} + X_{56} &= 450 \\
X_{47} + X_{57} &= 150 \\
X_{48} + X_{58} &= 300 \\
X_{14} + X_{24} + X_{34} &\leq 350 \\
X_{ij} \geq 0 \text{ for all } i \text{ and } j
\end{aligned}
$$

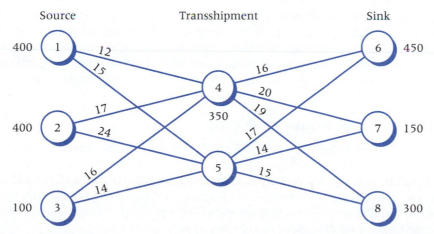

Figure 8.5 Network Representation of the Capacitated GS&G Transshipment Example

Node 4 now has more than one constraint. Because of this additional constraint, there are more than two nonzero coefficients in three columns. The additional limitations in the problem require the additional constraint. This is also true in the case of a capacitated arc. The variable associated with that arc would be expressed as a constraint with the limit on the RHS. If, for example, arc 4–6 had a capacity of 300 units, the constraint would be expressed

$$X_{46} \leq 300$$

As mentioned previously, transshipment problems represent one of four types of network models discussed in this chapter. Next, we will look at the shortest route problem.

8.3 *SHORTEST ROUTE*

The objective of a **shortest route problem** is to find the shortest route through a connecting network, from a source to one or more destinations. Since "shortest" does not refer only to physical distance, it is more descriptive to think of the objective as finding the least *cost* through a network where cost can be time, money, distance, etc. Thus, the objective is to find the least-cost route from a given node to any (or all) of the nodes in the network. We need to find an optimal set of routes that enable us to answer a variety of shortest route questions, depending upon the situation. For example, we may wish to find the shortest path from a source to a destination, when there are several possible combinations of arcs that can be traversed; or we may wish to find the shortest path from a specific node to every other node in the network. The procedure that we will demonstrate in the following problems will give us an all-inclusive solution; that is, it will give us the optimal set of routes.

Specialty Tours, Inc.

Specialty Tours, Inc. offers a combination Disney World–Caribbean Cruise package. After a short stay in the Magic Kingdom, guests are taken by bus to a cruise ship departing from Miami. Specialty would like to make this part of the vacation as comfortable and enjoyable as possible for guests. Therefore, they are providing the most luxurious land cruiser available. They would also like to minimize their cost. One part of this effort is to select the route with the shortest driving distance from Orlando to Miami. The network in Figure 8.6 represents possible routes.

Solving Shortest Route Problems

We have previously stated that, while network problems can be solved as LP problems, special-purpose algorithms often are better suited to the task. Moreover, these algorithms are easily converted to computer code. We will demonstrate the solution to shortest route problems, first using LP and then using the shortest route algorithm. Finally, we will increase the complexity of the problem in order to take advantage of the ease and speed of computer-based solutions.

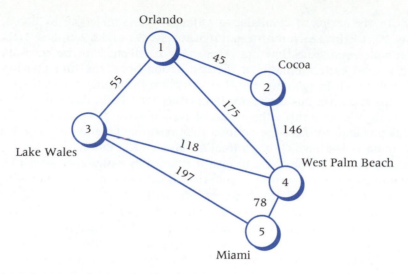

Figure 8.6 Routes from Orlando to Miami

LP Formulation of Shortest Route Problems

The complete formulation for the Specialty Tours problem is

$$\text{MIN } 45X_{12} + 55X_{13} + 175X_{14} + 146X_{24} + 118X_{34} + 197X_{35} + 78X_{45}$$

subject to

$$X_{12} + X_{13} + X_{14} = 1$$
$$X_{12} - X_{24} \qquad = 0$$
$$X_{14} - X_{45} \qquad = 0$$
$$X_{13} - X_{34} - X_{35} = 0$$
$$X_{35} + X_{45} \qquad = 1$$
$$X_{ij} \geq 0$$

Recall that a network model includes one variable for each arc. In this problem there are seven arcs, thus, there are seven variables. The cost associated with each arc, C_{ij}, is driving distance along that arc. The objective function indicates that these distances are to be minimized.

In a shortest route problem, at any node only one arc can be followed; in other words, it is an either/or situation. We can choose only one arc leaving any given node. For example, as the bus leaves Orlando (node 1), it can go either to Cocoa (node 2), to Lake Wales (node 3), or to West Palm Beach (node 4).

Recall that there is a constraint associated with each node. Thus there are five constraints that show the balance of flow through the network. To maintain consistency throughout our discussion of the LP formulations of network models, we will continue to think of the flow through the network, with a given supply available at a source and a demand to be met at the destination. There are, however, other ways to look at the problem—for example, in terms of arcs entering and leaving a node. For shortest route problems, flow is 1 unit. The first constraint is associated with the supply, 1, available at Orlando. The sum going to Cocoa, Lake Wales, or West Palm Beach must equal that supply. For nodes 2, 3, and 4, the flow into the node equals the flow out. These may be likened to the transshipment nodes discussed earlier. Finally, at the destination node, the sum arriving must equal the demand. In this case, the flow can come from only one of the two arcs entering the node; the bus can arrive from either West Palm Beach or Lake Wales, but not both. We force this either/or decision by making the sum = 1. When we solve this problem, we find the optimal solution to be Orlando to Lake Wales to Miami (route 1–3–5), which has a total distance of 252 miles.

This is a very simple problem. In fact, it is probably easier and faster to look at the diagram and select the correct route than it is to formulate the problem. With larger, more complex problems, however, this will not be the case. As problems increase in size and complexity, it becomes more difficult to find the solution intuitively. For example, in a network an arc can be directed or undirected. In the example problem, there are only directed arcs. In a problem involving arcs that can be traversed in either direction, each direction is considered a distinct arc and thus a distinct variable. That is, arc ij is separate and distinct from arc ji, and two variables X_{ij} and X_{ji} are required. Such situations can be incorporated into the formulation with varying degrees of ease. In the next sections, we will look at both the computationally efficient shortest route algorithm and solution by special-purpose computer software.

The Shortest Route Algorithm

The shortest route algorithm uses a labeling procedure to determine the shortest distance from a selected origin node to every other node. As the algorithm progresses, a label for each node is determined. The label indicates both the distance from the origin to that node and the immediate predecessor (the node that immediately precedes this node on the path). Then, by backtracking, the actual route from one node to any other node can be determined. This algorithm is iterative in nature, and in a network with n nodes it finds the optimal solution in n-1 steps. We will illustrate the shortest route algorithm with the following problem.

Greystock Canvas—a Shortest Route Problem   Greystock Canvas, located in Ocala, makes and repairs awnings for commercial customers located in seven other cities in Florida. The network is shown in Figure 8.7. The drive times are estimated drive times (in minutes). Greystock has built a reputation for fast, efficient service. It is company policy to arrive "on the spot" in as short a time as possible, making same-day repairs at the customer location if at all possible. If it is not possible to make the repair at the customer location, Greystock picks up the awning and returns it to Ocala. In any event, the company has to maintain a small, "ready to roll" fleet of repair vans. In order to minimize the travel time to each customer location, management needs to find the shortest route to each city serviced by Greystock.

The labeling procedure progresses in a stepwise fashion, beginning at the origin and fanning out to identify the shortest route to each node in ascending order of distance from the origin. Each label consists of an ordered pair of numbers. The first represents the distance from the origin to that node along a specified path.

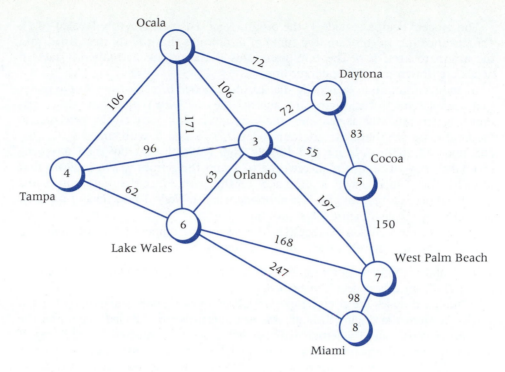

Figure 8.7 Greystock Shortest Route Problem

The second is the number of the node that precedes this node on the path. For example, consider node 6 below:

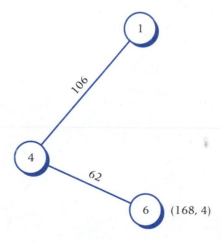

The label (168,4), shows us that the distance to 6 from node 1, the origin, is 168, and that node 4 immediately precedes node 6 on this path.

Initially each node is given a **temporary label.** When the best route is determined, the label becomes **permanent.**

The process begins at node 1, the origin. Node 1 is permanently labeled (0,1). The distance (or, in this case, the time) of 0 indicates that the shortest time from the origin to itself is 0. The 1 indicates this is the origin. Permanently labeled nodes are drawn in heavier, darker lines.

In the first iteration, each node that can be reached directly from 1 (the nodes that are adjacent to the origin) are labeled. The one with the shortest time (distance) is permanently labeled; the others are given temporary labels. Referring to Figure 8.7, we see that there are four nodes, 2, 3, 4, and 6, with times of 72, 106, 106, and 171, that can be reached directly from 1. We give each of these a temporary label, consisting of the direct time to 1 and the number 1, to indicate that node 1 is the immediately preceding node on this path. Since the route from 1 to 2 has the shortest time, we give it a permanent label. Node 1 and node 2 are now permanently labeled. Figure 8.8 shows these labels.

In the second iteration, we begin at this second permanently labeled node and fan out, labeling adjacent nodes. In general terms:

1. All nodes (both unlabeled and temporarily labeled) that can be reached directly from this node are identified.
2. Unlabeled nodes are given temporary labels, showing both the cumulative distance from the origin (through this new, permanently labeled node) and the predecessor node. The temporarily labeled nodes are evaluated for updating. If the distance component of a temporarily labeled node is less via this new node, the label is updated to show the better distance and the new predecessor node.
3. When the labeling is completed, all temporary labels are compared, and the one with the shortest distance is made permanent.

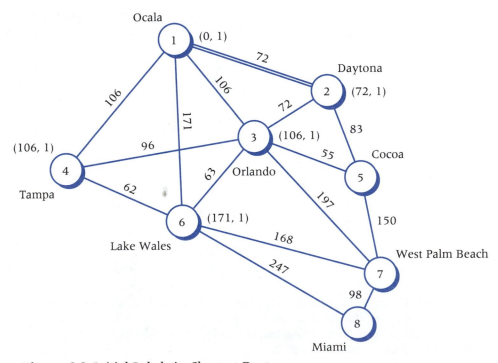

Figure 8.8 Initial Labels in Shortest Route

In the Greystock problem, permanently labeled node 2 is directly adjacent to nodes 3 and 5. Node 3 has a temporary label; node 5 is not yet labeled. We will first give node 5 the temporary label (155,2). The time is the cumulative time from the origin through node 2. We calculated it by adding the distance label at 2 (72) to the distance from node 2 to node 5 (83). The predecessor node, the node immediately preceding node 3 on this path, is 2. Next we will evaluate the temporary label at node 3. The label (106,1) shows a time of 106 minutes directly from node 1. Using the new path to get from the origin to node 3 through node 2 would require 144 minutes (72 + 72). Since 106 is the smaller number, we will not change this temporary label. Going through 2 offers no advantage; we leave node 3 unchanged. Finally, we compare all nodes with temporary labels, 3, 4, 5, and 6, and select the node with the smallest time to become permanently labeled. In this case there is a tie; both 3 and 4 have a time of 106 minutes. Ties can be broken arbitrarily. This time, we choose to give node 3 a permanent label. These labels are shown in Figure 8.9.

Each successive iteration continues to fan outward from the permanently labeled nodes to add another permanently labeled node. In a network with n nodes, there will be n-1 iterations. Thus, in our third iteration, we are fanning out from node 3. Nodes 4, 5, 6, and 7 are the adjacent nodes. We give node 7 the temporary label (303,3), the cumulative time 106 + 197, and the predecessor node 3. We evaluate the temporary labels at nodes 4, 5, and 6. Only the time at node 6 can be improved. The current label (171,1), showing the direct time from the origin, can be improved by going through node 3. The new label is (169,3). When we compare all

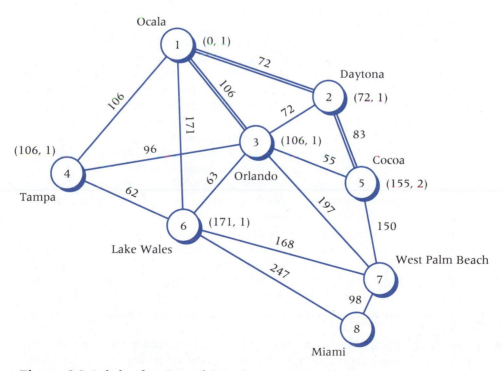

Figure 8.9 Labels after Second Iteration

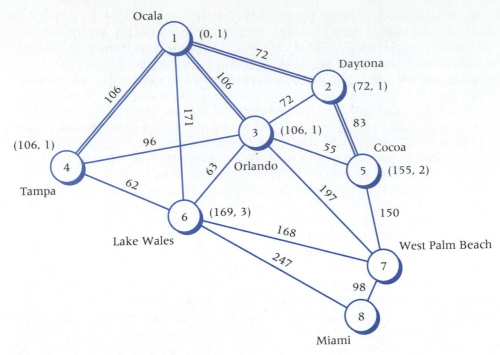

Figure 8.10 Labels after the Third Iteration

of the temporary labels, nodes 4, 5, 6, and 7, we see that the label at node 4, (106,1) has the shortest time. We give it a permanent label. Figure 8.10 shows the labels after the third iteration.

Figure 8.11 shows the labels for the remaining iterations. In the fourth iteration, moving out from node 4, we find only one non–permanently labeled adjacent node, node 6. The temporary label can be improved by going through node 4. The new temporary label becomes (168,4). The time represents the time in the label at node 4 plus the time from node 4 to node 6 (62). The new predecessor node is 4. After comparing all temporary labels, nodes 5, 6, and 7, we make the label with the smallest time permanent, that is, the label at node 5.

In the fifth iteration, we have only one node directly adjacent to node 5. Node 7 is temporarily labeled (303,3). Going through node 5, with a time of 155 + 150 = 305, will not improve upon this time, so the label is not changed. There are two nodes with temporary labels to compare, node 6 and node 7. Node 6 has the shorter time and is permanently labeled.

For the sixth iteration, we identify nodes 7 and 8 as directly reachable from the last permanently labeled node, 6. Node 8 is unlabeled. We temporarily label it (415,6); the time is 168 + 247 and the node immediately preceding it on the path is 6. Node 7 is temporarily labeled (303,3). We cannot improve upon this by going through node 6 (168 + 168 = 336). Node 7 has the shorter time, and is permanently labeled. Finally, there is one node left. The temporary label at 8 can be updated to (401,7).

To determine the shortest routes from the origin to all other nodes, or from the origin to a given destination, requires a backtracking procedure. Using the predecessor component of the permanent labels as follows:

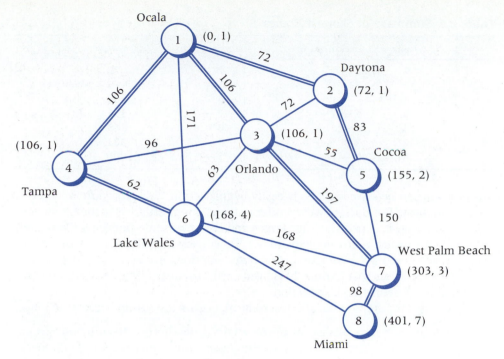

Figure 8.11 Labels for Iterations 4 through 7

1. At any node, check the predecessor.
2. Move to that node.
3. Again check the predecessor and move to that node.
4. Continue backtracking along the path via predecessor nodes until the origin is reached.

For example, to find the shortest route from the origin to node 8, begin at node 8. The label tells us that 7 is the node that immediately precedes 8 on the shortest path. Next, moving to node 7, we see that node 3 immediately precedes 7. At node 3, we find that node 3 is preceded directly by the origin. Thus we have this sequence of nodes:

$$8 \rightarrow 7 \rightarrow 3 \rightarrow 1$$

Table 8.6 summarizes the backtracking and gives the shortest route from the origin to all the nodes in this network. Notice that Greystock could make deliveries and pickups using three trucks: one from Ocala to Daytona to Cocoa, requiring 2 hours and 35 minutes driving time; one from Ocala to Orlando to West Palm Beach to Miami, requiring 4 hours and 41 minutes; and one from Ocala to Tampa to Lake Wales, requiring 2 hours and 48 minutes (notice that we converted minutes to hours and minutes and we do not consider stopping time in the cities visited).

Any node in a network can be the origin. For convenience, it is usually given the number 1. Using this backtracking method, it is possible to find the shortest route from the origin to any or all nodes. We could have used this method to find the shortest route from Orlando to Miami in the earlier Specialty tour problem. Since

Table 8.6 Summary of Shortest Routes

Node	Backtracking	Shortest route	Distance
2	$2 \rightarrow 1$	$1 - 2$	72
3	$3 \rightarrow 1$	$1 - 3$	106
4	$4 \rightarrow 1$	$1 - 4$	106
5	$5 \rightarrow 2 \rightarrow 1$	$1 - 2 - 5$	155
6	$6 \rightarrow 4 \rightarrow 1$	$1 - 4 - 6$	168
7	$7 \rightarrow 3 \rightarrow 1$	$1 - 3 - 7$	303
8	$8 \rightarrow 7 \rightarrow 3 \rightarrow 1$	$1 - 3 - 7 - 8$	401

this problem can be solved relatively easily by inspection, this procedure may seem overly complicated. It does, however, offer an excellent alternative to the LP formulation. Moreover, it is necessary for larger, more cumbersome problems. Computer solutions for shortest route problems frequently employ this algorithm because it is easily implemented on a computer. Computer solutions are especially helpful for the kind of problem that cannot be solved easily by inspection. We will demonstrate one of these in the next section.

Briefly, then the steps in the shortest route algorithm are summarized as follows:

1. Give each node that is adjacent to the origin (directly connected by one arc) a temporary label. The label has two components, an ordered pair of numbers. The first number shows the direct distance to the origin. The second number is the predecessor number. In this initial step, it is the origin, node 1.

2. Identify the temporarily labeled node having the shortest distance. Give it a permanent label. When all nodes have permanent labels, go on to step 4.

3. Identify all (non–permanently labeled) nodes adjacent to the last permanently labeled node. These nodes are either unlabeled or temporarily labeled. Give temporary labels to the unlabeled nodes and evaluate the temporarily labeled nodes for updating. The distance is cumulative from the origin and is computed by adding the distance along the arc to the distance shown on the permanent label at the preceding node. The predecessor component is the permanently labeled node number. Update temporary labels only if the distance through this new permanently labeled node is less than the distance currently showing in the label. The updated label shows the new distance and the new predecessor node. Return to step 2 and repeat the process.

4. To find the shortest distance from the origin to any node, start at that node and backtrack to the origin using the predecessor components of the labels. The predecessor number indicates the immediately preceding node on the shortest path.

COMPUTER SOLUTIONS FOR SHORTEST ROUTE PROBLEMS

Shortest route algorithms are easily implemented on a computer. For large-scale, complex network problems, a computer is essential. Numerous commercial packages are available for mainframe, mini, and personal computers.[1]

[1]For example, two frequently mentioned minimum cost/flow programs for mainframes are GNET, available from Gordon H. Bradely at the Navel Postgraduate School in Monterey, California, and PNET, available from Darwin Klingman at the University of Texas in Austin. Both can be used to solve shortest route problems.

The following example is a little larger than the previous ones. Although it can be solved using the shortest route algorithm, or even with LP, these methods obviously would take more time and thought and would be subject to careless errors. A computer solution is more efficient.

Big Red Cab—Shortest Route Example

Big Red Cab Company services a major tourist area. Most visitors arrive by plane and take a taxi to their hotel. Big Red would like to minimize travel time from the airport to each of several area hotels. The network in Figure 8.12 represents these locations and routes. Node 1 represents the airport; all other nodes are hotel sites. Each C_{ij} represents travel time in minutes.

The computer solution for this problem is shown in Figure 8.13.

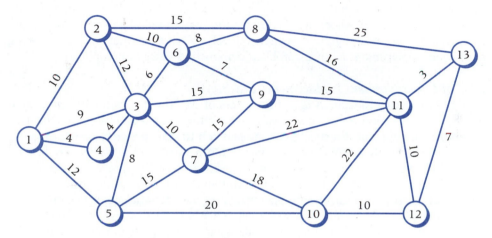

Figure 8.12 Big Red Cab Network of Routes

```
        SOLUTION - SHORTEST ROUTE NETWORK


                BRANCH
BRANCH          VALUE           PATH
------          ------          ----
1 — 2           10              1 — 2
1 — 3           8               1 — 4 — 3
1 — 4           4               1 — 4
1 — 5           12              1 — 5
1 — 6           14              1 — 4 — 3 — 6
1 — 7           18              1 — 4 — 3 — 7
1 — 8           22              1 — 4 — 3 — 6 — 8
1 — 9           21              1 — 4 — 3 — 6 — 9
1 — 10          32              1 — 5 — 10
1 — 11          36              1 — 4 — 3 — 6 — 9 — 11
1 — 12          42              1 — 5 — 10 — 12
1 — 13          39              1 — 4 — 3 — 6 — 9 — 11—13
```

Figure 8.13 Computer Solution for Big Red Cab Shortest Route

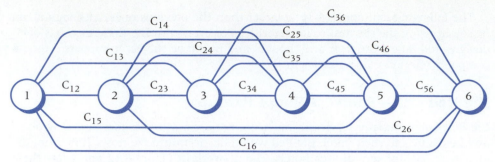

Figure 8.14 Network for Equipment Replacement Analysis

A Shortest Route Application

Earlier, we stated that many types of real-world problems that seemingly are not network problems, do in fact have a network structure and can be solved as network problems. The shortest route algorithm can, in fact, be used to solve problems that do not, at first glance, appear to involve a "shortest route." The following equipment replacement analysis problem demonstrates such an application.

Lord of Life Equipment Replacement (Leasing)

Lord of Life Lutheran Church is in the process of starting an adult day care center. For state certification, the center must provide a five-year spending plan. One item of required equipment is a specially equipped van to transport day care users with special needs. The Board of Governors has recommended leasing a new van. Several options are available: (1) lease a van at the beginning of the first year, thereby incurring minimal leasing costs but high maintenance and operating costs; (2) lease a new van each year, minimizing operating and maintenance costs but maximizing leasing costs; (3) lease a new van every other year, or in varying combinations of years. The governing board must decide what leasing pattern to follow in order to keep the van cost at a minimum.

Figure 8.14 shows the network representation for this equipment replacement problem. Each node represents a point in time. Node 1 is the beginning of year 1; node 6 is the beginning of year 6 or the end of year 5. The costs on each arc, here shown as C_{ij}, are the combined leasing/operating costs for that year. Leasing a new van each year would have a total cost of $C_{12} + C_{23} + C_{34} + C_{45} + C_{56}$. Leasing a van at the beginning of year 1 and keeping it for all five years would be C_{16}. We solve this problem by finding the shortest route from the origin to all nodes. Cost figures are supplied in an end-of-chapter question. The solution will be left to you.

8.4 *MINIMAL SPANNING TREE*

In network terminology, a **spanning tree** is a subset of the arcs in a given network that connects every node, but does not contain a **loop** (a loop is a path that connects a node to itself). Every node in the network may be reached from every other node through one or more arcs. The objective of a **minimal spanning tree** problem is to find the set of arcs that will connect all the nodes in the network at a minimum total distance; that is, to minimize the sum of the arc lengths used to connect all the nodes.

To demonstrate the minimal spanning tree, we will return to the Longboat Key Club security problem presented at the beginning of the chapter.

A Security System—A Minimal Spanning Tree Example Problem

The Longboat Key Club is an exclusive gulf-front resort on Longboat Key. Scattered among several pools, tennis courts, tropical gardens, and golf courses are private residences, a shopping mall, rental condominiums, restaurants, clubhouses, and a conference/visitor center. The resort is accessible only through a security checkpoint. Management is in the process of installing a new security system, including a television monitoring system, which will be connected to all residential, commercial, and recreational areas of the resort. To minimize disruption, management would like to use conduits (for telephone and electricity) that are already in place. It is even more important to reduce installation cost by minimizing the total length of cable used.

The network shown in Figure 8.15 represents this problem. Each node is a site to be connected, and the arcs show the conduits already in place. The objective is to connect all these sites, using the least amount of cable.

Solving Minimal Spanning Tree Problems

We will demonstrate an LP formulation, followed by the network flow algorithm and computer solution.

LP Formulation of a Minimal Spanning Tree Problem

The Longboat Key Club Security problem can be formulated as follows:

$$\text{MIN } 48X_{12} + 72X_{13} + 70X_{14} + 20X_{23} + 48X_{25} + 58X_{34} + 92X_{37} +$$
$$70X_{47} + 40X_{56} + 60X_{58} + 118X_{510} + 64X_{67} + 65X_{69} + 47X_{79} +$$
$$34X_{89} + 60X_{810} + 82X_{910}$$

subject to

$$X_{12} + X_{13} + X_{14} \geq 1$$
$$X_{12} + X_{23} + X_{25} \geq 1$$
$$X_{13} + X_{23} + X_{34} + X_{37} \geq 1$$

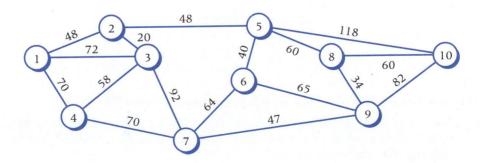

$$X_{14} + X_{34} + X_{47} \geq 1$$
$$X_{25} + X_{56} + X_{58} + X_{510} \geq 1$$
$$X_{56} + X_{67} + X_{69} \geq 1$$
$$X_{37} + X_{47} + X_{67} \geq 1$$
$$X_{58} + X_{89} + X_{810} \geq 1$$
$$X_{69} + X_{79} + X_{89} + X_{910} \geq 1$$
$$X_{510} + X_{810} + X_{910} \geq 1$$
$$X_{12} + X_{13} + X_{14} + X_{23} + X_{25} + X_{34} + X_{37} + X_{47} + X_{56} + X_{58} +$$
$$X_{510} + X_{67} + X_{69} + X_{79} + X_{89} + X_{810} + X_{910} = 9$$
$$X_{ij} = 1 \text{ or } 0$$

Again, one variable is associated with each arc and each node has an associated constraint. The spanning tree must connect all the nodes. At each node, a specific arc is selected or not selected. If on arc is selected, however, that does not mean another arc cannot also be used. In a minimal spanning tree the constraints must show that, for each node, at least one arc will be used. The constraints also must show that it is allowable and possible for more than one arc to enter or leave any given node. Since the arcs are undirected, it is possible to move from any node to any or all adjacent nodes. At least one arc must connect each node. For example, connections to node 1 are expressed by the constraint

$$X_{12} + X_{13} + X_{14} \geq 1$$

At node 2 it is possible to travel to node 1, node 3, and/or node 5. This is expressed as

$$X_{12} + X_{23} + X_{25} \geq 1$$

Note that the branches in this problem are symmetrical. The distance in either direction between two nodes is the same. Thus the distance from 1 to 2 is the same as the distance from 2 to 1. This is not always the case. In this constraint we could have used the variable X_{21} as equivalent to X_{12}, but if the distances were not the same, two arcs and therefore two variables would be required.

The final constraint limits the number of arcs. In a network with n nodes, there will always be n-1 arcs in the minimal spanning tree. This network has 10 nodes, so final constraint says that there must be exactly nine arcs in the solution.

The Greedy Algorithm Solution

The algorithm used for solving minimal spanning tree problems is an extremely simple optimizing technique. It is usually referred to as the **greedy algorithm** because at each step we make a "greedy" choice; that is, we choose the closest node. In this case, using the greedy algorithm results in an optimal solution.

Essentially, the technique requires only that at each iteration (n-1 for a network with n nodes) the closest node is joined. It is a two-step procedure:

1. Choose any node as the starting node. Join it to the closest node, forming a connected segment of two nodes. These nodes are termed connected. The remaining ones are unconnected.
2. Consider all nodes in the connected segment. Identify all arcs leading directly from the connected segment to unconnected nodes. Join the closest of these

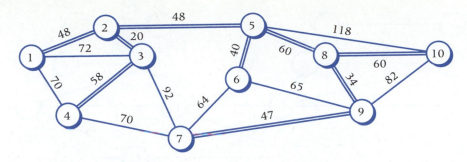

Figure 8.16 Longboat Key Club Network

nodes to the connected segment, making it part of the connected segment. Ties are broken arbitrarily. Repeat (n-1 times) until all nodes are connected.

We will use Longboat Key Club network, repeated in Figure 8.16, to demonstrate the greedy algorithm. The spanning tree is outlined in a darker line.

We begin at node 1 and join it to the closest node, node 2. We now consider those nodes directly connected to node 1 or node 2 (the connected segment). Node 3 is closest, so we join 2 to 3. Our spanning tree now consists of nodes 1, 2, and 3. Next, we consider unconnected nodes 4, 5, and 7, and make the connection from 2 to 5. As we repeat the process, connections are made in this sequence: from 5 to 6, from 3 to 4, from 5 to 8, from 8 to 9, from 9 to 7, and finally from 8 to 10. The total distance is 415. The starting node is arbitrary; we will arrive at the same solution starting at any node in the network. Note, however, that in a minimal spanning tree there may well be alternate optimal solutions.

Once again, this was an extremely simple problem. Things get a bit more difficult with problems having hundreds of nodes and even thousands of arcs. For these, computer solutions are essential.

COMPUTER SOLUTION FOR MINIMAL SPANNING TREE

To demonstrate the use of a computer solution for minimal spanning tree problems, let us consider a slightly larger problem.

Reilley Homes Cable Hookup—Minimal Spanning Tree Reilley Homes is building a new subdivision on rolling, wooded sites. Several ravines and a meandering creek necessitate the layout of homes shown in Figure 8.17. Home sites are represented by nodes. The numbers show the distance along a possible route to the next house. All Reilley homes come with cable hookups available. The cable contract has been awarded to Suburban Cable. Before construction begins, Suburban would like to run cable to each home site, keeping the cost to a minimum by minimizing the length of cable required.

This problem is not quite so easily solved by visual inspection. Even using the greedy algorithm is time-consuming. Figure 8.18 shows the computer output for this problem. From this we can see that the total number of feet required to connect all houses is 8070. The spanning tree has these branches: 1–5, 5–9, 9–13, 13–17, 17–18, 18–14, 14–15, 15–16, 16–19, 16–12, 12–8, 8–7, 7–3, 3–4, 5–10, 10–11,

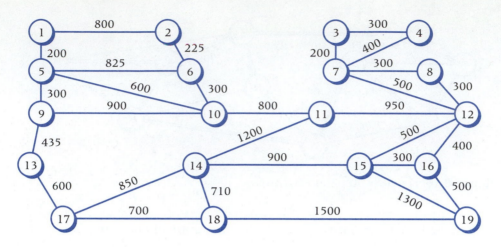

Figure 8.17 Reilly Homes Network

```
              BRANCH        VALUE
              ------        -----
               1 — 5         200
               5 — 9         300
               9 —13         435
               5 —10         600
              10 — 6         300
               6 — 2         225
              13 —17         600
              17 —18         700
              18 —14         710
              10 —11         800
              14 —15         900
              15 —16         300
              16 —12         400
              12 — 8         300
               8 — 7         300
               7 — 3         200
               3 — 4         300
              16 —19         500

          MINIMUM TOTAL SPAN = 8070
```

Figure 8.18 Reilley Home Minimal Spanning Tree Solution Using D&D Computer Solution

10–6, and 6–2. There are 18 branches, as we would expect with 19 nodes. Every node is connected, and there are no loops. In this problem, it takes longer to enter the data than to get a solution.

8.5 *MAXIMAL FLOW*

The objective in a **maximal flow problem** is to maximize the total amount of flow through a network in a given time period. All flows are transmitted from a single source to a single destination, a sink, through a network in which the branches have differing limited capacities. Examples include the flow of water, oil, or natural gas through pipelines; the flow of traffic through highway systems; and the flow of data through telecommunications systems. Compare this type of problem with the networks discussed thus far, in which the objective has been to determine the value (cost, time, distance, etc.) of the flow through a network. Now the objective is to determine the amount of flow across each arc, in a network composed of capacitated arcs, that will permit the maximum total flow from source to sink in a given amount of time.

The flow along an arc can be directed or undirected; that is, flow is allowed in one direction only or in both directions. Capacities on a given arc can be different for each direction. The capacities along an arc are shown by numbers adjacent to the node. The number immediately to the right of a node gives the capacity in the direction ij. The number to the left of a node gives the capacity in the opposite direction on that arc, ji. A zero indicates that no flow is allowed in that direction. For example, on arc 1,2

the 7 to the right of node 1 shows a flow capacity of 7 from 1 to 2; the 3 to the left of node 2 indicates a capacity of 3 from node 2 to node 1. If the 3 were changed to a 0, it would mean that no flow is permitted in the 2,1 direction.

Consider the following problem of transporting natural gas from a gas field in Oklahoma to a storage facility hundreds of miles away.

B-Low Cost Natural Gas Company—Maximal Flow Problem

B-Low Cost Natural Gas Company is using a system of pipes that has developed over a period of several decades. Because of varying pipe sizes, municipal rulings, and many other factors, flow capacities vary along the branches in the network. The pipe network and the flow capacities (in thousands of cubic feet per hour) are shown in Figure 8.19. Node 1 is the source node; node 7 is the sink node. B-Low wants to know not only the maximal flow per hour over this system, but the flow over each branch (for future replacement purposes).

Once again, for consistency and for comparison purposes, we will first demonstrate that this network problem can be solved using linear programming. Then we will discuss the maximal flow algorithm and use it to solve the B-Low Cost problem. Finally, we will demonstrate a computer solution for a more difficult problem.

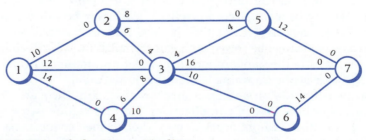

Figure 8.19 Network for B-Low Pipeline

LP Formulation of Maximal Flow Problems

The network problems considered thus far are variations of a minimum cost/ maximum flow problem. The maximal flow problem, while closely related, is slightly different. In the previous network problems, the objective was to determine the value (cost, time, distance, etc.) of the flow through a network. Here the objective is to determine the maximum *amount* of flow that can be transmitted through a network in a given amount of time. Furthermore, in a maximal flow problem, there are no supplies and no demands. These differences are reflected in the following LP formulation:

MAX FLOW

subject to

$$X_{12} + X_{13} + X_{14} = \text{FLOW}$$
$$X_{12} + X_{32} - X_{23} - X_{25} = 0$$
$$X_{13} + X_{23} + X_{43} + X_{53} - X_{32} - X_{35} - X_{34} - X_{37} = 0$$
$$X_{14} + X_{34} - X_{43} - X_{46} = 0$$
$$X_{25} + X_{35} - X_{53} - X_{57} = 0$$
$$X_{46} + X_{36} - X_{67} = 0$$
$$X_{37} + X_{57} + X_{67} = \text{FLOW}$$
$$X_{12} \leq 10$$
$$X_{23} \leq 6$$
$$X_{36} \leq 10$$
$$X_{53} \leq 4$$
$$X_{13} \leq 12$$
$$X_{32} \leq 4$$
$$X_{37} \leq 16$$
$$X_{57} \leq 12$$
$$X_{14} \leq 14$$
$$X_{34} \leq 8$$
$$X_{43} \leq 6$$
$$X_{67} \leq 14$$
$$X_{25} \leq 8$$
$$X_{35} \leq 4$$
$$X_{46} \leq 10$$

$$X_{ij} \geq 0 \text{ for all i and j}$$

This formulation does not look like the ones we have encountered previously in the other network models. Notice first that an unknown called FLOW is being maximized. (FLOW is a variable and could just as easily be called f or X_f.) This unknown, FLOW, appears both as the objective function variable and as a RHS value. The problem cannot be solved with this formulation. We will change it later so that it conforms to the standard formulation for minimum cost flow networks. For now, let's look at the reasoning behind this formulation.

Once, again, there is a variable associated with each arc. There are 15 variables, because some arcs have flow in two directions and thus require two distinct variables. Arc 2–3 is distinct from arc 3–2, even though they connect the same two nodes. Again, there is a constraint associated with each node and this constraint shows the balance of flow through that node.

The first constraint shows the flow entering the system, the flow at the source. By definition, the total flow through the system per unit of time is equal to the flow per unit of time leaving the source. Capacity restrictions on the arcs make it impossible for an unlimited amount of flow to leave the source and then just wander around somewhere in the system. Whatever leaves the source (whatever enters the system) has to exit the system at the sink. The objective is to maximize this amount (flow). The sum of the flows along the arcs originating at the source is equal to the flow, and is expressed

$$X_{12} + X_{13} + X_{14} = \text{FLOW}$$

or

$$X_{12} + X_{13} + X_{14} - \text{FLOW} = 0$$

The same is true of the flow exiting at the sink. The sum of the flows of the arcs converging on the sink is equal to the flow, and is expressed in the constraint

$$X_{37} + X_{57} + X_{67} = \text{FLOW}$$

or

$$X_{37} + X_{57} + X_{67} - \text{FLOW} = 0$$

For each node (other than the source and sink), what flows into a node must flow out of the node. This balance requirement, or "conservation of flow," must be satisfied. Each constraint for the intermediary nodes expresses this relationship or balance. For example, consider the flow balance at node 3. The amount of flow into node 3, along 4 arcs, is equal to the amount flowing out of the node, also along 4 arcs. This is expressed

$$X_{13} + X_{23} + X_{43} + X_{53} - X_{32} - X_{35} - X_{34} - X_{37} = 0$$

The additional constraints, not associated with the balance of flow at any node, express the arc capacities.

We can now make one additional change to the formulation. Recall that the flow entering the system, at the source, is equal to the flow exiting at the sink. Using this information, we can draw a dummy arc from the sink to the source, from node 7 to node 1, and call this variable X_{71}. The objective then is to maximize the flow along this arc. In the formulation, shown below, we simply substitute the variable X_{71} for the variable flow. You may sometimes see this referred to as a circular network.

MAX FLOW

subject to

$$
\begin{aligned}
X_{12} + X_{13} + X_{14} - \text{flow} &= 0 \\
X_{12} + X_{32} - X_{23} - X_{25} &= 0 \\
X_{13} + X_{23} + X_{43} + X_{53} - X_{32} - X_{35} - X_{34} - X_{37} &= 0 \\
X_{14} + X_{34} - X_{43} - X_{46} &= 0 \\
X_{25} + X_{35} - X_{53} - X_{57} &= 0 \\
X_{46} + X_{36} - X_{67} &= 0
\end{aligned}
$$

$$X_{37} + X_{57} + X_{67} - \text{FLOW} = 0$$

$$X_{12} \leq 10$$
$$X_{23} \leq 6$$
$$X_{36} \leq 10$$
$$X_{53} \leq 4$$
$$X_{13} \leq 12$$
$$X_{32} \leq 4$$
$$X_{37} \leq 16$$
$$X_{57} \leq 12$$
$$X_{14} \leq 14$$
$$X_{34} \leq 8$$
$$X_{43} \leq 6$$
$$X_{67} \leq 14$$
$$X_{25} \leq 8$$
$$X_{35} \leq 4$$
$$X_{46} \leq 10$$

$$X_{ij} \geq 0 \text{ for all i and j}$$

We will solve this problem in the following discussion of the maximal flow algorithm. We leave it up to you to solve it using LP and compare the two methods.

The Maximal Flow Algorithm

The maximal flow algorithm sequentially considers trial flows along continuous paths through the network. At each iteration, a continuous path, from source to sink, is arbitrarily chosen and "as much as possible" is transmitted along that path. "As much as possible" is the minimum capacity of any arc on the path (similar to reallocating along a stepping stone path). This limit ensures that, on any arc, the amount being shipped does not exceed the arc capacity. Also, as we discussed in the LP formulation, for all nodes except the source and sink, the flow entering a node must equal the flow leaving the node. No flow can be stored or deposited at a node for future use.

Let's consider the B-Low pipeline in Figure 8.19. There are several possible paths from 1 to 7, such as 1–2–5–7, 1–3–7, or 1–4–3–5–7. If we arbitrarily select 1–2–3–7, then the maximum amount that can be sent along the path is 6, the minimum capacity of any of the arcs on that path, arc 2–3.

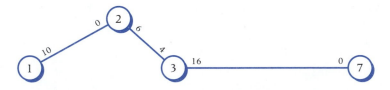

Merely selecting trial paths and assigned flows, however, does not guarantee optimality. To guarantee that an optimal solution is achieved in this process, the algorithm provides a method of revising the flows along the path to increase the overall flow through the network. As each trial path is selected, its arc capacities are revised to show the capacity remaining, that is, to indicate capacity available for flow along each arc on that path. There are two steps in the revision process:

(1) the amount of flow being transmitted is subtracted from the capacity in the direction of the assigned flow; (2) that amount is added to the capacity in the opposite direction (even if there can be no flow in that direction). For example, consider arc 3–7 shown below:

The flow capacity in the 3–7 direction is 16. In the 7–3 direction, the capacity is 0. We can assign only six units of flow to this arc (the minimum capacity of any arc on the path, as discussed above). According to the rules of the algorithm, to revise the flow capacities, we first subtract 6 from the capacity in the direction of the flow and then add this amount to the flow in the opposite direction. The revision can be shown in several ways. We choose to cross out the original capacity and write in the revised figures. It will help us keep track of successive revisions and compute the final flow on that arc.

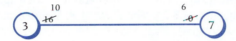

At each iteration, this procedure is followed for each arc in the trial path. The flow is tallied at the sink.

This process computes net flow along a path. The sum of the beginning and ending capacities should be equal. For this arc, the net flow at the start was 16 (16 + 0). After the revision, the net flow is still 16 (10 + 6). This process provides a way to undo previously assigned trial flows.

This process is repeated for different paths (each path tried constitutes one iteration) until there are no source-to-sink paths available with a positive capacity. In other words the optimal solution is achieved when every path from source to sink (in direction of the flow) has at least one arc with zero capacity.

Before we summarize the steps of the algorithm, let's demonstrate it on the B-Low Network, shown again in Figure 8.20.

First Iteration: We arbitrarily select the 1–3–7 path to begin. The minimum capacity on an arc on this path is 12 (on arc 1–3). We reduce all flow capacities, in the direction of the flow, *on the arcs on this path*, by 12. We increase capacities (on arcs on this path) in the opposite direction by 12. The flow of 12 for this path is tallied at the sink. Figure 8.21 shows this iteration.

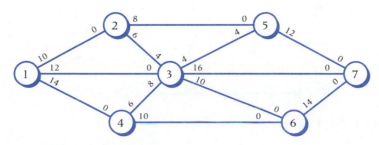

Figure 8.20 Network for B-Low Pipeline

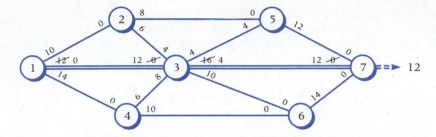

Figure 8.21 First Iteration B-Low Pipeline Flow

Second Iteration: Select path 1–4–6–7. The minimum capacity is 10, on arc 4–6. Reduce each capacity in the direction of the flow by 10 and increase the capacity in the opposite direction by 10. Tally the flow, 10, at the sink as shown in Figure 8.22.

Third Iteration: Select path 1–2–5–7. Subtract the minimum capacity of 8 from all capacities in the direction of the flow and add 8 to the capacities in the opposite direction, as shown in Figure 8.23. The flow of 8 is added at the sink.

Fourth Iteration: Select path 1–2–3–5–7. The minimum capacity is the revised capacity, 2, on arc 1–2. Subtract this from capacities in the flow direction, add it to capacity in the opposite direction, and tally it at the sink. The result is shown in Figure 8.24. Note that, after this iteration, only one arc leaving the source still has some capacity left.

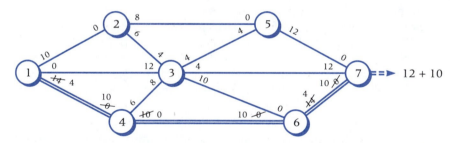

Figure 8.22 Second Iteration B-Low Pipeline Flow

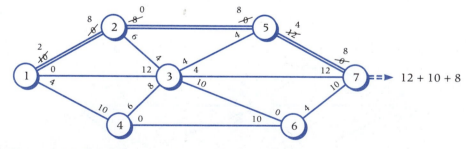

Figure 8.23 Third Iteration B-Low Pipeline Flow

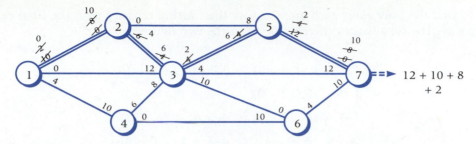

Figure 8.24 Fourth Iteration B-Low Pipeline Flow

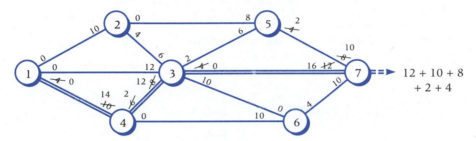

Figure 8.25 Fifth Iteration B-Low Pipeline Flow

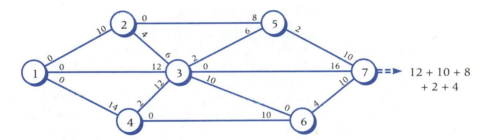

Figure 8.26 Maximum Flow Pattern B-Low Pipeline

Fifth Iteration: Select path 1–4–3–7 (there are other possibilities). The minimum, 4, is subtracted and added as shown in Figure 8.25. The flow of 4 is tallied at the sink. Note that now all arcs leaving the source have a zero capacity. There are no more paths with a positive flow capacity, so we have an optimal solution. The final network is shown in Figure 8.26.

The optimal flow is 36. Reconstructing the paths used at each iteration gives us the following paths:

$$1\text{--}3\text{--}7 \quad \rightarrow 12 \qquad 1\text{--}2\text{--}3\text{--}5\text{--}7 \rightarrow 2$$

$$1\text{--}4\text{--}6\text{--}7 \rightarrow 10 \qquad 1\text{--}4\text{--}3\text{--}7 \quad \rightarrow 4$$

$$1\text{--}2\text{--}5\text{--}7 \rightarrow \quad 8$$

To find the flow along each arc, compare the starting capacity with the final capacity. The flow is the difference between the two figures.

$$1\text{–}2 = 10\ (10 - 0) \qquad 3\text{–}6 = \ \ 0\ (10 - 10)$$
$$1\text{–}3 = 12\ (12 - 0) \qquad 3\text{–}7 = 16\ (16 - 0)$$
$$1\text{–}4 = 14\ (14 - 0) \qquad 4\text{–}3 = \ \ 4\ (6 - 2)$$
$$2\text{–}3 = \ \ 2\ (6 - 4) \qquad 4\text{–}6 = 10\ (10 - 0)$$
$$2\text{–}5 = \ \ 8\ (8 - 0) \qquad 5\text{–}7 = 10\ (12 - 2)$$
$$3\text{–}5 = \ \ 2\ (4 - 2) \qquad 6\text{–}7 = 10\ (14 - 4)$$

Note that it is possible to achieve the same optimal flow with different paths. Consider the solution shown in Figure 8.27.
The optimal flow is 36. Flows on each path are

$$1\text{–}3\text{–}7 \ \ \to 12 \qquad 1\text{–}4\text{–}3\text{–}5\text{–}7 \to 4$$
$$1\text{–}2\text{–}3\text{–}7 \to \ \ 4 \qquad 1\text{–}4\text{–}3\text{–}6\text{–}7 \to 2$$
$$1\text{–}2\text{–}5\text{–}7 \to \ \ 6 \qquad 1\text{–}4\text{–}6\text{–}7 \ \ \ \to 8$$

Summary of Steps in the Maximal Flow Algorithm

1. Locate any path from source node to sink node that has a positive flow capacity. In other words, when considering all arcs on the path, it must be possible to send some flow along the path in the direction of the flow. If there is no such path, stop. The optimal solution has been found.
2. Determine the arc in the path having the minimum flow capacity. This is the maximum amount that can be sent along this path. Increase the flow by this amount (tally this at the sink).
3. For all arcs on this path, decrease the capacities in the direction of the flow by this amount and increase the capacities in the opposite direction; in other words, calculate the net flow on each arc in the path. Go to step 1.

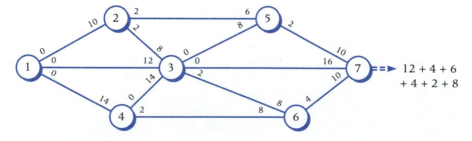

Figure 8.27 Alternative Optimal Solution

COMPUTER SOLUTION FOR MAXIMAL FLOW PROBLEMS

To demonstrate a computer solution, let's look at a slightly larger problem.

The Can of Worms—Maximal Flow Problem The "Can of Worms" connecting Interstates 490, 590 and 390 into and around Rochester, New York is going to be completely redesigned and reconstructed. The project will necessitate closing a large section of highway for two years. Before starting work, the DOT wants to look at the alternative routes that will be used as a detour. It may be necessary to make changes in these, such as widening or changing traffic patterns, in order to maintain the same level of traffic flow. For now, we will look only at the east-bound routes from the beginning to the end of the detour. Figure 8.28 shows the network of alternative routes around the closed Can. The DOT wants to find the maximal flow of traffic that can currently move over these routes during the morning rush hours, 7 to 9 AM.

Figure 8.29 shows the maximal flow pattern. Figure 8.30 shows the computer solution for this problem. The project manager can now spend his time more productively looking at the flow over the various branches to determine what kind of

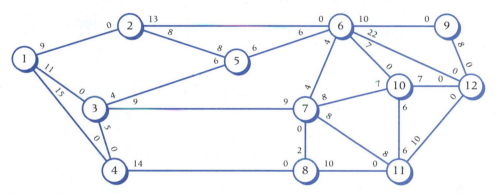

Figure 8.28 Alternative Routes Around Detour

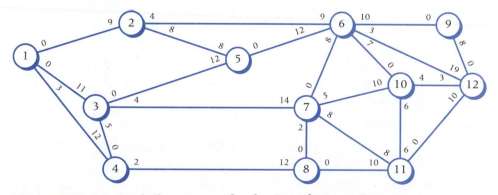

Figure 8.29 Maximal Flow Pattern for the Can of Worms Detour

```
                OPTIMAL SOLUTION—MAXIMAL FLOW NETWORK

             FLOW OVER EACH BRANCH:

                    BRANCH          FLOW
                    ------          ----
                    1 — 2            9
                    1 — 3           11
                    1 — 4           12
                    2 — 5            0
                    2 — 6            9
                    3 — 5            6
                    3 — 7            5
                    3 — 4            0
                    4 — 8           12
                    5 — 2            0
                    5 — 6            6
                    6 — 9            0
                    6 — 10           0
                    6 — 12          19
                    7 — 6            4
                    7 — 10           3
                    7 — 11           0
                    8 — 7            2
                    8 — 11          10
                    9 — 12           0
                    10 — 11          0
                    10 — 12          3
                    11 — 7           0
                    11 — 10          0
                    11 — 12         10

             FLOW THROUGH NETWORK:

             FLOW                PATHS:
             ----                ------
              9               1 — 2 — 6 — 12
              6               1 — 3 — 5 — 6 — 12
              4               1 — 3 — 7 — 6 — 12
              1               1 — 3 — 7 — 10 — 12
              2               1 — 4 — 8 — 7 — 10 — 12
             10               1 — 4 — 8 — 11 — 12

             MAXIMAL FLOW THROUGH NETWORK = 32
```

Figure 8.30 Computer Solution, Can of Worms Maximal Flow

changes to make to increase the flow, since the flow over the arcs leaving the source have a combined capacity of 35 and the combined capacities of the arcs entering the sink are 47. Various changes in capacities can be tried—tied to changes in the streets and highways involved.

Focus on Decision Making

George Johnson, plant manager for the Mariner Production Company in St. Petersburg, Florida, is currently wrestling with a maintenance problem. The company makes extensive use of high-speed, automated production equipment in its various production centers. Because of the impact on production when a machine malfunctions, it is extremely expensive to have a machine down for any period of time. Under the current operating system, when any of this equipment malfunctions, a worker in that particular production center calls the maintenance department and a repair person is dispatched as quickly as possible. For various reasons, this system is not performing satisfactorily. If the machine does not stop, the workers do not always detect a malfunction immediately. Furthermore, delays have been encountered when the telephones are already in use.

Mariner is considering the installation of an automated system. A monitoring device on each machine would be connected to a central monitor/alarm system in the maintenance office. This system would immediately detect a malfunction and sound an alert in the maintenance office. Mariner estimates that this system would save approximately $48,000 per year through faster maintenance response times. The cost of the system under consideration can be divided into three components: (1) the cost of purchasing and installing each monitor; (2) the cost of the central alarm system; and (3) the cost of connecting the machine monitors to the central alarm system.

In estimating the total costs of this system, George knows the cost of the central monitor is $23,000 and the cost to install a monitor on each machine is $7,500 per machine. The total connection cost is the unknown variable that George needs to determine to begin making his decision. Connection costs are estimated at $40 per foot if the wiring uses existing conduit and $85 per foot if new conduit must be installed.

Data Preparation/Problem Formulation

George had his electricians measure the wiring distances between machines and the maintenance department. Wiring could follow existing conduit paths, or where new conduit could be installed, it had to be accessible; therefore, wiring distances did not always follow the most direct routes between machines. The table below summarizes these distances.

From/To	Production Center									
	2	3	4	5	6	7	8	9	10	11
M	400	180*	540*							
2		300		500						
3			480		550					
4						700				
5					320*		400	300*		
6						460*			900	
7										560
8								450		
9									150*	
10										630*

(Distances are shown in feet. Distances followed by an asterisk (*) indicate new conduit requirements.)

George recognized this as a minimum spanning tree problem. In order to compare new conduit paths with existing paths, he first multiplied the distances by the cost per foot. Thus, he was minimizing total cost rather than distance.

Computer Solution

George entered these data into his PC and obtained the following results:

```
SOLUTION-


                                 BRANCH
           BRANCH                VALUE
           -------               ------
           1 — 3                 15300
           3 — 2                 12000
           3 — 4                 19200
           2 — 5                 20000
           5 — 8                 16000
           8 — 9                 18000
           9 — 10                12750
           3 — 6                 22000
           4 — 7                 28000
           7 — 11                22400


      MINIMUM TOTAL SPAN = 185650
```

Interpretation and Analysis of the Results

The results indicated that new conduit should be installed only between the maintenance department and machine center 3, and between machine centers 9 and 10. The remaining eight branches would use existing conduit. The total installation cost would be $185,650. Added to this would be the cost of installing the monitors on each machine (10 @ $7,500 = $75,000) and the cost of the central monitoring system ($23,000). Thus, the total cost of the system would be $283,650.

What Happens Next

Given this figure, George can now begin to decide whether this system is justified. This information constitutes just one input into the decision-making process. George must also consider certain other factors. For example, he must try to determine the reliability of the cost savings estimates; the availability of capital for this project; the internal rate of return on this investment; and the payback period. Other considerations might include the compatibility of the monitoring devices with new production equipment, and capacity limitations of the system relative to possible plant expansions. Certainly, George will want to consider these other factors before proceeding.

8.6 CONCLUDING REMARKS

The four network models presented here continued a discussion that was begun in Chapter 7 with the transportation and assignment models. Transshipment, shortest route, minimal spanning tree, and maximal flow models are all important variations of the LP problem. While the discussion of these models has been rather lengthy in an effort to reflect and emphasize the growing importance of these models, it has not even scratched the surface of the subject of network optimization models. A wide variety of real-world problems and subproblems can be modeled as networks, and network models are among the most important and popular optimization models being studied today by management scientists. There are consulting firms that deal only with such problems.

In general, the network models introduced here are applicable to physical distribution problems, scheduling problems, and design problems. Since "flow" can also encompass physical quantities, cash, distance, time, ideas, and so on, each model has wide applicability. The main difficulty may be in recognizing that a given problem can be modeled as a network problem. Many network problems are very large, with hundreds or thousands of nodes and arcs. Such problems are impossible to solve by inspection and are impractical to solve manually. Fortunately, computers and network software provide the means for solving such problems. Computers have become an essential component of these techniques.

Finally, a note about LP solution to network models. It is common practice to say these problems can be solved using LP, even though it may not be the technique of choice. We have chosen to demonstrate LP solutions to provide formulating practice; to demonstrate the special characteristics of network models; to help you understand networks; and to tie the models together as a class.

Management Science Application ────────────────────────────

PASSENGER-MIX AIRLINE SCHEDULING[2]

Prior to deregulation, airline routes and pricing were restricted by the Civil Aeronautics Board (CAB). Thus, competition among airlines was limited to frills such as special service and meals, and to the number of flights offered, which resulted in more convenient departure times. Deregulation brought new areas of competition for the carriers. New carriers offered low-cost, unrestricted fares in many of the major markets. Smaller regional lines began to offer either non-stop flights to major cities or reduced fares on multi-stop or connecting flights.

Much of the emphasis turned to filling seats that might otherwise go empty. This goal was accomplished through lower fares. These lower fares, however, could also be used by customers who would otherwise have travelled at higher fares against the gain of additional passengers at lower fares. Thus, the airlines were faced with balancing the loss of higher fares. Deregulation allowed the airlines to offer differentiated pricing, charging both full fares and discounted fares on the same flight. The airlines did this by restricting the number of seats offered at various discount prices. In order to maximize their revenue, however, they had to derive a method of determining the optimal number of seats to offer at each price. The determination of this mix provides the airline with two major outcomes: (1) the airline can

[2]Reprinted with permission of Fred Glover, Randy Glover, Joe Lorenzo, and Claude McMillan, "The Passenger-Mix Problems in the Scheduled Airlines," *Interfaces*, 12 (June, 1982): 73–79. Copyright (1982), The Institute of Management Sciences.

structure its reservation system more effectively by setting limits and priorities on the number of passengers travelling at different fares; and (2) airlines can evaluate different price/route scenarios in terms of profits generated from different passenger mixes.

The profitability of a passenger depends upon the length of the trip and the fare class. Although per-mile revenue is generally less for passengers traveling long distances, the total revenue to the carrier is greatest for those passengers. Airlines attempt to forecast the demand for passenger itineraries (PI) at various fare classes over the carrier's entire network. These forecasts indicate a theoretical optimal PI mix at the various fare classes. This mix can be expressed as the optimal occupancy of the available seats on each flight segment. Marketing managers attempt to design the airline's fare class structures based upon expected passenger itineraries so as to increase occupancy and, therefore, revenue.

Associated with special discount fares are two concepts: "spill" and "diversion." Spill refers to the movement of passengers to other flights with lower fares. Diversion occurs when a passenger who would have paid the higher fare for a given flight takes advantage of the discount fare. Carriers attempt to control spill and diversion by adding restrictions to discount fares, and by specifying a number of seats on each flight segment as reserved for each of the fare classes. Therefore, the airlines needed a system that would enable them to adjust fares to maximize occupancy and revenue without causing excess spill or diversion.

This problem was formulated for Frontier Airlines using a network flow model. In the network model, one set of arcs corresponds to flight segments and another to passenger itineraries differentiated by fare classes. Flow on the forward arcs represents the number of passengers on a flight segment and flow on the back arcs represents the number of passengers on each PI at each of the fare classes. Flow on each forward arc is limited by the capacity of the aircraft, and flow on the back arc is limited by the demand for the PI and the fare class that the back arc represents. These limits give simple upper bounds on the arcs. An increment of revenue is associated with each unit of flow on each back arc, equal to the price of the ticket at the fare class that arc represents. A network-optimizing component finds the flow on each arc that maximizes revenue on the carrier's network without violating the aircraft capacity constraints and the upper bounds posed by the demands forecast for the various passenger itineraries and their associated fare classes.

This system was built and implemented for Frontier Airlines. It was designed to accommodate a network of 600 flights and 30,000 passenger itineraries with up to five fare classes per PI. Following a run of the optimizer, a post-processor extracts and accumulates the flows representing fare-class loads among the passenger itineraries identified as optimal for each segment and reports the optimal fare class allocation for each flight segment. LP formulation of this problem would involve 200,000 variables and 3,000 constraints (excluding simple bounds), and would require several hours to solve. As demand forecasts are modified and updated, and revenue figures are changed to reflect various policies and operating conditions, this system makes it possible to provide rapid information for better pricing and reservation allocation decisions.

GLOSSARY

arc a connection (a line, a link) between two nodes in a network

arc capacity the maximum flow (U_{ij}) for an arc in a network

branch synonym for arc in network terminology

capacitated transshipment problem transshipment problem that has constraints or capacity limits on specific routes or transshipment points

directed arc permits flow or movement on a branch in a given direction only

greedy algorithm solution method used to solve minimal spanning tree problem, whereby sequentially making the best possible choice results in an optimal solution

loop series of arcs connecting a node to itself

maximal flow problem network problem that seeks to maximize the total amount of flow through a network in a given time period; all flows are transmitted from a single source to a single destination through a network in which the branches can have different capacities

minimal spanning tree problem network problem that seeks to determine the set of arcs that will connect all the nodes in the network at a minimum total distance, i.e., minimize the sum of the arc lengths used to connect every node in the network with all other nodes

network an arrangement of paths, connected at various points, through which items move from point to point along the connecting links; a network is drawn as a collection of nodes and arcs

network flow models class of models concerned with the flow of items through a network

nodes junction points or intersections in a network diagram, shown as circles

path sequence of arcs from a source (origin) to a destination (sink)

permanent label in shortest route algorithm, shows the shortest distance from the origin to that node and the predecessor node on the route

shortest route problem network problem that seeks to find the shortest route, through a connecting network, from a source to one or more destinations, in order to determine the least cost (time, money, distance, etc.) route

sink a destination node, where all flows end

source the origin node, point where all flows begin

spanning tree set of branches that connect every node in a network with all other nodes

temporary label in the shortest route algorithm, the intermediate label on a node, showing distance from the origin through a predecessor node

transshipment points node through which the flow can move, but which are neither origins nor destinations

transshipment problems network problems concerned with allocating the flow of a given product in such a way as to minimize total cost; allows shipment between sources, between destinations, and from destinations to sources; have intermediate points, transshipment points, through which items move

undirected arcs network branches permitted flow in either direction

PROBLEMS

1. Given the following network, with distances shown in miles, find the shortest route from node 1 to each of the other nodes.

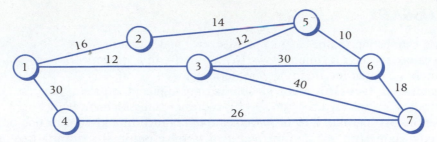

Formulate this as an LP problem.

2. Given the following network, with distances representing time in minutes, determine the fastest way to get from node 1 to node 15.

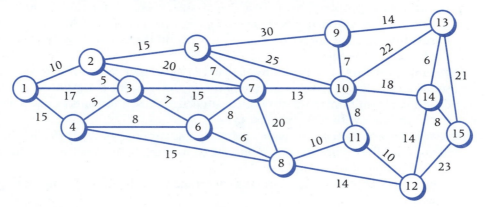

3. Develop a minimal spanning tree for the following network:

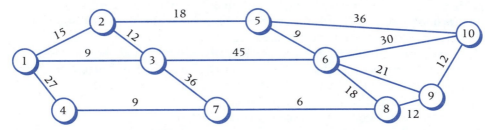

4. Given the following network, develop a minimal spanning tree:

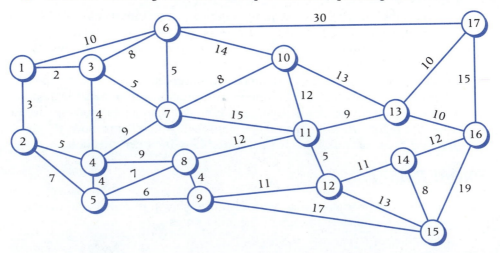

5. Given the following network, with flow capacities along each branch, determine the maximum flow from source node 1 to destination node 8 and the flow along each branch.

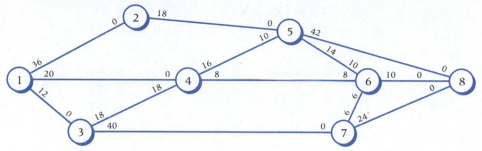

Formulate this as an LP problem.

6. Given the following network with flow capacities along each branch, determine the maximum flow from source node 1 to sink node 15, and the flow along each branch.

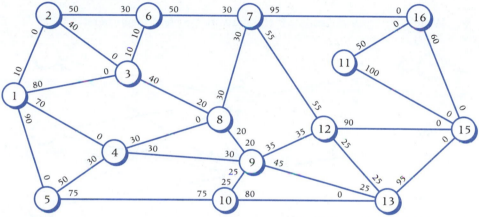

7. The following network represents a transshipment problem. Solve it as a transportation problem.

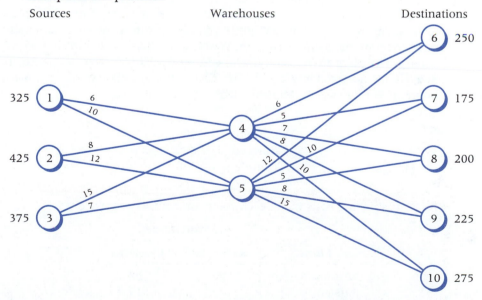

Formulate it as an LP problem.

8. Construct the network corresponding to the following LP formulation:

$$\text{MIN } 4X_{14} + 3X_{15} + 6X_{24} + 8X_{25} + 5X_{34} + 4X_{35}$$
$$+ 5X_{46} + 7X_{47} + 9X_{48} + 6X_{56} + 5X_{57} + 5X_{58}$$

subject to

$$
\begin{aligned}
X_{14} + X_{15} &\le 600 \\
X_{24} + X_{25} &\le 650 \\
X_{34} + X_{35} &\le 175 \\
X_{14} + X_{24} + X_{34} - X_{46} - X_{47} - X_{48} &= 0 \\
X_{15} + X_{25} + X_{35} - X_{56} - X_{57} - X_{58} &= 0 \\
X_{46} + X_{56} &= 675 \\
X_{47} + X_{57} &= 225 \\
X_{48} + X_{48} &= 450 \\
X_{14} &\le 300
\end{aligned}
$$

9. Write the LP formulation for the network problem given here.

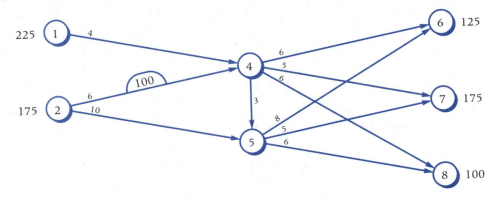

10. Old Acorn, Inc. manufactures oak trestle tables in Winston-Salem and Raleigh, North Carolina. The furniture is shipped monthly from these plants to warehouses in Richmond, Virginia and Charleston, West Virginia for shipment to retail outlets in Pittsburgh, Washington, Baltimore, Akron, and Harrisburg. The plant in Winston-Salem can produce 1,000 tables a month; the Raleigh facility produces 1,750. The Charleston warehouse has a capacity limitation of 900 pieces. Monthly demand is as follows:

Pittsburgh	575
Washington	600
Baltimore	625
Akron	450
Harrisburg	400

Per-unit shipping costs along each route are summarized below:

	Warehouse	
Plant	Richmond	Charleston
Winston-Salem	25	28
Raleigh	22	19

Warehouse	Pittsburgh	Washington	Baltimore	Akron	Harrisburg
Richmond	25	36	40	30	45
Charleston	30	44	28	45	42

Draw the network for this problem. What shipping pattern should be selected to minimize total monthly shipping costs?

11. Jellico Clothiers imports silk dresses from the Orient. Sara Jenine, scheduling manager for the southeastern U.S., wants to develop a monthly plan for shipping the dresses from their ports of entry, Miami and New Orleans, to several retailers in the southeast. Retailers in three cities, Fort Lauderdale, Atlanta and Jackson, also act as distribution centers. Monthly imports are 2,500 at Miami and 1,500 at New Orleans. Demand is 750 at Fort Lauderdale; 800 at Atlanta; 500 at Jackson; 300 at Tampa; 550 at Savannah; 650 at Charleston; and 450 at Montgomery. The available shipping routes and the per-unit shipping costs are shown in the following table (a line in the cell indicates that no direct route is available between these cities). Draw a network that represents these routes, and solve this problem so that shipping costs are minimized.

To

From	Ft. Ldle	Atlanta	Jackson	Tampa	Savana	Charleston	Montgomary
Miami	2.50	3.50	—	4.50	—	—	—
New Orl	—	6.50	3.00	—	—	—	5.00
Ft. Ldle	—	—	—	2.00	6.00	7.00	—
Atlanta	—	—	—	5.50	4.00	4.25	3.75
Jackson	—	—	—	—	9.00	2.75	5.25

The following map will be used in the next three questions. Approximate travel time by car, given in hours and minutes, is shown above the line; approximate distance in miles is shown below the line.

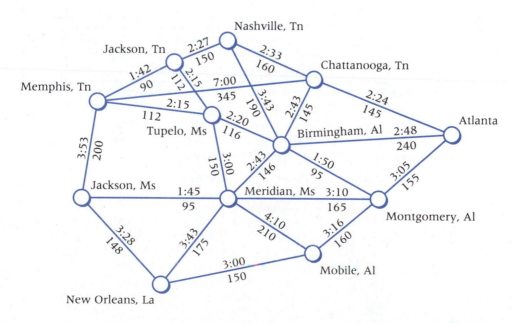

12. Once a week, Dr. Forbes-Bradford, a speech therapist in Nashville, Tennessee, travels by car to New Orleans to teach a course at the University. She would like to minimize her travel time. Using a map and the approximate traveling times given in hours and minutes, what route do you recommend she take?

13. SouthEast Telecommunications, Inc. plans to lay a new emergency communications cable in Georgia, Mississippi, Alabama, and Louisiana, following the major highways. Given the map above, how should this cable be laid in order to connect all the cities in these four states while minimizing the amount of cable used?

14. The Youth Soccer League would like to hold a pre-season soccer tournament for teams in Region Six (roughly the area shown on the map). In selecting a site for the tournament, they are working to ensure that those teams in Nashville and New Orleans travel about the same distance. What city should they select?

15. The G.B. Goldsmith department store is installing point-of-sale terminals at its downtown location. Letitia Weinstein, the computer consultant in charge of the switchover, has drawn the following representation of the current floor layout. The Xs show current registers; the dotted lines indicate a wiring path that can be used for the new terminals; and the numbers are distances between registers, given in feet.

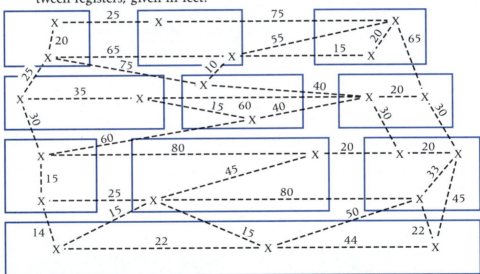

Draw this as a more traditional network. If she simply replaces each current register with a point-of-sale terminal, how should they be wired in order to minimize the total cable used? What kind of problem is this?

16. Lord of Life Church (example, page 274) is preparing to make its five-year leasing decision. The cost data they have gathered follows:

Length of Lease	Lease Cost	Maintenance Costs	Total
1	$ 6,500	$ 1,500	$ 8,000
2	11,000	3,500	15,000
3	16,000	6,500	22,500
4	20,000	10,500	30,500
5	24,500	14,500	39,000

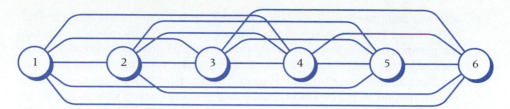

What leasing pattern should be selected to keep van costs at a minimum?

17. A work stoppage by carrier drivers in Canada has created a problem with deliveries of new cars in the U.S. There is a large backlog of cars waiting to be shipped, but no dealers in the U.S. can accept these cars. The Ford plant in Ontario has decided to transport the cars via railroad to New York City for shipment overseas. In the following network, node 1 represents the railhead at the plant and node 9 represents the port facility. The remaining nodes represent railroad junctions. There are limitations on the maximum numbers of carrier cars that can be included in the trains scheduled at specific junctions. These capacities are shown on the branches of the network. If three trains leave the plant each week, and each carrier can hold a maximum of 80 cars, what is the maximum number of cars that can reach NYC each week?

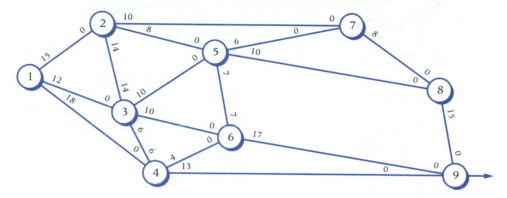

18. The RIT College of Business wishes to install a local area network to connect the dean's office; the accounting, management, marketing, finance, and decision sciences departments; the student services office; and the microcomputer lab. The table below shows the connection distances between areas.

	DO	Act	Mgt	Mkt	Fin	DSc	SSO	Lab
DO	0	23	52	46	19	27	35	118
Act	23	0	61	48	73	39	82	146
Mgt	52	61	0	55	90	41	78	157
Mkt	46	48	55	0	65	59	73	132
Fin	19	73	90	65	0	64	36	110
DSc	27	39	41	59	64	0	44	123
SSO	35	82	78	73	36	44	0	119
Lab	118	146	157	132	110	123	119	0

If the networking cable costs $36 per foot installed, how much will it cost to complete this network? (The objective is to keep cost to a minimum.)

19. The Wonderland theme park has a frontier dinner show nightly at the Outpost Dining Hall. After the show, Wonderland management wants the dinner patrons transported back to the theme park as quickly as possible. Since the Outpost is several miles from the theme park, customers must travel via the Wonderland transportation system. This transportation system comprises a combination of buses, trams, boats, and monorails that shuttle people between fixed points on the resort property. The figure below shows the routes traveled by each method of transportation. Determine the maximum number of guests the transportation system can move from dining hall (node 1) to the theme park (node 13).

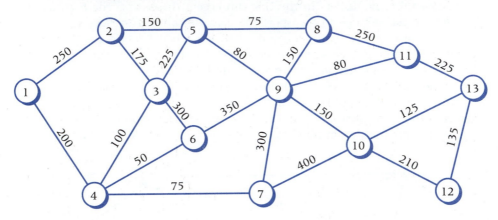

20. The Offtrack Betting Corporation has ten branches and a headquarters in Monroe County. Security would like to know the shortest distance route from headquarters to each of the branches. The following table summarizes these distances. Headquarters is number 1. Distances from point to point are the same in both directions; that is, from 2 to 3 is 8 miles and from 3 to 2 is also 8 miles. Both are represented in the table, but they are still only one branch. Draw the network and find the shortest distances.

From	To 1	2	3	4	5	6	7	8	9	10	11
1	—	5	14	18	—	—	—	—	45	—	—
2	5	—	8	12	—	15	—	—	—	—	—
3	14	8	—	4	4	—	16	—	—	—	—
4	18	12	4	—	—	16	5	—	25	—	—
5	—	—	4	—	—	—	12	7	—	—	12
6	—	15	—	16	—	—	—	—	24	17	11
7	—	—	16	5	12	—	—	9	—	15	11
8	—	—	—	—	7	—	9	—	—	14	3
9	45	—	—	25	—	24	—	—	—	11	22
10	—	—	—	—	—	17	15	14	11	—	9
11	—	—	—	—	12	—	11	3	22	9	—

21. The Orient Express Shipping Co. has the opportunity to ship olive oil from the Middle East to Japan. The company also has commitments to make deliveries of other commodities to other ports. Orient wants to know its present capacity for olive oil. The table below shows cargo capacities in barrels between the various ports. A is the source of olive oil; J is the port in Japan.

What is the maximum amount of olive oil that Orient can ship from port A to Port J at the present time?

Barrel Capacities (in 000's)

From	To A	B	C	D	E	F	G	H	I	J
A	—	10	20	15	—	—	—	—	—	—
B	—	—	5	—	7	10	—	—	—	—
C	—	5	—	—	—	24	—	—	—	—
D	—	—	8	—	—	5	12	—	—	—
E	—	—	—	—	—	—	—	12	—	19
F	—	5	—	—	—	—	28	17	—	—
G	—	—	—	—	—	14	—	—	23	—
H	—	—	—	—	16	—	—	—	24	3
I	—	—	—	—	—	—	—	6	—	17

Consultant's Report

Mid-Central Airline

Mid-Central Airline was founded in 1972 as a small commuter airline providing service to several cities in the midwestern, central plains, and mountain states. By 1986, the airline was servicing 15 cities: Cleveland, Ohio; Detroit, Michigan; Indianapolis, Indiana; Chicago, Illinois; Milwaukee, Wisconsin; Minneapolis/St. Paul, Minnesota; Des Moines, Iowa; St. Louis, Missouri; Kansas City, Missori; Omaha, Nebraska; Denver, Colorado; Bismarck, North Dakota; Casper, Wyoming; Salt Lake City, Utah; and Billings, Montana. Mid-Central has its main offices in Chicago, which also serves as its hub. Most of the airline's flights continue to be short hop, commuter-type flights offered once or twice daily between specific cities. There are, however, four daily direct flights between Chicago and Denver. Most passengers using Mid-Central are local traffic passengers, travelling primarily within the region serviced by Mid-Central. In addition, a fair number of Mid-Central passengers originate in flights from outside the region, fly to either Chicago or Denver, and transfer to a local flight to reach their destination. The following figure shows the routes flown by Mid-Central.

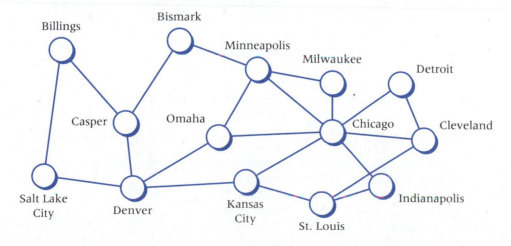

In 1988, Mid-Central applied for and received permission to add a direct route from Chicago to Salt Lake City. Service from Chicago to Salt Lake City was scheduled to begin on May 1, with service from Salt Lake City to Chicago to begin the following day. With much fanfare, the airline announced the new flight schedules and began booking passengers for these flights. Within a very short time. the flight for May 1 was fully booked (60 passengers).

On April 29, the FAA notified the airline that, because of a minor error in its application (which has since been corrected), the starting date for the new route must be delayed by one day. Now Mid-Central has 60 passengers who need to get to Salt Lake City on May 1. These passengers can be placed with other airlines that have service from Chicago to Salt Lake City, but Bud Collins, marketing director, would like to keep as many as possible on Mid-Central flights. He must consider both passenger goodwill and Mid-Central revenue. Accordingly, Bud has compiled a list showing the May 1 Mid-Central flights on which connections for Salt Lake City might be made, and the number of unoccupied seats on each of these flights. The list is shown in the following table. Bud has decided that passengers accepting rerouting with Mid-Central will be given a voucher for one free future flight on Mid-Central as compensation for the inconvenience.

Branch Flight		Seats Available
Origin	Destination	
Chicago	Detroit	15
Chicago	Cleveland	42
Chicago	Indianapolis	21
Chicago	Milwaukee	12
Chicago	St. Louis	16
Chicago	Kansas City	8
Chicago	Omaha	22
Chicago	Minneapolis	18
Detroit	Cleveland	10
Cleveland	St. Louis	20
Indianapolis	St. Louis	4
Milwaukee	Minneapolis	24
St. Louis	Cleveland	15
St. Louis	Kansas City	17
Kansas City	Omaha	11
Kansas City	Denver	19
Omaha	Kansas City	8
Omaha	Minneapolis	6
Omaha	Denver	17
Minneapolis	Milwaukee	14
Minneapolis	Bismark	27
Minneapolis	Omaha	14
Bismark	Casper	15
Casper	Denver	12
Casper	Billings	22
Casper	Salt Lake City	21
Denver	Kansas City	16

Denver	Omaha	19
Denver	Casper	16
Denver	Salt Lake City	20
Billings	Salt Lake City	17

You have been hired as a consultant to help Bud by applying management science techniques to this particular problem. Prepare a report for Bud Collins which addresses:

1. The number of these passengers that can be reassigned to other Mid-Central flights, and the flights to which they should be reassigned.
2. The number of connections these passengers must make to reach Salt Lake City on Mid-Central flights.
3. Any other factors you feel Mid-Central might want to consider before making these reassignments.

9

Integer Programming

By the end of this chapter, you should be able to:

1
recognize that a given problem requires one or more of the
variables to be integer;
2
formulate IP problems, including such special problems as
knapsack problems, capital budgeting problems, fixed cost problems,
and problems with logical conditions;
3
use the branch and bound method to reach an optimal
integer solution.

In previous chapters, we introduced linear programming as a management science technique that makes the best allocation of constrained resources in order to achieve an optimal objective. The divisibility assumption, discussed in Chapter 2, permits fractional (noninteger) solutions to linear programming problems, even though a fractional answer (3.5 tables or 5.25 airplanes) does not necessarily make sense in the real world. Simply rounding the solution is not necessarily the correct approach. Such solutions (as we will show later) may be either not feasible or not optimal. In this chapter, we introduce a mathematical programming method, integer programming (IP), that enables us to find an optimal integer solution without violating any of the LP constraints. We will describe three generic types of IP problems; discuss solution procedures; demonstrate in detail one of these solution procedures, the branch and bound method; and introduce some specific, well-known examples of problems requiring the use of integer constraints.

Williamson Suppliers

Williamson Suppliers purchases parts for resale from two vendors: Pear, Inc., and Apple Co. Williamson has to reorder two parts, X143 and X256. It currently needs 200 X143s and 120 X256s. The prices for these parts vary with the vendor. If purchased from Pear, Inc., part X143 costs $2.30 and part X256 costs $7.88. Apple charges $2.34 and $7.65 respectively for the two parts. In addition to the per-unit cost for these parts, however, certain fixed costs are associated with each order.

The purchasing manager estimates that it costs $35 to place an order with Pear and $45 to place an order with Apple. He now must decide how many parts to order from each supplier in order to minimize overall costs.

This is an example of a fixed cost problem that can be solved using IP. We will return to it later in the chapter.

9.1 *AN INTRODUCTION TO INTEGER PROGRAMMING*

Linear programming, as we have seen, does not guarantee integer solutions. Fractional answers are allowed; and what is allowed will occur. Obviously, there are situations in which we need whole number (integer) solutions. Frequently, non-integer solutions are adapted to the integer requirement by rounding, but the rounded solution is not always acceptable or practical. In some instances the solution is not optimal, but it might be acceptable, depending on the magnitude of the return or the cost of finding the optimal integer solution. In other instances, the rounded solution is not even feasible. We will demonstrate this later in our discussion of solution procedures.

A problem that fits all the assumptions of LP, with the exception of the divisibility assumption—that is, a problem in which some or all of the decision variables are required or constrained to be integer—is an **integer programming** (or integer linear programming) problem. The resulting models are widely used and are an important aid to decision makers in a variety of applications. The field of study that addresses this issue is called integer programming (IP). However, there is no one algorithm (like simplex for LP) that can solve all integer programming problems easily and practically. IP has become an important area of management science, with much attention given to developing better ways to solve IP problems. In this chapter, we can present only a simplified overview of some of the more commonly used solution procedures. Much of the work in IP is beyond the scope of this book.

Integer programming is important for two primary reasons: (1) in many real-world situations, non-integer answers simply do not make sense—whole number solutions are required; (2) integer programming enables the formulation of problems that cannot otherwise be modeled. Integer constraints can be used as a modeling tool in certain kinds of problems that are difficult or impossible to model without the use of the integer requirement. This will be demonstrated later in the chapter.

Types of Integer Programming Models

There are three basic or generic types of IP models, classified according to the type of variable or combination of variables used to formulate the problem: **all integer** models (also called pure, total, or general), **mixed integer** models, and **0–1** or **binary integer** models.

An all integer model requires all decision variables to be integer. Mixed integer models require some, but not all, decision variables to be integer. The 0–1 integer models restricts the integer variables to the values 0 or 1. Such binary integer models are particularly useful because the 0–1 variables can be used to represent dichotomous decisions; in other words, they can model yes/no or go/no-go situations. The following examples illustrate the three generic types of IP models.

All Integer

$$\text{MAX } 20X_1 + 30X_2$$

subject to

$$3X_1 + \ X_2 \le 150$$
$$4X_1 + \ 9X_2 \le 330$$
$$X_1, X_2 \ge 0 \text{ and integer}$$

Mixed Integer

$$\text{MAX } 60X_1 + 100X_2$$

subject to

$$40X_1 + \ 80X_2 \le 100$$
$$80X_1 + \ 40X_2 \le 120$$
$$X_1, X_2 \ge 0$$
$$X_1 \text{ integer}$$

0–1 Integer

$$\text{MAX } 20X_1 + 15X_2 + 23X_3 + 10X_4 + 27X_5$$

subject to

$$3.4X_1 + \ 3X_2 + \ 4X_3 + \ 3X_4 + \ 4X_5 \le 10$$
$$5X_1 + \ 4X_2 + 4.8X_3 + 3.7X_4 + \ 6X_5 \le 14$$
$$6X_1 + \ 6X_2 + \ 7X_3 + \ 6X_4 + \ 8X_5 \le 20$$
$$X_1, X_2, X_3, X_4, X_5 = 0 \text{ or } 1$$

Integer Programming Examples

In the following examples, we will explain which type of IP problem is being presented and formulate the model using the necessary integer constraints.

An All Integer Programming Problem

Compco, Inc., a computer training facility serving metropolitan Toronto, offers a variety of training packages at its downtown location. The company can teach several courses concurrently, using a staff of part-time instructors who can teach or assist in all workshops. At this time Compco is looking specifically at two of its courses: training in a highly sophisticated integrated software package, and an introduction to computers. Demand is such that both courses are sold out as soon as offered. Compco would like to maximize the daily profit from these two courses, because this profit enables Compco to offer certain other courses on a "goodwill" basis. Each workshop in the integrated program contributes a daily profit of $720, while the introductory course provides $300. Management must decide how many workshops in each subject to offer each week, in order to schedule and contract for the course instructors. Available instruction and preparation time for these two courses is limited to 56 hours a day. Each integrated workshop requires 7.5 hours, whereas the introductory workshop takes only 3 hours. The decision is further complicated by a restriction on the number of participants that can handled efficiently by the support staff. No more than 100 trainees can be accommodated on a daily basis without putting a strain on the staff and facility. Each of these two workshops has a class size restriction—6 per integrated workshop, 12 per introductory class.

Formulation This problem is very much like a linear programming problem, except that the decision variables must be integer. Since there is no way to offer part of a course, this is an all integer programming problem.

Compco is trying to determine how many workshops to offer for each course. Therefore, let

$$X = \text{number of integrated software workshops to offer}$$

$$Y = \text{number of introductory courses to offer}$$

Since the objective is to maximize the profit from these two courses, the objective function can be stated

$$\text{MAX } 720X + 300Y$$

The limitations or constraints on the system are the preparation and teaching time available and the class size. The time constraint can be formulated as

$$7.5X + 3Y \leq 56$$

The class size constraint can be formulated as

$$6X + 12Y \leq 100$$

Finally, the nonnegativity and integer constraints can be expressed

$$X, Y \geq 0 \text{ and integer}$$

Pulling all of this together, the entire problem can be modeled as follows:

$$\text{MAX } 720X + 300Y$$

subject to

$$7.5X + 3Y \leq 56$$

$$6X + 12Y \leq 100$$

$$X, Y \geq 0 \text{ and integer}$$

A Mixed Integer Programming Problem

Judy Jones, a young widow, has $100,000 to invest. She wants her investments to provide her with the maximum annual interest and dividend income possible. On the advice of her financial counselor, she has chosen two stock offerings and an interest-bearing brokerage account. Each share of Stock A, at $30.375 per share, has an anticipated annual dividend of $4.20. Stock B, costing $15.625 a share, has an annual dividend of $2.85. Interest on the brokerage account is currently 12 percent paid annually. For security, Judy wants at least 30 percent of her money in the brokerage account. She is also not too sure of Stock B, but her advisor has persuaded her by recommending she buy at least twice as many shares of Stock A as Stock B. Judy must now decide how many shares of each stock to purchase and how much to put in the account.

Formulation With the following decision variables:

A = number of shares of Stock A purchased

B = number of shares of Stock B purchased

I = dollars in brokerage account

the problem is formulated

$$\text{MAX } 4.2A + 2.85B + .12I$$

subject to

$$30.375A + 15.625B + I \leq 100000$$

$$A - 2B \geq 0$$

$$9.1125A + 4.6875B - .7I \leq 0$$

$$I \geq 0$$

$$A, B \geq 0 \text{ and integer}$$

The brokerage account constraint (at least 30 percent of the investment is to be in this account) would normally be expressed as $I \geq 0.3(30.375A + 15.625B + I)$ before being restated in standard form. Notice that, since it is not possible to purchase part of a share, the solution values for shares of stock (A and B) must be integers. It is possible, however, to invest a fractional part of a dollar in the brokerage account. Thus the solution value for this investment (I) does not have to be an integer, making this a mixed integer programming problem. One or more of the decision variables is required to be integer, but one or more of the other decision variables can take on any real value geater than or equal to zero.

A 0–1 Integer Programming Problem

Dom and Max are enrolled in a two-week wilderness survival camp, designed to build self-confidence, promote self-sufficiency, and identify leadership potential. The first week emphasizes group activities and experiences that require coopera-tion to achieve the goals. For the final exercise, each pair is transported to a se-cluded wilderness area with only what can be carried in their backpacks. They must make it back to headquarters within 72 hours. In selecting the items to take, Dom and Max have allotted only 650 cubic centimeters of space to food and drink, since they are supposed to fish and gather most of the items they need. They would like to take instant coffee, trail mix, water, chocolate bars, beef jerky, and hardtack. Unfortunately there is not enough space for all of these items. Their first step, then, was to measure each item, recognizing that the items canot be divided into smaller portions. Next, each man ranked the items in order of importance to him with 10 being high. They averaged these numbers to get the final ranks. The measurements and rankings are as follows:

Item	Measurement (cc)	Ranking
Water	200	9.5
Hardtack	205	6.0
Coffee	85	6.5
Chocolate	190	8.5
Trail mix	240	9.0
Jerky	125	5.5

They want to take as many of the high-ranked items as possible. Their goal is to maximize the total rank or utility value of the items selected, given the space restriction.

Formulation   This is a binary programming problem of a type known as a **knapsack problem.** A knapsack problem is an allocation problem that determines which items to select (from among several choices) to put in a restricted space, such that the total value of the items is maximized. The decision variables can have a value of zero (the item is not selected) or one (the item is selected). Each item must be selected in its entirety or not at all. The objective is to select, from the given set of items, a subset that maximizes the value of that subset subject to the given constraint (limited capacity). Decision variables represent the items, and the coefficients in the objective function are the rankings or utility values of the items. With the following decision variables,

$$X_1 = \text{selection of water}$$

$$X_2 = \text{selection of hardtack}$$

$$X_3 = \text{selection of coffee}$$

$$X_4 = \text{selection of chocolate}$$

$$X_5 = \text{selection of trail mix}$$

$$X_6 = \text{selection of jerky}$$

the problem is formulated

$$\text{MAX } 9.5X_1 + 6X_2 + 6.5X_3 + 8.5X_4 + 9X_5 + 5.5X_6$$

subject to

$$200X_1 + 205X_2 + 85X_3 + 190X_4 + 240X_5 + 125X_6 \leq 650$$

$$X_1, X_2, X_3, X_4, X_5, X_6 = 0 \text{ or } 1$$

This is just one of several special applications of binary integer programming. These are presented later in this chapter.

9.2 *INTEGER PROGRAMMING: A GRAPHICAL ILLUSTRATION*

In Chapter 3, we demonstrated that graphical analysis enhances understanding of linear programming problems and their solutions. By providing an intuitive feel for the problem, a graphical approach also is helpful in describing IP problems and in illustrating the relationship between LP and IP.

In the Compco Computer problem, Compco wished to determine how many of each of two computer training courses to offer in order to maximize profit. This all integer problem was formulated as follows:

$$\text{MAX } 720X + 300Y$$
subject to
$$7.5X + 3Y \leq 56$$
$$6X + 12Y \leq 100$$
$$X, Y \geq 0 \text{ and integer}$$

Except for the word "integer" in the constraints, this is a linear programming problem. We begin our analysis, then, by graphing the problem as if it were an LP problem, ignoring the integer requirements. This LP problem is referred to as the **LP relaxation** of the IP problem. Once the feasible set (area of feasible solutions) for the LP relaxation is determined, the integer points inside this feasible set must be identified. Recall that the set must be identified. Recall that the set of feasible solutions to an LP problem is seen as a space (an area that can contain numerous, continuous solutions) bounded by the linear constraints. The feasible solution set for the integer solution is the collection of integer points within this feasible set. These integer points are called **lattice points.**

Figure 9.1 shows the feasible set for the Compco problem. The shaded area is the feasible solution set for the LP relaxation. The dots are the lattice points, the integer points within this set. This is the set of feasible solutions to the IP problem. In other words, for a point to be a feasible integer point, it must satisfy the linear programming constraints *and* be a lattice point.

To solve the problem, it is necessary to determine which feasible point optimizes the objective function. We can demonstrate this graphically, just as with graphical LP, by graphing the objective function (isoprofit line) and moving it in an uphill or outward direction until it is no longer possible to move it further and still intersect a feasible point. Figure 9.2 shows this process. The optimal integer solution is 7,1—seven integrated workshops and one introductory course, for a profit of $5,340.

From Figure 9.2 it is possible to make some comparisons between LP and IP and gain some insight into their relationship. Notice that this optimal integer solution is not the optimal solution to the LP relaxation (remember, the optimal solution to

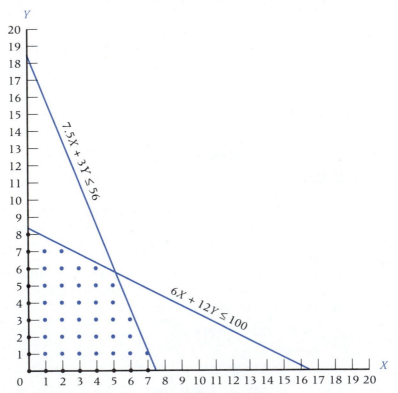

Figure 9.1 Feasible Integer Points—Compco Problem

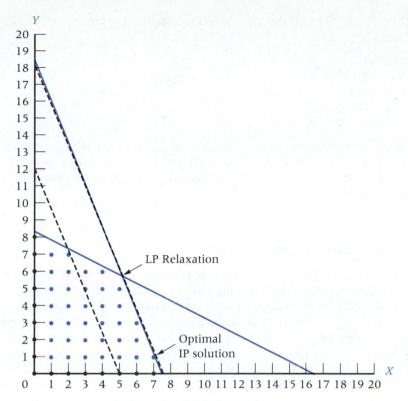

Figure 9.2 Graphical Solution for Compco Problem

an LP problem occurs at the intersection of binding constraints). The intersection is not an integer point, so it would not be a feasible integer solution. By continuing to push the objective function line outward to this intersection, we can find the optimal solution for the LP relaxation (noninteger solution). By solving two equations with two unknowns, we can find the value of the decision variables—5.17 integrated workshops and 5.75 introductory courses. The optimal value of the objective function is $5,447.40.

Comparing these two optimal values shows that the optimal integer value is lower than the optimal value for the LP relaxation. The integer (indivisibility) requirement adds a constraint. Adding a constraint usually reduces the optimal value for the objective function (at best it will give an "as good as" value). There is a cost to requiring integer variables, just as there is a cost to adding any additional constraints. The optimal value in our problem decreased with the addition of the integer constraint.

9.3 *INTEGER PROGRAMMING: SOLUTION METHODS*

A number of solution methods are available for solving IP problems, but no single algorithm (such as simplex for LP) has been developed to solve all IP problems. Moreover, none of the approaches used to solve IP problems is as efficient as simplex. The problems that can be solved using these methods generally are much smaller.

In this section, we will discuss the following primary procedures used to solve IP problems:

1. Graphical
2. Rounding LP solutions
3. Enumeration
4. Cutting Planes
5. Branch and Bound

Computer solutions are not included in this discussion, since they are usually computerized versions of one of the above methods. In a later section we will discuss the impact of the computer on IP solutions and present some example problems and solutions.

The Graphical Method

Recall from Chapter 3 that the graphical approach is useful primarily for problems with two unknowns. Despite this limitation, the graphical approach does provide a fairly simple solution procedure for very small problems—as demonstrated in the previous section. Solving an IP problem graphically is similar to the graphical approach for solving LP problems: the constraints are graphed in order to identify the feasible region for the LP relaxation; the integer points within this feasible space are identified; the feasible lattice points that yield the optimal solution are determined by moving the isoprofit line until it covers the last lattice point in the feasible area. Figures 9.1 and 9.2 showed a graphical solution.

Rounding LP Solutions

Frequently, in everyday practical situations, an integer programming problem is solved as a linear programming problem and the results are rounded. Obviously this approach can save time and the cost of formulating and solving an IP problem, but there are some serious disadvantages. A rounded solution may be infeasible, that is, it may violate one of the constraints. In the Compco problem, notice what happens if the LP solution is rounded to five integrated courses (X) and six introductory courses (Y). This solution is infeasible because it violates the class size restriction: $(6 \times 5) + (12 \times 6) = 102$, not ≤ 100. Always rounding down can help to avoid this infeasibility problem, however, that brings us to the second disadvantage of rounding solutions—rounded solutions are not necessarily optimal. It is also true that the optimal IP solution is not always near the rounded solution. We can see this in our Compco problem also. Rounding down gives us decision variables of 5, 5, with an objective function value of $5,100. Recall that the optimal IP value is $5,340. Nearby points 4,5 and 5,4 give objective function values of $4,380 and $4,800 respectively. Neither of these is close to the optimal value. With two decision variables, there are four neighbor solutions; with n decision variables there are 2^n neighbor points. Enumerating these to find an optimal value may not be practical or even guarantee an optimal solution.

In many situations, however, rounding does offer a practical, low-cost, time-saving solution method. It is possible to evaluate the difference between the value of the optimal relaxed LP solution and the rounded solution. If the difference between the LP relaxation and the rounded solution is not significant, and if it is not essential that the solution be optimal, then rounding down may indeed be the most practical solution procedure to use.

Enumeration

Complete enumeration requires listing all the feasible integer points, evaluating the objective function at each, and selecting the best one. Since every integer programming problem has a finite number of feasible solutions, complete enumeration is a possibility. Obviously, however, this is not a practical solution procedure for all problems. We have already seen how large some problems can become and what a difficult (if not impossible) solution approach this could become. Imagine listing all feasible points for even a simple example problem with five or six decision variables. Then imagine a real-life situation with 50 or 60 variables.

It is much more practical to attempt a partial enumeration, based on some selection criterion. This is similar to the trial-and-error approach mentioned in the discussion of rounding. Those points that seem most likely to provide an optimal solution are selected, that is, those points in the neighborhood of the optimal LP solution. Just as there is no guarantee that the optimal integer solution is in the neighborhood of the optimal LP solution, there is no guarantee that the selection criterion used will provide the optimal solution. The branch and bound solution that we discuss later uses an efficient, logical method of partial enumeration.

Cutting Planes

An in-depth discussion of the mechanics of cutting planes is beyond the scope of this text. We include it primarily to make you aware of it, and because the search for an efficient IP algorithm is concentrated on the cutting plane approach. A cutting plane is an additional constraint, called a cut, that is derived from the existing model constraints. The additional constraint is incorporated into the associated LP model by adding it to the constraint set. This new constraint, then, excludes the old LP solution, but does not exclude any lattice points. That is, a new feasible region is being constructed by cutting off areas that are infeasible for the integer problem. Thus, the new constraint has the effect of cutting off part of the LP feasible region *without eliminating an optimal integer point*. This "new" LP model (which will have a diminished optimal value) is then solved using simplex.

Cutting plane techniques search for the optimal IP solution by successively cutting off part of the LP feasible space until the optimal LP solution to this reduced problem is integer. The cutting plane method successively adds new constraints that reduce the feasible area in an attempt to find an optimal corner solution. Recall, from the graphical illustration of IP problems, that all feasible integer solutions can be represented by lattice points. It is possible to connect the outer points in order to describe the integer hull of the feasible area. Any optimal solution to an IP problem must be a lattice point on the convex hull of the feasible area (recall from the discussion in Chapter 3 that an optimal LP solution has to be a vertex). In order to locate the optimal integer solution, it is necessary to find the constraints that describe this convex hull. With these constraints, simplex can be used to determine the optimal integer solution, since the vertices would all be integers. The cutting plane method attempts to derive the additional constraints from the original model constraints. These constraints, which "cut" or remove pieces of the original constraint set, attempt to define the integer hull in order to form a vertex at the optimal lattice point.

Branch and Bound

Branch and bound is a quick, efficient method of partial enumeration. The technique logically partitions the area of feasible solutions into smaller areas (in such a way that the previous noninteger solution is excluded from the new feasible region), until the best solution is found. Partitioning or splitting the main problem in this way results in the creation of additional, smaller problems (subproblems) that must be solved. The solutions are systematically evaluated for optimality. The branch and bound procedure is discussed more fully in the next section.

9.4 *THE BRANCH AND BOUND METHOD*

There is no algorithm available that automatically and directly yields an optimum solution to an integer programming problem. Branch and bound is an intelligent search procedure for problem solving. The idea is to partition the set of all feasible solutions (the feasible space) into smaller solution subsets; compute upper and lower bounds on the value of the optimal solution in each subset; eliminate certain subsets from consideration; and continue partitioning and evaluating until the best integer solution is found.

The procedure begins with the relaxed LP solution and uses a tree-like diagram as a framework for the solution process, to help visualize and keep track of the partitioning and evaluation. In order to demonstrate this procedure, we will use a new problem—one that requires fewer branches than the Compco example.

Problem:

$$MAX\ 2X_1 + 3X_2$$

subject to

$$3X_1 + X_2 \le 150$$

$$4X_1 + 9X_2 \le 330$$

$$X_1, X_2 \ge 0 \text{ and integer}$$

The initial step is to solve for the LP relaxation; that is, we solve the problem as a linear programming problem without the integer restriction. Figure 9.3 shows an LP computer solution for this problem.

This initial solution establishes some limits, called the upper and lower bounds, for the solution being sought. The optimal value of the objective function (optimal Z), as indicated in the solution, establishes an **upper bound** for the optimal value of the integer solution. Recall, from the discussion of graphical interpretation of IP problems, that the integer requirement is an additional constraint and that the addition of a constraint cannot improve the value of the solution. The upper bound, UB, is the relaxed solution value, 139.58. A **lower bound,** LB, for this problem is determined by rounding down the solution variables and solving the

```
           AFTER 2 ITERATIONS,
           THIS SOLUTION IS OPTIMAL:

           VARIABLE          QUANTITY
           --------          --------
              X1              44.348
              X2              16.957

           OPTIMAL Z = 139.565
```

Figure 9.3 Solution—LP Relaxation

objective function using these values. The LB, which provides a feasible solution value, is 136. (Note that this is a maximization problem. For a minimization problem, the relaxed optimal solution is the lower bound, and the upper bound is found by rounding up the relaxed solution.) In a previous example, rounding down resulted in a suboptimal solution. At the present time, we do not know whether 136 (the solution obtained by rounding down) is optimal or suboptimal. Nor do we care that there might be an objective function somewhere in the feasible area with a value lower than 136, since we are maximizing.

The value of the optimal integer solution to the problem lies between these two values. To discover whether there is an improved solution, it is necessary to *branch*. As we proceed we will diagram the branch and bound solution, which helps us keep track of what we are doing and where we are in the solution process. The first node, with the upper and lower bounds (derived from the LP relaxation), is shown in Figure 9.4. Since this solution is not integer, it is infeasible. To begin searching for the optimal integer solution, we have to branch from this node.

Branching creates two new solution subsets. We have to divide the problem into two new, smaller subproblems to be solved and evaluated. We must select one of the decision variables on which to branch. It is an arbitrary decision, although the variable with the larger fractional part is frequently the designated choice. We will branch on X_2 (16.96). Since, in the optimal solution, X_2 must be an integer, we can develop two constraints from this value:

$$X_2 \leq 16$$

$$X_2 \geq 17$$

While we have not eliminated any possible integer values for X_2, we have eliminated the noninteger values between 16 and 17 from the feasible solution set. The

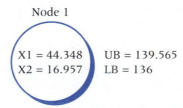

Node 1

$X1 = 44.348$ UB = 139.565
$X2 = 16.957$ LB = 136

Figure 9.4 Node 1 With Upper and Lower Bounds

two new problems are created by appending these two new constraints, one for each problem, as follows:

Problem 2	Problem 3
MAX $2X_1 + 3X_2$	MAX $2X_1 + 3X_2$
subject to	subject to
$3X_1 + X_2 \leq 150$	$3X_1 + X_2 \leq 150$
$4X_1 + 9X_2 \leq 330$	$4X_1 + 9X_2 \leq 330$
$X_2 \leq 16$	$X_2 \geq 17$
$X_1, X_2 \geq 0$ and integer	$X_1, X_2 \geq 0$ and integer

Figure 9.5 shows the output and solution for each of these two new problems. We know that all of the feasible integer solutions to the original problem are now contained in one of these two new problems (we eliminated only noninteger solutions). Since the problems all have the same objective functions, it is clear that either the optimal solution to problem 2 or the optimal solution to problem 3 is the optimal solution to the original problem. Thus, we no longer need to consider the original problem.

Figure 9.6 shows the new branch and bound diagram. The two new nodes reflect the addition of the new constraints. The upper bound at each of these nodes has been computed. Recall that the UB is the optimal value for the objective function for the LP relaxation. For problem 2, node 2, the UB is 137.34. For problem 3, node 3, the UB is 139.5. The lower bound remains the same as in the original problem, since neither solution is integer. We have not found a new feasible solution.

Evaluating the solutions at the descendant nodes 2 and 3 reveals that we do not have an optimal feasible integer solution (neither node has an integer solution). It is necessary to continue branching. In general, the solution at a node is optimal when it is integer and the UB at that node is greater than or equal to the UB at any other ending node. Recall that we have already discovered that the optimal solu-

```
        Problem 2                        Problem 3

   AFTER 2 ITERATIONS,              AFTER 3 ITERATIONS,
   THIS SOLUTION IS OPTIMAL:        THIS SOLUTION IS OPTIMAL:

   VARIABLE      QUANTITY           VARIABLE      QUANTITY
   ----------    ----------         ----------    ----------
      X1          44.667               X1          44.25
      X2          16                   X2          17
      S2           7.333               S1           .25

   OPTIMAL Z = 137.333               OPTIMAL Z = 139.5
```

Figure 9.5 Solution to Problems 2 and 3

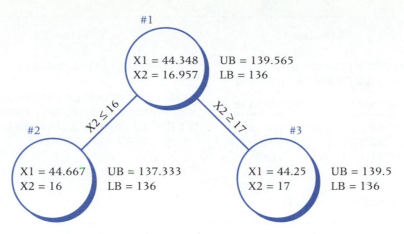

Figure 9.6 Nodes 2 and 3 with New Upper Bounds

tion to our problem lies either in problem 2 or in problem 3. Problem 3 has a higher
upper bound (139.5) than problem 2 (137.34). Thus in problem 3 we have already
found a better solution than we can possibly find in the feasible set for problem 2.
We can concentrate our efforts on problem 3, branching from it to create two more
subproblems. In general, we branch from the node that has the higher upper
bound. Again we arbitrarily select the variable with the greatest fractional part,
develop two new constraints, and solve for the new LP relaxations. At node 3, X_2 is
integer ($X_2 = 17$). We therefore branch on X_1, developing the two alternate constraints, $X_1 \leq 44$ and $X_1 \geq 45$. Remember that we are no longer working from the
original problem, but from the original problem with the additional constraint
$X_2 \geq 17$. The two new problems, 4 and 5, are shown below:

Problem 4	*Problem 5*
MAX $2X_1 + 3X_2$	MAX $2X_1 + 3X_2$
subject to	subject to
$3X_1 + X_2 \leq 150$	$3X_1 + X_2 \leq 150$
$4X_1 + 9X_2 \leq 330$	$4X_1 + 9X_2 \leq 330$
$X_2 \geq 17$	$X_2 \geq 17$
$X_1 \leq 44$	$X_1 \geq 45$

Figure 9.7 shows the solutions to these new problems. Figure 9.8 shows nodes 3, 4,
and 5 of the branch and bound diagram.

Once again we have to evaluate these solutions. The solution to problem 4 is still
noninteger. The upper bound at this point is 139.33. Problem 5, with the constraint
$X_1 \geq 45$, is infeasible. We do not yet have the optimal integer solution to the
problem; we must continue our search. We branch from node 4 (the problem at
node 5 is infeasible), branching on the noninteger value and developing two new

```
        Problem 4                          Problem 5

  AFTER 3 ITERATIONS,                 CALCULATING TABLEAU 4
  THIS SOLUTION IS OPTIMAL:
                                 THERE IS NO FEASIBLE SOLUTION TO
  VARIABLE          QUANTITY     THIS PROBLEM...OR SIMPLY BEYOND
  ---------         --------     MY LIMITED CAPABILITIES BESIDES,
    X1                44         I'M GETTING A HEADACHE!
    X2                17.111
    S1                .889            Press any key to continue
    S3                .111


  OPTIMAL Z = 139.333
```

Figure 9.7 Solutions to Problems 4 and 5

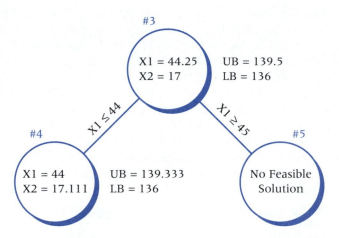

Figure 9.8 Nodes 4 and 5

problems, problem 6 and problem 7, from the additional constraints $X_2 \leq 17$ and $X_2 \geq 18$. The new problems are shown here:

Problem 6	*Problem 7*
Max $2X_1 + 3X_2$	Max $2X_1 + 3X_2$
subject to	subject to
$3X_1 + X_2 \leq 150$	$3X_1 + X_2 \leq 150$
$4X_1 + 9X_2 \leq 330$	$4X_1 + 9X_2 \leq 330$
$X_2 \geq 17$	$X_2 \geq 17$
$X_1 \leq 44$	$X_1 \leq 44$
$X_2 \leq 17$	$X_2 \geq 18$

Note that, in problem 6, we can combine the constraints $X_2 \geq 17$ and $X_2 \leq 17$ into one constraint $X_2 = 17$. In problem 7, the constraint $X_2 \geq 17$ is made redundant by the addition of the constraint $X_2 \geq 18$, and we can therefore drop it. Figure 9.9 shows the computer solution for each of these new problems; Figure 9.10 shows the diagram of nodes 4, 6, and 7.

When we evaluate the solutions at each of these nodes, we discover that there are two feasible integer solutions—not a frequent occurrence, but one you should be able to handle. Since we have an integer solution, it is necessary to recompute the lower bounds also. In each case we discover that the upper bound is equal to the lower bound, $UB = LB$. When the upper bound is equal to the lower bound it is not possible to achieve a better solution by continuing to branch on that node. In this case, with two such solutions, we clearly see that node 6 has the higher upper bound and is therefore a superior solution.

```
        Problem 6                          Problem 7

   AFTER 3 ITERATIONS,                 AFTER 4 ITERATIONS,
   THIS SOLUTION IS OPTIMAL:           THIS SOLUTION IS OPTIMAL:


   VARIABLE        QUANTITY            VARIABLE        QUANTITY
   --------        --------            --------        --------
     X1              44                  X1              42
     X2              17                  X2              18
     S1               1                  S1               6
     S2               1                  S3               1
     S3               0                  S4               2


   OPTIMAL Z = 139                     OPTIMAL Z = 138
```

Figure 9.9 Solutions to Problems 6 and 7

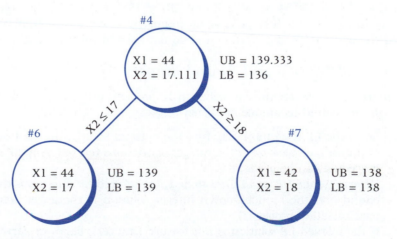

Figure 9.10 Nodes 6 and 7—Third Solution Subset

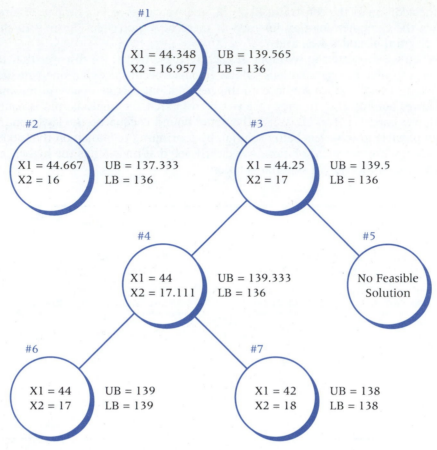

Figure 9.11 Node Diagram for Example Problem

In general, the optimal integer solution is reached when a feasible integer solution, and the upper bound at that node is greater than or equal to the upper bound at any other ending branch. From Figure 9.11, note that the ending nodes to be compared with node 6 are nodes 2, 5, and 9. The UB at node 6, UB = 139, is clearly greater than UB = 139.34 at node 2 and UB = 138 at node 7. The solution at node 5 is infeasible. By this process of comparison, we ensure that we have achieved the optimal integer solution and do not have to continue branching.

Summary of Branch and Bound Steps

In summary, the steps required to solve an IP problem using the LP model with the branch and bound technique are listed below:

Step 1: Solve the LP relaxation, i.e., find the optimal solution to the linear programming problem with the integer restrictions relaxed. Any LP solution procedure can be used.

Step 2: Determine the UB and LB. At node 1, the relaxed LP solution is the upper bound and the rounded-down integer solution is the lower bound (for maximization problems).

Step 3: If the relaxed LP solution is not feasible (integer), begin to partition the problem into smaller subproblems by branching on a selected variable.

The selection of the constraint on which to branch is arbitrary. We select the variable with the larger fractional part. Create two new constraints to reflect this partition (the $\geq$ and $\leq$ constraints created should eliminate fractional values for the variable).

Step 4: Branch to two descendant nodes, one for each new problem created by the new constraints (one for the $\geq$ constraint and one for the $\leq$ constraint).

Step 5: Solve the two new problems and determine the new upper bound at each node. (The existing maximum integer solution at any node is the lower bound. Until a new, higher integer solution is found, it remains the rounded-down solution from node 1.)

Step 6: Evaluate the solution for feasibility and optimality. If a feasible integer solution exists *and* its upper bound is greater than the upper bound at all other ending nodes (assuming they have been calculated), then the optimal integer solution has been found.

Step 7: Continue to branch, solve and evaluate the LP problem with newly developed constraints (i.e., steps 3–6) until the optimal feasible integer solution is reached.

Note that, for minimization problems, relaxed solutions are rounded *up* and upper and lower bounds are reversed, but the same procedure described and outlined above is used.

Using Branch and Bound with Mixed Integer and 0-1 Integer Problems

With only a few modifications, the basic branch and bound procedure, described above for the total integer problem, can be used to solve mixed integer programming problems and binary (0-1) problems. The differences are summarized below.

To solve mixed integer programming problems:

1. At node 1, to determine the lower bound, round down (for maximization problems) *only those variables with integer restrictions.*
2. When selecting which variable to branch from (usually the variable with the greatest fractional part), *consider only those variables that must be integer.* The optimal feasible solution has been reached at a node when it is the maximum upper bound of all ending nodes *and meets the specified integer requirements.*

In other words, with a mixed integer programming problem, the relaxed LP solution gives the optimal value for the variable(s) that are not restricted to integer values. We then concentrate (branch or partition) on those variables having integer requirements.

To solve 0-1 problems:

1. State 0-1 restrictions for variables in the model as constraints, such as $X_1 \leq 1, Y \leq 1$. Recall the following knapsack problem with Max and Dom:

$$\text{MAX } 9.5X_1 + 6X_2 + 6.5X_3 + 8.5X_4 + 9X_5 + 5.5X_6$$

subject to

$$200X_1 + 205X_2 + 85X_3 + 190X_4 + 240X_5 + 125X_6 \leq 650$$

$$X_1, X_2, X_3, X_4, X_5, X_6 = 0 \text{ or } 1$$

To apply the branch and bound method would require stating each 0-1 variable as a constraint instead of $X_1, X_2, X_3, X_4, X_5, X_6 = 0$ or 1, that is,

$$X_1 \leq 1$$
$$X_2 \leq 1$$
$$X_3 \leq 1$$
$$X_4 \leq 1$$
$$X_5 \leq 1$$
$$X_6 \leq 1$$

2. When branching on a selected variable, the two new constraints developed are $X = 1$ and $X = 0$. These two constraints form the branches at each succeeding node.

9.5 *INTEGER PROGRAMMING AND THE COMPUTER*

The tremendous recent advances in computer technology, both in hardware and software, have contributed to an increased ability to solve IP problems. Problems that can be solved easily by LP often become unsolvable for practical purposes when the integer restrictions are added. The time needed to compute the answers and the cost involved may be prohibitive. Computer solutions can alleviate (but not necessarily eliminate) this problem.

Solving even small total and mixed integer programming problems—with the possible exception of those modelled as network problems in Chapter 8—requires an extensive and sophisticatd computer program. This fact limits the size of the problem (the number of variables) that we can handle, even by computer. Many computer programs for solving IP problems are available from computer companies, software houses, book publishers, faculty members, computer consultants, students, and other sources. The programs vary in their capabilities and limitations, in their degree of sophistication and user friendliness, and in size and price. Some are teaching tools for demonstration purposes; some solve only 0-1 problems; some solve only very small problems; most severely restrict the number of variables that can be handled. Just as there is no one algorithm available for solving IP problems, there is no standard encoded solution approach. Some programs rely on enumeration, some use a branch and bound technique, and some use cutting planes. The IP program included with this book uses a branch and bound technique.

Figures 9.12 and 9.13 show the input and output respectively for the problem we introduced earlier in the discussion of the branch and bound technique. The problem was formulated as follows:

$$\text{MAX } 2X_1 + 3X_2$$

subject to

$$3X_1 + X_2 \leq 150$$
$$4X_1 + 9X_2 \leq 330$$
$$X_1, X_2 \geq 0 \text{ and integer}$$

Notice that input includes identifying the type of integer problem as pure integer, mixed integer, or 0-1. If the problem is mixed, then we must identify the integer

```
TYPE OF PROBLEM:  MAX /MIN


ENTER OBJECTIVE FUNCTION
MAX 2X1+3X2


ENTER THE CONSTRAINTS, ONE PER LINE, HERE. AFTER YOU HAVE
ENTERED THE LAST CONSTRAINT, ENTER THE WORD GO.


1    3X1+X2<150
2    4X1+9X2<330
3    GO




HERE IS WHAT YOU ENTERED:    (ILP)


0    MAX 2X1+3X2
     SUBJECT TO:
1       3X1+1X2≤150
2       4X1+9X2≤330


DO YOU WANT TO MODIFY THE DATA?  (YES/ NO )
```

Figure 9.12 Input with D & D Computer Solution

```
              SOLUTION AT NODE 1 (LP RELAXATION)

              VARIABLE      QUANTITY
              ----------    ----------
                 X1           44.35
                 X2           16.96

          UB = 139.565        LB = 136


          BRANCHING:  X2 <= 16
          SOLUTION AT NODE  2

              VARIABLE      QUANTITY
              ----------    ----------
                 X1           44.67
                 X2           16

          UB = 137.333        LP = 136


          BRANCHING:  X2 >= 17
          SOLUTION AT NODE  3
```

Figure 9.13 Output with D & D Computer Solution

```
VARIABLE                    QUANTITY
------------------          -----------------------
      X1                          44.25
      X2                          17

UB = 139.5              LB = 136


BRANCHING:  X1 <= 44
SOLUTION AT NODE  4

VARIABLE                    QUANTITY
------------------          -----------------------
      X1                          44
      X2                          17.11

UB = 139.333            LB = 139


BRANCHING:  X1 >= 45
SOLUTION AT NODE  5


THERE IS NO FEASIBLE SOLUTION


BRANCHING:  X2 <= 17
SOLUTION AT NODE  6

VARIABLE                    QUANTITY
------------------          -----------------------
      X1                          44
      X2                          17

UB = 139            LB = 139      FEASIBLE


BRANCHING:  X2 >= 18
SOLUTION AT NODE  7

VARIABLE                    QUANTITY
------------------          -----------------------
      X1                          42
      X2                          18

UB = 138            LB = 138      FEASIBLE


THIS IS THE OPTIMAL ILP SOLUTION:

VARIABLE                    QUANTITY
------------------          -----------------------
      X1                          44
      X2                          17


OPTIMAL Z VALUE =           139
```

Figure 9.13 Output with D & D Computer Solution

variables. In the solution, we have chosen to see each branch, but it is possible to skip this and see only the optimal solution. Notice that we have obtained the same optimal solution with the same branches.

Figure 9.14 shows the computer solution to the knapsack problem using LINDO, a computer program that was first mentioned in the LP chapter. Recall that the problem was formulated

$$\text{MAX } 9.5X_1 + 6X_2 + 6.5X_3 + 8.5X_4 + 9X_5 + 5.5X_6$$

subject to

$$200X_1 + 205X_2 + 85X_3 + 190X_4 + 240X_5 + 125X_6 \leq 650$$

$$X_1, X_2, X_3, X_4, X_5, X_6 = 0 \text{ or } 1$$

Notice that it is necessary to tell LINDO how many of the variables are integer. LINDO determines first the LP optimal solution and then, after branching, the integer solution. Now we know what Max and Dom will take in their backpack—water, coffee, trail mix, and jerky (X_1, X_3, X_5, and X_6).

```
                    OBJECTIVE FUNCTION VALUE

   1)    31.8750000


      VARIABLE      VALUE           REDUCED COST
           X1     1.000000            -2.000000
           X2      .000000             1.687500
           X3     1.000000            -3.312500
           X4     1.000000            -1.375000
           X5      .208333             .000000
           X6     1.000000             -.812500



       ROW  SLACK OR SURPLUS   DUAL PRICES
        2)        .000000          .037500


   NO. ITERATIONS =  5
   BRANCHES =  0  DETERM =  2.400E  2
   SET    X5 TO 0 AT    1 BND =  31.463420    TWIN =  30.592110
   SET    X2 TO 0 AT    2 BND =  30.000000    TWIN =  29.157890

   NEW INTEGER SOLUTION OF   30.0000   AT BRANCH   2 PIVOT   13

                    OBJECTIVE FUNCTION VALUE

   1)    30.0000000


      VARIABLE      VALUE           REDUCED COST
           X1     1.000000            -9.500000
           X2      .000000            -6.000000
           X3     1.000000            -6.500000
```

Figure 9.14 LINDO Input/Solution 0-1 Problem

```
              X4      1.000000            -8.500000
              X5       .000000            -9.000000
              X6      1.000000            -5.500000


         ROW  SLACK OR SURPLUS   DUAL PRICES
          2)     50.000000            .000000


NO. ITERATIONS =  13
BRANCHES =  2  DETERM =  1.000E  0
BOUND ON OPTIMUM:  30.59211
DELETE    X2 AT LEVEL 2
FLIP    X5 TO  1 WITH BOUND  30.59211
SET    X4 TO  0 AT  2 BND =  30.500000  TWIN =  30.592110


NEW INTEGER SOLUTION OF   30.5000   AT BRANCH   3 PIVOT   16


                   OBJECTIVE FUNCTION VALUE

  1)    30.5000000

     VARIABLE     VALUE         REDUCED COST
         X1      1.000000           -.700000
         X2       .000000           3.020000
         X3      1.000000          -2.760000
         X4       .000000           -.140000
         X5      1.000000           1.559999
         X6      1.000000            .000000


         ROW  SLACK OR SURPLUS   DUAL PRICES
          2)      .000000            .044000


NO. ITERATIONS =  16
BRANCHES =  3  DETERM =  1.250E  2
BOUND ON OPTIMUM:  30.59211
FLIP    X4 TO  1 WITH BOUND  30.59211
DELETE    X4 AT LEVEL 2
DELETE    X5 AT LEVEL 1
ENUMERATION COMPLETE. BRANCHES =    3 PIVOTS =    17

LAST INTEGER SOLUTION IS THE BEST FOUND
RE-INSTALLING BEST SOLUTION...
```

Figure 9.14 LINDO Input/Solution 0-1 Problem

9.6 *INTEGER PROGRAMMING: SPECIFIC 0-1 APPLICATIONS*

Certain binary integer programming problems, with basic structural similarities, occur frequently in real-world applications situations. It is important to recognize these problems when they occur and to be able to use 0-1 variables as a formulation tool in these specific situations. Being able to recognize a problem, and then being able to formulate it correctly, will enable you to solve the problem.

Binary (0-1) variables make it possible to incorporate dichotomous decision making into model formulation. We have selected the following examples to show how 0-1 variables are used to help make yes-no types of decisions and how they can be manipulated to enforce certain logical (either-or) conditions.

Capital Budgeting

Companies frequently make annual decisions on capital investments, selecting investment opportunities from among several recommended alternatives. The decision becomes one of choosing among these alternatives in order to maximize the return—subject to constraints on the amount available for investment over the given time frame. If projects can be partially funded, then linear programming can be used to model the problem. However, when a project must be funded in total or not at all (as is frequently the case), then integer programming is required. Consider the following example.

Ajax Manufacturing

Ajax Manufacturing is considering a number of alternative investments. Since its funds are limited, it wishes to choose those alternatives that will yield the greatest profits. The alternative investments, with their estimated net present values and their yearly capital requirements, are shown in the table below.

Investment Alternative	Net Present Value	Capital Requirements			
		Year 1	Year 2	Year 3	Year 4
New wing on plant	$57,000	$20,000	$12,000	$ 8,000	$ 6,000
Automated equipment	80,000	32,000	14,000	5,000	9,000
West Coast warehouse	95,000	5,000	21,000	33,000	10,000
New distribution center	68,000	7,000	10,000	16,000	28,000
Available capital		60,000	50,000	55,000	45,000

Formulation We use 0-1 integer variables to formulate this model, with 1 showing that the alternative has been selected and 0 indicating non-selection. The decision variables, then, are the investment alternatives:

$$X_1 = \text{new wing}$$

$$X_2 = \text{automated equipment}$$

$$X_3 = \text{warehouse}$$

$$X_4 = \text{distribution center}$$

The objective function is stated in terms of the net present value (in thousands) of each investment alternative:

$$\text{MAX } 57X_1 + 80X_2 + 95X_3 + 68X_4$$

The constraints control the capital to be used in each of the four years. For example, look at the first year. Ajax has budgeted $60,000; the new wing would require $20,000; the automated equipment would require $32,000; the warehouse would require $5,000; and the distribution center would require $7,000. The constraints, for each year, can be formulated:

$$20X_1 + 32X_2 + 5X_3 + 7X_4 \leq 60$$
$$12X_1 + 14X_2 + 21X_3 + 10X_4 \leq 50$$
$$8X_1 + 5X_2 + 33X_3 + 16X_4 \leq 55$$
$$6X_1 + 9X_2 + 10X_3 + 28X_4 \leq 45$$

In addition, the 0-1 integer requirements must be included, 1 for acceptance, 0 for rejection:

$$X_1, X_2, X_3, X_4 = 0 \text{ or } 1$$

The complete formulation, then is

$$\text{MAX } 57X_1 + 80X_2 + 95X_3 + 68X_4$$

subject to

$$20X_1 + 32X_2 + 5X_3 + 7X_4 \leq 60$$
$$12X_1 + 14X_2 + 21X_3 + 10X_4 \leq 50$$
$$8X_1 + 5X_2 + 33X_3 + 16X_4 \leq 55$$
$$6X_1 + 9X_2 + 10X_3 + 28X_4 \leq 45$$
$$X_1, X_2, X_3, X_4 = 0 \text{ or } 1$$

The important thing to remember, in a capital budgeting or investment problem in which a project must be funded in total or not at all, is that 0-1 variables allow each decision variable to assume one of two values—yes or no, select or reject. It is similar to the knapsack problem presented earlier, except that there are more constraints.

Logical Conditions

Binary 0-1 variables are also used to impose constraints that arise from logical conditions, and to offer multiple choices. We will first briefly discuss what this means and then present an example incorporating some of these constraints.

Multiple Choice Constraints

0-1 integer variables can be used to limit choices among competing alternatives. Again, 1 means yes or select and 0 means no or reject the alternative. If, for example, there are three investment alternatives (with all kinds of constraints so that the best alternative is not readily apparent), but only one investment is to be made, the constraint can be modelled as

$$X + Y + Z = 1$$

Since X, Y, and Z are 0-1 variables, only one of them can have a value of 1; the others must be 0.

k Out of n Alternatives

Sometimes it is necessary to limit the number of alternatives selected from among those recommended. Binary (0-1) variables enable us to do this also. Suppose, for example, that management is considering seven investment alternatives, but has decided to invest in only four projects right now. With 1 = yes and 0 = no (A, B, C, D, E, F, G = 0 or 1), this can be modelled

$$A + B + C + D + E + F + G = 4 \quad \text{[Select exactly 4 projects]}$$

These 0-1 variables can also be used to select at most k alternatives, or at least k alternatives, as follows:

$$A + B + C + D + E + F + G \geq 4 \quad \text{[Select at least 4 projects]}$$
$$A + B + C + D + E + F + G \leq 4 \quad \text{[Select at most 4 projects]}$$

If-Then

A dependency requirement is a logical condition that occurs frequently: *if* this is to happen, *then* this must happen. 0-1 variables can be used to tie alternatives together—to force a dependent relationship on two or more decision variables. For example, if in the Ajax example management did not want to build the new warehouse (X_3) unless the new distribution center (X_4) were also built, the following constraint would enforce the condition:

$$X_3 \leq X_4$$

or

$$X_3 - X_4 \leq 0$$

If the distribution center is not selected ($X_4 = 0$), the warehouse cannot be selected; it must also be 0. This still allows the option of selecting the distribution center project ($X_4 = 1$) and rejecting the warehouse project ($X_3 = 0$). The logical conditions are still met (X_3 is less than X_4, 0 is less than 1).

If management had decided to make the two projects co-requisite (one could not be accepted without the other), the constraint would be written as

$$X_3 - X_4 = 0$$

to reflect this condition.

If logical conditions present a problem for you, it might be helpful to use a trial-and-error approach in formulating the constraint. State or formulate the constraint in a way you think will work, and then test it by substituting the 0-1 values and seeing if the condition is met.

The following example utilizes some of the formulation tools discussed here.

Denneco, Inc.

Denneco, Inc. has decided to purchase new manufacturing equipment for one of its product lines. The following table shows information on the equipment:

Machine	Net Present Worth ($000)	Space Requirements (sq. ft.)
A	10	300
B	30	350
C	26	390
D	13	285
E	22	370
F	19	315

The production manager has provided the following additional information:

1. Only 1,000 square feet of space are available for the new machines.
2. Machines A and D perform the same function, so they should not both be purchased.
3. Machine E will work only on parts that have first been processed on machine B, so it should not be purchased unless machine B is also purchased (although machine B can be used without machine E).
4. Machines B, C, and E draw large amounts of power. The plant has the capacity to support the power requirements for only two of these machines.

Denneco has sufficient capital funds so that the machine costs are not a consideration. It wishes to select the equipment on the basis of net present worth.

Formulation　From what we have just discussed, the formulation of this problem should be clear. First, it is necessary to recognize that this is a 0-1 integer problem. It is integer because it is not possible to purchase part of a machine. It is binary because choices—dichotomous decisions—have to be made. The objective function is

$$\text{MAX } 10A + 30B + 26C + 13D + 22E + 19F$$

The initial constraint is one of limited floor space:

$$300A + 350B + 390C + 285D + 370E + 315E \le 1000$$

The remaining constraints are multiple-choice or logical conditions. A maximum of one of the two machines A and D should be purchased, each with a value of 0 or 1:

$$A + D \le 1$$

The third constraint states that machine E should not be purchased unless machine B is also purchased; that is, E is dependent upon B. The purchase of B is not, however, dependent on E; B can be purchased regardless of the decision on E. This is an if-then condition. If E is purchased, then B must also be purchased. Remembering that each has a value of either 1 or 0, then

$$E \le B$$

or

$$E - B \le 0$$

If E is selected (E = 1), then B must be 1 (selected) also. If E is not selected (E = 0), then B can be 1 or 0 and still satisfy the constraint. The fourth constraint states that the plant can support the power requirements, of, at most, two of the three machines B, C, and E. It does not say that two of these machines must be purchased. This is a "no more than k out of n" constraint:

$$B + C + E \leq 2$$

Finally, we add the binary integer requirement:

$$A, B, C, D, E, F = 0 \text{ or } 1$$

The model is formulated:

$$\text{MAX } 10A + 30B + 26C + 13D + 22E + 19F$$

subject to

$$300A + 350B + 390C + 285D + 370E + 315E \leq 1000$$

$$A + D \leq 1$$

$$E - B \leq 0$$

$$B + C + E \leq 2$$

$$A, B, C, D, E, F = 0 \text{ or } 1$$

Fixed Cost

A fixed cost problem is a slight variation of a linear programming or 0-1 problem. Fixed cost problems are problems in which certain costs are incurred if a particular action is taken. For example, the addition of a second shift in a plant usually has certain associated overhead costs that can be treated as fixed; video rentals usually are a function of the number of movies rented, but you must pay a one-time charge to become a member; a store can charge for each item ordered and then charge an additional fixed fee for home delivery, regardless of the number of items purchased. In each of these cases, the fixed cost can be treated as a 0-1 variable. The cost is either incurred (1) or it is not incurred (0), depending upon the situation. Let's return to the problem introduced at the opening of the chapter.

Williamson Suppliers

Recall that Williamson Suppliers purchases parts for resale from two vendors, Pear, Inc. and Apple Co. Williamson currently wishes to reorder two parts, X143 and X256. The part costs are shown below:

Supplier	X143	X256
Pear	$2.30	$7.88
Apple	2.34	7.65

Williamson currently needs 200 X143s and 120 X256s. The purchasing manager has found that, in addition to the per-unit cost for these parts, certain fixed costs are associated with placing an order with either of these suppliers. He estimates it costs $35 to place an order with Pear and $45 with Apple. He is trying to decide how many parts to order from each supplier in order to minimize his overall costs.

Formulation This problem is similar to a normal linear programming problem in that the purchasing manager wants to minimize costs subject to his need constraints. Ignoring the fixed costs associated with placing an order for a moment, the decision variables are:

$$P_1 = \text{number of X143 parts ordered from Pear}$$

$$P_2 = \text{number of X256 parts ordered from Pear}$$

$$A_1 = \text{number of X143 parts ordered from Apple}$$

$$A_2 = \text{number of X256 parts ordered from Apple}$$

and the formulation is:

$$\text{MIN}\quad 2.30P_1 + 7.88P_2 + 2.34A_1 + 7.65A_2$$

subject to

$$P_1 + A_1 = 200$$

$$P_2 + A_2 = 120$$

$$P_1, P_2, A_1, A_2 \geq 0$$

With this formulation, we minimize the cost per part subject to the requirement that 200 X143s and 120 X256s must be ordered. Next, we need to consider the fixed ordering costs. Since an order from a particular supplier is either made or it isn't , these variables are 0-1 and can be defined as:

$$PFC = \text{order placed with Pear, Inc.}$$

$$(1 = \text{fixed cost incurred; } 0 = \text{no order placed})$$

$$AFC = \text{order placed with Apple Co.}$$

$$(1 = \text{fixed cost incurred; } 0 = \text{no order placed})$$

The objective function then becomes:

$$\text{MIN}\ 2.30P_1 + 7.88P_2 + 2.34A_1 + 7.65A_2 + 35AFC + 45PFC$$

which is fairly straightforward.

Next, it is necessary to establish logical constaints such that, if any part is ordered from Pear, the Pear ordering cost is incurred ($PFC = 1$); and if any part is ordered from Apple, the Apple ordering cost is incurred ($AFC = 1$). Logically, $P_1 + P_2$ represents the number of parts ordered from Pear. If $P_1 + P_2$ is greater than 0, an order must have been placed with Pear and, therefore, PFC must equal 1.

[1] if $P_1 + P_2 > 0$, then $PFC = 1$

and [2] if $P_1 + P_2 \leq 0$, then $PFC = 0$

These logical conditions must be expressed as a constraint. Given $P_1 + P_2$ is the total number of parts ordered from Pear, it is possible to stae a third constraint as:

[3] $P_1 + P_2 \leq 320$

That is, the total number of parts ordered cannot exceed 320. This constraint simply states the portion of the total number of parts that will be ordered from Pear, and can take any value between 0 and 320. Note that constraint [3] is valid for both condition [1] and condition [2]. We can also restate constraint [3] such that, if no order is placed with Pear, it would be

[3a] $P_1 + P_2 \leq 0$ (and PFC would equal 0)

and if an order is placed with Pear, it would be

[3b] $P_1 + P_2 \leq 320$ (and PFC would equal 1)

since $P_1 + P_2$ could be any number between 1 and 320. Because these variations of [3] are a function of the value of PFC, we can restate constraint [3] as

$$P_1 + P_2 \leq 320PFC$$

If PFC $= 0$, then the constraint becomes [3a], and if PFC $= 1$, the constraint becomes [3b]. The same logic can be used to treat orders from Apple, giving the constraint

$$A_1 + A_2 \leq 320AFC$$

Adding these constraints, the model formulation becomes:

MIN $2.30P_1 + 7.88P_2 + 2.34A_1 + 7.65A_2 + 35AFC + 45PFC$

subject to

$P_1 + A_1 = 200$

$P_2 + A_2 = 120$

$P_1 + P_2 \leq 320PFC$

$A_1 + A_2 \leq 320AFC$

$P_1, P_2, A_1, A_2, PFC, AFC \geq 0$ and integer

PFC, AFC 0 or 1

Rewriting the logical constraints to place all decision variables on the LHS results in:

MIN $2.30P_1 + 7.88P_2 + 2.34A_1 + 7.65A_2 + 35AFC + 45PFC$

subject to

$P_1 + A_1 = 200$

$P_2 + A_2 = 120$

$P_1 + P_2 - 320PFC \leq 0$

$A_1 + A_2 - 320AFC \leq 0$

$P_1, P_2, A_1, A_2, PFC, AFC \geq 0$ and integer

PFC, AFC 0 or 1

This is an example of a fixed cost problem that requires the use of 0-1 decision variables in logical condition constraints. In this case, we used the coefficient 320, since we knew the total number of parts could not exceed that number. We could have used any arbitrary large number, as long as that number exceeded the total number of parts being ordered; for example, the constraint $P_1 + P_2 \leq 99999PFC$ would have worked equally well. Fixed cost problems are among the most difficult IP problems to formulate, since they depend upon intuitive reasoning.

The Fisher Company produces two products, A and B. Currently Fisher can sell all it produces of either product. Product A yields a profit contribution of $18 per unit and product B yields a profit contribution of $17 per unit.

The production of these products is limited, however, by the amount of production equipment that Fisher currently has available. Each product must pass through two departments, machining and polishing. The machining department uses an automatic lathe to machine aluminum blanks into the required shape for a particular product. The polishing department uses a polishing machine to grind and then polish the necessary surface finish onto the products. Product A requires 3 hours of machining and 4.5 hours of polishing time per unit. Product B requires 4 hours of machining and 3.75 hours of polishing time per unit. The company currently has 494 hours of machining time and 452 hours of polishing time available per week.

Additional hours of machining and polishing time can be obtained by leasing additional equipment on a weekly basis. Each leased automatic lathe increases machining time by 70 hours per week. Each leased polishing machine increases polishing time by 95.5 hours per week. The cost of leasing an additional lathe machine is $175 per week. The cost of leasing an additional polishing machine is $300 per week. Labor and other variable costs are constant and will not change if either or both additional machines are leased. That is, labor and material costs per unit have been deducted in determining the profit contribution per unit of each product. Additional labor is readily available to operate the machines. However, each leased lathe requires 150 square feet of floor space, and each leased polishing machine requires 90 square feet of floor space. Currently only 325 square feet of additional space are available. The leasing company has also informed Fisher that only two lathes and five polishing machines are available per week.

Fisher management wishes to determine the weekly production rate for each of these products that will maximize profit contribution. They also wish to know whether or not to lease additional lathes and/or polishing machines, and if so, how many of each.

Data Preparation/Problem Formulation

In this problem, Fisher management wishes to maximize the total profit contribution, which is a function of the number of each type of product produced. However, profit contibution will be reduced by the weekly lease costs if Fisher leases either or both of the machines. If A and B represent the units of each product produced, and ML and PL are integer variables representing the number of leased machines for the machining and polishing departments respectively, the objective function can be expressed as

$$\text{MAX } 18A + 16B - 175ML - 300PL$$

The constraint for the machine hours in the machining department can be expressed as

$$3A + 4B \leq 494 + 70ML$$

This means the hours required to produce products (3A + 4B) must be less than the 494 hours available plus 70 additional hours for each lathe is leased. We can restate this as

$$3A + 4B - 70ML \leq 494$$

The constraint for the polishing hours can likewise be stated as

$$4.5A + 3.75B - 95.5PL \leq 452$$

Available floor space would be represented by

$$150ML + 90PL \leq 325$$

and the maximum number of machines available for lease by

$$ML \leq 3$$

$$PL \leq 5$$

The complete formulation for this problem is

$$MAX\ 18A + 16B - 175ML - 300PL$$

subject to

$$3A + 4B - 70ML \leq 494$$

$$4.5A + 3.75B - 95.5PL \leq 452$$

$$150ML + 90PL \leq 325$$

$$ML \leq \quad 3$$

$$PL \leq \quad 5$$

$$A, B, ML, PL \geq 0 \text{ and } ML, PL \text{ integer}$$

Computer Solution

The computer solution to this mixed integer LP problem yields:

THIS IS THE OPTIMAL MILP SOLUTION:

VARIABLE	QUANTITY
A	50
B	86
ML	0
PL	1

OPTIMAL Z VALUE = 2062

Interpretation and Analysis of the Results

This solution tells Fisher management to produce 50 units of product A and 86 units of product B per week and to lease one polishing machine, but not to lease any automatic lathes. The total profit contribution associated with this solution is $2,062 per week.

What Happens Next

This solution assumes that there are no additional costs, such as wiring or plumbing costs, that would be required before the machine could be used. This may or may not be a reasonable assumption and should be verified.

The solution also suggests an optimal production schedule and leasing policy on a weekly basis. If no change in demand for these products is anticipated, management should consider a comparison of leasing costs versus purchase costs. Purchasing another polishing machine might be less expensive over an extended period of time if the payback period were long enough. Should demand (or any of the other parameters) change in the future, the company should reevaluate this policy.

9.7 *CONCLUDING REMARKS*

In this chapter we have introduced integer programming, an important mathematical programming approach for problems that do not satisfy the divisibility requirement of LP models. IP allows the additional requirement of whole-number solutions. Integer solutions are essential to many important real-world problems, including such strategic problem areas as capital budgeting and plant location. The binary integer models are particularly useful because the 0-1 variables can be used to represent dichotomous decisions.

Many real problems, however, cannot be solved by the solution methods described in this chapter. There is a gap between theory and the practice of IP. The difficulty has not been with the formulation but with efficient solution. As we have indicated, there is no single, all-purpose algorithm available to solve all IP problems. At best, there are "solution approaches." The techniques discussed in this chapter work well for problems with few variables. Until recently, even with the help of computers, most large IP problems could not be solved. The solution procedure was too costly in both memory and time requirements. Now, however, with the increased storage capacity and increased computational speed of the current generation of computers, larger problems can be solved successfully. This trend should continue as successive generations of computers are developed. At the same time, theoreticians continue to search for improved solution methods for IP problems. The gap between theory and practice will continue to narrow.

Management Science Application

TRUMBULL ASPHALT[1]

Trumbull Asphalt, a division of Owens-Corning Fiberglass, is the world's largest producer of industrial asphalt products. Trumbull has 22 production plants producing a variety of asphalt products. These production plants heat flux (the heavy end of petroleum refining that remains after the lighter ends have been removed) in an oxidation column and blend it with certain chemicals, depending upon the final product desired. The business is made volatile by the changing availability of flux and changes in customers' just-in-time requirements. In the early 1980s, Trumbull management attempted to develop a model to help them make decisions that would maximize their annual profit margin on operations.

Trumbull management faces a variety of complex and interrelated decisions. The complexity of these decisions is readily apparent in six operational areas: purchasing, transportation, plant operation, product blending, storage, and shipment of finished products. Decisions that must be made include:

1. Purchasing decisions. Flux is purchased from 30 to 40 different sources, with up to 60 additional potential sources available. Both the availability and price of flux changes constantly.

[1]Reprinted with permission from Clarence H. Martin and Sanford L. Lubin, "Optimization Modeling for Business Planning at Trumbull Asphalt," *Interfaces*, 15 (November-December, 1985), 66–72. Copyright 1985, The Institute of Management Sciences.

2. Transportation decisions. After purchase, the flux must be transported to Trumbull's processing plants by oceangoing tankers and barges, river and lake barge and towboat combinations, rail cars, trucks, and pipelines. All transportation systems must be equipped to keep the flux at high temperatures during shipment.

3. Plant operation decisions. The geographic dispersion of Trumbull's 22 plants provide many benefits, but fixed costs associated with each plant make the shutdown of any plant a strategic issue.

4. Raw material blending decisions. The production of its various products requires the selection of a particular grade or grades of flux. Finished products must meet rigorous customer specifications, but often can be blended from a combination of the eight grades of flux available. Differential pricing among flux grades makes optimal blending a major cost factor.

5. Storage decisions. Both the different grades of flux and the final products must be stored separately at high temperatures. Limited storage facilities contribute to a plant's capacity.

6. Distribution decisions. Once finished products are produced, they must be distributed to customers at elevated temperatures and in a specified period of time, since asphalt's physical characteristics can change over time.

The interaction of these various decisions has to be considered in any decision made. For example, a plant's ability to blend different grades of flux for a final product is dependent upon the grades and quantities of flux purchased.

To address these problems, two models were developed. The first was a strategic-tactical model, addressing flux purchasing and inbound shipment, operation curtailment at existing plants, blending, and shipments to customers. The second model was a more detailed operational model addressing spot market purchases of flux, storage capacity allocation, and weekly production schedules. This discussion will focus on the strategic-tactical model.

A 0-1 mixed integer programming model was selected with the objective of maximizing the annual margin for all Trumbull operations. Binary (0-1) variables represented the operation or closure of each plant. Continuous variables represented the quantity of each grade of flux to be (1) purchased from each source, (2) shipped from each source to each plant, and (3) processed into final products, thus representing the quantities of finished asphalt to be distributed from each plant to each customer. Constraints modelled the quantities of each grade of flux purchased and shipped; the maximum and minimum percentages of flux grades that could be blended for each finished product; the capacity of each plant; the quantities of asphalt shipped; the availability of flux; transportation capacities; customer demand; and distribution capabilities. The resulting model contained 1,696 variables and 886 constraints.

The results of this strategic-tactical model allowed better selection of flux grades for blending, thus saving on flux purchase costs and distribution costs. Production facility selection (operation or closure) also resulted in significant cost savings, and was not necessarily correlated with plant operating efficiency. Shadow prices from the LP results gave additional information on the desirability of the various flux sources. The use of this model resulted in cost reductions of over $1,000,000.

GLOSSARY

all integer type of IP problem in which all decision variables are required to be integer values

binary variables decision variables that must have a value of either 0 or 1

branch and bound method a solution method for solving integer programming problems that employs partial enumeration based upon a logical partitioning of the original problem into smaller subproblems, which are then solved and evaluated for optimality

capital budgeting problem a form of IP problem that uses binary decision variables and multiple constraints

complete enumeration a solution method for IP that involves enumerating all possible integer solutions and evaluating the objective function at each solution point to determine the optimal solution

cutting plane method a solution method for IP that adds constraints to the original problem excluding noninteger LP solutions until an all integer solution is found

fixed cost problem a form of IP problem that involves the addition of fixed costs to the objective function whenever certain decision variables have nonzero values

integer programming a subset of linear programming problems requiring some or all of the decision variables to have only integer (whole-number) values

knapsack problem a form of IP problem with binary decision variables that attempts to select as many of the decision variables as possible to fit into a limited space; a variation of the multiple-choice problem

lattice point an LP feasible solution where all decision variables have integer values

logical condition a constraint that expresses a logical condition, usually in the form of a multiple choice, k out of n selection, or if-then situation

lower bound the lowest acceptable value for an LP feasible solution in a maximization problem, usually obtained by rounding down the LP relaxation solution; in a minimization solution, the lower bound is the LP relaxation solution for the problem or subproblem

LP relaxation the LP solution to an IP problem that is obtained when the integer constraints are ignored

mixed IP type of IP problem in which some, but not all, of the decision variables are required to be integer values

rounded solution a feasible solution to an IP problem found by solving for the LP relaxation and then rounding each of the solution values (up or down) to integer values

round down a feasible solution to an IP problem found by truncating the LP relaxation solution values to integer values

upper bound the LP relaxation solution for a maximization problem or subproblem; the highest acceptable value for an LP feasible solution in a minimization problem, usually obtained by rounding up the LP relaxation solution

PROBLEMS

1.

$$\text{MAX } 3A + 2B$$

subject to

$$6A + 8B \leq 20$$
$$A, B \geq 0 \text{ and integer}$$

a. Solve the problem graphically.
b. Solve the problem using the branch and bound method.

2.

$$\text{MIN } X_1 + 2X_2$$

subject to

$$21X_1 + 9X_2 \geq 480$$
$$X_1, X_2 \geq 0 \text{ and integer}$$

a. Solve the problem graphically.
b. Solve the problem using the branch and bound method.

3.

$$\text{MAX } 18A + 10B$$

subject to

$$3A + 6B \leq 62$$
$$9A + 3B \leq 75$$
$$A + B \geq 12$$
$$A, B \geq 0 \text{ and integer}$$

a. Solve the problem graphically.
b. Solve the problem using the branch and bound method.

4. Solve the following problem using the branch and bound technique:

$$\text{MAX } 15A + 10B + 13C$$

subject to

$$4A + 2B + 3C \leq 35$$
$$2A + 2C \leq 25$$
$$3A + B \leq 30$$
$$A, B, C \geq 0 \text{ and integer}$$

5. Solve the following problem using the branch and bound technique:

$$\text{MAX } X_1 + X_2 + X_3$$

subject to

$$8X_1 + 16X_2 + 4X_3 \leq 490$$
$$20X_2 + 12X_3 \leq 600$$
$$X_1, X_2, X_3 \geq 0$$
$$X_1, X_2 \text{ integer}$$

6. Solve the following problem using branch and bound. Demonstrate the solution graphically.

$$\text{MIN } 10X + 8Y$$

subject to
$$4X + 10Y \geq 60$$
$$6X + 2Y \geq 50$$
$$2Y \geq 10$$
$$X, Y \geq 0$$
$$X \text{ integer}$$

7. Solve the following problem:

$$\text{MAX } 3A + 4B + 3C$$

subject to
$$A + B + C \leq 30$$
$$2B - 3C \geq 0$$
$$2A + 4B \leq 42$$
$$A, B, C \geq 0 \text{ and integer}$$

8. Solve the following problem:

$$\text{MAX } 3A + 4B + 2C + 3.5D$$

subject to
$$2A + 3B + C + 2D \leq 5$$
$$A + B + C + D \geq 2$$
$$A + D = 1$$
$$A, B, C, D = 0 \text{ or } 1$$

9. The commuter plane from Miami to West Palm Beach is a small twin-engine Cessna with a maximum weight allowance of 1,250 pounds. The plane carries up to eight passengers and freight. Passengers take priority. Each passenger pays $75 for the one-way flight. Freight charges are based (in part) on weight. This particular flight has six passenger reservations and nine packages that should go. The approximate weight of each passenger is given in the following table (passenger weight is needed in order to balance the seating on the small plane):

Passenger	Weight
1	110
2	175
3	215
4	125
5	160
6	180

The following table gives the weight and cost of each package:

Package	Weight	Profit
#1	35 lbs	$ 70
#2	80	140
#3	50	130
#4	10	30
#5	100	150
#6	25	50
#7	75	135
#8	60	130
#9	40	75

a. If the company wants to maximize its profit, what will the makeup of this flight be?

b. How much will the company gross?

10. A silversmith makes rings, bracelets, and necklaces especially for an annual Fall Craft sale held in the local shopping mall. For this project he wants to spend no more than 40 hours of labor. Moreover, he has only 2 pounds of silver allocated for these items. From experience he knows that each ring requires 0.5 ounce of silver, each bracelet requires 1 ounce, and each necklace requires 1.5 ounces of silver. He also knows that it takes him 2 hours of labor for each ring, 3 hours for each bracelet, and 2.5 hours for each necklace. The craftsman wants to maximize his profit. If he profits $3.00 per ring, $6.00 per bracelet, and $5.00 per necklace, how many of each should he make? Formulate this as an IP problem and solve.

11. Fred Hoff, Inc. has $170,000 to spend on new equipment for his refuse collection company. He is considering a trash compacting truck costing $75,000, an automatic conveyor system costing $90,000, a truck and equipment washer at a cost of $80,000, and a hydraulic lift truck costing $65,000. Labor- and time-saving considerations convince him that the purchases can help increase his annual profit as follows:

Purchase	Profit Increase
Compactor Truck	$4000
Conveyor	4500
Washer	3600
Hydraulic Truck	3800

Fred wants to purchase only one of the trucks (compactor or hydraulic lift). Moreover, he knows that if he purchases the equipment washer, he should buy the conveyor system. He has other uses for the conveyor and can purchase it independent of the washer. Which purchases should Fred make to maximize his profit?

12. Jane Cook has an inheritance of $75,000 to invest. She would like to invest the entire amount in order to maximize her annual income (interest and dividend). She has decided upon two stock offerings and a high-grade bond offering. Stock X, which costs $45, yields $7.00; stock Y costs $23 and yields $5.00. The bond investment yields 15 percent annually. Because of the low risk associated with the bond, Jane wants to invest a minimum of $10,000. Stock X appreciates 27 percent per year; stock Y grows 15 percent annually.

Jane wants a combined growth rate of at least 20 percent. Furthermore, she wants the bond investment to be at least 20 percent of the total money invested in stock.

a. How should she invest her money?
b. Compare the initial solution (the LP relaxation) and the round-down solution with this solution.
c. What changes occur in the solution if the stock can be purchased only in 100-share lots?

13. An independent trucker makes a daily trip from Olean to Buffalo carrying produce. He wants to make the trip as profitable as possible and has decided that, by being more selective in his cargo, he can increase his daily profit. His truck has a volume capacity of 2,000 cubic feet and can carry a maximum of 1,500 pounds. The following is a summary of the produce available at market, its weight, crated volume (crates cannot be divided), and profitability.

Product	Weight/crate (pounds)	Volume/crate (cubic feet)	Profit/crate
Eggs	35	50	$12.50
Apples	75	35	10.00
Cabbage	80	55	15.00
Honey	25	18	6.80
Cider	55	22	7.00

Formulate and solve this problem.

14. The Sheridan Company is expanding production capacity and is looking at six different machines, each costing about the same amount. The company can afford no more than three of the six machines. If they purchase machine A, however, they must also purchase C (the reverse is not true). Machines B, D, and E perform the same functions, so there is no need to purchase more than one of them, but at least one is essential. The net present value of each machine is shown below.

Machine	NPV (000s)
A	10
B	14
C	8
D	12
E	15
F	13

In order to maximize their net present worth, what decision should the company make?

15. The advertising manager of the Davis Company has two large jobs that must be printed: 150,000 brochures and 200,000 catalogs. The printing firm he normally uses charges $.06 for each brochure and $.08 for each catalog. The manager also has a second option: A local firm will lease the company a desktop publishing system for $8,000. Using this system, the manager estimates it will cost $.03 per brochure and $.04 per catalog (exclusive of lease costs). The system has a capacity of 300,000 pieces (brochures or catalogs). Any pieces not printed on the system can still be sent to the printer at the

rates quoted above. If the manager wants to minimize his total costs, should he lease this new system? How many of each piece should be sent to the printer and how many should be printed on the desktop publishing system?

16. The Williamson Company is considering the following capital investments: the introduction of two new products (A and B), a computerized billing system, and a new warehouse. Net present value of each alternative, capital requirements, and funds available are shown below.

Investment Alternative	Net Present Value	Capital Requirements			
		Year 1	Year 2	Year 3	Year 4
Product A	$56,000	$13,000	$10,000	$ 8,000	$14,000
Product B	73,000	21,000	16,000	12,000	9,000
Computerized billing	58,000	14,000	6,000	3,000	1,500
Warehouse	48,000	9,000	15,000	18,000	11,000
Available capital		55,000	45,000	40,000	35,000

Williamson wishes to choose the investment alternatives that will maximize its net present value. Should the company choose to introduce new product A, however, the warehouse must be built to give the company the necessary storage capacity. If product A is not introduced, the warehouse will still have a net present value of $48,000. What investments should Williamson recommend?

17. The town recreation department is considering a new recreation complex with a variety of features. Expected costs, space requirements, and daily usage figures are as follows:

Facility	Cost	Space Requirement	Expected Usage/day
Fitness center	$120,000	1,200 sq ft	60
Pool (indoor)	380,000	5,500	300
Pool (outdoor)	310,000	7,200	240
Movie theater	260,000	6,000	170
Gymnasium	190,000	10,200	140
Tennis courts (outdoor)	80,000	15,000	110
Baseball field	60,000	14,000	150
Soccer field	40,000	12,000	170
Skating rink (indoor)	210,000	10,100	165

The department has a total of $12 million to spend. The building will have a maximum size of 25,000 square feet allocated to these facilities (excluding offices, lobbies, and meeting rooms). In addition, there will be a maximum of 40,000 square feet of outdoor space available for these facilities. If the town leaders wish to maximize total daily usage of the facility, which components should be included? (Note: The use estimates on the pools are based on the assumption that only one pool will be built.)

18. If the town in Problem 17 wishes to minimize cost yet serve at least 850 people a day, how does the formulation change? What is the new solution?

19. The Omega Company is considering the purchase of a five-ton press, an eight-ton press, a radial trimmer, and a digital lathe. The following table shows the cost, the area occupied, the power required, and the contribution to profit for each machine:

Machine	Cost	Area Occupied (ft²)	Power Required (watts)	Profit Contribution
Five ton press	$ 70,000	140	500	$28,000
Eight ton press	106,000	160	700	45,000
Radial trimmer	80,000	185	800	40,000
Digital lathe	120,000	170	540	50,000

The plant manager wishes to know which of these machines he should purchase to maximize annual income, if the following conditions are all true:

a. His budget for new equipment is $250,000.
b. He has 370 square feet of floor space.
c. Existing plant wiring will allow only an additional 2,100 watts of power.
d. He does not need two presses.

20. The plant manager for the Omega company (problem 19) has been offered $80,000 for one of his existing machines. The machine currently has a contribution of $30,000 per year, occupies 150 square feet of floor space, and uses 775 watts of power. He wishes to include this possible sale in his new equipment purchase decision. How does this offer affect the decision in problem 19?

21. The Tin Tube Company purchases 15-inch rolls of tin, cuts them into narrow strips, and forms them into tubing. The rolls are cut into strips 2, 3, 4, or 5 inches wide. The cutting machine can make a maximum of four cuts per roll. This particular cutting machine offers only certain cutting settings:

Cutting Alternatives	2 in.	3 in.	4 in.	5 in.	Waste (inches)
	Number of Rolls				
1	2	0	0	2	1
2	0	3	0	1	1
3	0	1	3	0	0
4	0	0	0	3	0
5	1	1	1	1	1
6	1	0	2	1	0

If the company has orders for the following tubing:

Tubing Circumference	Rolls Required
2	1400
3	1100
4	700
5	800

a. What is the minimum number of rolls that Tin Tube must purchase to fill these orders?

b. How much waste is involved in the solution to part a?

c. If Tin Tube must place unused rolls in storage, how many rolls will have to be stored?

22. If Tin Tube's objective (problem 21) is to reduce the waste involved in cutting, how would your answer change?

23. The Chicken Little Company (CLC) is about to open a number of franchises in Monroe County. CLC wants to be sure that it selects locations in such a way that all major population centers have access to a CLC location. The following table shows the possible store locations and the population centers each location would serve.

Location	Population Centers Served
1	B, D, F
2	A, E, L, K
3	A, G, J, L
4	B, C
5	E, F, G, J
6	A, C, K
7	D, J, L
8	D, M

Which locations should CLC select if it wants to minimize the total number of locations?

24. The production manager of Ortiz Printing has two large jobs to run. The Jones company needs 150,000 brochures; the Rose Company needs 200,000 fliers. Both are within current press capacity. The manager estimates he will make $.03 per Jones brochure and $.04 per Rose flier with his current press. However, a sales representative recently showed him two new desktop publishing systems. One of these, the Venture System, would cost him $8,500, but would cut costs and enable him to make $.07 each on the Jones job and $.09 per piece on the Rose job. The Page Producer System would cost him $6,000, but would cut costs and allow him to make $.08 per piece on either job. The Venture System has a maximum capacity of 275,000 pieces and the Page Producer has a maximum capactiy of 175,000 pieces (over this time period). The manager feels his options are to purchase (a) one of the systems; (b) both of them; or (c) neither of them. Although not absolutely necessary, he would like to deduct any purchase costs from the income derived from these two jobs. What decision should the manager make? If he decides to purchase either system or both, how many of each job should be run on the new systems?

Consultant's Report _____

Warren and Associates

Warren and Associates was started in 1968 by Larry Warren, a consulting engineer. The firm, which began as a one-man operation serving Monroe County in western New York state, has grown into a large organization serving the northeastern United States. The company undertakes the engineering and construction of research facilities and office complexes for the electronics, telecommunications, and computer industries.

Over the years, the firm has gradually moved from providing primarily engineering, design, and project management services to providing turnkey operations that also include construction. Thus the company offers two basic services: (1) design, engineering, and project management, and (2) turnkey construction. Clients present their project proposals in various stages of development. The firm accepts client input, develops a plan, and prepares an estimate that is submitted to the client for review. In this proposal stage, there is no commitment or contract. The client is free to withdraw, delay, or give approval and issue a contract. Because of the uncertainty, Warren and Associates must prepare many such proposals to ensure future workloads. The firm has to make many more proposals than it can physically undertake, and has to bill a minimum number of man-days every year to cover overhead and proposal costs. Thus the firm must use care in planning its workload and in project selection.

The firm is currently considering eleven possible projects for the coming year. These projects, all of which have client approval, are listed in the table below. The table also indicates, for each project, its value (billings in millions of dollars); its estimated contribution margin (in thousands of dollars); the man-days required by the various disciplines to complete the project; whether or not the project is a telecommunications facility; and whether or not it is a turnkey operation. Warren and Associates must decide (within the framework of corporate objectives) which projects it should undertake for the coming year.

Projects for Consideration
Estimated Man-Days per Discipline

Proj #	Proj Billng	Contrb Margin	Engrg Dept	Plumbng Dept	Elec Dept	Arch Dept	Constr Dept	Proj Engr	Tel	Eng & Design
1	4.6	300	45	230	160	150	600	450		
2	4.2	275	86	120	40	42	371	215	x	
3	5.1	325	180	860	742	455	845	740		
4	2.0	200	236	20	35	155	0	80		x
5	2.4	184	410	140	135	144	270	320		
6	7.2	430	605	665	27	140	56	615		
7	6.6	485	40	73	956	36	302	455	x	
8	2.6	160	650	80	70	80	0	900		x
9	1.8	115	8	175	88	18	58	205	x	
10	9.2	490	215	190	870	160	235	625		
11	2.3	160	128	15	44	40	0	200	x	x
Manpower			1860	1890	2280	980	1910	3070		

One objective is to improve the firm's position in the burgeoning telecommunications industry. Warren's portion of this market is still relatively small—under $5 million. Thus one goal for the coming year is to increase telecommunications billings to $12.5 million.

Another objective is to concentrate on turnkey construction projects, which require maintaining general contracting personnel. To guarantee that this objective is met, the company has set a goal of a minimum of $30 million in client billings. Billings for the engineering, design, and project management service are not to exceed $5 million. The firm wants to maximize the total contribution margin for the year.

Since management is committed to providing quality service (despite the fact that much of its preliminary work represents unpaid services), the company must plan personnel development and work loads commensurate with good professional standards. It cannot do this using temporary help. It must also maintain a staff with the proper mix of disciplines, and do this with minimum turnover.

You have been hired as a consultant to help Warren & Associates by applying management science techniques to this particular problem. Prepare a report for Warren and Associates that addresses:

1. The projects that should be undertaken for the coming year, and the total expected profit contribution.
2. The extent to which the optimal solution meets the company's stated objectives.
3. Project 9 has been submitted by an old customer who has supplied substantial work in the past. Even if this project is not included in the optimal solution, the company might still wish to undertake it. Thus, if this project is not included in the optimal solution, include an alternate solution that includes it and discuss the opportunity cost (forgone contribution) of including it.

Chapter

10

Goal Programming

By the end of this chapter, you should be able to:

1

recognize a goal programming problem;

2

formulate goal programming problems with goals having different
priority levels, different weights, or both; and

3

solve goal programming problems using the modified simplex
method.

Goal programming, an extension of linear programming, enables decision makers to solve problems involving multiple criteria. Linear and integer programming are used to solve problems with a single objective function. Both attempt to find an optimal solution to linear problems by maximizing or minimizing the objective function subject to the problem's constraints. In some cases, however, decision makers have more than one goal or objective, and those goals may even be in conflict. Goal programming, a technique first introduced by Charnes and Cooper[1] and later refined by Ijiri[2], Lee[3], and others, makes it possible to solve those types of problems. Goal programming is also used when there is no feasible solution that satisfies all objectives; the decision maker seeks the best acceptable solution, given the various criteria that must be satisfied. In this chapter we will show how these problems are formulated. We will also explain how goal programming problems can be solved using a modified version of the simplex method.

ABC Investments — A Goal Programming Problem

Mary Thompson, a fund manager for ABC Investments, is currently working with a client who wishes to invest $1 million for a five-year period. There are three basic fund alternatives for this investment: stocks, bonds, and money market accounts.

---

[1]Abraham Charnes and William W. Cooper, *Management Models and Industrial Applications of Linear Programming*, Prentice-Hall, Inc., 1961.
[2]James P. Ignizio, *Goal Programming and Extensions*, D.C. Heath and Company, 1976.
[3]Sang M. Lee, *Goal Programming for Decision Analysis*, Auerbach Publishers, Inc., 1973.

Each of these alternatives has a different maturity period and a different yield. Money market accounts are the most liquid, stock fund investments have a two-year maturity, and bonds have a three-year maturity. The stock funds tend to have the largest yields, and the money markets have the smallest. Mary's investment strategy is both restricted and complicated by her client's wishes, which include: diversification of the investment on an annual basis; limited investment in the stock market; as large a yield as possible; and a minimum money market balance to cover the client's possible short-term cash needs. Mary knows that whatever plan she devises will probably involve moving a portion of the investment between the alternative accounts over the five-year period. The biggest question in her mind, however, is whether or not she can come up with a rational strategy that will satisfy all of her client's wishes at once.

We will return to Mary's problem later in the chapter.

10.1 *AN INTRODUCTION TO GOAL PROGRAMMING*

Linear programming is used to solve problems that have one specific goal or objective, finding the optimal solution that exists within the problem's constraints. Decision makers and organizations, however, are often faced with problems that have **multiple criteria** or many objectives. In problems involving multiple objectives, usually it is not possible to satisfy all objectives or goals. Frequently, one of these criteria is optimized at the expense of the remaining criteria. For example, companies often have a goal of maximizing profit, but may also wish to be good corporate citizens and employers. A solution that yields the greatest profit sometimes also has a negative impact on the environment or puts hundreds of people out of work. An oil company can maximize its profits by refining more aviation fuel and less home heating oil, but to do so in the middle of winter, when heating oil is in short supply, may be an unacceptable decision. Thus, companies often seek a solution that achieves "acceptable" profits while attempting to meet other criteria as well. Herbert Simon suggested an approach known as "satisficing," which means reaching a satisfactory solution to a problem with multiple criteria.

Goal programming (GP) involves a tradeoff among goals. An optimal GP solution minimizes the impact of these tradeoffs. It attempts to minimize the collective over- or underachievement of all goals. Under- or overachievement of a goal can be measured as a deviation from the desired objective. Thus, goal programming attempts to minimize the amount of deviation from all of the stated goals. It is possible that a solution that minimizes these deviations does not actually meet any of the stated multiple objectives. That is why the concept of satisficing, or reaching a statisfactory level of goal attainment, is important.

In some cases it is more important to meet some goals than others. In these cases, goals (actually the deviations from those goals) are given weights that signify the amount of importance attached to each goal. In other cases, some goals are so important that they preempt other goals completely; that is, these goals must be satisfied (or the deviation from them minimized) before any other goals are even considered. This is accomplished by establishing **preemptive priorities** for all goals. Because GP minimizes the deviation from the achievement of an objective, it can even be used with single-objective LP problems to determine the closest feasible solution on problems that would otherwise be infeasible. Goal programming has been widely applied to problems in business organizations, nonprofit organizations, and government agencies.

Because goal programming is a variation of the linear programming model (Chapter 2), all the same assumptions apply. Therefore, some simple GP problems can be solved using the simplex method discussed in Chapter 4. Others, such as those with multiple priority levels, require a modified version of the simplex method. While the solution method varies slightly from the LP method, the real key to solving goal programming problems is in formulating them properly. In the next section, we will examine a scheduling problem and show how it can be formulated as a goal programming problem.

10.2 *PROBLEM FORMULATION*

Consider the following problem faced by the Acme Manufacturing Company (AMC).

George Jenkins, production manager for AMC, must prepare weekly production schedules for three machine frames that AMC fabricates: X_1, X_2, and X_3. Each of the three frames passes through three departments: cutting, welding, and grinding. The accounting department has informed George that the profit contributions for the frames are $28, $40, and $32 respectively. George also knows that frame X_1 requires 3 hours of cutting time, 6 hours of welding time, and 3 hours of grinding time. Frame X_2 requires 7 hours of cutting time, 5 hours of welding time, and 6 hours of grinding time. Frame X_3 requires 5 hours of cutting time, 7 hours of welding time, and 5 hours of grinding time. Department labor schedules indicate that 210 hours are currently available in the cutting department, 280 hours in the welding department, and 250 hours in the grinding department. George knows that AMC can sell all the units of each frame that the company produces. His goal is to determine a weekly production schedule that will give AMC the largest profit contribution possible for the three products.

This problem can be solved as an LP problem, where the objective is to maximize profit contribution. The problem is formulated

$$\text{MAX } 28X_1 + 40X_2 + 32X_3$$

subject to

$$3X_1 + 7X_2 + 5X_3 \leq 210$$

$$6X_1 + 5X_2 + 7X_3 \leq 280$$

$$3X_1 + 6X_2 + 5X_3 \leq 250$$

$$X_1, X_2, X_3 \geq 0$$

The LP solution to this problem (with hours rounded to the nearest tenth and dollars rounded to the nearest penny) is

$$X_1 = 33.7$$

$$X_2 = 15.6$$

$$S_3 = 45.6$$

$$\text{Zmax} = 1565.93$$

where S3 represents the slack or unused hours in the grinding department.

The formulation of a goal programming problem is slightly different from the formulation of an LP problem. In a GP problem, the goals are stated as constraints rather than directly in the objective function. Thus, goal programming formulations contain two types of constraints: the structural or system constraints, which cannot be violated, and the more flexible goal constraints. Flexibility is introduced into the goal constraints through **deviational variables,** which represent the over- or underachievement of a particular goal. The deviational variable d_i^- represents a negative deviation or underachievement of goal i, and the deviational variable d_i^+ represents a positive deviation or overachievement of the goal. Each goal constraint includes both deviational variables (d_i^- and d_i^+), although at least one always is zero, since a goal cannot be simultaneously underachieved and overachieved.

Now, instead of the singular goal of maximizing profit, let's assume that top AMC management has instructed George Jenkins to incorporate the following criteria into his production schedule, as summarized in the earlier example.

1. Because of possible labor problems, AMC should avoid temporary layoffs. Since layoffs result when available labor hours are not fully utilized, George must seek to use all available labor hours.
2. Overtime results in higher costs and additional labor problems. Therefore, all overtime should be kept to a minimum.
3. A minimum weekly profit contribution of $1,250 is desired for these three products.

George Jenkins now has multiple criteria for this decision, and the problem becomes a goal programming problem. The structural constraints remain the same as in the original LP problem formulation. The goal constraints must be formulated from the information provided by top management.

With respect to labor utilization, goal 1 specifies no slack labor hours and goal 2 no overtime hours. Since unused or overtime hours occur on a department-by-department basis, there must be a goal constraint for each department. The company would like the production hours for each department to be equal to the hours available. For the cutting department, this can be stated mathematically as

$$3X_1 + 7X_2 + 5X_3 = 210$$

Letting d_1^- represent underachievement (unused hours) and d_1^+ represent overachievement (overtime) of this goal, this constraint can be restated as

$$3X_1 + 7X_2 + 5X_3 + d_1^- = 210 + d_1^+$$

Moving deviational variable d_1^+ to the left-hand side of the equation gives

[cutting] $3X_1 + 7X_2 + 5X_3 + d_1^- - d_1^+ = 210$

In similar fashion, the constraints for the welding and grinding departments are

[welding] $6X_1 + 5X_2 + 7X_3 + d_2^- - d_2^+ = 280$

and

[grinding] $3X_1 + 6X_2 + 5X_3 + d_3^- - d_3^+ = 250$

Thus, deviational variables d_1^-, d_2^-, and d_3^- represent the total underutilization of available hours, and d_1^+, d_2^+, and d_3^+ represent the total numbers of hours of overtime required.

The third goal, a minimum profit contribution of $1,250 per week, can be expressed by the constraint

$$28X_1 + 40X_2 + 32X_3 + d_4^- - d_4^+ = 1250$$

where d_4^- represents a profit shortfall and d_4^+ represents a surplus profit. It is important to note that, while deviational variables d_1, d_2, and d_3 all represent deviations in hours, the d_4 variables represent deviations in dollars. Normally, we would hesitate at mixing unlike variables. For the moment, however, we will assume that these different units are of equal value; AMC does not distinguish between a deviation of one hour and a deviation of one dollar.

To complete the formulation of the goal programming problem, we must complete the objective function. Since the objective in a GP problem is to minimize the overall deviations from these stated goals, the objective function can be expressed as

$$\text{MIN } d_1^- + d_1^+ + d_2^- + d_2^+ + d_3^- + d_3^+ + d_4^- + 0d_4^+$$

Note that deviational variable d_4^+ has been assigned a coefficient of zero. Since the goal states a minimum desired profit contribution, AMC would not wish to minimize the overachievement of this goal. The three decision variables representing the number of frames fabricated each week would also have zero coefficients in the objective function, since they are not being minimized. We can now state this GP problem in the traditional LP model form:

$$\text{MIN } 0X_1 + 0X_2 + 0X_3 + d_1^- + d_1^+ + d_2^- + d_2^+ + d_3^- + d_3^+ + d_4^- + 0d_4^+$$

subject to

$$
\begin{aligned}
3X_1 + 7X_2 + 5X_3 + d_1^- - d_1^+ &= 210 \\
6X_1 + 5X_2 + 7X_3 + d_2^- - d_2^+ &= 280 \\
3X_1 + 6X_2 + 5X_3 + d_3^- - d_3^+ &= 250 \\
28X_1 + 40X_2 + 32X_3 + d_4^- - d_4^+ &= 1250
\end{aligned}
$$

$$X_1, X_2, X_3, d_1^-, d_1^+, d_2^-, d_2^+, d_3^-, d_3^+, d_4^-, d_4^+ \geq 0$$

We can solve this problem as a normal LP problem using the simplex method. The rounded result is

$$
\begin{aligned}
X_2 &= 2.9 \\
X_3 &= 37.9 \\
d_3^- &= 42.9 \\
d_4^+ &= 80.0
\end{aligned}
$$

This result indicates that there is an underutilization or slack of 42.9 hours in the grinding department and that profit contribution is $1,330—the $1,250 minimum plus an overachievement of $80. Comparing this solution with the LP profit maximization solution, we can see the product mix changed from $X_1 = 33.7$, $X_2 = 15.6$, and $X_3 = 0$ to $X_1 = 0$, $X_2 = 2.9$, and $X_3 = 37.9$. The underutilization of hours in the grinding department was reduced from 55.6 to 42.9 hours, a change of 12.7 hours. This change also caused a drop in profit contribution from the $1,565.93 in the original solution to $1,330, a reduction of $235.93. Remember, however, that the d_4^+ deviation is not being minimized. Thus, the value of the objective function represents the total deviation from all goals—42.9 (hours) in this case.

Weighted Goals

In the AMC goal programming problem, all goals are considered to be of equal importance or weight. It is possible to adjust the relative importance of deviational variables, to reflect the importance of meeting certain goals, by assigning weights to the deviational variables. These weights become the objective function coefficients for the deviational variables. For example, assume that AMC equates one hour of goal 1, the utilization of all available hours, with $10.00 of profit contribution. That is, the company does not distinguish between falling one hour short of meeting goal 1 and falling $10.00 short in meeting the minimum profit contribution. Thus, AMC feels the underutilization variables (d_1^-, d_2^-, and d_3^-) are ten times as important as the profit shortfall variable (d_4^-). Assume further that goal 1 is twice as important as goal 2, the minimization of overtime. If profit underachievement is given a weight of 1, labor underutilization is therefore given a weight of 10 (ten times as great) and overtime hours are given a weight of 5 (half as important as goal 1). Using these weights as the objective function coefficients for the deviational variables, we can restate the GP model as

$$\text{MIN } 0X_1 + 0X_2 + 0X_3$$
$$+ 10d_1^- + 5d_1^+ + 10d_2^- + 5d_2^+ + 10d_3^- + 5d_3^+ + 1d_4^- + 0d_4^+$$

subject to

$$3X_1 + 7X_2 + 5X_3 + d_1^- - d_1^+ = 210$$
$$6X_1 + 5X_2 + 7X_3 + d_2^- - d_2^+ = 280$$
$$4X_1 + 6X_2 + 5X_3 + d_3^- - d_3^+ = 250$$
$$28X_1 + 40X_2 + 32X_3 + d_4^- - d_4^+ = 1250$$
$$X_1, X_2, X_3, d_1^-, d_1^+, d_2^-, d_2^+, d_3^-, d_3^+, d_4^-, d_4^+ \geq 0$$

A deviation of one hour for labor underutilization is the same as a deviation of $10.00 of profit underachievement or two hours of overtime. We can solve this problem using the simplex method or any LP computer program. The solution (rounded) is

$$X_2 = 20.6$$
$$X_3 = 25.3$$
$$d_1^+ = 60.6$$
$$d_4^+ = 382.94$$
$$\text{Zmin} = 303$$

Relating this solution to AMC's stated goals: goal 1 is totally achieved; goal 2 is underachieved by 60.6 hours; and goal 3 is overachieved by $382.94.

Altering the production schedule from the original LP maximization solution eliminated all unused hours in the grinding department. The only undesirable deviation is from goal 2, since 60.6 hours of overtime are necessary to achieve this solution. Total profit contribution for this solution is $1,632.94 (the $1,250 minimum plus the deviation of $382.94). This is an increase over both of the previous solutions and can be attributed to the additional overtime in the cutting department (d_1^+). Even with a weighting scheme, however, extreme care must be taken when the deviational variables are not in the same units. One way to avoid mixing unlike variables is to assign preemptive priorities to goals.

Goals with Preemptive Priorities

Assigning goals different **preemptive priorities** indicates that one goal is more important than another. When solving GP problems with preemptive priorities, the goal with the higher level priority is satisfied (as much as possible) before considering any other goals; in other words, the high-priority goal preempts all other considerations until it is satisfied. There is no tradeoff between goals with different priority levels. Once all level 1 (the highest level) goals have been satisfied, level 2 goals can then be addressed and so on. The term P_i will be used to represent a preemptive priority level, where $P_i >>> P_{i+1}$. Thus, by assigning different preemptive priorities to different goals, a clear order of preference or importance is created for the goals. The use of preemptive priorities is probably the most common approach to goal programming in practice today.

In the example problem, if the stated goals have preemptive priorities of P_1, P_2, and P_3 respectively, the objective function of the GP model may be stated as

$$\text{MIN } 0X_1 + 0X_2 + 0X_3$$
$$+ P_1d_1^- + P_2d_1^+ + P_1d_2^- + P_2d_2^+ + P_1d_3^- + P_2d_3^+ + P_3d_4^- + (0d_4^+)$$

Deviational variable d_4^+ is not given a priority level, since it has a zero coefficient. It is not really being minimized. The constraints for this problem do not change, but the solution procedure does. To solve problems involving preemptive priorities, the modified simplex method is used. We discuss this method in section 10.4 of this chapter. Deviational variable d_4^+ is shown in parentheses since it still has a zero coefficient (i.e., it is not really being minimized). The actual solution to this problem is identical to the weighted solution.

Weights can also be assigned to deviational variables within the same preemptive priority classification. For example, if AMC felt it was four times as important to minimize underutilization of hours and overtime in the cutting department (represented by variables d_1^- and d_1^+), the objective function would be

$$\text{MIN } 0X_1 + 0X_2 + 0X_3$$
$$+ 4P_1d_1^- + 4P_2d_1^+ + P_1d_2^- + P_2d_2^+ + P_1d_3^- + P_2d_3^+ + P_3d_4^- + 0d_4^+$$

The solution to this problem is

$$X_3 = 50$$
$$d_1^+ = 40$$
$$d_2^+ = 70$$
$$d_4^+ = 350$$

Thus, when we assign weights of 4 to the cutting department deviations, the solution changes. Product X_2 is dropped and production of X_3 increases. The 60.6 hours of overtime in the cutting department are reduced to 40 through the addition of 70 hours of overtime in the welding department. Profit contribution also changes to $1,600—an overachievement of the goal by $350.

Deviational Variable Constraints

When formulating a GP problem, it is possible to have constraints that contain only deviational variables. For example, if AMC formulated an additional objective of limiting total overtime in all departments to no more than 24 hours per week, we would add the constraint

$$d_1^+ + d_2^+ + d_3^+ \leq 24$$

Deviational variables d_1^+, d_2^+, and d_3^+ represent the total amount of overtime worked in all three departments. This constraint limits overtime to no more than 24 hours. But the limit of 24 hours is a goal, just like all the other goals, and it may or may not be met. To make this constraint accurately reflect the objective, therefore, we must add deviational variables d_5^- and d_5^+. The first, d_5^-, represents the difference between the actual number of hours of overtime worked and the goal of 24, where the actual number is less than 24. The second variable, d_5^+, represents the number of overtime hours worked in excess of 24 hours. The constraint that states this goal then becomes

$$d_1^+ + d_2^+ + d_3^+ + d_5^- - d_5^+ = 24$$

Assuming that AMC considers this to be a second-level priority goal, hours of overtime for each department to be third-level goals, and profit contribution a fourth-level goal (without weighting), the objective function would be

$$\text{MIN } 0X_1 + 0X_2 + 0X_3 + P_1d_1^- + P_3d_1^+ + P_1d_2^- + P_3d_2^+ + P_1d_3^- + P_3d_3^+$$
$$+ P_4d_4^- + 0P_4d_4^+ + 0P_2d_5^- + P_2d_5^+$$

To summarize, goal programming problems typically take one of four basic forms: (1) no weights, no priorities; (2) weights, no priorities; (3) priorities with no weights; and (4) priorities with weights. The first two forms can be solved as normal LP problems; the latter two require a modified solution procedure.

10.3 *FURTHER APPLICATIONS*

In the previous section, we illustrated the formulation of a goal programming problem using a manufacturing example. In this section, we will give examples of two additional types of goal programming problems—multiperiod investment problems and marketing media selection type problems—and their formulation. The first problem is the ABC Investment problem presented at the beginning of the chapter.

Multiperiod Investment Problem

Recall that Mary Thompson, a fund manager for ABC Investments, has $1 million available to invest. This money can be invested in any of three alternatives: money market accounts, stocks, and bonds. Money placed in money market accounts will yield 8 percent per year. Stock investments will yield 25 percent at the end of a two-year period. Bonds will yield 33 percent at the end of a three-year period. All investments are made at the beginning of each year; yields are realized at the end of the required investment periods. Any money not invested in stocks or bonds is automatically placed in a money market account. Mary, working with her client, has established the following objectives in the order of importance to the client:

1. The portfolio should be diversified. No more than $650,000 should be placed in any one alternative during any year.
2. No more than 40 percent of the total investment should be in stocks, since they have a higher risk.
3. The total yield should be maximized over the next five-year period.
4. At least $150,000 should be kept in the money market account to ensure short-term liquidity for the client.

Problem Formulation

Figure 10.1 uses bar graphs to show each possible investment, the year in which it orginates, and its duration.

Goal 1 Constraints   Goal 1 (no more than $650,000 placed in any alternative in any year) can be stated through a series of goal constraints. For year 1, the investment constraints for the three alternatives are

$$M_1 + d_1^- - d_1^+ = 650000$$

$$S_1 + d_2^- - d_2^+ = 650000$$

$$B_1 + d_3^- - d_3^+ = 650000$$

where

d_1^- is the amount by which the money market investment in year 1 falls short of the $650,000 goal.

d_1^+ is the amount by which the money market investment in year 1 exceeds the $650,000 goal.

d_2^- is the amount by which the stock market investment in year 1 falls short of the $650,000 goal.

d_2^+ is the amount by which the stock market investment in year 1 exceeds the $650,000 goal.

d_3^- is the amount by which the bond market investment in year 1 falls short of the $650,000 goal.

d_3^+ is the amount by which the bond market investment in year 1 exceeds the $650,000 goal.

In the second year, the total amount invested in stocks or bonds during the year is equal to the amount invested during the first year plus the amount invested at the beginning of the second year, since these are multiple-year investments. The amount invested in the money market, a one-year investment, is simply the amount invested in year 2. The goal constraints for the second year, therefore, are

$$M_2 \quad\ + d_4^- - d_4^+ = 650000$$

$$S_1 + S_2 + d_5^- - d_5^+ = 650000$$

$$B_1 + B_2 + d_6^- - d_6^+ = 650000$$

Deviational variables d_4 through d_6 are the same as those described for year 1.

In the third year, the amount invested in stocks in year 1 can be withdrawn. Thus, the total amount invested in stocks is the amount invested during years 2 and 3. The amount invested in bonds, which have a three-year maturity, is the

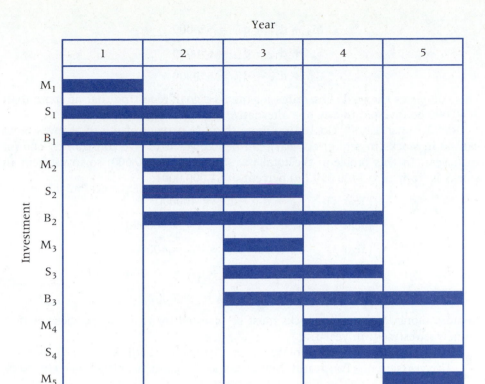

Figure 10.1 Possible Investments

amount invested in each of the first three years. Money market investments equal the amount invested during the third year. The goal constraints for year 3 are

$$M_3 \qquad\qquad + d_7^- - d_7^+ = 650000$$

$$S_2 + S_3 \qquad + d_8^- - d_8^+ = 650000$$

$$B_1 + B_2 + B_3 + d_9^- - d_9^+ = 650000$$

In year 4, the original bond investment (B_1) and the stock investment from year 2 (S_2) mature. No additional bond investment can be made in this year, since it would not mature until year 6. Thus, the goal constraints for year 4 are

$$M_4 \qquad\quad + d_{10}^- - d_{10}^+ = 650000$$

$$S_3 + S_4 + d_{11}^- - d_{11}^+ = 650000$$

$$B_2 + B_3 + d_{12}^- - d_{12}^+ = 650000$$

In year 5, no additional stock or bond investments can be made, since they will not mature by the end of the year. The investments equal the money market investments plus the stock market investment made in year 4 and the bond market investment made in year 3.

$$M_5 + d_{13}^- - d_{13}^+ = 650000$$

$$S_4 + d_{14}^- - d_{14}^+ = 650000$$

$$B_3 + d_{15}^- - d_{15}^+ = 650000$$

This completes the goal constraints for the first goal, requiring that no more than $650,000 be invested in any one alternative during any given year.

Goal 2 Constraints   Goal 2 (no more than 40 percent of the total investment can be in stocks in any given year) can be expressed in five constraints, one for each year. In this problem, the total investment is $1,000,000, so investment in stocks is limited to $400,000 (40 percent of $1,000,000):

[Year 1] $S_1 + d_{16}^- - d_{16}^+ = 400000$

[Year 2] $S_1 + S_2 + d_{17}^- - d_{17}^+ = 400000$

[Year 3] $S_2 + S_3 + d_{18}^- - d_{18}^+ = 400000$

[Year 4] $S_3 + S_4 + d_{19}^- - d_{19}^+ = 400000$

[Year 5] $S_4 + d_{20}^- - d_{20}^+ = 400000$

Because money invested in stocks must be invested for two-year periods, there is no new investment in year five.

Goal 3 Constraints   We can state the third goal, maximizing yield over the next five years, in one constraint. Money market investments yield 8 percent, stock investments 25 percent, and bonds 33 percent. This constraint takes the form

$$0.08\left(\sum M_i\right) + 0.25\left(\sum S_i\right) + 0.33\left(\sum B_i\right) + d_{21}^- - d_{21}^+ = 5000000$$

where the total yield is set equal to an arbitrarily large figure. Minimizing the deviation (d_{21}^-) from this figure ensures that the yield will be as large as possible. (Obviously, before using this constraint in a computer solution, we must convert it to its longer form of $0.08M_1 + 0.08M_2 + 0.08M_3 + \ldots$.)

Goal 4 Constraints   The fourth goal, keeping a minimum balance of $150,000 in the money market account each year, requires five goal constraints, one for each year:

$$M_1 + d_{22}^- - d_{22}^+ = 150000$$

$$M_2 + d_{23}^- - d_{23}^+ = 150000$$

$$M_3 + d_{24}^- - d_{24}^+ = 150000$$

$$M_4 + d_{25}^- - d_{25}^+ = 150000$$

$$M_5 + d_{26}^- - d_{26}^+ = 150000$$

These constraints complete the statement of the goals for this problem.

Structural Constraints   In addition to these constraints, several **structural constraints** are required. Structural constraints simply state other problem requirements and contain no deviational variables. In this case, the structural constraints represent the total amount of money available for investment in any given year. Thus, there are five structural constraints, one for each year. In year 1, we must divide the original $1,000,000 among the three alternatives:

$$M_1 + S_1 + B_1 = 1000000$$

In the second year, the money invested in the money market in year 1 plus the interest it earned are available for further investment. This can be expressed

$$M_2 + S_2 + B_2 = M_1 + 0.08M_1 = 1.08M_1$$

or

$$-1.08M_1 + M_2 + S_2 + B_2 = 0$$

In the third year, we have available the money from the money market investment for year 2 plus the money invested in stocks in year 1 plus accrued yields:

$$M_3 + S_3 + B_3 = 1.08M_2 + 1.25S_1$$

or

$$-1.08M_2 + M_3 - 1.25S_1 + S_3 + B_1 = 0$$

In year 4, we have available the money and accrued interest from the money market investment in year 3, the stock investment in year 2, and the bond investment in year 1. But the new investment is limited to the money market and stocks, since bonds purchased this year will not mature by the end of year 5. The constraint takes the form

$$M_4 + S_4 = 1.08M_3 + 1.25S_2 + 1.33B_1$$

or

$$-1.08M_3 + M_4 - 1.25S_2 + S_4 - 1.33B_1 = 0$$

In year 5, the money and accrued interest from the money market investment in year 4, the stock investment in year 3, and the bond investment in year 2 are all available. The new investment is limited to the money market, which matures at the end of the year. This constraint is

$$M_5 = 1.08M_4 + 1.25S_3 + 1.33B_2$$

or

$$-1.08M_4 + M_5 - 1.25S_3 - 1.33B_2 = 0$$

This is the last constraint for this problem.

Objective Function The objective function for this problem attempts to minimize the sum of all of the deviational variables. Using a preemptive priority ordering of the goals, the deviational variables d_1^+ through d_{15}^+ are given priority P_1 and minimized, since they represent investments over \$650,000 in a given alternative. The d_1^+ through d_{15}^+ variables have coefficients of zero, since they do not violate the goal and need not be minimized. We give deviational variables d_{16}^+ through d_{20}^+ a priority of P_2; they represent stock investments in excess of 40 percent of the total investment in any given year. Variables d_{16}^- through d_{20}^- have zero coefficients. We assign deviational variable d_{21}^- priority P_3, since it represents deviation from a high yield; d_{21}^+ has a coefficient of zero. We give variables d_{22}^- through d_{26}^- priority P_4, since they represent the deviation from the minimum money market investment of \$150,000. Variables d_{22}^+ through d_{26}^+ would have zero coefficients. The decision variables (M_i, S_i and B_i) all have zero coefficients, since they are not being minimized. Thus, the objective function can be stated as

$$\text{MIN } P_1\left(\sum_{i=1}^{15} d_i^+\right) + P_2\left(\sum_{i=16}^{20} d_i^+\right) + P_3(d_{21}^-) + P_4\left(\sum_{i=22}^{26} d_i^-\right) + 0\left(\sum_{i=1}^{5} M_i + \sum_{i=1}^{4} S_i + \sum_{i=1}^{3} B_i\right)$$

Bringing the objective function and the constraints together into the GP model, we can state the problem as

$$\text{MIN } P_1\left(\sum_{i=1}^{15} d_i^+\right) + P_2\left(\sum_{i=16}^{20} d_i^+\right) + P_3(d_{21}^-) + P_4\left(\sum_{i=22}^{26} d_i^-\right) + 0\left(\sum_{i=1}^{5} M_i + \sum_{i=1}^{4} S_i + \sum_{i=1}^{3} B_i\right)$$

subject to

$$M_1 + d_1^- - d_1^+ = 650000$$
$$S_1 + d_2^- - d_2^+ = 650000$$
$$B_1 + d_3^- - d_3^+ = 650000$$
$$M_2 + d_4^- - d_4^+ = 650000$$
$$S_1 + S_2 + d_5^- - d_5^+ = 650000$$
$$B_1 + B_2 + d_6^- - d_6^+ = 650000$$
$$M_3 + d_7^- - d_7^+ = 650000$$
$$S_2 + S_3 + d_8^- - d_8^+ = 650000$$
$$B_1 + B_2 + B^3 + d_9^- - d_9^+ = 650000$$
$$M_4 + d_{10}^- - d_{10}^+ = 650000$$
$$S_3 + S_4 + d_{11}^- - d_{11}^+ = 650000$$
$$B_2 + B_3 + d_{12}^- - d_{12}^+ = 650000$$
$$M_5 + d_{13}^- - d_{13}^+ = 650000$$
$$S_4 + d_{14}^- - d_{14}^+ = 650000$$
$$B_3 + d_{15}^- - d_{15}^+ = 650000$$
$$S_1 + d_{16}^- - d_{16}^+ = 400000$$
$$S_1 + S_2 + d_{17}^- - d_{17}^+ = 400000$$
$$S_2 + S_3 + d_{18}^- - d_{18}^+ = 400000$$
$$S_3 + S_4 + d_{19}^- - d_{19}^+ = 400000$$
$$S_4 + d_{20}^- - d_{20}^+ = 400000$$
$$.08M_1 + .08M_2 + .08M_3 + .08M_4 + .08M_5 + .25S_1 + .25S_2 + .25S_3 + .25S_4$$
$$+ .33B_1 + .33B_2 + .33B_3 + d_{21}^- - d_{21}^+ = 5000000$$
$$M_1 + d_{22}^- - d_{22}^+ = 150000$$
$$M_2 + d_{23}^- - d_{23}^+ = 150000$$
$$M_3 + d_{24}^- - d_{24}^+ = 150000$$
$$M_4 + d_{25}^- - d_{25}^+ = 150000$$
$$M_5 + d_{26}^- - d_{26}^+ = 150000$$
$$M_1 + S_1 + B_1 = 1000000$$
$$-1.08M_1 + M_2 + S_2 + B_2 = 0$$
$$-1.08M_2 + M_3 - 1.25S_1 + S_3 + B_1 = 0$$
$$-1.08M_3 + M_4 - 1.25S_2 + S_4 - 1.33B_1 = 0$$
$$-1.08M_4 + M_5 - 1.25S_3 - 1.33B_2 = 0$$
$$\text{all } M_i, S_i, B_i, d_i^-, d_i^+ \geq 0$$

Computer solutions to problems such as the one above frequently require more time to enter the data than to obtain a solution.

Marketing Research Problem

Widrick & Tyler, Inc. (WTI) has been hired to develop a promotional campaign for a new product. The media available for use on this campaign, with the cost of each, are shown below:

Advertising Media	Cost per Ad	Two-Parent Families Reached	Single-Parent Families Reached
Television	$4,000	5,000	1,300
Radio	250	400	150
Newspaper	600	3,500	1,000
Doorknob notice	2,400	6,000	2,000
Special-audience paper	300	200	900

The client wants this campaign to run over a four-week period and has stated his prioritized goals as follows:

1. Reach at least 40,000 single-parent families.
2. Reach at least 100,000 families overall.
3. Do not exceed an advertising budget of $70,000.
4. Do not use more than one TV spot per week; five radio spots per week; three newspaper ads per week; one doorknob notice per week per house; or one special-audience paper ad per week.

Problem Formulation

The formulation of this problem is considerably easier than the ABC Investment problem. We can state goal 1 (single-parent family audience of at least 40,000) with one constraint:

$$1300T + 150R + 1000N + 2000D + 900S + d_1^- - d_1^+ = 40000$$

where

$$T = \text{number of television ads}$$

$$R = \text{number of radio ads}$$

$$N = \text{number of newspaper ads}$$

$$D = \text{number of doorknob notices}$$

$$S = \text{number of ads in special audience paper}$$

$$d_1^- = \text{underachievement of 40,000 single family goal}$$

$$d_1^+ = \text{overachievement of 40,000 single family goal}$$

Goal 2 (100,000 families overall) also requires only one constraint:

$$6300T + 550R + 4500N + 8000D + 1100S + d_2^- - d_2^+ = 100000$$

The media coefficents are the sums of two-parent and single-parent families reached. The variable d_2^- represents underachievement of the goal, and d_2^+ represents overachievement.

Goal 3 (advertising budget of $70,000) uses the advertising costs per ad:

$$4000T + 250R + 600N + 2400D + 300S + d_3^- - d_3^+ = 70000$$

where d_3^- represents a cost savings, and d_3^+ is the amount over budget. We state goal 4 (media usage restrictions) in five constraints, each representing the maximum number of ads in a particular medium.

$$T + d_4^- - d_4^+ = 4$$
$$R + d_5^- - d_5^+ = 20$$
$$N + d_6^- - d_6^+ = 12$$
$$D + d_7^- - d_7^+ = 1$$
$$S + d_8^- - d_8^+ = 4$$

The objective function for this problem is

$$\text{MIN } 0T + 0R + 0N + 0D + 0S + P_1(d_1^-) + 0d_1^+ + P_2(d_2^-) + 0d_2^+ + P_3(d_3^+)$$
$$+ 0d_3^- + P_4(d_4^+ + 4d_5^+ + d_6^+ + d_7^+ + d_8^+)$$
$$+ 0(d_4^- + d_5^- + d_6^- + d_7^- + d_8^-)$$

which can be simplified as

$$\text{MIN } P_1(d_1^-) + P_2(d_2^-) + P_3(d_3^+) + P_4(d_4^+ + d_5^+ + d_6^+ + d_7^+ + d_8^+)$$

Combining the objective function and constraints, the goal programming model is

$$\text{MIN } P_1(d_1^-) + P_2(d_2^-) + P_3(d_3^+) + P_4(d_4^+ + d_5^+ + d_6^+ + d_7^+ + d_8^+)$$

subject to

$$1300T + 150R + 1000N + 2000D + 900S + d_1^- - d_1^+ = 40000$$
$$6300T + 550R + 4500N + 8000D + 1100S + d_2^- - d_2^+ = 100000$$
$$4000T + 250R + 600N + 2400D + 300S + d_3^- - d_3^+ = 70000$$
$$T + d_4^- - d_4^+ = 4$$
$$R + d_5^- - d_5^+ = 20$$
$$N + d_6^- - d_6^+ = 12$$
$$D + d_7^- - d_7^+ = 1$$
$$S + d_8^- - d_8^+ = 4$$
$$T, R, N, D, S, d_1^-, d_1^+ \geq 0$$

10.4 THE MODIFIED SIMPLEX METHOD

Goal programming problems that are stated without preemptive priorities can be solved using the simplex method. Problems with preemptive priorities require a different algorithm, known as the **modified simplex method.** The modified simplex method attempts to find a solution that minimizes the deviations from all priority 1 goals. Once this solution has been found, the method then attempts to find a solution that maintains this level 1 deviation while minimizing deviations from the priority 2 goals. It proceeds in this manner until the deviations at all the priority levels have been minimized as much as possible.

The modified simplex method uses a modified simplex tableau to solve preemptive priority GP problems. The tableau is similar to the normal simplex tableau, with one main exception: it has Z_j and C_j-Z_j rows for each priority level.

We will use an example problem to illustrate the solution of a GP problem using the modified simplex procedure.

The Williams Production Company manufactures two products, X_1 and X_2. These products are produced in three departments: A, B, and C. Product X_1 requires 5 hours in department A and 1 hour in department B. Product X_2 requires 2 hours in department A and 1 hour in department C. Currently 750 hours are available in department A, 100 in department B, and 100 in department C. The production manager wants to determine how many units of each product to produce next week, given the following goals in order of their priority:

1. Use all the hours available in department A.
2. Use no more than 20 hours of overtime in department B.
3. Use all the hours available in departments B and C; the use of all hours in department C is two-thirds as important as the use of all department B hours.
4. Keep overtime in departments B and C to a minimum. The overtime restriction for department B is three-fifths as important as that for department C.

When we formulate this problem, the GP model is

$$\text{MIN } 0X_1 + 0X_2 + P_1d_1^- + 3P_3d_2^- + 2P_3d_3^- + 0d_4^- + 0d_1^+ + 3P_4d_2^+$$
$$+ 5P_4d_3^+ + P_2d_4^+$$

subject to

$$5X_1 + 2X_2 + d_1^- - d_1^+ = 750$$
$$X_1 + d_2^- - d_2^+ \qquad = 100$$
$$X_2 + d_3^- - d_3^+ \qquad = 100$$
$$d_2^+ + d_4^- - d_4^+ \qquad = 20$$
$$X_1, X_2, d_i^-, d_i^+ \geq 0$$

where

d_1^- = underutilization of department A hours.
d_2^- = underutilization of department B hours.
d_3^- = underutilization of department C hours.
d_4^- = less than 20 hours of overtime in department B.
d_1^+ = overtime in department A.
d_2^+ = overtime in department B.
d_3^+ = overtime in department C.
d_4^+ = overtime in excess of 20 hours in department B.

We assign weights of 3 and 2 to underutilization of hours in departments B and C respectively, to establish the $1:\frac{2}{3}$ ratio stated in the problem. The variables representing overtime in these departments have weights of 3 and 5 to establish the $\frac{3}{5}:1$ ratio stated in the problem. Because all constraints are equalities and have both positive and negative deviations, there is no need to add slack, surplus, or

C(j)		0	0	P_1	$3P_3$	$2P_3$	0	0	$3P_4$	$5P_4$	P_2	
	Basis	X_1	X_2	d_1^-	d_2^-	d_3^-	d_4^-	d_1^+	d_2^+	d_3^+	d_4^+	RHS
P_1	d_1^-	5	2	1	0	0	0	−1	0	0	0	750
$3P_3$	d_2^-	1	0	0	1	0	0	0	−1	0	0	100
$2P_3$	d_3^-	0	1	0	0	1	0	0	0	−1	0	100
0	d_4^-	0	0	0	0	0	−1	0	1	0	1	20

Figure 10.2 Initial Tableau—First Step

artificial variables to this problem. The tableau form of this problem is shown in Figure 10.2.

Normally, the next step is to calculate Z row values. Note, however, that with preemptive priorities the Z value for the X_1 column is

Cj	Row	X_1		Z Value
P_1	d_1^-	5	=	$5P_1$
$3P_3$	d_2^-	1	=	$3P_3$
$2P_3$	d_3^-	0	=	0
0	d_4^-	0	=	0
				$5P_1 + 3P_3$

Since these are really unlike terms, we must add a separate Z row for each preemptive priority. These will be added in reverse order, from the lowest priority level (P_4) to the highest (P_1). We calculate each row in the following manner. For the Z row for priority P_4, treat any P_4 in the tableau as if it were a coefficient of 1; treat all other priorities as if they were zero. In situations where a weight is assigned, such as $3P_4$, the coefficient would be 3(1) or 3. Thus, to calculate the Z (P_4) row, the tableau would appear as shown in Figure 10.3.

We calculate each of the remaining rows in the same manner. Note that both the d_2^- and d_3^- rows are priority level 3. The Z rows for each priority level, with the Z values calculated, are shown in Figure 10.4.

Because there are four distinct Z rows in the tableau, there are four C − Z rows as well, one for each priority level. We are going to deviate from the normal C − Z form, however, and add Z − C rows instead. The only difference between the

C(j)		0	0	0	0	0	0	0	3	5	0	
	Basis	X_1	X_2	d_1^-	d_2^-	d_3^-	d_4^-	d_1^+	d_2^+	d_3^+	d_4^+	RHS
0	d_1^-	5	2	1	0	0	0	−1	0	0	0	750
0	d_2^-	1	0	0	1	0	0	0	−1	0	0	100
0	d_3^-	0	1	0	0	1	0	0	0	−1	0	100
0	d_4^-	0	0	0	0	0	1	0	1	0	−1	20
Z	P_4	0	0	0	0	0	0	0	0	0	0	0

Figure 10.3 Calculation of the Z_j Row for Priority P_4

C(j)		0	0	P_1	$3P_3$	$2P_3$	0	0	$3P_4$	$5P_4$	P_2	
	Basis	X_1	X_2	d_1^-	d_2^-	d_3^-	d_4^-	d_1^+	d_2^+	d_3^+	d_4^+	RHS
P_1	d_1^-	5	2	1	0	0	0	-1	0	0	0	750
$3P_3$	d_2^-	1	0	0	1	0	0	0	-1	0	0	100
$2P_3$	d_3^-	0	1	0	0	1	0	0	0	-1	0	100
0	d_4^-	0	0	0	0	0	1	0	1	0	-1	20
Z	P_4	0	0	0	0	0	0	0	0	0	0	0
Z	P_3	3	2	0	3	2	0	0	-3	-2	0	500
Z	P_2	0	0	0	0	0	0	0	0	0	0	0
Z	P_1	5	2	1	0	0	0	-1	0	0	0	750

Figure 10.4 Z Rows Added to Initial Tableau

normal C − Z rows and the Z − C rows will be the sign on each entry. The Z − C rows are added to the tableau in Figure 10.5. This completes the initial tableau. Because Z − C rows have been used rather than C − Z rows, the column with the largest (positive) Z − C value will be the pivot column. Since the priority 1 goals are satisfied first, we use the Z − C row for priority P_1 and ignore the other Z − C rows. An examination of the Z − C row reveals the pivot column is column X_1, with a Z − C value of 5. The pivot row and all other calculations are performed exactly as they are in the normal simplex tableau. Thus, X_1 enters the tableau and d_2^- leaves. The second tableau is shown in Figure 10.6.

Two additional modifications have been made to this tableau (and all following tableaus). We have omitted the Z rows to save space and have added the Z values for the RHS column at the end of the Z − C rows. These values indicate the total weighted amount of deviation from each goal—in other words, they show the value of the objective function for each goal taken separately.

C(j)		0	0	P_1	$3P_3$	$2P_3$	0	0	$3P_4$	$5P_4$	P_2	
	Basis	X_1	X_2	d_1^-	d_2^-	d_3^-	d_4^-	d_1^+	d_2^+	d_3^+	d_4^+	RHS
P_1	d_1^-	5	2	1	0	0	0	-1	0	0	0	750
$3P_3$	d_2^-	1	0	0	1	0	0	0	-1	0	0	100
$2P_3$	d_3^-	0	1	0	0	1	0	0	0	-1	0	100
0	d_4^-	0	0	0	0	0	1	0	1	0	-1	20
Z	P_4	0	0	0	0	0	0	0	0	0	0	0
Z	P_3	3	2	0	3	2	0	0	-3	-2	0	500
Z	P_2	0	0	0	0	0	0	0	0	0	0	0
Z	P_1	5	2	1	0	0	0	-1	0	0	0	750
Z−C	P_4	0	0	0	0	0	0	0	-3	-5	0	
Z−C	P_3	3	2	0	0	0	0	0	-3	-2	0	
Z−C	P_2	0	0	0	0	0	0	0	0	0	-1	
Z−C	P_1	5	2	0	0	0	0	-1	0	0	0	

Figure 10.5 Z − C Rows Added to Initial Tableau

C(j)		0	0	P_1	$3P_3$	$2P_3$	0	0	$3P_4$	$5P_4$	P_2	
	Basis	X_1	X_2	d_1^-	d_2^-	d_3^-	d_4^-	d_1^+	d_2^+	d_3^+	d_4^+	RHS
P_1	d_1^-	0	2	1	-5	0	0	-1	5	0	0	250
0	X_1	1	0	0	1	0	0	0	-1	0	0	100
$2P_3$	d_3^-	0	1	0	0	1	0	0	0	-1	0	100
0	d_4^-	0	0	0	0	0	1	0	1	0	-1	20
Z–C	P_4	0	0	0	0	0	0	0	-3	-5	0	0
Z–C	P_3	0	2	0	-3	0	0	0	0	-2	0	200
Z–C	P_2	0	0	0	0	0	0	0	0	0	-1	0
Z–C	P_1	0	2	0	-5	0	0	-1	5	0	0	250

Figure 10.6 Second Tableau

Since there are Z − C rows for each priority level, we will refer to each Z − C row by its priority number; for example, the P_1 row rather than the Z − C row for P_1. In the P_1 row, the largest value is 5 and the pivot column is column d_2^+. The pivot row is row d_4^-. The third tableau is shown in Figure 10.7.

The P_1 row still has a positive value, the 2 in column X_2. Thus, X_2 enters the next tableau. The pivot row is d_1^-. Figure 10.8 shows the completed fourth tableau.

C(j)		0	0	P_1	$3P_3$	$2P_3$	0	0	$3P_4$	$5P_4$	P_2	
	Basis	X_1	X_2	d_1^-	d_2^-	d_3^-	d_4^-	d_1^+	d_2^+	d_3^+	d_4^+	RHS
P_1	d_1^-	0	2	1	-5	0	-5	-1	0	0	5	150
0	X_1	1	0	0	1	0	1	0	0	0	-1	120
$2P_3$	d_3^-	0	1	0	0	1	0	0	0	-1	0	100
$3P_4$	d_2^+	0	0	0	0	0	1	0	1	0	-1	20
Z–C	P_4	0	0	0	0	0	3	0	0	-5	-3	60
Z–C	P_3	0	2	0	-3	0	0	0	0	-2	0	200
Z–C	P_2	0	0	0	0	0	0	0	0	0	-1	0
Z–C	P_1	0	2	0	-5	0	-5	-1	0	0	0	150

Figure 10.7 Third Tableau

C(j)		0	0	P_1	$3P_3$	$2P_3$	0	0	$3P_4$	$5P_4$	P_2	
	Basis	X_1	X_2	d_1^-	d_2^-	d_3^-	d_4^-	d_1^+	d_2^+	d_3^+	d_4^+	RHS
P_2	d_4^+	0	.4	.2	-1	0	-1	-.2	0	0	1	30
0	X_1	1	.4	.2	0	0	1	-.2	0	0	0	150
$2P_3$	d_3^-	0	1	0	0	1	0	0	0	-1	0	100
$3P_4$	d_2^+	0	.4	.2	-1	0	0	-.2	1	0	0	50
Z–C	P_4	0	1.2	.6	-3	0	0	-.6	0	-5	0	150
Z–C	P_3	0	2	0	-3	0	0	0	0	-2	0	200
Z–C	P_2	0	.4	.2	-1	0	-1	-.2	0	0	0	30
Z–C	P_1	0	0	-1	0	0	0	0	0	0	0	0

Figure 10.8 Fourth Tableau

In the fourth tableau, the P_1 row contains all zero or negative values. This indicates that the deviations from the priority 1 goal have been minimized. We will now shift our attention to the P_2 row. There are two positive values in this row, .4 in the X_2 column and .2 in the d_1^- column. The .4 in column X_2 is the largest positive value in the P_2 row. Column X_2 is, therefore, the pivot column. Note that, although column d_1^- has a positive value (.2) in the P_2 row, this column would never be the pivot column, even if the value were larger than the .4 in the X_2 column. Because the P_1 row has a value of -1 in this column, if d_1^- were to enter the tableau, the deviations from the priority 1 goal would increase. Thus, the negative value in the P_1 row preempts any positive values in the other priority rows for this variable. In examining the P_2 row, therefore, we will consider positive values only if the P_1 row for the column under consideration does not have a negative value. The X_2 column is the pivot column and the d_4^+ row is the pivot row. The fifth tableau is shown in Figure 10.9.

In this tableau, both the P_1 and P_2 row values are now zero or negative. This means we can now consider the P_3 row. The largest value is 5 in the d_4^- column, making this column the pivot column. The pivot row is the d_3^- row. The next tableau is shown in Figure 10.10.

C(j)		0	0	P_1	$3P_3$	$2P_3$	0	0	$3P_4$	$5P_4$	P_2	
	Basis	X_1	X_2	d_1^-	d_2^-	d_3^-	d_4^-	d_1^+	d_2^+	d_3^+	d_4^+	RHS
0	X_2	0	1	.5	-2.5	0	-2.5	-.5	0	0	2.5	75
0	X_1	1	0	0	1	0	1	0	0	0	-1	120
$2P_3$	d_3^-	0	0	-.5	2.5	1	2.5	.5	0	-1	-2.5	25
$3P_4$	d_2^+	0	0	0	0	0	1	0	1	0	-1	20
Z-C	P_4	0	0	0	0	0	3	0	0	-5	-3	60
Z-C	P_3	0	0	-1	2	0	5	1	0	-2	-5	50
Z-C	P_2	0	0	0	0	0	0	0	0	0	-1	0
Z-C	P_1	0	0	-1	0	0	0	0	0	0	0	0

Figure 10.9 Fifth Tableau

C(j)		0	0	P_1	$3P_3$	$2P_3$	0	0	$3P_4$	$5P_4$	P_2	
	Basis	X_1	X_2	d_1^-	d_2^-	d_3^-	d_4^-	d_1^+	d_2^+	d_3^+	d_4^+	RHS
0	X_2	0	1	0	0	1	0	0	0	-1	0	100
0	X_1	1	0	.2	0	-.4	0	-.2	0	.4	0	110
0	d_4^-	0	0	-.2	1	.4	1	.2	0	-.4	-1	10
$3P_4$	d_2^+	0	0	.2	-1	-.4	0	-.2	1	.4	0	10
Z-C	P_4	0	0	.6	-3	-1.2	0	-.6	0	-3.8	0	30
Z-C	P_3	0	0	0	-3	-2	0	0	0	0	0	0
Z-C	P_2	0	0	0	0	0	0	0	0	0	-1	0
Z-C	P_1	0	0	-1	0	0	0	0	0	0	0	0

Figure 10.10 Sixth Tableau

This tableau is the final tableau, since there are no positive $Z - C$ values that are not preempted by negative values in the higher priority rows. Column d_1^- has a value of .6 in the P_4 row, but it is preempted by the -1 in the P_1 row. The optimal solution to this problem can be summarized as follows: produce 110 untis of X_1 ($X_1 = 110$) and 100 units of X_2 ($X_2 = 100$); schedule 10 hours of overtime in department B ($d_2^+ = 10$), 10 hours under the limit of 20 hours of overtime for this department ($d_4^- = 10$); all first, second, and third priority level goals have been met; and there is a 10-hour deviation from the fourth level goal—which has a weight of 3—giving the objective function a value of 30 ($P_4 = 30$).

Summary of Steps for the Modified Simplex Method

1. Set up the initial tableau from the GP model. The objective function coefficients are the weighted priority levels (C_j row). Goal constraints does not have slack, surplus, or artificial variables added because the deviational variables serve the same purpose; they allow the initial solution to be at the origin. The d_i^- variables are entered first, in order, and since they have coefficients of $+1$, they are the variables in the initial tableau. Calculate the Z_j and $Z_j - C_j$ values for each priority level, entering the lowest priority level first and moving downward to the highest (P_1). The Z_j rows can be entered in the tableau or omitted to save space.

2. Determine the pivot column (the variable entering the new tableau). Begin by examining the highest-priority row. If this row has any positive values, the pivot column is the column with the largest value. If this priority row does not have any values greater than zero, move to the next lower priority row, and look for positive values that have not been preempted by negative values at higher priority levels. The largest positive, nonpreempted value in the highest priority level that has not already been optimized (no positive values in the row) determines the pivot column.

3. Determine the pivot row (the variable entering the solution in the new tableau). This procedure is identical to the LP simplex procedure. Select the smallest ratio of RHS value to pivot column coefficient.

4. Calculate the values for the new tableau using the LP simplex method. Calculate the new Z_j and $Z_j - C_j$ values for each priority row.

5. Check the solution for optimality. When an optimal solution has been reached, there are no positive $Z_j - C_j$ values at any priority level that have not been preempted by higher priorities. If the solution is not optimal, repeat steps 2 through 5.

10.5 *RESOLVING PROBLEMS*

When the modified simplex procedure is used to solve GP problems, a number of questions may arise. The following sections attempt to address those questions.

Tie for Pivot Column

When attempting to determine the pivot column, you may find that two or more variables (columns) have the same $Z - C$ value. When this occurs, look at the $Z - C$ values for the lower priority levels, in order. Break the tie in favor of the variable that has the higher $Z - C$ value for the lower priority level. If both variables are equal at all priority levels, arbitrarily select one of the variables.

Tie for Pivot Row

If the ratios used to determine the pivot row produce a tie—that is, two ratios that are the lowest nonnegative values—select the row that has the higher priority coefficient. If both rows have the same priority coefficient, select the row that is higher in the tableau.

Infeasible Problems

Infeasible GP problems are exactly like infeasible LP problems. They occur when the structural constraints cannot be satisfied and an artificial variable remains in the optimal solution with a nonzero value. Remember that, although slack, surplus, and artificial variables are not added to goal constraints, they must still be added to structural constraints.

Unbounded Problems

Unbounded GP problems are also like unbounded LP problems. They occur when one or more of the structural constraints imposes no limits on one of the decision variables. They are identified when the pivot column has no positive coefficients. And, like unbounded LP problems, they are usually caused by the omission of a structural constraint.

Alternate Optimal Solutions

Occasionally, a GP problem has more than one solution that minimizes the deviations from all of the goals. This situation exists when a variable not in the solution has $Z - C$ values of zero at all priority levels. Alternate optimal solutions are rare in GP problems, and do not occur at all if the goals are in conflict and (1) there is only one deviational variable at each priority level or (2) deviational variables with the same priority level are assigned different weights.

10.6 *COMPUTER SOLUTIONS*

Goal programming problems, like LP problems, usually are solved using a computer package. The numbers of variables and constraints in most GP problems make them unsuitable for manual solutions. Many computer-based solution procedures are available for GP problems. IBM's MPSX, discussed in Chapter 6, has a sequential solution procedure for these problems. Figure 10.11 shows the output from the Dennis and Dennis program, included with this text, for the Williams Production Company problem discussed in section 9.4. D4B represents variable d_4^- (B stands for below) and D2A represents variable d_2^+ (A stands for above).

```
                    AFTER 5 ITERATIONS,
                    THIS SOLUTION IS OPTIMAL:

                    VARIABLE              QUANTITY
                    ━━━━━━━━              ━━━━━━━━
                        X1                  110
                        X2                  100
                        D4B                  10
                        D2A                  10


                    ANALYSIS OF THE OBJECTIVE FUNCTION:

                    PRIORITY          NON-ACHIEVEMENT
                    ━━━━━━━━          ━━━━━━━━━━━━━━━
                        P1                   0
                        P2                   0
                        P3                   0
                        P4                  30
```

Figure 10.11 Dennis & Dennis GP Output

Focus on Decision Making

S & R Products distributes janitorial supplies to commercial and industrial cleaning services. The company has recently begun to sell its products to the retail market
through the Alway Corporation, a national door-to-door sales organization. Alway
has requested that S & R develop a detergent for automatic dishwashers to complete
this product line. Alway wants an initial order of 10,000 one-pound containers of
this product.

S & R has followed a very successful policy of purchasing excess production from
other suppliers at discount rates and blending as necessary to meet its own product
specifications. At this time, the company finds this approach more economical than
purchasing the raw ingredients directly from chemical suppliers. The company's
product manager has specified that S & R's dishwasher detergent should contain
26 percent sodium carbonate (±1.5 percent), 20 percent chlorine bleach (±1 percent),
and 8 percent sodium silicate (±0.5 percent). The remainder of the weight is composed of inert ingredients.

There are currently three suppliers from which S & R can purchase excess production. The composition of each supplier's product is shown in the table below. Costs per
pound are approximately equal for all three products.

Supplier	Sodium Carbonate	Chlorine Bleach	Sodium Silicate
Albertson	24%	30%	0%
Baldwin	34	14	8
Cimonetti	2	18	12

S & R management must now determine how much to purchase from each supplier.

Data Preparation/Problem Formulation

In discussing this problem, management decided that the most important factor was the production of exactly 10,000 pounds of this product, since the company wished to meet demand and had no ability to store excess production. Management felt the desired combination of ingredients was secondary to this production requirement. The problem was therefore formulated as a goal programming problem with two priority levels. Management assigned a priority level of 1 to achievement of the production goal and a priority level of 2 to the three ingredient goals. The problem formulation is shown below:

$$MIN \ 0A + 0B + P_1d_1^- + P_2d_2^- + 2P_2d_3^- + 3P_2d_4^- + P_1d_1^+ + P_2d_2^+$$
$$+ P_2d_3^+ + P_2d_4^+$$

subject to

$$1A + 1B + 1C + 1d_1^- - 1d_1^+ = 10000$$
$$.24A + .34B + .2C + 1d_2^- - 1d_2^+ = 2600$$
$$.3A + .14B + .18C + 1d_3^- - 1d_3^+ = 2000$$
$$.08B + .12C + 1d_4^- - 1d_4^+ = 800$$

where:

A	= pounds purchased from Albertson
B	= pounds purchased from Baldwin
C	= pounds purchased from Cimonetti
d_1^-	= underachievement of the production goal
d_2^-	= underachievement of the sodium carbonate goal
d_3^-	= underachievement of the chlorine bleach goal
d_4^-	= underachievement of the sodium silicate goal
d_1^+	= overachievement of the production goal
d_2^+	= overachievement of the sodium carbonate goal
d_3^+	= overachievement of the chlorine bleach goal
d_4^+	= overachievement of the sodium silicate goal

Computer Solution

The computer solution S & R management obtained for this problem follows:

```
AFTER 5 ITERATIONS,
THIS SOLUTION IS OPTIMAL:


VARIABLE            QUANTITY
--------            --------

   A                2826.087
   B                3478.261
   C                3695.652
   D4B                78.261


ANALYSIS OF THE OBJECTIVE FUNCTION:


PRIORITY          NON-ACHIEVEMENT
--------          ---------------

   P1                    0
   P2                  78.26
```

Interpretation and Analysis of the Results

These results suggest that S & R should purchase 2,826 pounds from Albertson, 3,478 pounds from Baldwin, and 3,696 pounds from Cimonetti. They also show that the sodium silicate goal (8 percent) is underachieved by 0.78 percent. Since this underachievement exceeded the tolerance of ±0.5 percent for sodium silicate, S & R management decided to weight the three ingredient deviations in reverse order; that is, they assigned the sodium carbonate deviation a weight of 1, the chlorine bleach deviation a weight of 2, and the sodium silicate deviation a weight of 3. The problem was then resolved with the following results:

```
AFTER 6 ITERATIONS,
THIS SOLUTION IS OPTIMAL:


VARIABLE                QUANTITY
--------                --------

   A                      2500
   B                      2500
   C                      5000
   D2B                     150


ANALYSIS OF THE OBJECTIVE FUNCTION:


PRIORITY            NON-ACHIEVEMENT
--------            ---------------

   P1                      0
   P2                     150
```

These results indicate that, if S & R purchases 2,500 pounds from Albertson, 2,500 pounds from Baldwin, and 5,000 pounds from Cimonetti, the second goal (sodium carbonate) will be underachieved by 1.5 percent and all other goals will be achieved. Since an underachievement of 1.5 percent is within the tolerance specified (±1.5 percent), this solution is satisfactory.

What Happens Next

After obtaining this acceptable result, S & R must ascertain that these quantities are available from each of the suppliers. S & R should also attempt to determine whether these quantities will be available in the future. Furthermore, changes in the prices of any of these products may cause S & R to look for other possible solutions.

10.7 CONCLUDING REMARKS

Goal programming is a decision making tool that enables managers to deal with problems involving multiple organizational objectives. GP also enables managers to find satisfactory solutions in situations where no optimal solution meets all goals. It helps managers to set priorities and to consider their impact prior to actual implementation. The availability of this tool provides decision makers a degree of flexibility not offered by pure LP.

BLUE HILLS HOME CORPORATION[4]

The St. Louis Division of Blue Hills Home Corporation (BHHC) provides remedial education services to private-school children in the eastern half of Missouri. Teacher assignments are made on a regional basis. BHHC employed 22 teachers to provide services eight hours a day over a nine-month period. The teachers were assigned to two different schools, working for four hours at each school each day. Part of the teacher reimbursement was based upon the distance teachers had to travel between their assigned schools.

While BHHC was interested in minimizing travel expenses, other criteria were also important in assigning jobs. BHHC also considered preferences expressed by the teachers, the teachers' supervisors, and the individual school principals. During the year prior to the assignment, each of these three groups expressed its pleasure or displeasure with particular job assignments. Supervisors also made recommendations based upon observed productivity and assessments of job attitude. Teachers expressed preferences based upon the working environment where they were teaching. Principals, who had the authority to discontinue BHHC's service, occasionally expressed preferences for or against particular teachers. Thus, BHHC attempted to consider all of the preferences of the teachers, supervisors, and school administrators in addition to minimizing travel costs. The final assignment of teachers to schools required a great deal of time on the part of BHHC administration. This problem was further complicated by the fact that preferences sometimes were in conflict.

In an effort to improve the assignment process, BHHC decided to attempt to apply goal programming to this assignment problem. A goal programming model with three priorities was selected.

The first priority goal was to cover all assignments, assigning each teacher to two different schools. Four hundred and sixty-two decision variables and 44 goal constraints were required to express these assignments.

The second priority goal dealt with the preferences of the teachers, supervisors, and school administrators. Weights were applied to these deviational variables, based upon a number of factors. Recommendations regarding appropriate teacher assignments, made by the three supervisors overseeing the teachers, were weighted based upon the number of years of managerial experience each supervisor had with BHHC. Teacher requests were given a weight, determined by multiplying the number of years of service the teacher had with BHHC times the current year's productivity index (a scale of 0 to 1.0 derived from a yearly evaluation). Requests from school administrators were weighted on the basis of an inverse ranking of the number of students being served; that is, larger numbers of students resulted in a higher ranking. These preferences added 17 goal constraints to the model. The weights ranged from 0.7 to 6.0.

The third priority goal was to minimize travel costs. The cost was obtained using the travel distance between schools at a standard cost of $0.185 per mile. Only one constraint was required for this goal.

[4]Reprinted by permission of Sang M. Lee and Marc J. Schniederjans, "A Multicriteria Assignment Problem: A Goal Programming Approach," *Interfaces,* 13 (August, 1983): 75–81. Copyright 1983, The Institute of Management Sciences.

This model enabled BHHC administrators to save an enormous amount of time in determining teacher assignments. In addition, since all parties (teachers, supervisors, and school administrators) were allowed to make some input, resistance to assignments was significantly reduced. During the first year, BHHC experienced an increase in the standard mileage costs (8.8 percent) and the number of schools serviced (10 percent). Based upon the past year's assignments, these increases should have resulted in an increase of about 20 percent in the transportation costs. Using the goal programming results, the actual increase was approximately 5 percent.

GLOSSARY

deviational variables variables introduced into GP problems that represent the over- or underachievement of the stated goals or objectives of the problem

goal constraints equality constraints that represent the achievement of a desired goal; contain deviational variables that permit deviations from the exact achievement of a particular goal

goal programming a special variation of LP that allows problems with multiple criteria to be formulated and solved

modified simplex method a modified form of the simplex solution procedure, used to solve problems with preemptive priorities; makes use of multiple $Z_j - C_j$ rows to minimize deviations from each of the priority levels

multiple criteria problems problems with more than one objective or goal

preemptive priorities priorities assigned to goals that ensure that deviations from the highest priority level are minimized before lower-level deviations are considered

satisficing meeting a certain acceptable or satisfactory level of goal attainment, as opposed to an "optimal" solution

structural constraints constraints that express limitations on decision variables in a GP problem, but are unrelated to stated goals or objectives

PROBLEMS

Note: In all of the following problems, the decision variables with zero coefficients have been omitted from the objective functions.

1.

$$\text{MIN } d_1^- + d_1^+ + d_2^- + d_2^+ + d_3^- + d_3^+ + d_4^- + d_4^+$$

subject to

$$7X_1 + 12X_2 + 4X_3 + d_1^- - d_1^+ = 600$$
$$3X_1 + 6X_2 + X_3 + d_2^- - d_2^+ = 280$$
$$4X_1 + 5X_2 + 2X_3 + d_3^- - d_3^+ = 280$$
$$6X_1 + 8X_2 + 2X_3 + d_4^- - d_4^+ = 280$$

a. Solve the above goal programming problem.
b. Modify the problem so that the negative deviational variables are given twice the importance of the positive deviational variables, and solve again.

2. Solve the following problem:

$$\text{MIN } P_1 d_2^- + P_2 d_1^+ + P_3 d_3^-$$

subject to

$$X_1 + X_2 + d_1^- - d_1^+ = 20$$
$$2X_1 + 3X_2 + d_2^- - d_2^+ = 16$$
$$X_2 + d_3^- - d_3^+ = 14$$

If the objective function to the above problem were

$$\text{MIN } 2P_1 d_1^- + P_1 d_2^- + P_3 d_3^- + P_2 d_1^+$$

how would the answer change?

3. A dry-cleaning chain wishes to locate the best location for its new branch store. The store should be located so that the distance from three nearby population centers is minimized. Overlaying a map of the area with an algebraic grid shows that the population centers are located as follows:

Population Center	Location Coordinates
A	$X_1 = 3, X_2 = 1$
B	$X_1 = 2, X_2 = 9$
C	$X_1 = 7, X_2 = 5$

All distances from the new location to the population centers are measured by the rectangular differences. For example, center A is located 9 blocks from center B ($|3 - 2| + |1 - 9| = 1 + 8 = 9$). Determine the location for the new store that minimizes the distances from the three population centers.

4. The dry cleaning chain in problem 3 has determined that population center A is twice the size of population center B and center B is three times the size of center C. If the chain wishes to locate its new store so that it minimizes the distances based upon the population densities—i.e., the distance from center A should be half as great as the distance from center B—where should the store be located?

5. The Bright Feather Bird Seed Company is blending a special 16-ounce box of parakeet seed mix using two different seeds, types A and B. Information on the two types of seeds is shown below:

Type	Cost/o	Protein	Fat	Fiber
A	$.04	8%	4%	6%
B	.07	15%	3%	8%

Bright Feather wants this blend to contain at least 2 ounces of crude protein and 0.5 ounce of fat. The company also wants it to contain no more than 1.5 ounce of crude fiber. They want to spend no more than $.90 per 16-ounce box. All goals have the same priority level, but Bright Feather management feels that keeping the cost below $.90 per box is three times as important as the other goals. How should the two types of seeds be blended to achieve these goals?

6. How does the answer to problem 5 change if Bright Feather decides that all the goals have equal priority and weight?

7. The Fairport Parks and Recreation Department has recently gathered information on a number of new projects that village residents have requested through signed petitions. The projects and related information are shown below:

Project	Cost	Number of Signatures	Acres Required
Baseball fields	$65,000	3,200	4
Soccer fields	62,000	4,300	5
Skating rink	67,000	3,500	1.5
Outdoor basketball courts	77,500	4,500	2
Lighted tennis courts	84,000	5,000	1

James Donahugh, Department Director, must now decide which of the projects to undertake. He has stated the following criteria to be used in the decision, in order of their importance.

1. Keep the total cost below $250,000.
2. Satisfy the largest number of people possible, using the number of signatures on a petition as a measure of the number of people satisfied.
3. Do not exceed a total of 10 acres of land for the complex.

Formulate this problem as a goal programming problem. (Do not solve.)

8. Savoy Sausages produces a special bulk sausage for a pancake restaurant franchise. The sausage is produced in 2,500-pound batches and contains a mixture of pork, at a cost of $3 per pound, beef, at $5 per pound, and cereal, at $1.75 per pound. According to the franchise specifications, each batch must contain at least 600 pounds of pork and at least 1,200 pounds of beef. The mix cannot contain more than 900 pounds of cereal. The production manager of Savoy wants to determine how many pounds of each ingredient to include in the next batch, given the following criteria:

1. Savoy has 800 pounds of pork on hand that must be either used in this batch or discarded. Any of this pork that is discarded will result in a loss of $3 per pound.
2. Savoy wishes to keep the total cost of the batch below $9,100.

Formulate and solve the goal programming solution for this problem, assuming that both criteria are equally important and that deviations should be weighted in proportion to their dollar value.

9. Wallister's Investment Counseling Service just received an investment order from a client. The client specified that the investment must be made in one or more of three stocks. Information on the stocks is shown below:

Stock	Price	Expected Growth (%)	Dividend
Hi-Tech Co.	$60	8%	$1.40
Sky Aerospace	80	12	1.10
Grandma's Rockers	20	2	3.50

The client has stated the following desires, with respect to the investment:

1. The total annual dividend from all stocks must be at least $20,000.
2. The expected growth from these stocks should be at least 7 percent.

3. No more than 6,000 shares of Sky Aerospace should be purchased.
4. The total investment should not exceed $600,000.

a. Formulate this problem as a goal programming problem (no priorities or weights) and solve.
b. Assuming the client's desires are stated in terms of their preemptive importance, resolve the problem.

10. Johnson Chemical Company produces two different novelty items for children: Silly Goo and Green Glop. The company makes a profit of $1 on each jar of Silly Goo and $1.25 on each jar of Green Glop. Both products pass through two production centers, mixing and curing. The mixing department can mix 50 jars of Silly Goo or 40 jars of Green Glop per hour. The curing department can cure 35 jars of Silly Goo or 40 jars of Green Glop per hour. There are currently 100 hours of mixing time and 80 hours of curing time available, although additional hours can be scheduled. Mr. Johnson, company president, has stated the following goals in the order of their priority:

1. Make at least $7,000 profit.
2. Schedule no more than 20 extra hours in the mixing department and no more than 25 extra hours in the curing department.

Formulate and solve this problem.

11. How would the solution to problem 10 change if Mr. Johnson changed his goals and priorities as follows:

1. Do not schedule more than a total of 35 extra hours.
2. Make at least $7,000 profit.
3. Schedule no more than 20 extra hours in the mixing department and no more than 25 extra hours in the curing department.

12. The Bilkmore Investment Company has $700,000 to invest. They are considering the following investments:

Investment	Yield (%)	Risk Factor/$1000
Treasury bonds	8	1
Industrial bonds	10	4
Real estate	15	8
New stock issues	20	17

Bilkmore's president has specified the following goals in order of importance:

1. The total yield should be at least $80,000.
2. At least 70 percent of the funds must be invested in bonds.
3. No more than 25 percent of the investment should be in new stock.
4. The total risk factor should not exceed 3,000 (note, risk factor is per $1000 invested).

What investments should Bilkmore make if it wishes to achieve these goals? Are all the goals achieved, and if not, which ones are not?

13. How is the solution to problem 12 affected if goals 2, 3, and 4 are reordered as follows:

2. The total risk factor should not exceed 3,000.
3. At least 70 percent of the funds must be invested in bonds.
4. No more than 25 percent of the investment should be in new stock.

14. Senator Briggston is planning the advertising campaign for his upcoming senatorial race. The senator's media advisor has provided the following information:

Medium	Cost/ad	Younger Audience/ad	Older Audience/ad
TV	$1500	5,000	3,500
Radio	150	3,000	1,000
Newspaper	400	2,500	6,000

The senator has established the following goals and priorities:

1. His total advertising budget should not exceed $25,000.
2. He wishes to reach at least 140,000 older voters and at least 125,000 younger voters. He feels it is twice as important to reach older voters as younger voters.
3. He does not wish to place more than 10 TV ads, 20 radio ads, or 15 newspaper ads.

Determine the number of ads the senator should place in each medium and the extent to which each of his goals is met.

15. How much does the solution to problem 14 change if the senator has only $17,500 to spend?

16. A manufacturing firm produces three products: A, B, and C. Products A and B each require 8 hours to produce; product C requires 8.5 hours. The plant has 4,800 hours of production capacity available per week. Product A contributes $27 per unit to profit, product B $25/unit, and product C $30/unit. The sales department estimates sales of 200, 240, and 220 units of products A, B, and C respectively. The firm wishes to determine the optimum production schedule for the coming week, given the following multiple goals, listed in order of their importance.

1. Achieve the stated sales goals. Use the profit contribution as weights.
2. Avoid the underutilization of normal production capacity.
3. Avoid overtime as much as possible.

17. Big Boy Manufacturing received an order for 600 units of its X3 widget. Two machines are currently available that can produce this widget. Machine A has 44 hours of available production time and machine B has 60 hours of available time. Machine A costs $15 per hour to operate and produces 6 units per hour. Machine B costs $17 per hour and produces 4.5 units per hour. Management goals, in order of importance, are:

1. Fill the order for 600 units.
2. Keep maximum overtime hours to 8 hours total.
3. Avoid underutilization of either machine.
4. Spend no more than $1,600 on production, excluding overtime and other costs.

18. Change problem 17 as follows:

4. Spend no more than $1,600 on production. Overtime hours are charged as follows: machine costs remain the same, but there is an additional charge of $12 per hour for machine A and $15 per hour for machine B.

19. Williamson Securities wishes to invest $3,000,000 in one or more of four possible investment alternatives over the next five years:

Alternative	Yield (%)	Maturity (years)
Stocks	12	2
Real Estate	15	4
Certificates of Deposit	9	3
Money Market	7	1

The investment manager has set the following criteria for the investment in order of their importance:

1. No more than $1,000,000 should be invested in any alternative in any given year.

2. At least $250,000 should be kept in the money market at all times.

3. Total yield should be maximized over the five-year period.

Assuming all investments are made on January 2 and mature on December 31, formulate the goal programming model necessary to solve this problem.

20. Western University has decided to award more athletic scholarships in an effort to improve its athletic teams. It has raised a total of $400,000 for the coming year. The amount of a scholarship is fixed according to category: in-state students receive $4,500 and out-of-state students receive $6,000. In addition, athletes designated "impact players" can be awarded an additional $1,500. The Board of Trustees has set the following guidelines for awarding the scholarships:

1. At least 60 percent of the scholarships should go to in-state students.

2. At least 35 percent of the scholarships should go to women athletes.

3. No more than 10 percent of the scholarship recipients can be designated as "impact players."

Formulate this problem as a goal programming model.

21. The Special Studies program at Western University has grown dramatically since the school's athletic teams won several conference championships. The department chairman now faces a dilemma with respect to hiring new faculty. Faculty fall into one of five groups: full professors, associate professors, assistant professors, instructors, and teaching assistants. The department chairman's primary goal is to maximize the number of professors (all ranks), since they have doctorates and publish scholarly articles—enhancing the school's academic image. His secondary goal is to spend as little as possible on salary, since the Board of Trustees is allocating more university funds to scholarships. And he must have sufficient faculty to teach the anticipated 3,000 students enrolled in departmental courses for the coming year. Teaching loads and salaries per semester are shown below:

Rank	Sections Taught	Average Salary
Full Professor	2	$25,000
Associate Professor	2.5	21,000
Assistant Professor	3	17,500
Instructor	3	12,000
Teaching Assistant	2	6,000

The average size of a class section is 30 students. The department currently has 2 Full Professors, 3 Associate Professors, and 5 Assistant Professors with tenure. Formulate the above problem as a goal programming model and solve.

22. Assume that, in problem 21, it costs the department chairman $3,500 to recruit and hire a full professor, $2,700 for an associate professor, $2,000 for an assistant professor, and $600 for an instructor. Assume further that teaching assistants cannot be used for more than 10 percent of the teaching load (as measured by the number of students taught per year). Also assume that the chairman's priorities are reversed, that is, the first priority is to spend as little as possible and the second priority is to maximize the number of professors (all ranks). How do these assumptions affect the goal programming model?

Consultant's Report _____

Comcon, Inc.

Comcon, Inc., is a manufacturer of computerized production and quality control systems. Comcon was founded in 1976 by three engineers, Wallace McRoy, Clinton Wilson, and Abraham Gardner. Prior to the founding of Comcon, Wallace and Clinton were employed as mechanical engineers by a large manufacturing firm. Both men recognized the need for some sort of automatic control process for high-speed, automated production equipment. Without such controls, it was not uncommon for hundreds of bad parts to be produced before the machine operator or quality control inspector discovered the problem. The men were discussing the problem at a neighborhood picnic one weekend when Abraham Gardner, an electrical engineer and computer hobbyist, overheard them. The three men spent the next several hours discussing possible solutions to this problem. The formation of Comcon was the result.

By 1989 Comcon, though small in size, had grown into a highly regarded manufacturer of customized computer control systems. The company sells primarily to small to medium-sized manufacturing companies that use high-speed production equipment. The systems measure product attributes such as length, diameter, and weight as the products are produced. If the attribute being measured does not meet product specifications, the machine is automatically adjusted. If the adjustment does not affect the product attribute, the machine is automatically shut down and an alarm is sounded.

All Comcon systems are custom-made in the firm's small production facility. Both production and storage space is at a premium at this facility. Systems are typically shipped as soon as they are completed. Production capacity is restricted to 10 systems per month, and there is room to store only one completed system. Production capacity can be increased by approximately 40 percent through the use of overtime, although Comcon has found this to be expensive.

Recently, Comcon signed a contract with a large, multi-plant manufacturer to produce and deliver 50 of its systems over a five-month period. The firm has agreed to pay Comcon $600,000 for each of these systems. The contract calls for Comcon to deliver 4, 8, 10, 14, and 14 systems per month during the five-month period beginning in April. Comcon also has contracts for four additional systems, two to be produced in April and two in June.

The owners, working with the firm's accountant, have arrived at the following cost estimates. Each system will cost Comcon $350,000 (variable and fixed costs) if produced during normal production time. The cost of each system produced on overtime is $410,000. While there is storage space for one completed system, Comcon estimates that the cost of holding a system is $8,000 per month. Although no cost estimates have been determined, the firm knows from past experience that adjusting to downturns in production by laying off employees becomes undesirable when the number of employees released exceeds 20 percent of the normal work-force in any given month. In addition to the direct costs associated with severance pay and unemployment benefits, there are the indirect costs associated with lower employee morale and declining productivity rates.

In bidding on this job, the partners determined that certain inefficiencies would be associated with the start-up on these systems. Thus, they estimate that normal production capacity in April will be limited to eight systems (including the two already scheduled). They further estimate that overtime capacity for April will be limited to three systems.

Once they gathered all of the necessary information, the partners sat down and listed all the considerations they would have to take into account when scheduling production over the five-month period. They first decided that they must meet their previous commitments for the four systems outside this contract, regardless of other considerations. After that, their production scheduling goals, listed in order of priority, are:

1. Meet the monthly delivery schedule called for by this contract.
2. Operate at or above 80 percent of normal capacity each month (6.4 units in April and 8 units in the remaining months).
3. Limit overtime production to one unit per month.
4. Make as much profit on this contract as possible.

You have been hired as a management consultant to help Comcon by applying management science techniques to this scheduling problem. Prepare a report for Comcon, Inc. that addresses:

1. The number of systems that should be produced each month, beginning in April and ending in August.
2. The deviations from any of the stated goals.
3. The amount of profit the firm can expect to make from this contract.

Chapter

11

Project Scheduling with PERT/CPM

By the end of this chapter, you should be able to:

1
recognize a project scheduling problem;

2
set up and draw a PERT/CPM network for a given project;

3
determine the critical path and project completion time;

4
determine expected start and completion times for all activities;

5
determine the slack on all activities;

6
determine the probability of completing the project within a given time;

7
crash a project manually and with LP; and

8
control cash flow throughout the duration of the project using PERT/cost.

PERT (project evaluation and review technique) and CPM (critical path method) are network analysis techniques used to plan, schedule, and control projects. These project management tools also aid in monitoring and reorganizing resources so that the project can be completed on time and within budget. Projects are characterized by their complexity, duration, cost, and the distinctive, unique, non-repetitive nature of the work involved. They can be modeled as networks to illustrate the interrelationship and sequential nature of the project parts. Thus, this chapter is a logical extension of the network approach presented in Chapter 8.

PERT and **CPM** provide a systematic, formalized approach to project management. These two techniques were developed independently and originally had some important differences, but the distinction between the two has become fuzzy with actual implementation. Features of both systems have been blended into a "PERT type" or **PERT/CPM** technique, especially with the increased use of computerized solutions. Firms today tend to merge the best features of both techniques in an effort to aid in the planning and control of their unique situations.

An Information Systems Lab

To support its new Information Systems major, Canandaigua Technology Institute wishes to establish a microcomputer lab for the exclusive use of the IS majors. A faculty committee has been created to determine the size of the lab and obtain the hardware and software needed. The committee needs to secure the room and turn it into a lab, by furnishing and wiring it and so on. The committee is also responsible for staffing the new lab. They would like this new lab available by the beginning of the next semester. Because of the number of different activities required to complete this project, the committee feels it will need to make use of some type of planning and scheduling tool if this project is to be completed on time.

11.1 AN INTRODUCTION TO PERT/CPM

Projects involve numerous interrelated activities that are sequential in nature; frequently require long periods of time to complete; may be extremely costly; and are usually a one-time effort. Given the nature of projects, their management is often a complicated and difficult process. Managers have utilized various tools to facilitate this process. One of the better-known planning tools, the Gantt bar chart, specifies the start and finish times for each activity on a horizontal time scale. It does not, however, show the interdependency between activities. It is this interdependency that controls the progress of the project. PERT/CPM is an effective scheduling tool that provides the systematic approach required by today's increasingly complex projects.

Both PERT and CPM were developed in the late 1950s—PERT by the Navy Special Projects Office and the management consulting firm Booz, Allen, and Hamilton—to support the planning of the Polaris Missile project and CPM by J.E. Kelly of Remington Rand and M.R. Walker of Dupont. As originally developed, the two techniques, while similar, differed in their treatment of time and cost. Both are time-oriented methods, but time estimates originally were assumed to be probabilistic for PERT and deterministic for CPM. Thus PERT was designed to handle the uncertainties that exist in predicting the time necessary to complete various project activities. Initially, PERT was applied mainly to research and development projects. CPM, which assumed that both time and costs are known with certainty, was concerned more with time/cost tradeoff—that is, the tradeoff between project completion date and project cost. CPM was used in more common and familiar projects, such as construction, in which costs and times could be estimated with some degree of certainty. As noted earlier, this usage distinction has largely disappeared. Computerized versions frequently include options for handling time uncertainties and time/cost tradeoff analysis. In this chapter, we refer to the methods collectively as PERT/CPM.

PERT/CPM is not an optimization technique. Rather, it is a descriptive or predictive tool whose value lies in the information it provides—determining project completion time and identifying those activities that are critical for on-time completion of the entire project. With this information, project managers can work toward completing the project on time and within (or close to) budget, with no sacrifice in quality. PERT/CPM is basically a three-part technique: (1) planning, which includes an in-depth analysis of the project and construction of the network to describe the project; (2) scheduling, which involves the analysis of the project network to determine completion time, critical activities, and start and finish times for each activity; and (3) controlling, which includes using the network and schedule to keep track of progress and making any revisions necessary to keep the project on schedule and within budget.

Since this is an introductory text, we will concentrate on the planning and scheduling procedures. We will use the Canadaigua Technical Institute Information Systems Lab problem, introduced at the beginning of the chapter, to illustrate discussion of PERT/CPM as a planning and scheduling tool.

11.2 *PERT/CPM PLANNING*

The planning stage involves three parts: (1) identifying and sequencing all activities of the project; (2) drawing the network to represent the project; and (3) estimating activity times and costs.

Identify Activities and Precedence Relationships

The initial step in the PERT/CPM approach is a thorough analysis of the project, resulting in the identification of all the activities associated with the project. In network terminology, an **activity** is a task or job that requires resources and takes time for completion. Once all the necessary activities have been identified it is essential to determine how these activities interrrelate. The interrelationship is indicated by identifying the **precedence relationships.** That means the immediately prior activity (or activities) for each activity in the project is identified. A subsequent activity cannot be started until its preceding activity has been completed. It is essential to compile a complete, accurate list of all activities and their **immediate predecessors.** For example, the IS committee determined that the following tasks had to be completed before the lab would be operational: evaluate and select software, comparison shop and obtain software, obtain hardware, secure room, wire the room, order furnishings, install tables, hire student lab workers, install hardware, and install software. Next, they had to sequence this list. The committee had to determine which activities must be completed before others could begin. That is, the committee had to determine the precedence relationship among the activities. Table 11.1 shows the results of this analysis. This step, by itself, makes a major contribution toward successful project completion. For some small projects, it may be all that is needed. In all cases, it helps to focus, clarify, and define the task facing the project manager and the project team. Once this step has been completed, it is possible to construct a PERT/CPM network.

Construct the Network

The PERT/CPM network depicts project activities and their interrelationships graphically, showing correct precedent relationships. The network has two components: activities, represented by arrows (directed branches or arcs), and events, represented by circles (nodes). As stated earlier, **activities** are tasks that consume time and resources and incur costs. **Events** are project milestones, occurring at points in time, and consume neither time nor resources. Events serve as connecting points for linking the activities; that is, they represent the termination of some activities and the beginning of other activities. A node is said to occur, or to be realized, when all activities entering it are completed. We use the terms node and event interchangeably throughout the discussion.

Table 11.1 Activity and Predecessor List for IS Lab Project

Activity Code	Activity	Immediate Predecessor
A	Evaluate and select hardware & software	—
B	Order hardware	A
C	Obtain room	—
D	Comparison shop/purchase software	A
E	Prepare/wire room	C
F	Acquire tables	C
G	Install tables/furnishings	E, F
H	Hire workers	—
I	Install hardware	B, G
J	Install software	D, H, I

Figure 11.1 shows some typical representations of simple network relationships. 11.1 (a) shows an activity (A) beginning at node 1 and ending at node 2. 11.1 (b) shows a sequential network, with activity C immediately preceded by activity B, which is immediately preceded by activity A. 11.1 (c) shows simultaneous activities A and B, both beginning at the same node, but terminating at different nodes. 11.1 (d) shows a precedence relationship, in which activity F can start only after both C and D are completed.

Given an inclusive and accurate list of activities and predecessors, organized in a logical fashion, the network can be constructed. We do not advise attempting to draw the network without the activity/predecessor list. Rules and suggestions for drawing the PERT/CPM network are summarized below.

1. Each activity is represented by only one arrow—that is, no activity can be represented twice. (This is sometimes referred to as AOA or activity on arrow.)
2. Arrows imply precedence only; the length has no meaning, that is, length is not proportional to duration. Arrows need not be drawn as straight lines, but generally should move from left to right.

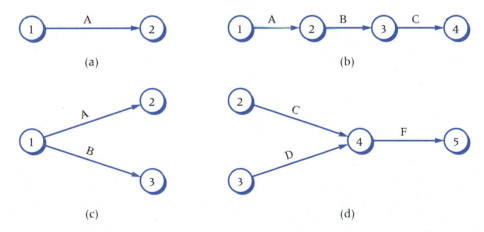

Figure 11.1 Typical Representations of Network Relationships

3. Every activity (arrow) must begin and end with an event (node). The network begins with a single node and ends with a single node.
4. Each activity must start at the node in which its immediate predecessor(s) ended; that is, before an activity can begin, all preceding activities must be completed.
5. Two events (nodes) can be directly connected by *no more* than one activity (arrow). Or to say it another way, two or more activities cannot simultaneously share the same start and finish nodes. Dummy activities must be used when there are concurrent activities in order not to violate this rule. We will discuss dummy activities later in this chapter.

Network construction begins with any activity or activities having no precedent (the beginning of the project). The network grows to the right. Numbering is arbitrary; numbers identify events and imply nothing about precedence. The usual practice, however, is to number the nodes such that the node representing the completion of an activity has a higher number than the node at the beginning of the activity. In fact, some software packages require this convention. For large networks, it may be best to number nodes in multiples of 10 or to leave gaps in the numbering so that additions or changes can be incorporated later. The alternative is to renumber as changes are made.

As each activity is added to the network, it is necessary to consider what activities have to be completed before this activity can start; what activities follow this activity; and what activities occur concurrently with this activity. Looking at each activity this way helps ensure that the correct precedence relationships are represented in the network.

Before continuing, let's look at the construction of a simple project. Table 11.2 shows the activities and predecessors for building a small backyard deck. This is not an all-inclusive activity list; we are using it to illustrate a common error made in network logic. Figure 11.2 shows the resulting network. The deck-building activities are in a serial sequence, based on when they are likely to occur. This is the time sequence one is likely to consider when visualizing building the deck. It indicates how the activities might be ordered. According to the list and network, however, the materials cannot be ordered until the layout has been finished. This is not necessarily true. It is possible to order the materials concurrently with laying out

Table 11.2 Activity/Predecessor List for Building Deck

Activity	Description	Immediate Predecesor
A	design/plan	—
B	layout deck	A
C	order materials	B
D	build deck	C

Figure 11.2 Network for Building Deck

Table 11.3 Revised Activity/Predecessor List for Deck

Activity	Description	Immediate Predecesor
A	design/plan	—
B	layout deck	A
C	order materials	A
D	build deck	B, C

the deck, since planning and designing the deck involves taking the measurements necessary to place the order. Table 11.3 shows the revised activities and predecessors list, which allows for these concurrent activities.

Activities should not be placed in series unless absolutely necessary. Whenever possible, the network should reflect the possibility that activities can occur simultaneously (concurrently). Doing so makes the project more flexible, and may even shorten completion time. Figure 11.3 (a) depicts the relationship between the concurrent activities B and C. However, since it links two nodes with more than one activity (activities B and C share the same starting and ending nodes, 2 and 3), violating rule 5, it is an incorrect network representation.

We represent concurrent activities in the network with dummy activities. The broken or dashed line in Figure 11.3 (b) is a dummy activity.

Dummy activities are used in the construction of a network to ensure that proper precedence is maintained, and to avoid having two nodes directly connected by more than one activity. Dummy activities, represented with a broken line as shown in Figure 11.3, keep activities and events in proper sequence. Dummies use no resources, incur no cost, and have a time duration of zero. The important point to remember is that dummies designate a precedence relationship. Thus, in the deck example, the broken line from node 3 to node 4 is a dummy activity that shows that both activities B and C must be completed before activity D can be started.

Figures 11.3 (c) and (d) show additional network representations using dummies. In Figure 11.3 (c), activity E is preceded by both activities B and C. Activity D is preceded only by B. In 11.3 (d), activity F is preceded by both B and C.

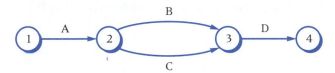

Figure 11.3(a) Incorrect representation of concurrent activity

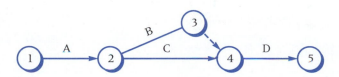

Figure 11.3(b)

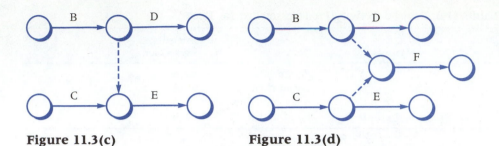

Figure 11.3(c)   **Figure 11.3(d)**

Activity D is preceded by B, and E is preceded by C. These activities and precedents are listed as follows:

Activity	Immediate Predecessor		Activity	Immediate Predecessor
D	B		D	B
E	B, C		E	C
			F	B, C

Now let's return to the IS Lab and draw the network for this problem. There are no hard and fast rules for drawing networks; the process is as much art as science. Frequently, it takes several attempts before the network emerges without unnecessary dummy activities and with no lines crossing each other. (Note, however, that it may be impossible to draw some networks without lines that cross.) Our advice is to work in pencil and to look ahead—realizing that, whenever an activity is preceded by two or more activities, those preceding activities probably all terminate at the same node.

In drawing the network for the IS Lab, we begin by drawing a beginning node and labelling it node 1. Since this is our beginning point, all activities with no immediate predecessors (activities A, C, and H) must originate at this node. We can draw three lines coming out of node 1 and label them A, C, and H as shown in Figure 11.4.

The ending node for any of these activities will also be the beginning node for any activities that follow them. In other words, activities emanate from, or begin at, the node at which their immediate predecessors terminate. Looking ahead, we see that activities B and D are preceded by activity A. Thus we can draw node 2 at the end of activity A and show activities B and D originating from it, as shown in Figure 11.5.

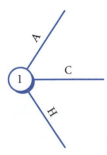

Figure 11.4

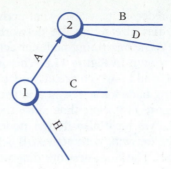

Figure 11.5

Since activities E and F are preceded by activity C, we add node 3 as the ending node for activity C and the beginning node for activities E and F. The network at this point is shown in Figure 11.6.

Looking ahead again, we see that the only activity preceded by activities currently on the network is activity G—which is preceded by activities E and F. Because G is the only activity preceded by these activities, the beginning node for activity G (node 4) will be the terminating node for E and F. But E and F are concurrent activities that both originate at the same node (node 3). Since we cannot have two activities originate from the same node and end at the same node, we must use a dummy activity. This is shown in Figure 11.7.

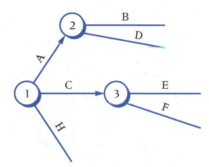

Figure 11.6

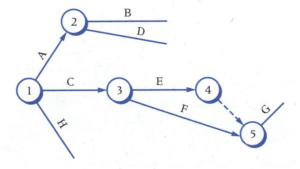

Figure 11.7

Looking at our list of predecessors, we see that activity I is the only remaining activity preceded by activities already on the network—activities B and G. That means we can make node 6 the beginning node for activity I and the ending node for activities B and G, as shown in Figure 11.8. The only remaining activity, J, is preceded by activities D, H, and I—which are all now on the network. Thus we can add node 7 as the beginning node for activity J and the terminating node for D, H, and I. This is shown in Figure 11.9. Note that, since there are no other activities to be added to this network, we have also drawn node 8 as the ending node for activity J. By redrawing the network with activity B below activity D at node 2, we can eliminate crossing lines. The final network diagram is shown in Figure 11.10.

We have spent a considerable amount of time in compiling the activities and immediate predecessor list and drawing the network, because we think it is a crucial step in project management with PERT/CPM. Omitting activities or predecessors, or establishing incorrect precedence, can distort the project, thus resulting in costly mistakes (decisions based on erroneous information). The network provides a visual verification of the activity relationships. These steps are analogous to the observation, formulation, and information gathering steps we have emphasized in the management science process. This is especially true since computer programs can easily handle the solution step, the network analysis used to identify the critical path and project completion time, and to determine starting and completion times for the activities. If the computer input is in error—for example, if it contains incorrect precedence relationships—the output can be worthless. The output is only as good as the input.

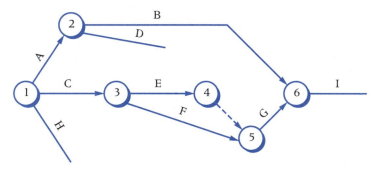

Figure 11.8

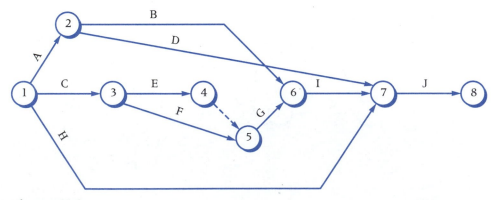

Figure 11.9

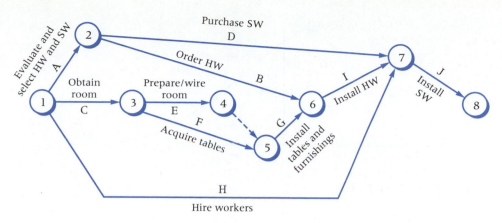

Figure 11.10

Estimate Activity Times and Costs

Every activity has an expected completion time, an activity duration time, and a cost associated with it. PERT/CPM allows for two possibilities—deterministic times and stochastic times. Deterministic times are much more likely to occur in projects that are repeated (although not necessarily in exactly the same way), such as construction jobs, for which historical data and a stable technology or methodology are available. Experience sometimes can provide accurate time estimates. For example, a building contractor who installs thousands of windows in new homes every year can estimate with a fair degree of certainty how long it will take to install the windows in a new house.

It is much more likely, however, that times are uncertain. This is especially true for research and development projects. The original version of PERT allowed for this uncertainty by assuming that activity time is a random variable with a beta probability distribution. The developers of PERT selected the **beta distribution** because it is unimodal (a single peak); it has finite and nonnegative end points (a continuous, bounded range of values); and it is not necessarily symmetrical (it can be skewed in either direction). Although questions have been raised as to the suitability of this distribution to describe time variability in specific projects, no all-inclusive alternative has been selected. Using this distribution provides a reasonable approximation in most situations, and it continues to be the distribution most employed.

The procedure employs three estimates of each activity time: an **optimistic time,** a **pessimistic time,** and a **most likely time.** The optimistic time (denoted by a) is the minimum time, unlikely but possible. There is an extremely small probability that the activity time will be less than or equal to the optimistic time. It is the lower bound of the probability distribution. The pessimistic time (denoted by b) is the maximum time, also unlikely but possible. There is an extremely small probability of the activity time being greater than or equal to the pessimistic time, b, which is the upper bound of the probability distribution. The most likely time (denoted by m) is the most probable time, or the most realistic time estimate. If the same activity were completed many times, this is the time that would occur most frequently; it is the mode of the probability distribution. Figure 11.11 shows a typical beta distribution.

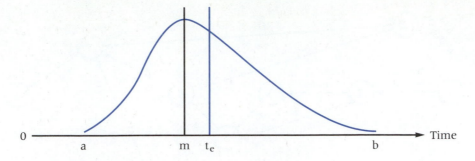

Figure 11.11 Beta Distribution

An expected time can be calculated using the following formula:

$$\text{Expected time } (t_e) = \frac{a + 4m + b}{6}$$

If the three time estimates for activity C (obtain room) are

$$\text{optimistic time} = 3$$
$$\text{most likely} = 6$$
$$\text{pessimistic time} = 9$$

then the expected time would be

$$t_e = \frac{3 + 4(6) + 9}{6}$$

$$t_e = \frac{36}{6}$$

$$t_e = 6$$

The times for each activity are shown in Table 11.4. Figure 11.12 repeats the network with expected activity times shown below each activity line.

The three time estimates represent the best guesses of the people most closely associated with the project, those who are most knowledgeable about it. Since these estimates are subjective, why is the estimated duration for each activity

Table 11.4 Activity Times

Activity	Start & End node	Optimistic Time	Most Likely	Pessimistic Time	Mean Time (t_e)
A	1, 2	3	4	11	5
B	2, 6	5	8	11	8
C	1, 3	3	6	9	6
D	2, 7	4	8	12	8
E	3, 4	2	4	12	5
F	3, 5	1	3	5	3
G	5, 6	2	3	4	3
H	1, 7	7	10	13	10
I	6, 7	2	2	2	2
J	7, 8	1	2	3	2

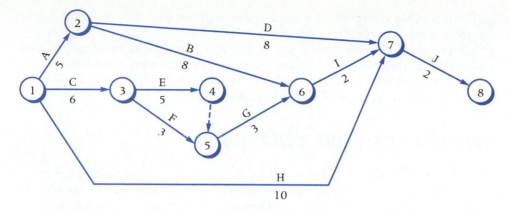

Figure 11.12 Network with Estimated Times

based on three time estimates rather than one best guess? The three times are useful to assess the reliability of the estimated time. If the range of estimates from pessimistic to optimistic is very large (highly variable), representing greater uncertainty in the times, then management probably will have less confidence in the resulting estimated time. If the range of estimates is narrow, the times are probably more certain, and confidence in the estimated time is greater.

The variability of the activity times (variance) can be determined using the formula

$$\text{Variance} = \sigma^2 = \left[\frac{b - a}{6}\right]^2$$

Using this formula, the variance for activity C can be calculated as follows:

$$\sigma^2 = \left[\frac{9 - 3}{6}\right]^2$$

$$\sigma^2 = 1$$

Table 11.5 shows the calculated variances for each activity. In the following discussion of network analysis, we are using the calculated estimated times. If our times were deterministic instead, the analysis procedure would be identical. We

Table 11.5 Activity Time Estimates with Mean and Variance Calculated

Activity	Start & End Node	Variance (σ^2)
A	1, 2	1.78
B	2, 6	1.00
C	1, 3	1.00
D	2, 7	1.78
E	3, 4	2.78
F	3, 5	.44
G	5, 6	.11
H	1, 7	1.00
I	6, 7	0.00
J	7, 8	.11

will return to the discussion of variance later when we evaluate the probability of completing the project on schedule.

It is extremely important for a project manager to gather accurate information concerning activity times, associated costs for the activities, availability of resources, and cost/time tradeoffs. Obviously, the accuracy of further analysis is dependent upon the accuracy of this information.

11.3 PERT/CPM SCHEDULING

Once the network has been drawn and the expected times have been determined, it is possible both to determine the minimum completion time for the project and to schedule each activity (beginning and ending times). This stage is handled very nicely by computer and is discussed later in the chapter. The manual solutions discussed here provide the basis for understanding the computer solution.

Project Completion Time—Critical Path

Obviously, completion of the project requires that all activities be completed. One way to determine completion time, then, might be to add up all activity duration times. However, since not all activities are completed in series (some activities occur simultaneously), this time would be in error. In networks with concurrent activities, more than one path can be traced through the network. In order to complete the project, all paths must be completed (or traversed). In the IS Lab network in Figure 11.11, there are five such paths. Thus, since simultaneous activities are represented on different paths, it is possible to determine project completion time by identifying the paths and computing the length of each by summing its activity times. The path with the longest completion time, called the **critical path**, gives the project completion time.

To understand this procedure, look again at the IS Lab network and the five paths with corresponding times that are summaried in Table 11.6. Notice that the third path listed, C–E–G–I–J, includes the dummy activity.

The only path with a duration long enough to ensure that all other paths will be completed is path C–E–G–I–J. Every other path is shorter, so it would be impossible to complete all activities on this longest path. The activities on this critical path, the longest path through the network, are critical activities. If any of these activities is delayed, the entire project will be delayed.

In summary, the completion of a project requires that all paths of a network be completed. To determine project completion time requires identifying the critial path (the longest path). Delaying any activity on this path delays the entire project.

Table 11.6 Alternative Paths and Their Times in IS Network

PATH	ACTIVITY TIMES	TOTAL PATH TIME
A–D–J	5 + 8 + 2	17
A–B–I–J	5 + 8 + 2 + 2	17
C–E–G–I–J	6 + 5 + 3 + 2 + 2	18
C–F–G–J–I	6 + 3 + 3 + 2 + 2	16
H–J	10 + 2	12

The discussion above shows one method for identifying the critical path—enumeration, in which all paths through the network are identified and their duration or length is computed in order to identify the longest one, that is, the critical path. With all but the simplest networks, this method is impractical and inefficient. The following discussion presents a methodology for developing a schedule that includes start and finish times for each activity and a method for determining a network's critical path.

Network Analysis

There are two basic algorithms for analyzing a network—**activity analysis** and **event analysis.** Both are based on establishing time boundaries and are similar in their approach. We present our personal preference—activity analysis—followed by a brief discussion of event analysis.

Activity Analysis

Activity analysis focuses upon times associated with each activity. These times indicate the earliest and latest times that an activity can be started or finished.

Earliest Start and Earliest Finish Times We begin by defining two terms associated with an activity: the **earliest start time** (ES) and the **earliest finish time** (EF). Let

$$ES_i = \text{the earliest start time for activity i}$$

$$EF_i = \text{the earliest finish time for activity i}$$

For any activity, the earliest start time indicates the earliest time that an activity can begin. The earliest finish time indicates the earliest time that an activity can end or be completed. The relationship between these terms can then be defined as

$$EF_i = ES_i + t_{ei}$$

where t_{ei} is the expected time for activity i. All time units are elapsed times from the beginning of the project. Thus, the project is considered to begin at time zero. All activities with no immediate predecessors, therefore, will have an earliest start time of zero. Referring to the IS Lab example, activity A would have an earliest start time of zero and an expected time of five weeks. Its earliest finish time can be calculated as

$$EF_A = 0 + 5 = 5$$

This result indicates that the earliest activity A can be finished is at the end of week 5. The earliest start and earliest finish times can be displayed within square brackets above the activity arrow, as shown in Figure 11.13.

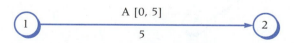

Figure 11.13 Earliest Start and Earliest Finish Times

Activity B, which originates at event node 2, cannot begin until activity A (which precedes it) has been completed. Since the earliest finish time for activity A is 5, this becomes the earliest starting time for activity B. The expected time for activity B is eight weeks. Thus, the earliest finish time for activity B would be

$$EF_B = 5 + 8 = 13$$

Since all activities terminating at a given node must be completed before any activities beginning at that node can start, the earliest starting time for all activities emanating from a node is equal to the greatest earliest finish time for any activity ending at that node. Figure 11.14 shows that activity E has an earliest finish time of 11 weeks and activity F has an earliest finish time of 9 weeks. Thus, the earliest start time for activity G must be the larger of these two times, or 11 weeks.

The process of moving from the beginning or starting node on a network to the ending node is known as a **forward pass** through the network. The complete network is shown in Figure 11.15, which includes all earliest start and earliest finish times. Note that the earliest finish time at node 8 is 18 weeks. Since node 8 is the ending node for this network, the earliest expected completion time for the total network is 18 weeks.

Latest Start and Latest Finish Times   The next step in the algorithm requires the definition of two additional terms: the latest start time (LS) and the latest finish time (LF). Let

$$LS_i = \text{the latest start time for activity i}$$

$$LF_i = \text{the latest finish time for activity i}$$

The **latest start time** for any activity is the latest time that an activity can be started without delaying the expected completion time for the project. Similarly,

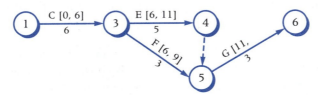

Figure 11.14 Earliest Start Time for Activity G

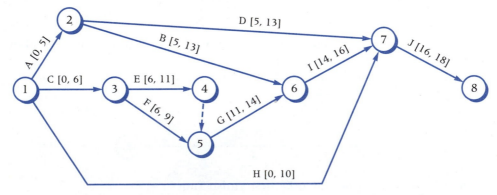

Figure 11.15 IS Lab Network Showing Earliest Start and Earliest Finish Times

the **latest finish time** for any activity is the latest time that an activity can be completed without extending the expected project completion time. The relationship between these terms can be defined as

$$LS_i = LF_i - t_{ei}$$

Latest start and latest finish times are determined by making a **backward pass** through the network. This means starting at the ending node and moving backward through the network to the beginning node.

The forward pass through the network determined that the expected project duration time was 18 weeks. Since the latest finish for activity J is the latest time this activity can be completed without extending the expected project duration, the latest finish can be set equal to 18 weeks. The expected time for activity J is 2 weeks. Thus, the latest start time can be calculated as

$$LS_J = 18 - 2 = 16$$

The latest finish and latest start times can be displayed within square brackets below the activity arrow, as shown in Figure 11.16. Activities D, I, and H all terminate at node 7. This means we must complete these activities in time for activity J to begin at time 16 at the latest. Thus, the latest finish times for these activities must be equal to 16. Working backwards, we determine their latest start times to be 8, 14, and 6 weeks respectively. These times are shown in Figure 11.17.

When two or more activities begin at the same node, the smaller latest start time must be used to determine the latest finish time for any activities terminating at that node. For example, Figure 11.18 shows that activities B and D both begin at node 2. Activity B has a latest start time of 6 and activity D has a latest start time of 8. Since activity A must finish in time for both activities to start on time, activity A must have a latest finish time of 6, the smaller of the latest start times.

Figure 11.19 shows the complete network, with all earliest start and finish times and latest start and finish times.

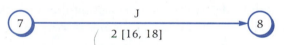

Figure 11.16 Latest Start and Latest Finish Times

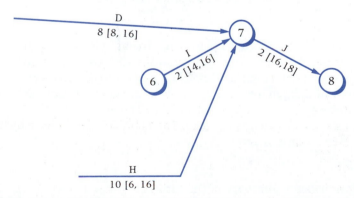

Figure 11.17 Latest Start and Latest Finish Times for Activities D, I and H

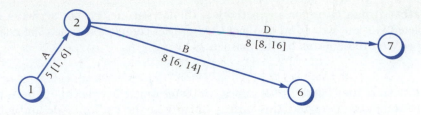

Figure 11.18 Determination of Latest Finish Time for Activity A

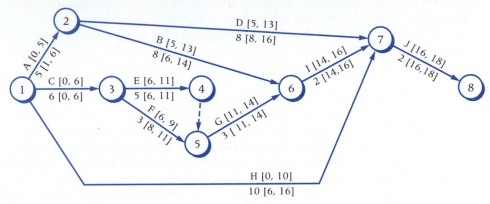

Figure 11.19 IS Lab Network Showing Earliest Start, Earliest Finish, Latest Start and Latest Finish Times

In addition to determining the earliest start, earliest finish, latest start, and latest finish times for each activity, the algorithm provides additional information about the network.

Slack Time   Whenever the earliest and latest start or finish times differ, this implies that the beginning or completion of an activity can be delayed without delaying the completion of the project. The amount of time that a particular activity's start or finish can be delayed without increasing the completion time for the project is known as **slack** time. Slack (S_i) for any activity can be determined by the relationships

$$S_i = LS_i - ES_i \quad \text{or} \quad S_i = LF_i - EF_i$$

For example, the slack time associated with activity D is

$$LS_D - ES_D = 8 - 5 = 3$$

Thus, activity D can be delayed up to three weeks without delaying the entire project. In general, activities not on the critical path can be delayed for some period of time without delaying the completion of the project. Activities on the critical path cannot be delayed, because if any of the activities on this path are delayed, the project can no longer be completed on time. Therefore, activities on the critical path have no slack associated with them. For example, activity E, which is on the critical path, has a slack of zero:

$$LS_E - ES_E = 6 - 6 = 0$$

Table 11.7 provides a summary of the earliest and latest start times, the earliest and latest finish times, and the slack times for all activities. Activities witth zero slack time have been identified as being on the critical path.

Table 11.7 IS Lab Activity Schedule

Activity	Earliest Start	Earliest Finish	Latest Start	Latest Finish	Slack	Critical Path?
A	0	5	1	6	1	
B	5	13	6	14	1	
C	0	6	0	6	0	YES
D	5	13	8	16	3	
E	6	11	6	11	0	YES
F	6	9	8	11	2	
G	11	14	11	14	0	YES
H	0	10	6	16	6	
I	14	16	14	16	0	YES
J	16	18	16	18	0	YES

In the previous discussion, we defined slack as the amount an activity can be delayed without delaying the completion of the project. We could have called this total slack, because it is actually a combination of two separate types of slack: **shared slack** and **free slack.** Shared slack is slack time that is shared with preceding activities. Since slack represents the maximum delay time available, it must be shared whenever two or more noncritical activities are connected in series. Free slack is slack that is not shared with any other activities. Free slack for any activity can be defined as the amount of slack for that activity minus the amount of slack for the immediately preceding activity. If there is more than one preceding activity, the free slack is the slack for that activity minus the maximum slack associated with all immediately preceding activities.

In the example, activity A has one week of slack and is not preceded by any other activities. This means activity A has one week of free slack. If this activity is delayed by one week, the completion time for the network will not be delayed. Activity B also has one week of slack, but it is preceded by activity A. Thus, activity B has no free slack ($S_B - S_A = 1 - 1 = 0$). The week of slack calculated for activity B is shared slack. If activity A is delayed for one week, its earliest finish time is 6. Thus, the earliest start time for activity B is delayed by one week (becomes 6 instead of 5) and there is no longer any slack associated with activity B. Activity D has three weeks of slack and is preceded by activity A. Thus, activity D has two weeks of free slack ($S_D - S_A = 3 - 1 = 2$). The slack and free slack for each activity on the example project are shown in Table 11.8.

Table 11.8 Slack and Free Slack for IS Lab Activities

Activity	Slack	Free Slack
A	1	1
B	1	0
C	0	0
D	3	2
E	0	0
F	2	2
G	0	0
H	6	6
I	0	0
J	0	0

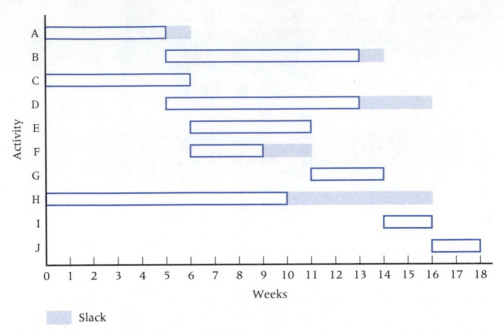

Figure 11.20 Gantt Chart

Note that the activity schedule table indicates not only which activities lie on the critical path and the project duration, but also the amount of slack time associated with noncritical activities. Knowing the earliest and latest start and finish times for each activity can help a manager keep a project on schedule. Careful monitoring of the project as it progresses, and comparing actual activity times with those expected, will alert a project manager of any discrepancies or delays.

Heretofore we have shown project networks using PERT diagrams. Projects can also be displayed using Gantt charts, which show activities as horizontal bars with the X-axis representing time. Figure 11.20 is a Gantt chart for the IS Lab project, with the solid bars representing the times for each activity and the shaded areas representing the amount of slack time associated with each activity.

Event Analysis

An alternative to the activity analysis just discussed is event analysis. Event analysis focuses on times associated with events rather than activities. This procedure also establishes time boundaries, **earliest time** (ET) and **latest time** (LT) for each event. From these times, slack can be determined and the critical path identified.

Earliest Time The earliest time at which an event can occur is immediately after *all* the preceding activities have been completed. This is also the earliest possible starting time for all activities emanating from that node. The earliest time for any given event (j) is analogous to the earliest start time for all activities beginning at that event (node).

Earliest times are calculated by making a forward pass through the nework:

$$ET_j = \text{Max} \{ET_i + t_{ij}\} \quad \text{for all (i, j) activities ending at node j where } t_{ij}$$
is the estimated time duration for activity (i, j) and ET_i is the

earliest time for node 6 is computed as

$$ET_6 = \text{Max} \{ET_2 + t_{26}, ET_5 + t_{56}\}$$

$$= \text{Max} \{5 + 8, 11 + 3\}$$

$$= \text{Max} \{13, 14\}$$

$$= 14$$

Table 11.9 summarizes the ET calculations for all the IS Lab events. The project termination or completion node, 8, has an earliest start of 18 weeks. This indicates the project duration is 18 weeks, the same completion time found using activity analysis.

Latest Time The latest time for an event to occur is the latest allowable time an event can occur without causing a delay in the project completion time. The latest time for event (j) is analogous to the latest finish time for all activities ending at this event (node).

Latest times are calculated using a backward pass through the network:

$$LT_i = \text{Min} \{LT_j - t_{ij}\}$$

for all (i, j) activities emanating from node i where t_{ij}, is the estimated time duration for activity (i, j) and LT_j is the latest time that activity (i, j) can end, or the latest time succeeding activities can begin. For example, the latest time at node 2 is computed as

$$LT_2 = \text{Min} \{LT_7 - t_{27}, LT_6 - t_{26}\}$$

$$= \text{Min} \{16 - 8, 14 - 8\}$$

$$= \text{Min} \{8, 6\}$$

$$= 6$$

Table 11.9 Calculation of Earliest Times for IS Lab

Ending Node (Event)	Start Node (immediately preceding event)	Earliest + Activity Time Time $(ET_i + t_{ij})$		Maximum = earliest time ET_i
1	—	—		0
2	1	0 + 5	5	5
3	1	0 + 6	6	6
4	3	6 + 5	11	11
5	4	11 + 0	11	11
	3	6 + 3	9	
6	2	5 + 8	13	
	5	11 + 3	14	14
7	2	5 + 8	13	
	1	0 + 10	10	
	6	14 + 2	16	16
8	7	16 + 2	18	18

The calculations of latest times for all events in the IS Lab network are shown in Table 11.10.

Event Slack Event slack indicates how much "free time" is available in reaching that event. In other words, it indicates how much delay (among the activities terminating in that event) can be tolerated before the project is delayed. Event slack is the difference between the latest and earliest times at that event:

$$\text{Event Slack for event (node) } i = LT_i - ET_i$$

For example, we calculate slack for event 5 as

$$\text{Slack}_5 = LT_5 - ET_5$$

$$= 11 - 11$$

$$= 0$$

Table 11.11 shows the event slack time for this network.

For those events having zero slack, no delay can be tolerated. These are critical events. For our network, events 1, 3, 4, 5, 6, 7, and 8 have zero event slack and are thus critical. Not all activities terminating at a critical event have to be critical. Thus, just having the critical events identified does not necessarily identify the critical activities. Notice that events 3, 4, and 5 are all critical, but that activity F, which begins at event 3 and ends at event 5, is not critical. All events with zero

Table 11.10 Calculation of Latest Times for IS Lab

Start Node (Event)	End Node (immediately following event)	Latest − Activity Time Time ($LT_j - t_{ij}$)		Minimum = latest time LT_i
8	—		—	18
7	8	18 − 2	16	16
6	7	16 − 2	14	14
5	6	14 − 3	11	11
4	5	11 − 0	11	11
3	4	11 − 5	6	6
	5	11 − 3	8	
2	6	14 − 8	6	6
2	7	16 − 8	8	
1	2	6 − 5	1	
	3	6 − 6	0	0
1	7	16 − 10	6	

Table 11.11 Event Slack

Event	Slack
1	0 − 0 = 0
2	6 − 5 = 1
3	6 − 6 = 0
4	11 − 11 = 0
5	11 − 11 = 0
6	14 − 14 = 0
7	16 − 16 = 0
8	18 − 18 = 0

slack time are on the critical path, but it is sometimes confusing to try to identify the critical path using only critical events.

Probability of Completing the Project Within a Specified Time

Recall that activity times are expected times based on three time estimates—pessimistic, most likely, and optimistic times for each activity. Therefore, the project completion time is an *expected* time. Obviously, there is potential variability in this overall time. If the activity times are random variables, then overall completion time is also a random variable. There is no guarantee that the project will be completed within that expected time. It is useful to be able to determine the probability that the project will be completed within a specified time. For the IS example, the college wants the lab available at the start of the fall term, which is 20 weeks away. The expected completion time is 18 weeks. The committee wants to know the probability that the lab will be ready within 20 weeks.

The procedure for determining this probability is based on certain assumptions. The first assumption is that activity times are statistically independent random variables that are identically distributed. Therefore, the means and variances of activity times along any path, including the critical path, can be added to give the mean expected time and variance of that path. The second assumption is that there are sufficient activities involved such that the total time (T) will have an approximately normal distribution. The latter assumption is based on the central limit theorem (the sum of independent variables is approximately normally distributed). Another assumption is that the actual project completion time is the time required for the critical path. That is, the critical path as determined remains the longest path through the network as the project moves to completion, even if the actual time required changes. If this last assumption does not hold, calculation of this probability becomes much more complex, involving joint probabilities of all paths through the network.

To begin the process of determining the probability of completing the project within a certain time, it is necessary to determine the overall variance on the critical path. Just as the expected times (mean time, t_e) of the activities on the critical path were totaled to determine expected completion time, overall variance can be determined by summing the variances on these critical activities. Thus, referring to Table 11.12 (which repeats the mean and variance calculations in

Table 11.12 Activity Time Estimates with Mean and Variance Calculated

Activity	Start & End Node	Optimistic Time	Most Likely	Pessimistic Time	Mean Time	Variance
A	1, 2	3	4	11	5	1.78
B	2, 6	5	8	11	8	1.00
C	1, 3	3	6	9	6	1.00
D	2, 7	4	8	12	8	1.78
E	3, 4	2	4	12	5	2.78
F	3, 5	1	3	5	3	.44
G	5, 6	2	3	4	3	.11
H	1, 7	7	10	13	10	1.00
I	6, 7	2	2	2	2	0.00
J	7, 8	1	2	3	2	.11

Table 11.5), we determine the variance on the critical path as follows:

$$\text{Variance, project time } V(T) = v_{13} + v_{34} + v_{56} + v_{67} + v_{78}$$

$$V(T) = 1.00 + 2.78 + .11 + 0 + .11$$

$$V(T) = 4.00$$

The variance on the critical path, or the variance on the project completion time, is 4.00. The standard deviation is equal to the square root of the variance. Therefore, the standard deviation for the project completion time is 2.00:

$$\sigma = \sqrt{V(T)}$$

$$\sigma = \sqrt{4}$$

$$\sigma = 2$$

With the mean and standard deviation for the expected project time known, it is possible to determine the probability of a completion time using a probability table for a standard normal distribution (Appendix A). To do this, we must first calculate a Z value as follows:

$$Z = \frac{x - T_E}{\sigma}$$

where x = the completion time for which the probability statement is being made, T_E = the expected project completion time, and σ = standard deviation for the project completion time. Thus for an x value of 20 weeks, and the expected time of completion of 18 weeks, the Z value is

$$Z = \frac{20 - 18}{2}$$

$$Z = 1$$

The corresponding probability in the table for the standard normal distribution is .84134. There is about an 84 percent chance that the IS Lab will be ready within 20 weeks. Figure 11.21 illustrates this probability on a normal curve.

The information generated in the analysis of the network can be invaluable for project management. The manager now knows the expected total time required for the project; the specific start and completion dates for each activity; which ac-

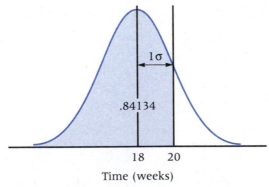

Figure 11.21 Probability of Completion within 20 Weeks

tivities are critical; and what slack time is available on noncritical activities. This information gives the manager a powerful tool for monitoring and controlling the progress of the project. Among other things, management can use this information to establish a schedule, calendar, or time chart; reevaluate the activities and their relationships to determine if there is a more effective way to do things; consider shifting resources or reallocating resources to speed up completion, that is, look at the possibility of spending more money in order to reduce time; or exert tighter control over critical activities. The following sections will discuss some techniques used to adjust the schedule and the project plan and to exert control over the implementation.

11.4 *TIME/COST TRADEOFF*

Once a project network has been analyzed and the project duration has been determined, it may be necessary or desirable to shorten completion time—for example, to avoid late penalties or to collect incentives for being ahead of schedule. In the case of the IS Lab, if the next term were to begin in 16 weeks, the 18-week duration would have to be shortened to ensure that the lab would be available to students on time. Project duration usually can be shortened by allocating additional resources to critical activities, with the understanding that (1) there exists a minimum duration for the project and continued expenditures cannot reduce project completion below this minimum, and (2) efficient allocation of resources requires further analysis of the project, looking at time/cost tradeoffs in order to achieve the greatest time reduction per dollar expended.

PERT and CPM, as originally developed, were time-oriented. They were designed to enable project managers to develop schedules for planning and monitoring projects. CPM also introduced cost as a companion factor, using the dual viewpoint of time and cost to bring cost into the planning and control process. CPM assumes that both time and cost are known with certainty and that cost is a linear function of time. Thus, there is a tradeoff between the time it takes to complete an activity and the cost of the resources used in the activity. In other words, certain (not necessarily all) activities in a project can be shortened, but only by increasing costs. Costs are direct costs only, such as labor, equipment, and materials. Figure 11.22 represents the time/cost tradeoff relationship in a typical project. Notice that the minimum completion time has the highest project cost, and the minimum cost occurs at the expected project completion time. The only feasible completion times (with corresponding costs) for the project lie on the curve between and including these two points.

Shortening the project duration is called **project crashing.** Obviously, if additional money is to be spent to shorten a project, it should be done as economically as possible. A cost analysis of the project, which looks at the tradeoff between time and cost, must be undertaken to determine which activities to crash and by how much.

Project Crashing

Crashing a project requires sequentially reducing activity times in such a way that each dollar spent results in a maximum time reduction. To achieve this, it is necessary to know the following for each activity: the expected activity time under

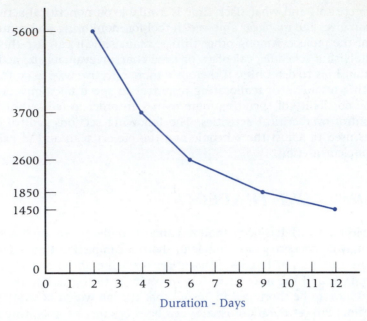

Figure 11.22 Example Time/Cost Tradeoff Curve

normal circumstances, **normal time** (t_n); the cost under normal circumstances, **normal cost** (c_n); the least possible time it can take to complete the activity, **crash time** (t_c); and cost under expedited or crash circumstances, **crash cost** (c_c). Figure 11.23 shows the relationship between normal and crash time and cost for an activity.

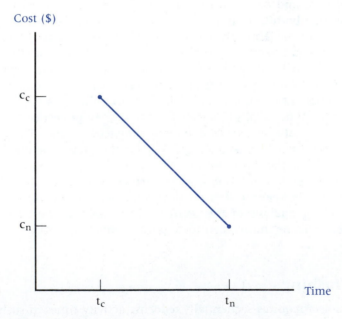

Figure 11.23 Relationship of Normal and Crash Time Cost

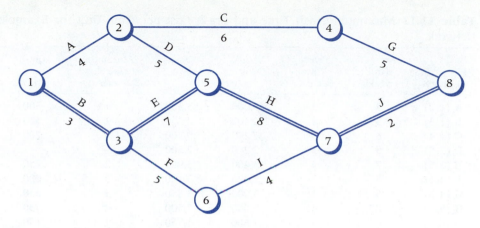

Figure 11.24 Network Used for Crashing Demonstration

These figures indicate the maximum time reduction for each activity and the cost of each time reduction. The maximum time reduction is calculated as follows:

$$\text{Maximum time reduction} = \text{normal time} - \text{crash time}$$

$$= t_n - t_c$$

Crashing cost per unit of time is calculated as follows:

$$\text{Crashing cost/time} = \frac{\text{crash cost} - \text{normal cost}}{\text{normal time} - \text{crash time}}$$

$$\text{Crashing cost/time} = \frac{c_c - c_n}{t_n - t_c}$$

We will use the network in Figure 11.24 to demonstrate the crashing technique. The critical path B–E–H–J, with a completion time of 20 weeks, is shown with darker lines. If activity E has a normal time of 7 weeks and a crash time of 5 weeks, then the maximum allowable time reduction (t_r) is

$$t_r = t_n - t_c$$

$$= 7 - 5$$

$$= 2 \text{ weeks}$$

Assuming the normal cost for this activity is $3,400 and the crash cost is $3,900, then the crashing cost per unit of time is

$$\text{Crashing cost/time unit} = \frac{c_c - c_n}{t_r}$$

$$= \frac{3900 - 3400}{2}$$

$$= \$250 \text{ per week}$$

Table 11.13 summarizes normal and crash costs, normal and crash times, and crash cost per week for each activity in the network shown in Figure 11.24.

Table 11.13 Maximum Crash Time and Crash Cost per Time Unit for Example Network

Activity	Normal Time (weeks)	Crash Time (weeks)	Normal Cost (per week)	Crash Cost	Maximum Crash Time (weeks)	Crash Cost per week
A (1,2)	4	3	$3,000	$3,300	1	300
B (1,3)	3	2	2,100	2,450	1	350
C (2,4)	6	3	7,200	9,300	3	700
D (2,5)	5	5	2,200	2,200	—	—
E (3,5)	7	5	3,400	3,900	2	250
F (3,6)	5	2	2,800	3,400	3	200
G (4,8)	5	4	3,000	3,650	1	650
H (5,7)	8	6	6,000	7,500	2	750
I (6,7)	4	3	1,600	1,750	1	150
J (7,8)	2	2	800	800	—	—
		$32,100	$38,250			

With this information, it is possible to crash the network. We will do so first manually and then using LP. Crashing can be approached from two directions: crashing to a predetermined stopping point or goal (e.g., a deadline date); or crashing the network until it can be reduced no further. The results are plotted on a curve, showing the possible reductions and costs, and, finally, the completion date that best satisfies the time and cost requirements is selected. We will demonstrate the latter method.

The network in Figure 11.24 has a project completion time of 20 weeks (critical path B-E-H-J) at a total cost of $32,100. Using all crash times and analyzing the project again, we determine a project completion time of 16 weeks (the critical path would be A-D-H-J) at a total maximum cost of $38,250. The actual crash cost may be less, however, since no additional money is spent to crash activities unnecessarily; that is, noncritical activities are not crashed. The project can be crashed only to 16 weeks.

Since the objective of project crashing is to reduce the project duration time, and project duration can be shortened only by shortening critical activities, we start the crashing process by looking at the critical activities. Although this implies that not all activities must be crashed, be aware that, as the critical activities are crashed, the critical path may change and previously noncritical activities may become critical and thus require crashing.

To crash a project network, at each iteration:

1. Identify, from the critical path, the activity with the minimum crash cost per unit of time. If there is more than one critical path, select the activity or activities with the minimum aggregate crash cost (either a common activity or one from each path).
2. Crash the selected activity(ies) as much as possible, that is, to the crash limit or to the point where another path becomes critical, whichever comes first.
3. Revise the network (adjust the network for the time and cost changes made to the crashed activity(ies), determine the critical path(s), and repeat the process until either a critical path is completely crashed or the desired goal is reached.

Thus for this network, we select that activity on the critical path having the minimum crash cost per week—activity E with a per-week crash cost of $250. This is crashed as far as possible without causing another path to become critical—one week. According to Table 11.13, activity E has a maximum crash time of two weeks. Since path A-D-H-J becomes critical at 19 weeks, however, activity E is crashed only one week. Thus at iteration 1, we have reduced critical activity E by one week, reducing the project duration to 19 weeks, at an increased cost of $250. This result is shown in Figure 11.25(a).

Next, we must once again identify the activity to crash. Since there are now two critical paths, we need an activity from each. The two critical paths have an activity in common, H, which could be crashed, shortening both paths simultaneously. It has a crash cost per week of $750, however, which is higher than the combined costs of two different activities—A at $300 and E at $250. We crash each of these to its limit, one week. At iteration 2, critical activities A and E have each been crashed by one week, reducing the project completion time to 18 weeks and increasing total cost by an additional $550. Figure 11.25(b) shows this outcome.

For the next iteration, the same two paths remain critical. For path A-D-H-J, only activity H can be crashed, since activity A has been crashed to its limit and activities D and J cannot be crashed. Activity H is common to both paths. We can crash it to the limit (two weeks) without another path becoming critical. Thus, at the end of this iteration, we have reduced the completion time to 16 weeks, increasing the cost by another $1,500. This result is shown in Figure 11.25(c).

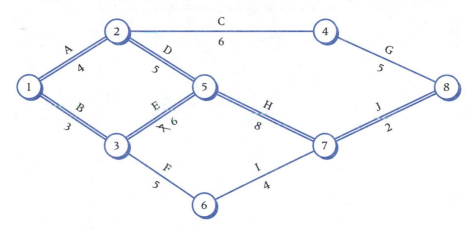

Figure 11.25(a) Crashing the Project Network

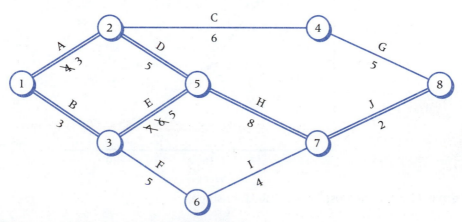

Figure 11.25(b) Crashing the Project Network

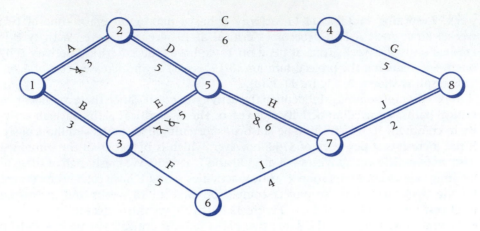

Figure 11.25(c) Crashing the Project Network

Table 11.14 Summary of Crashing Process

Iteration	Changes	Completion Time	Project Cost	Critical Path
—	—	20	$32,100	B–E–H–J
1	Crash activity E 1 week	19	32,350	B–E–H–J
				A–D–H–J
				B–E–H–J
2	Crash activities (1,2) and (3,5) each 1 week	18	32,900	A–D–H–J
3	Crash activity (5,7) 2 weeks	16	34,400	B–E–H–J
				A–D–H–J

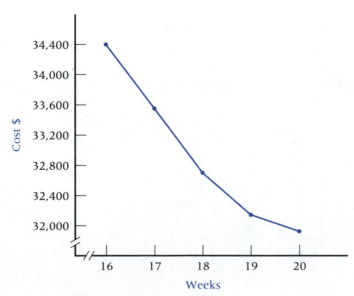

Figure 11.26 Time/Cost Tradeoff Relationship

With this iteration, we have reached the crashing point. Notice that the critical path A-D-H-J has been completely crashed. The total additional cost is $2,300. There are two critical paths, A-D-H-J and B-E-H-J. Three of the 10 activities were crashed. Table 11.14 summarizes these changes.

Figure 11.26 shows the time/cost tradeoff relationship for this network. With this information, the project manager can select the plan that best satisfies both time and cost requirements. The costs considered in crashing are the direct costs only. To make a decision on the best completion time, given time and cost considerations, the manager also must take into account indirect costs (overhead, interest, utilities) and penalties assessed.

From even this short demonstration of manual crashing, you can see that crashing a project manually can be cumbersome and time consuming. On large projects, it is virtually impossible. Manual crashing has been included in this chapter to help you better understand the crashing process. LP provides an alternative method that is more practical for larger problems.

Project Crashing with Linear Programming

When formulating a crashing problem using linear programming, the network is crashed to a predetermined time. We will use the same problem we crashed manually and assume the network will be crashed to 16 weeks. The objective is to crash the network to 16 weeks while keeping the crashing costs to a minimum. Let CT_k be the number of weeks activity k is crashed. The objective function for this problem can then be stated as

$$\text{MIN } 300CT_A + 350CT_B + 700CT_C + 0CT_D + 250CT_E + 200CT_F$$
$$+ 650CT_G + 750CT_H + 150CT_I + 0CT_J$$

The maximum amount of time each activity can be crashed (CT_k) is known and can be expressed as a constraint. The maximum crash time constraints for this problem are

$$CT_A \leq 1$$
$$CT_B \leq 1$$
$$CT_C \leq 3$$
$$CT_D = 0$$
$$CT_E \leq 2$$
$$CT_F \leq 3$$
$$CT_G \leq 1$$
$$CT_H \leq 2$$
$$CT_I \leq 1$$
$$CT_J = 0$$

The next constraints will represent the latest finish times for all activities terminating at a particular node j. More than one activity can end at a given node, but recall that all activities that end at the same node have the same latest finish times, since the latest finish times are all set equal to the latest start time for the successor activity. Thus, if we use the variable LF_j to represent the latest finish time at node j, it will represent the latest finish time for all activities terminating at that node. In the example, node 8 is the last node in the network. Since we wish to crash the network to 16 weeks, we set LF_8 equal to 16. The latest start for activity J is then equal to 14 ($16 - 2 = 14$) plus any time that activity J is crashed. The latest start time can be expressed by

$$LS_7 \leq LF_8 - t_{eJ} + CT_J \quad [11.1]$$

and since the latest finish for all activities at node 7 is equal to this latest start time,

$$LF_7 = LS_7 \quad [11.2]$$

that is, the latest finishes for activities H and I are equal to the latest start for activity J. Substituting equation 11.2 into equation 11.1, we can state the relationship as

$$LF_7 \leq LF_8 - t_{eJ} + CT_J \quad [11.3]$$

We can generalize this expression for any activity beginning at node i and ending at node j as follows:

$$LF_i \leq LF_j - t_{eij} + CT_{ij} \quad [11.4]$$

This inequality can be rewritten in terms of the latest finish at node j as

$$LF_j \geq LF_i + t_{eij} - CT_{ij} \quad [11.5]$$

Using this form, the constraints for activities G and J, which both end at node 8, are as follows:

$$LF_8 \geq LF_7 + 2 - CT_J \quad [J]$$

$$LF_8 \geq LF_4 + 5 - CT_G \quad [G]$$

The activity represented by each constraint is shown in brackets following the constraint. Activities H and I both end at node 7. These activities are represented by the constraints

$$LF_7 \geq LF_5 + 8 - CT_H \quad [H]$$

$$LF_7 \geq LF_6 + 4 - CT_I \quad [I]$$

The constraints for the remaining activities are shown below.

$$LF_6 \geq LF_3 + 5 - CT_F \quad [F]$$

$$LF_5 \geq LF_3 + 7 - CT_E \quad [E]$$

$$LF_5 \geq LF_2 + 5 - CT_D \quad [D]$$

$$LF_4 \geq LF_2 + 6 - CT_C \quad [C]$$

$$LF_3 \geq LF_1 + 3 - CT_B \quad [B]$$

$$LF_2 \geq LF_1 + 4 - CT_A \quad [A]$$

We can rearrange each of these inequalities to place all variables on the LHS and all constants on the RHS. For example,

$$LF_2 \geq LF_1 + 4 - CT_A$$

becomes

$$LF_2 - LF_1 + CT_A \geq 4$$

The problem can be simplified somewhat. Variables CT_D and CT_J are both equal to zero and can be dropped from the objective function and constraints. The complete LP formulation is then

MIN $300CT_A + 350CT_B + 700CT_C + 250CT_E + 200CT_F + 650CT_G$
$+ 750CT_H + 150CT_I$

subject to

$$CT_A \leq 1$$
$$CT_B \leq 1$$
$$CT_C \leq 3$$
$$CT_E \leq 2$$
$$CT_F \leq 3$$
$$CT_G \leq 1$$
$$CT_H \leq 2$$
$$CT_I \leq 1$$
$$LF_2 + CT_A \geq 4$$
$$LF_3 + CT_B \geq 3$$
$$LF_4 - LF_2 + CT_C \geq 6$$
$$LF_6 - LF_3 + CT_F \geq 5$$
$$LF_5 - LF_2 \geq 5$$
$$LF_7 - LF_3 + CT_E \geq 7$$
$$LF_7 - LF_5 + CT_H \geq 8$$
$$LF_7 - LF_6 + CT_I \geq 4$$
$$LF_8 - LF_4 + CT_G \geq 5$$
$$LF_8 - LF_7 \geq 2$$
$$LF_8 = 16$$

$$\text{all } LF_i \text{ and } CT_{ij} \geq 0$$

The computer solution to this problem is

$$CT_A = 1$$
$$CT_E = 2$$
$$CT_H = 2$$
$$LF_2 = 3$$
$$LF_3 = 3$$
$$LF_4 = 9$$
$$LF_5 = 8$$
$$LF_6 = 8$$
$$LF_7 = 14$$
$$LF_8 = 16$$
$$Zmin = 2300$$

This solution is identical to the solution obtained when crashing the network manually. Activity A is crashed 1 week and activities E and H are crashed 2 weeks each. The normal cost for the network was $32,100. That cost has been increased by $2,300 (the cost of crashing) to $34,400.

11.5 *PERT/COST*

In addition to the scheduling and monitoring of the project, a project manager must also be concerned with cost management. For most organizations, the need to pay for individual project activities creates a demand on both the overall budget and the day-to-day cash flow. In order to handle these budget demands effectively, management must know when the demands will occur. For any project, the times when activities are scheduled determines when the budget demands occur. Effective cost management also requires the periodic review of expenditures, comparing actual costs to budgeted costs, and undertaking corrective action when necessary to reduce overruns. The **PERT/Cost** system is used both to predict cash flow and to monitor and control project costs.

PERT/Cost is essentially an accounting system that is organized on a project basis, using the project activities as the basic element of control. The cost of each activity is known (or should be). This cost is generally assumed to be expended at a constant rate during that activity's duration. That is, costs are assumed to be linear over time. For example, if an activity cost is $2,000 and it takes five weeks to complete the activity, we assume there is a $400-per-week expenditure. With some computer packages, this assumption may not be necessary.

The PERT/Cost procedure requires the construction of two tables showing budgeted cash expenditures: one with all activities starting at the earliest start times, and one with all activities starting at the latest start time. Each assumes that activity costs are expended at a uniform rate. For this discussion, we will use the same project we used to demonstrate project crashing, shown above in Figure 11.23.

Table 11.15 shows weekly cash expenditures with activities beginning at their early start times. Notice that rows in the table represent the activities (one row for each activity) and columns represent weeks. Budget demands are recorded in the appropriate weeks, as determined by the earliest start time. Note that earliest start refers to the end of the appropriate week. For example, activity E, which has an early start time of three weeks, begins at the end of three weeks. It is shown in the table begining after week 3 ends (i.e., at week 4). The final two rows show total weekly cost (column total) and cumulative cost to date. Total cost of the project is the total cumulative cost at the end of the project (week 20). Table 11.16 shows weekly cash expenditures for this project assuming that each activity will start at its latest start time.

This information, which is summarized in Table 11.17 and graphed in Figure 11.27, shows the range between the expected cumulative outflow depending on starting time. The shaded area between the lines on the graph shows the area of feasible budgets for total budget costs—if the project is completed on time. Since actual budget demands should fall within this shaded area, management can anticipate budget demands.

Since a time/cost tradeoff usually is associated with the expenditure of money, if activities are not begun until their late start times, the expenditures are deferred and an interest savings may be realized. This can be done only with projects that have fairly deterministic times, so that waiting to begin activities (at late start times) does not increase the risk of delaying the project.

In addition to predicting cash outflows, effective cost management requires monitoring and controlling costs. That is, management must compare actual ex-

Table 11.15 Weekly Expenditures, Early Start Times

	\multicolumn{20}{c}{Week}

	1	2	3	4	5	6	7	8	9	10	11	12	13	14	15	16	17	18	19	20
A	750	750	750	750																
B	700	700	700																	
C					1200	1200	1200	1200	1200	1200										
D					440	440	440	440	440											
E				500	500	500	500	500	500	500										
F				560	560	560	560	560												
G											600	600	600	600	600					
H											750	750	750	750	750	750	750	750		
I									400	400	400	400								
J																			400	400
Weekly Total	1450	1450	1450	1810	2700	2700	2700	2700	2540	2100	1750	1750	1350	1350	1350	750	750	750	400	400
Cumulative	1450	2900	4350	6160	8860	11560	14260	16960	19500	21600	23350	25100	26450	27800	29150	29900	30650	31400	31800	32200

Table 11.16 Weekly Expenditures, Late Start Times

	\multicolumn{20}{c}{Week}

	1	2	3	4	5	6	7	8	9	10	11	12	13	14	15	16	17	18	19	20
A		750	750	750	750															
B	700	700	700																	
C									1200	1200	1200	1200	1200	1200						
D						440	440	440	440	440										
E				500	500	500	500	500	500	500										
F										560	560	560	560	560						
G																600	600	600	600	600
H											750	750	750	750	750	750	750	750		
I															400	400	400	400		
J																			400	400
Weekly Total	700	1450	1450	1250	1250	940	940	940	2140	2700	2510	2510	2510	2510	1150	1750	1750	1750	1000	1000
Cumulative	700	2150	3600	4850	6100	7040	7980	8920	11060	13760	16270	18780	21290	23800	24950	26700	28450	30200	31200	32200

Table 11.17 Range of Weekly Cash Demands

Week	Cash Outflow w/LS	Cash Outflow w/ES
1	700	1450
2	2150	2900
3	3600	4350
4	4850	6160
5	6100	8860
6	7040	11560
7	7980	14260
8	8920	16960
9	11060	19500
10	13760	21600
11	16270	23350
12	18780	25100
13	21290	26450
14	23800	27800
15	24950	29150
16	26700	29900
17	28450	30650
18	30200	31400
19	31200	31800
20	32000	32200

penditures with planned expenditures and take any remedial action necessary to reduce cost overruns. Monitoring project costs is facilitated by a PERT/Cost report comparing actual to budgeted costs, which is produced at regular intervals. This report identifies activities that are projected to have cost overruns (or underruns). Table 11.18 shows a PERT/Cost report for our example, assuming 12 weeks have elapsed. We prepare the report by comparing, for each activity, actual cost to date with budgeted cost to date. We calculate budgeted cost to date for each activity using the formula

$$\text{Budgeted Cost to date} = \frac{\text{Percentage of work completed}}{100} \times \text{Budget}$$

In other words, we assume that the percentage of the budget used up by an activity is the same as the percentage of that activity that is completed.

The table shows the percentage of each activity completed; total budget for each activity; budgeted cost to date (figured as shown above); the amount that has actually been expended to date; and the cost overrun to date. Cost overrun is figured by subtracting column 3 (budgeted cost to date) from column 4 (actual cost to date). If there is a surplus, or underrun, the figure is negative (in parenthesis). Thus, after 12 weeks have been completed, we can determine that the situation is well under control for the four completed activities, A, B, D, and E, with a total overrun of only $50. For activity C, however, which is two-thirds completed, notice that there is a significant cost overrun ($700). Some managerial intervention will be necessary to keep the project cost within budget.

PERT/Cost can be an effective control procedure, but there can be certain problems with implementation. For example, if some overhead costs are common to

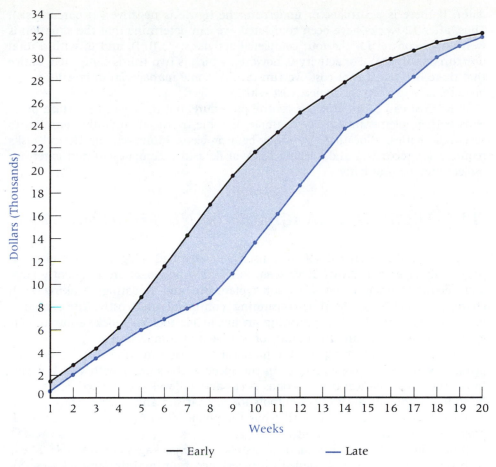

Figure 11.27 Graph of Cumulative Weekly Expenditures

Table 11.18 Pert/Cost Report after 12 weeks

Activity	Percent Complete	Budget	Budgeted To Date	Actual To Date	Overrun To Date
A	100	3000	3000	2900	(100)
B	100	2100	2100	2300	200
C	66.66	7200	4800	5500	700
D	100	2200	2200	2200	—
E	100	3500	3500	3450	(50)
F	60	2800	1680	1800	120
G	0	3000	0	0	0
H	25	6000	1500	1400	(100)
I	0	1600	0	0	0
J	0	800	0	0	0

several activities, allocating them may be a problem. Moreover, the clerical tasks required for recording and keeping track of data in a complicated and extensive project may be prohibitive.

date). If there is a surplus, or underrun, the figure is negative (in parenthesis). Thus, after 12 weeks have been completed, we can determine that the situation is well under control for the four completed activities, A, B, D, and E, with a total overrun of only $50. For activity C, however, which is two-thirds completed, notice that there is a significant cost overrun ($700). Some managerial intervention will be necessary to keep the project cost within budget.

PERT/Cost can be an effective control procedure, but there can be certain problems with implementation. For example, if some overhead costs are common to several activities, allocating them may be a problem. Moreover, the clerical tasks required for recording and keeping track of data in a complicated and extensive project may be prohibitive.

11.6 *PROJECT MANAGEMENT AND THE COMPUTER*

Computers and specialized software packages have had a significant impact on project management. As we have seen, PERT/CPM networks are frequently large and require numerous revisions for replanning and updating. Making such changes manually can be time-consuming, confusing, and costly. The computer has changed that situation, providing an invaluable tool for quick, accurate network analysis and easing the burden of change and comparison.

The computer cannot replace the manager's decision making role. Rather, the primary value of the computer lies in the speed and accuracy with which it performs the mathematical computations necessary to develop the schedules, and in its ability to provide a variety of outputs for comparison and control. Thus, project management software is a tool that has the potential to help management with project scheduling and cost control.

Today, hundreds of project management software packages are available. Many such programs have been designed (or redesigned from mainframe packages) for the self-contained desktop computer. For instance, the *Project Management Software Directory* by Jack Gido, published in 1985 by Industrial Press (listed in our bibliography), which does not claim to be all-inclusive, compares the features of over 100 packages. These packages vary widely with respect to cost, features, ease of use, and type of computer required.

In a recent article for *P&IM Review and APICS News*[1], Smith and Gupta identify certain functions and programs that should be a basic part of any project management program. These include calculation of network times; evaluation and checking of network logic; optimizing capability in the tradeoff of cost and resources; resource leveling and balancing; and scheduling using calendar times. Furthermore, according to Smith and Gupta, the ideal system would require these five items of input data: the work breakdown structure; immediate predecessors for each activity; immediate successors of each activity; time estimates for each activity and an estimate of required resources; and other direct costs. These inputs would enable the program to generate:

1. An on-screen and plotter or printer network
2. A schedule using calendar dates
3. A budget

[1]Larry A. Smith and Sushil Gupta, "Project Management Software in P&IM," *P&IM Review and APICS News* (June, 1985): 66–68.

4. A baseline plan for control
5. A resource histogram

While the ideal has not been achieved, the state of the art for project management software is at an advanced stage. Another study, by Smith and Mills, was published in *Project Management Quarterly*.[2] The authors compared 40 packages and reported that over 85 percent had the following features:

1. Gantt charts
2. Calendar dating
3. Flexible report generation
4. Networks generated by plotters
5. Cost control and cost reporting
6. Resource allocation (enabling the user to balance resources and at the same time adjust the schedule)
7. Capability for easy updating

Despite the many packages available and the advanced state of the art, using project management software is not without problems. Using more advanced software may require a great deal of training and support, and may prove too costly. Furthermore, updating the data files may be too difficult for clerical help. Management must decide whether the need justifies the cost of using the computer and advanced software.

Figure 11.28 shows the output for the IS Lab problem using the instructional software that accompanies this book. Figure 11.29 shows the same problem output using Harvard Total Project Manager, one of the earlier and more popular products on the market.

[2]Larry A. Smith and Joan Mills, "Project Management Network Programs," *Project Management Quarterly* (June, 1982): 18–29.

ACTIVITY	IMMEDIATE PREDECESSOR	EXPECTED (t)	VAR
A		5.00	1.78
B	A	8.00	1.00
C		6.00	1.00
D	A	8.00	1.78
E	C	5.00	2.78
F	C	3.00	0.44
G	E,F	3.00	0.11
H		10.00	1.00
I	B,G	2.00	0.00
J	D,H,I	2.00	0.11

Press any key to continue.

ACT	EARLY START	LATE START	EARLY FINISH	LATE FINISH	SLACK (LS-ES)	CRITICAL PATH
A	0.0	1.0	5.0	6.0	1.0	
B	5.0	6.0	13.0	14.0	1.0	
C	0.0	0.0	6.0	6.0	0.0	YES
D	5.0	8.0	13.0	16.0	3.0	

ACT	EARLY START	LATE START	EARLY FINISH	LATE FINISH	SLACK (LS-ES)	CRITICAL PATH
E	6.0	6.0	11.0	11.0	0.0	YES
F	6.0	8.0	9.0	11.0	2.0	
G	11.0	11.0	14.0	14.0	0.0	YES
H	0.0	6.0	10.0	16.0	6.0	
I	14.0	14.0	16.0	16.0	0.0	YES
J	16.0	16.0	18.0	18.0	0.0	YES

CRITICAL PATH: C–E–G–I–J

NETWORK COMPLETION TIME = 18
VARIANCE ON CRITICAL PATH = 4
STANDARD DEVIATION ON CRITICAL PATH = 2

Press any key to continue.

Figure 11.28 PERT Computer Output

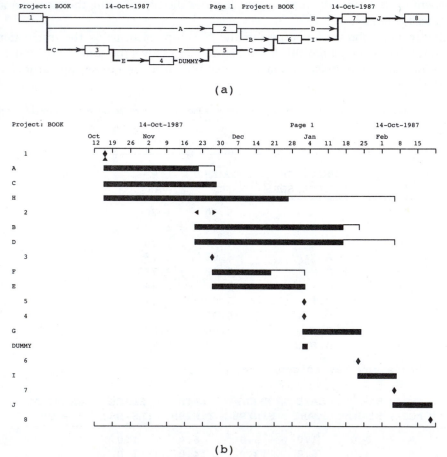

(a)

(b)

Figure 11.29 Output from Harvard Total Project Manager

The research and development department at Markham-Rogers, a manufacturer of spectrographic testing equipment, has recently developed a new model. M-R management feels this new model will fill an existing void in its current product line, and wishes to bring it to market as soon as possible. Since this new model is a variation of current models, using existing technology, M-R can begin production almost immediately. The marketing department is responsible for introducing new products. Management recognizes, however, that in the past the marketing campaign has lagged behind the production schedule. That is, the marketing department has not been entirely reliable. When a new product has been developed and readied for marketing, the marketing campaign has not been completed. As a result, M-R has lost valuable time. This time, management insists that the marketing department be better prepared and that the marketing campaign and production be synchronized.

Data Preparation/Problem Formulation

A marketing project for introducing new products includes a myriad of activities—preparing the necessary promotional material, conducting and evaluating marketing studies, developing brochures, setting prices, and so on. George McGuire, a project manager for M-R, met with the marketing people. Together they developed a list of marketing activities that must be accomplished, along with immediate predecessors and estimated durations. The table below summarizes this information.

ACTIVITY	IMMEDIATE PREDECESSORS	OPTIMISTIC TIME	MOST LIKELY TIME	PESSIMISTIC TIME
A	—	6	7	14
B	—	5	7	9
C	—	4	6	8
D	A	3	5	7
E	D	4	12	14
F	B	6	7	11
G	C	2	3	10
H	C	1	1	4
I	G	9	12	15
J	H	12	15	18
K	F	2	3	7
L	E	2	3	4
M	K, L	2	8	20
N	I, J	5	6	7
O	E	2	9	10
P	M, N, O	11	13	15

M-R management has instructed George to create a project schedule that includes starting dates for each activity. Moreover, the project should begin as soon as possible (the following Monday, April 16). M-R works a five-day week, and is closed on Memorial Day (May 28) and July 4. Management wants to know the likelihood the project will be completed by the end of June 29, for a July 2 (Monday) release date.

Computer Solution

ACTIVITY	IMMEDIATE PREDECESSOR	EXPECTED (t)	VAR
A	—	8.00	1.78
B	—	7.00	0.44
C	—	6.00	0.44
D	A	5.00	0.44
E	D	11.00	2.78
F	B	7.50	0.69
G	C	4.00	1.78
H	C	1.50	0.25
I	G	12.00	1.00
J	H	15.00	1.00
K	F	3.50	0.69
L	E	3.00	0.11
M	K,L	9.00	9.00
N	I,J	6.00	0.11
O	E	8.00	1.78
P	M,N,O	13.00	0.44

ACT	EARLY START	LATE START	EARLY FINISH	LATE FINISH	SLACK (LS–ES)	CRITICAL PATH
A	0.0	0.0	8.0	8.0	0.0	YES
B	0.0	9.0	7.0	16.0	9.0	
C	0.0	7.5	6.0	13.5	7.5	
D	8.0	8.0	13.0	13.0	0.0	YES
E	13.0	13.0	24.0	24.0	0.0	YES
F	7.0	16.0	14.5	23.5	9.0	
G	6.0	14.0	10.0	18.0	8.0	
H	6.0	13.5	7.5	15.0	7.5	
I	10.0	18.0	22.0	30.0	8.0	
J	7.5	15.0	22.5	30.0	7.5	
K	14.5	23.5	18.0	27.0	9.0	
L	24.0	24.0	27.0	27.0	0.0	YES
M	27.0	27.0	36.0	36.0	0.0	YES
N	22.5	30.0	28.5	36.0	7.5	
O	24.0	28.0	32.0	36.0	4.0	
P	36.0	36.0	49.0	49.0	0.0	YES

CRITICAL PATH: A–D–E–L–M–P
NETWORK COMPLETION TIME = 49
VARIANCE ON CRITICAL PATH = 14.55
STANDARD DEVIATION ON CRITICAL PATH = 3.81

Interpretation and Analysis of the Results

The computer solution indicates that this network has an expected completion time of 49 days. It also shows that activities A, D, E, L, M, and P are on the critical path. Given that the time estimates are probabilistic, George can determine the probability of completion of this project by July 2. There are 54 working days between April 16 and July 2. The computer solution shows the standard deviation on the critical path to be 3.81 days. Therefore, 54 days is 1.312 standard deviations to the right of the mean (49 days). Using a table for the area under the normal curve, George can determine the probability of completion within 54 days to be approximately 90.52 percent. If this probability is not satisfactory, one or more of the activities on the critical path can be shortened. (A probability of completion of 99 percent would require an expected completion time of approximately 45 days.)

What Happens Next

After meeting with management and informing them of the probability of completion by July 2 (90.5 percent), George received approval to begin the project. George began by setting up a schedule of start and completion dates for each activity. This schedule is shown in the table below. All times are as of 8:00 AM on the given day; in other words, an activity that will be completed at 5:00 PM on April 25 is shown as being finished at 8:00 AM on April 26.

Activity	Early Start Date	Early Finish Date	Late Start Date	Late Finish Date
A	4/16	4/26	4/16	4/26
B	4/16	4/25	4/26	5/ 7
C	4/16	4/24	4/25	5/ 3
D	4/26	5/ 3	4/26	5/ 3
E	5/ 3	5/18	5/ 3	5/18
F	4/25	5/ 7	5/ 7	5/17
G	4/24	4/30	5/ 4	5/10
H	4/24	4/26	5/ 3	5/ 7
I	4/30	5/16	5/10	5/29
J	4/26	5/17	5/ 7	5/29
K	5/ 7	5/11	5/17	5/23
L	5/18	5/23	5/18	5/23
M	5/23	6/ 6	5/23	6/ 6
N	5/17	5/25	5/29	6/ 6
O	5/18	5/31	5/24	6/ 6
P	6/ 6	6/25	6/25	6/25

George also used an available software package to create a Gantt chart for this project. It is shown below.

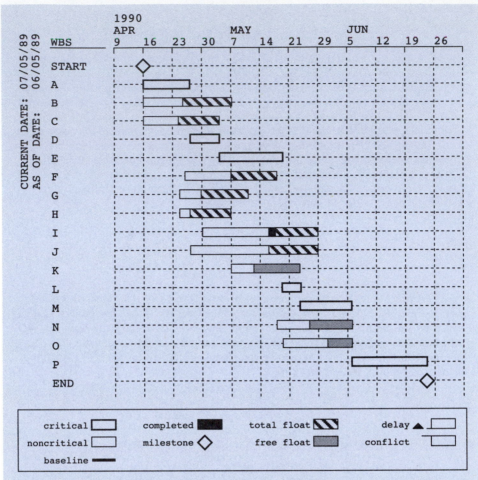

George's next step was to notify each marketing staff member responsible for a particular activity about that activity's start and completion times. He also told marketing to notify him immediately if any delays occurred. George then set the first and third Monday in each month as review points. On these days, he would formally review the project's progress with all the people involved in the project.

After reviewing the Gantt chart, George also scheduled a meeting with the marketing manager. He had noticed that activities E, I, J, and K all would occur simultaneously during the second week in May, and he was concerned that some of the same marketing people would be assigned to more than one of these tasks. He knew such assignments would cause these people to be overloaded. While he knew that some of the work on activities I, J, and K could be delayed, he wanted to ensure that the project was not delayed due to careless scheduling of staff.

11.7 *CONCLUDING REMARKS*

Managing large, complex projects is a significant problem in society today. Because of the unique, complex, and costly nature of most projects, their management presents special difficulties. PERT/CPM is one of the most frequently used management planning tools, providing a systematic technique that can aid in the planning, scheduling, and controlling of projects. Seat-of-the-pants project management is rapidly giving way to highly sophisticated computer programs that integrate the best features of PERT and CPM with other software, including spreadsheet functions. In this chapter, we have barely been able to scratch the surface of project management.

PERT/CPM is a valuable tool because (1) it requires those involved to analyze and understand the project thoroughly in order to identify the project activities, establish predecessor relationships, and estimate activity durations and resource requirements; (2) the network concisely displays the complex interrelationship among the project activities; (3) the planning and scheduling stages not only identify critical activities but also indicate the degree to which the other activities are noncritical; and (4) the fundamental concepts are fairly easy to understand.

The computer has had a major impact on the use of PERT/CPM. Large projects, often requiring thousands of nodes, may require a network diagram that covers several walls. Changes are time-consuming and can be confusing. Today, computer programs provide an invaluable tool for quick, accurate network analysis, performing the mathematical computations necessary to develop the schedules. Multiple runs that span the life of the project are common and are accomplished with relative ease.

Finally, we should note that the use of PERT/CPM (or any project management tool) does not guarantee the success of a project. When combined with the qualitative tools of those involved in the project—their experiences, common sense, and intuition—PERT/CPM will increase the likelihood of success.

Management Science Application _____

MILTON ROY ANALYTICAL PRODUCTS DIVISION[3]

The Analytical Products Division of Milton Roy manufactures spectrophotometers, refractometers, and diffraction gratings. The spectrophotometers, produced under the SPECTRONIC trademark, enable users to perform spectroscopic analysis of their products to ensure product quality. Milton Roy is a major producer of this equipment and has some instruments that have been on the market for over 38 years. There are currently eleven different models in the SPECTRONIC series, covering a broad market range in terms of price and performance. These instruments vary in the spectroscopic technique used (Milton Roy is a pioneer in the use of diode array technology in compact bench-top instruments) and the amount of computer integration built into the product. Basic instruments contain preprogrammed microprocessors, while the more complex instruments are integrated with fully programmable PCs. This paper focuses upon Milton Roy's use of project management techniques to evaluate the feasibility of introducing new products into the market.

The development and introduction of new products in the SPECTRONIC line is based upon a number of factors, but two primary questions must be answered:

1. What value will this product have in the marketplace?
2. How long will it take to bring this product to the market?

[3]The authors are indebted to Cornelius J. McCarthy and the management of the Milton Roy Analytical Products Division for providing this application. Because this information pertains to proprietary Milton Roy development, the details have been modified somewhat for clarity and to protect proprietary information.

The value in the marketplace determines the potential sales of the product and the price that will be charged for it. The time required to bring the product to the market has an impact on its cost and on the ability and/or willingness of the company to undertake the project. Thus, new products undergo careful analysis to determine the answers to these key questions. This analysis also includes the determination of such factors as the technical design of the product; possible configurations; the amount of computer integration; and the time required to build and test a prototype, to begin actual production of the product, to prepare manuals and marketing brochures, and so on. In many cases, tradeoffs between higher costs and shorter times can play a significant part in a product's eventual development.

Before proceeding with new products, however, the company must have a fairly good estimate of how long it will take and how much it will cost to bring a new product to market. Once these questions have been answered, management can make the decision to proceed or not to proceed with this product. The following discussion describes how project management techniques were used to facilitate the introduction of a new product.

Cornelius McCarthy, Director of Instrument Research and Development, uses interdisciplinary teams to develop project plans for new products. But instead of simply assigning one group to develop the project plans for a proposed product, he attempts to have multiple teams working independently to develop these plans.

For this product, McCarthy began by providing training in the techniques of project management for all personnel who would be involved in these planning teams. This training provided a common knowledge base and approach to project planning. He then allowed several people to purchase and use different project management software packages. After these packages were tested and compared, one package was selected as the common package to be used in developing project plans. This package has the ability to prepare both Gantt charts and PERT networks and to track both costs and the use of resources. Training was then provided that integrated this particular software package with the typical project management techniques.

At the conclusion of this training, the class was divided into four different teams, and each team was given the task of preparing a project plan for the introduction of a new product that would fill a perceived gap in the existing product line. The basic technological approach and the resources available were predefined, to ensure that each group would be using common terminology and resources in planning this product. A joint meeting was also held with all teams. This meeting addressed the major questions regarding the technological approach and the product performance and marketing considerations. The meeting concluded with all teams in agreement on the major controlling factors for this project. When teams determined that additional or new resources were required, they requested them from McCarthy. If he agreed, those resources were added to the list and were made available to all teams.

The team efforts culminated in a meeting where each team was given the opportunity to present its proposed plan. These plans included timelines for the project, the anticipated product cost, and the projected development costs. After each team made its presentation, the plans were compared and discussed, with the teams moving toward consensus on the project plan. The result of this meeting was agreement on a plan with accompanying time estimates and costs. These figures were then used to perform net present value analysis. On the basis of this analysis, it was decided that this particular product could be brought to market in a timely fashion with a reasonable expected return, and the product was approved.

One of the major advantages of this multiple team approach lies in the time estimates produced by each team. As plans from the multiple teams are compared, some elements are in common while others are dependent upon the design selected by each team. With regard to these common elements, if all teams are in relative agreement on the amount of time necessary to perform a given project task, it can be assumed that the time estimate is fairly accurate. The times required for instrument castings and covers and for items purchased externally are examples of time estimates that normally have a high degree of agreement. Conversely, for some common tasks there may be wide disagreement on the time estimate that cannot be resolved during the meeting. This disagreement is typically due to one of the following causes: (1) a misunderstanding of the input definitions or requirements; (2) uncertainty regarding a new technological approach (including whether or not it will actually work); or (3) a history of difficulty with this particular task. If the cause of the disagreement is differing assumptions or poor input definitions, clarification and subsequent recycling of the planning process should resolve these differences. Normally, however, this variance is related to the latter two causes. These indicate that the tasks have associated risks that will require closer attention and control during the actual project.

Tasks that are plan-specific—that is, tasks that are dependent upon a team's choice of approach or design—have different time estimates associated with them. These estimates often have a major impact upon the project's total estimated completion time. In these cases, the differences in estimated times can affect the product design chosen for implementation. For example, if time required to bring a product to market is considered crucial, the design plan with the shorter completion time may be chosen, assuming performance factors are acceptable.

An additional advantage of this multi-team approach is that it involves a larger number of people. While working on the project plans, those people tend to become committed to the project. When the project is approved, therefore, the staff is already motivated to see it through to completion.

GLOSSARY

activity a task or job, having a cost and a duration, that must be completed as part of a project; in a PERT/CPM network it is represented by an arrow or directed branch

activity slack length of time an activity can be delayed without affecting the duration of the entire project

backward pass procedure moving backward through the network, beginning at project termination node, used to determine latest start and finish times

beta distribution a continuous, unimodal, not necessarily symmetrical probability distribution used to determine expected activity times in network analysis

CPM (critical path method) project management technique, similar to PERT, which adds the concept of cost

crash cost cost to complete activity under crash or expedited conditions (c_c)

crash time least possible time it can take to complete an activity, using special efforts and concentrating resources (t_c)

crashing method used to shorten an activity duration; time/cost tradeoff analysis used to reduce project time at minimum cost

critical activities activities on the critical path; delaying completion of any of these will delay entire project, as they have zero slack

critical path longest path through a network; the sum of times of activities on critical path gives project completion time

dummy activity used in the construction of a network to ensure that proper precedence is maintained and to avoid having two nodes directly connected by more than one activity; represented with a broken line; uses no resources, incurs no cost, and has a time duration of zero

earliest (event) time (ET) earliest time an event can occur, immediately after all preceding activities have been completed

earliest finish time earliest time at which an activity can be completed

earliest start time earliest time at which an activity can start

event project milestones, nodes in a network, points in time, representing the termination of all activities leading into the node and beginning of all activities emanating from the node

expected time average time for an activity, calculated as weighted average $(a + 4m + b)/6$

forward pass procedure moving forward through network, beginning at project initiation; used to determine earliest start and finish times

gantt chart bar chart showing on a horizontal time line the start and finish times of each activity in a project

immediate predecessor an activity that immediately precedes a given activity; immediately prior activity that has to be completed before the given activity can start

latest finish time latest time at which an activity can be completed without delaying the completion of the entire project

latest start time latest time at which an activity can begin without delaying completion of the project

latest (event) time (LT) latest time an event can occur without delaying entire project

most likely time time that an activity would take under normal conditions, or if it were repeated numerous times (denoted by m)

nodes connections or junctions of a network; the circles that represent the beginning and ending of activities

normal cost cost to complete an activity under normal or ordinary conditions (c_n)

normal time time to complete an activity under ordinary conditions (t_n)

optimistic time minimum time for completing an activity if everything goes well (denoted by a)

PERT (program evaluation review technique) a project management technique used for scheduling and controlling projects, based on representing the project as a network

PERT/Cost project management accounting system used to measure and control project costs throughout duration of project

PERT/CPM term used to describe the project management procedure merging or blending useful features from PERT and CPM

pessimistic time longest possible time for completing an activity, under the most unfavorable conditions when everything goes wrong (denoted by b)

precedence relationship specifies the immediately prior activity or activities for each activity, thus identifying the interrelationship of network activities in a project

slack free time or allowable delay in a network

PROBLEMS

1. Given the following activity and predecessor list, construct a PERT/CPM network.

Activity	Immediate Predecessor
A	—
B	—
C	—
D	A
E	C
F	B, D, E

2. Given the following activity and predecessor list, construct a PERT/CPM network.

Activity	Immediate Predecessor
A	—
B	A
C	A
D	B
E	C
F	C
G	D, E

3. Given the following activity and predecessor list, construct a PERT/CPM network.

Activity	Immediate Predecessor
A	—
B	—
C	A
D	A
E	B
F	C
G	E
H	E
I	D, F, H
J	H

4. Given the following activity and predecessor list, construct a PERT/CPM network.

Activity	Immediate Predecessor
A	—
B	—
C	—
D	A, B
E	A
F	A, B
G	C, D
H	E
I	H, F
J	G

5. Given the following activity and predecessor list, construct a PERT/CPM network.

Activity	Immediate Predecessor
A	—
B	A
C	A
D	A
E	B
F	C
G	C, D
H	B
I	B
J	E, F, G
K	C, D
L	C, D
M	J, K
N	I, L, M
O	I, L, M
P	H, O

6. Computer Operations, Inc., a Rochester, New York–based computer training center, has decided to offer a computer workshop in Miami in February. Since the managers want to ensure that everything goes smoothly, and thereby escape the cold weather for several days, they have listed all the activities that will have to be completed before the conference can begin. Their list is reproduced below:

- Arrange for the conference location with a Miami hotel (A).
- Arrange for computer rentals in Miami (B).

Once the arrangements for the location and computers have been made:

- Have the advertising agency design and place the workshop advertisements (C).
- Prepare a workshop schedule and an outline of the presentation (D).

- Design the brochure to be used in the mass mailing (E).
- Begin to take reservations for the workshop (F).

When the workshop schedule and presentation outline are completed:

- Prepare the handouts and notebooks (G).
- Prepare the disks to be used by the participants (H).
- Prepare the slides to be used to support the presentation (I).

Once the brochure has been designed:

- Have the brochures printed (J).

And after they have been printed:

- Mail the brochures (K).

When all of the reservations have been taken:

- Reserve sufficient guest rooms with the hotel (L).
- Make arrangements for meals for the participants (M).
- Schedule the breaks and snacks with the hotel (N).
- After the workshop schedule is ready, hire additional facilitators for the workshop (O).

Once the additional facilitators have been hired:

- Train the facilitators (P).

After the handouts, notebooks, and disks have been prepared:

- Duplicate them in sufficient quantities for all of the registered participants (Q).

a. Set up a list of all activities and their immediate predecessors.
b. Draw a PERT/CPM network for this project.

7. Identify all the paths in the following network, and indicate the critical path and project duration (activity times are in months).

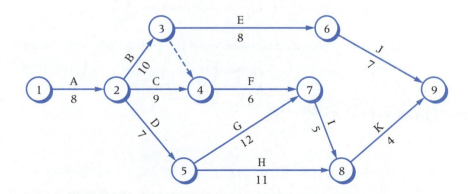

8. For the network in problem 7, determine the earliest and latest start and finish times and slack times. How can you determine the critical path from this information?
9. For the network in problem 7, determine early and late times for each event.

10. Given the following network with activity times in weeks, determine earliest and latest start and finish times and slack times for each activity. Identify the critical path and indicate the expected project duration.

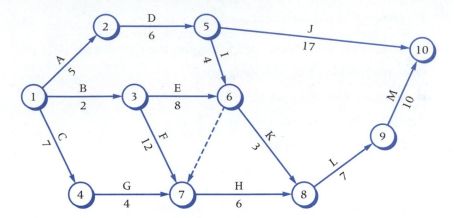

11. Given the following network with activity times in weeks, determine earliest and latest start and finish times and slack times for each activity. Identify the critical path and indicate the expected project duration.

How would the project completion time be affected if the expected time for activity (E) were shortened to 5 weeks?

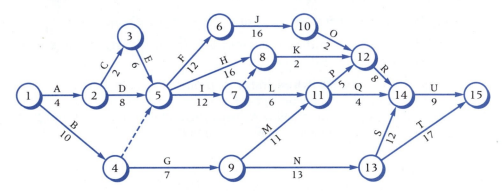

12. Given the following activity and predecessor list with activity time in days:

Activity	Immediate Predecessor	Duration
A	—	34
B	—	8
C	—	10
D	B	4
E	C	8
F	D, E	12
G	D, E	35
H	F, G	6
I	H	10
J	F	14
K	F	40

L	A, J	43
M	A, J	28
N	H	12
O	N	18
P	I, K, M	22

a. Draw the network.
b. Determine event times.
c. Determine activity times.
d. Identify the critical path.
e. Determine the expected completion time for the project.

13. Given the following network, with optimistic, most likely, and pessimistic times given in weeks:

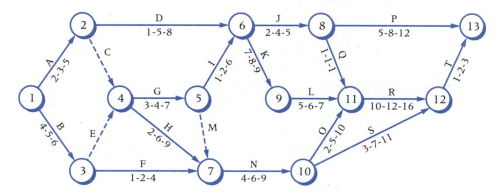

a. Identify the critical path.
b. Determine the expected project completion time.
c. How much slack time is associated with the activity beginning at node 10 and terminating at node 11?
d. Is this slack shared or free slack? If it is shared, with which activities is it shared?
e. What is the standard deviation of the time on the critical path?
f. What is the probability that the project will be completed within 45 weeks?

14. Each year the local Rotary presents a special fund-raising "Follies." Since such a production involves a number of activities, it requires a great deal of planning to ensure that the opening-night performance goes off as scheduled. Looking at the following list of activities (listed in random order as the planners think of them), we can see that the presentation can be modelled as a PERT/CPM project. The anticipated times to complete each activity (in days) are shown in parentheses.

Tryouts for singers and dancers (5 days)
Select musical pieces (14)
Write special music (30)
Write program/story line (30)
Select director (2)
Select choreographer (2)
Choreograph dances (15)

Teach performers dance steps (20)
Select stage manager (2)
Design scenery (10)
Obtain props (21)
Initial rehearsals (16)
Advanced rehearsals (16)
Dress rehearsal (1)
Construct scenery (21)
Make/obtain costumes (40)
Erect scenery (7)
Obtain auditorium (5)
Print tickets (18)
Sell tickets (31)
Select business manager (2)
Sell ads for program (50)
Print program (15)
Get ushers, ticket takers, ad sellers (2)
Train ushers, ticket takers, ad sellers (1)

Rearrange this list, ordering activities as you feel they should be performed. Indicate precedence relationships (immediate predecessors). Draw the network. Compare your list and network with those prepared by others in the class. What does the result tell you?

15. Using the activities and predecessors list shown in your network for problem 14, and using the times given in parentheses, find early start, late start, early finish, and late finish for each activity. What activities are critical? How far ahead should the Rotary begin preparing for its annual Follies?

16. The following table lists the activities of a network, with time estimates given in weeks:

Activity	Immediate Predecessors	Optimistic Time	Most Likely Time	Pessimistic Time
A	—	2	3	4
B	—	2	5	8
C	—	7	8	12
D	B	6	7	9
E	A	3	10	12
F	A	11	12	13
G	C, D	2	4	8
H	E	4	7	10
I	F, G	5	9	19
J	H	3	5	15

a. Draw the network.
b. Calculate the activity times.
c. Determine the critical path.
d. Determine the variance on the critical path.
e. What is the probability that the project will be completed on time? Within 30 weeks?

17. A construction project consists of 22 activities, A to V as described here:

- A, B, and C are initial activities that can be performed simultaneously.
- F can start immediately after A is completed.
- D can start only after both B and C have been finished.
- Once both A and B are completed, activity E can be started.
- G cannot begin until E has been finished.
- Activities H and K can start immediately after F is completed.
- Activities I and J begin after D, G, and H have all been completed.
- Activities L and M immediately follow I.
- Activities N, O, and P succeed K.
- Q follows L.
- R follows M, J, and N.
- S follows R.
- U begins after both Q and S have been completed.
- T follows O and V follows O and P.

Draw up an activities and predecessor list for this project and construct the network.

18. Given the following times for problem 17, determine the critical path, completion time, and variance on the critical path.

Activity	Optimistic Time	Most likely Time	Pessimistic Time
A	14	16	24
B	4	10	16
C	12	15	18
D	16	20	24
E	6	20	24
F	8	8	8
G	6	8	16
H	9	14	18
I	16	18	23
J	16	26	40
K	30	36	42
L	4	9	10
M	6	15	24
N	11	13	15
O	20	24	28
P	12	16	20
Q	10	13	26
R	6	6	7
S	5	11	17
T	8	10	16
U	4	8	14
V	10	14	18

19. Given the project information shown below in the network and time/cost table:

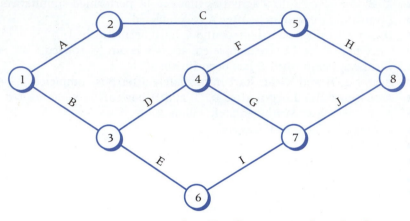

Activity	Normal Time	Crash Time	Normal Cost	Crash Cost
A (1, 2)	5	4	800	950
B (1, 3)	3	2	600	780
C (2, 5)	8	6	1,200	1,440
D (3, 4)	7	5	750	1,150
E (3, 6)	8	6	1,120	1,440
F (4, 5)	2	2	460	460
G (4, 7)	11	8	1,300	1,900
H (5, 8)	9	6	1,080	1,410
I (6, 7)	6	5	500	690
J (7, 8)	4	2	650	930

a. Determine the critical path and completion time for the project.
b. Determine the allowable crash time for each activity.
c. Determine the crash cost per day for each activity.
d. Crash this project to its minimum length at the lowest possible direct cost.
e. Identify the critical path for the crashed project.

20. If the company in problem 19 wishes to crash the project to 20 days, which activities should be crashed? What will the total project cost be?

21. Given the project information shown below in the network and time/cost table:

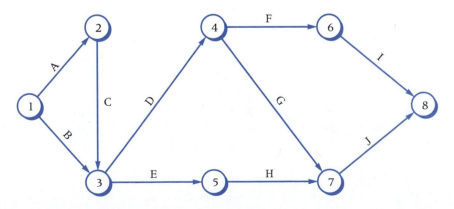

Activity	Normal Time	Crash Time	Normal Cost	Crash Cost
A (1,2)	7	5	1,400	2,000
B (1,3)	10	9	1,650	1,850
C (2,3)	4	3	900	1,260
D (3,4)	8	5	1,200	2,700
E (3,5)	3	2	750	1,000
F (4,6)	5	3	800	2,000
G (4,7)	7	5	1,140	1,980
H (5,7)	10	6	2,000	3,320
I (6,8)	7	6	1,350	1,900
J (7,8)	6	3	1,000	1,780

a. Determine the critical path and completion time for the project.
b. Determine the allowable crash time for each activity.
c. Determine the crash cost per day for each activity.
d. Crash this project to its minimum length at the lowest possible direct cost.
e. Identify the critical path for the crashed project.

22. If the company in problem 21 wishes to crash the project to 25 days, which activities should be crashed? What will the total project cost be?

23. Formulate the LP crashing model for problem 21.

24. Given the following project information:

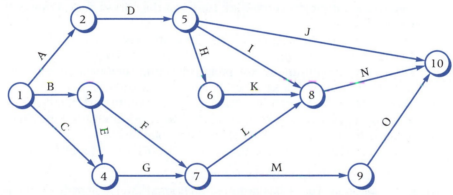

Activity	Normal Time (days)	Crash Time (days)	Normal Cost	Crash Cost
A (1,2)	20	18	$11,000	$12,000
B (1,3)	14	12	8,000	9,400
C (1,4)	18	16	12,000	14,200
D (2,5)	15	12	14,000	17,000
E (3,4)	9	8	6,000	6,600
F (3,7)	18	15	18,000	21,600
G (4,7)	12	9	8,000	9,350
H (5,6)	10	8	10,000	14,000
I (5,8)	15	12	25,000	27,400
J (5,10)	30	25	29,000	32,250
K (6,8)	7	6	20,000	21,250
L (7,8)	19	15	16,000	18,400
M (7,9)	21	18	14,000	16,700
N (8,10)	16	14	12,000	12,700
O (9,10)	11	10	16,000	16,800

a. Determine the normal completion time and cost for this project.

b. Crash this project to its minimum length at the lowest possible direct cost.

c. If the company wishes to crash the project to 65 days, which activities should be crashed? What will the total project cost be?

25. Formulate the LP crashing model for problem 24.

26. Given the normal and crash times and costs for the following project activities.

Activity	(i, j)	Time Estimates (weeks) Normal	Crash	Project Costs $000's Normal	Crash
A	1, 2	22	18	250	530
B	1, 3	21	18	120	390
C	2, 4	12	6	80	440
D	2, 5	8	7	110	155
E	3, 5	6	4	225	335
F	3, 6	9	6	100	340
G	4, 7	15	10	375	575
H	4, 6	5	5	650	650
I	5, 6	6	5	470	535
J	6, 7	15	11	500	800

a. Determine the project completion time and the critical path. What is the cost of this project?

b. Determine the allowable crash time for each activity.

c. Determine the crashing cost per week for each activity.

d. Determine the minimum cost project-crashing solution (crash the project all the way and determine the new project cost).

e. What is the cost differential between the solution to part d and the project cost, if all activities were crashed to their minimum (crash) time?

f. What is the critical path for the crashing solution?

g. Illustrate, with a graph, the time/cost tradeoff for this problem.

27. Formulate the LP crashing model for problem 26.

28. Allegheny National Forest has acquired additional land that will be opened to visitors this summer. Before the area can be opened, however, a new fire tower must be erected. If the tower is not completed by opening day, 10 weeks away, the park will not be opened and the park service will lose approximately $1,500 per week in visitors' fees. The fire tower construction project is described in the following table:

Activity	Description	Immediate Predecessor	Opt. Time	Most L Time	Pess. Time	Cost
A	Order steel	—	2	5	8	$25,000
B	Clear land	—	1	2	3	5,000
C	Pour footings	B	1	1	1	1,300
D	Erect tower	A, C	2	3	7	12,000
E	Build shed	B, H	.5	1	1.5	2,500
F	Install generator	E	2	2	2	7,600
G	Order equipment	—	1	4	7	3,700
H	Obtain lumber	—	1	2	3	7,200

I	Add observation room	D, H	1	1.5	2	3,400
J	Wire tower	F, I	1	2	3	2,200
K	Install equipment	G, J	1	1	1	1,500

a. Construct the network.
b. Identify the critical path, project completion time, and variance on the critical path.
c. What is the probability that the park will be open on time?
d. Given the expected completion time, how much will the park service lose if the project is completed as scheduled?
e. What is the cost of constructing the tower? How many weeks will it take for entrance fees to cover the construction costs?

29. Using the calculated expected activity times as normal times, the activity costs given in problem 28, and the table of crash times and costs given here, crash the fire tower project so that it will be completed on time.

Activity	Crash time	Crash cost
A	3	28,000
B	1	5,500
C	1	1,300
D	2	13,800
E	1	2,500
F	2	7,600
G	1	3,100
H	1	5,100
I	1	4,100
J	.5	4,600
K	1	1,500

a. What is the total project cost when crashed?
b. Would this be economically justified?

30. The Frimbee Company has developed the following PERT/CPM network for an upcoming project:

Activity	Duration	Cost
A (1,2)	2	$2,000
B (1,3)	3	1,950
C (1,4)	8	4,000
D (2,4)	3	2,700
E (2,5)	4	4,800
F (3,4)	1	400
G (4,5)	1	1,500
H (4,6)	2	2,600
I (4,7)	7	4,900
J (5,7)	3	2,250
K (6,7)	2	1,800

a. Solve this problem, determining project completion time *and* times for all activities.
b. Construct PERT/Cost tables (early start/late start cost tables) and a graph of the budget demands versus time.

31. The following table shows costs incurred to date by the Frimbee Company after 4 weeks:

Activity	Activity Cost to Date	Completed?
A (1,2)	$2,100	Yes
B (1,3)	1,900	Yes
C (1,4)	2,200	No
D (2,4)	1,750	No
E (2,5)	2,540	No
F (3,4)	380	No

(All remaining activities have not begun yet.)

a. Prepare a PERT/Cost report based on these figures, assuming an earliest start schedule, and assuming that budgeted cost is equal to the budget for the completed activity times the proportion of the activity that has been completed.
b. Where does the total project stand relative to budget?
c. Where do the activities shown above stand relative to budget?
d. Are any actions suggested by this information?

32. The following table shows costs incurred to date by the Frimbee Company after 11 weeks:

Activity	Activity Cost to Date	Completed?
A (1,2)	$2,100	Yes
B (1,3)	1,900	Yes
C (1,4)	4,150	Yes
D (2,4)	2,600	Yes
E (2,5)	4,820	Yes
F (3,4)	410	Yes
G (4,5)	1,500	Yes
H (4,6)	2,600	Yes
I (4,7)	2,000	No
J (5,7)	1,650	No
K (6,7)	1,900	No

a. Prepare a PERT/Cost report based on these figures, assuming an earliest start schedule, and assuming that budgeted cost is equal to the budget for the completed activity times the proportion of the activity that has been completed.
b. Where does the total project stand relative to budget?
c. Where do the activities shown above stand relative to budget?
d. Are any actions suggested by this information?

33. Motion Oil Company has undertaken a major renovation project in Monroe County, modernizing every station and creating mini-markets. The associated activities, with their immediate predecessors, times, and costs, are shown in the following table:

Activity	Description	Immediate Predecessor	Activity Duration	Activity Cost
A	Remove pumps	—	3 weeks	$ 500
B	Renovate office	—	7	3,000
C	Excavate	A	5	1,000
D	Remove tanks	C	2	500
E	Install footings	C	3	900
F	Install new tanks	D	2	4,750
G	Install structural steel	E	5	3,800
H	Put up new sign	E	1	4,500
I	Install roof	G	5	1,400
J	Wiring/lights	I	4	1,500
K	Install pump controls	G, B	3	2,800
L	Fill and pave	F, J, K	7	3,200
M	Install new pumps	L	2	9,000
N	Landscape	L	6	1,500

a. Solve this problem, determining project completion times for all activities.
b. Construct PERT/Cost tables (early start/late start cost tables) and a graph of the budget demands versus time.

34. The following table shows costs incurred to date (after 18 weeks) for the Motion Oil renovation:

Activity	Activity Cost to Date	Completed?
A	475	Yes
B	3,150	Yes
C	990	Yes
D	1,550	Yes
E	900	Yes
F	4,810	Yes
G	3,750	Yes
H	4,575	Yes
I	700	No
J	0	No
K	1,750	No
L	0	No
M	0	No
N	0	No

a. Prepare a PERT/Cost report based on these figures, assuming an earliest start schedule, and assuming that budgeted cost is equal to the budget for the completed activity times the proportion of the activity that has been completed.
b. Where does the total project stand relative to budget?
c. Where do activities I and K stand relative to budget?

Anderson and Sons Construction Company

Anderson and Sons Construction Company has been awarded the contract for construction of the new Perinton Town Hall. According to the contract, construction must begin by March 27 and be completed by July 3—in time for a special dedication during the July Fourth weekend festivities. There is a $5,000-per-week delay penalty.

Bob Anderson has been in the construction business for close to 40 years, and this project is similar to several other office complexes he has worked on over the years. It calls for preparing the site and constructing a single-story wooden structure with rough-sawn cedar siding and shake shingle roof. The building is to be situated on the side of a small incline, such that the rear of the basement/lower level has a walk-out to the lower-level parking lot. The contract also calls for laying the parking lots and landscaping the property. Because of his experience, Bob is confident that his bid is accurate and that the project can be completed within the allotted 14 weeks (70 working days). He does not want to have to work on weekends.

However, late winter and early spring weather conditions have conspired to delay the project. A late winter storm, followed by a quick thaw and two weeks of heavy spring rains, have already delayed the start of the project by one week. This delay has raised serious doubts in the minds of his three sons, who are now in the business with Bob. Furthermore, a strike at the supplier's plant could have an effect on the delivery of the shake shingles. It threatens another one- to two-week delay in the project.

The sons—who, in the past, have paid little attention to the initial project planning stage—are now anxious to review their father's estimates. Bob has laid out the project as follows:

Job	Description	Immediate Predecessors	Duration
1	Clear and prepare the site	—	6 days
2	Excavate the cellar (lower level)	1	4
3	Pour the concrete for the cellar	2	2
4	Erect wooden frame, including roof	3	10
5	Fasten exterior sheathing	4	5
6	Install rough plumbing & wiring	5	7
7	Rough carpentry including door and window frames	4	9
8	Shingle roof	4	5
9	Insulate outside walls	6, 7, 8	2
10	Sheet rock and plaster inside walls	9	7
11	Do finish carpentry inside	10	20
12	Sand, stain and varnish wood trim, etc.	11	6
13	Lay tile in bathrooms	10	8
14	Install remaining plumbing fixtures	13	2
15	Paint interior	14	8
16	Lay flooring	15	6
17	Install hot water heater	6	1

18	Install heating and cooling ducts	4	6
19	Install heat pump	6, 18	3
20	Stain exterior	5, 8	2
21	Finish exterior including gutters and downspouts	5, 8	1
22	Place insulation in attic	10	1
23	Grade and lay forms for walks, driveways, and parking lots	21	3
24	Pour walks, driveways, and parking lots	23	3
25	Landscape yard	24	5
26	Install electrical outlets, switches, etc. and hook up electrical system	17, 19	3
27	Clean up exterior and interior	12, 16, 22, 25, 26	1

Bob's seat-of-the-pants estimate is 13 weeks (65 working days). His sons are concerned that this estimate is inaccurate, and the weather delays and delivery delays have intensified the problem of completing the work on schedule.

You have been hired as a consultant to help Bob by applying management science techniques to this particular problem. Prepare a report for Anderson and Sons that addresses:

1. A visual presentation of the precedence relationships through the use of a PERT network diagram.
2. The expected length of time required to complete this project.
3. Suggested tasks that might be candidates for overtime work if a reduction in the expected completion time is required.
4. The impacts of a one-week (five working days) or two-week (ten working days) strike by the shake shingle manufacturer's employees.

Chapter

12

Inventory Management

By the end of this chapter, you should be able to:

1
describe the functions and importance of inventory;

2
define the important components of an inventory situation;

3
analyze relevant inventory costs;

4
list the assumptions of the EOQ model;

5
solve problems using the EOQ formula;

6
demonstrate the applicability of EOQ to production lot size
situations, discussing the necessary relaxation in assumptions;

7
use the EOQ model to solve problems involving quantity discounts;

8
discuss the concept of shortages and solve problems involving
allowable shortages;

9
discuss the concept of safety stock and service levels;

10
solve simple problems having stochastic demand and/or lead time;
and

11
explain the concepts and application of MRP and JIT.

In this chapter, we discuss mathematical
techniques used for inventory analysis. More specifically, we show how inventory
models can help in making decisions concerning the basic inventory questions of
how much to order and when to order, usually with the objective of minimizing
total inventory costs. Because inventories are an integral part of most organizations, often representing a significant investment in the firm's capital, inventory
management is one of the most popular and important topics in management science. Inventory models are also among the oldest management science techniques,
dating to 1915, when F.W. Harris developed the economic order quantity model.

We will concentrate on the basic, fundamental models wherein demand is
known with certainty and is constant over time: the classical economic order
quantity (EOQ) model. As the chapter progresses, we will relax various assump-

tions of the EOQ model in order to apply the model to different inventory situations. Since demand is seldom known with certainty, we will also introduce inventory models that can be used to compensate for uncertain demand. Throughout the chapter our emphasis is on the importance of inventory, the functions it performs, and the necessity for skillful inventory management.

Bare Wood Furniture

Bare Wood Furniture sells unfinished furniture in the Los Angeles area. Bare Wood purchases the fully assembled furniture pieces directly from a number of manufacturers. Normally, a given type or style of furniture is purchased entirely from one manufacturer. In reviewing the items that Bare Wood carries, Martin Marino, the assistant manager, has found the 42-inch-wide, three-shelf bookcase to be Bare Wood's best-selling item. The company purchases this product from a manufacturer in North Carolina. Bare Wood has found that this manufacturer produces fully assembled, sound-quality bookcases at a reasonable price. The manufacturer also ships orders promptly, so that Bare Wood usually receives an order approximately one week after placing the order. Recently, Martin has been under some pressure from the warehouse to reduce the number of bookcases purchased in each order. Because Bare Wood has been expanding the number of furniture lines it carries, the warehouse manager is becoming concerned about the lack of available space. He feels that a large amount of warehouse space is currently taken up by this particular bookcase.

While Martin understands the warehouse manager's concern, he knows that Bare Wood places fairly large orders for these bookcases for two reasons. First, the company sells 90 of them per week; and second, the office manager has estimated that it costs Bare Wood about $55 to place each order with this manufacturer. For these reasons, Bare Wood typically places orders for these bookcases once a quarter, ordering 1,170 units per order.

When Martin attempted to explain why such large orders were placed, the warehouse manager informed him that, based upon the space required, the insurance costs, and the value of capital tied up in the inventory, he estimated it cost Bare Wood $12.61 a year for each bookcase held in inventory. He stated that, at this rate, it costs more to store five units than it costs to place an order ($63.05 versus $55). On this basis, he felt that it would be cheaper to place orders weekly and to keep the inventory level as low as possible.

Although the warehouse manager has not convinced him to change the company's ordering policy on this item, Martin decides he had better take a closer look at all the costs involved and the company's policy.

12.1 AN INTRODUCTION TO INVENTORY ANALYSIS

Inventory is broadly defined as any quantity of items, or economic resources, being held in storage for some future use. In the more traditional view of inventory, associated with manufacturing and retail organizations, inventory takes the form of raw materials, spare parts, semi-finished or in-process goods, and finished goods. Inventory also takes a wide variety of other forms, however, including equipment and supplies, cash, and labor or personnel. Thus it is found to some extent in almost all organizations.

Businesses carry inventories for a number of reasons to serve a variety of purposes. Inventories serve as a protection against fluctuating demand, thereby meeting future demand quickly to prevent slowdowns in production or the loss of sales and customer goodwill. They are also used to smooth out the time gap between supply and demand. For example, while certain food crops are harvested only once or twice a year, the demand for products using these foods is steady throughout the year. Inventories can be carried as a hedge against strikes or inflation. They can be used to store labor. For example, by producing at a smoother constant rate and storing excess production, a company frees labor for alternative uses in periods when labor is a constraint on production. Furthermore, in some instances, working at a smooth rate can reduce labor costs. Inventories help smooth out irregularities in the supply process, serving as a hedge against uncertain lead times (the time between placing and receiving an order). Sometimes there are economic advantages to buying or producing in large batches. There may be quantity discounts on purchases; also, it is often more economical to produce in large batches, storing the excess for future demand, rather than producing at a more costly lower rate. In general, inventories can increase the operating flexibility of an organization.

Inventory represents a significant cost for many organizations, sometimes as much as 30 to 40 percent of total invested capital. This is a non-earning asset. Viewed as a claim on an organization's capital, inventory should be reduced. As we have just seen, however, there are frequently excellent reasons for maintaining high inventory levels. Any reduction in inventory can have an effect on other aspects of the organization. That is, there is a cost to carrying inventory, but there is also a cost associated with insufficient inventory. Careful management of inventory can contribute to an organization's profit.

The goal of inventory management, then, is to find the proper balance between the higher cost associated with carrying higher inventory levels and the losses associated with lower inventory levels. It is necessary to decide, for every item in inventory, how much to order and when to order it. This task involves making tradeoffs between the cost of holding inventory and the cost of ordering inventory. While reducing inventory reduces the cost of holding inventory (carrying cost), it also means that more orders must be placed and the cost associated with placing orders (ordering cost) increases. Good inventory management can be supported by quantitative models. Using only basic, fundamental inventory models, we will demonstrate the use of quantitative models in deciding when to order and how much to order. First, however, it is necessary to take a closer look at inventory systems and to make an important point concerning inventory models.

Inventory Systems

An inventory system is the environment in which items are removed from inventory (called depletion) and added to inventory (called replenishment). It involves a cyclical process, whereby inventory is depleted as demand for the item occurs, and is replenished periodically, either when the inventory level reaches a certain level (called the reorder point) or at specified time intervals. Inventory systems are characterized by a variety of properties. There does not exist just one inventory model that is applicable to all inventory situations. Rather, there are a number of models, dependent upon the characteristics or properties of the specific system. Inventory systems are frequently described by the following properties:

Manner in Which Replenishment Occurs

Replenishment may occur all at once, scheduled such that the entire replenishment order arrives exactly when the demand level reaches zero (instantaneous receipt), or it may occur gradually over a specific period of time. Instantaneous receipt is typical of a retail inventory system. Gradual replenishment, referred to as noninstantaneous receipt, is usual for production systems in which replenishment inventories are produced internally. These systems also are described as ordering versus production inventories, depending on whether the firm replenishes its inventory by ordering from a vendor or by producing inventory items internally.

Demand can be deterministic or stochastic. In the first case, demand is known with certainty. Deterministic demand can be constant or variable. When demand is not known with certainty (i.e., it is probabilisitic in nature), it is governed by a specified probability distribution. The rate of demand, the demand over a given time period, also can be deterministic, constant or variable, or stochastic. In general, while demand seldom is absolutely deterministic, many models assume deterministic demand. It is very important to use demand forecasts or estimates that have a high degree of confidence.

Demand can be dependent or independent. With dependent demand, the demand for an item is determined by the demand for the final product for which this item is a component. For example, the demand for 10-speed gear shifts is dependent upon the demand for 10-speed bicycles. The demand for the bikes, however, is independent. Independent demand is typical of finished products. While this chapter deals mainly with independent demand inventory items, later in the chapter we will briefly discuss a system for handling dependent-demand items.

Ordering Policy

An ordering policy is necessary to make the when-to-order decision. Two basic approaches to ordering—fixed quantity or order point, and fixed time or periodic review—are used by most organizations. The ordering policy employed depends upon how closely the organization monitors its inventory levels. It is important to note that good inventory management includes two necessary and interrelated components: a method for keeping track of inventory levels, and the decision making component.

A fixed quantity system, also called a perpetual inventory system, requires a continuous review policy. Every depletion is recorded immediately, and the inventory level is known at all times. With this system, the company places a fixed-quantity order each time the inventory level reaches a predetermined level, called a reorder point. While this is generally a more expensive policy, computerized systems have made it increasingly popular and accessible to a greater number of organizations.

A fixed time or periodic review system involves periodically auditing inventory levels. At each check, the inventory on hand is compared with a desired maximum inventory level or target. The difference between the inventory on hand and the target is the quantity ordered, and it can vary each time an order is placed. It is possible to have variations and combinations of these two basic approaches. Although this chapter will briefly introduce a no inventory system, we are concerned only with order point systems.

Lead Time

Lead time is the time between the initiation of a replenishment order and its receipt. As with demand, it can be deterministic (constant or variable) or stochastic and is governed by a specified probability distribution.

Treatment of Stockout

A stockout or shortage occurs when demand exceeds the quantity of inventory on hand. That is, demand for an item cannot be met because the inventory level for that item has reached zero. Stockouts can be allowed or disallowed, planned or accidental. In any event, since there is a cost (stockout cost) involved with shortages, there must be a policy that addresses the issue of shortages. When the consequence of a shortage would be too great in monetary or human terms (for example, running out of essential medical supplies), shortages are disallowed. The organization keeps inventory at a level that minimizes the probability of a stockout. In certain instances, it is more economical to plan for shortages with backordering (backlogging) than to maintain high inventory levels. In most cases, however, stockouts are accidental.

Whether planned or accidental, a stockout policy must involve consideration of backordering and lost sales. With backordering, all demand that cannot be met is filled when inventory has been replenished. Essentially, backordering is a policy of allowing a negative inventory level. There are costs associated with backordering, which we will discuss later. There are also instances when backordering is not possible—for example, if customers refuse to wait, or if the organization has a policy of not taking orders when there is no inventory. Lost sales are costly in terms of both lost revenue and loss of goodwill.

As a protection against unplanned stockouts, especially given uncertain demand or lead times, an organization can add a buffer—a safety stock level—to the reorder point. That is, an order is computed and placed so that replenishment will occur when a certain level of inventory is still remaining, rather than at zero inventory level. The problem for management thus becomes one of determining the proper level of safety stock, since it affects carrying and stockout costs.

A number of other properties must be taken into consideration when describing an inventory system, such as the structure of the system (single-stage versus multistage systems); the type or nature of the item (perishable or non-perishable, single item or multiple items); the time or planning horizon over which inventory decisions are made; and any constraints on the system (for example, space restrictions). It is extremely important that the system properties be identified and fully considered in order to use the appropriate inventory model.

12.2 *INVENTORY DECISIONS*

Effective inventory control has two basic components. There must be a method for keeping track of inventory (an inventory accounting system). There must also be a decision making component, usually supported by quantitative techniques such as the ones described here. Although management must make a number of decisions concerning inventory, including such factors as location, staffing, and the type of accounting system, the basic inventory decisions concern the quantity to order and when to order. In general, these decisions are based upon an evaluation of inventory-related costs; in other words, inventory-related costs are the most frequently used criteria for evaluating inventory decisions. Note that a number of other factors sometimes are used to make decisions in inventory analysis, such as product life cycle or return on investment. Most basic inventory models, however, seek to minimize the total cost of the inventory system.

Inventory Costs

Inventory costs include ordering costs, carrying or holding costs, stockout or shortage costs, and item purchase or production costs. Each of these is discussed in greater detail below.

Ordering cost is simply the cost of placing an order. This includes all the clerical and administrative costs associated with all activities needed to replenish inventory. Thus, ordering costs include some or all of the following components: requisitioning and purchasing costs (processing a purchase order, recordkeeping, etc.); transportation costs (getting the order from the supplier); receiving costs (unloading and placing the order in storage); inspection costs; accounting and auditing costs; and all related overhead costs (for example, telephone, postage, and computer time).

In production situations, setup costs are analogous to ordering costs. Here, however, the primary costs are the labor and material costs associated with setting up the machines for production. Setup costs also include the clerical and administrative costs associated with production support.

Ordering cost is assumed to be a fixed cost per order. The cost is the same each time an order is placed, regardless of the size of the order. Therefore, annual ordering costs vary with the number of orders placed per year, and are usually expressed in terms of dollar cost per order.

Carrying cost, also called holding cost, is the cost associated with keeping inventory on hand. These costs include the direct and indirect (or explicit and implicit) costs associated with owning and maintaining inventory. Total carrying cost includes some or all of the following components: cost of capital (deferred or forgone profit on the investment tied up in inventory, opportunity cost of doing something else with the money, interest paid on the capital invested in inventory); direct storage costs (including rent, utilities, security, maintenance, recordkeeping, and so on); obsolescence and deterioration of the inventory items; and taxes, insurance, and depreciation.

Carrying costs are usually expressed in one of two ways: in terms of the dollar cost of carrying one unit in inventory per unit of time (typically dollar cost per item per year), or as a percentage of the value of the inventory value. For example, a certain table has a cost of $300. Carrying cost can be expressed as a dollar amount per year, such as $30. Alternatively, the holding cost, expressed as a percentage of the value of the item, would be 10 percent of the value of the item. Carrying costs vary with the level of inventory held and sometimes with the length of time an item is held (for example, with perishable or seasonal items).

Stockout cost, also referred to as shortage cost, occurs when an item is out of stock and current demand cannot be met. As we said previously, stockouts can be planned or accidental. Moreover, they can be temporary if items are backordered, or permanent if sales are lost. Temporary shortages are eliminated when the supply arrives. Stockout costs are sometimes difficult to assess, as it is often difficult to accurately estimate the value of customer ill will. Moreover, the magnitude of the cost depends upon whether or not backordering is allowed. If backordering is not allowed, the cost includes both the lost-sale cost and a customer ill-will cost. If backordering is allowed, the shortage cost includes the relevant clerical and administrative costs and could also include some lost-sales and ill-will costs. In the case of production stockouts, the cost may be very high. Stockout costs typically include some of the following components: costs of idled production (including idle labor, idle machine, shutdown and setup costs); product spoilage; lost sales; customer ill will; all costs associated with placing special orders; and all clerical and administrative costs.

Stockout costs are usually expressed as a cost per unit of inventory per unit of time. It is also possible, however, to assume a fixed cost per shortage, regardless of the size of the shortage or the length of time of the shortage.

Item cost is the purchase price of the item. In production situations, it is the cost to produce the item. In either case, it is generally assumed to be a constant and is not really a direct inventory cost. The firm must procure the items in any event, so item cost usually is not included in the total inventory cost analysis. The assumption that the price is a constant is sometimes relaxed if there are quantity discounts for specific order quantities, or if it is possible to reduce unit cost for large production runs. In these cases, total inventory costs include a consideration of the item cost. Although we will examine this situation later, the major focus of this chapter is on models with constant per-unit cost. We will begin our discussion of basic inventory models with deterministic inventory models.

DETERMINISTIC INVENTORY MODELS

12.3 *ECONOMIC ORDER QUANTITY (EOQ) MODEL*

The economic order quantity (EOQ) model is the most widely known inventory model. The objective of this model is to minimize total inventory costs. Since inventory costs are a function of the quantity ordered, the model determines the order quantity that results in the lowest total cost. The EOQ model is the most elementary of all the inventory models. It makes the following assumptions:

1. Only one item is being considered. If EOQ levels are desired for several items, each level must be determined independently.
2. Demand for the item is known with certainty. For example, the annual demand is known and will not vary.
3. Demand is constant over time, for example, 72 units per day, 20 units per week, or 85 units per month.
4. The cost of placing an order and the per-unit carrying cost are constant and independent of the quantity ordered.
5. The entire order quantity arrives at one time (no partial orders are received), and the entire order can be processed at once.
6. Order receipt is instantaneous. Orders are received as soon as the order is placed. In some cases, where the time required to fill an order is known and constant, this assumption may not be necessary.
7. The inventory on hand is depleted (the inventory level reaches zero) just before each new order arrives. There are never any extra units left over nor any shortages.
8. The quantity ordered is constant. The same number of units is ordered each time an order is placed.

The effects of these assumptions on inventory levels over time are shown in Figure 12.1. The downward slope of the inventory level indicates a constant usage over time. As the inventory level reaches zero, a new order is received and the cycle begins again. Since there is no remaining inventory when a new order arrives, and since the order receipt is instantaneous, the maximum inventory level is achieved when an order arrives. This level is equal to the quantity ordered (Q).

Recall that, in the Bare Wood Furniture example presented earlier, Martin Marino was trying to determine the number of bookcases to order. The company was ordering 1,170 bookcases at a time, and the warehouse manager suggested that an order quantity of 90 units (a week's supply) would be better. Figures 12.2 and 12.3 show the effect of these order sizes on the inventory level and the number of orders placed. Large order sizes increase the size of the inventory and reduce the number of orders placed; small order sizes reduce the inventory level and increase the number of orders placed.

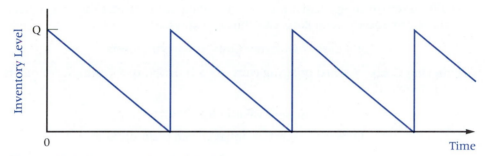

Figure 12.1 Inventory Level Over Time

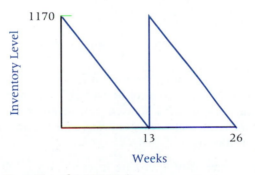

Figure 12.2 Order Quantity of 1,170 Units

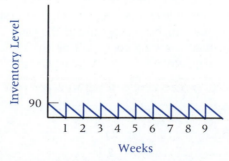

Figure 12.3 Order Quantity of 90 Units

Both figures show demand as constant. In many inventory situations, the assumption of constant demand is not valid. Whenever demand is approximately constant, however, the EOQ model provides a satisfactory solution.

Development of the EOQ Model

The objective of the EOQ model is to minimize total inventory costs over time. We will begin the development of this model by examining those costs in terms of the quantity ordered (Q).

Total Inventory Costs

The total inventory costs (TC) include all costs associated with ordering and carrying the item over a period of time. For purposes of this explanation, we will use a time period of one year. Thus, all costs will be annual costs. Total inventory costs normally have two components: the cost of placing an order and the cost of holding units in inventory. Total costs can thus be expressed as

$$\text{Total Cost} = \text{Ordering Costs} + \text{Carrying Costs}$$

Ordering Costs Annual ordering costs are a function of the number of orders placed per year. If

$$D = \text{the annual demand for the item}$$

$$Q = \text{the number of units ordered per order}$$

$$C_o = \text{the cost of placing an order}$$

the number of orders placed per year can be expressed as D/Q and the annual ordering costs (OC) are

$$OC = \frac{D}{Q} \times C_o$$

Carrying Costs Since carrying costs are a function of the inventory level over time, we must first address the concept of average inventory.

Average Inventory Figure 12.1 showed that inventory declined from a maximum of Q units to zero units at a constant rate. The average inventory during this period can be determined as

$$\frac{(\text{beginning inventory} + \text{ending inventory})}{2} \quad \text{or} \quad \frac{Q + 0}{2} = \frac{Q}{2}$$

This is illustrated in Figure 12.4, and can also be proven geometrically.

Once the average inventory level has been established and the cost of carrying a unit of inventory over time has been determined the total carrying costs can also be determined. The annual carrying costs will be the average inventory level for the year times the carrying cost per unit per year. Letting

$$C_c = \text{carrying cost per unit per year}$$

the annual carrying costs (CC) can be expressed as

$$CC = \frac{Q}{2} \times C_c$$

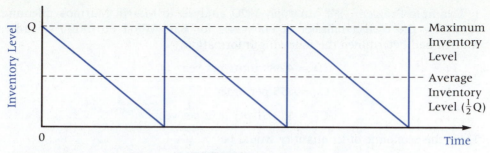

Figure 12.4 Average Inventory Level Over Time

These cost components can then be combined to determine the total annual cost as

$$TC = OC + CC$$

or

$$TC = \frac{D}{Q} \times C_o + \frac{Q}{2} \times C_c$$

Figure 12.5 shows graphically the annual ordering costs, carrying costs, and total costs as a function of the number of units per order. To minimize the total cost, the lowest point on the total cost curve must be found. This point occurs when the quantity ordered is equal to Q^* (the optimal order size). The point can be determined mathematically using differential calculus (see Appendix D for a discussion of this approach). The optimal order size, Q^*, is given by the formula

$$Q^* = \sqrt{\frac{2DC_o}{C_c}}$$

This optimal order size quantity is also known as the **economic order quantity** or EOQ.

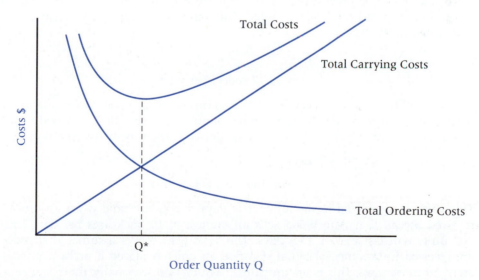

Figure 12.5 Annual Ordering Costs, Carrying Costs, and Total Costs

Example Problem We can apply EOQ analysis to Martin Marino's dilemma regarding the correct number of bookcases for Bare Wood Furniture to order. Martin had determined the following information:

$$D = 4{,}680 \text{ units per year}$$

$$C_O = \$55 \text{ per order}$$

$$C_C = \$12.61 \text{ per unit per year}$$

Thus, the economic order quantity would be

$$Q^* = \sqrt{\frac{2(4680)\,(55)}{12.61}}$$

$$= 202.05 \approx 202$$

If Martin orders 202 units each time he places an order, the total annual costs associated with this bookcase will be

$$TC = \frac{4680}{202}(55) + \frac{202}{2}(12.61)$$

$$= 1{,}274.26 + 1{,}273.61$$

$$= 2{,}547.87$$

This annual cost of $2,547.87 is less than either the total cost of $7,596.85 associated with ordering 1,170 units per order (current policy), or the total cost of $17,254.58 that would be associated with ordering 15 units per order as suggested by the warehouse manager.

Note, on the graph in Figure 12.5, that the ordering costs and carrying costs are equal at the economic order quantity Q^*. The total cost calculations confirm this. The slight variation in the costs ($1,274.26 versus $1,273.61) is caused by rounding the actual Q^* value of 202.05 to 202.

Additional Information

Once the economic order quantity is known the number of orders that will be placed in a year (N) can be determined. This value is equal to D/Q^*. In the example, this would be

$$N = D/Q = 4680/202$$

$$= 23.17 \text{ orders per year}$$

The time between orders (cycle time) also can be determined as the total number of days worked divided by the number of orders per year. If Bare Wood Furniture is open six days per week, or 312 days per year, the time between orders (t) is

$$t = 312/23.17$$

$$= 13.5 \text{ working days between orders}$$

This value is also equal to the number of days' supply on hand when an order is received. Recall that Bare Wood sells an average of 15 bookcases per day. Thus, 202 units will last $202/15$ or 13.5 days. The basic EOQ model assumes that orders are received instantaneously, that is, when an order is placed it arrives immediately. In most cases, this is an unrealistic assumption. Normally there is a delay between the time an order is placed and the time it is actually received. When this is the case, a second decision must be made as well. That decision is when to reorder an item.

When To Order—Reorder Point

In order to determine when to reorder, one additional piece of information is needed: the time required for a supplier to process an order and ship the item. This elapsed time between the time an order is placed and the time it is received is known as **lead time.** Figure 12.6 illustrates the lead time for an order. If a firm knows the lead time for an order is five days, it must place the order five days before the inventory level reaches zero. Normally this is done by monitoring the current inventory level and placing an order when five days' supply of inventory remains. This inventory level is known as the **reorder point** (RP) and is shown in Figure 12.6. Given the assumption that demand is constant, the reorder point is easily calculated as the product of the lead time and the daily usage (d):

$$RP = L_T(d)$$

In the case of Bare Wood Furniture, d is 15 units per day. If the lead time is five days, then the reorder point is

$$RP = (5)(15) = 75 \text{ units}$$

Thus, an order would be placed when the existing inventory level reached 75 units on hand. Note that the value of Q^* is not dependent upon the length of the lead time. Lead time and order quantity are independent values. In some cases, however, lead time is so long that the reorder point is greater than Q^*. When this occurs, the inventory on hand is added to the number of units currently on order, and this total is compared to the reorder point.

Sensitivity of the EOQ Model

In developing the EOQ model, we made assumptions about costs and demand being known and constant. Using those figures, we determined an EOQ value that resulted in the minimum total cost. But what if there was an error in the cost or demand estimates? What if we do not choose to order the exact EOQ? How sensitive are total costs to errors in input values or deviations from the resulting EOQ?

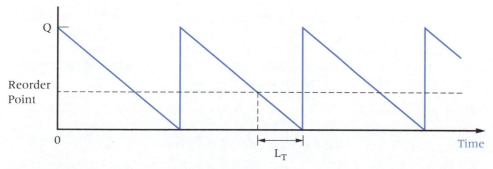

Figure 12.6 Lead Time and Reorder Point

Table 12.1(a) Effect of Changes in Demand, Ordering Costs, or Carrying Costs Upon Total Cost

Percent Change in demand or ordering costs	Total Costs	Percent Change in Total Costs
−50	$2,702.42	5.72
−25	2,574.27	1.03
−10	2,551.40	0.14
+10	2,550.76	0.11
+25	2,563.74	0.62
+50	2,600.41	2.02

Table 12.1(b) Effects of Change in Quantity Ordered Upon Total Cost

Order Quantity	Percent Change in Order Quantity	Total Cost	Percent Change in Total Costs
100	−50.5	$3,204.50	25.77
150	−25.8	2,661.75	4.47
200	− 0.01	2,548.00	0.00
EOQ 202	—	2,547.87	—
250	+23.7	2,605.85	2.28
300	+48.5	2,749.50	7.91

Using the Bare Wood Furniture figures as an example, Table 12.1(a) shows the effects of an error in annual demand, ordering costs, or carrying costs upon total costs. Table 12.1(b) shows the effects of ordering less or more than the calculated EOQ value. (Note: Figure 12.5 illustrated the total cost curve for various order quantities. Since this curve was relatively flat near the minimum point, it suggested that slight changes in the quantity ordered would not make major differences in the total cost. Table 12.1(a) and (b) illustrate this fact using the figures for Bare Wood Furniture.) As these tables show, an error or change in the demand, ordering cost, or carrying cost of up to 50 percent results in a change of less than 6 percent in the total annual costs. A deviation from the calculated EOQ value of 25 percent results in a change of less than 5 percent in the total annual costs. Thus, the EOQ model is relatively insensitive to errors or changes in demand or cost figures or to deviations from the calculated EOQ value.

An EOQ Variation

In the previous EOQ explanation, we expressed carrying cost in dollars per unit. It is also possible to calculate EOQ when carrying cost is expressed as a constant percentage of the inventory value. Since many of the carrying costs, such as insurance costs and the cost of capital tied up in inventory, may be a function of the amount invested in inventory, this is not an unusual variation.

If that carrying cost is a constant percent of the inventory value, where

$$C_i = \text{the percentage of the inventory value}$$

$$P = \text{the purchase price of the item}$$

the carrying cost per item, C_c, can be expressed as

$$C_c = C_i(P)$$

Substituting this into the EOQ formulas, the total cost would be

$$TC = \frac{D}{Q}(C_o) + \frac{Q}{2}(Ci)(P)$$

and the economic order quantity would be

$$Q^* = \sqrt{\frac{2DC_o}{C_iP}}$$

Assuming Bare Wood pays $45 for each bookcase and carrying cost is calculated to be 8 percent of the average inventory value, the economic order quantity is

$$Q^* = \sqrt{\frac{2(4680)(55)}{.08(45)}}$$

$$= 378.15 \approx 378$$

and the total cost is

$$TC = \frac{4680}{378}(55) + \frac{378}{2}(.08)(45)$$

$$= 680.96 + 680.40$$

$$= 1,361.36$$

Thus, the economic order quantity can be calculated when carrying cost is expressed as either a dollar value per item or a percentage of the item's value.

12.4 *PRODUCTION LOT SIZE MODEL*

In the EOQ model, one of the assumptions is that inventory receipt is instantaneous. This assumes that inventory is ordered from an outside vendor and is received in one shipment at one point in time. Many times, however, items sold or used by a firm are either produced within the firm or received as they are produced by another firm. When the production rate for these items is the same as the use rate, a continuous production facility may be practical. In many cases, however, items are produced at a rate greater than the use rate. When this happens, the extra items are placed in inventory. If this were to continue indefinitely, the inventory level would grow very large. To prevent this, production of the item is suspended at some point and then resumed later when the inventory level falls. In these cases, ordering costs are replaced with setup costs, which we discussed previously. Since the firm still wishes to minimize its total costs, the goal of this model is to determine the number of units it should produce in each production run to achieve minimum total costs. This model is referred to as the production lot size (PLS) model.

This model retains all the assumptions of the basic EOQ model, with the exception of the instantaneous receipt assumption. Two additional parameters also are required for this model: the production or receipt rate (the rate at which the item is produced or delivered) and the demand rate. Let

  p = the production rate per unit of time (or the receipt rate per unit of time for non-production cases)

  d = the demand or use rate per unit of time

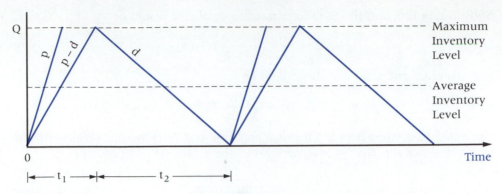

Figure 12.7 Inventory Level for Noninstantaneous Receipt–PLS Model

where the production rate exceeds the demand rate (p > d). Figure 12.7 shows the inventory level over time for noninstantaneous receipt situations. Demand (use) is constant over the entire period.

Model Development

During time period t_1, units are produced at rate p and used at rate d, where p > d. Thus, the inventory grows at a rate of p − d. At the end of this period, production (or receipt) ceases. The inventory is then used at a rate of d during time period t_2. At the end of this period, production begins again and the cycle is repeated.

The PLS model determines the optimum number of units (Q) to produce each time to minimize total costs. Referring to Figure 12.7, if Q units are produced during time t_1, at a production rate p, then

$$Q = p(t_1)$$

and

$$t_1 = \frac{Q}{p}$$

During this production period, the items are also being used at a rate d. The total number of units used or demanded can be expressed by $d(t_1)$. Substituting $(\frac{Q}{p})$ for t_1, the units used during this period would be $d(\frac{Q}{p})$. If Q units are produced and $d(\frac{Q}{p})$ units are used, the maximum inventory level would be

$$\text{maximum inventory} = Q - d(\tfrac{Q}{p})$$

$$= Q(1 - \tfrac{d}{p})$$

The average inventory would be one-half of this maximum inventory value over the period $t_1 + t_2$ or

$$(\tfrac{Q}{2})(1 - \tfrac{d}{p})$$

Using this average inventory value, total carrying cost can be expressed as

$$CC = (\tfrac{Q}{2})(1 - \tfrac{d}{p})(C_c)$$

Set up (or ordering) cost would be

$$SC = (\tfrac{D}{Q})C_s$$

and total costs per year would be

$$TC = SC + CC$$

$$= \frac{D}{Q}(C_s) + \frac{Q(1 - d/p)}{2}(C_c)$$

Using differential calculus, the optimal production lot size can be determined to be

$$Q^* = \sqrt{\frac{2(D)(C_s)}{C_c(1 - d/p)}}$$

Example Problem

The Wilson Company produces a drive shaft used in its small electric motors. The lathe used to machine this drive shaft is capable of producing 150 shafts per week. Current motor production is a constant 100 motors per week. The cost of setting up the lathe for drive shaft production is $65 per setup. The cost of carrying a drive shaft in inventory is $3.60 per shaft per year. Annual demand for the motors is 3,900. Wilson management wishes to determine the most economical number of drive shafts to produce each time the lathe is set up.

The optimal production lot size is

$$Q^* = \sqrt{\frac{2(3900)(65)}{3.60(1 - (100/150))}}$$

$$= \sqrt{422,500}$$

$$= 650$$

and the total annual cost associated with this production lot size is

$$TC = \frac{3900}{650}(65) + \frac{650(1 - (100/150))}{2}(3.60)$$

$$= 390 + 390$$

$$= 780$$

Additional Information

Since units are used during the production process, the maximum inventory is less than the production lot size. The maximum inventory can be calculated by subtracting the quantity used from Q, the quantity produced. The quantity used is equal to the demand rate (d) times the production period (t_1) which can be expressed as d/p. Thus, the maximum inventory for this problem is

$$\text{maximum inventory} = Q - d(d/p)$$

$$= 650 - 100(650/150)$$

$$= 606.67 \approx 607 \text{ units}$$

The number of production runs per year (N) would be

$$N = D/Q^*$$

$$= 3900/650$$

$$= 6 \text{ runs per year}$$

Assuming 260 working days per year, the time between production runs (cycle time) would be

$$t = {}^{260}\!/_{N}$$

$$= {}^{260}\!/_{6}$$

$$= 43.33 \text{ days between production starts}$$

Thus, the optimal solution to this problem would be for Wilson to produce 650 drive shafts in each production run. Since the shafts are produced at a rate of 150 per week, it will take 4.33 weeks before the lathe can be switched to another product.

12.5 *INVENTORY MODEL WITH BACKORDERS (SHORTAGES)*

In most cases, a firm carries an adequate inventory so that it has enough items on hand to meet demand. Frequently, when customers wish to buy an item and the firm does not have it available, the customers go to a competitor for the product and the sale is lost. On occasion, however, items are backordered, with the customer taking delivery when the item arrives. Although backordering (allowing shortages in inventory) can reduce the amount of inventory on hand, typically there are costs associated with backordering an item. The inventory model that represents this situation includes the ordering costs, the carrying costs, and the cost of backordering items. Except for the assumption that inventory is received as the current inventory level reaches zero, this model retains all the other assumptions associated with the basic EOQ model. The goal of this model is to determine the number of items that should be ordered each time to minimize total inventory costs, including backordering costs. The inventory model with backorders or shortages is illustrated in Figure 12.8.

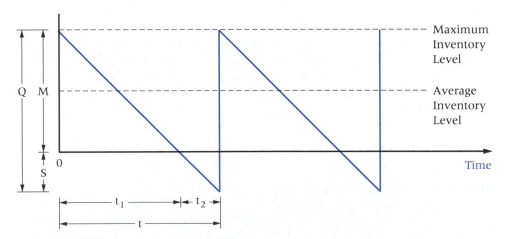

Figure 12.8 Inventory Level for Noninstantaneous Receipt–Backorders

Model Development

Inventory is used at a constant rate until it runs out at the end of time t_1. At this point, shortages occur until the firm receives the order at the end of time t_2. When a new order is received, the firm uses some of the units immediately to fill the backorders and places the remaining units in inventory. The maximum shortage or maximum number of units backordered equals S. The maximum inventory level, M, is equal to the quantity ordered, Q, minus the quantity backordered: $M = Q - S$.

The average inventory during period t_1 can be expressed as $M/2$. Using geometry with similar triangles, it can be shown that

$$\frac{t_1}{M} = \frac{t}{Q}$$

and

$$t_1 = \frac{t(M)}{Q}$$

If the average carrying cost per time period t is expressed as

$$CC_t = (M/2)(t_1)(C_c)$$

the value of t_1, can be substituted giving

$$CC_t = \left(\frac{M}{2}\right)\left(\frac{t(M)}{Q}\right)(C_c)$$

If t is expressed in a fractional part of one year, the number of order cycles per year can be expressed as $1/t$. Multiplying the average carrying cost per period times the number of order cycles per year yields the annual carrying cost:

$$CC = \left(\frac{M}{2}\right)\left(\frac{t(M)}{Q}\right)(C_c)\left(\frac{1}{t}\right)$$

$$= \frac{C_c(M)^2}{2Q}$$

The average number of units short or backordered during period t_2 is $S/2$. Using similar triangles, it can be shown that

$$\frac{t_2}{S} = \frac{t}{Q}$$

and

$$t_2 = \frac{t(S)}{Q}$$

Thus, the average shortage cost during the reorder period will be

$$CS_t = (S/2)(t_2)(C_s)$$

Substituting the value for t_2,

$$CS_t = \left(\frac{S}{2}\right)\left(\frac{t(S)}{Q}\right)(C_s)$$

Multiplying this value by ¼, the number of order cycles per year, yields the annual cost of shortages or backorders per year:

$$CS = \left(\frac{S}{2}\right)\left(\frac{t(S)}{Q}\right)(C_s)\left(\frac{1}{t}\right)$$

$$= \frac{C_s(S)^2}{2Q}$$

Ordering costs remain unchanged from the basic EOQ model. Thus, total costs for this model can be expressed as

$$TC = \frac{C_o(D)}{Q} + \frac{C_c(M)^2}{2Q} + \frac{C_s(S)^2}{2Q}$$

Unlike the basic EOQ model, this cost function contains two unknown values, Q and M. To find the optimal values of Q and M, the partial derivatives with respect to Q and M can be taken and set equal to zero. Solving these resulting equations for Q and M yields the following equations:

$$Q^* = \sqrt{\frac{2(C_o)(D)}{C_c}}\sqrt{\frac{C_c + C_s}{C_s}}$$

$$M^* = \sqrt{\frac{2(C_o)(D)}{C_c}}\sqrt{\frac{C_s}{C_c + C_s}}$$

The value of S can then be determined from the relationship

$$S = Q - M$$

Example Problem

The Telephone Shop sells 9,000 Mickey Mouse telephones per year. The cost of placing an order for these telephones is $25 per order, and carrying costs are $2.30 per telephone per year. Because the Telephone Shop is one of the few stores in the area that carries this particular specialty item, customers are willing to wait when the store is out of stock. The store estimates it costs $40 each time it backorders these items.

To determine the optimum number of these telephones to order each time it places an order, the telephone store will use the formula

$$Q^* = \sqrt{\frac{2(C_o)(D)}{C_c}}\sqrt{\frac{C_c + C_s}{C_s}}$$

Substituting the appropriate values

$$Q^* = \sqrt{\frac{2(25)(9000)}{2.30}}\sqrt{\frac{2.30 + 40}{40}}$$

$$= 454.86 \approx 455 \text{ units per order}$$

The maximum number of telephones that will be in inventory will be

$$M^* = \sqrt{\frac{2(25)(9000)}{2.30}}\sqrt{\frac{40}{2.30 + 40}}$$

$$= 430.13 \approx 430 \text{ units}$$

The number of units backordered during each reorder cycle will be

$$S = 455 - 430$$

$$= 25 \text{ units}$$

We can calculate the total cost associated with this policy as

$$\text{TC} = \frac{25(9000)}{455} + \frac{2.30(430)^2}{2(455)} + \frac{40(25)^2}{2(455)}$$

$$= 494.51 + 467.33 + 27.47$$

$$= 989.31$$

Note that the number of units ordered when backorders are acceptable will be higher than the number of units ordered under the basic EOQ formula. The total cost, however, will be lower. (The Q* value using the basic EOQ formula, with no backorders, would be 442 units and the total cost would be $1,017.34.)

12.6 *QUANTITY DISCOUNTS*

In some situations, a supplier offers a customer a price break or discount if the customer agrees to purchase a specified minimum quantity of an item. There may even be more than one price break or minimum quantity. The main advantages of buying larger quantities per order are lower per-unit cost and lower annual ordering costs (since larger order quantities result in fewer orders per year). Other possible advantages are a smaller risk of stockouts and lower transportation costs. The main disadvantages of ordering larger quantities are higher holding costs, greater capital requirements, and the increased risk of obsolescence.

When a price discount is offered to induce larger purchases, the item cost (IC) is no longer constant and must be considered in the total cost function. If P is the item price per unit, the total cost function is

$$\text{TC} = \text{OC} + \text{CC} + \text{IC}$$

$$\text{TC} = \frac{D}{Q}(C_o) + \frac{Q}{2}(C_i)(P) + D(P)$$

Note that the holding cost in this equation is expressed as a percentage of the purchase price rather than as a constant (as discussed in Section 12.2). While holding cost can be expressed in terms of dollars per unit, some components of carrying costs can, in fact, change as the price paid for the product changes. Thus, we have chosen to use carrying cost as a percentage of item value.

Figure 12.9 shows the total cost function graphically for a base price and a discounted price. As Figure 12.9 shows, the total cost function is now noncontinuous. Below the minimum discount quantity, the cost function TC_R applies. Above the minimum quantity, the cost function TC_D applies. The manager's goal is still to purchase the quantity that results in the lowest total cost. Depending upon the shape of the cost curves, this may be at C_R or it may be at C_D.

Note that, due to lower item costs, the discount cost function will always be below the normal or non-discount cost function. Thus, Q_D^* will always have a lower cost if it is feasible (that is, if Q_D^* is greater than the minimum discount

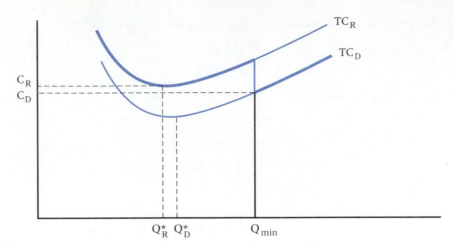

Figure 12.9 Total Cost Function for Base and Discounted Prices

quantity). If Q_D^* is not feasible, the total cost associated with purchasing the discount quantity must be compared with the cost of purchasing Q_R^* units per order with no discount.

When multiple discounts are offered, the EOQ value is determined for the lowest price (greatest discount) available first. If this quantity is not feasible, the order quantity is set equal to the minimum discount quantity and EOQ is then calculated for the next lowest price. This is repeated for all available prices until a feasible EOQ value is found. Total costs are then compared for orders equal to the feasible EOQ value and all the other order quantities previously determined (that is, the minimum order quantities).

The following example illustrates the determination of the optimal quantity to be ordered when quantity discounts are offered.

Example Problem

The Racheson Company uses 60,000 microswitches per year in its products. Ordering costs are estimated at $55 per order and carrying costs are 20 percent of the item cost. While Racheson normally pays the supplier $3 per switch, the supplier has recently offered Racheson the switches at $2.85 each if it orders at least 10,000 per order, or $2.80 each if it orders 30,000 per order.

To determine the optimum number of switches to order, Racheson must first find the EOQ value for each price. Beginning with the lowest price (greatest discount), each EOQ value is calculated. At a price of $2.80, EOQ_3 is

$$EOQ_3 = \sqrt{\frac{(2)\,(60000)\,(55)}{(2.80)\,(.2)}} \approx 3{,}433$$

Since the price of $2.80 is granted only for purchases of at least 30,000 units, this quantity is not feasible. This means that the minimum discount quantity must be used as the order quantity at a price of $2.80. This results in a total cost of

$$TC_3 = \frac{60000(55)}{30000} + \frac{30000(280)\,(.2)}{2} + 60000(2.80)$$

$$= 110.00 + 8{,}400.00 + 168{,}000$$

$$= 176{,}510.00$$

The EOQ value for a price of $2.85 ($EOQ_2$) is

$$EOQ_2 = \frac{(2)(60000)(55)}{(2.85)(.2)} \approx 3{,}403$$

This value also is not feasible, so the minimum quantity of 10,000 units must be used as the order quantity when calculating total costs at a price of $2.85. This results in a total cost of

$$TC_2 = \frac{60000(55)}{10000} + \frac{10000(2.85)(.2)}{2} + 60000(2.85)$$

$$= 330.00 + 2{,}850.00 + 171{,}000$$

$$= 174{,}180.00$$

The EOQ for the base price of $3 ($EOQ_1$) is

$$EOQ_1 = \frac{(2)(60000)(55)}{(3.00)(.2)} \approx 3{,}317$$

This value is feasible and is used in calculating the total cost associated with a $3 price. The total cost associated with this order quantity is

$$TC_1 = \frac{60000(55)}{3317} + \frac{3317(3)(.2)}{2} + 60000(3)$$

$$= 995.10 + 994.87 + 180{,}000$$

$$= 181{,}989.97$$

Table 12.2 summarizes these costs for each of the three switch prices.

From these figures, it is clear that purchasing a minimum quantity of 10,000 switches per order at a discounted price of $2.85 results in the lowest annual cost. While these calculations allow the determination of the optimum order quantity, remember that larger quantities can be ordered only if space is available to store them and the capital is available to pay for them.

While other variations of the EOQ model exist, we will limit our discussion to the four models described. We will now continue the discussion of inventory systems by considering two models with stochastic demand.

Table 12.2 Costs Associated with Each Price Level

Price	Quantity Ordered	Ordering Costs	Carrying Costs	Item Costs	Total Costs
$3.00	3,317	$995	$ 995	$180,000	$181,990
2.85	10,000	330	2,850	171,000	174,180*
2.80	30,000	110	8,400	168,000	176,510

STOCHASTIC INVENTORY MODELS

12.7 *REORDER POINT MODELS WITH STOCHASTIC DEMAND*

In the inventory models discussed previously, we assumed that demand was constant and known and that lead time was either zero or constant. Unfortunately, these assumptions do not always hold. In actual practice, the demand rate and/or lead time often fluctuate over time. In these cases, the demand and lead time values are stochastic or probabilistic; that is, they can be described by a probability distribution. As with deterministic demand, there are a number of different models or heuristic procedures that can be used in stochastic situations, but most of these are complex and beyond the scope of this book. In this and the following section, we will describe some models or procedures that provide fairly accurate approximations of the optimal solutions. In the models presented, we will consider situations where demand is stochastic in nature, but we will retain the assumption of a constant lead time. The assumption of instantaneous receipt will also be retained.

Figure 12.10 illustrates a situation where the inventory demand rate is not constant. Using the average demand rate over time, the reorder point can still be calculated as the product of demand times lead time. But when demand exceeds the average rate, as shown in the case of the first and third reorder periods, a stockout will occur. When demand is less than the average demand, there will still be inventory left on hand when the new order arrives, as in the case of the second reorder period.

Safety Stocks

One way to prevent these stockouts is to carry extra units of inventory in what is known as a **safety stock** or buffer. This is shown in Figure 12.11. When the demand rate exceeds the average or expected demand during the reorder period, the safety stock provides protection against stockouts.

The size of the safety stock will determine the amount of protection provided. The larger the safety stock, the greater the level of protection and the fewer stockouts. Since stockouts cost money, a large safety stock reduces the number of stockouts and, therefore, their annual cost. The disadvantage of safety stocks is that they raise carrying costs. The larger the safety stock, the larger the carrying cost.

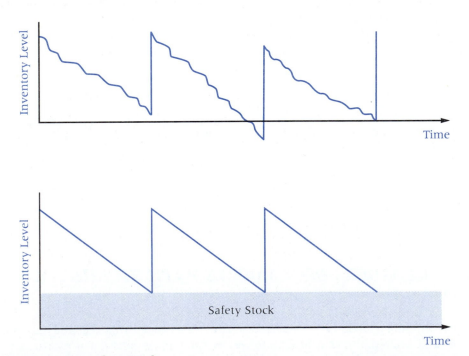

Figure 12.11 Safety Stock

Assuming ordering costs, carrying costs, and annual demand are known, the economic order quantity will not change. The size of the safety stock will affect only the reorder point. The reorder point in this case can be expressed as the average demand times the lead time plus the desired level of safety stock (SS):

$$RP = d(LT) + SS$$

The purpose of the model, therefore, is to attempt to balance the cost of stockouts against the cost of carrying a safety stock so that the total costs of both are minimized. Since demand in this model can be described by a probability distribution, we will consider the situation where the demand rate during the reorder period can be described by a discrete distribution.

Determining Reorder Points and Safety Stocks with Discrete Demand Distributions

This procedure first determines the average or expected demand during the reorder period. Based upon this figure and the distribution of past demand, safety stock levels can be determined for all discrete demand points that exceed the average demand, using the reorder point formula restated as

$$SS = RP - d(LT)$$

The total costs associated with each of these safety stock levels (expected stockout costs and carrying costs) can then be calculated. The safety stock that results in the lowest combined cost is then chosen. This procedure can be demonstrated through the following problem.

Example Problem

J&M Manufacturing sells an item that has an annual demand of 13,000 units and an EOQ of 3,250 units per order. It costs J&M $15 per year for each unit it carries in inventory and $55 per unit each time there is a stockout. Although demand per day varies, average demand is 50 units per day (13,000 units/260 working days). The lead time for this item is 5 days. Company records indicate the following demand during past reorder periods:

Demand (units)	Probability of demand
150	.12
200	.17
250	.44
300	.17
350	.06
400	.04

Average demand during a reorder period can be determined to be 250 units (50 units per day times 5 days lead time). Possible safety stocks associated with demands of at least 250 units are

Demand	Safety Stock
250	0
300	50
350	100
400	150

With a carrying cost of $15 per unit, the costs associated with each of these safety stocks are shown below.

Safety Stock	Carrying Cost
0	$ 0
50	750
100	1,500
150	2,250

Stockout costs are a function of the cost of stocking out, the number of units short, the probability of stocking out, and the number of times per year the stockout may occur. Since the risk of a stockout is greatest during the reorder period, we calculate the number of orders placed per year. As shown earlier, this figure is the annual demand divided by the economic order quantity. In this case, the number of reorders per year is

$$N = {}^{13,000}/_{3,250} = 4 \text{ order per year}$$

We can now calculate the expected annual stockout costs. The number of units short is a function of the demand and the safety stock carried. For example, if zero units of safety stock are carried, J&M will stockout whenever demand during lead time is 300, 350, or 400 units. The number of units short is equal to the demand less 250, and the probability of a stockout is equal to the probability of the actual demand. The costs for each possible stockout are summed to obtain the total expected cost associated with the particular level of safety stock. The calculations for a safety stock of zero are shown below.

Demand	Stockout (units)	Probability of stockout	Cost per unit	Orders per year	Stockout cost
300	50	0.17	$55	4	$1,870
350	100	0.06	55	4	1,320
400	150	0.04	55	4	1,320
				Total cost =	4,510

If the safety stock is set at 50 units, stockouts will occur only when demand exceeds 300 units (250 + 50).

Demand	Stockout (units)	Probability of stockout	Cost per unit	Orders per year	Stockout cost
350	50	0.06	55	4	$ 660
400	100	0.04	55	4	880
				Total cost =	1,540

When the safety stock is 100 units, stockouts occur when demand is 400 units.

Demand	Stockout (units)	Probability of stockout	Cost per unit	Orders per year	Stockout cost
400	50	0.04	55	4	$440

With a safety stock of 150 units, no stockouts will occur and the stockout cost will be zero. We can then determine total annual costs for each level of safety stock.

Safety Stock	Carrying Cost	Stockout Cost	Total Costs
0	$ 0	$4,510	$4,510
50	750	1,540	2,290
100	1,500	440	1,940
150	2,250	0	2,250

This summary shows that the lowest total cost ($1,940) is associated with a safety stock of 100 units. Thus, we would set the reorder point at 350 units (RP = 50(5) + 100 = 350).

Determining Reorder Point and Safety Stock using a Service Level Policy

In some situations where demand can be approximated by a continuous function, the determination of stockout and carrying costs becomes more difficult. In these situations, the use of a **service level** approach may be more practical. When using this approach, management defines an acceptable service level, which specifies the percentage of time that management wishes to have sufficient inventory on hand to meet customer needs. Too high a service level will result in larger inventories and higher carrying costs; too low a service level will result in more stockouts.

In these situations, demand during the reorder period can be described by the mean demand during the lead time and the standard deviation of demand during the lead time. Economic order quantities can still be used, where annual demand is estimated from the mean demand per reorder period. The reorder point can be expressed as

$$RP = \mu + z(\sigma)$$

where

μ = average demand during the reorder period

z = the number of standard deviations required for a specified service level

σ = the standard deviation of demand during the reorder period

The value of $z(\sigma)$ represents the amount of safety stock that will be carried to ensure the desired service level. This procedure is illustrated by the following example.

Example Problem

The Walters Company wishes to establish a 95 percent service level policy for an item. Mean demand during the reorder period is 300 units, with a standard deviation of 14 units. Lead time is one week.

The number of standard deviations associated with a service level of 95 percent (or a stockout rate of 5 percent) can be determined to be 1.645 from Appendix A. We then calculate the reorder point as

$$RP = 300 + 1.645(14)$$

$$= 300 + 23$$

$$= 323 \text{ units}$$

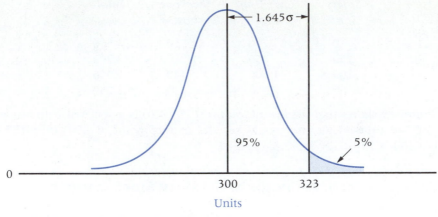

Figure 12.12 Reorder Point for 95% Service Level

Thus, if Walters uses a reorder point of 323 units, it should meet demand during the reorder period 95 percent of the time. This result is illustrated in Figure 12.12.

In some cases, the mean and standard deviation may be known for a period of time that is less than the lead time. For example, the mean demand may be 60 units per day with a standard deviation of 7 units per day. If lead time is 5 days, the mean demand during the reorder period is

$$\mu = 60(5) = 300$$

Since daily demand is independent, we can estimate the standard deviation during the reorder period. The variance per day is 49 units (7^2) and the variance during the reorder period is 245, or 5(49). Thus, the standard deviation during the reorder period is

$$\sigma_{LT} = \sqrt{5(49)} = 15.65$$

Using these values, we calculate the reorder point (assuming a 95 percent service level) as

$$RP = 300 + 1.645(15.65) = 325.74$$

This value can be rounded to 326 units. Note, however, that if the value were 325.44 units, it should still be rounded to 326. Rounding down to 325 units would not ensure a 95 percent service level (although it might be close enough to satisfy management's goals).

12.8 *SINGLE PERIOD MODEL AND MARGINAL ANALYSIS*

In the previous inventory models, it was assumed that the inventory cycle was repetitive and that any items not used during a given period could be carried forward into the next period or cycle. This is not true in all cases, however. In certain situations, a **single-period inventory model** is more appropriate. A single-period problem, also known as the **newsboy problem,** has the following characteristics: (1) orders are placed for a single time period with no opportunity to reorder during that period; (2) the item being ordered is perishable or has a limited life; and (3) demand is stochastic. Examples of this type of problem include a newsboy buying papers to sell at a newsstand; a grocery store ordering perishable fruit to sell during the week; and a souvenir stand ordering a special commemorative item for an upcoming event.

The following problem is an example of the newsboy type of problem. In this example, the stochastic demand distribution is discrete.

A Newsboy Problem: Discrete Demand

George's Novelty Shop wishes to carry a special plaque commemorating the 25th reunion for the Class of 1965 at a nearby state university. George feels he will be able to sell these plaques for $12 each during an upcoming alumni weekend. He can order the plaques for $4.80 each from a supplier. The supplier has agreed to buy back any unsold plaques for $1.20 each, since the wooden frames can be reused. Records of plaque sales at past alumni weekends show the following demand distribution:

Plaques Sold	Sales Frequency	Cumulative Frequency
30	.15	.15
31	.20	.35
32	.30	.65
33	.25	.90
34	.10	1.00

Solving the Newsboy Problem

We will first show the solution to newsboy problems using a table of expected profits. This method involves enumeration of conditional profits for each combination of stocking action and actual demand, and the calculation of expected profits for each stocking action. We will then show how to use a form of marginal analysis related to the service level approach to solve these problems.

Using Expected Value Analysis

George makes a profit of $7.20 ($12.00 − $4.80) on each plaque sold. If he buys a plaque and cannot sell it, however, he loses $3.60 ($4.80 − $1.20), his cost less the salvage value. Table 12.3 shows conditional profits for various stocking levels versus demands, and the expected profit for each stocking level based upon the sales

Table 12.3 Conditional and Expected Profits

Stocking Level	Actual Demand					Expected Profit
	30	31	32	33	34	
30	216.00	216.00	216.00	216.00	216.00	$216.00
31	212.40	223.20	223.20	223.20	223.20	221.58
32	208.80	219.60	230.40	230.40	230.40	225.00
33	205.20	216.00	226.80	237.60	237.60	225.18
34	201.60	212.40	223.20	234.00	244.80	222.66
Probability	.15	.20	.30	.25	.10	

frequency probabilities. The conditional profits show the profit that will occur if a particular stocking action is chosen and a particular demand occurs. For example, if George stocks 31 units and demand is for 30 units, 30 units will be sold and one unit will remain unsold. This will result in a conditional profit of $212.40 $(7.20(30) - 3.60(1))$.

We obtain the expected profit figures for the stocking actions by summing the product of the conditional profit and its associated probability for each possible demand. For example, the expected profit associated with stocking 32 units is $208.80(.15) + 219.60(.20) + 230.40(.30) + 230.40(.25) + 230.40(.10) = 225.00$.

From Table 12.3, the largest profit, $225.18, is obtained with a stocking level of 33 units. Thus, if George wishes to maximize his profits, he should stock 33 of the plaques. While we can use this approach—calculating all the conditional profits and the expected profit for each stocking level—to determine the optimal stocking action, another approach can produce the same result with considerably less effort.

A Marginal Analysis Approach

An approach known as marginal analysis can also be used to determine the optimal stocking action in newsboy type problems. This approach can be described as follows:

Let

Q = the quantity stocked

D = the quantity actually demanded

C_U = the cost of understocking, i.e., the profit per item lost when demand exceeds the quantity stocked

C_{OS} = the cost of overstocking, i.e., the per unit loss incurred when the quantity stocked exceeds demand

The probability that demand is less than or equal to the quantity stocked can be expressed as

$$P(D \leq Q)$$

If, instead of stocking Q units, we were to stock one additional unit (Q + 1 units), the expected cost of this stocking action (overstocking) could be expressed as

$$C_{os}P(D \leq Q)$$

The probability that demand exceeds the quantity Q can be expressed as

$$P(D > Q)$$

Since

$$P(D \leq Q) + P(D > Q) = 1$$

this probability can be restated as

$$P(D > Q) = 1 - P(D \leq Q)$$

Whenever demand is greater than the quantity stocked, the expected cost of this stocking action (understocking) can be expressed as

$$C_U[1 - P(D \leq Q)]$$

If the cost of overstocking is less than the cost of understocking, we will continue to stock additional units until we reach a quantity (Q*) where the cost of overstocking is equal to the cost of understocking. This point is expressed mathematically as

$$C_{os}P(D \leq Q^*) = C_U[1 - P(D \leq Q^*)]$$

Solving this equation for the value of $P(D \leq Q^*)$, we find

$$(C_{os} + C_U)(P(D \leq Q^*)) = C_U$$

$$P(D \leq Q^*) = \frac{C_U}{C_{os} + C_U}$$

This means that we will continue to stock additional units until the probability that the demand is less than or equal to the quantity stocked reaches (or exceeds) this value. In George's Novelty Shop, the cost of understocking was $7.20 and the cost of overstocking $3.60. Thus,

$$P(D \leq Q^*) = \frac{C_U}{C_{os} + C_U} = \frac{7.20}{3.60 + 7.20} = \frac{7.20}{10.80} = 0.6667$$

Looking at the cumulative frequency of demand for this problem,

Plaques Sold	Sales Frequency	Cumulative Frequency
30	.15	.15
31	.20	.35
32	.30	.65
33	.25	.90 ←
34	.10	1.00

we can see that $P(D \leq Q)$ exceeds 0.6667 when 33 units are stocked ($P(D \leq Q)$ = 0.90). This is the same result that we achieved using the expected profit value method. This method can also be applied to problems where the demand distribution is continuous. We will illustrate this through an example problem where demand can be described by the normal probability distribution.

A Newsboy Problem: Normal Probability Distribution

Assume that the demand for George's Novelty Shop is normally distributed, with a mean demand of 40 plaques and a standard deviation of 7 plaques. Since the costs of overstocking and understocking remain unchanged, the $P(D \leq Q^*)$ is still 0.6667. The quantity (Q*) that provides this level can be determined from the normal probability distribution shown in Figure 12.13.

The shaded area under the curve represents a probability of 0.6667. This represents a z value of 0.435 standard deviations. With this information, we can calculate the value of Q as

$$Q = \mu + z\sigma = 40 + (.435)(7) \approx 43$$

Thus, George should order 43 plaques if he wishes to maximize his expected profits, given this distribution.

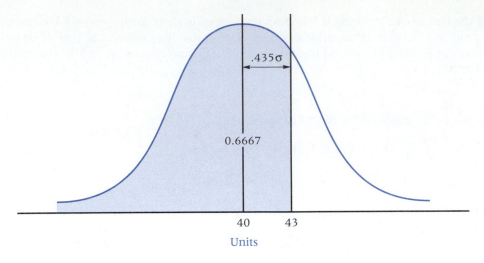

.435σ

0.6667

40   43

Units

Figure 12.13 Normal Demand Distribution for George's Novelty Shop

12.9 *SIMULATION IN INVENTORY CONTROL*

In some stochastic situations, many decisions are interdependent in nature, such as order quantity, reorder point, safety stock, and lead time. In these cases, an optimal inventory level policy can sometimes be determined through the use of simulation techniques. Simulation enables a manager to model a probabilistic inventory situation and to test the impact of various policies. Since simulation is discussed in detail in Chapter 15, including the simulation of an inventory system, we will not discuss it further at this point.

12.10 *A-B-C, AN INVENTORY CONTROL CONCEPT*

Throughout this chapter, we have stressed that effective inventory management requires an effective inventory information system to keep track of inventory and demand levels, and the use of the appropriate quantitative model to support inventory decision making. In the introduction to inventory analysis, we briefly discussed the concept of periodic and continuous review systems. Thus far our discussion and the inventory models we have described have all dealt with single-item inventories. In reality, however, many organizations carry large numbers of items (sometimes thousands) in inventory. It would be highly impractical to use a sophisticated inventory information or accounting system to maintain control over every inventory item. Recall, for example, that the EOQ model is used for single-item inventory, and every time the input is changed in any way, the EOQ has to be recalculated. Imagine using EOQ on thousands of inventory items and having to redo the calculations every time demand or costs change. Therefore, many organizations use a classification scheme to differentiate those items that require tight control from those requiring minimal control. In this way, money and time are spent controlling only important items. The cost of closely controlling relatively unimportant inventory items generally cannot be justified.

The A-B-C classification scheme is frequently used to categorize inventory items. With this scheme, inventory items are grouped according to some control criterion, usually annual inventory value. Note that other criteria can be used, such as frequency of use, item cost, or importance of the item. Different degrees of control (different inventory systems) could be used within each category. Figure 12.14 is a representation of the concept.

Group A includes a small percentage (10 to 15 percent) of the items that constitute a large percentage (70 percent or more) of the annual dollar value of the inventory. This group is tightly controlled. Accordingly, each item in this group should receive special attention. Organizations generally use detailed quantitative techniques, such as EOQ analysis, with each of the items in the group. Group B accounts for another small percentage (approximately 10 percent) of the items in inventory, and constitutes approximately 20 percent of total inventory value. These items merit less control than items in group A. Category C includes the remainder of the inventory items (approximately 75 to 80 percent) and accounts for only 10 percent (or less) of the total inventory value. Inventory control of these items should be minimal, since the expense of tighter control cannot be justified by the value of the items. Frequently, group C items are controlled by some "rule of thumb system" or seat-of-the-pants decision making. Items in group C can be ordered on the basis of experience or when stock is depleted.

In general, as described here, categories A and B together account for 20 to 25 percent of the total number of inventory items and approximately 90 percent of total inventory value. However, depending upon the situation, the number of categories can be varied as required by the circumstances. It may also be necessary to place items in groups arbitrarily, regardless of their inventory dollar value, depend-

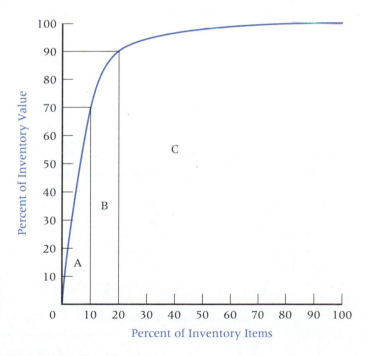

Figure 12.14 A-B-C Classification System

ing on their perceived importance to the organization. The important point is to recognize that some inventory items warrant detailed and continuous planning and control, whereas others do not. A classification system can be utilized to distinguish them.

12.11 *MATERIAL REQUIREMENTS PLANNING (MRP)*

Up to this point, we have been considering inventory systems with independent demand. Many items carried in inventory, however, are components or subassemblies of end products. Demand for these items is dependent upon the demand for the end products. MRP (Material Requirements Planning) is a system that was developed to deal with dependent demand situations, where the finished product is an assembly made up of many component parts. Figure 12.15 illustrates one of the basic principles upon which MRP is based. Figure 12.15(a) shows the inventory level for a finished product that was determined using the production lot size

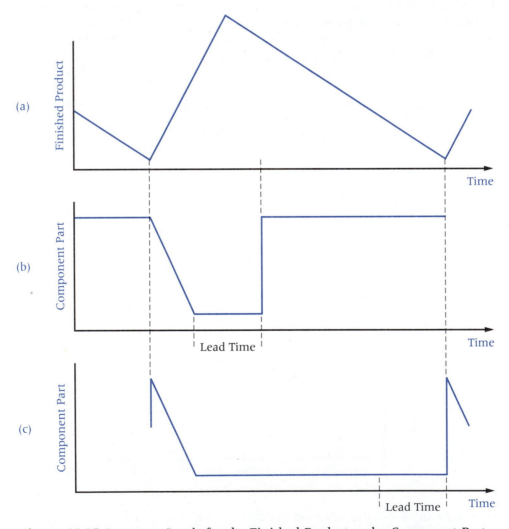

Figure 12.15 Inventory Levels for the Finished Product and a Component Part

model. Production of this product begins at time A and continues until 1,000 units (the production lot size) are completed at time B. Units are then drawn from inventory until time C, when the cycle is repeated.

Figure 12.15(b) shows the inventory level for one of this product's purchased component parts, where inventory is ordered on an EOQ basis (Q* = 1,200 units) whenever the inventory level falls below the reorder point (RP = 200 units). Note that the inventory level for this part begins to fall at time A. When the reorder point is reached, the part is reordered and the new units arrive at time B. These parts are then carried in inventory unused until time C.

Figure 12.15(c) shows the inventory level for the same purchased part, but in this case, we recognize the fact that the part will not be needed until time C. The reorder occurs not when a reorder point is reached, but at a point in time prior to time C. The time between the reorder and time C is equal to the lead time for this part. As this diagram illustrates, the latter ordering procedure substantially reduces the inventory level for the component part. When a finished product is made up of several different component parts, this procedure reduces the inventory level for all these parts. This is the principle upon which the MRP system is based. Items subject to dependent demand are ordered using a time-phased system.

An MRP system has the following components:

1. a master production schedule;
2. a bill of material file;
3. an inventory status file;
4. a computer-based MRP program.

Each of these components is discussed in greater detail in the following sections.

The **master production schedule** (MPS) provides information on the independent demand for the finished product over time. This is often determined from firm customer orders and forecasts of upcoming demand. The master production schedule can be revised as necessary when demand changes.

The **bill of materials** (BOM) is a structured parts list for the finished product that also shows the hierarchial relationship between the finished product and all the components. The BOM also includes lead times for all manufactured and purchased parts.

The **inventory status file** contains information on the current inventory levels for the finished product and all component parts. This file is updated constantly as parts are added to or drawn from inventory. Accurate inventory records are crucial to the successful operation of an MRP system.

The MRP program is a computer program capable of using input from the master production schedule, the bill of materials, and the inventory status file to determine time-phased requirements and scheduled work or purchase order releases for all parts. The sheer number of calculations required make the computer a necessity for MRP systems. The relationships among these components in an MRP computer system are shown in Figure 12.16.

The MRP process and calculations are demonstrated through the following simple example.

Example Problem

The Acme Skateboard Company produces a variety of skateboards that it sells to sporting goods and department stores. The production schedule for the company's "Professional" model for the coming month are shown on the master production

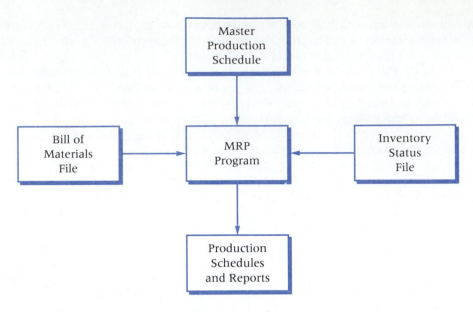

Figure 12.16 MRP Computer System

schedule (Table 12.4). A partial bill of materials for this skateboard is shown in Figure 12.17. The figure shows that the skateboard is assembled by attaching two wheel assemblies to the board assembly. The board assembly is made up of various components that have been laminated together; a wheel assembly consists of a wheel bracket, an axle, two wheels, and various other components (a spring,

Table 12.4 Acme Master Production Schedule

Week	1	2	3	4	5	6	7	8
Units ordered					100	50	0	100

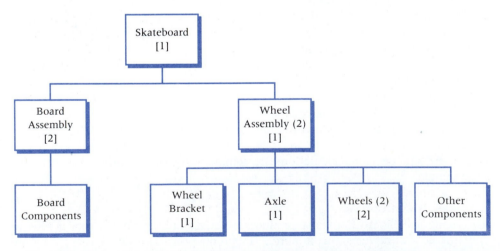

Figure 12.17 Partial Bill of Materials for "Professional" Model

plunger, wheel nuts, etc.). Quantities per assembly, when greater than one, are shown in parentheses. Lead times are shown in square brackets. The current inventory status of three items is shown in Table 12.5.

The MRP time-phased calculations for skateboards, wheel assemblies, and wheels are shown in Table 12.6. Gross requirements for skateboards, derived from the MPS, show that 100 skateboards are needed in week 5, 50 in week 6, and 100 in week 8. Since the inventory status report shows there are currently 20 of these boards on hand, the net requirement for week 5 is 80 skateboards. This exhausts the inventory and leaves net requirements of 50 skateboards for week 6 and 100 for week 8. With an assembly lead time of one week, the work orders must be released in weeks 4, 5, and 7. This means 160 completed wheel assemblies (80 × 2) must be available in week 4, 100 in week 5, and 200 in week 6. There are currently 200 wheel assemblies on hand. This inventory level will satisfy the requirements for week 4 with 40 units remaining. One hundred assemblies are required in week 5. Subtracting the 40 units on hand leaves a balance (net requirement) of 60 for week 5 and 200 for week 7. With a one-week lead time on the wheel assemblies, the work orders must be released in weeks 4 and 6. There are two wheels per assembly, so 120 (60 × 2) wheels will be needed in week 4 and 400 in week 6. Sub-

Table 12.5 Partial Inventory Status Report

Item	On-hand
Skateboard	20
Wheel Assembly	200
Wheels	75

Table 12.6 MRP Calculations for Three Levels

	Week							
	1	2	3	4	5	6	7	8
Skateboards (LT = 1)								
Gross requirements					100	50	0	100
Remaining inventory	20	20	20	20	20			
Net requirements					80	50		100
Scheduled receipts					80	50		100
Planned order release				80	50		100	
Wheel assembly (LT = 1)								
Gross requirements				160	100		200	
Remaining inventory	200	200	200	200	40			
Net requirements					60		200	
Scheduled receipts					60		200	
Planned order release				60		200		
Wheels (LT = 2)								
Gross requirements				120		400		
Remaining inventory	75	75	75	75				
Net requirements				45		400		
Scheduled receipts				45		400		
Planned order release		45		400				

tracting the 75 currently on hand, the net requirement for week 4 is for 45 wheels. The net requirement for week 6 is 400. A two-week lead time for the wheels means that the orders must be released in week 2 (45 units) and week 4 (400 units).

As these limited calculations demonstrate, a computer is absolutely necessary for any practical use of MRP. This discussion is not meant to be a complete description of an MRP system, but it should give you an idea of how the system works. Because the accuracy of the MRP calculations is dependent upon the inputs into the system, it is extremely important that all input figures be accurate.

While the planned order releases in the example reflect actual requirements, orders sometimes are combined to achieve more economic production or order quantities by some form of economic analysis, such as EOQ models or a part-period balancing method.

12.12 *JUST-IN-TIME INVENTORY MANAGEMENT*

In this chapter we have been discussing inventory systems. No such discussion would be complete without at least a mention of the just-in-time system (JIT). The JIT system is used by a number of Japanese firms and is, in reality, more of a production philosophy than a simple inventory control system. The primary goal of the system is to reduce in-process inventory levels as much as possible. This is accomplished by producing in small lot sizes. As with the MRP system, demand for a finished good creates demand for its component parts. Thus, parts are purchased or manufactured only as they are needed for the next stage of production. In order for this small lot size approach to be effective, setup costs must be low. The Japanese have spent a great deal of effort in this area; the results have been new production methods and equipment with very low setup or changeover costs.

The JIT system also incorporates an emphasis on quality. In a system where parts flow into the production process only as needed and when needed, defective parts can halt the process unless safety stocks exist. Since the reduction of in-process inventory includes the reduction or elimination of safety stocks, a zero-defects approach to quality control is a necessary component of JIT. The JIT system cannot be effective when parts or work in process is defective.

The same principle applies to production problems or bottlenecks. Without inventories to act as buffers, any production problems caused by equipment breakdowns or workers falling behind will disrupt the entire system. Rather than using safety stocks to minimize the impact of such disruptions, the JIT philosophy suggests that such disruptions highlight problems in the production process that can then be studied and eliminated.

The JIT approach also includes relationships with vendors. Inventory is reduced by receiving a more continuous flow of parts on an as-needed basis from suppliers. Thus, there must be a strong correlation between the manufacturing schedule and vendor deliveries. In Japan, a vendor might make several deliveries per week or even per day. And as previously mentioned, the delivered parts must be of extremely high quality.

While the JIT system offers some real benefits, its introduction requires some major changes in philosophy regarding the entire production process. JIT has been a major success in Japan, but only time will tell whether it will work as well in other countries with different cultures.

12.13 *THE ROLE OF THE COMPUTER IN INVENTORY MANAGEMENT*

Today, computerized inventory systems play an integral role in the effective management of inventory. These systems can be categorized into three primary areas: (1) recordkeeping; (2) decision making tools; and (3) advanced, integrated systems such as MRP and JIT. Moreover, the areas of recordkeeping and decision making can be combined within a computer system.

A large part of inventory management is recordkeeping. No inventory system can function properly without accurate inventory status records. In manual recordkeeping systems that require a periodic physical count of items, the inventory status records are up to date only immediately following the count. Computerized systems can eliminate this problem, often enabling management to monitor inventory levels daily. For example, many retail operations now use point-of-sale (POS) terminals that immediately update the inventory status as each sale is made or an order is received. The computer can also prepare periodic or exception reports for managers.

Decision making involves the use of models similar to or including those covered in this chapter to make EOQ and reorder point decisions. These models can be integrated into the computerized system, automating the reordering of parts as inventory levels fall below the reorder point. Because these automated computer systems are faster and more accurate than manual systems, they enable management to expand the scope of inventory management to more items.

The use of inventory systems such as MRP and JIT has grown dramatically in the past decade. Such systems would not be feasible without the computer, as discussed previously.

The computer has increased the size and scope of inventory management in most firms today. It has allowed managers to move beyond simple recordkeeping and EOQ analysis to totally new approaches to inventory management.

Focus on Decision Making

Joe Bonatelli, owner of Joe's Discount Beach Supplies, has four stores located on Florida's Long and Sand Keys between St. Petersburg Beach and Clearwater Beach. All supplies are received at Joe's main store in St. Petersburg Beach. The orders are then divided and shipped to the remaining stores in Joe's delivery van. Joe has an undergraduate degree in business and attempts to use good management practices, including the use of EOQ analysis on most of his major purchases. Joe keeps all relevant inventory information on his PC. Among the many items Joe carries is a 32-quart insulated ice chest.

Recently, the distributor who supplied Joe with these ice chests went out of business. Joe has found two new distributors who will supply him with this product. The first, Ajax, has offered to sell Joe any quantity he wants at a price of $15.50 per unit. The second distributor, Wyndham, has offered Joe the following price structure:

Quantity Purchased	Price
1–149	$16.00
150–249	15.65
250 or more	15.15

Joe must now make the decision as to which of these distributors to use.

Data Preparation/Problem Formulation

Joe's records indicate that he sells 1,150 of these ice chests each year. The former distributor charged Joe $14.25 per unit. His calculations show that it costs him 20 percent of his cost per chest per year in storage costs and $38 per order in ordering and receiving costs (part of the receiving cost is the reshipment to the other three stores). The EOQ on this item has been 175 units per order. Joe estimates the ordering and storage costs will remain unchanged with the new distributor. Since he wants to continue ordering at an EOQ level, Joe calculated his costs for both distributors.

Computer Solution

The results for Ajax were as follows:

```
THE OPTIMAL EOQ VALUE = 167.91 UNITS
ANNUAL COSTS (EXCLUDING ITEM COSTS):
     CARRYING COST =        $260.26
     ORDERING COST =        $260.26
     TOTAL COSTS   =        $520.52
THE REORDER POINT IS 44.11 UNITS
THE NUMBER OF ORDERS PER YEAR IS 6.85
THE CYCLE TIME IS 53.29 DAYS
```

Joe added the item cost of $17,825 (1,150 items at $15.50) to the total inventory costs of $520.52. This gave him a total cost of $18,345.52 for Ajax.

The computer results for Wyndham were:

```
TOTAL COST SUMMARY FOR EACH PRICE AVAILABLE:
```

CAT	COST	QUANT	CARRY	ORDER	ITEM	TOTAL
1	THIS PRICE/QUANTITY NOT FEASIBLE					
2	15.650	167	261.36	261.68	17,997.50	18,520.53
3	15.150	250	378.75	174.80	17,422.50	17,976.05

```
PURCHASE 250 UNITS AT A PRICE OF $15.15
THE NUMBER OF ORDERS PER YEAR IS 4.6
THE CYCLE TIME IS 79.35 DAYS
```

Interpretation and Analysis of the Results

The results indicate that, if Joe wishes to minimize his total costs, he should purchase this item from Wyndham. He should purchase 250 units per order, taking advantage of the quantity discount and paying $15.15 per unit. This alternative will save $369.47 over his second best alternative, purchasing from Ajax at a cost of $15.50 (an EOQ of 168 units per order). However, there are other questions to be answered before Joe makes his final decision.

What Happens Next

Joe has been using EOQ analysis to make his inventory decisions because he wants to minimize costs. Implicit in the use of this analysis is the assumption that his demand for this product is fairly constant throughout the year. If Joe has not already done so, he should verify the fact that there are not large seasonal swings for this item. A further consideration in this problem is the amount of space available to store the larger quantities of this item that Joe will be ordering—approximately a 43 percent increase in the number of units that will need storing. He might want to consider the sales distribution of this item by store when evaluating storage space. Joe should also investigate the amount of lead time required on his orders, the reliability of this distributor, and the distributor's payment terms.

12.14 *CONCLUDING REMARKS*

Inventory represents a major cost in most firms' operations. In this chapter we presented a number of basic inventory models, both deterministic and stochastic, that attempt to help management reduce those costs. Each model is based upon a specific set of assumptions, and the choice of model depends upon how closely these assumptions are met. These models are merely an introductory subset of the many variations that exist. The trend in this area is toward more sophisticated, computerized systems, which, in the case of JIT, introduce concepts that extend far beyond basic inventory decisions.

Management Science Application _____

BLUE BELL TRIMS ITS INVENTORY[1]

Blue Bell, Inc. is one of the world's largest apparel manufacturers. It has three major businesses: Wrangler Group, which manufactures denim and corduroy jeans and several other product lines; Red Kap, which makes a variety of durable garments for on-the-job wear; and Jantzen, which manufactures a variety of sports and casual apparel lines, including swimwear and sweaters. In 1982, Blue Bell management became concerned about its high investment in working capital. In this business, inventory and accounts receivable constitute about 75 percent of a company's assets. Inventory averaged over $371 million from April 1981 to March 1982 and represented more than 50 percent of Blue Bell's assets. Annual charges for maintaining this inventory (carrying costs) totaled more than 25 percent of the inventory investment. Net interest expenses had gone from $1.1 million in 1979 to $21.9 million in 1982.

Two major changes were also taking place in the industry at this time. First, the lead time on orders placed with Blue Bell was decreasing. Retailers, sensitive to the increasing costs of their own inventories, were waiting longer to place orders, but wanted the same shipment dates. This shortened the production time available, increasing the pressure to produce inventories and increasing the level of uncertainty in the production planning process. The second change was an increase in the service demands placed on Blue Bell by its customers. The retail apparel industry was becoming increasingly concentrated, as major chains and discounters gained larger market shares. These

[1]Reprinted by permission of Jerry R. Edwards, Harvey M. Wagner and William P. Wood, "Blue Bell Trims Its Inventory," *Interfaces* 15, No. 1 (January–February, 1985). Copyright 1985, The Institute of Management Sciences.

larger accounts expected higher product availability, more on-time shipments, and shipments of complete orders. Thus, Blue Bell faced an increased pressure to maintain superior customer service for competitive reasons.

In response to these pressures, Blue Bell organized a working capital task force. This task force was headed by the vice president of finance and included a manager from the data processing systems group, a chief engineer from manufacturing, and a profit center controller. Work began at the Wrangler Group, which makes 35 million pairs of jeans a year in 37 plants. Wrangler manufactures and stocks over 10,000 individual SKUs [stock keeping units], which indicates the magnitude of the problem faced by the task force.

The task force developed a simulation model for inventory planning which focused, initially, on finished goods inventories. In developing this model, the task force had to recognize that Blue Bell management wanted a production policy that would maintain an even workforce throughout the year. The results of the simulation showed management that inventory levels could be reduced by 50 percent without affecting service levels. This led the task force to identify two key analytic tasks that would lead to inventory reduction. The first was to determine a better approach for managing and allocating capacity. The second was to find a better balance between carrying costs and the risk of shortages. Data showed that inventory levels were not well balanced at the SKU level. Some SKUs had several months supply on hand, while others were out of stock.

The team constructed seven models to address these tasks: (1) sales forecasting; (2) safety stock planning; (3) product line planning; (4) lot planning; (5) size planning; (6) net requirements planning; and (7) marker design and selection. The forecasting model weighted historical demand with bookings to date, producing 12 monthly forecasts that were updated each month. The safety stock model used monthly forecasts, production lead times, target service levels, and a normal distribution of forecast errors to determine the appropriate safety stock. The product line planning model indicated cumulative production for each of the next twelve months, and reflected the desire to maintain a level workforce. The lot planning model disaggregated the production plan and planned safety stocks to lots, such as men's straight-leg blue denims. The size model apportioned the planned lot inventory to sizes or SKUs (designated by waist and inseam measurements). The net requirements model determined the net requirements based upon the gross requirements for each SKU, the current inventory, and the work in progress. The seventh model, market design and selection, was aimed at addressing the fact that there was considerable variation in the net SKU requirements from week to week. This variation made inventory balance extremely difficult.

Fabric is cut to meet each week's requirements. The fabric is placed on a cutting table in layers, depending upon the demand. A "marker" or pattern containing the parts of garments is then placed over the fabric, and it is cut following the marker. The cutting department can vary the number of layers and the marker used, depending upon demand. The task force discovered that the markers frequently contained not only patterns for SKUs that were needed, but also patterns for SKUs not needed that week. Markers were designed to minimize the amount of fabric wasted by cutting. New markers were expensive and had a lead time of up to two weeks. Since the cost of fabric represents over 50 percent of the cost of a garment, reducing fabric waste was an important consideration in marker design. Two design elements that reduced waste were increasing the number of garments in a marker and increasing the number of different sizes in a marker. Waste is usually 15 percent. The task force found that Blue Bell had a library of very efficient markers with low waste percentages, but that the library was not flexible in the number and sizes of garments produced. This resulted in the cutting of sizes that were not needed. Recognizing the possible tradeoff between flexibility and waste, the task force increased the library of markers. They also developed a marker selection model that would choose the best subset of markers from the library and determine the number of layers of fabric for the week's requirements.

The task force tested and then implemented the use of these models. This implementation was strongly supported by top management at Blue Bell. The implementation began with a single profit center at Wrangler and was then rolled out to all divisions.

The result of this implementation was a reduction in inventory levels from $371 million in the second quarter of 1982 to $256 million in the first quarter of 1984. This $115 million reduction was achieved without any reduction of sales volume or narrowing of product lines. Short-term debt decreased approximately $64 million over this period. Net interest expenses in 1983 were $16 million lower than in 1982. The program also resulted in an annual fabric cost savings of about $1 million, despite some expectation that fabric cost might increase. In addition, service levels have remained the same or have been increased by this program. In the test division, on-time shipments increased and order cancellations declined despite significantly lower inventory levels.

GLOSSARY

backorder order that has not been filled due to lack of an item, but that will be filled at a later date as the item becomes available

bill of materials (BOM) file list of components, subassemblies, and raw materials used in a product, including the quantities of each required; used in conjunction with an MRP system, lead times are also included

carrying cost all costs associated with holding an item in inventory for a period of time

cycle time time between the placement or receipt of two consecutive orders

economic order quantity order quantity that will result in the minimum total periodic cost for a particular inventory item

item cost purchase price of an item

inventory status records records showing current levels of inventory

just-in-time (JIT) method of inventory control designed to reduce inventory levels to minimum number required for succeeding demand, theoretically one unit

lead time time between the placement of an order and the receipt of the ordered items

material requirements planning (MRP) dependent demand inventory control system; "MRP system" can also refer to necessary computer software

ordering cost cost of placing an order with a vendor or supplier

production lot size quantity that should be produced in order to minimize total annual inventory costs; applies to situations where production rate is greater than demand rate

quantity discount price discount offered by supplier to induce larger purchases

reorder point inventory level at which an order is placed to replenish existing inventory

safety stock quantity of inventory that exceeds normal requirements; carried as a protection against unexpected stockouts

service level proportion of time that demand should be met by existing inventory levels

setup cost cost of initiating a production run

single-period model classic inventory model where decision is made for a single time period, demand is stochastic, and the item has a limited useful life; also referred to as Newsboy problem

stockout cost cost associated with having insufficient inventory to meet current demand; sometimes referred to as opportunity cost

PROBLEMS

1. The Winter Company sells 8,640 industrial pumps each year. Each of the pumps has a built-in filter that Winter purchases from a supplier. It costs Winter $20 to place an order for these filters and $1.50 per unit to hold them in inventory. What is the economic order quantity for this product? What is the total annual cost associated with this EOQ?

2. The Speedy Cart Company manufactures go-carts. Annual demand is estimated to be 12,500 carts for the coming year. The company purchases tires for its carts from a local tire manufacturer, paying $15 per tire. If it costs Speedy $30 each time it places an order and carrying costs are 20 percent of the average inventory value, determine the economic order quantity for these tires. What is the minimum total annual cost associated with this inventory?

3. Alberson Manufacturing orders 18,000 components a year from a subcontractor. The company estimates that it costs $45 to place each order and that carrying costs are $.50 per unit per year.

    a. Determine the EOQ for this product.
    b. Determine the minimum total cost per year associated with this inventory.
    c. Determine the cycle time for this product.

4. The Hobby Shop (THS) sells a model rocket kit. This kit is very popular, and THS estimates it will sell about 600 over the coming year. Given that the demand for this kit is fairly constant over the year, THS is trying to determine an inventory policy for this kit. Ordering costs are $48 per order. Carrying costs are 5 percent of the item's cost, which is $36 per kit. The vendor is very reliable and normally delivers the kit six days after the order is placed.

    a. Determine the EOQ for this kit.
    b. Determine the minimum total annual cost.
    c. If THS is open six days a week, 50 weeks per year, determine the reorder point that should be used.

5. The Winter Company in problem 1 has decided to produce the filters itself rather than purchasing them from an outside vendor. Setup costs are estimated to be $140, and the filters can be produced at a rate of 12,000 units annually. Carrying costs will still be $1.50 per unit per year.

   a. Determine the production lot size for this filter.
   b. Determine the maximum inventory level.
   c. Determine the minimum total annual cost associated with the optimal production lot size.

6. Given the following inventory information for a noninstantaneous situation:

$$d = 1,000 \text{ units per month}$$

$$p = 4,000 \text{ units per month}$$

$$C_O = \$60 \text{ per order}$$

$$C_C = \$3 \text{ per unit per order}$$

   a. Determine the PLS for this product.
   b. Determine the minimum total annual cost associated with the PLS found in part (a).
   c. Determine the maximum inventory level for this product.
   d. Determine the cycle time for this product.

7. The Ajax Manufacturing Company purchases 48,000 units of a particular item per year. It costs the company $36 to place an order and $2.40 to carry a unit in inventory for a year. The company works 200 days per year and lead time for this item is 8 working days.

   a. Determine the EOQ for this item.
   b. Determine the minimum total annual cost associated with the optimum EOQ value.
   c. Determine the reorder point for this item.

8. The Anderson Company is facing a dilemma. They must decide whether to continue to purchase a key part from a vendor or to begin manufacturing it.

   They are currently purchasing a part from a vendor for $9.00 per unit. The cost of placing an order with this vendor is $54, and carrying costs are 20 percent of the average inventory value.

   The production manager has informed them that this part could be produced internally at a cost of $8.50 per unit. He estimates setup costs at $220 per setup, and production capacity at 64,000 units per year. Anderson uses 16,000 of these parts annually.

   a. Determine the EOQ Anderson should use if it continues to purchase the part.
   b. Determine the minimum total annual cost of inventory using this EOQ value.
   c. Determine the PLS Anderson should use if it decides to manufacture the part.
   d. Determine the minimum total annual cost of inventory using this PLS.
   e. Should Anderson continue to purchase this part, or should they begin manufacturing it themselves?
   f. What other factors, other than cost, might Anderson wish to consider before making this decision?

9. The Williamson Company produces pocket radios. Annual demand for these radios is 30,000 units. Each radio takes two AA batteries, which Williamson purchases from a battery manufacturer. The cost of placing an order for these batteries is $75 and the cost of holding them in inventory is $.60 per battery per year.

   a. Determine the EOQ for this battery.
   b. Determine the minimum total annual cost of inventory.
   c. Because the batteries contain acid, a possible hazard, the state recently levied a $.03 charge on batteries held in inventory. This charge applies to the maximum number of batteries held at any given time during the year (rather than the average number). Formulate a new EOQ formula that will take this charge into consideration.
   d. Using the formula developed in (c), determine the new EOQ for these batteries.

10. The Maxville Company sells 12,000 portable CD players each year. The company estimates that ordering costs are $108 per order, carrying costs are $4 per player per year, and backorder costs are $35 per player backordered.

    a. Determine the economic order quantity for these CD players.
    b. Determine the minimum total annual cost associated with this order quantity.
    c. Determine the maximum inventory level for this player.

11. The Winter Company (problem 1) has developed a reputation for extremely reliable pumps. Because of this reputation, Winter's customers are willing to wait for its pumps even when the company is temporarily out of stock. Winter estimates the cost of backordering is $12 per unit.

    a. Determine the economic order quantity for these pumps when backordering is permitted.
    b. Determine the minimum total annual cost associated with this order quantity.
    c. Determine the maximum inventory level.

12. Pro-Sport Sporting Goods sells a special custom-made tennis racquet. Demand for this racquet is a fairly constant 40 units per month. The racquets sell for $200 each. Pro-Sport can place only one order per month, and delivery takes approximately three weeks. Ordering costs are estimated at $45 per order and carrying costs are estimated to be 4 percent of the retail price of the racquet. While customers are willing to wait when these racquets are not available, Pro-Sport estimates the cost of the paperwork involved and the loss of customer goodwill is $33 for each racquet not available when a customer wants to buy.

    a. Determine the economic order quantity for these racquets.
    b. Determine the minimum total annual cost associated with this order quantity.
    c. Determine the maximum inventory level for this racquet.

13. Speedy Cart (problem 2) has been offered a $.10 per tire discount by its tire supplier, on the condition that it order a minimum of 6,000 tires per order. Should Speedy Cart take advantage of this offer?

14. The Hobby Shop (problem 4) has been offered the following quantity discounts on the rocket kits it sells:

Price	Minimum Order
$35.90	200
35.85	350
35.80	600

What is the optimal purchase quantity for this kit?

15. The Winter Company (problem 1) uses a special gasket in its industrial pumps. Each pump requires four of these gaskets. Ordering costs are $65 per order and carrying costs are 10 percent of the cost of the gasket. The cost of the gasket is dependent upon the size of the order placed. The price list for this gasket follows.

Price	Minimum Order
$.50	1
.48	5,000
.46	10,000

What is the optimal purchase quantity for this kit?

16. How would the answer to problem 15 change if the price list for this gasket were as follows:

Price	Minimum Order
$1.50	1
1.49	7,500
1.48	15,000

17. The LeGrange Company carries an item in inventory that has a carrying cost of $4 per unit per year. The company orders using an economic order quantity and orders four times per year. The number of units used during the re-order period is shown below:

Number of Units	Probability
210	.52
220	.18
230	.14
240	.10
250	.06

a. If this company incurs a $15 stockout cost on each item, determine the optimum safety stock that should be carried for this item.
b. Determine the optimum reorder point for this item.

18. The Telephone Shop sells a portable telephone with a number of special features. This telephone is very popular, so TTS stocks a large number of them. Because there is a long lead time on orders for this telephone, TTS orders only six times per year. They estimate carrying costs at $7 per telephone and stockout costs at $32 per stockout. Past data show the following sales and frequencies during the reorder period:

Quantity Sold	Frequency
80	40
90	36
100	12
110	8
120	4

Determine the optimal safety stock and reorder point for TTS. What costs are associated with this reorder point level?

19. Assume that The Telephone Shop (problem 18) cannot determine the cost associated with a stockout and decides to adopt a service level policy. What reorder point should TTS use if it wishes to meet 85 percent of all demand during the reorder period?

20. A firm has developed the following probability distribution for demand during lead time:

Demand During Lead Time	Probability
200	.10
300	.25
400	.30
500	.25
600	.10

Carrying costs are $1.50 per unit per year and stockout costs are estimated at $4.50 per unit. The firm places orders for this item on an optimal basis, 10 times per year. Determine the appropriate level of safety stock and the cost associated with this level.

21. Larimore Manufacturing uses large quantities of a particular part. The firm estimates carrying costs for this part are $3 per unit per year and it costs the company $8 per stockout. Lead time demand for these parts is randomly distributed, with a mean of 240 parts and a standard deviation of 20 parts. Determine the optimum reorder point for this part.

22. Jones & Sons Software purchases floppy disks from a large manufacturer. Carrying costs on these disks are $1 per box per year and shortage costs are $3.60 per box. Lead time on reorders is one week. If the firm uses 1,200 boxes per week, with a standard deviation of 100 boxes per week, determine the optimal reorder point for these disks.

23. A firm that has a mean reorder period demand of 550 units, with a standard deviation of 30 units, wishes to provide a service level of 96 percent for this item. Determine the reorder point for this item.

24. Frank's Furniture sells a popular student desk. Frank has decided to establish an inventory policy that will ensure that he meets demand 90 percent of the time. Past data show that means sales of this desk are 20 units per day, normally distributed, with a standard deviation of 4 units per day. Lead time on this desk is 5 working days. Determine the reorder point Frank should use to meet his desired inventory policy.

25. A group of investors is planning to rebuild a local dinner theater that was destroyed by fire. Old records show a mean attendance of 200 patrons per performance, with a standard deviation of 25. If the investors wish to build a

theater large enough to accomodate 97 percent of the demand for any given performance, what seating capacity should they use?

26. Lou's Lunchwagon sells sandwiches and other luncheon items to factory workers in an industrial park several miles from town. Every morning, Lou stops at a bakery and picks up some small apple pies that are popular with the workers. Unfortunately, the pies do not keep well, and any pies not sold must be discarded at the end of the day. Lou has the following record of pie sales over the past month:

Number of Pies	Days Sold
15	6
16	12
17	18
18	10
19	4

Lou feels the above demand is randomly distributed. If Lou pays $2.40 each for the pies and sells them for $4 each, how many pies should Lou buy at the bakery every morning if he wishes to maximize his income?

27. How would the answer to problem 26 change if a local plant cafeteria offered to buy any of Lou's unsold pies at the end of the day for $1.50 each?

28. Mary's Fashion Boutique is preparing its order for a line of summer slacks. The vendor sells the slacks only in even dozens of pairs and does not accept reorders or returns. Thus, Jane, the manager of MFB, must order for the entire season. MFB purchases the slacks for $264 per dozen and resells them for $432 per dozen. Any slacks not sold by the end of the season are marked down and sold at half price. Jane's best estimate of sales for the coming season are as follows:

Dozens of Pairs Sold	Estimated Probability
7	.06
8	.15
9	.21
10	.23
11	.18
12	.12
13	.05

Determine the optimal number of these slacks (dozens) Jane should order by developing a conditional profit table and then determining expected profits for each stocking action.

29. Determine the number of slacks (dozens) Jane (problem 28) should order using marginal analysis.

30. The R&S Computer Store sells a software package called "The Tax Accountant" for $125. R&S pays $80 for the package. Almost all sales are made in the first quarter of the year. The vendor will accept returns, but will give R&S only a $60 credit on each returned package. The following table shows past sales for this product:

Number Sold	Frequency
20	4
21	8
22	10
23	14
24	16
25	12
26	10
27	6

Determine the number of packages of this software R&S should order if it wishes to maximize its profit on this product.

31. The R&S Computer Store has the opportunity to purchase any or all of the remaining inventory of a personal computer that has been discontinued by the manufacturer. R&S must pay the manufacturer $500 for each of the computers and plans to resell them for $795 each. Any computers not sold by Christmas will be sold for $400. Estimated demand between now and Christmas is as follows:

Demand	Probability
0	.10
1	.15
2	.30
3	.20
4	.15
5	.10

a. Construct a conditional profit table for this problem.
b. Determine the expected profit for each stocking action.
c. Determine the number of computers R&S should purchase.

32. Determine the number of computers R&S (problem 31) should purchase using marginal analysis.

33. The Lindahlt Company has gathered the following information on the items it holds in inventory:

Item	Annual Demand	Cost per Unit
A	5,000	$28
B	750	30
C	1,200	35
D	1,800	15
E	2,600	44
F	2,400	8
G	1,150	16
H	350	22
I	800	50
J	100	35
K	250	32
L	2,750	75
M	200	18
N	500	25

Perform an A-B-C analysis on these inventory items.

34. Mavis Corporation manufactures product A5. The product tree structure for this product is shown below, with the number of subcomponents shown in parentheses (if greater than 1). Determine the gross requirements for each part (by part number) if 350 A components are required.

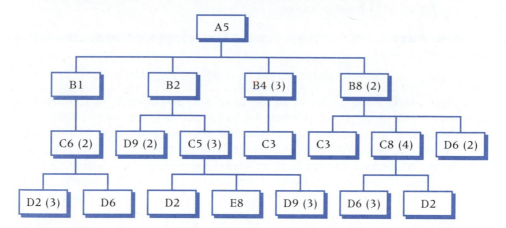

35. Given the following information for the Mavis Corporation (problem 34):

Master Production Schedule (A5)

Week	1	2	3	4	5	6	7	8	9	10	11	12
Requirements							100	50	150	200	50	200

Lead Times		Inventory on Hand	
Pdt No.	Weeks	Pdt No.	Quantity
A5	1	A5	20
B1	1	B1	50
B2	2	B2	190
B4	2	B4	200
B8	1	B8	400

Determine the net product requirements and planned order release dates for all level B components.

36. Given the following additional information for Mavis Corporation (problems 34 and 35):

Lead Times		Inventory on Hand	
Pdt No.	Weeks	Pdt No.	Quantity
C3	2	C3	250
C5	1	C5	50
C6	1	C6	300
C8	3	C8	600
D2	1	D2	500
D6	2	D6	0
D9	3	D9	450
E8	3	E8	350

a. Determine the net product requirements and planned order release dates for all level C components.
b. Determine the net product requirements and planned order release dates for all level D components.
c. Determine the net product requirements and planned order release dates for all level E components.

Consultant's Report ———————————————————————————————

HYPER-FAST COMPUTER COMPANY

In 1980, Mark Stein, a pioneer in the birth and development of the personal computer, retired from the corporation he had founded in the early 1970s. Once again he turned his attention to his first and true love—research and development. He wanted to concentrate his efforts on building a relatively low-cost computer for the educational market in order to make computers truly accessible to all schoolchildren. He understood it was also necessary that this computer be highly competitive in the business market. He needed to ensure sufficient sales to permit him to offer educational grants and discounts to public schools.

In 1985 his new company, Hyper-Fast, introduced the Libra computer, which met with rave reviews, numerous awards, and instantaneous success. The Libra 386/325 is one of the most technically advanced personal computers on the market. It runs either the MS-DOS, OS/2, or UNIX operating system. Standard features include the Intel 80386 microprocessor, running at 25 MHz; a choice of 1 MB or 4 MB of RAM—expandable to 16 MB using a dedicated high-speed, 32-bit memory slot; the Intel 82385 Cache Memory Controller with 32 KB of high-speed static RAM cache; VGA systems, including a high-performance 16-bit video adapter; a socket for 25 MHz Intel 80387 or 25 MHz WEITEK 3167 math coprocessor; 5.25″ 1.2 MB or 3.5″ 1.44 MB diskette drive; dual diskette and hard disk drive controller; hard disk; enhanced 101-key keyboard; one parallel and two serial ports; 200-watt power supply; and eight industry-standard expansion slots. Its options include: 25 MHZ Intel 80387 math coprocessor; 25 MHz WEITEK 3167 math coprocessor; 1 MB or 4 MB RAM upgrade kit; and 2 MB or 8 MB memory expansion board kit.

Each computer sold can be individually configured to meet the needs of its owner. One of the breakthrough features of the system is its modular design. Many of the components parts, including the system board, power supply, and disk drives, have snap-in installation. Moreover, the start-up diagnostic program identifies any problem areas or malfunctions in easily understood English words rather than cryptic computer terms.

Since 1985, Hyper-Fast has introduced several other models, including a special low-cost school version and a laptop. However, the Libra 386/325 has remained its leading seller. Demand has been fairly constant from month to month, with an annual demand of 84,000 units.

The computer and all parts are available only from the factory through direct sales. This policy permits individualized configuration and keeps the cost below $5,000 ($4,875). Hyper-Fast guarantees delivery within three working days on all items. All components except the disk drives are manufactured by Hyper-Fast and stored in inventory until needed. Annual carrying cost is 20 percent for all modules. Disk drives are supplied by Eastern Digital Corporation. The time required to receive an order on these drives has been 12 working days and the cost is $75 each.

Peggy Northry, Purchasing Director, has become increasingly dissatisfied with the delivery of the EDC drives. The 12-day delivery time has recently been stretched to 15 to 25 days. This is making it impossible to plan inventory reorders or to schedule production with any regularity. Discussions with EDC management left Peggy with the impression that the situation will not get any better in the near future. Thus, after discussion with Mark Stein, Peggy decided to look for alternate sources for these drives. She found what she considers to be three viable options.

1. American Electronics Corporation (AEC). The cost to place an order is estimated at $75 per order, and the time required to receive an order is approximately 4 working days. AEC offers quantity discounts as follows:

Quantity	Price
0– 2,499	$75.00
2,500–12,999	74.75
over 13,000	74.50

2. Mizu Electronics, a Japanese electronics firm with a production plant located in California. The delivery times are longer—9 working days, and the ordering costs are $10 greater ($85 per order). The quantity discounts offered by Mizu are as follows:

Quantity	Price
0– 1,999	$76.00
2,000– 7,499	75.50
7,500–14,999	75.00
over 15,000	74.25

3. Purchase Beta Company, a small, local manufacturing company with the capacity to make disk drives and produce the drives internally. The firm could be purchased on the following basis: $2,000,000 in cash this year and annual payments of $500,000 for the next 9 years. The firm would be operated as an independent subsidiary, with the exception of disk drive production. It is estimated that setup costs would be $265 per setup. The firm has the capacity to produce 125,000 drives per year. Carrying costs would still be 20 percent of the drive cost per unit per year. The estimated production cost of the drives is $71 per drive. The net present value of the purchase cash flow is $4,435,920. Lead time on orders would be 15 working days (three weeks).

You have been hired as a consultant to help Peggy by applying management science techniques to this particular problem. Prepare a report for Hyper-Fast that addresses:

1. The total annual costs associated with alternative (1), using AEC as the supplier of the disk drives and assuming a minimum cost ordering strategy.
2. The total annual costs associated with alternative (2), using Mizu Electronics as the supplier of the disk drives and assuming a minimum cost ordering policy.
3. The total annual costs associated with alternative (3), acquiring the Beta Company and producing the drives at that site. Mark Stein feels that, while the company will still be operated as an independent subsidiary, the purchase cost should be included in the cost of the disk drives over the next 10 years. It is assumed the Beta Company will operate at a break-even level over the next 10 years.
4. The non-monetary advantages and disadvantages of purchasing the Beta Company.

13

Decision Analysis

By the end of this chapter, you should be able to:

1
recognize the three basic conditions under which decisions
are made;

2
determine the recommended decision for a problem under
conditions of uncertainty, using any of several different criteria;

3
determine the recommended decision for a problem under
conditions of risk, using the expected value criterion;

4
understand the role utility theory plays in decision making under
conditions of risk, and how decisions can be affected by utility;

5
represent a sequential decision making situation through the use of
a decision tree;

6
determine revised probabilities of outcomes based upon additional
or sample information, using Bayesian analysis; and

7
determine the expected value of perfect information and the
expected value of sample information.

In Chapter 1, we said this book was about making decisions and solving problems. We pointed out that decision making was a part of life, and an important part of a manager's life. The succeeding chapters continued that theme, illustrating how quantitative tools can be used as a tool to help managers make "better" decisions. This chapter focuses on specific types of problems or decisions that cannot be resolved using one of the other types of models discussed in this book, and provides a structure for examining these decision making situations.

George's Sporting Goods

George Murphy, owner and manager of George's Sporting Goods, sells a wide variety of sporting equipment. Although most of the sales are retail sales made to customers coming to the store, George also has a contract with the local recreation department. This contract stipulates that the recreation department will buy soccer balls only from George, and that it will buy them in lots of one dozen. It also specifies that George will sell the soccer balls at a fixed price (set by the contract) and that he will supply enough soccer balls to meet the needs of the department. The manufacturer that supplies George with soccer balls requires him to place his order for the coming season in February, and to order in even dozens of balls. Unfortunately, the recreation department doesn't place its order until after the April program registration. This means that George must place his order before he knows how many soccer balls the recreation department is going to buy.

If the recreation department's order exceeds the number of balls that George purchases, he must place a special order for the additional balls. Even though special orders cost more, he still must sell the balls at the agreed-upon fixed price. If he orders too many balls, he must reduce the price on any balls still in stock at the end of the season to get rid of them through the retail store, since he does not have sufficient storage space to hold them until the next season.

George's problem is to decide how many dozens of soccer balls to order in February, given an objective of maximizing the profit he makes on this contract. We will examine this problem further in the context of decision theory at a later point in this chapter.

13.1 *AN INTRODUCTION TO DECISION ANALYSIS*

All the previous chapters in this book have focused on some form of managerial decision making. In Chapter 1, the decision making process was outlined as follows:

1. Clearly identify and define the problem.
2. Collect any necessary data.
3. Identify alternative courses of action.
4. Evaluate the alternatives using the data.
5. Make the decision, i.e., choose an alternative, based upon the previous analysis and evaluation.

The methods used to analyze the data and evaluate the alternatives have varied from chapter to chapter. In several of the chapters, we have used an optimizing model to determine an optimal solution, thus enabling the decision maker to make the best decision possible. Some problems, however, cannot be solved using optimization models. In such cases, the manager may use a model to provide additional data, which can then be used to aid the decision-making process. In this chapter we describe decision-making situations in which the decision maker must choose from a number of alternatives wherein the outcome of the decision is affected by nature. In other words, at the time the decision is made, the decision maker does not know what will happen.

Let's use a simple example to illustrate this type of problem. A student looks at the sky and sees dark clouds, and must decide whether or not to carry an umbrella to class. If it doesn't rain, the student will experience the inconvenience of carrying the awkward umbrella unnecessarily. If he or she decides not to carry the umbrella, and it does rain, then the student will get soaked returning to the dorm. Thus, the alternative decisions and the possible outcomes are clear. But once the decision is made, the true outcome is decided by nature. Whether it rains or doesn't rain is beyond the control of the decision maker. In these cases, the "best" decision may not be the "right" or correct decision. If getting soaked far outweighs the inconvenience of carrying an umbrella needlessly, the decision will be to carry the umbrella—but later, if it doesn't rain, the decision may be viewed as the "wrong" one. This example simply suggests that good decisions do not necessarily ensure good results. By using the decision-making models discussed in this chapter, however, the manager can avoid making inconsistent or arbitrary decisions. While this may not lead to the best decision in any given situation, it should lead to better decisions on the average.

Decision Matrix

When confronted with this type of problem, the decision maker must be able to identify the various choices available. These will be referred to as **decisions** or **decision alternatives.** We assume that the decision maker can correctly identify all the possible decision alternatives available. The decision maker should also be able to identify all the possible outcomes that might occur. Since these are controlled by nature, we will refer to them as **states of nature.** In reality, any outcome that is unpredictable or uncontrollable is referred to as a state of nature. Once all the decision alternatives and states of nature are defined, a **decision matrix** or **payoff table** can be constructed as follows:

Decision Alternatives	*States of Nature*				
	S_1	S_2	S_3	·	S_n
d_1	C_{11}	C_{12}	C_{13}	·	C_{1n}
d_2	C_{21}	C_{22}	C_{23}	·	C_{2n}
d_3	C_{31}	·	·	·	·
·	·	·	·	·	·
d_m	C_{m1}	·	·	·	C_{mn}

where

d_i represents the decision alternatives from 1 to m;

S_j represents the states of nature from 1 to n;

C_{ij} represent the conditional outcomes or payoffs that result from jth state of nature occurring when decision i has been made.

The decision matrix shows the conditional outcomes that result when a specific decision is made and a particular state of nature occurs. These outcomes are frequently in the form of monetary payoffs—profits or losses. We will illustrate this with the Sporting Goods example.

Recall that George Murphy, manager of George's Sporting Goods, must decide how many soccer balls to order for the coming recreation department season. George has to place his order in February, but the recreation department will not order from him until April. All orders must be in dozens of soccer balls. The balls cost George $11 each ($132 per dozen). The recreation department has agreed to pay $24 per ball ($288 per dozen). In reviewing data from previous years, George has found that the recreation department orders either five, six, or seven dozen balls per year on a seemingly random basis. George's decision is complicated by two additional factors. First, if the recreation department's demand is greater than the number of balls he purchases, he must place a special order for the additional balls, and his cost is then $14 per ball ($168 per dozen). Second, if he orders too many balls, he must reduce the price on any balls still in stock at the end of the season to $9 per ball ($108 per dozen) and sell them through the retail store to get rid of them.

In making this decision, George will attempt to maximize his profits on the contract. Since George has demand information from prior years, he has three decision alternatives, d_1, d_2, and d_3, which correspond to purchases of 5, 6, or 7 dozen balls. There are also three states of nature, S_1, S_2, and S_3, representing the dozens of balls the recreation department is expected to order during the coming season.

We can determine the conditional payoffs for this problem as follows. If George purchases five dozen soccer balls, he pays $660 (5 × 132). If demand is for five dozen balls, he receives $1,440 (5 × 288) and makes a profit of $780 (1,440 − 660). If demand is for six dozen balls, he receives $1,728 but must purchase an additional dozen balls at $14 each for a total cost of $828 (5 × 132 + 168) and a profit of $900. If demand is for seven dozen balls, his net profit is $1,020: ((7 × 288) − (5 × 132) − (2 × 168)).

If Max purchases six dozen balls and the demand is for five dozen, he has to sell one dozen at $9 each. His cost is $792 (6 × 132) and his revenue $1,548, or ((5 × 288) + (1 × 108)). Profit is $756. If demand is for six dozen balls, his net profit is $936, or ((6 × 288) − (6 × 132)). If demand is for seven dozen balls, his net profit is $1,056: ((7 × 288) − (6 × 132) − (1 × 168)).

If Max purchases seven dozen balls, his net profits are $732 ((5 × 288) + (2 × 108) − (7 × 132)), $912 ((6 × 288) + (1 × 108) − (7 × 132)), or $1,092 ((7 × 288) − (7 × 132)) depending upon demand. Placing these conditional payoffs in the matrix gives the result shown in Table 13.1. We will use this decision matrix (Table 13.1) to structure this problem. Decision trees can also be used to illustrate decision-making problems, as we will explain later in the chapter.

Decision Making Conditions

Decision making problems fall into one of three categories—certainty, risk, or uncertainty—depending upon the circumstances under which the decision is made.

Conditions of certainty exist when all the information necessary to make the decision is known. This category can be subdivided into two situations:

1. In the first, the decision maker has perfect information. Not only are all decision alternatives, all possible states of nature, and all conditional payoffs known, but also the actual state of nature that will occur is known. Under these circumstances, the decision is easy to make.

Table 13.1 Decision Matrix for George's Sporting Goods Problem

Decision Alternatives (dozens ordered)	States of Nature (dozens sold)		
	S_1 (5)	S_2 (6)	S_3 (7)
d_1 (5)	$780	900	1,020
d_2 (6)	756	936	1,056
d_3 (7)	732	912	1,092

2. In the second situation, the decision maker has all the input information and wishes to make an optimal decision for a specific, static situation. In this situation, he or she can use one of the optimizing models discussed previously (linear programming, for example).

Because decision making under conditions of certainty is virtually automatic in the first situation, and employs one of the models already discussed in the second situation, we will not discuss conditions of certainty further in this chapter.

Conditions of risk exist when the decision maker does not know which state of nature will occur, but can determine or estimate the probability of occurrence for each state. These probabilities are either derived empirically using past data (e.g., over the past eight years George sold five dozen balls in two of the years, or 25 percent of the time); or they are estimated, based upon experience or "best guesses." Obviously, to be useful, there should be some confidence in the accuracy of these probabilities.

Conditions of uncertainty exist when the decision maker does not know which state of nature will occur and cannot determine or estimate probabilities of occurrence for the states of nature. Note that the decision maker's uncertainty is not total—the decision alternatives, states of nature, and conditional payoffs are known or can be determined.

13.2 *DECISION MAKING UNDER CONDITIONS OF UNCERTAINTY*

Decision making under conditions of uncertainty is difficult, since probabilities cannot be assigned to the states of nature. In these situations, there are a number of alternative decision-making criteria which can be applied. We will present five different approaches or criteria for decision making. No decision-making approach guarantees good results if good results are measured after the fact. A good decision is the one that is best, given the information available at the time. Thus, all decision-making techniques under conditions of uncertainty guarantee equally good decisions. That is, none of these approaches is guaranteed to achieve good results, but all enable the decision maker to make consistent decisions following specific criteria. If nothing else, this method avoids decisions that are arbitrary or inconsistent. We will use George's Sporting Goods to illustrate each approach. The decision matrix for this problem is repeated below.

Decision Alternatives (dozens ordered)	States of Nature (dozens sold)		
	S_1 (5)	S_2 (6)	S_3 (7)
d_1 (5)	$780	900	1,020
d_2 (6)	756	936	1,056
d_3 (7)	732	912	1,092

Laplace Criterion

The **Laplace criterion** assumes that, in the absence of information to the contrary, all states of nature are equally likely to occur. In this problem, therefore, we can assume that there is a one-third chance of selling 5, 6, or 7 dozen balls in any year. Since George wants to make as much profit as he can over time, the Laplace criterion simply uses the average payoff for each decision alternative, as shown below.

Decision Alternative	Average Payoff	
d_1 (5)	$900	[(780 + 900 + 1020)/3]
d_2 (6)	916	
d_3 (7)	912	

The largest average profit ($916) occurs when George orders six dozen balls each year. This would be George's decision using the Laplace criterion.

Maximin Criterion

The **maximin criterion** is a pessimistic decision-making criterion. It assumes that whatever decision is made will probably result in the lowest payoff, once a state of nature occurs. With that in mind, the decision maker finds the minimum payoff that can occur for each decision alternative and then selects the alternative that gives the maximum of those minimum payoffs. In other words, the decision maker is attempting to make the best of a bad situation. Using the example, we identify the minimum payoff for each alternative:

Decision Alternatives (dozen ordered)	States of Nature (dozens sold)			Minimum
	S_1 (5)	S_2 (6)	S_3 (7)	
d_1 (5)	$780	900	1,020	780
d_2 (6)	756	936	1,056	756
d_3 (7)	732	912	1,092	732

We then select the maximum of these minimums ($780). Using this criterion, George would order five dozen balls each year. This decision ensures that George will make a minimum of $780 per year (and, looking at the payoff table, a maximum of $1,020 per year). Thus, the maximin criterion is a conservative or pessimistic approach to decision making.

Maximax Criterion

The **maximax criterion** is an optimistic decision-making criterion. It examines the matrix for the maximum payoffs associated with each decision alternative and then selects the alternative that maximizes those maximums. Referring to the example, we identify the maximum payoff for each alternative:

Decision Alternatives (dozen ordered)	States of Nature (dozens sold)			Maximum
	S_1 (5)	S_2 (6)	S_3 (7)	
d_1 (5)	$780	900	1,020	1,020
d_2 (6)	756	936	1,056	1,056
d_3 (7)	732	912	1,092	1,092

The maximum of those maximums ($1,092) is then used to determine the best decision. In this case, George should order seven dozen balls when using the maximax criterion. Note that, in two of the three possible occurrences (states of nature), George does not make the highest profit with this alternative. But the choice is based upon the fact that, if seven dozen balls are ordered (sold), the yearly profit is maximized. The maximax criterion, therefore, is an optimistic decision strategy.

Hurwicz Criterion

The **Hurwicz criterion** attempts to find a middle ground between the maximin and maximax criterion. Decision makers are, on the whole, neither totally pessimistic nor totally optimistic. Hurwicz introduced a **coefficient of optimism** (α) that attempts to measure the decision maker's degree of optimism. The coefficient can vary from zero to 1, such that $0 \leq \alpha \leq 1$. A coefficient of zero indicates the decision maker is totally pessimistic, while a coefficient of 1 indicates the decision maker is totally optimistic.

The Hurwicz criterion first identifies the maximum and minimum payoffs for each decision alternative. It then multiplies the maximum payoff by the coefficient of optimism, α, and the minimum payoff by $1 - \alpha$ (also known as the coefficient of pessimism) and adds the results together. The maximum of those resulting values is then used to select the best decision. In the example, we identify the maximum and minimum payoffs for each alternative:

| Decision Alternatives (dozen ordered) | States of Nature (dozens sold) | | | Maximum | Minimum |
	S_1 (5)	S_2 (6)	S_3 (7)		
d_1 (5)	$780	900	1,020	1,020	780
d_2 (6)	756	936	1,056	1,056	756
d_3 (7)	732	912	1,092	1,092	732

We then multiply these values by α and $1 - \alpha$. George's coefficient of optimism is 0.5, meaning that he is neither optimistic nor pessimistic. Thus

Alternative		Resulting Value
d_1 (5)	$(1,020 \times .5) + (780 \times .5) = 510 + 390 =$	900
d_2 (6)	$(1,056 \times .5) + (756 \times .5) = 528 + 378 =$	906
d_3 (7)	$(1,092 \times .5) + (732 \times .5) = 546 + 366 =$	912

The results show that the maximum value, $912, is associated with the third alternative, ordering seven dozen balls. Thus, using the Hurwicz criterion, George would choose to order seven dozen balls per year. One problem associated with the use of the Hurwicz criterion is the selection of an appropriate value for α. Estimating a decision maker's degree of optimism is a highly subjective undertaking.

Minimax Regret or Savage Criterion

The **minimax regret criterion,** also referred to as the **Savage criterion,** is based upon the concept of **opportunity loss.** Opportunity loss refers to the fact that there is a cost in terms of lost profit associated with making the wrong decision, given a certain state of nature. This is also known as the decision maker's regret. The Savage criterion first determines the amount of regret associated with each decision and state of nature. It then identifies the maximum regret for each alternative, and the decision is made based upon the alternative that minimizes this maximum regret. In the example,

Decision Alternatives (dozen ordered)	States of Nature (dozens sold)		
	S_1 (5)	S_2 (6)	S_3 (7)
d_1 (5)	$780	900	1,020
d_2 (6)	756	936	1,056
d_3 (7)	732	912	1,092

if actual demand were for five dozen balls and George had ordered seven dozen balls, he would make a profit of $732. Had he chosen to order five dozen balls, his profit would be $780. Thus, his regret at not choosing to order five dozen balls is the difference between those two values, or $48. In effect, we determine the opportunity loss for each column by subtracting each value in the column from the largest value in that column. For the first column, this gives

Maximum Value in Column		Column Value		Regret
780	–	780	=	0
780	–	756	=	24
780	–	732	=	48

We calculate the second and third columns in the same manner.

2nd Column				3rd Column			
Maximum Value in Column	Column Value		Regret	Maximum Value in Column	Column Value		Regret
936	–	900	= 36	1,092	–	1,020	= 72
936	–	936	= 0	1,092	–	1,056	= 36
936	–	912	= 24	1,092	–	1,092	= 0

Placing each of these values in a table yields the **regret table** or **opportunity loss table** shown in Table 13.2. Selecting the maximum regret for each decision (row) yields

Decision Alternative	Maximum Regret
d_1 (5)	$72
d_2 (6)	36
d_3 (7)	48

Table 13.2 Opportunity Loss Table for George's Sporting Goods

Decision Alternatives (dozens ordered)	States of Nature (dozens sold)		
	S_1 (5)	S_2 (6)	S_3 (7)
d_1 (5)	$ 0	36	72
d_2 (6)	24	0	36
d_3 (7)	48	24	0

Table 13.3 Summary of Decisions Under Different Criteria

Criterion	Decision (dozens of balls)
Laplace	6
Maximin	5
Maximax	7
Hurwicz ($\alpha = 0.5$)	7
Savage	6

We then select the minimum of these regrets, $36. This result indicates that George should order six dozen balls per year.

Summary of Decisions

Table 13.3 summarizes the decisions made using the various decision-making criteria. The summary shows that the decision is dependent upon the decision criterion chosen. Each criterion attempts to help the decision maker choose the best alternative, yet the summary table shows this best choice, for the example, can vary from five to seven dozen. What this really says is that the decision criterion chosen depends upon the decision maker's outlook. Pessimistic decision makers often use maximin because it offers a "safe" decision, and optimistic decision makers tend to use maximax because the results are more in line with their viewpoint. When making decisions under uncertainty, selecting *one* of the decision-making criteria *and using it every time* does not necessarily guarantee the best results, but it does ensure consistency.

13.3 *DECISION MAKING UNDER CONDITIONS OF RISK*

Expected Value

Recall that conditions of risk indicate that the decision maker can assign probabilities of occurrence to each state of nature. Using these probabilities, an **expected value** of the payoffs for any decision alternative can be calculated. The expected value of a particular outcome is equal to the value of that outcome times the probability of its occurrence. For example, if a lottery has a payoff of $1,000,000 and 10,000,000 chances are sold, the expected value associated with purchasing a lottery ticket is

$$\$1,000,000 \times \frac{1}{10,000,000} = 10¢$$

This can be expressed as OV, the outcome value, times p, the probability of that outcome occurring. Expected value, EV, is then equal to OV(p) for any outcome. When considering the expected value for any decision alternative, the expected values for all outcomes associated with that alternative must be summed to find the expected value for the alternative. This can be expressed as

$$EV(d_i) = \sum_{j=1}^{n} OV_{ij}(p_j) \quad [13.1]$$

where

$EV(d_i)$ = the expected value associated with decision alternative i.

OV_{ij} = the outcome value for decision i and state of nature j.

p_j = the probability of occurrence of state for nature j.

n = the number of states of nature.

Let's look at expected value applied to the example problem. Assume George has the following data on the recreation department's soccer ball purchases over the past 10 years. The purchases seem to be randomly distributed, in that there is no discernable pattern or trend.

Dozens Purchased	Number of Years Purchased
5	2
6	5
7	3

By dividing the number of years each quantity was purchased by the total number of years for which data exists, a relative frequency or probability of purchase can be determined. Since the total number of years is 10, the probabilities are .2, .5, and .3. These probabilities can be entered into the payoff table as shown below.

Decision Alternatives (dozens ordered)	States of Nature (dozens sold)		
	S_1 (5)	S_2 (6)	S_3 (7)
d_1 (5)	$780	900	1,020
d_2 (6)	756	936	1,056
d_3 (7)	732	912	1,092
Probability	0.2	0.5	0.3

To determine the expected payoff value for the first decision alternative (five dozen), we multiply the payoffs times the probabilities for each state of nature and sum the results. We repeat the process for the remaining alternatives.

EV(5 dozen) = (780 × .2) + (900 × .5) + (1,020 × .3)

= 156 + 450 + 306

= 912

EV(6 dozen) = (756 × .2) + (936 × .5) + (1,056 × .3)

= 151.2 + 468 + 316.8

= 936

EV(7 dozen) = (732 × .2) + (912 × .5) + (1,092 × .3)

= 146.4 + 456 + 327.6

= 930

The expected value of $936 is the largest. This result indicates that George should order six dozen balls each year. The expected value implies that, over a long period of time, George can expect to make an average profit of $936 per year on this contract. Thus, expected value decisions do not ensure that the decision maker will receive the largest payoff for any given decision. Rather it suggests that, by using this criterion for many decisions over time, the decision maker will achieve better results *on the average*. When dealing with monetary payoffs, the expected value is often referred to as **expected monetary value** or EMV.

Opportunity Loss

The concept of opportunity loss or regret was discussed previously in the section on the minimax regret criterion. The regret table also can be used to determine the best solution using the expected value criterion. The opportunity loss table is repeated below, with the probabilities of occurrence added.

Decision Alternatives (dozen ordered)	States of Nature (dozens sold)		
	S_1 (5)	S_2 (6)	S_3 (7)
d_1 (5)	$ 0	36	72
d_2 (6)	24	0	36
d_3 (7)	48	24	0
	0.2	0.5	0.3

Expected opportunity loss values (EOL) are calculated in the same manner as expected values—the probabilities are multiplied times the opportunity losses and summed for each row.

$$EOL(5) = (\ 0 \times .2) + (36 \times .5) + (72 \times .3) = 39.6$$

$$EOL(6) = (24 \times .2) + (\ 0 \times .5) + (36 \times .3) = 15.6$$

$$EOL(7) = (48 \times .2) + (24 \times .5) + (\ 0 \times .3) = 21.6$$

The decision alternative that offers the lowest expected opportunity loss is the best decision. In this case, that decision is the purchase of six dozen balls with an EOL of $15.60. Note that this is the same decision determined by the expected value criterion. This is always the case. Any decision that maximizes expected value also minimizes expected opportunity loss.

Expected Value of Perfect Information

In the EMV example, George is making his decision under conditions of risk. Suppose, however, that a market research company offered to forecast the number of soccer balls the recreation department would buy during the coming years with 100 percent accuracy. These forecasts do not affect the expected distribution of demand, that is, the probabilities that states of nature will occur; they simply forecast which state of nature will occur in any given year. Thus, if the forecast predicted demand for five dozen balls in a given year, George would order five dozen balls and make $780 profit in that year. If the forecast were for six dozen balls, George would order six dozen and make $936. And if the forecast were for seven dozen, George would order that number and make it $1,092 profit. Given that the probabilities of occurrence for each state of nature have not changed, we can determine the expected profit with perfect information:

Forecast	Conditional Profit	Probability of Occurrence	Expected Profit
5	$ 780	0.2	$156.00
6	936	0.5	468.00
7	1,092	0.3	327.60
			$951.60

Thus, if George has perfect information about demand, he can make an expected profit of $951.60 per year. Note that he will never actually make $951.60 in a given year; his profit will be $780, $936, or $1,092. The $951.60 figure represents the average profit that can be expected over the coming years, given perfect information.

Recall that, using the expected value criterion, George expected an average profit of $936. Thus, with perfect information, he can make an average of $15.60 more ($951.60 − 936). This figure is known as the **expected value of perfect information** or **EVPI.** With the perfect information provided by the forecasts, George expects to make an additional $15.60 in profit. If the market research company were to charge George for the forecast information, this amount ($15.60) should be the maximum amount that George would be willing to pay for that information. The expected value of perfect information is based upon the assumption that the information is, indeed, perfect or completely accurate. Since few forecasts offer that degree of accuracy, the expected value of perfect information can be used as a benchmark against which the cost of information can be compared.

Note that the expected value of perfect information is exactly the same as the minimum EOL value determined earlier. These values are always identical, since with perfect information the EOL would be zero.

Dominated Alternatives—A Special Case

Some decision making situations have an alternative that is inferior to another alternative for all states of nature. For example, in the following situation, with three alternatives and three states of nature

Decision Alternatives	States of Nature		
	S_1	S_2	S_3
d_1	50	50	50
d_2	15	40	80
d_3	20	45	90
Probability	0.30	0.45	0.25

alternative d_2 is said to be **dominated** by alternative d_3, because the conditional payoffs for alternative d_3 are superior to those for alternative d_2 for all states of nature. When a situation of dominance exists, the dominated alternative can be dropped from the analysis without affecting the solution.

13.4 *DECISION MAKING USING UTILITY*

In some decision making cases, expected monetary value is not the best criterion on which to base a decision. There are several reasons for this. Monetary considerations are frequently not the only considerations that are used in making a decision. Job candidates from small communities sometimes turn down higher-paying jobs in large cities simply because they don't like the hectic city pace. Similarly, candidates from large cities sometimes turn down more lucrative job offers in smaller cities because those cities do not offer the breadth of cultural and sports activities found in large cities.

Many people buy state lottery tickets for which the expected monetary payoff does not justify the cost of the ticket. It is not that those people who buy tickets are not rational, or do not realize the low expected value; the size of the payoff is simply sufficiently large to entice people to spend the small amount required to buy the lottery ticket. The ticket enables the holder to fantasize until the drawing is held.

Consider the following situation. A small company has a choice between two investments, A and B, as shown in the decision matrix below:

Investment	Favorable Market	Unfavorable Market	EMV
A	$500,000	−$250,000	$50,000
B	$ 50,000	$ 30,000	$38,000
Probability	0.40	0.60	

On the basis of expected monetary value, the decision should be investment A, since it has the higher EMV ($50,000 versus $38,000). But a small company might think twice about any investment with a 60 percent chance of losing $250,000. If a loss of that magnitude would bankrupt the company, alternative B might be the wiser decision, despite the lower expected monetary value. In this case, individuals who choose investment B over investment A are called "**risk avoiders,**" since they would choose a decision resulting in a lower EMV to avoid the risk of a large loss.

Now consider the same company faced with two different investment alternatives.

Investment	Favorable Market	Unfavorable Market	EMV
A	$1,000,000	−$200,000	$40,000
B	$ 60,000	$ 50,000	$52,000
Probability	0.20	0.80	

In this situation, the expected monetary value favors investment B ($52,000 versus $40,000). But some individuals would choose investment A because it has such a large potential payoff ($1,000,000), despite the relatively small probability of that payoff occurring. These individuals are referred to as "**risk takers,**" since they would choose a decision with a lower EMV in an effort to achieve a large gain. Decision makers who choose solely on the basis of EMV are referred to as "risk neutral." They are neither risk takers nor risk avoiders.

The Concept of Utility

In situations where expected monetary value is not a valid criterion for choosing between alternatives, the concept of **utility** may help. Utility is an alternative method of measuring the decision maker's satisfaction with the results of a decision. This satisfaction can be measured in units called **utiles**. Utility can also be compared to monetary values as a method of evaluating the attractiveness of different monetary payoffs. For example, if you had $10 and had an opportunity to gain an additional $100, that opportunity might have a fairly high utility for you. If, on the other hand, you had $10,000 and had an opportunity to gain an additional $100, that opportunity might not have the same utility as the first case. Monetarily, the gain is exactly the same in both cases ($100); but in terms of utility, we might expect greater satisfaction (utility) in the first case than in the second.

Assigning Utility Values to Monetary Outcomes

Utility values can be determined for any monetary decison-making situation. This is accomplished by first assigning utility values to the highest and lowest monetary payoffs. Utility values ranging from 0 to 1 are customarily used, although other values are sometimes used. If, for example, the decision maker faces decisions that result in payoffs ranging from a $10,000 loss to a $90,000 gain, the loss has a utility value of 0 and the gain has a value of 1. Thus, the utility associated with a monetary payoff can be expressed as follows:

$$U(-10,000) = 0$$

$$U(90,000) = 1$$

The next step is to select intermediate points along the monetary scale and determine the decision maker's indifference point between a given payoff with certainty and a second expected payoff with a probability of p. For example, the decision maker might be offered the choice between (1) a guaranteed $10,000 gain, or (2) a gain of $90,000 with a probability of occurrence, p, and a loss of $10,000 with a probability of occurrence of $1 - p$. We adjust the value of p until the decision maker is indifferent between these two alternatives. At that point,

$$U(10,000) = U(90,000)(p) + U(-10,000)(1 - p)$$

Assume this hypothetical decision maker is indifferent between these alternatives when p is equal to 0.25. Since U(90,000) equals 1 and U(−10,000) equals zero, we can restate the above equation as

$$U(10,000) = (1)(p) + (0)(1 - p)$$

Substituting $p = .25$ into this equation, we can state the utility of $10,000 as

$$U(10,000) = (1)(.25) + (0)(1 - .25)$$

$$U(10,000) = .25 + 0 = .25$$

This process can then be repeated for other monetary values between −$10,000 and $90,000. Table 13.4 shows possible results of this questioning process for our hypothetical decision maker. Figure 13.1 is a graph comparing these utility values

Table 13.4 Indifference Probabilities
and Utility Values for
Imaginary Decision Maker

Certain Payoff	Indifference Probability	Utility Value
$ 0	0.05	.05
10,000	0.10	.10
30,000	0.22	.22
40,000	0.28	.28
50,000	0.37	.37
70,000	0.56	.56
80,000	0.70	.70

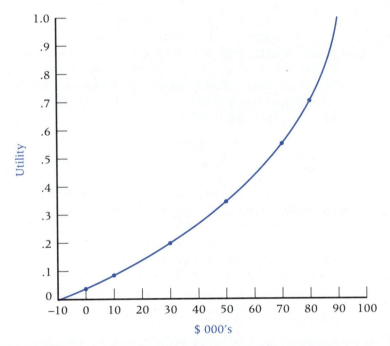

Figure 13.1 Utility Function for Hypothetical Decision Maker

and payoffs. The function shown by the graph is known as a **utility function.** It illustrates the attractiveness of monetary outcomes for this hypothetical decision maker.

Using Utility Values to Measure Risk Preferences
Utility also can be used to measure the amount of risk that a decision maker is willing to take when making a decision. Using the previous example, if p = .50, the expected monetary value of the outcome can be calculated as

$$EMV = (90,000)(.5) + (-10,000)(.5)$$

$$= 45,000 - 5,000$$

$$= 40,000$$

Thus, the decision maker might be expected to be indifferent between this opportunity, with a probability of .5, and a guaranteed payoff of $40,000. The expected monetary value of the outcome is the same in both cases. If, however, the decision maker assigned an indifference probability of less than .5 to U(40,000), the EMV would be less than $40,000. For example, with a p of .28, the EMV would be (90,000)(.28) + (−10,000)(.72) or $18,000. This would suggest that, despite the fact that the guaranteed payoff was greater than the EMV, the decision maker preferred to take the chance that the actual payoff would be $90,000. A decision maker who prefers taking a chance when the EMV is less than the guaranteed payoff is a risk taker. A decision maker who will not take a chance unless the EMV is greater than the guaranteed payoff is an example of a risk avoider. Someone who chooses indifference probabilities, such that the EMV is exactly equal to the guaranteed income, is risk neutral. Figures 13.2 and 13.3 show utility functions for decision makers who are risk takers and risk avoiders respectively.

Expected Utility Value

When the payoffs for various alternatives are expressed in terms of utility, the best alternative can be selected using expected utility value instead of expected monetary value. The expected utility value is given by the formula

$$EUV(d_i) = \sum_{j=1}^{n} U_{ij}(p_j) \qquad [13.2]$$

where

$EUV(d_i)$ = the expected utility value associated with decision alternative i.

U_{ij} = the utility of the outcome for decision i and state of nature j.

p_j = the probability of occurrence for state of nature j.

n = the number of states of nature.

When the decision-making problem has conditional outcomes expressed in terms of utility, the formula can be used with a decision matrix, just as it was when calculating expected monetary value. For example, the matrix below illustrates a

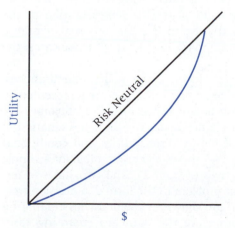

Figure 13.2 Utility Function for Risk Takers

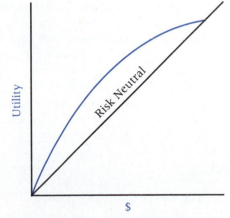

Figure 13.3 Utility Function for Risk Avoiders

decision-making situation where there are three alternatives and three states of nature. All payoffs are in utiles.

Decision Alternatives	States of Nature S_1	S_2	S_3
d_1	.8	.6	.5
d_2	.4	.7	.8
d_3	.2	.6	1.0
Probability	0.2	0.5	0.3

We calculate the expected utility values for each alternative using equation [13.2] as follows:

$$EUV(d_1) = (.8 \times .2) + (.6 \times .5) + (.5 \times .3) = .61$$

$$EUV(d_2) = (.4 \times .2) + (.7 \times .5) + (.8 \times .3) = .67$$

$$EUV(d_3) = (.2 \times .2) + (.6 \times .5) + (1.0 \times .3) = .64$$

In this example, the second decision alternative (d_2) is the best choice, since it has the largest expected utility value (.67). Note that risk avoidance or risk taking characteristics are inherent in the utility values assigned, so the decision determined using the EUV is the best decision, given the decision maker's risk preferences.

The problem with using utility as a decision making criterion is the difficulty in determining utility values for all of the possible outcomes. Not only is it a time-consuming task, but different decision makers are likely to assign different utility values to the same outcomes, leading to different decisions. However, in cases where the decision maker feels that expected monetary value is not a suitable decision-making criterion, but still wants to use quantitative analysis, expected utility values may offer a viable alternative.

13.5 DECISION TREES

Recall that decision-making problems can be illustrated using either decision matrices or decision trees. **Decision trees** provide a graphic representation of the decision-making situation. They are especially useful in situations that require a series of interrelated sequential decisions to be made over time. In these cases, the use of matrices would be cumbersome.

Decision trees are constructed in network form, using nodes and branches. Decision points are represented by square nodes, and alternatives are represented by the branches emanating from these decision nodes. When different outcomes are possible, they are represented by a circle or chance node. The branches emanating from them represent the different states of nature. Probabilities and conditional payoffs are shown on these branches. Table 13.5 shows a decision table for a simple decision problem with two decision alternatives (d_1 and d_2) and two states of nature (S_1 and S_2). Figure 13.4 shows the same problem in the form of a decision tree.

The two decision alternatives (d_1 and d_2) are shown as the branches emanating from decision node D1. The states of nature are the branches emanting from chance nodes C1 and C2. The probabilities for each state of nature and the conditional payoffs are shown on the state-of-nature branches.

Table 13.5 Decision Matrix for Example Problem

Decision Alternatives	States of Nature S_1	S_2
d_1	150	200
d_2	400	100
Probability	0.3	0.7

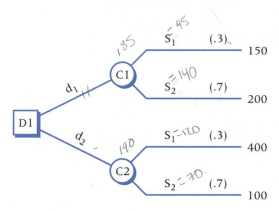

Figure 13.4 Decision Tree for Example Problem

Solving Decision Problems Using Decision Trees

Decision trees are constructed moving from left to right, beginning with a decision node and adding decision and state-of-nature branches. Decision trees are solved working backwards, from right to left. The probabilistic outcomes for each state-of-nature branch are calculated first. These expected values are then summed for each chance node to give the expected value associated with each decision alternative. Once expected values have been determined for each alternative, the best decision can be selected from among the alternatives based upon these expected values. In the example problem, therefore, we calculate the expected values for each branch and then sum them for each chance node. For branch S_1, emanating from choice node C1, the EMV is $45 (.3 × 150). For branch S_2, emanating from choice node C1, the EMV is $140 (.7 × 200). These values are summed, and the resulting value is placed above node C1. For branch S_1, emanating from choice node C2, the EMV is $120 (.3 × 400). For branch S_2, emanating from choice node C2, the EMV is $70 (.7 × 100). These values are summed, and the result is placed above node C2 as shown in Figure 13.5. Once we have calculated these expected values, they are displayed above the chance nodes and the decision is made. Alternatives that are not selected, based upon these expected values, are "pruned" from the tree by drawing two vertical lines (∥) through the decision branch as shown in Figure 13.6. In this example, we select decision alternative d_2 with an expected value of 190 as the best alternative. Decision alternative d_1, with an expected value of 185, is pruned from the tree.

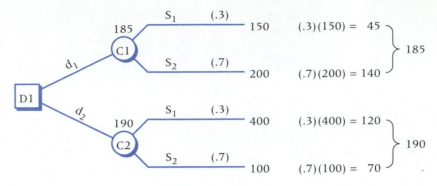

Figure 13.5 Calculation of Expected Values Associated with Chance Nodes

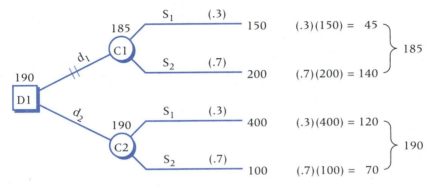

Figure 13.6 Decision Tree Solution

Sequential Decisions

Decision trees offer an advantage over decision matrices in problems involving sequential decisions. Sequential decision making is a process that involves two or more interrelated decisions that must be made in stages, one after the other. Consider the following problem.

Example Problem

The Wellington Company is an oil and gas exploration company. The company drills wells, and if it finds oil or gas, it then sells the rights to a producing company. Wellington has recently been offered $100,000 for the exploration rights it now holds on a particular parcel of land. Since these exploration rights expire soon, Wellington must decide whether to sell the rights or to drill a well on the land. If Wellington drills and finds oil, the rights can be sold for $16,000,000. If gas is found, the rights are worth $9,500,000. If neither gas nor oil is found, the rights are worthless. On any given site, the chance of finding oil is 2.5 percent and the chance of finding gas is 3.75 percent. It costs $800,000 to drill a well. Prior to drilling, the company also has the option of conducting a seismic test, at a cost of $180,000. These tests indicate positive or negative geological formations. If the test yields positive results, the chance of finding oil is increased to 6 percent and the chance of finding gas becomes 9 percent. If the results are negative, the chance of finding oil drops to 1 percent and the chance of finding gas is 1.5 percent. Positive

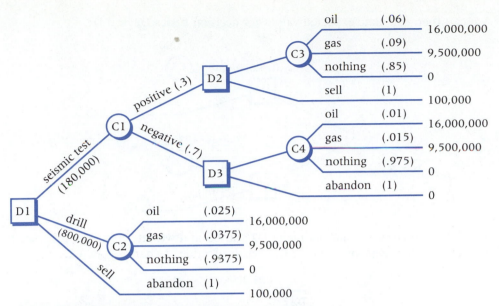

Figure 13.7 Decision Tree for Wellington Company

results are obtained in 30 percent of all tests. If Wellington conducts a seismic test and obtains negative results, however, Wellington will no longer be able to sell the rights.

Wellington is thus faced with sequential decisions. At the first stage, it can sell the rights to the land, drill, or conduct a seismic test. If it decides to conduct the seismic test, the second-stage decision must be made: whether or not to drill a well based upon the test results. The decision tree representing this problem is shown in Figure 13.7. The cost associated with each decision is shown below the decision. Working backwards, we can calculate the expected values for chance nodes C3, C4, and C2. Since each of these chance nodes follows a decision to drill with a cost of $800,000, we deduct the cost of drilling from the expected value to give the net expected value at each of these nodes.

	oil	(.06)	16,000,000	= 960,000	
1, 015,000					1,815,000
C3	gas	(.09)	9,500,000	= 855,000	−800,000
	nothing	(.85)	0	= 0	1,015,000

	oil	(.01)	16,000,000	= 160,000	
−497,500					302,500
C4	gas	(.015)	9,500,000	= 142,500	−800,000
	nothing	(.975)	0	= 0	−497,500

	oil	(.025)	16,000,000	= 400,000	
−43,750					756,250
C2	gas	(.0375)	9,500,000	= 356,250	−800,000
	nothing	(.9375)	0	= 0	−43,750

We can then calculate expected values for decision nodes D2 and D3.

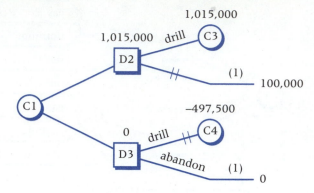

Once the decisions are made at nodes D2 and D3 and we determine the associated expected values, we can calculate the expected value at chance node C1.

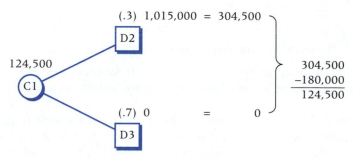

At chance node C1, the cost of testing is deducted from the expected value of $304,500 to determine the net expected value. All the necessary calculations are now complete and we can make decision D1.

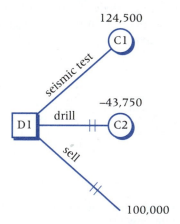

As these results show, Wellington should: (1) make the decision to conduct a seismic test; and, if the test results are positive, (2) drill a well. If, on the other hand, the test results are negative, Wellington should not drill. The expected monetary value of these decisions is a profit of $124,500 for this site.

While the decision tree in this example has been segmented and abbreviated as the calculations were performed, in most cases all calculations can be performed on the original, complete decision tree. Again, decision trees are one method of displaying the decision-making problem visually. Problems involving sequential decisions are more easily illustrated using a decision tree than with a series of decision matrices.

13.6 *BAYESIAN ANALYSIS—DECISION MAKING WITH SAMPLING*

In most cases, managers attempt to use the best information available to make their decisions. Frequently, managers can obtain additional information that will allow them to make better decisions, but this additional information is not without cost in terms of both time and money. Managers often make decisions based upon the information at hand simply because the cost of obtaining additional information exceeds the benefits derived by it.

When we use expected value to make decisions, the probabilities assigned to the various states of nature are sometimes subjective in nature. The accuracy of these probability estimates sometimes can be improved by obtaining additional information through market research, experimentation, or sampling. When such additional information can be obtained, the original probability estimates, known as **prior probabilities**, can be revised through the use of Bayes's theorem. These revised probabilities are known as **posterior probabilities.**

Bayes's theorem states that, if the probability of a state of nature occurring, $P(S_i)$, is known, and the conditional probability of an experimental result occurring given that a particular state of nature exists, $P(R_j|S_i)$, is also known, then it is possible to determine the probability that a given state of nature exists based upon the experimental result obtained. This can be stated as

$$P(S_i|R_j) = \frac{P(S_i)P(R_j|S_i)}{P(R_j)} \quad \text{or} \quad \frac{P(S_i \cap R_j)}{P(R_j)} \quad [13.3]$$

$\left.\begin{array}{c} \\ \\ \\ \\ \end{array}\right\}$ Bayes theory.

where $P(R_j)$ can be expressed as

$$P(R_j) = \sum_{j=1}^{n} P(S_i)P(R_j|S_i) \quad [13.4]$$

The use of Bayes's theorem to revise probability estimates, and the use of those posterior probabilities in the decision-making process, will be illustrated through the following example.

Example Problem

Mr. Williams is considering the purchase of one of three different machines. All three machines can be used to produced the company's primary product, but the cost savings associated with each machine varies with the extent to which the machine is utilized. Thus, machine 1 is most economical at low production volumes, machine 2 at moderate volumes, and machine 3 at higher volumes. The volume at which the machines will operate is a function of the market for the company's new product. The company has prepared estimates that the market will be poor, moderate, or good: poor—40 percent; moderate—35 percent; and good—25 percent. Table 13.6 shows the cost savings associated with each of these machines for each market condition. Also shown are the EMV calculations for each alternative.

Table 13.6 Conditional Payoffs and EMVs

Decision Alternatives	States of Nature S_1 Poor	S_2 Moderate	S_3 Good	EMV
d_1	6,000	10,000	14,000	9,400
d_2	−2,000	18,000	18,000	10,000
d_3	−5,000	12,000	29,000	9,450
Probability	0.40	0.35	0.25	

Based upon the EMV calculations, Mr. Williams would choose to buy the second machine (d_2), since it offers the greatest expected savings ($10,000).

A market research firm has offered to conduct a survey and make an assessment of market conditions with regard to the company's new product. The cost of this research would be $1,500, and the assessment would indicate whether the market is unfavorable or favorable toward this product. The market research firm has provided the following conditional probabilities associated with this assessment:

Assessment	Existing State of Nature S_1 Poor	S_2 Moderate	S_3 Good
Unfavorable	0.8	0.6	0.1
Favorable	0.2	0.4	0.9

This table shows that, if poor market conditions actually exist, the assessment will be unfavorable 80 percent of the time and favorable only 20 percent of the time. If moderate market conditions exist, the assessment will be unfavorable 60 percent of the time and favorable 40 percent of the time. And if market conditions are good, the assessment will be unfavorable 10 percent of the time and favorable 90 percent of the time.

From the initial problem, the prior probabilities for the states of nature are

$$P(S_1) = 0.40$$

$$P(S_2) = 0.35$$

$$P(S_3) = 0.25$$

The table of market research assessment results gives the following conditional probabilities. (UR indicates an unfavorable result and FR a favorable result.)

$$P(UR|S_1) = 0.80 \qquad P(FR|S_1) = 0.20$$

$$P(UR|S_2) = 0.60 \qquad P(FR|S_2) = 0.40$$

$$P(UR|S_3) = 0.10 \qquad P(FR|S_3) = 0.90$$

However, Mr. Williams really wants to know how the probabilities associated with each state of nature will change as a result of the market research information. To determine this, the joint probabilities (state of nature and unfavorable results) must first be calculated. To do so, we multiply the probabilities of occurrence for each state of nature by the conditional probabilities for a particular assessment, given that state of nature. Thus, if the assessment is unfavorable, the joint probabilities, $P(S_i \cap R_j)$, are

$$P(S_1 \cap UR) = P(S_1)P(UR|S_1) = (.40)(.8) = 0.320$$

$$P(S_2 \cap UR) = P(S_2)P(UR|S_2) = (.35)(.6) = 0.210$$

$$P(S_3 \cap UR) = P(S_3)P(UR|S_3) = (.25)(.1) = 0.025$$

Recall from equation [13.4] that the probability of a result $P(R_j)$ is equal to the sum of these values. Thus, the probability of the market research returning an unfavorable assessment $P(UR)$ is 55.5 percent (0.320 + 0.210 + 0.025).

We can now use equation [13.3] to determine the posterior probability of a state of nature given an unfavorable assessment, $P(S_1|UR)$.

$$P(S_1|UR) = \frac{0.320}{0.555} = 0.577$$

$$P(S_2|UR) = \frac{0.210}{0.555} = 0.378$$

$$P(S_3|UR) = \frac{0.025}{0.555} = 0.045$$

Thus, if the market research were to be conducted and if the assessment were unfavorable, we would revise the probabilities of the states of nature occurring from 0.4, 0.35, and 0.25 to 0.577, 0.378, and 0.045 respectively. Since the EMVs are calculated using the probabilities for the states of nature, once we revise these probabilities, we must revise the EMVs. Thus, if an unfavorable assessment occurs, we recalculate the EMVs using these new conditional probabilities. The results of those calculations are shown in Table 13.7. If the market research yields an unfavorable market assessment, Mr. Williams should select the first machine (d_1), with an expected monetary value of $7,872.

We can perform similar calculations to determine the joint probabilities when the market research assessment is favorable:

$$P(S_1 \cap FR) = P(S_1)P(FR|S_1) = (.40)(.2) = 0.080$$

$$P(S_2 \cap FR) = P(S_2)P(FR|S_2) = (.35)(.4) = 0.140$$

$$P(S_3 \cap FR) = P(S_3)P(FR|S_3) = (.25)(.9) = 0.225$$

Summing these results, we obtain the probability of the market research yielding a favorable assessment, $P(FR)$. This probability is equal to 44.5 percent (0.080 + 0.140 + 0.225).

Table 13.7 Expected Monetary Values When Result is Unfavorable

Decision Alternatives	States of Nature S_1 Poor	S_2 Moderate	S_3 Good	EMV
d_1	6,000	10,000	14,000	7,872
d_2	−2,000	18,000	18,000	6,460
d_3	−5,000	12,000	29,000	2,956
Probability	0.577	0.378	0.045	

We then use equation [13.3] to determine the posterior probability of a state of nature given a favorable assessment, $P(S_1|FR)$.

$$P(S_1|FR) = \frac{0.080}{0.445} = 0.180$$

$$P(S_2|FR) = \frac{0.140}{0.445} = 0.315$$

$$P(S_3|FR) = \frac{0.225}{0.445} = 0.506$$

We then use these probabilities to calculate the expected monetary values associated with a favorable assessment. The results of those are calculations shown in Table 13.8. Thus, if the market research yields a favorable market assessment, Mr. Williams should select machine 3 (d_3), with an expected monetary value of $17,554. Note that Mr. Williams should select machine 1 if the market research assessment is unfavorable and machine 3 if the assessment is favorable; but it has not yet been decided whether or not he should actually hire the market research firm to make the assessment. We can show this decision (whether or not to hire the market research firm) using the decision tree in Figure 13.8. Decision D1 is to hire

Table 13.8 Expected Monetary Values When Result is Favorable

Decision Alternatives	States of Nature S_1 Poor	S_2 Moderate	S_3 Good	EMV
d_1	6,000	10,000	14,000	11,314
d_2	−2,000	18,000	18,000	14,418
d_3	−5,000	12,000	29,000	17,554
Probability	0.180	0.315	0.225	

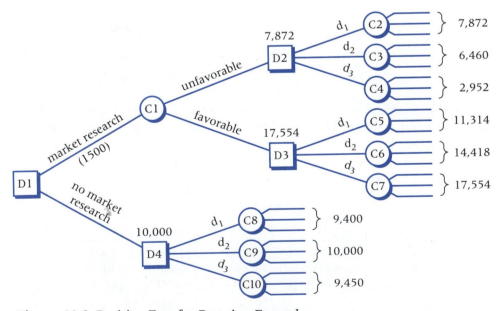

Figure 13.8 Decision Tree for Bayesian Example

the market research firm or not to hire the firm. If the firm is hired, the results are either unfavorable (55.5 percent of the time) or favorable (44.5 percent of the time). If the results are unfavorable, decision D2 is to buy machine 1 with an EMV of $7,872. If the results are favorable, decision D3 is to buy machine 3 with an EMV of $17,554. Decision node D4 represents the original problem with an EMV of $10,000. We calculate the EMV at chance node C1 as the sum of the probability of a particular assessment multiplied by the EMV associated with that result for each result. We then subtract the cost of the research ($1,500) from this value to determine the net expected monetary value of $10,680.49.

$$\text{EMV} = (.555)(7,872) + (.445)(17,554)$$
$$= 4,368.96 + 7,811.53 = 12,180.49$$

$$\text{net EMV at C1} = 12,180.49 - 1,500 = 10,680.49$$

Since hiring the firm has the greater EMV ($10,680.49 versus $10,000), the decision is made to hire the firm. The full **decision policy** for this problem can be stated as: (1) hire the firm to perform the market research and assess the market for the company's new product; and (2) if the assessment is unfavorable, purchase machine 1; if the assessment is favorable, purchase machine 3.

Using a Tabular Approach to Calculate Posterior Probabilities

The calculations necessary to develop posterior probabilities can also be performed by organizing the data into tabular form. This tabular form is sometimes easier to work with than the formulas. One table must be constructed for each possible sample result (R_j). The table has five columns. Column (1) contains the states of nature (S_i). Column (2) contains the prior probabilities $P(S_i)$ associated with each state of nature. Column (3) contains the conditional probabilities showing the result of the sample (research or experiment), given the particular state of nature $P(R_j | S_i)$. Column (4) shows the joint probability $P(R_j \cap S_i)$, which equals the product of columns (2) and (3), $P(S_i)(P(R_j | S_i))$. The sum of the values in column (4) is the probability of the sample result $P(R_j)$. Column (5) contains the posterior probabilities $P(S_i | R_j)$; these values are determined by dividing the joint probabilities in column (4) by the probability of the sample result (as in equation [13.3]). Table 13.9 shows the tabular form of the calculations for unfavorable and favorable results for the example problem.

Expected Value of Sample Information

As this problem illustrates, it is possible to determine the expected monetary values associated with the assessment results before the market research is performed. Those expected monetary values are, in fact, used to make the decision on whether or not to do the research. While the results of such research often enables a manager to make a better decision, the information gained usually is far from perfect. Earlier in the chapter we determined the expected value of perfect information (EVPI). The **expected value of sample information** (EVSI) can also be determined. The EVSI indicates how much this imperfect sample information is worth to the manager. In the example, Mr. Williams can make an expected $10,000

Table 13.9 Calculation of Posterior Probabilities Using Tabular Form

UNFAVORABLE RESULTS

(1) S_i	(2) $P(S_i)$		(3) $P(UR \mid S_i)$		(4) $P(UR \cap S_i)$	(5) $P(S_i \mid UR)$		
S1	0.40	×	0.8	=	0.320	0.577	=	$.320/.555$
S2	0.35	×	0.6	=	0.210	0.378	=	$.210/.555$
S3	0.25	×	0.1	=	0.025	0.045	=	$.025/.555$

$$P(UR) = 0.555$$

FAVORABLE RESULTS

(1) S_i	(2) $P(S_i)$		(3) $P(FR \mid S_i)$		(4) $P(FR \cap S_i)$	(5) $P(S_i \mid FR)$		
S1	0.40	×	0.2	=	0.080	0.180	=	$.080/.445$
S2	0.35	×	0.4	=	0.140	0.315	=	$.140/.445$
S3	0.25	×	0.9	=	0.225	0.506	=	$.225/.445$

$$P(FR) = 0.445$$

without the sample information and $12,180.49 (prior to paying the market research firm) with the sample information. Thus, the value of that information is the amount by which Mr. Williams can increase his expected gain (EMV) if he has it. In this case, that value is $2,180.49 ($12,180.49 − 10,000). This means that Mr. Williams would be willing to pay up to $2,180.49 for this information. Since the actual cost of the research is $1,500, it is worthwhile for Mr. Williams to purchase it. Note that, if the expected value of the outcomes with the research had been less than $10,000, it would have indicated that the additional information had no value to the company.

13.7 *COMPUTER APPLICATIONS*

Commercially developed decision analysis software is now available for both personal computers and mainframes, although its growth has been slow. This software covers a broad range of decision analysis topics. Some of it is aimed at simply reducing the computational burden associated with large decision matrices or Bayes analysis. Other software provides color-graphic displays of decision trees. Packages that solve large, complex decision tree problems are also available. Some of these packages are able to prune thousands of branches in a matter of seconds.

Software that attempts to quantify the subjective inputs of the process has also been developed, and there are interactive packages that attempt to estimate the decision maker's risk preferences and develop an indifference function. Other interactive software packages aid probability estimates through the use of pie charts and other graphic displays. Finally, packages exist that attempt to quantify multiple-criteria decision-making inputs and to help the decision maker select an alternative.

▮ Focus on Decision Making ▮

The management of the Rochester Savings and Loan Association (RSL) has been under increasing pressure from its board of directors to ensure that all its loans are in compliance with both RSL operating procedures and Federal savings and loan regulations. These procedures include establishing the debtor's credit rating, determining the appropriate collateral, and setting the required interest rate and payment period. The loan agreement must then be signed by the debtors and approved and signed by the authorized loan officers of RSL.

After granting the loan, the loan department is then required to review each loan periodically to ensure that the proper payments are being made on time and that RSL's records continue to be accurate and up to date. Moreover, new Federal regulations require that savings and loans conduct periodic audits of all loans to ensure that proper procedures are being followed. The government considers loan departments that meet these regulations to be "in compliance." Loan departments that do not meet the regulations are said to be "out of complicance" and are subject to further audits by Federal auditors. As a rule of thumb, 90 percent of all loans must be in compliance to avoid Federal penalties.

Based upon previous audits, Elaine Davis, vice president of RSL, feels that the loan department conforms to all rules and regulations and is in compliance 95 percent of the time, despite occasional lapses in procedures. George Swartz, a board member, feels less certain. Based upon much of the unfavorable publicity savings and loans have been receiving nationally, George feels the percentage of compliance is much lower.

To convince George that RSL's loan department is in compliance, Elaine invited him to sit in on an upcoming audit. Elaine explained to George that the audit was based upon a random sampling of the outstanding loans. She further explained that, based upon national statistics furnished by the government, if a loan department is in compliance, there is still a 3 percent chance that an audit may discover a discrepancy. For departments out of compliance, that chance is 40 percent.

Elaine began by selecting five loans at random. She and George then examined the papers prepared by the loan officers when the loans were granted and the records of payment amounts and dates. The first three loans were in order, causing Elaine to comment that everything was in compliance, as she had suggested. The fourth loan they examined, however, contained a discrepancy. A recent loan payment was made three weeks late and the account had not been flagged to indicate possible problems. The fifth loan contained no discrepancies. George immediately stated that four out of five loans was only 80 percent, well below the government guidelines, and therefore the loan department was out of compliance. Elaine responded by saying a computer program was available that could be used to perform further analysis on this problem, and that they should look at the results before jumping to any conclusions. She was sure the results of the program would show that there was nothing to be concerned about. Elaine entered the data into an office PC and obtained the results discussed in the next section.

Data Preparation/Problem Formulation

Elaine felt this problem could be represented as a Bayesian decision analysis problem. She let state of nature S1 represent "in compliance" and S2 represent "out of compliance." She let I, the result, be the probability of finding a discrepancy on the fourth loan examined, assuming the department is in compliance. The probability that the department is in compliance is .95, based upon past audit data, and the probability it is out of compliance is .05. If there is a 3 percent chance of a discrepancy if the department is in compliance, then there is a 97 percent chance of no discrepancy. Thus the probability of finding a discrepancy in the fourth loan if the department is in compliance is the joint probability for the five results or

$$(.97)(.97)(.97)(.03)(.97) = .02656$$

The probability of finding the discrepancy in the fourth loan if the department is out of compliance is the joint probability

$$(.6)(.6)(.6)(.4)(.6) = .05184$$

Thus, Elaine knows $P(S1) = .95$ and $P(S2) = .05$. She also knows $P(I \mid S1) = .02656$ and $P(I \mid S2) = .05184$.

Computer Solution

Elaine entered this data into the computer and obtained the following solution.

S	P(S)	P(I|S)	P(I,S)	P(S|I)
S1	.95	.02656	0.0252	0.907
S2	.05	.05184	0.0026	0.093
			0.0278	

Interpretation and Analysis of the Results

The results show that the probability of obtaining a discrepancy on only the fourth loan to be 2.8 percent. The revised probability estimates show the probability of being in compliance as 90.7 percent and the probability of being out of compliance as 9.3 percent. While this indicated that things were probably not as bad as George had assumed (20 percent discrepancies), neither were they as good as Elaine had assumed (5 percent discrepancies). Although the probability of being in compliance meets the government requirements, both agreed that the sample size should be expanded and the program rerun.

Examination of five additional loans found all to be correct. Elaine reran the program, using the probability of one discrepancy in ten (the fourth loan), and obtained the following results.

S	P(S)	P(I|S)	P(I,S)	P(S|I)
S1	.95	.02281	0.0217	0.991
S2	.05	.00403	0.0002	0.009
			0.0219	

As these results show, the revised probability of being in compliance has changed to 99.1 percent. While the audit results still show discrepancies in 10 percent of the examined loans, Bayes analysis takes into account the results of past experience, which indicates that the loan department has been in compliance 95 percent of the time.

What Happens Next

While the above results from a sample of 10 loans strongly suggest that the department is in compliance, the entire audit procedure should be clearly defined. This should include the number of audits per year, the number of loans that should be checked in any audit, and the number of discrepancies from this sample that would make the loan department out of compliance. And, of course, there should be procedures for dealing with discrepancies in order to help the loan department avoid them in the future.

13.8 *CONCLUDING REMARKS*

The problems addressed in this chapter cannot be solved using one of the optimization techniques introduced in previous chapters, because both multiple alternatives and multiple states of nature exist. Some management scientists feel decision theory has limited practical value because of the often highly subjective nature of the probability estimates. While it is true that the probabilities are often subjective, it is important to remember that managers are often working with the best information available at the time. The fact that some of that information may be subjective does not relieve them of the decision-making responsibility; it simply indicates that they should be cautious. Despite possible shortcomings, the use of decision analysis, especially decision trees, seems to be growing in popularity as a method of dealing with these types of problems.

Management Science Application

USING DECISION ANALYSIS IN FOREST MANAGEMENT[1]

Prescribed fire—fire ignited under controlled conditions to achieve a particular set of objectives—is an important tool in modern forest management. Prescribed fires are used to reduce fire hazards created by heavy volumes of logging slash (branches, chips, etc.) or naturally accumulated forest residues; to enhance wildlife habitat by eliminating decadent vegetation and stimulating new growth; to facilitate site preparation prior to planting seedlings; to control diseases and insects; and to improve range forage. Uncertainties in weather, fire behavior, and other factors make the planning and executing of fires challenging. A fire that burns too "hot" may fail to meet desired objectives or may escape the prescribed area, causing damage to forest resources or nearby structures. A fire that burns too "cool" may not fully meet its objectives and could leave dangerous residual fuels. Decision analysis techniques enable forest managers to incorporate key uncertainties explicitly in the planning and decision-making process. Conceptual decision models were developed for prescribed fire planning and execution. These models were then implemented as prototype software models on computers and used to evaluate prescribed fire decisions in national forests in California, Arizona, and Washington.

A simple example of the use of decision analysis would be the commitment of resources (personnel and equipment) to a burn. The two decision alternatives are: (1) commit resources, with an unavoidable cost if the burn is subsequently cancelled, and (2) postpone the burn, with a smaller cost associated with the delay in meeting burn objectives. This decision deals with two uncertainties, the weather conditions on the day of the burn and the results of the actual burn. Weather conditions determine whether a burn should be carried out or postponed. The burn results define the success of the burn in meeting management's objectives.

[1]Reprinted by permission of David Cohan, Stephen M. Haas, David L. Radloff, and Richard F. Yancik, "Using Fire in Forest Management: Decision Making Under Uncertainty," *Interfaces,* 14, No. 5 (September–October, 1984): 8–19. Copyright (1984), The Institute of Management Sciences.

Figure 1 shows the decision tree for this decision. Note that, in this case, committing resources is preferable to postponement, even with significant uncertainties about the weather and the outcome of the burn.

The decision analysis techniques developed were then applied to prescribed fire planning and execution decisions in three national forests, in each case with different management objectives. Each of these will be discussed separately.

Tahoe National Forest

This study was carried out on the Downieville Ranger District of the Tahoe National Forest. A significant amount of timber is produced in this forest, and prescribed burning is used to prepare sites for planting new stands and to reduce the hazard of wildfire caused by heavy concentrations of logging slash. The decision alternatives were either (1) broadcast burning or (2) yarding of unmerchantable material (YUM) followed by broadcast burning. Yarding involves piling and removing large slash material prior to burning. Yarding costs about $100 per acre, but reduces the cost and difficulty of controlling the burn. Figure 2 (page 528) shows a decision tree for this problem.

The expected monetary value supports the decision to burn without yarding. The probability of an escaped fire without YUM would have to be more than triple the estimate before YUM and burn would be the preferred alternative. This analysis helped convince the district specialist, who initially had a strong preference for the YUM and burn alternative, that burning without yarding would be the best choice. While the difference in expected monetary value is relatively small, a large number of such decisions are made annually in the Downieville district alone.

Prescott National Forest

This study was conducted in the Chino Valley Ranger District of the Prescott National Forest. The vegetation is primarily a mix of chaparral and pine. The forest is used for recreation, as a wildlife habitat, as a watershed, and for grazing livestock. Burns are conducted in the district to rehabilitate riparian zones in order to improve domestic range and wildlife habitat, with a secondary objective of reducing the hazard of wildfire. Decision analysis was used in conjunction with a major burning program in a 150,000-acre area near a population center with about 2,000 homes and other structures. These structures faced a considerable risk of loss from wildfire. While prescribed burning could reduce this risk, there was also risk from escaped prescribed fires. The analysis examined the choice between prescribed burning and the status quo. Based upon data from a 20-year period, probability distributions for losses were determined and incorporated into the decision tree. This tree is shown in Figure 3 (page 529).

Since the objective was to minimize expected cost plus losses, the major burn program is preferable in spite of the risk of losses caused by escaped prescribed fires. The analysis suggested that, following this decision, costs plus losses could be reduced by almost half over a 20-year period.

A further question was whether or not losses from escaped prescribed fires should be given more weight than losses from wildfires, given legal and political considerations. Using the analysis, it was found that, if prescribed losses

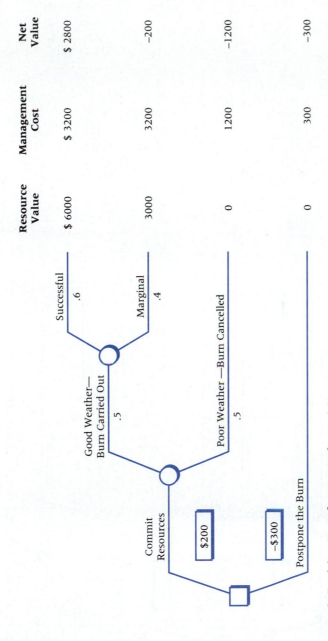

	Resource Value	Management Cost	Net Value
Successful .6	$ 6000	$ 3200	$ 2800
Marginal .4	3000	3200	−200
	0	1200	−1200
	0	300	−300

Figure 1 Decision Tree for Example Decision

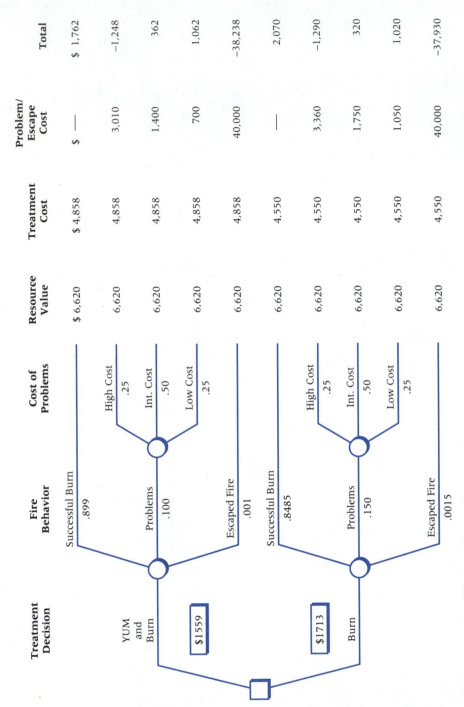

Treatment Decision	Fire Behavior	Cost of Problems	Resource Value	Treatment Cost	Problem/ Escape Cost	Total
	Successful Burn .899		$ 6,620	$ 4,858	$ —	$ 1,762
	Problems .100	High Cost .25	6,620	4,858	3,010	−1,248
		Int. Cost .50	6,620	4,858	1,400	362
YUM and Burn		Low Cost .25	6,620	4,858	700	1,062
$1559	Escaped Fire .001		6,620	4,858	40,000	−38,238
	Successful Burn .8485		6,620	4,550	—	2,070
	Problems .150	High Cost .25	6,620	4,550	3,360	−1,290
		Int. Cost .50	6,620	4,550	1,750	320
Burn		Low Cost .25	6,620	4,550	1,050	1,020
$1713	Escaped Fire .0015		6,620	4,550	40,000	−37,930

Figure 2 Tahoe National Forest Decision Tree

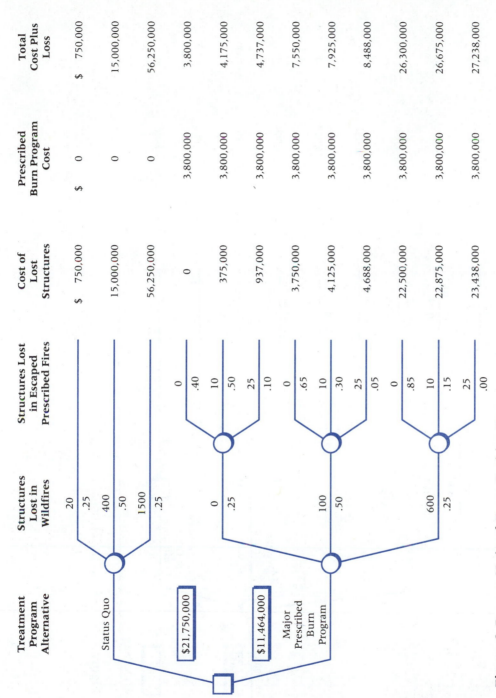

Figure 3 Prescott National Forest Decision Tree

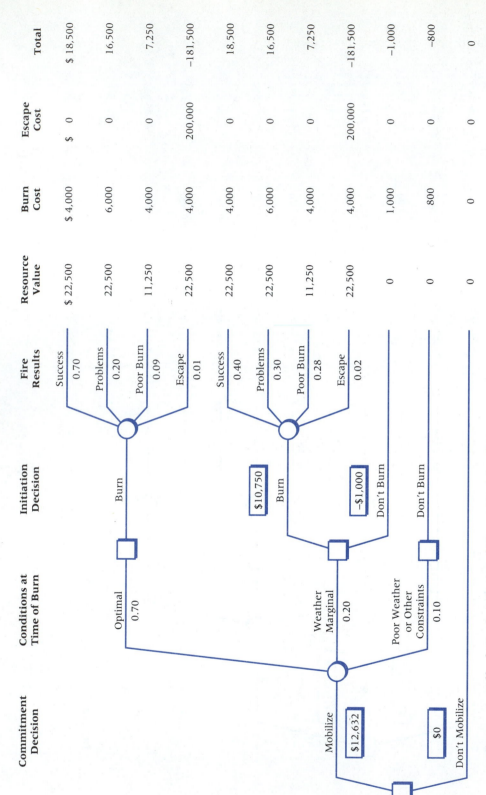

	Resource Value	Burn Cost	Escape Cost	Total
Success 0.70	$ 22,500	$ 4,000	$ 0	$ 18,500
Problems 0.20	22,500	6,000	0	16,500
Poor Burn 0.09	11,250	4,000	0	7,250
Escape 0.01	22,500	4,000	200,000	–181,500
Success 0.40	22,500	4,000	0	18,500
Problems 0.30	22,500	6,000	0	16,500
Poor Burn 0.28	11,250	4,000	0	7,250
Escape 0.02	22,500	4,000	200,000	–181,500
	0	1,000	0	–1,000
	0	800	0	–800
	0	0	0	0

Figure 4 Gifford Pinchot National Forest Decision Tree

were assessed as being 10 times the direct economic loss, the burn alternative would still be considerably less expensive than the status quo.

Gifford Pinchot National Forest

Two districts of this forest were included in this study. Large lumbering operations create heavy volumes of logging slash (up to several hundred tons per acre). The rugged terrain makes prescribed fires the only practical alternative for preparing planting sites and reducing the hazard of wildfire. In these cases, the decision is whether or not to mobilize for a burn and whether or not to actually initiate the burn under marginal conditions. Since burns usually cover about 50 acres surrounded by standing timber, considerable losses can result from escaped prescribed fires. The decision on whether or not to mobilize and, given conditions, whether or not to initiate the burn, are shown in Figure 4 (page 530). As the decision tree shows, the best choices are to mobilize for a burn and to initiate the burn even if weather conditions are marginal. In this case, moderate changes in the value of a successful burn, or in the chance of unfavorable outcomes, can change the decision.

This work illustrated that decisions considered difficult became easier to make when using decision analysis. The explicit assessment of probabilities associated with key uncertainties helped managers understand their implications and relative importance. Sensitivity analysis also illustrated which assumptions were critical to the decision. Finally, the use of decision analysis gave managers a clear and concise rationale for important decisions.

GLOSSARY

decision alternatives list of all alternative choices available to the decision maker

decision matrix see payoff table

decision policy strategy statement of decision alternatives to be selected at each decision point; some decisions may be conditional upon the outcome of prior decisions

decision tree graphical or pictorial representation of the decision-making problem, including decision nodes (squares) and chance nodes (circles); begins with first-stage decision and ends with conditional payoffs

dominance situation where payoffs associated with one or more alternatives are inferior to the payoffs from some other alternative

expected opportunity loss expected value of the opportunity loss associated with a given decision alternative

expected value decision criterion that determines a weighted average of the payoffs associated with any decision alternative; the weight assigned to each payoff is its probability of occurrence

expected value of perfect information expected value of information that would allow decision maker to make correct decision each time; expected value with perfect information minus best expected value under risk

expected value of sample information expected value of information gained from sampling or experimentation; expected value of optimal decision policy with sampling less best expected value without the information

Hurwicz criterion decision-making criterion (conditions of uncertainty) that determines a weighted average of the maximum and minimum payoffs associated with any decision alternative; the weight for the maximum payoff is α, the coefficient of optimism, and the weight for the minimum payoff is $(1 - \alpha)$

Laplace criterion decision-making criterion (conditions of uncertainty) that assumes all states of nature are equally likely to occur and takes the average value of the payoffs associated with each decision alternative

maximax criterion optimistic decision-making criterion (conditions of uncertainty) that selects decision associated with maximum payoff in table

minimax regret criterion decision-making criterion (conditions of uncertainty) that selects decision based upon the smallest of the maximum regrets associated with each decision alternative

maximin criterion pessimistic decision-making criterion (conditions of uncertainty) that selects the largest of the minimum payoffs associated with each decision alternative

payoff table table showing all conditional payoffs, i.e., payoffs that occur for each combination of decision alternative and state of nature

posterior probabilities conditional probabilities determined by using Bayes theorem to revise prior probabilities based on additional information (sample or experiment results)

prior probabilities probabilities of occurrence of states of nature prior to revision

regret table table that expresses the decision maker's regret at making the wrong decision associated with each state of nature

risk preference measure of decision maker's willingness to take a risk for a potential payoff as expressed in the decision maker's utility function

states of nature all possible outcomes associated with a decision that may occur

utility measure of satisfaction with an outcome; can be used to measure risk preference of decision maker

utility function graph that shows the relationship between utility (utiles) and money for a particular decision maker; a concave utility function implies the decision maker will avoid risk, a convex utility function implies the decision maker will seek risk.

PROBLEMS

1. A decision maker has four decision alternatives. There are four possible states of nature and the conditional payoffs are as follows:

Decision Alternative	States of Nature			
	S_1	S_2	S_3	S_4
d_1	24	24	22	25
d_2	24	23	27	19
d_3	25	24	22	26
d_4	22	23	25	21

   a. If the decision maker is facing conditions of uncertainty, what decisions would be made using the Laplace, maximin, maximax, and Savage criteria?

   b. What decision would be made using the Hurwicz criterion with an α of 0.4?

c. Would the answer to part b change if α were 0.7?

d. Which of these decision criteria provides the best decision? Explain.

2. Assume the decision maker in problem 1 obtains the following probability estimates for the states of nature: $P(S_1) = 0.2$; $P(S_2) = 0.3$; $P(S_3) = 0.4$; and $P(S_4) = 0.1$.

a. What decision would be made using the expected monetary value as the criterion?

b. Determine the expected opportunity loss for this problem.

3. Consider the following payoff table, where the payoffs are in dollars of profit and the decision maker cannot determine probabilities for the states of nature:

Decision	States of Nature			
Alternative	S_1	S_2	S_3	S_4
d_1	40	44	38	45
d_2	36	42	39	43
d_3	42	46	40	36
d_4	43	45	41	44

What decisions would be made using the Laplace, maximin, maximax, Hurwicz ($\alpha = 0.5$), and Savage criteria?

4. If the values given in the payoff table in problem 3 were costs instead of profits, how would the decisions change under each criterion?

5. If the following probability estimates for the states of nature in problem 3 were obtained, what decision would be made using expected monetary value as the criterion? $P(S_1) = 0.3$; $P(S_2) = 0.2$; $P(S_3) = 0.3$; and $P(S_4) = 0.2$.

6. Consider the following payoff table:

Decision	States of Nature					
Alternative	S_1	S_2	S_3	S_4	S_5	S_6
d_1	6	5	8	10	9	11
d_2	7	6	11	6	5	9
d_3	11	9	5	7	8	11
d_4	6	13	10	5	6	10
d_5	5	5	7	9	10	12
d_6	8	11	11	8	7	7

a. If the decision maker is facing conditions of uncertainty, what decision would be made using the Laplace, maximin, maximax, and Savage criteria?

b. What decision would be made using the Hurwicz criterion with an α of 0.6?

7. Assume that the following probability estimates for the states of nature in problem 6 were obtained: $P(S_1) = 0.1$; $P(S_2) = 0.2$; $P(S_3) = 0.05$; $P(S_4) = 0.2$; $P(S_5) = 0.25$; and $P(S_6) = 0.2$.

a. What decision would be made using expected monetary value as the criterion?

b. What is the EVPI?

8. Fred Miller recently started a small computer company in his garage. Fred now has the opportunity to sign one of two contracts for the sale of his machines. The payoffs from each of these contracts will depend upon how well Fred's machines perform over the first year. If the machine's performance is rated unacceptable, Fred will lose $500,000 with contract A and $20,000 with contract B. If the machine's performance is rated acceptable, he will make $700,000 with contract A and $475,000 with contract B.

    a. If Fred estimates there is a 70 percent chance his machines will be rated acceptable, which contract should he sign, based upon the expected monetary value criterion?
    b. Is there any reason that Fred should use some criterion other than expected monetary value? Explain.

9. The ACME Corporation must borrow $2,000,000 for the coming quarter. The current interest rate the company must pay is 12 percent. ACME is currently one of the leading bidders on a major government contract. If ACME is awarded the contract, it will be considered a low-risk company and the interest it will have to pay will drop to 10 percent. If, on the other hand, ACME does not win the contract, lenders will consider the loan much riskier and raise the rate to 15 percent. The government's decision on the bid will be announced in three days, and ACME feels it has a 75 percent chance of winning the contract.

    a. Should ACME take the loan today or wait until the government contract award is announced?
    b. One of ACME's officers has suggested that ACME take a loan for $1,000,000 today and the additional $1,000,000 after the government announcement is made. Evaluate this proposal.

10. Alice Fisher sends information to various clients via express delivery companies. In all cases, it is important that the client receive the information by the next day. Alice has the following information on each company:

Company	Cost per shipment	Probability of next day arrival
Republic Express	$18.00	0.99
United Package	12.00	0.97
Eagle Mail	6.00	0.89

Alice makes an average profit of $200 when her information arrives on time; if it arrives late, she makes nothing. If Alice wishes to maximize her profits, which delivery company should she use?

11. The John & Red Company sells long underwear. They have found that, when winter is very cold, they sell 4,000 pairs; when the winter is average, they sell 3,200 pairs; and when the winter is mild, they sell 2,500 pairs. The long underwear sells for $30 a pair and costs the company $18 per pair. Any pairs not sold during the season are sold to a discount chain at half price ($15). The company recently saw a forecast for the coming winter that said there was a 20 percent chance the winter would be very cold, a 45 percent chance it would be average, and a 35 percent chance it would be mild. How many pairs of long underwear should the company manufacture if it wishes to maximize its profits?

12. Caroline Murphy has enrolled at a local community college and has an eight o'clock class on Monday, Wednesday, and Friday. She lives several miles from the campus and can take either of two routes to get to school. The first involves using interstates 490 and 390, but the second is on local roads. The interstates are faster when there are no construction delays or accidents. She has determined the following driving times (in minutes) for each route under each condition.

Decision Alternative	Interstates clear	Construction or accident
Interstates	20	46
Local roads	35	35

If Caroline estimates that the interstates will be clear 65 percent of the time, what is the latest time she can leave her apartment and still make her eight o'clock class on time? What other factors might Caroline want to consider in making this decision?

13. The Kranston Corporation is considering the introduction of a new product. The company can use one of two designs on this product. Design A will be more profitable if consumer preferences remain basically unchanged. Design B will be more profitable if consumer preferences change. Initial estimates indicate there is a 60 percent chance consumer preferences will remain unchanged. The payoff table for this decision is shown below. All figures are in dollars of net profit.

Decision Alternative	Consumer preferences Unchanged	Changed
Design A	43,000	10,000
Design B	35,000	19,000
Probability	0.6	0.4

a. Determine the optimal decision for Kranston if management wishes to maximize profit.
b. What is the EVPI?

14. The Willmark Company must decide whether to place a small, medium, or large order. Possible demands are low, moderate, and high. The following payoff table shows their expected profit figures in thousands of dollars.

Decision Alternative	States of Nature (Demand) Low	Moderate	High
Small	600	300	0
Medium	−500	1,000	800
Large	−1,000	0	1,200

If the probabilities associated with each level of demand are P(low) = 0.2, P(moderate) = 0.3, and P(high) = 0.5, which decision should Willmark choose based upon an EMV criterion?

15. The Groff Corporation faces a make-or-buy decision on a subcomponent for one of its products. Profit for this product will depend upon market conditions for the product. Market estimates indicate the market conditions will be either poor, fair, good, or excellent. Groff management has constructed

the following payoff table, showing profits in thousands of dollars and the probability estimates for the various market conditions.

Decision Alternative	Market conditions			
	Poor	Fair	Good	Excellent
Make	10	75	150	350
Buy	25	100	125	200
Probability	0.2	0.2	0.5	0.1

Should Groff management decide to make or buy this subcomponent, based on an EMV criterion?

16. Fuzzy's Cheeses sells large wheels of a special cheese to a local grocery chain. Because of the time required to make each wheel, Fuzzy's must decide how many wheels to produce each month before the chain places its order. The chain pays $400 for each 200-pound wheel purchased. It costs Fuzzy's $300 to produce a wheel. If Fuzzy's produces more wheels than the chain buys in a given month, Fuzzy's sells the remaining wheels to a local discount store for $300 each. If, however, the chain orders more wheels than Fuzzy's has produced, Fuzzy's buys enough wheels to fill the order from a specialty store in Vermont (placing its own labels on the wheels before delivery). The cost of these wheels to Fuzzy's (including shipping) is $460 each. Upon reviewing past records of sales, Fuzzy's finds the chain has purchased the following number of wheels each month over the past 10 months: 6 wheels—4 months; 7 wheels—4 months; and 8 wheels—2 months. Sales appear to be randomly distributed.

   a. Set up the payoff table for this problem.
   b. Determine the optimum number of wheels of this cheese that Fuzzy's should produce each month using the expected monetary value criterion.
   c. How much should Fuzzy's be willing to offer as a discount to induce the grocery chain to make its purchase decision before Fuzzy's begins production? Explain.

17. A manufacturer is considering the purchase of special-purpose equipment to manufacture a product. His choices are:

   ■ Continue with present methods, which cost $9 per unit produced.
   ■ Purchase a machine for $10,000 that has a one-year useful life and will reduce costs to $6 per unit.
   ■ Purchase a machine for $60,000 that has a four-year life (assume straight-line depreciation of 25 percent) and will reduce costs to $4.50 per unit.

   Annual demand for this product has the following distribution:

Demand (units)	Probability
2,000	.15
3,000	.40
4,000	.35
5,000	.10

   a. Which decision should this manufacturer make if he wishes to maximize his annual profits on this product?
   b. What is the EVPI?

18. Dr. Marple has an opportunity to rent out his condominium in Miami for the week prior to and including New Year's Day for $3,000. The potential renter wants an answer within the hour, however. Dr. Marple is hesitant because it has been announced that, if Notre Dame University wins its last football game of the season against USC on the coming weekend, Notre Dame will be invited to play in the Orange Bowl on New Year's Day. If this happens, he is sure he can rent the condominium to a ND alumnus for $5,500. Pigskin prognosticators indicate the chance of ND beating USC is 37 percent. Dr. Marple realizes that, if he turns down his current offer and Notre Dame loses the game, there will not be another chance to rent.

a. Draw a decision tree that represents this problem.
b. State Dr. Marple's decision policy based upon EMV.

19. Given the following decision tree, find the best decision policy and its expected monetary value. All values are in dollars of profit and values shown in parentheses are the costs associated with a decision.

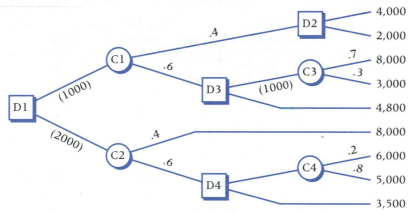

20. Given the following decision tree, find the best decision policy and its expected monetary value. All values are costs in dollars and values shown in parentheses are the costs associated with a decision.

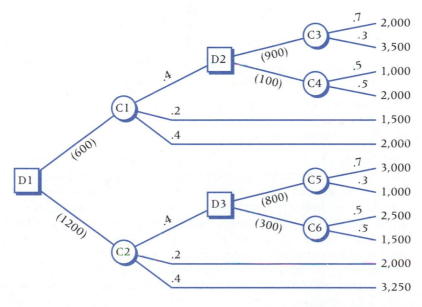

21. State lottery tickets cost $1 each. The following payoff table illustrates the decision to purchase a ticket:

Decision Alternative	States of Nature	
	S_1 Win	S_2 Lose
Purchase	$1,500,000	−$1
Don't Purchase	0	0

a. If the state sells three million lottery tickets, what is the best decision using the EMV criterion?

b. If a particular decision maker was indifferent between winning the lottery with a probability of winning of 0.000,000,25 and not purchasing, would this decision maker purchase a ticket?

22. A firm has two divisions, each of which faces the same decision alternatives. The payoffs associated with the decision alternatives are as follows:

Decision Alternatives	Potential Sales		
	Low	Moderate	High
d_1	0	75	200
d_2	50	100	150
d_3	75	100	125
Probabilities	0.35	0.35	0.30

a. Which decision alternative should each division choose, using an EMV criterion?

b. The managers of the two divisions (A and B) have expressed their indifference between certain payoffs and the given payoffs with probabilities p and (1 − p) as follows:

Payoff	Indifference of Manager	
	Division A	Division B
50	0.10	0.35
75	0.20	0.50
100	0.30	0.65
125	0.45	0.80
150	0.60	0.90

Find each manager's decision using the expected utility value criterion.

c. Draw a utility function for each division manager.

d. Which manager is a risk taker? A risk avoider?

23. B&L Inc. has been invited to bid on a government contract for a lens system for a satellite camera. B&L management estimates the cost of preparing a bid will be $50,000. They also estimate that, if they bid on this contract, there is a 60 percent chance they will win the contract. The contract calls for the delivery of a working lens system 10 months after the awarding of the bid. B&L researchers feel that three possible designs can be used for this system. Design A is a mechanical system that would cost $60,000 and would have a 55 percent probability of working. Design B is a mechanical system that would cost $90,000 and would have a 70 percent chance of working.

Design C is an electronic system that would cost $125,000 and, since B&L has built such a system before, would have a 100 percent chance of working. The government will pay the contractor $250,000 upon delivery of a working system. The researchers feel that there is only enough time to build two systems; in other words, if mechanical system A or B is built and does not work, B&L will have to build the electronic system to ensure delivery.

a. Draw the decision tree for this problem.
b. Determine which decision(s) B&L should make and the expected monetary value of those decisions.

24. The John & Red Company (problem 11) can hire a meteorologist who will study the weather patterns in the local area and predict whether the coming winter will be above average temperature or below average temperature. The table below shows the relationship between the meterologist's past predictions and the actual temperatures for the winter.

Prediction	Mild	Average	Very Cold
Above average	0.7	0.5	0.15
Below average	0.3	0.5	0.85

a. If the meterologist charges $500 to conduct the study and make a prediction, what decision should the John & Red company make?
b. What is the expected value of sample information?

25. Caroline Murphy (problem 12) has discovered that a local radio station makes an assessment of traffic conditions on the interstates each morning at 7:00 AM. She has found that, if the radio station reports the interstates will be clear, they actually are clear 80 percent of the time. If the station reports the interstates will be backed up, they actually are clear 10 percent of the time.

a. What is the probability that the radio station will report that the interstates will be clear?
b. How would such a report affect the decision made in problem 12?

26. A market research firm has offered to conduct a survey on consumer preferences for the Kranston Corporation (problem 13). Past experience shows that, when consumer preferences are unchanged, the survey will reveal that fact 85 percent of the time. When consumer preferences have changed, the survey reveals that fact 75 percent of the time.

a. What is the probability the research will reveal a change in consumer preferences?
b. Draw a decision tree for this problem.
c. If the market research firm charges $5,000 to conduct the survey, state a decision policy for Kranston management.

27. The Willmark Company (problem 14) can purchase additional information on market demand for $750. This information will yield one of two results, R_1 and R_2. The conditional probabilities associated with these results are as follows:

$$P(R_1|S_1) = 0.7 \qquad P(R_1|S_2) = 0.5$$

$$P(R_1|S_3) = 0.1 \qquad P(R_2|S_1) = 0.3$$

$$P(R_2|S_2) = 0.5 \qquad P(R_2|S_3) = 0.9$$

a. State a decision policy for Willmark.

b. What is the EVSI?

28. The Groff Corporation (problem 15) can purchase market research for $3,000 that will enable them to estimate expected market conditions more accurately. The research will yield strong or weak predictions. The conditional probabilities associated with these results are as follows:

Research Predictions	Poor	Fair	Good	Excellent
Strong	.10	.20	.75	.95
Weak	.90	.80	.25	.05

a. What decision should Groff management make if the research yields strong predictions?

b. What decision should Groff management make if the research yields weak predictions?

c. Should Groff management hire the firm to conduct the research? Why or why not?

29. The Washington Company is considering the introduction of a new product. They know from past data that 50 percent of all new products in this area fail to break even, 30 percent just break even, and 20 percent produce a reasonable profit. One option is to test-market this product before making a final decision. In the past, good test market results have been achieved with products that fail to break even only 5 percent of the time, with products that break even 30 percent of the time, and with products which yield a reasonable profit 78 percent of the time. If Washington management decides to test-market this product and the results are good, what is the probability that the product will yield a reasonable profit?

30. Mike Tessoni, production manager for Wilco Manufacturing, has an automated production machine that tends to go out of adjustment easily. Records show that the machine is properly adjusted 70 percent of the time. When the machine is properly adjusted, it produces good parts 90 percent of the time. When it is out of adjustment, however, it produces good parts only 30 percent of the time. Unfortunately, it is impossible to tell whether the machine is properly adjusted or out of adjustment by inspecting it. Mike has just come up to the machine and has examined the last three parts produced by the machine. He found the first two parts to be bad and the third part to be good. What is the probability the machine is properly adjusted?

31. Mike Tessoni has three machine operators, Sam, Alice, and Will, who all produce a particular part. Based on past experience, Mike knows that the production rate and the proportion of good parts produced by each operator varies as follows:

Operator	Number of Parts Produced	Quality of Work (Percent Good Parts)
Sam	200	98
Alice	350	90
Will	450	80

A basket of finished parts has just arrived at the assembly line, and the tag stating which operator produced the parts has been lost. Mike takes a sample of five parts from the basket and finds two are defective.

a. What is the probability the parts in the basket were produced by Sam?
b. What is the probability they were produced by Alice?
c. What is the probability they were produced by Will?

Consultant's Report _____

Wilson Company[2]

The Wilson Baby Food Company has been a nationally recognized producer of baby foods for over 45 years. Over these years it has been fortunate to be participating in a growing market. But this will probably not be true in the future.

Recently, sales have been falling along with the drop in the birthrate. In fact, most long-term predictions foresee this lower birthrate as a permanent phenomenon.

Two months ago at a corporate long-range planning session it was agreed that the company should consider the expansion of its product line beyond baby foods. It was unanimously decided that the first move should be to change the name to the Wilson Company.

Shortly after the meeting, a proposal was made to produce and market a line of geriatric foods. These prepared foods would be aimed at the 65-and-over age bracket. Preliminary analysis indicated that this market had above-average growth potential over the next 30 years, and at present few firms competed in this market.

In addition, this analysis showed that if sales were high, an average profit of $6 million per year could be realized over the first five years of the project's life. If, on the other hand, sales were low, the company could incur an average loss of $3 million per year over the same time period.

On the basis of historical experience, the management of the Wilson Company thought that the likelihood of high sales from any project was .3 and the likelihood of low sales was .7.

The manager of marketing, Janet Collinge, was unclear as to what she should do next. She felt she had two alternatives. The first would be to undertake a market survey which would yield additional information from which a better decision could be made. The second alternative would be to omit the survey and base the decision on current information.

If a survey was undertaken, the result would predict either success for the product (high sales), inconclusive results, or product failure (low sales).

Survey results are by no means perfect. Ms. Collinge has conducted countless surveys in the past and has some information which may be helpful in reaching a decision alternative. First, if one considers all those products which have achieved a high level of sales in the marketplace, the results indicate that in 60 percent of the cases the survey forecast success, in 30 percent of the cases the result was inconclusive, and in 10 percent of the cases the survey forecast failure. Next, if one

[2]Barry Shore, *Quantitative Methods for Business Decisions: Text and Cases* (New York: McGraw-Hill, 1978), pp 139–140. Reprinted by permission of McGraw-Hill.

considers all those products which have achieved a low level of sales, these surveys showed that in 20 percent of the case the survey forecast success, in 30 percent the result was inconclusive, and in 50 percent the survey forecast failure.

You have been hired as a consultant to help Ms. Collinge by applying management science techniques to this particular problem. Prepare a report for Wilson Company that addresses:

1. The action Wilson should take if the survey is not conducted, and the expected value of the project.
2. A visual representation of this problem, illustrating the decisions and outcomes.
3. The action Wilson should take if the survey is conducted, and the expected value of the project.
4. The maximum amount Wilson should pay to have the survey conducted.

Chapter

14

Queuing Analysis

By the end of this chapter, you should be able to:

1

identify a queuing situation, recognizing its major components and structure;

2

discuss the managerial problems involved in a given queuing system;

3

identify the costs associated with a specific queuing system;

4

discuss the assumptions underlying the basic single-server and multiple-server models;

5

compute the operating characteristics of the models introduced in the chapter; and

6

use a computer program to solve the more complex models introduced here.

A queue is simply a waiting line, and waiting in line is a fact of life. We are all familiar with waiting in line for course registration, at banks, and at checkout counters of all sorts. Queues, of course, are not restricted to humans. Objects can also wait in lines. Airplanes wait for clearance to take off and land. Machines wait in a queue for repair. Computer programs wait their turn to be run. Moreover, there are costs associated with waiting lines, and managerial decisions must be made concerning the operation of queuing systems. The analysis of waiting line situations is an important area of study for management scientists.

In this chapter, we describe queuing theory, the mathematical analysis of waiting lines. The results of a queuing analysis can help managers make decisions concerning the operation of specific waiting line situations. Queuing theory is a highly mathematical discipline that incorporates elements of statistics and probability theory, to construct models that provide a statistical description of the queuing system. In this chapter, however, we are going to provide a more qualitative overview of queuing theory.

A Parking Garage Problem

The city of Rochester owns and operates several parking garages in the downtown area. For the past several years, skeleton crews have maintained these garages after 7 PM, because so few people remained in the city or ventured downtown after dark. Now, however, there has been a rejuvenation in what is being called the Cultural District. Restaurants, theaters, and museums in this area are attracting crowds of people to evening events. The city operates one garage in the area, and Mr. Esposito, manager of the garage, has been receiving complaints from patrons and from City Hall regarding long waiting lines at the cashier's booth and heavy congestion in the garage. The county manager, the mayor, the city council, and the county legislature all have a stake in the success of the cultural area. If they are successful at renewing this area, there are hopes of bringing the downtown area back to life. Theater owners, the Philharmonic, and restaurant owners all have a special interest in this situation. Unhappy patrons will not return.

The garage has two exits (west and east), each with three exit booths. Currently, only one booth, at the west exit of the garage, is in operation at night. Mr. Esposito has several options available to him, including opening one booth at each exit; opening two or three booths at one exit; or opening two or three booths at each exit. There is also a cost consideration to his problem. There is a budget crunch in the city, and Mr. Esposito must keep operating costs down. In addition, union requirements state than an employee must work a minimum of four hours at a time. Thus, Mr. Esposito must try to maintain a decent level of service (not yet defined) and at the same time keep his operating cost within a strict budget. This is the problem frequently faced by managers of queuing systems. We will return to Mr. Esposito later in the chapter.

14.1 AN INTRODUCTION TO QUEUING ANALYSIS

A queue forms whenever some unit, or customer, demands some type of service and that demand is not immediately met. That is, the current demand for service exceeds the current service capacity. This is generally the result of a fluctuating demand. During periods of peak demand a queue forms. At other times the service facility may be idle. Queuing analysis, or queuing theory, is a mathematical method for analyzing waiting line problems. Queuing analysis enables the analyst to compute certain operating characteristics that describe the behavior of the queue.

Queuing models are a descriptive rather than an optimizing technique. The results of queuing analysis are **operating characteristics** or measures of performance. Rather than providing an optimal solution, these statistics describe the operation or behavior of the queuing system under particular conditions. Operating characteristics include such information about the queue as the average length of the queue, the average time spent in the queuing system, and the amount of system idle time. Queuing models are stochastic. Many of the parameters of the queuing model are not known with certainty. Thus, the parameters used to compute the operating statistics are described by a probability distribution. Average or expected values are used in the computations. Queuing models are also static and nonlinear. It is assumed that the parameters do not vary with time, and that changes in the operating characteristics are not proportional to changes in the model parameters.

Management of a queuing system involves much more than merely describing the queue. The manager generally uses the operating statistics as input into a broader framework, within which the manager can make decisions concerning the queue. The objective is to determine the appropriate level of service, but achieving this can be difficult. Providing too great a service capacity is costly in terms of machinery or employee idle time. Providing too little service is also costly, although the cost of customer waiting time is frequently more difficult to assess. It may involve such factors as customer dissatisfaction or lost business. Determining an acceptable level of service may involve attempting to minimize total costs (the cost of service plus the cost of waiting), or it may involve meeting a predetermined level of service. We will discuss this very important topic further in a later section on economic analysis of waiting lines.

There are a very large number of different queuing models, each related to a different type of situation. In any queuing system, customers from a calling population arrive at the queuing system and join the queue. There is a decision rule that determines the order in which customers are served. Some kind of service facility performs the required service. After being served, the customers leave the system. In this text we refer to any member of a queue as a "customer," although they are also known as units or calling units. The queuing system is depicted in Figure 14.1, and is discussed in more detail in the following section.

14.2 *QUEUING SYSTEM COMPONENTS*

In order to analyze a queuing system, it is necessary to fully recognize and describe the system components and structure. In this section, we will discuss the basic components of the queuing system—arrivals, queues, and service facility.

Arrivals

The arrival element, frequently referred to as the input source, includes the **calling population** (the source of arrivals) and the manner in which arrivals occur (the arrival pattern). The size of the population and a precise description of the pattern of arrivals is required in order to analyze the problem.

Size of the Calling Population
The calling population may be considered either infinite (basically an unlimited source) or finite (a limited source). Queues with an infinite calling population are generally more amenable to analytical modeling. Examples of queues with infinite calling populations include most customers at checkout counters or teller windows. Examples of queuing systems with a finite source include a fleet of six emergency vehicles that must be maintained by a crew of automotive mechanics.

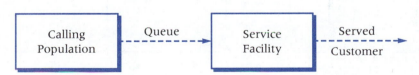

Figure 14.1 Queuing System

The key consideration in determining whether a source is infinite or finite is whether or not the arrival rate is significantly affected when one or more of the customers is being served. For example, if there are only five customers in the source, and one is being served, the probability of another customer arrival is cut significantly (the size of the population that can arrive has been cut by 20 percent).

The basic models that we consider in this chapter assume an infinite calling population. However, the finite source queue is a sufficiently common occurrence that we have included an example.

The Arrival Pattern

Customers can arrive in batches or groups (couples or families at a theater) or individually. In this chapter, we are concerned only with individual arrivals. Customers can arrive on a scheduled basis (by appointment) or randomly on an unscheduled basis. With scheduled arrivals, such as patients at a physician's office, analytical queuing models may not be the appropriate tool. When customers arrive unexpectedly, the arrival times are random variables and the arrival pattern can be described by some frequency distribution (which must be determined). Recall that random means that each arrival is independent of other arrivals.

The arrival process can be described by either the mean **interarrival time,** the time between two consecutive arrivals, or the mean **arrival rate,** the average number of arrivals per time period. Figure 14.2 shows the difference between arrival rate and interarrival time. The figure shows six arrivals in a one-hour period, an arrival rate of six per hour. The interarrival times vary (as they do for most queuing systems). It is assumed that arrivals are described by a specific probability distribution. In the figure, there are 8 minutes between the arrivals of customers C_1 and C_2, 2 minutes between customers C_2 and C_3, and 5 minutes between customers C_3 and C_4. The average or mean interarrival time for this hour is $^{60}/_6 = 10$ minutes or $\frac{1}{6}$ of an hour. Note that the mean interarrival time is the inverse of the mean arrival rate. The arrival rate is designated by λ (lambda). Interarrival times are designated by $1/\lambda$.

Probability Distribution of the Arrival Process   It is very common in queuing situations for the arrival rate to be described by the Poisson probability distribution. This distribution assumes that arrivals are completely independent of one another and of the state of the system. It further assumes that the probability of an arrival occurring during any specific time does not depend upon when the time period occurs.

Given the arrival rate, it is possible to calculate probabilities about the number of arrivals that will occur in a specific time period using the Poisson probability density function. The mathematical form for the Poisson probability function is given by

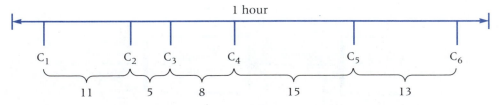

Figure 14.2 Customer Arrivals in One-Hour Time Span

$$P_n = \frac{\lambda n e^{-\lambda}}{n!}$$

where

n = the number of arrivals in the time period

λ = expected or average number of arrivals for the time period

e $\approx$ 2.71828

Values of $e^{-\lambda}$ are given in Table 3 of Appendix A, and the cumulative Poisson probabilities P_n are given in Table 4, Appendix A.

For example, if there are six random arrivals per hour on average, the probability of four arrivals during a given hour is

$$P_4 = \frac{6^4(2.71828)^{-6}}{4(4-1)(4-2)(4-3)} = \frac{1296(.0025)}{24} = .135$$

It is useful to recognize that, if the arrival rate has a Poisson distribution, the interarrival time $\frac{1}{\lambda}$ has an exponential (sometimes called negative exponential) distribution. This is because of the relationship between the continuous exponential distribution and the discrete Poisson distribution. It is possible to think of them as being dual distributions. Figure 14.3 shows the Poisson distribution and Figure 14.4 shows the exponential distribution, both for arrivals at a bank teller window recorded over several hours.

The Queue

The existence of a queue is related directly to the nature of the arrival and service patterns. In our discussion of the queue, we include customer attitude, queue discipline, and queue length, although customer attitude is often included as a characteristic of the calling population and queue discipline is sometimes referred to as service discipline.

Customer attitude describes the behavior of the customers, which can be categorized as patient or impatient. A patient customer enters the queue and remains in the queue until served, regardless of the state of the system. An impatient cus-

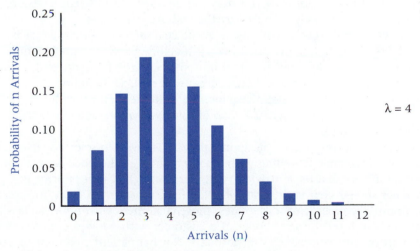

Figure 14.3 Poisson Distribution for Arrivals

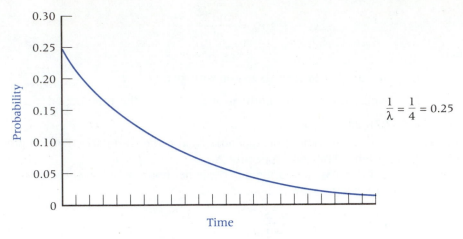

$$\frac{1}{\lambda} = \frac{1}{4} = 0.25$$

Figure 14.4 Exponential Distribution of Interarrival Times

tomer may show impatience in a number of ways: **balking**—refusing to join the queue; **reneging**—growing tired and leaving the queue before being served; or **jockeying**—switching between lines. If the customer is not patient and engages in any of these behaviors, the queuing situation can become very complex. In this chapter, we assume patient customers.

Queue length or capacity refers to the maximum number of customers a queue can contain at any given time. Queues are classified by length as either infinite, meaning unlimited in capacity, or finite, meaning limited to a specified number. Generally, any queue capacity that is a large, finite number is considered infinite. That means a customer is able and willing to join the queue regardless of its length. Problems with infinite queues are more amenable to analytical queuing models.

Queue discipline, sometimes referred to as service discipline, is the decision rule that determines which customer in the queue is selected for service. Among the alternative disciplines are:

First-come, First-served (FCFS). This self-explanatory discipline is most frequently used with humans. Even when it may not be the most efficient decision rule, it is the one most easily tolerated by the waiting customers.

Last-come, First-served (LCFS). In this case, the customer who arrived last is served first. This frequently occurs when machine parts, or other inanimate customers, are stacked and the item on top is selected for service. It is common with materials in a warehouse, because it reduces handling.

Random. With a random queue discipline, the customer served is chosen randomly. This might occur when a mob of fans wait at a stage door for an autograph or souvenir.

Priority. With a priority queue discipline, priority is given to selected customers. For example, people travelling with small children are boarded first. Priority queuing means that each arriving customer is assigned to a priority class. The customer served next is the one with the highest priority class. With preemptive priority or emergency disciplines, those customers with priority classification can also interrupt the service of a customer with a lower classification. This occurs with emergencies in hospitals. Normal patient treatment is preempted for emergency treatment.

Service Facility

An analysis of the service facility requires describing its structure (the number and arrangement of servers), the manner in which they are served (the distribution of service times), and the behavior of the server.

Queuing System Structure

The structure of the service facility is described in terms of numbers of service **channels** or **servers** and the physical arrangement or configuration of the servers. The number of servers is the number of parallel identical servers available to service the arriving customers. (Note that parallel here means performing the same service.) Queuing systems are classified as **single-server** or **multiple-server.** In a multiple-server queuing system, a single queue is serviced by two or more parallel servers. This occurs frequently in banks, with customers lining up in one queue awaiting the next available teller. In the case of multiple servers, each having its own separate queue, the system is analyzed as identical single-server queues. This situation occurs in grocery stores that have more than one full-service checkout counter open at one time.

A queuing system is also classified by the number of phases, or sequential steps, through which each customer must pass. In a **single-phase system,** each customer must pass through only one service point. That is, the customer receives service from only one type of server. In a **multiple-phase system,** the customer must pass through more than one service point. That is, the customer receives service from two or more different types of servers, arranged in series. For example, a patient being admitted to the hospital must first wait to check in at admissions, where a number of forms are filled out. The patient must then go through a series of tests before finally getting a bed. In a multiple-phase queuing system, the served customers from one stage (output) become the source of customers (input) for the next phase.

Queuing systems can be in any combination of servers and phases—some of which can be quite complex. Figure 14.5 shows four *basic* queuing system structures: single-server, single-phase; single-server, multiple-phase; multiple-server, single-phase; and multiple-server, multiple-phase.

Probability Distribution of the Service Times

Service time is the length of time a server spends servicing a customer. This time can be constant or random in nature. While it may take exactly 30 seconds every time a cup of soda is dispensed from a machine, the time it takes to get a cup of soda at a drive-up service window will probably fluctuate. Non-human service times are more likely to be constant; human service times are more likely to be random. When the service times are random, it is necessary to determine how that random variable is distributed. As with arrival rates, service times may fit any of a number of probability distributions. The most commonly assumed distribution for random service times is the exponential distribution. Like the Poisson distribution, the exponential distribution corresponds to the assumption that service times are completely independent and memory less. However, research based upon empirical evidence has raised doubts concerning the validity of this assumption in many cases. It is important that assumptions concerning the distributions of service times and arrivals be carefully checked using appropriate statistical tests. One

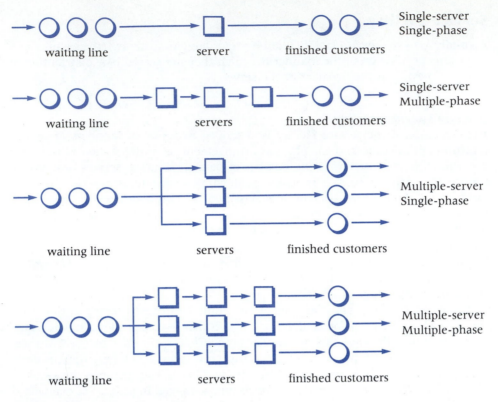

Figure 14.5 Basic Queuing Structures

quick way to rule out distributions that are not Poisson or exponential is to compute the mean and standard deviation. In the exponential distribution, mean and standard deviation are equal. In the Poisson, mean and variance are equal.

Service can be described in terms of service time (for example, service takes an average of 5 minutes) or in terms of **service rate,** the average number of customers served per time period (e.g., an average of 12 customers are served per hour). Mean service rate is designated by μ; mean service time is $1/\mu$. The mean service rate is the inverse of the mean service time. It is a generally accepted convention that rate is used to describe arrivals and mean time is used to describe service. It is essential that both be in the same units of time measurement.

The probability density function for an exponential distribution is given by

$$f(t) = \mu e^{-\mu t}$$

With an exponential service time distribution, the probability of a service being completed within a specific period of time is given by

$$P(t) = 1 - e^{-\mu t}$$

where

$$\mu = \text{mean service rate}$$

$$t = \text{specific time period}$$

Figure 14.6 shows the graph of an exponential probability density function. Recall that the total area under any probability density function equals 1. The shaded

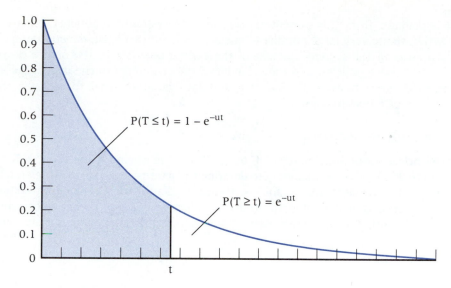

Figure 14.6 Exponential Probability Distribution

area under the exponential probability function and to the left of t equals $1 - e^{-\mu t}$ and represents the probability of service being completed within time period t. The unshaded area to the right of t equals $e^{-\mu t}$, or the probability that service will take longer than the specified time period t. For example, assume that an average of four customers an hour are serviced at a checkout counter, or an average of one customer is serviced every ¼ hour (average service time of 15 minutes). We can determine the probability of service being completed in 12 minutes (⅕ hour) using the equation and values from the table for $e^{-\mu}$ as follows:

$$P(.2) = 1 - e^{-4(.2)} = 1 - e^{-.8} = 1 - .4493 = .5507$$

Thus, with an exponential distribution of service times, it is probable that 55.07 percent of the customers will be serviced in 12 minutes or less.

Note that the graph in Figure 14.6 demonstrates an additional property of an exponential distribution. Observe that most of the area under the probability density function is concentrated in the left portion. Short service times have the highest probability of occurrence. As service times increase, the probability function tails off toward zero probability. With an exponential distribution, a random variable is most likely to take on a small value.

Behavior of the Server

While it is usually assumed that a server serves one customer at a time, and that service time is unaffected by such considerations as length of the waiting line, it is possible for servers to exhibit unusual behavior. For example, a server might fail while serving a customer (especially when machinery is involved). It is also possible for service rates to change (speed up or slow down), depending on the number waiting in line. Batch processing (serving several customers at one time) is also possible. For example, at an amusement park, when the ride ends and new customers are allowed on, they enter simultaneously. Such situations are not amenable to an analytic queuing model. For this chapter, we assume no unusual service behavior.

It is obvious, from this presentation of queuing system components and their properties, that a very large number of queuing systems can exist, depending upon the structure of the system, the size of the calling population, the nature of arrivals, the service policies, and the behavior of the customers in the queue. Before leaving this section we will look at a standard notation used to describe the parameters of a queuing system.

The Kendall Notation

The **Kendall notation,** developed by a British mathematician named D. G. Kendall in 1953, offers a taxonomy to describe the parameters of a queuing system succinctly. It provides a means for specifying or identifying the queuing system being studied and enables students and researchers in queuing theory to communicate easily with one another. In Kendall notation, a queuing system is designated

$$A/B/s$$

where

A is replaced by the code denoting the arrival distribution.

B is replaced by the code denoting the service distribution.

s is replaced by an integer denoting the number of servers.

To denote arrival and service distributions, Kendall notation uses

M for Markovian to describe random occurrences that have no memory of past events (Poisson and exponential distributions).

D for deterministic to describe random events that occur in a constant, unchanging manner.

G for general to describe any other probability distribution with a known mean and variance (also referred to as arbitrary or undefined).

For example, M/M/1 describes a basic queuing system having Poisson arrivals, exponential service times, and a single server.

It is possible for the arrival pattern to be governed by one probability distribution and the service pattern by another. A queuing system having Poisson arrivals, deterministic or constant service times, and two servers is shown as

$$M/D/2$$

The notation allows for further description of the system. For example, a system having random arrivals, random service, three servers, and a finite queue length is noted

$$(M/M/3): \text{Finite queue}$$

14.3 *SOLVING QUEUING PROBLEMS*

Queuing analysis is a descriptive tool whose major objective is predicting the behavior of the system, as reflected in specific measures of performance referred to as operating characteristics. The information may then be used as input into a decision making process, which can be based either on providing a specified level of service (a service level approach) or on minimizing the total waiting and service costs (a cost minimization approach). The operating characteristics are frequently used in selecting a solution from among the alternatives studied. In this case, operating characteristics are computed for each alternative being considered. In general, solving a queuing problem involves formulating the model of the problem, deciding upon the measures of performance that are needed, computing these operating characteristics, and analyzing the results. We will look more closely at the cost minimization approach in the later section on the economic analysis of queuing problems.

Basically, there are two solution approaches to queuing problems, analytic and simulation. So called "commonsense solutions" are not desirable in queuing problems. For example, doubling the number of servers usually will not halve the waiting time.

Analytic Solution Versus Simulation

The analytic approach, the subject of this chapter, uses formulas to determine the operating characteristics of the system. These statistical performance measures are computed from three input variables: the arrival rate, λ; the service rate, μ; and the number of servers, s. Some queuing situations are so complex, however, that it is not practical or possible to use an analytic approach. In these situations, simulation may be used. Simulation, discussed in the next chapter, studies the queuing system by imitating its behavior in an artificial environment. Since this approach requires fewer simplifications and assumptions concerning the system being studied, more complex queuing problems can be solved using simulation. The results, however, are still in the form of operating statistics or performance measures that describe the operation of the queuing system under specific conditions.

The analysis depends upon the situation. With either solution technique, solving a queuing problem requires a careful analysis of the queuing system, identifying and verifying the system components and parameters as discussed previously. The queuing model (the formula for determining the system's operating characteristics) varies with the type of system being studied. The more complex the system, the more complex the formulas. We present the specific formulas as we present specific queuing situations later in the chapter. Here, we are discussing operating characteristics in general to familiarize you with the terms and notation.

Operating Characteristics

The operating characteristic upon which queuing systems are evaluated include the following performance measures:

W = Average or expected waiting time spent in the queuing system, i.e., time spent in line and being served.

W_q = Average or expected waiting time in the queue before service starts.

L = Average number of customers in the queuing system, i.e., the number of customers in line and being served.

L_q = Average number of customers in the queue; the average length of the queue.

P_n = The probability of finding exactly n units in the queuing system.

ρ = The probability of the system being busy, referred to as the **utilization factor**; the percentage of the time the server can be expected to be busy and the customer will have to wait.

P_0 = The probability of an empty or idle facility, i.e., the probability that there are no customers in the system.

Recall that:

λ = Mean arrival rate (number of customers per unit of time).
μ = Mean service rate (number of customers served per unit of time).
$1/\mu$ = Mean service time.
s = Number of parallel service facilities in the system.

For the models discussed in this chapter, the service rate must exceed the arrival rate ($\mu > \lambda$ or $1/\mu < 1$). If the arrival rate exceeds or is equal to the service rate, the queuing system is said to explode. That is, theoretically the queue can continue to grow to an infinite length. In a system with equivalent parallel servers, the combined service rate, $s\mu$, has to exceed the arrival rate ($s\mu > \lambda$).

Queuing theory provides many measures of a queuing system's performance. The decision maker must select the operating characteristics relevant to the specific problem. Before discussing specific models, we need to make one more important point concerning operating characteristics and steady state.

Steady State

When a queuing system begins operation, its operating characteristics are greatly affected by initial conditions and time elapsed since the system began operation. For example, when a bank opens its doors there may be no customers waiting to be served. Such operating characteristics as length of time spent in the system and average number of customers in the queue may be understated as a result. This startup period is referred to as a **transient state.** Operating characteristics in the transient state do no reflect long-term expected values. After a sufficient period of time, the operating characteristics may become independent of the initial conditions and elapsed time. The system then reaches equilibrium or **steady state** and the operating characteristics fluctuate about their "true" values. In other words, in steady state, the operating characteristics are not a function of time. Steady-state statistics reflect the long-term condition of the system. Figure 14.7 graphically depicts a system's transient and steady-state stages. Almost all basic queuing models assume that the operating characteristics describe the system in steady state. All the models we describe in this chapter make that assumption.

14.4 *BASIC QUEUING MODELS (M/M/1 AND M/M/s)*

In this section, we describe the elementary single-server and multiple-server queuing models. This discussion emphasizes model assumptions and operating characteristics, and explains how these models are used. We do not show the derivations of the formulas used to determine operating characteristics.

Assumptions

The assumptions for the basic single-server and multiple-server models are identical except for the number of equivalent parallel servers. These assumptions are:

- The calling population is infinite.
- The arrivals have a Poisson distribution with a mean rate of λ.
- There is a single queue having an infinite capacity.
- The customer behavior is patient; there is no balking or reneging.

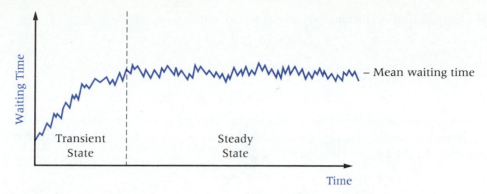

Figure 14.7 Transient and Steady State Conditions

- The queue discipline is on a first-come, first-served basis.
- The service mechanism is single-phase.
- The service facility has s identical servers, each capable of serving any customer. Note that s can represent a single server or multiple servers.
- Service time has an exponential distribution, with a mean service rate of μ or a mean service time of $1/\mu$. For a multiple-server system, each server is assumed to have the same rate of service.
- There is no unusual server behavior.
- A steady-state situation exists.
- Overall service rate exceeds arrival rate ($s\mu > \lambda$).

Operating Characteristics

Recall that operating characteristics are determined using arrival rate, λ, and service rate, μ. The operating characteristics for these basic models are given by the following formulas.

Single-server Model
- Probability that the system is busy (utilization factor)

$$\rho = \lambda/\mu$$

- Probability that the system is idle

$$P_0 = 1 - (\lambda/\mu) \quad \text{or}$$

$$= 1 - \rho$$

- Probability of n customers in the system

$$P_n = P_0 (\lambda/\mu)^n \quad \text{or}$$

$$= P_0(\rho)^n$$

- Average number of customers in the system

$$L = \lambda/(\mu - \lambda)$$

- Average number of customers waiting to be served

$$L_q = \lambda^2/[\mu(\mu - \lambda)]$$

- Average time a customer spends in the system

$$W = \frac{1}{(\mu - \lambda)}$$

- Average time a customer waits before being served

$$W_q = \frac{\lambda}{\mu(\mu - \lambda)}$$

It has been proven that, in a steady-state queuing process, a relationship exists between the arrival rate (λ), the average number in the system (L), and the average time in the system (W) such that

$$L = \lambda W$$

That is, if there are λ arrivals per time period, and if each of these arrivals spends W average time in the system, then the total time in the system for λ arrivals is λW. This relationship is known as Little's Law. For example, if there are six arrivals per hour and each arrival spends one-half hour in the system, then the total number of customer hours is 3. This implies that, on the average, there are three customers in the system.

It also follows, based on the same rationale, that the relationship between number in the queue and waiting time in the queue can be given by

$$L_q = \lambda W_q$$

Expected time in the system (W) is equal to average time in the queue (W_q) plus the time it takes to be serviced or mean service time ($\frac{1}{\mu}$):

$$W = W_q + \frac{1}{\mu}$$

These relationships are extremely important:

$$L = \lambda W$$

$$L_q = \lambda W_q$$

$$W = W_q + \frac{1}{\mu}$$

When any one of the operating characteristics L, L_q, W, or W_q has been found, it is possible to determine the other three directly.

Now let's look at a simple example of an M/M/1 queue.

M/M/1 Example   The local savings and loan has one drive-up teller window in operation. Cars arrive at the window in a Poisson fashion at a rate of 15 customers per hour. It takes the teller an average of 2 minutes to service each customer. Service is on a FCFS basis and times are exponentially distributed. There is an infinite calling population and an infinite queue capacity. Management is interested in the operating characteristics of the current system.

First, it is necessary to express λ and μ in the same units of time: $\lambda = .25$ cars per minute, $\mu = .5$ cars per minute. Then

$$\rho = \frac{\lambda}{\mu} = \frac{.25}{.5}$$

$$= .5 \quad \text{(proportion of time server is busy)}$$

$$P_0 = 1 - \left(\frac{\lambda}{\mu}\right) = 1 - .5$$

$$= .5 \quad \text{(probability of an empty system)}$$

$$L = \frac{\lambda}{(\mu - \lambda)} = \frac{.25}{(.5 - .25)}$$

$$= 1 \quad \text{(expected number of cars in the system)}$$

$$L_q = \frac{\lambda^2}{[\mu(\mu - \lambda)]} = \frac{(.25)^2}{[.5(.5 - .25)]}$$

$$= .5 \quad \text{(expected number of cars in the queue)}$$

$$W = \frac{1}{(\mu - \lambda)} = \frac{1}{(.5 - .25)}$$

$$= 4 \text{ min.} \quad \text{(expected time in the system for each car)}$$

$$W_q = \frac{\lambda}{[\mu(\mu - \lambda)]} = \frac{.25}{[.5(.5 - .25)]}$$

$$= 2 \text{ minutes} \quad \text{(expected time waiting to be served)}$$

A 2-minute wait is not unreasonable for a drive-up teller. It is not necessary, under current conditions, to consider adding another teller.

Multiple-server Model

The calculation of operating characteristics for M/M/s models is more complicated than the calculations for the M/M/1 model. For computational convenience, tables developed from these formulas are frequently used to make the calculations. The use of software packages for queuing problems has greatly eased the computational burden.

- Probability that the system is busy (utilization factor)

$$\rho = \frac{\lambda}{s\mu}$$

- Probability that the system is idle

$$P_0 = \frac{1}{\left[\displaystyle\sum_{n=0}^{s-1} \frac{(\lambda/\mu)^n}{n!}\right] + \left(\frac{(\lambda/\mu)^s}{(s - 1)!}\right)\left(\frac{\mu}{s\mu - \lambda}\right)}$$

- Probability of n customers in the system

$$P_n = \frac{(\lambda/\mu)^n}{s!\,s^{n-s}}P_0 \quad \text{for } n > s$$

$$P_n = \frac{(\lambda/\mu)^n}{n!}P_0 \quad \text{for } 0 \le n \le s$$

- Average number of customers waiting to be served

$$L_q = \frac{(\lambda/\mu)^s \lambda\mu}{(s - 1)!\,(s\mu - \lambda)^2}P_0$$

- Average number of customers in the system

$$L = L_q + \frac{\lambda}{\mu}$$

- Average time a customer waits before being served

$$W_q = \frac{L_q}{\lambda}$$

- Average time a customer spends in the system

$$W = W_q + \frac{1}{\mu}$$

Notice that, with the multiple-server formulas, the computations must be performed in sequence. P_0 has to be calculated first. This value is then used to compute L_q. L_q is used to compute L and W_q; W_q is used to compute W.

M/M/s Example Mrs. Kroft is manager of the savings and loan in the previous example. She has noted that on Friday evenings there are still sometimes several cars in line when two teller windows are open from 5 to 9 PM. She is considering opening the third teller window for this time period. She has noted that cars arrive on these nights at a rate of 54 per hour. Service time still averages 2 minutes per car at each window. For now, she is interested only in comparing the operating characteristics of the system using two teller windows and three teller windows. For the two-teller system, λ has changed to .9 customers per minute. Arrival rate is .5 customers per minute per window. Thus $s\mu$ is 1.0 for two windows and 1.5 for three windows.

$$\rho = \lambda/s\mu$$

$$= 90\% \text{ with two tellers}$$

$$= 60\% \text{ with three tellers}$$

$$P_0 = \cfrac{1}{\left[\displaystyle\sum_{n=0}^{s-1} \frac{(\lambda/\mu)^n}{n!}\right] + \left(\frac{(\lambda/\mu)^s}{(s-1)!}\right)\left(\frac{\mu}{s\mu - \lambda}\right)}$$

$$= 5.3\% \text{ with two}$$

$$= 14.6\% \text{ with three}$$

$$L_q = \frac{(\lambda/\mu)^s \lambda \mu}{(s-1)!\,(s\mu - \lambda)^2} P_0$$

$$= 7.7 \text{ customers with two}$$

$$= .53 \text{ customers with three}$$

$$L = L_q + \lambda/\mu$$

$$= 9.5 \text{ customers with two}$$

$$= 2.3 \text{ customers with three}$$

$$W_q = Lq/\lambda$$

$$= 8.6 \text{ minutes with two}$$

$$= .6 \text{ minutes with three}$$

$$W = W_q + 1/\mu$$

$$= 10.6 \text{ minutes with two}$$

$$= 2.6 \text{ minutes with three}$$

Notice that, with two tellers, a customer must wait more than 8 minutes to be served. With three tellers, this drops to under 1 minute. If Mrs. Kroft feels that an 8.6-minute customer wait is too long, she may decide to open the third window.

Now that we have presented the assumptions and formulas for our two basic models, we return to Mr. Esposito's parking garage problem.

Analysis of Parking Garage Problem

Recall that Mr. Esposito is considering making changes in the operation of the parking garage in the downtown cultural district. His options include (1) maintaining the status quo by operating one booth at the west exit; (2) opening a second booth at that same exit; (3) operating two booths, one at each exit; or (4) operating multiple booths at each exit.

After several months of data collecting, Mr. Esposito has determined that, for the hours from 7 to 11 PM, cars leave the parking garage at a rate of 114 per hour or 1.9 cars per minute ($\lambda = 1.9$). The average time to collect the flat $2.00 fee is 30 seconds, or 2 cars per minute service rate ($\mu = 2.0$).

Option One: Status Quo

Realistically, this is not an option. There is too much political pressure on him to lessen the waiting time and ease the congestion. We are going to determine the operating characteristics only as a starting place for comparisons. The status quo is a single-server basic queuing system with $\lambda = 1.9$ and $\mu = 2.0$. Using the formulas presented earlier, we obtain the following results:

$$\rho = \lambda/\mu$$
$$= 1.9/2.0$$
$$= .95$$

$$P_0 = 1 - (\lambda/\mu) \quad \text{or}$$
$$= 1 - \rho$$
$$= 1 - .95 = .05$$

$$L = \lambda/(\mu - \lambda)$$
$$= 1.9/(2.0 - 1.9)$$
$$= 19$$

$$L_q = \lambda^2/[\mu(\mu - \lambda)]$$
$$= (1.9)^2/[2(2 - 1.9)]$$
$$= 3.61/[2(.1)]$$
$$= 18.05$$

$$W = 1/(\mu - \lambda)$$
$$= 1/(2.0 - 1.9)$$
$$= 10$$

$$W_q = \lambda/[\mu(\mu - \lambda)]$$
$$= 1.9/[2(2 - 1.9)]$$
$$= 9.5$$

From these statistics Mr. Esposito knows that, on the average, there are 18 cars waiting to be served and that a car must wait an average of 9.5 minutes to be served. This is rather excessive in the confines of a parking garage with people anxious to get on with their evening. Furthermore, the server is busy 95 percent of the time.

Option Two: Open a Second Booth at the Same Exit

With this option, the system becomes a multiple-server basic queuing system. The arrival rate and the service rate remain the same. That is, $\lambda = 1.9$ and $\mu = 2.0$. There are now two servers (s = 2). The operating characteristics for this option are summarized below:

$$\rho = \lambda/s\mu$$

$$= \frac{1.9}{((2)(2))} = .475$$

$$P_0 = \frac{1}{\left[\displaystyle\sum_{n=0}^{s-1} \frac{(\lambda/\mu)^n}{n!}\right] + \left(\frac{(\lambda/\mu)^s}{(s-1)!}\right)\left(\frac{\mu}{s\mu - \lambda}\right)}$$

$$= .356 \quad \text{(interpolating from the table of } \lambda/\mu \text{ values in}$$
$$\text{table 4 in appendix A)}$$

$$L_q = \frac{(\lambda/\mu)^s \lambda\mu}{(s-1)!(s\mu - \lambda)^2} P_0$$

$$= \frac{.95^2(1.9)(2)}{(2-1)![(2)(2) - 1.9]^2}(.356)$$

$$= \frac{.9025(3.8)}{1(4-1.9)^2}(.356)$$

$$= \frac{3.43}{4.41}(.356)$$

$$= .277$$

$$L = L_q + \lambda/\mu$$

$$= .277 + .95$$

$$= 1.227$$

$$W_q = L_q/\lambda$$

$$= .277/1.9$$

$$= .146$$

$$W = W_q + 1/\mu$$

$$= .146 + \frac{1}{2}$$

$$= .646$$

The statistics for this system are obviously much improved over the single-server system currently in existence. Cars have almost no waiting time at all, and there is almost no line of cars causing congestion in the garage. Furthermore, this option may be attractive because the two servers can utilize the same booth. To open the east exit might entail additional costs, such as utility and security costs.

Option Three: Open an Additional Booth at the Opposite Exit

This option provides two distinct single-server systems, one at the east exit and one at the west exit. For each exit, we assume that the average arrival rate will be 57 cars per hour or .95 per minute ($\lambda = .95$). That is, half of the cars will use the east exit and half will use the west exit. The service rate will remain the same, 2 cars per minute ($\mu = 2$). The operating characteristics for this option are summarized below:

$$\rho = {}^{.95}\!/_{2.0} = .475$$

$$P_0 = 1 - .475 = .525$$

$$L = {}^{.95}\!/_{(2.0 - .95)} = .9$$

$$L_q = {}^{.95^2}\!/_{[2(2 - .95)]} = {}^{.9}\!/_{2.1} = .43$$

$$W = {}^{1}\!/_{(2 - .95)} = {}^{1}\!/_{1.05} = .95$$

$$W_q = {}^{.95}\!/_{[2(2 - .95)]} = {}^{.95}\!/_{2.1} = .45$$

Since there are two booths, we must double the number of people in the system ($L = .9$) for the garage as a whole. These statistics are also an improvement over the first option. On the average, no one has to wait even 1 minute to pay at the booth, and there is almost no line of cars.

Compare this option (two identical single-server systems) with the multiple-server system of option 2. Notice that W_q is much lower for the multiple-server model. From the standpoint of customer time, it is always better to have a single queue serviced by s multiple-servers than to have s distinct queues, each serviced by its own server. In Mr. Esposito's situation, the time differential is really not a factor in the decision. There are other situations where s single queues might be preferable to a single queue with s servers. Consider a supermarket checkout system. While a single queue would reduce customer waiting time, it would also increase the congestion in the shopping aisles. The layout of grocery stores would have to be altered to accommodate a single queue. In Mr. Esposito's case, option 3—booths at opposite exits—might be preferable for the customers as well. It might ease the congestion in the garage, and a choice of exits might also ease the traffic situation outside the garage as drivers head homeward. As we shall see in the next section, operating characteristics are only an input into the decision making process.

Option 4: Two Servers at each Exit

Considering the results from these options, there is really no need for Mr. Esposito to consider additional booths at either exit. However, we have determined the operating characteristics for comparison purposes. At each exit, $\lambda = .95$, $\mu = 2.0$, and s = 2. Thus, there would be an average of .02 cars in the queue. Cars would wait in line for .03 minutes, so there would be virtually no waiting time. On the negative side for Mr. Esposito, the server idle time would be nearly 62 percent. Four employees would be paid to stand around most of the time.

14.5 ECONOMIC ANALYSIS OF QUEUES

Thus far, we have shown how queuing theory can be used to determine operating characteristics of a queuing system. We have also indicated that to solve queuing problems—to make decisions using these operating characteristics as input—we must establish decision criteria. Previously we have alluded to two different decision criteria: (1) minimizing total cost, where total cost is the sum of service cost and waiting cost (cost minimization approach), and (2) achieving a specified level of service in terms of a minimum waiting time or queue length (service level approach). In this section, we are going to take a closer look at cost analysis, the economic analysis of queuing systems.

In order to minimize total cost, TC, it is necessary to define the two costs: the cost of waiting, C_w, and the cost of service (or facility cost), C_s.

$$TC = C_w + C_s$$

Figure 14.8 shows that these two costs are in direct opposition to each other. As the cost of waiting decreases, the cost of service increases. If the cost function, shown as the total cost curve, can be defined, finding the best solution is not a difficult matter. Note that costs can be computed either as cost per unit of time or as cost per customer served. In this text, cost per unit of time is used.

Service Cost, C_s, is composed of both fixed and variable costs. Annual fixed costs include such costs as amortization, insurance, and taxes. Variable costs include employee costs. In some cases, only variable costs (notably employee costs) are used to determine service costs. Total service cost per unit of time is expressed as service cost per channel or server (C_s) multiplied by the number of servers (s). Thus, in a two-server system, if the cost per employee is $6.00 per hour, the total service cost (sC_s) is $12.00. Cost must be converted to the same units of time as waiting time so the cost components can be added.

Waiting Cost, C_w, can be time spent waiting in the queue to be served or in the system. In this text, waiting is the time spent in the system. Thus, cost is a function of W. It is also assumed that waiting cost is proportional to waiting time: if it costs $5.00 to wait one hour, it costs $10.00 to wait two hours. The waiting cost per unit of time for the whole system is equal to the cost of one customer waiting one unit of time multiplied by the average number of units in the system (L):

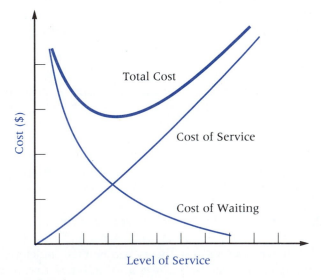

Figure 14.8 Queuing Costs

$$C_w = LC$$

where

C = cost per unit of time for one customer

L = number of customers in the system

This is equivalent to

$$C_w = \lambda WC$$

Recall that the arrival rate, λ, multiplied times the time spent in the system, W, yields the length of the queue (number of units in the queue).

Thus, total cost is given by the formula

$$TC = LC + sC_s$$

A Cost Analysis Example

Engineers and other employees of the New Products Division at ITEL frequently work from patents, blueprints, and schematics that are housed in a climate-controlled environment. The librarian, Ms. Oldham, is responsible for maintaining these documents. Employees check them out as needed and check them in when they are not being used. All items must be returned to the vault each evening. Mr. Lohr, Vice President for Product Design, has noticed that there is frequently a backup as individuals wait in line to check out or check in documents. Furthermore, Ms. Oldham sometimes has to leave the document desk to answer calls or to help in other areas, adding to the congestion at the documents desk. She is also concerned because she feels that too much of her time is spent on this clerical task, to the neglect of clients requiring other services and her other professional duties. It is clear to everyone involved that the situation has to change. Ms. Oldham has suggested that two clerks be hired to maintain the documents desk, clearing up the problem of the long lines and freeing her to handle all the other library duties. Mr. Lohr is not sure that this is necessary. He wants to look at the problem solely on a cost basis in order to provide the level of service that will minimize the cost of waiting and service. Mr. Lohr has collected the following data: $\lambda = 14$/hour; $\mu = 15$/hour. Ms. Oldham's salary and benefit package is $14 per hour. The salaries of those waiting for service average $17 per hour, and each clerk could be hired for $7.50 per hour. Now Mr. Lohr can compare his options.

Option 1: Status Quo
Operating statistics for the single-server system:

$$\rho = 93.3\%$$

$$L = 14$$

$$L_q = 13.1$$

$$W = 1 \text{ hour}$$

$$W_q = 56 \text{ minutes}$$

Cost of waiting is equal to the number of units in the system multiplied by the hourly cost of waiting per customer ($C_w = LC$). The waiting cost per customer is equivalent to their salary. Thus

$$C_w = (14)(17) = \$238$$

Service cost for the single-server system is Ms. Oldham's hourly salary, $14. Total cost for the status quo is

$$TC = C_w + C_s$$

$$= 238 + 14 = \$252$$

Operating characteristics (14 people in line and a waiting time of one hour) and total hourly costs ($252) strongly indicate a need for change.

Option 2: Hire One Clerk

The option to hire one clerk assumes that the librarian will remain as the second server in a multiple-server queuing system. Operating characteristics for the two-server system:

$$\rho = 46.7\%$$

$$L = 1.19$$

$$L_q = .26$$

$$W = 4.8 \text{ minutes}$$

$$W_q = 1.2 \text{ minutes}$$

Cost of waiting:

$$C_w = (1.19)(17) = \$20.23$$

Cost of serving: the total serving cost, is the combined hourly salary of Ms. Oldham and the clerk,

$$C_s = 14 + 7.50 = \$21.50$$

Note that this is slightly different from two servers with the same salary sC_s. It is still the combined salaries of the two servers, however. The total cost is

$$TC = 20.23 + 21.50 = \$41.73$$

Option 3: Hire Two Clerks

This option assumes that the librarian will not continue to serve at the document desk. It is a two-server system, but the total cost must include Ms. Oldham's salary. The operating characteristics remain the same as in option 2. Waiting cost is the same, only service cost changes. The two clerks' combined hourly salary is $15 ($sC_s = (2)(7.50)$). Total service cost is

$$TC_s = \text{clerk 1} + \text{clerk 2} + \text{librarian}$$

$$= 7.50 + 7.50 + 14 = \$29$$

Total cost for this option is

$$20.23 + 29.00 = \$49.23$$

Based on total cost only, Mr. Lohr would choose option 2. However, if Ms. Oldham could show him the cost benefits of freeing her for other professional duties, he might choose option 3 with a marginal cost of $7.50 per hour.

Because the cost of waiting is not always easy to estimate, the cost minimizing approach is difficult to implement. The difficulty with estimating waiting costs is frequently a function of the relationship between customer and server. When customers are internal to the organization operating the queuing system, it is usually possible to estimate the cost of waiting accurately. "Internal" implies that customers are employed or owned by the organization that operates or is responsible for the queuing system. For example, consider a queue that develops as machines wait to be repaired by an in-house service person, or as secretaries wait to use the duplicating machine. Both customer and server are part of the same organization. In either case, it should not be difficult to estimate a waiting cost. When the customers are external to the organization operating the queuing system, however, estimating waiting costs is difficult. "External" implies that the customers and servers do not have common interests. The organization operating the queuing system does not own or employ the queue customers. Mr. Esposito at the parking garage and Mrs. Kroft at the savings and loan both recognize that long lines cause problems for them. Customers might switch banking institutions; people might not come downtown at night and the city would suffer. However, it is impossible for either one to estimate the cost associated with one customer waiting one minute. In such a situation, as we have seen, the service level approach is a viable alternative. The decision maker may have to specify a desired service goal. He or she can use the results of the queuing analysis to determine the system design that best achieves the specified goal.

14.6 *OTHER QUEUING MODELS*

Recall that there are a very large number of queuing models, and that the choice depends upon the situation being modelled. The formulas can quickly become complicated and computationally burdensome. The use of tables for $P(0)$ and P_n values, and the use of computer software packages to handle the computations, both have eased this difficulty. Nevertheless, only a very few queuing models can be demonstrated in an introductory text. Anyone interested in learning more about queuing models should read one of the specialized queuing texts listed in the references for this chapter.

Poisson Arrivals, Arbitrary Service Times (M/G/1)

Recall that, in many cases, service time cannot be assumed to fit an exponential distribution. In this section we consider the situation wherein the service time distribution is undefined or arbitrary, but the mean ($1/\mu$) and standard deviation (σ) are known. Furthermore, service times are assumed to be independent and the probability distribution holds for all services. Specifically, the model has the following assumptions: (1) Poisson arrivals; (2) arbitrary service time distribution with known mean and standard deviation; (3) infinite calling population; (4) infinite queue; (5) FCFS queue discipline; (6) single server. The system's operating characteristics are determined from these model equations.

$$\rho = \lambda/\mu$$

$$P_0 = 1 - \lambda/\mu$$

$$L_q = \frac{\lambda^2\sigma^2 + (\lambda/\mu)^2}{2(1 - \lambda/\mu)}$$

$$L = L_q + \lambda/\mu$$

$$W_q = L_q/\lambda$$

$$W = L/\lambda \quad \text{or} \quad W_q + 1/\mu$$

Notice that it is first necessary to calculate L_q, number of customers waiting to be served. From this it is then possible to calculate L, number of customers in the system. In order to determine L_q, the standard deviation, σ, must be known.

An M/G/1 Example

The savings and loan discussed earlier is considering opening a branch office in a local mall. The branch is expected to need only one drive-up teller during daytime banking hours. Management wants to determine queuing statistics to confirm this decision. Mrs. Kroft plans to transfer one of the village office tellers to the branch office. Data collected on this teller indicates that her service times, not exponentially distributed, have a mean of 3 minutes per customer ($1/\mu = 1/20$ hour) and a standard deviation of 4 minutes ($\sigma = 1/15$ hour). Customers are expected to arrive in a Poisson manner at a rate of 12 per hour. Is Mrs. Kroft correct that only one drive-up teller is needed?

$$\rho = \lambda/\mu = 12/20 = .60 \quad \text{(percent teller utilization)}$$

$$P_0 = 1 - \lambda/\mu = .40 \quad \text{(probability teller idle)}$$

$$L_q = \frac{\lambda^2\sigma^2 + (\lambda/\mu)^2}{2(1 - \lambda/\mu)} = \frac{144(1/15)^2 + .60^2}{2(1 - .60)}$$

$$= \frac{144(.0044) + .3600}{.80} = \frac{.9936}{.8}$$

$$= 1.24 \text{ customers in waiting line}$$

$$L = L_q + \lambda/\mu = 1.24 + .6$$

$$= 1.84 \text{ customers in system}$$

$$W_q = L_q/\lambda = 1.84/12 = .15 \text{ hrs} = 9 \text{ minutes waiting}$$

$$W = L/\lambda \quad \text{or} \quad W_q + 1/\mu$$

$$= .15 + .05 = .20 \text{ hrs} = 12 \text{ minutes in system}$$

Note that the variance (σ^2) has an important effect on the performance of the queuing system. As the variance increases, L_q, L, W_q, and W also increase. Performance is not dependent only on the mean service time. A server with a lower mean service time can be less productive than one with a higher service time who is also more consistent. Mrs. Kroft could note the fairly low number of customers who are in line on the average and the disproportionate length of time they have to wait, and work to reduce the variance in the service time.

Poisson Arrivals, Constant Service Times (M/D/1)

The queuing situation with constant service times is a special case of the (M/G/1) model with a standard deviation equal to zero (0). This situation most frequently occurs with mechanically performed services. The model assumes an infinite calling population, Poisson arrivals, infinite queue, FCFS discipline, and a constant service time. The operating characteristics are determined using the formulas for the (M/G/1) model, using a standard deviation of zero ($\sigma = 0$).

A (M/D/1) Example

The manager of the snack concession at the local community college is thinking of placing a snack vending machine in the hallway outside the faculty offices. Those faculty members with offices near there are concerned about the noise and congestion that would result. The manager assures them that there will be no long lines, hence no congestion and no noise. At a similar location, students arrive at the machine at a rate of one per minute (Poisson distribution). The snacks are dispensed at a constant rate of 20 seconds.

Using this data, the manager has determined the following operating characteristics:

$$\rho = \frac{1}{3} \quad \text{or} \quad \text{a 33.3\% utilization rate}$$

$$P_0 = 66.7\%$$

$$L_q = .0833 \text{ customers waiting in line}$$

$$L = .4167 \text{ customers in the system}$$

$$W_q = .0833 \text{ min.} \approx 5 \text{ sec.}$$

$$W = .4167 \text{ min.} \approx 24 \text{ sec.}$$

Thus, based upon these figures he knows there should be an average of only 0.08 students in line at any given time. (Of course, these figures disregard possible behavioral patterns such as meeting a friend at the machine and stopping to talk.)

Finite Source Queues (M/M/s): Finite Source

In many real-life situations, the number of customers is small and the calling population cannot be considered infinite. For example, consider the situation in which two in-house maintenance men are responsible for the repair and upkeep of 10 machines. In this situation, with the machines as customers, the source is limited or finite. Using a queuing model that assumes an infinite calling population is not appropriate. In the earlier discussion concerning calling populations, we pointed out that with a finite population, the probability of arrivals is affected by the number of arrivals that have already occurred. In the case of finite populations, the customer alternates between being in the system and being out of the system. The arrival rate, λ, is each customer's individual arrival rate (identical for each customer).

This model assumes Poisson arrivals, exponential service times, and FCFS queue discipline. The operating characteristics for the multiple-server system are determined using the following formulas

where:

N = number of customers in the calling population

s = number of servers

λ = mean arrival rate for each individual customer

μ = mean service rate

n = number of customers in the system

$$P_0 = \cfrac{1}{\left[\displaystyle\sum_{n=0}^{s-1} \frac{N!}{(N-n)!\,n!} \left(\frac{\lambda}{\mu} \right)^n + \displaystyle\sum_{n=s}^{N} \frac{N!}{(N-n)!\,s!\,s^{n-s}} \left(\frac{\lambda}{\mu} \right)^n \right]}$$

$$P_n = \frac{N!}{(N-n)!\,n!} \left(\frac{\lambda}{\mu} \right)^n P_0 \quad \text{for } 0 \le n \le s$$

$$P_n = \frac{N!}{(N-n)!\,s!\,s^{n-s}}\left(\frac{\lambda}{\mu}\right)^n P_0 \quad \text{for } s < n \le N$$

$$L_q = N - \frac{\lambda + \mu}{\lambda}(1 - P_0)$$

$$L = \sum_{n=1}^{N} nP_n = L_q + (1 - P_0)$$

$$W_q = \frac{L_q}{\lambda(N - L)}$$

$$W = W_q + \frac{1}{\mu}$$

For single-server systems (s = 1), the formulas for P_0 and P_n reduce to:

$$P_0 = \frac{1}{\displaystyle\sum_{n=0}^{N} \frac{N!}{(N-n)!}\left(\frac{\lambda}{\mu}\right)^n}$$

$$P_n = \frac{N!}{(N-n)!}\left(\frac{\lambda}{\mu}\right)^n P_0$$

The formulas for L_q, L, W_q, and W are the same.

Now we are beginning to see complicated formulas and burdensome computations. Recall that tables have been developed to yield system operating characteristics for various combinations of input parameters. Even more efficient is the use of queuing software packages that are programmed with various queuing formulas. Using the computer to solve queuing problems is much faster and less susceptible to error than doing the calculations by hand. We will solve the next example using such a program.

A Finite Source Example

The Periwinkle Manufacturing Company has six machines that operate 12 hours each day. In the course of the day, each machine has to be realigned an average of three times (Poisson distribution). Two mechanics are responsible only for realignment. A realignment takes a mechanic an average of 2.4 hours per machine. Records confirm that this service time follows an exponential distribution. Management is concerned about the amount of lost time when the machines are being realigned. Mr. Steele wants to know the probability that four or more of his machines will be out of commission at one time. He also wants to know the number of machines waiting for realignment at any given time. He is considering adding a third mechanic and wants to know how this would change the operating statistics.

Figure 14.9 shows the computer output for this problem with two mechanics and with three mechanics. Notice that, with two mechanics, four machines are out of commission 21.7 percent of the time; five machines are out of commission 13.0 percent of the time; and 3.9 percent of the time all six machines are being realigned. Thus, with two mechanics, at least four machines will be out of commission over 38 percent of the time. On average, three machines are out of service and 1.2 machines are waiting for service. With three mechanics, there are four or more machines out of commission just over 21 percent of the time. On average, 2.4 machines are out of service and 0.29 machines are waiting for service. Al-

```
        (1) MULTIPLE SERVER, FINITE POPULATION
        (2) MEAN ARRIVAL RATE = 3
        (3) MEAN SERVICE RATE = 5
        (4) NUMBER OF SERVERS = 2
        (5) POPULATION SIZE = 6

         *** MULTIPLE SERVER, FINITE POPULATION ***

    NUMBER OF UNITS IN SYSTEM = 3.0141

    NUMBER OF UNITS IN QUEUE = 1.2226

    TIME IN SYSTEM = .3365

    TIME IN QUEUE = .1365

    PROBABILITY SERVICE FACILITY IS IDLE = 3.72%

    P( 4 ) = .217    ( 21.7% )
    P( 5 ) = .13     ( 13% )
    P( 6 ) = .039    ( 3.9% )

        (1) MULTIPLE SERVER, FINITE POPULATION
        (2) MEAN ARRIVAL RATE = 3
        (3) MEAN SERVICE RATE = 5
        (4) NUMBER OF SERVERS = 3
        (5) POPULATION SIZE = 6

         *** MULTIPLE SERVER, FINITE POPULATION ***

    NUMBER OF UNITS IN SYSTEM = 2.432

    NUMBER OF UNITS IN QUEUE = .2912

    TIME IN SYSTEM = .2272

    TIME IN QUEUE = .0272

    PROBABILITY SERVICE FACILITY IS IDLE = 5.51%

    P( 4 ) = .143       ( 14.3% )
    P( 5 ) = .057       ( 5.7% )
    P( 6 ) = .011       ( 1.1% )
```

Figure 14.9 Output for Two and Three Mechanics With Finite Source

though Mr. Steele can compare operating statistics, he will really have to do a cost analysis to help him make his decision. This is possible in this situation, since both the service cost and the cost of waiting can be computed.

Finite Queue Model (M/M/1): Finite Queue

In many queuing situations, the queue length is limited either by the physical facility or by customer attitude. Queue length places a constraint on the queuing system. For example, in many instances, the queue length for a drive-up concession window at a fast-food restaurant is limited to the capacity of the drive-up lane. Customers arriving while the waiting area is full have to leave without being served. The situation is referred to as a finite queue. Notice that the probability that a customer will not (or cannot) join the system is an important consideration in a queue with a finite capacity.

This model has the same assumptions as the basic single-server model, except that the queue length is finite. In this situation, it is not necessary for service rate to be greater than arrival rate ($\lambda/\mu < 1$). The operating characteristics are determined as follows:

$$P_0 = \frac{1 - (\lambda/\mu)}{1 - (\lambda/\mu)^{M+1}} \quad \text{for } \rho \neq 1$$

$$P_0 = \frac{1}{M + 1} \quad \text{for } \rho = 1$$

$$P_n = (\lambda/\mu)^n P_0 \quad \text{for } n \leq M$$

$$L = \frac{\lambda/\mu}{1 - (\lambda/\mu)} - \frac{(M + 1)(\lambda/\mu)^{M+1}}{1 - (\lambda/\mu)^{M+1}} \quad \text{for } \rho \neq 1$$

$$L = M/2 \quad \text{for } \rho = 1$$

$$L_q = L - (1 - \rho)$$

$$W = \frac{L}{\lambda(1 - P_M)}$$

$$W_q = W - 1/\mu$$

where

M = the maximum number in the system and $M - 1$ = maximum queue length

P_M = value of P_n for $n = M$ (probability that a customer will not enter the system)

Note that this model can also be used when customers balk when there are M customers in the system.

A Finite Queue Example

The new drive-up window at the Jayhawk Diner can service 12 customers per hour. Customers arrive at a rate of 10 per hour. Unfortunately, the drive-up lane can accommodate only six cars (including the one being served). The drive-up lane is directly off a busy street, and cars that cannot fit in the lane must pass by without being served. How many cars drive by without being served each hour? If management estimates it loses $5.00 in sales per car that drives by, how much do they lose per hour? Figure 14.10 shows the output for this problem.

Based upon the balking rate of 7.74 percent approximately 0.774 cars will drive by each hour (10 × .0774). At a cost of $5 per car this comes to lost sales of $3.87 per hour.

```
        *** SINGLE SERVER, FINITE QUEUE LENGTH ***

    NUMBER OF UNITS IN SYSTEM = 2.2902

    NUMBER OF UNITS IN QUEUE = 1.5213

    TIME IN SYSTEM = .2482

    TIME IN QUEUE = .1649

    PROBABILITY SERVICE FACILITY IS IDLE = 23.12%

    BALKING RATE = 7.74%
```

Figure 14.10 Finite Queue Operating Characteristics

 ## 14.7 *QUEUING MODELS AND THE COMPUTER*

As we have indicated several times in this chapter, computers are ideal for solving queuing problems. Because of the closed form of the queuing models (the queuing formulas), most models are easily adapted to a computer. The computer easily handles queuing computations that might otherwise prove difficult. In this section, we will solve a multiple-priority queuing problem using a computer. This problem might otherwise prove extremely burdensome.

Priority Queuing

Recall that, in our previous discussion concerning the queue (or service) discipline, we mentioned that it is possible to place arriving customers in priority queues. That is, each customer can be assigned to a specific classification, and those having a higher classification or priority are served before those with a lower classification. In a queuing system with m classifications or queues, it is assumed that queue 1 has the highest priority for service and queue m has the lowest. Rates of arrival and service can vary within each classification. It is also possible that, within classifications, service may follow any queue discipline. While it is possible for a priority discipline to be preemptive, as mentioned earlier, we will not consider preemptive priority queues in this chapter.

Poisson Arrival, Exponential Service, Multiple-Server, Priority Queue (M/M/s): NPRP/Infinite source/Infinite queue

The model described here has the same assumptions as the (M/M/s) system described earlier, except that there is a priority queue discipline. That is, the system has a Poisson arrival distribution, infinite source, infinite queue, priority queue discipline, with FCFS within each classification, a single server, and an exponen-

Chapter 14   *Queuing Analysis*   571

tial service time distribution for each priority class. Operating characteristics are determined using the following formulas:

$$\rho = \lambda/\mu \quad \text{where } \lambda = \sum_{i=1}^{m} \lambda_i$$

$$W_{qk} = \frac{1}{A \cdot B_{k-1} \cdot B_k}$$

where

$$A = s! \left(\frac{s\mu - \lambda}{(\lambda/\mu)^s} \right) \left(\sum_{j=0}^{s-1} \frac{(\lambda/\mu)^j}{j!} \right) + s\mu,$$

$$B_0 = 1,$$

$$B_k = 1 - \frac{\sum_{i=1}^{k} \lambda_i}{s\mu}, \quad \text{for } k = 1, 2, \ldots, m,$$

and

$$W_k = W_{qk} + \frac{1}{\mu}$$

$$L_k = \lambda_k W_k$$

$$L_{qk} = L_k - \lambda/\mu$$

where

λ_i = mean arrival rate for priority class i

μ = mean service rate per server

W_{qk} = the expected waiting time in line for a customer in priority class k

W_k = the expected waiting time in the system for a customer in priority class k

m = number of priority classes

An Example of a Queuing System with Priority Queue Discipline   Sonship Press gives one of three categories to a printing job: rush order, normal, and odd lots (or low priority). Rush orders are run before either of the other two. Normal orders take precedence over the odd lots. However, once a run has been started, the printer completes it before starting any new job. Management is sure that the arrival rates for the jobs are Poisson distributed with means of 5, 8, and 3 per day for the rush, normal, and odd lots respectively. Service time distributions are exponential with a mean of 3 per hour. The jobs are run eight hours a day. Management wants to know the time for each priority so that the sales force can promise realistic delivery times. Figure 14.11 shows the computer solution, giving the operating characteristics for the priority discipline. Times are in hours. Thus, a rush job should be in the system for approximately 35 minutes on the average, a normal job for 53 minutes, and an odd-lot job for 99 minutes.

```
              *** PRIORITY QUEUING SYSTEM ***

              A  = 36.000
              B0 =  1.
              B1 =  0.792
              B2 =  0.458
              B3 =  0.333


          PRIORITY      NUMBER OF UNITS IN SYSTEM
            (1)              0.175
            (2)              0.612
            (3)              0.545


          PRIORITY      TIME IN SYSTEM
            (1)              0.077
            (2)              0.118
            (3)              0.223


          PRIORITY      TIME IN QUEUE
            (1)              0.035
            (2)              0.077
            (3)              0.182
```

Figure 14.11 Operating Characteristics for Priority Discipline

Focus on Decision Making

Murphy Manufacturing uses ten multi-function, automated in-line machines in its manufacturing processes. These machines are integral to Murphy's production process. They are highly complex, are in use eight hours per day, and tend to malfunction frequently. Because the operation of these machines is critical to Murphy's production, the company employs five full-time, skilled mechanics to maintain them. The union that represents the mechanics recently negotiated a wage increase to $22 per hour. Given the high cost of these mechanics, and the fact that most of them appear to be idle part of each day, management would like to determine whether reducing the number of mechanics would achieve a cost savings. This problem has been turned over to Roberta Turner, an industrial engineer, for further analysis.

Data Preparation/Problem Formulation

Roberta began by gathering information on the breakdown pattern of the machines. She found that, on average, each machine broke down once every 4 days. In other words, approximately 2.5 of the machines malfunctioned on any given day. She also found that the lost production time while a machine was down cost the company $3,400 per day. The interarrival times for the malfunctions seemed to follow an exponential probability distribution (a Poisson-distributed rate of arrivals).

She then discovered that a mechanic required an average of six hours to repair a machine. Generally, one mechanic was assigned to any malfunctioning machine. The foreman informed her that all mechanics were of equal ability. It also appeared that repair times were random and exponentially distributed. All repairmen were paid $22 per hour or $176 per day. The personnel office estimated fringe benefits to be worth an additional $65 per day for each mechanic. Once Roberta gathered the data, she used a computer program for multiple server/finite population queuing problems to determine operating characteristics of the system. She felt that, once she had this information, she could make reasonable cost comparisons for various staffing levels.

Computer Solution

Using an arrival rate of 0.25, a service rate of 1.333, 5 servers, and a finite population of 10, the following results were obtained:

```
        *** MULTIPLE SERVER, FINITE POPULATION ***
    NUMBER OF UNITS IN SYSTEM = 1.5815
    NUMBER OF UNITS IN QUEUE = .0027
    TIME IN SYSTEM = .7515
    TIME IN QUEUE = .0013
    PROBABILITY SERVICE FACILITY IS IDLE = 17.92 %
    SERVICE COST = $ 1205
    WAITING COST = $ 5377.18
    TOTAL COST = $ 6582.18
```

Roberta then reran the problem with 4, 3, and 6 servers. A summary of all results is shown below:

	Servers			
	3	4	5	6
Number of units in system	1.6929	1.5972	1.5815	1.5795
Number of units in queue	0.1349	0.0212	0.0027	0.0002
Time in system	0.8152	0.7603	0.7515	0.7503
Time in queue	0.0650	0.0101	0.0013	0.0001
Prob. facility idle	17.3%	17.85%	17.92%	17.93%
Service cost	$ 723	$ 964	$1,205	$1,446
Waiting cost	$5,756	$5,430	$5,377	$5,370
Total cost	$6,479	$6,394	$6,582	$6,816

Interpretation and Analysis of the Results

The results indicate that, on a cost basis, the optimum number of mechanics is four. With four mechanics, the average number of machines down at any given time is 1.6; the average time each machine is down is .76 days or 6.08 hours. The total cost of mechanics and down time is $6,394 per day. Reducing the number of mechanics from five to four will reduce overall costs $188 per day.

What Happens Next

Although using only four mechanics will save the company $188 per day, Roberta must consider several other factors before making the final decision. She knows that, when a machine malfunctions and more than one mechanic is idle, they sometimes work on the machine together. This shortens the service time somewhat and can alter the results. If idle mechanics, working in teams, can shorten a machine's down time significantly, the cost of the extra mechanic may be more than offset by the high cost of machine down time ($425 per hour). Furthermore, assumptions basic to the analysis might be inaccurate. For example, all mechanics may not be equally skilled on all machines, and not all the machines may malfunction at the same rate. In addition, management may want to consider the anticipated union reaction to a reduction in this skilled labor group. More importantly, the company should make sure it is attempting to solve the correct problem. Rather than focusing on the optimal number of mechanics, perhaps the company should be looking at ways to reduce the occurrence of malfunctions. Given the high cost of machine down time, a preventative maintenance program during off hours might be a better solution; or they might want to consider replacing the machines if they are aging.

14.8 *CONCLUDING REMARKS*

In this chapter, we have given a brief introduction to queuing models. We have been able to examine only a very small number of queuing situations, representing only a fraction of the almost infinite number of queuing models that exist. Our purpose has been to give you some insight into how queues are formed and how queuing analysis can provide information that is useful for the management of queuing systems. We have omitted the mathematical analysis necessary to derive the formulas for the operating characteristics. Instead, we have chosen to present a more qualitative overview.

Sometimes queuing situations are so complex that the analytical queuing models cannot be used to compute the operating characteristics. In fact, there is a large probability that no analytical model will fit a given situation. Simulation, discussed in the next chapter, is often used to analyze such queuing systems.

Management Science Application _____

MACHINE-SERVICE IN AN ELECTRONICS COMPANY[1]

This study applied the use of quantitative techniques to determine the optimal staffing of a machine-service crew in an electronics manufacturing and testing company. The company operates 24 hours a day (three shifts), 5 days a week. When a machine breakdown occurs, the machine operator records the time of the breakdown and calls the machine-service crew to repair the machine.

A multi-channel (server) queuing system was used to model the machine-service operation for this firm. The four major components of this system were: (1) source population; (2) queuing discipline; (3) arrival pattern; and (4) service pattern. The source population consisted of 50 machines. The

[1]Reprinted with permission. H. L. Ong, T. N. Goh, and H. K. Sim, "A Modelling Study of Machine-Service Operation in an Electronics Industry," *Journal of the Operations Research Society,* 36 (11) (November, 1985), 993–998. Copyright 1985, Pergamon Press.

source population was considered infinite in this study because it was not seriously affected by the finite number of potential breakdowns. The queuing discipline was first-come-first-served. The arrival pattern of machine breakdowns followed a Poisson distribution. Breakdowns range from 3 to 6 machines per hour. The arrival pattern in the first hour was significantly different from the remaining hours in each shift because some machine breakdowns which occurred at the end of one shift were carried over to the beginning of the next shift. The arrival rates for the remaining seven hours of a shift were not significantly different (although the last hour of each shift had the lowest arrival rate—due to the carryover already discussed). The service pattern followed an Erlang probability distribution with a mean service time of 18.84 minutes. Service patterns for the three shifts were not significantly different.

Because of the difficulty of using an Erlang service distribution, the standard multi-channel queuing model (M/M/s) was used in the analysis to provide an approximate solution. Using the formula for the probability that at least one server is available

$$1 - \frac{\left(\frac{\lambda}{\mu}\right)^s \cdot P_0}{s!\,[1 - (\lambda/\mu s)]}$$

where

$$P_0 = \frac{1}{\left[\sum_{n=0}^{s-1} \frac{1}{n!}\left(\frac{\lambda}{\mu}\right)^n\right] + \frac{1}{s! \cdot [1 - (\lambda/\mu s)]} \cdot \left(\frac{\lambda}{\mu}\right)^s}$$

Using these formulas, the number of servers needed for a β percent chance that a server will be available when a breakdown occurs, i.e., the minimum number of servers s_i needed to meet the demand for period i β percent of the time. The value of s_i can be determined from the inequality:

$$\sum_{k=0}^{s_i=1} P_k \geq \beta\%$$

where P_k is the probability of k customers in the queuing system. Since the machine-service times were not exponentially distributed, this model provided only an approximate solution. A simulation was then run to determine the actual number of servers required. The results from the simulation were found to be very close to the results found by the queuing model.

Once the minimum manpower requirements were determined, an optimal manpower schedule was determined for each shift. Here, two different approaches were used. The first was mixed integer programming, which took into account meal breaks by the machine repair crew. This approach will not be discussed further. The second approach was an economic analysis of the queuing results. The total operation cost is the sum of the cost of service and the cost of lost production due to machine breakdowns. It is formulated as

$$TC(s) = sC_s + W_s(\lambda)(u)(C_u)$$

where

s = number of servers per shift

C_s = cost of one server per hour

W_s = average waiting time for a faulty machine in the system

u = total number of units of the product tested per hour

C_u = cost per unit of product not tested due to machine breakdown

This can be approximated as

$$TC(s) = sC_s + \frac{1}{\mu}\left[1 + \frac{\left(\dfrac{\lambda}{\mu}\right)^s}{s!\,s\left(1 - \dfrac{\lambda}{\mu s}\right)^2}P_0\right](\lambda)(u)(Cu)$$

The optimal number of servers needed is then calculated by

1. For a given set of values of λ, μ, C_u, C_s, u and s, compute the TC(s).
2. Compute the TC for s = s + 1, s + 2, ..., 7.
3. Determine the optimal value of s that minimizes the total cost TC.

For this company, $C_s \approx \$8.25/\text{hour}$, $C_u \approx \$0.08/\text{unit}$, and $u \approx 2{,}875$ units per hour.

The results of these calculations revealed that one additional server was required during the first hour of every shift. Asking one server from the previous shift to work overtime during the first hour of the present shift seemed the most justifiable solution. This resulted in a more than 85 percent availability of servers when a breakdown occurred.

GLOSSARY

arrival rate (λ) average number of customers entering a queuing system in a given time period

calling population set of all customers that can enter the queuing system, the source of arrivals; described as **infinite**, a very large or unlimited number, or **finite**, a small or limited number

channel synonymous with server

customer attitude describes the customer behavior in the queue, either patient or impatient; impatient behavior includes **balking** (refusing to join the queue), **reneging** (leaving the system before being served), and **jockeying** (switching back and forth between queues)

interarrival times ($\frac{1}{\lambda}$) amount of time between two consecutive arrivals entering a queuing system.

Kendall notation a shorthand notation, or taxonomy, for describing a queuing system; succinctly describes the parameters of a queuing system and provides a means of identifying queuing systems

multiple-phase queuing system a queuing system that is configured in sequential steps; a customer must pass through more than one service point, receiving service from two or more different types of servers, arranged in series

multiple-server system a system having a single queue with two or more parallel identical servers

operating characteristics average values that describe (statistically) how the queuing system performs under specific conditions; measures of performance that describe the operation of the queuing system include such quantities as L_q (length of the queue), L (number of customers in the system), W (waiting time in the system), W_q (waiting time in the system), and ρ (the percentage of the time the system is busy)

queue a waiting line, one or more customers or calling units waiting to be served

queue discipline decision rule or policy used to determine the manner in which customers in the queue are selected for service; includes such decision rules as **FCFS** (first come, first served), **LCFS** (last to come, first served), and **priority** (served in order of some category designations)

queue length maximum number of customers that a queue can contain at any given time; a capacity constraint

queuing theory the mathematical study of queues

service facility the component of the queuing system which performs the service

service rate (μ) the average number of customers that can be served by one server per given time period

service time amount of time a server spends servicing a customer; a random quantity

single-phase queuing system queuing mechanism having only one stage; each customer must pass through only one service point

single-server system a system having only one server (one service facility)

steady state a condition in which the behavior of the system is not a function of time; equilibrium, or constant level of performance, usually achieved after a system has been operating long enough so that operating characteristics are independent of the conditions present when the system began operation and of the time elapsed since the system began operation

system utilization the percentage of time the queuing system is busy, $\rho = \lambda/s\mu$

transient state startup condition of a queuing system, wherein the operating characteristics are dependent upon the initial conditions (conditions present when the system began operation) and on the time that has elapsed since the system began operation; operating characteristics in the transient state do not reflect long-term expected values

utilization factor ratio of the mean arrival rate (λ) to the product of the number of servers (s) and the mean service rate (μ)

PROBLEMS

1. Describe 10 queuing situations with which you are familiar in real life. Identify the components of each (for the most part, assume Poisson arrivals and exponential service times). Try to include at least one system having a finite queue, one with a finite population, and one with a constant service time. Are you familiar with any priority queuing systems?

2. For each of the following situations, identify the components and/or structure of the queuing system. Use Kendall notation as much as possible.

   a. A fast-food restaurant has several service channels available, each with its own line. Arriving customers usually join the shortest line. Arriving customers average 60 per hour. An order usually takes three minutes to fill, with a standard deviation of 30 seconds.

b. Customers arrive randomly at a coffee vending machine at an average of 30 per hour. The coffee is dispensed at a constant rate of 20 seconds per cup.

c. A lab assistant is responsible for the maintenance of a computer lab with seven computers. In general the computers break down at a rate of two per week. It takes an average of three days to return the computer to functioning.

d. Customers arriving at a customer service desk average four per hour. Mean service time is 9 minutes, with a standard deviation of 3 minutes.

e. A national fast-food chain has changed the configuration of its drive-up windows. Arriving cars place their order at a speakerphone, then drive to the first window to pay and to the next window for pickup. Both arrivals and service times are random.

3. Customers arrive randomly at an automatic teller machine at an average rate of 6 per hour. What is the probability that no customers will arrive in any given hour? What is the probability that exactly six customers will arrive in any given hour? That more than 3 will arrive?

4. Consider a single-server queue that meets the following assumptions: infinite calling population, Poisson arrival, infinite queue, FCFS queue discipline, exponential service times, and steady-state conditions. If the mean arrival rate is ten per hour and mean service rate is 12 per hour, answer the following questions:

a. What is the mean interarrival time in minutes? Mean service time in minutes?

b. What is the probability of exactly one arrival during the first hour? Three arrivals? No arrivals? What is the probability that there will be more than six arrivals in the first hour?

c. What is the probability that the service time for the first arrival will be at least four minutes? Less than two minutes?

d. What is the utilization factor? Explain what this means.

e. How much time (in minutes) can a customer expect to wait before being served?

f. How long a waiting line will there be (on average)?

5. Given an M/M/1 queuing system with an arrival rate of 48 per hour and a service time of one minute, determine the operating characteristics for the system. How do these change if a second channel is opened up? If the service cost is $25 per hour per channel and the waiting cost is $30, is a second channel justified on a cost basis?

6. Given an M/M/s queuing system with six servers, an interarrival time of .25 minutes, and a service time of one minute, identify λ and μ. Determine the operating characteristics of this system. Each server is paid $6.50 per hour. Waiting costs are estimated at $85 per hour. Is it economically justifiable to add a seventh server?

7. The reserve book desk at the university library is manned by student helpers. During the week, one student works at a time in four-hour shifts. Students arrive randomly to request reserve items at an average of 20 per hour. It takes the student clerk an average of two minutes to locate and check out the requested items. Service time is exponentially distributed.

a. On the average, how many students are waiting to request an item? How long can they expect to wait?

b. When the student workers are not filling requests, they are expected to do certain recordkeeping chores. These chores are assumed to take about 25 percent of the student's time. Is it reasonable to assume that the workers will have time to finish the recordkeeping? Discuss this.

8. During the final two weeks of each semester (problem 7), the arrival rate increases to 32 requests per hour. Is it possible for the one student to meet this level of demand? How do you know? How do the operating characteristics change if a second student is added for these weeks?

9. Joe Trau is concerned about the amount of time and money that is being lost each day by employees standing around waiting for service. An average of 25 machinists per hour arrive at the tool crib at Trau and Sons. It takes an attendant an average of two minutes for each request.

   a. How much time is lost each day by employees waiting at the tool crib? Assume an eight-hour day, a Poisson arrival, and exponential service time distributions.

   b. If the machinists are paid $18 per hour and the tool crib attendant receives $9.50, what is the optimum number of attendants to have in the crib?

10. Mr. Trau (problem 9) has also noticed that the six secretaries appear to spend a great deal of time at the copier. If each secretary makes 8 trips to the copier a day, and each visit averages 15 minutes, is any time lost waiting to use the copier? If each secretary earns $8.00 per hour, how much does it cost in waiting time only?

11. Both the machinists and the secretaries (problems 9 and 10) always use their trips to the crib or the copier as an excuse for a trip to the coffee machine. This machine brews each cup of coffee individually, taking a constant 1.5 minutes to brew and serve the coffee.

   a. How long will each employee spend at the coffee machine (in line and waiting for coffee)?

   b. If the coffee machine serves 40 cups per hour, with a standard deviation of .02, how does this affect lost time?

12. Mobil Mart sells to customers in a hurry. An average of 38 customers arrive per hour. Checkout averages 1.5 minutes. There is normally only one clerk on duty at a time. Because customers are in a hurry, they will not wait if there are more than three people at the checkout counter. How many customers does Mobile Mart lose each day? Assume a 12-hour day.

13. Dimeco has four large presses, each of which breaks down an average of once every other day. There is one mechanic responsible for getting the machines functional again. This mechanic has an expected repair time of two hours per machine. If the mechanic is paid $25 per hour, and machine time is worth $60 per hour, what is the cost associated with repairing the machines? If a two-man team can repair a machine in one hour, should Dimeco hire another mechanic? Assume an 8-hour day.

14. At Tranco Electronics, components arrive at a workstation at a rate of 60 units per hour. Processing time averages .75 minute per component, with a standard deviation of .02. If it costs the company $3.00 per day for each unit of in-process inventory at the workstation, how much (on average) does it cost the company? A temporary employee at this workstation required

.9 minutes to process each component, but the standard deviation was reduced to .01. Which employee had the higher in-process inventory at the end of each day?

15. Panorama Car Wash is a large automatic car wash that can wash 6 cars at one time. They have recently added a facility for vans and trucks. This channel has its own waiting line. However, there is room in the queue for only three waiting vehicles. Trucks and vans arrive at a rate of 12 per hour, and it takes an average of four minutes to wash them. Assume Poisson/exponential distributions. When an arriving customer sees a full waiting line, he or she is forced to drive on. Panorama loses an average of $7.00 for each customer that it loses. The car wash is open six days a week from 9 AM to 7 PM. How much does Panorama lose each week?

16. MotoPhoto has added a new service, Quick Passport Photos, at its Midtown Mall location. Photographs take an average of three minutes from start to finish. It is a totally automated procedure. The picture itself takes a constant two minutes, once the customer presses the take button. However, it takes time for individuals to adjust themselves. Mr. Terrell, manager of the store, thought this service would appeal to a limited number of people who needed a fast but not high-quality photo. However, it has become very popular with teenagers, young couples, and parents with small children. What was intended as a convenience, and as a way to bring more people into the store, is fast becoming a major nuisance—but a lucrative one. During after-school hours (3–9 PM Monday through Friday), and on weekends (10 AM until 9 PM on Saturdays and noon to 5 PM on Sundays), arrivals at the machine average 18 an hour. The clerk is overwhelmed with requests for change for the machine. To continue as things are, Mr. Terrell would have to hire another clerk at a rate of $4.00 an hour.

   a. What exactly is the situation facing Mr. Terrell? How many people are usually waiting in line to use the machine? How long must they wait?

   b. Mr. Terrell is considering cordoning off a waiting area. However, this would limit the size of the waiting line to five people. How would this affect the system?

   c. Mr. Terrell now makes a profit of $1.00 on each picture. As things now stand, however, he is losing some of his other customers, who will not enter the store when there are large crowds waiting for a picture. He figures he may be losing up to $125 a day in other sales. If he limits the size of the waiting line, he will probably make up his lost sales, but he will lose the revenue from the lost picture sales. Based on this information, what do you think Mr. Terrell should do? Why? Can you see any other options open to him? Would a second machine help?

   d. There is another photo booth available that has a constant service time of 90 seconds. With this one, the configuration of the system would change. The arriving customers would pay a clerk, then enter the booth. Thirty seconds after they sat down, the picture would be taken automatically, and 60 seconds later they would have a finished product. Do you have some ideas about analyzing this situation? Assume arrivals remain the same, 18 per hour with a Poisson distribution. Assume service time for payment is at a rate of 45 per hour, exponentially distributed.

17. Five pediatricians have recently formed a partnership. Each doctor currently employs a lab technician for in-office testing. Jobs arrive to each technician at a rate of 3 per hour. It takes an average of ten minutes to accomplish each task. The doctors are now ready to form a technician pool. Compare the amount of time spent waiting for lab results under the current situation with one in which the five doctors utilize five technicians. Compare the probability of having to wait with the two systems. If the doctors wish to have a utilization factor of around 85 percent, how many technicians should they retain? If they wish to keep waiting time in the system to under 15 minutes, how many should they retain? Can this decision be made on an economic basis? What information do you need?

18. Hoff Brothers owns six refuge disposal trucks. The company has one mechanic who is responsible for routine maintenance and for minor breakdowns. Trucks arrive randomly at the garage for this work at an average of six per week. Mean service time is six hours, with a standard deviation of one hour. Mechanics work an 8-hour day. On any given workday (M–F), optimum route coverage requires five trucks. Can Fred expect to have five trucks in operation on any given day?

   a. When five trucks are not available, the other trucks must cover the missing truck's route, resulting in an overtime cost of $160 a day. The mechanic receives $15 an hour. Hoff Brothers is considering adding a mechanic to create a two-man team. This should reduce service time to 4 hours. Should the second mechanic be added?

19. The city school district has developed a homework hotline. From 6 to 10 o'clock each night, students can call to receive help with their homework. The hotline has been set up in two distinct districts. Students in District one call one number; students in District two call another number. Each district has 7 helpers on line. Surprisingly, the statistics for each district are almost identical. Calls come in at an average of 25 per hour. Help requires an average of 15 minutes per call. The Board of Education is very proud of this innovative effort to help individual students. In public service announcements and advertisements for the service, they claim that there is never a wait; calls are taken immediately. Is this correct?

   a. Unfortunately, this is a very costly program. The district would like to eliminate some of the tutors. At this arrival and service rate, can they cut back on the tutors and still maintain a waiting time of fifteen minutes or less?

   b. What happens if they combine the two systems and reduce the number of tutors to 13? 12?

20. The Beutel Trucking company has one loading dock at its Daytona warehouse. Trucks are loaded and unloaded by a three-person team. On average, 4 trucks arrive randomly each hour. It takes a team an average of 12 minutes to load or unload a truck. On average how many trucks are waiting to be serviced? How long does the truck have to wait? Management would like to have three trucks or fewer in line at any given time. What is the probability of this occurring?

   a. If it costs $9.00 per person per hour to service the truck, and $65.00 is the estimated cost of keeping a truck off the road for one hour, what is the total cost associated with loading or unloading a truck?

b. Beutel's is considering an increase to a four-member team. This would reduce unloading time to 9 minutes. How does this affect the operating characteristics? What are the total costs now?

c. A new warehouse and loading dock are being constructed by Beutel's in Orlando. This facility would probably average six trucks an hour. The company is considering a two-channel arrangement, with each channel using a two-man team. Each team is expected to average 15 minutes to service each truck. Do you recommend this over the one-channel system with a three-man team?

21. Al's Barber Shop is a small, one-chair operation that currently averages 15 customers a day. A haircut averages 20 minutes. In this small shop, Al has noticed that, if there are three customers currently waiting, there is a lot of customer dissatisfaction and customers sometimes choose not to wait. Analyze this situation. How long is the average waiting line? How long can a customer expect to wait? Consider a seven-hour day, six days a week. Is there a difference if you analyze it as having an infinite queue and as having a finite queue of three?

   a. Al would like to move, expanding to become Al and Son. At the new location, with the second barber available, Al would probably average 25 customers a day. How does this change his operating characteristics?

   b. Assume the overhead costs would remain the same. Each haircut costs $6.00 at the old location, but can be raised to $6.50 in the new location. Considering that Al and his son would split the income, and considering that he loses sales when there are more than three waiting at the old location, do you recommend that Al make the change?

22. The congestion at the New York–Canadian Niagara Frontier border on weekends and Holidays was extremely heavy this past summer. The Ontario Provincial government, in an attempt to alleviate the problem, has established flying squads of agents. These agents are located in a central location and are ready to move to any of the three bridges in the Niagara Falls area. On July Fourth weekend, 190 cars an hour arrived at the bridge. The average time to interview occupants was 1.5 minutes. There are normally 4 agents on duty. What would happen to the line under these circumstances? How many agents should be moved in to keep the line under 5 cars?

23. Monroe Community College offers a free dental cleaning and checkup service to its students, faculty, and staff, and to residents in a nearby senior citizens' residence. All service is walk-in, but service is prioritized. Senior citizens are first, faculty and staff second. Thus, the school's students are given the lowest priority. Arrival rates at the dental clinic are random and they vary with the group. Senior citizens arrive at a rate of 4 per day. Faculty/staff average 3 per day, while students average 7 a day. Only one student hygienist is on duty at a time, and the clinic is open eight hours a day. Cleaning time averages 30 minutes and is exponentially distributed. On the average, how long must a student wait for service? If the priorities were to be switched, such that students were first and senior citizens second, would this affect the waiting time for each group?

24. If the sales department for Sonship Press (priority queuing example, page 572) advertised that rush jobs would be completed in less than one hour (average expected time in the system was approximately 35 minutes), and this increased the number of rush jobs per day from 5 to 7, how would the time in the system be affected for each priority?

Life Line

Life Line is a social service referral and intervention agency funded by the United Way of Greater Rochester. It began operation in the early 1970s as a logical extension to the reference desk at the public library, providing an information/referral service for local social service organizations. People called the reference library when they had no idea who else to call when they were looking for a source of help for their problems. The need for such a service became quickly apparent, and it soon outgrew the library. Within two years, it was a not-for-profit organization in its own right with a board of directors, a paid coordinator, and a staff of volunteers to answer the telephone and keep track of all agencies providing needed services in the county. Start-up monies came from grants from the Gannett Foundation and the Daisy Marquis Jones Foundation. As a result of a massive public-service advertising campaign on local TV, radio, billboards, newspapers, posters, and other media, the target population soon became familiar with the Life Line number, 222-HELP.

Soon callers were seeking help for an ever-increasing variety of problems—from legal and medical problems to garbage pickup and snow removal complaints; from requests for day care services to housing problems. More and more agencies were added to the referral services, including hotlines for abused children and battered women, and shelters for runaways and the homeless. Sometimes life and death calls were received—cries for help from potential suicides and accidental poisonings. The poison control center and suicide help lines were tied into the Life Line number, with trained professionals available for intervention counseling. Volunteer staffs manned the phone lines 24 hours a day, 7 days a week.

By the mid 1980s, it became increasingly difficult to find volunteers, and Life Line, like many other social service agencies, had to begin paying its staff or drastically reduce service. It soon became infeasible to attempt to maintain a combination of paid and unpaid telephone personnel. Employee cost became a factor in this vital service, and the Board of Directors began to collect and analyze the pertinent data in an attempt to offer the maximum service at a minimum cost. Thus, they began to look at the number and frequency rates of the calls and the length of time required to handle the calls. Accordingly, the day was divided into the three 8-hour shifts worked by the staff. Data on incoming calls revealed the following patterns:

Shift	Arrivals of Calls
midnight–8 AM	1 call every 45 sec (Poisson Distribution)
8 AM–4 PM	1 call every 60 sec (Poisson Distribution)
4 PM–midnight	1 call every 100 sec (Poisson Distribution)

The data on the service times indicated the following patterns:

Shift	Service Times
midnight–8 AM	1.5 minutes/call (exponential distribution)
8 AM–4 PM	55 seconds/call (exponential distribution)
4 PM–midnight	1 minute/call (exponential distribution)

Data also indicate that Friday and Saturday nights, during the midnight to 8 AM shift, calls come in at a rate of one every 30 seconds, with the majority requiring some form of intervention. The service time increases to 2 minutes per call, exponentially distributed.

The telephone staff members are paid at varying rates, dependent upon the shift time. Those working the 8 AM to 4 PM and 4 PM to midnight shifts receive $7.50 per hour. The midnight to 8 AM shift receives $9.00 per hour Sunday through Thursday, with an additional $2.50 per hour for Friday and Saturday. The staff works on a rotating basis of six nights on followed by two off, so that everyone works some weekends. Intervention staff are provided and paid by their sponsoring agencies and, in fact, are not housed in the same facility. When a Life Line staff person ascertains that a caller needs some form of intervention, the call is immediately switched to the line designated for that particular service, such as poison control. The lengthy time required by this kind of help is therefore not part of the service times assessed to Life Line calls.

The Board of Directors feels that the service provided by Life Line is vital to the community. A busy line or an overloaded system with long waiting times is potentially life-threatening. The Board wants to continue providing immediate service, but cannot afford to overstaff the operation. After much heated argument, they have agreed that a service goal is to immediately answer 95 percent of the incoming calls.

You have been hired as a consultant to help the Life Line Board of Directors by applying management science techniques to this particular problem. Prepare a report for the board that addresses:

1. The number of staff members required on the midnight to 8:00 AM shift, Monday through Friday, to meet the board's stated service goal.
2. The number of staff members required on the 8:00 AM to 4:00 PM shift to meet the board's stated service goal.
3. The number of staff members required on the 4:00 PM to midnight shift to meet the board's stated service goal.
4. The number of staff members required on the midnight to 8:00 am shift, Friday and Saturday, to meet the board's stated service goal.
5. The cost of staffing each of the above shifts.
6. The impact of a change in the service goal from 95 percent immediate answers to 90 percent. This impact should be measured in terms of staff levels, cost per shift, utilization rates, and time spent waiting for someone to answer the call.

By the end of this chapter, you should be able to:

1

define simulation, describing its major characteristics and usefulness;

2

understand when simulation is the appropriate tool to use;

3

define and use the Monte Carlo method;

4

explain the use of random or pseudorandom numbers in a simulation;

5

understand the concept of sampling from a given probability distribution;

6

design or formulate a simple manual simulation;

7

understand the role of the computer and special purpose languages in simulation.

Management science models are selective abstractions of reality. They simplify reality by ignoring or assuming away extraneous or irrelevant factors, in order to create a framework within which the problems can be analyzed mathematically. All of the solution techniques presented thus far have specific, restrictive assumptions. However, in reality there are situations in which these assumptions do not hold (lead time is not deterministic, the arrival pattern does not fit a Poisson distribution, etc.). Furthermore, there are situations where the system under study is too complex or dynamic to permit the development of an analytical model. Simulation provides a flexible alternative form of analysis. It is a descriptive process that involves first developing a model to represent (imitate) the system being studied, and then performing sampling experiments on the model to establish measures of the system's performance. The system is modeled with the intention of evaluating and predicting its behavior by seeing how it performs under various circumstances. In this chapter we provide an overview of the nature and characteristics of a simulation study, and a description of the mechanics and methodology involved in a simulation study.

An Inventory Problem

The Micro Store, which sells equipment and supplies for personal computers, is reevaluating its inventory policies. The store manager, John Topping, is especially concerned about the inventory for PC keyboards. After reviewing sales records for the past 40 weeks, he has a fairly clear picture of the demand distribution for keyboards. He also has records of lead time on reorders for the same period. Taking into consideration holding costs ($0.50 per week per keyboard), a $65.00 ordering cost, and an estimated $25 opportunity loss cost when keyboards are out of stock, he has decided to adopt a policy of ordering 35 each time he reorders keyboards, and also placing an order whenever the total number of keyboards in inventory and on order at the end of the week is below 35. However, he is concerned that this may not be the correct decision, and he cannot use an analytical model because of the variability in demand and lead time.

Later in this chapter, we will return to Mr. Topping's problem to see how simulation can help him with this decision.

15.1 AN INTRODUCTION TO SIMULATION

Broadly defined, **simulation** is an experimental process that enables the user to understand how the system under study will behave in reality by imitating its behavior in an artificial environment. Simulation is a technique used to imitate the operation of a real-world system as it evolves over time. The basic idea is to construct a model that approximates the system of interest as closely as possible, and then to conduct sampling experiments on the model over a period of time in order to evaluate its performance under various circumstances. Running the simulation generates representative samples of the measures of performance. Thus, it is a descriptive rather than a normative (optimization) technique. With this definition it is easy to imagine one of the more familiar analog or physical simulations, such as a model airplane in a wind tunnel. The term also encompasses computerized mathematical simulation, which is the focus of the chapter. In this context (quantitative analysis), simulation means experimentation based on a mathematical model. In simulation, the input is in the form of decision alternatives being considered and system parameters that describe the system's operational factors. Output is in the form of performance descriptors that measure the effectiveness of the system. By running the simulation, it is possible to explore the characteristics of the system. Figure 15.1 illustrates this concept.

Simulation is one of the most, if not the most, popular and useful management science tools in practice today. Recall the 1983 study described in Chapter 1, which indicated that over 87 percent of the survey respondents made either moderate or frequent use of simulation. In an earlier study, simulation received a utility ranking of 1. The popularity of simulation is due to these advantages:

1. Simulation requires fewer simplifications and assumptions concerning the problem environment. Real-life complexities can be incorporated into the model. It can be used in situations where the assumptions underlying the analytical model do not hold, or in situations that are too complex to be solved using an analytical procedure.

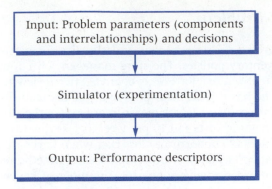

Figure 15.1 Input-Output for Simulation Model

2. Simulation can be used when experimentation with the real system is impractical or impossible. For instance, it would be impractical to try various lead times with an inventory problem, because this approach would require a great deal of time and could be very costly. Using simulation and the computer, decision makers can experiment with alternative courses of action, variables, and policies relatively quickly and inexpensively and with less risk.

3. Simulation can be used in situations in which there is a crucial dependence upon time. Whenever a system is operating in a dynamic environment, wherein time must be taken into consideration when analyzing the problem, simulation is an appropriate technique to use. Furthermore, with simulation a great deal of time compression can be attained, allowing long-term effects to be realized in a matter of minutes.

4. Simulation is an extremely flexible tool that can handle a wide variety of problem types. It has been successfully applied to a number of diverse systems, including queuing systems, production systems, financial systems, and inventory systems. It can be used to predict both the effect of change on an existing system and the performance of new systems under varying circumstances.

5. Simulation theory is relatively straightforward, and the simulation approach is fairly easy to understand and to explain to others.

Simulation is more than a technique of last resort, to be used when an analytical model cannot be used. However, there are certain disadvantages or cautions associated with simulation:

1. Because simulation is so flexible and easy to apply, an analytical procedure that could yield a better solution may be overlooked.

2. There is no guarantee that an optimal solution will be achieved.

3. Constructing the simulation study can be a slow and costly process.

4. The accuracy of the results may be difficult to validate, particularly with simulations of extremely complex systems.

Types of Simulation

There are several types of simulation, which can be classified in several ways. Simulations are either discrete (called discrete event simulation) or continuous. **Discrete event simulations** are appropriate for systems whose variables change at distinct points in time. Discrete event simulation outputs typically represent a number of occurrences, such as number of items sold or number of customers in line. **Continuous simulations** are appropriate for systems whose variables are continually changing. Continuous simulation outputs can take any value (integer or noninteger) over a given range. These outputs typically represent measurable values such as time or weight. In this chapter, we are concerned with discrete event simulations. Simulation models also can be classified as static, representing a system at a particular point in time, or dynamic, representing a system as it evolves over time.

Within these broad classifications, simulation models are either deterministic or stochastic. In a **deterministic simulation** the values of all the variables are known. A deterministic simulation is used primarily to provide a way to change the parameters of a model and to predict the behavior of a system for different sets of conditions (when it may be impossible to use any other analytical or optimization technique). We do not discuss deterministic simulation in this chapter. In a **stochastic simulation** model, one or more of the inputs is a random variable. The behavior of such probabilistic variables can be represented by a probability distribution. Note that random inputs result in random outputs. Such results can be considered only as estimates of the true characteristics of the system. In this chapter, we are concerned primarily with stochastic simulations. This means we are interested in simulations used to analyze decisions made under uncertainty.

Simulations also are categorized by time. Thus, simulations can be **time-independent** or **time-dependent.** Time-independent simulations are concerned with the number of occurrences within a given period of time. Therefore, it is not necessary to know when an event occurred. The simulation of daily product demand, where only the quantity demanded per day is of interest, is an example of a time-independent simulation. In time-dependent simulations, the time an event occurs is important. An example of a time-dependent simulation is a simulation of machine repair, for it is important to know when a machine breaks down and how long it takes to repair it.

In a time-dependent simulation, it is necessary to track the occurrence of events over time. Two approaches can be used to accomplish this, a **fixed-time increment** and a **variable-time increment.**

A fixed-time increment simulation advances the system clock a fixed amount of time, such as one minute. Once the system clock advances, the system is checked to see if any event occurs at that point in time. If an event does occur, the system is updated and the clock advances again. If an event does not occur at that time, the clock is simply advanced. Fixed-time increment simulations require that the time increment be shorter than the event times, and this often results in system checks when no events occur.

In a variable-time increment simulation, or **next-event simulation,** the clock is advanced to the point in time when the next event occurs. If, for example, we are simulating a variable production process where a worker assembles a part, the simulation records when the worker starts to assemble the part, determines how long the assembly process takes, and then advances the clock to the completion time. Although it is necessary to keep track of the beginning and ending of each event in a variable-time increment simulation, this is often more efficient than using a fixed-time increment. Most simulations use the variable-time increment approach. The Micro Store problem introduced at the beginning of this chapter is a discrete event, stochastic simulation and is time-independent.

The Simulation Process

Simulation is a process that involves setting up a model of a real system and performing sampling experiments on it. This process is a systematic approach that can be divided into several distinct phases or stages. However, while these phases are discussed as distinct, there is in reality a great deal of overlap among the steps, and not all simulation studies necessarily follow the same order. The phases are summarized in Figure 15.2. As the chapter progresses, we will discuss some of the specific concerns and operational problems in greater detail.

Starting with the identification of a problem, the initial step or phase in the simulation process requires clearly defining and formulating the problem. The problem is explicitly stated and the variables, model parameters, performance criteria, and decision rules are specified. This process includes identifying the problem components or events, collecting data that describe the input variables, and identifying the relationship among the components. It requires clearly understanding why a simulation is necessary and stating the objectives of the study.

The second phase includes (1) model construction and data collection; (2) computerization of the model; and (3) validation and verification of the model. Once the components and their interrelationships have been fully identified, the model is developed. The goal here is to construct a model that sufficiently imitates the system while keeping the cost (both in human and computer terms) to a minimum. When the data has been collected and the model developed, the computer

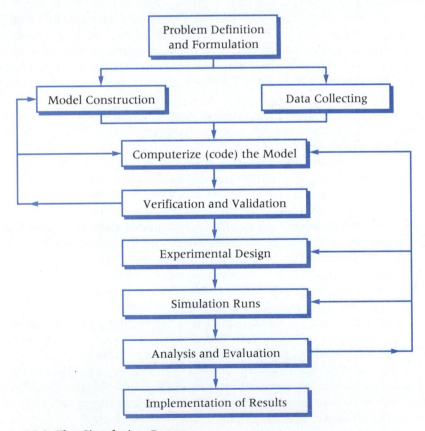

Figure 15.2 The Simulation Process

program representing the model is coded. The model is then validated and the computer code verified. Validation ensures that the model accurately represents the real-world system being simulated. This process involves making sure that the inputs are accurately modelled and that the model responds to these inputs as the actual system does. If the model does not adequately simulate the response of the system, the model formulation and construction must be reexamined. Verification ensures that the model is correct in terms of logic and programming, that is, the program is performing correctly. Validation is a major operational concern in simulation and will be discussed in greater detail later.

In the third phase, the experiments must be (1) designed, (2) run, and (3) analyzed and evaluated. Experimental design requires defining the statistical procedures that will be used in exercising the model. Included here is the determination of such operational concerns as run time, sample size, and initialization periods. Recall that the experiments are sampling experiments on a model of the real system. The model is then run and the results are analyzed and evaluated. Output will be performance descriptors in the form of operating statistics for the sample. It is necessary to ensure that the problem is addressed in a statistically sound manner. In other words, it is essential that sample size and run time are sufficient for drawing valid statistical inferences from the results.

Once the preceding phases have been completed, the last phase—implementation of a course of action, based upon the results of a simulation model—is fairly straightforward. However, successful implementation does depend upon the successful completion of all the other steps in the process.

Good documentation is important at all steps of the simulation . Anyone using the simulation should be able to understand the assumptions that have been made, the input required to run the model, and the meaning of the output. Furthermore, good documentation enables users to change the parameters of the model more easily in order to determine the relationship between input parameters and output measures of performance.

In the next section, we discuss some specific concerns involved in the construction of the simulation model.

15.2 *SIMULATION OF STOCHASTIC SYSTEMS*

Recall that, in a stochastic system, some of the system components are represented by random variables. These random variables are represented in the simulation model by probability distributions. In a simulation of the stochastic system, there must be a method for generating the probabilistic inputs.

Sampling from a Probability Distribution

In developing a simulation, the randomness that occurs in the real system must be duplicated in the simulation model. This requires drawing random samples from the probability distribution that represents the real system. For example, if we wish to simulate the demand for keyboards in the Micro Store problem, we need a way to generate demand that replicates the probabilities of occurrence of demand.

Recall that Mr. Topping has decided to adopt a policy of ordering 35 each time he reorders keyboards, and also placing an order whenever the total number of keyboards in inventory at the end of the week and currently on order is below 35. He is concerned that this may not be the correct decision.

Demand	Number of Weeks Demand Occurred
9	4
10	10
11	14
12	8
13	4

It costs the store $65 to place an order with the distributor and $0.50 to hold a keyboard in inventory for a week. Furthermore, Mr. Topping has estimated that, each time a customer enters the store to buy a keyboard and there are none in inventory, the store loses the opportunity to make $25 profit. Lead time on reorders ranges from 2 to 5 weeks, with the following distribution:

Lead Time (Weeks)	Number of Weeks Lead Time Occurred
2	8
3	16
4	12
5	4

The store currently has 36 keyboards in inventory. The probabilities of occurrence are shown in Table 15.1. Notice that, to find the probabilities from the observed occurrences, we simply divide the number of occurrences by the total number of occurrences (40).

It is fairly simple to visualize a physical device that would generate a demand of 10 keyboards with a probability of .25. For example, we could take 100 identical slips of paper; label them (10 with 9 keyboards, 25 with 10 keyboards, 35 with 11 keyboards, 20 with 12 keyboards, and 10 with 13 keyboards); place the slips in a bowl; and stir them up and draw slips at random (with replacement). With a physical device of this kind, we are generating values for x by randomly selecting from the probability distribution p(x). This is an example of random variable generation, and is known as the **Monte Carlo** sampling method. The Monte Carlo method can be defined as a technique for selecting numbers randomly according to a probability distribution. These random samples are used as inputs in a simulation. Thus, Monte Carlo is not a simulation, but rather a procedure used within a simulation.

Of course, such physical devices are not used in a simulation. In practice, the process of generating random events or occurrences (the random variables) is accomplished using **random numbers.** A random number has two important statistical properties, uniformity and independence. Each random number is an

Table 15.1 Demand Probabilities

Demand	Number of Weeks Demand Occurred	Probability of Demand
9	4	.10
10	10	.25
11	14	.35
12	8	.20
13	4	.10

independent sample drawn from a continuous uniform distribution, between 0 and 1. In a uniform distribution, each value has an equal likelihood of occurrence. A random number table, like the one in Appendix A at the end of the text, is usually used for manual simulation. Computerized simulation models generate pseudorandom numbers using a mathematical procedure, as discussed later in this chapter.

The Monte Carlo Method

The Monte Carlo Method uses random numbers to generate random variables that are used as the probabilistic inputs. That is, it is a technique for selecting variables randomly from a probability distribution. It is possible to generate a random variable (x) that corresponds to a given probability distribution by first selecting a random number between 0 and 1, then finding the range in the cumulative probability distribution within which that random number falls, and then identifying the associated variable (x).

To demonstrate this process, let's look again at the Micro Store example. Table 15.2 shows the cumulative probabilities for this example. The table shows that the cumulative distribution is defined over the interval $(0, 1)$ and represents the probability that the keyboard demand will be less than or equal to x. For example, the probability that the demand will be less than or equal to 10 keyboards, $F(10) = P(x \le 10) = .35$.

Once we have determined the cumulative probabilities, we can establish a range of random numbers that corresponds to that probability distribution. Table 15.3 shows this range. Since the cumulative probability values are two-digit values, such as .35, we use two-digit random numbers to ensure correspondence between the random numbers and the cumulative probabilities. Note that the first range of random numbers in Table 15.3 (00–09) contains 10 two-digit numbers out of a possible 100 (00–99). These 10 random numbers represent 10 percent of all the random numbers in this distribution. This corresponds to the p(x) of 0.10 associ-

Table 15.2 Cumulative Probabilities for Demand

Demand (x)	Number of Weeks Demand Occurred	p(x) Probability of Demand	F(x) Cumulative Probability
9	4	.10	.10
10	10	.25	.35
11	14	.35	.70
12	8	.20	.90
13	4	.10	1.00

Table 15.3 Range of Random Numbers

(x) Demand	F(x) Cumulative Probability	Range of Random numbers
9	.10	00–09
10	.35	10–34
11	.70	35–69
12	.90	70–89
13	1.00	90–99

Table 15.4 Random Numbers

572374
091041
707671
820328
053294

Table 15.5 Determination of Random Variable Values

Week	Random Number	Range	Demand
1	57	35–69	11
2	25	10–34	10
3	74	70–89	12
.			
.			
.			

ated with the random variable x = 9. The random number range for the first variable (x = 9) begins with the number 00 (the smallest possible random number) and ends with 09 (one less than the cumulative probability value represented as an integer, 10). The next range begins with the next random digit (10) that is equal to the cumulative probability of the previous variable and again ends with a value (34) that is one less than the current cumulative probability (35). We repeat these assignments for all random variable values.

We can now determine the random variables by using a computer to generate random numbers or by taking them from a random number table. These random numbers can be used in conjunction with the graph of the cumulative probability distribution or with the cumulative probability table.

Table 15.4 shows a group of random numbers generated by a computer program (although they could have been taken from a random number table instead). Each digit in the table is a random number. The digits shown are whole numbers, but they can be used in decimal form instead, such as .572374. They can also be taken in any combination—for example, 572, 374; 57, 23, 74; or 5, 7, 2, 3, 7, 4. In the above examples, we have taken the numbers from the first row of the table, moving from left to right. They can also be taken moving vertically in the table (50, 78, 07, 90, etc.). We will use them in pairs, moving from left to right. The first random number is 57. Referring to Table 15.3, the number 57 falls in the range 35–69. This means that the first random variable is 11, so 11 keyboards are demanded the first week of the simulation. The second random number is 23. This falls in the 10–34 range, so the second week's demand is for 10 keyboards. The third random number is 74, which falls in the 70–89 range. Thus, the demand for the third week is 12 keyboards. This is summarized in Table 15.5. A procedure that uses a random-number with a cumulative probability distribution to determine a value for a random variable is known as a **random process generator.** While we have shown this process manually, it is usually computerized, as discussed further later in the chapter.

Table 15.6 Lead Time Probabilities and Random Number Ranges

Lead Time (Weeks)	Number of Weeks Lead Time Occurred	Probability of Occurrence	Cumulative Probability	Range of Random Numbers
2	8	.2	.2	0–1
3	16	.4	.6	2–5
4	12	.3	.9	6–8
5	4	.1	1.0	9

Table 15.7 Random Digits for Micro Store Manual Simulation

Random Numbers for Demand	Random Numbers for Lead Time
57 23 74	7 8 6
09 10 41	6 8 5
70 76 71	5 7 5
82 03 28	7 2 4
54 32 94	4 6 3

Manual Solution Steps

We will use the Micro Store example, in simplified form, to demonstrate a manual simulation. Given the information in the Micro Store example, we will determine weekly demand, inventory levels, and costs. Notice that there are two random variables in this problem, demand and lead time. Lead time probabilities and the corresponding random number ranges are shown in Table 15.6.

Note that one-digit random numbers are used in this range, since the probabilities have only one decimal place. We will use two sets of random numbers, one for demand and one for lead time. These random numbers, divided into two-digit groupings for demand and single digits for lead time, are shown in Table 15.7.

The first random number for demand is 57. Demand during the first week is for 11 keyboards. The beginning inventory is 36 keyboards, and no orders are received during this week. This gives an ending inventory of 25 keyboards. Since this inventory level is below the reorder point of 35, we place an order for 35 additional keyboards, incurring an order cost of $65. The random number for lead time on this order is 7. This means the lead time on this order will be 4 weeks. The ending inventory of 25 keyboards results in a carrying cost of $12.50. There are no stockouts, so total costs for this week are $77.50. We set the beginning inventory in week 2 equal to the ending inventory in week 1 (25) and repeat the process for week 2. The random number 23 gives a demand of 10 keyboards and an ending inventory of 15. This ending inventory, combined with the 35 keyboards on order, exceeds the reorder point of 35, so no additional order is placed. The carrying cost this week is $7.50. Since there are no stockouts, the total cost is also $7.50.

In the third week, the beginning inventory is 15 keyboards. The random number 74 gives a demand of 12, resulting in an ending inventory of 3 keyboards. This inventory, together with the 35 keyboards on order, exceeds the reorder point, so the carrying cost and total cost for this week are both $1.50. In the fourth week, the demand is for 9 keyboards, but only 3 are available. This results in a stockout of 6 keyboards and an opportunity cost of $150. In the fifth week, we receive the order placed in week 1, making 35 keyboards available. Demand is for 10 key-

Table 15.8 Manual Simulation of the Micro Store Inventory Problem

Week	Beg Inv	Order Recpt	RN	Demand	End Inv	RN	Lead Time	Order Cost	Inv. Cost	Stock-out Cost	Total Cost
1	36	0	57	11	25	7	4	$65	$12.50	$ 0	$ 77.50
2	25	0	23	10	15			0	7.50	0	7.50
3	15	0	74	12	3			0	1.50	0	1.50
4	3	0	09	9	0			0	0.00	150	150.00
5	0	35	10	10	25	8	4	65	12.50	0	77.50
6	25	0	41	11	14			0	7.00	0	7.00
7	14	0	70	12	2			0	1.00	0	1.00
8	2	0	76	12	0			0	0.00	250	250.00
9	0	35	71	12	23	6	4	65	11.50	0	76.50
10	23	0	82	12	11			0	5.50	0	5.50
11	11	0	03	9	2			0	1.00	0	1.00
12	2	0	28	10	0			0	0.00	200	200.00
13	0	35	05	9	26			0	13.00	0	13.00
										Average =	$ 66.77

Table 15.9 Average Weekly Cost

Simulation Number	Number of Weeks Simulated			
	13	52	260	520
1	$35.42	$47.32	$58.06	$59.44
2	31.88	44.40	53.38	49.97
3	44.88	73.94	56.32	51.11
4	67.08	59.04	55.15	50.83
5	41.46	60.06	53.31	50.85
6	45.73	45.33	48.63	54.48
7	85.12	48.18	52.95	57.70
8	77.88	75.41	50.77	49.49
9	43.46	57.90	52.85	49.78
10	58.54	53.33	58.09	51.27

boards, reducing the ending inventory to 25 and triggering the placement of another order. The simulation is carried out in this fashion for the desired 13 weeks of operation. Table 15.8 summarizes this process.

The simulation results show that the average cost of this policy, over the 13 weeks simulated, would be $66.77. Each time we perform the simulation, we might obtain a different result. Since the demand and lead time are random, the average cost will have random components. Recall that simulation is a descriptive model rather than an optimization model. Thus, every simulation can have different average costs. Table 15.9 shows the average costs for simulations of 13, 52, 260, and 520 weeks.

Based upon the distribution of costs for this example, the average cost would be approximately $53 per week for this policy. Statistically, we would expect (and Table 15.9 demonstrates) that larger simulation sample sizes give values closer to the expected cost.

When simulating an event for an actual application, care should be taken to simulate a sufficient number of occurrences to ensure that the results are truly representative of the actual situation. While there are methods for determining the number of simulations necessary for a desired level of accuracy, these methods are beyond the scope of this introductory chapter.

15.3 *GENERATING RANDOM VARIABLES (PROBABILISTIC INPUT)*

In the previous section, we demonstrated a technique for taking random numbers and transforming them into input variables such that the historical probability distribution was replicated. It is also possible to sample from known theoretical distributions, such as the exponential, Poisson, or uniform distribution. In these situations, it is necessary to identify the probability distribution appropriate for the data. There are a number of goodness-of-fit tests to help ensure that a fit has been attained. For more information, you should consult a good statistics text or one of the specialized simulation texts in the bibliography. Once the distribution has been specified, samples from this distribution can be generated automatically, using uniform random numbers, to provide input to the simulation model. In this section we will describe the procedures (called process generators) for sampling from both discrete and continuous distributions.

Recall that discrete random variables are used to describe variables that change at distinct or discrete points in time. Discrete distributions describe events having only a finite number of alternative outcomes. A number of theoretical discrete probability distributions exist, such as Bernoulli, geometric, and discrete uniform. However, for simulation modeling, the binomial and the Poisson are the most frequently used discrete distributions.

In a continuous distribution, the variables of interest can take on any value in some interval. Continuous distributions include (among others) the uniform, exponential, geometric, beta, Weibull, Erlang, gamma, and triangular distributions.

Note that the empirical distribution can be either discrete or continuous. It is used by the simulation modeler when it is not possible to identify a known theoretical distribution for the input data. At times, it is unnecessary to specify a theoretical distribution and the empirical distribution is used. The Micro Store problem used empirical data.

Many computer languages, especially simulation languages, have built-in process generation routines. In practice, most simulation modelers use these existing routines and do not have to worry about constructing a generation routine. Appendix F lists specialized simulation texts that provide further information on the application of probability distributions to simulation.

In this section, we use brief examples to demonstrate sampling from the discrete Poisson distribution and from the continuous uniform and exponential distributions.

Generating Random Variables from a Discrete Distribution (Poisson)

Most discrete distributions can be generated using an inverse transformation technique. This can be done using either a table-lookup procedure or (in some cases) an algebraic technique, with the final generation scheme in terms of a formula. We previously described the concept of using a table lookup to generate a random variable. The process begins with the generation of a random number. The number is then located in the appropriate table or on a vertical axis of a graph, and then the input variable is read from the table or the graph. In a computerized version of the table-lookup generation scheme, given a value for r, the computer program must search an array of inputs to find the interval where r lies. The process is performed with either a table or an analytic representation of a graph. In the following example, we will create and then use a lookup table.

CompuNet

CompuNet provides computer network services on a subscription basis. CompuNet wants to ensure that it has enough call-in ports allocated during off-peak hours to support expected demand. This demand can be represented by a Poisson distribution with a mean of 0.9 calls per hour. The company wishes to simulate 5 hours of off-peak operation.

The first step is to set up a cumulative probability distribution table using the Cumulative Poisson Probabilities Table (Appendix A, Table 4). We then determine random number ranges based upon the cumulative probability distribution. The table shows that a mean of 0.9 has cumulative probabilities for up to 6 calls associated with it. (Note that there are 7 probabilities, but one of them represents 0 calls.) Thus, the calls, cumulative probabilities, and random number ranges are

x Calls per Hour	$F(x)$ Cumulative Probability	Number Range
0	.4066	0000–4065
1	.7725	4066–7724
2	.9371	7725–9370
3	.9865	9371–9864
4	.9977	9865–9976
5	.9997	9977–9996
6	1.0000	9997–9999

Since the Poisson table expresses the numbers to four decimal places, we use four-digit random numbers. The next step is to obtain five four-digit random numbers (one for each of the five hours). Normally we would use the computer to generate these numbers, but in this example we will draw them from the random number table in Appendix A to illustrate its use. These numbers drawn from the first row of the table are

$$7687 \quad 0833 \quad 9163 \quad 9744 \quad 5539$$

Five hours are simulated using these random numbers. The random number 7687 falls within the range 4066 to 7724, which corresponds to 1 call during the first hour. The second random number, 0833, falls within the range 0000 to 4065 and corresponds to 0 calls during the second hour. The results for all five hours are

Hour	Random Number	Simulated Number of Calls
1	7687	1
2	0833	0
3	9163	2
4	9744	2
5	5539	1

Thus, it appears from this relatively small sample that two call-in ports would be sufficient during off-peak hours. Obviously, the company would want to simulate many more hours before drawing any firm conclusions. However, the example was meant only to demonstrate how to use the Poisson distribution in a discrete simulation.

Generating Random Variables from Continuous Distributions (Uniform and Exponential)

There are a number of generation techniques that are used to generate samples from continuous distributions. However, some of these methods are highly specialized and beyond the scope of this text. In this section we will briefly describe the **inverse transformation technique,** which can be used to sample from the exponential, uniform, and Weibull distributions. It is a relatively straightforward technique.

Recall that every random variable x has an associated cumulative distribution function F(x), whose values are in the interval 0 to 1. The random variable r, given by r = F(x), is uniformly distributed over this interval. The solution of x in terms of r is called taking the inverse of F(x), and is denoted $x = F^{-1}(r)$. The procedure requires generating a random number, r, uniformly distributed on the interval zero to 1, and applying the inverse transformation $F^{-1}(r)$ to obtain a random variable x with the appropriate distribution.

We will illustrate the inverse transformation technique with two examples, a uniform distribution and an exponential distribution. In the uniform distribution, a random variable can assume any value over a specified range. Each value in the range has an equal probability of occurrence.

The Cable Company provides cable TV service for a large metropolitan area. When a relay fails and must be replaced, the company finds the replacement time to be uniformly distributed between a minimum time of 10 minutes and a maximum time of 15 minutes. Cable wishes to simulate a number of relay replacements.

For a random variable x, uniformly distributed in the interval from a to b, the probability density function (pdf) is given by the function

$$f(x) = \frac{1}{b - a} \quad \text{for } a \leq x \leq b \text{ and } 0 \text{ otherwise}$$

The cumulative density function (cdf) is

$$F(x) = \frac{x - a}{b - a} \quad \text{for } a \leq x \leq b \text{ and } 0 \text{ otherwise}$$

Using the inverse transformation technique, a random number r, is generated and F(x) is set equal to it. Thus

$$\frac{x - a}{b - a} = r$$

Solving for x yields

$$x = a + r(b - a)$$

Thus, a random number of .38 gives a replacement time of

$$x = 10 + .38(15 - 10) = 11.9 \text{ minutes}$$

This figure by itself is meaningless. Again, the example was used to demonstrate the simulation process rather than to solve a problem. In the next problem we demonstrate the generation of a random variable using the exponential distribution.

George's Glass Shop finds that the time required to produce a special glass laboratory instrument can be described by an exponential distribution with a mean of 40 minutes. George wishes to simulate the production of a number of these instruments.

The exponential distribution has a probability density function of

$$f(x) = \lambda e^{-\lambda x} \quad \text{when } x \geq 0$$

and a cumulative density function of

$$F(x) = 1 - e^{-\lambda x}$$

where λ is the mean number of occurrences per time period and $1/\lambda$ is the mean time between completions. Setting $F(x)$ equal to a random number, r, yields

$$1 - e^{-\lambda x} = r$$

which can be expressed as

$$1 - r = e^{-\lambda x}$$

Note that, since r is uniformly distributed on the interval zero to 1, $1 - r$ is also uniformly distributed on the interval between zero and 1. Thus, r can be substituted for $1 - r$ so that

$$r = e^{-\lambda x}$$

Taking the natural log of both sides of the equation, the result is

$$\ln(e^{-\lambda x}) = \ln(r)$$

$$-\lambda x = \ln(r)$$

Solving for x gives

$$x = -\frac{1}{\lambda} \ln(r)$$

This equation is the random variable generator for the exponential distribution. Using a new random number, such as .02, we can use the formula to produce the value of the random variable, x.

$$x = -(40) \ln(.02)$$

$$x = 156.5$$

Thus, in this simulation, it would take 156.5 minutes to produce the first instrument. Note that this is an extremely long time relative to the average time of 40 minutes. The next random number, .78, would result in a production time of 9.9 minutes. Next, we will look at a simulation with two continuous distributions, one exponential and one uniform.

A Continuous Probability Distribution Example with More than One Distribution

A bank is remodeling one of its branch offices and wants to make sure there is enough space for customers waiting in line for its drive-up window. Past data show that the drive-up window is busiest from 11:30 AM to 1:00 PM. During that period, customer interarrival time averages 5 minutes, exponentially distributed, and the teller service time is uniformly distributed between 2 minutes and 6 minutes. The bank has decided to conduct a simulation of this period to determine the maximum number of customers it can expect to be waiting in line.

The interarrival time (IAT) can be generated by the inverse transformation function

$$x = -\lambda \ln(r)$$

where λ is the average interarrival rate and r is a random number. The service time can be generated by the function

$$x = a + (b - a)r$$

where a is the minimum time required, b is the maximum time required, and r is a random number. An example simulation is shown below in Figure 15.3. We use the first random number, .94, to generate an interarrival time. This random number is substituted into the inverse transformation function for the exponential distribution to give an interarrival time of 0.31 minutes. Thus, the first customer arrives at 11:30.31 (times are given to the nearest hundredth of a minute rather than in seconds). Next, we need to determine the service time for this customer. The random number .63 (drawn from a separate random number distribution) is used to generate a service time. We substitute this random number into the inverse transformation function for the uniform distribution, yielding a service time of 5.35 minutes. This means the first customer departs at 11:34.83 (11:30.31 + 4.52).

Cust.	Rand Num.	IAT	Arrival Time	Length of Line	Rand Num.	Service Time	Departure Time
1	0.94	0.31	11:30.31	0	0.63	4.52	11:34.83
2	0.34	5.39	11:35.70	0	0.98	5.92	11:41.62
3	0.88	0.64	11:36.34	1	0.81	5.24	11:46.86
4	0.47	3.78	11:40.12	2	0.93	5.72	11:52.58
5	0.69	1.86	11:41.97	2	0.21	2.84	11:55.42
6	0.93	0.36	11:42.34	3	0.26	3.04	11:58.46
7	0.80	1.12	11:43.45	4	0.51	4.04	12:02.50
8	0.19	8.30	11:51.76	4	0.15	2.60	12:05.10
9	0.08	12.63	12:04.38	2	0.87	5.48	12:10.58
10	0.74	1.51	12:05.89	2	0.61	4.44	12:15.02
11	0.60	2.55	12:08.44	2	0.17	2.68	12:17.70
12	0.90	0.53	12:13.94	3	0.99	5.96	12:23.66
13	0.37	4.97	12:13.94	3	0.62	4.48	12:28.14
14	0.08	12.63	12:26.57	1	0.53	4.12	12:32.26
15	0.99	0.05	12:26.62	2	0.73	4.92	12:37.18
16	0.01	23.03	12:49.65	0	0.76	5.04	12:54.69
17	0.66	2.08	12:51.72	1	0.52	4.08	12:58.77
18	0.72	1.64	12:53.37	2	0.42	3.68	1:02.77
19	0.58	2.72	12:56.09	2	0.91	5.64	1:08.09
20	0.44	4.10	1:00.19	2	0.59	4.36	1:12.45

Figure 15.3 Bank Drive-Up Window Simulation Results

The process is repeated for the second customer. Thus, the second customer arrives at 11:35.70 and begins service immediately, departing at 11:41.62. The third customer arrives at 11:36.34 and must wait in line until the second customer departs.

Based upon the results shown, 19 customers arrive between 11:30 AM and 1:00 PM (the 20th customer does not arrive until 1:00.19). The maximum number of cars in line during this period, excluding the car being served, is 4. Remember that the above results represent a sample from the population and may or may not be truly representative.

This introduction to simulation suggests that manual simulation is often impractical and sometimes impossible. In the following section, we will discuss the role of the computer in the simulation process and will briefly describe some of the special-purpose simulation languages available.

15.4 *COMPUTERIZED SIMULATION*

The increased popularity of simulation can be attributed partly to the increased availability of the computer and special simulation languages. Without the aid of a computer, many simulations would be impossible to run. However, computerizing the simulation process requires more than a one-to-one translation of the manual procedure described previously. For example, it is not practical to use valuable computer storage for a random number table. Therefore, a computerized simulation should include an automatic procedure for generating random numbers. It should also include a process generator—a procedure for generating the random (input) variables that correspond to the specific probability distribution—as discussed in the previous section.

Generating Pseudorandom Numbers

Recall that only a physical process can generate true random numbers. This approach is highly impractical for use in a computer program. Most computer languages have a subroutine to generate random numbers using a mathematical procedure. These are called pseudorandom numbers, to imply that the mathematical procedure removes true randomness. There are a number of mathematical schemes used to generate random numbers. The goal of any such scheme is to produce a sequence of numbers between 0 and 1 that imitates the ideal properties of uniformity and independence as closely as possible. To determine if the generated numbers do, in fact, possess these properties, there are a number of statistical tests that can be performed, e.g., the Kolmogorov-Smirnov or the chi-squared test. Once again, we refer the interested reader to a good statistics text or to one of the simulation referrals in the bibliography.

A numerical method should have certain other characteristics: (1) it should be fast (that is, cost-effective in terms of computer time); (2) it should not require much core storage space; (3) there should be a sufficiently long cycle (the length of the random number sequence before previous numbers begin to repeat); and (4) it should be replicable—that is, it should be possible, given the starting point, to generate the same set of numbers. For the latter reason, it is desirable to use pseudorandom rather than pure random numbers. The simulation model is easier to validate when a given sequence can be repeated.

In actual practice, the individual designing the model or running the simulation often never works directly with random number generation or with testing the generated random numbers, since most computer and simulation languages have built-in random number generators. However, some generators that have been used for years have been found to be inadequate. Others, also available in widely used simulation languages, have been tested and validated. In the next section we discuss simulation languages.

Simulation Languages

As we have indicated previously, the complexity of the relationships being studied and the computational burden usually make it necessary to use a computer for but the simplest simulation studies. It is possible to develop the model and run the simulation using a general-purpose programming language, such as BASIC or FORTRAN. It is also possible to perform simulations using spreadsheet packages, such as Lotus 1-2-3 or Excel. However, numerous special-purpose simulation languages have been developed that offer certain advantages for many simulation studies. Most simulation languages are oriented toward either event scheduling or process interaction. With the event scheduling (or next event) modeling approach, characteristic events of the system are identified and the simulation model describes the changes that take place at the time of each event. That is, the program updates the clock at each event. In a process interaction approach, the system is modeled as a series of activities that each entity must undertake as it passes through the system.

These languages are intended to simplify and assist in model formulation, thus reducing program preparation time and cost. Although different languages have different strengths and may be intended for different types of problems or simulation studies, most of the languages have such features as: random number generators; process generators; automatic statistical data gathering; good debugging and error diagnostic capabilities; report generation capabilities (both fixed-format and flexible design); list processing capabilities; and a master scheduling routine to keep track of events as they occur. There is an ever-increasing number of such languages available. Examples of commonly used simulation languages are GPSS/H, GASP IV, SLAM, SIMSCRIPT, and DYNAMO.

Deciding which language to use often requires expert advice. The advantages of a special simulation language must be weighed against the fact that general-purpose languages typically allow greater programming flexibility and are much more widely used and available. In the following section, we will demonstrate a simulation using a program written in BASIC and in GPSS. These examples are intended only for demonstration purposes, to show the reader what can be done, not how to do it.

AEROSPACE ELECTRONICS CORPORATION

Aerospace Electronics Corporation (AEC) supplies an electronic component for aircraft guidance systems. The manufacturing process involves assembling the component from the various electronic parts and then testing it on a special testing machine. Because the testing machines are expensive to purchase and maintain, several assemblers share a single test machine. The machine can test only one component at a time, however. An assembler cannot begin assembling a new component until the completed component has been tested.

Thus, each assembler assembles a component and then moves to the test machine. If the machine is being used, the assembler joins a first-come, first-served queue until it is free. When the test machine is free, the assembler tests the component. Once the testing is completed, the assembler begins assembling the next component.

Studies indicate the following assembly and testing times:

Assembly Time (minutes)	Number of Occurrences	Testing Time (minutes)	Number of Occurrences
30	3	8	12
31	9	9	48
32	10	10	80
33	21	11	50
34	33	12	10
35	48		
36	31		
37	22		
38	11		
39	8		
40	4		

Assemblers are paid $7.50 per hour and the test machine cost is $20 per hour (based on an 8-hour day), regardless of utilization. The profit contribution for each component is $12, exclusive of assembly and testing costs.

The production scheduling department must determine the number of assemblers to assign to each test machine in order to maximize profit contribution. It also wishes to determine the expected number of components produced per week for each test machine.

To determine the number of assemblers to assign to each test machine, we can simulate the daily operation with different numbers of assemblers and compare the results. In this case, an appropriate measure would be profit contribution over a period of time, which we can determine using the number of components produced and the assembler and machine costs. We will simulate the problem twice, once using a program written in BASIC and once using GPSS.

AEC Simulation Using a BASIC Program

Figure 15.4 shows a flowchart for this simulation. Figure 15.5 shows a partial program listing written in Microsoft QuickBASIC. Random numbers were generated using the language's built-in random number generator.

Figure 15.6 shows a diagram of the simulation results for the first 122 minutes of one simulation run with four assemblers. This diagram uses a Gantt chart to illustrate the assembly, testing, and idle time for each assembler and the test machine. The random numbers and the associated random variable times are shown on the diagram. Note the large amount of idle time during the first 57 minutes, while the test machine waits for the first assembler to finish and then the assemblers wait for the test machine to be available. This result is based on the assumption that the assemblers begin work with no partially completed components left from the previous shift or the previous day.

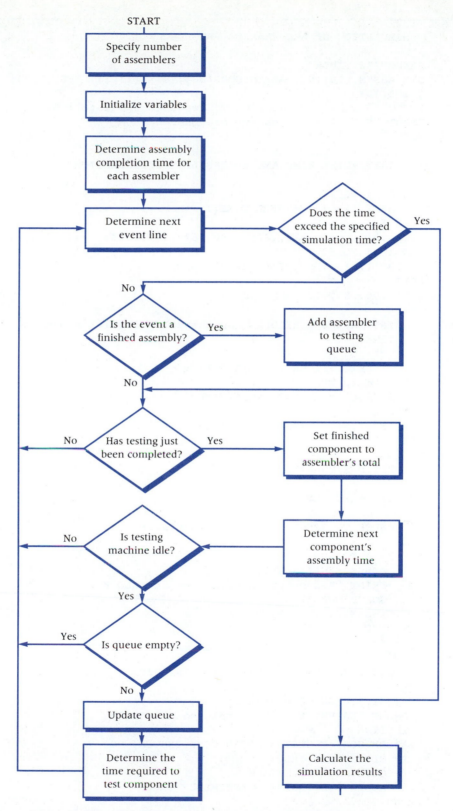

START

Specify number
of assemblers

Initialize variables

Determine assembly
completion time for
each assembler

Determine next
event line

Does the time
exceed the specified
simulation time?   Yes

No

Is the event a
finished assembly?   Yes   Add assembler
                                    to testing
                                    queue

No

Has testing just   Yes   Set finished
been completed?   component to
No   assembler's total

Is testing   Determine next
machine idle?   component's
No   assembly time

Yes

Is queue empty?   Yes

No

Update queue

Determine the   Calculate the
time required to   simulation results
test component

Figure 15.4 Flowchart for Manual Simulation of AEC Problem

```
'     SIMULATION OF AEC EXAMPLE PROBLEM
'
RANDOMIZE TIMER
DIM ASSEM.FIN(10), ASSEM.COMP(10), TIME(11,2), TEST(5,2),
QUEUE(10)
INPUT "How many minutes do you want to simulate"; MIN
INPUT "How many assemblers are there"; NUM
CLS
'
'     INITIALIZE TIME AND PROBABILITY DISTRIBUTIONS
'
FOR I = 1 TO 11
   TIME(I,1) = I + 24:READ TIME(I,2)
NEXT I
DATA .015,.060,.110,.215,.380,.620,.775,.885,.940,.980,1.0
FOR I = 1 TO 5
   TEST(I,1) = I + 7:READ TEST(I,2)
NEXT I
DATA .06,.30,.70,.95,1.00
'
'     INITIALIZE VARIABLES AND DETERMINE INITIAL ASSEMBLY
      TIMES
'
TEST.IDLE = 1:CLOCK = 0:TEST.FINISH = -1
FOR I = 1 to NUM
   TESTER = I:GOSUB ASSEMBLE.TIME
   TESTER = 0
   ASSEM.FIN(I) = ASSEMBLE + CLOCK
NEXT I
'
'     BEGIN SIMULATION
'
10 CLOCK = NEXT. EVENT
'
'     CHECK TO SEE IF ASSEMBLER IS FINISHED
'
FOR I = 1 TO NUM
   IF ASSEM.FIN(I) = CLOCK THEN
      PRINT "Assembler";I;"finished at";CLOCK
      GOSUB QUEUE.ADD
      ASSEM.FIN(I) = 9999
   END IF
NEXT I
'
'     CHECK TO SEE IF TESTING IS FINISHED
'
IF TEST.FINISH = CLOCK THEN
   PRINT TESTER;"testing completed at";CLOCK
   TESTING = 0
   ASSEM.COMP(TESTER) = ASSEM.COMP(TESTER) + 1
   IF CLOCK < MIN THEN
      GOSUB ASSEMBLE.TIME
      ASSEM.FIN(TESTER) = ASSEMBLE + CLOCK
   END IF
```

```
      TESTER = 0:TEST.FINISH = -1
      END IF
      '
      '    IF TEST MACHINE IS IDLE, UPDATE QUEUE
      '
      IF TESTING = 0 THEN
      IF QUEUE(1) > 0 THEN
          TESTER = QUEUE(1)
          PRINT "Assembler";TESTER;"using test machine"
          TESTING = 1
          GOSUB QUEUE.ADJ
          GOSUB TEST.TIME
          TEST.FINISH = TEST + CLOCK
      END IF
      END IF
      IF CLOCK < MIN THEN GOTO NEXT.EVENT.TIME
      '    CALCULATE PROFIT
      TOTAL.COMP = 0
      FOR I = 1 TO NUM
      TOTAL.COMP = TOTAL.COMP + ASSEM.COMP(I)
      NEXT I
      PROFIT = TOTAL.COMP * 12
      LABOR = 7.50 * NUM * (MIN/60)
      MCOST = 20 * (MIN/60)
      PRINT "Assemblers = ";NUM,"minutes = ";MIN
      PRINT "Net profit = ";PROFIT - LABOR - MCOST
      END
      .
      .
      .
      .
```

Figure 15.5 BASIC Program Listing for AEC Simulation

Table 15.10 illustrates the results obtained for 5 simulation runs of 8 hours each with 3, 4, 5, and 6 assemblers. All figures are in dollars of profit contribution. As Table 15.10 shows, the most profitable number of assemblers to assign to each testing machine per day is 4, with an average profit of $116.00. When the simulation was run for 8 hours, and then run for a second 8-hour period with the partially assembled components from the first run being completed in the second run, the average profit for the second 8-hour period jumped to $152. This illustrates that the assumptions can have a major impact upon the results of the simulation. The first 8-hour period is based on the assumption that assemblers do not leave partially assembled components for the next shift or next day; there is a definite startup period for each shift or day. The second 8-hour period is based on the assumption that a more continuous operation, with partially assembled components completed during the next shift or day, is the norm. This second assumption eliminates the initial idle time in the simulation and results in an average of three additional components being completed during an 8-hour period. The assumptions used in the simulation should approximate reality as closely as possible. The impact of initial conditions is discussed further in section 15.5.

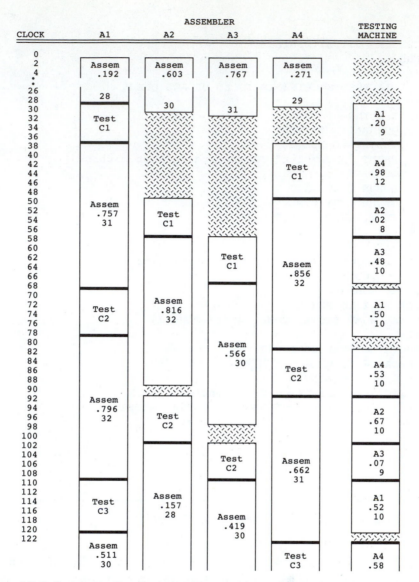

Figure 15.6 Computer Simulation with Four Assemblers

Table 15.10 Profit Contribution for AEC Simulation

Simulation	Number of Assemblers per Test Machine			
Number	3	4	5	6
1	$56	$116	$80	$20
2	56	128	80	8
3	68	116	80	20
4	56	116	80	20
5	56	104	92	20
Average	$58.40	$116.00	$66.40	$17.60

AEC Simulation Using GPSS

Figure 15.7 shows the GPSS program listing for this simulation, with 3 to 6 assemblers per testing machine over an 8-hour day. The program output from the GPSS simulation is shown in Figure 15.8.

GPSS simulates components that are generated by the assemblers and flow through the testing machine. The number of entries in the output indicates the number of components that entered the testing machine. Since any components still in the testing machine at the end of the simulation are not finished, the number of entries is reduced by 1. We determine the profit by multiplying the number of completed components by the profit contribution of $12 and then subtracting

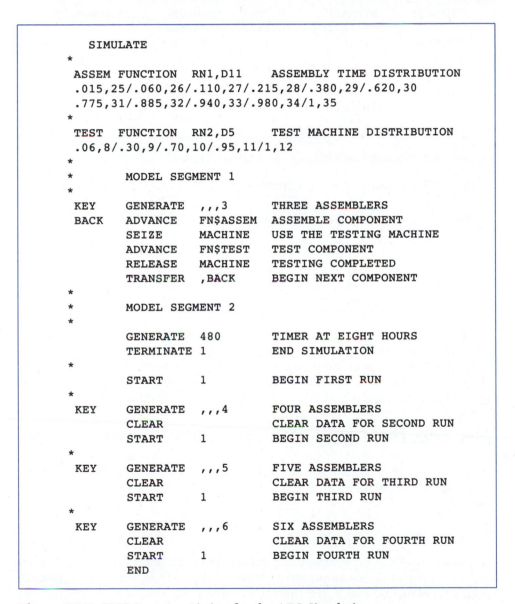

```
      SIMULATE
*
 ASSEM FUNCTION  RN1,D11     ASSEMBLY TIME DISTRIBUTION
 .015,25/.060,26/.110,27/.215,28/.380,29/.620,30
 .775,31/.885,32/.940,33/.980,34/1,35
*
 TEST  FUNCTION  RN2,D5      TEST MACHINE DISTRIBUTION
 .06,8/.30,9/.70,10/.95,11/1,12
*
*      MODEL SEGMENT 1
*
 KEY    GENERATE   ,,,3        THREE ASSEMBLERS
 BACK   ADVANCE    FN$ASSEM    ASSEMBLE COMPONENT
        SEIZE      MACHINE     USE THE TESTING MACHINE
        ADVANCE    FN$TEST     TEST COMPONENT
        RELEASE    MACHINE     TESTING COMPLETED
        TRANSFER   ,BACK       BEGIN NEXT COMPONENT
*
*      MODEL SEGMENT 2
*
        GENERATE   480         TIMER AT EIGHT HOURS
        TERMINATE  1           END SIMULATION
*
        START      1           BEGIN FIRST RUN
*
 KEY    GENERATE   ,,,4        FOUR ASSEMBLERS
        CLEAR                  CLEAR DATA FOR SECOND RUN
        START      1           BEGIN SECOND RUN
*
 KEY    GENERATE   ,,,5        FIVE ASSEMBLERS
        CLEAR                  CLEAR DATA FOR THIRD RUN
        START      1           BEGIN THIRD RUN
*
 KEY    GENERATE   ,,,6        SIX ASSEMBLERS
        CLEAR                  CLEAR DATA FOR FOURTH RUN
        START      1           BEGIN FOURTH RUN
        END
```

Figure 15.7 GPSS Program Listing for the AEC Simulation

```
       FACILITY     AVERAGE      NUMBER     AVERAGE       [3 Assemblers]
                    UTILIZATION  ENTRIES    TIME/TRAN
       MACHINE      .702         34         9.912


       FACILITY     AVERAGE      NUMBER     AVERAGE       [4 Assemblers]
                    UTILIZATION  ENTRIES    TIME/TRAN
       MACHINE      .894         43         9.977


       FACILITY     AVERAGE      NUMBER     AVERAGE       [5 Assemblers]
                    UTILIZATION  ENTRIES    TIME/TRAN
       MACHINE      .946         46         9.870


       FACILITY     AVERAGE      NUMBER     AVERAGE       [6 Assemblers]
                    UTILIZATION  ENTRIES    TIME/TRAN
       MACHINE      .948         47         9.681
```

Figure 15.8 Selected GPSS Output for AEC Simulation

Table 15.11 Summary of Profit Contribution Calculations for AEC Simulation

Number of Assemblers	Completed Components	Profit Contr.	Labor Costs	Test Costs	Total Costs	Net Profit Contr.
3	33	$396	$180	$160	$340	$ 56
4	42	504	240	160	400	104
5	45	540	300	160	460	80
6	46	552	360	160	520	32

the labor costs ($7.50 per hour × 8 hours × n assemblers) and the testing machine costs ($22 per hour × 8 hours). These calculations are summarized in Table 15.11. As this table shows, the GPSS results agree with the results obtained when running the simulation in BASIC. The optimal number of assemblers to assign to a test machine is four.

15.5 SPECIAL CONCERNS WHEN USING SIMULATION

Certain issues, problems, or areas of concern must be given consideration when undertaking any simulation. In this section, we will briefly present some of these issues.

Optimization

As a descriptive technique, simulation reflects the operation of a system. The results or output of a simulation study represent the state of the system, given a specific set of inputs. That is, the simulation model measures the output of the system for predetermined values of the decision variables. If a simulation contains random events, each simulation run generally yields different values for the measure of effectiveness.

While simulation output is always descriptive, it may be possible to use a search technique (trial and error) to obtain a near-optimal or quasi-optimal solution. This involves systematically changing the values of the decision variables and observing the effect on the output. The results are then searched for the best solution. This approach can yield the best solution for the inputs used, but there is no guarantee that the values considered for the decision variables include the optimal values. Achieving optimality is even more difficult because of sampling error. That is, variations in output measures can be the result of sampling error rather than changes in the input values of the decision variables. Thus, there is really no guarantee that the solution achieved using a search procedure will be optimal. A systematic search technique is easier when only one decision variable is being tested. With more than one, the process is much more complex.

The Validation Process

Validation of the simulation model is an integral but difficult part of model development. The two components of the validation process, verification and validation, are conducted simultaneously.

Verification involves comparing the conceptual model to the computer code written to implement the conceptualization. That is, the purpose of verification is to ensure that the computer code accurately reflects the conceptual model. This requires examining the program for logic and programming errors. A verification process uses some commonsense practices and standard program testing techniques.

Validation is the overall process of comparing the behavior of the model to the behavior of the real system. That is, validation refers to the process of determining that a model accurately represents the real system. This is usually achieved through a calibration procedure, an iterative process of comparing the model behavior to the actual system, behavior-making adjustments in the model, comparing the revised model to reality, making additional revisions, and so on. The validation procedure uses both informal, subjective comparisons and more objective statistical tests. The subjective comparisons usually involve using individuals who are knowledgeable about one or more aspects of the system to make subjective judgments about the model and its output. Objective tests compare model data to corresponding system data using statistical tests. These can include tests to ensure that the real-world variables and the simulated variables are distributed in the same manner, and tests to compare model output with historical data to see if the model can accurately predict the past.

In general, no model ever totally represents the system being studied. Revisions of the model involve a cost in time and effort. Therefore, in the validation process, the modeler is usually searching for an acceptable level of discrepancy between model and system behavior. That is, the modeler must compare the possible increase in accuracy against the cost associated with increased validation effort. Although absolute validation might not be possible, the modeler must attempt to achieve an acceptable level of confidence in the model.

Output Analysis

Once the simulation has been run, the output data must be analyzed in order to predict the performance of the system. Statistical analysis of the output is required, since the output data will exhibit random variability. This variability occurs because the output data are a function of randomly generated inputs. If we run a simulation twice, two different sets of random numbers will produce two different inputs that are likely to result in different outputs. Thus, the simulation results provide an estimate of the system's performance. The purpose of statistical analysis is to determine the accuracy of this estimate. Statistical analysis can also be used to determine the number of observations required for a desired level of accuracy.

This analysis is complicated by the fact that the observations within the simulation are not completely independent. For example, in a queuing simulation, the time a customer spends waiting is dependent upon prior customers; in an inventory simulation, the ending inventory for a given period is the beginning inventory for the next period. This relationship is known as **autocorrelation,** and it implies a lack of independence that makes traditional statistical analysis (which assumes independence) not applicable to the analysis of simulations.

In addition to the problem of autocorrelation, the initial conditions that exist when the simulation is started affect the results. For example, in the AEC problem, if all component assemblers begin by assembling a component, the machine sits idle until the first component assembly is completed. And since all assemblers begin at the same time, and the assembly times are approximately equal, the assemblers all finish their first assembly at approximately the same time. This means that, while the assembler who finished first is using the testing machine, the other assemblers are waiting (they are idle). However, once the simulation has been running for a period of time, the component completion points become more evenly distributed over time and the idle time drops for both the machine and the assemblers. Since the intent frequently is to measure the system performance as an ongoing system, the initial conditions can distort this measurement. During the startup period, the system's performance is time dependent. This initial period of time or startup period is called the transient period. Once the simulation results are no longer time-dependent, the system is said to have reached steady state.

Two ways of reducing the errors associated with the transient period are (1) to specify initial conditions that are close to those encountered at steady state, or (2) to disregard the data generated during the transient period. The difficulty with specifying initial conditions similar to steady-state conditions is that, until the simulation is run, steady-state conditions are generally not known. The difficulty with beginning the simulation after the transient period is that the length of the transient period is not known and is not easily determined. Although statistical methods that estimate the length of the transient period are available, these methods are not included here because they are beyond the intended scope of this chapter.

Simulations are classified as either terminating simulations or steady-state simulations. A terminating simulation is one that is run for a predetermined time period or until a predetermined event occurs. When the simulation clock reaches the specified time, or the specified event occurs, the simulation is stopped. Examples of terminating simulations include a queuing simulation that is run for eight hours or 480 minutes, or an inventory simulation that terminates when a stockout occurs. A steady-state simulation is one that runs over a very long period of time, so that the behavior of the system in steady state can be observed. The method of analysis used depends upon which category of simulation is used. For a discussion of either type of analysis, you should read one of the specialized texts listed as references for this chapter.

Obviously, the longer the simulation is run and the more observations that are included in the data, the better will be the estimate of the system's performance. Thus, the error in this estimate can be reduced by running very long simulations, or by running repeated replications of the simulation with different sets of random numbers. This desire for greater accuracy must be balanced, however, against the time and cost of running longer simulations and gathering additional data. Again, this topic is discussed in greater detail in some of the reference books listed at the end of the chapter.

The point that you should remember is that simulation output data contains some random variability. Without some assessment of the magnitude of the error between the estimate of the system's performance and its actual performance, use of the output data to make managerial decisions could lead to the wrong decision.

Focus on Decision Making

Wilson Magnet, owner of the On-the-Spot Photo Developing Company, was considering the installation of a photo booth at a large shopping mall. After comparing figures from other photo booths in the city and the normal customer traffic at this mall, Wilson estimated that the proposed booth would have an average of 20 customers per hour. Based upon past experience, Wilson knew a clerk in the booth can process an average of 25 customers per hour. He felt that the arrival rate could be approximated by the Poisson distribution and that the service rate was exponentially distributed. He therefore felt that he could use a single-channel queuing model to determine the operating characteristics for the booth. Using the standard queuing formulas, he determined that the number of cars in line at the booth, including the car being served, was 4; that the average wait for service was 9.6 minutes; and that a customer would be at the booth an average of 12 minutes.

Wilson was unsure of his assumptions regarding the statistical distributions of arrivals and services, however. Given the heavy traffic at the mall, he also wished to know the maximum number of cars that might be waiting for service at the booth. He felt this figure would be more important than the average number of cars waiting, since the booth must have sufficient space to accommodate any customers who choose to wait. Past experience at other locations indicated that customers do not seem to balk (leave) when the line gets long.

To obtain answers to these questions, Wilson decided to simulate the traffic at this booth. He felt the results of the simulation might confirm the results obtained with the queuing formulas, thereby validating those results. He also felt a simulation would indicate the maximum number of cars that might reasonably be found in line.

Data Preparation/Problem Formulation

Wilson used a mean interarrival time of 0.05 ($\frac{1}{20}$) with an exponential distribution, and a mean service time of 0.04 ($\frac{1}{25}$), also with an exponential distribution. In the simulation, he used times to the nearest minute and assumed that service would begin and end, and the new customers would arrive, at the beginning of the minute. He also assumed that a service was completed before new customers arrived; that is, if a service was completed and a customer arrived at minute 17, the service was completed prior to the customer's arrival. If a customer arrived and the service facility was busy, the customer joined the queue. Wilson also assumed that the customers were infinitely patient and there was no balking.

Computer Solution

Using a queuing simulation with Poisson arrivals and exponential service rates of 20 and 25 per hour, Wilson ran 10 computer simulations of 10 hours each. An example output from one of the simulations is shown below.

```
SIMULATION SUMMARY:

                                                       HOURLY
                                    TOTAL             AVERAGE
                                    -----             -------

    TOTAL ARRIVALS        =          216                21.6
       NUMBER SERVED      =          214                21.4
       NUMBER BALKING (LOST) =         0                 0.0
       NUMBER STILL IN LINE =          2
       MAXIMUM LENGTH OF LINE   =    18
    AVERAGE LENGTH OF SERVICE   = 2.3 minutes
    AVERAGE TIME SPENT WAITING  = 9.6 minutes
    AVERAGE NUMBER IN LINE      = 4.1
    AVERAGE INTERARRIVAL TIME   = 2.9 minutes
```

Interpretation and Analysis of the Results

Wilson noticed some variability in the results. He summarized the results of all 10 of the simulations in the following table.

	Minimum Average	Maximum Average	Average for 10 Outputs
Length of Service	2.1	2.7	2.5
Time Spent Waiting	4.8	15.8	9.9
Number in Line	2.0	7.4	4.1
Interarrival Time	2.7	3.7	3.0
Maximum Number in Line	9	20	14

After reviewing the results, Wilson felt that they validated the use of the queuing formulas. He also felt, however, that the simulation results provided him with additional information. While the queuing formula had indicated there would be an average of four cars in line at the booth, the simulation showed that at some point during the day there would be up to 20 cars in line. This would definitely be unacceptable to the mall managers. He also knew that customers were unlikely to join a line with over six cars in it.

What Happens Next

Given the results of the simulation, Wilson knows he will have to make some adjustments. He may have to (1) modify the booth so that customers can drive up from either side, and use two employees in the booth to reduce the maximum line length; (2) relocate the booth to a less convenient location, where there will be less traffic tie-up; or (3) assume customers will balk if the line is too long, and risk the loss of some repeat business.

15.6 *CONCLUDING REMARKS*

Simulation is an extremely flexible tool that can be applied to many different types of problems. As indicated previously, simulation studies are generally applied in situations where the assumptions underlying the analytical model do not hold; in situations that are too complex to be solved analytically; in situations in which there is a critical dependence upon time; and in situations wherein experimenting on the real system is impossible or impractical.

The decision to use a simulation study rather than an analytical technique must come after the problem has been fully defined and formulated. Then, if an analytical model is available (or one can be adapted to the problem), it should probably be used. In fact, many practitioners believe that, if at all possible, all problems should first be modeled and solved analytically (even if it means introducing simplifying assumptions). This approach gives the modeler a feel for the model and the system and helps ensure the validity of the model.

It is also necessary to consider whether or not the decision being made is important enough to justify the cost of a simulation study. However, as computer costs continue to decrease, simulation studies become more economically feasible, and as special-purpose simulation languages continue to proliferate, the simulation process becomes less time-consuming as well.

In this chapter, we have applied simulation to an inventory problem and a scheduling problem. These are just two business areas where simulation has been applied successfully. Among other applications are queuing problems of all types; PERT networks with distributions other than the beta distribution; machine breakdown and maintenance problems; public service operations; and many strategic management and marketing situations where managers want to assess the impact of changes in one or more decision variables upon the system's performance.

Management Science Application ————————————————————————

STALKING THE ENDANGERED CAT:
A QUEUING ANALYSIS OF CONGESTION AT
AUTOMATIC TELLER MACHINES[1]

The introduction of automatic teller machines (ATMs) capable of carrying out many routine banking transactions makes the use of queuing or simulation modeling in retail banking more attractive, if not essential. Customer demands occur at random, service times are unpredictable, and under most conditions, customers form and maintain reasonably orderly queues.

Bank management wished to set service standards at ATMs and to determine which ATM locations were overloaded or congested. Management also wanted to identify which ATM locations would benefit most from additional terminals. The particular ATM studied was called a CAT (Customer Activated Terminal). An overloaded CAT was referred to as "endangered."

[1]Reprinted by permission from Peter Kolesar, "Stalking the Endangered CAT: A Queueing Analysis of Congestion at Automatic Teller Machines," *Interfaces*, 14 (November–December 1984): 16–26. Copyright (1984), The Institute of Management Science.

The bank has nearly 500 ATMs, most located in New York City. The ATMs (one or more) are located in bank vestibules. The vestibules are open throughout the day during banking hours and can be accessed after banking hours by inserting the plastic bank card in the vestibule door's slotted lock. In an effort to establish "service standards" for customer delay at the ATMs, management chose the waiting time in line as the parameter of interest.

At the time of the study, most ATM locations had two machines in a vestibule of rather limited size. Customers usually formed a single queue on a first-come-first-served basis that fed both machines. This suggested that the classic M/M/c/K limited queue model might be appropriate. In real ATM facilities, however, none of the assumptions associated with this model were precisely true. It was felt that the model was still a useful statistical descriptor of the actual ATM facility performance.

Students were used to collect data at several ATM locations. They measured service times by recording the time a customer "occupied" an ATM. These times were substantially longer than computer measured service times, since they also included the time required to shuffle papers, find the bank card, etc. Whenever a queue existed, the next service began when the customer at the ATM stepped away. When no queue existed, service began when a customer stepped up to the ATM. Over 90 percent of the observed services took place when a queue existed. Data were collected in one-hour intervals at several branches during hours and days when high-traffic was anticipated. While large amounts of data on service times during congested periods was obtained, only censored information was obtained on arrivals and queue lengths because of the size of the vestibules and the difficulty in gathering data on customer balking. The customer arrival process was also complicated by the fact that people frequently arrived in groups. Sometimes all of the people in the group became customers and at other times, although the entire group stood in line, only one member of the group actually used the ATM. When a queue existed, some customers were observed to balk, that is, to begin to join the line and then turn away. Other customers, when interviewed, admitted that they often balked by simply walking past the bank when they saw a long line through the vestibule window. Still other customers balked by not even attempting to seek service at the times they knew to be busiest.

Service times were not observed to be exponentially distributed. The mode was not zero and there appeared to be a minimum service time of almost half a minute. To test whether the exponential distribution would still be a useful model of service times, the M/G/2/12 model was simulated using the empirical data. The simulation generated estimates of the probability of delay and the mean delay. These were then compared to the M/G/2/12 model outputs over a broad range of traffic intensities. There appeared to be no practical difference.

Mean service times also differed by site and by ATM. These differences appear to have been caused by the population of users at each site and differences in the hardware. The queuing model also assumes servers are always available, but this was not always the case. ATMs sometimes go down for a number of reasons—the ATM may have failed, the computer supporting the ATM may have gone down, or the ATM may have simply run out of cash.

One of the key factors affecting the queue length was the size of the vestibule. Even during peak hours, there were rarely more than a dozen persons in line. But in reality, more customers couldn't fit into the vestibule. A model with a balking probability tied to the length of the queue would be more accurate—if its parameters could be estimated. Once the simulation verified that the M/G/2/12 model would provide reasonably good results, statistics were calculated for arrival rates varying from 10 customers per hour to 200. The results showed that there is remarkably little waiting per delayed customer at any arrival rate. At an arrival rate of 50 customers per hour, the average delay was only 0.46 minutes. When the arrival rate is 100 customers per hour, the utilization rate rose to 94 percent but the average delay was only 3.26 minutes. (An infinite waiting room would saturate at this arrival rate.) Even at a super saturated rate of 200 arrivals per hour, average delay was only 5.67 minutes.

Until these figures were revealed, bank management had focused upon line wait. A related important observation was that substantial numbers of customers were probably being "lost," i.e., they were balking. The calculated figures indicated that at an arrival rate of 100 customers per hour approximately 10 percent of the arriving customers would be lost, and at an arrival rate of 130 per hour, this loss rate would increase to approximately 27 percent. Although hard proof was not available, the researchers were convinced that during some hours as many as 50 percent of arriving customers may have been lost. While lost customers may, in fact, simply defer their transaction to another time or place, if the system becomes congested during desirable hours, what had been a minor inconvenience could easily become a major problem, causing customers to switch to another bank.

With these considerations in mind, bank management attempted to define the percentage of lost customers that would represent an undesirable situation—an endangered CAT. This information was then used to aid in the selection of actual sites for upgrading. Bank management observed that after increasing the number of ATMs in the system, substantial increases in completed transactions occurred at the upgraded facilities and modest increases occurred at others. From this information, they concluded that the lost customer hypotheses and their actions to increase capacity have been validated.

GLOSSARY

autocorrelation situation wherein dependency exists among data, implying a lack of statistical independence

continuous simulation model used to model systems whose variables are continually changing

deterministic simulation model simulation in which there are no probabilistic events; values of all the variables are known

discrete event simulations used to model systems whose variables change at distinct or discrete points in time

fixed-time increment in a simulation experiment the system clock is advanced a fixed amount of time; at each advance, the system is checked to see whether an event occurred in that time and the system is updated as necessary

inverse transformation technique a mathematical technique used to generate random variables from specific probability distributions; it can be used to sample from certain continuous distributions and from empirical distributions, and it is the underlying principle for sampling from a wide variety of discrete distributions

Monte Carlo sampling method a technique used for selecting numbers randomly from a probability distribution; a generation technique that uses random numbers to create the probabilistic inputs used in a simulation

next event simulation a type of simulation that proceeds by repeatedly advancing the clock from the time of one event to the time of the next event; also called variable-time increment

process generator a mathematical procedure that automatically generates random variables that correspond to a specific distribution

pseudorandom number a random number generated using a mathematical formula rather than by a physical process; "pseudo" implies that the number is not truly random

random number an independent sample drawn from a continuous uniform distribution, between 0 and 1; each value has an equal likelihood of occurrence

simulation a descriptive technique used to study the behavior of a real-world system over time by imitating its behavior in an artificial environment

stochastic simulation simulation model in which one or more of the inputs is a random variable

time-dependent simulation simulation in which the time an event occurs is important

time independent simulation simulation concerned with the number of occurrences within a given period of time; it is not necessary to know when an event occurred

transient period the initial period of time; the startup or warmup period in a simulation in which output is a function of time

validation process for determining how closely the model predicts the behavior of the system, i.e., how adequately the simulation represents the system being modelled

variable-time increment simulation simulation experiment in which the clock is advanced to the point in time when the next event occurs (see next event simulation)

verification part of the validation process that seeks to ensure that the computer code accurately reflects the conceptual model

PROBLEMS

1. Simulate demand for 20 weeks using the following probability distribution for the demand. Use the third column of random numbers from Table 2 of Appendix A.

Weekly Demand (Product A)	Probability of Demand
6	.10
7	.15
8	.25
9	.30
10	.15
11	.05

2. The following data indicate the number of hematology laboratory arrivals each hour at General Hospital during the period from 7 AM to 12 noon.

Number of Patients	Frequency
0	3
1	4
2	7
3	8
4	10
5	14
6	15
7	11
8	9
9	6
10	1

a. Simulate 25 hours of lab activity, using the second column of random numbers in Table 2 of Appendix A.

b. Compute the average number of patients per hour from the simulation results and compare this value with the expected average number of patients obtained using the frequency distribution. How do you explain the results?

3. The Hess Service Station at the corner of Routes 31 and 250 has recorded the time between arrivals of cars over the past several weeks, and has determined the following probability distribution.

Interarrival Times (min)	Probability
1	.05
2	.20
3	.35
4	.30
5	.10

a. Simulate the arrival of cars for 20 arrivals and compute the average time between arrivals.

b. Compare this average time with the average time determined from the frequency distribution (3.2 minutes).

c. Simulate the arrival of cars at the station for one hour, using a different stream of random numbers.

4. The process of manufacturing Widgets at Denneco requires the operation of four machines. The weekly frequency of machine breakdown is described by the following probability distribution.

Machine Breakdowns per week	Probability
0	.10
1	.15
2	.30
3	.35
4	.10

a. Simulate machine breakdown per week for 15 weeks.
b. Based on the simulation results, how many machines will break down per week on the average?

5. It requires 1, 2, 3, or 4 hours to repair a machine at Denneco. The following probability distribution for repair times has been recorded.

Repair time (hrs.)	Probability
1	.15
2	.30
3	.35
4	.20

Simulate repair times for 20 machines. What is the average repair time per machine, based on the simulation results?

6. a. Using the first five weeks of operation from problem 4 (breakdowns), and the repair times per machine from problem 5, determine the total time spent repairing machines during a five-week period.
b. If it costs $50 per hour to repair a machine, determine the average repair cost per week.

7. Denneco is considering a preventive maintenance program that would alter the probability of machine breakdown as follows:

Machine Breakdowns per week	Probability
0	.15
1	.20
2	.30
3	.30
4	.05

The cost of the preventative maintenance is $150 per week. Simulate five weeks of operation, using the repair times from problem 5.

a. Determine whether or not the preventive maintenance program should be instituted.
b. Should the same set of random numbers that were used to determine breakdowns in problem four be repeated here? Discuss.

8. The local savings and loan's drive up facility has three drive-up windows. The cars wait in a single line before proceeding to the first available window. There is space in the line for only 6 cars waiting for service (there can be a total of 9 cars in the system). If there is no space in line, there is nowhere else for the cars to wait, and they cannot enter the system. The directors are trying to determine whether to operate two or three teller windows on Friday nights, when the S&L is open from 5—9 PM. The following probability distributions for interarrival times and service times have been determined from historical data.

Interarrival times (min)	Probability
1	.20
2	.35
3	.25
4	.15
5	.05

Service Time (min)	Probability
1	.15
2	.30
3	.35
4	.10
5	.10

a. Simulate the system operation for 1 hour for both 1 and 2 tellers. Compute the following operating characteristics: average queue length, waiting time in the system, and utilization for each system. Assume there are no cars in line at 5 PM, but that each window begins a service at that time.

b. For now, we are interested only in comparing the operating characteristics of the two systems. What additional information should we have in order to make an informed decision?

9. Dr. Foster is presenting a paper at a national conference for pediatric dentists. His flight is scheduled to leave at 3:30 PM. He knows from experience that, to make it to the airport on time, he must leave his office by 2:00 PM. Looking over his scheduled appointments for that day, Dr. Foster is trying to decide whether or not to cancel any appointments. Patients are scheduled 15 minutes, 30 minutes, or 60 minutes apart. Based on his experience, Dr. Foster has estimated the following duration times for these patients and the scheduled procedures.

Patient	Appointment	Expected Duration
1	9:00	35 min
2	9:30	20
3	9:45	20
4	10:00	50
5	11:00	20
6	11:15	30
7	11:45	15
8	12:00	60
9	1:00	20
10	1:30	30

From experience he knows that the patient has a 5 percent chance of being 10 minutes early; a 15 percent chance of being 5 minutes early; a 50 percent chance of being on time; a 15 percent chance of being 5 minutes late; a 10 percent chance of being 10 minutes late; and a 5 percent chance of not arriving. He also knows that the duration of the visit is probabilistic, and he has estimated the following distribution for expected duration.

5 min under	.10
10 min under	.10
expected time	.35
5 min over	.30
10 min over	.10
15 min over	.05

Should Dr. Foster cancel any of his appointments?

10. For years, Wagor Drug Store in the village of Victor has sold 500 copies of the local weekly newspaper each week. However, a change in newspaper ownership and resulting format changes has affected sales. Now Mr. Wagor is attempting to determine how many copies to stock each week. For the past three months, he has been keeping track of sales, and has recorded the following probability distribution.

Number Sold	Probability
400	.10
420	.15
440	.25
460	.30
480	.15
500	.05

Mr. Wagor pays $.75 per newspaper and sells them for $1.25. If he has papers left at the end of the week, he discards them and loses the purchase cost. Using marginal analysis (probabilistic inventory):

a. Determine an acceptable stocking policy.
b. Simulate 20 weeks of business using this policy.
c. If there is a goodwill cost of $.10 for each paper demanded but not available, how would this change the answer to part (b), using the same stocking policy?

11. The March of Dimes Foundation has been gathering data over the past five years on donations received in the suburban Chicago area during the Mothers March. The data indicates that there is a 22 percent chance that, when the volunteer mother calls, there is someone home and that person is willing to contribute. The dollar amount can be described by the following distribution.

$ Contributed	Probability
1.00	.15
2.00	.30
3.00	.40
4.00	.10
5.00	.05

Simulate calls on 100 houses.

a. At how many houses were people home and willing to contribute?
b. What is the simulated amount contributed?

12. J&R Barbershop presently has two barbers working. However, there are three chairs in the shop. Ronnie, the proprietor, is trying to decide whether or not to hire another barber. He has noticed that, if there are four customers waiting, a new customer will not wait. Assume that customers arrive in a Poisson manner at a rate of four per hour, and that the time it takes to give a haircut is exponentially distributed with a mean of 20 minutes. Haircuts cost $6.50. A new barber would cost $200 per week ($5 per hour for 40 hours) plus a $2.00 commission on each haircut. Ronnie wished to simulate 8 hours of operation to determine whether or not to hire another barber.

a. Discuss the assumptions that must be made before performing this simulation. What assumptions would be reasonable?
b. Using simulation data for 8 hours of operation only, is a third barber justified?

13. Ronnie, the proprietor of R&J Barbershop, has noticed that certain times and days are much busier than others. He has recorded the following data on arrival rates and service rates for Saturday mornings (9 AM–12 noon).

Arrivals per hour	Frequency
20	.10
15	.20
12	.35
10	.20
6	.10
4	.05

Haircuts per hour	Frequency
7	.05
6	.20
5	.35
4	.25
3	.15

On Saturday mornings, a customer will wait as long as there is waiting space available. There is room for six customers to wait comfortably. There are presently two barbers working. The third barber chair is not being used. Use the figures given in problem 12 for haircut price and barber costs. Use a simulation to determine whether Ronnie should hire a barber for Saturday mornings.

14. The time between arrivals at the post office can be described by an exponential distribution. If the mean interarrival time is 6 minutes, simulate the arrival of 20 customers using the exponential process generator.

15. The time required to serve a customer is uniformly distributed between 37 and 43 minutes. Simulate the time required to service 15 customers. If a clerk begins waiting on the first customer at 10:00 AM, what time will he/she finish with the fifteenth customer, assuming there is a continuous queue of customers waiting to be served?

16. Ed's Computer Supplies sells printer ribbon to three local institutions: University of Fairport, Henrietta Institute of Technology, and Gates College. Weekly demand figures for ribbons have the following distributions:

U. of Fairport		H.I.T.		Gates College	
Number	Frequency	Number	Frequency	Number	Frequency
20	.14	10	.20	5	.10
25	.21	20	.35	10	.20
30	.32	30	.25	15	.30
35	.24	40	.20	20	.25
40	.09			25	.15

Ed orders new ribbons every Friday afternoon and receives delivery on Monday morning. He is currently considering three stocking actions: (1) stock 75 ribbons; (2) stock 85 ribbons; and (3) stock 90 ribbons. If Ed wishes to have enough ribbons on hand to meet the total weekly demand of these institutions at least 90 percent of the time (9 out of 10 weeks), which of these stocking actions should he adopt?

17. Paula Graham, director of data processing for Acme Corporation, has three jobs that must be run on the computer after normal working hours. Each run involves loading the data tape, running the program, and then printing the output. Probabilistic time distributions for each of these activities are given below (in minutes).

Load Tape		Run Job		Print Output	
Time	Probability	Time	Probability	Time	Probability
4	.1	9	.15	12	.05
5	.2	10	.21	13	.10
6	.2	11	.28	14	.20
7	.3	12	.22	15	.25
8	.1	13	.14	16	.20
9	.1			17	.15
				18	.05

The computer's operating system does not permit any activities for a new job to begin until the current job has finished printing. Paula wishes to use simulation to estimate how long the operator will have to stay to run these jobs.

18. Ralph's Repair Service repairs Alpha and Beta computers. The distribution of service times for these two models are as follows:

Alpha		Beta	
Time	Frequency	Time	Frequency
20	.15	30	.10
25	.25	35	.20
30	.30	40	.25
35	.20	45	.20
40	.10	50	.15
		55	.10

a. If 55 percent of the computers brought in for repair are Alphas (randomly distributed), simulate 20 repairs and determine the total time Ralph will spend repairing those computers.

b. How does the distribution of computer models arriving for repair compare with the expected distribution?

19. The activities on the PERT network shown below have the following probability distributions for completion times.

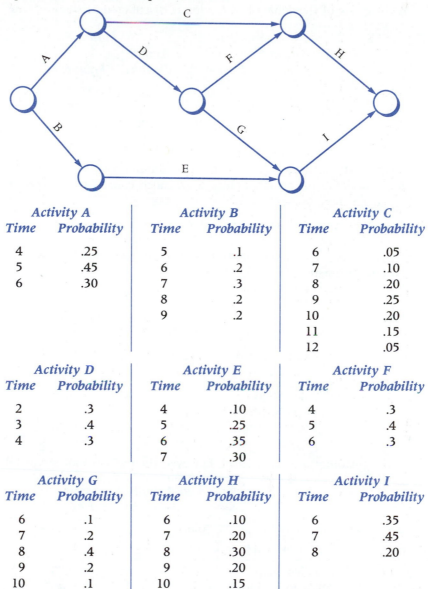

Activity A	
Time	Probability
4	.25
5	.45
6	.30

Activity B	
Time	Probability
5	.1
6	.2
7	.3
8	.2
9	.2

Activity C	
Time	Probability
6	.05
7	.10
8	.20
9	.25
10	.20
11	.15
12	.05

Activity D	
Time	Probability
2	.3
3	.4
4	.3

Activity E	
Time	Probability
4	.10
5	.25
6	.35
7	.30

Activity F	
Time	Probability
4	.3
5	.4
6	.3

Activity G	
Time	Probability
6	.1
7	.2
8	.4
9	.2
10	.1

Activity H	
Time	Probability
6	.10
7	.20
8	.30
9	.20
10	.15
11	.05

Activity I	
Time	Probability
6	.35
7	.45
8	.20

Use a simulation to determine the critical path in this network and the expected completion time.

20. Erwin Frome is collecting door-to-door for the Save the Whales Foundation. Data from past years show that:

- No one is home at 40 percent of the houses called upon.
- When someone is home, a woman answers the door 65 percent of the time and a man answers the door 35 percent of the time.
- Women make a donation 37 percent of the time and men make a donation 26 percent of the time.
- The size of the donation is randomly distributed as shown below:

Woman		Man	
Amount Donated	Frequency	Amount Donated	Frequency
$3	.4	$2	.25
5	.4	3	.35
10	.2	5	.30
		10	.10

a. Construct a flowchart showing this simulation.

b. Simulate calls on 100 homes. How much could Erwin expect to collect from those homes?

21. Cantor Surveys has recently conducted a survey of customer preferences among three video rental establishments: Video Shop, Video Business, and Movie House. The survey found that, if a customer is satisfied with a particular establishment, there is a greater chance the customer will return there for his or her next rental. These probabilities are shown below:

	Probability Next Movie Will Be Rented At		
Last Movie Was Rented At	Video Shop	Video Business	Movie House
Video Shop	.80	.15	.05
Video Business	.10	.75	.15
Movie House	.10	.10	.80

If the customer was dissatisfied, however, the probabilities are as follows:

	Probability Next Movie Will Be Rented At		
Last Movie Was Rented At	Video Shop	Video Business	Movie House
Video Shop	.30	.45	.25
Video Business	.25	.35	.40
Movie House	.25	.25	.50

The survey also found that 80 percent of Video Shop's customers were satisfied, 75 percent of Video Business's customers were satisfied, and 85 percent of Movie House's customers were satisfied.

a. Draw a flowchart that describes the simulation process, indicating where a customer will rent his or her next movie.

b. Assume a customer just rented a movie from the Video Shop. Simulate his or her next 15 rentals. What proportion of rentals will each outlet receive?

c. Repeat part (b), assuming the most recent rental was from Video Business.

d. Repeat part (b), assuming the most recent rental was from Movie House.

Consultant's Report ─────────────────────────────────

Somerville Fabrication Company[2]

"Sorry," said the voice over the intercom system, "the overhead crane is backlogged with requests and will be unable to pick up your job for at least 15 minutes." Marie LeBlanc, a machinist for the Somerville Fabrication Company, lit up a cigarette and prepared for the long wait.

This condition was becoming more frequent lately. The shop was so busy that the crane was unable to keep pace with the demands for service.

The Problem

Somerville Fabrication Company specializes in the machining of large castings which generally weigh from 100 pounds to several tons. It is therefore impossible for these jobs to be moved or positioned by hand. Instead an overhead mobile crane is used.

The crane runs on tracks and is positioned 100 feet above the shop floor. The operator sits inside the cab and receives instructions through a mobile radio which keeps him in contact with the central dispatcher on the shop floor. The dispatcher, on the other hand, receives requests for crane service from the 135 machinists who are scattered throughout the 40,000-square-foot shop floor. Unless the machinists receive prompt service from the crane, they are unable to perform any additional work on their current job or other jobs. An unavailable crane always means lost production time.

The Alternatives

The manager of the machine shop, Dan Gurney, has been concerned about these delays for several months and has collected some information from two sales representatives who specialize in materials handling equipment. The first recommended that the use of the present crane be discontinued and that it be replaced by a new one capable of performing the jobs 50 percent faster. The present crane is leased for $5000 per year; the faster one could be leased for $12,000 per year. The present crane has an annual operating cost including fuel, maintenance, and labor or $30,000. It is expected that the new crane would incur the same costs. The shop is on a two-shift schedule, each one 8 hours long, and the company is open 200 days per year.

[2]Barry Shore, *Quantitative Methods for Business Decisions: Text and Cases* (New York: McGraw-Hill, 1978), pp. 363–365. Reprinted by permission of McGraw-Hill.

The second sales representative recommended that a second crane identical to the present one be used. He felt that this would meet the needs of the shop more than adequately. The cost of leasing the second crane would be the same as the present one.

Priority Calls

The demand for crane service is initiated when a machinist places a call to the dispatcher. The call is then put into one of two categories. The first is the routine category, and as calls arrive, they are scheduled on a first come, first served basis. The second is a priority category, consisting of all calls whose jobs are behind schedule. All priority jobs are taken ahead of routine jobs, but a job which is already being serviced cannot be interrupted for a priority job. The priority job however, would be next.

Relevant Cost Savings

Dan Gurney met with the accounting department for the purpose of determining the possible savings that could be accrued by the addition of crane capacity. Working together, they estimated that it cost the company $1 for every minute of waiting time on routine jobs and $2 for every minute on priority jobs.

Discussion of Problem

Dan Gurney was presenting this information to the vice president of finance, Betty Wilson. "Betty, it's very difficult to determine the total cost associated with either of these alternatives because there doesn't seem to be any pattern associated with calls for service. Sometimes calls arrive one right after the other and a large backlog occurs. Why, on Wednesday of last week one routine job had to wait 1 hour for the crane. On other occasions the crane is idle. I just can't seem to uncover any pattern."

Betty Wilson added, "It looks to me as if you already have enough crane capacity on the average, but I think this is one of those situations where the averages don't tell the whole story."

They were both silent for a moment, and then Betty Wilson continued, "Dan, I'll bet that our management science group can help us with some estimates. Why don't you familiarize them with this problem and ask them to report to us in 2 weeks with some preliminary comparisons?"

Data Collection

The management science group decided that the easiest way to compare the costs of the various alternatives was to simulate the process. To do this, they needed some data.

The crane operators on both shifts were asked to record the time it took to service each call. Early during this data collection process it was determined that service times seemed to be independent of arrival rates, the time of day, or the shift. The results of 200 calls for service are given in Exhibit A.

In addition, the dispatcher was asked to record the time between calls. After careful analysis it was determined that the pattern was the same throughout the day and on each shift. It was also discovered that approximately 30 percent of all calls were in the priority category. There was no pattern to these priority calls; they seemed to occur on a random basis. The results of the 200 calls which the dispatcher recorded are given in Exhibit B.

With the data collected, the next step was to simulate each of the alternatives and determine the cost of each of them.

Exhibit A Service Times

Service times (minutes)	Number of observations
3	40
4	80
5	50
6	30
	200

Note: Service times include the length of time it takes for the crane to travel from one job to the next.

Exhibit B Time between Arrivals

Time between arrivals, minutes	Number of observations
2	4
3	20
4	100
5	40
6	20
7	10
8	6
	200

You have been hired as a consultant to help Dan Gurney by applying management science techniques to this particular problem. Prepare a report for Summerville Fabrication Company that addresses:

1. The results of a simulation of 2 hours of operation using the present crane.
2. The results of a simulation of 2 hours of operation, assuming a new crane is leased from the first sales representative (50 percent faster crane operation).
3. The results of a simulation of 2 hours of operation, assuming that a second crane identical to the first is leased from the second sales representative.
4. A recommendation based upon estimated annual costs associated with each alternative.
5. A discussion of the factors that should be considered when making any decision based upon these simulations.

Markov Analysis

By the end of this chapter, you should be able to:

1

discuss the basic assumptions of Markov analysis, including those
that characterize homogeneous Markov chains and first-order
Markov processes;

2

define and discuss the necessary elements in Markov analysis,
initial conditions and transition probabilities;

3

determine the probability of finding a system in any particular
state at any specified time;

4

determine steady-state probabilities;

5

recognize and solve problems involving absorbing states;

6

understand Markov application in marketing, production,
and finance.

Markov analysis belongs to a family of
models that are stochastic and time dependent. These models provide a method for
analyzing the behavior of a system in a dynamic situation, describing and predicting the movement of the system among different system states over time. Thus,
Markov analysis is not an optimization tool, but rather a descriptive tool that can
provide information useful for decision making. Markov analysis (or Markov processes) can be applied to any situation that seeks to determine, in a sequential
manner, the probability of certain events happening or not happening. Although
the procedure was originally developed early in this century by the Russian mathematician Andrei Markov to describe and predict the behavior of particles of gas in
closed containers, Markov analysis has been successfully applied to a wide variety
of managerial decision making situations. These include applications in marketing,
such as market share analysis; production, such as machine maintenance; and finance, for example, the aging of accounts receivable.

A Listener Share Problem

Leon Satterlee has been station manager for radio station WAAA in Corning,
New York for only four months. He would like to make the station the number-one

listened-to station in the area. He realizes that he has a lot of catching up to do, and he will have to proceed one time slot at a time. After examining the last several Arbitron ratings, he has decided that his best chance at turning things around is in the early morning time slot. There are three FM radio stations with early morning drive-to-work programming. The total listening audience for these stations (a core audience that remains stable) is 100,000. The most recent ratings survey, released on May 1, shows that the first-place station (WBBB) has a market share of 44.1 percent. WAAA is in second place with 32.4 percent of the market. The third-place station, WCCC, has 23.5 percent of the early morning audience.

We will look more closely at Mr. Satterlee's problem as we proceed with the chapter.

16.1 *AN INTRODUCTION TO MARKOV ANALYSIS*

Markov analysis is used to study the evolution of systems in which there is probabilistic movement from one condition to another condition over repeated periods of time, in order to predict the behavior of the system. The condition of the system at any point in time is called the state of the system or the system state. Markov analysis can be used to make such predictions as the probability that the system will be in any particular state at any specified time (called **state probabilities**), and the long-run probability of the system being in each state (called **steady state** or **equilibrium**).

Markov Properties

In this chapter we are restricting our discussion to Markov processes that meet the following assumptions:

1. The system being studied has a finite number of discrete states (conditions).
2. The **transition probabilities** (the probabilities of moving from one state to another) remain constant over time.
3. The probability of being in one particular state after a specified period of time is dependent only on the current state and the transition probabilities, and not on any earlier conditions.

This third assumption, known as the memoryless Markov property, limits our discussion to first-order Markov processes. Given these assumptions, we are concerned with homogeneous Markov chains.

In order to construct a model of the system, it is necessary to determine the initial states of the system and the transition probabilities. The initial states of the system describe the condition or system state at the point in time at which the analysis begins. Transition probabilities measure the probability of the system moving from one state to another state during a specified time period.

Since the number of possible states is finite, it is possible to construct a square matrix, P, made up of all the probabilities of possible movements from state to state, denoted as p_{ij}. That is, p_{ij} denotes the probability of going from one state, i, to another state, j, in one time period.

$$
\begin{array}{c}
\text{To State} \\
\begin{array}{cccccc}
1 & 2 & \cdots & j & \cdots & n
\end{array}
\end{array}
$$

$$
P = \begin{array}{c} \text{From} \\ \text{State} \end{array}
\begin{array}{c}
1 \\ 2 \\ \cdot \\ i \\ \cdot \\ n
\end{array}
\left[
\begin{array}{cccccc}
p_{11} & p_{12} & \cdots & p_{1j} & \cdots & p_{1n} \\
p_{21} & p_{22} & \cdots & p_{2j} & \cdots & p_{2n} \\
\cdot & \cdot & \cdots & \cdot & \cdots & \cdot \\
p_{i1} & p_{i2} & \cdots & p_{ij} & \cdots & p_{in} \\
\cdot & \cdot & \cdots & \cdot & \cdots & \cdot \\
p_{n1} & p_{n2} & \cdots & p_{nj} & \cdots & p_{nn}
\end{array}
\right]
$$

In this matrix, the states from which the system moves are shown along the left-hand side, and the states to which the system moves are shown along the top. Let's look more closely at the transition probability matrix in the context of Mr. Satterlee's listener share problem.

Mr. Satterlee realizes he needs more and better information on viewer listening habits and patterns before he can begin to make changes at the station. Thus he has been conducting some research of his own, tracking the movement of listeners from station to station over the past several months. Once a month, he has determined such important data as listener loyalty to each station and how many listeners switch from each station to each of the other stations. From these data, he has compiled the following probabilities that a listener will move from one station to another, from one month to the next (note that the station call letters are abbreviated, e.g., WAAA = A):

		To Station		
		A	*B*	*C*
From	A	.6	.2	.2
	B	.2	.7	.1
	C	.2	.3	.5

We can use this **transition probability matrix** (which we will also refer to as the transition matrix) to describe single-period conditional probabilities, p_{ij}. **Conditional probabilities** describe the probability that a specific event will occur, given that another event has already occurred. We can use the transition matrix to make predictions into the future, one period at a time. For example Mr. Satterlee can predict that, if a particular listener is currently listening to station A, there is a 60 percent probability that listener will be listening to station A in the next month. He can also predict what his market share will be in the next month, given the current market share and the transition probabilities. He will retain 60 percent of his current market share and gain 20 percent each from the current market share held by stations B and C. Thus he will have $(.60 \times .324) + (.20 \times .441) + (.20 \times .235) = .3296$ or 32.96 percent of the market on June 1.

Mr. Satterlee can use these initial conditions (the market shares) and the transition probabilities to predict his share of the market in future months. He can predict the **state probability**, the probability that the system will be in state i at period t. If he is not satisfied with the predicted outcome, he can decide what steps to take to change the situation (to change the transition probabilities).

Thus, the essential elements in the Markov analysis are the transition probabilities and the initial conditions. These are the components needed to compute the state probabilities at any specified time. In the following section, we discuss these elements in more detail.

Transition Probabilities

The Markov process describes an uncertain system. The transition probability concept is a key element in Markov analysis. The assumption that the movement from each state to every other state is known with certainty is essential to developing the transition probability matrix shown above. Developing the transition probabilities requires careful research and recordkeeping, as well as a detailed analysis of the data describing the movement of the system from state to state over time. For example, in the radio station switching example, where the stations are the states of the system, Mr. Satterlee should look not only at the net gain or loss of listeners each month, but also at the underlying pattern of the switching process. He must consider the listeners retained by each station, lost by each station to the other stations, or gained by each station from the other stations. Table 16.1, representing the results of listener surveys conducted one month apart, shows the net change in listening audience for each station. According to these data, station A gained 1,400 listeners, station B gained 1,100 listeners, and station C lost 2,500 listeners. However, this information is superficial and is inadequate for Mr. Satterlee's needs. Table 16.2 shows the additional data that Mr. Satterlee has gathered, showing listeners retained, gained, and lost by each station. From Table 16.2 we can see that the net gain of 1,400 listeners to station A (shown in Table 16.1) was, in reality, the result of a pattern of gains and losses. Station A retained 18,600 listeners, gained 8,600 listeners from B, gained 5,200 listeners from C, and lost 6,200 customers each to B and C. Notice that Table 16.2 shows the retention of listeners as the intersection of row A and column A, while losses to other stations are shown in the remaining cells in row A, and the gains from other stations are shown in the remaining cells in column A. The table shows this same information for stations B and C.

Table 16.1 Net changes in Listening Audience

	Month 1 (April)	Month 2 (May)	Net Gains/ Losses
A	31,000	32,400	+1,400
B	43,000	44,100	+1,100
C	26,000	23,500	−2,500

Table 16.2 Customers Retained, Gained, and Lost at Time 2 (May)

From	To Stations		
	A	B	C
A	18,600	6,200	6,200
B	8,600	30,100	4,300
C	5,200	7,800	13,000

With such detailed analysis, it is possible to predict the rate, or probability, at which the stations will retain, gain, or lose listeners in the future (assuming the system is stable). We can calculate the transition probabilities for the radio system by dividing the value in each particular state by the total initial listening audience for the station. Thus, for Station A the rate of retention is equal to the audience retained in the next month (May) divided by the initial listening audience (in April):

$$^{18,600}\!/_{31,000} = .6$$

The probability that station A will lose listeners to station B is $^{6,200}\!/_{31,000} = .2$, and the probability that the station will lose listeners to station C is also $^{6,200}\!/_{31,000}$ or .2. The same approach can be used to determine the transition probabilities for stations B and C. Transition probabilities in each row of a transition matrix sum to 1. Also, recall that each probability in the transition matrix is a conditional probability. That is, the condition at any time in the future is dependent only on the current condition. The transition probabilities for the radio system are shown again in Table 16.3.

In each row of the transition matrix, P, the transition probabilities must also sum to 1:

$$p_{i1} + p_{i2} + \ldots + p_{in} = 1 \quad \text{for } i = 1, 2, \ldots n.$$

In the example, these probabilities express the movement or switching of a particular station's audience. Since those listeners are either retained or lost to other stations, the transition probabilities in each row must sum to 1. For example,

$$p_{AA} + p_{AB} + p_{AC} = 1 \quad (.6 + .2 + .2 = 1)$$

The transition probabilities can be used to predict state probabilities. That is, they can predict the probability, p, of the system being in a particular state, i, in any given time period, t. We will denote state probabilities as follows:

$$p_i(t)$$

where
$$p = \text{probability}$$

$$i = \text{a particular state, } 1, 2, 3, \ldots n$$

$$t = \text{a given time period}$$

Since the system must occupy one and only one of the possible states at any given period, the sum of all p_i values must equal 1:

$$p_1(t) + p_2(t) + \ldots + p_n(t) = 1 \text{ for every } t$$

where n = number of states in the system.

In other words, total market share must add to 1. Thus, in the example,

$$.324 + .441 + .235 = 1$$

Table 16.3 Transition Matrix for the Radio Station System

From		To Station		
		A	B	C
	A	.6	.2	.2
	B	.2	.7	.1
	C	.2	.3	.5

Initial Conditions

Initial conditions, which describe the system as it currently exists, are usually described by a one-dimensional matrix called a row vector. In the example, the market share is divided 32.4 percent to A, 44.1 percent to B, and 23.5 percent to C. The initial conditions are thus described by the row vector

$$[.324 \quad .441 \quad .235]$$

Initial conditions can also be used to describe the condition of a single listener. For example, using the example, the vector [0 0 1] would indicate that a single listener is currently listening to station C. In general, it shows that the entire system is in state C. Thus, a system can represent an entire market or a single listener.

16.2 *PREDICTING FUTURE STATES*

In this section we will demonstrate two techniques that can be used to predict state probabilities two or more periods in the future—tree diagrams and matrix multiplication.

Tree Diagrams

Probability trees, with the transitions shown as the paths through the tree, provide a logical and convenient way to illustrate the transitions of a Markov process. The probabilities associated with the pathways are joint probabilities, which are calculated as the product of the probabilities on each branch. It is possible to construct either a tree showing the state of the system, given a particular starting state, or a more complicated tree showing all the possible paths. In the following figures, we will demonstrate both.

Figure 16.1 illustrates the probabilities of the system states after two months, May and June, for a single listener who on May 1 was listening to Station A. In this situation, the initial condition vector would be [1 0 0].

To determine the probability of a listener remaining with station A for two time periods, through May and June until July 1, we trace a path from A on May 1 to A on June 1 to A on July 1. Since this probability is a joint probability, we calculate

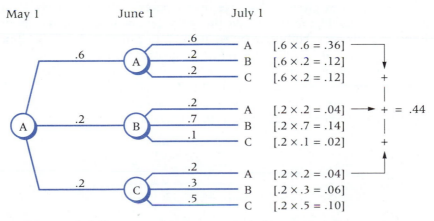

Figure 16.1 Probability Tree Showing a 2 period Transition from State A

it as the product of the probabilities on each branch. Thus the probability of a listener (or listeners) being with station A on June 1 and July 1, given that he or she listened to A on May 1, is .6 × .6 or .36.

$$P(A) = .6$$

$$P(A|A) = .6$$

$$P(A \cap A) = P(A)\,P(A|A) = (.6)(.6) = .36$$

To determine the probability being in state A on July 1, given an initial listening condition of A, we must also consider additional possibilities. It is possible that the listener switched to either B or C on June 1 and then back to A for the July 1 survey. Thus it is necessary to calculate the joint probabilities along these paths also. To determine the probability of being in state A on July 1, we add the joint probabilities of the paths that end in state A as follows:

$$A \text{ to } A \text{ to } A = .6 \times .6 = .36$$

$$A \text{ to } B \text{ to } A = .2 \times .2 = .04$$

$$A \text{ to } C \text{ to } A = .2 \times .2 = \underline{.04}$$

$$.44$$

Adding these probabilities shows that there is a 44 percent probability that a listener tuned to station A on May 1 is still tuned to A on July 1. This applies to each individual listener or to the audience as a whole. Thus, 44 percent of the audience listening to station A on May 1 is probably listening to A on July 1. This same tree can be used to determine the probability of being in either state B or state C on July 1, given the initial condition of listening to station A. It requires calculating the joint probabilities on each path, and summing those paths ending in the particular state of interest, B or C. In this case, the probability of being in state B after two transitions, given a starting state A, is

$$.12 + .14 + .06 = .32$$

Similarly, the probability of being in state C, given a starting state A, is

$$.12 + .02 + .10 = .24$$

It is also possible to construct a tree diagram that shows the probabilities of each state occurring, given each state as the beginning state—that is, showing all possible ending states given all possible initial states. This tree shows all paths through the system. Figure 16.2 shows the radio station system for two months.

We can use the probability tree in Figure 16.2 to compute the probabilities of being in each state two periods in the future, given each state of the system on May 1. The tree and the joint probabilities can be used to construct a table or matrix showing these probabilities. This is referred to as a two-step transition probability matrix. The tree is divided into three sections, one for each possible initial state, A, B, or C. These correspond to the rows in the matrix below.

	To State Time 2		
From State	A	B	C
A	.44	.32	.24
B	.28	.56	.16
C	.28	.40	.32

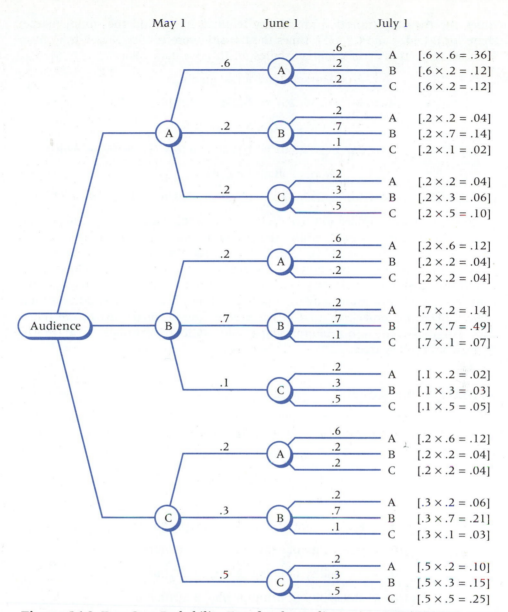

Figure 16.2 Two-Step Probability Tree for the Radio Station System

Note that the tree in Figure 16.2 has been constructed to show the probabilities as they relate to one listener. The original market shares could have been included on the branches from audience to station A, B, and C and used in the computations of the joint probabilities. Instead, we will convert these figures to market shares after determining the two-step transition probabilities. That is, we will determine market shares on July 1 using the market share values as of May 1 and the two-step transition probabilities.

Recall that the predicted market share for each station includes the listeners retained plus the listeners gained from each of the other stations. Thus, the market share on July 1 for station A equals the sum of the initial market share for A (.324)

times the two-step transition probability retained by A, and the initial market share for B (.441) and C (.235), times the transition probability gained by A from B and C respectively. Thus, market shares on July 1 are as follows:

Market share for A equals

$$.324(.44) + .441(.28) + .235(.28) = .14256 + .12348 + .0658 = .33184$$

Market share for B equals

$$.324(.32) + .441(.56) + .235(.40) = .10368 + .24696 + .09399 = .44464$$

Market share for C equals

$$.324(.24) + .441(.16) + .235(.32) = .07776 + .07056 + .0752 = .22352$$

When these are rounded to three decimal places, the market shares are .332 for A, .445 for B, and .224 for C. Notice that, when rounded to three decimal places, the market shares do not add to 1.00. This is simply a rounding discrepancy.

While the probability tree provides a logical and convenient way to look at the transitions, it should be obvious from even this small example that trees can become very cumbersome and tedious, especially as they become larger. Matrix multiplication, which provides a more efficient procedure for predicting future states, uses essentially the same multiplication and addition technique used in the Markov probability tree.

A Matrix Approach

The matrix approach uses matrix multiplication on the initial conditions and the transition matrix to predict future states of the system. The system state at time 0 is a vector

$$p(0) = [p_1(0), p_2(0), p_3(0), \ldots, p_n(0)]$$

where

$p(0)$ = vector of initial conditions (all $p_i(0)$ values)

$p_1(0)$ = probability of being in state 1 at time 0

$p_2(0)$ = probability of being in state 2 at time 0

$p_3(0)$ = probability of being in state 3 at time 0

$p_n(0)$ = probability of being in state n at time 0

The transition probability matrix is given by

		To State				
From State	*1*	*2*	$\cdots$	*j*	$\cdots$	*n*
1	p_{11}	p_{12}	$\cdots$	p_{1j}	$\cdots$	p_{1n}
2	p_{21}	p_{22}	$\cdots$	p_{2j}	$\cdots$	p_{2n}
.	.	.	$\cdots$	.	$\cdots$	.
$P =$ i	p_{i1}	p_{i2}	$\cdots$	p_{ij}	$\cdots$	p_{in}
.	.	.	$\cdots$	.	$\cdots$	.
n	p_{n1}	p_{n2}	$\cdots$	p_{nj}	$\cdots$	p_{nn}

where

P = the transition matrix (matrix of transition probabilities)

p_{ij} = the probability of going from state i to state j

For a review of matrix multiplication, refer to Appendix B of this text.

Predicting Future States

In this section we will demonstrate two methods for computing future state predictions using matrix multiplication. We begin by calculating state probabilities after one time period, that is, the probability of being in state j at time 1 when the system is currently in time 0. This is computed by multiplying the initial condition vector by the transition matrix.

$$p(1) = p(0)P$$

That is, the vector of state probabilities at time 1 is equal to the vector of state probabilities at time 0 times the transition matrix.

Recall that it is possible to specify the initial vector in several ways. For example, since in many Markovian systems the system is in only one of the possible system states, the initial vector could be [1 0 0], meaning the system is in state 1. It is also possible for the state vector to be in whole numbers, representing customers or listeners, for example ([3100 4300 2600]) or in fractions ([⅙ ⅓ ½]). For the radio station system, the system state is

$$p(0) = [.324 \quad .441 \quad .235]$$

The transition matrix for the radio station system described earlier is repeated in Table 16.4. Thus, for the radio station system, the market shares on June 1 are calculated as

$$[.324 \quad .441 \quad .235] \begin{bmatrix} .6 & .2 & .2 \\ .2 & .7 & .1 \\ .2 & .3 & .5 \end{bmatrix} = [.330 \quad .444 \quad .226]$$

Probabilities After Two or More Periods

Method 1

Now, to determine state probabilities at time 2, we continue the procedure used above:

$$p(2) = p(1)P$$

Table 16.4 Transition Matrix for Radio Station System

From	To Station		
	A	B	C
A	.6	.2	.2
B	.2	.7	.1
C	.2	.3	.5

Thus for the radio system example

$$[.330 \quad .444 \quad .226] \begin{bmatrix} .6 & .2 & .2 \\ .2 & .7 & .1 \\ .2 & .3 & .5 \end{bmatrix} = [.332 \quad .4446 \quad .2234]$$

= market shares of .332, .445, .223.

It is possible to continue using this approach for additional time periods. To determine state probabilities after three time periods, which would have made the tree more unwieldy, simply continue computing

$$p(3) = p(2)P$$

as above. In the example, after three time periods the result is

$$[.332 \quad .445 \quad .223] \begin{bmatrix} .6 & .2 & .2 \\ .2 & .7 & .1 \\ .2 & .3 & .5 \end{bmatrix} = [.3328 \quad .4448 \quad .2224]$$

= market shares on August 1 of .333, .445, .222.

With this method, in order to predict the state of the system at each time period, the transition matrix is multiplied by the most recently determined system vector. That is, to predict the system state after one time period, we multiplied the state vector at time 0 by the transition matrix. Then to determine the system state at time 2, we multiplied the state vector for time 1 by the transition matrix. This process was repeated to determine the system state for time 3, and could have continued for as many months (t) as desired.

This method shows the changes in the system on a period-by-period basis. We can see, for example, that the market share for station B appears to have stabilized at 44.5 percent of the audience, and that while the market share for station A is continuing to increase, it is doing so at a slower rate than at first. However, there is another method that is more efficient for predicting the state of the system t time periods in the future. This is explained in the next section.

Method 2

Recall that the state of the system at time 1 equals the state of the system at time 0 times the transition matrix:

$$p(1) = p(0)P$$

Recall also that the state of the system at time 2 equals the state of the system at time 1 times the transition matrix:

$$p(2) = p(1)P$$

Introducing the value of p(1) into the equation for p(2) results in the following expression:

$$p(2) = p(1)P = p(0)(P)(P) = p(0)P^2$$

Similarly, since the state of the system at time 3 equals the state of the system at time 2 times the transition matrix,

$$p(3) = p(2)P$$

it follows that

$$p(3) = p(0)(P)(P)(P) = p(0)P^3.$$

In general, the system state at any time in the future (in time t) is equal to the state vector at time 0 multiplied by the transition matrix raised to the power t (called a t-step transition matrix):

$$p(t) = p(0)P^t$$

Thus for the market share example, we can determine the market shares in time 2 as follows:

$$p(2) = p(0)P^2$$

$$[.324 \quad .441 \quad .235] \begin{bmatrix} .6 & .2 & .2 \\ .2 & .7 & .1 \\ .2 & .3 & .5 \end{bmatrix}^2 =$$

$$[.324 \quad .441 \quad .235] \begin{bmatrix} .44 & .32 & .24 \\ .28 & .56 & .16 \\ .28 & .40 & .32 \end{bmatrix} = [.332 \quad .445 \quad .224]$$

The new matrix

$$\begin{bmatrix} .44 & .32 & .24 \\ .28 & .56 & .16 \\ .28 & .40 & .32 \end{bmatrix}$$

is a two-step transition matrix. Notice that this is essentially the way we chose to perform the calculations with the probability tree. However, because of rounding during the calculations, these market shares do not add to 1.00. For time 3, this procedure gives

$$[.324 \quad .441 \quad .235] \begin{bmatrix} .6 & .2 & .2 \\ .2 & .7 & .1 \\ .2 & .3 & .5 \end{bmatrix}^3 =$$

$$[.324 \quad .441 \quad .235] \begin{bmatrix} .38 & .38 & .24 \\ .31 & .50 & .19 \\ .31 & .43 & .26 \end{bmatrix} = [.333 \quad .445 \quad .223]$$

This method is computationally more efficient. It is not always easy to multiply matrices together, but this is a simple computation for a computer. While there are computer programs designed especially for Markov processes, there are also numerous packages available that perform matrix multiplication, including many commercial spreadsheet programs.

16.3 *STEADY STATE*

In the long run, the majority of Markov processes stabilize. In a stabilized system, the operating characteristics are time independent, and the system is said to be in **steady state** or **equilibrium**. It is logical to conclude that, as t grows larger, the

state values could stabilize, since the initial state conditions tend to lose significance in the distant future. Steady state occurs when additional transitions do not
affect the probability of finding the system in any particular state. That is, when
steady state is reached, multiplication of the state condition by the transition matrix does not change the state condition. This is expressed as

$$p(t) = p(t - 1)P$$

where

$$t = \text{any time after steady state is reached.}$$

Steady state probabilities are average probabilities that the system will be in a
certain state after a number of transitions. Within the system there will be continued movement from state to state, but the average probability of being in a given
state will remain constant. Not all Markov chains reach steady state. However, if
there is some time period for which every element in the t-step transition matrix
has no zero elements (every element of $P^t > 0$), the process will reach steady state.

It is possible to determine steady state by multiplying the transition matrix by
itself a number of times. When the elements in the matrix no longer change (when
the t-step transition matrix equals the $t - 1$ step transition matrix), steady state
has been achieved. As indicated in Figure 16.3, the radio station system reaches
equilibrium in time 12. Actually, in this case, $p(t) = p(t - 1)P$ (carried to three

Transition Matrix	Period	System State
	0	[0.324 0.441 0.235]
$\begin{bmatrix} 0.600 & 0.200 & 0.200 \\ 0.200 & 0.700 & 0.100 \\ 0.200 & 0.300 & 0.500 \end{bmatrix}$	1	[0.330 0.444 0.226]
$\begin{bmatrix} 0.440 & 0.320 & 0.240 \\ 0.280 & 0.560 & 0.160 \\ 0.280 & 0.400 & 0.320 \end{bmatrix}$	2	[0.332 0.445 0.224]
$\begin{bmatrix} 0.376 & 0.384 & 0.240 \\ 0.312 & 0.496 & 0.192 \\ 0.312 & 0.432 & 0.256 \end{bmatrix}$	3	[0.333 0.445 0.223]
$\begin{bmatrix} 0.333 & 0.444 & 0.222 \\ 0.333 & 0.445 & 0.222 \\ 0.333 & 0.444 & 0.222 \end{bmatrix}$	11	[0.333 0.444 0.222]
$\begin{bmatrix} 0.333 & 0.444 & 0.222 \\ 0.333 & 0.444 & 0.222 \\ 0.333 & 0.444 & 0.222 \end{bmatrix}$	12	[0.333 0.444 0.222]

Figure 16.3 Reaching Steady State

decimal places) after six periods, but the matrix probabilities do not reach equilibrium until period 12, although the changes between periods 6 and 12 are extremely small (.001 or less). Notice that, as the number of time periods increases, the matrix of transition probabilities approaches a limit whereby all rows are identical and equal to the steady state vector.

This example also demonstrates that steady state is independent of the initial state vector. That is, the steady state matrix shows that the probability of being in a given state in the distant future is not dependent on where the process started. The steady state depends only on the transition probabilities. For example, the radio stations began at time 0 with market shares of .324, .441, and .235. Multiplying these initial shares by steady state conditions results in steady state market shares.

$$[.324 \quad .441 \quad .235] \begin{bmatrix} .333 & .444 & .222 \\ .333 & .444 & .222 \\ .333 & .444 & .222 \end{bmatrix} = [.333 \quad .444 \quad .222]$$

If the beginning market shares were .25, .35, and .40, the market shares would be equal to

$$[.25 \quad .35 \quad .40] \begin{bmatrix} .333 & .444 & .222 \\ .333 & .444 & .222 \\ .333 & .444 & .222 \end{bmatrix} = [.333 \quad .444 \quad .222]$$

Thus if no action is taken to influence listener choice, and the transition probabilities remain unchanged, in the long run Mr. Satterlee will have a market share of 33.3 percent of the listening audience. Knowing this can help him decide what, if any, action to take. If he wants to become number 1, he will have to do something to draw listeners from the other stations and retain them once they switch.

Algebraic Computation of Steady State

The method just demonstrated for determining the steady state transition matrix is rather tedious. Fortunately, steady state values can also be determined algebraically. To gain a better understanding of the algebraic determination of steady-state values, it is helpful to review some of the earlier findings that are used in developing the algebraic solution.

First, recall from the previous discussions that the transition of the system state from one time period to the next is described by the equation

$$p(t) = p(t - 1)P$$

which has been generalized to

$$p(t) = p(0)P^t$$

That is, the state probabilities in period t are equal to the initial state probabilities multiplied by the t-step transition matrix.

At steady state, the state probabilities in a given time period t are the same as in the previous time period, t − 1, and multiplication of the system state by the transition matrix yields the same system state:

$$p(t) = p(t - 1)P$$

If the steady-state values are represented by the symbol π, and the steady-state vector as $[\pi_1 \ \pi_2 \ \pi_3]$, then at steady state

$$\pi = p(t) = p(t - 1)P \quad \text{or}$$

$$\pi = \pi P$$

That is, the steady-state values remain the same after a one-step transition. This can also be presented as

$$[\pi_1 \ \pi_2 \dots \pi_n] \begin{bmatrix} p_{11} & p_{12} & \cdots & p_{1n} \\ p_{21} & p_{22} & \cdots & p_{2n} \\ \cdot & \cdot & & \cdot \\ \cdot & \cdot & & \cdot \\ p_{n1} & p_{n2} & \cdots & p_{nn} \end{bmatrix} = [\pi_1 \ \pi_2 \dots \pi_n]$$

Using matrix multiplication, a system of n linear equations results as follows:

$$\pi_1 = \pi_1 p_{11} + \pi_2 p_{21} + \dots + \pi_n p_{n1}$$

$$\pi_2 = \pi_1 p_{12} + \pi_2 p_{22} + \dots + \pi_n p_{n2}$$

$$\pi_n = \pi_1 p_{1n} + \pi_2 p_{2n} + \dots + \pi_n p_{nn}$$

Recall that the sum of the state probabilities must be 1:

$$\pi_1 + \pi_2 + \dots + \pi_n = 1$$

This equation must be used to ensure that the sum of the steady state probabilities do not exceed 1. When this equation is added, there are $n + 1$ equations and n unknowns. Thus, one of the initial equations is redundant and can be dropped. (For example, if all values of π are known except for π_n, then π_n can be determined from $\pi_1 + \pi_2 + \dots + \pi_n = 1$ and the equation $\pi_n = \dots$ is redundant).

Using the market shares example

$$[\pi_1 \quad \pi_2 \quad \pi_3] \begin{bmatrix} .6 & .2 & .2 \\ .2 & .7 & .1 \\ .2 & .3 & .5 \end{bmatrix} = [\pi_1 \quad \pi_2 \quad \pi_3]$$

gives the following system of equations:

[1] $\pi_1 = .6\pi_1 + .2\pi_2 + .2\pi_3$

[2] $\pi_2 = .2\pi_1 + .7\pi_2 + .3\pi_3$

[3] $\pi_3 = .2\pi_1 + .1\pi_2 + .5\pi_3$

If we replace equation 3 with the equation showing that the sum of state probabilities must sum to 1, the result is

[1] $\pi_1 = .6\pi_1 + .2\pi_2 + .2\pi_3$

[2] $\pi_2 = .2\pi_1 + .7\pi_2 + .3\pi_3$

[3] $1 = \pi_1 + \pi_2 + \pi_3$

Rewriting the equations gives

[1] $-.4\pi_1 + .2\pi_2 + .2\pi_3 = 0$

$$[2] \qquad .2\pi_1 - .3\pi_2 + .3\pi_3 = 0$$

$$[3] \qquad \pi_1 + \pi_2 + \pi_3 = 1$$

Solving these equations simultaneously yields

$$\pi_1 = .333$$

$$\pi_2 = .444$$

$$\pi_3 = .222$$

which are the steady-state conditions. These are the same values we obtained earlier in Figure 16.3 in the 12th time period. Recall that, as t grows larger, the matrix of transition probabilities to the power of t approaches a limit whereby all rows are identical and equal to the steady state vector.

16.4 *ABSORBING STATES: A SPECIAL CASE*

A system is in an **absorbing** or trapping state if it is impossible to exit that state and move to some other state. That is, if any transition probability p_{ij} is equal to 1.0, and it is possible to go from each state to an absorbing state in a finite number of steps, the system is absorbing. Once that absorbing state is reached, it cannot be left (there is zero probability of moving from that state to any other state). Table 16.5 shows a transition matrix with an absorbing state (state 3). Once state 3 is achieved, there is a 1.0 probability that it will be achieved in succeeding time periods. The system ends when state 3 is reached, since there is no movement from state 3 to the other two states. In this case, with only one absorbing state, the steady state distribution is [0   0   1].

When a system is in an absorbing or trapping state, the normal methods of Markov analysis that we have been discussing cannot be used. It is no longer a question of what proportion of the total will reach a given state (all of the total will actually be in the absorbing states). With the presence of absorbing states, it is possible to determine:

1. The average number of periods the various state categories will spend in each nonabsorbing state before finally becoming absorbed.
2. The average number of periods it will take for the state categories (the system) to move from any beginning nonabsorbing state to an absorbing state.
3. The probability of moving from any given nonabsorbing state to each of the absorbing states.
4. The proportion of the system that will end up in each of the absorbing states.

Table 16.5 Transition Matrix with an Absorbing State

		To Station		
From		1	2	3
	1	.6	.2	.2
	2	.2	.7	.1
	3	0	0	1

There are many practical examples of absorbing states, including such currently important environmental concerns as the irreversible destruction of fish and game by pollution and acid rain. We will demonstrate an absorbing state matrix by using a debt example, an accounts receivable application, which is perhaps the most popular absorbing state application example.

A Bad Debt Example

Harold Kroft, manager of Best Built Cabinets, has divided the accounts receivable into two categories, 0 to 30 days old and 31 to 60 days old. Any accounts that are more than 60 days old are written off as bad debts. Mr. Kroft uses the total balance method of aging accounts. Accordingly, he classifies a customer's total balance in the aging category of the account's oldest unpaid bill. This means he places the total account balance in the age classification that corresponds to the oldest unpaid amount. This method of aging allows an account that is currently in the 31–60 day category to appear in the 0–30 day category in the next month if the customer pays an older bill during the month. Thus, at any time, there are four possible categories for an account: paid in full, 0–30 days, 31–60 days, and bad debt. Based on an analysis of past transitions of accounts receivable dollars, Mr. Kroft has developed the following transition matrix for Best Built.

	1	2	3	4
1	1	0	0	0
2	0	1	0	0
3	.5	0	.2	.3
4	.4	.4	.1	.1

where

state 1 = paid in full

state 2 = bad debt

state 3 = 0–30 days old

state 4 = 31–60 days old

Mr. Kroft recognizes that all accounts eventually end up either as paid in full or as bad debts. However, he would like to determine how much of the $6,500 now in accounts receivable will eventually be collected and how much will become bad debts.

The Fundamental Matrix

When a system has an absorbing state, the normal methods of Markov analysis cannot be used. Instead, through some matrix manipulations, a special matrix called a **fundamental matrix** is designed. The fundamental matrix F is defined using the following procedure.

1. Arrange or rearrange the transition matrix so that the absorbing states are first.
2. Partition the rearranged transition matrix into four parts

I	O
A	N

where

>   I = the **identity matrix**, having ones in a diagonal from upper left to lower right and zeros elsewhere

>   O = a matrix of zeros

>   A = a matrix of the transition probabilities of the remaining states of the system being absorbed in the next period

>   N = a transition matrix for the nonabsorbing states showing movement among these states

Notice that the vertical partition of the transition matrix divides the matrix into two groups, absorbing and nonabsorbing states.

3. Compute the fundamental matrix as the inverse of the difference between the identity matrix and the nonabsorbing transition matrix, N

$$F = (I - N)^{-1}$$

Where the exponent -1 stands for the inverse and I and N are of the same dimension (recall Appendix B reviews matrix algebra).

Using the bad debt example to demonstrate the concept of the fundamental matrix gives the following:

	1	2	3	4
1	1	0	0	0
2	0	1	0	0
3	.5	0	.2	.3
4	.4	.4	.1	.1

$$I = \begin{bmatrix} 1 & 0 \\ 0 & 1 \end{bmatrix} \qquad O = \begin{bmatrix} 0 & 0 \\ 0 & 0 \end{bmatrix}$$

$$A = \begin{bmatrix} .5 & 0 \\ .4 & .4 \end{bmatrix} \qquad N = \begin{bmatrix} .2 & .3 \\ .1 & .1 \end{bmatrix}$$

Then

$$F = (I - N)^{-1}$$

$$= \left(\begin{bmatrix} 1 & 0 \\ 0 & 1 \end{bmatrix} - \begin{bmatrix} .2 & .3 \\ .1 & .1 \end{bmatrix} \right)^{-1}$$

$$= \begin{bmatrix} .8 & -.3 \\ -.1 & .9 \end{bmatrix}^{-1}$$

$$= \begin{bmatrix} 1.30 & .44 \\ .15 & 1.16 \end{bmatrix}$$

The fundamental matrix shows the average number of periods the system will be in each nonabsorbing state before absorption occurs. In this case, if an account is in state 3 (0–30 days old), it will be in state 3 for 1.3 periods before being paid in full. Similarly, if an account is in state 3, it will spend .44 periods in state 4 before being paid in full or becoming a bad debt. By summing the rows in the fundamental matrix, it is also possible to determine the average number of periods to absorption. In this example, if an account is 31 to 60 days old (state 4), it will take, on average, 1.31 periods (.15 + 1.16) until it is either paid in full or written off as a bad debt.

It is also possible to determine the probabilities of moving from any nonabsorbing state to each absorbing state, by multiplying the fundamental matrix by the A matrix, (F)(A). Mr. Kroft can compute the probability that a given debt (accounts receivable dollars) will eventually end up in each of the absorbing states. Thus, we have

$$FA = \begin{bmatrix} 1.30 & .44 \\ .15 & 1.16 \end{bmatrix} \times \begin{bmatrix} .5 & 0 \\ .4 & .4 \end{bmatrix}$$

$$FA = \begin{bmatrix} .83 & .17 \\ .54 & .46 \end{bmatrix}$$

The FA matrix shows the probability that the debt for any given period will be absorbed. Recall that the first row shows the debts in the 0–30 day category and the second row shows debts in the 31–60 day category (categories 3 and 4 of the rearranged matrix). Columns 1 and 2 represent the paid and bad debt categories respectively. Thus, if a debt is currently in the first month (0–30 days), there is a .83 probability that it will eventually be paid off and a .17 probability that it will become a bad debt. Similarly, if a debt is in the second month, there is a .54 probability that it will be paid off and a .46 probability that it will become a bad debt.

Finally, using this information, Mr. Kroft can determine how much of the $6,500 now in accounts receivable will eventually be collected and how much will become bad debts. The accounts receivable is currently divided, with $4,000 in month 1 and the remaining $2,500 in month 2. This vector [4000 2500] is an initial vector or state of the system. To determine how much will be collected and how much will be written off, we simply multiply this initial vector by the FA matrix as follows:

$$[4000 \quad 2500] \begin{bmatrix} .83 & .17 \\ .54 & .46 \end{bmatrix} = [4670 \quad 1830]$$

Thus, $4,670 of the current accounts receivable will eventually be paid in full and $1,830 will become a bad debt. If Mr. Kroft considers the latter too high—as would seem likely—he will have to investigate the possibilities of reducing the amount of bad debts. To do so would require taking action to change the probabilities, and then deciding whether or not it is economically viable to make the necessary changes. The Markov process is only a tool that can provide information useful for reaching a decision.

16.5 *MARKOV ANALYSIS AND THE COMPUTER*

In this chapter, we have kept the problems small and simple to ensure that the matrix computations are manageable and easily understood. While the basic matrix computations are not difficult, it is obvious that with large problems they can quickly become burdensome. In fact, as the number of states increases, both the computational difficulty and the chance for making computational mistakes increase exponentially. Moreover, matrix inversion cannot be described as a simple or easy procedure even for small problems. Fortunately, the kinds of Markov analysis that we have been discussing are easily programmed using special-purpose programs. Such programs are available for most computers, from the mainframe to the personal computer. Moreover, some Markov computations are also available in several statistical packages and as functions in some spreadsheet packages. The Markov computations available in these programs generally include the multiplication of vector by matrix and the multiplication of a matrix by itself (raising a matrix to the power of t). In the remainder of this section, we will demonstrate additional business and managerial applications of Markov analysis, using the computer to solve the problems.

A Car Rental Example

The Discount Dollar Car Rental Company rents cars throughout Florida. Cars are rented either locally, which means they are returned to the same city, or one-way, which means they are returned to one of the other cities. Currently there are 350 cars in Miami, 275 cars in Orlando, 225 cars in Tampa, 400 cars in Jacksonville, and 175 cars in Fort Myers. Management has determined that the following minimum number of rental cars should be available in each city:

Miami	350
Orlando	250
Tampa	200
Jacksonville	250
Ft. Myers	150

An analysis of rental records has revealed the following weekly transition probabilities:

	Miami	*Orlando*	*Tampa*	*Jacksonville*	*Ft. Myers*
Miami	.28	.27	.14	.21	.10
Orlando	.22	.35	.23	.11	.09
Tampa	.23	.25	.30	.07	.15
Jacksonville	.18	.22	.12	.35	.13
Ft. Myers	.21	.18	.19	.10	.32

Management wishes to determine if the minimum allocations will be met after four weeks of operations, if no cars are reallocated between cities.

The computer output showing the number of cars available in each city after four weeks is given in Figure 16.4. From this, management can see that some action must be taken in order to meet the minimum requirements in Miami and Jacksonville.

Without these minimum numbers of cars available, Discount Dollar loses rental income. One course of action would be the use of incentive rental rates for cars returned to Miami and Jacksonville. Management has determined that, if such in-

```
        TRANSITION MATRIX AFTER 4 TRIALS (PERIODS)

              1     2     3     4     5
          _____
       1   .227  .266  .199  .164   .143
       2   .228  .267  .2    .161   .143
       3   .228  .266  .201  .161   .144
       4   .227  .266  .199  .165   .144
       5   .228  .265  .2    .161   .146
          _____


    RESULTING VECTOR (MATRIX) — AFTER 4 PERIODS:

    324.356      379.239      284.501    231.914    204.99

    STEADY STATE PROBABILITIES:

              1     2     3     4     5
          _____
           .228  .266   .2   .162   .144
          _____


    STEADY STATE DISTRIBUTION:

    324.52       379.39       284.84     231.26     204.98
```

Figure 16.4 D&D Computer Output

centives were offered, it would be possible to change the transition matrix as follows:

	Miami	*Orlando*	*Tampa*	*Jacksonville*	*Ft. Myers*
Miami	.28	.27	.14	.21	.10
Orlando	.26	.30	.21	.14	.09
Tampa	.28	.22	.28	.09	.13
Jacksonville	.18	.22	.12	.35	.13
Ft. Myers	.21	.18	.19	.10	.32

Figure 16.5 shows the system state after four weeks, given the new transition probabilities and the original initial conditions. Obviously, the minimum numbers have
all been met. Before making a decision on the incentive program, Discount Dollar
must consider all the costs involved in the incentive program, including a possible
decrease in revenue from decreased rates, or a possible increase because more cars
are now available for rent. These factors will probably also be weighed against
other options, which might include the cost of transporting cars from one location
to another.

A Training Problem

East Rochester Technical College is a proprietary, two-year college offering a specialized technical training program. In order to plan for the future, the adminis-

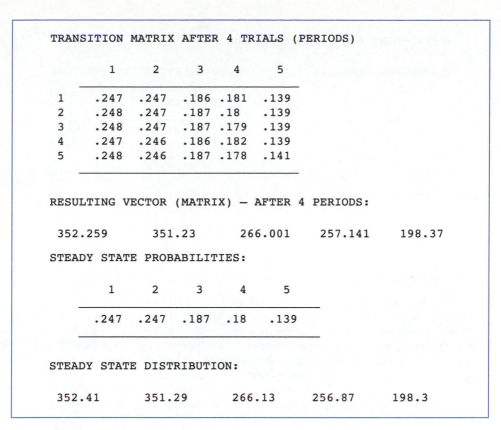

```
   TRANSITION MATRIX AFTER 4 TRIALS (PERIODS)


           1     2     3     4     5
         _____
    1    .247  .247  .186 .181   .139
    2    .248  .247  .187 .18    .139
    3    .248  .247  .187 .179   .139
    4    .247  .246  .186 .182   .139
    5    .248  .246  .187 .178   .141
         _____


   RESULTING VECTOR (MATRIX) — AFTER 4 PERIODS:

    352.259      351.23      266.001      257.141     198.37

   STEADY STATE PROBABILITIES:

           1     2     3     4     5
         _____
         .247  .247  .187  .18   .139
         _____


   STEADY STATE DISTRIBUTION:

    352.41       351.29      266.13       256.87      198.3
```

Figure 16.5 Computer Output Using New Transition Matrix

tration is interested in knowing how many students will graduate each year, continue in the program, or drop out. The administration has developed the following transition probabilities. Notice that, at the conclusion of the first year (row 1, first year), a student may either continue (taking second-year courses or first-year courses) or leave school (transferring as well as dropping out). It is not possible to graduate from the first year. At the conclusion of the second year, a student can graduate, drop out, or repeat second-year courses. With this program, it is not possible to take first-year courses after the second year. A student's status in the next school year depends only upon his or her status this year.

	1st	2nd	Grad	Leave
1st	.25	.57	0	.18
2nd	0	.13	.68	.19
Grad	0	0	1	0
Leave	0	0	0	1

The school's administration needs to know what proportion of students in the first and second year will eventually graduate and what proportion will drop out. Figure 16.6, showing the computer output for this problem, reveals that 59 percent of current first-year students will graduate and 41 percent will drop out. Of the current second-year students, 78 percent will graduate and 22 percent will drop out. Thus if there are currently 2,000 first-year students and 1,800 second-year students, 2584 will graduate.

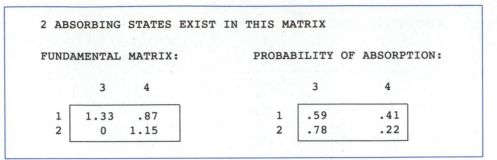

```
2 ABSORBING STATES EXIST IN THIS MATRIX

FUNDAMENTAL MATRIX:              PROBABILITY OF ABSORPTION:

         3      4                          3        4

   1   1.33    .87                 1     .59      .41
   2      0   1.15                 2     .78      .22
```

Figure 16.6 Computer Output for Training Example

Focus on Decision Making

Olympus Lumber Products uses a number of saws in its mill to cut rough lumber into various-sized boards for its many products. Because the saw blades are used continuously throughout the day, they become progressively duller over time. The blades can be categorized into one of four states (1–4) depending upon sharpness, with state 1 indicating a very sharp blade and state 4 indicating a dull blade in need of replacement. While a saw is running, it is difficult to determine the blade's state. Operators can detect dull blades over time, however, because they are less efficient and produce more scrap. Once an operator determines that the blade is dull, he must shut down the machine and have the blade replaced. At the end of the day, when the saws are shut down, all the blades are inspected and those that are dull (state 4) are replaced. Blades that are replaced are then sharpened so that they can be used as replacements.

It costs $65 to replace (remove and sharpen) a saw blade at the end of each day. However, if a blade becomes dull while in use, the estimated cost of the lost efficiency, extra scrap, and down time while the blade is being replaced is $300.

John Zebraski, mill supervisor, is considering alternative policies for replacing blades. He would like to establish a policy that will result in the lowest daily costs for the company and that is relatively easy for his maintenance people to follow. The two alternative policies he is considering are: (1) replacement of all blades found to be at state 3 or higher at the end of the day; or (2) replacement of all blades found to be at state 2 or higher at the end of each day.

Data Preparation/Problem Formulation

Mr. Zebraski has collected data that indicate a saw that is sharp (state 1) at the end of the day has an 85 percent probability of being at state 2 at the end of the next day and a 15 percent chance of being at state 3. A saw blade in state 2 has a 55 percent probability of staying in that condition, a 30 percent probability of moving to state 3, and a 15 percent probability of moving to state 4 by the end of the next day. A saw blade classified in state 3 has a 65 percent probability of staying in that condition and a 35 percent probability of moving to state 4 by the end of the next day.

Mr. Zebraski has decided that he can use Markov analysis to solve this problem. He has therefore placed the above data into the following transition matrix, which illustrates the current policy—that is, blades are replaced only as they become dull:

State at the end of the previous day	State at the end of the day			
	1	2	3	4
1		.85	.15	
2		.55	.30	.15
3			.65	.35
4	1.00			

State at the end of the previous day	State at the end of the day			
	1	2	3	4
1		.85	.15	
2		.55	.30	.15
3	1.00			
4	1.00			

State at the end of the previous day	State at the end of the day		
	1	2	3
1		.85	.15
2	1.00		
3	1.00		

State 4 is not required in this matrix, since all blades are replaced before becoming dull (there is a zero percent probability of moving from state 1 to state 4). Mr. Zebraski entered each of these matrices into a Markov computer program and obtained the following results.

Computer Solution

The first matrix, replacement of dull blades (current policy), resulted in:

STEADY STATE PROBABILITIES:

1	2	3	4
.168	.318	.345	.168

The second matrix, replacement of state 3 or higher blades (alternative 1), resulted in:

STEADY STATE PROBABILITIES:

1	2	3	4
.257	.486	.184	.073

The third matrix, replacement of state 2 or higher blades (alternative 2), resulted in:

STEADY STATE PROBABILITIES:

1	2	3
.500	.425	.075

Interpretation and Analysis of the Results

Mr. Zebraski next used these outputs to determine the costs associated with each policy. Dull blades discovered during the day cost $300 per blade, and blades replaced at the end of the day cost $65 each. The calculations were:

Current policy:
Daytime replacements:	16.8% × $300	= $50.40
End-of-day replacements:	16.8% × $65	= $10.92
		$61.32

Alternative 1:
Daytime replacements:	7.3% × $300	= $21.90
End-of-day replacements:	(25.7% + 18.4%) × $65	= $28.67
		$50.57

Alternative 2:
End-of-day replacements:	(42.5% + 7.5% + 50%) × $65	= $65.00

These results indicate that, from a cost standpoint, it would be best to replace all blades at state 3 or higher at the end of each day. The cost incurred would be $50.57 per saw per day. Thus, it appears that alternative 1 should be adopted.

What Happens Next

While this problem may seem fairly straightforward, there are other factors which Mr. Zebraski might want to consider. For example, have all of the conditions necessary for the use of Markov analysis been met? While the transitional probabilities may be an accurate reflection of actual wear on the average, individual blade wear could be a function of the type of wood being cut (hardwood versus softwood) or the thickness of the pieces being cut. If certain saws are used repeatedly for one type of wood or one thickness, different policies for different uses may be more appropriate.

16.6 CONCLUDING REMARKS

In this chapter, we have introduced Markov analysis as a descriptive tool that is used to describe the state of a given system at some time in the future. Markovian models provide a way to determine the probability that a given event will occur as the result of a transition, or recurring transitions, from one situation to another. Markov does not provide a direct optimal solution to a problem, but the information provided can be used in the decision making process.

While Markov analysis does have certain managerial applications, its value is not limited to the direct application to real-world problems. Markov processes form the foundation for some queuing and inventory models. However, there are certain challenges to applying Markov analysis to real-world problems. A key difficulty lies with the transition probabilities. The historical data needed to develop them may not be available. Moreover, it may prove somewhat difficult to find decision problems that meet the rather restrictive assumptions. Douglas J. White has authored two excellent articles on the applications of Markov decision processes.[1]

Management Science Application ————————————————————

DETECTING SPONTANEOUS COMBUSTION IN COAL MINES[2]

Coal mines in the United Kingdom are particularly liable to spontaneous combustion, known as heating. Early detection is vital to protect human life and to prevent heavy losses in both equipment and coal reserves. Inspection by mine officials before and after each shift is the primary method of detection. This is backed up by a system that conducts regular analysis of mine ventilating air. This system, known as a tube bundle system, continuously draws out mine air samples from various important points in the pit and analyzes them about every twenty minutes for traces of carbon monoxide (CO), which is generated in heatings. The background level of CO is in the range of 4–20 parts per million. As a heating grows, more CO tends to be given off, but the amount and rate are variable. Effective detection can be provided from calculations based on measurements of CO in the ventilating air. However, the sampling picture can be confused because CO levels vary as a result of such factors as the presence of CO from shotfiring and diesels, weather conditions on the surface, and changes in the workload. While trained people can pick out a significant rise against a noisy background, they may not always be available.

Remedial measures are much more likely to be successful with early recognition of a significant rise. However, in any automatic alarm system there is also a need to compromise between speed and reliability. Many alarm systems tend to generate repeated false alarms, and for an alarm to be taken seriously it is necessary for the automatic alarm system to avoid this. The advent of computer-based monitoring systems raised the possibility of developing more sophisticated alarms, and this project was undertaken with the support and cooperation of the National Coal Board (N.C.B.) and the European Coal and Steel Community (E.C.S.C.).

As the project developed, the following requirements were defined: instrumentation should be accurate to 1 ppm and should have a stable baseline; a computer alarm should detect heatings as rapidly as possible in the presence of "noise"; it should have a low false-alarm rate; it should be applicable with intermittent sampling of only one parameter, CO; alarm settings should be objectively calculated, and should not require more attention from mine officials than can realistically be provided; the computer should also detect open fires; the system should be comprehensible to ventilation officers and mine-

[1]See Douglas J. White, "Real Applications of Markov, Decision Processes," *Interfaces*, 15 (November–December, 1985): 73–83; "Further Real Applications of Markov Decision Processes," *Interfaces*, 18 (September–October, 1988): 55–61.
[2]Reprinted with permission of *Journal of the Operations Research Society*, 37 (June, 1986): 591-602. G. McCormick, "Algorithms for the Detection of Spontaneous Combustion in Coal Mines," Copyright 1986, Pergamon Press.

air scientists, i.e., they should be able to get an intuitive grasp of what the computer is doing; it should be possible for mine officials to override computer suggestions when they are aware of events that alter the interpretation of the statistics.

At the beginning of this study, development of an algorithm was hampered by the lack of data in digital form. Eventually, however, the increased availability of digital data and the development of a method to evaluate and compare algorithms led to a surge in algorithm development. Initial algorithms were based upon exponential smoothing with trend. These were abandoned in favor of exponentially smoothed regression. All of these smoothing alarms performed about equally well, but were effective only with slow heatings. Non-smoothing algorithms that were used include the "Basic Discriminating Alarm" (B.D.A.) and "Filter." The B.D.A. is based on the occurrence of continued CO levels above a threshold (dependent upon local conditions) for more than a selected number of observations. It was found to be effective for fast heatings, but not for slow heatings. An ad hoc method, called "Filter," was also developed. Using the crude heuristic: "If CO comes down, higher values can't have been due to a heating, so ignore earlier higher results," this method attempted to simulate the pattern detection capability of a human observer. It worked as well as any other method on both fast and slow heating. The performance of these alarms was encouraging, but testing with real data made it clear that an algorithm without an objective technique for setting the alarm levels was incomplete. An alarm setting technique had to be included to allow the alarm system to be applied to different environments.

For statistical reasons, it was diffiicult to set alarm levels for "Filter." While alarm level calculations were easily performed for the smoothing methods, they were simply not adequate for this kind of problem.

A change in approach led to the development of the Multiple Discriminating Alarm (M.D.A.), which in turn led to the development of a much more sophisticated stochastic model. The M.D.A. selects a number of threshold values of CO and for each of them keeps track of how long (in number of observations) the CO has exceeded the threshold. Since shotfirings and diesels cause the CO level to exceed the threshold, the problem becomes one of determining the number of observations that the CO level can remain above the threshold before the alarm is given. Markov analysis provided the answer to this problem. Studies determined that the probability of CO which was above a threshold falling below the threshold was a constant and vice versa. Thus, the probability of the CO level remaining above the threshold for a given period of time (or number of observations) could be predicted. The states were defined as "below" (state 0) and "above" (state 1) threshold levels. Thus,

$P_{ij}(t)$ = probability of being in state j at time t if initially in state i at time zero,

L = the mean length of time spent in state 1 (above threshold) each time it is entered,

R = the proportion of time spent in state 0 (below threshold),

where

$$P_{00}(t) = 1 - R + R \exp(-t/LR)$$

$$P_{11}(t) = R + (1 - R) \exp(-t/LR)$$

This analysis can also be used to determine sampling frequency. Given the high cost of the analyzers, this information can be used to help establish the number and frequency of observations and whether more frequent observations should be taken at certain points in the mine.

At the time this study was published, the M.D.A. was operational at eight collieries and the more sophisticated version was operational at two collieries. Experience has shown that it works; a number of heatings have been successfully detected. The alarm was expected to be installed in more collieries. However, development of M.D.A. is not complete. For example, more work can be done on irregular and continuous sampling, on estimation and on alarm levels, and other matters such as combining M.D.A. with data from other sources. The model allowed the most to be made of a minimal knowledge of rare events (heatings). The algorithms proposed are simple enough to allow a microcomputer to monitor several points while simultaneously revising alarm levels. At the same time, they are effective and adaptable. While other computerized alarms have been developed, none of them has met all of the requirements defined in this study.

GLOSSARY

absorbing state state that, if once entered is impossible to exit (there is 0 probability of moving from that state to any other state); a trapping state, $p_{ij} = 1$ (where $i = j$), that has no losses to other states but can have gains from other states

bad debt example popular example of an application of Markov analysis that includes the absorbing states, bad debt, and paid in full, in the transition matrix

brand switching problem a very popular Markov application example that is concerned with the probabilities of customers switching from one brand to another

conditional probability probability that one event will occur, given that another event has already occurred

equilibrium see steady state

first-order Markov processes use information from only the immediately preceding period to predict behavior in the future; that is, the probability of moving from one state to another is dependent only on the current condition, not on any earlier conditions

fundamental matrix specially defined matrix $F = (I - N)^{-1}$ which indicates the expected number of times the system will be in any nonabsorbing state before absorption

homogeneous Markov chains Markov process wherein the transition probabilities remain constant over time, the number of states is finite, and time periods are of equal length

identity matrix matrix that has ones in a diagonal from upper left to lower right and zeros elsewhere

initial conditions state of the system at time 0

Markov analysis stochastic technique used to study the evolution of systems in which there is probabilistic movement from one state to another state over repeated periods of time; a method that analyzes the current behavior of a system in order to predict the future behavior of that system

Markovian "memoryless" property assumption that the condition of the system at any time depends only upon its condition in the immediately preceding period

state of the system condition of the system at any given time period

state probability the probability that the system will be in a given state; e.g., the probability that the system will be in state i in period t is stated $p_i(t)$

steady state a constant value that the system achieves after an extended period of time, regardless of the starting state; an equilibrium condition where the probability of being in a given state does not change from period to period

transition matrix a table of transition probabilities for the system, describing conditional probabilities between states

transition probability probability that the system will move from state i to state j in one step; describes the movement or transition from one state to another in one time period

PROBLEMS

1. A survey of the three lawn care firms in Fairfield showed that, on June 1, there was a total of 2,000 customers with 500 for firm A, 900 for firm B, and 600 for firm C. On July 1 the breakdown was 525 for firm A, 885 for firm B, and 590 for firm C. These net changes were analyzed further and showed that firm A retained 420 customers during the month, gained 105 customers (63 from B and 42 from C), and lost 80 customers (45 to B and 35 to C). Firm B retained 810 customers, gained 75 customers (45 from A and 30 from C), and lost 90 customers (63 to A and 27 to C). Firm C retained 528 customers, gained 62 customers (35 from A and 27 from B), and lost 72 customers (42 to A and 30 to B).

   a. Display this pattern of gains and losses in a table.
   b. Compute monthly transition probabilities and construct the transition matrix.

2. Referring to problem 1, how many customers would each of the three lawn care firms have on August 1? September 1?

3. Given the following transition matrix:

	A	B
A	.7	.3
B	.4	.6

   a. Use a decision tree to determine the probability of an entity being in state A after 2 periods (time 2) if it starts in state A at time 0.
   b. Given an initial state of [.4 .6], compute the system state after two periods (time 2).

4. If the initial system state is [3,000 4,000 3,500], compute the system state after two periods, given the following transition matrix.

	A	B	C
A	.4	.3	.3
B	.5	.4	.1
C	.2	.2	.6

5. **a.** Determine the state of the system in problem 4 after three periods.
   b. Determine the steady-state probabilities for A, B, and C.

6. Using the matrix of transition probabilities developed in problem 1, determine the steady state for the system.

7. A marketing vice-president for Sansonic Corporation, a Japanese manufacturer of inexpensive miniature radios, would like to estimate the equilibrium state for the U.S. market. The market is broken down into three categories: U.S. models (domestic), other import models, and Sansonic models. If the following transition probabilities have been determined,

	D	I	S
D	.75	.15	.10
I	.10	.65	.25
S	.15	.10	.75

what will Sansonic's equilibrium share of this market be (assuming no change in the transition probabilities)?

8. A recent survey of a market with only two brands serving 50,000 customers showed the following results: 70 percent of brand A customers remain loyal each week and 30 percent switch to brand B; 75 percent of brand B's customers remain loyal and 25 percent switch to brand A. At the time of the survey, brand A had 26,000 customers and brand B had 24,000 customers.

   a. Display this information as a transition matrix.
   b. If a customer is currently buying brand A, use a decision tree to determine the probability that this customer will buy product B (1) next week; (2) at the end of two weeks.
   c. Determine the share of the market that will be held by brand A after three weeks.
   d. Determine the steady-state probabilities.

9. Built Better Construction has been awarded the contract to remodel Old Town in Center City. Much of the interior work will involve demolishing or renovating plaster walls. The plaster dust frequently clogs the filter on the ventilating system and causes the system to shut down. The filter is classified as clean, partially clogged, or totally clogged. When the system becomes completely clogged, work must stop until the filter is replaced and the system is restarted. Prior experience has shown that a clean filter has a .15 probability of remaining clean, a .65 probability of becoming partially clogged, and a .2 probability of becoming totally clogged. A partially clogged filter has a .4 probability of remaining that way and a .6 probability of becoming totally clogged. A totally clogged filter must be replaced with a clean filter.

   a. Set up the transition matrix showing this situation.
   b. If a system shutdown costs the company $150 in lost work time and filter costs, how much will it cost BBC to follow a policy of not replacing filters until the system stops?

10. If BBC in problem 9 decides to adopt a policy of replacing partially clogged filters (at a cost of $20), how will these costs compare with those found previously?

11. The fruit wine cooler market is shared by five brands: C&G, Appleton, Georgia Peach, Sun Valley, and Great Outback. The competition among these brands is intense. Great Outback, the newest entry into the market, hired a market research firm to study customer preferences over a five-month period. The results showed a relatively constant rate of brand switching on a monthly basis. C&G retained 45 percent of its customers, while 20 percent switched to Appleton, 12 percent to Georgia Peach, 18 percent to Sun Valley, and 5 percent to Great Outback. Appleton retained 39 percent of its customers, while 15 percent switched to C&G, 17 percent to Georgia Peach, 13 percent to Sun Valley, and 16 percent to Great Outback. Georgia Peach retained 42 percent of its customers, while 19 percent switched to C&G, 8 percent to Appleton, 21 percent to Sun Valley, and 10 percent to Great Outback. Sun Valley retained 50 percent of its customers, while 10 percent switched to C&G, 10 percent to Appleton, 10 percent to Georgia Peach, and 20 percent to Great Outback. Great Outback retained 48 percent of its customers, while 12 percent switched to C&G, 10 percent to Appleton, 16 percent to Georgia Peach, and 14 percent to Sun Valley.

   a. Set up the transition matrix for this problem.
   b. Find the steady state percentage of customers for each brand of cooler.
   c. If this market has annual sales of $500,000,000, what sales volume can Great Outback expect?

12. Great Outback (problem 11) is considering a special advertising campaign costing $25,000,000. The market research firm has indicated that, as a result of this campaign, the transition probabilities would be as follows:

	C&G	A	GP	SV	GO
C&G	.45	.17	.11	.17	.10
A	.14	.35	.15	.12	.24
GP	.18	.08	.42	.10	.22
SV	.10	.09	.08	.49	.24
GO	.12	.09	.15	.14	.50

   Should Great Outback proceed with this advertising campaign?

13. The housing council in Fairfield County has classified housing in the county into rentals, single-family homes, and privately owned, multiple-occupancy buildings (condominiums, townhouses, duplexes, etc.). A recent study has shown the following trends in housing moves: Sixty percent of renters stay in apartments, 20 percent move to single-family homes, and 20 percent move to private multiple-occupancy dwellings. Eighty percent of single-family dwellers remain in their homes, 5 percent move to apartments, and 15 percent move to private multiple-occupancy dwellings. Seventy-two percent of private multiple-occupancy dwellers remain there, 23 percent buy single-family homes, and 5 percent move to apartments. If the current housing distribution for the county is 20 percent rental apartments, 50 percent single-family homes, and 30 percent private multiple-occupancy buildings, what will the distribution be in five years?

14. If the occupancy level of the units in Fairfield County (problem 13) is 75 percent for apartments, 96 percent for single-family homes, and 85 percent for private multiple-occupancy buildings, will there be a potential housing problem in the next five years if no new building occurs and the population remains stable?

15. Each weekday Denneco Company inspects its production machines, classifying their condition as excellent, good, fair, or down. Machines that are down are repaired immediately and returned to the excellent category. Company records show the following transition probabilities between categories:

	Excellent	Good	Fair	Down
Excellent	.25	.60	.15	0
Good	0	.55	.35	.10
Fair	0	0	.50	.50
Down	1.0	0	0	0

The company has 150 machines. Machines that are down cost the company $300 in lost production and repair costs before they are fixed. Machines in fair condition cost the company $80 per day in lost production.

a. How much is lost, on average, due to machines being in fair condition or down?

b. The company is considering a preventive maintenance program that would require servicing all machines found to be in fair condition. Assuming this would cost $40 per machine serviced, would this policy be justified?

16. An extensive study on a new brand of PCs being used in a college computer laboratory shows that, on an hourly basis, 97 percent of the PCs that are running (up) will still be running the next hour. Those PCs that do break down normally have to be sent out for repair, although it has been discovered that the student lab assistant can easily restart 1 percent of those machines by the next hour.

a. If a PC is up and running at noon, what is the probability that it will be up at 2:00 PM?

b. What are the steady-state probabilities for this PC?

17. Dr. Joseph is scheduled to give his 6:00 PM class a hands-on exam in the PC lab and will require 23 working computers. He checks the lab at 8:00 AM and finds 27 of the 30 PCs are running; the remaining 3 are down. Using the information given in problem 16, how many PCs will be running when Dr. Joseph returns to give his exam?

18. Real Leather, Inc., a manufacturer of leather clothing, classifies its sewing machine operators according to their productivity in the preceding month. Records of the past five years indicate that the work force has been distributed across five productivity categories (with category 1 being the most productive) as follows: 1—10 percent; 2—18 percent; 3—35 percent; 4—22 percent; and 5—15 percent. A new organizational system introduced six months ago groups operators into voluntary units. These units elect their own supervisors and set their own work schedules. Production records under the new system have shown month-to-month changes in employee productivity. These changes are shown in the transition matrix below.

	1	2	3	4	5
1	.60	.20	.15	.05	0
2	.30	.45	.18	.05	.02
3	.10	.25	.50	.10	.05
4	0	.10	.20	.45	.25
5	0	0	.15	.25	.60

a. The new plant manager wants to know what the long-run productivity distribution will be under the new production system.

b. If operators earn an average of $1,100 per month, and if productivity losses for each category are 1—5 percent; 2—10 percent; 3—25 percent; 4—28 percent; and 5—32 percent, what is the long-term benefit of this new system for the company on a monthly basis?

19. Given the transition matrix below, find the appropriate fundamental matrix.

$$\begin{bmatrix} 1 & 0 & 0 & 0 \\ .2 & .2 & .3 & .3 \\ .5 & .2 & .1 & .2 \\ 0 & 0 & 0 & 1 \end{bmatrix}$$

20. Ruby Groton, a large regional furniture store, makes most of its sales on the installment plan. The accounts are classified each month as paid, current (being paid on time), overdue (one payment behind), or bad debt. Experience has shown that, when a customer is two or more payments behind, the account will probably turn into a bad debt. At that point, the customer's credit is cancelled and the account is written off as a bad debt. Store records indicate that each month 40 percent of the accounts classified as current are paid in full, 50 percent remain current, and 10 percent become overdue. On the overdue accounts, 10 percent are paid in full, 30 percent become current (the customer pays for two months), 45 percent remain overdue (the customer pays one payment), and 15 percent become bad debts. If Ruby Groton now has $900,000 in accounts receivable ($840,000 current and $60,000 overdue), how much should the company be prepared to write off as a bad debt?

21. Wilson Widgets has an automatic widget maker that can produce 10 good widgets per hour when it is in proper adjustment. If the machine goes out of adjustment, however, all widgets must be reworked at a cost of $2 each. It cost $40 to adjust the machine. Unfortunately, it is impossible to tell whether the machine is properly adjusted without shutting it down for maintenance. The widget maker exhibits the following hourly transition matrix.

	Adjusted	Out of Adjustment
Adjusted	.8	.2
Out of Adjustment	.4	.6

At steady state, what proportion of the time will the machine be out of adjustment? What will be the average rework cost?

22. Wayco Products carries a variety of mail-order products. When Wayco receives an order, it may find that product is on-hand, discontinued, on-order, or replaced with a new, improved product. The transition probabilities showing movement between categories are as follows:

	On-hand	Discontinued	On-order	Replaced
On-hand	.50	.10	.35	.05
Discontinued	0	1	0	0
On-order	.35	.05	.45	.15
Replaced	0	0	0	1

a. Over time, what percentage of on-hand products will be discontinued?

b. How many periods will an on-hand product be on-hand before being absorbed?

23. Best Buy Department Store has done an analysis of its accounts receivable and finds they fall into four categories: paid-in-full (PIF), 30 days, 60 days, and bad debt. The store bills on a monthly basis. People who pay within the billing period (the month) are considered paid-in-full. Those accounts that are not paid-in-full during the month are categorized as 1–30 days overdue. The accounts that are 1–30 days overdue can be paid-in-full or moved to the 31–60 days overdue category. Anyone who has not paid by the end of the second month—past 60 days overdue—is considered a bad debt. An analysis of past transactions and accounts receivable has shown the following probabilities of change in the accounts from month to month.

	PIF	30	60	BD
PIF	.89	.11	0	0
30	.73	0	.27	0
60	.98	0	0	.02
BD	0	0	0	1

a. If there are 1,000 PIF accounts this month, what distribution of accounts can Best Buy expect after five months?

b. Can you see any long-term problems for Best Buy if they consider a 3 percent bad debt rate to be acceptable?

24. The University of Fairport has developed the following transition matrix showing movement of its students between the following categories: freshman, sophomore, junior, senior, graduate, and early leave.

	F	S	J	Sr	G	EL
F	.2	.6	0	0	0	.2
S	0	.15	.7	0	0	.15
J	0	0	.1	.8	0	.1
Sr	0	0	0	.03	.96	.01
G	0	0	0	0	1	0
EL	0	0	0	0	0	1

If the University of Fairport currently has 1,500 freshman, 1,200 sophomores, 1,000 juniors, and 800 seniors, how many of these students will graduate over the next four-year period?

25. Rossville General Hospital has compiled daily information on 146 patients admitted to the hospital through its emergency room. (Patients treated, but not actually admitted to the hospital, are not included in this data.) Analysis of the records shows the following:

■ Of the 146 patients admitted, 90 were in satisfactory condition, 40 were in fair condition, and 16 were in critical condition.

■ Of the 90 patients in satisfactory condition, 72 remained in the hospital in satisfactory condition the following day, while 6 were discharged and 12 had deteriorated to fair condition.

■ Of the 40 in fair condition, 17 remained in fair condition the following day, while 16 had improved to satisfactory condition and 7 had deteriorated to critical condition.

- Of the 16 in critical condition, 6 remained in critical condition the following day, while 4 had improved to satisfactory condition, 4 had improved to fair condition, and 2 had died.

The hospital administrator feels this data is typical for all patients admitted through the emergency room.

a. If the emergency room just admitted a patient, what is the probability he will be discharged in the next three days?

b. What is the average number of days patients spend in each condition until discharged?

c. What is the probability a patient will be discharged?

Consultant's Report

Cable Week

Until 1989 there were three national weekly television viewing magazines—TV News, TV Week, and Cable Guide—with TV News, the pioneer in the market, having a steady 50 percent of the market and the other two fighting for the remaining 50 percent. These figures held for both subscription buyers and over-the-counter buyers. The entrance of Cable Week into the market upset this balance. Through a combination of aggressive advertising, sensational news "scoops," and a low introductory subscription rate, Cable Week quickly grabbed 15 percent of the market (1 percent from TV News, 6 percent from TV Week, and 8 percent from Cable Guide). It appeared to be difficult to shake the loyalty of TV News subscribers, many of whom had subscribed to the magazine for over 20 years.

There are approximately 18 million TV magazines sold per week. Of these, 8 million are sold through subscription and 10 million are sold over-the-counter. Buyers do not purchase more than one title each week. Market research has indicated that weekly over-the-counter sales are based on a combination of factors, including name recognition and regular features. However, the most important selection criteria seem to be cover art and cover story (which are usually related). Thus, the magazine with the cover and/or lead article that "grabs" the individual reader is the one selected at the checkout counter or newsstand. While this decision is highly individualized, there does seem to be a pattern. Readers tend to prefer the profiles and interviews of TV celebrities over hard news stories. Price does not seem to be a major factor in over-the-counter sales, since all four magazines are priced competitively, within $.25 of each other.

Profit for the magazine publishers comes from both sales income and advertising income. The publishers make approximately $.05 per sale. Advertising rates increase with readership. The base is $25,000 for a minimum readership of 500,000. This increases by $2,500 for each 100,000 additional readers. These are full-page ads. Half-page and quarter-page ad prices are proportional. The TV magazines average 10 pages of ads per issue (this total includes combinations of whole-page, half-page, and quarter-page ads).

Sean McGraff, marketing manager for Cable Week, is ready to attack the over-the-counter sales market. For the past six months, he has been researching the buying habits of these readers. On June 1, the market for the 10 million buyers in this market segment was 48 percent for TV News, 19 percent for TV Week, 18 percent for Cable Guide, and 15 percent for Cable Week. His research has been tracking the movement of readers from month to month to assess the pattern of gains and losses. The following tables show these movements for the first and last months.

| | January 1 | | | |
From To	TV News	TV Week	Cable Guide	Cable Week
TV News	4,080,000	240,000	288,000	192,000
TV Week	285,000	1,349,000	133,000	133,000
Cable Guide	216,000	198,000	1,260,000	126,000
Cable Week	210,000	120,000	90,000	1,080,000

| | June 1 | | | |
From To	TV News	TV Week	Cable Guide	Cable Week
TV News	4,061,078	238,887	286,664	191,110
TV Week	287,152	1,359,186	134,004	134,004
Cable Guide	207,405	190,121	1,209,864	120,986
Cable Week	221,135	126,363	94,772	1,137,267

Sean wants to improve Cable Week's overall share of the market, and is considering two alternatives for increasing readership:

1. Create a magazine within a magazine by adding a mini–soap opera digest to the magazine, consisting of weekly plot summaries and a weekly article featuring some aspect of the soaps (characters, actors/actresses, stories). Market research indicates that this would not be sufficient to pull in readers who currently purchase the soap opera magazines on the market; that is, it would not increase the overall TV magazine audience. However, it would allow them to gain an extra 1 percent per month from each competitor and simultaneously reduce their losses to each competitor by 1 percent per month. It would cost Cable Week approximately $22,500 per week in production and salaries.
2. Add a weekly consumer column offering an in-depth review of the audio and visual equipment currently on the market, such as VCRs, TVs, and CDs. This would not be a consumer advocacy column; instead each week the magazine would review one item in much the same way it currently reviews programs, movies, and concerts. This would allow them to gain an additional .5 percent per month from each competitor and simultaneously reduce their losses to each competitor by .5 percent per month. The weekly cost of this alternative would be $6,000.

Either of these alternatives would be introduced by a major advertising campaign, which would cost approximately $100,000.

You have been hired as a management consultant to help Sean by applying management science techniques to this particular problem. Prepare a report for Cable Week that addresses:

1. The total share of the market Cable Week can expect in the long run, assuming no price or format changes by any of its competitors and no further actions by Cable Week.
2. The desirability of each of the alternatives being considered, including any potential profit increases on an annual basis.
3. The reasonableness of the assumptions upon which this analysis is based.

Chapter

17

Forecasting

By the end of this chapter, you should be able to:

1
describe the need for forecasting and its role in decision making;

2
discuss the manager's role in the forecasting process;

3
understand the difference between qualitative and quantitative forecasting methods, listing several of each;

4
describe the applicability of each type of forecast;

5
select the correct technique given the specific problem parameters;

6
forecast (solve problems) using the time series and causal techniques introduced in the chapter;

7
measure the forecast error, using both MAD and MSE, and be able to discuss the accuracy of various forecasting methods;

8
determine the strength of the relationship between the variables in a regression model; and

9
discuss the role of the computer in making forecasts and the decisions based upon the forecasts.

Many important decisions made by individuals and organizations depend on an assessment of the future—demand for products and services, sales levels, cost trends, manpower needs. Management must predict the future in order to make decisions in the present. The need to deal with the future, efficiently and accurately, is a part of every management decision and can make the difference between success and failure.

Individuals predict the future in a number of ways, including past experience, intuition, and best guesses. Organizations forecast using a variety of techniques, informal and formal, qualitative and quantitative. The decision maker can forecast based on gut feeling or intuition, on past experience or personal judgement, or by relying on the opinion or judgement of "experts." There are also quantitative forecasting techniques available to help the decision maker. With the increased use of computers and the easy availability of forecasting packages, these quantitative techniques are becoming ever more important to modern organizations and are among the most widely used quantitative models. While no forecast can make perfect predictions, forecasts can provide guidelines for making the decision. Decisions are made by the manager or decision maker with the best information that is available.

Acme Compressor's Production Schedule

Carlos Montoya, production manager for the Acme Compressor Company, must schedule production of the company's new model I100 industrial compressor one week in advance. Mr. Montoya feels he must schedule as accurately as possible, since underproduction could cost the company sales and overproduction does not properly utilize the company's already strained labor resources and limited storage facilities. The company currently averages 500 to 600 hours of overtime per week, spread over all products. Overproduction of the new product would be needlessly expensive. Mr. Montoya knows how many hours of labor are required to manufacture each model I100 (87 labor hours). If he had an accurate demand figure for the I100, he thinks it would help him schedule production for the coming week. He has the I100 sales figures for the first 11 weeks of its production and also sales during the same period for the older H90 model. He wants to forecast demand for the I100, and feels he should be able to do so using this data. However, he is not quite sure how to go about it.

17.1 *AN INTRODUCTION TO FORECASTING*

A forecast is a prediction of the future. Organizations must predict the future in order to make decisions in the present that will ensure their continued success. Since the future is an implicit part of every management decision, it is essential that organizations have accurate and timely forecasts.

Many forecasting techniques, each with its own special use, are available to help with the decision making. These models can be grouped or classified in a variety of ways—judgemental forecasts, extrapolation techniques, regression models, conditional methods, and so on. In this chapter we will classify forecasting techniques as qualitative (subjective) or quantitative (objective), and will further subdivide quantitative models into time series and causal. **Qualitative** models, ranging from "best guesses" or "hunches" to highly structured methods for reaching a consensus from a group of experts, are all based on subjective data—ultimately, someone's opinion. **Quantitative** models, which range from a simple extension of the past into the future to highly complex multiple regression and econometric models, are based on hard data, either historical or obtained through experimentation. Figure 17.1 shows a breakdown of some of the common forecasting techniques. Discussion of the Box-Jenkins and econometric models is beyond the scope of this text. Before we discuss specific forecasting techniques, let's look at the forecasting process or system.

The Forecasting Process

The forecasting process begins when the need to obtain a forecast is identified at the appropriate managerial level. Next, management identifies the objective of the forecast and establishes the planning horizon (the period over which the forecast

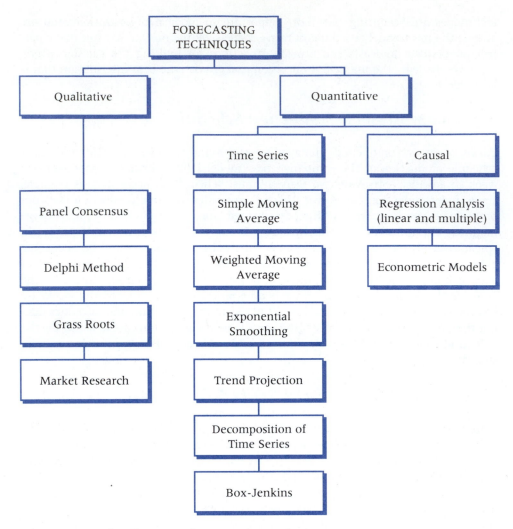

Figure 17.1 Classification of Forecasting Techniques

will be made). Under ideal circumstances, the data necessary for the forecast are compiled and then analyzed. Among other things, the analysts look for discernible patterns and/or relationships among variables. They structure an appropriate model, based on these data, and choose a forecasting procedure that behaves well under the model. In many cases, however, a procedure is selected without any thought to the form of the actual underlying model. Selecting the forecasting technique is a crucial part of the process, depending ultimately upon the parameters of the problem.

Selecting a Forecasting Technique
The following considerations influence the choice of forecasting method:

1. The accuracy required. In general, the greater the accuracy required, the greater the need for more sophisticated techniques. The planning horizon also can influence the level of accuracy required (short-term forecasts, affecting day-to-day operations, require greater accuracy).

2. The time available to make the forecast. Less sophisticated methods are more likely to be used when time is short.
3. The cost involved. Cost includes two types of cost—the cost of the forecast itself, and the cost to the firm of making an inaccurate forecast (the cost of inaccuracy). It would be foolish to spend large sums of money on a forecast of little significance, when intuition or judgement based on past experience would work as well. Ideally, the technique selected minimizes the total of these two costs.
4. The availability of hard data. Quantitative techniques depend on hard data. If historical data are not available and no experiment can provide the data, it will probably be necessary to use a qualitative technique.

The forecasting technique selected should be the one most likely to produce the information needed, with the desired level of accuracy, in the time available, at the right (minimal) cost. Thus, the decision maker must also understand the comparative advantages, costs, and applications of the alternatives available.

Consideration should also be given to the time period over which the forecast is to be made. Forecasts are frequently categorized by the time horizon of the forecast: short-range (concerned with the daily operations of the organization); medium-range (used for those decisions needing the additional lead time); and long-range (for decisions that affect the organization further in the future, such as new product planning, building projects, and long-term financing). Time designations are arbitrary and depend upon the organization. In general, short-term refers to anything up to one year and long-term refers to more than three years. However, for some organizations, long-term can be one year. For others, long-term is 10 to 20 years (or even longer in some cases).

The increased availability of computerized forecasting programs has greatly reduced the cost and time required for some of the more sophisticated techniques. More organizations are able to undertake more sophisticated forecasts. Under these circumstances, the time and cost considerations often do not play as important a part in the selection process. The existence of computer routines also helps to explain why simplistic forecasting techniques are sometimes selected (often naively) without first structuring the model based on the available data.

We begin our discussion of forecasting techniques by taking a cursory look at qualitative forecasts.

17.2 *QUALITATIVE FORECASTING TECHNIQUES*

Qualitative forecasts are generally based on the opinion or judgement of one or more experts. They are often used in situations where historical data is lacking (introducing a new product or service), or in situations where quantitative methods are either inappropriate or cannot be used. This includes situations where time and/or money constraints prohibit using a quantitative forecasting technique. Qualitative forecasts are used at both extremes of importance—for forecasts of little importance, and for forecasts of great importance. They are used in situations where it just doesn't pay to expend resources for a formal model (the potential return is not high enough). And they are used when the decision is extremely important and complex, requiring a wide variety of input (which includes data from quantitative forecasting models). In these situations, after all the available information has been gathered, the final forecast is usually made based on the judgement of the chief executive officer and his advisory staff. Qualitative forecasts are also used in situations where external factors play a significant role, but not necessarily in a clearly defined way—for example, the impact of proposed trade-restricting legislation.

Qualitative forecasting includes certain useful, informal techniques based on human experience, including best guesses, gut feelings, or intuition. However, formalized technical procedures have been designed to incorporate human experience and expertise into the forecasting process. In the remainder of this section we describe some qualitative forecasting methods that elicit and combine forecasts from groups of experts: panel consensus, the Delphi method, grass roots forecasting, and market research.

Panel concensus is a jointly developed forecast, arrived at by assembling a panel or group of experts and openly presenting information to them. It is based on the assumption that two or more heads are better than one. However, since group dynamics inevitably play a role and the configuration of the group strongly affects the outcome, the forecast might not reflect a true consensus. As a result, the accuracy of such forecasts is generally considered poor. However, the forecast can be arrived at in a relatively short period of time for a modest cost. These forecasts are typically applied to the introduction of new products and services.

The **Delphi method,** which was developed by the Rand Corporation, also relies on a panel of experts, but its structure removes the group dynamic drawbacks. The experts do not meet together, but are interrogated by a sequence of questionnaires. After the organization receives the responses to the first questionnaire, it compiles them and uses them to produce another questionnaire. The results from both questionnaires are then sent to the group members. In this way, information available to one expert is made available to the rest of the group. Based upon the results of the two questionnaires, the decision makers can usually make a forecast (although another round may sometimes be necessary). The key to the Delphi method is the feedback mechanism. The accuracy of the forecast depends upon the quality of the design of the questionnaires. While forecasts using the Delphi method are considered to be fairly accurate over most time frames, the procedure can be costly and requires more time than most other procedures.

Grass roots forecasting uses those people closest to the problem to make forecasts. These individuals (experts) are asked to make a forecast. For example, sales personnel often are asked to forecast demand in their district. Management then combines the individual forecasts into one overall forecast. The quality and accuracy of these forecasts depends upon the quality of the individual forecasts. If done conscientiously, these forecasts offer the advantage of bringing detailed, first-hand knowledge into the forecast. However, these forecasts can be costly. For example, the cost can include such items as sales that are not made while sales personnel undertake this administrative task. In addition, those closest to the problem, such as sales people, may not have the proper motivation or expertise necessary to develop a forecast. Grass root forecasts can be effective. If they are done well, they can provide fairly accurate short-term forecasts.

Market research, the most quantitative of the qualitative forecasting methods, encompasses a variety of techniques, including telephone surveys, test marketing, mail questionnaires, personal interviews, and consumer panels. These devices can determine the perceived quality of a product or service and its potential demand. Market research is helpful in predicting the size, configuration, and structure of the market for various products or services. As with grass roots forecasting, these techniques are based on the concept of "going to the source." Highly sophisticated statistical procedures are used to analyze consumer responses and make a forecast. Market research techniques require the greatest amount of time and are probably the most expensive qualitative technique. However, if applied properly, they have the highest degree of accuracy, especially for short-term forecasts.

We will now turn our attention to quantitative forecasts, which are based on hard data and are therefore more objective. We look first at time series models.

17.3 *TIME SERIES FORECASTING*

A statistical time series is the set of values that a random variable takes on over a period of time. It is a description of the past. The temperature taken daily at the same time for the past week; the number of customers served during the lunch hour for a month at Lou's Diner; sales of used cars by Holsworth Motors in each of the preceding 12 months—all these are everyday examples of time series. The behavior of a time series is usually displayed in graph form, because this is most descriptive of the pattern of behavior of the series.

Time series forecasting techniques relate the forecast to only one factor—time. A time series forecast uses the past to predict what will happen in the future. The forecaster undertakes an analysis of a time series with the assumption that the past is a good guide to the future; what has occurred in the past will continue to happen. It does not assume that history will repeat itself, but that past tendencies or past patterns will continue. Understanding the patterns, or the behavior, of the series in the past often is helpful in understanding the behavior of the series in the future.

Time Series Components

The time series pattern is assumed to be the result of certain component parts: trend, seasonal variations, cyclical variations, and random variations.

Trend (T) is the pattern of the variable observed over a fairly long period of time. It is the long-run direction of the series of data. The values can increase or decrease at various rates; the trend can remain constant, or it can change. Figure 17.2 shows examples of two common types of trend lines. Figure 17.2(a) shows a linear trend that indicates a constant increase. Figure 17.2(b) shows a nonlinear trend line. This one is decreasing at a constant percentage change.

The **seasonal variation** (S) is a fluctuation in the value of the variable that recurs at regular, periodic intervals over one year or less. It is a movement or variation that is repetitive and periodic—a regular pattern of variability. Seasonal variations can be the result of nature, such as snow tire sales in the winter; or of human behavior, such as Poinsettia plant sales in December. Seasonal variations are not limited only to the seasons of the year. For example, the number of traffic accidents peaks each day at 5:30 PM in the can-of-worms on Interstate 490. Figure 17.3 presents an example of a time series showing seasonal peaks (Saturday and Sunday) for pizza sales over a three-week period for a neighborhood pizza delivery service.

Cyclical Variation (C) refers to cycles, long-term swings of data points about the trend line. Cyclical fluctuations cover a fairly substantial period of time, usually requiring a time series that spans several years. Moreover, the length and am-

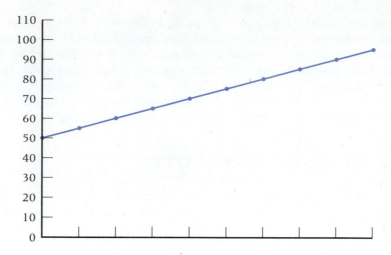

Figure 17.2(a) Trend—Constant Change

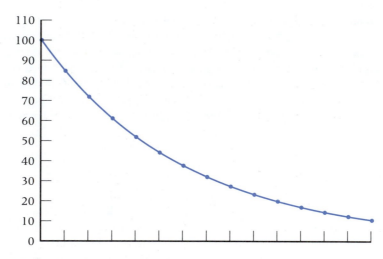

Figure 17.2(b) Trend—Constant Percentage Change

plitude of their oscillation are variable (neither constant nor symmetrical). All this makes cycles difficult to identify. For most short-term forecasts, the cyclic component is not considered. Cyclical variations or cycles are often the result of business or economic cycles—as the economy swings from prosperity to recession. Figure 17.4 shows two cycles oscillating or fluctuating around the trend line.

Random variations (R) are irregular fluctuations that occur by chance, having no specific identifiable or assignable cause (that is, they result from unanticipated, nonrecurring factors). Because they cannot be predicted in a systematic way, they are not included in forecasting models.

Forecasting with Time Series

Since time series forecasting models try to predict the future based on a set of past data, and these past data can contain a variety of components, the decision maker must decide how deeply to analyze the data.

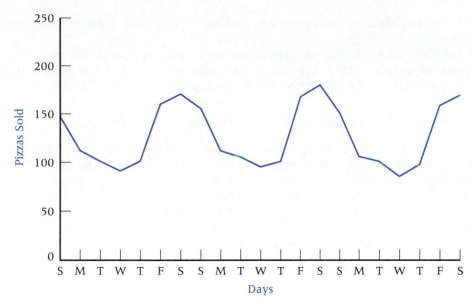

Figure 17.3 Seasonal Variation in a Pizza Sales Time Series

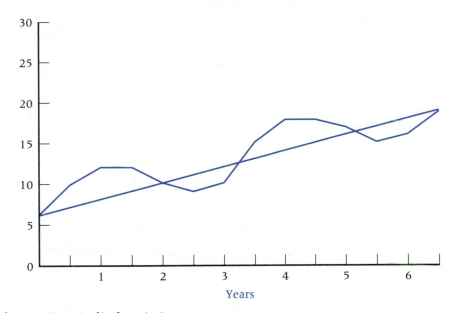

Figure 17.4 Cyclical Variation

There are a number of techniques available that use the data as observed. These methods are typically used with fairly stable time series, those having no significant trend, cycle, or seasonality. These methods use averaging techniques designed to smooth out random fluctuations to provide a "good enough" forecast.

Classical time series forecasting, by contrast, uses more complicated techniques to analyze the data, decomposing the time series into its component parts (T, S, C, and R), and then recombining them in such a way that a better forecast is produced.

We now turn our attention to the averaging techniques that use the data as observed. In the appendix to this chapter, we look at a time series technique that makes adjustments for the component parts, the decomposition of a time series.

Time Series Forecasting Using Averaging Techniques

In this section we are going to discuss averaging techniques that smooth out random fluctuations—moving average, weighted moving average, and exponential smoothing. These methods are best used for short-term forecasts, in the absence of seasonal and cyclic variations. A simple average of all the observed variable values can be used under similar circumstances. This method gives satisfactory results if the variations around the mean value are small, and it has the advantage of minimal cost and ease of use. However, if the base level changes during the time period covered, the simple average is very slow in responding. Thus we do not include it in our discussion.

Simple Moving Average

A **moving average** generates a forecast for the next period by averaging the actual values of the forecast variable for the most recent n time periods. To compute a simple moving average, requires first deciding upon the number of data points or time periods (n) to include in the average. The most recent n observed values are then averaged to obtain a forecast for the next immediate period. As each period evolves, data for the new time period is added and the value of the oldest time period is subtracted and a new average is calculated. Moving averages can also be centered so that only values in the middle of a sequence can have a moving average. Centered moving averages are discussed in the appendix to this chapter.

The simple moving average (SMA) equals the summation of the most recent n data values divided by n:

$$SMA = \frac{\sum (\text{most recent n variable values})}{n}$$

The forecast for the next period (F_{t+1}) can be expressed as

$$F_{t+1} = \frac{\sum_{i}^{t} X_i}{n}$$

where

F_{t+1} = the forecast for the next immediate period

X_i = the individual variable values, i.e., the actual observed data points for the immediately preceding n periods

t = the most recent period

n = the number of periods included in calculating the average

$i = t - n + 1$

To illustrate the SMA method, we return to Mr. Montoya's problem. Recall that Carlos Montoya is the production manager for the Acme Compressor Company. He has to schedule production of the company's new model I100 industrial compressor one week in advance. He has sales figures for both the I100 model and the older H90 model. He would like to use these data in some way to arrive at an accurate demand forecast for the I100 in order to avoid overproduction.

Table 17.1 shows I100 sales for the first 11 weeks of its production, and also shows sales during the same period for the older H90 model. These data are graphed in Figure 17.5. Mr. Montoya's first choice is to try a simple moving average.

The following calculations are for a three-period moving average used to forecast demand for week 12:

$$F_{12} = \frac{10 + 7 + 16}{3} = 11$$

Table 17.1 I100 and H90 Sales Data

Week	I100 Sales	H90 Sales
1	13	7
2	7	5
3	14	11
4	15	7
5	9	14
6	18	12
7	8	13
8	15	18
9	10	10
10	7	19
11	16	16

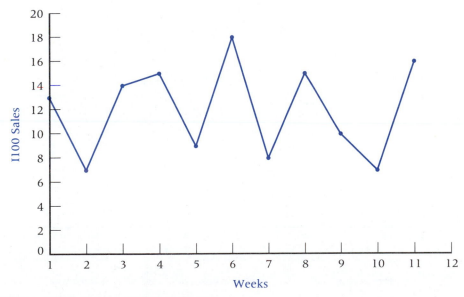

Figure 17.5 Graph of I100 Sales Data

Using a five-period moving average gives the following results:

$$F_{12} = \frac{8 + 15 + 10 + 7 + 16}{5} = 11.2$$

In this case, there is not much difference between the two forecasts. The five-period SMA shows a slightly higher forecasted demand. We will continue to consider Mr. Montoya's problem. Table 17.2 compares Mr. Montoya's data, showing actual values for sales, and forecasts using three- and five-period moving averages. The error column shows the difference between the actual observed value and the forecast value. Figure 17.6 is a graph showing these data.

Selecting the number of time periods (n) to use for the moving average requires care. The effects of different period lengths may be conflicting. The longer the

Table 17.2 Comparison of Moving Averages

Period Sales	Actual	3 period SMA	Error	5 period SMA	Error
1	13				
2	7				
3	14				
4	15	11.33	3.67		
5	9	12.00	−3.00		
6	18	12.67	5.33	11.6	6.40
7	8	14.00	−6.00	12.6	−4.60
8	15	11.67	3.33	12.8	2.20
9	10	13.67	−3.67	13.0	−3.00
10	7	11.00	−4.00	12.0	5.00
11	16	10.67	5.33	11.6	4.40
12		11.00		11.2	

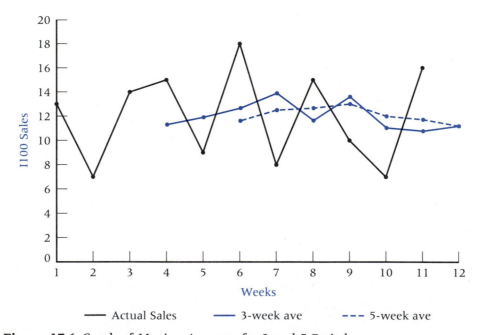

Figure 17.6 Graph of Moving Averages for 3 and 5 Periods

moving average period, the smoother the pattern, because the random elements are smoothed out more and there are fewer fluctuations. That means, if there is a trend, the moving average with more periods will lag behind it. Thus, moving averages with larger n values are less sensitive to random variations, but slower in responding to any underlying trend. Moving averages using shorter time spans are more sensitive to random variation, producing more oscillations, which may be distracting or misleading; however, they respond more quickly to trends. Notice, in Figure 17.6, the relatively smooth pattern of the five-period moving average. The three-period average, by contrast, exhibits more fluctuation and responds more quickly to the variations in the actual values. However, we do not know whether these variations are random noise. It may be a matter of trial-and-error experimentation to find the best n.

The simple moving average is a mechanical method that is quick, easy, and relatively inexpensive to use. It provides a fair to good forecast for the immediate future. However, a simple moving average does not react well to variations that occur for a reason, such as seasonality. Moreover, because the simple moving average gives equal weight to every period selected, it always lags behind any underlying trend. It also requires large amounts of data that must be gathered and stored. This can create problems, and is considered a disadvantage of the SMA. We now turn our attention to the weighted moving average, which partially eliminates the lagging problem.

Weighted Moving Average

In a **weighted moving average**, weights are used to vary the effects of past data. Thus, weights are assigned to each data point and a weighted mean is calculated as the forecast for the next immediate period. Weighted moving averages (WMA) are generally used on data that show a trend. The most recent observations usually have the most weight, with decreasing weights assigned to older data points:

$$WMA = \frac{\sum (\text{weight} \times \text{variable value for most recent n periods})}{\sum (\text{weights})}$$

or if the weights that are assigned to the various observations must sum to 1, then

$$WMA = \sum (\text{weight} \times \text{variable value for most recent n periods})$$

The forecast for the next period is expressed

$$F_{t+1} = \sum_{i=t-n+1}^{t} W_i X_i$$

where

F_{t+1} = the forecast for the next immediate period

X_i = the individual variable values, i.e., the actual observed data points for the immediately preceding n periods

W_i = the weights given to each period

and $\sum W_i = 1.0$

Now let's return to Mr. Montoya's problem and see what happens when weights are assigned. The data we used previously did not show any trend. Therefore, we will use the H90 sales data from Table 17.1, which appear to have an upward trend. Mr. Montoya has chosen to forecast for period 12, the next week, using a three-period weighted moving average and the following weights: ⅙ (.17) for period 9, the oldest period to be used; ⅓ (.33) for period 10, the immediately preceding period; and ½ (.5) for period 11, the most recent period. Thus,

$$F_{12} = (⅙ \times 10) + (⅓ \times 19) + (½ \times 16) = 15.97$$

results in a forecasted demand of 15.97 for the coming week. A simple three-period moving average for this forecast yields a forecast of 15 units for period 12.

Table 17.3 compares the weighted three-period forecast with a simple three-period moving average. The table also includes a three-period weighted average using weights of .1, .15, and .75. The graph in Figure 17.7 compares the simple and weighted three-period moving averages. Figure 17.8 compares weighted averages using different weights. The weighted average responds more quickly to recent changes or variations in the pattern (which may or may not be desirable, depending on the causes of the fluctuations).

There is an almost infinite number of possible weighting schemes. Finding the correct weights, like finding the right number of periods for the moving average, is a matter of judgement and trial-and-error experimentation. If more recent periods are weighted too heavily, the resulting forecast might be an overreaction to what issimply a random fluctuation. On the other hand, weighting too lightly might result in an underreaction (lagging) to an actual change in the pattern. Comparingthe forecast errors (the differences between the observed values and the forecast values) using different weighting schemes provides one way of checking the effect of different weights. Forecast error will be discussed later.

The weighted moving average, like the simple moving average, requires the retention of large amounts of data. This requirement can be a serious drawback in problems with large numbers of variables. The next technique, exponential smoothing, overcomes this problem.

Table 17.3 Comparison of Simple and Weighted Moving Averages

Period	Actual Sales	3 period SMA	3 period WMA .17, .33, .5	3 period WMA .1, .15, .75
1	7			
2	5			
3	11			
4	7	7.67	8.34	9.70
5	14	7.67	7.98	7.40
6	12	10.67	11.18	12.65
7	13	11.00	11.81	11.80
8	18	13.00	12.84	12.95
9	10	14.33	15.33	16.65
10	19	13.67	13.15	11.50
11	16	15.67	15.86	17.55
12		15.00	15.97	15.85

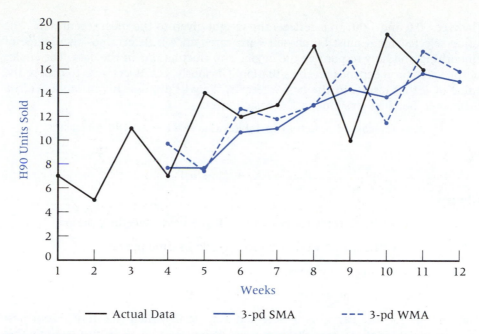

Figure 17.7 Graph Comparing Weighted and Simple Moving Averages

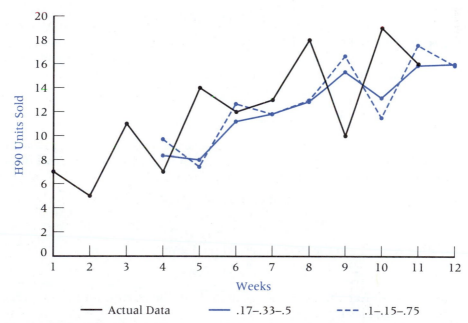

Figure 17.8 Comparison of 3 Period Weighted Moving Averages with Weights of .17, .33, .5 and .1, .15, .75

Exponential Smoothing

Exponential smoothing is a moving average technique that requires only three pieces of data: the forecast for the most recent period, the actual value for that period, and a smoothing constant, α. The smoothing constant is a weighting factor (between 0.0 and 1.00) that reflects the weight given to the most recent data. The value selected for α must be chosen with care, since it determines the degree of smoothing and how responsive the model is to fluctuations in the data. The choice of the value for α depends on the situation. Obviously, the objective is to choose the value of α that results in the best forecasts. We will discuss this in more detail a little later, but first let's look at the basic model:

$$\text{New forecast} = \alpha \text{ Actual variable value} + (1 - \alpha) \text{ Old forecast}$$

or

$$F_{t+1} = \alpha X_t + (1 - \alpha)F_t$$

where

F_{t+1} = The forecast for period $t + 1$, the next suceeding period

X_t = The actual value for the variable in time period t

F_t = Forecast for period t

α = The smoothing constant $(0 \leq \alpha \leq 1)$

The forecast for any period is a weighted average in which the most recent past data are weighted more strongly than more distant past data. We demonstrate this in the following way:

Assuming three periods of data, X_1, X_2, X_3, the forecast for period 4 is

$$F_4 = \alpha X_3 + (1 - \alpha)F_3$$

The forecast for period 4 is a weighted average of the actual value for period 3 (X_3) and the forecasted value for that same period 3 (F_3), with weights of α and $1 - \alpha$ respectively. Using the same formula, the forecasts for periods 3 and 2 are

$$F_3 = \alpha X_2 + (1 - \alpha)F_2$$
$$F_2 = \alpha X_1 + (1 - \alpha)F_1$$

There is no forecast for the initial period F_1 (it may be a guess). It makes sense to take the initial observed value as the initial forecast, that is, $F_1 = X_1$. Substituting X_1 for F_1 in the forecast for period 2, F_2 can be expressed

$$F_2 = \alpha X_1 + (1 - \alpha)X_1$$
$$F_2 = X_1$$

Substituting X_1 for F_2 in the forecast for period 3 gives

$$F_3 = \alpha X_2 + (1 - \alpha)X_1$$

We can now substitute this new expression for F_3 in the forecast for period 4 (F_4), with the following result:

$$F_4 = \alpha X_3 + (1 - \alpha)F_3$$
$$F_4 = \alpha X_3 + (1 - \alpha)[\alpha X_2 + (1 - \alpha)X_1]$$
$$= \alpha X_3 + \alpha(1 - \alpha)X_2 + (1 - \alpha)^2 X_1$$

This expression can be generalized to

$$F_{t+1} = \alpha X_t + \alpha(1 - \alpha)X_{t-1} + (1 - \alpha)^2 X_{t-2} + \ldots + \alpha(1 - \alpha)^{t-1}X_1 + (1 - \alpha)^t F_1$$

Thus, the forecast for period 4 is a weighted average of the first three values, with the most recent period, period 3, weighted most heavily. The coefficients of the variables decrease as the data becomes older. Exponential smoothing is especially useful because, in many applications, the importance of past data decreases as the past becomes more distant. In other words, recent data are generally more important. The method is intended for essentially stable situations where the deviations over time are caused by random effects, that do not follow a regular pattern.

The value of α affects the performance of the model. It is the weight given to the most recently observed data. The larger the α, the more strongly the model reacts to the most recent data. If a time series is fluctuating erratically, as a result of random variability, a small α value is appropriate in order not to overreact. Larger α values are better for stable time series, which show little random fluctuation, in order to react more quickly to those fluctutations that are really turning points, representing changing conditions in the time series.

To demonstrate the exponential smoothing, let's look again at Mr. Montoya's data for I100 compressor sales. Beginning with period 1, we set F_1 equal to 13, the actual value for the first period (there is no forecast available for the first period). Using the exponential smoothing formula

$$F_{t+1} = \alpha X_t + (1 - \alpha)F_t$$

with $X_1 = 13$ and an α of .3, the forecast for period 2 is

$$F_2 = .3(13) + (1 - .3)13 = 13$$

The actual value for period 2 is 7. Forecast error is $X_t - F_t$ (actual value minus forecast value). Thus the forecast error here is -6. Continuing for period 3 yields

$$F_3 = .3(7) + (1 - .3)13 = 11.2$$

which has a forecast error of 2.8. Table 17.4 shows a summary of the exponential smoothing calculations, using α values of .3 and .6. Figure 17.9 shows a plot of the data comparing the different smoothing constants. Notice that, with $\alpha = .6$, the forecast for period 12 is 13.09 versus 12.15 for $\alpha = .3$.

Table 17.4 Summary of Exponential Smoothing Forecasts for I100 Sales Using $\alpha = .3$ and $\alpha = .6$

Period	Actual Value	Forecast $\alpha = .3$	Error	Forecast $\alpha = .6$	Error
1	13	13.00	0.00	13.00	0.00
2	7	13.00	−6.00	13.00	−6.00
3	14	11.20	2.80	9.40	4.60
4	15	12.04	2.96	12.16	2.84
5	9	12.93	−3.93	13.86	−4.86
6	18	11.75	6.25	10.95	7.05
7	8	13.62	−5.63	15.18	−7.18
8	15	11.94	3.06	10.87	4.13
9	10	12.86	−2.86	13.35	−3.34
10	7	12.00	−5.00	11.34	−4.34
11	16	10.50	5.50	8.74	7.26
12		12.15		13.09	

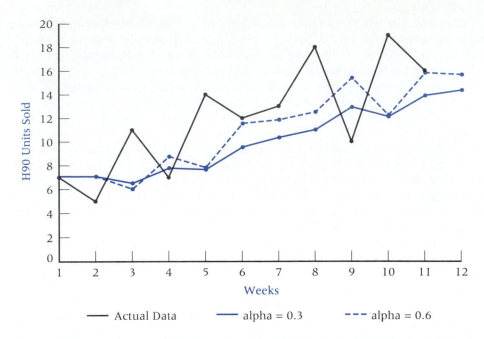

Figure 17.9 Graph of Actual Data and Forecasts with $\alpha = .3$, and $\alpha = .6$

In general, simple exponential smoothing is superior to the other moving average techniques discussed earlier. This technique has both small computational costs and storage requirements and produces better short-term forecasts. However, it does have a tendency to lag behind actual trends. A variation, exponential smoothing that adjusts for trend, is available for use when this is a serious problem.

Adjusted Exponential Smoothing

As stated previously, trend is a long-term movement, and exponentially smoothed forecasts always lag behind trend. In other words, the forecast values are above or below the actual observed values. However, exponentially smoothed forecasts can be adjusted to correct for a trend lag. The adjusted forecast consists of the exponentially smoothed forecast with a trend adjustment factor added to it:

Trend Adjusted Forecast = Forecast + Trend Factor

The trend adjusted forecast uses a smoothing constant (β) to smooth the trend, preventing erratic responses to random fluctuations. Like α, β takes on a value between 0.0 and 1.0 that is often determined subjectively. It also reflects the weight given to the most recent data.

Mathematically, the trend adjusted model is

$$\text{Adjusted } F_{t+1} = F_{t+1} + \left(\frac{1 - \beta}{\beta}\right) T_{t+1}$$

where

β = the smoothing constant for trend

T = an exponentially smoothed trend factor

F_{t+1} = the exponentially smoothed forecast for time period t + 1

The exponentially smoothed trend factor (T_{t+1}) is calculated using the formula

$$T_{t+1} = \beta(F_{t+1} - F_t) + (1 - \beta)T_t$$

where

$$T_t = \text{the last period trend factor}$$

When there is no initial trend factor, the choice is subjective (frequently a zero trend factor is used initially). As an example, let's compute the third period sales for the H90 model for Mr. Montoya, using the exponentially smoothed forecast for $\alpha = .3$. The initial forecast is set equal to the actual sales of 7 ($F_1 = X_1$). We then determine F_2 and F_3 as follows:

$$F_2 = .3(7) + (1 - .3)(7) = 7$$

$$F_3 = .3(5) + (1 - .3)(7) = 6.40$$

The trend factor for period 3 (T_3) is computed next. Normally the initial trend, T_1, is set equal to zero. For this probelm, we will give β a value of 0.1. The trend factor, T_2, is then

$$T_2 = \beta(F_2 - F_1) + (1 - \beta)T_1$$

$$= .1(7 - 7) + (.9)(0)$$

$$= 0$$

Note that, when the initial forecast is set equal to actual sales and the initial trend is set equal to zero, the trend factor for the next period is always zero. Trend factor T_3 is then calculated as

$$T_3 = \beta(F_3 - F_2) + (1 - \beta)T_2$$

$$= .1(6.4 - 7) + (.9)(0)$$

$$= -0.06$$

Now we can use this figure in the adjusted forecast formula.

$$\text{Adjusted } F_3 = F_3 + \left(\frac{1 - \beta}{\beta}\right)T_3$$

$$\text{Adjusted } F_3 = 6.4 + \left(\frac{1 - .1}{.1}\right)(-0.06)$$

$$= 6.4 + 9(-.06)$$

$$= 5.86$$

Table 17.5 shows the adjusted forecasts for the H90 sales data. Figure 17.10 compares the graphs.

Forecast Error

Almost all forecasts contain some error. **Forecast error** is defined as the difference between the actual observed value and the forecast value:

$$\text{Forecast error} = \text{Actual} - \text{Forecast}$$

It follows that the objective of any forecasting method should be to provide a forecast with a sufficient or acceptable degree of accuracy, at the least possible cost.

Table 17.5 Comparison of Smoothed Forecast and Trend Adjusted Forecast

Period	Actual Value	Forecast $\alpha = .3$	Error	Adjusted Forecast $\beta = .1$	Error
1	7	7.00	0.00	7.00	0.00
2	5	7.00	−2.00 7.00	−2.00	
3	11	6.40	4.60 5.86	5.14	
4	7	7.78	−0.78 8.54	−1.54	
5	14	7.55	6.45 8.02	5.98	
6	12	9.48	2.52 11.65	0.35	
7	13	10.24	2.76 12.87	0.13	
8	18	11.07	6.93 14.18	3.82	
9	10	13.15	−3.15 17.82	−7.82	
10	19	12.20	6.80 15.56	3.44	
11	16	14.24	1.76 19.10	−3.10	
12		14.77	19.61		

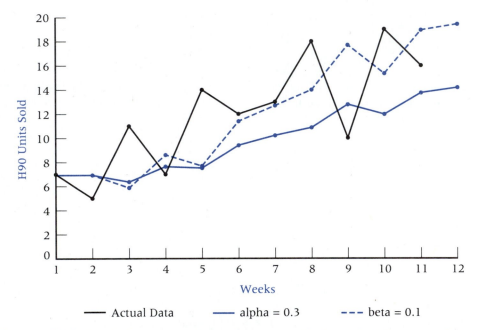

Figure 17.10 Graph Comparing Simple Exponentially Smoothed Forecast with Adjusted Forecast

Forecast errors influence decisions. Recall that forecast accuracy is one criterion used in selecting a forecasting technique. It is necessary to look at both the performance of the forecast over time (the historical error performance) and the ability of the forecast to respond to change. Forecast error can also be used to help determine such things as number of periods to use in a moving average, which weights to use, and which smoothing constants give a better forecast. Forecast error is also used to evaluate the success or failure of the technique in use.

In this section we describe two commonly used methods for measuring error, mean absolute deviation (MAD) and mean squared error (MSE), and a method for tracking forecast error in order to ensure that the forecast is performing adequately. Both MAD and MSE are measures for summarizing the historical errors of a forecast.

MAD is the average of the absolute deviations for all the forecast errors. That is, all the errors are treated as positive values, ignoring + and − signs. All errors are weighted evenly. MAD is computed using the formula

$$MAD = \frac{\sum |Actual - Forecast|}{n}$$

where

n = the number of periods for which errors may be determined (periods having both an actual and a forecast value).

For the five-period moving average, shown in Table 17.2, the MAD is

$$MAD = \frac{6.4 + 4.6 + 2.2 + 3.0 + 5.0 + 4.4}{6}$$

$$= \frac{25.6}{6}$$

$$= 4.27$$

MSE is the average of the squared errors. Thus, MSE weights errors according to squared values. The formula for MSE is

$$MSE = \frac{\sum (Actual - Forecast)^2}{n}$$

where

n = the number of periods for which there is a forecast error, i.e., periods having both an actual and a forecast value.

For the same five-period moving average, the MSE is

$$MSE = \frac{(40.96 + 21.16 + 4.84 + 9.00 + 25.00 + 19.36)}{6}$$

$$= \frac{120.32}{6}$$

$$= 20.05$$

Table 17.6 summarizes the computation of these measures for Mr. Montoya's I100 forecasts using three-week and five-week moving averages. These comparisons would help Mr. Montoya determine the better moving average to use. Table 17.7 uses MSE to compare the results of exponential smoothing with three different values for α, for both the I100 and the H90 models. Notice that, with data that are primarily random (I100), a smaller alpha gives a more accurate forecast. With data that exhibit a trend (H90), a larger alpha is slightly better. This is a very important use for error measures.

Table 17.6 Summary of MAD and MSE Computations for Three- and Five-Period Moving Averages

Period Sales	Actual	3 period SMA	Error	5 period SMA	Error
1	13				
2	7				
3	14				
4	15	11.33	3.67		
5	9	12.00	−3.00		
6	18	12.67	5.33	11.6	6.40
7	8	14.00	−6.00	12.6	−4.60
8	15	11.67	3.33	12.8	2.20
9	10	13.67	−3.67	13.0	−3.00
10	7	11.00	−4.00	12.0	5.00
11	16	10.67	5.33	11.6	4.40
12		11.00		11.2	
			MAD = 4.29		MAD = 4.27
			MSE = 19.49		MSE = 20.02

Table 17.7 Summary of Exponential Smoothing Forecasts with $\alpha = .1$, $\alpha = .3$, and $\alpha = .6$

	MSE $\alpha = .1$	MSE $\alpha = .3$	MSE $\alpha = .6$
I100	15.929	19.229	26.367
H90	27.948	17.152	16.698

There is wide disagreement among forecasting experts on which measure of forecast error to use. Indeed, selecting a measure of forecast error is not necessarily a simple matter. It is really a matter of personal choice and is frequently influenced by what is currently in vogue. Computationally, MAD weights all errors evenly and MSE weights errors according to their squared values. Therefore, MSE is influenced much more by large forecast errors. MAD is much easier to calculate. While both measures provide a sense of accuracy, actually interpreting the significance of either value is largely judgmental. We will leave it to you to look at all the figures and decide which, if any, forecast Mr. Montoya should use.

Tracking Forecast Error

It is frequently as important to measure and track forecast error as it is to maximize forecast accuracy. That is, it is necessary to monitor forecast error to make sure that the forecast is performing as it should be, and that it responds adequately to changes in data patterns. This becomes a matter of comparing the cost of not responding to real changes in trend with the cost of responding to random fluctuations. One way to monitor forecasts is by the use of a **tracking signal.** A tracking signal compares the ratio of cumulative forecast error to the corresponding value of MAD to predetermined limits. If the ratio falls within the limits, the forecast is probably (not definitely) performing adequately.

$$\text{Tracking Signal} = \frac{\sum (\text{Actual} - \text{Forecast})}{\text{MAD}}$$

Mathematically this is expressed as

$$\text{TS}_n = \frac{\sum\limits_{t=1}^{n} (A_t - F_t)}{\text{MAD}_n}$$

where

TS_n = tracking signal for time period n

$(A_t - F_t)$ = forecast error in time period t

MAD_n = mean absolute deviation as of time period n

We can use the forecast error and MAD figures from Table 17.7 to calculate the tracking signal for the eleventh week:

$$\text{TS}_{11} = \frac{(6.4 - 4.6 + 2.2 - 3.0 - 5.0 + 4.4)}{4.27}$$

$$= \frac{0.4}{4.27}$$

$$= 0.094$$

Setting the limits for the tracking signal is a managerial decision that depends on a number of factors, including the importance of the forecast and cost effectiveness.

Time Series Forecasting Using Trend Projection

We previously defined trend as the long-run direction of the series of data. This trend line can be linear or nonlinear. However, in this chapter we will consider only linear trend. If a plot of the data, called a **scatter diagram**, indicates that there is a trend, and if it appears to follow a straight line with respect to time, then this trend can be projected into the future and used to forecast. The basic idea with **trend projection** is to fit a function to a set of time series data in which the independent variable is time and the dependent variable is the variable being forecast. This requires determining the Y-axis intercept (at X = 0, the value of Y where the trend line crosses the Y axis) and the slope of the line (the amount of change in Y for a one-period change in X). The intercept and slope are the parameters of a straight line.

There are several procedures for fitting the function to the time series data— that is, for estimating the Y intercept and the slope. When the forecast is needed quickly, the line can be drawn, or fit "by eye." The objective is to find a straight line that comes close enough to all the points in the scatter diagram. Note that it is not necessary actually to touch any of the points, but rather to find a good fit. Consider the scatter diagram in Figure 17.11(a). The straight line shown in Figure 17.11(b) appears to be a reasonable fit. However, when fitting the line by eye, there is no mesure for the goodness of fit.

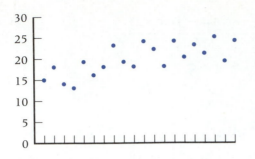

Figure 17.11(a) Scatter Diagram

Figure 17.11(b) Good Fit (Line Drawn by Eye)

The method of **least squares** regression is the most widely used formal procedure for estimating the Y intercept and slope of the line of best fit. Again, note that it is possible to have a nonlinear trend line and use the same basic methodology. However, we are considering only linear or straight-line functions. The function is determined such that the sum of the squared deviations between the trend line and the observed data points is minimized. That is, the equations that are used to estimate the parameters of the trend line minimize the sum of the squares of the vertical deviations between the trend line and the data points.

The estimated regression equation, used to forecast trend into the future is

$$Y' = a + bx$$

where

Y' = the dependent variable, i.e., the variable being forecast

b = slope of the line

a = y intercept

x = the period number (the independent variable)

This is also the equation for a straight line. The values for a and b must be determined. However, since the objective is to find the equation for the best fit, the values to be determined are those that minimize the difference between the points on the line and the actual observations (minimize forecast error).

$$\sum_{t=1}^{n} (Y_t - Y'_t)^2$$

where

n = number of periods

Y_t = actual observed value for time period t

Y'_t = Forecast value in time period t

or since $Y'_t = a + bx_t$

$$\sum_{t=1}^{n} (Y_t - [a + bx_t])^2$$

where

Y_t = actual observed data

x_t = time period

a = y intercept

b = slope of the line

The formulas that can be used to compute the values of a and b are shown below. These formulas, derived using calculus, can be found in any elementary statistics book dealing with regression analysis.

$$b = \frac{\sum xY - n\bar{x}\bar{Y}}{\sum x^2 - n\bar{x}^2}$$

$$a = \bar{Y} - b\bar{x}$$

where

$\bar{x}$ = the average of the x values (x = time periods)

$\bar{Y}$ = average of the Y values (Y = observed values)

$\sum xY$ = x times Y for each period, summed over all periods

$\sum x^2$ = x squared for each period, summed over all periods

n = number of periods used in the analysis.

From these formulas, it is apparent that we must make several calculations: summations of products, products of averages, summations of squared values, and so on. In the following example, we will demonstrate how the data can be set up in tabular form and used to make these computations.

Consider the scatter diagram in Figure 17.12, and the monthly sales figures in Table 17.8. We can find the linear equation of best fit for these data using the above formulas for a and b. Arranging the data into the four columns shown in Table 17.9 simplifies the computations. Column 1 shows the time periods (x). Column 2 shows the sales figures (Y). Column 3 is the product of Y and x, or column 2 multiplied by column 1. Column 4 is x^2, or the column 1 values squared. Each column is also summed. The average of x($\bar{x}$) and Y ($\bar{Y}$) is simply their sums divided by the number of periods. Thus

$$\bar{x} = \sum \frac{x}{n} = \frac{66}{11} = 6$$

$$\bar{Y} = \sum \frac{Y}{n} = \frac{185}{11} = 16.82$$

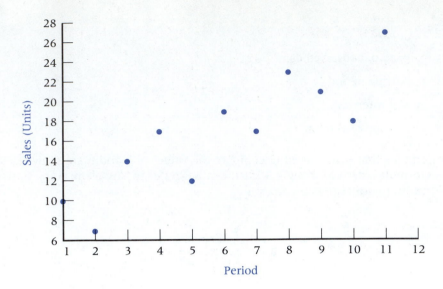

Figure 17.12 Scatter diagram

Table 17.8 Monthly Sales Figures

Period	Sales
1	10
2	7
3	14
4	17
5	12
6	19
7	17
8	23
9	21
10	18
11	27

Table 17.9 Calculations

x	Y	(x)(Y)	x^2
1	10	10	1
2	7	14	4
3	14	42	9
4	17	68	16
5	12	60	25
6	19	114	36
7	17	119	49
8	23	184	64
9	21	189	81
10	18	180	100
11	27	297	121
$\sum$ 66	185	1,277	506

The slope, b, can now be computed.

$$b = \frac{\sum xY - n\bar{x}\bar{Y}}{\sum x^2 - n\bar{x}^2}$$

$$b = \frac{1277 - 11(6)(16.82)}{506 - 11(6)^2}$$

$$= \frac{1277 - 1110}{506 - 396}$$

$$= 1.52$$

The slope indicates that sales are increasing, on the average, by $1,518 every month. We can now compute the Y intercept using

$$a = \bar{Y} - b\bar{x}$$

$$a = 16.82 - 1.52(6)$$

$$= 7.70$$

The equation for the best fit linear trend is

$$Y' = a + bx$$

$$Y' = 7.70 + 1.518x$$

We can now use this equation to forecast sales for period 12.

$$Y' = 7.70 + 1.52 (12)$$

$$Y' = 25,940$$

The least squares procedure will be used again in the section on causal models. However, before we leave the subject of trend projection with time as the independent variable, it is necessary to make a few observations concerning the assumptions underlying this procedure. The basic underlying assumption is that historical trends continue. Time is the surrogate for a number of factors in the underlying system that are hard to measure and/or identify. These factors affect the dependent variable, and the overall process or system is assumed to be regular or consistent. That is, the model assumes that the system that is producing or causing Y (the dependent variable) is essentially stable. Therefore, it will continue to act in the future as it has acted in the past. However, if the system changes significantly, the underlying assumption is invalid and the forecast will be inaccurate. It is important to use time as the independent variable only when the underlying system is, in fact, identifiable and stable.

Our discussion of times series forecasting has not been all-inclusive. In an introductory text, we can barely manage to scratch the surface. Some excellent models, like the Box-Jenkins model, are beyond the scope of this text and have not even been mentioned. We encourage the interested reader to read about these more advanced models in the sources mentioned in the reference section of this text. We now turn our attention to causal forecasting techniques.

17.4 *CAUSAL FORECASTING TECHNIQUES*

In the earlier section on linear trend projection, we demonstrated a relationship between sales and time. With each succeeding time period (as time increased), sales increased. In that example, time was the independent variable and sales was the dependent variable. It is also possible for there to exist a similar relationship between variables, when time is not one of the variables. That is, in certain situations there is a linear relationship between variables wherein one variable can be identified as a dependent variable that seems to react in a predictable way to changes in one or more independent variables. There is a logical association between these variables; one depends on the other. However, this does not mean that one variable causes the other. **Causal forecasting** models attempt to establish a functional relationship between the variable to be forecast (the dependent variable) and one or more independent or predictor variables. These models do not prove causality.

In using a causal model, the plausible relationship between variables must be established. An independent variable can affect the value of the dependent variable, but the independent variable's value is not affected by the value of the dependent variable. If this relationship does exist, and if it can be adequately defined mathematically, a very accurate forecast might be made. Causal forecasts require more time, more data, and more money than other methods. However, the forecasts can be superior. The most common causal models are regression (linear and multiple) and econometric models. In this section we will discuss regression models, emphasizing simple linear regression.

Regression Analysis

Regression analysis is a method for measuring the relationship between the dependent variable and one or more independent variables. The regression equation is the measure of this relationship, and is ultimately used to predict future values of the dependent variable. We introduced this concept in the discussion of linear trend projection. The basic assumption is that a relationship exists between these variables, and that regression measures this relationship. We begin our presentation with simple linear regression, which measures the relationship between one dependent variable and one independent variable.

Simple Linear Regression

Consider the following figures compiled by Fairport Savings and Loan, shown in Table 17.10. Loan officers have noticed that new home mortgage loan applications increase the month following the announcement of Eastman Kodak's annual employee bonus. One of the directors of the S & L, Jake Fiske, would like to know if he can use the bonus announcement to predict loan applications.

First, we must establish a plausible linear relationship between the variables. This can be done using a scatter diagram (as discussed earlier), or through the calculation of certain statistics that indicate the correlation between the two variables (we will discuss the correlation coefficient and the coefficient of determination later). Many computer programs are available that calculate these figures. The scatter diagram is useful as a screening device for problems with only two variables. Figure 17.13 shows the scatter diagram for the FS & L data. It is probably safe

Table 17.10 Loan Applications Compared to Bonus Amount

Employee Bonus (per 000/yr)	Mortgage Applications
15	6
22	11
19	7
25	11
14	8
18	10
30	13
21	9
29	16
27	15

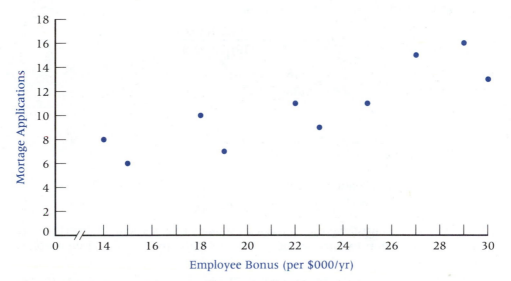

Figure 17.13 Scatter Diagram of Loan Application Data

to say that a linear relationship does exist. Using these figures, we will first do the regression analysis and will discuss some of the assumptions associated with the analysis. Recall the regression equation

$$Y' = a + bx$$

where

Y' = the dependent variable (loan applications)

b = slope of the line

a = y intercept

x = the independent variable (amount of bonus)

and the normal equations to find a and b:

$$b = \frac{\sum xY - n\bar{x}\bar{Y}}{\sum x^2 - n\bar{x}^2}$$

$$a = \bar{Y} - b\bar{x}$$

where

$\bar{x}$ = the average of the x values

$\bar{Y}$ = average of the Y values (Y = observed values)

$\sum xY$ = x times Y for each period, summed over all periods

$\sum x^2$ = x squared for each period, summed over all periods

n = number of periods used in the analysis

The calculations necessary to use the equations are shown in Table 17.11. Substituting in the normal equations for a and b

$$b = \frac{2480 - (10)(22)(10.6)}{5126 - (10)(22)(22)}$$

$$= \frac{148}{286}$$

$$= .5175$$

$$a = 10.6 - .5175(22)$$

$$= -.785$$

Thus the regression equation is

$$Y' = -.785 + .5175(x)$$

This equation, of course, represents the least squares line or the line of best fit. We can use this equation to forecast the number of loan applications, given a bonus amount.

Table 17.11 Tabulations for regression equation

x	Y	xY	x^2
15	6	90	225
22	11	242	484
19	7	133	361
25	11	275	625
14	8	112	196
18	10	180	324
30	13	390	900
21	9	189	441
29	16	464	841
27	15	405	729
$\sum$ = 220	106	2,480	5,126
n = 10			
Avg = 22	10.6	248	

We now return to the discussion of the underlying assumptions for simple linear regression.

Linear Regression Assumptions

1. The linear relationship between the variables is persistent and stable. Linear regression does not react to significant positive or negative changes in trend, i.e., the line does not change directions.
2. The average of all forecast errors is zero, and the variance (MSE) is constant. This can be true only when the errors are evenly distributed about the regression line. Recall that forecast errors are any deviations in the observed data from the regression line values, and are equal to the difference between the actual or observed points and the forecast results obtained using the regression equation.
3. The deviations from the line are independent of one another; that is the deviations are random. Thus no patterns should be apparent in the plotted data.
4. The deviations are normally distributed. If the values are concentrated close to the line, with a small proportion of larger deviations, this assumption is probably met. This, of course, implies that there are sufficient observations for a normal distribution (usually 20 or more in practice).
5. Predictions are being made only within the range of observed values.

While it is possible to fit a regression line to almost any set of data, unless these assumptions are met we cannot interpret the results intelligently and ensure forecast accuracy. In the next section, we will measure closeness of fit and the relationship between two variables.

Coefficient of Determination

The **coefficient of determination** can be used to measure the closeness of fit of the regression line. Before giving you the formula used most often for determining the coefficient, we want to explain briefly where the measure comes from. For a more complete discussion of this subject, we refer the reader to any good statistics text.

The closeness of fit can be measured by comparing unexplained differences between observed values Y and the forecasted values Y' (the sum of the squared deviations from the regression line Y − Y') to the total variations or differences, which are defined as the difference between the observed value and the mean of the observed value. That is, total variation is the sum of the squared differences between Y and $\overline{Y}$. This procedure compares the vertical dispersion of points around the regression line to the dispersion of points around the mean. If the vertical dispersion is smaller, then a better forecast can be obtained by using the regression line than merely using the average of the observed values. The ratio

$$\frac{\text{unexplained variation}}{\text{total variation}}$$

or

$$\frac{\sum (Y - Y')^2}{\sum (Y - \overline{Y})^2}$$

yields the percentage of variation that is *not* explained by the value of the independent variable. This unexplained variation can be the result of a variety of factors, including random fluctuations.

The coefficient of determination, r^2, is this percentage subtracted from 1. The value of r^2 can range from 0 to 1. The result is the precentage of variation that can be explained by changes in the independent variable, or the closeness of fit of the regression line.

$$r^2 = 1 - \frac{\sum (Y - Y')^2}{\sum (Y - \bar{Y})^2}$$

Having said all this, in order to explain what the coefficient of determination is, we now present a formula for r^2, which can be used with the same calculations that have been made and tabulated to determine the regression equation.

$$r^2 = \left[\frac{n\sum xY - \sum x \sum Y}{\sqrt{\left[n\left(\sum x^2\right) - \left(\sum x\right)^2\right]\left[n\sum Y^2 - \left(\sum Y\right)^2\right]}} \right]^2$$

Now let's use this with the home loan applications data available in Table 17.10. All necessary values are in this table except $\sum Y^2$, which is 1222.

$$r^2 = \left[\frac{(10)(2480) - (220)(106)}{\sqrt{[10(5126) - (220)(220)][(10)(1222) - (106)(106)]}} \right]^2$$

$$r^2 = \left[\frac{1480}{\sqrt{2,814,240}} \right]^2$$

$$r^2 = .778$$

For these data, the r^2 value means that 78 percent of the variation in loan applications (over the data range) can be explained by the amount of the announced bonus. The remaining 22 percent is due to unexplained factors, which could be random factors or the result of other variables. If r^2 were 1, it would indicate that 100 percent of the change in the dependent variable could be explained by the change in the independent variable. Having variation that is not explained by the independent variable ($r^2 < 1$) indicates that there will be some amount of forecast error when the regression equation is used. The fit is not perfect.

Correlation Coefficient

Correlation is a measure of the strength of the relationship between the independent variable and the dependent variable. In order for the forecast from a regression equation to be reliable, this relationship has to be relatively strong. The coefficient of correlation, used to measure this relationship, is the square root of r^2. That is, the formula is

$$r = \frac{n\sum xY - \sum x\sum Y}{\sqrt{\left[n\left(\sum x^2\right) - \left(\sum x\right)^2\right]\left[n\sum Y^2 - \left(\sum Y\right)^2\right]}}$$

Possible values for r vary from −1 to +1. The closer it is to −1 or +1, the stronger is the relationship between the dependent and independent variables, and more reliable is the regression equation (given a sufficient sample size). The sign of r is the sign of the regression coefficient b. If r is positive, it indicates that Y increases as x increases. If r is negative, it means that Y decreases as x increases. Thus the correlation coefficient not only measures the strength of the relationship between the variables, it also indicates the direction of the relationship. For our example, then,

$$r = .882$$

which might be an acceptable correlation. As the bonus amount increases, the loan applications also will increase.

Standard Error of the Estimate

The **standard error of the estimate,** like the coefficient of determination, is a measure of how well the regression line fits the data. If the dispersion of the data around the regression line is small, the standard error of the estimate will be small; if the dispersion is large, the standard error of the estimate will be large. The standard error of the estimate can be determined from the formula

$$s_e = \frac{\sum Y^2 - a\sum Y - b\sum xY}{\sqrt{n-2}}$$

where

n = the number of periods for which data exist

Note that all the figures needed to compute the standard error of the estimate have been calculated previously.

Multiple Regression

In the discussion of the coefficient of determination, we mentioned that the percentage of deviation or variation that could not be explained by the changes in the independent variable might be the result of another variable or variables that influenced the dependent variable. In other words, it is possible that the dependent variable might depend on two or more independent variables. The inclusion of additional variables might improve the forecast. In the FS & L loan application problem, it might well be that the number of applications is a function of the bonus amount and also other variables, such as interest rate and leading economic indicators. Regression analysis can easily be extended to handle more than one independent variable.

Multiple regression, the method that reflects the relationship between one dependent variable and a number of independent variables, is an extension of linear regression. The general form for the multiple regression equation is

$$Y' = \sum_{i=1}^{n} a + b_i x_i$$

where

> Y' = the dependent variable, i.e., the variable being forecast
>
> b_i = slope of the line for each independent variable (also called regression coefficient)
>
> a = Y intercept
>
> x_i = the independent variables

If the FS & L loan application problem had two independent variables, such as bonus amount and interest rate, we would have

$$Y' = a + b_1 x_1 + b_2 x_2$$

where

> Y' = the number of loan applications
>
> x_1 = bonus amount
>
> x_2 = interest rate
>
> b_1, b_2 = regression coefficient for x_1 and x_2 respectively
>
> a = Y intercept

There is one additional underlying assumption. In order for the results of multiple regression to be valid, it is assumed that the independent variables are not correlated with one another. Thus the changes in the dependent variable Y caused by changes in one independent variable, x_1, and the changes in Y caused by changes in another independent variable, x_2, are not related.

As variables are added, regression analysis becomes much more complex. As the computations become more complicated and difficult, the computer becomes the only viable means for developing the regression coefficients. With the widespread availability of specialized computer programs, the computational difficulty is no longer a major problem or obstacle to the use of multiple regression. In addition to the problem of computational complexity, multiple regression has an additional difficulty: the amount of data required can be huge, and data gathering can be a real problem. In this introductory text, we cannot present a thorough discussion of multiple regression.

In our discussion of causal models thus far, we have indicated that regression models are generally sophisticated models, requiring extensive data in order to obtain meaningful relationships. Regression models give good to excellent short- and medium-range forecasts at a reasonably low cost. Increased availability of computer programs makes regression analysis a viable forecast tool for most organizations. In practice, regression techniques are among the most used quantitative techniques. The econometric model, a system of interdependent regression equations that describe an economic system, is another of the more common causal models. While it can provide superior forecasts, the data requirements are the same as for regression analysis, and it is much more complex and costly. We mention it here to emphasize once again that we are merely scratching the surface of a very large and important topic.

17.5 *FORECASTING AND THE COMPUTER*

In our discussion of the various forecasting techniques, we have demonstrated manual solutions. We have done so in order to give you a better understanding of each technique. In order to select a model for a specific situation, it is essential to know the usefulness, data requirements, cost, time requirements, and limitations of the various models. In practice, however, computer solutions have largely replaced manual solutions.

The computer is an extremely important tool in the forecasting procedure, both in the selection or derivation of the model and in performing the mathematical computations necessary for the forecast. Although the computations are not difficult, as the amount of data increases the calculations can become tedious, time-consuming, and cumbersome. For the more sophisticated causal models, like multiple regression and econometric models, the computations are so complex that the computer offers the only practical solution procedure. As the number of forecasting programs available has increased and the cost has decreased, more businesses are using sophisticated forecasting techniques.

There are a large number of forecasting programs available, including programs that are part of computer libraries; special-purpose programs from vendors; off-the-shelf, multipurpose programs that perform certain techniques such as regression; and preprogrammed functions. Among the most widely used packages are BMDP (Biomedical Computer Programs), SAS (Statistical Analysis System), Minitab, and SPSS (Statistical Package for Social Sciences). Most colleges and organizations have access to one of these. Among the larger, more sophisticated packages are General Electric's Time Series Forecasting programs (Fcst1 and Fcst2, used for projecting linear trends over time and for exponential smoothing) and IBM's Consumer Goods System, COGS, and IMPACT, which are oriented specifically to manufacturing and distribution systems. Many of these packages are also available in PC versions. In addition, there are a variety of teaching packages available for colleges and universities, as well as in-house programs available within departments and firms.

Obviously, the programs vary greatly not only in features, size restrictions, and data input and output, but also in the size of the computer required, cost, and time involved. For example, some multiple regression programs check for the underlying assumption that independent variables are not correlated with one another. It is necessary to be aware of the features that a program provides. The following examples illustrate computer solutions, using the D&D software that accompanies this text.

The first example, shown in Figure 17.14, demonstrates the use of trend adjusted exponential smoothing ($\alpha = .3$ and $\beta = .2$) to forecast sales for the next month. Figure 17.15 shows the results when the search option is used to find the best forecast.

The second example, shown in Figure 17.16, shows a simple linear regression that forecasts snowblower sales as a function of predicted snowfall (x = predicted snowfall, Y = snowblower sales). The output gives the regression equation, r and r^2 values, and the trend line points.

```
CALCULATION RESULTS:

ALPHA = .3          BETA = .2

                                                ADJUSTED
PERIOD   ACTUAL   FORECAST   ERROR    TREND    FORECAST    ERROR
------   ------   --------   -----    -----    --------    ------
  1       70.00     70.00     0.000    0.000     70.00       0.00
  2       68.00     70.00    -2.000    0.000     70.00      -2.00
  3       78.00     69.40     8.600   -0.120     68.92       9.08
  4       84.00     71.98    12.020    0.420     73.66      10.34
  5      102.00     75.59    26.414    1.057     79.81      22.19
  6      112.00     83.51    28.490    2.431     93.23      18.77
  7       90.00     92.06    -2.057    3.654    106.67     -16.67
  8       98.00     91.44     6.560    2.800    102.64      -4.64
  9       95.00     93.41     1.592    2.633    103.94      -8.94
 10      100.00     93.89     6.114    2.202    102.69      -2.69
 11      110.00     95.72    14.280    2.129    104.23       5.77
 12      128.00    100.00    27.996    2.560    110.24      17.76
 13      132.00    108.40    23.597    3.728    123.31       8.69
 14      120.00    115.48     4.518    4.398    133.07     -13.07
 15      115.00    116.84    -1.837    3.789    131.99     -16.99
 16      125.00    116.29     8.714    2.921    127.97      -2.97
 17      120.00    118.90     1.100    2.860    130.34     -10.34
 18      100.00    119.23   -19.230    2.354    128.65     -28.65
 19      118.00    113.46     4.539    0.729    116.38       1.62
 20      128.00    114.82    13.177    0.856    118.25       9.75
 21                 118.78              1.475    124.68

        MSE          =      201.425                      167.115
        MAD          =       10.642                       10.547
        TRACKING SIGNAL =    15.278                       -0.286

FORECAST FOR PERIOD 21 = 118.78   ADJUSTED FORECAST = 124.68
```

Figure 17.14 D&D Trend Adjusted Exponential Smoothing

```
SEARCH OPTION:

CALCULATION RESULTS:

ALPHA = .9          BETA = .9

                                                ADJUSTED
PERIOD   ACTUAL   FORECAST   ERROR    TREND    FORECAST    ERROR
------   ------   --------   -----    -----    --------    ------
  1       70.00     70.00     0.000    0.000     70.00       0.00
  2       68.00     70.00    -2.000    0.000     70.00      -2.00
  3       78.00     68.20     9.800   -1.620     68.02       9.98
  4       84.00     77.02     6.980    7.776     77.88       6.12
  5      102.00     83.30    18.698    6.431     84.02      17.98
  6      112.00    100.13    11.870   15.789    101.88      10.12
  7       90.00    110.81   -20.813   11.193    112.06     -22.06
  8       98.00     92.08     5.919  -15.739     90.33       7.67
```

9	95.00	97.41	−2.408	3.220	97.77	−2.77
10	100.00	95.24	4.759	−1.629	95.06	4.94
11	110.00	99.52	10.476	3.692	99.93	10.07
12	128.00	108.95	19.048	8.855	109.94	18.06
13	132.00	126.10	5.905	16.314	127.91	4.09
14	120.00	131.41	−11.410	6.414	132.12	−12.12
15	115.00	121.14	−6.141	−8.600	120.19	−5.19
16	125.00	115.61	9.386	−5.834	114.97	10.03
17	120.00	124.06	−4.061	7.019	124.84	−4.84
18	100.00	120.41	−20.406	−2.588	120.12	−20.12
19	118.00	102.04	15.959	−16.788	100.18	17.82
20	128.00	116.40	11.596	11.248	117.65	10.35
21		126.84		10.518	128.01	

MSE	=	136.070		135.796
MAD	=	9.882		9.816
TRACKING SIGNAL =		6.391		5.933

Figure 17.15 D&D Search Option To Find Best Forecast

OUTPUT SUMMARY:

X	Y	X * Y	X^2	Y^2
85.00	10.00	850.00	7,225.00	100.00
125.00	24.00	3,000.00	15,625.00	576.00
130.00	24.00	3,120.00	16,900.00	576.00
90.00	16.00	1,440.00	8,100.00	256.00
75.00	10.00	750.00	5,625.00	100.00
90.00	18.00	1,620.00	8,100.00	324.00
80.00	16.00	1,280.00	6,400.00	256.00
140.00	30.00	4,200.00	19,600.00	900.00
135.00	26.00	3,510.00	18,225.00	676.00
120.00	22.00	2,640.00	14,400.00	484.00
100.00	20.00	2,000.00	10,000.00	400.00
95.00	17.00	1,615.00	9,025.00	289.00
100.00	21.00	2,100.00	10,000.00	441.00
1,365.00	254.00	28,125.00	149,225.00	5,378.00

THE REGRESSION EQUATION IS:

$$Y = -6.356 + .247 X$$

STANDARD ERROR OF THE ESTIMATE, S(e):

$$S(e) = 2.265$$

CORRELATION COEFFICIENT, R:

$$R = .93 \qquad (R^2 = .864)$$

```
      X            Y'
  ----------   ----------
     85.00        14.606
    125.00        24.471
    130.00        25.704
     90.00        15.839
     75.00        12.140
     90.00        15.839
     80.00        13.373
    140.00        28.170
    135.00        26.937
    120.00        23.238
    100.00        18.305
     95.00        17.072
    100.00        18.305
```

Figure 17.16 Regression Analysis Using D&D

Focus on Decision Making

Superstar Video is an independently owned video rental franchise operation, with several hundred outlets across the eastern United States. Because viewer preferences vary slightly with geographic location, each location is responsible for placing its own orders for both rental and sale videos. Seventy percent of the store's income is derived from rentals. The remainder comes from sales of new and used videos, blank tapes, and other video accessories. Purchase of movies for rental purposes is based upon a fairly standard formula calculated by Superstar Video franchise headquarters. Local owners can modify these figures if they wish.

Classic movies, recent releases that did not do well at the box office, and made-for-TV specials are usually sold as special-order items. Superstar purchases new releases of hit movies in quantity for sale. Demand for these movies is usually of short duration; customers will not wait for a special order on these movies, since they can go to other outlets to purchase them. The stores make a large proportion of sales of blockbuster hits on a pre-order basis prior to the actual release of the video. Each store generally purchases some additional copies to sell to customers who chose not to pre-order. Other movies, not sold on a preorder basis, are purchased in quantities determined by the local store owner.

Susan McVee, new owner of the Harrisburg franchise, is currently attempting to develop a method of forecasting sales of new releases. The previous owner based his purchases solely upon the amount the movie grossed at the box office. While there was clearly a relationship between these figures, Susan felt that she could make better forecasts.

Data Preparation/Problem Formulation

Over the past quarter, Susan has gathered relevant data on the movies ordered for sale. She feels that video sales are related not only to box office gross, but also to the ratings given the movie by the local movie critics and the amount of pre-release advertising in Superstar Video's monthly news magazine, which is mailed to all Superstar members. The local critics rate movies on a scale of 1 to 4, with 4 being the top rating. Pre-release advertising can be classified as full page, half page, or no advertisement in the month prior to a video's release. Susan recorded these in terms of the number of half pages devoted to a video: 0, 1, or 2. The following table shows the data she gathered on the 16 movies ordered over the past quarter.

Box Office Gross (000's)	Critic Rating	Advertising Half pages	Units Sold
42,000	3	2	280
19,000	1	0	120
25,100	1	0	145
44,800	4	2	295
22,600	1	0	135
14,000	2	1	140
37,900	4	2	215
49,500	4	2	310
22,300	3	1	160
28,300	2	1	180
27,400	2	1	230
24,600	2	0	130
39,000	3	2	255
16,400	1	0	110
29,700	4	2	300
33,100	2	1	210

Susan decided to use simple and multiple regression analysis to test the relationships among the data.

Computer Solution

Susan first ran a simple regression, with sales as the dependent variable and box office gross as the independent variable. She obtained the following results:

```
Gross    Regression Output:
Constant                      26.52396
Std Err of Y Est              35.63309
R Squared                     0.759818
No. of Observations                 16
Degrees of Freedom                  14

X Coefficient(s)  0.005866
Std Err of Coef.  0.000881
```

She then used multiple regression analysis with the following groupings of independent variables: (1) box office gross and critical ratings; (2) box office gross and advertising half pages; (3) critical ratings and advertising half pages; and (4) box office gross, critical ratings, and advertising half pages. The following table summarizes the standard error of the estimate for each set of independent variables she used.

Independent Variables Included	Standard Error of the Estimate
box office gross critic rating	30.516
box office gross advertising half pages	25.625
critic rating advertising half pages	32.100
box office gross critic rating advertising half pages	26.657

The complete output for the multiple regression resulting in the smallest standard error of the estimate (the one using box office gross and advertising half pages as independent variables) is shown below.

```
Total    Regression Output:
Constant                    67.03217
Std Err of Y Est            25.62543
R Squared                   0.884657
No. of Observations               16
Degrees of Freedom                13

X Coefficient(s)  0.002813  47.29744
Std Err of Coef.  0.001031  12.60916
```

Interpretation and Analysis of the Results

Based upon these results, Susan felt she had a fairly reliable forecasting tool. The equation

$$\text{Sales} = 67.0 + .0028X_1 + 47.2974X_2$$

where:

X_1 = box office gross in thousands of dollars

X_2 = half pages of advertising in Superstar Newsletter

gave results with a standard error of estimate of 25.6 and an r squared of 0.885. While she felt more comfortable with this formula, she felt there was still a higher degree of error than she would prefer. Using this formula to forecast past sales, she discovered that in one case she would have purchased 53 too many videos and in another, 55 too few.

What Happens Next

While Susan recognizes that there is probably no perfect forecasting tool, she still wants to improve her accuracy. She has decided, therefore, to begin collecting data on other factors as well. Additional factors she is considering include movie ratings (R, PG, etc.), nominations and awards, and discount coupons. While all of these movies

17.6 *CONCLUDING REMARKS*

Forecasts are an important part of the decision making process, helping managers anticipate and plan for the future by reducing uncertainty and providing some decision making guidelines. As indicated in the surveys shown in Chapter 1, forecasting techniques are among the most widely used quantitative techniques. All firms forecast in some way or another. Yet, no technique can provide totally accurate predictions of the future; they all have some degree of inaccuracy. Furthermore, each technique works best under a particular set of circumstances. Choosing the best technique for a situation—or building the model that represents the situation—involves selecting a technique that will serve its intended purpose at an acceptable level of accuracy and cost. Forecasting techniques range from very simple to extremely complex. The manager has to know what the technique can and cannot accomplish. Moreover, it is important to note that, while the forecasting technique provides a prediction of the future, the forecast is only a tool to be used as part of the decision making process. Part of the decision is approval of the forecast. That is, the manager must decide whether to accept the forecast, or to devote more resources to obtaining a better forecast. Ultimately, the decision maker makes the decision, usually based on a number of sources of information, both subjective and objective.

Management Science Application ─────────────────────────────

POLISHING THE BIG APPLE[1]

The New York City Department of Sanitation employs over 10,000 people and has a budget of approximately one-half billion dollars. One of the department's duties involves cleaning the city's streets. During the late 1970's, the city experienced a rapid deterioration in the cleanliness of its streets as measured by Scorecard, a street cleanliness rating system. In 1980, this rating reached an all-time low score of 53 percent. This low rating created several problems for the Department of Sanitation: (1) the command staff placed little confidence in Scorecard results due to a natural bureaucratic aversion to being measured and a lack of understanding of the system; (2) morale in the

[1] Reprinted by permission of Lucius J. Riccio, Joseph Miller and Ann Litke, "Polishing the Big Apple: How Management Science Has Helped Make New York City Streets Cleaner," *Interfaces,* Volume 16, Number 1 (January–February, 1986): 83–88. Copyright (1986), The Institute of Management Sciences.

department was lowered; (3) the department had no knowledge base to explain the relationship between the use of department resources and the cleanliness levels; (4) there was no coordination with other city agencies; and (5) the city council rejected a proposal to expand the cleaning force citing a lack of confidence in the department's ability to manage the additional resources to achieve a sufficient payoff for the public.

In 1981, in an attempt to remedy these problems, the department began to analyze the street cleaning problem from a management science perspective. Fortunately, extensive data were available. The city had monthly Scorecard ratings for each of the city's 59 community districts. It also had detailed records of the use of manpower, the status of mechanical equipment, the percentage of collection loads not picked up, and the weather conditions. Using this data, the department built regression models which clearly proved the relationship between manpower and cleanliness levels. Using the regression models and the worker-to-Scorecard ratios, the department could make projections for individual districts and use those projections for performance evaluation systems and for budget proposals.

The department also discovered that some districts had a much better payoff for manpower allocations than others. For example, the analysis showed that five times as many cleaners were required to raise the Wall Street area rating one percentage point as were required for a district in Staten Island. Given the department's ability to clearly demonstrate these relationships, its credibility rose and it was able to justify additional manpower. Scorecard ratings increased as predicted.

The department also used parametric models to determine why cleaners were more effective in some areas than others. In some areas, cleaners picked up much more litter, but achieved lower ratings. This seemed counter intuitive. The models showed a strong relationship between ratings and the litter rate for a particular area. It wasn't that the cleaners were doing a bad job; the streets simply didn't stay clean. The department found that by altering the time between cleanings based upon the litter rate for a given area, it could attain higher ratings.

Finally, a Monte Carlo simulation model was developed to predict the relationship between ratings and illegally parked cars on the streets being cleaned. This simulation showed that sometimes one less car parked illegally could increase the probability of receiving an acceptable rating by 20 percent or more. Using this information, the department was able to obtain cooperation from the Department of Transportation. The Department of Transportation now coordinates its ticketing program with the Department of Sanitation, helping the cleaners to improve their efficiency.

Once a valid relationship was established between the Scorecard ratings and departmental efforts, the department also structured an employee recognition program based upon Scorecard ratings. Districts were grouped into eleven administrative zones. Employees in the district which achieved the greatest increase in ratings were given free tickets to a New York sporting event (Knicks, Rangers, etc.). Three employees were also drawn randomly from the district with the greatest citywide improvement and given an all-expense-paid trip to the Super Bowl (using outside funding).

The results of the departments efforts are an ability to predict Scorecard ratings with a high degree of accuracy and an increased department credibility. Cleanliness ratings are near record levels, but are being achieved with 700 fewer cleaners. The department estimates a savings of approximately $12 million in annual recurring costs.

GLOSSARY

adjusted exponential smoothing time series forecasting method that uses a smoothing constant, β, to adjust an exponentially smoothed forecast for changes in trend

causal forecasting techniques forecasting methods that try to establish a functional relationship between the variable to be forecast and one or more independent or predictor variables

coefficient of determination r^2, measures the strength of the relationship of the variables in the regression equation, i.e., measures "closeness of fit"

correlation coefficient r, measures the strength and direction of relationship between the dependent and independent variables, with values in the range -1 to $+1$

cyclical variation C, long-term variation around the trend line

Delphi method qualitative forecasting technique that develops a forecast by eliciting opinions from a group of experts through a series of questionnaires, eliminating problem of group dynamics

decomposition of a time series time series forecasting technique that breaks a time series into its component parts (trend, seasonal, cyclic, random) and then recombines them in order to forecast

econometric forecasting technique a sophisticated causal technique that uses a series of interdependent equations to describe an economic system

exponential smoothing a moving-averages forecasting technique that uses only a single weight factor, a smoothing constant α; recent data are weighted more heavily, and weighting declines exponentially as data age

forecast error the difference between the actual observed values or data points and the forecast values $(A_t - F_t)$

grass roots forecasting a qualitative forecasting technique that relies on "going to the source," using those people closest to the problem to make forecasts; the individual forecasts are then added together to get a forecast

least squares method method of fitting a line (curve) to a set of data so that the sum of squares of the deviations between observed values and calculated values on the line is minimized; a method of deriving a function that best fits a set of data

market research a group of qualitative marketing techniques using such techniques as customer surveys and personal interviews, to consult the consumer; highly sophisticated statistical procedures use these responses to make a forecast; probably the most expensive, most time-consuming, most quantitative, and most accurate qualitative technique

MAD (mean absolute deviation) a measure of forecast error, computed as the average absolute deviation; MAD weights all deviations evenly, $MAD = (\Sigma|A - F|)/n$

MSE (mean squared error) a measure of forecast error that is the average of the squared errors; MSE weights deviations according to their squared value, $MSE = \Sigma(A - F)^2/n$

moving average time series forecasting method using averages calculated from a fixed number of most recent observations

panel consensus qualitative forecasting technique using an assembled group of experts to reach a forecast agreement

qualitative forecast subjective forecast based upon judgement, experience, expert opinion

quantitative forecast forecast based on the analysis of hard data, either historical observation or arrived at from experimentation

random unpredictable variation in a time series, occurring by chance

regression analysis statistical technique for measuring the relationship of one variable to one or more other variables

scatter diagram plot of the dependent variable to be forecast against a single predictor or independent variable

seasonal variation variation or movement in a time series that occurs periodically and is repetitive

standard error of the estimate measures the scatter of the data around the regression line as a measure of accuracy of the regression line

time series forecasting quantitative forecasting technique that assumes the past is a good predictor of the future and time is the only relevant factor; uses observed historical data to extrapolate future data

tracking signal measure used to control forecasts; identifies forecasts that are not keeping pace with trend

trend long-term behavior of the item being forecast

trend projection time series forecasting method, using least squares method to fit a function in which time is the independent variable

weighted moving average time series forecasting technique that calculates averages by assigning weights, with most recent data usually being weighted more heavily

PROBLEMS

The data in the following three tables, I, II, and III, will be used in questions 1 through 11.

TABLE I		TABLE II		TABLE III	
Wk	Amount	Month	Amount	Yr.	Amount
1	26	Jan	1700	79	35,560
2	30	Feb	1760	80	40,100
3	54	Mar	1860	81	38,900
4	26	Apr	1540	82	43,200
5	32	May	1740	83	46,700
6	42	Jun	1500	84	45,000
7	38	Jly	1640	85	45,800
8	28	Aug	1520	86	46,300
9	40	Sep	1500	87	44,500
10	44	Oct	1840	88	46,000
11	50	Nov	1700		
12	58				
13	32				

TABLE I		TABLE II		TABLE III	
Wk	Amount	Month	Amount	Yr.	Amount
14	36				
15	32				
16	40				
17	40				
18	36				

1. **a.** Using the weekly data in Table I, compute a three-period moving average forecast for periods 4–19.
   b. Plot the actual values and the forecasts graphically, and compare them.

2. What is the difference in the forecast for period 19 if you use a six-period moving average? Plot these forecast values on the graph from problem 1 and compare the results.

3. **a.** Using a three-period moving average and the data in Table II, forecast monthly demand for December.
   b. Use a five-period moving average to forecast demand for December.
   c. Plot the actual demand and the three-period and five-period moving average forecast values and compare the graphs.

4. Determine the MAD for the three-period moving average and the five-period moving average in problem 3. What does this information suggest?

5. Determine the MSE for the three-period and the five-period moving averages in problem 3. What does this information suggest? How does this compare with your answer for problem 4? Explain.

6. For the weekly sales figures in Table I, calculate the three-period weighted moving average using weights of .2, .3, and .5 from oldest to most recent week. How does the forecast for week 19 compare to the three-period simple moving average calculated in problem 1? Which method do you think works better with these data? Why?

7. **a.** For the monthly data in Table II, compute a weighted four-period moving average using weights of .1, .2, .3, and .4 from oldest to most recent respectively. What is the forecast for December with this weighting scheme?
   b. Compare this with the results using weights of .4, .3, .2, and .1 from oldest to most recent.

8. Determine the MAD for each weighting scheme in problem 7. What can you conclude?

9. **a.** For the annual attendance figures shown in Table III, compute an exponentially smoothed forecast for year 11 using an alpha of .2. Use 35,560 as the initial forecast.
   b. Try an alpha of .4 and compare the results.

10. **a.** Plot the annual data used in problem 9. Is there a recognizable trend? Compute a trend adjusted exponentially smoothed forecast for year 11, using an alpha of .2 and a beta of .1. Use an initial trend of 0. How does this forecast compare to the forecast obtained in problem 9a?
    b. What happens if you use an alpha of .2 and a beta of .5?
    c. Use the search option in the D&D software to find the best alpha and beta.

11. Compare the MAD determined with the best alpha and beta in problem 10 to the MAD computed using alpha = .2 and beta = .1.

12. The monthly annual tonnage carried by Leo's Cartage Company for the years 1977–1986 have been recorded as follows:

Year	Tons
1977	5500
1978	5400
1979	5700
1980	6200
1981	6400
1982	6500
1983	6300
1984	6400
1985	6300
1986	6200

In attempting to forecast tonnage for 1987, Leo wants to compare forecasts using moving average and exponentially smoothed forecasts.

a. Compute a three-period moving average for 1980–1987. What is the MSE?

b. Compute an exponentially smoothed forecast for the years 1980–1987. Use an alpha of .35 and 5500 for the initial forecast. What is the MSE?

c. Plot the raw data, the moving averages, and the exponentially smoothed values on the same graph and compare.

13. a. Using the data from problem 12 forecast again, using trend adjusted exponential smoothing with an alpha of .4 and a beta of .4. Use 0 for the initial trend. What is the MSE?

b. Use the search procedure to find the best alpha and beta.

14. a. It has been suggested that Leo (problem 12) might obtain a better forecast with linear trend projection using least squares regression. Find the forecast for 1987 using least squares regression.

b. What is the coefficient of determination for this line? Do you consider it a good fit?

c. Is regression a good method for these data? Why or why not?

15. Draw a scatter diagram for the following data:

X	Y
1	26
2	30
3	27
4	31
5	35
6	32
7	33
8	36
9	38
10	36
11	39
12	44

Fit a line by eye to these data. Use the method of least squares regression to find the regression equation for the data. Use the equation to forecast for period 13. Plot the forecast values on the same graph.

16. Develop a liner regression equation to predict demand in the next period from the following data:

Year	1980	81	82	83	84	85	86	87
Demand	268	272	293	284	287	290	300	296

   a. What is the regression equation and the forecast for 1988?
   b. What is the standard error of estimate and the correlation coefficient?

17. Sounds Great, Inc. has recorded the following monthly sales figures for compact disc players over a two-year period:

	1986	1987
Jan	16	30
Feb	15	28
Mar	20	32
Apr	20	35
May	19	34
June	18	39
July	22	39
Aug	24	40
Sept	23	40
Oct	28	38
Nov	35	48
Dec	40	60

Forecast sales for January 1988 using:

   a. Linear trend projection using least squares regression.
   b. Exponential smoothing using an alpha of .25 and an initial forecast of 16 for January 1986.
   c. Trend adjusted exponential smoothing with an alpha of .25 and a beta of .15 (use 0 for initial trend).
   d. Trend adjusted exponential smoothing using the D&D search for best alpha and beta.

   Which method would you use?

Note: The following questions (18-22) require information covered in the appendix to this chapter.

18. a. Determine the linear trend equation and seasonals for the following quarterly data:

Qtr:	1	2	3	4	5	6	7	8	9	10	11	12	13	14
Sales:	25	40	45	30	28	42	46	33	30	43	49	35	34	45

   b. Plot the data.
   c. Plot the regression line for the data.
   d. Calculate the seasonal relatives for this data.
   e. Forecast sales for period 15 using the seasonal index.

19. What is the correlation coefficient for the trend line in problem 18c? If the sales figures in problem 18 are deseasonalized by dividing the actual figures by the seasonal relatives, what is the correlation coefficient for this deseasonalized data?

20. Using the data from problem 18, determine the seasonals using a centered moving average.
21. Use the seasonal relatives determined in problem 20 to deseasonalize the time series data in problem 18. Plot these new values. Use least squares regression on these data to identify the trend. Forecast sales for period 15 using this regression equation and the seasonal relative for that quarter.
22. What is the coefficient of determination for this trend line (problem 21)? Can you recommend which forecast to use for period 15?
23. Compare the seasonal relatives obtained in problem 18d with those calculated in problem 20.

APPENDIX: TIME SERIES FORECASTING USING DECOMPOSITION

Classical **decomposition** isolates and measures the various components of the time series, identified previously as trend (T), seasonality (S), cyclical variations (C), and random or irregular variations (R). That is, the effect of each component is studied separately. The components are then recombined into a model that describes the behavior of the series. The purpose of this kind of time series analysis is to build a model that is used to forecast. There are two basic models, additive and multiplicative, used to describe how these components are combined. Our discussion will be limited to the multiplicative model. However, we will note that, in the additive approach, each component is an actual amount, and the series is the sum of the components:

$$Y = T + S + C + R$$

In the multiplicative model, only T is an actual amount. The seasonal, cyclical, and random components are all measured in relative terms (usually a percentage of trend). The series is the product of the components:

$$Y = T \times S \times C \times R$$

For example, if there were a trend projection of 250 units, a seasonal factor of 1.10, a cyclical factor of .90, and a random factor of 1.03, then the forecast value would be

$$Y = 250 \,(1.10)(.90)(1.03) = 254.925$$

In this Appendix we present two methods for identifying trend and seasonality.

Multiplicative Model using Linear Trend Projection

The first step in decomposing the time series is to identify the trend. This is simply the trend line which has been projected using least squares regression to find the line of best fit.

Identifying Trend
Consider the quarterly sales data for Al's Previously Owned Sport Cars, shown in Table 17.12 and Figure 17.17. Al wishes to forecast sales for the remainder of 1990. Figure 17.18 shows the computational values and the regression equation for these data. Using the equation, Al would forecast third-quarter 1990 sales of 22.154. Fig-

Table 17.12 Quarterly Sport Car Sales

Year	Period	Quarter	Cars Sold
1987	1	1	6
	2	2	14
	3	3	20
	4	4	10
1988	5	1	14
	6	2	18
	7	3	28
	8	4	14
1989	9	1	15
	10	2	21
	11	3	30
	12	4	15
1990	13	1	13
	14	2	22

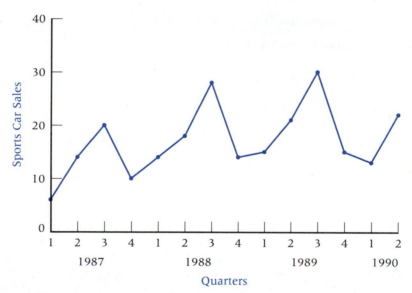

Figure 17.17 Graph of Quarterly Sport Car Sales

ure 17.19, shows the plot of the forecasted data. However, when we compare this figure with Figure 17.17, we can see that actual sport car sales tend to be seasonal. Therefore, Al must determine the effects of seasonality before he can make his forecast.

Determining the Seasonal Relative Components

The seasonal relatives indicate the extent of deviation from the trend line because of seasonal variations. There is one relative for each season. Thus, there are 12 relatives for monthly data and four relatives for quarterly data. Al has quarterly sales figures. Assuming that the series consists only of a linear trend with seasonal and random components (no cyclic element), this series can be represented as Y =

```
OUTPUT SUMMARY:

     X            Y          X * Y          X^2           Y^2
  --------     --------    ----------    ----------    ----------
     1.00         6.00         6.00          1.00         36.00
     2.00        14.00        28.00          4.00        196.00
     3.00        20.00        60.00          9.00        400.00
     4.00        10.00        40.00         16.00        100.00
     5.00        14.00        70.00         25.00        196.00
     6.00        18.00       108.00         36.00        324.00
     7.00        28.00       196.00         49.00        784.00
     8.00        14.00       112.00         64.00        196.00
     9.00        15.00       135.00         81.00        225.00
    10.00        21.00       210.00        100.00        441.00
    11.00        30.00       330.00        121.00        900.00
    12.00        15.00       180.00        144.00        225.00
    13.00        13.00       169.00        169.00        169.00
    14.00        22.00       308.00        196.00        484.00
  --------     --------    ----------    ----------    ----------
   105.00       240.00     1,952.00      1,015.00      4,676.00

              Press any key to continue.

THE REGRESSION EQUATION IS:

   Y = 12.132 + .668 X
```

Figure 17.18 Output Showing Regression Computations and Regression Equation

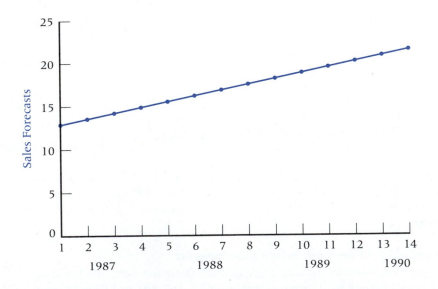

Figure 17.19 Graph of Forecasted Values

$T \times S \times R$. We can remove the trend component by dividing both sides of the equation by T:

$$Y = T \times S \times R$$

$$\frac{Y}{T} = \frac{T \times S \times R}{T}$$

$$\frac{Y}{T} = S \times R$$

This operation produces a series made up entirely of seasonality and random variations. Consider the data in Table 17.13, which shows the actual data for the sport car sales (Y) and the forecast values (Y' or trend). The seasonal/random component ($S \times R$) for each period can be determined by dividing the actual by the trend. For example, for the first quarter in 1987 (period 1), Y = 6 and Y' = 12.8. Since trend (T) is represented by the forecast value (Y'), we calculate $S \times R$ as

$$\frac{Y}{T} = S \times R$$

$$\frac{6}{12.8} = .469$$

The final column in Table 17.13 shows these calculations. Note that there are 14 calculated ($S \times R$) values. However, there can be only one seasonal relative value for each like period (quarter). The fluctuations in the like period seasonal/random values can be attributed to the random component. To remove some of this random factor and obtain an estimate of the seasonal relative for each quarter, we must average the $S \times R$ figures for all like periods. Grouping the $S \times R$ values by like periods and averaging them yields the seasonal relatives for each like period. For Al's sales data this yields

		Quarter		
	First	Second	Third	Fourth
	.469	1.040	1.415	.676
	.905	1.115	1.663	.801
	.827	1.116	1.540	.745
	.625	1.024		
$S \times R$ =	.7065	1.0738	1.5393	.7407

The multiplicative model requires that the average seasonal factor equal 1. Therefore, the sum of the factors for four quarters must equal 4 and the sum for 12 months must equal 12. It is sometimes necessary to make another adjustment when determining seasonal factors. Since the sum of the seasonal relatives in this problem is 4.053 (probably because of rounding), we must adjust the seasonals by multiplying each one by $^{4.00}/_{4.053}$. Thus the adjusted seasonal relatives are as follows:

$$\text{Quarter } 1 = .6972 = 70\%$$

$$\text{Quarter } 2 = 1.0597 = 105\%$$

Table 17.13 Computation of the seasonal x random (S × R)

Period	Actual (Data)	Forecast (Trend)	Data/trend
1	6	12.800	0.469
2	14	13.468	1.040
3	20	14.136	1.415
4	10	14.804	0.676
5	14	15.473	0.905
6	18	16.141	1.115
7	28	16.809	1.663
8	14	17.477	0.801
9	15	18.145	0.827
10	21	18.813	1.116
11	30	19.481	1.540
12	15	20.149	0.745
13	13	20.818	0.625
14	22	21.486	1.024

$$\text{Quarter 3} = 1.5191 = 152\%$$

$$\text{Quarter 4} = .7310 = 73\%$$

These figures indicate that, for the first and fourth quarters of each year, sales are below the average or trend line by approximately 30 percent and 27 percent respectively. The third quarter, with sales at 152 percent of the trend value, appears to be the best quarter for sales of sports cars.

These seasonal relatives and the projected trend line can be used to forecast sales in the future. First we use the regression equation

$$Y' = 12.132 + .668x$$

to forecast sales for periods 15 and 16:

$$\text{Period 15} \quad Y' = 12.132 + .668(15) = 22.154$$

$$\text{Period 16} \quad Y' = 12.132 + .668(16) = 22.822$$

Next, we adjust the forecast for seasonality. The adjusted forecast equals the trend (Y') multiplied by the seasonal relative (S):

$$Y = T \times S = Y' \times S$$

Period 15 is a third quarter; period 16 is a fourth quarter. Thus, Al's seasonally adjusted sales forecasts are

$$\text{Forecast for Period 15} = 22.154 (1.52) = 33.67$$

$$\text{Forecast for Period 16} = 22.822 (.73) = 16.66$$

Recall that we assumed the absence of cycles for these calculations. If cycles were in fact present, the computation of the seasonal relatives would obviously be distorted. In the next section, we describe the centered moving average method for determining seasonal relatives, which handles the cyclic component better. Furthermore, the centered moving average method can handle changes in trend. Linear projection of the trend line using least squares regression is unable to compensate for changes in trend.

Using Centered Moving Average to Eliminate Trend

Recall that, in our discussion of moving average, we used the average of a certain number of periods (n) to project or forecast the next period. A centered moving average is positioned in the middle of the data used to compute the average. For example, with a three-period moving average, the average is positioned at period 2. For a five-period moving average, the average of the five values is positioned at period 3. It is not a projection for the next period, but rather an average of the series or season, positioned in the center. Table 17.14 illustrates this. Note that the first period for which there can be a centered moving average is period 2, centered between 1 and 3.

$$\frac{25 + 30 + 50}{3} = 35$$

Since it is a moving average, we drop the first period and add the next to give

$$\frac{30 + 50 + 30}{3} = 36.7$$

There can be no average positioned at period 6 because there is no value following it; that is, 6 is not in the center of any periods. The same it true of the five-period moving average. In Table 17.14 the periods for which no average is given are not in the middle period of a five-period series. Only period 3 fits this requirement. However, there is a computational problem with centered moving averages that use an even number of periods. There is no middle period where the average can be positioned. For example, the middle period in a four-period moving average is somewhere between periods 2 and 3. This has important computational ramifications, since to find seasonal relatives, the moving average must be divided into the original value next to which it is positioned. This difficulty can be overcome by an additional computation, taking a centered two-period moving average of the original even-period moving average. Table 17.15 illustrates this for a four-period moving average. In order to remove trend from the time series using a centered moving average, the length of the period must equal the length of the season.

Using these centered moving average figures for the trend and cyclic components, the seasonal relatives can be found using the equation

$$Y = T \times C \times S \times R$$

$$\frac{Y}{T \times C} = S \times R$$

Table 17.14 Three Period and Five Period Moving Average

| | Three Period | | | Five Period | |
Period	Value	Average	Period	Value	Average
1	25		1	25	
2	30	35	2	30	
3	50	36.7	3	50	43
4	30	38.3	4	65	
5	35	41.7	5	45	
6	60				

Table 17.15 Centered Moving Average for a Four-Period Average

Period	Value	First MA	Second MA
1	25		
2	30		
3	45	33.75	34.375
4	35	35	35.25
5	30	35.5	35.875
6	32	36.25	36.375
7	48	36.5	
8	36		

Again using the sales data for Al's Previously Owned Sport Cars, let's determine the seasonal relatives using the centered moving average technique. Table 17.16 shows all the calculations. Notice in the table that the moving average is not placed in the middle, but just below it. To complete the calculations, we average the like periods to find the seasonal relatives. The random variations tend to be averaged to zero over a number of periods and are therefore considered to be eliminated.

Quarter	1	2	3	4
			1.482	.667
	.849	1.000	1.503	.732
	.759	1.043	1.500	
average	.8040	1.022	1.495	.6995
$\times \dfrac{4.00}{4.02} =$	.8	1.02	1.49	.70

Notice that these seasonal relatives are comparable (but not identical) to the ones calculated earlier.

Table 17.16 Centered Moving Average and $Y/(T \times C)$ Calculations

Yr	Per	Qtr	Value	MA_1	MA_2	Sales/Ma_2
1	1	1	6			
	2	2	14			
	3	3	20	12.5	13.5	1.482
	4	4	10	14.5	15.0	0.667
2	5	1	14	15.5	16.5	0.849
	6	2	18	17.5	18.0	1.000
	7	3	28	18.5	18.63	1.503
	8	4	14	18.75	19.13	0.732
3	9	1	15	19.5	19.75	0.759
	10	2	21	20.0	20.13	1.043
	11	3	30	20.25	20.0	1.500
	12	4	15	19.75		
4	13	1	13			
	14	2	22			

Once these seasonal relatives have been determined using centered moving averages, their values can be used to deseasonalize the time series data. This results in a value that is the combined trend, cyclical and random components.

$$\frac{Y}{S} = T \times C \times R$$

That is, dividing the actual observed values in the time series by the seaonsal factors results in a value for the combined trend, cyclical, and random components. Table 17.17 shows the deseasonalized values for Al's data. Sometimes, as in this case, when the values (T × C × R) are plotted, a linear trend is shown. This trend can then be identified using the least squares regression technique:

$$Y' = a + bx$$

That is, the deseasonalized values are used in calculating the regression equation.

We have presented two alternative ways to decompose a time series and then recombine the components to make a forecast. In practice, the centered moving average is probably the method of choice for determining seasonal relatives.

Table 17.17 Deseasonalized Sales Figures

Yr	Per	Qtr	Sales	SI	Deseasonalized Y/S
1	1	1	6	0.80	7.50
	2	2	14	1.02	13.73
	3	3	20	1.49	13.42
	4	4	10	0.70	14.29
2	5	1	14	0.80	17.50
	6	2	18	1.02	17.65
	7	3	28	1.49	18.79
	8	4	14	0.70	20.00
3	9	1	15	0.80	18.75
	10	2	21	1.02	20.59
	11	3	30	1.49	20.13
	12	4	15	0.70	21.43
4	13	1	13	0.80	16.25
	14	2	22	1.02	21.56

Consultant's Report

Carry-Out Container Corporation

Carry-Out Container Corporation (CCC), a small company located in Buffalo, New York, serves customers in upstate New York, eastern Pennsylvania, and southern Ontario, Canada. It began operation in 1983, as the brainchild of four MBA students—John Schmeelk, who is CEO of the company; Judy Gustafson, who is now Vice President in charge of production and distribution; Fred Schmidt, who is

now Comptroller; and Keith Kuehn, who is Vice President in charge of Sales and Marketing. Stock in the company is evenly divided among the four founding friends.

The Company began as a project for an MBA course in entrepreneurship. While discussing ideas for the class project, the group stopped one night for coffee at a small off-campus sandwich shop. While sitting there, John noticed that several customers had asked for their orders "to go." The friends began comparing the advantages and disadvantages of various take-out places and the success or lack thereof of take-out packaging—including soggy or stale sandwiches, Chinese cartons, pizza boxes, and the burger boxes used by national burger chains. They concluded that whoever had devised these take-out containers had a great idea. They decided that, for their class project, they would "start" a carry-out container company. The more they researched the idea, the more excited they became. Various futurists and trend spotters in newspaper and magazine columns predicted a trend in the eating habits of the modern family. Yuppies would continue their munching and grazing eating habits. Young working couples were turning more and more to the ease and convenience of take-out food of all kinds. Busy families with hectic schedules were eating out more and more. A large percentage of those eating out were also taking out. Two years after graduation, the four classmates had turned their fictional company into CCC.

The carry-out container manufactured by CCC is a one-piece, preformed styrofoam box that looks like two connected square bowls. The connection point between the bowls is a hinge. When the bowls are folded along the hinge, a box is formed. A tab on one bowl fits into a slot on the second bowl to secure the box in a closed position. The foam acts as an insulator, to keep the food warm or cold. The one-piece construction allows the boxes to be easily shipped and stored. CCC currently produces only one size container (the sandwich/burger size, ($3\frac{1}{2}'' \times 3\frac{1}{2}'' \times 3''$) in a cream color, with no design or printing on the box. Expansion ideas include adding a second (dinner) size and offering color options and customized printing. However, this is still in the future.

CCC customers are generally small, independent restaurants, coffee shops, bagel shops, delicatessens, and specialty food stores. They currently have 700 customers, but the number increases weekly, as the small sales staff develops new customers and old customers change their orders. Not one of these customers accounts for more than 2 percent of their business.

Forecasting demand has not been an easy task for Judy Gustafson, because of the increasing number of accounts, the changing order sizes, and the apparent seasonality of the demand. It appears that demand increases at holiday time and during summer months, when more people opt to eat outside. The number of backorders is increasing, late orders are becoming commonplace, and inventory levels fluctuate wildly. It is difficult to set up an accurate production schedule or to maintain inventory control without accurate forecasts for demand. Judy wants to develop an improved forecasting method that will take the seasonality and customer growth into consideration. She has compiled the following data concerning sales over the past three and one-quarter years:

Month	Sales 1986	1987	1988	1989
January	3,000	2,900	3,600	4,800
February	3,300	3,800	4,200	5,700
March	2,900	3,500	4,800	5,600
April	3,500	4,300	4,900	
May	3,500	4,200	5,700	
June	3,900	4,800	6,000	
July	4,500	5,500	6,200	
August	5,000	5,750	7,000	
September	5,000	5,600	6,800	
October	4,400	5,650	6,900	
November	5,500	6,000	7,000	
December	7,500	7,950	10,000	

You have been hired as a consultant to help Judy by applying management science techniques to this particular problem. Prepare a report for Carry-Out Container Corporation that addresses:

1. The most appropriate technique for CCC to use to forecast future monthly demand.
2. Monthly sales forecasts for the remainder of the year.
3. Seasonal indices for each month.
4. The annual rate of growth in container sales.
5. The amount of confidence Judy should be able to place in these forecasts.

Chapter
18

Decision Support Systems

By the end of this chapter, you should be able to:

1
define a decision support system;
2
enumerate the characteristics of a DSS;
3
describe the components of a DSS;
4
explain how management science models relate to DSS; and
5
define an expert system.

Over the past decade, a specialized area of management information systems (MIS) known as decision support systems (DSS) has become increasingly popular. These systems are computer-based tools that support managers in making decisions in unstructured and semi-structured situations. These systems often include management science models such as those discussed in the previous chapters of this book. This chapter will provide a brief overview of DSS.

18.1 *MANAGEMENT INFORMATION SYSTEMS*

By the mid-1960s, most firms had successfully installed and were using computers. Large amounts of data had been entered into computerized databases or databanks. Businesses were using the computer in **transaction processing systems** (TPS) to assist in day-to-day operations. Payroll processing and inventory control recordkeeping are examples of these applications. During this period, the emphasis was on using the computer to process large amounts of data rapidly, and the key focus was upon the efficient use of the firm's computer resources.

As computer use grew, however, managers began to realize that if all of the data stored in the computer could be put into some usable form, it could provide valuable information on which to base management decisions. This led to the development of **management information systems** (MIS), computer-based systems that provide managers with relevant information that can be used to support decision making. In some cases, this information is integrated from several different sources. The purpose of management information systems is to provide relevant, timely information to decision makers. This means that the MIS must be able to process the available data and to provide the decision maker with only those data that are pertinent to the particular decision making situation. This information is frequently provided through computer-generated reports. These reports can be scheduled periodically, produced upon request, or triggered by some special circumstances.

Periodic Reports

Periodic reports normally are issued at given points in time—the end of a week, month, or quarter. They include information used by management to monitor and review performance or to plan for upcoming periods. Different reports are generally produced for each functional area. Production reports, sales reports, inventory status reports, income statements, and production schedules are examples of such reports.

Demand Reports

On occasion, management requests additional information that is not contained in the periodic reports. These reports, sometimes referred to as demand reports, provide management with more detailed information concerning a specific topic. For example, the sales department might wish to concentrate more of its efforts on the firm's largest customers and might request a list of all customers whose purchases exceed $100,000 per year. These reports may take longer to prepare, since they are approaching the data in a new or nonstandard manner.

Exception Reports

A third type of report is known as the exception report. Exception reports are prepared automatically whenever a predetermined situation occurs. Accident reports and machine breakdown reports fall into this category, when a report is prepared each time an accident occurs or there is a major machine breakdown. The computer can also be programmed to generate reports that flag or highlight situations that deviate from a plan or expectations. Reports generated whenever production falls 15 percent behind schedule, or when the rate of defects increases by 5 percent, are examples of exception reports. These reports acknowledge that certain situations require immediate management decisions or intervention, and they alert the manager to the fact that such a situation exists.

Thus, management information systems process data into relevant, timely information that managers can use in making decisions. Often, however, the information provided by MIS reports is not sufficient to support management decision making in less structured situations. This fact has led to the development of DSS. As stated previously, decision support systems are specialized systems designed to support managers in semi-structured and unstructured decision making situations. They go beyond the traditional MIS reports or information generation tasks.

In a 1983 study of information systems and their effectiveness in supporting managers' needs, Alloway and Quillard[1] grouped information systems into four categories: (1) operational systems, which prepare standardized reports on a peri-

---

[1] Robert Alloway and Judith Quillard, "User Managers' System Needs," *MIS Quarterly,* 7 (No. 2, 1983): 32.

odic schedule; (2) exception reports systems, designed to support tactical decision making when deviations from plans occur; (3) inquiry systems, which enable decision makers to make ad hoc inquiries to obtain specialized information on particular topics; and (4) analytical systems, which include analytical capabilities using modeling, simulation, or statistical routines. Sixty-three percent of the systems studied were categorized as operational systems, 16 percent as exception reporting systems, 12 percent as inquiry systems, and 9 percent as analytical systems. The first two categories clearly fall into the traditional MIS report generation area. The last two categories fall into the DSS area.

The study found that 66 percent of the managers rated the operational systems appropriate and 60 percent rated the exception reporting systems appropriate. Thus, while a majority of managers found the MIS reporting systems appropriate for their needs, more than a third of those responding had additional information needs that were not being met. The ratings for the inquiry and analytical systems were 81 percent and 97 percent respectively. This suggests that decision support systems are better able to satisfy managers' needs for information required to make decisions. The analytical system is especially critical in more complex or unstructured situations because it enables the decision maker to use the information in conjunction with management science models. An earlier study by Rockart and Treacy[2] found that senior managers want to be able to manipulate and analyze existing databases in order to obtain needed decision making information.

18.2 *DSS CHARACTERISTICS AND CLASSIFICATIONS*

While management information systems provide managers with better and more timely information, recent trends in technology, organizational size and complexity, increasing competition, and international markets have put pressure on managers to make better decisions in shorter periods of time. Fortunately, at the same time, changes in computer technology have provided greater computing power at a fraction of the previous cost. The combination of the increased pressures and changes in technology have resulted in a new, specialized type of information system known as a **decision support system** (DSS). Developed in the 1970s and 1980s, these systems enable managers to use the computer as an aid to making semi-structured and unstructured decisions as well.

Like the management science models we have discussed throughout this book, decision support systems are simply tools that aid managers in making decisions. It is still the manager who must make the decision. With the help of DSS, however, the quality and productivity of management decision making has been improved. As it has evolved and continues to evolve, the term decision support system means different things to different people. While most agree on the basic concepts of DSS, there is no universally accepted definition. Scott-Morton articulated the concepts of DSS under the term management decision systems in the early 1970s. He defined such systems as "interactive, computer-based systems which help decision makers utilize data and models to solve unstructured problems."[3] While more re-

---

[2]John Rockart and Michael Treacy, "Executive Information Support Systems," *Sloan Working Paper 1167-80,* Center for Information Systems Research, Massachusetts Institute of Technology (April, 1981).
[3]D. S. Scott-Morton, *Management Decision Systems: Computer-Based Support for Decision Making,* Cambridge, MA: Division of Research, Harvard University, 1971.

cent definitions have expanded the scope to include semi-structured as well as un-structured problems, this basic definition still incorporates most of the appropriate information about DSS. Turban provides the following working definition: "A DSS is an interactive CBIS [computer-based information system] that utilizes decision rules and models coupled with a comprehensive database and the decision maker's own insights, leading to specific, implementable decisions in solving problems that would not be amenable to management science optimizing models per se."[4]

DSS Characteristics

Since there is no common agreement on exactly what a DSS is, there is also no agreement on the characteristics of a DSS. An "ideal set" of characteristics and ca-pabilities for a DSS is summarized in the list that follows:

1. DSS should provide support for decision makers in semi-structured and un-structured situations, where EDP, MIS, or management science alone cannot solve the problem.
2. DSS should provide support for both individuals and groups.
3. DSS should support all phases of the decision making process: problem defini-tion, data preparation, problem formulation, solution, analysis, and implemen-tation.
4. DSS should be adaptive over time. DSS must be flexible so users can add, delete, combine, change, or rearrange basic elements (providing fast response to unexpected situations).
5. DSS should be easy to use. It should be interactive, use an English-like dialog, support graphics capabilities, and generally be user-friendly.
6. DSS should attempt to improve the effectiveness of decision making (accuracy, timeliness, quality) rather than its efficiency (cost of making the decision, in-cluding the charges for computer time).
7. The decision maker should have complete control over all steps of the decision making process. A DSS should support rather than replace the decision maker.[5]

Most DSS have only some of the characteristics included in the above list. We have chosen to combine and summarize these characteristics into four primary charac-teristics of decision support systems. They are:

1. DSS are designed to assist managers in making semi-structured or unstruc-tured decisions.
2. DSS support all phases of the decision making process, but do not replace managerial judgement.
3. DSS are interactive in nature.
4. DSS incorporate both data and quantitative models.

We have said that DSS should support all phases of the decision making process and that they should incorporate both data and quantitative models. We will illus-trate this through the use of Figure 18.1, which shows the four phases of decision making that have been discussed under the "Focus on Decision Making" sections of previous chapters. These phases are: (1) data preparation; (2) problem formula-tion; (3) computer solution; and (4) interpretation and analysis of the results.

---

[4]Efraim Turban, *Decision Support and Expert Systems: Managerial Perspectives,* Macmillan Publishing Company, (New York, 1988), p. 73.
[5]Adapted from Turban, pp. 73–75.

Phases of Decision Making

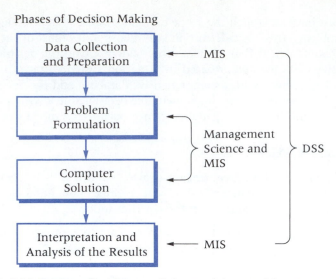

Figure 18.1 DSS Support for Phases of the Decision Making Process

In the data preparation phase, the decision maker gathers information or data from internal and external sources. In a DSS, this information can be obtained from reports or from customized queries. In the problem formulation phase, the decision maker formulates the problem and/or selects the appropriate model. In the computer solution phase, the decision maker uses a computerized model or solution procedure to find an optimal solution (normative models) or to test various alternatives and identify those that are acceptable (descriptive models). In the interpretation and analysis phase, the decision maker compares the results of the computer solution with company standards or with management expectations and reaches a decision. Using a DSS, this comparison could be performed against computerized standards or norms, and reports and recommendations can be generated automatically. It is also possible for the decision maker to use the computer to input the solution into "what if?" scenarios and to prepare appropriate analytical reports. This phase may even incorporate much of the "what happens next" discussion. As the figure shows, MIS supports the data preparation phase; management science and MIS support the problem formulation and computer solution phases; and MIS supports the interpretation and analysis of the results phase. Thus, DSS—incorporating both MIS and management science—supports all four phases.

The objective of DSS is to improve the quality and effectiveness of the managerial decision making process. Alter[6] suggests that DSS increases effectiveness by:

1. Improving personal efficiency. This means allowing decision makers either to perform decision making tasks in less time or to perform the same tasks more thoroughly. A DSS may even enable the decision maker to perform a more appropriate task. (It should be noted that it is not inconsistent to say that a DSS attempts to improve effectiveness rather than efficiency, but that effectiveness may be increased by improving personal efficiency. By improving the efficiency of the decision maker, better decisions can often be made. For example,

[6]Steven L. Alter, *Decision Support Systems: Current Practice and Continuing Challenges,* Addison-Wesley Publishing Company (Reading, MA, 1980), pp. 95–104.

in some cases a DSS may automate intrinsically clerical tasks that are performed by people who are not clerks.)

2. Expediting problem solving. This is accomplished by providing faster turnaround, improving consistency and accuracy, and providing better ways of viewing or solving problems.

3. Facilitating interpersonal communication. This may be achieved by providing individuals with tools of persuasion or by providing the organization with a vocabulary and a discipline that facilitates negotiations across subunit boundaries.

4. Promoting learning or training. Learning can occur when the decision maker develops a better understanding of how the system or process works; training can be facilitated when DSS enables trainees to gain more experience by making many more decisions in a given period of time.

5. Increasing organizational control. Organizational control is increased when additional data are provided upon which to make and evaluate decisions.

DSS Classifications

There are a number of different ways in which to classify DSS. We present one introduced by Alter[7] based upon categorization by the generic operations performed, independent of the type of problem, functional area, or decision perspective. This classification scheme places decision support systems into one of seven distinct types:

1. File drawer systems, which allow immediate access to data.
2. Data analysis systems, which allow the manipulation of data.
3. Analysis information systems, which provide access to databases and small models.
4. Accounting models, which calculate the consequences of planned actions on the basis of accounting definitions.
5. Representational models, which estimate the consequences of actions on the basis of models that are partially nondefinitional.
6. Optimization models, which provide guidelines for action by determining the optimal solution subject to given constraints.
7. Suggestion models, which perform mechanical work leading to specific suggested decisions for fairly structured tasks.

Management science models exist in several of these categories.

18.3 *DSS COMPONENTS*

Decision support systems are composed of both software (programs) and hardware (equipment). The software can be divided into the following three components:

- Communication subsystem
- Data management subsystem
- Model management subsystem

Figure 18.2 illustrates a generalized DSS structure, showing the relationships among these three subsystems and between the user and the DSS.

[7]Alter, *op. cit.*, pp. 73–88.

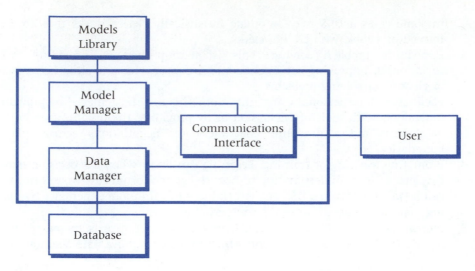

Figure 18.2 DSS Structure Showing Components

Communication Subsystem

The communications subsystem provides the interface between the user and the DSS. This interface is normally interactive in nature. The communications subsystem also frequently supports graphics display capabilities.

Model Subsystem

The model subsystem normally consists of a model manager and a models library. The model manager selects, or allows the user to select, the appropriate model to be used in the analysis of the problem. The model library contains computerized quantitative and financial models. Assignment, goal programming, inventory, linear programming, network, transportation, and queuing models are frequently included in a model library.

Data Subsystem

The data subsystem contains a database and a data manager. The data manager is a database management system that enables the user to query the database and/or input parameters for a given model to be determined from the database.

Individual versus Group Decision Support Systems

Decision support systems were originally designed as individual systems, that is, systems designed to support individual decision makers. Recently, however, **group decision support systems** (GDSS) have also emerged. These systems support decision making by groups of managers. The structure of a GDSS is similar to that of a DSS, but the communications subsystem is designed to support a number of users. The users of a GDSS sometimes are connected to the system through a local area network, where each user has a terminal for input, and output is displayed on a large screen; or they can be spread over a wide geographic area and connected using the teleconferencing capabilities of a wide-area network. The term **group-**

ware has also been popularized recently to describe the adaptation of computing and telecommunications to support the special needs of business teams. Again, the focus of this software is on issues related to collaborative work and decision making.

18.4 *DESIGN OF A DECISION SUPPORT SYSTEM*

Because a DSS supports semi-structured and unstructured problems, the development of a decision support system differs somewhat from other applications software development. DSS development usually follows what is known as an adaptive systems development process. The application is frequently developed in subcomponents using an iterative process. This process is shown in Figure 18.3.

Decision support systems can be developed in-house or purchased from an outside vendor. In-house systems typically fall into one of two groups. Systems in the first group are developed using either a procedural language, a modeling or simulation language, or a fourth-generation language. BASIC, COBOL, FORTRAN, and C are examples of procedural languages. GPSS and SLAM are examples of simulation languages. RAMIS and FOCUS are examples of fourth-generation languages.

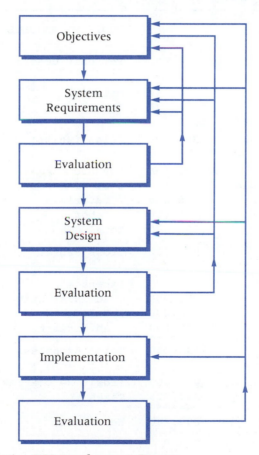

Figure 18.3 Adaptive DSS Development Process

Systems in the second group normally are developed using a collection of off-the-shelf software. This software would include a spreadsheet, such as Lotus 1-2-3 or Excel; a database management system, such as dBASE IV or R:BASE; a graphics display and/or presentation package, such as Harvard Graphics or IBM Storyboard Plus; a word processor or desktop publishing package; a special-purpose statistical package, such as SAS or SPSS; and management science software. When developing a DSS using off-the-shelf software, the developer must be sure that data can be passed between the different pieces of the system.

Spreadsheet packages are particularly popular in designing DSS because they are relatively easy to use and enable the manager to design models that incorporate "what if?" analysis. Figure 18.4 shows a spreadsheet that contains two pro forma income statements. The second column shows the impact of a 5 percent change in labor costs per unit and a 10 percent change in material costs.

DSS packages also can be purchased from vendors. A number of DSS packages are available, each supporting a particular class of problem. Table 18.1 contains examples of this type of DSS software.

Mainframe DSS software costs between $25,000 and $500,000, depending upon its capabilities. Whether a company designs its own DSS or purchases it from an outside vendor frequently depends upon how well the purchased packages meet the

INITIAL RESULTS:		MODIFIED RESULTS:	
Per Unit Costs:		Per Unit Costs:	
Material	$2.40	Material	$2.64
Labor	$3.25	Labor	$3.41
Sales (units)	300,000	Sales (units)	300,000
Revenue	$4,200,000	Revenue	$4,200,000
Cost of Goods Sold		Cost of Goods Sold	
Materials	720,000	Materials	792,000
Labor	975,000	Labor	1,023,000
Total CGS	1,695,000	Total CGS	1,815,000
Gross Profit	$2,505,000	Gross Profit	$2,385,000
Expenses		Expenses	
Administration	252,000	Administration	252,000
Sales	42,000	Sales	42,000
Advertising	350,000	Advertising	350,000
Total Expenses	$644,000	Total Expenses	$644,000
Profit Before Taxes	$1,861,000	Profit Before Taxes	$1,741,000
Taxes	967,720	Taxes	905,320
Net Profit	$893,280	Net Profit	$835,680

Figure 18.4 Example Spreadsheet Showing "What If?" Analysis

Table 18.1 Examples of Decision Support Software

DSS	Description	Developer
BRANDAID	Models market systems and marketing plans for packaged goods.	J. D. C. Little
GADS	Geographical planning and problem analysis concerning territorial planning or definition.	IBM
MAPP	Supports financial planning and budgeting for a set of products.	Citibank
CIS	Models the manufacturing process for trucks, including all component parts.	Ztrux
EIS	Supports financial planning and modeling.	Boeing Computer

needs of its decision makers. Because vendors are trying to reach as large a market as possible, commercial DSS packages tend to be broad in nature, while still focusing on specific types or classes of problems. Customized DSS developed in-house can be more specific to the organization's problem, but may take longer to develop, program, and test.

Remember, however, that a successful computer-based DSS should have most of the ideal characteristics listed previously. To be effective, a DSS must be used. Thus, a successful DSS should be: (1) easy to use; (2) robust; (3) adaptive to changes; (4) complete on major issues; and (5) easy to understand.

18.5 *EXPERT SYSTEMS*

An **expert system** is a knowledge-based system that uses an artificial intelligence program and a database containing detailed knowledge in a particular area to support decision making. The expert system functions much like a human expert, acting as a consultant to help the decision maker in solving a problem. Initially, these systems were developed to replicate the abilities of human experts.

The use of expert systems generally offers the following advantages:

- A reduced need for highly paid or scarce human experts.
- Improved consistency and accuracy in decision making. (Some expert systems have demonstrated that they produce more accurate decisions than recognized human experts.)
- Better documentation of the rationale for a decision than that provided by human decision makers.
- Training in a particular area of expertise for those attempting to develop specialized knowledge.

An expert system typically has the following components:

1. A **user interface** that enables the user to communicate with the expert system. This interface is usually interactive and frequently uses a natural language combined with word or pattern recognition. This lets the user communicate with the expert system without the need to understand specialized commands.

2. An **inference engine** that provides a computer-based reasoning ability. The inference engine is usually based upon a series of "if...then" decision rules.
3. A **knowledge base** that contains the data pertinent to the particular subject area.
4. A **development engine** that can be used by experts and systems analysts to create or modify the expert system and/or the knowledge base.

Early applications of expert systems were in such areas as medical diagnosis, automobile repair, and circuit design. Expert systems are generally more difficult and time-consuming to develop than other software. Most expert systems also have a fairly narrow area of focus. While these problems have limited the number of actual business applications thus far, current trends indicate that, like MIS and DSS, expert systems will continue to grow in both use and usefulness.

18.6 *CONCLUDING REMARKS*

Decision support systems combine the information gathering capabilities of a management information system, the modeling and optimization techniques of management science, and the judgement of the manager, to support decision making in unstructured or semi-structured situations. In the future, management science models such as those discussed in this text will be an integrated part of such decision support systems. They will be readily available, easy to use, and as close as the desktop terminal, personal computer, or even the portable laptop computer.

GLOSSARY

decision support systems interactive, computer-based systems that help decision makers utilize data and models to solve unstructured problems

expert systems knowledge-based systems that use an artificial intelligence program and a database containing detailed knowledge in a particular area to support decision making

group decision support systems decision support systems designed to facilitate decision making by groups; GDSS include communication capabilities that allow all members of the group to communicate with the DSS and with one another

management information systems computer-based systems that provide managers with needed information, usually provided in the form of reports

transaction processing systems computer-based systems used to process large amounts of data; typically run in batch mode with emphasis upon the efficient use of the computer

REVIEW QUESTIONS

1. Computer-generated reports can be classified as: (1) periodic reports; (2) demand reports; and (3) exception reports. Explain the difference between these reports.
2. In your own words, what is a decision support system?

3. What are the four primary characteristics of a DSS as defined by this chapter?
4. What is the objective of DSS?
5. Identify the seven distinct types of decision support systems as defined by Alter.
6. What are the components of a DSS? Illustrate the structure of a DSS, showing its three subsystems, through the use of a diagram. What purpose does each subsystem serve within the DSS?
7. Illustrate the adaptive systems development process through the use of a diagram.
8. It is sometimes said that spreadsheet software is the primary DSS used by managers today. Why would this be so?
9. What is an expert system?
10. Describe each of the components of an expert system.

Cases

Alcan (X)[1]

Mr. J. Kade of the Industrial Engineering Department of the Aluminum Company of Canada, Limited was considering a request from the production control group in the Foil Mill for a re-assessment of the current inventory policy. Space limitations required that a limited number of standard widths of aluminum foil be carried in stock from which customers' orders were slit. The production control group's request resulted from low turnover on some standard widths and large scrap losses when filling customers' orders of certain widths.

Background

As an integrated producer of aluminum products, Alcan mined bauxite ore in various countries and shipped the ore to several smelters where the aluminum was refined. Although the largest portion of its sales was in ingot form to other fabricators, the company was moving more and more into fabricating semifinished and finished products such as aluminum foil. The Foil Mill, part of the Kingston works, produced aluminum foil of different widths for a variety of different end uses. Forty percent of the output of the Foil Mill was classed as converter foil and used by other manufacturers, thirty percent was for household foil while the final thirty percent, classed as rigid container foil, was used by subsidiary companies for containers.

Process

Customers ordered foil specifying the width, gauge and surface finish required. A coil was selected from stock in the Foil Mill which was rolled to the desired thickness and finish. The coil was then sent either to a separator or a slitter where it was slit to the desired width. The separator was used to slit and then separate coils which had been pack rolled in two layers. This was done for thinner gauge orders to give sufficient strength to the foil for slitting. Both the separator and the slitter could be used for single layer foil. It was possible to produce up to eight usable widths on the separator and twelve on the slitter. However, the machines required that all the widths be equal.

[1]From Christoph Haehling von Lanzenauer, *Cases in Operations Research* (London, Ontario: The University of Western Ontario, 1975), pp. 17–21. Reproduced with Special Permission from The University of Western Ontario.

Slitting Operation

A number of difficulties were encountered during the slitting operation. A minimum of $\frac{1}{4}''$ must be trimmed from each edge of the standard widths in order to guarantee clean edges. Another difficulty was the tendency of two adjacent widths to interlock as they were being coiled. To break them apart required the use of a special tool and a sledge hammer which damages the outer edges of the foil. To overcome this, the core on which the foil was wound extended $\frac{1}{8}''$ on either side of the coil. This resulted in a "centre cut" of at least $\frac{1}{4}''$ between two widths. The edge trim and centre cut were fed into air hoses which blew the foil into scrap boxes. The maximum width the air hose could handle was $1\frac{1}{2}''$.

Furthermore, it was not possible to re-coil foil of less than $3\frac{1}{2}''$ width. If a customer's order called for a width less than $3\frac{1}{2}''$, a final slitting was done on a special purpose slitter on which narrow widths can be coiled. This special slitter did not require a centre cut but still required the $\frac{1}{4}''$ edge trim.

The limitations of re-coiling to widths $3\frac{1}{2}''$ or more and blowing to widths of $1\frac{1}{2}''$ or less restricted the slitting of customer order widths from some standard inventory widths. For example, there was no combination of edge trims that would allow a customer order of $35\frac{1}{2}''$ width to be slit from a standard inventory width of $39''$ in one pass. An edge trim of $\frac{1}{4}''$ taken on one side would leave a trim of $3\frac{1}{4}''$ on the other side which was too wide for the air hoses and too narrow for re-coiling. The $3\frac{1}{4}''$ strip could not be slit into two strips and blown away as there would be insufficient tension on the outer strip for proper slitting. No more than one edge trim per side could be taken. The customer order width of $35\frac{1}{2}''$ could therefore not be slit from a standard inventory width of $39''$ unless more than one pass were made which the Foil Mill foreman was reluctant to do. If the trim strip of the foil was between $1''$ and $1\frac{1}{2}''$, the machine operated at roughly one-half of normal speed in order to allow the air hose to remove the trim.

Selection of Standard Widths

Due to the two-week delay in receiving replenishment of stock from the Sheet Mill, the Foil Mill re-ordered a three-week supply of aluminum foil when the inventory was insufficient to satisfy demand during the next three weeks. The type of inventory carried was constrained by space limitations which restricted the number of different standard widths that could be held and the Sheet Mill wanted the number of widths it produced kept to a minimum. In light of these restrictions, currently only seven standard widths were being carried in inventory. This was felt to provide sufficient stock widths to minimize scrap loss while keeping the number fairly low. Obviously, the selection of standard widths depended on the composition of the customers' orders and had to be reviewed periodically. In making this selection, three questions had to be answered.

1. How many standard widths should be carried in the Foil Mill?
2. Which standard widths should be carried in the Foil Mill?
3. Which standard width should be used in slitting a customer's order?

Scrap Loss

In order to answer the three questions regarding which widths to stock, it was necessary to determine the scrap loss which resulted when a standard width was slit into a customer order width. The customers could order any width from $1''$ to $53''$

in increments of ⅛". Since some of possible widths had never been ordered, only 175 different widths were considered. Standard widths were available in ¼" increments up to 54". However, it was not necessary to stock standard widths less than 26" because orders for narrow widths can be slit in multiples from wider standard widths. Slitting multiple widths from wider standard widths resulted in less scrap than cutting a single width from a narrower standard width. There was a computer program available which calculated the amount of scrap which would result from slitting any customer's order from any stock width.

As a sample calculation for the scrap loss using projected sales of 24" foil of 20,000 lbs., the scrap resulting from using 52" standard width was:

$$\text{Scrap} = \frac{(52 - 2 \times 24)}{52} \times 20,000 \text{ lbs.} = 1,538 \text{ lbs.}$$

If the order was slit from 24½" standard width, the resulting scrap was:

$$\text{Scrap} = \frac{(24½ - 24)}{24½} \times 20,000 \text{ lbs.} = 408 \text{ lbs.}$$

Since 24" foil cannot be slit from a 27½" standard width in one pass because of too large an edge trim, the scrap resulting from this combination would be a large number.

The Montreal office supplied Mr. Kade with a six-month forecast of sales which he could use to aid him in deciding on the stock widths to be carried in inventory. Demand for household foil and converter foil was quite stable. However, requirements for rigid container foil did vary as it was sold to the packaging industry whose specifications were continuously modified. However, the forecasts supplied by the Montreal office had in the past been quite accurate.

Development of a Solution Procedure

Due to the rather large problem involving 175 customer order widths and 120 possible standard widths and the necessity to re-evaluate the inventory policy periodically, an efficient procedure would be required to determine an appropriate inventory policy. Mr. Kade approached the Operations Research Group in the company's head office in Montreal and asked for advice in solving this problem. For the development of the procedure the Operations Research Group decided to work with a small sample problem. After consulting with Mr. Kade they developed a sample with a scrap loss matrix as given in Table 1. The numbers in the body are the weights of scrap in pounds which will result from slitting the estimated cus-

Table 1 ALCAN (X) Scrap Loss Matrix

		Standard Widths						
		A	B	C	D	E	F	G
	I	61	19	69	4	46	26	45
Customer	II	15	M	44	52	66	95	27
Widths	III	94	55	M	85	65	67	M
	IV	42	48	11	62	13	M	M
	V	23	M	M	58	M	M	M

tomer orders of each width on the left from the standard widths shown in the column heading. M indicates that a customer width cannot be slit from a standard width in one pass or at all.

American Brands, Inc.[2]

Brad Holgate's early interest in soaps began when he discovered that he could make small amounts of it with his chemistry set. After graduating from college, Brad could not find a suitable job and decided it was time to go back to making soaps. Brad's uncle, Mr. Wilfred, who was running a drugstore in his hometown, agreed to put on his store shelves any soap that Brad might manufacture, provided he was satisfied with the quality and only after informal trials had been carried out.

Soap manufacture in small quantities does not require an elaborate setup—a few vats, ladles, a hearth, and the ability to judge when the soap is just right. Brad started with an initial investment of $350 to buy the necessary equipment and chemicals. After a few spoiled batches, Brad came out with a quality of bath soap satisfactory to him and he distributed these as free samples. The response was quite gratifying. The next batch was again distributed as free samples and the comments confirmed the results of the first trial. Two weeks later, in July 1964, "Bradbar" soap made its appearance at the corner drugstore. As Brad was his favorite nephew, Mr. Wilfred made special efforts to induce trial by his customers, particularly by those whose business he was confident of not losing even if the soap proved unsatisfactory. Things moved slowly for the first three weeks and Brad's soap looked like another "also ran," when suddenly, in the next three days, not only the same customers started coming back for a repeat purchase but also their friends to whom it had been recommended. The shelves were swept clean within the week and Brad had to make a rush repeat order. Business began to grow until five years later Mr. Bradley Holgate, President, Holgate & Co. was selling bath soaps in five different brand names. Holgate and Company could now boast of twenty-three employees including one salesman and one salesman-cum-accountant. A large number of drug stores in Northeastern Delaware now carried Holgate products. However, Brad found the going tougher than ever before. Though he firmly believed in, as he called it, the intrinsic worth of his product, he felt that the growth of his company was limited. He realized that he needed better organization and a stronger financial base. He would also be entering into a market where much larger and established companies were operating. Sandy, an old school friend and a successful businessman, was visiting him on a summer evening and, on listening to Brad's problems, he hinted that it might be worthwhile to investigate possible relations with some other company that might be in a similar situation. He knew of just such a company in the southern part of the state and offered to discuss the matter with them. In spite of Brad's earlier misgivings, Holgate and Lashley merged in 1968 to form American Brands, Inc., with a 65–35 partnership between Brad and Mr. Lashley. Mr. Lashley was getting on in years and was content with being the minority partner.

[2]From Aggarwal and Khera, *Management Science: Cases and Applications*, 1st. ed. (Oakland, Calif.: Holden-Day, Inc.,)

From 1969 onwards the sales of American Brands grew rapidly and so did their problems. (See Table 1). Although they had become larger, with gross sales at $8.2 million, and had a full-time Marketing Manager, Production Supervisor, and Controller, they were finding it difficult to meet the seasonal demands for their bath soaps. (See Figure 1). The consumption of bath soaps became particularly heavy during the summer months and rose considerably above winter month requirements. This heavy imbalance placed a severe strain on the production facilities in the one month preceding summer and caused production to slack off abruptly with the onset of winter. The problem was further complicated by the fact that American Brands had been marketing two product lines, regular and luxury. While the regular line had four product items, the luxury line had three. The projected demand for 1979 for the two product lines is given in Table 2.

Anthony Seagram, the Production Supervisor, frequently complained about losses incurred from the switching in production between the luxury and the regular lines of soap because of the seemingly capricious demands made by the Marketing Manager, Jack Daniels. No sooner did Anthony settle down to the production of one line, when Jack would come out with a change of priorities. Not only did this result in frequent stockouts of raw materials (as proper inventory

Table 1 American Brands, Inc. Gross Sales*

1969	1970	1971	1972	1973	1974	1975
1.6	2.7	3.5	4.9	6.1	7.2	8.2

*Millions of dollars.

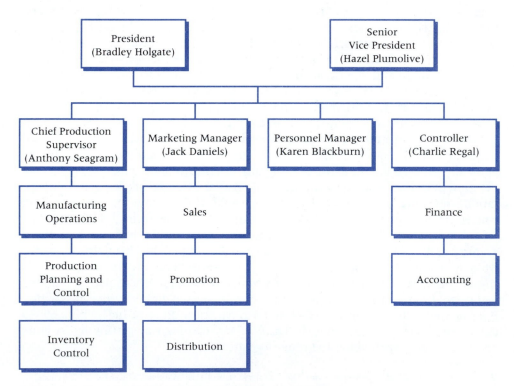

Figure 1 American Brands Inc. Organizational Chart

Table 2 American Brands, Inc. 1979 Sales Forecasts*

Month	Regular	Luxury	Total
January	40	24	64
February	61	27	88
March	64	61	125
April	83	109	192
May	88	126	214
June	106	137	243
July	124	165	289
August	135	161	296
September	97	147	244
October	84	114	198
November	76	62	138
December	51	46	97
Total	1,009	1,179	2,188

*Sales given in thousands of cases.

planning was not possible) but it also caused a loss in production capacity. Each time the product line had to be changed from regular to luxury, some additional equipment had to be put in place, temperature control devices installed, and molds changed. It was Anthony's estimate that the changeover from regular to luxury meant a loss of two hours forty-five minutes and the change from luxury to regular caused a one hour loss. Additional time lost in trial runs when the product line was changed was, on the average, one hour for the luxury line, and one-half hour for the regular line. Frequent trial runs also resulted in a rise in the percentage of waste. Jack put the blame on Anthony and his production department who "were never able to produce enough and on time." He felt he had no control over demand and simply conveyed what the market demanded. He felt it was up to Anthony to figure out the ways and means to produce it. As it was, he complained, sales could easily be pushed up by at least 7 percent if only Anthony could produce orders on time, particularly those for the luxury items. Jack felt that the sales of luxury soaps could be increased by at least 5 percent, starting immediately. Not only did he feel that opportunities were being missed but also that sales were getting hurt by another 5 percent due to the ill will generated by delayed shipments. Charlie Regal, the Controller, was opposed to the idea of increasing production without an accurate estimate of expected sales. He regarded Jack's attitude as being unrealistic and wanted some additional long-term orders before he would okay any proposals for increased production. He contended that if Jack could forecast the demand better, loss in capacity could be reduced. Anthony tended to agree and said that he could produce, given proper batch runs, up to 180,000 cases per month, and with overtime he could produce another 30,000 cases. Charlie, however, would not agree to overtime as this meant an additional cost per hour of $1.20. This increased cost would push up the costs per case by 80¢ for regular and $1.00 for luxury items. With storage charges at 10¢ per case per month, and the deterioration that might take place while in storage he felt the total cost may have become too high. Anthony, however, pointed out that bath soaps have a reasonably long shelf life (though the humidity in the warehouse would have to be increased slightly at a negligible cost) and consequently no deterioration was likely to occur. Jack was also opposed to overtime, as he feared that the increased manufacturing costs would necessitate higher prices which would, in turn, make his task even more difficult. If any overtime had to be resorted to, he did not want it during production of luxury items. It was his belief that any increase in its price in the present market would make it practically unsaleable. Anthony pointed out that it would not be possible for him to change to regular line production at the end of each day just so luxury soap would not be produced during overtime. The luxury brands would have to take their share of the overtime premium. However, he would try to avoid it as best as he could. Anthony, on the other hand, believed that the luxury line should be dropped altogether as the per case productivity for the regular line was 10 percent higher. Jack felt that it would be suicidal to drop the luxury items as it would have repercussions on the sales of the regular product also. Many of the stores would find it more convenient to drop both if one was discontinued and their main competitor in the region was looking for just such an opportunity. It was therefore decided not to drop the luxury line.

American's profits had increased by only 3 percent in 1978 whereas sales for the same year had increased by 14 percent. Anthony Seagram had to develop a production schedule that would indicate the number of cases of the regular and the luxury lines that should be produced each month during 1979. The objective was to have available enough soap of each grade to meet each month's forecasted demand while minimizing capacity loss, overtime production, and storage charges.

Labatt's Breweries[3]

During June, 1969, Mr. Barry Davidson, an analyst for Labatt's Ontario Breweries, was faced with a question posed by the warehouse manager concerning the repair and replacement policy for pallets used in the shipment of beer. Should the pallets be repaired at all and if so, how often? This question always arose in early summer when the supply of pallets became tighter as a result of increased summer shipments.

Company Background

Labatt's Breweries Ltd., of which Labatt's Ontario Breweries was a wholly owned subsidiary, was one of Canada's largest brewing companies with operations all across Canada. Labatt's Ontario Breweries had one brewery in London, Ontario with a capacity of 1.5 million barrels annually and a new brewery under construction in Toronto with a projected capacity of 500,000 barrels annually. Labatt's also had a brewery in LaSalle, Quebec with a capacity of 1.3 million barrels as well as smaller breweries in St. John's, Winnipeg, Saskatoon, Edmonton, New Westminster, Victoria.

Pallet Pool

Labatt's belonged to a pallet pool with the other breweries in Ontario and Quebec and their common retail outlets, the Brewers' Warehousing Company in Ontario

[3]From Christoph Haehling von Lanzenauer, *Cases in Operations Research* (London, Ontario: The University of Western Ontario, 1975), pp. 82–84. Reproduced with Special Permission from The University of Western Ontario.

and the independent wholesalers in Quebec. The pallets were used for shipments to the retail outlets from the breweries and the return of empties. Each brewery shipped its products to many locations throughout both provinces. The use of a common bottle and pallet by breweries in Canada allowed the return of empties to any brewery.

New bottles, when shipped to the breweries from the glass manufacturers, were shipped on new pallets. The bill for the new pallets was included with the bill for the new bottles. From time to time, additional pallets could be ordered by the individual breweries, if required. The number of new pallets purchased by each brewery was recorded and at the end of each fiscal year, breweries that had purchased more than their share of new pallets were compensated by those breweries that had purchased less than their share. A brewery's share of new pallets purchased was determined by the number of new pallets purchased times its share of the market.

Damaged pallets were repaired by individual breweries if feasible. If a center block had been damaged, the pallet was not repaired. When questioned, the foreman at Labatt's in charge of pallet repair said: "Pallets are damaged through abuse by the handlers." Often in repairing a pallet, the new nails would split a center block which would necessitate scrapping of the pallet. Approximately 10 percent of the damaged pallets were unrepairable. All pallets were identified as to time of purchase.

There were approximately 150,000 pallets in the pool as of May 1, 1969, the end of fiscal 1969. In 1969F, 59,925 new pallets had been purchased at an average cost of $4.47, 32,050 had been sold as scrap for an average price of $0.55 and 7,771 had been repaired by members of the pool. The average cost of repairing a pallet at Labatt's in 1969F was $2.07. 1,721,000 pallets of beer were moved in Ontario and Quebec in 1969F. Labatt's share of the Ontario and Quebec market was approximately 33 percent.

Using the records for pallet repairs at Labatt's, Mr. Davidson was able to obtain the average damage rates for the pallets, which, he felt could be applied to the entire pallet pool.

Description of Pallets	Percentage of Pallets Damaged in Year			
	One	Two	Three	Four
New Pallets	22	45	33	—
Pallets repaired in Year One	—	47	48	5
Pallets repaired in Year Two	—	—	83	17

The foreman in charge of pallet repairs considered pallets over two years old not worth repairing and they were scrapped.

Although $0.75 was the most ever received for damaged pallets, the warehouse manager thought that as much as $1.50 could be obtained if the scrapped pallets were in a better condition.

With changes in the price of pallets, and cost of repairing pallets which, due to the high labour content, was rising rapidly, Mr. Davidson wanted to implement the most economical pallet replacement policy. He was willing to carry out the analysis and discuss the results with other members of the pallet pool.

Pierre Cardigan of Paris[4]

Pierre Cardigan, after returning from World War II where he served as a sergeant, decided to go into business for himself. Before the war he had worked as a fashion designer for a small firm located on the outskirts of Paris. Pierre was certain that he would be most successful if he remained in this line of business.

Realizing that a good location would be important to his firm's success, he acquired a shop in the most fashionable district of Paris. After remodeling, Pierre Cardigan of Paris was opened as an haute couturier for women's fashions. Pierre Cardigan was the featured designer of the house. His designs were so well accepted by the world of high fashion that his label soon became synonymous with fine styling and good quality.

In order to capitalize on this phenomenal success, Pierre decided to expand his product line, relying on the company name and label to insure a successful expansion. He first expanded into the women's pret-a-porter (ready-to-wear) clothing market area and, in the late 50's, into the men's ready-to-wear garments.

Pierre Cardigan has grown rapidly in the last ten years and has become one of the world's leading manufacturers of men's clothing. The company's production facilities are scattered in several Western countries. In addition to supplying countless retail outlets, Pierre Cardigan of Paris now also owns and operates 300 retail stores in the United States. Mr. Cardigan no longer has time to be directly involved with the fashion design aspect of his company. Instead, he has a staff of designers and fashion coordinators who create and design all the styles of the company's products. They are under the direction of the production department and are responsible for consulting with fabric manufacturers to stay current with emerging trends in colors, patterns, and textures of new fabrics. This is necessary to develop the new styles that have made the company a leader in the fashion industry. Pierre still maintains the right to approve new styles since he feels that this is necessary to insure continued excellence in the product line.

The laying out of patterns, cutting, sewing, assembling, and finishing are all done in company plants, as well as the inspecting, packing, and shipping. Mr. Cardigan feels that such complete in-house operations are necessary to insure a high level of quality control. Pierre feels that the production department has done an outstanding job in producing quality garments while keeping costs to a minimum. Much of the company's financial success is considered to be due to the production department's efficiency.

The primary reason for the company's great and rapid expansion has been Pierre Cardigan's ability to anticipate economic and style trends. His company has undergone three major reorganizational changes since its inception and there are indications that another change is in the making.

Thus, growth has not come without its problems. Expansion has caused the firm to become highly levered with debt. The company has often found itself without sufficiently qualified internal personnel to fill managerial positions for the expanding facilities, thereby forcing Pierre to hire outside personnel. This, in some cases, has caused personnel conflicts within the company. In order to alleviate this problem a management development program has been started.

---

[4]From Aggarwal and Khera, *Management Science: Cases and Applications*, 1st. ed. (Oakland, Calif.: Holden-Day, Inc.,)

Because the sales of the company are greatly influenced by consumer tastes, an erroneous prediction of the fashion trend could spell disaster. Pierre Cardigan of Paris minimizes this risk by maintaining a conservative, yet well-tailored and stylish approach. The men's clothing industry has other problems to contend with besides changing consumer tastes. For example, when there is a downturn in the economy, men's clothing is one of the first areas to feel the crunch. In these times men will forego the purchase of a suit in order to reallocate the funds towards other needs. Additionally, the clothing industry faces periodic material shortages. Hedging on the textile market, energy crisis, climate conditions, and even political conditions can all affect the availability of material.

Another problem area that has developed along with rapid expansion is the managerial decision-making process within the company. When the company was small, the management was fairly successful with the intuitive approach to decision making. Now, due to the size of the company and the highly competitive market in which it operates, new and more objective methods for decision making are needed.

For instance, one such problem is the control of proper allocation of units between the Pierre Cardigan retail stores and the independent retailers in such a way as to maximize corporate profits. To bring the problem into better focus, consider one garment category, suits, and one fabric category, woven, both categories making one division. Within the woven category there are six ranges, each range being distinguished by certain fabric characteristics common to that range, thus making each range distinct. These ranges are used when determining price. Garments made from fabrics within a specific range share a common price.

For all practical purposes, however, manufacturing costs are identical for all garments in a specific category, regardless of range. Consequently, there are varying mark-up percentages on ranges in a certain category. In the woven category, mark-ups vary from 47–59 percent. As a result some ranges are more profitable than others. (See Table 1). In view of the wide difference between mark-up percentages and the resulting gross profit, it has been the company's policy to allocate as many of the higher profit-producing units as possible to Pierre Cardigan's own retail outlets.

Table 1 Pierre Cardigan of Paris Breakdown of Woven Range Suits

Range	Description	Units Manufactured	Cost	Retail Price	Gross Profit Per Unit	Minimum Unit Sales Forecast for Own Division
101	Saxonies	41,200	$ 87.50	$165	$ 77.50	16,480
102	Heritage Flannels	10,500	88.25	170	81.75	4,725
103	Heritage Worsteds	74,400	89.25	170	80.75	33,480
111	Silver Trumpeter Worsteds	15,100	103.50	225	121.50	11,325
130	Silver Trumpeter Tropicals	3,800	92.75	195	102.25	2,800
446	British Mohair	400	109.75	215	105.25	180
		Total 145,400				Total 68,990

Of the 145,000 units manufactured for the woven category, no less than 68,990 units must be sold by their own retail stores in order to meet target profit goals. These figures were determined by past performance along with current market trends and forecasts. Management must work within the constraint of a maximum budget of $8.1 million to be allocated among the retail stores for purchases in the woven category.

A market survey among recent buyers of the company's suits had shown that, in the worsted category, customers purchased three times as many Heritage suits as the Silver Trumpeter suits; in the Heritage series, worsted suits were preferred over the flannels by a margin of six to one; and in the Silver Trumpeter series, seven worsted suits were purchased for every two flannels.

The situation is not as obvious as it seems. The retail stores must have an adequate selection for the customers to choose from, while keeping the end-of-the-season inventory to a minimum so that they will not be forced to take excessive markdowns on unsold goods at that time.

Shale Oil Company [5]

The Shale Oil Company contains several operating units that comprise its Aston, Ohio, manufacturing complex. These units process the crude oil that is pumped through and transform it into a multitude of hydrocarbon products. The units run 24 hours per day, seven days per week, and must be shut down for maintenance on a predetermined schedule. One such unit is Distillation Unit No. 5, or DU5. Studies have shown that DU5 can operate only 3½ years without major equipment breakdowns and excessive loss of efficiency. Therefore, DU5 is shut down every 3½ years for cleaning, inspection, and repairs.

DU5 is the only distillation unit for crude oil in the Aston complex, and its shutdown severely affects all other operating units. Some of the production can be compensated by Shale refineries in other locations, but the rest must be processed before the shutdown and stored. Without proper planning, a nationwide shortage of Shale gasoline could occur. The timing of DU5's shutdown is critical, and the length of time the unit is down must be kept to a minimum to limit production loss. Shale uses PERT as a planning and controlling tool to minimize shutdown time.

The first phase of a shutdown is to open and clean the equipment. Inspectors can then enter the unit and examine the damage. Once damages are determined, the needed repairs can be carried out. Repair times can vary considerably depending on what damage the inspection reveals. Based on previous inspection records, some repair work is known ahead of time. Thorough cleaning of the equipment is also necessary to improve the unit's operating efficiency. Table 1 lists the many maintenance activities and their estimated completion times.

[5]From Professor Barry Render, University of New Orleans, in *Cases and Readings in Quantitative Analysis for Management* by Barry Render and Ralph M. Stair, Jr. (Boston: Allyn & Bacon, 1982). ©1982 by Allyn and Bacon, Inc. Reprinted by permission.

Table 1 Preventive Maintenance of DU5

Activities		Time Estimates (in days)		
		Optimistic	Most Likely	Pessimistic
1-2	Circulate wash water throughout unit	1	2	2.5
2-3	Install blinds	1.5	2	2.5
3-4	Open and clean vessels and columns	2	3	4
3-5	Open and clean heat exchangers, remove tube bundles	1	2	3
3-6	Open and clean furnaces	1	2	4
3-7	Open and clean mechanical equipment	2	2.5	3
3-8	Inspect instrumentation	2	4	5
4-9	Inspect vessels and columns	1	2	3
5-10	Inspect heat exchanger shells	1	1.5	2
5-11	Inspect tube bundles	1	1.5	2
6-12	Inspect furnaces	2	2.5	3
6-17	Retube furnaces	15	20	30
7-13	Inspect mechanical equipment	1	1.5	2
7-18	Install new pump mechanical seals	3	5	8
8-19	Repair instrumentation	3	8	15
9-14	Repair vessels and columns	14	21	28
10-16	Repair heat exchanger shells	1	5	10
11-15	Repair tube bundles, retube	2	5	10
12-17	Repair furnaces	5	10	20
13-18	Repair mechanical equipment	10	15	25
14-20	Test and close vessels and columns	4	5	8
15-16	Install tube bundles into heat exchanger shells	1	2	3
16-20	Test and close heat exchangers	1	2	2.5
17-20	Test and close furnaces	1	2	3
18-20	Test and close mechanical equipment	1	2	3
19-20	Test instrumentation	2	4	6
20-21	Pull blinds	1.5	2	2.5
21-22	Purge all equipment with steam	1	3	5
22-23	Start up unit	3	5	10

Red Brand Canners[6]

On Monday, September 13, 1965, Mr. Mitchell Gordon, Vice-President of Operations, asked the controller, the sales manager, and the production manager to meet with him to discuss the amount of tomato products to pack that season. The tomato crop, which had been purchased at planting, was beginning to arrive at the cannery, and packing operations would have to be started by the following Monday. Red Brand Canners was a medium-sized company which canned and distributed a variety of fruit and vegetable products under private brands in the western states.

[6]Reprinted with permission of Stanford University Graduate School of Business, © 1965 by the Board of Trustees of the Leland Standord Junior University.

Mr. William Cooper, the controller, and Mr. Charles Myers, the sales manager, were the first to arrive in Mr. Gordon's office. Dan Tucker, the production manager, came in a few minutes later and said that he had picked up Produce Inspections's latest estimate of the quality of the incoming tomatoes. According to their report, about 20 percent of the crop was Grade "A" quality and the remaining portion of the 3,000,000-pound crop was Grade "B".

Gordon asked Myers about the demand for tomato products for the coming year. Myers replied that they could sell all of the whole canned tomatoes they could produce. The expected demand for tomato juice and tomato paste, on the other hand, was limited. The sales manager then passed around the latest demand forecast, which is shown in Table 1. He reminded the group that the selling prices had been set in light of the long-term marketing strategy of the company, and potential sales had been forecasted at these prices.

Bill Cooper, after looking at Myers's estimates of demand, said that it looked like the company "should do quite well (on the tomato crop) this year." With the new accounting system that had been set up, he had been able to compute the contribution for each product, and according to his analysis the incremental profit on the whole tomatoes was greater than for any other tomato product. In May, after Red Brand had signed contracts agreeing to purchase the grower's production at an average delivered price of 6¢ per pound, Cooper had computed the tomato products' contributions (see Table 2).

Dan Tucker brought to Cooper's attention that, although there was ample production capacity, it was impossible to produce all whole tomatoes as too small a

Table 1 Red Brand Canners Demand Forecasts

Product	Selling Price per Case	Demand Forecast (Cases)
24 cans of size 2½ whole tomatoes	$4.00	800,000
24 cans of size 2½ choice peach halves	5.40	10,000
24 cans of size 2½ peach nectar	4.60	5,000
24 cans of size 2½ tomato juice	4.50	50,000
24 cans of size 2½ cooking apples	4.90	15,000
24 cans of size 2½ tomato paste	3.80	80,000

Table 2 Red Brand Canners Product Item Profitability

Product	24-2½ Whole Tomatoes	24-2½ Choice Peach Halves	24-2½ Peach Nectar	24-2½ Tomato Juice	24-2½ Cooking Apples	24-2½ Tomato Paste
Selling price	$4.00	$5.40	$4.60	$4.50	$4.90	$3.80
Variable costs:						
Direct labor	1.18	1.40	1.27	1.32	0.70	0.54
Variable overhead	0.24	0.32	0.23	0.36	0.22	0.26
Variable selling	0.40	0.30	0.40	0.85	0.28	0.38
Packaging material	0.70	0.56	0.60	0.65	0.70	0.77
Fruit*	1.08	1.80	1.70	1.20	0.90	1.50
Total variable costs	3.60	4.38	4.20	4.38	2.80	3.45
Contribution	0.40	1.02	0.40	0.12	1.10	0.35
Less allocated overhead	0.28	0.70	0.52	0.21	0.75	0.23
Net profit	0.12	0.32	(0.12)	(0.09)	0.35	0.12

Table 2 Red Brand Canners Product Item Profitability, continued

*Product usage is as given below:

Product	Pounds per Case
Whole tomatoes	18
Peach halves	18
Peach nectar	17
Tomato juice	20
Cooking apples	27
Tomato paste	25

portion of the tomato crop was "A" quality. Red Brand used a numerical scale to record the quality of both raw produce and prepared products. This scale ran from zero to ten, the higher number representing better quality. Rating tomatoes according to this scale, "A" tomatoes averaged nine points per pound and "B" tomatoes averaged five points per pound. Tucker noted that the minimum average input quality for canned whole tomatoes was eight and for juice it was six points per pound. Paste could be made entirely from "B" grade tomatoes. This meant that whole tomato production was limited to 800,000 pounds.

Gordon stated that this was not a real limitation. He had been recently solicited to purchase 80,000 pounds of Grade "A" tomatoes at 8½¢ per pound and at that time had turned down the offer. He felt, however, that the tomatoes were still available.

Myers, who had been doing some calculations, said that although he agreed that the company "should do quite well this year," it would not be by canning whole tomatoes. It seemed to him that the tomato cost should be allocated on the basis of quality and quantity rather than by quantity only as Cooper had done. Therefore, he had recomputed the marginal profit on the basis (see Table 3), and from his results, Red Brand should use 2,000,000 pounds of the "B" tomatoes for paste, and the remaining 400,000 pounds of "B" tomatoes and all of the "A" tomatoes for juice. If the demand expectations were realized, a contribution of $48,000 would be made on this year's tomato crop.

Table 3 Red Brand Canners Marginal Analysis of Tomato Products

Z = cost per pound of A tomatoes in cents.
Y = cost per pound of B tomatoes in cents.
1. $(600,000 \text{ lb} \times Z) + (2,400,000 \text{ lb} \times Y) = (3,000,000 \text{ lb} \times 6)$.
2. $\dfrac{Z}{9} = \dfrac{Y}{5}$.
   $Z = 9.32¢$ per pound.
   $Y = 5.18¢$ per pound.

Product	Canned Whole Tomatoes	Tomato Juice	Tomato Paste
Selling price	$4.00	$4.50	$3.80
Variable cost			
(excluding tomato costs)	2.52	3.18	1.95
	$1.48	$1.32	$1.85
Tomato cost	1.49	1.24	1.30
Marginal profit	($0.01)	$0.08	$0.55

Southern Hydraulic Supplies Company[7]

The Southern Hydraulic Supplies Company was a distributor of hydraulic supplies in the Gulf states area. Southern handled standard hydraulic fittings, tubing, and similar items. Generally Southern carried an entire line for each manufacturer whose products it handled and provided local stock for rapid delivery to customers. The items that Southern stocked were mainly used in the maintenance, modification, and manufacture of trucks, off-highway construction equipment, and machine tools.

Southern had grown from a small two-person operation to a $75-million-per-year business in a span of 25 years. The growth of its dollar volume was based on an excellent reputation for good service coupled with the general expansion of industry in the Gulf states. From its inception Southern had been a profitable business in sound financial condition.

Despite the continued growth of profits in absolute terms, however, Southern found that profits as a percentage of sales had declined from 11.3 percent of sales to 6.4 percent of sales. When management became aware of the seriousness of the problem, it was decided to undertake a thorough review of policies and procedures in the areas that could have significant influence on costs and profits—namely, product line, sales methods, stock handling and storage methods, billing and record keeping, and inventory replenishment. The last area was included as a major area for study because the company had been experiencing increasing difficulty with out-of-stock situations and unbalanced inventories.

Inventory Replenishment Procedures

Up until the time that the review of the inventory replenishment policies and procedures was begun, there had been no formal study of this phase of the company's operations. Since maintaining inventories was one of the company's major functions, Southern had always used experienced personnel to control the placing of orders and had relied on their judgment to make correct decisions. One thing that became immediately apparent as this phase of Southern's operations came under scrutiny was that the inventory replenishment problem had become vastly more complicated in recent years as the variety of items carried had tripled from what it had been five years previously to more than 15,000 separate stock items. Because no formal study had been made previously of the inventory replenishment operations, it was decided as a first step to get some general information about order placement costs and inventory carrying costs and also to analyze in detail several typical items of inventory.

Several years earlier Southern had installed a small computer for maintaining inventory records, writing purchase orders, and other record keeping functions. To use this equipment, efficiently, the master inventory records were updated only once weekly. Purchase orders were also prepared on a schedule of once each week. Purchase requisitions were turned in by the supervisors responsible for various types of stock, and these were accumulated until Friday when they were used to initiate purchase orders. In effect this meant that review of the inventory levels occurred once every five days as the supervisors turned in most of their purchase requisitions only once each week immediately before the scheduled machine run. In

[7]From Meier/Johnson/Newell/Schrieber, CASES IN PRODUCTION 7 OPERATIONS MANAGEMENT, © 1982, PP. 232–235. Reprinted by permission of Prentice Hall, Inc., Englewood Cliffs, New Jersey.

total, the cost of preparing and processing a requisition, preparing a purchase order, and making necessary record changes was estimated to be $12.50 per order.

Analysis of company records indicated that the following were reasonable estimates of the variable cost per year of carrying inventories (as a percentage of dollar value of average inventory):

Cost Category	% of Total
Capital cost	18
Obsolescence	5
Insurance	3
Taxes	2
Storage and handling	11
Total	39

One of the typical items of inventory analyzed in detail was a small hydraulic fitting. The fitting was purchased for $14.00 and sold for $19.50. The manufacturer from whom Southern procured the fitting did not offer any quantity discount on the fitting, but it would not fill orders for less than 50 fittings without adding a flat charge of $25.00 to the order. For this particular item, there were other distributors in Southern's immediate vicinity that could supply a comparable fitting made by another manufacturer. Because of this, orders that Southern could not fill immediately were lost.

The fitting was ordered from the manufacturer located about 1,500 miles away and shipped to Southern by truck. An analysis of the time taken to receive the fittings from the day the purchase order was prepared until the fittings were received indicated that this varied between 5 and 14 working days. The historical record of the time between the preparation of the purchase order and receipt of the fittings is shown in Table 1. It was estimated that inspection of the shipments, preparation of receiving reports, and related activities cost Southern $12.25 per order.

Table 1 Analysis of Procurement Lead Times[1] (working days between order issue and delivery of fittings)

8	11
12	14
6	9
5	8
7	9
8	7
8	6
9	8
13	13
9	10
10	7
8	7
11	12
7	10
8	9
5	10
7	7
6	8
9	14
7	6

[1]Average lead time = 8.7 days.

Table 2 Analysis of Orders for One Year[1] (orders filled per day)

35	9	17	16	20	0
0	8	4	0	0	19
0	0	28	11	13	29
17	17	25	16	7	18
36	0	27	0	0	11
6	28	20	13	14	29
0	0	0	24	0	14
5	29	7	11	10	0
11	9	0	0	41	19
18	0	8	27	8	31
0	0	0	26	0	10
4	0	18	0	9	16
16	23	28	6	22	0
25	0	20	0	0	27
0	17	22	26	0	18
19	8	0	13	44	14
14	13	0	0	24	0
32	31	16	21	0	0
15	8	31	17	7	38
0	0	24	22	40	3
17	25	16	0	9	17
18	11	0	10	0	0
10	0	0	42	0	21
30	43	14	0	0	15
15	9	36	18	21	0
0	0	11	0	16	9
12	12	0	12	0	14
21	22	3	27	23	0
23	15	30	4	19	6
15	0	12	19	25	23
12	7	0	17	0	12
0	15	10	0	2	22
19	10	0	34	15	0
37	33	20	17	12	34
0	26	14	21	0	5
13	0	21	0	32	
0	6	0	18	8	
18	20	17	13	0	
20	13	37	24	5	
14	7	19	33	15	
19	0	0	26	20	
18	0	0	0	30	
0	39	35	18	23	
10	19	16	0	0	
15	16	13	16	11	

[1]Average orders filled per day = 13.1.

Customer orders filled each day for one year (260 working days) were tabulated for this fitting and are shown in Table 2. No record was kept of customer orders that were cancelled because the fitting was out of stock. Further analysis of the records pertaining to this fitting revealed the fact that replenishment orders for the fitting were always for lots of 750 and that the amount of stock on hand averaged about 115 units on the days that purchase orders were issued for replenishment stock.

Teaneck Construction Company[8]

The Teaneck Construction Company is a small organization operating in Northwestern Florida. Ninety percent of the company's dollar volume is obtained from contracts for municipal work.

Management has decided to submit a bid for the construction in April of a mile-long extension to the main sewer system in the nearby town of Deerfield. The extension is going into a residential area that until now has used septic tanks. The bidding is expected to be competitive, because whoever gets this contract will have some advantage in obtaining a contract that is to be awarded by the town later in the year, and that is worth approximately $1 million. In order to submit the most competitive bid possible, the project managers of Teaneck decided to evaluate the alternatives of using one, two, or three work shifts.

Table 1 shows time and cost estimates made by Teaneck's engineers. The trunk sewer extension is to be laid in a tunnel for one-third its length; the remaining two-thirds is to be constructed in trenches. To build the tunnel, a primary shaft must be excavated first. After this, the secondary shafts can be driven and the tunnel can be dug simultaneously. The trench is to be started at the same time as the primary shaft. Another crew of workers follows the trench workers, laying the pipes, pouring the concrete, and refilling the trenches as far as they have been excavated. The excavators lose no time as a result of this follow-up. A third group would be performing a similar function in the tunnel.

[8]From Martin K. Starr/Irving Stein, THE PRACTICE OF MANAGEMENT SCIENCE, © 1976, pp. 62–63. Reprinted by permission of Prentice Hall, Inc., Englewood Cliffs, New Jersey.

Table 1

	Activity	1 Shift		2 Shifts		3 Shifts	
		Time (days)	Cost ($)	Time (days)	Cost ($)	Time (days)	Cost ($)
A	Move in machinery & equipment	12	3,000	6	3,300	4	3,600
B	Excavate primary shaft	12	6,250	12	6,600	12	6,950
C	Excavate secondary shafts	60		24		12	
D	Excavate trenches	300	33,700	150	42,500	100	44,700
E	Excavate tunnel	305	36,150	155	39,100	105	40,000
F	Backfill (trenches only)	50	1,000	25	1,500	17	2,000
G	Pipelaying in trenches	50	8,500	25	8,200	17	8,900
H	Pipelaying in tunnel	46	5,500	25	5,700	16	6,000
J	Pour concrete in trenches	70	11,400	35	11,650	25	11,850
K	Pour concrete in tunnel	60	11,000	30	11,250	20	11,500
L	Landscape	10	2,000	8	2,900	6	3,000
M	Move out	6	500	3	750	2	1,000
	Total direct costs	$119,000		$133,450		$139,500	
	Total indirect costs	$140/day		$160/day		$180/day	

There is an additional complication that may have serious effects on the profitability of this job. There is a strong chance that the local Excavators Union will strike on the inception date of the project. At the last meeting of the project managers, there was consensus that the probability of such a strike fell somewhere close to 80 percent; at least, it was decided to use this figure for planning purposes. In case of a strike, the direct costs associated with the project would remain unchanged, since the issue involved was not one of wages; but indirect costs would accrue for the duration of the strike at the same daily rate as indicated in Table 1. Teaneck's direct labor is hired from union pools, the common practice of all construction companies in the area. General and administrative costs are put at 40 percent of the sum of direct and indirect costs. Normally, Teaneck aims at making a profit equal to 10 percent of total costs.

There was also a recognized need to develop some kind of estimate to describe the probability of the strike's duration. With a great deal of misgiving, the project managers came up with the following guesses:

Table 2

Length of strike in days	20	30	40
Probability of a strike of n days, on the condition that a strike occurs	.25	.25	.50

United Rail Equipment Co.[9]

With the growing worldwide energy crisis, considerable effort is being expended to more efficiently use available energy resources. One area which can offer considerable savings is mass transit as an alternative to automobile travel.

The largest manufacturer of rail transportation in the United States is United Rail, a division of URE, Inc., which was incorporated in 1927 as a holding company for United-Equipment and the United Car & Manufacturing Company. United Rail Equipment was the name later given to the United Car & Manufacturing Company when it was made a division of URE, Inc.

URE, Inc. is a heavy industrials company principally engaged in the manufacture for sale or lease of railroad rolling stock, the design and construction of petroleum refining and chemical processing plants; the manufacture for sale or lease of commercial truck trailers and shipping containers, and the design and manufacture of industrial furnaces, tunnel kilns, and oxygenlacing equipment. Its worldwide operations are carried on through subsidiaries located in Western Europe, Canada, and Latin America. The United Rail Equipment Division manufactures freight and passenger cars, forgings, various railroad car parts, and miscellaneous medium to heavy weldments. In 1977, the company sold over 1,700 freight cars and a much smaller number of passenger cars. Recent orders have created a two-year backlog in orders worth over $1 billion to the company's future production.

[9]From Aggarwal and Khera, *Management Science: Cases and Applications*, 1st. ed. (Oakland, Calif.: Holden-Day, Inc.,)

The two-year backlog is particularly pleasing to Eugene Farrell, Marketing Vice President for the Division. After being discharged from the Navy, Farrell joined the company as a salesman in 1948. He rose to the position of marketing manager in 1964 and was elected Vice President in 1969. During his time with the company, he had seen many years when the company had to look far and wide to secure enough orders to keep its production lines going. The two-year backlog, the first in Farrell's reign as Vice President, gave him a comfortable feeling.

However, Farrell's contentment with the status quo was challenged by Frank Evans, the company's chief industrial engineer. Evans, a much younger man with a degree in mechanical engineering from MIT and one in industrial and systems engineering from Stanford, believed that a two-year backlog was detrimental to the company's image. He felt the company was being unresponsive to the critical social need for urban mass transit. He felt also that in the long run such slow deliveries would be detrimental to United Rail since cities shopping for new mass transit cars might turn to foreign suppliers in order to get faster deliveries. He was particularly concerned about competition from French and Japanese manufacturers of such equipment. On April 17, 1977, Evans sent a memo to Edward Crown, the Executive Vice President, expressing his views and asking for authorization to conduct a study to explore the possibilities of speeding up the production process.

Ed Crown had a great deal of respect for Evans' capabilities but he wanted to consider additional factors before making any decisions. Consequently, he called a meeting to consider the matter with Evans, Farrell, and Arthur Conway, Controller. The meeting was scheduled for 9:30 a.m. on May 14. Evans was the first to speak and talked of the potential dangers of long backlogs. This immediately brought arguments from Eugene Farrell, who pointed to the fallacy of speeding up deliveries when the public transportation "boom" might not last as long as some had expected. He also said that it might be very costly to hire the additional manpower that would be needed if production were increased. Evans argued back that no more personnel need be hired since he intended to study the company's practice regarding "make or buy" decisions. His study therefore would determine which materials, subassemblies, and assemblies to *make* within the company's manufacturing facilities, and which ones to *buy* from subcontractors in order to minimize the time required to build a rapid transit car.

Ed Crown, who had so far remained silent, spoke next. He liked Evans' idea of optimizing production but did not want to antagonize Farrell, with whom he had a very close relationship. He argued that Farrell was right in his appraisal of the potential of the rapid transit market, and that the fear of foreign competition was unfounded. However, a closer look at "make or buy" decisions was justified from a cost point of view. He looked to Art Conway for support and found a ready ally. Conway argued that if manufacturing costs could be reduced, the possible effects of an uncertain market could be minimized. This compromise helped Evans and Farrell avoid a confrontation, and Evans set about the task of optimizing the company's "make or buy" practices.

He started by investigating the overall rapid transit vehicle, which is made up of several subsystems such as car body structure, propulsion, suspension, braking, interior finish, air conditioning, and automatic train control. He found that each of these systems is comprised of numerous subsystems; thus, the "make or buy" decision must be made for each system and subsystem.

Evans believed that the suspension system is a vital system in the modern rapid transit car. This system provides a safe and comfortable ride at all speeds and accommodates the propulsion motor-drive and brake units. The suspension system is also utilized for housing the automatic train control functions and the parking brake (handbrake). Evans therefore decided to first evaluate the "make or buy" decision in regard to those subassemblies which make up the suspension system and are a bottleneck in increasing in-house production.

Since the major structural parts used in the suspension system are usually steel castings, and the company does not have its own foundry facilities, United Rail would have to obtain these castings from an outside foundry. There have been occasions when United Rail has purchased this system, completely assembled, from a supplier. However, more often United Rail has chosen to buy a quantity of the subsystems and do a considerable amount of the assembly in-house. In this case, the system supplier is first asked to quote the cost of supplying the complete system. Costs are then obtained from the system supplier for the deletion of certain items of *work content* and certain items of *supply*. The cost of these same items of work content and supply are also obtained for internal production so that the cost of performing the work internally can be compared to that of having it done by the supplier.

For the suspension system, there were eleven different items of work content and supply which were being considered. For each of these items, the amount by which United Rail's costs varied from the costs of the supplier were determined.

The cost differential for each of the items in question is presented in Table 1. A negative number in the cost differential column indicates that it would cost United Rail more to perform the function in-house. (A positive number in the cost differential column indicates how much United Rail will save if it produces it in-house). Table 1 also illustrates the time it would take the company to perform each activity.

Since there is normally a limitation on the length of time which a partially completed system can be retained in the shop prior to its becoming a part of the transit car, there is a constraint on the amount of time which can be spent in-house in completing each system. These times are shown in Table 2.

Table 1 Cost Differentials and Completion Times for Various Suspension System Functions

Function No.	Item	Cost Differential ($)	Completion (Hours)
1	Side Bearing Assembly	24.90	4.25
2	Radial Bar Supports	−12.30	1.28
3	Radial Bar	22.12	4.25
4	Handbrake Kit	37.12	3.22
5	Trip Cocks	4.90	1.42
6	Brake Units	−35.20	4.67
7	Brake Piping	−10.18	5.72
8	Axle Generator	24.20	4.21
9	Current Collector	10.18	1.24
10	Wiring	−42.18	6.97
11	Wheel Axle Assembly	−12.81	2.58

Table 2 Maximum Time Allowed for the Completion of Each System

System No.	Item Nos.	Total Maximum Time
1	2, 4, 7, 8, 9, 10	20 hours
2	1, 3, 7, 8	12 hours
3	9, 10, 11	10 hours
4	5, 7, 11	8 hours
5	1, 3, 6	7 hours

Warner-Lambert Canada Limited (X)[10]

In April 1968, Warner-Lambert Canada Limited was considering introducing throat lozenges to the Canadian pharmaceutical market. Lozenges distributed under the company brand name had sold well in the U.S. and had become a profitable venture. Consequently, the Canadian subsidiary was contemplating launching a throat lozenge on the Canadian market.

Warner-Lambert Canada Limited was a wholly owned subsidiary of the U.S. parent. The company had two factories in Canada, both located in Toronto, one making candy and chewing gum and the other producing pharmaceuticals and health and beauty aids.

One of the products sold throughout the world by the parent company and its subsidiaries was Listerine Antiseptic, a well-known mouthwash. It had been on the market for many years and was highly regarded both by dealers and consumers. Distributed through both food and drug stores, Listerine mouthwash held nearly 40 percent of the Canadian mouthwash market.

In the fall of 1965 the U.S. parent decided to test market a throat lozenge under the Listerine brand name. The lozenges were designed to provide temporary relief from sore throats caused by coughs and colds. As the test market was successful, national distribution in the U.S. was undertaken the following year and 9.5 percent of the total throat lozenge market was achieved. In the fall of 1967 two additional flavours, orange and lemon-mint, were added. By February 1968, Listerine was second in throat lozenge sales with 16.5 percent of the total U.S. market.

In April 1968, Mr. R.T. DeMarco, Product Manager in the Consumer Products Division of Warner-Lambert Canada Limited, decided to investigate the possibilities of manufacturing and distributing Listerine Throat Lozenges in Canada. He assigned Chris Seymour, an Assistant Brand Manager in the Consumer Products Division, the task of recommending to the company an action plan for the proposed product.

The Market

Mr. Seymour's first step was to investigate the Canadian throat lozenge market. At that time there were about 40 brands of the product being sold in Canada at prices ranging from 35¢ to $1.49 per package. There were no unique product claims since all brands offered the same benefit (i.e., temporary relief from sore throat pain). Mr. Seymour was surprised to find out that there was virtually no media advertising in this product field. About 85 percent of the throat lozenges sold in Canada

[10]From Christoph Haehling von Lanzenauer, *Cases in Operations Research* (London, Ontario: The University of Western Ontario, 1975), pp. 172–182. Reproduced with Special Permission from The University of Western Ontario.

Table 1

	1963	1964	($ in Millions) 1965	1966	1967	Est. 1968
U.S. Food/Drug*	$27.8	$29.4	$33.6	$33.8	$32.1	$34.5
% Change	+11%	+7%	+15%	+1%	−4%	+7%
Canada Food/Drug**	—	$ 2.9	$ 3.5	$ 3.4	$ 3.3	$ 3.5
% Change	—	—	+12%	−3%	−3%	+6%

*U.S. (A.C. Neilsen)
**Estimated on Canadian Davee, Koehnlein and Keating Company (D. K. & K.) (retail sales)

were sold through drug stores while the remainder were distributed through food stores or other mass merchandisers. In the U.S. only 70 percent were sold by drug stores. Mr. Seymour collected the growth data in the Canadian and U.S. markets for the previous few years as shown in Table 1.

Pharmaceutical products which were available to Canadian consumers without a prescription could be classified into two categories.

1. Antibacterial/Antibiotic Throat Lozenges

(Sometimes called OTC or Over-The-Counter products.) These contained active ingredients which were either antibiotic in nature or which worked against specific kinds of bacteria. Canadian sales of lozenges in this category had declined 13 percent in the years 1964–67.

2. Proprietary Throat Lozenges

These did not contain this kind of active drug ingredient; rather they contained ingredients which relieved throat irritation temporarily without specifically acting on the cause of the irritation. Canadian sales of lozenges in this category had increased 55 percent in the year 1964–67.

The Canadian sales volumes for each category were as shown in Table 2.

In analyzing the sales drop in Canada of the antibiotic lozenges Mr. Seymour learned that in March, 1966, the U.S. Federal Drug Administration had banned the sale of all antibiotic throat lozenges in the U.S. As far as he could determine there was no such legislation being contemplated in Canada at that time.

Mr. Seymour also gathered information on the distribution of sales across Canada. In 1967 the Maritimes accounted for 7 percent of the total throat lozenge market, Quebec for 26 percent, Ontario for 42 percent, the Prairies for 15 percent

Table 2 Share of Lozenge Market By Product* (000's)

	1964		1965		1966		1967	
Anti/Anti	$ 862	58%	$ 975	55%	$ 817	47%	$ 746	45%
% vs. 1964								
Base	100%		110%		95%		87%	
Proprietary	$ 620	42%	$ 809	45%	$ 940	54%	$ 958	55%
% vs. 1964								
Base	100%		130%		150%		155%	
Total	$1,482	100%	$1,784	100%	$1,757	100%	$1,704	100%

*Based on D. K. & K. drug wholesale figures

and B.C. for 10 percent. Mr. Seymour obtained data on the 10 leading brands which accounted for more than 50 percent of the market (Table 3).

Mr. Seymour noted that in the first two months of 1968 Listerine throat lozenges in the U.S. had achieved second position with 16.5 percent of lozenge sales while market leading Sucrets held 35 percent. Both brands were proprietary products.

One difference between the Canadian and the U.S. markets was the amount of media advertising. While there was virtually no advertising in Canada, Warner-Lambert in the U.S. spent $1.25 million on throat lozenges, Sucrets spent $1.92 million and the total industry expenditures on advertising reached $5.8 million. Mr. Seymour believed that if a new product were to be introduced it should be supported by a strong marketing campaign.

Market Packaging and Pricing

On the Canadian throat lozenge market there were several different types of packages (Table 4) with the number of throat lozenges per package ranging from 10 to 50. Each company in the throat lozenge market offered only one flavour. Prices varied from 35¢ to $1.49 a box but the average price range for the main competitors was between 59¢ and 89¢.

The Product

Listerine Throat Lozenges manufactured and sold in the U.S.A. were classified as proprietary and were packaged 18 to a small pocket sized box. The lozenge itself was a candy disk about ¾" in diameter and about ¼" thick. A "bunch wrapper" was used to "bunch" foil around the lozenge. The wrapped lozenges were placed in holes in a rectangular piece of cardboard, a backing was applied and finally a plastic bubble was placed over each lozenge on the front of the card. This process was referred to a blister packaging. Each card held 6 lozenges and there were 3 cards per cardboard box. The user, after withdrawing the card from the box, simply pressed his thumb on the plastic bubble and the lozenge dropped out of the back of the card.

Table 3 Competitive Share of Canadian Market 1964–1967**

Product	Company	Product Category	1964	% Share of Market 1965	1966	1967
Bradosol	Ciba	Proprietary	11.8%	11.7%	15.5%	16.3%
Cepacol	Merrill	Proprietary	7.0	7.6	8.5	7.7
Formalid	Wampole	OTC	7.0	6.7	7.2	6.7
Dequadin	Glaxo	OTC	5.2	4.8	5.7	6.3
Bionets	Horner	OTC	5.5	3.8	6.0	5.5
Strepsils	W-C	Proprietary	–*	–*	1.1	5.3
Sucrets	M.S. & D.	Proprietary	4.2	5.0	4.0	5.2
Spectrocin-T	Squibb	OTC	2.2	3.6	7.7	4.9
Meggazones	Meggasson	Proprietary	3.5	4.1	4.3	4.7
Spectrocin-C	Squibb	Proprietary	1.0	2.9	3.6	2.9
% Total Above Products			47.4%	50.2%	63.6%	65.5%
% All Others			52.6%	49.8%	36.4%	34.5%
% Total Market			100%	100%	100%	100%

*Not on Market
**D.K. & K.

Table 4 Representative Sample of Throat Lozenge Market Packaging & Pricing

Product	Packaging Type	# of Lozenges	Retail Price	Retail Price Per Lozenge
Bradosol	Plastic Case	20	$0.91	4.6¢
Cepacol	Carton	20	.59	3.0
Contac	Carton	18	.89	4.9
Coricidin	Carton	20	1.39	7.0
Dequadin	Tube Carton	20	1.13	5.7
Formolid	Carton	50	.35	.7
Meggezones	Tin Box	25	.79	3.2
Krylex	Tube Carton	10	.90	9.0
Spectrocin-C	Tube Carton	10	.89	8.9
Spectrocin-T	Tube Carton	10	.89	8.9
Orlenta	Tube Carton	12	.90	7.5
Benylin	Tube Carton	10	.60	6.0
Soothettes	Carton	20	1.49	7.5
Strepsils	Tin	24	1.52	5.2
	AVERAGE	19.2	$ .926	4.8¢

Warner-Lambert management believed the product could obtain either antibacterial/antibiotic or proprietary classification since Listerine Throat Lozenges acted to some degree directly against the cause of irritation. Mr. Seymour, after consulting other marketing officials in the company, felt that the Listerine Throat Lozenge introduced in Canada should be classified as proprietary and should be the same product as was being sold in the U.S. This would eliminate any product development cost and would allow the Canadian market to be supplied initially by the U.S. parent if desired. The Canadian division obtained the necessary proprietary number to allow distribution of the lozenges in food stores. Warner-Lambert expected to obtain quick, wide penetration by capitalizing on the existing distribution channels between the company salesmen and the food stores which handled Listerine mouthwash.

Mr. DeMarco was in general agreement with the proposals but he urged Mr. Seymour to find out if the U.S. parent could indeed supply the Canadian market. The production planner in the U.S. informed Mr. Seymour that the U.S. could supply a limited quantity of the lozenges bunch wrapped and inserted into the cards. In order to print the Canadian proprietary number and to have bilingual printing however, it would be necessary to do the boxing in Canada.

Mr. Seymour learned that the Canadian plant could manufacture the lozenges but the Canadian plant did not have the specialized equipment necessary to bunch wrap and insert the lozenges in the holes in the cards. They did have, however, the equipment required to print the boxes and to insert the cards in the boxes. Ten months would be required for delivery and installation of the specialized equipment for bunching and blister packing.

The Test Market

Warner-Lambert often conducted a test market study before introducing a new product. Mr. Seymour realized that a national campaign could not be undertaken before the fall of 1969 but time and facilities existed to conduct a test market in one area during the 1968–69 season if management felt it was desirable. Mr. Seymour believed the prairie provinces would be an easily isolated geographical region with a minimum of advertising spillover from media in other areas. Management chose to price the product in direct competition with market leading Bradosol's price of 91¢ and accordingly set the price of Listerine lozenges at 89¢ per package of 18. Retailers would purchase the lozenges from Warner-Lambert for 55¢ a box. Mr. Seymour originally estimated that test market sales would be $60,500 (net factory value) which would represent 12.8 percent of the prairie market for lozenges. Because they could not have the necessary equipment for the test period between September 16, 1968 and August 15, 1969 the blister packaged lozenges would have to be imported from the U.S. and would be boxed in Canada in bilingual boxes.

The cost of the test was estimated to be:

Advertising	$ 43,900
Promotion	20,000
Research	10,000
Direct Selling	5,000
Direct Operating	4,600
Lozenge Cost (Including Packaging)	30,800
	$114,300

The lozenge cost was fixed since none of the imported product could be salvaged if it was not sold. Mr. Seymour used three volume estimates to represent the possible sales outcomes. He defined a successful test market as sales of 110,000 boxes ($60,500) of lozenges and he assessed the chance of achieving this level at 70 percent. He realized that even if they did not sell 110,000 boxes during the test year, they might sell a sufficient amount to be able to label the test as inconclusive. He believed there was a 20 percent chance that an inconclusive test having sales of about 90,000 boxes ($49,500) would occur. He would label the test a failure if sales were as low as 60,000 boxes ($33,000).

In order to give the product an adequate test and to be operating efficiently during the cold season it would be necessary to have the product on the store shelves by the end of October 1968. This would require shipments from the factory to start by September 16th. Mr. L. J. O'Keefe, Sales Manager, informed Mr. Seymour that the very latest his salesmen could begin to take orders for September delivery was August 12th. This meant that July 15 would have to be the deadline for a decision to test market the product. If the order for the bunch wrapped and carded lozenges was sent to the U.S. before that date, however, there would be sufficient time to have them placed in bilingual boxes in Canada and delivered to the stores for the fall cough/cold season.

Equipment Decision

The machinery necessary for Canadian production would cost $88,000 with an additional $8,000 for installation expenses. If the order was placed in October 1968 the equipment would be ready to produce the lozenges for the introduction of the national campaign in the fall of 1969. Equipment ordered in October would require a deposit of $25,000 that would be forfeited if the order was cancelled during or before February 1969. After February the order could not be cancelled. Mr. Seymour felt that by the end of February the company would know whether the test market was going to be successful, inconclusive or a failure. An alternative choice to ordering in October was to hold the original order until the end of February 1969 when the test market outcome could be determined. Under this alternative the equipment would not be ready for the start of the 1969 campaign and if Warner-Lambert decided to go national 85 percent of the first year sales would have to be imported. The total variable cost to the Canadian division for lozenges imported from the U.S. was 28¢ per box whereas this would be reduced to 14¢ if the product was made entirely in Canada. Since Warner-Lambert Canada based their decisions on the profit contribution to the Canadian division only, and since the U.S. division would only guarantee to supply 85 percent of the first year demand, it was decided that the equipment should be ordered no later than February 28, 1969 if a national campaign was to be launched.

Profit Potential

Mr. Seymour estimated before the test market that there was a 50 percent chance of achieving high sales of 800,000 boxes from the national campaign. He believed medium sales of 650,000 boxes and low sales of 400,000 boxes had a 30 percent and 20 percent chance of occurrence respectively. National introduction would increase fixed costs due to advertising, research, and direct operating and selling expenses. Initial forecasts suggested these costs would be approximately $255,000 a year. This does not include equipment or test marketing costs. The product would be dropped after one year if national sales were medium or low. If the product reached the high sales forecast in the first year, Mr. Seymour felt it was conservative to assume that that level would be maintained for the expected ten year life of the equipment.

The test market results would allow Mr. Seymour to make more accurate estimates for the sales outcome of the national campaign. He did not think there was any chance of achieving medium or high sales nationally if the test market sales volume was considered a failure. On the other hand, a successful test would suggest a 90 percent chance for high sales nationally and a 10 percent chance for medium sales. Although an inconclusive test result was the most difficult to evaluate, Mr. Seymour estimated it would suggest a 65 percent chance of low national sales and a 35 percent chance for high sales.

Mr. Seymour learned that the new equipment had no other use and would have negligible value if the new product was dropped. He decided to make his initial projections on a before tax basis since all the revenues and expenses with the exception of the equipment purchase were period flows and were subject to the same tax rate. If his analysis did not make the optimum course of action obvious he planned to recalculate considering the tax effects.

At the same time he realized that a dollar received in the future was of less value than a dollar received immediately. Since the company looked for new projects that returned 10 to 15 percent after taxes he decided to discount the before tax income figures for the national campaign at 22 percent (Table 5). With these assumptions he felt he could determine the best strategy for the new product.

Table 5 Profit Contribution From National Sales

		Sales	
	High	**Medium**	**Low**
I. *Equipment Ordered October 1968*			
Sales (boxes)	800,000	650,000	400,000
Contribution Margin			
per box (55¢-14¢)	41¢	41¢	41¢
Contribution Margin	$328,000	$266,500	$164,000
Fixed Costs	255,000	255,000	255,000
Profit	$ 73,000	$ 11,500	−$ 91,000
Years	10	1	1
Present Value Discount			
Factor at 22%	3.923	.82	.82
Present Value of			
Expected Profit	$286,379	$ 9,430	−$ 74,620
II. *Equipment Ordered February 1969*			
A. Year 1			
Sales (boxes)	800,000	650,000	400,000
Contribution Margin			
per box year 1	29.1¢	29.1¢	29.1¢
55¢ − ([.85 × .28] +			
[.15 × .14])			
Year 1 Contribution	$232,800	$189,000	$116,400
Fixed Costs	255,000	255,000	255,000
Profit from Year 1	−$22,200	−$65,850	−$138,600
Present Value			
Year 1 Profit	−$18,204	−$53,997	−$113,652
(Profit × .82)			
B. Years 2 to 10			
Contribution Margin			
per box years 2–10	41¢		
Contribution Margin			
per year	$328,000		
Fixed Cost	255,000		
Profit per year	$ 73,000		
Discount Annuity from			
years 2 to 10, to time zero	3.104		
3.786 × .82			
Present Value Profit			
years 2 to 10	$226,592		
Present Value of			
Expected Profit	$208,388	−$53,997	−$113,652

Wilton Toy Company[11]

In May 1971, Mr. Brian Cunningham, President of Wilton Toy Company, was evaluating two new product proposals to determine which one his company should accept. After the two proposals had each reached the final planning stages, Mr. Cunningham reviewed the company's financial position and decided that only one new product could be undertaken at that time. He wanted to select the most profitable venture, but he hoped to avoid incurring a great deal of risk.

Wilton had just experienced two years of declining profit. Since accepting the top position at Wilton after Mr. Art Wilton's death in December 1970, Mr. Cunningham had continued to operate the business based on the policies and procedures formed by his predecessor, but he was beginning to re-examine existing practices in order to reverse the downward profit trend. With the exception of a few standard products, most toys had a limited product life cycle. The first few years were extremely important since the company that produced an innovative idea often was able to make substantial profits before the completion became too keen. In the past, Wilton had competed successfully because it had introduced many popular new products. In recent years, however, Wilton had shown a decline in new product introductions. The problem was compounded by disappointing sales levels for a remote control battery operated model car that was introduced for the 1970 Christmas season.

In the past, Wilton Toys had always calculated the before tax return on investment that could be expected for a new venture. When two or more proposals were in the final planning stages and were competing for the same funds, the R.O.I. was used as the determining factor. The two proposals being considered in May recommended that Wilton produce a toy pistol and a plastic mini motorcycle replica. The toy pistol suggestion had been submitted by the new product design team which was formed by management personnel. The team believed the toy should be modeled after the U.S. Army pistols used in Vietnam. Sales estimates for the gun were made with considerable confidence since the market potential was well known for this type of product. The sales manager believed that 30,000 guns could be sold at Wilton's price of $4.00. The project would require an investment of about $110,000 and would incur $4,000, fixed costs and $3 per gun, variable costs.

Wilton had always attempted to utilize the potential of its work force by encouraging company employees to submit new product ideas. The motorcycle proposal was the direct result of a suggestion by Mr. Larry Bradshaw, a production foreman. Mr. Bradshaw believed a small replica of the mini motorcycle would be very popular and could be produced economically. The sales manager, however, experienced considerable difficulty in making a sales estimate due to the novelty and the uniqueness of the toy. After considerable discussion and deliberation, the sales manager set the best estimate for motorcycle sales at 6,000 units for Wilton's $11.50 selling price. The required investment would be $116,000 while fixed costs would be $5,000 and variable cost would be $6 per cycle.

Mr. Cunningham realized the R.O.I. forecast for the motorcycle proposal was 24.1 percent compared to 23.6 percent for the gun suggestion, but the small spread combined with the uncertainty of the motorcycle sales volume concerned him. These doubts prompted Mr. Cunningham to hire Mr. Julian Davis on a consulting

[11]From A.A. Grindlay, "Wilton Toy Company," in MANAGEMENT SCIENCE AND THE MANAGER, Newson ed., © 1980, pp. 151–154. Reprinted by permission of Prentice Hall, Inc., Englewood Cliffs, New Jersey.

basis. Mr. Cunningham asked Mr. Davis to examine the R.O.I. calculations for each proposal and to make some sound recommendations suggesting how the uncertainty should be handled.

Mr. Davis spent some time studying the background of the selection problem. Then he confronted the men responsible for making the forecasts used in the R.O.I. calculations. He learned that the selling price and the fixed costs could be accurately predetermined. The sales volume, the variable cost, and the investment expense, on the other hand, were the best estimates of the sales manager, the production manager and the vice president respectively. All three men admitted that there could be considerable variation from their forecasted values.

When Mr. Davis returned to the sales manager, he had little difficulty in extracting a sales range for each project. Using the sales range for the upper and lower limits, Mr. Davis asked at what sales estimate would there be a 75 percent chance that actual pistol sales would be less than the estimate. The sales manager figured that there was a 75 percent chance that pistol sales would be less than 31,000 units. Continuing in this manner Mr. Davis and the sales manager were able to set the odds for sales being equal to or less than six specific volumes for each project (Table 1). Mr. Davis noted that the sales volume for the motorcycle proposal might vary over 90 percent from the figure used in the original R.O.I. calculations.

Mr. Davis used the same technique when he met again with the production manager and the vice president. The production manager was initially quite reluctant to make cost estimates for specific probabilities. Mr. Davis asked him what the greatest possible variable cost would be. Next he asked what chance existed that the production manager's original forecast to Mr. Cunningham might be exceeded. By graphing the estimates, Mr. Davis was able to ask about intermediate values between these forecasts. As the distribution began to take shape, the production manager's confidence developed and Mr. Davis was finally able to draw a representative curve for the possible outcomes.

Mr. Davis planned to calculate the expected value for each variable for both alternatives from the forecasts he had received (Tables 1 and 2). The expected values could be used to determine an R.O.I. figure for both proposals. All possible results would then have an effect on the R.O.I. figures, rather than just the most likely value. Mr. Davis hoped to illustrate the risk by revealing the spread of possible outcomes for each proposal. He planned to run a computer simulation to calculate the R.O.I.'s for both alternatives. The simulation results could be plotted to show the frequency distribution which would reveal the possibilities of all levels of return for each project.

Table 1 Wilton Toy Company Sales Forecasts

	Toy Pistol		Motorcycle	
Estimate (units)	Probability Actual Less than Estimate		Estimate (units)	Probability Actual Less than Estimate
24,000	5%		2,500	5%
28,000	30		3,500	30
30,000	50		6,000	50
31,000	75		7,500	80
33,000	95		9,000	95
36,000	100		11,000	100

Table 2 Wilton Toy Company Investment and Variable Cost Distributions

Estimate	Toy Pistol Probability Actual Less than Estimate	Estimate	Motorcycle Probability Actual Less than Estimate
Investment			
$106,000	5%	$113,000	5%
108,000	15	115,000	25
109,000	30	116,000	50
110,000	50	118,000	70
112,000	95	120,000	90
115,000	100	123,000	100
Variable cost			
$2.94	5	$5.85	5
2.96	25	5.90	20
2.98	40	5.95	40
3.00	50	6.00	50
3.02	70	6.05	75
3.04	90	6.10	90
3.07	100	6.15	100

Appendix A

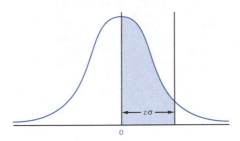

Table 1 Area under the Normal Curve, where z represents the number of standard deviations from the mean.

z	.00	.01	.02	.03	.04	.05	.06	.07	.08	.09
0.0	.0000	.0040	.0080	.0120	.0160	.0199	.0239	.0279	.0319	.0359
0.1	.0389	.0438	.0478	.0517	.0557	.0596	.0636	.0675	.0714	.0753
0.2	.0793	.0832	.0871	.0910	.0948	.0987	.1026	.1064	.1103	.1141
0.3	.1179	.1217	.1255	.1293	.1331	.1368	.1406	.1443	.1480	.1517
0.4	.1554	.1591	.1628	.1664	.1700	.1736	.1772	.1808	.1844	.1879
0.5	.1915	.1950	.1985	.2019	.2054	.2088	.2123	.2157	.2190	.2224
0.6	.2257	.2291	.2324	.2357	.2389	.2422	.2454	.2486	.2517	.2549
0.7	.2580	.2611	.2642	.2673	.2703	.2734	.2764	.2794	.2823	.2852
0.8	.2881	.2910	.2939	.2967	.2995	.3023	.3051	.3078	.3106	.3133
0.9	.3159	.3186	.3212	.3238	.3264	.3289	.3315	.3340	.3365	.3389
1.0	.3413	.3438	.3461	.3485	.3508	.3531	.3554	.3577	.3599	.3621
1.1	.3643	.3665	.3686	.3708	.3729	.3749	.3770	.3790	.3810	.3830
1.2	.3849	.3869	.3888	.3907	.3925	.3944	.3962	.3980	.3997	.4015
1.3	.4032	.4049	.4066	.4082	.4099	.4115	.4131	.4147	.4162	.4177
1.4	.4192	.4207	.4222	.4236	.4251	.4265	.4279	.4292	.4306	.4319
1.5	.4332	.4345	.4357	.4370	.4382	.4394	.4406	.4418	.4429	.4441
1.6	.4452	.4463	.4474	.4484	.4495	.4505	.4515	.4525	.4535	.4545
1.7	.4554	.4564	.4573	.4582	.4591	.4599	.4608	.4616	.4625	.4633
1.8	.4641	.4649	.4656	.4664	.4671	.4678	.4686	.4693	.4699	.4706
1.9	.4713	.4719	.4726	.4732	.4738	.4744	.4750	.4756	.4761	.4767
2.0	.4772	.4778	.4783	.4788	.4793	.4798	.4803	.4808	.4812	.4817
2.1	.4821	.4826	.4830	.4834	.4838	.4842	.4846	.4850	.4854	.4857
2.2	.4861	.4864	.4868	.4871	.4875	.4878	.4881	.4884	.4887	.4890
2.3	.4893	.4896	.4898	.4901	.4904	.4906	.4909	.4911	.4913	.4916
2.4	.4918	.4920	.4922	.4925	.4927	.4929	.4931	.4932	.4934	.4936
2.5	.4938	.4940	.4941	.4943	.4945	.4946	.4948	.4949	.4951	.4952
2.6	.4953	.4955	.4956	.4957	.4959	.4960	.4961	.4962	.4963	.4964
2.7	.4965	.4966	.4967	.4968	.4969	.4970	.4971	.4972	.4973	.4974
2.8	.4974	.4975	.4976	.4977	.4977	.4978	.4979	.4979	.4980	.4981
2.9	.4981	.4982	.4982	.4983	.4984	.4984	.4985	.4985	.4986	.4986
3.0	.4987	.4987	.4987	.4988	.4988	.4989	.4989	.4989	.4990	.4990

Table 2 Random Number Table

76870	83391	63974	45539	64151	54333	73292	70139	38283	45363	74477
79143	62027	76667	13714	16297	02788	75628	89703	05057	71682	20482
53130	17606	95574	17615	83603	06362	03703	37249	91646	63989	78853
57461	20206	86223	19863	64780	66506	25967	15217	60328	76616	81811
67835	86676	75158	73471	91534	79500	10142	68200	41868	03841	59999
58471	92768	56322	25177	50896	58141	22364	75010	04470	06423	91008
04114	26969	31633	84436	43029	37079	61819	31048	45203	08129	14404
19976	92047	13814	69021	55459	77334	62282	89821	78591	01215	14002
52194	74833	84743	30964	26772	33578	39887	70903	93257	44379	19779
07475	45035	78354	17023	95578	26930	75563	93231	95778	65376	84660
13790	75119	19295	87688	73876	97187	53360	88292	79119	68348	78915
57130	75880	43070	66016	93582	23079	24138	53419	92366	72267	28178
09777	47990	36412	64159	94412	56866	36888	70872	56449	14297	89248
82966	13418	42998	25944	71331	81806	44371	33323	45080	33476	61216
14774	81340	15642	24751	26327	00835	79132	12071	09164	89172	30450
43773	72227	98512	47612	72949	89520	24849	36124	20393	81494	09206
75725	18444	57204	95049	10236	88576	43879	09078	30720	93154	26000
50199	22499	55724	30853	73854	44572	70488	13856	98802	07672	97351
95288	30506	88792	99976	49732	64002	22300	63507	77209	89708	66280
60257	65944	67636	99050	30234	80587	13083	51832	29958	06146	62632
14945	20929	25499	86087	40881	63689	11712	45555	27135	10362	75328
35992	90797	94968	59993	81567	71504	35387	20583	86243	90247	86302
84639	86218	55977	33004	95499	02875	99146	17718	81268	04386	39700
40003	41975	94037	70034	58677	38216	59565	59671	35052	71679	67550
65971	54700	16479	03840	33407	98151	99260	56482	40760	41789	39567
62300	46505	98312	67218	51224	48506	63400	74953	96264	34683	56505
78315	41692	28366	21435	78746	28038	39555	93151	56761	59150	97488
54574	45665	19045	34737	42556	44370	41185	18084	23574	07203	92017
90635	47918	47994	92981	99476	32124	92598	36883	48283	89852	76558
80715	75029	58166	69669	42398	96885	06205	88816	87443	69481	62373
51949	29509	23074	21249	56545	15201	87171	08687	31936	87765	55675
31038	14599	80825	36819	13875	59548	14257	18199	53602	07318	86093
35169	27652	14370	30642	87979	15654	29657	84309	62016	74289	79977
31526	27047	64540	75906	14422	40377	52192	38230	46679	58413	62421
20815	89618	51951	70524	72200	50903	73140	97393	39724	93394	70950
13187	39336	81415	41537	31043	48123	14598	90446	67115	04746	44321
94234	95015	81376	80508	91635	62102	03583	66054	47680	71525	45803
33129	48975	02385	75042	41035	69616	34563	35610	55391	03444	93653
40935	04801	06457	96912	16238	21881	46714	97134	63932	68211	72565
33273	46795	09218	20320	15589	81051	69315	60864	01866	49265	97109
99814	64231	53539	97878	46514	04759	63906	36943	08867	45153	61541
08247	18140	33999	84813	80938	93176	50239	70922	92529	08519	12872

Table 3 Values of $e^{-\lambda}$

λ	$e^{-\lambda}$	λ	$e^{-\lambda}$	λ	$e^{-\lambda}$
0.0	1.00000	4.0	0.01832	8.0	0.00034
0.1	0.90484	4.1	0.01657	8.1	0.00030
0.2	0.81873	4.2	0.01500	8.1	0.00027
0.3	0.74082	4.3	0.01357	8.3	0.00025
0.4	0.67032	4.4	0.01228	8.4	0.00022
0.5	0.60653	4.5	0.01111	8.5	0.00020
0.6	0.54881	4.6	0.01005	8.6	0.00018
0.7	0.49659	4.7	0.00910	8.7	0.00017
0.8	0.44933	4.8	0.00823	8.8	0.00015
0.9	0.40657	4.9	0.00745	8.9	0.00014
1.0	0.36788	5.0	0.00674	9.0	0.00012
1.1	0.33287	5.1	0.00610	9.1	0.00011
1.2	0.30119	5.2	0.00552	9.2	0.00010
1.3	0.27253	5.3	0.00499	9.3	0.00009
1.4	0.24660	5.4	0.00452	9.4	0.00008
1.5	0.22313	5.5	0.00409	9.5	0.00007
1.6	0.20190	5.6	0.00370	9.6	0.00007
1.7	0.18268	5.7	0.00335	9.7	0.00006
1.8	0.16530	5.8	0.00303	9.8	0.00006
1.9	0.14957	5.9	0.00274	9.9	0.00005
2.0	0.13534	6.0	0.00248	10.0	0.00005
2.1	0.12246	6.1	0.00224		
2.2	0.11080	6.2	0.00203		
2.3	0.10026	6.3	0.00184		
2.4	0.09072	6.4	0.00166		
2.5	0.08208	6.5	0.00150		
2.6	0.07427	6.6	0.00136		
2.7	0.06721	6.7	0.00123		
2.8	0.06081	6.8	0.00111		
2.9	0.05502	6.9	0.00101		
3.0	0.04979	7.0	0.00091		
3.1	0.04505	7.1	0.00083		
3.2	0.04076	7.2	0.00075		
3.3	0.03688	7.3	0.00068		
3.4	0.03337	7.4	0.00061		
3.5	0.03020	7.5	0.00055		
3.6	0.02732	7.6	0.00050		
3.7	0.02472	7.3	0.00045		
3.8	0.02237	7.8	0.00041		
3.9	0.02024	7.9	0.00037		

Table 4 Cumulative Poisson Probabilities $P(\lambda \leq c)$

λ	c: 0	1	2	3	4	5	6	7	8	9	10	11	12	13	14	15	16	17	18	19	20
0.05	0.9512	0.9988	1.0000																		
0.10	0.9048	0.9953	0.9998	1.0000																	
0.15	0.8607	0.9898	0.9995	1.0000																	
0.20	0.8187	0.9825	0.9989	0.9999	1.0000																
0.25	0.7788	0.9735	0.9978	0.9999	1.0000																
0.30	0.7408	0.9631	0.9964	0.9997	1.0000																
0.35	0.7047	0.9513	0.9945	0.9995	1.0000																
0.40	0.6703	0.9384	0.9921	0.9992	0.9999	1.0000															
0.45	0.6376	0.9246	0.9891	0.9988	0.9999	1.0000															
0.50	0.6065	0.9098	0.9856	0.9982	0.9998	1.0000															
0.55	0.5769	0.8943	0.9815	0.9975	0.9997	1.0000															
0.60	0.5488	0.8781	0.9769	0.9966	0.9996	1.0000															
0.65	0.5220	0.8614	0.9717	0.9956	0.9994	0.9999	1.0000														
0.70	0.4966	0.8442	0.9659	0.9942	0.9992	0.9999	1.0000														
0.75	0.4724	0.8266	0.9595	0.9927	0.9989	0.9999	1.0000														
0.80	0.4493	0.8088	0.9526	0.9909	0.9986	0.9998	1.0000														
0.85	0.4274	0.7907	0.9451	0.9889	0.9982	0.9997	1.0000														
0.90	0.4066	0.7725	0.9371	0.9865	0.9977	0.9997	1.0000														
0.95	0.3867	0.7541	0.9287	0.9839	0.9971	0.9995	0.9999	1.0000													
1.00	0.3679	0.7358	0.9197	0.9810	0.9963	0.9994	0.9999	1.0000													
1.10	0.3329	0.6990	0.9004	0.9743	0.9946	0.9990	0.9999	1.0000													
1.20	0.3012	0.6626	0.8795	0.9662	0.9923	0.9985	0.9997	1.0000													
1.30	0.2725	0.6268	0.8571	0.9569	0.9893	0.9978	0.9996	0.9999	1.0000												
1.40	0.2466	0.5918	0.8335	0.9463	0.9857	0.9968	0.9994	0.9999	1.0000												
1.50	0.2231	0.5578	0.8088	0.9344	0.9814	0.9955	0.9991	0.9998	1.0000												
1.60	0.2019	0.5249	0.7834	0.9212	0.9763	0.9940	0.9987	0.9997	1.0000												
1.70	0.1827	0.4932	0.7572	0.9068	0.9704	0.9920	0.9981	0.9996	0.9999	1.0000											
1.80	0.1653	0.4628	0.7306	0.8913	0.9636	0.9896	0.9974	0.9994	0.9999	1.0000											
1.90	0.1496	0.4337	0.7037	0.8747	0.9559	0.9868	0.9966	0.9992	0.9998	1.0000											
2.00	0.1353	0.4060	0.6767	0.8571	0.9473	0.9834	0.9955	0.9989	0.9998	1.0000											
2.10	0.1225	0.3796	0.6496	0.8386	0.9379	0.9796	0.9941	0.9985	0.9997	0.9999	1.0000										
2.20	0.1108	0.3546	0.6227	0.8194	0.9275	0.9751	0.9925	0.9980	0.9995	0.9999	1.0000										
2.30	0.1003	0.3309	0.5960	0.7993	0.9162	0.9700	0.9906	0.9974	0.9994	0.9999	1.0000										
2.40	0.0907	0.3084	0.5697	0.7787	0.9041	0.9643	0.9884	0.9967	0.9991	0.9998	1.0000										
2.50	0.0821	0.2873	0.5438	0.7576	0.8912	0.9580	0.9858	0.9958	0.9989	0.9997	0.9999	1.0000									
2.60	0.0743	0.2674	0.5184	0.7360	0.8774	0.9510	0.9828	0.9947	0.9985	0.9996	0.9999	1.0000									
2.70	0.0672	0.2487	0.4936	0.7141	0.8629	0.9433	0.9794	0.9934	0.9981	0.9995	0.9999	1.0000									
2.80	0.0608	0.2311	0.4695	0.6919	0.8477	0.9349	0.9756	0.9919	0.9976	0.9993	0.9998	1.0000									

λ	c: 0	1	2	3	4	5	6	7	8	9	10	11	12	13	14	15	16	17	18	19	20
2.90	0.0550	0.2146	0.4460	0.6696	0.8318	0.9258	0.9713	0.9901	0.9969	0.9991	0.9998	0.9999	1.0000								
3.00	0.0498	0.1991	0.4232	0.6472	0.8153	0.9161	0.9665	0.9881	0.9962	0.9989	0.9997	0.9999	1.0000								
3.20	0.0408	0.1712	0.3799	0.6025	0.7806	0.8946	0.9554	0.9832	0.9943	0.9982	0.9995	0.9999	1.0000								
3.40	0.0334	0.1468	0.3397	0.5584	0.7442	0.8705	0.9421	0.9769	0.9917	0.9973	0.9992	0.9998	0.9999	1.0000							
3.60	0.0273	0.1257	0.3027	0.5152	0.7064	0.8441	0.9267	0.9692	0.9883	0.9960	0.9987	0.9996	0.9999	1.0000							
3.80	0.0224	0.1074	0.2689	0.4735	0.6678	0.8156	0.9091	0.9599	0.9840	0.9942	0.9981	0.9994	0.9998	1.0000							
4.00	0.0183	0.0916	0.2381	0.4335	0.6288	0.7851	0.8893	0.9489	0.9786	0.9919	0.9972	0.9991	0.9997	0.9999	1.0000						
4.20	0.0150	0.0780	0.2102	0.3954	0.5898	0.7531	0.8675	0.9361	0.9721	0.9889	0.9959	0.9986	0.9996	0.9999	1.0000						
4.40	0.0123	0.0663	0.1851	0.3594	0.5512	0.7199	0.8436	0.9214	0.9642	0.9851	0.9943	0.9980	0.9993	0.9998	0.9999	1.0000					
4.60	0.0101	0.0563	0.1626	0.3257	0.5132	0.6858	0.8180	0.9049	0.9549	0.9805	0.9922	0.9971	0.9990	0.9997	0.9999	1.0000					
4.80	0.0082	0.0477	0.1425	0.2942	0.4763	0.6510	0.7908	0.8867	0.9442	0.9749	0.9896	0.9960	0.9986	0.9995	0.9999	1.0000					
5.00	0.0067	0.0404	0.1247	0.2650	0.4405	0.6160	0.7622	0.8666	0.9319	0.9682	0.9863	0.9945	0.9980	0.9993	0.9998	0.9999	1.0000				
5.20	0.0055	0.0342	0.1088	0.2381	0.4061	0.5809	0.7324	0.8449	0.9181	0.9603	0.9823	0.9927	0.9972	0.9990	0.9997	0.9999	1.0000				
5.40	0.0045	0.0289	0.0948	0.2133	0.3733	0.5461	0.7017	0.8217	0.9027	0.9512	0.9775	0.9904	0.9962	0.9986	0.9995	0.9998	0.9999	1.0000			
5.60	0.0037	0.0244	0.0824	0.1906	0.3422	0.5119	0.6703	0.7970	0.8857	0.9409	0.9718	0.9875	0.9949	0.9980	0.9993	0.9998	0.9999	1.0000			
5.80	0.0030	0.0206	0.0715	0.1700	0.3127	0.4783	0.6384	0.7710	0.8672	0.9292	0.9651	0.9841	0.9932	0.9973	0.9990	0.9996	0.9999	1.0000			
6.00	0.0025	0.0174	0.0620	0.1512	0.2851	0.4457	0.6063	0.7440	0.8472	0.9161	0.9574	0.9799	0.9912	0.9964	0.9986	0.9995	0.9998	0.9999	1.0000		
6.20	0.0020	0.0146	0.0536	0.1342	0.2592	0.4141	0.5742	0.7160	0.8259	0.9016	0.9486	0.9750	0.9887	0.9952	0.9981	0.9993	0.9997	0.9999	1.0000		
6.40	0.0017	0.0123	0.0463	0.1189	0.2351	0.3837	0.5423	0.6873	0.8033	0.8858	0.9386	0.9693	0.9857	0.9937	0.9974	0.9990	0.9996	0.9999	1.0000		
6.60	0.0014	0.0103	0.0400	0.1052	0.2127	0.3547	0.5108	0.6581	0.7796	0.8686	0.9274	0.9627	0.9821	0.9920	0.9966	0.9986	0.9995	0.9998	0.9999		
6.80	0.0011	0.0087	0.0344	0.0928	0.1920	0.3270	0.4799	0.6285	0.7548	0.8502	0.9151	0.9552	0.9779	0.9898	0.9956	0.9982	0.9993	0.9997	0.9999	1.0000	
7.00	0.0009	0.0073	0.0296	0.0818	0.1730	0.3007	0.4497	0.5987	0.7291	0.8305	0.9015	0.9467	0.9730	0.9872	0.9943	0.9976	0.9990	0.9996	0.9999	1.0000	
7.20	0.0007	0.0061	0.0255	0.0719	0.1555	0.2759	0.4204	0.5689	0.7027	0.8096	0.8867	0.9371	0.9673	0.9841	0.9927	0.9969	0.9987	0.9995	0.9998	0.9999	1.0000
7.40	0.0006	0.0051	0.0219	0.0632	0.1395	0.2526	0.3920	0.5393	0.6757	0.7877	0.8707	0.9265	0.9609	0.9805	0.9908	0.9959	0.9983	0.9993	0.9997	0.9999	1.0000
7.60	0.0005	0.0043	0.0188	0.0554	0.1249	0.2307	0.3646	0.5100	0.6482	0.7649	0.8535	0.9148	0.9536	0.9762	0.9886	0.9948	0.9978	0.9991	0.9996	0.9999	1.0000
7.80	0.0004	0.0036	0.0161	0.0485	0.1117	0.2103	0.3384	0.4812	0.6204	0.7411	0.8352	0.9020	0.9454	0.9714	0.9859	0.9934	0.9971	0.9988	0.9995	0.9998	0.9999
8.00	0.0003	0.0030	0.0138	0.0424	0.0996	0.1912	0.3134	0.4530	0.5925	0.7166	0.8159	0.8881	0.9362	0.9658	0.9827	0.9918	0.9963	0.9984	0.9993	0.9997	0.9999
8.20	0.0003	0.0025	0.0118	0.0370	0.0887	0.1736	0.2896	0.4254	0.5647	0.6915	0.7955	0.8731	0.9261	0.9595	0.9791	0.9898	0.9953	0.9979	0.9991	0.9997	0.9999
8.40	0.0002	0.0021	0.0100	0.0323	0.0789	0.1573	0.2670	0.3987	0.5369	0.6659	0.7743	0.8571	0.9150	0.9524	0.9779	0.9875	0.9941	0.9973	0.9989	0.9995	0.9998
8.60	0.0002	0.0018	0.0086	0.0281	0.0701	0.1422	0.2457	0.3728	0.5094	0.6400	0.7522	0.8400	0.9029	0.9445	0.9701	0.9848	0.9926	0.9966	0.9985	0.9994	0.9998
8.80	0.0002	0.0015	0.0073	0.0244	0.0621	0.1284	0.2256	0.3478	0.4823	0.6137	0.7294	0.8220	0.8898	0.9358	0.9647	0.9816	0.9909	0.9957	0.9981	0.9992	0.9997
9.00	0.0001	0.0012	0.0062	0.0212	0.0550	0.1157	0.2068	0.3239	0.4557	0.5874	0.7060	0.8030	0.8758	0.9261	0.9585	0.9780	0.9889	0.9947	0.9976	0.9989	0.9996
9.50	0.0001	0.0008	0.0042	0.0149	0.0403	0.0885	0.1649	0.2687	0.3918	0.5218	0.6453	0.7520	0.8364	0.8981	0.9400	0.9665	0.9823	0.9911	0.9957	0.9980	0.9991
10.00	0.0000	0.0005	0.0028	0.0103	0.0293	0.0671	0.1301	0.2202	0.3328	0.4579	0.5830	0.6968	0.7916	0.8645	0.9165	0.9513	0.9730	0.9857	0.9928	0.9965	0.9984

Appendix B
Review of Matrix Algebra

A matrix may be defined as a rectangular array of numbers in m rows and n columns. It is described by the number of rows and columns used. Thus, a matrix with m rows and n columns is described as an $m \times n$ matrix, or a matrix of $m \times n$ dimension (order). This describes the size of the matrix. The number of elements in a matrix can be found by multiplying the number of rows times the number of columns.

A matrix is designated by either a single capital letter or a small bracketed letter with subscripts for rows and columns. It takes the following form:

$$A = [a_{ij}] = \begin{bmatrix} a_{11} & a_{12} & \cdots & a_{1n} \\ a_{21} & a_{22} & \cdots & a_{2n} \\ \vdots & \vdots & & \vdots \\ a_{m1} & a_{m2} & \cdots & a_{mn} \end{bmatrix}$$

where A is an $m \times n$ matrix.

Brackets are the usual notation for a matrix, but they may be replaced by ( ) or $\| \ \|$.

An individual element is located by specifying its row and column position, using two subscripts. The first subscript is for the row; the second subscript is for the column. Thus a_{12} is the element in row 1, column 2. Matrices as a whole have no numerical value. However, the numbers in the matrices represent useful data.

Special Matrices

A number of special matrices are often encountered. A square matrix has an equal number of rows and columns ($m = n$). In a zero or null matrix (denoted by 0) the elements are all zero (0). The identity matrix (denoted by I) is a square matrix in which all elements along the diagonal where $i = j$ (top left corner to bottom right corner) are equal to 1. All other elements are zero.

$$I = \begin{bmatrix} 1 & 0 & 1 \\ 0 & 1 & 0 \\ 0 & 0 & 1 \end{bmatrix}$$

A matrix with only one row ($m = 1$) and two or more columns is a row vector or an n-component (dimension) row vector. A matrix with only one column ($n = 1$) and two or more rows is a column vector or an m-component (dimension) column vector. Vectors are written with only one subscript (a_n). Thus

$$X = [2 \quad 4 \quad 8 \quad 6]$$

is a four-dimensional row vector and

$$Y = \begin{bmatrix} 91 \\ 82 \\ 75 \end{bmatrix}$$

is a three-dimensional column vector. A null vector has all zero elements and a unit vector has one unit (1) with the remaining elements all zero.

Matrix Operations

The Transpose of a Matrix

The transpose of a matrix, denoted A^T, is obtained by interchanging the row and column of the original matrix. Thus the ith row of matrix A becomes the ith column of the matrix A^T. For example, if

$$A = \begin{bmatrix} 4 & 8 & 5 \\ 6 & 3 & 7 \end{bmatrix}$$

then

$$A^T = \begin{bmatrix} 4 & 6 \\ 8 & 3 \\ 5 & 7 \end{bmatrix}$$

Addition and Subtraction of Matrices

Matrices can be added and subtracted only if they are of the same order, i.e., exactly the same size. Then the corresponding elements in each matrix are added and subtracted as shown here for a 2×2 matrix.

$$\begin{bmatrix} a_{11} & a_{12} \\ a_{21} & a_{22} \end{bmatrix} + \begin{bmatrix} b_{11} & b_{12} \\ b_{21} & b_{22} \end{bmatrix} = \begin{bmatrix} a_{11} + b_{11} & a_{12} + b_{12} \\ a_{21} + b_{22} & a_{22} + b_{22} \end{bmatrix}$$

For example,

$$\begin{bmatrix} 5 & 6 \\ 7 & 8 \end{bmatrix} + \begin{bmatrix} 3 & 3 \\ 4 & 4 \end{bmatrix} = \begin{bmatrix} 8 & 9 \\ 11 & 12 \end{bmatrix}$$

Matrix Multiplication

Scalar multiplication is the multiplication of a matrix by a constant, accomplished by multiplying every element in the matrix by the constant. If A = the matrix and c = a constant, then

$$cA = \begin{bmatrix} ca_{11} & ca_{12} & ca_{13} \\ ca_{21} & ca_{22} & ca_{23} \\ ca_{31} & ca_{32} & ca_{33} \end{bmatrix}$$

For example, let

$$A = \begin{bmatrix} 4 & 8 & 2 \\ 12 & 9 & 6 \\ 7 & 5 & 15 \end{bmatrix}$$

Then

$$4A = \begin{bmatrix} 16 & 32 & 8 \\ 48 & 36 & 24 \\ 28 & 20 & 60 \end{bmatrix}$$

Vector multiplication of an n-component row vector times an n-component column vector is accomplished by multiplying their corresponding elements and adding the products. Obviously, each vector must have the same number of elements. The result of vector multiplication is always a number. If

$$A = [a_1 \quad a_2 \quad a_3] \quad \text{and} \quad B = \begin{bmatrix} b_1 \\ b_2 \\ b_3 \end{bmatrix}$$

then

$$AB = a_1 b_1 + a_2 b_2 + a_3 b_3$$

or

$$AB = \sum_{i=1}^{n} a_i b_i$$

For example, if

$$A = [5 \quad 8 \quad 4] \quad \text{and} \quad B = \begin{bmatrix} 6 \\ 7 \\ 3 \end{bmatrix}$$

then

$$AB = (5 \times 6 + 8 \times 7 + 4 \times 3) = 98$$

Multiplying a matrix by a matrix is more complex than the two techniques just demonstrated. First, in order to multiply two matrices, the number of columns in the first matrix must be equal to the number of rows in the second matrix. If this condition is not met, the matrices are not "conformable." Multiplication is not defined. That is, if A is an $a \times b$ matrix and B is a $c \times d$ matrix, they can be multiplied only if $b = c$. Then AB is defined. The product matrix has as many rows as the first matrix and as many columns as the second matrix. That is, the order, or size, of the product matrix AB is $a \times d$. For example, if A is a 2×3 matrix and B is a 3×4 matrix, the two can be multiplied and the product AB is a 2×4 matrix. If A is a 3×4 matrix and B is a 2×3 matrix, the two cannot be multiplied because the number of columns of A are not equal to the number of rows of B ($4 \neq 2$).

In general, when multiplying matrices, each element in the resulting or product matrix is the sum of the products of the elements of the ith row of the first matrix and the jth column of the second matrix. That is, an entry in the ith row and jth column of the new matrix is obtained by adding the products formed by multiplying, in order, each entry in the ith row of the first matrix by the corresponding entry in the jth column of the second matrix. If

$$A = \begin{bmatrix} a_{11} & a_{12} & a_{13} \\ a_{21} & a_{22} & a_{23} \\ a_{31} & a_{32} & a_{33} \end{bmatrix} \quad \text{and} \quad B = \begin{bmatrix} b_{11} & b_{12} \\ b_{21} & b_{22} \\ b_{31} & b_{32} \end{bmatrix}$$

then

$$AB = \begin{bmatrix} a_{11}b_{11} + a_{12}b_{21} + a_{13}b_{31} & a_{11}b_{12} + a_{12}b_{22} + a_{13}b_{32} \\ a_{21}b_{11} + a_{22}b_{21} + a_{23}b_{31} & a_{21}b_{12} + a_{22}b_{22} + a_{23}b_{32} \\ a_{31}b_{11} + a_{32}b_{21} + a_{33}b_{31} & a_{31}b_{12} + a_{32}b_{22} + a_{33}b_{32} \end{bmatrix}$$

A simple way to find each element is to think in terms of vector multiplication (the result of vector multiplication is always a number). In the above matrices, the first element in row 1 of AB is the product of the multiplication of the row vector (the first row of matrix A):

$$[a_{11} \quad a_{12} \quad a_{13}]$$

and the column vector (the first column of matrix B):

$$\begin{bmatrix} b_{11} \\ b_{21} \\ b_{31} \end{bmatrix}$$

The second element in the first row of matrix AB is the product of the row 1 vector from matrix A:

$$[a_{11} \quad a_{12} \quad a_{13}]$$

and the vector for column 2 of matrix B:

$$\begin{bmatrix} b_{12} \\ b_{22} \\ b_{32} \end{bmatrix}$$

The process is then repeated for rows 2 and 3. In other words, the first matrix, A, is subdivided into row vectors and the second matrix, B, is subdivided into column vectors. Each element in the new matrix is then the product of vector multiplication.

Consider the following matrices, A and B:

$$A = \begin{bmatrix} 4 & 5 & 7 \\ 3 & 6 & 6 \end{bmatrix} \quad \text{and} \quad B = \begin{bmatrix} 1 & 0 \\ 8 & 3 \\ 5 & 2 \end{bmatrix}$$

The resulting product matrix AB will be a 2×2 matrix. The element in row 1, column 1 is given by the vector product of the first row of A times the first column of B. Thus

$$ab_{11} = [4 \quad 5 \quad 7] \begin{bmatrix} 1 \\ 8 \\ 5 \end{bmatrix} = 4 \times 1 + 5 \times 8 + 7 \times 5 = 79$$

The element in row 1, column 2 is given by the vector product of the first row of A times the second column of B. Thus

$$ab_{12} = [4 \quad 5 \quad 7] \begin{bmatrix} 0 \\ 3 \\ 2 \end{bmatrix} = 4 \times 0 + 5 \times 3 + 7 \times 2 = 29$$

Since AB is a 2×2 matrix, the calculations for the row 1 elements are complete. Row 2 is similarly accomplished, with the row 2 vector being used. Thus, the first element in row 2, column 1 is given by the vector product of the second row of matrix A times the first column of matrix B. The final element is the result of multiplying the second row of A times the second column of B.

$$ab_{21} = [3 \quad 6 \quad 6] \begin{bmatrix} 1 \\ 8 \\ 5 \end{bmatrix} = 3 \times 1 + 6 \times 8 + 6 \times 5 = 81$$

and

$$ab_{22} = [3 \quad 6 \quad 6] \begin{bmatrix} 0 \\ 3 \\ 2 \end{bmatrix} = 3 \times 0 + 6 \times 3 + 6 \times 2 = 30$$

Thus

$$AB = \begin{bmatrix} 79 & 29 \\ 81 & 30 \end{bmatrix}$$

It should be clear that in general $A \times B$ does not give the same result as $B \times A$. The multiplication of matrices is not commutative. It may also be true that AB is defined and BA is not. For example, if A is a 3×2 matrix and B is a 2×4 matrix, AB is defined, but BA is not.

Matrix multiplication does satisfy the associative and distributive laws of algebra:

$$A \times (B \times C) = (A \times B) \times C \qquad \text{[associative law]}$$
$$A \times (B + C) = (A \times B) + (A \times C) \quad \text{[distributive law]}$$

The Inverse of a Matrix

The inverse of any square matrix, A, can be denoted by A^{-1}. The inverse of a matrix may be found using the Gauss-Jordan elimination process. The matrix to be inverted (A) is first placed next to an identity matrix (I). The original matrix is then converted to an identity matrix through the use of elementary row operations. Identical operations are also performed on the identity matrix. This method will be used to invert the following 3×3 matrix:

$$
\begin{array}{cc}
A & I \\
\begin{bmatrix} 4 & 2 & 1 \\ 3 & 4 & 3 \\ 6 & 6 & 5 \end{bmatrix} &
\begin{bmatrix} 1 & 0 & 0 \\ 0 & 1 & 0 \\ 0 & 0 & 1 \end{bmatrix}
\end{array}
$$

The first step is to convert element a_{11} to 1. This is done by dividing the first row of the matrix by 4.

$$\begin{bmatrix} 1 & \tfrac{1}{2} & \tfrac{1}{4} \\ 3 & 4 & 3 \\ 6 & 6 & 5 \end{bmatrix} \quad \begin{bmatrix} \tfrac{1}{4} & 0 & 0 \\ 0 & 1 & 0 \\ 0 & 0 & 1 \end{bmatrix}$$

The next step is to change element a_{21} to zero. To accomplish this, row 1 is multiplied times 3 and subtracted from row 2.

$$\begin{bmatrix} 1 & \tfrac{1}{2} & \tfrac{1}{4} \\ 0 & \tfrac{5}{2} & \tfrac{9}{4} \\ 6 & 6 & 5 \end{bmatrix} \quad \begin{bmatrix} \tfrac{1}{4} & 0 & 0 \\ -\tfrac{3}{4} & 1 & 0 \\ 0 & 0 & 1 \end{bmatrix}$$

Element a_{31} is changed to zero next by multiplying row 1 times 6 and subtracting it from row 3.

$$\begin{bmatrix} 1 & \tfrac{1}{2} & \tfrac{1}{4} \\ 0 & \tfrac{5}{2} & \tfrac{9}{4} \\ 0 & 3 & \tfrac{7}{2} \end{bmatrix} \quad \begin{bmatrix} \tfrac{1}{4} & 0 & 0 \\ -\tfrac{3}{4} & 1 & 0 \\ -\tfrac{3}{2} & 0 & 1 \end{bmatrix}$$

This completes the first column. The next step is to convert element a_{22} to 1. This is done by dividing row 2 by $\tfrac{5}{2}$.

$$\begin{bmatrix} 1 & \tfrac{1}{2} & \tfrac{1}{4} \\ 0 & 1 & \tfrac{9}{10} \\ 0 & 3 & \tfrac{7}{2} \end{bmatrix} \quad \begin{bmatrix} \tfrac{1}{4} & 0 & 0 \\ -\tfrac{3}{10} & \tfrac{4}{10} & 0 \\ -\tfrac{3}{2} & 0 & 1 \end{bmatrix}$$

Element a_{12} is now changed to zero by multiplying row 2 times $\tfrac{1}{2}$ and subtracting it from row 1.

$$\begin{bmatrix} 1 & 0 & -\tfrac{2}{10} \\ 0 & 1 & \tfrac{9}{10} \\ 0 & 3 & \tfrac{7}{2} \end{bmatrix} \quad \begin{bmatrix} \tfrac{4}{10} & -\tfrac{2}{10} & 0 \\ -\tfrac{3}{10} & \tfrac{4}{10} & 0 \\ -\tfrac{3}{2} & 0 & 1 \end{bmatrix}$$

Element a_{13} is changed to zero next. This is achieved by multiplying row 2 times 3 and subtracting it from row 3.

$$\begin{bmatrix} 1 & 0 & -\tfrac{2}{10} \\ 0 & 1 & \tfrac{9}{10} \\ 0 & 1 & \tfrac{8}{10} \end{bmatrix} \quad \begin{bmatrix} \tfrac{4}{10} & -\tfrac{2}{10} & 0 \\ -\tfrac{3}{10} & \tfrac{4}{10} & 0 \\ -\tfrac{6}{10} & -\tfrac{12}{10} & 1 \end{bmatrix}$$

This completes the second column. The next step is to convert element a_{33} to 1. Multiplying the row by $\tfrac{10}{8}$ accomplishes this change.

$$\begin{bmatrix} 1 & 0 & -\tfrac{2}{10} \\ 0 & 1 & \tfrac{9}{10} \\ 0 & 0 & 1 \end{bmatrix} \quad \begin{bmatrix} \tfrac{4}{10} & -\tfrac{2}{10} & 0 \\ -\tfrac{3}{10} & \tfrac{4}{10} & 0 \\ -\tfrac{3}{4} & -\tfrac{3}{2} & \tfrac{5}{4} \end{bmatrix}$$

Element a_{13} is now changed to zero by multiplying row 3 times $\tfrac{2}{10}$ and adding it to the first row.

$$\begin{bmatrix} 1 & 0 & 0 \\ 0 & 1 & \tfrac{9}{10} \\ 0 & 0 & 1 \end{bmatrix} \quad \begin{bmatrix} \tfrac{1}{4} & -\tfrac{1}{2} & \tfrac{1}{4} \\ -\tfrac{3}{10} & \tfrac{4}{10} & 0 \\ -\tfrac{3}{4} & -\tfrac{3}{2} & \tfrac{5}{4} \end{bmatrix}$$

The last step is to convert element a_{23} to a zero. This is accomplished by multiplying row 3 times $\frac{9}{10}$ and subtracting it from row 2.

$$
\begin{array}{cc}
\mathbf{I} & \mathbf{A^{-1}} \\
\begin{bmatrix} 1 & 0 & 0 \\ 0 & 1 & 0 \\ 0 & 0 & 1 \end{bmatrix} &
\begin{bmatrix} \frac{1}{4} & -\frac{1}{2} & \frac{1}{4} \\ \frac{3}{8} & \frac{7}{4} & -\frac{9}{8} \\ -\frac{3}{4} & -\frac{3}{2} & \frac{5}{4} \end{bmatrix}
\end{array}
$$

This completes the matrix inversion using the Gauss-Jordan procedure.

Appendix C
Review Of Selected
Probability Topics

Probability provides a numerical method of expressing the chance or likelihood that an event will occur. We frequently hear expressions of probability such as "a 30 percent chance of rain." Thus, probability is used to express the uncertainty about the occurrence of an event. The forecaster does not know whether it will rain or not, but is saying that under similar meteorological circumstances, rain can be expected about 30 percent of the time. Probability theory is frequently useful to managers dealing with situations having uncertain outcomes.

Probability Concepts

An **experiment** or random experiment is used to describe a situation whose outcome is unknown at a given point in time. An experiment can have many possible outcome which can be defined, but only one of those outcomes will occur. An **event** is a possible outcome of the experiment. A set of all possible events that may occur is referred to as the **event space** or sample space. For example, on the roll of a die, the set $\{1, 2, 3, 4, 5, 6\}$ would express the event space. Each possible outcome is expressed as an **element** of the event space. Events may be defined in such a way that each event is an element, for example, rolling a 1, or they may be defined as a combination of elements, for example, rolling an odd number. The former case would be referred to as an elementary event, the latter as a composite event. The **probability** of an event occurring, which is expressed as the proportion of time that a particular event is likely to occur, is expressed numerically as a value between zero and one. Thus, if **E** is used to define an event, the probability of that event can be expressed as P(E) where

$$0 \leq P(E) \leq 1$$

If $P(E) = 0$, there is no chance the event will occur and if $P(E) = 1$, the event is certain to occur.

Determination of Event Probabilities

Probabilities assigned to events are determined using one of three methods: (1) classical (a priori); (2) empirical; or (3) subjective.

The classical method assumes that all elements have an equal chance of occurring. Thus, the probability of an element occurring can be expressed as

$$P(\text{element}) = \frac{1}{\text{number of elements in the event space}}$$

and the probability of a composite event can be expressed as

$$P(\text{event}) = \frac{\text{number of elements in the event set}}{\text{number of elements in the event space}}$$

Thus, the probability of rolling a 1 on a die can be expressed as

$$P(1) = \frac{1}{\{1,2,3,4,5,6\}} = \frac{1}{6}$$

and the probability of rolling an odd number can be expressed as

$$P(\text{odd}) = \frac{\{1,3,5\}}{\{1,2,3,4,5,6\}} = \frac{3}{6} = \frac{1}{2}$$

The probability of a composite event can also be expressed as the summation of the probabilities of occurrence of each element contained in the event set. For example, the probability of rolling an odd number can also be expressed as

$$P(\text{odd}) = P(1) + P(3) + P(5) = \frac{1}{6} + \frac{1}{6} + \frac{1}{6} = \frac{3}{6} = \frac{1}{2}$$

Sometimes more complex experiments do not have such straightforward elements. For example, if a coin is tossed twice, what is the probability of a Tail occurring on each toss, i.e., the probability of obtaining two Tails? On the first toss, either a Head or a Tail may occur. On the second toss, the identical outcomes exist. The following table summarizes the results of the two tosses.

Element	First Toss	Second Toss
1	Head	Head
2	Head	Tail
3	Tail	Head
4	Tail	Tail

Assuming all elements are equally likely to occur, two Tails are obtained one time out of four results or 25 percent of the time. This may also be shown through the use of a tree diagram that enumerates the resulting elements. Figure 1 illustrates the use of the tree diagram.

The empirical method uses historical data to estimate the probability of an event. If, for example, a merchant discovered that 70 out of the last 100 customers had purchased a particular product, the probability that a customer entering the store would purchase that product could be estimated as

$$P(\text{purchase}) = \frac{70}{100} = 0.70$$

Empirical or historical estimates of probability can be good or bad. They are based on the assumption that things will continue as they were in the past. If the merchant collected data during a sale or while competitors were out of stock on that product, the probability might not be an accurate estimate.

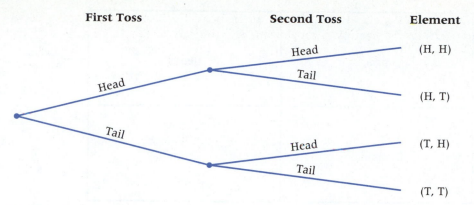

First Toss   **Second Toss**   Element

Head   Head   (H, H)

Tail   (H, T)

Tail   Head   (T, H)

Tail   (T, T)

Figure 1 Tree Diagram

The subjective method of determining probabilities relies on subjective estimates based on experience, intuition, or other factors influencing the estimator. Since individuals differ, we would expect their subjective probability estimates to vary as well. This suggests that these estimates may not be accurate, but they may be the only estimates available. A firm attempting to estimate the success of a new product is unlikely to assume that success and failure are equally likely (classical approach), and the firm would not have empirical data on this product, so the probability of success estimate would have to be subjective (although it would probably be influenced by empirical data on other new products).

Mutually Exclusive and Collectively Exhaustive Events

When events that are part of an event set have no elements in common, those events are said to be **mutually exclusive**. For example, if events were defined as drawing either a spade, a heart, a diamond, or a club from a deck of cards, these events would be mutually exclusive. If, however, we defined events as drawing either a spade or a face card from a deck of cards, these events are not mutually exclusive since the king, queen, and jack of spades are both spades and face cards.

Events existing within an event space can be shown in a **Venn diagram**. Figure 2 illustrates the use of a Venn diagram to show two events, A and B, which exist in a sample space. The sample space is represented by the rectangular box

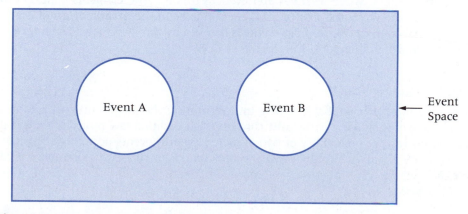

Event A   Event B   ← Event Space

Figure 2 Venn Diagram Showing Events A and B

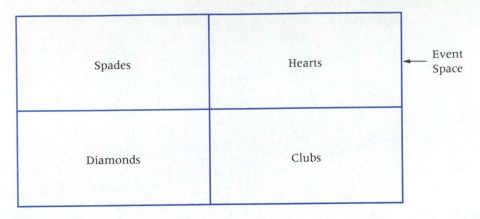

Figure 3 Collectively Exhaustive Events

and the events are represented by the circles. Since these events share no common elements, they are mutually exclusive.

If the list of events contains all possible events that may occur in an experiment, the list is referred to as being **collectively exhaustive**. Thus, the events in a collectively exhaustive list of events contain all the elements in the sample space. For example, if events are defined as the suits in a deck of 52 cards (spades, hearts, diamonds, clubs), Figure 3 illustrates that this is a collectively exhaustive list of events.

Unions and Intersections of Event Sets

As we have seen, some composite events are a combination of elementary events, for example, rolling an odd number on a die. If we wish to describe all the elements that belong to two or more events, we refer to them as the **union** of the event sets. Thus, all the elements belonging to events A or B or both can be represented as the union of A and B. A union of events is designated with the ∪ symbol. The union of A and B is therefore A ∪ B. In Figure 2, A ∪ B is represented by all elements within event A and all elements within event B.

In some cases, two or more events may share common elements. This is illustrated in Figure 4, where event A and event B overlap. The elements common to both events, shown by the shaded area, are said to be in the **intersection** of A and B. An intersection to two or more events is denoted by the ∩ symbol. The intersection of A and B is therefore expressed as A ∩ B.

Addition Law

A number of laws of probability help in determining the probabilities of complex events. One of these laws is the **addition law**. The addition law provides a method of determining the probability of two or more (or both) events occurring. This law is used to calculate the union of two or more events; our two-event example would be expressed as

$$P(A \cup B) = P(A) + P(B) - P(A \cap B)$$

This indicates that the probability of the union is determined by first adding the probability of each event, then subtracting the intersection of the two events. Since

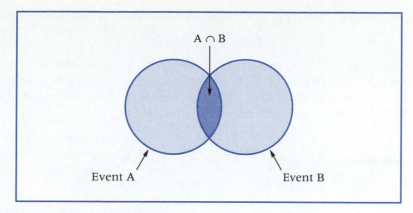

Figure 4 Intersection of Events A and B

both events contain the elements of the intersection, the intersection probability is subtracted to prevent double counting.

When events are mutually exclusive, however, there are no common elements or intersection. In this case, the addition law is simplified as

$$P(A \cup B) = P(A) + P(B)$$

Furthermore, when events are both mutually exclusive and collective exhaustive, the addition law may be generally stated as

$$P(A \cup B \cup C...) = P(A) + P(B) + P(C) + ... = 1$$

Addition Law and Complementary Events

Figure 5 shows an event space and the event A. All elements lying within the circle belong to event A and all elements outside the circle (shaded area) do not belong to event A. The elements in the shaded area are referred to as the complement of event A, denoted as $\tilde{A}$.

Because event A and its complement are both mutually exclusive and collectively exhaustive, the probability of the union is

$$P(A \cup \tilde{A}) = P(A) + P(\tilde{A}) = 1$$

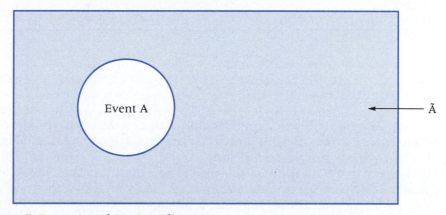

Figure 5 Event A and Its Compliment

Using this known relationship, the probability of event A can be expressed as

$$P(A) = 1 - P(\tilde{A})$$

Thus, if we know either the probability of event A or the probability of $\tilde{A}$, we can easily compute the remaining value. For example, if we wished to compute the value of the probability of rolling something other than a six on the roll of a die, we could first compute the probability of rolling a six as

$$P(6) = \frac{1}{6}$$

and then determine the probability of not rolling a 6 as

$$P(\tilde{6}) = 1 - P(6) = 1 - \frac{1}{6} = \frac{5}{6}$$

Conditional Probabilities

In some experiments, two or more events occur jointly. This may be due to sequential activities such as tossing a coin repeatedly, or it may be due to the simultaneous occurrence of several events, such as a student being male or female and a sophomore or junior and passing or failing, etc. In some cases, the occurrence of one event may in some way affect the occurrence of some other event. When this happens, we say the effected event has a **conditional probability**. A conditional probability is one that is affected by the occurrence of some other event. Conditional probabilities are expressed as $P(A|B)$ or the probability of event A occurring given that event B occurs.

This can be illustrated by an example. Two coin tosses are to be made in sequence. Two coins will be used for the tosses. The first coin is unbiased and results in a Head 50 percent of the time. The second coin is biased and results in a Head 30 percent of the time. The unbiased coil will be used for the first toss. If the result of the first toss is a Head, the second coin will be used for the second toss. If the result of the first toss is a Tail, the first coin will be used again for the second toss. The probability of obtaining a Head on the first coin toss can be expressed as

$$P(H) = .5$$

But the probability of a Head on the second toss is dependent on the result of the first toss. If a Head occurs on the first toss, the probability of a Head on the second toss is expressed as

$$P(H|H) = .3$$

If a Tail occurs on the first toss, however, the probability of a Head on the second toss is expressed as

$$P(H|T) = .5$$

Joint Probabilities

Recall that when two or more events occur and share common elements, the common elements are referred to as the intersection, for example, $A \cap B$. The probability that two events share common elements is referred to as a **joint probability** and is expressed as $P(A \cap B)$. The following example illustrates joint probabilities.

The Mihal Company has required all new hires to take an aptitude test. All new hires are placed on probationary status for a six-month period. At the end of that period, they are either discharged or made permanent employees, based on their performance. The company has kept records on the performance of all new hires over the past year. The data are summarized in the following table.

Test Score	Postprobationary Action		
	Discharge	Permanent	Total
Below 40	48	18	66
Above 40	27	57	84
Total	75	75	150

The joint probabilities can be calculated as follows:

$$P(B40 \cap D) = \frac{48}{150} \div .32 \qquad P(B40 \cap P) = \frac{18}{150} = .12$$

$$P(A40 \cap D) = \frac{27}{150} = .18 \qquad P(A40 \cap P) = \frac{57}{150} = .38$$

The following table shows these joint probabilities.

Test Score	Postprobationary Action		Marginal Probability
	Discharge	Permanent	
Below 40	.32	.12	.44
Above 40	.18	.38	.56
Marginal Probability	.50	.50	1.00

The marginal probabilities are calculated using the addition law for mutually exclusive events. For example,

$$P(B40) = P(B40 \cap D) + P(B40 \cap P) = .32 + .12 = .44$$

Using Joint Probabilities to Calculate Conditional Probabilities

Figure 6 shows a Venn diagram illustrating a situation with two events, A and B, which share common elements.

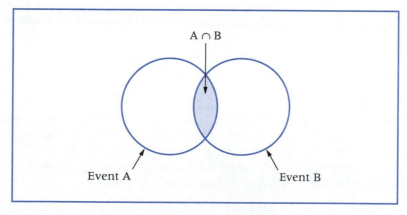

Figure 6 Events A and B with Shared Elements

The probability of the intersection is $P(A \cap B)$ and the probability of B occurring is $P(B)$. Thus, if B occurs and we want to determine the probability of A occurring, we must determine the conditional probability $P(A|B)$. Given that B has already occurred, the probability of A occurring can be expressed by the proportion of $P(B)$ represented by the intersection $P(A \cap B)$. This relationship can be expressed as the conditional probability of A given B

$$P(A|B) = \frac{P(A \cap B)}{P(B)}$$

The conditional probability of B given A is expressed

$$P(B|A) = \frac{P(A \cap B)}{P(A)}$$

Using this relationship, let's return to the Mihal Company's information. We saw that 44 percent of all new hires scored below 40 on the test and 56 percent scored above 40. If a job applicant is given the test and scored above 40, what is the probability that he or she will become a permanent employee? To determine this conditional probability (permanent employee given a score above 40), we use the formula

$$P(P|A40) = \frac{P(A40 \cap P)}{P(A40)} = \frac{.38}{.56} = .68$$

Thus, if the applicant scores above 40 on the test, there is a 68 percent chance that the applicant will become a permanent employee. This compares favorably with the 50 percent chance of becoming a permanent employee when the test results are not used in selection.

Multiplication Law

Just as it is possible to determine a conditional probability from a joint probability and marginal probability, the joint probability can be determined from a conditional probability and a joint probability. This relationship is expressed by

$$P(A \cap B) = P(A|B)P(B) \quad \text{and} \quad P(A \cap B) = P(B|A)P(A)$$

For example, if we know the probability that a machine is out of adjustment is .2 and the probability of the machine producing a bad part if it is out of adjustment is .4, the probability that the machine is out of adjustment and has produced a bad part is

$$P(BP \cap OA) = P(BP|OA)P(OA) = (.4)(.2) = .08$$

Independent Events
In some cases, events are independent of one another. In these cases, the probability of event B, given that event A has occurred, $P(B|A)$, is exactly the same as the probability of event B, $P(B)$. For example, the probability of tossing a Head on a coin is .5. The probability of obtaining a Head on a second toss of the same coin, given that the first toss resulted in a Head, is still .5. Therefore,

$$P(H|H) = P(H) = .5$$

When this is the case, the events are said to be independent and the multiplication law can be modified to

$$P(A \cap B) = P(A|B)P(B) = P(A)P(B)$$

Thus, the probability of obtaining a Head on both tosses is

$$P(H \cap H) = P(H)P(H) = (.5)(.5) = .25$$

Bayes's Theorem

We have discussed how probability estimates are determined. We have also shown that for dependent events, the occurrence of one event may alter the probability of occurrence of a second event (conditional probability). Frequently, it is possible to revise a priori probability estimates based on additional information. These revised probability estimates are referred to as posterior probabilities. Bayes's theorem provides a means of calculating these posterior probabilities.

This can be illustrated through the following example. There are two events, A_1 and A_2, with probabilities of occurrence of $P(A_1)$ and $P(A_2)$. Given the occurrence of a related event B, the conditional probabilities can be calculated as follows

$$P(A_1|B) = \frac{P(B|A_1)P(A_1)}{P(B|A_1)P(A_1) + P(B|A_2)P(A_2)}$$

and

$$P(A_2|B) = \frac{P(B|A_2)P(A_2)}{P(B|A_1)P(A_1) + P(B|A_2)P(A_2)}$$

(Bayes's theorem is discussed further in Chapter 13.)

Determining the Number of Possible Events

We have frequently looked at the toss of a coin when discussing probability. The number of possible outcomes for each toss is 2. If the coin is tossed four times in sequence, the number of possible outcomes may be expressed as

$$(2)(2)(2)(2) = 2^4 = 16$$

Now consider a second example in which there are five playing cards, the ace, king, queen, jack, and ten of spades. If one card is selected, there are five choices or outcomes. If cards selected are not replaced and a second card is drawn, there are four choices on the second draw. The total number of possible outcomes can be expressed as

$$(5)(4)(3)(2)(1) = 120$$

This is known as a factorial product and can be denoted as 5 factorial or 5! In general, the factorial for any whole number n can be expressed as n! where

$$n! = (n)(n-1)(n-2)\ldots(2)(1)$$

Note: By definition, 1! = 1 and 0! = 1.

Permutations
Using this information, we can now determine the number of different ways of taking r items from a group of n items, where the sequence of selection is consid-

ered. Each different possibility is called a **permutation**. The number of possible permutations of r items from a group of n items can be denoted by P_r^n and is expressed as

$$P_r^n = \frac{n!}{(n - r)!}$$

For example, if we select any three items from a group of five items, the number of permutations is

$$P_3^5 = \frac{5!}{(5 - 3)!} = \frac{5!}{2!} = (5)(4)(3) = 60$$

Combinations

With permutations, the sequence of events is considered. For example, if we select three items from among four, A, B, C, and D, one at a time, we can obtain any of the following results

ABC	ACB	BAC	BCA	CAB	CBA
ABD	ADB	BAD	BDA	DAB	DBA
ADC	ACD	DAC	DCA	CAD	CDA
DBC	DCB	BDC	BCD	CDB	CBD

There are 24 unique results, or permutations $(4!/(4 - 3)! = 4! = 24)$. If, however, the specific sequence of selection does not matter, that is, ABC and CBA are considered identical, then the number of different combinations of n items taken r at a time can be denoted by C_r^n which can be calculated from

$$C_r^n = \frac{n!}{r!(n - r)!}$$

Using the example of four items, A, B, C, and D, taken three at a time, the number of different combinations would be

$$C_3^4 = \frac{4!}{3!(4 - 3)!} = \frac{4!}{3!} = 4$$

Using these combinations and permutations, we can see that the probability of drawing the three letters A, B, and C would be one in four or .25. However, the probability that those three letters would be drawn in ABC order would be one in twenty-four or approximately .042.

Appendix D
Review of Selected
Differential Calculus Topics

The following material is a brief review of differential calculus. It deals with derivatives of simple functions and the determination of maximum and minimum points. For a more detailed discussion, the reader is referred to any basic calculus text.

A mathematical model typically consists of a dependent variable expressed as a function of one or more decision variables. When the relationship between the dependent variable and the decision variables(s) is linear, a technique such as linear programming may be used to find an optimal solution. When the relationship is not linear, however, and the objective is to maximize or minimize the function (dependent variable), differential calculus may be used to find the optimal solution.

FINDING THE FIRST DERIVATIVE OF A SIMPLE FUNCTION WITH ONE VARIABLE

The **first derivative** of a function with respect to X may be expressed as $f'(x)$ or $df(x)/dx$. To find the first derivative of a function with respect to a variable, x, two rules are applied.

1. If a term does not contain the variable x, its first derivative is equal to zero.
2. If a term does contain the variable x, multiply the term by the exponential value of x and reduce the exponent by 1. For example, if a function contains the term X^3, the first derivative of this term would be $3X^2$.

The application of these rules can be illustrated with the following function:

$$f(x) = 5X^3 - 2X^2 + 40X - 135$$

The first derivative of the first term, $5X^3$, is $3(5)X^2$ or $15X^2$. The derivative of the second term is $-2(2)X^1$ or $-4X$. The derivative of the third term is $1(40)X^0$. Since X^0 is equal to 1, this derivative is equal to 40. The derivative of the fourth term is 0 (rule 1). Thus,

$$f'(x) = 15X^2 - 4X + 40$$

Table 1 Example Functions and Their First Derivatives

f(x)	f'(x)
6	0
X	1
$3X^2$	$6X$
$4/x$	$-4/x^2$
$8/x^3$	$-24/x^4$

Table 1 shows examples of functions and their first derivatives with respect to X. The term $1/x$ can be expressed X^{-1}. The first derivative of this term would be X^{-2} or $-1/x^2$.

USING THE FIRST DERIVATIVE TO FIND A MAXIMUM OR MINIMUM POINT

The first derivative is equal to the slope of the function at a point (x). A concave function will have a zero slope at its maximum point and a convex function will have a zero slope at its minimum point. Thus, the point at which the maximum occurs on a concave function can be found by taking the first derivative of the function, setting it equal to zero, and solving for the value of X. Likewise, the point at which the minimum occurs on a concave function can be found by taking the first derivative of the function, setting it equal to zero, and solving for the value of X. This can be illustrated using the total inventory cost function from Chapter 12. The total cost was expressed as a function of Q, the quantity ordered, by the mathematical function

$$TC = (D/Q)C_0 + (Q/2)C_c$$

This cost curve is shown graphically in Figure 1.

To minimize its total annual inventory costs, a firm must order Q* units each time it places an order, since this quantity results in the minimum total cost. To the left of this point, the slope of the function is negative; to the right of this point, the slope of the function is positive. At the point, the slope of the cost function is zero.

To determine the value of Q*, it is therefore necessary to take the first derivative of the cost function with respect to Q, set it equal to zero, and then solve for the value of Q (Q*). Recognizing that $1/Q$ may be restated as Q^{-1}, the total cost function

$$TC = f(Q) = (D/Q)C_0 + (Q/2)C_c$$

may be restated as

$$f(Q) = D(C_0)Q^{-1} + (C_c/2)Q^1$$

Taking the first derivative with respect to Q yields

$$f'(Q) = -1(D)(C_0)Q^{-2} + 1(C_c/2)Q^0$$

Since Q^0 is equal to 1, the first derivative may be expressed as

$$f'(Q) = -(D)(C_0)Q^{-2} + C_c/2$$

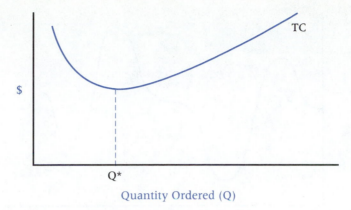

Quantity Ordered (Q)

Figure 1 Total Annual Inventory Cost Function

By setting this derivative equal to zero, the value of Q at the point on the cost curve where its slope is equal to zero, i.e., where Q is equal to Q*, can be determined:

$$-1(DC_0)Q^{-2} + {}^{C_c}/_2 = 0$$

$$-1(DC_0)Q^{-2} = {}^{-C_c}/_2$$

$$Q^{-2} = \frac{-({}^{C_c}/_2)}{-DC_0} = \frac{C_c}{2DC_0}$$

$$Q^2 = \frac{2DC_0}{C_c}$$

$$Q = \sqrt{\frac{2DC_0}{C_c}}$$

This is the formula for the economic order quantity discussed in Chapter 12.

NONLINEAR FUNCTIONS WITH MAXIMUM AND MINIMUM POINTS

The minimum point on the total cost curve was relatively easy to determine because the function was a convex function with one minimum point. Consider the function shown in Figure 2. This nonlinear function has two maximum points (a) and (d) and two minimum points (b) and (e). It also has what is known as a point of inflection (c). This point has a zero slope, but is neither a maximum nor minimum point on the curve. Points (a), (b), (d), and (e) are know as extreme points on the curve. They are also **local** or **global** maximum or minimum points. Local maximum or minimum points [(a) and (e)] are maximum or minimum points on the curve, but are not the absolute maximum or minimum points. Global maximum and minimum points [(b) and (d)] represent the absolute maximum and minimum points on the curve.

When solving for maximum profit or minimum cost, it is important to find the global maximum or minimum. Since points (a) through (e) all correspond to points where the first derivative is equal to zero, simply finding these points is not enough. Taking the first derivative of the function, setting it equal to zero, and

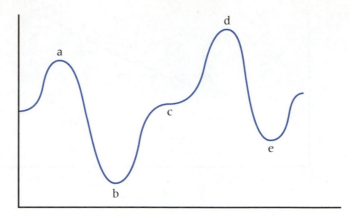

Figure 2 A Nonlinear Function

solving identifies values for these extreme points, but the extreme points are not necessarily global maximum or minimum points. The fact that the slope of the function at a maximum or minimum point is equal to zero is referred to as a **necessary condition.** To determine whether an extreme point is a maximum or minimum point, however, we must take the second derivative of the function.

The Second Derivative

The **second derivative** is found by taking the derivative of the first derivative of the function, and is represented as f"(x). Thus, if the first derivative of a function is equal to

$$f'(x) = 5X^2$$

the second derivative is

$$f''(x) = 2(5)X = 10X$$

Substituting the extreme point values into the second derivative, if the value is greater than zero, the point is a minimum. If the value is less than zero, the point is a maximum. And if the value is equal to zero, the point is an inflection point. This is known as a **sufficient condition** for determining a local maximum or local minimum point.

   To determine a global maximum or minimum point, the values identified when the first derivative was set equal to zero are substituted back into the original function. When a function exists between limits or end points, the values of the end points should also be compared to determine if either of these points may also be a global maximum or minimum.

An Example

Consider the function $f(x) = X^3 - 6X^2 + 40$ over the interval $0 \leq x \leq 5$ shown in Figure 3. This function has both a maximum and minimum point. Taking the first derivative with respect to X gives

$$f(x) = X^3 - 6X^2 + 40$$

$$f'(x) = 3X^2 - 12X = X(3X - 12)$$

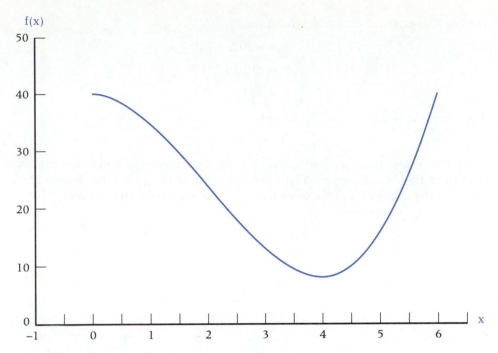

Figure 3 Graph of the Function $f(x) = X^3 - 6X^2 + 40$

Setting this equal to zero and solving yields

$$X(3X - 12) = 0$$

$$X = 0 \quad \text{and} \quad X = 4$$

The second derivative is

$$f''(x) = 6X - 12$$

Thus,

$$f''(0) = -12 \qquad f''(4) = 12$$

The value of the second derivative at $X = 0$ is -12, which is less than zero and therefore a local maximum. The maximum value is $f(0) = 40$. The value of the second derivative at $X = 4$ is 12, which is greater than zero and therefore a local minimum. The minimum value is $f(4) = 8$. Since $0 \leq X \leq 5$, the value $X = 5$ must also be evaluated. At $X = 5$, the value of the function is 15. Since this value is neither a maximum nor minimum, the global maximum is found at $X = 0$ and the global minimum is found at $X = 4$.

A Profit Maximization Example

The profit made on a particular product is a function of the price (P) of that product. The profit function has been found to be expressed by

$$f(P) = -15P^2 + 210P - 1,450$$

Taking the first derivative gives

$$f'(P) = -30P + 210$$

Setting this equal to zero and solving for P:

$$0 = -30P + 210$$

$$30P = 210$$

$$P = 70$$

The second derivative of the function is

$$f''(P) = -30$$

Since this is less than zero, the point P = 70 must represent a maximum point. And since there is only one solution point, it must be the global maximum. Thus, the firm maximizes its profit by charging a price of $70 for this product.

Appendix E
A Guide to Using
Dennis & Dennis
Software

Note: the Dennis and Dennis software may have been updated, modified, or enhanced after this book was printed. To ensure that you are aware of any changes made since this material was printed, place Disk 1 in the default drive and examine the READ.ME file. At the DOS prompt, enter:

```
TYPE READ.ME
```

then press the ⟨RET⟩ key. To obtain a printed copy of this file, make sure the printer is ready and enter:

```
TYPE READ.ME>PRN:
```

followed by the ⟨RET⟩ key. (For serial printers, use COM1: instead of PRN:)
The Dennis & Dennis programs are all menu driven.

The Main Menu provides access to all the programs. To select a model program to run from the Main Menu, use the up or down arrow keys to highlight the model to be run and press the ⟨RET⟩ key to complete the selection.

The Model Selection Menu permits selection of the type of problem to be solved. Most programs have a secondary or subprogram model selection menu, since the program can be used to solve different types of problems.

The Data Entry Menu allows you to select the manner in which the data will be entered.

The Ending Menu, which appears after the solution, offers several options:

1. *Modify Data and Run Again* returns to either an input summary ("HERE IS...") or a completed entry table, allowing you to modify the data and solve the problem again (useful for performing **postoptimality analysis).**
2. *Run Again with New Data* clears all current data entries and returns you to the beginning of the data entry section of the program to run a new problem using the same model.

3. *Save to a Disk File* lets you save the data used in the just completed problem to a disk file. This option prompts for a filename.
4. *Print Problem* allows you to print a summary of the problem input and the problem output to either a disk file or a printer. Selecting the printer option sends the output to a printer (if one is connected and turned on). With the disk file option, the output is written as a DOS text file to the specified disk. Note that output files can be printed without entering the D&D Models programs, using either the DOS **PRINT** command (e.g., at the DOS prompt, type **PRINT B:MYFILE)** or the DOS **TYPE** command (e.g., **TYPE B:MYFILE> PRN:).** In these examples, **MYFILE** represents the file name and **B:** represents the disk drive. The latter command will redirect the output from the screen to a parallel printer. (If you are using a serial printer, enter **COM1:** instead of PRN:.)
5. *Return to Main Menu* exits the program and returns to the Main Menu.
6. *Return to DOS* exits the D&D Models completely and returns to the DOS prompt.

DATA ENTRY

Data can be entered from the keyboard or from a disk file. *Keyboard Entry* takes one of two forms (many models use a combination): (1) Prompted input. Each entry is prompted by a question, e.g., "HOW MANY VARIABLES ARE THERE?" Type the appropriate response and then press the ⟨RET⟩ key. (2) Tabular entry. Type the correct responses into the blank cells of the table and then use the ⟨RET⟩ key or one of the arrow keys on the numeric keypad to move to another cell. Press the FIO key when all entries are completed.

Entering a problem *from a disk file* can be done only *after* a problem has been entered and then saved to a disk file. When this menu selection has been made, the program prompts for the filename of the problem. Legitimate filenames begin with the disk drive designation, use the letters of the alphabet (A–Z) or digits (0–9), are no more than eight characters in length (not counting the drive designation), and do not include a suffix. They take the form d:xxxxxxxx or d:\ssssss\xxxxxxxx (where d: = disk drive and ssssss is an existing subdirectory). If the file exists, the data is read from that file and displayed on the screen, where it can be accepted and used as it exists or it can be modified.

Making Entries

All programs have size limitations, e.g., number of rows, number of variables, etc. Pay attention to these when entering problems.

Limit variable names to no more than 5 characters in length. Almost any variable names can be used as long as they begin with a letter (A–Z). Certain letters are used for specific purposes. For example, LP uses A and S for surplus and artificial variables. Variable names using subscripts take the form X2, Y3, etc.

Enter a zero (0) and not the letter O in numeric entries.

Drop the trailing zeros after the decimal place, e.g., 7.9, not 7.90 and 63, not 63.00. It won't make any difference to the computer and it will save you keystrokes.
In tabular form, a blank is treated as a zero (0).

Enter large numbers (more than 6 significant digits) in scientific notation, e.g., 6.5E6, not 6500000. Note that in most cases PCs work only with values up to seven digits and only the first six digits will be accurate.

Scale your input (if possible) so that the number of significant digits is consistent throughout the problem. It does not change the correct answer, and it affects the computer's ability to determine the correct answer by avoiding the loss of significant digits in the calculations.

Press ⟨RET⟩ after each *prompted* entry.

The monitor displays only 80 characters and 25 lines at a time. Therefore, for tabular entries, a larger table will scroll one row or column at a time as entries are made. The size of table that can be displayed varies with the program, e.g., for the transportation program, the screen can display only 7 columns and 10 rows at a time.

Program output may be rounded to whole numbers or to two or three decimal places. Thus, there may be minor discrepancies between these solutions and manual solutions.

Output tableaus may not always fit on the screen (because of the 80-character display limit). Tableaus that are too large to fit are displayed in segments.

Output that is longer than 25 lines will scroll off the screen. Some programs have an automatic pause that holds a given number of lines on the screen for 5 seconds before scrolling. Output can be frozen using the [Ctrl]-[NumLock] keys or the [Pause] key (PS/2s) as described in the special keys section.

Do not enter dollar signs ($), commas (,), or the percent sign (%). Enter 14.95, not $14.95; 6000, not 6,000.

Special Keys

Keys listed together with a hyphen are pressed simultaneously.

Caps Lock is a soft switch that toggles from lowercase to uppercase and back each time you press the key.

Num Lock is a soft switch that turns the numeric keypad on and off. When the key is "on," the numbers are activated. When the key is "off," the arrow keys are in use.

TAB can be used with tabular entries as a ⟨RET⟩ key to enable you to complete entries from either side of the keyboard.

Ctrl-Num Lock temporarily suspends the computer's operations. As output scrolls off the screen, pressing these keys freezes the screen until you press the space bar or another alphanumeric key. PS/2s use a [Pause] key.

Ctrl-Scroll Lock is the program termination key. Pressing these keys stops the program execution and gives you the DOS prompt. To run the Main Menu program again type START.

Shift-PrtSc allows you to send the image currently on the screen to the printer. It works at any time during program execution and is independent of the program command to send output to the printer. PS/2s use a [PrintScreen] key.

Function keys ([F3]-[F10]) are used to make changes in tabular entry. They are listed in a footer at the bottom of the screen. The [F3] key alters the type of problem, e.g., from maximization to minimization; [F5] deletes a row; [F6] adds a row; [F7] deletes a column; [F8] adds a column; and [F10] accepts the entries and exits the table.

Cursor movement keys are used with tabular input. Arrow keys move in the direction indicated (right, left, up, down); [TAB] and ⟨RET⟩ emulate the right arrow key; the [Home] key moves the cursor to the first column in the current row (left-hand edge of the line); the [End] key moves the cursor to the last column in the row (right hand edge of the line). [PgUp] moves the cursor to the top row of the tableau and [PgDn] moves the cursor to the bottom row of the tableau.

CORRECTING MISTAKES AND MODIFYING DATA

Before Completing an Entry. If you catch a mistake while typing the entry (before pressing the ⟨RET⟩ key), correct it using the backspace/erase key (←) located above the ⟨RET⟩ key. This key deletes characters to the left of the prompt, one character at a time.

A slight variation is used for long prompted entries such as the objective function and constraints used in Linear Programming, Integer Programming, and Goal Programming. If a mistake is discovered while making entries, the [Home] key can be used to move to the beginning of the line, the [End] key to move to the end of the line, or the left and right arrow keys can be used to move one character at a time to the left or right. Characters above the cursor may be replaced by simply typing over them or deleted by pressing the [Del] (delete) key. To insert additional text within the entry, position the cursor and then press the [Ins] (insert) key. Whatever you type will be inserted at that point. Pressing the ⟨Ret⟩ key completes the entry. (Caution: pressing cursor keys other that the right or left arrow keys will also terminate the entry.)

Completed Entries. Correcting completed entries depends on whether the input form is prompted or tabular. Prompted input uses an input summary and an error correction routine. The tabular input procedure permits use of cursor movement keys and designated function keys to make changes.

The editing features discussed above for entering objective functions or constraints also can be used when modifying that data.

Prompted Input

1. Check the inputs at the "HERE IS..." input summary. If you find a mistake, select "YES" in response to the "DO YOU WANT TO MODIFY THE DATA?" prompt.
2. Enter the line number on which the mistake appears and press ⟨RET⟩. If there is more than one mistake, each must be corrected independently.
3. Enter the correct value when prompted to do so and press ⟨RET⟩.
4. You will return to step 1. If all the entries are correct, press ⟨RET⟩ while the "NO" response is highlighted.

Tabular Input

1. After completing your entries, but before pressing the [F10] key, check the entries for accuracy. If you find no mistakes, press the [F10] key; otherwise proceed to steps 2–3.
2. If the mistake is in a table entry, use the cursor movement keys to move to the entry and reenter the correct value.

3. If the mistake is in the type of problem or the size of the problem, use the appropriate function key to change the problem type or to add or delete a row or column. Any row or column added must be filled in.

SPECIFIC PROGRAM GUIDELINES

Linear Programming

Solves either maximization or minimization problems. Identifies decision variable values, slack, surplus, reduced costs, and shadow prices. Performs sensitivity analysis on the objective function coefficients and the right-hand sides. Uses the Simplex algorithm.

To Use the LP Program

1. Data entry may be free-form (prompted input) or tabular (spreadsheet style).
2. Problems are limited to 30 variables and 30 constraints.
3. All variables must appear in the objective function (even those with a 0 coefficient). If a variable name is repeated in the objective function, an error message will indicate that it is a duplicate and allow you to change the entry.
4. Constraints can be entered in any order. Variables with 0 coefficients do not have to be entered. If a constraint contains a variable not found in the objective function, an error message indicates this and allows you to make the correction. Constraints may not have negative right-hand sides (multiply by -1 to convert them before entering). When entering inequalities using $<$ or $>$, it is not necessary to add the equal sign ($=$). Nonnegativity constraints are assumed and do not have to be entered.
5. When making a tabular entry be sure to enter only the coefficients (not the variable).
6. A coefficient of -900000 or 900000 appears in tableaus with artificial variables (not the more familiar letter M).

Transportation and Assignment

Solves either maximization or minimization problems, balanced or unbalanced problems (automatically adds dummies), and problems with unacceptable routes or assignments. Determines optimal distribution and cost/profit.

To Use the Transportation and Assignment Programs

1. Data entry is a two-part procedure, a combination of prompted input and tabular entry.
2. Tableaus are limited to 40 rows, 40 columns (not including dummies, which are added automatically).
3. Use M (or $-M$ for maximization problems) for an unacceptable route or assignment.
4. Default variables for supply and demand (S1, S2, D1, D2, etc.) and for assignments (1, 2, 3, etc.) can be changed in the table by typing the variable name of choice over the default name.
5. Messages in the output indicate the existence of alternate optima, and identify unbalanced and infeasible problems.

Network Models

Solve shortest route, maximal flow, and minimal spanning tree problems. Determines least cost route from a given node to any (or all) of the nodes (shortest route). Maximizes the total amount of flow from an origin to a destination (sink) in a given period of time (maximal flow). Finds the set of arcs that will connect all the nodes in the network at a minimum total distance (minimum spanning tree).

Problem formulation and data preparation are important. It is helpful to analyze the problem and prepare the data by drawing the network and creating a table for all the data.

To Use the Network Programs

1. Data entry is a combination of an initial prompted entry to define the size of the network, and tabular input to describe the network.
2. All networks are limited to 30 nodes and 30 branches.
3. Node numbers must be *consecutive* integers from 1 to 30. For maximal flow, the source is node 1 and the sink will have the highest node number.
4. Shortest route and minimal spanning tree are assumed to be symmetrical (branch value is constant, independent of direction). Thus, a branch is entered only once. Maximal flow is assumed to be asymmetrical (flow can vary with direction). Thus, branch values must be entered for flow in each direction, with a beginning and ending node given in the direction of the flow. Branches with flows of 0 are not entered.

Integer Programming

Solves pure integer, mixed integer, and 0,1 problems; maximization or minimization. The IP program uses a branch-and-bound technique (branching only on the node with the higher upper bound for maximization problems or the lower bound for minimization problems).

To Use the IP Program

1. Data entry is free-form (prompted).
2. Pure integer and mixed integer problems are limited to 25 variables and 25 constraints; 0,1 problems are limited to 12 variables and 12 constraints.
3. All variables must appear in the objective function (even those with a 0 coefficient).
4. Constraints can be entered in any order. Variables with 0 coefficients do not have to be entered. Constraints may not have negative right-hand sides (multiply by −1 to convert them). When entering inequalities using < or >, it is not necessary to add the equal sign (=). Nonnegativity constraints are assumed and do not have to be entered.
5. The IP program does not perform sensitivity analysis. The modify data option from the ending menu can be used to do postoptimality analysis.

Goal Programming

Solves problems having deviational variables with either/or both different priority levels and different weights. Determines optimal feasible solution by minimizing the deviations from stated goals, based on assigned priority level. Uses the modified simplex method.

To Use the GP Program

1. Data entry may be free-form (prompted) or tabular and is a slightly modified version of the entry routine used with LP, with the addition of several prompts necessary to fully describe the goal programming problem, e.g., real variables, deviational variables, priorities, and weights.
2. Goal programming problems are limited to 25 variables (decision variables plus deviational variables) and 30 constraints (system plus goal).
3. With free-form entry, it is not possible to use + and − with the deviational variables. Use A for above and B for below, e.g., D1A, D1B, etc.
4. When entering the names of the deviational variables, all the *negative* deviational variables *must be* entered first.
5. It is possible to have problems with priorities and weights, with priorities but no weights (all weight 1), with neither priorities (all priority 1) nor weights, with no priorities but with weights. The program allows 5 priority levels. Entering a weight of 0 eliminates the variable from the objective function. Therefore, *you must enter a weight of at least one* (≥ 1) for any deviational variable to be minimized. If the problem is not weighted, all the deviational variables that are to appear in the objective function have a weight of 1. If there are no priority levels, enter a priority level of 1 for each deviational variable.
6. It is not necessary to enter the objective function for either entry method (the program automatically minimizes the undesirable deviations). Once you have moved on to part 2 of the data entry, it is not possible to change the objective function. However, it is possible to use the modify data option of the ending menu to make changes (after the problem is solved).
7. Variables with 0 coefficients do not have to be entered. Constraints may not have negative right-hand sides. When entering inequalities using < or >, it is not necessary to add the equal sign (=). Nonnegativity constraints are assumed and do not have to be entered.

PERT

Solves PERT networks described using either: (1) beginning and ending node numbers for each activity or (2) identified activities and their immediate predecessors. Determines project completion time (and variability where applicable); the activities lying on the critical path; early and late start and finish times, and slack for each activity; the completion time, variance, and standard deviation on the critical path. Identifies when a problem has more than one critical path (delineates two of the paths and determines critical path variance for each of those paths).

To Use the PERT Program

1. Data entry is a combination of prompted input (to describe the problem) and tabular input (to define the network).
2. Networks can have no more than 52 activities. Node numbers can be no more than 3 digits. There can be a maximum of 10 predecessors for any given activity (large entries are truncated for display purposes only).
3. Node numbers must be integers. Activities must be in alphabetic order, i.e., an activity leaving a node must have a letter greater than an activity entering the node.
4. For problems entered using predecessors, the predecessor letters have to be less than the activity letter, i.e., for each activity its predecessors must be letters that come before it.

5. When entering predecessors, use a hyphen (-) or make no entry when there are no predecessor activities. Use a comma to separate letters when there is more than one predecessor.
6. For probabilistic problems, the times must be $a < m < b$, i.e., optimistic times are lower than most-likely times and most-likely times are lower than pessimistic times. Units of time must be consistent, e.g., all in days, weeks, etc.
7. Output indicates when there are multiple critical paths and identifies two such paths. The existence of additional critical paths is so noted. Moreover, the output summary indicates when an activity lies on a critical path.

Deterministic Inventory

Solves EOQ, production lot size, EOQ with backorders, quantity discount problems and MRP schedules. Identifies the reorder point. Calculates carrying (holding) and ordering costs, total annual cost, the number of orders per year, and the cycle time. For specific models, identifies maximum inventory, quantity to order when a quantity discount is offered, or backorder quantity and cost.

To Use the Deterministic Inventory Program

1. Data entry is from prompted input.
2. Carrying cost can be expressed either as a dollar/unit value or as a percentage of inventory value. Data entry is in two prompted steps, first describing the way carrying cost is expressed ($/%) and then, depending on the method of expression, either carrying cost in dollars and cents or the price per unit and percent of inventory value.
3. In the Production Lot Size Model, production and demand rate have to be in the same unit of time, e.g., daily, weekly, etc. Any time period can be used as long as it is used consistently throughout the problem.
4. In the EOQ with Backorders Model, it is not possible to use a zero (0) backorder cost to show no backorder cost. This model can be used only if there is a backorder cost.
5. In the Quantity Discount Model, there is a limit of 20 prices (price ranges) that can be compared. This number (prices being compared) includes the unit price for orders less than the discount quantities. This original price/cost is entered first. The minimum quantity of zero (0) is entered automatically. If the program already knows this unit price (entered as part of carrying cost entry), it is also entered automatically by the program as PRICE 1.

Probabilistic Inventory

Solves Discrete Demand Distribution—ROP Determination; Continuous Demand Distribution—Mean and Standard Deviation of Use Known; and Single Period Model—Marginal Analysis. Identifies either the minimum total inventory cost under conditions of uncertainty or a specified service level. Identifies, depending on the model, optimal safety stock and reorder point that will minimize the sum of stockout cost and safety stock carrying cost: either the probability of being out of stock at a given reorder point (i.e., the service level achieved with that reorder point, or the safety stock and the reorder point necessary to achieve a desired service level) or the stocking level (order quantity) that maximizes expected profits using marginal analysis.

To Use the Probabilistic Inventory Program

1. Data entry is from prompted input.
2. With the Discrete Demand Model, the time frame used for demand and lead time has to be consistent (it is not necessary that daily figures be used). To use average demand during lead time, use a lead time of 1.
3. With the Discrete Demand Model, frequency can be entered either as a whole number or as a probability of occurrence (decimal), but has to be consistent throughout the problem. Probabilities do not have to add to one (1.00). The program will normalize.
4. With the Discrete Demand model and the Single Period Model, quantities and demand levels (which must be listed when prompted) are limited to *20* entries, and must be entered in *ascending* order.
5. With the Continuous Demand Model—ROP/Safety Stock Option, the service level desired is for that particular reorder period. The service level entered is the stockout risk (the % of orders/period) subtracted from 1. This is the percentage of orders that will not have a stockout. For example, if you are willing to be out of stock 10% of the time (a stockout risk of 10%), enter 90.

Decision Theory

Solves problems in situations of uncertainty where probabilities cannot be assigned to future occurrences (choice of maximin, maximax, minimax regret, Laplace, and Hurwicz as decision criteria), and where probabilities can be assigned (uses expected value as the decision criterion). Also gives the option of using a Bayesian procedure to develop posterior probabilities from those probabilities previously assigned. Identifies (depending on the model) the optimal alternative; expected opportunity loss (the expected value of perfect information); an optimal decision strategy; the expected value of sample information (EVSI); and the efficiency of sample information. The decision-making criteria used here are based on monetary value.

Before entering the data for this program, analyze the decision situation and, depending on the nature of the decision to be made, set up a decision tree, payoff table, or decision matrix.

To Use the Decision Theory Program

1. Data entry is a combination of prompted input to describe the matrix and tabular input to fill in the matrix.
2. The decision matrices are limited to 20 (decisions) by 20 (states of nature).
3. For minimization problems, enter the negative of the value, i.e., multiply all outcomes (costs) by -1.
4. Enter probabilities as decimal values ($0 \leq P \leq 1$). The sum of the probabilities of the states of nature must equal 1.
5. Enter conditional probabilities, e.g., $P(I1|S1)$, in decimal form such that $0 \leq P \leq 1$ and the sum of each column is 1 (when there is more than one row).
6. To use a Bayesian procedure to calculate posterior probability without decision alternatives, simply enter a zero (0) in response to the number of decision prompts and proceed as usual, following on-screen directions.

Queuing Models

Solves single server (infinite source, random arrival pattern described by a Poisson distribution, random service time pattern described by a negative exponential distribution, and an infinite queue); multiple server (single waiting line, infinite source, Poisson arrival, exponential service, infinite queue); single server (infinite source, Poisson arrival, variable service, infinite queue); single server (infinite source, Poisson arrival, exponential service, finite queue); single server (finite source, Poisson arrival, exponential service, infinite queue); multiple server (finite source, Poisson arrival, exponential service, infinite queue length); and nonpreemptive multiple priority queuing. Identifies various operating characteristics, such as the average number of customers waiting in line or in the system (both in line and being serviced), the average time a unit waits (again both in line or in the system), and system utilization. Also calculates total cost to allow the user to make an economic evaluation (to help determine the level of service that will balance the cost of providing service with the cost of customers waiting for that service). The models all assume that the customers arrive individually and randomly, that no balking or reneging occurs (except in the case of finite queues), and that the queue discipline is FCFS.

To Use the Queuing Program

1. Data entry is in the form of prompted input.
2. Mean arrival rate (the average level that a system realizes over a period of time), mean service rate (the average length of time it takes to service a customer), service cost, and waiting cost must be given for the same time units, e.g., per hour, per day, etc.
3. Number of servers refers to number of service channels and must be an integer.
4. Maximum queue length for a finite queue and size of the finite population are integers.

Simulation

The simulation program is designed to give users the opportunity to perform simple simulations through the use of the Monte Carlo technique. It solves (1) Monte Carlo; (2) an inventory simulator; and (3) a queuing simulator.

The *Monte Carlo* determines a cumulative probability distribution (from observed values and their associated probabilities, which are entered), and using that distribution and randomly generated numbers, simulates a number of expected occurrences. The *inventory simulation* (discrete, time-independent simulation) allows users to make decisions regarding the reorder quantity and reorder point for an inventory system with stochastic demand. Lead time can be constant or variable. Users may define a discrete demand distribution, use a uniform distribution, or use a distribution built into the program. The *queuing simulation* (a discrete, time-dependent simulation) illustrates the operation of a service facility with stochastic arrivals and service times. The program generates random interarrival times using either a preset distribution or a user-defined distribution. As customers arrive, a second distribution determines the service time required. Balking may be included as desired. The program has two built-in service distributions, "Fast" and "Normal." Output is in the form of a minute-by-minute description of the system and summary statistics.

To Use the Simulation Program

1. Data entry from the keyboard is from prompted input. The discrete distribution is in a modified tabular form.
2. The discrete distribution table is limited to a maximum of 30 observations, i.e., 30 observed values and 30 corresponding frequencies of occurrence or probabilities.
3. The Monte Carlo simulation is limited to the simulation of 1000 periods; the inventory simulation to 104 periods (two years); and the queuing simulation to 8 hours, each hour containing 60 simulated minutes.
4. Selecting a repeatable sequence of random numbers always begins the simulation with the same random number and generates the same sequence of random numbers; responding NO to the prompt causes the computer to generate a different sequence of random numbers each time the simulation is run.
5. When a non-repeatable sequence of random numbers is chosen and you later choose to send the output to a printer or DOS text file, the results will differ from those displayed on the screen because a new sequence of random numbers is used.

Markov Analysis

Identifies the transitional probabilities for a given period or periods, the probability or quantity in the resulting vector in that period, and the steady state probabilities and quantities. Where absorbing states exist, it provides the fundamental matrix.

To Use the Markov Program

1. Data entry is a combination of prompted input and tabular entries to fill in the matrix.
2. The matrix size is limited to 2 to 12 states (integer only). Anything over 10 scrolls.
3. Transition probabilities should be given as decimal values; each row must add to 1.0.
4. Number of trials can be integers only.
5. Initial vector values can be decimals or whole numbers.

Forecasting Models

Solves moving averages (simple and weighted); exponential smoothing (simple and trend adjusted); and linear regression (simple and seasonally adjusted). Time series models determine a forecast and MAD. The regression model derives a regression equation and then uses this relationship to determine the forecast values, and also determines the standard deviation of regression and the correlation coefficient.

To Use the Forecasting Programs

1. Data entry is a combination of prompted and tabular input.
2. Limits are 100 periods for moving averages and exponential smoothing problems, 20 periods in the moving average, 100 pairs (of X Y values) for regression analysis.

3. With a WMA, the weight for the most recent time period is entered last. Weights are entered as decimal or integer values (weights are normalized prior to any calculations).
4. Alpha and Beta (exponential smoothing) are entered as decimal values between 0 and 1.
5. For the initial period forecast (exponential smoothing), use the actual period 1 value if no beginning forecast is given.
6. X (independent variables) and Y (dependent variables) (regression analysis) have to be entered in pairs; do not enter the variable for which you are forecasting.
7. It is not necessary to zero the years if time is the independent variable (regression analysis).

COMPUTER IRREGULARITIES

Values are stored in microcomputers using binary notation, which can occasionally produce some strange results. For example, the value 0.9 is sometimes stored (and later displayed) as .9000001 or .8999999 (or 9.000001E-1). Most of the output values have been formatted or rounded to avoid this problem.

Common Problems/Errors

It is impossible to anticipate all possible problems. However, some of the more common problems are discussed below.

To Stop a Program While It Is Running
Press the Ctrl-Scroll Lock key (terminates the program to the DOS prompt).
Never open the disk drive door or turn the computer off while the red light on the disk drive is lit.

"Compatibility" Problems
These may occur because a computer may not be totally "IBM compatible." Check to make sure you have booted the system with the correct version of DOS. If you are still having problems, check the computer's user manual. These programs also require a video controller that supports graphic output.

Printer Errors
Occur when printed output is specified and the printer is not turned on, when there is no paper in the printer, and when the printer is not "online" (the Online or Ready light is off). If you press the Shift and PrtSc keys simultaneously and nothing happens, the problem is probably with the cable or printer.

Disk Drive Errors
There are several disk drive error messages, most of which are self-explanatory:

```
DISK OR DRIVE NOT READY. CHECK DRIVE DOOR.
```

Make sure there is a disk in the drive specified and the drive door is closed, then press the space bar.

```
                    DISK IS WRITE PROTECTED.
```

Remove the write-protect tab or replace the disk with a formatted but not write-protected disk.

```
                    PATH/FILE ACCESS ERROR.
```

or

```
                    PATH NOT FOUND.
```

or

```
                    FILE NOT FOUND.
```

The computer cannot find the specified disk drive or subdirectory path. Retype the correct drive/path designation and filename.

```
                    DISK FULL.
```

There is no room on the specified disk. Replace with another formatted disk or press the ⟨RET⟩ key.

```
FILE ALREADY EXISTS. DO YOU WANT TO OVERWRITE IT? (YES/ NO )
```

There is already a file with the name you specified. Answering YES will replace it with your current problem. Answering NO will result in a prompt to "ENTER A DIFFERENT FILENAME BELOW" and a repetition of the original filename request prompt.

```
THERE ARE NO FILES FOR THAT MODEL ON THE DISK/PATH SPECIFIED.
```

The computer could find no files for that type of model on the disk specified. If you specify a filename that cannot be found, but there are other files for that type of model on the disk, you will see "CURRENT FILES ARE:" followed by a list of the available files. You will then be given another opportunity to enter a filename.

Cannot find ... Errors

This usually results when the program cannot find a run-time module or library file it needs. These files are all on the D&D Models Disk 1. If you get this message, make sure disk 1 is in one of the disk drives and specify which one if prompted to do so.

Program Termination Errors

These stop the program and return you to DOS. You will be instructed to press any key to return to the DOS system. To begin again, you must return to the Main Menu. Type **START** and press ⟨RET⟩. The most common program termination messages with explanations are:

Division by Zero   An unusual set of entries may sometimes produce a situation in which the computer attempts to divide by zero. In that case, you will see a message similar to DIVISION BY ZERO or OVERFLOW ERROR, and the output will contain the machine's equivalent of infinity. Usually this is the result of erroneous input. Check your values carefully and try again. If the same result occurs, try another problem; you may have an atypical problem/situation.

Memory Problem Errors   These usually result in the program either not running at all or terminating after beginning to run. These errors result from having insufficient memory (RAM) installed in the computer. Common error messages are: OUT OF MEMORY or OUT OF STRING SPACE IN MEMORY. A similar problem is the OVERFLOW problem. It means that the values entered, when used in the necessary calculations, produced a result that was too large to be represented in the computer's floating point notation.

Appendix F
Selected References

The Management Science Approach to Decision Making (Chapter 1)

Borsting, J., et al. "A Model for a First Course in Management Science/Operations Research." *Interfaces* 18 (September-October 1988): 72–80.

Churchman, C.W., R.L. Ackoff, and E.L. Arnoff. *Introduction to Operations Research*. New York: John Wiley & Sons, 1957.

Forgionne, G.A. "Corporate Management Science Activities: An Update." *Interfaces* 13 (May-June 1983): 20–23.

Gaither, N. "The Adoption of Operations Research Techniques by Manufacturing Organizations." *Decision Sciences* 6 (September 1975): 797–813.

Hillier, F.S., and G.J. Lieberman. *Introduction to Operations Research*. 4th ed. Oakland: Holden-Day, 1986.

Kleijnen, J.P.C. "Computers and Operations Research: A Survey." *Computers and Operations Research* 3 (1976): 327–335.

Klingman, D., N. Phillips, D. Steiger, and W. Young. "The Successful Deployment of Management Science throughout Citgo Petroleum Corporation." *Interfaces* 17 (1987): 4–25.

Shannon, R.E., S.S. Long, and B.P. Buckles. "Operations Research Methodologies in Industrial Engineering: A Survey." *AIIE Transactions* 12 (1980): 364–367.

Simon, Leonard S. "What Is a Management Scientist?" *Interfaces* 1 (1971): 25–36.

Linear Programming (Chapters 2, 3, 4, 5, 6)

Anderson, D.R., D.J. Sweeney, and T.A. Williams. *Linear Programming for Decision Making*. St. Paul: West Publishing, 1974.

Avramovich, D., et al. "A Decision Support System for Fleet Management: A Linear Programming Approach." *Interfaces* 12 (1982): 1–19.

Balbirer, S.D., and D. Shaw. "An Application of Linear Programming to Financial Planning." *Interfaces* 11 (1981): 77–83.

Bradley, S.P., A.C. Hax, and T.L. Magnanti. *Applied Mathematical Programming*. Reading, MA: Addison-Wesley, 1977.

Carino, H.F., and C.H. LeNoir, Jr. "Optimizing Wood Procurement in Cabinet Manufacturing." *Interfaces* 18 (March-April 1988): 10–19.

Daellenbach, Hans G., and J. Bell. *User's Guide to Linear Programming*. Englewood Cliffs, NJ: Prentice-Hall, 1970.

Dantzig, G.B. *Linear Programming and Extensions*. Princeton: Princeton University Press, 1963.

Emmons, Hamilton, et al. *Storm User's Manual.* Oakland: Holden-Day, 1986.

Gass, S. *Linear Programming: Models and Applications.* 5th ed. New York: McGraw-Hill, 1985.

Hillier, F. S., and G. J. Lieberman. *Introduction to Operations Research.* 4th ed. Oakland: Holden-Day, 1986.

Hooker, J. N. "Karmarkar's Linear Programming Algorithm." *Interfaces* 16 (July-August 1986): 75–90.

Karmarkar, N. "A New Polynomial Time Algorithm for Linear Programming." *Combinatorica* 4, no. 4 (1984): 373–95.

Lee, Sang M. *Linear Optimization for Management.* New York: Mason/Charter, 1976.

Schrage, L. *User's Manual for Linear, Integer, and Quadratic Programming with LINDO.* Redwood City, CA: Scientific Press, 1987.

Smith, B. D. "A Lease Portfolio Planning Model." *Interfaces* 12 (1982): 53–65.

Winston, Wayne L. *Operations Research: Applications and Algorithms.* Boston: Duxbury Press, 1987.

Wagner, H. M. *Principles of Operations Research.* 2d ed. Englewood Cliffs, NJ: Prentice-Hall, 1975.

Network Models—Transportation, Assignment, Transshipment, Network Flow, and PERT/CPM (Chapters 7, 8, 11)

Bazaraa, M., and J. Jarvis. *Linear Programming and Network Flows.* New York: Wiley, 1977.

Choypeng, P., P. Puakpong, and R. E. Rosenthal. "Optimal Ship Routing and Personnel Assignment for Naval Recruitment in Thailand." *Interfaces* 16 (August 1986): 47–52.

Evarts, H. F. *Introduction to PERT.* Boston: Allyn & Bacon, 1964.

Gass, S. *Linear Programming: Models and Applications.* 5th ed. New York: McGraw-Hill, 1985.

Glover, F., et al. "The Passenger-Mix Problem in Scheduled Airlines." *Interfaces* 12 (June 1982): 73–79.

Halpern, J., E. Sarisamlis, and Y. Wand. "An Activity Network Approach for the Analysis of Manning Policies in Firefighting Operations." *Management Science* 28 (October 1982): 1121–1136.

Jensen, P., and W. Barnes. *Network Flow Programming.* New York: Wiley, 1980.

Klingman, D., et al. "The Challenges and Success Factors in Implementing an Integrated Products Planning System for Citgo." *Interfaces* 16 (June 1986): 1–19.

Minieka, E. *Optimization Algorithms for Networks and Graphs.* New York: Decker, 1978.

Moder, J., E. W. Davis, and C. Phillips. *Project Management with CPM and PERT.* New York: Van Nostrand-Reinhold, 1983.

Phillips, D., and A. Diaz. *Fundamentals of Network Analysis.* Englewood Cliffs, NJ: Prentice-Hall, 1981.

Wiest, J., and F. Levy. *A Management Guide to PERT/CPM.* 2d ed. Englewood Cliffs, NJ: Prentice-Hall, 1977.

Integer Programming (Chapter 9)

Boykin, R. F. "Optimizing Chemical Production at Monsanto." *Interfaces* 15 (February 1985): 88–95.

Eaton, D., et al. "Determining Emergency Medical Service Vehicle Deployment in Austin, Texas." *Interfaces* 15 (1985): 96–108.

Garfinkel, R. S., and G. L. Nemhauser. *Integer Programming.* New York: Wiley, 1972.

Gelb, B., and B. Khumawala. "Reconfiguration of an Insurance Company's Sales Regions." *Interfaces* 14 (1984): 87–94.

Martin, C. H., and S. L. Lubin. "Optimization Modeling for Business Planning at Trumbull Asphalt." *Interfaces* 15 (December 1985): 66–72.

Plane, D. R., and C. McMillan, Jr. *Discrete Optimization: Integer Programming and Network Analysis for Management Decisions*. Englewood Cliffs, NJ: Prentice-Hall, 1971.

Schrage, L. *Linear, Integer, and Quadratic Programming with LINDO*. Palo Alto, CA: Scientific Press, 1986.

Shapiro, J. *Mathematical Programming: Structures and Algorithms*. New York: Wiley, 1979.

Taha, H. *Integer Programming: Theory, Applications, and Computations*, Orlando, FL: Academic Press, 1975.

Wagner, H. M. *Principles of Operations Research*. 2d ed. Englewood Cliffs, NJ: Prentice-Hall, 1975.

Zionts, Stanley. *Linear and Integer Programming*. Englewood Cliffs, NJ: Prentice-Hall, 1974.

Goal Programming (Chapter 10)

Ignizio, J. P. *Goal Programming and Extensions*. Lexington, MA: D.C. Heath, 1976.

Lee, S. M. *Goal Programming for Decision Analysis*. Philadelphia: Auerbach, 1972.

Lee, S. M., and L. Moore. "Optimizing University Admissions Planning." *Decision Sciences* 5 (1974): 405–414.

Lee, S. M., and M. J. Schniederjans. "A Multicriteria Assignment Problem: A Goal Programming Approach." *Interfaces* 13 (August 1983): 75–81.

Inventory Models (Chapter 12)

Brown, R. *Decision Rules for Inventory Management*. New York: Holt, Rinehart and Winston, 1967.

Buffa, E. S., and W. Taubert. *Production-Inventory Systems: Planning and Control*. 3rd ed. Homewood, IL: Irwin, 1979.

Edwards, J., H. M. Wagner, and W. P. Wood. "Blue Bell Trims Its Inventory." *Interfaces* 15 (February 1985): 34–52.

Hadley, G., and T. M. Whitin. *Analysis of Inventory Systems*. Englewood Cliffs, NJ: Prentice-Hall, 1963.

Hillier, F. S., and G. J. Lieberman. *Introduction to Operations Research*. 4th ed. Oakland: Holden-Day, 1986.

Kleutghen, P. P., and J. C. McGee. "Development and Implementation of an Integrated Inventory Management Program at Pfizer Pharmaceutical." *Interfaces* 15 (February 1985): 69–87.

Naddor, E. *Inventory Systems*. New York: Wiley, 1966.

Orlicky, J. *Material Requirements Planning*. New York: McGraw-Hill, 1975.

Peterson, R., and E. Silver. *Decision Systems for Inventory Management and Production Planning*. 2d ed. New York: Wiley, 1984.

Schonberger, R. J. *World Class Manufacturing*. New York: The Free Press, 1986.

Stockton, R. S. *Basic Inventory Systems: Concepts and Analysis*. Boston: Allyn & Bacon, 1965.

Tersine, R. *Principles of Inventory and Materials Management*. New York: North-Holland, 1982.

Decision Analysis (Chapter 13)

Barron, F. H. "Payoff Matrices Pay Off at Hallmark." *Interfaces* 15 (August 1985): 20–25.

Bunn, D. *Applied Decision Analysis*. New York: McGraw-Hill, 1984.

Cohan, D., S. M. Haas, D. L. Radloff, and R. F. Yancik. "Using Fire in Forest Management: Decision Making Under Uncertainty." *Interfaces* 14 (October 1984): 8–19.

Dunford, R. R. "Decisions, Decisions." *Industrial Research* 16 (July 1974): 27–30.

Eilon, S. "What Is a Decision?" *Management Science* 16 (December 1970): B172–B189.

Lindgren, B.W. *Elements of Decision Theory*. New York: MacMillan, 1971.

Schlaifer, R. *Analysis of Decisions under Uncertainty*. New York: McGraw-Hill, 1969.

Winkler, R. *Introduction to Bayesian Inference and Decision*. New York: Holt, Rinehart, and Winston, 1972.

Waiting Lines (Chapter 14)

Cooper, R. *Introduction to Queueing Theory*. 2d ed. New York: North-Holland, 1981.

Gross, D., and C. M. Harris. *Fundamentals of Queueing Theory*. New York: Wiley, 1974.

Krell, B. E., and M. Arminio. "Queueing Theory Applied to Data Processing Networks." *Interfaces* 12 (August 1982): 21–33.

Karlin, S., and H. Taylor. *A First Course in Stochastic Processes*. 2nd ed. Orlando, FL: Academic Press, 1975.

Kolesar, P. "Stalking the Endangered CAT: A Queueing Analysis of Congestion at Automatic Teller Machines." *Interfaces* 14 (December 1984): 16–26.

Lee, A. *Applied Queueing Theory*. New York: St. Martin's Press, 1966.

Newell, G. F. *Applications of Queueing Theory*. London: Chapman & Hall, 1971.

Ong, H. L., T. N. Goh, and H. K. Sim. "A Modelling Study of Machine-Service Operation in an Electronics Industry." *Journal of the Operations Research Society* 36 (November 1985): 993–998.

Stevenson, W. J. *Production/Operations Management*. 2d ed. Homewood, IL: Irwin, 1986.

Vogel, M. "Queueing Theory Applied to Machine Manning." *Interfaces* 9 (1979): 1–8.

Simulation (Chapter 15)

Banks, J., and J. Carson. *Discrete-Event System Simulation*. Englewood Cliffs, NJ: Prentice-Hall, 1984.

Fishman, G. *Principles of Discrete Event Simulation*. New York: Wiley, 1978.

Glovin, L. B. "Product Blending: A Simulation Case Study in Double-Time." *Interfaces* 9 (December 1979): 64–76.

Kolesar, P. "Stalking the Endangered CAT: A Queueing Analysis of Congestion at Automatic Teller Machines." *Interfaces* 14 (December 1984): 16–26.

Naylor, T. H., et al. *Computer Simulation Techniques*. New York: Wiley, 1968.

Schreiber, T. *Simulation Using GPSS*. New York: Wiley, 1974.

Watson, H. *Computer Simulation in Business*. New York: Wiley, 1981.

Markov Analysis (Chapter 16)

Flamholtz, E., and G. Glasser. "A Markovian Analysis for the Valuation of Human Assets Acquired by an Organizational Purchase." *Interfaces* 14 (1984): 11–15.

Isaacson, D., and R. Madsen. *Markov Chains: Theory and Applications*. New York: Wiley, 1976.

Karlin, S., and H. Taylor. *A First Course in Stochastic Processes*. 2nd ed. Orlando, FL: Academic Press, 1975.

Kemeny, J., and L. Snell. *Finite Markov Chains*. Princeton: Van Nostrand, 1960.

McCormick, G. "Algorithms for the Detection of Spontaneous Combustion in Coal Mines." *Journal of the Operations Research Society* 37 (June 1986): 591–602.

White, D. J. "Real Applications of Markov Decision Processes." *Interfaces* 15 (November–December 1985): 73–83.

White, D. J. "Further Real Applications of Markov Decision Processes." *Interfaces* 18 (September–October 1988): 55–61.

Forecasting (Chapter 17)

Ashley, R., and J. Guerard. "Applications of Time Series Analysis to Texas Financial Forecasting." *Interfaces* 13 (August 1983): 46–55.

Box, G. E. P., and G. M. Jenkins. *Time Series Analysis: Forecasting and Control*. Rev. ed. San Francisco: Holden-Day, 1976.

Chambers, J., S. K. Mullich, and D. D. Smith. "How To Choose the Right Forecasting Technique." *Harvard Business Review* 49 (July–August 1971): 55–64.

Hanke, J. E., and A. G. Reitsch. *Business Forecasting.* 2d ed. Boston: Allyn & Bacon, 1986.

Makridakis, S., S. C. Wheelwright, and V. E. McGee. *Forecasting: Methods and Applications.* 2d ed. New York: Wiley, 1983.

Parker, G. C., and E. L. Segura, "How to Get a Better Forecast." *Harvard Business Review* 49 (March–April 1971): 99–100.

Riccio, L. J., J. Miller and A. Litke. "Polishing the Big Apple: How Management Science Has Helped Make New York City Streets Cleaner." *Interfaces* 16 (January–February 1986): 83–88.

Wheelwright, S. C., and S. Makridakis. *Forcasting Models for Management.* 4th ed. New York: Wiley, 1985.

Decision Support Systems (Chapter 18)

Blanning, R. "What Is Happening in DSS?" *Interfaces* 13 (October 1983): 71–80.

Davis, G. B. *Management Information Systems: Conceptual Foundations, Structure and Development.* New York: McGraw-Hill, 1974.

Fordyce, K., P. Norden, and G. Sullivan. "Review of Expert Systems for the Management Science Practitioner." *Interfaces* 17 (April 1987): 64–77.

Hicks, J. O. *Management Information Systems: A User Perspective.* 2d ed. St. Paul, MN: West, 1987.

Mann, R. I., and H. J. Watson. "A Contingency Model for User Involvement in DSS Development." *MIS Quarterly* (March 1984): 27–38.

McLeod, R. *Introduction to Information Systems: A Problem Solving Approach.* Chicago: Science Research Associates, 1989.

Schultheis, R., and M. Sumner. *Management Information Systems: The Manager's View.* Homewood, IL: Irwin, 1989.

Sprague, R. H., Jr., and E. D. Carlson. *Building Effective Decision Support Systems.* Englewood Cliffs, NJ: Prentice-Hall, 1982.

Sullivan, R. S., and S. C. Secrest. "A Simple Optimization DSS for Production Planning at Dairyman's Cooperative Creamery Association." *Interfaces* 15 (October 1985): 46–53.

Turban, Efraim. *Decision Support and Expert Systems: Managerial Perspectives.* New York: Macmillan, 1988.

Appendix G
Selected Problem Solutions

Chapter 2

1. Let A = number of A chairs
      B = number of B chairs

$$MAX\ 15A + 35B$$

subject to

$$
\begin{aligned}
20A + 32B &\leq 10000 \\
2A + 2B &\leq 800 \\
2A + 8B &\leq 2000 \\
A, B &\geq 0
\end{aligned}
$$

3. Let X = units of product X
      Y = units of product Y

$$MAX\ 6X + 4Y$$

subject to

$$
\begin{aligned}
3X + 3Y &\leq 45 \\
2X + 3Y &\leq 48 \\
4X + 2Y &\leq 54 \\
X, Y &\geq 0
\end{aligned}
$$

5. Let P = pounds of pork
      B = pounds of beef
      C = pounds of cereal

$$MIN\ 3P + 5B + 1.75C$$

subject to

$$
\begin{aligned}
P + B + C &= 2500 \\
P &\geq 600 \\
B &\geq 1200 \\
C &\leq 900 \\
P, B, C &\geq 0
\end{aligned}
$$

7. Let F = number of football jerseys
   S = number of soccer shirts

$$\text{MAX } 6F + 4.5S$$

subject to

$$
\begin{aligned}
8F + 5S &\le 1935 \\
2F + 2S &\le 600 \\
2F + 3S &\le 685 \\
F, S &\ge 0
\end{aligned}
$$

9. Let G = number of gliders
   C = number of chairs

$$\text{MAX } 100G + 40C$$

subject to

$$
\begin{aligned}
40G + 25C &\le 900 \\
1.5G + .67C &\le 30 \\
-2G + C &\ge 0 \\
G, C &\ge 0
\end{aligned}
$$

11. Let X1 = number of 8″ skillets
    X2 = number of 12″ skillets
    X3 = number of 2 quart pans

$$\text{MAX } 1.4X1 + 0.9X2 + 1.1X3$$

subject to

$$
\begin{aligned}
.5X1 + .6X2 + .4X3 &\le 48 \\
1X1 + 1.5X2 + .5X3 &\le 90 \\
X1, X2, X3 &\ge 0
\end{aligned}
$$

15. Let R = number of radio ads
    D = number of daytime TV ads
    P = number of prime-time TV ads
    N = number of newspaper ads

$$\text{MAX } 7000R + 25000D + 60000P + 4000N$$

subject to

$$
\begin{aligned}
1000R + 5000D + 12000P + 500N &\le 60000 \\
R &\le 8 \\
D &\le 5 \\
P &\le 3 \\
N &\le 20 \\
R &\ge 1 \\
D + P &\ge 1 \\
N &\ge 1 \\
-.6R - .6D - .6P + .4N &\le 0 \\
R, D, P, N &\ge 0
\end{aligned}
$$

17. Let L = gallons of Lite Cooler
R = gallons of Regal

$$MAX\ 2.6L + 3.1R$$

subject to

$$
\begin{aligned}
4L + 3R &\leq 1200 \\
2L + 3R &\leq 1000 \\
4R &\leq 1100 \\
L &\geq 150 \\
R &\geq 100 \\
L, R &\geq 0
\end{aligned}
$$

21. Let W = bottles of light white
C = bottles of Chablis
P = bottles of summer pink

$$MAX\ 2W + 1.70C + 1.25P$$

subject to

$$
\begin{aligned}
W &\leq 650 \\
C &\leq 750 \\
P &\geq 300 \\
W + C + P &\leq 1500 \\
W, C, P &\geq 0
\end{aligned}
$$

23. Let C = acres of corn to plant
P = acres of pumpkins to plant

$$MAX\ 250C + 125P$$

subject to

$$
\begin{aligned}
C + P &\leq 500 \\
100C + 75P &\leq 40000 \\
P &\geq 100 \\
C, P &\geq 0
\end{aligned}
$$

25. Let R = ounces of raisins; B = ounces of bananas
C = ounces of coconut; S = ounces of sunflower seeds

$$MIN\ .04R + .03B + .06C + .02S$$

subject to

$$
\begin{aligned}
R + B + C + S &\geq 16 \\
2R + 3B &\geq 16 \\
3R + C + S &\geq 18 \\
2B + 2C + S &\geq 15 \\
3R + 2C + S &\geq 22 \\
4B + 3S &\geq 17 \\
R, B, C, S &\geq 0
\end{aligned}
$$

27. Let D = number of deluxe units
  B2 = number of two-bedroom units
  B3 = number of three-bedroom units

MAX 20000D + 7000B2 + 12000B3

subject to

2000D +	1200B2 +	1500B3 ≤	400000	(sq. feet)
D		≤	30	(max sales)
−.2D +	.8B2	−.2B3 ≥	0	(20% agreement)
−.4D +	.6B2	−.4B3 ≤	0	(40% limit)
D		≥	10	(seller option)
		B3 ≥	10	(seller option)

D, B2, B3 ≥ 0

31. Let Rij = units produced on regular hours in month i and shipped in month j;
  thus, RJJ represents units produced in month J (January) and
  shipped in month J (January)
  Oij = units produced on overtime hours in month i and shipped in month j

MIN 8RJJ + 12OJJ + 11RJF + 15OJF + 14RJM + 18OJM + 8RFF +
  12OFF + 11RFM + 15OFM + 8RMM + 12OMM

subject to

$$RJJ + RJF + RJM ≤ 1800$$
$$OJJ + OJF + OJM ≤ 400$$
$$RFF + RFM ≤ 1800$$
$$OJF + OJM ≤ 400$$
$$RMM ≤ 1800$$
$$OJM ≤ 400$$
$$RJJ + OJJ = 1500$$
$$RJF + OJF + RFF + OFF = 2500$$
$$RJM + OJM + RFM + OFM + RMM + OMM = 2000$$
$$RJM, OJM, RJF, OJF, RJM, OJM, RFF, OJF, RFM, OJM, RMM, OJM ≥ 0$$

32. Let Z = pretzels packages   C = chex & nuts packages
  N = peanuts packages   P = party mix packages

Since each package is 8 ozs, there are two packages per pound. Thus, 200
pounds of pretzels will produce 400 packages, etc.

MAX .30Z + .45N + .26C + .54P

subject to

Z +		.2P ≤	400	(pretzels)
	N + .15C +	.1P ≤	800	(peanuts)
	.85C +	.7P ≤	1000	(chex cereal)

Z, N, C, P ≥ 0

Chapter 3

2. Moving clockwise around the feasible region, the extreme points are:
$(0,5)$ $(5/3,5)$ $(80/13, 30/13)$ $(8,0)$

4. $X_1 = 20$, $X_2 = 20$, Zmax $= 180$

6. $X_1 = 6$, $X_2 = 2$, Zmax $= 36$

8. $A = 120{,}000$, $B = 80{,}000$, Zmax $= 240{,}000$

10. $X_1 = 4$, $X_2 = 4$, Zmax $= 48$

12. $F = 170$, $S = 115$, Zmax $= 1537.5$

14. **a.** MAX $6X_1 + 4X_2 + 0S_1 + 0S_2 + 0S_3$

subject to

$$X_1 + 2X_2 + 1S_1 \qquad\qquad = 6$$
$$2X_1 + 3X_2 + \qquad 1S_2 \qquad = 12$$
$$3X_1 + 3X_2 + \qquad\qquad 1S_3 = 12$$
$$X_1, X_2, S_1, S_2, S_3 \geq 0$$

b. $X_1 = 4$, $X_2 = 0$, Zmax $= 24$

c. $S_1 = 2$, $S_2 = 4$, $S_3 = 0$

16. $X_1 = 10$, $X_2 = 6$, Zmax $= 26$

18. $X = 4$, $Y = 2$, Zmin $= 400$

20. $X_1 = 6$, $X_2 = 12$, Zmax $= 84$

22. $X_1 = 2$, $X_2 = 6$, Zmin $= 34$

24. MAX $X_1 + X_2 + X_3 + 0S_1 + 0S_2 + 0S_3$

subject to

$$3X_1 + 4X_2 + 2X_3 + 1S_1 \qquad\qquad = 100$$
$$5X_1 + 3X_2 + 6X_3 + \qquad 1S_2 \qquad = 160$$
$$4X_1 + \qquad 5X_3 - \qquad\qquad 1S_3 = 85$$
$$X_1, X_2, X_3, S_1, S_2, S_3 \geq 0$$

26. $X_1 = 39/8$, $X_2 = 11/8$, Zmin $= 361/8$ (45.125)

28. $X_1 = 15/7$, $X_2 = 26/7$, Zmin $= 537/14$ (38.357)

30. $X_1 = 3$, $X_2 = 2.5$, Zmin $= 5.5$

32. Solution is unbounded.

34. $X_1 = 14.86$, $X_2 = 12.86$, Zmax $= 138.60$

36. $X_1 = 47.5$, $X_2 = 7.5$, Zmax $= 157.5$

Chapter 4

1. Final Solution.

C_j	BASIC	5	3.5	3	0	0	
	VAR	X_1	X_2	X_3	S_1	S_2	RHS
5	X_1	1	0	1.167	.833	$-.083$	237.5
3.5	X_2	0	1	.667	$-.667$	.167	25
	Z	5	3.5	8.167	1.833	.167	1275
	$C - Z$	0	0	-5.167	-1.833	$-.167$	

4.

C_j	BASIC VAR	5 X_1	-3 X_2	4 X_3	2.5 X_4	0 S_1	0 S_2	-M A_1	0 S_3	-M A_2	0 S_4	RHS
0	S_1	3	2	1	3	1	0	0	0	0	0	6
0	S_2	2	4	0	-3	0	1	0	0	0	0	5
-M	A_1	-4	3	5	4	0	0	1	-1	0	0	3
-M	A_2	1	0	2	1	0	0	0	0	1	-1	1
	Z	3M	-3M	-7M	-5M	0	0	-M	M	-M	M	-51M
	$C-Z$	5-3M	-3+3M	4+7M	2.5+5M	0	0	0	-M	0	-M	

6. **a.** MAX $6X_1 + 5X_2 + 0S_1 + 0S_2$

subject to

$$1.5X_1 + 2X_2 + \ S_1 \qquad\qquad = 30$$
$$8X_1 + 4X_2 \qquad\quad + \ S_2 = 80$$
$$X_1, X_2, S_1, S_2 \geq 0$$

b.

C_j	BASIC VAR	6 X_1	5 X_2	0 S_1	0 S_2	RHS
0	S_1	1.5	2	1	0	30
0	S_2	8	4	0	1	80
	Z	0	0	0	0	0
	$C-Z$	6	5	0	0	

C_j	BASIC VAR	6 X_1	5 X_2	0 S_1	0 S_2	RHS
0	S_1	0	1.25	1	-.187	15
6	X_1	1	.5	0	.125	10
	Z	6	3	0	.75	60
	$C-Z$	0	2	0	-.75	

C_j	BASIC VAR	6 X_1	5 X_2	0 S_1	0 S_2	RHS
5	X_2	0	1	.8	-.15	12
6	X_1	1	0	-.4	.2	4
	Z	6	5	1.6	.45	84
	$C-Z$	0	0	-1.6	-.45	

8.

C_j	BASIC VAR	4 A	6 B	M A_1	0 S_1	M A_2	0 S_2	RHS
M	A_1	4	6	1	-1	0	0	12
M	A_2	4	2	0	0	1	-1	18
	Z	8M	8M	M	-M	M	-M	30M
	$C-Z$	4-8M	6-8M	0	M	0	M	

C_j	BASIC VAR	4 A	6 B	M A_1	0 S_1	M A_2	0 S_2	RHS
4	A	1	1.5	.25	−25	0	0	3
M	A_2	0	−4	−1	1	1	−1	6
	Z	4	6−4M	1−M	M−1	M	−M	12+6M
	C−Z	0	4M	2M−1	−1−M	0	M	

C_j	BASIC VAR	4 A	6 B	M A_1	0 S_1	M A_2	0 S_2	RHS
4	A	1	.5	0	0	.25	−.25	4.5
0	S_1	0	−4	−1	1	1	−1	6
	Z	4	2	0	0	1	−1	18
	C − Z	0	4	M	0	M	1	

10. a. Final Tableau:

C_j	BASIC VAR	1 A	3 B	2 C	5 D	−M A_1	−M A_2	0 S_1	RHS
2	C	.8	0	1	0	−.2	.467	−.067	1.333
3	B	.6	1	0	0	−.4	.267	.033	1.333
5	D	0	0	0	1	1	−.667	.167	4.667
	Z	3.4	3	2	5	3.4	−1.6	.8	
	C − Z	−2.4	0	0	0	−M−3.4	−M+1.6	−.8	

b. All constraints are binding.

c. A = −$2.40

d. Constraint 1 = $3.40; constraint 2 = $1.60; constraint 3 = $0.80.

e. Constraint 1, because it has the largest shadow price.

12. a. MAX 1250D386 + 900D286 + 800L286

subject to

$$D386 + \quad D286 \qquad\qquad \le 100$$
$$L286 \le 60$$
$$D386 \qquad\qquad\qquad\qquad \le 45$$
$$D286 + L286 \le 120$$
$$4D386 + \quad 3D286 + 2.5L286 \le 290$$
$$D386, D286, L286 \ge 0$$

b. Final Tableau:

C_j	BASIC VAR	1250 D386	900 D286	800 L286	0 S_1	0 S_2	0 S_3	0 S_4	0 S_5	RHS
0	S_1	0	.25	0	1	.625	0	0	−.25	65
0	S_3	0	−.75	0	0	.625	1	0	−.25	10
1250	D386	1	.75	0	0	−.625	0	0	.25	35
0	S_4	0	1	0	0	−1	0	1	0	60
800	L286	0	0	1	0	1	0	0	0	60
	Z	1250	937.5	800	0	18.75	0	0	312.5	91750
	C−Z	0	−37.5	0	0	−18.75	0	0	−312.5	

c. Constraints 2 (laptop capacity) and 5 (labor hours) are binding.
d. Constraint 2 = $18.75 and constraint 5 = $312.50.

14. a. MIN
    b. A and A_2
    c. TABLEAU

C_j	BASIC VAR	4 A	6 B	M A_1	0 S_1	M A_2	0 S_2	RHS
4	A	1	1.5	.25	−.25	0	0	3
M	A_2	0	−4	−1	1	1	−1	6
	Z	4	6−4M	1−M	M−1	M	−M	6M+12
	C−Z	0	4M	2M−1	−1−M	0	M	

d. S_1 column is the pivot column; A_2 row (second row) is the pivot row.

e.

C_j	BASIC VAR	4 A	6 B	M A_1	0 S_1	M A_2	0 S_2	RHS
4	A	1	.5	0	0	.25	−.25	4.5
0	S_1	0	−4	−1	1	1	−1	6
	Z	4	2	0	0	1	−1	18
	C − Z	0	4	M	0	M−1	1	

16. a. MAX
    b. A, D and B
    c. TABLEAU

C_j	BASIC VAR	5 A	6 B	5 C	4 D	0 S_1	0 S_2	0 S_3	RHS
5	A	1	0	.2	0	.2	0	−.2	4
4	D	0	0	1	1	−.2	.133	.367	30
6	B	0	1	.6	0	.2	−.067	−.033	10
	Z	5	6	8.6	4	1.4	.13	.27	200
	C−Z	0	0	−3.6	0	−1.4	−.13	−.27	

d. Yes, this solution is optimal.
e.

VARIABLE	QUANTITY	VARIABLE	DUAL COST/SHADOW PRICE
A	4	A	0
B	10	B	0
D	30	C	−3.6
		D	0
Zmax = 200		S1	−1.4
		S2	−.13
		S3	−.27

f. All constraints are binding.
g. It would decrease by 14.4 [(4)(3.6)].

18. **a.** A, A_1 and B

b.

C_j	BASIC VAR	6 A	5 B	3 C	0 S_1	$-M$ A_1	0 S_2	RHS
6	A	1	0	1	2	0	3	45
$-M$	A_1	0	0	0	0	1	0	10
5	B	0	1	1	-1	0	0	25
	Z	6	5	11	7	$-M$	18	$-10M+390$
	C$-$Z	0	0	-8	-7	0	-18	

c. Yes, this solution is optimal.

d. This is an infeasible solution (problem). An artificial variable (A_1) remains in the solution.

20. **a.** S_1, S_2 and A

b.

C_j	BASIC VAR	8 A	6 B	7 C	0 S_1	0 S_2	0 S_3	RHS
0	S_1	0	0	3	1	0	2	20
0	S_2	0	0	-1	0	1	-3	75
8	A	1	.75	2	0	0	2	80
	Z	8	6	16	0	0	16	640
	C$-$Z	0	0	-9	0	0	-16	

c. Yes, this solution is optimal.

d. This problem has an alternate optimal solution. Variable B has a reduced cost of zero, indicating it can enter the solution with no change in the objective function.

Chapter 5

1. **a.** $X_1 = 4.8$, $X_2 = 9.6$, Zmax $= 14.4$
b. $4/3 \geq C_1 \geq \frac{1}{2}$ and $2 \geq C_2 \geq \frac{3}{4}$

3. **a.** $X_1 = 9$, $X_2 = 4$, Zmax $= 228$
b. No Limit $\geq C_1 \geq 16$ $15 \geq C_2 \geq 0$

5. $5.333 \geq C_1 \geq 2$ and $6 \geq C_2 \geq 2.25$
6. $60 \geq b_1 \geq 30$, $130 \geq b_2 \geq 75$, and No Limit $\geq b_3 \geq 68$
9. $28 \geq C_1 \geq 9.33$ and $18 \geq C_2 \geq 6$
10. $124 \geq b_1 \geq 60$, $120 \geq b_2 \geq 40$, and No Limit $\geq b_3 \geq 5$
13. **a.** A $= 60$, B $= 45$, $S_2 = 120$, Zmax $= 480$
b. No Limit $\geq C_1 \geq 2$ and $10 \geq C_2 \geq 0$
c. $380 \geq b_1 \geq 120$, No Limit $\geq b_2 \geq 810$, and $160 \geq b_3 \geq 0$

15. **a.** A maximization problem. The objective function coefficient for the artificial variable is $-M$.
b. There are four constraints. Since the slack, surplus, and artificial variables are added in order, the first three constraints are $\leq$ constraints (S_1, S_2, and S_3). The last constraint must be $\geq$ ($A_1 - S_4$).
c. $6 \geq C_1 \geq 2$ and $10 \geq C_2 \geq 3.333$
d. $420 \geq b_1 \geq 180$, $810 \geq b_2 \geq 450$, No Limit $\geq b_3 \geq 60$, $270 \geq b_4 \geq$ No Limit

17. a.
$$X_1 = 9 \qquad S_1 = 0$$
$$X_2 = 0 \qquad S_2 = 50$$
$$X_3 = 12 \qquad S_3 = 0 \qquad \text{Zmax} = 3000$$
$$\qquad\qquad S_4 = 5$$

b. There are four constraints.

c. 100. Since $Z = 200(9) + C_2(12) = 3000$, $C_2 = 100$.

d. The first and third constraints are binding. S_1 and S_3 are equal to zero.

e. The -6 for X_2 is a reduced cost, indicating that for every unit of X_2 produced, the value of the objective will be reduced by 6. A unit of the resource 1 is worth 15 (one more unit of this resource would increase the objective function value by 15); one less unit would reduce the objective function value by 15. A unit of resource 3 is worth 12.

18. a. Add one more unit of the second constraint. It has the highest shadow price—8.

b. Yes. The reduced cost for variable X_1 is 0, indicating an alternate optimal solution exists. Both solutions have an optimal Z value of 6,800.

20.

$$\text{MIN } 200Y_1 + 210Y_2$$

subject to

$$6Y_1 + 4Y_2 \geq 3$$
$$4Y_1 + 7Y_2 \geq 5$$
$$Y_1, Y_2 \geq 0$$

21. PRIMAL: $X_1 = 21.538$, $X_2 = 17.692$, Zmax $= 153.077$
Shadow prices: $S_1 = 0.38$, $S_2 = .692$
DUAL: $Y_1 = 0.38$, $Y_2 = .692$, Zmin $= 153.077$
Shadow prices: $S_1 = 21.538$, $S_2 = 17.692$

23. $Y_1 = .5$, $Y_2 = .5$, $Y_3 = 0$, Zmin $= 490$
Shadow prices: $S_1 = 45$, $S_2 = 35$, $S_3 = 20$

26.

$$\text{MIN } 400Y_1 - 120Y_2 + 540Y_3$$

subject to

$$9Y_1 - 4Y_2 + 6Y_3 \geq 1$$
$$7Y_1 - 5Y_2 + 11Y_3 \geq 2$$
$$8Y_1 - 3Y_2 + 9Y_3 \geq 1.5$$
$$Y_1, Y_2, Y_3 \geq 0$$

28.

$$\text{MIN } 1200Y_1 - 300Y_2 + 1100Y_3 + 600Y_4 - 600Y_4'$$

subject to

$$14Y_1 - 3Y_2 + 15Y_3 \qquad\qquad \geq 12$$
$$12Y_1 \qquad + 10Y_3 + Y_4 - Y_4' \geq 9$$
$$16Y_1 - 4Y_2 + 18Y_3 \qquad\qquad \geq 15$$
$$13Y_1 + \qquad 10Y_3 + 2Y_4 - 2Y_4' \geq 11$$
$$Y_1, Y_2, Y_3, Y_4, Y_4' \geq 0$$

29. $Y_1 = 0$, $Y_2 = 0$, $Y_3 = .182$, Zmin $= 98.182$
Dual Prices: $Y_1 = 203.636$, $Y_2 = 125.455$
Shadow Prices: $S_1 = 0$, $S_2 = 49.091$, $S_3 = 0$

Chapter 6

1. A = 500,000; B = 200,000; C = 0; D = 300,000; Zmax = 260,000
3. M = 0; N = 40; TV = 0; Zmax = 1,000,000
5. **a.** Variables A, C, D, and S_2 are basic.
   b. Constraints 1 and 3 are binding.
   c. It will change by 2.5, to 37.5.

7. NE = 15; C = 45; DC = 20; SE = 15; Zmax = 13,050,000
9. **a.** Variables A and B are basic.
   b. The first and third constraints are binding.
   c. 415.20 (assuming a maximization problem).

11. FGF = Fast Grow produced at Fairport, etc.
    FGF = 500; GTF = 2500; FGB = 3000; MGB = 2000; Zmin = 34,200
15. J = 22,784.81; P = 12,151.899; C = 25,063.291; Zmin = 49,329.11
20. The optimal solution to this problem (basic variables and quantities) will not change as long as the objective function coefficient for the decision variables remains between the lower limit and the upper limit (assuming only one coefficient is changed). Assuming this is a maximization problem, decision variable C is probably not basic, since it has no lower limit.

    The shadow prices for all constraints will remain the same as long as the RHS values do not decrease below the lower limit or increase above the upper limit.
23. A = 3687.5; B = 562.5; C = 750; Zmin = 3121.25
25. OJ = 45; GR = 250; P = 30; GUAVA = 20, MANGO = 6; ORPINE = 425; TRDEL = 400; HMANG = 20; HGUAV = 28; Zmax = 14,336
    Shadow Prices: ORANGE = 8.96; GRAPEFRUIT = 8.96; TANGERINE = 7.936; PINEAPPLE = 21.76; GUAVA = 14.08; MANGO = 16.64
29. TWOSHELF = 20; THREESHELF = 20; PLANTER = 10; Zmax = 345.5

Chapter 7

1. A,1 = 150; A,3 = 350; B,2 = 350; B,3 = 450; C,1 = 600; COST = 36,250
4. 1,D = 80; 1,E = 40; 2,B = 110; 2,C = 40; 3,A = 50; 3,C = 100; DUMMY,A = 30; DUMMY,E = 35; PAYOFF = 2,115
6. A → 1, B → 2, C → 3, D → 6, E → 5, F →4, COST = 145
8. Northwest Corner: 1,A = 105; 2,A = 15; 2,B = 45; 3,B = 90; 3,C = 90; Cost = 2,107.50
   Least Cost method: 1,B = 15; 1,C = 90; 2,B = 60; 3,A = 120; 3,B = 60; Cost = 1,762.50
   The least cost initial solution is also the final solution. The MODI values for the unoccupied cells are: 1,A = .5; 2,A = 1.5; 2,C = .5; and 3,C = 3
10. **a.** Add a dummy column.
    b. 1 → A, 2 →DUMMY, 3 → B, 4 →C, COSTS = 44

12. Pastore → C, Ruiz → A, Jackson → B, and Willis unassigned or Willis → B and Jackson unassigned. 18 hours.
14. **a.** 3,400
    b. 3,400

16. **a.** Pedersen → 1, Ruiz → 2, Murphy → 3, Levy → 5, Rullon → 4 and Crestuk unassigned. Alternative solutions exist. (9.8)

  b. Crestuk

  c. Ruiz → 4, Murphy → 1, Crestuk → 5, Levy → 3, Rullon → 2 and Pedersen unassigned. Alternative solutions exist. (11.35)

18. **a.** 1 → NAPOLEON, 2 → ECLAIR, 3 → CHEESECAKE, DUMMY → STRUDEL, PROFIT = .35

  b. Strudel

  c.

$$\text{MAX } .10N_1 + .12E_1 + .06S_1 + .05C_1 + .07N_2 + .15E_2 + .10S_2 + .05C_2 + .11N_3 + .08E_3 + .07S_3 + .10C_3$$

subject to

$$N_1 + E_1 + S_1 + C_1 = 1$$
$$N_2 + E_2 + S_2 + C_2 = 1$$
$$N_3 + E_3 + S_3 + C_3 = 1$$
$$N_1 + N_2 + N_3 \le 1$$
$$E_1 + E_2 + E_3 \le 1$$
$$S_1 + S_2 + S_3 \le 1$$
$$C_1 + C_2 + C_3 \le 1$$
$$N_1, N_2, \ldots C_2, C_3 \ge 0$$

20. **a.** A, S = 200; B, T = 250; B, U = 250; C, R = 200; D, R = 250; D, U = 150; COST = 4,687.50 (Alternate Optima exist.)

  b. A, S = 200; A, U = 100; B, T = 250; B, U = 250; C, R = 150; C, U = 50; D, R = 300; COST = 4,702.50

  c. No, the savings is only $15.

22. Kristen → checkups, Rachel → tighten, and Sara → instruction (23 patients per hour)

24. Wright, Perez and Sharp to 1st grade; Smith and Zenid to 2nd grade; Jacobs to 3rd grade; and Garman and Mateo are unassigned. Effectiveness = 23.4

26. **a.**

$$\text{MIN } 200X_{11} + 230X_{12} + 180X_{13} + 330X_{14} + 190X_{21} + 300X_{22} + 250X_{23} + 200X_{24} + 325X_{31} + 175X_{32} + 225X_{33} + 185X_{34}$$

subject to

$$X_{11} + X_{12} + X_{13} + X_{14} = 20$$
$$X_{21} + X_{22} + X_{23} + X_{24} = 18$$
$$X_{31} + X_{32} + X_{33} + X_{34} = 59$$
$$X_{11} + X_{21} + X_{31} \le 21$$
$$X_{12} + X_{22} + X_{32} \le 14$$
$$X_{13} + X_{23} + X_{33} \le 12$$
$$X_{14} + X_{24} + X_{34} \le 15$$
$$X_{11}, X_{12}, \ldots, X_{33}, X_{34} \ge 0$$

  b.

	1	2	3	4	SUPPLY
1	200	230	M	330	20
2	190	300	250	200	18
3	325	175	225	185	21
DEMAND	21	14	12	15	

c. $W_1, S_1 = 20$; $W_2, S_1 = 1$; $W_2, S_3 = 2$; $W_2, S_4 = 15$; $W_3, S_2 = 14$; $W_3, S_3 = 7$; COST = 11,715

28. a. B → 3, D → 2, E → 1, F → 4, Customers served = 149
    b. Clerks A and C are unassigned.

Chapter 8

1. a.

Branch	Branch Value	Path
1–2	16	1–2
1–3	12	1–3
1–4	30	1–4
1–5	24	1–3–5
1–6	34	1–3–5–6
1–7	52	1–3–7

b. MIN $16X_{12} + 12X_{13} + 30X_{14} + 14X_{25} + 12X_{35} + 30X_{36} + 40X_{37} + 26X_{47} + 10X_{56} + 18X_{67}$

subject to

$$X_{12} + X_{13} + X_{14} = 1$$
$$X_{12} - X_{25} = 0$$
$$X_{13} - X_{35} - X_{36} - X_{37} = 0$$
$$X_{14} - X_{47} = 0$$
$$X_{25} + X_{35} - X_{56} = 0$$
$$X_{36} + X_{56} - X_{67} = 0$$
$$X_{37} + X_{47} + X_{67} = 1$$
$$X_{12}, X_{13}, X_{14}, X_{25}, X_{35}, X_{36}, X_{37}, X_{47}, X_{56}, X_{67} \geq 0$$

3.

Branch	Branch Value
1–3	9
3–2	12
2–5	18
5–6	9
6–8	18
8–7	6
7–4	9
8–9	12
9–10	12

Minimum Total Span = 105

5. Flow over each branch:

Branch	Flow
1–2	18
1–3	12
1–4	20
2–5	18
3–4	4
3–7	8
4–5	16
4–6	8
5–8	42
6–5	8
6–8	6
7–6	6
7–8	2

Flow through network:

Flow	Paths:
18	1–2–5–8
16	1–4–5–8
4	1–4–6–5–8
4	1–3–4–6–5–8
6	1–3–7–6–8
2	1–3–7–1–8

Maximal Flow through Network = 50

LP Formulation:

MAX FLOW

subject to

$X_{12} + X_{13} + X_{14} - \text{FLOW} = 0$

$X_{12} - X_{25} = 0$

$X_{13} + X_{43} - X_{34} - X_{37} = 0$

$X_{14} + X_{34} + X_{54} - X_{43} - X_{45} - X_{46} = 0$

$X_{25} + X_{45} - X_{54} - X_{56} - X_{58} = 0$

$X_{46} + X_{56} + X_{76} - X_{65} - X_{67} - X_{68} = 0$

$X_{37} + X_{67} - X_{78} = 0$

$X_{58} + X_{68} + X_{78} - \text{FLOW} = 0$

$X_{12} \leq 36$

$X_{13} \leq 12$	$X_{45} \leq 16$	$X_{65} \leq 10$
$X_{14} \leq 20$	$X_{46} \leq 8$	$X_{67} \leq 6$
$X_{25} \leq 18$	$X_{54} \leq 10$	$X_{68} \leq 10$
$X_{34} \leq 18$	$X_{56} \leq 14$	$X_{76} \leq 6$
$X_{37} \leq 40$	$X_{58} \leq 42$	$X_{78} \leq 24$
$X_{43} \leq 18$	$X_{64} \leq 8$	

$X_{12}, X_{13}, \ldots, X_{76}, X_{78}, \text{FLOW} \geq 0$

8.

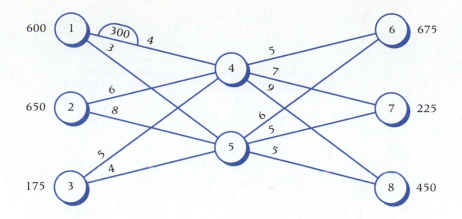

10.

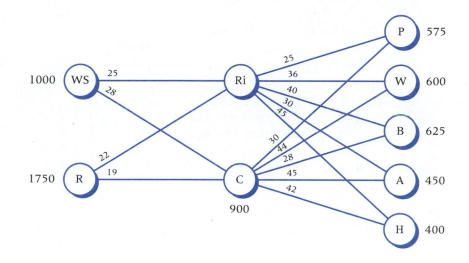

Solution:

X_{13}	900
X_{23}	850
X_{24}	900
X_{35}	575
X_{36}	600
X_{38}	450
X_{39}	125
X_{47}	625
X_{49}	275

Minimum Cost = 142,450

12. Nashville, TN to Birmingham, AL to Meridian, MS to New Orleans, LA (10 hours and 9 minutes).

14. Solution from Nashville (node 1):

Branch		Branch Value	Path
1–2	(Jackson, TN)	150	1–2
1–3	(Memphis, TN)	240	1–2–3
1–4	(Jackson, MS)	431	1–8–10–4
1–5	(Chattanooga, TN)	160	1–5
1–6	(Atlanta, GA)	305	1–5–6
1–7	(Tupelo, MS)	262	1–2–7
1–8	(Birmingham, AL)	190	1–8
1–9	(Montgomery, AL)	285	1–8–9
1–10	(Meridian, MS)	336	1–8–10
1–11	(Mobile, AL)	445	1–8–9–11
1–12	(New Orleans, LA)	511	1–8–10–12

Solution from New Orleans (node 1):

Branch		Branch Value	Path
1–2	(Mobile, AL)	150	1–2
1–3	(Meridian, MS)	175	1–3
1–4	(Montgomery, AL)	310	1–2–4
1–5	(Birmingham, AL)	321	1–3–5
1–6	(Tupelo, MS)	325	1–3–6
1–7	(Atlanta, GA)	465	1–2–4–7
1–8	(Chattanooga, TN)	466	1–3–5–8
1–9	(Jackson, MS)	148	1–9
1–10	(Memphis, TN)	348	1–9–10
1–11	(Jackson, TN)	437	1–3–6–11
1–12	(Nashville, TN)	511	1–3–5–12

The city closest to being equidistant from both Nashville and New Orleans is Montgomery, AL, 285 miles from Nashville and 310 miles from New Orleans. This criterion alone, however, may result in a poor choice of cities relative to the other possible participants.

16. Lease for two years and then for three years. The minimum cost will be $37,500.

18.

Branch	Branch Value
DO–Fin	19
DO–Act	23
DO–DSc	27
DO–SSO	35
DO–Mgt	41
DO–Mkt	46
DO–Lab	110

Minimum Total Span = 301 feet

Total Cost = (301)($36) = $10,386

21. Flow over Each Branch:

Branch	Flow
A–B	10
A–C	17
A–D	12
B–E	7
B–F	8
C–B	5
C–F	12
D–C	0
D–F	0
D–G	12
E–J	19
F–G	5
F–H	15
G–I	17
H–E	12
H–I	0
H–J	3
I–H	0
I–J	17

Flow through Network:

Flow	Paths:
7	A–B–E–J
3	A–B–F–H–J
12	A–D–G–I–J
5	A–C–B–F–G–I–J
12	A–C–F–H–E–J

Maximal Flow through Network = 39 (000 barrels)

Chapter 9

1. a. LP Relaxation: A = 3.333, B = 0, Zmax = 10
IP Solution: A = 3, B = 0, Zmax = 9
b. Solution at Node 1 (LP Relaxation)

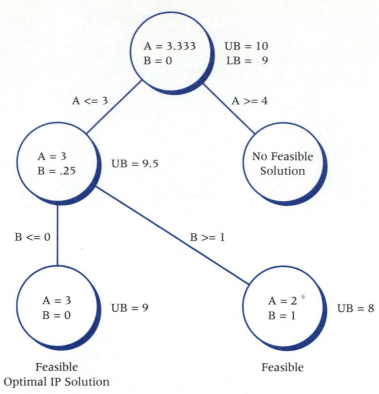

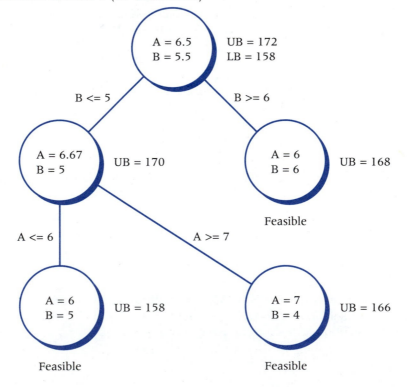

3. **a.** LP Relaxation: A = 6.5, B = 5.5, Zmax = 172
   IP Solution: A = 6, B = 6, Zmax = 168
   b. Solution at Node 1 (LP Relaxation)

5.

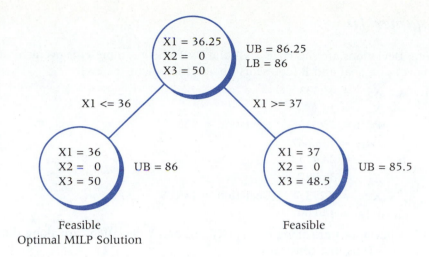

Feasible
Optimal MILP Solution

Feasible

7. There are two alternate optimal solutions:

A = 21, B = 0, C = 0, Zmax = 63; and
A = 3, B = 9, C = 6, Zmax = 63

9. **a.** The company should take all passengers and packages 1, 3, 6, 7, 8, and 9.
   b. $450 on passengers and $590 on packages; $1,040 total.

11. Fred should purchase the compactor truck and the conveyor for a net profit of $8,500.

13.

$$MAX\ 12.5E + 10A + 15C + 6.8H + 7CI \leq 1500$$

Subject to

$$35E + 75A + 80C + 25H + 55CI \leq 1500$$
$$50E + 35A + 55C + 18H + 22CI \leq 2000$$
$$E, A, C, H, CI \geq 0\ and\ INTEGER$$

Solution:
   E = 37
   A = 0
   C = 0   Optimal Z Value = 516.9
   H = 8
   CI = 0

16. Williamson should invest in Product B, computerized billing, and the warehouse. The net present value of this investment is $179,000.

19. Omega should purchase the eight-ton press and the digital lathe for a profit contribution of $95,000.

21. **a.** 1,184 rolls
   b. 1,184 inches (the equivalent of 78.9 15-inch rolls)
   c. 4 4-inch rolls and 732 5-inch rolls.

24. The manager should purchase desktop system A. He should then schedule 75,000 of the Jones' brochures on the current press and 75,000 on the new system. He should schedule all 200,000 fliers on the new system. This will yield a profit of $17,000.

Chapter 10

Note: Deviations are shown as DxA and DxB where A represents overachievement (above) of a goal and B represents underachievement (below).

1. **a.** X_2 = 43.333

X_3 = 20

D3B = 23.333   Deviation = 130

D4A = 106.667

b. X_1 = 25.455

X_2 = 32.727

X_3 = 7.273   Deviation = 149.09

D4A = 149.091

3. X deviations are along the X_1 (X) axis and Y deviations are along the X_2 (Y) axis. Thus, the constraint
$$X_1 + DAXB - DAXA = 3$$
expresses the X_1 coordinate, DAXB expresses the amount the coordinate is to the left of population center A, and DAXA expresses the amount the coordinate is to the right of population center A. The optimal solution is:

X_1 = 3

X_2 = 5

DBYB = 4

DCXB = 4   MIN Deviation = 13

DAYA = 4

DBXA = 1

5. A = 7.333, B = 8.667, D2B = 0.133, D4B = 0.367, D3A = 0.053 and the minimum deviation is 0.11 (0.11 ounces of crude protein less than the 2 ounces desired).

7. MIN 0D1B + P1D1A + P2D2B + 0D2A + 0D3B + P3D3A

Subject to

6500BF + 62000SF + 67000SR + 77500BC + 84000TC + D1B − D1A = 250000

3200BF + 4300SF + 3500SR + 4500BC + 5000TC + D2B − D2A = 25000

4BF + 5SF + 1.5SR + 2BC + 1TC + D3B − D3A = 10

9. **a.**   MIN P1D1B + P1D2B + P1D3A + P1D4A

Subject to

1.4HT + 1.1SA + 3.5GR + 1D1B − 1D1A = 20000

.6HT + 4SA − 1GR + 1D2B − 1D2A = 0

1SA + 1D3B − 1D3A = 6000

60HT + 80SA + 20GR + 1D4B − 1D4A = 600000

Solution:

SA   =   1324.503

GR   =   5298.013

D3B   =   4675.497   MIN Deviation = 0

D4B = 388079.473

b. Change objective function to:

$$\text{MIN } P1D1B + P2D2B + P3D3A + P4D4A$$

Solution:

$$
\begin{aligned}
SA &= 1324.503 \\
GR &= 5298.013 \\
D3B &= 4675.497 \quad \text{MIN Deviation} = 0 \text{ (All} \\
&\hspace{3.8cm}\text{priority levels)} \\
D4B &= 388079.473
\end{aligned}
$$

11. Change the objective function to:

$$\text{MIN } P2D1B + P3D4A + P3D5A + P1D6A$$
and add the following constraint:
$$D2A + D3A + D6B - D6A = 35$$

Solution:

$$
\begin{aligned}
GG &= 4300 \\
D1B &= 1625 \\
D4B &= 12.5 \\
D2A &= 7.5 \\
D3A &= 27.5 \\
D5A &= 2.5
\end{aligned}
$$

Analysis of the Objective Function:

Priority	Non-Achievement
P_1	0
P_2	1625
P_3	2.5

14. He should place 10 TV ads, 15 radio ads, and 15 newspaper ads. He will be $1,750 below budget and reach 132,500 younger voters (7,500 over his goal).

16. The firm should produce 200 units of A, 240 units of B, and 220 units of C. They must schedule 590 hours of overtime to meet this schedule. (Their priority level 3 goal will not be achieved by 590 hours.)

17. Big Boy should schedule 55 hours of machine A time and 60 hours of machine B time. Goal 2 is not achieved (excess overtime = 3 hours) and goal 4 is not achieved (excess costs = $245). Priority levels 1 and 3 goals are achieved.

20. $\text{MIN } P1D1B + P2D2B + P3D3A$

Subject to

1. $.4ISM + .4ISW + .4ISIPM + .4ISIPW - .6OSM - .6OSW - .6OSIPM - .6OSIPW + D1B - D1A = 0$

2. $.65ISW + .65ISIPW + .65OSW + .65OSIPW - .35ISM - .35ISIPM - .35OSM - .35OSIPM + D2B - D2A = 0$

3. $.9ISIPM + .9ISIPW + .9OSIPM + .9OSIPW - .1ISM - .1ISW - .1OSM - .1OSW + D3B - D3A = 0$

4. $4500ISM + 4500ISW + 6000OSM + 6000OSW + 1500ISIPM + 1500ISIPW + 1500OSIPM + 1500OSIPW \le 400000$

Chapter 11

1.

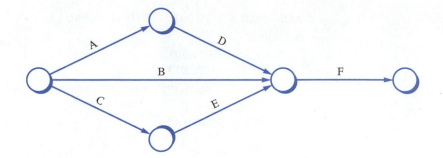

3.

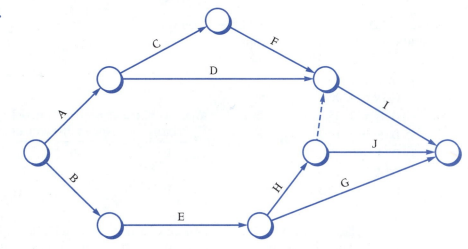

7.	Path	Duration
	1–2–3–6–9	33
	1–2–3–4–7–8–9	33
	1–2–4–7–8–9	32
	1–2–5–7–8–9	36 = Critical Path
	1–2–5–8–9	30

9.

Event	Early Time	Late Time
1	0	0
2	8	8
3	18	21
4	18	21
5	15	15
6	26	29
7	27	27
8	32	32
9	36	36

11.

Act	Early Start	Late Start	Early Finish	Late Finish	Slack (LS-ES)	Critical Path
A 1–2	0.0	0.0	4.0	4.0	0.0	Yes
B 1–4	0.0	2.0	10.0	12.0	2.0	
C 2–3	4.0	4.0	6.0	6.0	0.0	Yes
D 2–5	4.0	4.0	12.0	12.0	0.0	Yes
E 3–5	6.0	6.0	12.0	12.0	0.0	Yes
— 4–5	10.0	12.0	10.0	12.0	2.0	
F 5–6	12.0	12.0	24.0	24.0	0.0	Yes
I 5–7	12.0	19.0	24.0	31.0	7.0	
H 5–8	12.0	24.0	28.0	40.0	12.0	
J 6–10	24.0	24.0	40.0	40.0	0.0	Yes
— 7–8	24.0	40.0	24.0	40.0	16.0	
L 7–11	24.0	31.0	30.0	37.0	7.0	
K 8–12	28.0	40.0	30.0	42.0	12.0	
G 4–9	10.0	18.0	17.0	25.0	8.0	
M 9–11	17.0	26.0	28.0	37.0	9.0	
N 9–13	17.0	25.0	30.0	38.0	8.0	
O 10–12	40.0	40.0	42.0	42.0	0.0	Yes
P 11–12	30.0	37.0	35.0	42.0	7.0	
Q 11–14	30.0	46.0	34.0	50.0	16.0	
R 12–14	42.0	42.0	50.0	50.0	0.0	Yes
S 13–14	30.0	38.0	42.0	50.0	8.0	
T 13–15	30.0	42.0	47.0	59.0	12.0	
U 14–15	50.0	50.0	59.0	59.0	0.0	Yes

Critical Paths: A–C–E–F–J–O–R–U and A–D–F–J–O–R–U

Network Completion Time = 59 weeks

If activity E was shortened to 5 weeks, path A–C–E–F–J–O–R–U would no longer be critical. The project duration would remain 59 weeks with one critical path, A–D–F–J–O–R–U.

13. a. Critical Path: B–E–G–I–K–L–R–T

  b. Network Completion Time = 40.2 weeks

  c. 3.5 days

  d. Shared slack; shared with activities N and H

  e. Standard deviation on critical path = 1.6 days

  f. $Z = (45 - 40.2)/1.6 = 3.00$

  From the standard normal table, there is a 99.86% probability that the project will be completed within 45 weeks.

16. a.

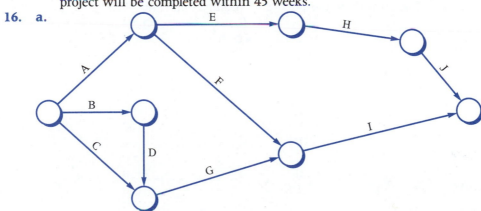

b.

Activity	Expected (t)	Var
A	3.00	0.11
B	5.00	1.00
C	8.50	0.69
D	7.17	0.25
E	9.17	2.25
F	12.00	0.11
G	4.33	1.00
H	7.00	1.00
I	10.00	5.44
J	6.33	4.00

Act	Early Start	Late Start	Early Finish	Late Finish	Slack (LS-ES)	Critical Path
A	0.0	1.0	3.0	4.0	1.0	
B	0.0	0.0	5.0	5.0	0.0	Yes
C	0.0	3.7	8.5	12.2	3.7	
D	5.0	5.0	12.2	12.2	0.0	Yes
E	3.0	4.0	12.2	13.2	1.0	
F	3.0	4.5	15.0	16.5	1.5	
G	12.2	12.2	16.5	16.5	0.0	Yes
H	12.2	13.2	19.2	20.2	1.0	
I	16.5	16.5	26.5	26.5	0.0	Yes
J	19.2	20.2	25.5	26.5	1.0	

c. Critical Path: B–D–G–I
Network Completion Time = 26.5

d. Variance on Critical Path = 7.69
Standard Deviation on Critical Path = 2.77

e. The probability of completing the project on time is 50%.
$Z = (30 - 26.5)/2.77 = 1.2635$
From the standard normal table, the probability of completing the project within 30 weeks is approximately 89.7%.

18. Critical Path: A–E–G–I–M–R–S–U
Network Completion Time = 103.33
Variance on Critical Path = 31.73
Standard Deviation on Critical Path = 5.63

19. a. Critical path = 1–3–4–7–8   Completion time = 25

Activity	(b) Crash Time	(c) Cost/Day
A	1	150
B	1	180
C	2	120
D	2	200
E	2	160
F	0	—
G	3	200
H	3	110
I	1	190
J	2	140

d. Minimum time (1–3–4–7–8) = 17

On path 1–3–4–7–8:

Activity	Days	Cost
B (1–3)	1	180
D (3–4)	2	400
G (4–7)	3	600
J (7–8)	2	280

On path 1–2–5–8:

Activity	Days	Cost
C (2–5)	2	240
H (5–8)	3	330

On path 1–3–4–5–8:
Activities B (1) and H (3) have already been crashed.

On path 1–3–6–7–8:
Activities B (1) and J (2) have already been crashed.

Activity	Days	Cost
E (3–6)	1	160

Crash cost = $2,190 + $8,460 (Normal Cost) = $10,650

e. Paths A–C–H (1–2–5), B–D–G–J (1–3–4–7–8), and B–E–I–J (1–3–6–7–8) are critical.

23. LP crashing formulation:
MIN 300A + 200B + 360C + 500D + 250E + 600F + 420G + 330H + 550I + 260J + 0LF8 + 0LF7 + 0LF6 + 0LF5 + 0LF4 + 0LF3 + 0LF2

Subject to

A ≤ 2	LF8 − LF7 + J ≥ 6
B ≤ 1	LF8 − LF6 + I ≥ 7
C ≤ 1	LF7 − LF5 + H ≥ 10
D ≤ 3	LF7 − LF4 + G ≥ 7
E ≤ 1	LF6 − LF4 + F ≥ 5
F ≤ 2	LF5 − LF3 + E ≥ 3
G ≤ 2	LF4 − LF3 + D ≥ 8
H ≤ 4	LF3 − LF2 + C ≥ 4
I ≤ 1	LF3 + B ≥ 10
J ≤ 3	LF2 + A ≥ 7
	LF8 = 23 (days desired)

27. LP crashing formulation:
MIN 70A + 90B + 60C + 45D + 55E + 80F + 40G + 0H + 65I + 75J + 0LF7 + 0LF6 + 0LF5 + 0LF4 + 0LF3 + 0LF2

Subject to

A ≤ 4	LF7 − LF6 + J ≥ 15
B ≤ 3	LF7 − LF4 + G ≥ 15
C ≤ 6	LF6 − LF5 + I ≥ 6

$$D \leq 1 \qquad LF6 - LF4 + H \geq 5$$
$$E \leq 2 \qquad LF6 - LF3 + F \geq 9$$
$$F \leq 3 \qquad LF5 - LF3 + E \geq 6$$
$$G \leq 5 \qquad LF5 - LF2 + D \geq 8$$
$$H = 0 \qquad LF4 - LF2 + C \geq 12$$
$$I \leq 1 \qquad LF3 + B \geq 21$$
$$J \leq 4 \qquad LF2 + A \geq 22$$
$$LF7 = 41$$

31. a.

Activity	Actual Cost	Budget To Date	Over/Under Budget
A	$2,100	$2,000	100
B	1,900	1,950	(50)
C	2,200	2,000	200
D	1,750	1,800	(50)
E	2,540	2,400	140
F	380	400	(20)
	10,870	10,550	320

b. The project is currently $320 over budget.

c. Activities B, D, and F are under budget and activities A, C, and E are over budget (see table).

d. Yes, activity C is currently 10 percent over budget and activity E is 5.8 percent over budget. These activities should be monitored.

34. a.

Activity	Actual Cost	Budget To Date	Over/Under Budget
A	475	500	(25)
B	3,150	3,000	150
C	990	1,000	(10)
D	1,550	1,500	50
E	900	900	0
F	4,180	4,750	60
G	3,750	3,800	(50)
H	4,575	4,500	75
I	700	560	140
J	0	0	0
K	1,750	1,867	(117)
L	0	0	0
M	0	0	0
N	0	0	0
	22,650	22,377	273

b. The total project is $273 over budget at this time.

c. Activity I is 25 percent ($140) over budget at this time.
Activity K is 6.3 percent ($117) under budget.

Chapter 12

1. EOQ Value = 480 units

   Annual Costs (excluding item costs):

   Carrying cost = $360.00
   Ordering cost = $360.00
   Total Costs   = $720.00

3. a. EOQ Value = 1800 units
   b. Annual costs (excluding item costs):

      Carrying cost = $450.00
      Ordering cost = $450.00
      Total Costs   = $900.00
   c. The cycle time is 36.5 days.

5. a. Optimal Lot Size = 2400 units
   b. Maximum Inventory = 672 units
   c. Annual Costs (excluding item costs):

      Carrying Cost = $504.00
      Setup Cost   = $504.00
      Total Costs   = $1,008.00

7. a. EOQ Value = 1200 units
   b. Annual Costs (excluding item costs):

      Carrying Cost = $1,440.00
      Ordering Cost = $1,440.00
      Total Costs   = $2,880.00
   c. The reorder point is 1920 units.

9. a. EOQ Value = 3872.98 units
   b. Annual Costs (excluding item costs):

      Carrying Cost = $1,161.90
      Ordering Cost = 1,161.90
      Total Costs   = $2,323.80
   c.
   $$TC = (D/Q)C_o + (Q/2)C_c + (Q)(.03)$$
   $$dTC/dQ = -D(C_o)/Q^2 + \tfrac{1}{2}C_c + .03 = 0$$
   $$Q^* = \sqrt{(2D(C_o))/(C_c + 2(.03))}$$
   $$Q^* = \sqrt{2(60000)(75)/(.6 + .06)}$$
   $$Q^* = 3692.74 \text{ units}$$

11. a. EOQ with Backorders = 509.12 units
    b. Carrying Cost = $301.70
       Ordering Cost = 339.41
       Backorder Cost =   37.71
       Total Costs   = $678.82
    c. Maximum Inventory = 452.55

13. Total cost summary for each price available:

Cat	Cost	Quant	Carry	Order	Item	Total
1	15.00	1000	1,500.00	1,500.00	750,000.00	753,000.00
2	14.90	6000	8,940.00	250.00	745,000.00	754,190.00

15. Total cost summary for each price available:

Cat	Cost	Quant	Carry	Order	Item	Total
1	This price/quantity not feasible					
2	0.48	9675	232.20	232.19	16,588.80	17,053.19
3	0.46	10000	230.00	224.64	15,897.60	16,352.24

Purchase 10000 units at a price of $.46.

17. Summary of total costs at various safety stock levels:

Safety Stock	Carrying Cost	Stockout Cost	Total Costs
0	$0	$312	$312
10	$40	$132	$172
20	$80	$36	$116
30	$120	$0	$120

Optimal Safety Stock = 20 units
Optimal reorder point = 240 units

21. Treat this problem as a marginal analysis problem attempting to offset carrying costs ($3) and stockout costs ($8). Thus,

$P(D < Q^*) = .7273$ and $Z = 0.6047$

$ROP = 240 + 20(.605) = 252.1$ units

23. Safety Stock = 52.5 units
Reorder Point = 602.5 units

25. Safety Stock = 47 units
Reorder Point = 247 units

27. The optimum quantity to stock is 17 units.
Expected profit at this stocking level = $26.00.

29. The optimum quantity to stock is 11 units.
Expected profit at this stocking level = $1,558.56.

33. The following is one possible allocation to the three categories:

Item	Annual Demand	Cost per Unit	Inventory Value	Category
L	2,750	$75	$206,250	A
A	5,000	28	140,000	A
E	2,600	44	114,400	A
C	1,200	35	42,000	B
I	800	50	40,000	B
D	1,800	15	27,000	B
B	750	30	22,500	B
F	2,400	8	19,200	C
G	1,150	16	18,400	C
N	500	25	12,500	C
K	250	32	8,000	C
H	350	22	7,700	C
M	200	18	3,600	C
J	100	35	3,500	C
			$665,050	

(These figures do not add to 100% due to rounding.)

69.3%	A	
19.8%	B	
11.0%	C	

35.

Component	WEEK 1	2	3	4	5	6	7	8	9	10	11	12
A5 LT = 1												
Gross requirements							100	50	150	200	50	200
Remaining inventory	20	20	20	20	20	20	20					
Net requirements							80	50	150	200	50	200
Scheduled receipts							80	50	150	200	50	200
Planned order release						80	50	150	200	50	200	
B1 LT = 1												
Gross requirements							80	50	150	200	50	200
Remaining inventory	50	50	50	50	50	50						
Net requirements							30	50	150	200	50	200
Scheduled receipts							30	50	150	200	50	200
Planned order release						30	50	150	200	50	200	
B2 LT = 2												
Gross requirements							80	50	150	200	50	200
Remaining inventory	190	190	190	190	190	190	110	60				
Net requirements									90	200	50	200
Scheduled receipts									90	200	50	200
Planned order release							90	200	50	200		
B4 LT = 2												
Gross requirements							240	150	450	600	150	600
Remaining inventory	200	200	200	200	200	200						
Net requirements							40	150	450	600	150	600
Scheduled receipts							40	150	450	600	150	600
Planned order release					40	150	450	600	150	600		
B8 LT = 1												
Gross requirements							160	100	300	400	100	400
Remaining inventory	400	400	400	400	400	400	240	140				
Net requirements									160	400	100	400
Scheduled receipts									160	400	100	400
Planned order release								160	400	100	400	

Chapter 13

1. **a.** LAPLACE — d_3, 24.25
   MAXIMIN — d_1 & d_3, 22
   MAXIMAX — d_2, 27
   SAVAGE   — d_1, d_3, & d_5, 5
   b. HURWICZ — d_3, 23.6
   c. HURWICZ — d_3, 24.8
   d. None of these criteria provide a best decision. They provide a consistent approach to decision making and a rationale for making a particular decision.

3. LAPLACE   — d_4, 43.25
MAXIMIN — d_4, 41
MAXIMAX — d_3, 46
HURWICZ — d_4, 43
SAVAGE   — d_4, 1

5. d_4, 43

7. EMV — d_3, 8.75
EOL — d_3, 2.4
EVPI = 2.4

9. **a.** Acme should take the loan today, with an expected interest payment of $225,000.
b. This proposal will always have an expected interest charge between the cost of taking the loan today and the cost of waiting. It will, therefore, never be the optimal choice.

11. The company is indifferent between manufacturing 3,200 and 4,000 pairs (EMV = $34,725).

13. **a.** Design A, EMV = $29,800.
b. EVPI = $3,600

15. The company should make (EMV = $127,000).

17. **a.** Purchase the $60,000 machine. Expected costs = $30,300.
b. EVPI = $1,500

19. EMV = 4,320

23. **a.**

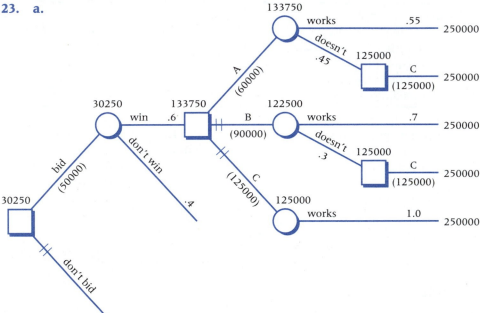

b. Bid. If bid is won, build system A; if system A does not work, build system C. EMV = $30,250.

25. **a.** The radio station will report that the interstate is clear 55.5 percent of the time.
b. If the radio reports clear, she should take the interstate; if it reports back-ups, she should take local roads. (Versus taking the interstate all the time—problem 12 solution.)

28. **a.** If strong prediction, Groff should make (EMV = 174,855).
    b. If weak prediction, Groff should buy (EMV = 79,025).
    c. Groff should not purchase the market research, since the cost of $3,000 exceeds the EVSI of $2,810.

30. P (properly adjusted) = 12.5 percent.

Chapter 14

3.
$$P(0) = 0.0025$$
$$P(6) = 0.1606$$
$$P(\leq 3) = P(0) + P(1) + P(2) + P(3)$$
$$= (.0025 + .0149 + .0446 + .0892) = .1512$$
$$P(> 3) = (1 - .1512) = 0.8488$$

5. Yes, the second channel is justified on a cost basis ($78.58 versus $145).

7. **a.** On the average, there are 2 students waiting, including the student being helped. Students can expect to wait an average of 6 minutes before receiving the reserve material (or 4 minutes in line).
   b. Given the utilization rate of 66.7 percent, the helpers will be idle about one-third of the time. Therefore, it may be reasonable to expect them to complete the recordkeeping. However, even though the expected idle time exceeds the time required, it may be broken up into such small parts that the workers spend time just finding where they left off.

9. **a.** Each employee spends approximately 10 minutes waiting (excluding service) or 12 minutes total. Thus, over an 8-hour day, 33.3 hours are lost waiting.
   b. The optimum number of attendants is two.

11. **a.** Assuming a mean arrival rate of 31 (25 machinists and 6 secretaries per hour), each employee will spend approximately 4.09 minutes at the coffee machine.
    b. This would change the time at the coffee machine to 5.74 minutes per employee.

13. The cost is $486.60. With a two-mechanic team, the cost is $533.64. The second mechanic is not justified.

15. The balking rate is 12.18 percent. Thus, Panorama loses $613.87 per week.

17. Under the current system, each doctor would wait approximately 20 minutes for the lab results. Using a pool with 5 technicians, each doctor would have to wait an average of 10.52 minutes for results. With 3 technicians, the utilization rate would be 83.3 percent. Four technicians should be retained if they wish to keep waiting time in the system under 15 minutes (expected time with 4 technicians = 12 minutes). To make this decision on an economic basis, we would need the rate of pay for the technicians, the rate of pay for the doctors, and information on whether the doctors wait for results or simply proceed to the next patient(s) while waiting.

19. No, this claim is incorrect. The average caller must wait approximately 14 minutes before receiving help.

a. No. By combining the two districts, they could cut the waiting time to approximately 6 minutes (5.9) with 14 tutors. But with 13 tutors, the waiting time is over 25 minutes and 12 tutors would result in an infinite queue.

23. A student would have to wait .778 days or 6.22 hours for service. With the change in priorities, students would wait approximately 47 minutes for service.

Chapter 15

Note: Answers for some problems will vary depending on the random numbers selected.

1. Demand for weeks 1 through 20:

9, 11, 8, 9, 9, 11, 9, 8, 9, 7, 9, 7, 10, 9, 7, 8, 9, 8, 8, 7

3. a. Demand for weeks 1 through 20:

3, 4, 1, 4, 3, 4, 5, 3, 3, 3, 5, 4, 4, 3, 3, 3, 3, 3, 4, 4, 3

Average IAT = 3.4 minutes,

b. The average for this simulation is higher than the expected value.

c.

Period	RN	Sim IAT	Time	Period	RN	Sim IAT	Time
1	25	3	0:03	10	64	4	0:33
2	09	2	:05	11	64	4	:37
3	85	4	:09	12	21	2	:39
4	40	3	:12	13	71	4	:43
5	24	2	:14	14	78	4	:47
6	47	3	:17	15	31	3	:50
7	93	5	:22	16	22	2	:52
8	81	4	:26	17	95	5	:57
9	30	3	:29	18	57	3	1:00

5. Average time is 2.75 hours based on the following random numbers: 65, 89, 59, 69, 44, 95, 36, 78, 24, 61, 44, 59, 89, 64, 56, 74, 10, 28, 14, 84.

7. a.

Week	Breakdowns	Repair Times
1	3	3
		4
		3
2	1	3
3	3	2
		4
		2
4	2	3
		2
5	3	3
		2
		3
		34 hours

6.8 hours × $50 + 5 weeks × $150 = $340 + $750 = $1,090 total or $490 per week. Based on these results, the program does not appear to be justified.

b. Using the same random numbers would give a better comparison over this small sample. However, different sets of random numbers should be used with a larger number of samples to obtain more accurate results.

9. Using two sets of random numbers, one set for arrivals (04, 64, 14, 68, 18, 73, 58, 46, 72, 65) and one for service times (09, 04, 57, 75, 10, 81, 07, 06, 94, 22), Dr. Foster should cancel his 1:30 appointment.

11. a. Based on computer-generated random numbers, 21 people were home and willing to contribute.

b. Based on a second set of random numbers, total contributions were $51.

15.

Period	Random Number	Simulated Value	Finish Time
1	06	37	10:37
2	38	39	11:16
3	46	40	11:56
4	33	39	12:35
5	79	42	1:17
6	92	43	2:00
7	94	43	2:43
8	79	42	3:25
9	96	43	3:58
10	00	37	4:35
11	14	38	5:13
12	14	38	5:51
13	30	39	6:30
14	06	37	7:07
15	04	37	7:44

17.

Job	RN	Load Time	RN	Run Time	RN	Print Time	Total Time
1	9	9	59	11	32	14	34
2	0	4	80	12	81	17	33
3	7	7	67	12	32	14	33

The total time required to process all three jobs would be 1 hour and 40 minutes (based on a sample of one).

19. Using nine different random number groups (one for each activity), expected completion times ranged from 21 to 26 for five simulations. Each path was critical at least once.

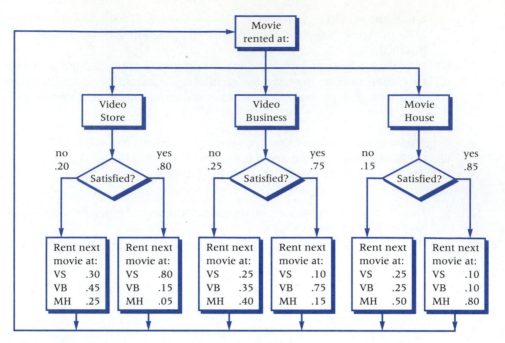

VS = Video Store
VB = Video Business
MH = Movie House
S = satisfied
D = dissatisfied

Chapter 16

1. a.

	A	B	C
$^6/_1$:	500	900	600
$^7/_1$:	525	885	590

	A	B	C
A	420	45	35
B	63	810	27
C	42	30	528

b.

	A	B	C
A	.84	.09	.07
B	.07	.90	.03
C	.07	.05	.88

3. a. 0.61
   b. A = 55.6% and B = 44.4%

5. a.

A	B	C
3807	3110	3583

   b.

A	B	C
3787	3098	3615

7. 39.7% of the market.

9. a.

$$
\begin{array}{c}
 & \begin{array}{ccc} C & P & TC \end{array} \\
\begin{array}{c} C \\ PC \\ TC \end{array} &
\left[
\begin{array}{ccc}
.15 & .65 & .2 \\
0 & .4 & .6 \\
1 & 0 & 0
\end{array}
\right]
\end{array}
$$

b. At steady state:
S1 = .341, S2 = .369, S3 = .290
.29(150) = $43.50 per day

11. a.

$$
\begin{array}{c}
 & \begin{array}{ccccc} C\&G & A & GP & SV & GO \end{array} \\
\begin{array}{c} C\&G \\ A \\ GP \\ SV \\ GO \end{array} &
\left[
\begin{array}{ccccc}
.45 & .2 & .12 & .18 & .05 \\
.15 & .39 & .17 & .13 & .16 \\
.19 & .08 & .42 & .21 & .1 \\
.1 & .1 & .1 & .5 & .2 \\
.12 & .1 & .16 & .14 & .48
\end{array}
\right]
\end{array}
$$

b. Steady state distribution:
[.199 .164 .187 .249 .201]

c. $100,500,000

15. a. Steady state = [.232 .309 .286 .174]
At steady state, 42.9 machines will be in fair condition and 26.1 will be down. Thus, the loss will be $11,262.

b. Changing the transition matrix would result in the following steady state: [.324 .432 .200 .043]. Out of the original 150 machines, this means that 30 would be in fair condition and 6.5 would be down. Costs would be $4,335.
Adding the cost of the preventive maintenance ($1,200) would result in a total cost of $5,535. Thus, the preventive maintenance would be justified.

19. Fundamental matrix:

$$
\begin{array}{c}
 & \begin{array}{cc} 1 & 4 \end{array} \\
\begin{array}{c} 2 \\ 3 \end{array} &
\left[
\begin{array}{cc}
1.36 & .45 \\
.30 & 1.21
\end{array}
\right]
\end{array}
$$

21. At steady state, the machine will be out of adjustment 33.3% of the time. Rework costs will average $6.67 per hour.

23. a. PIF   30   60   BD
[876 96 26   2]

b. In the short term, there does not seem to be a cause for concern. At the end of the year, less than 1 percent of these accounts will have become bad debts. However, based solely on the transition probabilities, all accounts could become bad debts since a sink exists.

25. a. 16.7%

b.

Condition	Days to Discharge
Satisfactory	13.12
Fair	12.21
Critical	10.13

c. The probability of discharge is a function of the entering condition, but the average probability for all entering patients is 84.2%.

Chapter 17

1.

Period	Forecast	Period	Forecast
4	36.67	12	44.67
5	36.67	13	50.67
6	37.33	14	46.67
7	33.33	15	42.00
8	37.33	16	33.33
9	36.00	17	36.00
10	35.33	18	37.33
11	37.33	19	38.67

3. December forecast = 1680 (3 period)
December forecast = 1640 (5 period)

5. MSE (3 period) = 25,666.67
MSE (5 period) = 25,640.00
The difference in the MSE values is not significant.

7. December forecast = 1684
December forecast = 1596 (reversed weights)

9. 43,698.07 with an $\alpha = .2$
45,359.25 with an $\alpha = .4$

11. MAD $(\alpha \ldots) = 2506.253$ (exclude pd 1—2784.725)
MAD (search...) = 1822.781 (exclude pd 1—2025.312)

14. Y' = 6640
$r^2 = .569$ (The goodness of fit depends on the data we are trying to forecast. This coefficient seems moderate at best.) Examination of a plot of this data (not shown) suggests seasonal or cyclical variations.

16. Y' = 268.571 + 3.929(X)
1988 forecast = 304
Se = 6.289
r = .856

18. Y' = 33.165 + .578(X)
(plots not included)

Quarter	Seasonal Relatives
1	.7781
2	1.1185
3	1.2459
4	.8576

Period 15 forecast = 52 (52.122)

20.

Quarter	Seasonal Relatives
1	.777
2	1.122
3	1.245
4	.857

22. $r^2 = .832$

Index